Ch

a travel survival kit

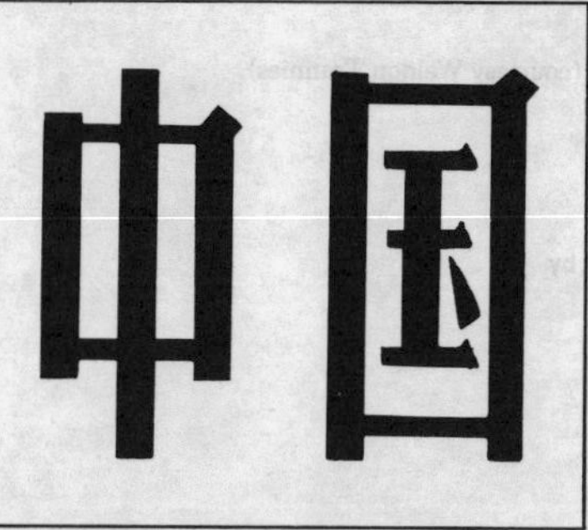

Alan Samagalski
Robert Strauss
Michael Buckley

China - a travel survival kit
2nd edition

Published by
Lonely Planet Publications
Head Office: PO Box 88, South Yarra, Victoria 3141, Australia
US Office: PO Box 2001A, Berkeley, CA 94702, USA

Printed by
Colorcraft, Hong Kong

Photographs by
Alan Samagalski (AS)
Robert Strauss (RS)
Jim Hart (JH)
Front cover: Leo Meier (courtesy Weldon Trannies)

Cartoons by
Graham Harrop
Tony Jenkins

Chinese Characters typeset by
Polyprint, Melbourne
Colorcraft, Hong Kong

First Published
October 1984

This Edition
May 1988

National Library of Australia Cataloguing in Publication Data

Samagalski, Alan
China, a travel survival kit.

2nd ed.
Includes index.
ISBN 0 86442 003 X.

1. China - Description and travel - 1976 - Guide Books.
I. Strauss, Robert. I. Title.

915. 1'0458

Alan Samagalski came to Lonely Planet after a lengthy stay on the Indian subcontinent, having gone astray from the Melbourne University Genetics Department and a stumbling career at Melbourne's legendary 'Last Laugh' and 'Comedy Cafe'. Alan subsequently disappeared into China and emerged several months later with an armful of material for the first edition of *China – a travel survival kit*. He returned to China to help research the new edition. He has also written *Chile & Easter Island*, co-authored *Indonesia* and has contributed to the *Hong Kong, Macau & Canton* and *South-East Asia on a Shoestring* guides, all for Lonely Planet.

Robert Strauss, gentleman and scholar, author of the *Trans-Siberian Rail Guide* and co-author of *Tibet – a travel survival kit*, made some considerable contributions to the first edition of *China* and spent many months travelling and researching the country for the second edition. Born in England, Robert moved out in the '70s to travel in Europe and Asia, including a visit to the Tibetan communities in Dharamsala (India) and Nepal. After completing a degree in oriental languages in 1981, Robert made several trips to China and spent his time teaching, travelling and writing between England, Germany, Portugal and China.

Michael Buckley was raised in Australia, but is now a resident in Vancouver, Canada, making a living from freelance journalism and teaching English to immigrants. Michael kicked off his travelling days with a years overland trip through Asia, India and the Middle East to Europe in the '70s. He first fell into the Middle Kingdom through the Hong Kong trapdoor in 1981 when solo travel became possible. Lonely Planet sent him back to help research the first edition of *China*. Although he did not take part in the second edition he has since co-authored Lonely Planet's *Tibet – a travel survival kit*.

Lonely Planet Credits

Editors	Katie Cody Elizabeth Kim Nicky Klempfner Debbie Lustig
Maps	Chris Lee Ack Graham Imeson
Cover design	Chris Lee Ack
Design & illustrations	Vicki Beale Joanne Ryan
Typesetting	Ann Jeffree Debbie Lustig

Thanks also to Lindy Cameron for proofing and index, Peter Turner for proofing, Mark Balla for language section editing, Todd Pierce for map keys and Richard Nebesky for additional photos.

THE FIRST & SECOND EDITIONS

The first edition of this book appeared after myself and Michael spent many months on the road in China in 1983, followed by many more at our desks and failing typewriters and exhausted word-processors in Melbourne and Vancouver.

Reaction to the book was mostly favourable. On my update trip through the country I was neither lynched by angry backpackers nor did I find too many discarded copies of the book floating down the Yangtse River.

For the second edition, Robert Strauss handled the peripheral areas of the Middle Kingdom: stocking up on some more of the local lingo in Tibet and Qinghai, freezing his bum off in Xinjiang, searching for lost tribes in the South-West, getting sandblasted in Inner Mongolia and struggling once again with the idiosyncratic hotel staff of the far North-East. I added another centimetre or two to the lengthening tourist trails of eastern China, dosed up on banana pancakes and muesli in Yangshuo, investigated bomb-shelter subterranean cultures in Xian, gathered strange souvenirs in Beijing, and somehow wound up back in Hong Kong via Shanghai and the south-east coast.

We were helped by a host of people and thanks must go to those who wrote notes, letters, or simply recognised us somewhere along the line and told us about their experiences. Special thanks to: Clare, who made me find out what was over the next hill and around the next corner in Hong Kong and Canton; Geoff Bonsall, Lonely Planet's Hong Kong distributor, whose flat became a storehouse for packets of notes and whose taste in Hong Kong restaurants is always appreciated; Graham Harrop, a troglodyte from Vancouver and perpetrator of some of the cartoons which appear in this book; Anthony Jenkins whose cartoons have graced the pages of many other LP books; Rocky Dang of Phoenix Travel, Hong Kong; and to journalist Bob Leamen for his article defending the book.

Thanks also to many travellers along the way, including Nan Cameron (USA) for moral support; the Theory of Cardboard, the Mad Hatter, Sally and Scarlet Wheat for fine company, enormous meals and translation work in Beidaihe (they'll know what I'm talking about); Regien Hasperhoven (Holland) and Konstanze Unlig (West Germany) for their charming company in Beijing; Lorelei Cotovsky (USA) for more moral support; Ester (West Germany) and his Canadian friend (sorry, forgot your name) who took me caving in Yangshuo; H.Wei and Lao Liu for fine spirits and friendship, sadly arrested; X. Ke, who survived, for the wonderful evening of minority detail; Laurie Fullerton for spark and support; Amicar Carvalho ('I came to Asia to look at all the colourful people and all they do is stand looking at me!') and Sofia Cibrao for the Portuguese Tibet connection and Macanese Christmas; Teresa van Rijswijk, cyclist extraordinaire.

– **Alan Samagalski**

Contents

Introduction

After being closed for repairs for almost 30 years the Middle Kingdom suddenly swung open its big red doors – but not quite all the way. Comrades! We must increase the production of tourists! China desperately needs the foreign exchange that tourism so conveniently provides, and it has done very well out of the deal so far. With several million tourists flocking in every year, the tallest buildings in China are, appropriately, hotels. Come back in five years time and there'll be Marco Polo Pizza Bars dotting the Great Wall.

In the late 1970s the tour groups started rolling in but the prospects for individual travel looked extremely dim. It has always been possible for individuals to travel to the PRC, but by invitation only, and until the late 1970s few managed an invite. The first regulars were people from Sweden and France (nations favoured by China) who stepped off the Trans-Siberian in 1979 when it reopened after 30 years.

In 1981 the Chinese suddenly started issuing visas to solo and uninvited travellers through a couple of their embassies overseas, but mainly through various agencies in Hong Kong. Just about anyone who wanted a visa could get one, but since there was no fanfare, news spread slowly by word of mouth. By 1983 it seemed that just about everyone who landed in Hong Kong was going to China. After all, we'd been waiting over 30 years to travel in the country unfettered by tour guides.

Nowadays the vague travellers' trails of China have been worn down to gullies tramped by baffled westerners, who notice that the image of the late '60s and early '70s – hardy peasants and sturdy workers in blue uniforms building a Communist heaven – has changed. Today they see lepers begging in Qingdao; the Shaolin Monastery selling handkerchiefs sporting kung fu fighting monks; Mao Zedong key-rings and hand-towels sold outside his mausoleum in Beijing; Shandong peasants churning up the fields with primitive ploughs; old women making offerings in Taoist temples on Tai Shan; a Christian church in Tianjin packed to the steeple for a Sunday-night service; tarts inside the Beijing Hotel; and a burgeoning black market in almost every tourist town.

Nor did China turn out to be the easiest of countries to travel in – at least not on your own. Although many early guidebooks spoke of the country in glowing terms, a lot of people quickly discovered that travel in China has its own share of hassles. Travelling in China is much easier than it used to be, and most westerners seem to be staying longer and enjoying the place much more than those who went there a few years ago. But at some stage you'll probably find yourself at the end of your tether with both the place and the people; a lot depends on where you go, how long you stay and how you travel.

Many of the hassles stem from the same problems that afflict other Asian countries: too few resources and too many people. Yet the outstanding feature of China is that, after what seems like several hundred years of stagnation, it is now making a determined effort to modernise and catch up with the west. The size of the task is staggering, and now is a unique opportunity to get some whiff of what the Communists have been doing for the last 40 years. The sleeping giant stood up in 1949 and, whatever you feel about the place, China is a country that cannot be ignored.

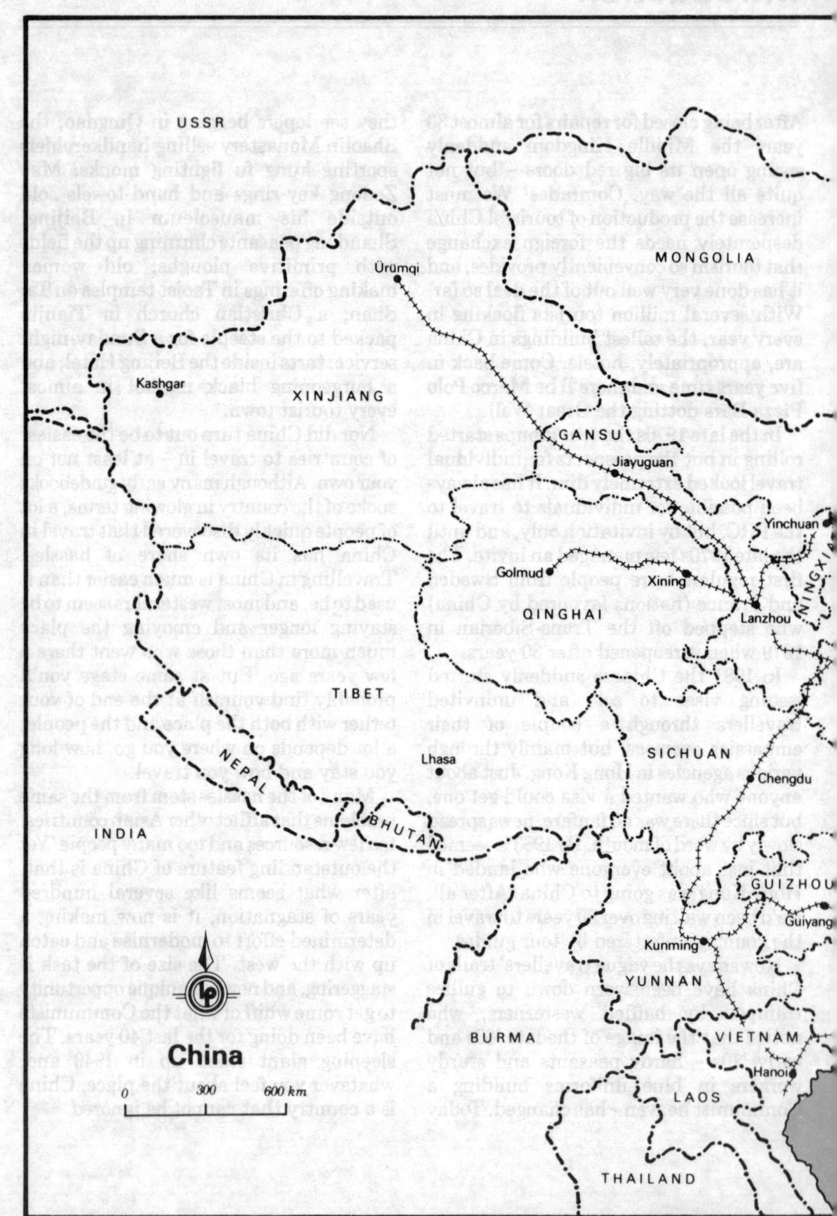
USSR
MONGOLIA
Ürümqi
Kashgar
XINJIANG
GANSU
Jiayuguan
Yinchuan
NINGXIA
Golmud
Xining
Lanzhou
QINGHAI
TIBET
NEPAL
Lhasa
SICHUAN
Chengdu
BHUTAN
INDIA
GUIZHOU
Guiyang
Kunming
YUNNAN
BURMA
VIETNAM
Hanoi
LAOS
THAILAND
China
0
300
600 km

To Ulan-Ude
To Chita
Manzhouli
HEILONGJIANG
Ulan-Bator
Harbin
INNER
MONGOLIA
Vladivostok
Changchun
JILIN
Erlian
Shenyang
LIAONING
Sea of Japan
Hohhot
Beijing
KOREA
Tokyo
HEBEI
Tianjin
Shijiazhuang
JAPAN
Taiyuan
Jinan
Yellow Sea
SHANXI
SHANDONG
Xi'an
Zhengzhou
JIANGSU
SHAANXI
HENAN
Nanjing
Hefei
HUBEI
Shanghai
SHANGHAI
ANHUI
Wuhan
ZHEJIANG
East China Sea
Nanchang
Changsha
HUNAN
JIANGXI
Fuzhou
FUJIAN
Taipei
GUANGDONG
Guangzhou
(Canton)
TAIWAN
GUANGXI
Hong Kong
Nanning
Macau
South China Sea
Haikou
Sanya
Hainan Island

Facts about the Country

CHINESE DYNASTIES

Xia	2200 – 1700 BC
Shang	1700 – 1100 BC
Zhou	1100 – 221 BC
Western Zhou	1100 – 771 BC
Eastern Zhou	770 – 256 BC
Spring & Autumn Period	770 – 476 BC
Warring States Period	476 – 221 BC
Qin	221 – 207 BC
Han	206 BC – 220 AD
Western Han	206 BC – 24 AD
Eastern Han	25 – 220 AD
Three Kingdoms Period	220 – 280
Wei	220 – 265
Shu Han	221 – 263
Wu	222 – 280
Jin	265 – 420
Western Jin	265 – 316
Eastern Jin	317 – 420
Southern & Northern Dynasties	420 – 589
Southern	
Song	420 – 479
Qi	479 – 502
Liang	502 – 557
Chen	557 – 589
Northern	
Northern Wei	386 – 534
Eastern Wei	534 – 550
Western Wei	535 – 556
Northern Qi	550 – 577
Northern Zhou	557 – 581
Sui	581 – 618
Tang	618 – 907
Five Dynasties	907 – 960
Later Liang	907 – 923
Later Tang	923 – 936
Later Jin	936 – 946
Later Han	947 – 950
Later Zhou	951 – 960
Liao	916 – 1125
Song	960 – 1279
Northern Song	960 – 1127
Southern Song	1127 – 1279
Western Xia	1038 – 1227
Jin	1115 – 1234
Yuan (Mongol)	1271 – 1368
Ming	1368 – 1644
Qing (Manchu)	1644 – 1911

CHINESE REPUBLICS

Republic of China	1912 – 1949
People's Republic of China	1949 –

HISTORY

The Chinese have traditionally claimed a history of 5000 years, yet ancient legends tell of both celestial and mortal emperors who ruled China for tens of thousands of years before this. First came the 'Three Sovereigns' who had human heads and the bodies of snakes. Next came the mortal 'Five Sovereigns' who are credited with inventing writing, establishing the institutions of marriage and family, and teaching people about agriculture and herbal medicines.

The Xia & Shang Dynasties

One of these mortal sovereigns, Yu, is said to have founded the Xia Dynasty, which held power from the 21st to the 16th century BC. The story goes that the last Xia sovereign was so tyrannical that his subjects rebelled against him. The leader of this revolt founded the Shang Dynasty which ruled until the 11th century BC. Whether the Xia actually existed is uncertain, but archaeological evidence has shown that the Shang had full-fledged urban societies built on the sites of rural villages, which in turn had developed on the sites of even older settlements of prehistoric tribes. The last despotic Shang ruler was overthrown by the king of the subject Zhou people in the west, who founded the Zhou Dynasty.

The Zhou Dynasty
The Zhou period is important for the establishment of some of the most enduring Chinese political concepts. Foremost is the 'mandate of heaven' in which heaven gives wise and virtuous leaders a mandate to rule and removes it from those who are evil and corrupt. The concept of the emperor as the 'Son of Heaven' probably originated during the Zhou Dynasty. Later, the concept of the mandate of heaven was extended to incorporate the Taoist theory that heaven expresses disapproval of bad rulers through natural disasters such as earthquakes, floods and plagues of locusts. Another refinement is the 'right of rebellion' which says that the will of heaven is expressed through the support of the people for their ruler or through their withdrawal of support. This justified rebellions against tyrannical rulers and allowed successful rebel leaders to claim the mandate of heaven to rule.

The concept of the 'dynastic cycle' followed from this. It maintains that as the moral quality of the ruling family declines, heaven passes power on to another dynasty. Thus there is an endless cycle in which governments rise, pass through a period of prosperous and just rule but gradually grow weak and corrupt until heaven has no alternative but to hand its mandate over to a new, strong and just ruler.

During the Zhou period the Chinese also developed the concept of a separate identity. Though split into separate kingdoms, they were united by a common belief in the superiority of the Shang-Zhou culture. These kingdoms came to be known as the Chung-kuo or Central States, while outsiders were considered barbarians.

The Warring States
The Zhou dominated the areas north and south of the Yellow River, and formed a feudal society which included over 1700 semi-independent feudal states. Their lords swore allegiance to the emperor and gave military aid when required. However, as the power of the Zhou royal family declined, that of the feudal states increased. Big states swallowed little ones and by 700 BC only 200 independent states existed. Continuing annexations during the Warring States Period reduced the number to a handful.

The Warring States Period was one of turmoil, incessant wars, unbridled power and great extremes of wealth and poverty – but an important time in Chinese history. One of China's most influential philosophers, Confucius, lived during this time. His attempts to find a solution to its troubles led him to uphold the Zhou Dynasty as the golden age of good government on which all rulers should model themselves. Confucius' ideas resulted in the Chinese custom of venerating the alleged good government, people and literature of a distant past.

The Chinese social structure was also changing. From 500 BC onwards a landlord class developed, distinct from the long-established aristocracy of the feudal states. One explanation for the development of the landlord class is that feudal rulers rewarded their soldiers with grants of land. Another is that the defeat of feudal lords freed large numbers of serfs and allowed them to start farming on their own. As poorer farmers foundered under the burden of increased taxes, they sold out to wealthier farmers who then rented the land to tenant farmers. The trend continued in the succeeding Qin Dynasty, during which heavy taxes ruined the peasants while the landlord class grew.

The Empire of Qin Shihuang
The Warring States Period ended in the 3rd century BC when the state of Qin united the Chinese, for the first time, into a single

empire. However, the rule of the First Exalted Emperor Qin Shihuang lasted only from 221 to 207 BC and is remembered mainly for his tyranny and cruelty.

Centralised control increased dramatically. The power of the aristocracy was broken by apportioning their land to private farmers. Books written before the Qin period were destroyed to wipe out ideas which conflicted with the emperor's. Prisoners of war and peasants who had lost their land were drafted into gangs to build public works like the Great Wall, which snaked across northern China and was designed to keep the northern nomads at bay. A network of roads was built connecting the capital with distant parts of the empire. Weights, measures, coinage and the writing system were standardised. The foundations of a large, unified Chinese empire were laid.

When Qin Shihuang died a rebellion broke out and the Qin capital (near modern-day Xian) was captured by an army led by the commoner Liu Pang. Liu took the title of emperor and established the Han Dynasty.

The Han Dynasty
The Han Dynasty lasted from 206 BC to 220 AD. During this period the pattern of the modern Chinese state was established and the empire reached its zenith.

The Han emperors were rarely, if ever, able to rule with the same degree of absolute power as Qin Shihuang. Their power was shared with powerful regional governors and princes, wealthy merchant families, the landed gentry, the emperor's immediate family, relatives, servants, palace eunuchs, and the remarkably well-developed and precisely ranked government bureaucracy.

The fifth Han emperor, Wu, came to power in 147 BC and expanded the empire to its furthest boundaries with far-flung military campaigns. Wu was an intensely autocratic monarch. He decreed that knowledge of Confucian texts and teachings be a prerequisite for appointment to government positions. A university was

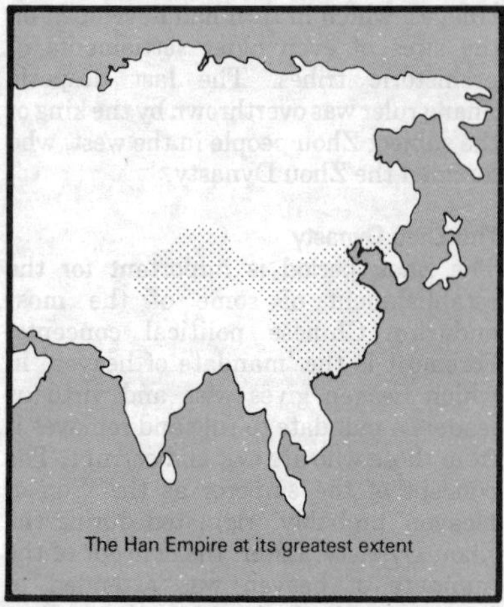
The Han Empire at its greatest extent

set up in the capital to teach Confucianism, and examinations in the Confucian classics were instituted. Confucianism became the basis of education and admission to the Chinese civil service for the next 2000 years.

The Problem of Foreigners
Mountains and deserts isolated China from continental neighbours, but the expansion of the empire into Central Asia brought the Han Chinese into contact with numerous foreigners. Diplomatic missions even introduced the Han to the Roman Empire, and to the Greek settlements left over from Alexander's invasion in the mountains of north-west India. However, these contacts had little or no impact on the Chinese world.

The Shang and Zhou had their own customs for dealing with those outside the Central States. The 'barbarians' were expected to 'come and be transformed' by contact with the 'higher' Chinese civilisation. They were expected to 'observe the rites' of the Chinese court and to 'offer tribute'. In return they would be treated courteously and presented with gifts.

The Chinese continued to view themselves as a superior race through the later Han period, but the awkward fact remained that the Han armies could never quite defeat the barbarians who plagued the empire's boundaries. Often they were forced to receive the barbarian ambassadors as guests or equals, but these receptions were still officially recorded as the visits of vassals who brought tribute.

Invasions & Migrations

Strains on the empire's economy and a succession of weak rulers led to power struggles between powerful regional rulers and their armies. The Han empire finally split into three separate kingdoms in 220 AD.

The rivalry between these kingdoms invited invasion by China's northern neighbours and caused great migrations of Chinese people. However, the concept of a unified empire remained and there were always rulers who aspired or claimed to be China's legitimate sovereign. During this period the north came under the control of the Turkish-speaking Tobas, while the south split into separate Chinese kingdoms.

The conquest of northern China by the foreigners resulted in two interesting developments. The first was the growing power of Buddhism, probably introduced to China by Indian merchants accompanied by Buddhist priests. It boomed between the 3rd and 6th centuries when the northern invaders (many of whom were acquainted with the religion before they came to China) patronised the Buddhist monks, partly to build up a group of educated officials who were not Confucians.

The second development was the absorption of the northern 'barbarians' into Chinese culture. The Toba eventually disappeared as a race, either rejoining the Turkish tribes in the north or successfully assimilating the Chinese way of life. The seduction of the northern invaders by the 'civilised' style of Chinese life was repeated later with the Manchus and Mongols.

The Sui & Tang Dynasties

The country was finally reunited in the 6th century under the Sui Dynasty, founded by a general of Chinese-Toba descent who had usurped the northern throne and conquered southern China.

The Sui Dynasty was short lived and in 618 AD the throne was again usurped, this time by a noble family of Chinese-Toba descent who founded the Tang Dynasty. The Chinese now look on the Tang Dynasty as a golden age of Chinese power and prosperity, and a high point in culture and creativity.

At the height of Tang power, their capital at Changan (on the site of modern-day Xian) was one of the greatest cities in the world. It held a million people within its walls and perhaps another million outside, and was a thriving imperial metropolis of commerce, administration, religion and culture. The Chinese empire covered the greatest area since the Han Dynasty. The government was highly centralised, with power concentrated increasingly in the hands of the emperor.

The Sui had instituted a nationwide examination system which enabled people from all over China to serve in the government bureaucracy in Changan; this system

The Tang Emperor Li Shih-Min

was continued and developed by the Tang. The Sui had also improved communications by building canals linking strategic parts of the empire. Canal links were further developed during the Tang Dynasty, and roads and inns were built for officials, travellers, merchants and pilgrims.

These communication systems radiated out to the sea ports and caravan routes which connected China to the rest of the world. The capital became a centre for international trade and the home of a large foreign community. Numerous religions established temples and mosques, including Islam, the Zoroastrian sect of Persia, and the Nestorian Christian sect of Syria. During this period China was exposed to a greater variety of foreign cultures than at any time until the present. Nevertheless the foreigners had to comply with the tribute system, and the Tang government recorded official meetings with foreigners in terms of vassals giving tribute.

The Tang system of government was to have a profound influence on future dynasties. The Ming modelled themselves on the Tang and in turn were scrupulously copied by the Qing. At the apex of the social order was the emperor, the Son of Heaven who maintained the balance between people and the forces of nature. He was the 'first farmer' of a peasant empire and the ceremonial head of a ruling class. He was the guardian of the state ideology of Confucianism as well as the patron of Buddhism and Taoism. He presided over government policy and state affairs with his ministers and other high officials, and honoured officials and foreign dignitaries with audiences and banquets. He took part in devising strategy and issued orders and commissions to his officers during wartime. He was also the stud of the well-stocked harem. The day-to-day task of government was handled by the emperor's personal staff, the palace eunuchs and the huge government bureaucracy.

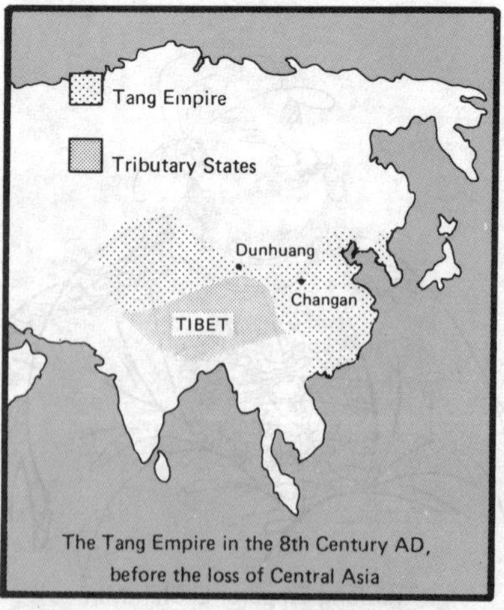

Tang Empire
Tributary States
Dunhuang
Changan
TIBET

The Tang Empire in the 8th Century AD, before the loss of Central Asia

China's Economic Revolution

Towards the end of the 8th century the Tang Dynasty started to decline. Tang armies suffered defeats at the hands of provincial warlords and Tibetan and Turkish invaders. The Tang gradually began to lose control of the transport networks and the tax collection system on which their power and prosperity depended, and the dynasty finally fell in 907 AD. China once again split into a number of independent states.

Nevertheless there was rapid economic development. When Marco Polo arrived in China in the 13th century he found huge, prosperous cities on a scale unlike any in Europe, an orderly society and large scale inter-regional trade. The south had split into separate kingdoms but remained peaceful, and trade and commerce developed rapidly in the absence of central government controls.

The empire was reformed in 960 AD by a southern general who founded the Song Dynasty using political skill rather than military means. Peace helped maintain the prosperous economic structure. In the wake of another invasion from the north in the 12th century, the Song court was forced to flee south, where Hangzhou became a highly developed commercial, political and cultural centre.

Throughout the 'Southern Song' period the south remained under the control of the Han Chinese, and the north in the hands of the northern invaders. Secure behind the Great Wall, both parties were oblivious to the fury that was about to be unleashed with the beginning of the Mongol invasion.

The Mongol Reign (Yuan Dynasty)

Beyond the Great Wall lay the Gobi Desert. Beyond that lay only slightly more hospitable grassland stretching all the way from Manchuria to Hungary, inhabited by nomadic Turk and Mongol tribes who endured a harsh life as shepherds and horse-breeders. The Mongols, despised for what was considered their ignorance and poverty, occasionally went to war with the Chinese but were always defeated.

In 1206 after 20 years of internal war, Genghis Khan united the roaming Mongol tribes into a new nation, the 'Blue Mongols', under the protection of the heavenly sky. He began the invasion of China in 1211, penetrated the Great Wall two years later and took Beijing in 1215. Stubborn resistance from the Chinese rulers, conflict within the Mongolian camp, and campaigns in Russia delayed the conquest of Song China for many years. Not until 1279 did the grandson of Genghis, Kublai Khan, bring southern China under his sway.

The Mongols made Beijing their capital, and Kublai Khan became the first emperor of the Yuan Dynasty. Kublai's government in China concentrated power in the cities and towns. The Mongols improved the road system linking China with Russia and promoted trade throughout the empire and with Europe. They instituted a famine relief scheme and expanded the canal system which brought food from the countryside to the cities.

Overall the Mongols had little effect on the Chinese and like the Toba before them, adopted many of the ways of their conquered subjects. The Mongol rule was, however, significant because it generated European interest in the Far East. The Mongol armies had swept into Eastern Europe and the whole continent was on the verge of an invasion. The invasion was called off at the last minute but it forced the Europeans to take notice of Asia. Trade and contacts across Asia were made easier by Mongol supremacy since the boundaries between nations were cut. It was the China of the Mongols that Europeans like Marco Polo visited, and their books revealed the splendours of Asia to an amazed Europe.

The Ming Dynasty

Kublai Khan died in 1294, the last Khan to rule over a united Mongol empire. The Mongol reign over China was rapidly disintegrating by the 1350s, and several rebel armies vied for power. The chief contender was Zhu Yuanzhang, a man of poor peasant origins, whose powerful army secured most of southern China before attacking Beijing and driving out the Mongols.

Zhu Yuanzhang proclaimed himself the first emperor of the Ming Dynasty and

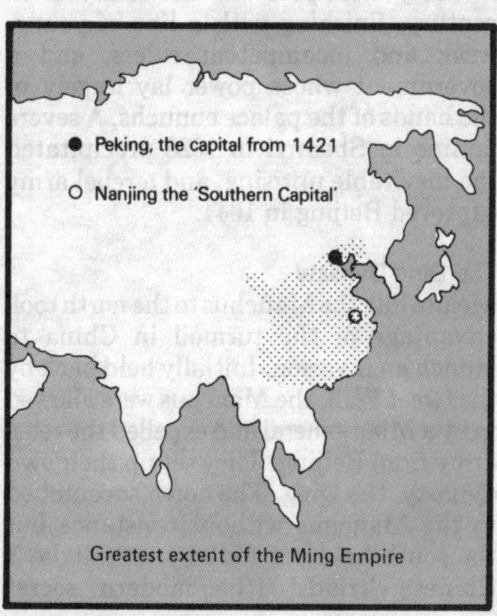

Greatest extent of the Ming Empire

took the name Hong Wu. He established Nanjing as the capital, far from the north and safe from attack. Hong Wu set about organising a new government structure. Buddhism and Taoism were made state religions, the competitive examination system to select officials was revived, and the civil government was modelled on the Tang Dynasty system.

Hong Wu's rule is noted, however, for two developments which ultimately weakened China. The first was a dramatic increase in the power of the emperor versus the bureaucracy; Hong Wu's rule was almost totalitarian, stifling intellectual thought and personal initiative. The second was the increased isolation of China from the rest of the world; the Ming emperors saw China as culturally superior and economically self-sufficient, with nothing to learn from other countries. The chief exception was the third Ming emperor, Yong Le, who launched massive maritime expeditions to distant parts of the world. These came to an end when he died, and no more colonies, commercial bases or permanent contacts with other countries were established.

China was beginning to stagnate just as Europe was entering its most dynamic phase since the Roman Empire. The Ming Dynasty collapsed in the early 17th century, finishing with a line of young, weak and incompetent rulers, and a government whose power lay largely in the hands of the palace eunuchs. A severe famine in Shaanxi in 1628 precipitated the inevitable uprising, and a rebel army captured Beijing in 1644.

The Qing Dynasty

Meanwhile the Manchus to the north took advantage of the turmoil in China to launch an invasion. Initially held back by the Great Wall, the Manchus were allowed in by a Ming general and expelled the rebel army from Beijing. They set up their own dynasty, the Qing. The north succumbed to the Manchus without resistance but the south held out for 20 years. Today's Chinese 'triads' (the modern secret societies generally thought to be involved in criminal activity, especially drug trafficking), are actually the descendants of secret societies originally set up to resist the northern barbarians.

Although the Manchus concentrated power in their own hands and alienated the Han Chinese, the reign of the Qing emperors from 1663 to 1796 was a period of great prosperity. The throne was occupied by three of the most able rulers China has known: Kangxi, Yongcheng and Qianlong. The Qing expanded the empire to its greatest limits since the Han Dynasty, and Mongolia and Tibet came under Qing suzerainty. Reduced taxation and massive flood control and irrigation projects benefited the peasants.

The emperors' exceptional competence led to a further concentration of power in their hands, but the responsibilities of the throne became too great for the successors of Qianlong. Like the Mongols, the Manchu rulers succumbed to the ways of the Chinese and soon became culturally indistinguishable from them, modelling their government on the Ming Dynasty. Thus the isolationism and intellectual conservatism of the Ming was passed on to

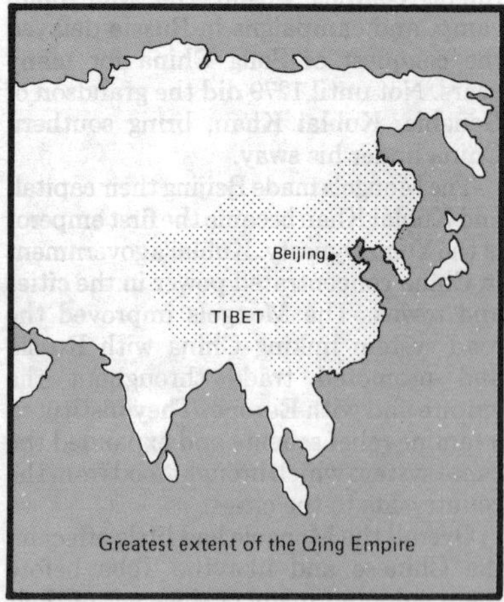

Greatest extent of the Qing Empire

the Qing. China continued to be an inward-looking nation, oblivious to the technological and scientific revolutions taking place in Europe. The coming of Europeans to China hastened the fall of the Qing and helped mould the China we know today.

The Coming of the West

The Europeans couldn't be held back by the Great Wall – they came by sea. The first European ships to land in China were those of the Portuguese who arrived in 1516. Possibly as a reward for clearing nearby waters of pirates, they were permitted to set up base at Macau in 1557. Over the following century the British, Dutch and Spanish all landed in China.

The trade overtures of the foreign merchants were initially rebuffed by the Qing government, but it finally opened the port of Canton to foreign trade in 1685. The foreigners were kept at arm's length, far from the political centre in the north. Trade flourished mainly in China's favour – although the foreigners had other ideas.

In 1773 the British started selling Indian opium to the Chinese in an effort to even up the balance of trade, since Britain was selling China some wool and spices while buying great quantities of tea, silk and porcelain. With opium addiction increasing and Chinese silver fast disappearing from the country, the emperor thundered an edict in 1800 banning the trade, which the foreigners, Chinese merchants and corrupt officials duly ignored.

More drastic measures were taken in 1839 when the Chinese seized 20,000 chests of opium in Canton. When subsequent negotiations broke down the British attacked Canton in the first of what became known as the 'Opium Wars'. Altogether there were four Opium Wars, each launched by the westerners on some minor pretext. French troops joined the British in the Third Opium War, and the Russians and Americans lent naval support. The fourth and last Opium War was fought from 1859 to 1860.

Each war was ended by an 'Unequal Treaty'. These, along with subsequent treaties, opened more Chinese ports to foreign ships, gave foreigners the right to settle in certain areas and later let them travel freely in China. The Chinese were forced to pay large war indemnities, customs tariffs on imported western goods were severely reduced, western diplomats were permitted to take up residence in Beijing, freedom of movement was eventually accorded to missionaries, and foreigners were granted immunity to Chinese laws. The Russians seized the area of Siberia east of the Amur River in 1860, and the French seized Cochin-China from Annam, part of Vietnam today and over which the Chinese claimed suzerainty. By 1860 the opening of China was virtually complete.

The Taiping Rebellion

In the second half of the 19th century there were two dramatic events which could have halted this process of decay. One was the Boxer movement, a patriotic peasant uprising. The other was the Taiping movement founded by Hong Xiuquan, a native of Guangdong. Convinced he was on a mission from God and professing to be the younger brother of Jesus Christ, Hong and his followers preached Christianity while smashing Buddhist, Taoist and Confucian idols and razing their temples to the ground. Hong called his movement the 'Heavenly Kingdom of the Great Peace', and attempts by the Qing to suppress it only led him to declare open rebellion in 1851.

Marching north from Guangdong, the Taipings captured numerous towns on the Yangtse River; by 1853 they had captured Nanjing and brought southern China under their control. The army comprised 600,000 men and 500,000 women, and was a highly organised and strictly disciplined movement that adhered only to the Christian god. Gambling, opium, tobacco and alcohol were forbidden. Women were appointed as administrators and officials, and the practice of foot-binding was

Taiping coin

abolished along with slavery, prostitution, arranged marriages and polygamy. The peasants were attracted by their policy of agrarian reform and fairer taxation. In many ways the Taipings were a forerunner of the Communist movement.

However, the Taipings failed to gain the support of the western powers, who until then had remained neutral. In fact, the success of the Taipings probably worried the westerners. It was more expedient for them to deal with a corrupt and weak Qing government than with the strong, united Taipings. After 1860 the western powers allied with the Qing and a counter-offensive began. By 1864 the Taipings had retreated to their capital city of Nanjing. A Qing army aided by British army regulars and European and American mercenaries besieged and captured the city, slaughtering the defenders. Hong Xiuquan committed suicide and the rebellion ended.

Decline of the Qing

The years after the Taiping Rebellion were a time of further intrusion into China by the foreign powers. The Qing government grew progressively weaker and the lot of the peasants became increasingly miserable.

In 1861, a time when China needed a strong government more than ever, six-year-old Emperor Guangxu ascended the throne. Real power remained in the hands of his aunt the Empress Dowager Wu Cixi, a former concubine. Wu Cixi saw reform and modernisation as a threat to the conservative power base of the Qing Dynasty. Clinging to this belief, she spent the next 48 years presiding over the disintegration of China.

China's own colonial empire began to break up. A war with France from 1883 to 1885 ended Chinese suzerainty in Indo-China and allowed the French to maintain control of Vietnam and eventually gain control of Laos and Cambodia (Kampuchea). The British occupied Burma. In 1895 Japan forced the Chinese out of Korea and made them cede Taiwan. Britain, France, Germany and Russia rushed in to map out 'spheres of influence' in a spree of land-grabbing. By 1898 they were on the verge of carving up China; this was prevented by an American proposal for an 'open-door' policy which would leave all of China open to trade with any foreign power.

Economically the Chinese government fared disastrously. China was in debt to the western powers and Japan, and began to raise taxes, which added to the general misery of the peasants. Coastal trade by foreign ships developed at the expense of the Chinese junk trade. Foreigners built railways and telegraph lines and opened coal mines and ironworks but used them to exploit the country. Missionaries arrived in large numbers, threatening traditional Chinese society with foreign religion, science, education and morals. Chinese students returning from study abroad brought anti-Manchu sentiment and European-influenced political ideologies.

An attempt at 'self-strengthening' in 1881 resulted in the building of naval yards, arsenals and railways, proved a failure when the supposedly modern Chinese army was defeated in the Sino-Japanese War of the mid-1890s. Then in 1898 the imperial court made a dramatic attempt to halt China's disintegration. Emperor Guangxu had come under the influence of the reformer Kang Youwei, who pressed for modernisation and liberalisation of China if it were to survive intact. The 'Hundred Days Reform' of 1898 was opposed by Cixi. The emperor tried to have her arrested but his military officials changed sides, imprisoned him, returned Cixi to power, and executed the emperor's supporters. Kang escaped to Japan.

The Boxer Rebellion
For almost 40 years the foreigners in China had been doing very much as they pleased. Bizarre retribution came with the Boxer Rebellion, the second event which might radically have changed the course of history.

The Chinese name for the Boxers clumsily translates as 'Righteous and Harmonious Fists'. They began in Shandong Province in the last years of the 19th century as an anti-Manchu organisation supported by the peasantry. At that time Shandong was in the grip of severe economic misery caused by war, floods, drought and famine. The 'boxers' developed a form of exercise aimed at harmonising mind and body in preparation for combat, and added rituals so that spirits would possess their bodies and make them invincible in battle.

The Qing failed to help the Shandong peasants, and the foreigners were blamed for disregarding the gods and angering the spirits. The slogan of the Boxers, 'Overthrow the Qing; destroy the foreigner', had immediate appeal. The Boxers suffered a heavy defeat by government troops in October 1899, but the Qing court saw the strength and popularity of the Boxers as an instrument to throw the foreigners out of China.

Towards the end of 1899 the Boxers and the government formed an anti-foreigner alliance. The Boxers began to massacre Chinese Christians, missionaries and other foreigners, destroying churches and ripping up railroads. They converged on Beijing in 1900 and laid siege to the foreign legations' compound. The imperial government declared war on the allied armies of Russia, Britain, Germany, France, the US, Japan, Italy and Austria.

The legations, however, held out until a relief force of foreign troops arrived to end the siege and put down the rebellion. The imperial court fled to Xian, and the Boxers were dispersed. Although the foreign powers punished China with executions of government officials and Boxer leaders and exacted a huge indemnity, they did not break up the Chinese empire. Instead they preserved the dynasty with Cixi as ruler, thus maintaining their own supremacy. The Chinese had once again been defeated and foreign privileges preserved.

The Fall of the Qing
With the defeat of the Boxers even the empress realised that China was too weak to survive without reform. The civil service examinations based on the irrelevant 1000-year-old Confucian doctrines were abolished, but other court-sponsored reforms proved to be a sham. By now secret societies aimed at bringing down the Qing Dynasty were being set up all over the country and by Chinese abroad. In 1905 several of these merged to form the Alliance for Chinese Revolution, headed by the Cantonese Dr Sun Yatsen.

The empress dowager died in 1908 and the throne was ascended by two-year-old Emperor Puyi. The power of the central government rapidly fell apart. When the court announced the nationalisation of the railways in 1911, the move was viewed by provincial governors and wealthy merchants as an attempt to restrict their autonomy. An army coup in Wuhan seized control of the city, and the heads of many other provinces declared their loyalty to the rebels. By the year's end, most of southern China had repudiated Qing rule and given its support to the Alliance for Chinese Revolution. On 1 January 1912,

Sun Yatsen was proclaimed president of the Chinese Republic.

Early Days of the Republic

When China became a republic in 1912 it was in name only. Sun's government in Nanjing had no substantial army with which to enforce its authority. In the north power was held by the former chief of the imperial armies, Yuan Shikai, who planned to set himself up as emperor until his grandiose ambitions were cut short by his sudden death in 1916.

The combination of internal upheaval and foreign imperialism began to make China's survival as an autonomous nation seem unlikely. The gravest threat came from Japan. During WW I Japan had joined the Allies and taken Germany's port of Qingdao along with German ships, railways and industries in the Shandong Peninsula. In 1915 Japan presented China with the 'Twenty-One Demands' which would have reduced China to a Japanese colony. Under the threat of a Japanese military advance out of Shandong, Yuan Shikai was forced to accept the economic concessions. However, some of the more extreme political demands, such as attaching Japanese 'political advisers' and 'police' to the provincial governments, were resisted.

Meanwhile the warlords, provincial military leaders left over from the Qing, controlled much of China and were backed by their own armies. Supplies and requisitions for their armies were taken from the peasants, the people least able to resist. As they became increasingly destitute, the peasants were forced to join the warlord armies in order to survive by looting others. Militarism and the consequent decline in productivity led to increasing poverty – a familiar situation in China.

The Intellectual Revolution

The intelligentsia in China continued to search for solutions to China's crisis. Following Yuan's death, his opponents returned from abroad. The conservative Confucian order came under attack once again and the struggle for a new ideology which could save China resumed.

The mainstream of the intellectual revolution came from Beijing University, although in nearly all the major cities and towns there were many political organisations with their own journals. One of the leaders of the movement, Li Dazhao, worked as a librarian at Beijing University. Li became a founding member of the Chinese Communist Party and is still regarded as one of the best Chinese interpreters of Marxism; he also gave the young Mao Zedong a job in the university library and influenced Mao's political beliefs.

In 1918 Li started a society for the study of Marxism which was joined by Mao and by Zhang Guodao, a student leader at the university and later a founder of the Communist Party. Chen Duxiu, dean at the university until 1919, was another Beijing intellectual who organised Marxist study groups throughout China and also became a founder of the Chinese Communist Party.

In Tianjin a Marxist study group was started by a young scholar, Zhou Enlai. When Mao returned from Beijing to his native Changsha he started his own Marxist study group, whose members included Liu Shaoqi. In Hebei Province the 'Social Welfare Society' was formed with Lin Biao as a member.

In May 1919, the intellectual revolution was given impetus when the news reached China that the Allies at the Versailles Peace Conference had agreed to support Japan's claims to German concessions on Chinese territory. Student protests against the Japanese, and against the warlord regime in Beijing which had supported the treaty, were broken up by the police but did not end there. A wave of nationalist, anti-Japanese, anti-foreign, anti-warlord feeling swept through the country's intellectuals. The aims of the movement were clear: unite China, destroy the powerful warlords, establish a central government, throw off the shackles of the unequal treaties forced on China in the 19th century, and modernise sufficiently to cope with foreign powers. The question of how this was to be done, however, remained unanswered.

The Kuomintang & the Communists

After initial setbacks Sun Yatsen and the Kuomintang (Nationalist) Party – the political party which had emerged as the dominant political force after the fall of the Qing – managed to establish a secure base in southern China, and began training a National Revolutionary Army with which to challenge the northern warlords.

Since 1920 Russians who had taken part in the Bolshevik Revolution came to China as representatives of the Soviet government and the Communist International (Comintern), the international body dedicated to world revolution. Talks between the Comintern representatives, Li Dazhao and Chen Duxiu, eventually resulted in several Chinese Marxist groups banding together to form a Chinese Communist Party (CCP) at a meeting in Shanghai in 1921.

In 1922 the CCP members were urged by the Moscow Comintern representatives to join the Kuomintang. There was a great deal of uneasiness within the CCP about doing this since they feared the Kuomintang was interested only in a national revolution which would unify the country and eliminate foreign interference, not in a wider social revolution. The Russians insisted that a social revolution could not occur without a national revolution first. Russian military, economic and political advisers were sent to China between 1923 and 1927 to help the Kuomintang, perhaps primarily to help form a buttress against aggressive Japanese ambitions on the Soviet Union's eastern flank. Under threat of the withdrawal of Russian support, the CCP joined the Kuomintang.

Sun Yatsen's death from cancer in 1925 removed the unifying influence in the faction-ridden Kuomintang Party. A power struggle emerged between those in the political wing who were sympathetic to the social reform policies of the Communists, and those in the military wing led by Chiang Kaishek. Chiang commanded the National Revolutionary Army and had strengthened his claim as Sun's legitimate heir by marrying the sister of Madame Sun Yatsen. He opposed social reform and wished to preserve the capitalist state, dominated by a privileged elite of wealthy family members and their associates, and supported by a military dictatorship.

Chiang Kaishek

The Peasant Movement

Under the direction of Communist Party member Peng Bai, the Kuomintang set up a Peasant Training Institute in Canton where hundreds of potential peasant leaders from Guangdong, Hunan and other provinces trained for six months before returning to their home provinces to organise the peasants. The peasant organisations grew much faster than their urban industrial counterparts, and began pressing for radical changes. They demanded that land rent be reduced to only 25% of the crop, that high taxes be removed, that taking land as payment for debts be prohibited, that farm labourers be paid more, and that the landlords' private armies and gangs be abolished. Impressed by the strength of the peasant movement, Mao Zedong, who taught at the Institute around 1925 or 1926, tried to persuade the Kuomintang leadership that the greatest potential for social revolution lay in the countryside. He was ignored as attention was focused on the impending 'Northern Expedition'.

The Shanghai Coup

In 1926, in an effort to unify China, the Kuomintang embarked on the Northern Expedition to wrest power from the remaining warlords. Chiang Kaishek was appointed commander in chief by the Kuomintang and the Communists. One force of the National Revolutionary Army (NRA) moved up through Hunan to take the city of Wuhan, which became the seat of the Kuomintang government. Meanwhile Chiang Kaishek's force captured Nanchang.

Following this victory Chiang tried to persuade the Russian advisers and the political and military leaders of the Kuomintang to join him, excluding the Communists. There was now an obvious struggle for power within the Kuomintang. With the NRA about to move on Shanghai, Chiang took the opportunity to put down both the Communists and his opponents in the Kuomintang.

Shanghai was under the control of a local warlord, but his strength was being undermined by a powerful industrial movement organised in the city by the Communists under Liu Shaoqi and Zhou Enlai. Kuomintang strategy called for the Shanghai workers to take over key installations in the city while the Kuomintang armies advanced on it. In March 1927 a general strike was called and Shanghai industry shut down; police stations and military arsenals were seized and 5000 workers were armed. The Kuomintang Army then entered the city.

Supported by the Shanghai industrialists who were worried about the trade union movement, and by foreigners who feared the loss of trade and privileges, Chiang let loose a reign of terror against the Communists and their sympathisers. With the help of Shanghai's underworld leaders and with financial backing from Shanghai bankers and foreigners, Chiang armed hundreds of gangsters, dressed them in Kuomintang uniforms and launched a surprise attack overnight on the workers' militia. About 5000 Shanghai Communists were killed. Massacres of Communists and various anti-Chiang factions followed in other Chinese cities. Zhou Enlai managed to escape by a hair's breadth. Li Dazhao was executed by slow strangulation.

The political leadership of the Kuomintang was thrown into turmoil once again. Since the military supported Chiang Kaishek, the Wuhan government was forced to bow to him. By the middle of 1928 the Northern Expedition had reached Beijing and a national government was established with Chiang holding both military and political leadership.

The Kuomintang Government

Even at the end of the Northern Expedition only about half the country was under direct Kuomintang control; the rest was ruled by local warlords. Despite these and other problems Chiang was obsessed with his campaigns against the Communists, which he continued in the 1930s.

Any prospects of social and rural reform under the Kuomintang were lost. In the cities labourers were treated little better than beasts of burden; children were used as slave labour in factories, standing at machines for 12 or 13 hours a day and sleeping under them at night; women and children were sold as concubines, prostitutes or domestic slaves; the destitute and starving died on the streets of Chinese cities and strikes were ruthlessly suppressed by foreign and Chinese factory owners.

In the countryside the Kuomintang 'government' consisted of a Kuomintang-appointed county magistrate who ruled in collusion with the landlords and moneylenders and their private armed guards.

Attempts at reform were blocked because it was not in their interest to reduce rents or allow the establishment of rural banks with low interest rates for peasants. They used money made available by the government at low interest and lent it at higher interest to the poor farmers. If rural reformers persuaded farmers to use fertiliser to increase yield, the farmers had to borrow money at high interest rates to buy fertiliser – and if a better crop resulted the local merchants simply lowered the buying price. Peasant protests were often dealt with by the private armies and gangs retained by many landlords, while the peasants' wives and children were taken into the landlords' households as domestic slaves in lieu of debts.

Tax collectors had police powers and could imprison peasants for failing to pay taxes and rent. Peasants who did not want to go to jail were forced to borrow money at interest rates of up to 700% a year. In some instances land taxes were collected 60 years in advance. Not only were most peasants destitute, they were terrified of taking any step which would bring them into conflict with armed authority. The Communists quickly realised that the only way to win a social revolution was with guns.

The Civil War

After the massacre of 1927 the remaining Communist forces staged insurrections in several towns. Rebel units of the Kuomintang under Zhou Enlai and Zhu De (who held a high-ranking post in the Kuomintang Army but was sympathetic to the Communists) seized Nanchang and held it for several days until they were driven out by loyal Kuomintang troops. The revolt was a fiasco, but it marked the beginning of the Red Army.

In Changsha, Mao Zedong organised an uprising of the peasantry, miners and rebel Kuomintang soldiers. Mao's army moved south through Hunan, fighting Kuomintang troops, and climbed into the Jinggang Mountains on the Hunan-

Stamps showing the 90th anniversary of the birth of Mao Zedong

Jiangxi border. They were reinforced by Zhu De's troops, and a strategy was mapped out to first consolidate control over the Jinggang area and then slowly expand from there.

However, the Party hierarchy, which was led by Li Lisan and followed orthodox Marxist theory that revolution must be based in the cities and towns, ordered the Communist army to attack Nanchang and Changsha. After two costly defeats at Changsha in 1930, Mao and Zhu refused to obey Li's orders to attack Changsha again. There ensued a brief Party war in which a number of anti-Maoists were killed or imprisoned. From then on the power base of the revolution was moved squarely to the countryside and the peasants.

Communist-led uprisings in other parts of the country brought various parts of the country under their control. However, the Communist armies were still small, with limited resources and weapons. The Communists adopted a strategy of guerrilla warfare, emphasising mobility and rapid concentration and deployment of forces for short attacks on the enemy, followed by swift separation once the attack was over. Pitched battles were avoided except where their force was overwhelmingly superior. The strategy was summed up in a four-line slogan:

The enemy advances, we retreat;
The enemy camps, we harass;
The enemy tires; we attack;
The enemy retreats; we pursue.

By 1930 the ragged Communist forces had been turned into an army of perhaps 40,000 and such a serious challenge to the Kuomintang, that Chiang had to hurl a number of extermination campaigns against them. He was defeated each time, and the Red Army expanded its territory.

The Long March

Chiang's fifth extermination campaign began in October 1933, when the Communists suddenly changed their strategy. Mao and Zhu's authority was being undermined by other members of the Party who advocated meeting Chiang's troops in pitched battles, but this strategy proved disastrous. By October 1934 the Communists had suffered heavy losses and were hemmed into a small area in Jiangxi.

On the brink of defeat, the Communists decided to retreat from Jiangxi and march north to Shaanxi. In China's northern mountains the Communists controlled an area which spread across Shaanxi, Gansu and Ningxia, held by troops under an ex-Kuomintang officer who had sided with the Communists after the 1927 massacres.

There was not one 'Long March' but several, as various Communist armies in the south made their way to Shaanxi. The most famous was the march from Jiangxi Province which began in October 1934, took a year to complete and covered 5000 miles over some of the world's most inhospitable terrain. On the way the Communists confiscated the property of officials, landlords and tax-collectors, redistributed the land to the peasants, armed thousands of peasants with weapons captured from the Kuomintang, and left soldiers behind to organise guerrilla groups to harass the enemy. Of the 90,000 who started in Jiangxi only 20,000 made it to Shaanxi. Fatigue, sickness, exposure, enemy attacks and desertion all took their toll.

The march proved, however, that the Chinese peasants could fight if they were given a method, an organisation, leadership, hope and weapons. It brought together many people who later held top positions in the People's Republic after 1949, including Mao Zedong, Zhou Enlai, Zhu De, Lin Biao, Deng Xiaoping and Liu Shaoqi. It also established Mao as the paramount leader of the Communist movement; during the march a meeting of the Communist Party hierarchy recognised Mao's overall leadership and he assumed supreme responsibility for strategy.

The Japanese Invasion

In September 1931 the Japanese occupied the potentially wealthy but underdeveloped area of Manchuria, setting up a puppet state with the last Chinese emperor, Puyi, as the symbolic head.

Despite the Japanese invasion Chiang was obsessed with putting down the Communists. 'Pacification first, resistance afterwards' was his slogan. The Communists believed that unless the Japanese were defeated there would be no China left at all, and advocated an anti-Japanese alliance with the Kuomintang. Instead, Chiang launched his extermination campaigns, the last of which forced the Communists to retreat to Shaanxi.

At the end of 1936 Chiang flew to Xian to oversee yet another extermination campaign against the Communists. The deadlock was broken in an unexpected manner. In what became known as the 'Xian Incident' Chiang was taken prisoner by his own generals, led by Marshal Zhang Xueliang who commanded an army of Manchurian troops. Chiang was forced to call off his extermination campaign and to form an anti-Japanese alliance with the Communists. In 1937 the Japanese launched an all-out invasion and by 1939 had overrun eastern China. The Kuomintang government retreated west to Chongqing.

At the end of 1941 America entered the war, after the Japanese bombed Pearl Harbor. The Americans hoped to use the Chinese to tie up as many Japanese troops as possible, and to use China as a base for attacking Japanese shipping and troops in South-East Asia. Chiang hoped the Americans would win the war against the Japanese and provide him with the munitions he required to finally destroy the Communists.

From 1938 until the end of the war the Japanese were never seriously harassed by the Kuomintang troops, as Chiang attempted to save his troops for renewed attacks on the Communists once the Americans had defeated the Japanese. The American General Joseph Stilwell, who was sent to China in 1942 by President Roosevelt to improve the combat effectiveness of the Chinese army, concluded that 'the Chinese government is a structure based on fear and favour in the hands of an ignorant, arbitrary and stubborn man . . .' and that its military effort since 1938 was 'practically zero'.

Defeat of the Kuomintang

Since the defeat of Japan was in America's interest, Chiang saw no need to maintain his alliance with the Communists, reasoning that the Americans would support him regardless.

The alliance collapsed in 1941 when Kuomintang troops ambushed the rear detachment of one of the Communist armies. This non-combat detachment was annihilated and its commander, Ye Ding, was imprisoned in Chongqing. Chiang then blockaded Communist forces to prevent them from receiving supplies. Although the Communists did not directly retaliate, clashes between the Kuomintang and the Communists were frequent, often developing into all-out civil war.

Nevertheless the Communist armies and guerrillas expanded into areas occupied by the Japanese. When the war against Japan ended in 1945 the Communist army numbered 900,000 and was backed by militia and active supporters numbering millions. With the surrender of Japan in 1945, a dramatic struggle for position began as the Kuomintang and Communist forces gathered in Manchuria for the final showdown.

By 1948 the Communists had captured so much American-supplied Kuomintang equipment and recruited so many Kuomintang soldiers that they equalled the Kuomintang in both numbers and supplies. Three great battles were fought in 1948 and 1949 which saw the Kuomintang defeated and hundreds of thousands of Kuomintang troops join the Communists. The Communists moved south and crossed the Yangtse; by October all the major cities in southern China had fallen to them.

In Beijing on 1 October 1949, Mao Zedong proclaimed the foundation of the People's Republic of China. Chiang Kaishek fled to the island of Formosa (Taiwan), taking with him the entire gold reserves of the country and what was left of his air force and navy. Some two million refugees and soldiers from the mainland crowded onto the island. President Truman ordered a protective American naval blockade to prevent an attack from the mainland, as the United States continued to recognise Chiang's delusions as the legitimate ruler of all China.

Early Years of the People's Republic

The People's Republic started as a bankrupt nation. The economy was in chaos following Chiang's flight to Taiwan with China's gold reserves. The country had just 12,000 miles of railways and 48,000 miles of usable roads, all in bad condition. Irrigation works had broken down and livestock and animal populations were greatly reduced. Industrial production fell to 50% of the pre-war days and agricultural output plummeted.

With the Communist takeover China seemed to become a different country. Unified by the elation of victory and the immensity of the task before them, and further bonded by the Korean War and the necessity to defend the new regime from possible American invasion, the Communists made the 1950s a dynamic period. The country's obsessive haste to catch up with history and become a great nation was awesome.

By 1953 inflation had been halted, industrial production had been restored to pre-war levels and the land had been confiscated from the landlords and redistributed to the peasants. In the mid-1950s industry was nationalised and farmers were encouraged to pool land and equipment in mutual-aid teams and co-operatives with a view to using resources more efficiently and increasing production.

35th anniversary of the founding of the People's Republic of China

The Great Leap Forward

Despite the rapid advances China was making in both agricultural and industrial output, the Chinese government embarked on the ill-fated 'Great Leap Forward', an ambitious plan to transform the country into a developed nation at one stroke.

The seasonally under-employed peasantry were to work on local small-scale industrial projects like steel furnaces and fertiliser plants, as well as on labour-intensive dams and irrigation networks.

While industry was being decentralised, gigantic rural communes, which would supposedly allow a more efficient use of land and resources, were being established. Having won their land, the peasants now found it being taken away again.

The factors of inefficient management, little incentive to work on the common field, and large numbers of the rural work force engaged in industrial projects, resulted in a massive slump in agricultural output. With industry in confusion and agriculture at an all-time low, China was struck by two disasters: the floods and droughts which ruined the harvests of 1959 and 1960, and the sudden withdrawal in 1960 of all aid by the Soviet Union.

Prelude to the Cultural Revolution

The withdrawal of Soviet aid, the failure of the Great Leap Forward and of the communes, unprecedented bad weather and poor harvests all contributed to the severe food shortages and famine of 1959 and 1960 to 1961.

By 1964 to 1965 the economy had recovered some of its equilibrium and the hardship years were past. Industry and agriculture started to pick up and there was a general sense of optimism, clouded only by a growing fear of war with the USA spreading from Vietnam. The economic disasters, however, had opened a rift between Mao and the rest of the Communist Party. Mao found himself in a political recession with much of the responsibility for the failure of the Great Leap Forward laid on him.

A new period began in which Liu Shaoqi and Deng Xiaoping were in the ascendancy. Ownership of land was turned over to the individual villages; family ownership of land and small private plots was guaranteed; limited free markets were permitted; bonus systems and material incentives were introduced into industry. Agriculture took priority over heavy industry.

To put their policies into effect Liu and Deng built up an enormous government and Party bureaucracy, labour unions, Party schools and Communist Youth Leagues over which Mao had little or no influence. However, Mao did have one power base – the Army. Mao was still chair of the Military Affairs Commission, a post he had held since 1935. Lin Biao, his faithful disciple, was its vice-chair. Together they controlled the Army – the trump card in any showdown.

1966-1970: The Cultural Revolution
With the rise of the bureaucratic elite, Mao believed that China was losing the spirit of the revolution and returning to the capitalist past. Their policies reeked of 'revisionism' in which a new breed of capitalist opportunists would lead China back into the misery and oppression which the revolution had sought to destroy. China needed a 'Cultural Revolution' to put it back on track.

In August 1966 the Party Central Committee adopted a programme for the Cultural Revolution. The resolution stated that the bourgeoisie was attempting to stage a comeback using 'old ideas, culture, customs and habits of the exploiting class to corrupt the masses and capture their minds'.

The aim of the Cultural Revolution was 'to struggle against and crush those persons in authority who are taking the capitalist road ... and to transform education, literature, and art and all other parts of the superstructure that do not correspond to the socialist economic base, so as to facilitate the consolidation and development of the socialist system'.

There was no doubt as to the ideological basis of the campaign; the resolution declared that 'in the Great Proletarian Cultural Revolution, it is imperative to hold aloft the great red banner of Mao Zedong's thought and put proletarian politics in command ... Mao Zedong's thought should be taken as the guide for action in the Cultural Revolution'.

The 'Revolution' rapidly turned into political mayhem personally directed by Mao. Backed by his supporters in the Army, he purged officials who opposed him in the Party, Army and government. Thousands of government officials lost their jobs and most of these were sent to the countryside for re-education in socialism, the thought of Mao Zedong and labour on commune farms. The Young Communist League and the Party Training Schools were disbanded; the Army was to be the source of new cadres.

In 1967 Liu was named China's 'Khrushchev' and in 1968 he was expelled from the Communist Party, dismissed from all offices and declared a traitor; he died in prison in 1969. Deng Xiaoping was purged as the second-ranking 'Capitalist Roader'. Peng Dehuai was accused of being a counter-revolutionary and disappeared; he died in 1974. Peng Zhen, the powerful mayor of Beijing, also disappeared. Even Zhou Enlai and Zhu De were attacked in the occasional Red Guard wall poster.

The Red Guards The Red Guards changed the face of the Cultural Revolution. Exactly how they started is unknown, but it seems that no one planned or foresaw their appearance at Beijing University in May 1966. The group was initially suppressed but Mao was quick to recognise their potential. He gave his official support to the movement and unleashed a madness that may have surprised even him. Millions of teenagers were given an opportunity to physically and psychologically attack and humiliate teachers, professors, cadres and others in authority.

Where conflicts about leadership arose, the Red Guard factions fought each other as well. Arms, even mortars, were seized from local militia, and the Red Guards fought each other until civil war was close. In 1967 Mao was forced to call in the Army to end the chaos, using weapons when necessary to disarm the Guards and end the factional fighting.

The Cultural Dissolution The Cultural Revolution was really a time of cultural dissolution, reminiscent of the book-burning of Qin Shihuang 2000 years before. This time it was Mao's wife, Jiang Qing, a former Shanghai B-grade film actress, who became the cultural supremo.

The dissolution of art and culture originated at least as far back as 1942 in Yanan when Mao delivered his 'Talk on Arts & Letters'. He laid down the principles which were to govern the Communist Party's approach to culture. Mao said there is no such thing as art for art's sake, no art which transcends class or party, and no art independent of politics. All art and literature serve political ends and were to be made to serve the interests of the Communist Party.

The Cultural Revolution produced a cultural sterility which could only have been matched by the Nazis or the Khmer Rouge. Universities and secondary schools were closed; intellectuals were dismissed, killed, persecuted or sent to labour in the countryside. Publication of scientific, artistic, literary and cultural periodicals ceased. Movies, plays and operas from before the Cultural Revolution disappeared and movie studios closed. Library collections were destroyed.

Theatres, movies, radio, television and loudspeakers in train carriages were dominated by Jiang Qing's 'Revolutionary Model Operas' which portrayed themes from the Chinese revolution or the post-1949 period. Connoisseurs of music could enjoy compositions like *The Chuang Minority Loves Chairman Mao with a Burning Love* and *The Production Brigade Celebrates the Arrival in the Hills of the Manure Collectors*.

Bookstores sold the works of Mao Zedong and little else. In 1964 Lin Biao summarised Mao's teachings in the 'little red book' of Mao quotations for the Army and peasants; in 1966 copies flooded the cities. Literally hundreds of millions of 'little red books' rolled off the presses in every major language.

The Red Guards attacked writers, artists and intellectuals, destroying their works and sending them to labour in the countryside. Temples were ransacked, monasteries disbanded and monks sent to the countryside or sometimes killed. Any physical reminder of China's past – temple, monument, work of art – was considered bound up with exploitation, capitalism or feudalism and was consequently destroyed.

The Fall of Lin Biao

Three years after Mao began his revolution, the Red Guards had risen and been suppressed, Liu Shaoqi had been locked away, and millions of people had been sent to labour in the fields. Mao's victory was so complete that at the Ninth National Party Congress in 1969, Lin Biao stated that 'whoever opposes Chairman Mao Zedong's thought, at any time or under any circumstances, will be condemned and punished by the whole Party and the whole country'. Mao Zedong and the Thought of Mao Zedong were the unifying

Stamps from the Cultural Revolution

forces behind the Party-government-military, and the man was raised virtually to the level of emperor. It was no accident that Mao hailed his people from the Gate of Heavenly Peace which the Son of Heaven had presided over in ages past.

The 1969 National Congress also adopted a new constitution, reportedly drafted by Mao himself. It designated Lin Biao, who was defence minister and vice-chairman of the Party and who was referred to as Mao's 'closest comrade in arms', as Mao's successor. It therefore came as a shock in 1972 when it was announced that Lin Biao had been killed in a plane crash in September 1971 while fleeing to the Soviet Union after a failed assassination attempt and coup against Mao.

With the Army firmly in power and Lin designated as Mao's successor, it seems unlikely that he should have tried to wrest command from a man in the last few years of his life. It's possible that Lin may have been planning a coup or that Mao feared he was and had him executed. Whatever the truth, the story of the plane crash was effective on two counts: it suggests that Lin actually attempted a coup and was therefore a traitor, and that in Mao's China political foes were not disposed of in an offensive manner.

The Rise of Zhou Enlai

With Lin dead and Mao's health steadily deteriorating as he approached 80, Premier Zhou Enlai now exercised the most influence in the day-to-day governing of China. Zhou was a remarkable survivor of the Cultural Revolution, though he tended to support the same economic policies as Liu Shaoqi. His loyalty to Mao, however, appears never to have wavered since Mao assumed supreme leadership of the Party in the 1930s. As premier, Zhou's main preoccupation during the Cultural Revolution was to hold together the administrative machinery of the government.

After the 1969 Congress Zhou set about reorganising the government structure and restoring and expanding China's diplomatic and trade contacts with the outside world – including the USA. Despite attempts at reconciliation by the Chinese in the 1950s, the US continued to follow a policy of armed 'containment' of China which aimed to isolate and eventually bring about the collapse of the Communist government.

In 1969 the Nixon administration finally cancelled most of the restrictions against trade, travel, and cultural and newspaper contacts with China, and Chinese and American diplomats discussed terms of peaceful coexistence and the ceasing of American armed protection of Taiwan. The Bamboo Curtain finally parted in 1972 when Nixon stepped of the plane at Beijing Airport, to be greeted by Zhou.

The Second Coming of Deng Xiaoping

In 1973 Zhou was able to return to power none other than Deng Xiaoping, vilified as China's Number Two Capitalist Roader during the Cultural Revolution.

There were now two factions vying for power in the Chinese leadership. The first was the 'moderates' or 'pragmatists' led by Zhou Enlai and Deng Xiaoping. The second was the 'radicals', 'leftists' or 'Maoists'. Yet there was no open conflict between Zhou and Mao, and certainly Deng must have been brought back with Mao's approval.

The 'Maoist' faction was led by Mao's wife Jiang Qing, who rode to power during the Cultural Revolution on Mao's name and her marriage certificate. With their power threatened by the resurgence of Zhou and Deng, the radicals mounted the oddly named 'Criticise Lin Biao and Confucius' campaign – in reality an attack on Zhou and Deng.

While Zhou lived, the inevitable power struggle was kept at bay. However, his health rapidly deteriorated and in the midst of the radical resurgence he died in early January 1976. A memorial service was held in the Great Hall of the People in Beijing, from which Mao was absent.

After the memorial service the period of mourning was unexpectedly declared over. Deng Xiaoping suddenly disappeared from public view and the newspapers started to propagate the line that China was once again threatened by people in authority who were taking the 'capitalist road'. The post of acting premier went to the fifth-ranking Vice-Premier Hua Guofeng, little known in the west. Deng had been passed over for what appeared to be a compromise candidate for the job.

The Tiananmen Incident

In March 1976, during the Qing Ming Festival when the Chinese traditionally honour the dead, people began to lay wreaths dedicated to Zhou on the Heroes Monument in Tiananmen Square. More and more people came to honour Zhou with wreaths and eulogies until the square was filled with thousands of people. Wreaths were sent by ministries of the central government, departments of the central command of the People's Liberation Army and other military units as well as factories, schools, stores and communes in the Beijing area.

For the Chinese, Zhou represented the antithesis of the madness and fanaticism of the Cultural Revolution and its instigators, and the last vestige of goodness and justice in the government; without him everything seemed lost. Though there was some scattered official support for the demonstration in Tiananmen, on the whole it was a rare, spontaneous display of how the Chinese felt about what was happening. Indirectly it was an attack on Mao and an open defiance of the leftists who had commanded that there be no more mourning for Zhou.

In the early hours of 5 April, the wreaths and poems in Tiananmen were torn down from the square and carted away. Those who tried to prevent the removal of the tributes were arrested, and guards surrounded the monument. The same day tens of thousands of people swarmed into the square demanding the return of the wreaths and the release of those arrested, only to be attacked and dispersed by thousands of men wearing the armbands of the Workers Militia armed with staves. The subsequent demonstrations and riots became known as the 'Tiananmen Incident'. The demonstrations were declared counter-revolutionary and the blame was laid on Deng. On 7 April a meeting of the Politburo stripped Deng of all his offices and Hua Guofeng was made vice-chairman of the Party and continued as premier.

Mao was still in public view but disappeared in the middle of the year. Who had access to him, what he was being told, whether he still had the capacity to grasp or influence any of the events taking place, is unknown. The Chinese were now going through another struggle. Mao had led them against the Kuomintang, the Japanese and the Americans in Korea, and then into the depths of the Cultural Revolution. Finally at Tiananmen his own people turned against him, just a few blocks from his home behind the walls of the Zhongnanhai government compound.

In late July the massive Tangshan earthquake struck northern China, claiming half a million lives. For the Chinese great natural disasters foreshadow the end of dynasties, and once again it seemed like the cycle of Chinese history had come full swing. With the portentous sign from heaven that he had lost the mandate to rule, Mao died in the early hours of the morning on 9 September 1976.

The Gang of Four

With Mao gone the two factions had to stand on their own feet. The meat in the sandwich was Hua Guofeng, whose authority rested largely on his status as the chosen successor to Mao Zedong.

Change came swiftly and dramatically. Less than a month after the death of Mao, Hua Guofeng had Jiang Qing and a number of other leftist leaders and their supporters arrested. She and three other principal allies of Mao – Yao Wenyuan,

Zhang Chunqiao and Wang Hongwen – were selected as scapegoats for this latest ideological change and became known as the 'Gang of Four'.

Yao Wenyuan, a relatively young writer in the late 1950s, first won praise from Mao in 1957 after writing an article against bourgeois influence in the arts and journalism; during the Cultural Revolution Yao became a Politburo member, responsible for Party propaganda and mass media. Zhang Chunqiao, for most of his career, was involved in literary propaganda work; during the Cultural Revolution he became vice-premier. Wang Hongwen was a political activist at factory floor level in Shanghai at the beginning of the Cultural Revolution; by 1973 and before he was 40 years of age he was a vice-chairman of the Communist Party.

The Third Coming of Deng Xiaoping

In the middle of 1977 Deng Xiaoping returned to power for the third time and was appointed to the positions of vice-premier, vice-chairman of the Party and chief of staff of the PLA. His return heralded yet another battle royal for the leadership – this time between Deng and Hua.

Hua did not have the unequivocal support of the Party since he was really a compromise leader for both left and right factions. Yet it was not until September 1980 that Hua finally relinquished the post of premier to Zhao Ziyang. Zhao is a long-standing member of the Communist Party whose economic reforms in Sichuan in the mid-1970s overcame the province's bankrupt economy and food shortages and won him Deng's favour. In June 1981 Hu Yaobang, a protégé of Deng's for several decades, was named Party chairman in place of Hua.

Final power now passed to the collective leadership of the six-member Standing Committee of the Communist Party, which included Deng, Hu and Zhao. The China they took over was racked with problems. A backward country had to be modernised and the material standard of living improved. Ways had to be found to rejuvenate and replace an aged leadership (themselves) and to overcome the possibility of leftist backlash. The wasteful and destructive power struggles plaguing the Communist Party since its inception had to be eliminated. The need for order had to be reconciled with the popular desire for more freedom; those with responsibility had to be rewarded but watched over for the misuse of privilege; the crisis in faith in the Communist ideology had to be overcome; and a regime now dependent on the power of the police and military for its authority had to be legitimised.

The Trial of the Gang of Four

The first dramatic step taken to guard against a leftist backlash was the trial of the Gang of Four and a number of its supporters at the end of 1980.

Jiang Qing was accused of framing and persecuting to death Liu Shaoqi and other high-ranking Party members as well as making false charges against others. She was labelled a 'ringleader of the Lin Biao and Jiang Qing counter-revolutionary cliques' and was accused of working to overthrow the government and of 'tyrannizing the people'.

The others were accused variously of working 'hand in glove' with Jiang Qing to seize power; of making false charges against Party members; of plotting an armed rebellion in Shanghai; of agitating for a counter-revolution and being instrumental in creating violent disturbances across China in 1976; of smearing people who mourned Zhou Enlai's death as counter-revolutionaries; of falsely charging Deng Xiaoping of being the person behind the Tiananmen Incident; of engineering several incidents during the Cultural Revolution which led to the death, wounding or maiming of many innocent people; of framing Peng Dehuai; and of conspiring with Lin Biao to seize power and assassinate Mao.

The trial was reminiscent of Stalin's

show-trials of the 1930s. 'Guilty' was a foregone verdict, as one political faction wreaked revenge on another, though the demise of the 'leftists' provided general relief. Jiang Qing and Zhang Chunqiao were sentenced to death but were given a two-year reprieve in which to repent their sins; their sentences were commuted to life imprisonment. The others were sentenced to long prison terms.

Resolution of a Theological Crisis

Deng was able to ward off immediate threats from the leftists by locking them up, but he still had to deal with a major crisis – what to do with Mao Zedong. One step taken was the resolution on the historical roles of Mao Zedong and Liu Shaoqi issued in 1981 by the Central Committee of the Communist Party.

Deng had every intention of pulling Mao off his pedestal and making a man out of the god. However, he couldn't denounce Mao as Khrushchev had denounced Stalin, since Mao had too many supporters in the Party and too much respect among the common people. An all-out attack would have provoked those who would otherwise begrudgingly fall in line with Deng and his supporters. Instead a compromise stand was taken.

The resolution cited Mao as 'a great Marxist and a great proletarian revolutionary, strategist and theorist. It is true that he made gross mistakes during the Cultural Revolution, but, if we judge his activities as a whole, his contributions to the Chinese revolution far outweigh his mistakes'. The resolution went on to blame Mao for initiating and leading the Cultural Revolution which 'was responsible for the most severe setback and the heaviest losses suffered by the Party, the state and the people since the founding of the People's Republic'. Liu Shaoqi (who had died in prison in 1969) and his economic policies were given unequivocal rehabilitation.

The Purge of the Party

The trial of the 'Gang of Four' was a major step towards breaking the power of Deng's opponents. However, there were still large numbers of Maoists in the bureaucracy who could obstruct the implementation of Deng's new policies. In 1983 the Central Committee of the Communist Party launched a three-year campaign referred to as an 'overall rectification of Party style and consolidation of Party organisations' – a purge by any other name but without the violence of previous purges. Between two to four million people lost their Party membership in an effort to remove those who still supported the 'Gang of Four' and to ensure the survival of Deng's policies beyond his grave. Deng has also elevated a number of younger supporters to the Politburo and other high-ranking government and Party positions.

Foreign Policy

Chinese relations with foreign countries are largely determined by the government's present economic policies, which aim to rapidly modernise China by importing technology and teachers. A number of pressing foreign policy problems remain. These include the continued occupation of Taiwan by the Kuomintang, the status of Hong Kong after 1997, the continued occupation of Macau by Portugal, and the continuing conflict between the Vietnamese and the Khmer Rouge in Kampuchea.

The Taiwan problem is not ancient history but the scars of the bitter civil war run deep. Today the Beijing government no longer talks of liberating Taiwan but of a peaceful solution which would allow it to join the People's Republic, and perhaps even allow the Kuomintang to govern the island and retain its own military.

Hong Kong became a British possession as a result of the treaties forced on China in the 19th century. In 1898 the large area known as the New Territories, which joined China to the Kowloon Peninsula, was leased by Britain for 99 years. In 1984, with the lease due to expire, Britain agreed to hand the entire colony lock, stock and skyscrapers back to China in 1997.

The position of Macau is simpler. In 1974 the new left wing government in Portugal tried to give Macau back to China as part of their drive to pack up the ragtag Portuguese empire, but the Chinese refused to take it. The Portuguese constitution now regards Macau as Chinese territory under Portuguese administration, and 1999 is the date that has been set for its official return to China.

On China's southern borders the 'Communist monolith' theory of the 1950s and 1960s took another beating with the (disastrous) Chinese invasion of Vietnam in 1979. In their desperation to drum up support against the Vietnamese, the Chinese allied themselves with the Khmer Rouge regime of Pol Pot, responsible for the death of perhaps as many as two million Kampucheans – making the Chinese accomplices in one of the greatest mass murders of modern history. The Chinese have continued their support for the Khmer Rouge and appear willing to fight to the last Kampuchean.

The Chinese also have a serious 'foreign policy' problem in Tibet (Xizang in Chinese). Although since the 1950 invasion it has been administered as an autonomous region of China, many Tibetans are resentful of the Chinese for their dismantling of Tibetan political and economic systems and especially, Tibetan Buddhism. Its leader, the Dalai Lama, has been in exile in northern India since 1959, when anti-Chinese feeling led to riots. Thousands of Tibetan Buddhist monasteries were destroyed by the Chinese during the Cultural Revolution.

But the worst violence of recent years occurred late in 1987, when 27 monks were arrested for demonstrating against China outside Lhasa's Jokhang Temple. Four days later, at least eight Tibetans and six Chinese police were killed when a mob of 2000 Tibetans stoned and set fire to a police station in the capital.

The Dalai Lama refuses to return to his homeland until the Chinese withdraw and recognise his claims, both to religious leadership and as head of the Tibetan 'government in exile'.

Dissidence, Privilege & the Future

One common characteristic of the top Communist leaders (including Mao, Zhou, Hua and Deng) is that they are essentially authoritarian and do not accept challenges to their power. The right to set up political parties in opposition to the Communist Party, the right to publish independent opposition newspapers, and the right to voice ideas or philosophies in opposition to the Party's official line have all been suppressed, to varying degrees, by the Communist leaders.

The first major suppression resulted from the 'Hundred Flowers' campaign of 1956. In that year the Communist leadership encouraged the Chinese to speak out and voice their opinions of the new government. To their horror many intellectuals challenged the Party's right to be the sole political force in the country. The following year untold numbers of people who had voiced opposition to the Communists were arrested and imprisoned. The second great suppression was, of course, the Cultural Revolution, which raised the thoughts of Mao to a state religion and smashed those who questioned it.

Then came the 'Democracy Wall Movement' in November 1978, in which political wall posters were glued to a wall in the middle of Beijing by anyone with an opinion to air. The movement was initially supported by Deng Xiaoping, possibly to drum up mass support for his campaign against Hua Guofeng, possibly to make a good impression in the USA which Deng was about to visit and with which full diplomatic relations would be established in January 1979. Later that year Deng moved to close down Democracy Wall; plain clothes police were sent in to disrupt the crowds that gathered at the wall each day, and the leading activists were arrested and imprisoned. In January

1980 Deng gave an important speech in which he insisted that the right to put up wall posters be stripped from China's constitution because it had been exploited by a 'handful of reactionaries with ulterior motives' to undermine China's 'stability and unity' and threaten plans for economic development.

At the end of 1986 the general mood of impatience with the speed of reform was dramatically highlighted in the streets in Hefei, Wuhan, Shanghai and Beijing. In these and other cities thousands of students and workers marched and used wall posters to press for more liberty, democracy and better living conditions.

The government was quick to counter these demands with honeyed words. These were followed by an all-out attack on 'bourgeois liberalism' (essentially the western political concepts of democracy and freedom), and on those seeking 'all-round westernisation'. The government deemed this incompatible with the 'four basic principles' of Party policy, which are adherence to the socialist road, Marxism-Leninism-Mao Zedong thought, leadership of the Communist Party and the dictatorship of the proletariat.

Within days, the vice-president of Hefei University, Fang Lizhi (commonly known as the 'Sakharov of China'), was sacked from his post; Liu Binyan, one of China's leading intellectuals and a renowned crusader against corruption, was expelled from the Communist Party; and a liberal paper in Shanghai was placed under direct censorship. Rumours quickly circulated about the role of Hu Yaobang, general secretary of the Communist Party, whose outspoken support of reform allegedly once included the comment: 'Marx never saw a light bulb, Engels never saw an airplane, and neither of them ever visited China'. With conservative factions clamouring for sacrifice, Hu disappeared from official functions for several weeks until he made world news in January 1987 by resigning from his post.

At the time many observers took this as evidence of a conservative backlash against the reform process. But in November 1987 at the CCP's 13th Congress, Deng became the first Chinese leader to freely abdicate power when he stood down from most of his posts, paving the way for the election of Zhao Ziyang as Party general secretary. The next Premier is Soviet-educated 59-year-old Li Peng; the two have been described as 'reformers with reservations'. With the appointment of several members of the new generation to the Politburo's Standing Committee, and Deng's success at persuading his fellow octogenarian Long March veterans (the 'old comrades') to follow him into retirement, it looks like China may be headed for a new period of openness and market-oriented reform.

Able to suppress most political opposition, the Communist Party has established itself as a privileged group supported by the police and military and requiring unquestioning obedience from those lower down the ranks. The higher up the scale, the greater the number of privileges – such as the provision of cars or better quality housing – and the better the standard of living. The system of ranking was established in the 1950s and has remained largely unchanged since then. Arguably, its roots lie in the careful ordering of society prescribed by Confucianism.

Privilege is a dilemma for a government which espouses egalitarianism. Mao realised that there was a growing elite of fat bureaucrats and tried to wipe them out with the Cultural Revolution. But those who were thrown out of their apartments and mansions were simply replaced by others, and Mao and his entourage continued to live their own privileged lifestyle. It remains to be seen whether the gap between the haves and the have-nots will be closed, but it should be remembered that Deng's economic policies are aimed at significantly raising the ordinary people's standard of living.

It should also be remembered that the problems that faced the Communists were and are immense, and for China to have come as far as it has today is a remarkable achievement. Perhaps the Communists have not delivered all they promised, yet it seems unlikely that anyone else could have done a better job.

GOVERNMENT

Precious little is known about the inner workings of the Chinese government, but westerners can make educated guesses.

The highest authority rests with the Standing Committee of the Communist Party Politburo. The Politburo comprises 25 members. Below it is the 210-member Central Committee, made up of younger Party members and provincial Party leaders. At grass roots level the Party forms a parallel system to the administrations in the Army, universities, government, and industries. Real authority is exercised by the Party representatives at each level in these organisations. They, in turn, are responsible to the Party officials in the hierarchy above them, thus ensuring strict central control.

Between 1921 and 1935 the general secretary of the Central Committee and the Politburo held overall leadership of the Party. The significance of this title changed during the Long March when Mao became the Party chairman, assuming power over both Party and government. The post of general secretary was subordinated to him and eventually abolished in 1945. Provision was then made for a chair and four vice-chairs to constitute a Standing Committee of the Politburo.

The Standing Committee of the Politburo still retains supreme power but its members are now accorded a hodgepodge of titles. Foremost on the Standing Committee is general secretary Zhao Ziyang. Diminutive Deng Xiaoping is still chair of the Military Affairs Commission, which gives him overall command of the Army. He was also chair of the Central Advisory Commission, whose function is to deal with elderly leaders stepping down from their posts. This post is now held by Chen Yun. Another member of the Standing Committee is Premier Li Peng. The post of general secretary was restored in 1956 as a top administrative job and seems to be regaining its original mantle as the foremost leadership position in the Party. However, in the Chinese political sphere titles and appearances are slippery things and often belie the holder's real power. Hu Yaobang was general secretary until he was suddenly dropped or, to put it officially, resigned the post in yet another political upheaval in 1987. He has, however, kept his seat on the Politburo and may again become influential.

The day-to-day running of the country lies with the State Council, which is directly under the control of the Communist Party. The State Council is headed by the premier. Beneath the premier are four vice-premiers, 10 state councillors, a secretary-general, 45 ministers and various other agencies. The State Council implements the decisions made by the Politburo: it draws up quotas, assesses planning, establishes priorities and organises finances. The ministries include Public Security, Education, Defence, Culture, Forestry, Railways, Tourism, Minority Affairs, Radio & Television, the Bank of China and Family Planning.

Rubber-stamping the decisions of the Communist Party leadership is the National People's Congress (NPC). In theory the NPC is empowered to amend the constitution and to choose the premier and members of the State Council. The catch is that all these must first be recommended by the Central Committee, and thus the NPC is only an approving body. The composition of NPC members is surprising: there is a sizeable number of women, non-Communist Party members, intellectuals, technical people and industrial managers. The Army is not well represented and the rural areas supply only a small fraction of the total. Exactly why so much effort is made to maintain the NPC and give it publicity through television and newspapers is unknown, but it seems important for the Chinese government to maintain the illusion of democracy.

If the NPC is a white elephant, then the great stumbling block of the Chinese political system is the bureaucracy. There are 24 ranks on the ladder, each accorded its own particular privileges. The term 'cadre' is usually applied to all bureaucrats but that term includes both the lowliest clerks and the political leaders with real power (from the work-unit leaders to Zhao Ziyang) as well as Party and non-Party members. Despite attacks on the bureaucratic system by the Red Guards the system survived intact, if many of its former members did not. Deng's three-year purge (headed by Hu Yaobang) weeded the bureaucracy of many officials who might slow down implementation of his new economic policies. Other offenders, according to the *Selected Works of Deng Xiaoping* published in 1983, include the despotic, the lazy, the megalomaniac, the corrupt, the stubborn and the unreliable.

Problems with the Chinese bureaucracy really began with the Communist takeover in 1949. When the Communist armies entered the cities the peasant soldiers were installed in positions of authority as Party representatives in every office, factory, school and hospital. Once in power these revolutionaries, who had rebelled against the despotism of the Kuomintang, reverted to the inward looking, conservative values of their rural homes: respectful of authority, suspicious of change, interested in their families' comfort, sceptical of the importance of technology and education, and suspicious of intellectuals. Their only real training had been in the Red Army, which had taught them how to fight, not how to run a modern state. During the 1950s Liu Shaoqi and Deng Xiaoping tried to build up a competent bureaucracy, but their training organisations were decimated by Mao's Cultural Revolution. The bureaucratic system survived but new officials had neither the technical competence nor the ideological zeal which was supposed to push China on to greater glories. The slothfulness, self-interest, incompetence and preoccupation with the pursuit of privilege continued.

At grass roots level the basic unit of social organisation outside the family is the *danwei* or work unit. Every Chinese is a member of one, whether he or she works in a hospital, school, office, factory or village. Many westerners may admire the cooperative spirit this system is supposed to engender, but they would cringe if their own lives were so intricately controlled. Nothing can proceed without the work unit. It issues ration coupons for grain, oil, cotton and coal, and it decides if a couple may marry or divorce and when they can have a child. It assigns housing, sets salaries, handles mail, recruits Party members, keeps files on each unit member, arranges transfers to other jobs or other parts of the country, and gives permission to travel. The work unit's control extends into every part of the individual's life.

The Chinese political scene is made up of white elephants, stumbling blocks and work units. There is even a bogeyman to contend with – the Army. The People's Liberation Army covers the land forces, the Navy and the Air Force, and developed from the Chinese Workers and Peasants Red Army of the 1920s and 1930s. The army is currently being trimmed down from about 4.2 million members to around three million. There are also several million workers and peasants in the local militia, which can be mobilised in time of war.

In 1949 the Army took control of every institution in China; the Cultural Revolution strengthened its grasp and there is still a considerable overlap between the Party, Army and State. The death of Lin Biao was a major blow to the Army's power. Deng dealt another major blow by putting on trial, and subsequently imprisoning, a number of high ranking military leaders who had supported the Gang of Four. In a delicate transfer of power he has also tried to wean the Army away from participation in the political scene and towards target practice and modernisation of equipment and fighting techniques.

Mao held that 'political power grows out of the barrel of a gun'. He also maintained that 'the Party commands the gun and the gun must never be allowed to command the Party'. The gun (or armed forces) has been a burden in Chinese politics because whoever had control of it could do away with their opponents. Mao lost almost all influence in the civilian government during the early 1960s but his command of the Army was the deciding factor in the showdown with Liu Shaoqi. Likewise, Deng Xiaoping couldn't have made a comeback after Mao's death if the military had completely supported Jiang Qing. As to the other manipulations involved, if you can work out how Deng could come back three times from the political grave then you have probably unlocked the secrets of political power in China today.

Political Dissidence & Repression

> If you close the people's mouths and let them say only nice things, it keeps the bile inside.
>
> from one of the last posters to appear on Democracy Wall.

As the events in 1986 showed, not everyone in China is content with the political system, which clearly lacks channels allowing constructive criticism to reach the higher levels of government. In the last decade a handful of extraordinarily courageous political dissidents spoke their minds and paid the price. Many such dissidents, though labelled 'counter-revolutionaries' were, ironically, devoted Communists. Once a dissident is convicted as a counter-revolutionary, there is next to no legal recourse since he or she is stripped at the same time of political and civil rights.

There are several categories of dissident: members of 'democracy and human rights' movements; individuals protesting unjust treatment by officials, arbitrary arrest, or miscarriage of justice; members of religious organisations; and members of minorities protesting for political or religious reasons.

Wei Jingsheng, a leading figure in the Democracy Wall Movement, was arrested during the 'Beijing Spring' of 1979. After a seven-hour trial Wei was sentenced to 15 years imprisonment. He spent the following years in solitary confinement in Beijing Prison No 1. Wei was reportedly transferred in 1983 to a psychiatric clinic as his mental health had suffered; it was rumoured that he was then moved to a camp in Qinghai Province. In 1986 it was reported that Wei had died in a psychiatric hospital in Jilin Province. Many other activists in the democracy movement such as Ren Wanding, Liu Qing, Wang Xizhe and Xu Wenli were imprisoned. In 1986 there was an unconfirmed report of a government document stating that Wei Jingsheng's death should serve as a reminder of the fate of counter-revolutionaries.

Catholics in China have repeatedly been arrested and imprisoned for refusing to break with the Vatican and join the independent Roman Catholic Church in China. The Roman Catholic Bishop of Shanghai, Ignatius Gong Pinmei, consistently supported independence of the church from the government. Reportedly still detained in Shanghai's main prison, Bishop Gong was arrested in 1955, sentenced to life imprisonment in 1960 and has thus spent well over 30 years in prison. Many other Roman Catholic priests and lay Catholics have been arrested and imprisoned. Father Francis Xavier Zhu Shude was first detained in a labour camp in 1953, and was repeatedly sentenced to further imprisonment for carrying out religious duties in the camp. He died there in 1983 at the age of 70, after more than 30 years in detention.

Tibetan dissidents such as Kalsang Tsering, Lobsang Chodag and Thubten

Kelsang Thalutsogentsang have been arrested in Lhasa for expressing support for the Dalai Lama and Tibetan independence.

Prisoners are held in a variety of institutions, including prisons, detention centres, labour camps and corrective labour camps. Remote areas such as Tibet, Qinghai, Xinjiang and some provinces in the north-east contain large numbers of such camps, which serve as the equivalent of political exile for dissidents sent there.

The Chinese government rigorously ignores requests for information on dissidents on the grounds that this topic is beyond 'foreign interference' and strictly an 'internal affair'. Quite possibly South Africa, which has received much criticism from China, could argue that apartheid qualifies as an internal matter. The truth is that any country which denies access to such topics invites conjecture as to the validity of its claims of justice.

More details on this topic can be found in publications such as Amnesty International's China report or *Seeds of Fire – Chinese Voices of Conscience*, edited by Geremie Barme and John Minford.

POPULATION & PEOPLE

The national census of 1982 revealed that the population of mainland China (excluding Taiwan, Hong Kong and Macau) had reached a staggering 1,008,000,000 people. Han Chinese make up about 93% of the total; the rest is composed of China's 55 or so minority nationalities, including Mongols and Tibetans. Only about one-fifth of the total population live in the cities and towns; the rest live in the villages.

These billion people have to be fed with the produce of just 15% of the land they live on, the sum total of China's arable land. The rest is barren wasteland or can only be lightly grazed. Much of the productive land is also vulnerable to flood and drought caused by the vagaries of China's summer monsoons or unruly rivers. Since the revolution, irrigation and flood control schemes have improved the situation but the afflictions of the weather cannot be completely overcome. In 1981, for instance, there were devastating floods in Sichuan Province and drought in the Beijing area. Despite these problems the Communists have managed to double food production since 1952. Unfortunately the population has increased by almost the same amount, leaving the quantity of food available per person pretty much what it was 30 years ago.

Of China's billion people, more than a quarter were rated by the census as illiterates (people 12 years of age and over who cannot read or who can only read a few words). Those with school education number a respectable 600 million, but more than half that figure have been to primary school only. There are 4.4 million university graduates and a paltry 1.6 million undergraduates. Given the formidable nature of the task, the Communists have certainly made considerable improvements in education. However, the statistics indicate that the staggering population still has very little technical and scientific expertise to draw upon. Even if the Chinese can be adequately fed, the prospect of substantially improving their lot and modernising the country without foreign help is a poor one – as the Chinese government has realised.

Birth Control

Birth control programmes instituted by the Communist government in the 1950s met with some success, but were abandoned during the Cultural Revolution. The responsibility lies with Mao Zedong, whose decision was probably his greatest mistake. He believed that birth control was a capitalist plot to make China weak and that the country would find strength in a large population. His ideas very much reflected his background – that of the peasant farmer who wants many hands to make light work in the fields.

It was not until 1973 that population growth targets were again included in China's economic planning, and campaigns like 'Longer, Later, Fewer' were launched. Planning for the future is a nightmare. Chinese estimates of how many people the country can support range up to 1.4 billion. The current plan is to limit growth to 1.2 billion by the year 2000, hold steady somehow, and allow birth control and natural mortality to reduce that figure.

Huge billboards in Chinese cities spell out the goals for the year 2000 – modernisation and population control. The posters look like ads for a Buck Rogers sci-fi movie re-run or Fritz Lang's *Metropolis*: planes, UFOs and helicopters fill the skies, strange vehicles glide down LA-type freeways, and skyscrapers poke out of futuristic cities. Often the only people visible are a smiling couple with their one child, often a girl. The figure on the poster is 1.2 billion, the quota set for the year 2000.

So what will life be like then? A western teacher put this question to his university students in China and got back the following predictions in writing. Most of them envisaged a quiet family-oriented life: husband, wife and one child, living in a roomy apartment with no granny or other relatives (they'll be retired and kept busy elsewhere). People will have private telephones, travel abroad will be easy, large meals will be prepared in modern kitchens equipped with labour saving devices like fridges and washing machines. The bicycle will be a museum piece replaced by private cars, cities will be full of skyscrapers, and colour TVs and picnics will occupy leisure time. The CCP will still be in charge but politics were expected to play a minor role in peoples' lives, and there will be a free press. Progress will, of course, bring about pollution and traffic congestion, but generally the place will be quiet and orderly. Few envisage war.

The one-child campaign is bound up with this vision of materialistic splendour, but how do you get a billion people to procreate at a government-designated quota? In recent years the main thrust of the campaign in the cities is to encourage couples to sign a one-child pledge by offering them an extra month's salary per year until the child is 14, plus housing normally reserved for a family of four (a promise often not kept because of the acute housing shortage). If the couple have a second child then the privileges are rescinded, and penalties such as demotion at work or even loss of job are imposed. If a woman has an abortion it entitles her to a vacation with pay. The legal age for

marriage is 22 for men and 20 for women, but if the woman delays marriage until after the age of 25 then she is entitled to longer maternity leave. Material incentives are also applied in rural areas, sometimes meaning that farming couples get a double-sized plot if they only have one child. All methods of birth control are free; the most common are the IUD, female sterilisation and abortion. Forcing women to have abortions and falsifying figures are two methods taken by some local officials in their enthusiasm to meet the 'quotas' in their area.

The birth control measures appear to be working in the cities, but it's difficult to say what's happening in the villages or if the target of zero growth can ever be reached. The catch is that Chinese agriculture still relies on human muscle and farmers find it desirable to have many children. As late as 1971 the yearly rate of increase stood at 2.3%, which would have doubled the population again in another 30 years. By 1979 the rate was down to 1.2%, though that would still double the population in 59 years.

If the Chinese can be convinced or pressured into accepting birth control, the one thing they cannot agree to accept is the sex of their only child. The desire for male children is deeply ingrained and the ancient custom of female infanticide continues to this day – as the Chinese government and press will freely admit. In 1982 a young man in Liaoning was sentenced to 13 years imprisonment for smothering his two-month-old daughter and throwing her body down a well. According to one Chinese news source 195 female infants in a county in Anhui Province were drowned between 1978 and 1979. The *People's Daily* has even called the imbalance of the sexes a 'grave problem' and reported that in one rural area of Hebei Province the ratio of male to female children (under the age of five) was five to one. The paper also reported a case in Zhengzhou (Henan Province), in which two applications for divorce were rejected, having been made by husbands on the grounds that their wives had given birth only to female children. In one attempt to counter this age-old prejudice against female offspring the family planning billboards depict, almost without fail, a rosy-cheeked little girl in the ideal family.

Minorities

The Chinese government officially recognises 55 national minorities. They account for a bit less than 7% of the population but are distributed over some 50% of Chinese-controlled territory, mostly in the sensitive border regions.

Some minorities, like the Zhuang and the Manchu, have become so assimilated over the centuries that to the western eye they look indistinguishable from their Han counterparts; only language and religion separate them. Other minority groups no longer wear their traditional clothing except on market or festival days. Some have little or nothing in common with the Han Chinese, like the Turkish-descended Uygurs of Xinjiang who are instantly recognisable by their swarthy Caucasian appearance, Turkish-related language, use of Arabic script and adherence to Islam.

Han migrations and invasions over the centuries have pushed many of the minorities into the more isolated, rugged areas of China. Traditionally the Han have regarded them as barbarians. Indeed, it was only with the formation of the People's Republic that the symbol for 'dog' – which was included in the characters for minority names – was replaced with the symbol for 'man'.

Minority separatism has always been a threat to the stability of China, particularly amongst the Uygurs and the Tibetans who have poor and often volatile relations with the Han and whose homelands form the border regions of China. The minority regions provide China with the greater part of its livestock and hold vast untapped deposits of minerals.

Keeping the minorities under control

has been a continuous problem for the Han Chinese. Tibet and Xinjiang are heavily garrisoned by Chinese troops, partly to protect China's borders and partly to prevent rebellion among the local population (as happened in Tibet in 1959 and again in 1987). Chinese migration to minority areas has been encouraged as a means of controlling them by sheer weight of numbers. For example, 50 years ago, Inner Mongolia had a population of about four million and Xinjiang had 2.5 million. Today those figures are 19 and 13 million respectively. The Chinese government has also set up special training centres, like the National Minorities Institute in Beijing, to train loyal minority cadres for these regions. Since 1976 the government has tried to diffuse discontent by relaxing some of its grasp on the day-to-day life of the minority peoples, in particular allowing temples and mosques closed during the Cultural Revolution to reopen.

ECONOMY

When the Communists came to power in 1949, some change in the economic conditions of the people and the country was inevitable, for the old China could not have been worse off. The cessation of war, the setting up of a stable government and redistribution of the fat of the past regimes could only improve China for the better. The official Chinese press readily describes China as a developing nation; it still has enormous difficulties to overcome before it catches up with countries like Japan, the United States and West Germany.

China's economic policies have undergone a radical change since the death of Mao Zedong and the fall of the so-called Gang of Four. Mao had largely isolated China from the world economy, apprehensive that economic links with other countries would make China dependent on them. Believing that private enterprise would return China to the oppressive capitalism of the past, he used the Cultural Revolution to put an end to even the most basic forms of private enterprise. All aspects of the economy, from barber shops and restaurants to steel mills and paddy fields, came under state ownership and rigid state control.

Deng has reversed these policies. Modernisation of the country is to be achieved by turning away from the narrow path of self-reliance and centralised planning of the Mao era, and by importing foreign technology and expertise. Essentially these policies are a continuation of the work done in the early 1960s by Deng Xiaoping and Liu Shaoqi. The aim is to achieve the 'Four Modernisations' (industry, agriculture, defence, and science and technology), quadruple production of everything, boost individual income dramatically and turn China into a modern state by the year 2000.

Today the PRC's centrally planned economy has moved to a three-tier system. On the first rung is the state, which continues to control consumer staples (such as grains and edible oils) and industrial and raw materials. On the second rung come private purchases or sales of services and commodities within a price range set by the state. On the third rung is the rural and urban 'free marketing' in which prices are established between buyer and seller, except that the state can step in if there are unfair practices.

Industrial Reform

Prior to 1979 a factory would be allotted a certain amount of raw material and told to produce a certain number of units by the appropriate ministry in Beijing. Any profit had to be remitted to the central government. It was then up to the ministry to determine how much of that profit should be returned to the factory in the form of subsidies for repairs, retooling or expansion. Factory managers were essentially cogs in a machine controlled from above.

Following decisions made at the end of 1978, centralised control was relaxed and state-controlled enterprises were thrown back on their own resources, having to find their own raw materials, set production targets, and hire and fire their own labour force instead of accepting workers assigned to them by state labour bureaus. The state gets its share of the profits through taxation, and what's left is retained by the factory to be reinvested or spent. Workers are paid overtime, and can receive bonuses if the factory does well. Early in 1983 the government began testing a system whereby workers are hired on contract, though they can be fired for causing economic losses or breaking rules.

In Shenyang, the capital of Liaoning Province, three major reforms have been introduced: leasing of companies to individuals or collectively-run businesses; shareholding by factory workers; and, rather surprisingly, official recognition of bankruptcy.

Rural Reform

In 1978 the government introduced an agricultural 'responsibility' system which replaced the rigidly collectivised agriculture system instituted under Mao. The system is applied differently from province to province, retaining state-owned farms in the north-east where mechanised agriculture prevails, while in the south-west 'market gardening' controlled by individual villages or families is more appropriate, given the difficult terrain.

Under the system a work team or family was contracted to work a plot of state land. They decided what to grow and when, provided the government with its quota, and were then allowed to sell any surplus at rural free markets and keep the profit. In 1984 a new system was initiated whereby peasants would be granted long land leases with the right to transfer and renew their leaseholds, although it is not possible for peasants or anyone else to actually own land.

Around the end of 1984 it was decided to do away with the quota system which required peasants to sell a certain percentage of their produce to the state. The idea now is that if peasants can get more for their produce in free markets it will encourage them to increase production. The two exceptions are grain and cotton, over which the state maintains control. The state contracts for grain and cotton then purchases its requirements for more than the market price and permits the rest of the crop to be regulated by the market price. In theory, when the market price is high the state sells its reserves to bring the price down.

In early 1985, after more than 35 years of rigid price controls, the government took the crucial step of lifting those controls in Canton and Shanghai. This applied to all consumer goods in those cities including meat, eggs, fish, poultry, dairy products, fruits and vegetables. Controls continued on grain, edible oils, cotton and a few other products. Some cities had already had price controls lifted and it appears the government will extend this policy to all urban areas and perhaps the whole country over a period of several years.

Foreign Investment

In sharp contrast to the extreme self-reliance of the Maoist period is China's present open-door policy on foreign investment and joint-venture enterprises with foreign companies.

In an attempt to attract foreign investment to China, the government has set up 'Special Economic Zones' such as Shenzhen County which borders Hong Kong. Low wages, reduced taxation and abundant labour have been used to encourage foreign companies to set up industries in the SEZs. Low production costs mean that Chinese goods can be competitive on the world market. Since 1984 when 14 coastal cities were opened to foreign investment along similar lines, just about every major city and town has been seeking foreign investment. There are hundreds of joint-venture enterprises, from oil and gas exploration in the South China Sea to the construction of several commercial nuclear power plants. Not all goes smoothly – foreign businesspeople are sometimes driven mad by the Kafkaesque paperwork for contracts, by the overcharging, or by just plain inefficiency in the use of equipment and even unwillingness on the part of the Chinese to accept advice on increasing production.

The money to finance China's modernisation comes from a number of sources: foreign investment, loans from foreign banks and financial organisations, and the booming tourist industry. The Chinese even seem willing, for a price, to allow the Gobi Desert to be used as a dumping ground for nuclear waste from foreign reactors. China also has vast untapped oil and mineral deposits, particularly in the outlying regions of Qinghai, Tibet and Xinjiang. Another source of foreign money are the Overseas Chinese, who are courted with appeals to patriotism and encouraged to invest in the motherland. Most of the foreign money invested in the Pearl River Delta in Guangdong Province and in the Shenzhen SEZ comes from Hong Kong and Macau and from Overseas Chinese.

Private Enterprise

Besides the peasants who bring their produce to sell in the free markets, there's a new breed of entrepreneur in China – the private urban businessperson and its subspecies the pedlar. Faced with the return of rusticated youth sent away to work during the Cultural Revolution, and growing unemployment amongst young people, the government has even tended to encourage the peddling trades.

The total work force numbers about 450 million. A quarter of these are urban employees in state-run and collective enterprises. Almost all the rest are rural workers. Statistics for 1982 put the number of self-employed people in the cities and towns at 1.4 million. This number has probably increased greatly over the last few years, but even if it tripled or quadrupled it would still represent a tiny fraction of the total work force. The success of the new economic policies should therefore be measured in terms of their benefits to the rural population, the vast majority of Chinese.

The private businesses and street pedlars may not seem so extraordinary, but barely more than 10 years ago, during the Maoist era, they did not exist. Free enterprise was a dirty word from the mid-60s until the death of Mao, and during that time there were no curbside restaurants, no pedlars and no throngs of shoppers browsing and haggling with merchants on the sidewalks.

Today private enterprise comes in every form. Cooks, maids and nannies are becoming commonplace in the homes of middle and upper-income families. At least one Chinese company in Canton has been exporting cooks and cleaning women to Hong Kong since 1984. There are numerous privately run inns and hotels, restaurants and pedicabs. Even prostitution has made a comeback (if it really was suppressed during the Maoist era). Pedlars sell just about anything: shoes, clothing, produce from distant provinces, tickets to sporting events and shows, and often goods from state stores.

Consumerism

An ordinary urban Chinese income is around Y60 (about US$20) per month, although in some ways that figure is deceptively low. Housing rental is fixed at between 3 to 6% of income (but that could mean a tiny house or flat inhabited by several people per room), and various perks go with some jobs, such as bus passes, free child care services, non-staple food allowances, haircut and public bath allowances, and bonuses. Education and medical care are free, and personal income tax is nonexistent or negligible. Up to 50% of a person's income can be spent on food. Smaller bills include bicycle parking at Y0.02, bus maps Y0.30 and inter-city letter postage around Y0.08.

It's when you look at the cost of luxury or

high quality goods or household appliances that you notice the huge gap in the buying power between the Chinese and comparatively wealthy westerners. In China a bicycle starts from around Y150, or two to three months' wages; a sewing machine is around Y150; a multi-speed desk fan is Y150 to Y200; a poor quality digital watch costs Y6 or three days' wages.

Nevertheless, over the past few years there's been a boom in the quantity and availability of luxury consumer goods in China; the Four Modernisations may not be industry, agriculture, defence and science but cassette players, washing machines, TV sets and electric fans.

The Back Door

Production of consumer goods still cannot meet demand. The country's industries have been unable to keep pace with the new demand for household appliances, colour TVs, fashionable clothes and other luxury goods by the *nouveau riche* class of farmers, urban traders and skilled workers which has arisen in the last few years. Nor are they satisfied with Chinese merchandise; they want high status foreign cigarettes, liquor, cameras, cassette players and watches.

Because of the shortages many Chinese still rely on their connections (*guanxi*) to supply them with luxury items. Hong Kong relatives troop over the border laden down with all sorts of presents for their relatives in the People's Republic. Connections also open the 'back door'– the unauthorised means whereby goods made in state-owned factories and intended for sale in state-owned shops pass into private hands in return for favours or bribes.

The system of privilege is another means by which a few Chinese are able to accumulate a disproportionate share of available luxuries. While few individuals could afford to buy a car, a high-ranking cadre will have a car placed at his disposal by the state – which amounts to much the same thing as owning one for as long as he retains his position. Likewise, better quality housing, even hot running water, is still very much the domain of the Chinese elite.

The black market in foreign currency is another product of China's new economic policies. At lower levels currency is bought from foreigners and resold to other Chinese who use it to buy imported consumer goods. At higher levels the buyers are usually Chinese enterprises and individuals who use foreign currency to import consumer goods or finance their children's education overseas; the sellers are usually Hong Kong and Macau residents who, having sold their foreign currency at a much higher rate than the official exchange rate, will then buy large quantities of Chinese products which they export for profit.

Results

Figures are constantly produced to prove that these new policies are working. Nationwide annual increases in production of various goods from 1980 to 1984 are said to be about 6% for grain, 22% for millet, 5% for coal, about 2% for oil, about 6% for electricity and 4% for steel. The Chinese press is full of remarkable success stories of prosperous peasants and hard-working entrepreneurs who got rich because of the new economic policies.

With the increase in quantity there has been a dramatic rise in defective goods, or 'dirty radishes', to use the Chinese expression. In 1986, *China Daily* reported that at least one-third of goods produced in China were defective or did not conform to national standards. 'Red Flag' limousines continued to do nearly four km to the litre, faulty electric blankets electrocuted sleeping grannies, and hair conditioners left women bald. Members of the 1984 Chinese expedition to the Antarctic revealed that they suffered extreme discomfort when their parkas, made in Shanghai, proved neither cold-resistant nor waterproof.

The Chinese press recently also blasted

counterfeiting and copyright piracy, which have become rampant. Fake Chinese and foreign cigarettes are common, as are counterfeit medicines, wines and watches.

Overall the Chinese government seems confident that living standards are rising because of the new economic policies. However, Deng's policies have not gone unchallenged within the Communist Party leadership. As late as 1985 the Chinese press was still carrying articles criticising economic policy under Mao and exhorting officials to fall in line with Deng's new policies, while reassuring them that (somehow) these policies do not conflict with Marxism nor represent a renunciation of socialism and a return to capitalism as they fear.

Even top Party leaders have been critical. In a speech in 1985, the octogenarian Chen Yun, as a member of the Standing Committee of the Politburo, criticised the relaxation of central planning and the view that supply and demand could blindly determine production. He said that some media reports about growing prosperity amongst the peasants were 'divorced from reality' and that 'some people, including some Party members . . . are getting rich by illegal means like speculation, swindling, graft and bribe taking'.

Against these problems has to be weighed the argument that the Chinese people are poor and the country backward, requiring some radical new policies which might work in the long run regardless of the short-term consequences. It should be remembered that Deng's policies are being applied with the intention of raising the living standard of the great mass of Chinese, both urban and rural.

GEOGRAPHY

The insularity of the Chinese is very much a product of geography; the country is bounded to the north by deserts and to the west by the inhospitable Tibetan plateau. The Han Chinese, who first built their civilisation around the Yellow River, moved south and east towards the sea. The Han did not develop as a maritime nation so expansion was halted at the coast; they found themselves in control of a vast plain cut off from the rest of the world by oceans, mountains and deserts.

China is the third largest country in the world, after the Soviet Union and Canada. Only half of China is occupied by Han Chinese; the rest is inhabited by Mongols, Tibetans, Uygurs and a host of other 'national minorities' who occupy the periphery of Han China, in the strategic border areas. Distance, isolation and inhospitable terrain have made Han control of these people a tenuous affair, and the boundaries of the empire often changed during the Han expansion. Beyond this periphery of 'barbarians' lies a multitude of other powers with whom China has shared borders for centuries, not always happily: North Korea, Mongolia, the Soviet Union, Afghanistan, Pakistan, India, Nepal, Sikkim, Bhutan, Burma, Laos and Vietnam.

From the capital of Beijing the government rules 21 provinces and the five 'autonomous regions' of Inner Mongolia, Ningxia, Xinjiang, Guangxi and Tibet. Beijing, Tianjin and Shanghai are administered directly by the central government. China also controls about 5000 islands and lumps of rock which occasionally appear above water level; the largest of these is Hainan off the southern coast. Taiwan, Hong Kong and Macau are all firmly regarded by the People's Republic as Chinese territory, and under the 1984 agreement with Britain, Hong Kong will be handed back to China in 1997. There is conflict with Vietnam concerning sovereignty over the Nansha and Xisha island groups in the South China Sea; Vietnam claims both and has occupied some of the Nansha Islands.

China's topography varies from mountainous regions with towering peaks to flat, featureless plains. The land surface, like a staircase, descends from west to east.

Sino-British Joint Declaration on Hong Kong

At the top of the staircase are the plateaux of Tibet and Qinghai in the south-west, averaging 4500 metres above sea level. Tibet is referred to as the 'Roof of the World.' At the southern rim of the plateau is the Himalayan mountain range, with peaks averaging 6000 metres high; 40 peaks rise 7000 metres or more. Mt Everest, known to the Chinese as Qomolangma Feng, lies on the China-Nepal border.

Melting snow from the mountains of western China and the Tibet-Qinghai plateau provides the headwaters for many of the country's largest rivers: the Yangtse (Chang), Yellow (Huang), Mekong (Lancang) and Salween (or Nu, which runs from eastern Tibet into Yunnan Province and on into Burma).

Across the Kunlun and Qilian mountains on the northern rim of the Qinghai-Tibet plateau and the Hengduan Mountains on the eastern rim, the terrain drops abruptly to between 1000 and 2000 metres above sea level. The second step of the staircase is formed by the Inner Mongolia, Loess and Yunnan-Guizhou plateaux, and the Tarim, Sichuan and Junggar basins.

The Inner Mongolia Plateau has open terrain and expansive grasslands. Further south, the Loess Plateau is formed of loose earth 50 to 80 metres in depth – in the past the soil erosion which accompanied a torrential rainfall often choked the Yellow River. The Yunnan-Guizhou Plateau in China's south-west has a lacerated terrain with numerous gorges, rapids and waterfalls, and is noted for its limestone pinnacles with large underground caverns such as those at Guilin and Yangshuo.

The Tarim Basin is the largest inland basin in the world and is the site of the Xinjiang Autonomous Region. Here you'll find the Taklamakan Desert (the largest in China) as well as China's largest shifting salt lake, Lop Nur, where nuclear bombs are tested. The Tarim Basin is bordered to the north by the Tian Mountains. To the east of this range is the low-lying Turpan Depression, known as the 'oasis of fire' and the hottest place in China. The Junggar Basin lies in the far north of Xinjiang Province, beyond the Tian Mountains.

As you cross the mountains on the eastern edge of the second step of the staircase, the altitude drops to less than 1000 metres above sea level. Here, forming the third step, are the plains of the Yangtse River Valley and northern and eastern China. These plains – the homeland of the Han Chinese, their 'Middle Kingdom' – are the most important agricultural areas of the country and the most heavily populated. It should be remembered that two-thirds of China is mountain, desert, or otherwise unfit for cultivation. If you exclude the largely barren regions of Inner Mongolia, Xinjiang and the Tibet-Qinghai plateau from the remaining third, all that remains for cultivation is a meagre 15 to 20%. All this to feed a billion people!

In such a vast country, the waterways quickly took on a central role as communication and trading links. Most of China's rivers flow east. At 6300 km the Yangtse is the longest in China and the third longest in the world after the Nile and the Amazon. It originates in the snow-covered Tanggula Mountains of south-western Qinghai, and passes through Tibet and several Chinese provinces before emptying into the East China Sea. The Yellow River, about 5460 km long and the second longest river in China, is the birthplace of Chinese civilisation. It originates in the Bayan Har Mountains of Qinghai and winds its way through the north of China into the sea east of Beijing. The third great waterway of China, the Grand Canal, is the longest man-made canal in the world. It originally stretched 1800 km from Hangzhou in south China to Beijing in the north, though most of it is no longer navigable.

CLIMATE

Spread over such a vast area, China is subject to the worst extremes in weather, from the bitterly cold to the unbearably hot. There isn't really an 'ideal' time to visit the country, so use the following information as a rough guide to avoid temperature extremes. The warmest regions in winter are in the south and south-west such as Xishuangbanna, the south coast and Hainan Island. In summer, high spots like Emei Shan are a welcome relief from the heat.

North

Winters in the north fall between December and March and are incredibly cold. Beijing's temperature doesn't rise above 0°C (32°F), although it will generally be dry and sunny. North of the Great Wall, into Inner Mongolia or Heilongjiang, it's much colder with temperatures dropping well below freezing, and you'll see the curious sight of sand dunes covered in snow.

Summer in the north is around May to August. Beijing temperatures can rise to 38°C (100°F) or more. July and August are also the rainy months in the city. In both the north and south most of the rainfall is in summer.

Spring and autumn are the best times for visiting the north. Daytime temperatures are 20°C to 30°C (70°F to 85°F) and there is less rain. Although it can be quite hot during the day, night can be bitterly cold and bring frost.

Central

In the Yangtse River Valley area (including Shanghai) summers are long, hot and humid. Wuhan, Chongqing and Nanjing have been dubbed 'the three furnaces' by the Chinese.

You can expect very high temperatures any time between April and October. Winters are short and cold, with temperatures dipping well below freezing – almost as cold as Beijing. It can also be wet and miserable at any time apart from summer. While it is impossible to pinpoint an ideal time to visit, spring and autumn are probably best.

South

In the far south, around Canton, the hot, humid periods last from around April through September, and temperatures can rise to 38°C (100°F) as in the north. This is also the rainy season. Typhoons are liable to hit the south-east coast between July and September.

There is a short winter from January to March, nowhere near as cold as in the north, but temperature statistics don't really indicate just how cold it can get so bring warm clothes. If you flop into China around this time wearing thongs, shorts and a T-shirt, you'll see what I mean!

Autumn and spring can be good times to visit, with day time temperatures in the mid-20°C (70°F to 80°F)range. However, it can be miserably wet and cold, with perpetual rain or drizzle, so be prepared.

North-West

Try to avoid China's north-west at the height of summer. Industrial Ürümqi is dismal at this time (although it's a good time to visit the Lake of Heaven in the mountains east of the city), and Turpan (worse off for being situated in a depression) has unbearable maximums of around 47°C (118°F).

In winter this region is as formidably cold as the rest of northern China. In Ürümqi the average temperature in January is around -10°C (-50°F), with minimums down to almost -30°C (-86°F). Temperatures in Turpan are only slightly more favourable to human existence.

Tibet

For details of this special region see the Tibet chapter in this book.

RELIGION

Chinese religion has been influenced by three great streams of human thought: Taoism, Confucianism and Buddhism. Each is more a philosophy than a religion, but all have been inextricably entwined in popular Chinese religion along with ancient animist beliefs. The founders of Taoism, Confucianism and Buddhism have been deified and the Chinese worship them and their disciples as fervently as they worship their own ancestors and a pantheon of gods and spirits – the worship closely bound up with sorcery and magic.

Taoism

According to tradition, the founder of Taoism is a man known as Lao Tzu. He is said to have been born around the year 604 BC, but some doubt that he ever lived at all. Almost nothing is known about him, not even his name. 'Lao Tzu' translates as 'the old boy' or the 'Grand Old Master'.

Legends depict Lao Tzu as having been conceived by a shooting star, carried in his unfortunate mother's womb for 82 years, and born as a wise old man with white hair. Another story goes that he was the keeper of the government archives in a western state of China, and that Confucius visited him.

At the end of his life, Lao Tzu is said to have climbed on a water buffalo and ridden west towards what is now Tibet, in search of solitude for his last few years. On the way, he was asked to leave behind a record of his beliefs. The product was a slim volume of only 5000 characters, the *Tao Te Ching* or *The Way and its Power*. He then rode off on his buffalo.

At the centre of Taoism is the concept of *Tao*. Tao cannot be perceived because it exceeds senses, thoughts and imagination; it can be known only through mystical insight which cannot be expressed with words. Tao is the way of the universe, the driving power in nature, the order behind all life, the spirit which cannot be exhausted. Tao is the way people should order their lives to keep in harmony with the natural order of the universe:

There is a being, wonderful, perfect;
It existed before heaven and earth.
How quiet it is!
How spiritual it is!
It stands alone and it does not change.
It moves around and around, but does
not on this account suffer.
All life comes from it.
It wraps everything with its love as in a
garment, and yet claims no honour, and
does not demand to be Lord.
I do not know its name, and so I call it
Tao, the Way, and
I rejoice in its power.

Just as there have been different interpretations of the 'way', there have also been different interpretations of *Te* – the power of the universe. This has led to the development of three distinct forms of Taoism in China.

One form held that 'the power' is philosophical. The philosophical Taoist, by reflection and intuition, orders his or her life in harmony with the way of the universe and achieves the understanding or experience of Tao. Philosophical Taoism has many followers in the west.

The second form held that the power of the universe was basically psychic in nature, and by practising yogic exercises and meditation a number of individuals could become receptacles for Tao. They could then radiate a healing, psychic influence over those around them.

The third form is the 'popular Taoism'

which took hold in China. The power of the universe is the power of gods, magic and sorcery. Because popular Taoism has been associated with alchemy and the search for immortality, it often attracted the patronage of Chinese rulers before Confucianism gained the upper hand. It's argued that only philosophical Taoism actually takes its inspiration from the *Tao Te Ching*, and that the other labels under which 'Taoism' has been practised used Lao Tzu's name to give themselves respectability.

Confucianism

With the exception of Mao, the one name which has become synonymous with China is Confucius. He was born of a poor family around the year 551 BC – during the chaotic Warring States Period – in what is now Shandong Province. His ambition was to hold a high government office and to reorder society through the administrative apparatus. At most he seems to have had several insignificant government posts, a few followers and a permanently blocked career. At the age of 50 he perceived his 'divine mission' and for the next 13 years tramped from state to state offering unsolicited advice to rulers on how to improve their governing, while looking for an opportunity to put his own ideas into practice. That opportunity never came, and he returned to his own state to spend the last five years of his life teaching and editing classical literature. He died in 479 BC, at the age of about 72.

The glorification of Confucius began after his death, and eventually his ideas permeated every level of Chinese society. Government offices presupposed a knowledge of the Confucian classics, and spoken proverbs trickled down to the illiterate masses. During the Han Dynasty Confucianism effectively became the state religion; his teachings were made the basic discipline for training government officials and remained so until almost the end of the Qing Dynasty in 1911. In the 7th and 8th centuries temples and shrines were built to Confucius and his original disciples. During the Song Dynasty the Confucian bible *The Analects* became the basis of all education.

It is not hard to see why Confucianism took hold in China. The perpetual conflict of the Warring States Period had inspired Confucius to seek a way which would allow people to live together peacefully. His solution was Tradition. Like others of his time, he believed that there had once been a period of great peace and prosperity in China. This had been brought about because people lived by certain traditions which maintained peace and social order.

Confucius advocated a return to these traditions and also devised values which he thought were necessary for collective well-being. He aimed to instil a feeling of humanity towards others and respect for oneself, as well as a sense of the dignity of human life. Courtesy, selflessness, magnanimity, diligence and empathy would naturally follow. His ideal person was competent, poised, fearless, even-tempered and free of violence and vulgarity. The study of 'correct attitudes' became the primary task. Moral ideas had to be driven into the people by every possible means – at temples, theatres, homes, schools and festivals, and in proverbs and folk stories.

All people rendered homage to the emperor, who was regarded as the embodiment of Confucian wisdom and virtue, the head of the great family-nation. For centuries administration under the emperor lay in the hands of a small Confucian scholar class. In theory anyone who passed the examinations qualified, but in practice the monopoly of power was held by the educated upper classes. There has never been a rigid code of law because Confucianism rejected the idea that conduct could be enforced by some organisation; taking legal action implied an incapacity to work things out by negotiation. The result, however, was arbitrary justice and oppression by those who held power. Dynasties rose and fell but the Confucian pattern never changed.

There are several bulwarks of Confucianism but the one which has probably had the most influence on the day-to-day life of the Chinese is *Li*, which has two meanings. The first meaning of Li is 'propriety' – a set of manners or a knowledge of how to behave in a given situation – and presumes that the various roles and relationships of life have been clearly defined. The second meaning of Li is 'ritual' – when life is detailed to Confucian lengths it becomes completely ordered.

Confucian codes of conduct and clearly defined patterns of obedience became inextricably bound up in Chinese society. Women obey and defer to men, younger brothers to elder brothers, sons to fathers. Respect flows upwards, from young to old, from subject to ruler. Age is venerated since it gives everything (including people, objects and institutions) their dignity and worth; the elderly may be at their weakest physically, but they are at the peak of their wisdom.

The family retains its central place as the basic unit of society; Confucianism reinforced this idea, but did not invent it. The key to family order is filial piety – children's respect for and duty towards their parents. Teaming up with traditional superstition, Confucianism reinforced the practice of ancestor-worship. Confucius himself is worshipped and temples are built for him. The strict codes of obedience were held together by these concepts of filial piety and ancestor worship, as well as by the concept of 'face' – to let down the family or group is a great shame for a Chinese.

Buddhism

Buddhism was founded in India in the 6th century BC by Siddhartha Gautama of the Sakyas. Siddhartha was his given name, Gautama his surname and Sakaya the name of the clan to which his family belonged.

The story goes that though he was a prince brought up in luxury, Siddhartha became discontented with the world when he was confronted with the sights of old age, sickness and death. He despaired of finding fulfilment on the physical level, since the body was inescapably subject to these weaknesses.

Around the age of 30 Siddhartha broke from the material world and sought 'enlightenment'. After several failed attempts he devoted the final phase of his search to meditation and mystic concentration. One evening, so the story goes, he sat beneath a bo tree, slipped into a deep meditation and emerged having achieved enlightenment.

Buddha founded an order of monks and preached his ideas for the next four decades until his death around 480 BC. To his followers he was known as Sakyamuni, the 'silent sage of the Sakya clan', because of the unfathomable mystery that surrounded him. Gautama Buddha was not the only Buddha, but the fourth, and is not expected to be the last.

The cornerstone of Buddhist philosophy is the view that all life is suffering. Everyone is subject to the traumas of birth, sickness, decrepitude and death; to what they most dread (an incurable disease or an ineradicable personal weakness), as well as separation from what they love. The cause of suffering is desire – specifically the desires of the body and the desire for personal fulfilment. Happiness can only be achieved if these desires are overcome, and this requires following the 'eight-fold path'. By following this path the Buddhist aims to attain *nirvana*, a condition beyond the limits of mind and feelings; a state of bliss.

The first pathway is 'right knowledge': the recognition that life is suffering, that suffering is caused by desire for personal gratification and that suffering can be overcome by following the eight-fold path. The second pathway is 'right aspiration' – involvement with the knowledge of what life's problems basically are. The other pathways require that one refrain from abuse and deceit; that one show kindness and avoid self-seeking in all actions; that one develop virtues and curb passions; and that one practise yoga.

There are several varieties of yoga, each designed to unite humans with the universal 'god'. The *raja yoga* which Buddha studied under his Hindu teachers at the outset of his search for enlightenment uses mental exercises to penetrate deep into the psyche where it is believed the real problems and answers lie, and to achieve a personal experience of what lies hidden within.

Buddhism developed in China during the 3rd to 6th centuries AD. It was probably introduced by Indian merchants who took Buddhist priests with them on their land and sea journeys to China. Later, an active effort was made to import Buddhism into China. In the middle of the 1st century AD the religion had gained the interest of the Han Emperor Ming, who sent a mission to the west; the mission returned in 67 AD with Buddhist scriptures, two Indian monks and images of the Buddha. Centuries later, other Chinese monks like Xuan Zang journeyed to India and returned with Buddhist scriptures which were then translated from the original Sanskrit to Chinese – a massive job involving Chinese as well as foreign scholars from Central Asia, India and Sri Lanka.

Buddhism spread rapidly in the north of China where it was patronised by various ruling invaders, who in some cases had been acquainted with the religion before they came to China. Others patronised the Buddhist monks because they wanted educated officials who were not Confucians. In the south Buddhism spread more slowly, carried down during Chinese migrations from the north. There were several periods in which Buddhists were persecuted and their temples and monasteries sacked and destroyed, but the religion survived. To a people constantly faced with starvation, war and poverty its appeal probably lay in the doctrines of reincarnation and nirvana which it had borrowed from Indian Hinduism.

Buddhist monasteries and temples sprang up everywhere in China, and played a similar role to the churches and monasteries of medieval Europe. Monasteries were guest houses, hospitals and orphanages for travellers and refugees. With gifts obtained from the faithful, they were able to amass considerable wealth, which enabled them to set up moneylending enterprises and pawn shops. These pawn shops were the poor man's bank right up to the mid-20th century.

Buddha wrote nothing, and the writings that have come down to us date from about 150 years after his death. By the time these texts came out, divisions had already appeared within Buddhism. Some writers tried to emphasise Buddha's break with Hinduism, while others tried to minimise it. At some stage Buddhism split into two major schools: *Hinayana* and *Mahayana*.

The *Hinayana* or 'little raft' school holds that the path to nirvana is an individual pursuit. It centres on the monks, individuals who make the search for nirvana a full-time profession. This school maintains that people are alone in the world and must tread the path to nirvana on their own; Buddhas can only show the way. The Hinayana school is the Buddhism of Sri Lanka, Burma, Thailand and Kampuchea.

The *Mahayana* or 'big raft' school holds that since all existence is one, the fate of the individual is linked to the fate of others. The Buddha did not just point the way and float off into his own nirvana, but continues to offer spiritual help to others seeking nirvana. The Mahayana school is the Buddhism of Vietnam, Japan, Tibet, Korea, Mongolia and China.

The outward difference between the two schools is the cosmology of the Mahayana school. Mahayana Buddhism is replete with innumerable heavens, hells and descriptions of nirvana. Prayers are addressed to the Buddha, combined with elaborate ritual. There are deities and *bodhisattvas*, a rank of supernatural beings in their last incarnation before nirvana. Temples are filled with images such as the future Buddha Maitreya, often portrayed as fat and happy over his coming promotion, and Amitabha, a saviour who rewards the faithful with admission to a sort of Christian paradise. The ritual, tradition and superstition that Buddha rejected came tumbling back in with a vengeance.

An interesting form of Buddhism is the Tantric (Lamaist) Buddhism of Tibet. This has been the religion of Tibet since the early 7th century AD and is heavily influenced by Tibet's pre-Buddhist Bon religion which relied on priests or shamans to placate spirits, gods and demons.

Chinese Religion

Taoism combines with old animistic beliefs to teach people how to maintain harmony with the universe. Confucianism takes care of the political and moral aspects of life. Buddhism takes care of the afterlife. But to say that the Chinese have three religions – Taoism, Buddhism and Confucianism – is too simple a view of their traditional religious life. At the first level Chinese religion is animistic, with a belief in the innate vital energy in rocks, trees, rivers and springs. At the second level people from the distant past, both real and mythological, are worshipped as gods. Overlaid on these beliefs are popular Taoism, Mahayana Buddhism and Confucianism.

On a day-to-day level the Chinese are much less concerned with the high-minded philosophies and asceticism of Buddha, Confucius or Lao Tzu than they are with the pursuit of worldly success, the appeasement of the dead and the spirits, and the seeking of hidden knowledge about the future. Chinese religion incorporates what the West regards as superstition; if you want your fortune told, for instance, you go to a temple. The other important thing to remember is that Chinese religion is polytheistic. Apart from Buddha, Lao Tzu and Confucius there are many other divinities such as house gods and gods and goddesses for particular professions.

The most important word in the Chinese popular religious vocabulary is *joss* (luck), and the Chinese are too astute not to utilise it. Gods have to be appeased, bad spirits blown away and sleeping dragons soothed to keep joss on one's side. *Fung-shui* (literally wind-water) is the Chinese technique of manipulating or judging the environment. Fung-shui uses unseen currents that swirl around the surface of the earth and are caused by dragons which sleep beneath the ground. In Hong Kong, if you want to build a house or find a suitable site for a grave then you call in a fung-shui expert; the wrath of a dragon which woke to find a house on his tail can easily be imagined! In Hong Kong some villages even have groves of trees planted for good spirits to live in.

Integral parts of Chinese religion are death, the afterlife and ancestor-worship. At least as far back as China's Shang Dynasty there were lavish funeral ceremonies involving the internment of horses, carriages, wives and slaves. The more important the person the more possessions and people had to be buried with him since he would require them in the next world. The deceased had to be kept happy because his powers to inflict punishments or to grant favours greatly increased after his death. Even today a traditional Chinese funeral can still be a lavish event.

The Chinese Temple

Architecturally, the roof is the dominant feature of a Chinese temple. It is usually green or yellow and is decorated with figures of divinities and lucky symbols such as dragons and carp. Stone lions often guard the temple entrance.

Inside is a small courtyard with a large bowl where incense and paper offerings are burnt. Beyond is the main hall with an altar table, often with an intricately carved front. Here you'll find offerings of fruit and drinks. Behind is the altar with its images framed by red brocade embroidered with gold characters. Depending on the size and wealth of the temple there are gongs, drums, side altars and adjoining rooms with shrines to different gods, chapels for prayers to the dead and displays of funerary plaques. There are also living quarters for the temple keepers. There is no set time for prayer and no communal service except for funerals. Worshippers enter the temple whenever they want to make offerings, pray for help or give thanks.

The dominant colours in a Chinese temple are red, gold or yellow, and green. The orange to red colour range represents joy and festivity. White stands for purity and is also the colour of death. Green signifies harmony, of fundamental importance to the Chinese. Yellow and gold herald heavenly glory. Grey and black are the colours of disaster and grief.

The most striking feature of the Buddhist temple is the pagoda. It was probably introduced from India along with Buddhism in the 1st century AD. Because the early pagodas were constructed of wood, they were easily destroyed by fire and subject to corrosion, so materials such as brick, stone, brass and iron were substituted. They were often built to house religious artefacts and documents, to commemorate important events, or as monuments. The Big Goose Pagoda in Xian is a monolithic example of pagoda construction.

During the Northern Wei period the construction of cave temples began, and was continued during later dynasties. The caves at Longmen near Luoyang, at Mogao near Dunhuang, and at Yungang near Datong are some of the finest examples.

In Buddhist art the Buddha is frequently displayed in a basic triad, with a bodhisattva on either side. The latter are Buddhist saints who have arrived at the gateway to nirvana but have chosen to return to earth to guide lesser mortals along righteous paths. Their faces tend to express joy, serenity or compassion. Sometimes the bodhisattvas are replaced by the figures of Buddha's first two disciples, the youthful Ananda and the older Kasyapa.

Islam

The founder of Islam was the Arab prophet Mohammed. Strictly speaking, Muslims believe it was not Mohammed who shaped the religion but God, and Mohammed merely transmitted it from God to his people. To call the religion 'Mohammedanism' is also wrong, since it implies that the religion centres around Mohammed and not around God. The proper name of the religion is Islam, derived from the word *salam* which primarily means 'peace', and in a secondary sense 'surrender'. The full connotation is something like 'the peace which comes by surrendering to God'. The corresponding adjective is 'Muslim'.

The prophet was born around 570 and came to be called Mohammed, which means 'highly praised'. His ancestry is traditionally traced back to Abraham, who had two wives, Hagar and Sarah. Hagar gave birth to Ismael, and Sarah had a son named Isaac. Sarah demanded that Hagar and Ismael be banished from the tribe. According to Islam's holy book the *Koran*, Ismael went to Mecca, where his line of descendants can be traced down to Mohammed. There have been other true prophets before Mohammed, but he is regarded as the culmination of them and the last.

Mohammed said that there is only one God, Allah. The name derives from joining *al* which means 'the' with *Illah* which means 'God'. His uncompromising monotheism conflicted with the pantheism and idolatry of the Arabs. Also, his moral teachings and vision of a universal brotherhood conflicted with what he believed was a corrupt and decadent social order based on class divisions. The initial reaction to his teachings was hostile. He and his followers were forced to flee from Mecca to Medina in 622 AD, where Mohammed built up a political base and an army which eventually defeated Mecca and brought all of Arabia under his control. He died in 632 AD, two years after taking Mecca. By the time a century had passed the Arab Muslims had built a huge empire which stretched all the way from Persia to Spain. Though the Arabs were eventually supplanted by the Turks, the strength of Islam has continued to the present day.

Unlike in many other countries, Islam was brought to China peacefully. Arab traders who landed on the southern coast of China established their mosques in great maritime cities like Canton and Quanzhou, and Muslim merchants travelling the 'Silk Road' through Asia to China won converts among the Han Chinese in the north of the country. There are also large populations of Muslim Uygur people (of Turkish descent) whose ancestors first moved into China's Xinjiang region during the Tang Dynasty.

Christianity

The earliest record of Christianity in China dates back to the Nestorians, a Syrian Christian sect. They first appeared in China in the 7th century when a Syrian named Raban presented Christian scriptures to the Chinese imperial court at Chang'an (Xian). This event and the construction of a Nestorian monastery in Chang'an are recorded on a large stone stele made in 781 AD, now displayed in the Shaanxi Provincial Museum in Xian.

The next major Christian group to arrive in China were the Jesuits. The priests Matteo Ricci and Michael Ruggieri were permitted to set up base at Zhaoqing in Guangdong Province in the 1580s, and eventually made it to the imperial court in Beijing. Large numbers of Catholic and Protestant missionaries established themselves in China following the invasion of China by the western powers in the 19th century.

Judaism

One of the curiosities of China are the Chinese Jews. Kaifeng in Henan Province was the home of their largest community. Their religious beliefs and almost all the customs associated with them have died out, yet the descendants of the original Jews still consider themselves Jewish. Just how the Jews got to China is unknown. They may have come as traders and merchants along the Silk Road when Kaifeng was the capital of China, or they may have emigrated from India. For more details, see the Kaifeng section in this book.

Religion, Culture & Communism

Today the Chinese Communist government professes atheism. It considers religion to be base superstition, a remnant of old China which was used by the ruling classes to keep power. For whatever reason, perhaps partly in an effort to improve relations with the Muslim, Buddhist and Lamaist minorities, the Chinese government is once again permitting open religious activity.

Traditional Chinese religious beliefs took a battering during the Cultural Revolution when monasteries were disbanded, temples destroyed and the monks sometimes killed or sent to the fields to labour. Many temples and monasteries are now derelict or used for other functions. Although traditional Chinese religion is strong in places like Macau, Hong Kong and Taiwan, it's difficult to determine the situation in China itself.

Since the death of Mao, the Chinese government has allowed many temples (sometimes with their own contingent of monks and novices) to reopen as active places of worship. All religious activity is firmly under state control and many of the monks function as caretakers within renovated shells. Pilgrimages to burn incense, throw *sing pui* (fortune-telling sticks) and make offerings to the gods by burning fake paper money appear to be common practice in temples once more. There are also stories of peasants rebuilding shrines to local gods, consulting fung-shui experts before constructing buildings and graves, and burying deceased relatives with traditional religious ceremonies. A common sight in southern China is paper pictures of gods pasted on the doors of houses.

Confucius has often been used as a political symbol, his role 'redefined' to suit the needs of the time. At the end of the 19th century he was upheld as a symbol of reform because he had worked for reform in his own day. After the fall of the Qing Dynasty, Chinese intellectuals vehemently opposed him as a symbol of a conservative and backward China. In the 1930s he was used by Chiang Kaishek and the Kuomintang as a guide to proper, traditional values. During the Cultural Revolution Confucius was attacked as a symbol of the decadence and oppression of old China. Just what line to take with Confucian teachings remains a problem for the Chinese government, though he is now making something of a comeback as the government emphasises stability and respect for order and authority.

Christianity is a reminder of foreign intrusion and imperialism on Chinese soil. The western powers in the 19th century used the missionaries as an excuse to expand the areas under their control, claiming the need to protect the missions. Besides winning religious converts, the missions posed a threat to traditional Chinese society since they introduced an alien religion, science, education and morals.

A common criticism is that many early Chinese Christians were 'rice Christians' – attracted to the power and wealth of the church rather than to the faith itself. True or not, the Chinese Christian churches survived the Communist takeover in 1949. Like the Buddhist temples, they were closed down during the Cultural Revolution; many have since been restored and are once again active places of worship. There are around three million Catholics and probably an equal number of Protestants in China today.

Freedom of religion is guaranteed under the Chinese constitution, but it carries a crucial rider that 'Religious bodies and religious affairs are not subject to any foreign domination'. In the late 1950s the Chinese government moved to sever the churches from foreign influence and to place them under the control of the government. The 'Three-Self Patriotic Movement' was set up as an umbrella organisation for the Protestant churches, and the 'Catholic Patriotic Association' was set up to replace Rome as the leader of the Catholic churches.

There is much friction between the government and the Chinese Catholic church because the church refuses to disown the Pope as its leader, and because the Vatican maintains diplomatic relations with Taiwan. In March 1983, four elderly priests who had already spent long terms in prison were again sentenced to long terms of imprisonment on charges which included subversion and collusion with foreign countries, though it's thought their main offence was maintaining illicit contacts with the Vatican.

The Cultural revolution resulted in the closure of Muslim mosques (even in distant Xinjiang where the non-Chinese population is predominantly Muslim), though many of these have since reopened. Of all people in China the Tibetans felt the brunt of Mao's mayhem. The Dalai Lama and his entourage fled to India in 1959 when the Tibetan rebellion was put down by Chinese troops. During the Cultural Revolution the monasteries were disbanded (some were levelled to the ground) and the theocracy which had governed Tibet for centuries was wiped out overnight. Some Tibetan temples and monasteries have been reopened and the Tibetan religion is still a very powerful force among the people.

THE ARTS

Chinese art is like Chinese religion – it has developed over a period of more than 2000 years and absorbed many influences. Two of China's most revered arts, calligraphy and painting, have been inspired by the Taoist respect for nature and deeply influenced by Confucian morality.

Calligraphy

Calligraphy has traditionally been regarded in China as the highest form of visual art. A fine piece of calligraphy was often valued more highly by a collector of art than a good painting. Children were trained at a very early age to write beautifully, and good calligraphy was a social asset. A scholar, for example, could not pass his examination to become an official if he was a poor calligrapher. A person's character was judged by his or her handwriting; if it was elegant it revealed great refinement.

Chinese calligraphy brushes

The basic tools of calligraphy are paper, ink, ink-stone (on which the ink is mixed) and brush. These are commonly referred to as the 'four treasures of the scholar's study'. A brush stroke must be infused with the creative or vital energy which, according to the Taoists, permeates and animates all phenomena of the universe: mountains, rivers, rocks, trees, insects and animals. Expressive images are drawn from nature to describe the different types of brush strokes – for example, 'rolling waves', 'leaping dragon', 'startled snake slithering off into the grass', 'dewdrop about to fall' or 'playful butterfly'. A beautiful piece of calligraphy therefore conjures up the majestic movements of a landscape. The qualities of the brush strokes are described in organic terms of 'bone', 'flesh', 'muscle' and 'blood'. Blood, for example, refers to the quality of the ink and the varied ink tones created by the degree of moisture of the brush.

Calligraphy is regarded as a form of self-cultivation as well as self-expression. It is believed that calligraphy should be able to express and communicate the most ineffable thoughts and feelings, which cannot be conveyed by words. It is often said that looking at calligraphy 'one understands the writer fully, as if meeting him face to face'. All over China, decorative calligraphy can be found in temples, adorning the walls of caves, and on the sides of mountains and monuments.

Painting

Looking at Chinese paintings for the first time, the Italian Jesuit priest Matteo Ricci (who reached China in 1582) criticised Chinese painters for their lack of knowledge of the illusionistic techniques of shading, with the result that their paintings 'look dead and have no life at all'. The Chinese were in turn astonished by the oil paintings brought by the Jesuits, which to them resembled mirror images – but they rejected them as paintings because they were devoid of expressive brushwork.

Chinese painting is the art of brush and ink. The basic tools are those of calligraphy, which influenced painting in both technique and theory. The brush line, which varies in thickness and tone, is the important feature of a Chinese painting. Shading is regarded as a foreign technique (introduced to China via Buddhist art from Central Asia between the 3rd and 9th centuries), and colour plays only a minor symbolic and decorative role. As early as the 9th century, ink was recognised as being able to provide all the qualities of colour.

Although you will see artists in China painting or sketching in front of their subject, traditionally the painter works from memory. The painter is not so interested in imitating the outward appearance of the subject as in capturing its lifelike qualities and imbuing the painting with the energy that permeates all nature.

From the Han Dynasty until the end of the Tang Dynasty, the human figure occupied the dominant position in Chinese painting, as it did in pre-modern European art. Figure painting flourished against a Confucian background, illustrating moralistic themes. Landscape painting for its own sake started in the 4th and 5th centuries. The practice of seeking out places of natural beauty and communing with nature first became popular among Taoist poets and painters. By the 9th century the interest of artists began to shift away from figures, and from the 11th century onwards landscape has been the most important aspect of Chinese painting.

The function of the landscape painting was to substitute for nature, allowing the viewer to wander in imagination. The painting is meant to surround the viewer, and there is no 'viewing point' as there is in western painting. Guo Xi, a painter of the 11th century, wrote:

> Contemplation of such pictures arouses corresponding feelings in the breast; it is as if one has really come to these places . . . without leaving the room, at once, he finds himself among the streams and ravines.

Guo spoke of landscape elements in organic terms: the watercourses were the arteries of mountains, the grass and trees its hair, the mist and haze its complexion.

In the 11th century a new attitude towards painting was formulated by a group of scholar-painters led by Su Dongpo (1036-1101). They recognised that painting could go beyond mere representation; it could also serve as a means of expression and communication in much the same way as calligraphy.

Painting became accepted as one of the activities of a cultured person, along with poetry, music and calligraphy. The scholar-amateur painters, who were either officials or living in retirement, did not depend on painting for their income. They painted for pleasure and became their own patrons and critics. They were also collectors and connoisseurs of art, and the arbiters of taste. Their ideas on art were voiced in voluminous writings and in inscriptions on paintings.

Moralistic qualities appreciated in a virtuous person (in the Confucian frame of things) became the very qualities appreciated in paintings. One of the most important was the 'concealment of brilliance' under an unassuming exterior, since any deliberate display of technical skill was considered vulgar. Creativity and individuality were highly valued, but only within the framework of tradition. Artists created their own style by transforming the styles of the ancient masters, seeing themselves as part of the great continuity of the painting tradition. This art-historical approach became a conscious pursuit in the late Ming and early Qing dynasties.

Funerary Objects

As early as neolithic times (9000-6000 BC), offerings of pottery vessels and stone tools or weapons were placed in graves to accompany the departed.

During the Shang Dynasty, precious objects such as bronze ritual vessels, weapons and jade were buried with the dead. Dogs, horses and even human beings were sacrificed for burial in the tombs of great rulers. When this practice was abandoned, replicas (usually in pottery) were made of human beings, animals and precious objects. A whole repertoire of objects was produced especially for burial, making symbolic provision for the dead without waste of wealth or human sacrifice.

Burial objects made of earthenware were very popular from the 1st to the 8th centuries AD. During the Han Dynasty, pottery figures were cast in moulds and painted in bright colours after firing. Statues of attendants, entertainers, musicians, acrobats and jugglers were made, as well as models of granaries, watchtowers, pigpens, stoves and various other things.

Close trade links with the west were illustrated by the appearance of the two-humped Bactrian camel, which carried merchandise along the Silk Road, amongst funerary objects. Warriors with west Asian faces and heavy beards appeared as funerary objects during the Northern Wei Dynasty, a foreign dynasty founded by the Turkish-speaking Tobas of Central Asia. The cosmopolitan life of Tang China was illustrated by its funerary wares; western and central Asians flocked to the capital at Chang'an and were portrayed in figurines of merchants, attendants, warriors, grooms, musicians and dancers. Tall western horses with long legs, introduced to China from Central Asia at the beginning of the 1st century BC, were also popular subjects for tomb figurines.

Other funerary objects commonly seen in Chinese museums are fearsome military figures dressed in full armour, often trampling oxen underfoot. The figures may have served as tomb guardians and may represent the four heavenly kings. These kings guard the four quarters of the universe and protect the state; they have been assimilated into Buddhism and you see statues of them in Buddhist temples.

Guardian spirits are some of the strangest funerary objects. Common ones have bird wings, elephant ears, a human face, the body of a lion, and the legs and hooves of a deer or horse, all rolled into one. One theory is that these figures represent Tubo, the earth-spirit or lord of the underworld who was endowed with the power to ward off demons and evil spirits. He was entrusted with guarding the tomb of the deceased. Those figures with human faces may have represented the legendary Emperor Yu. He is said to have been the founder of the legendary Xia Dynasty, and was transformed into Tubo after his death.

Ceramics

Earthenware production has a long history in China. As long as 8000 years ago Chinese tribes were making artefacts with clay. The primitive 'Yangshao' culture (so named because the first excavation of an ancient agricultural village was made in the region of Yangshao near the confluence of the Yellow, Fen and Wei rivers) is noted for its distinctive pottery painted with flowers, fish, animals, human faces and geometric designs. Around 3500 BC the 'Lungshanoid' culture (so named because evidence of this ancient culture was first found near the village of Lungshan in Shandong Province) was making white pottery and eggshell-thin black pottery.

Pottery-making was well advanced by the Shang period; the most important development occurred around the middle of the dynasty with the manufacture of a greenish glaze applied to stoneware artefacts. During the Han Dynasty the custom of glazing pottery became fairly common. However, the production of terracotta pottery – made from a mixture of sand and clay, fired to produce a reddish-brown colour, and left unglazed – continued.

During the Southern and Northern Dynasty periods, a type of pottery halfway between Han glazed pottery and true porcelain was produced. The proto-porcelain was made by mixing clay with quartz and the mineral feldspar to make a hard, smooth-surfaced vessel. Feldspar was mixed with traces of iron to produce an olive-green glaze. The technique was perfected under the Tang but few examples survive. Tri-colour glazed vessels were also produced during the Tang Dynasty.

By the 8th century, Tang proto-porcelain and other types of pottery had found an international market, and were exported as far afield as Japan and the east coast of Africa. Chinese porcelain did not reach Europe until the Ming period, and was not manufactured there until the 17th century.

Chinese pottery reached its artistic peak under the Song rulers. During this time true porcelain was developed. It was made of fine kaolin clay and was white, thin, transparent or translucent. Porcelain was produced under the Yuan but gradually lost the delicacy and near-perfection of the Song. However, it was probably during the Yuan Dynasty that 'blue-and-white' porcelain made its first appearance. This porcelain had blue decorations on a white background; it was made of kaolin clay quarried near Jingdezhen, and mixed with a type of cobalt imported from Persia.

During this period tri-colour and five-colour porcelain, with floral decorations on a white background, was produced. Another noted invention was mono-coloured porcelain, in ferrous red, black or dark blue. A new range of mono-coloured vessels was developed under the Qing.

During the Qing Period the production of coloured porcelain continued with the addition of new colours and glazes and more complex decorations. This was the age of true painted porcelain, decorated with delicate landscapes, birds and flowers. Elaborate designs and brilliant colouring became the fashion. Porcelain imitation of other materials such as gold and silver, mother of pearl, jade, bronze, wood and bamboo, also became popular.

Bronze tripod

Bronze Vessels

Bronze is an alloy, the chief elements being copper, tin and lead. Tradition ascribes the casting of bronze to the legendary Xia Dynasty of 4000 years ago. Emperor Yu, the founder of the dynasty, is said to have divided his empire into nine provinces and then cast nine bronze tripods to symbolise the dynasty. However, the 1928 discovery of the last Shang Dynasty capital at Anyang in Henan Province provided the first evidence that the ancient Chinese used bronze.

The Shang ruler and the aristocracy are believed to have used a large number of bronze vessels for offerings of food and wine in sacrificial ceremonies. Through ritual sacrifices the spirits of ancestors were prevailed upon to look after their descendants. The vessels were often buried with the deceased, along with other earthly provisions. Most of the late Shang funeral vessels have short, pictographic inscriptions recording the names of the clan, the ancestor and the vessel's maker, along with important events. Zhou Dynasty bronze vessels tend to have longer messages in ideographic characters, and describe wars, rewards, ceremonial events and the appointment of officials.

The early bronzes were cast in sectional clay moulds, an offshoot of the advanced pottery technology's high-temperature kilns and clay-mould casting. Each section of the mould was impressed, incised or carved with the required designs. By the 5th century BC, during the Eastern Zhou period (771-256 BC), bronzes with geometric designs and scenes of hunting and feasting were inlaid with precious metals and stones.

Bronze mirrors were used as early as the Shang Dynasty and had already developed into an artistic form by the Warring States period. Ceramics gradually replaced bronze utensils by the Han Dynasty, but bronze mirrors were not displaced by glass mirrors until the Qing Dynasty.

In China, the mirror is a metaphor for self-inspection in philosophical discussion. The wise man has three mirrors: a mirror of bronze in which he sees his physical appearance, a mirror of the people by which he examines his inner character and conduct, and a mirror of the past by which he learns to emulate successes and avoid the mistakes of earlier times. The backs of bronze mirrors were inscribed with wishes for good fortune and protection from evil influence. Post-Han writings are full of fantastic stories of the supernatural powers of mirrors. One of them relates the tale of Yin Zhongwen, who held a mirror to look at himself but found that his face was not reflected; soon after he was executed.

Jade

The jade stone has been revered in China since neolithic times. While the pure white form is the most highly valued, the stone varies in translucency and colour, including many shades of green, brown and black. To the Chinese, jade symbolises nobility, beauty and purity. Its physical properties have become metaphors for the Confucian ideal of the *junzi*, the noble or superior man. A Chinese dictionary of the 2nd century AD defines the character of jade in this way:

> Jade is the fairest of stones.
> It is endowed with five virtues.
> Charity is its lustre, bright yet warm;
> Recitude is its translucency, revealing
> the colour and markings within;
> Wisdom is its pure and penetrating note when struck.
> It is courage, for it can be broken but does not bend;
> Equity is its sharp edges which injure none.

Jade is also empowered with magical and life-giving properties. Taoist alchemists, hoping to become immortal, ate an elixir of powdered jade. The stone was thought to be a guardian against disease and evil spirits. Plugs of jade were placed over the orifices of corpses to prevent the life force from escaping. Opulent jade suits, meant to prevent decomposition, have been found in Han tombs; examples can be seen in the Nanjing Museum and in the Anhui Provincial Museum in Hefei.

LANGUAGE

The official language of the People's Republic is the Beijing dialect, usually referred to in the west as 'Mandarin'. It's spoken mainly in the north-east and south-west. In China it's referred to as *putonghua* or 'common speech' and the Chinese government set about popularising it in the 1950s.

Spoken

China has eight major dialects, though about 70% of the population speaks Mandarin. The other major dialect is Cantonese, spoken in the south and basically the same as that spoken in Hong Kong. However, Cantonese is almost unintelligible to the northerners and vice-versa.

To further confuse the issue, Chinese is a 'tonal' language. The difference in intonation is the deciding factor in the meaning of the word. For example, Cantonese *gaai* can mean 'chicken', 'street' or 'prostitute' depending on the way you say it. Another phrase in Chinese means 'grass for your horse' unless you get the tones wrong, in which case it means 'fuck your mother'.

For all its thousands of characters, Chinese has only a bit more than 400 syllables to pronounce them, so the tones are used to increase the number of word sounds available. There are few phonetic similarities between any of the Chinese dialects and the European languages – which makes it difficult for both sides to learn the other's language. Thus the Chinese have come up with the saying 'nothing is more terrible above or below than a foreigner speaking Chinese'.

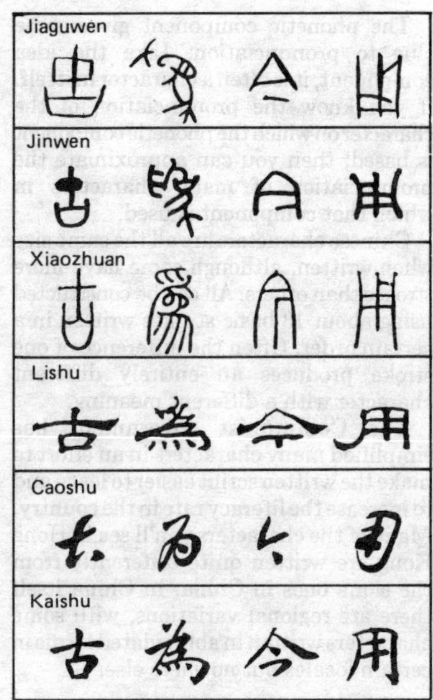

Written

Written Chinese has something like 50,000 'pictographs' – characters which symbolise objects or actions. About 5000 are in common use and you need about 1500 to read a newspaper easily.

The story goes that Chinese characters were invented by the official historian of China's mythical 'Yellow Emperor', who is supposed to have ruled over the country 4000 years ago. The earliest known characters are the *jiaguwen*, simple inscriptions carved on bones and tortoise shells by primitive Chinese tribes; about 4500 such characters have been discovered. Some of these are still in use.

A system of pictographs known as *dazhuan* continued under the Emperor Qin Shihuang, but under the succeeding Han dynasties these gave way to a system known as *lishu*, which used constructions of dashes and dots, and horizontal and vertical strokes. The succeeding *caoshu* script was written with swift brush strokes, many of them joined together to make handwriting easier. The *kaishu* script shaped during the Wei and Jin dynasties was further simplified for ease of handwriting.

In the early stages of developing the script, each character stood for a single word. Later, two or more characters were combined to form new characters. Today, 90% of the characters in common use are made up of two or more original characters; that is, each character has two or more components.

The idea component, called a radical, gives a clue to the meaning and is often written on the character's left-hand side. Characters with related meanings will all contain the same radical. For example, the characters for mud, lake, river and oil all contain the radical which represents the character for water. There are over 200 radicals, according to which Chinese dictionaries are often arranged.

The phonetic component gives some clue to pronunciation. Like the idea component, it is often a character in itself. If you know the pronunciation of the character on which the phonetic component is based, then you can approximate the pronunciation of many characters in which that component is used.

Chinese characters are all the same size when written, although some have more strokes than others. All can be constructed using about 13 basic strokes written in a certain order. Often the difference of one stroke produces an entirely different character with a different meaning.

The Communist government has simplified many characters in an effort to make the written script easier to learn and to increase the literacy rate in the country. Many of the characters you'll see in Hong Kong are written quite differently from the same ones in China. In China itself there are regional variations, with some characters written in abbreviated forms in certain locales but nowhere else.

Pinyin

In 1958 the Chinese officially adopted the 'pinyin' system to write their language using the Roman alphabet. Since the official language of China is the Beijing dialect, this pronunciation is used.

The popularisation of this spelling is still at an early stage, so don't expect Chinese to be able to use pinyin. In the countryside and the smaller towns you may not see a single pinyin sign anywhere, so unless you speak Chinese you'll need a phrasebook with Chinese characters if you're travelling in these areas. Though pinyin is helpful, it's not an instant key to communication since westerners usually don't get the pronunciation and intonation of the romanised word correct.

Pinyin is often used on shop fronts, street signs and advertising billboards. It is of help to have a passing knowledge of the system. Basically the sounds are read as they're pronounced in English. There are a few exceptions:

c is pronounced 'ts' as in *its*
q is pronounced 'ch' as in *choose*
x is pronounced as 'sh' as in *short*
z is pronounced as 'ds' as in *bids*
zh is pronounced as the initial *j*

For example, the second syllable of *Guangzhou* is pronounced 'joe'. *Xian* is pronounced 'Shi-arn'. *Chongqing* is pronounced 'Chong ching'.

Since 1979 all translated texts of Chinese diplomatic documents and Chinese magazines published in foreign languages have used the pinyin system of spelling names and places. The system replaces the old Wade-Giles and Lessing systems of romanising Chinese script. Thus under pinyin, 'Mao Tse-tung' becomes *Mao Zedong*; 'Chou En-lai' becomes *Zhou Enlai*; and 'Peking' becomes *Beijing*. The name of the country remains as it has been generally written: 'China' in English and German, and 'Chine' in French.

Tones

The four basic tones used in pinyin are usually indicated by the following marks:

— high level
ˊ rising
˘ falling-rising
ˋ falling

An unmarked syllable is unstressed and is pronounced lightly and quickly with no particular tone.

Communication Problems

With so many people learning English, communicating in China is not as difficult as it appears. Someone who speaks even a little of the language will always emerge from the crowd to help you. There are lots of Chinese who speak English extremely well and their numbers increase year to year. In the tourist hotels and at the CITS offices someone nearly always speaks at least communicable English.

Hong Kongers are usually very friendly

and helpful despite their reputation in Hong Kong itself. There are lots of foreign students in China, and even those who have been studying there for only a year can be surprisingly fluent; the African students reputedly speak the best Chinese. By the way, the good nature of many of these people is sometimes abused by non-Chinese speakers who seem to regard them as having been placed on earth to sort out every minor communication problem. Don't use people as interpreters unless you absolutely have to!

Gestures

Hand signs are well-used in China. The following observations are random – there are hundreds more gestures and interpretations if you watch and ask. The 'thumbs-up' sign has a long tradition as an indication of excellence or, in Chinese, *gua gua ting hao*. Another way to indicate excellence is to gently pull your own earlobe between thumb and index finger.

Food and cigarettes can be refused by gently pushing away with your upraised palm. It is polite to refuse something three times before accepting. The offerer keeps repeating *bu ke qi* (literally: don't stand on ceremony). A good way to refuse cigarettes or food is to place your right hand over your heart and keep repeating *bu hui* (I'm physically unable), *duzi bu hao* (My stomach's not good) or *chi baole* (I've had enough to eat).

When it comes to numbers, there is often confusion between four *(si)* and 10 *(shi)*. When referring to the number 10, use your two index fingers to form the shape of a cross which is also the shape of the Chinese character for 10. There are lots of other finger signs for numbers.

I was pleasantly surprised several times in China to receive an old gesture which I'd previously only seen in kungfu movies to show gratitude or as a farewell. One fist is clenched against the outstretched palm of the other hand and both are raised together to the forehead. Another time, after I'd checked a restaurant bill and questioned a blatant mistake, the manager suddenly appeared and gave the old sign to solicit forgiveness or express regret. The hands were pointed outwards, palms pressed together, and then swung up and down from the forehead to the waist. One of the strangest things I noticed when asking my way was that Chinese would often point by pouting and moving their lips in the right direction!

Behaviour

Many of the hassles in China can be mitigated with a smattering of language and appreciation of the different psychological reflexes. In their daily life, Chinese often have to compete for goods or services in short supply and many have been assigned jobs for which they have zero interest and often no training. Those who have *guanxi* (connections) usually get what they want because the 'connections' network is, of course, reciprocal. Obtaining goods or services through connections is informally referred to as *zou hou men* (going through the back door). Cadres are well placed for this activity: foreigners are not.

Another convention affecting communication between foreigners and Chinese is 'face'. 'Face' can be loosely considered as status and most Chinese will go to great lengths to avoid 'losing face'. For example, a foreigner may front up at a hotel desk and have a furious row with the receptionist over dorm beds which the foreigner knows exist/are vacant while the receptionist firmly denies all knowledge of the fact. Regardless of who is right or wrong, the receptionist is even less likely to back down (and 'lose face') if the foreigner throws a fit or becomes violent. Persistent waiting may lead to a 'compromise' whereby the receptionist suddenly goes off duty to be replaced by a colleague who coincidentally finds a spare dorm bed or, after the foreigner tactfully refers to a possible 'misunderstanding', discovers a cheaper alternative. There are many such social mores which can severely maul the nerves of even the most patient of foreigners. It is pointless to steer a collision course toward these barriers, but it is often possible to manipulate your way around them.

One way to ask a question in Chinese is to place the verb together with the negative of the verb. One of the commonest examples is *you mei you?* (literally: have not have?). Although grammatically correct, this form of question makes it very easy for the person asked to give the reply that requires the least possible effort, namely, *mei you* (not have). Nobody leaves China without having learnt this phrase! *Mei you* can mean many things, such as 'not available today', 'not available for you', 'not available because I'm resting' or 'not available because I don't give a cuss who you are!' To stave off this response for as long as possible, it's worth diving straight in with *wo yao* (I want)

Mafan ni (literally: cause bother for you) is a useful way to butter up someone to get them to do something for you or to express gratitude for a favour they've just done you. When you've reached an impasse by peaceful means, it often helps to ask *zenmo ban?* (literally: what to do?). Since many Chinese only respond to a specific question, this provides them scope to tell you about a room, bus, flight, etc you didn't know about (and were thus unable to request). Sometimes the simplest things seem mighty complicated!

Phrasebooks

Phrasebooks are invaluable – but it's better to copy out the appropriate sentences in Chinese rather than show someone the book; otherwise they'll take it and read every page. Reading place names or street signs is not difficult since the Chinese name is accompanied by the pinyin form; if not you'll soon learn lots of characters just by repeated exposure. A small dictionary in English, pinyin and Chinese characters is also useful for learning a few words.

PHRASE LIST

Places

airport
fēi jī chǎng
飞机场

CAAC
zhōng gúo mín yòng háng kōng zǒng jú
中国民用航空总局

China International Travel Service
zhōng kúo kúo jì lǚ xíng shè
中国国际旅行社

long-distance bus station
cháng tū qì chē zhàn
长途汽车站

main train station
hūo chē zǒng zhàn
火车总站

post office
yóu zhèng jú
邮政局

Public Security Bureau
gōng ān jú
公安局

Time

tonight
jīn wǎn
今晚

today
jīn tiān
今天

tomorrow
míng tiān
明天

the day after tomorrow
hòu tiān
后天

three days ahead
dà hòu tiān
大后天

in the morning
zài shàng wǔ
在上午

during the day
yì zhěng tiān
一整天

in the afternoon
zài xìa wǔ
在下午

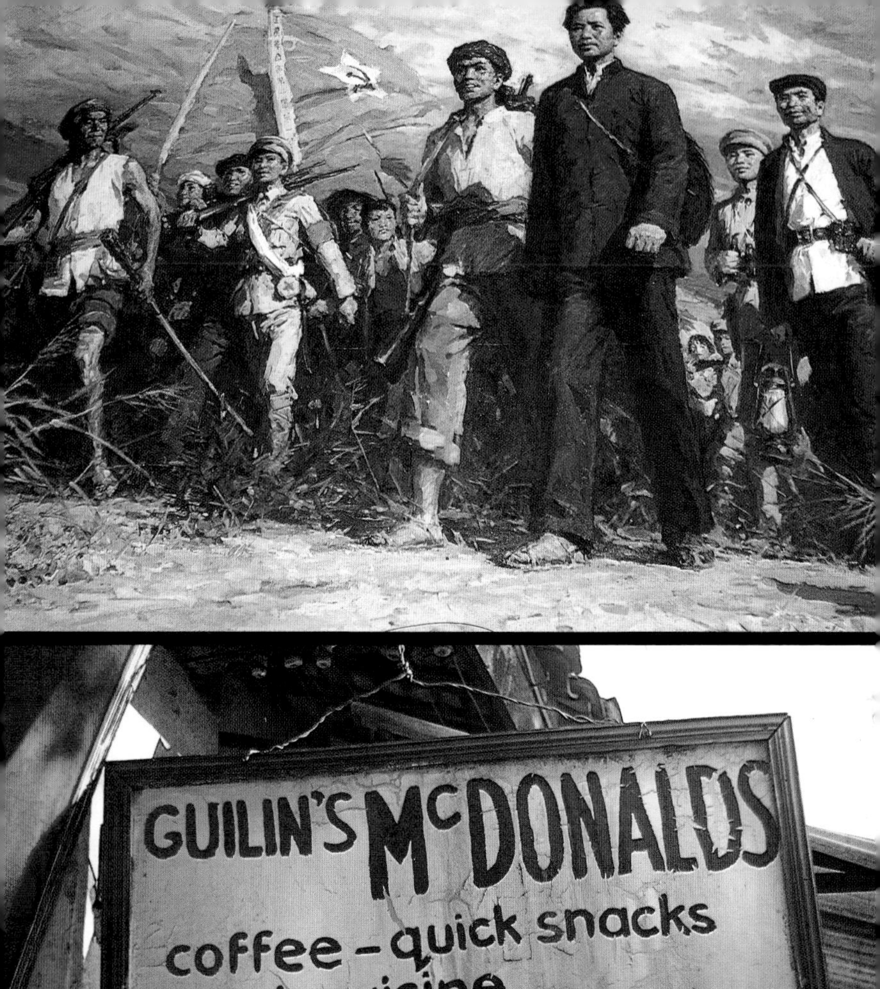

Top: Painting in Mao museum, Changsha (AS)
Bottom: Sign in Guilin (AS)

in the evening
zài wăn shàng
在晚上

at night
zài wăn shàng
在晚上

Toilets

toilet
cè sŭo
厕所

men
nán rén
男人

women
nŭ rén
女人

Hotels

guest house
zhāodàisuŏ
招待所

tourist hotel
bīnguăn or *fàndiàn* or *lŭguăn*
宾馆或饭店或旅馆

local hotel
lŭ shè
旅舍

Useful Phrases

I want a........
wŏ yào........
我要

single room
yí jiān dān rén fáng
一间单人房

multi-person room
dūo rén fáng jiān
多人房间

double room
shuāng rén fáng
双人房

dormitory bed
chúang wèi
床位

how much is a........?
........yào dūo shăo qián?
要多少钱

per night
měi wăn
每晚

Is there anything cheaper?
yŏu pián yi de yì diăn ma?
有便宜一点的吗？

That's too expensive.
tài gùi le
太贵了

I am a student.
wŏ shì yí ge xué shēng
我是一个学生

I cannot read or write Chinese.
wŏ bú hùi kàn huò xiě zhōng wén
我不会看或写中文

yes
shì
是

no
bù
不

thank you
xiè xie
谢谢

sorry
duì bù qĭ
对不起

What's to be done now?
xiàn zài zěnmo bàn?
现在怎么办？

Would you mind........?
máfan nĭ........?
麻烦您

It doesn't matter.
méi shì
没事

How much does it cost? (lit. how much money?)
dūo shăo qián?
多少钱？

Public Security

I want to extend my visa.
wŏ yào yán cháng wŏ de qiān zhèng
我要延长我的签证

by two weeks
dào liăng ge xīng qī
到二个星期

by one month
dào yí ge yuè
到一个月

by two months
dào liăng ge yuè
到二个月

I need an Alien's Permit for the following places.
wŏ xū yào yí fèn yún xŭ wài gúo rén lŭ yóu de zŭn zhèng dào yĭ xià de dì fāng qù
我需要一封允许外国人旅游的准证到以下的地方去

Post Office

I want to send this letter by air mail to........
wŏ yào jì zhè fēng háng kōng xìn dào........
我要寄这封航空信到

letter
xìn
信

package
bāo gŭo
包裹

air mail
háng kōng
航空

surface mail
píng yóu zhèng
平邮政

Bicycles

I want to hire a bicycle.
wŏ yào zū yí liàng zì xíng chē
我要租一辆自行车

How much is it per day?
duō shăo qián yì tiān?
多少钱一天

How much is it per hour?
dūo shăo qián mĕi xiăo shí?
多少钱每小时

Transport

I want to go to........
wŏ yào dào........
我要到

I want to see........
wŏ yào kàn........
我要看

I want to buy........
wŏ yào măi........
我要买

I want to buy one/two/three tickets to........
wŏ yào yì/liăng/sān zhāng qù........de piào
我要一/二/三能去...的票

I want to go at........(time)
wŏ yào zài........diăn dào
我要在...点到

Could you buy a ticket for me?
ke yi ti wo mai yi zhang piao ma?
可以替我买一张票吗？

What time does the train leave?
huŏ chē jĭ diăn zhōng kāi?
火车几点钟开？

What time does the bus leave?
qì chē jĭ diăn zhōng kāi?
汽车几点钟开？

What time does the boat leave?
chuán jĭ diăn zhōng kāi?
船几点钟开？

What time does the plane leave?
fēi jī jĭ diăn zhōng qĭ fēi?
飞机几点钟起飞？

When is the first bus?
tóu bān qì chē jĭ diăn zhōng kāi?
头班汽车几点钟开？

When is the last bus?
mò bān qì chē jĭ diăn zhōng kāi?
末班汽车几点钟开？

When is the next bus?
xià yì bān qì chē jĭ diăn zhōng kāi?
下一班汽车几点钟开？

Where can I buy a bus map?
nălĭ kĕ yĭ măi jiāo tōng dìtú?
那里可以买一张交通地图？

How long does the trip take?
zhècì lŭxíng yào duō jiŭ?
这次路行要多久？

How much is a hard-seat?
yìng xí yào duō shăo qián?
硬席要多少钱？

How much is a soft-seat?
ruăn xí duō shăo qián?
软席要多少钱？

How much is a hard-sleeper?
yìng wò duō shǎo qián?
硬卧要多少钱？

How much is a soft-sleeper?
ruǎn wò duō shǎo qián?
软卧要多少钱？

I'd like a middle berth.
wǒ xiǎng yào ge zhōng pù
我想要个中铺

train number
chē hào
车号

Where is the 1st-class waiting room?
tóu děng hòu chē shì zài nǎr?
头等候车室在哪儿？

Where is the left-luggage room?
xíng lǐ shì zài nǎr?
行李室在哪儿？

I want to refund this ticket.
wǒ yào tùi diào zhè zhāng piào
我要退掉这张票

Food

I'm vegetarian.
wǒ chī sù
我吃素

bean curd
dòu fu
豆腐

beef
níu ròu
牛肉

chicken
jī
鸡

crab
xiè
蟹

duck
yā
鸭

dumplings
jiǎo zi
饺子

eel
shàn yú
鳝鱼

fish
yú
鱼

frogs
qīng wā or *tián jī*
青蛙

mushrooms
mó gu
磨菇

octopus
zhāng yú
章鱼

pepper
hú jiāo
胡椒

pork
zhū ròu
猪肉

prawns
xiā
虾

rice
mǐ fàn
米饭

snake
shé
蛇

soup
tāng
汤

squid
yóu yú
尤鱼

vegetables
shū cài
蔬菜

Drinks

beer
pí jiǔ
啤酒

fizzy drink
qìshuǐ
汽水

orange juice
júzi shuǐ
桔子水

tea
chá
茶

water
shuǐ
水

wine
pútao jiŭ
葡萄酒

Numbers

1 *yī* 一
2 *èr* 二
3 *sān* 三
4 *sì* 四
5 *wŭ* 五
6 *lìu* 六
7 *qī* 七
8 *bā* 八
9 *jĭu* 九
10 *shí* 十
11 *shí yī* 十一
12 *shí èr* 十二
20 *èr shí* 二十
30 *sān shí* 三十
100 *yì băi* 一百
120 *yì băi èr shí* 一百二十
200 *èr băi* 二百
221 *èr băi èr shí yì* 二百二十一

Countries

Australia
ào dà lì yà
澳大利亚

Britain
yīng guó
英国

Canada
jīa ná dà
加拿大

France
fă guó
法国

Germany
dé guó
德国

New Zealand
xīn xī lán
新西兰

Sweden
rùi diăn
瑞典

Switzerland
rùi shì
瑞士

USA
mĕi guó
美国

Street Names & Nomenclature

street
dà jiē
大街

road
lù
路

north
bĕi
北

south
nán
南

east
dōng
东

west
xī
西

People's
rénmín
人民

Liberation
jiĕfàng
解放

Streets and roads are usually split up into sectors. Each sector is given a number or (more usually) is labelled according to its relative position to the other sectors using compass points. For example, Zhongshan Lu (Zhongshan Rd) might be split into an east and a west sector. The east sector will be designated Zhongshan Donglu and the west will be Zhongshan Xilu.

Facts for the Visitor

VISAS

Visas for individual travel in China are easy to get. The only people automatically excluded from entering China are holders of South Korean, South African and Israeli passports. Don't worry if you have a Taiwanese visa in your passport; it doesn't turn heads any more.

Visas are readily available in Hong Kong, from Chinese embassies in most western countries and from Chinese embassies in many other countries. If you can't wait until you get to Hong Kong or if you want to fly direct to China, then enquire first at the nearest Chinese embassy.

In Hong Kong a number of agents issue Chinese visas. Generally they offer a choice of a visa by itself, or a package deal including visa and transport to China. The best agencies are:

Travellers Hostel, 16th floor, Block A, Chungking Mansions, Nathan Rd, Tsimshatsui, Kowloon (tel 3-687710 or 3-682505). Popular because of their cheap prices and because many travellers stay here.

Phoenix Services, Room 603, Hanford House, 221D Nathan Rd, Tsimshatsui, Kowloon (tel 3-7227378 or 3-7233006). Lots of people have spoken very highly of this place, which has friendly and exceptionally helpful staff who really deserve a plug from this guidebook!

Wah Nam Travel, Room 1003, Eastern Commercial Centre, 397 Hennessy Rd, Wanchai, Hong Kong Island (tel 5-8911161). There is a second office in Room 602, Sino Centre, 582-592 Nathan Rd, Kowloon (tel 3-320367).

Guangdong (HK) Tours Company Ltd in the Seaview Commercial Building (diagonally opposite the Macau Ferry Terminal), Connaught Rd, Central (tel 5-497194). Low prices, extremely friendly and helpful staff, lots of useful free maps.

Visa Office of the Ministry of Foreign Affairs of the PRC, 5th floor, Low Block, 26 Harbour Rd, Wanchai, Hong Kong Island (tel 5-8939812). Open Monday to Friday, 9 am to 12.30 pm and 2 to 5 pm, Saturday 9 am to 12.30 pm. This place has been dispensing some of the cheapest visas around; some people got three-month visas here for just HK$50 (single entry) or HK$80 (double entry).

Visa applications require two passport-size photos. Your application must be written in English, and you're advised to have one entire blank page in your passport for the visa.

The visa application form asks you to specify your travel itinerary and your means of transport, but you can deviate from this as much as you want. You *don't* have to leave from the place you specify on your visa application form.

The cost of visas and the types of package deal you get in Hong Kong change quite frequently, so use this information as a rough guide only. The best deals include a three-month visa for HK$70 issued in two working days, three-month visa for HK$110 issued in one working day, three-month visa for HK$170 issued same day, one-month visa for HK$50 issued after one week.

If you want more flexibility to enter and exit China several times, multiple-entry visas are available from some agencies. This is particularly useful if you intend to follow complicated routings in and out of China via Nepal, Pakistan, Thailand or Burma. Multiple-entry visas cost, on average, HK$500 for three months and HK$600 for six months.

Some agencies in Hong Kong are now able to obtain your visa on a separate paper which you present at the Chinese border. All that is required is your passport number, nationality, date of birth and full name. The visa costs HK$300, takes three days to obtain and is valid for two months. Certain ports of entry such as Shenzhen are experimenting with issuing five-day visas at the border.

It should be possible to get a visa for stays longer than six months. All visas are valid from the date of issue, *not* from the date of entry.

Foreign Students

Many Chinese universities take foreign students, usually for Chinese-language courses. Most students stay a year or two, but six-week summer courses and all sorts of other programmes are also available. Once you're accepted by a Chinese university you're automatically given a visa. You can then go to China to study, do your course, and be free to travel. Foreign students in China are entitled to student prices for hotel rooms and train fares. Students or Foreign Experts who have a resident's permit and need to leave China briefly can usually obtain a re-entry permit inside China at a Public Security Office for Y5. If you're a foreign student in Taiwan you'll also get student discounts, since Taiwan is considered to be part of China.

Extensions

Visa extensions are handled by the Foreign Affairs Section of the local Public Security Bureaus (the police force). The Chinese government travel organisation, China International Travel Service, has nothing to do with extensions. Extensions cost Y5 (a bit more than US$1). The general rule is that you can get one extension of one month's duration, though at an agreeable Public Security Bureau you may be able to wangle more, for longer, with cogent reasons like illness, or transport delays, etc.

Embassies

Following are the addresses and telephone numbers of Chinese embassies in major cities around the world.

Australia
247 Federal Highway, Watson, Canberra, 2602 ACT

Canada
411-415 Andrews St, Ottawa, Ontario KIN 5H3

England
31 Portland Place, London WIN 3AG

France
11 George V Avenue, 75008, Paris

West Germany
5307 Wachtbergniederbachen, Konrad-Adenauer St, 104, Bonn

Italy
Via Giovanne, Paiseillo 39, Roma 00198

Japan
15-30 Minami-Azabu, 4-Chome, Minato-ku, Tokyo

Netherlands
Adriaan Goehooplaan 7, Den Haag

Sweden
Bragevagen 4, Stockholm

Switzerland
Kalcheggweg 10, Berne

USA
2300 Connecticut Avenue NW, Washington, DC 20008. Consulates: 3417 Montrose Boulevard, Houston, Texas 77006; 104 South Michigan Avenue, Suite 1200, Chicago, Illinois 60603; 1450 Laguna St, San Francisco, California 94115; 520 12th Avenue, New York, New York 10036

CUSTOMS

Immigration procedures are so streamlined they're almost a formality these days. The third-degree at customs seems to be reserved for Seiko-smuggling Hong Kongers who are much more of a problem than the stray backpacker.

Customs require that you declare on the 'Baggage Declaration for Incoming Passengers' the number of cameras, wristwatches, recorders (including multi-purpose combination sets), radios, calculators, electric fans, bicycles, sewing machines, TV sets and cine-cameras you're taking into China; this is to prevent you from selling them in the country or giving them away as presents.

They also ask you to declare the quantity of foreign currency and travellers' cheques you're carrying, and any gold, silver, jewellery, antiques, calligraphy and other works of art. When you leave China, you'll be asked to show that you still have all the items listed. If any items you list on your form are stolen in China, you should ask Public Security to provide a Certificate of Loss (see theft section for details). Don't lose the declaration form!

You're allowed to import 600 cigarettes or the equivalent in tobacco products, two litres of alcoholic drink and one pint of perfume. You're allowed to import only 3000 feet of movie film, and a maximum of 72 rolls of still film. Importation of fresh fruit is prohibited.

It's illegal to import any printed material, film, tapes, etc 'detrimental to China's politics, economy, culture and ethics'. But don't be too concerned about what you take to read.

As you leave China, any tapes, manuscripts, books, etc 'which contain state secrets or are otherwise prohibited for export' can be seized – as in any other country. Cultural relics, handicrafts, gold and silver ornaments, and jewellery purchased in China have to be shown to customs on leaving. You'll also have to show your receipts; otherwise the stuff may be confiscated. Don't get paranoid – they usually check only that you've still got your Walkmans and your camera with you and that you're not departing with large doses of Chinese currency.

Lastly, an item for the travelling herbalist: export of musk, toad-cake, cinnabar, euconmia, gastrodia-elata, pianzihuang, caterpillar fungus, Liu-Shen pills and Angongniuhuang pills is prohibited.

MONEY

The basic unit of Chinese currency is the *yuan* – designated in this book by a capital 'Y'. The yuan is divided into *jiao* and *fen*. Ten fen make up one jiao, and 10 jiao make up one yuan. Jiao and yuan are commonly referred to in spoken Chinese as *mao* and *kuai* respectively. There are, in fact, two types of currency in use in China: Renminbi and Foreign Exchange Certificates.

Renminbi

RMB or 'People's Money' is issued by the Bank of China. Paper notes are issued in denominations of one, two, five and 10 yuan; one, two and five jiao; and one, two and five fen. Coins are in denominations of one yuan; five jiao; and one, two and five fen. The one-fen note is small and yellow, the two-fen note is blue, and the five-fen note is small and green.

Foreign Exchange Certificates

FEC or 'Tourist Money' is issued in China for use by foreign tourists, diplomats, Overseas Chinese and Chinese from Hong Kong and Macau. FEC comes in seven denominations: 100 yuan, 50 yuan, 10 yuan, five yuan, one yuan, five jiao and one jiao. There are no coins.

You're meant to use FEC in places which serve foreigners only, such as some large hotels and foreign trade centres. It is also supposed to be used for payment of such things as through-train fares to Hong Kong or ship fares to Hong Kong or Macau, international and domestic air fares, international telecommunications charges and parcel post. Ever since the inception of FEC in 1980, there have been rumours that it will be abandoned or phased out, and the enthusiasm with which the Chinese enforce the regulations regarding its use varies greatly from place to place. One plan to phase out FEC in November 1986 was abandoned due to 'co-ordination' problems in the bank network.

In practice, some foreign visitors have managed to pay their whole way through China using only RMB, but to be on the safe side you need a mixture of both RMB and FEC. Although there is no basis, for example, for the common scam of three-wheeler (San Lun Che) drivers demanding fares in FEC, some shops and hotels like to operate an interesting 'price differential'.

1 Yuan Renmibi

1 Yuan Foreign Exchange Certificate

You may be asked if you want to pay a given price in FEC or pay about 30% more in RMB. Some hotels simply will *not* accept payment in RMB no matter how hard you plead, cry or rant. Some railway stations have separate booking offices for foreigners which insist on payment in FECs, and air tickets can only be bought in FECs.

On the other hand, in smaller towns and in the countryside where few foreigners go you'll probably find that the locals have absolutely no idea what FECs are, and you'll have to pay in RMB.

Changing Money

Foreign currency and travellers' cheques can be changed at the main centres of the Bank of China or at its branch offices in the tourist hotels, some Friendship Stores, and some of the big department stores. You'll be issued FECs and small change will be made up of RMB one, two and five-fen notes and coins.

Travellers' cheques from most of the world's leading banks and issuing agencies are now acceptable in China – stick to the major companies such as Thomas Cook, American Express and Bank of America, and you'll be OK.

Australian, Canadian, US, UK, Hong Kong, Japanese and most West European currencies are acceptable in China. The exchange rates are approximately:

A$1	=	Y2.49
C$1	=	Y2.71
DM1	=	Y1.94
HK$1	=	Y0.47
Y1000 (yen)	=	Y24.0
UK£1	=	Y5.53
US$1	=	Y3.71

Credit Cards

In general, credit cards are gaining more acceptance in China for use by foreign visitors in major tourist cities. Useful cards include Visa, Federal Card, Mastercard, American Express and Diners Club.

It wouldn't be worthwhile to get a credit card especially for your trip to China, but if you already have one you might find it useful. Banks in some of the outlying regions of China can take a long time to debit your account overseas.

Black Market

Getting hold of RMB (which you'll need if you want to buy things at the little street-stalls, restaurants or markets) is no trouble. There is a booming black market in almost every major tourist town. The black-marketeers will just about change your underpants for you, sell you railway tickets and swap your FECs for RMB at a premium. A few years ago the black market was very small and fairly restricted. Guilin was the place to go for the best rates and the business was fronted by 'change money' women, who hung out in the main street murmuring 'fifatee/sicksatee' as you wandered past. In Beijing and Shanghai it's now fronted by sleazy Uygur mobsters who flog hashish as a sideline.

The exchange rate consistently hovers around the 125 RMB for 100 FECs mark, with occasional fluctuations either up or down depending on location and rumours of the FECs being done away with. Always try bargaining. Travellers have reportedly experienced short-changing (faked alert or 'paper' replacement). Always agree first on the price, count what you are given and only then hand over your part. If real or 'engineered' danger appears in mid-transaction, don't be flustered into a hasty exchange only to find later that you've lost out. Either hand back what you have been given or hang onto it and walk away coolly. The changers will find you again – vested interest! In some places there even appears to be some scope for changing Hong Kong and US dollars.

If there's no black market you should still be able to find Chinese who'll swap on a one-to-one basis; try staff in the hotels and shops. Banks may also give you RMB if you ask for it. Some people seem to think it's illegal for foreigners to have RMB – it's not.

Some Chinese may ask you to buy goods from the Friendship Stores for them. Other dealers buy the goods with the FECs they've bought from you and then resell them to Chinese customers at a mark-up. As for bringing things into China to sell, you'll probably find that the Chinese strike too much of a hard bargain to make it worth the trouble – and you could probably make just as much profit off the cash black market anyway.

Money-Exchange Vouchers

Whenever you change foreign currency into Chinese currency you'll be given a money-exchange voucher recording the transaction. If you've got any leftover Chinese currency when you leave the country and want to reconvert it to hard currency you must have those vouchers – not all of them, but at least equal to the amount of RMB you want to change.

Foreign Exchange Certificates can be taken in and out of the country as you please, but RMB is not supposed to be taken out. If you do get stuck with a heap of RMB, ask around at the travellers' hang-outs in Hong Kong, as someone who's going to China will probably buy it. The Bank of China in Central, Hong Kong will also exchange RMB.

COSTS

How much will it cost to travel in China? That's largely up to the degree of comfort you desire – and what's cheap to one person may be expensive to another. It also depends on how much travelling you do and where you go, and on which country you come from. At the time of writing Americans and West Germans were enjoying very favourable rates of exchange for their currencies – Australians not so good.

If you want to do China on a bottom-of-the-barrel shoestring budget then you have to sleep in dormitories at every hotel, get local price on all train tickets and forego sleepers. Travelling, however, is *not* an endurance test. If you want to find out how long you can stay away and how little money you can spend doing it, go ahead, but you won't get gold stars or rabbit stamps each time you sleep on the floor of a train. Your journey can be a miserable experience if you're constantly worried about how far the money is going to stretch and if you force yourself to live in perpetual discomfort. Travelling on too low a budget only allows for a limited experience of a country – you get a one-sided view just like those people who take expensive tours and stay in posh hotels.

China just isn't going to be as cheap and as comfortable as India or South-East Asia; if you want to have a good time in the PRC then spend a bit more money. If you care about your sanity take a sleeper. Train trips in China are almost always long; it's no fun to sit for 30 hours in a hot, crowded hard-seat carriage where the lights are on all night and people stare at you while constantly spitting on the floor.

Most low-budget travellers do China on less than US$10 a day, and much of this gets spent on accommodation and transport. Develop a toleration for dormitories. If you're sharing with Chinese then you'd better be able to cope with a language that's spoken late into the night at 140 decibels, a television turned to full volume and spitting from five paces. Dorm beds are cheap (usually no more than Y10) and most hotels will readily dispense them. Rooms are invariably expensive – particularly if you're travelling alone, since most Chinese hotels only provide double rooms and it's unlikely they'll give you half price. Food costs decrease if you're with somebody else. 'Eating Chinese' with a few other people not only gives you a greater variety of food to choose from, it brings the price down.

Costs also vary from place to place. Beijing has an acute shortage of cheap accommodation, but in small, obscure towns you can get a room for just a few yuan. In heavily touristed places it is often virtually impossible to get local price on the trains, but in other places it can be easy. Taking buses and boats is a good idea since you pay the same as the locals and you get to see more of the countryside as well. Foreigners are often charged double for transport in Tibet. Travelling at night on the trains will also save on hotel bills. But if money is no object, you'll get plenty of opportunity in China to use it up.

Tipping

China is one of those wonderful countries where tipping is not done and almost no one asks for it.

INFORMATION

Officialdom & Paperwork

Of all the striking Chinese sayings a particularly applicable one is 'With one monkey in the way, not even 10,000 men can pass'. Three of the major monkeys in China today are CITS (China International Travel Service), the PSB (Public Security Bureau) and the mass of little bits of paper collectively referred to as 'red tape'.

China International Travel Service (CITS)

CITS deals with China's foreign tourist hordes, and mainly concerns itself with organising and making travel arrangements for group tours. It is known in Chinese as Luxingshe. CITS existed as far back as 1954 when there were few customers; now they're inundated with a couple of hundred thousand big-noses a year and it will take a while for them to get their act together.

CITS will buy train and plane tickets for you (and some boat tickets), reserve hotel rooms, organise city tours, and even get you tickets for the cinema, opera, acrobatics and other entertainment as well as organise trips to farms and factories, and provide vehicles (taxis, minibuses) for sightseeing or transport.

All rail tickets bought through CITS will be tourist-priced (an extra 75% on top of the Chinese price) and there will usually be a Y2 or Y3 service charge added on to the price of rail, boat or plane tickets. CITS has nothing to do with issuing travel permits or visa extensions – for that you must go directly to the Public Security offices.

CITS offices and desks are usually located in the major tourist hotels in each town or city open to foreigners; sometimes they are located elsewhere but you can get the hotel reception desk to phone them.

Service varies. Some CITS people are friendly and full of useful information about the places they're stationed in; others can be downright rude. In some cases you'll even find CITS offices staffed by people who speak sparse or zero English. Getting information out of CITS is sometimes pot-luck; again, it depends on who you're dealing with. Generally speaking, though, solo travellers will rarely have to deal with them.

Following are the addresses and telephone numbers of China International Travel Service offices in Beijing and other major cities around the world:

Beijing
: 6 East Changan Avenue, Beijing (tel 551031; cable Lüxingshe, Beijing; telex 22350 CITSH CN).

Britain
: 24 Cambridge Circus, London WC2 H8HD (tel 01-8369911)

France
: 7 Rue Jean Goujon, 75008, Paris (tel 359-74-85)

Hong Kong
: Unit 601/605/606, 6th Floor, Tower II, South Sea Centre, Tsimshatsui East, Kowloon (tel 3-7215317, cable 2320 Hong Kong, telex 38449 CITC HX)

Japan
: 1st Floor, A K Building, 6-1, 5 Ban-cho, Chiyoda-ku, Tokyo (tel 03-234-5366)

USA
: 60E, 42nd St, Suite 465, New York, New York 10165 (tel 212-867-0271)

China Travel Service (CTS)

CTS is concerned with tourists from Hong Kong, Macau and possibly Taiwan, and with foreign nationals of Chinese descent (Overseas Chinese).

CTS doesn't deal with western tourists, but in Hong Kong, where English is spoken, they do issue visas and you can use their services to book trains, planes, hovercraft and other transport to China.

In China CTS is sometimes mixed in with the CITS offices and desks in the tourist hotels, particularly in towns with only one major tourist hotel where westerners and Overseas Chinese stay.

CTS seems to have a wider range of services than CITS; one advantage is that they will book transport that CITS won't, such as boats plying routes not normally used by western tourists. You may be more likely to get cheap tickets out of them.

Following are the addresses for the China Travel Service in Beijing and Hong Kong:

Beijing
: 8 Dongjiaomin Xiang, Beijing (tel 557070, cable 2464 Beijing, telex 22487 CTSHO CN).

Hong Kong
: China Travel Building, 77 Queens Rd, Central, Hong Kong Island (tel 5-259121, telex 73344 KKCTS HX).

CAAC

The overseas offices of the China National Aviation Corporation, the domestic and international carrier of the People's Republic are in the countries that follow.

There are also offices in Addis Ababa, Baghdad, Belgrade, Bucharest, Sharjah, Teheran and, for academic interest, in Pyongyang.

Australia
: 104 The Waldorf, 57-67 Liverpool St, Sydney (tel 2679403, airport 6698445)

Burma
: 67 Prome Rd, Rangoon (tel 75714, airport 40113)

England
: 153 Auckland Rd, Upper Northwood, London SE19 2RH (tel 01-7714052). Gatwick Airport office: Room 601, North Roof Office Block (tel 02 93502021)

France
47, Rue Pergolese 75016 Paris (tel 450 1994, airport 864-21-17)
Japan
Minato Ku Motoazabu 3-4-38 Tokyo (tel 4043700 or Narita Airport (0476) 323941); 4F Matsufuji Building, 3-25 Gotomachi, Nagasaki (tel 281510)
Pakistan
25/C, 24th St, Block 6, PECHS Karachi-29 (tel 435570)
Philippines
7 Cabildo Corne, Cerrada St, Urdaneta Village, M Manila (tel 817-9898, airport 8316351)
Switzerland
CH-8058 Zurich Airport, terminal B 1-101, Zurich (tel 8163090 or 8163091)
Thailand
134/1-2 Silom Rd, Bangkok (tel 2356510-1, 2351880-2)
USA
2500 Wilshire Boulevard, Los Angeles, California 90057 (tel 3842703, airport 6468104); 51 Grant Avenue, San Francisco, California 94108 (tel 3922156, airport 8770750); 45E, 49th St, New York, New York 10017 and at 4230E Pan Am Terminal Building, JF Kennedy International Airport (tel 3719898-9 and 3552222, airport 6564722)
USSR
Leninskye Gory UL, Druzhby 6 (tel 143-15-60, airport 578-27-25)
West Germany
Duesseldorferstr. 4, D-6000 Frankfurt/M. 1, (tel 069/233/038-039, airport 069/690 5214)

Public Security Bureau (PSB)

The Public Security Bureau (Gong An Ju) is the name given to China's police, both uniformed and plain-clothes. Its responsibilities include suppression of political dissidence, crime detection, mediating family quarrels and directing traffic. A related force is the Chinese People's Armed Police Force (CPAPF), which was formed several years ago to absorb cuts in PLA manpower.

The Foreign Affairs Branch (Wai Shi Ke) of the Public Security Bureau deals with foreigners. This branch is responsible for issuing visa extensions and Alien Travel Permits.

What sets the Chinese police aside from their counterparts in, say, Mexico and South America, is their amiability towards foreigners (what they're like with their own people may be a different story). They'll sometimes sit you down, give you a cup of tea and practise their English – and the frequency of competent English-speakers is surprisingly good. The PSB is responsible for introducing and enforcing regulations concerning foreigners. So, for example, they bear responsibility for exclusion of foreigners from certain hotels. If this means you get stuck for a place to stay, they can offer advice. Don't pester them with trivia or try to 'use' them to bully a point. Do turn to them for mediation in serious disputes with hotels, restaurants, taxi drivers, etc. This often works, if only as a 'face-saving' device since the PSB wields considerable power – especially in remote areas.

The only run-in you may have with the PSB is when you end up in a 'closed' place and the PSB must put you on your way. For misdemeanours such as being in a town without a permit, or being off-course without a good alibi, there could be a fine which can usually be bargained down. You may even have to write a 'self-criticism' confessing your guilt. There appear to be no set rules for dealing foreigners who have wandered into 'closed' areas. If there are, then many Public Security staff are unaware of them, so how you're treated is up to the discretion of the individual police.

One traveller covered up an expulsion order issued to him by Guiyang PSB. The Wuhan PSB caught up with him, kept him for six days, fined him US$100 and slung him out via Canton. The expulsion was not so much for visiting closed places as for overstaying his visa. (He also used an unusual device to get into Chinese hotels on the way – telling them he was from Xinjiang, where a different language is spoken and a Caucasian face is the norm. Chinese, however, carry all sorts of odd ID like swimming licences, work-unit cards, bicycle licences and probably travel authorisation.) Some people get fined; some are told to move on; some are allowed to stay in the 'closed' area or never catch sight of Public Security. The worst you can expect is ejection from the country at your own expense.

Alien's Travel Permit

A few years ago only 130 places in China were officially open to foreign tourists. Then the number swept to 244 and at the time of writing was in the 400s. With the number of open places increasing so quickly, the following list is only a rough guide of ideas for your own itinerary. As a rule of thumb, most of the places described in this book are open to foreigners; a few have been prised open before their time. To find out about newly opened areas, it's best to check with the PSB in provincial capitals. Remote PSBs are often more helpful with visas, but tend to be the last to receive lists of new openings.

To travel to closed places you officially require an 'Alien's Travel Permit' (*Lüxing Zheng*), obtainable from the Public Security Bureau in each place open to foreigners. They use their discretion in issuing you with a permit to a closed place. However, the choice of open places is now so extensive that the majority of travellers will have no need for this type of permit. Foreign academics and researchers usually need to front up with the right credentials or letter of introduction (*jie shao xin*) and may then be given a free hand to pursue their lizards, steam trains, donkeys or whatever in remote places.

One PSB turned down my request with the straight-faced logic that such permits are for places foreigners can't visit. Like the best of bureaucrats PSB does not want to step out of line, and if they think you're asking for an unusual permit they'll just say no. There's no harm in at least asking for a permit to a strange place – you just might get it.

Alien Travel Permits can be demanded from you at hotel registration desks, PSB offices, boat or bus ticket offices, and unusual areas during spot checks by police. If you're off the track but heading towards a destination for which you have a permit, PSB will either stop you and cancel the destination, or will let you continue on your way.

The permit also lists the modes of transportation you're allowed to take: plane, train, ship or car – and if a particular mode is crossed out then you can't use it. If a mode is cancelled it can be reinstated at the next PSB, but that may only be for a single trip from Point A to Point B. You could try and carry on regardless – or you could lose the permit in the next open city and start again.

If you manage to get a permit for an unusual destination, the best strategy is to get to that destination as fast as you can (by plane if possible). Other PSBs do not have to honour the permit and can cancel it and send you back. Take your time getting back – you're hardly likely to be hassled if you're returning to civilisation. Transit points usually don't require a permit and you can stay the night.

Open Cities & Areas

* indicates provincial capital

Anhui Province

Anqing, Bengbu, Bozhou, Chaohu, Chuxian, Fengyang county, Fuyang county, Hefei*, Huaibei, Huainan, Huangshan county, Jingxian county, Jiuhuashan (Qingyang), Lu'an, Ma'anshan, Shexian county, Suzhou, Tongling county, Tunxi, Wuhu, Xiuning county

Beijing Municipality

Fujian Province

Chong'an, Fuzhou*, Putian, Quanzhou, Xiamen, Zhangzhou

Gansu Province

Anxi county, Chengxian, Dangchang county, Dunhuang county, Jiayuguan, Jinchang, Jiuquan county, Lanzhou*, Linxia, Minqin county, Minxian, Pingjiang, Qingyang county, Têwo (Dêngkagoin) county, Tianshui county, Wenxian, Wudu county, Wuwei, Xiahe

(Labrang monastery), Xifeng, Yongjing county, Yumen, Zhangye, Zhugqu county

Guangdong Province, including Hainan Island
Anding county, Baisha county, Baoting county, Boluo county, Changjiang county, Chaozhou, Chengmai county, Danxian county, Dapu county, Deqing county, Ding'an county, Dongfang county, Dongguan county, Fengkai county, Fengshun county, Foshan, Gaoyao county, Guangzhou (Canton)*, Haifeng county, Haikou, Heyuan county, Huaiji county, Huidong county, Huiyang county, Huizhou, Jiangmen, Ledong county, Lingao county, Lingshui county, Lufeng county, Luoding county, Maoming, Meixian, Nanhai county, Qionghai county, Qiongshan county, Qiongzhong county, Sanya, Shantou, Shaoguan, Shenzhen, Shunde county, Sihui county, Tunchang county, Wanning county, Wenchang county, Xingning county, Xinxing county, Yunfu county, Zhanjiang, Zhaoqing, Zhongshan, Zhuhai

Guangxi Province
Beihai, Beiliu county, Binyang county, Guilin (and Yangshuo), Guiping county, Guixian county, Hepu county, Jinxiu Yao autonomous county, Lingshan county, Liuzhou, Long'an county, Longsheng multinational autonomous county, Luchuan county, Nanning*, Qinzhou, Rongshui Miao autonomous county, Rongxian county, Sanjiang Dong autonomous county, Wuming county, Xing'an county, Yulin

Guizhou Province
Anshun, Guiyang*, Huangguoshu Falls (Zhenning autonomous county), Kaili, Liupanshui, Qingzhen county, Shibing county, Zhenyuan county, Zunyi

Hebei Province
Baoding, Botou, Cangzhou, Chengde, Handan, Langfang, Qinhuangdo (including Beidaihe & Shanhaiguan), Shijiazhuang, Tangshan, Wanping county (Jinshan Ling Chang Cheng), Xingtai, Zhao county, Zhouxian county, Zunhua county (Dongling Tombs)

Heilongjiang Province
Anda, Bei'an, Daqing, Fangzheng county, Hailun, Harbin*, Hegang, Heihe, Ichun, Jagdaqi (Da Hinggan Ling), Jiamusi, Jixi, Zhaodong, Mudanjiang, Nenjiang county, Qiqihar, Qitaihe, Shuangcheng county, Shuangyashan, Suifenhe, Suihua, Tongjiang, Wudalianchi

Henan Province
Anyang, Gongxian, Hebi, Huixian, Jiaozuo, Kaifeng, Linxian, Luohe, Luoyang (and Longmen Caves), Nanyang, Pingdingshan, Puyang, Sanmenxia, Shangqiu, Wenxian county, Xinxiang, Xinyang (Jigong Shan), Xuchang, Yuxian Sanmenxia, Zhengzhou*, Zhoukou, Zhumadian

Hubei Province
Danjiangkou, Ezhou, Honghu county, Huanggang county, Huangshi, Jiangling county, Jianli county, Jingmen, Puqi, Shashi, Shiyan, Suizhou, Wuhan*, Xiangfan, Xianning, Yichang

Hunan Province
Anren county, Anxiang county, Changde, Changde county, Changsha*, Chenxian, Chenzhou, Dayong, Fenghuang county, Guidong county, Guiyang county, Hanshou county, Hengshan county, Hengyang, Jinshi, Jishou, Lengshuijiang, Lengshuitan, Lianyuan county, Linli county, Lixian, Loudi, Nanxian, Qiyang county, Rucheng county, Sangzhi county, Shaoyang, Taojiang county, Taoyuan county, Xiangtan, Xiangtan county (and Shaoshan), Xinhuang Dong autonomous county, Xupu county, Yiyang, Yizhang county, Yongshun county, Yongxing county, Yongzhou, Yuanjiang county, Yuanling county, Yueyang, Zhijiang county, Zhuzhou

Jiangsu Province
Changshu, Changzhou, Huai'an county, Huaiyin, Lianyungang, Nanjing*, Nantong, Suzhou, Wuxi, Xuzhou, Yangzhou, Yixing county, Zhenjiang

Jiangxi Province
Anyuan county, Chongren county, Dexing county, Fengxin county, Fuzhou, Ganzhou, Ganzhou county, Ji'an, Ji'an county, Jingdezhen, Jinggangshan county, Jiujiang (and Lushan), Le'an county, Nanchang*, Nanfeng county, Pengze county (Dragon Palace Cave), Pingxiang, Quannan county, Shanggao county, Wanzai county, Xinyu, Xunwu county, Yanshan county, Yichun, Yifeng county, Yihuang county, Yingtan, Yiyang county

Jilin Province
Antu county (Changbai Shan area), Baicheng, Changchun*, Gongzhu Ling, Hunjiang, Jilin, Liaoyuan, Longjing, Meihekou, Siping, Tonghua, Tumen, Yanji

Liaoning Province
Anshan, Benxi, Chaoyang, Dalian, Dandong, Fushun, Fuxin, Jinzhou, Liaoyang, Shenyang*, Tieling, Yingkou

Nei Menggu (Inner Mongolia) Autonomous Region
Baotou, Chifeng, Dalad Banner (Xiangshawan), Dongsheng, Erenhot, Hailar, Hohhot*, Manzhouli, Tongliao, Ulan Hot, Xilinhot (Abagnar Qi), Zalantun (Butna Qi)

Ningxia Autonomous Region
Guyuan county, Haiyuan county, Lingwu county, Pingluo county, Qingtongxia, Tongxin county, Wuzhong, Xiji county, Yanchi county, Yinchuan*, Zhongning county, Zhongwei county

Qinghai Province
Gangca county (Qinghai Lake: Bird Island/Niaodao), Golmud, Gonghe county, Huangzhong county (and Taersi monastery), Ledu, Lenghu, Mangya, Xining*

Shaanxi Province
Baoji, Hancheng, Hanzhong, Huangling county, Huayin county, Lintong county, Liquan county, Liuba county, Lüeyang county, Mianxian, Nanzheng county, Pucheng county, Qianxian county, Tongchuan, Xi'an*, Xianyang, Xingping county, Yan'an, Yangling

Shandong Province
Dezhou, Dongying, Jinan*, Jining (including Qufu & Yanzhou counties), Kenli (Shengli oilfield), Linyi, Qingdao, Rizhao, Tai'an (and Taishan), Weifang, Weihai, Yantai, Zaozhuang, Zibo

Shanghai Municipality
Shanxi Province
Changzhi, Datong, Fanzhi county, Hongtong county, Linfen, Pingyao county, Ruicheng county, Taiyuan*, Wutai county, Yangquan, Yuncheng

Sichuan Province
Barkam county, Chengdu*, Chongqing, Dazu county, Deyang, Dukou, Emei county, Fengdu county, Fengjie county, Fuling, Guangyuan, Guanxian county, Hongya county, Jiang'an county, Leshan, Luzhou, Maowen Qiang autonomous county, Meishan county, Mianyang, Nanchong, Nanping county, Neijiang, Songpan county, Wanxian county, Wushan county, Wuxi county, Xichang, Xindu county, Xingwen county, Yibin, Yunyang county, Zhangning county, Zhongxian county, Zigong

Tianjin Municipality
Tibet Autonomous Region
Lhasa*, Nagqu, Nêdong county, Shigatse county, Zhangmu (Nyalam)

Yunnan Province
Chuxiong, Dali, Jinghong county, Kunming*, Lijiang (Naxi autonomous county), Menghai county, Qujing, Shilin (Lunan), Simao county, Tonghai county, Yuxi

Xinjiang Autonomous Region
Aksu, Artux, Changji, Hami, Kashgar, Korla, Shihezi, Turfan county, Ürümqi*

Zhejiang Province
Deqing county (Mogan Shan), Hangzhou*, Huzhou, Jiaojiang, Jiaxing, Jinyun county, Lishui, Ningbo, Putuo county (Putuo Shan & Shenjiamen), Qingtian county, Quzhou, Shaoxing, Tiantai county, Wenzhou

Other Useful Papers

Given the Chinese preoccupation with impressive bits of paper, it's worth carrying around a few business cards, student cards and anything else that's printed and wrapped in a plastic envelope.

These additional ID are useful for leaving with bicycle-renters who often want a deposit or other security for the bikes. Sometimes they ask you to leave your passport but you should insist on leaving another form of ID or a deposit. Some hotels also require you to hand in your passport as security – offer to pay in advance.

It's worth hanging on to cheap room or dormitory hotel receipts – the fact that you've been allowed to stay cheaply at some other hotel will weigh in your favour at the next place. Likewise, hang on to any Chinese-price tickets you happen to buy.

Officially, the only foreigners who qualify for student discounts in China are those studying in China or Taiwan. They have their own ID cards. Some travellers have received student discounts using driver's licences, youth hostel cards, international student cards, forgeries, made-in-Hong Kong imitations and the like. Surprisingly enough, these lies and tricks have been going on for several years but often still work. However, they don't benefit bona fide students who sometimes have their genuine cards knocked back because the Chinese behind the hotel desk has seen so many forgeries about. One French student had a ding-dong battle in Zhengzhou station with a smug booking clerk who threw her absolutely genuine card into the rubbish bin and told her it was a fake! In early 1987 there were rumours that foreign student cards were to be abolished and replaced with a letter of introduction from the student's embassy.

A supply of passport photos is useful. Although they're obtainable in China, it's more convenient if you bring them along. They're particularly useful if you're going to Europe on the Trans-Siberian, as that may require three visas (Mongolian, Soviet and Polish).

GENERAL INFORMATION

Post

As well as the local post offices there are branch post offices in just about all the major tourist hotels, from where you can send letters, packets and parcels. (The contents of packets and parcels are checked by the post office staff before mailing.) In some places, you may only be able to post printed matter from these branch offices. Other parcels may require that a customs form be attached at the town's main post office, where their contents will be checked.

The international postal service seems efficient, and air-mailed letters and postcards will probably take around five to 10 days to reach their destinations. An International Express Mail Service now operates in many Chinese cities. If possible, write the country of destination in Chinese, as this should speed up the delivery.

Large envelopes are a bit hard to come by; try the department stores. If you expect to be sending quite a few packets then stock up when you come across such envelopes. A roll of strong, sticky tape is a useful item to bring along and serves many purposes. String, glue and sometimes cloth bags are supplied at the post offices. The Friendship Stores will sometimes package and mail purchases for you, but only goods actually bought at the store.

International Post The ordinary postal rates for international mail (other than to Hong Kong or Macau) are listed below. There is a slightly reduced postage rate for letters and postcards to certain countries.

Letters Surface mail is Y0.80 up to 20 g, and Y1.50 above 20 g and up to 50 g. Air mail letters are an additional Y0.30 for every 10 g or fraction thereof.

Postcards Postcards are Y0.60 by surface mail and Y0.90 by air mail to anywhere in the world.

Aerogrammes are Y1.00 to anywhere in the world.

Printed Matter Surface mail is Y0.50 up to 20 g, Y0.80 above 20 g and up to 50 g, Y1.40 above 50 g and up to 100 g, Y2.70 above 100 g and up to 250 g, Y5.10 above 250 g and up to 500 g, Y8.10 above 500 g and up to one kg, Y13.50 above one kg and up to two kg, and for each additional kg or fraction thereof the charge is Y5.70.

Air mail for printed matter is an additional Y0.20 for every additional 10 g or fraction thereof.

Small Packets Surface mail charges are Y1.80 up to 100 g, Y3.60 above 100 g and up to 250 g, Y6.50 above 250 g and up to 500 g, Y10.80 above 500 g and up to one kg. Air mail for small packets is an additional Y0.20 for every 10 g or fraction thereof.

Parcels Rates vary depending on the country of destination. Charge for a one-kg parcel sent surface mail from China to the UK is Y27, to the USA Y15.30, to West Germany Y17.80. Charge for a one-kg parcel sent air mail to the UK is Y41, to the USA Y38.50, to West Germany Y35.30.

Post offices are very picky about how you pack

things; don't finalise your packing until the thing has got its last customs clearance. If you have a receipt for the goods then put it in the box when you're mailing it, because it may be opened again by customs further down the line.

Registration Fees The registration fee for letters, printed matter and packets is Y0.50. Acknowledgement of receipt is Y0.40 per article.

Some of the restrictions on what you can post out of the country reach the point of comical absurdity. In Wuhan I picked up a copy of *Acta Academiae Medicinae Wuhan*, a journal of medical research published (in English) by the Wuhan Medical College, freely available from the pamphlet shelf of the Jianghan Hotel dining room. I scurried off to the post office to send it back to Hong Kong but the staff there looked at it dubiously and telephoned someone who obviously told them that it wasn't to be posted. No doubt it was some sort of secret research which wasn't to leave the confines of hotel dining rooms. In the next town I posted it, no questions asked.

Poste Restante There's a post restante in just about every city and town, and they seem to work OK. Apart from these you can receive mail at some of the major tourist hotels, such as the Peace Hotel in Shanghai. Some of the hotels have a mail box or desk where incoming mail for foreigners is kept (you don't have to be staying at the hotel). Other hotels have noticeboards where letters are displayed (one letter I saw in Canton was for Mr Wolf-doctor Kunler . . . hmmmh, strange people roaming these parts). Many places will hold mail for several months if you write such an instruction on the outside of the letter.

It's worth noting that some foreigners living in China have had their mail opened or parcels pilfered before receipt – and some have their outgoing mail opened and read. This seems to affect tourists less, although letters with enclosures will almost certainly be opened. Your mail is less likely to be opened if it's sent to cities that handle high volumes of mail, like Beijing. Officially, the People's Republic prohibits several items from being mailed to it, including books, magazines, notes and manuscripts.

Domestic Services Internal post is very cheap and, by all accounts, very fast – say one or two days from Canton to Beijing. I sent one letter in Shanghai to another address in the city and it arrived on the same day.

Telephone

Many hotel rooms are equipped with phones from which local calls are free. Local calls can also be made from public phones (yes there are some around – though not many) and there are also long-distance phone services.

Direct dialling for international calls is gradually being introduced at top hotels in the major cities. You can also use the main telecommunications offices. Lines are a bit faint but usually OK and you generally don't have to wait more than half an hour before you're connected.

The usual procedure is to fill out a form with the relevant information concerning who you want to call, and hand it to the attendant at the telephone desk.

Charges for telephone calls to western countries vary. Rates for station-to-station calls are: Y9.70 per minute to Australia; Y10.90 per minute to West Germany, the UK and the USA; Y13.60 per minute to Canada; Y6 to Hong Kong.

There is a minimum charge of three minutes. Collect calls are cheaper than calls paid for in China. Time the call yourself; the operator will not break in to tell you that your minimum period of three minutes is approaching. After you hang up, the operator will ring back to tell you how much it cost. There is no call cancellation fee.

If you are expecting an international call, try to advise the caller beforehand of your hotel room number; the operators frequently have difficulty understanding western names, and the hotel receptionist may not be able to locate you.

The phone system in Beijing has improved but Li Binsheng, a well-known cartoonist, once drew a satirical cartoon which depicted an old man standing with a telephone receiver in his hand while his son and grandson waited beside him. The caption for the old man said: 'If I fail to get through, my son will follow; if he fails too, he has his son to follow'.

Telex & Telegraph

International telexes and telegrams can be sent from some of the major tourist hotels and the central telegraph offices in some of the bigger cities.

Telexes (other than those to Hong Kong of Macau) cost about Y9.20 per minute, with a three-minute minimum. International telegram rates are usually around Y1.90 per word; more for the express service. Rates to Hong Kong are less. There are also internal services.

Time

Time throughout China is set to Beijing time. When it's noon in Beijing it's also noon in far-off Lhasa, Ürümqi and all other parts of the country.

When it's noon in Beijing the time in cities around the world is:

Frankfurt	5 am
Hong Kong	12 noon
London	4 am
Los Angeles	8 pm
Melbourne	2 pm
Montreal	11 pm
New York	11 pm
Paris	5 am
Rome	5 am
Wellington	4 pm

The General Office of the State Council experimented with daylight saving in 1986 and was so pleased with the reduction in traffic accidents and savings in electricity that it intends to continue with the idea. The Chinese public became mighty confused figuring out what was happening. Chinese working for foreigners thought the time change only applied to Chinese, not foreigners; long-distance buses, trains and boats kept to old time; CAAC decided to postpone all flights, including those of foreign airlines, by one hour. Since Chinese consider regular hours for mealtimes a prerequisite for good health, there was considerable concern that this experiment was detrimental to health and could alter the time-balance intervals between meals.

The State Council has decreed that in the future clocks will be set back one hour at 2 am on the first Sunday of the second 10 days of April, and will be advanced one hour at 2 am on the first Sunday of the second 10 days of September.

Electricity

Electricity is 220 volts, 50 cycles AC. Plugs are usually two-pin American type, so take conversion plugs if you're bringing any electrical equipment with you. Battery chargers are available in some major department stores in Canton, Beijing and Shanghai. Many of the top-class hotels cater for various makes and models of foreign electrical goods. Chinese cities are thankfully free of the frequent power black-outs which afflict countries like India and the Philippines.

Weights & Measures

The metric system is widely used in China. However, the traditional Chinese measures are often used for domestic transactions and you may come across them:

1 metre	=	3 shichi	=	3.28 feet
1 kilometre	=	2 shili	=	0.62 miles
1 hectare	=	15 mu	=	2.47 acres
1 litre	=	1 sheng	=	0.22 gallons
1 kilogram	=	2 jin	=	2.20 pounds

Business Hours

Banks, offices, government departments and Public Security Bureaus are open

Monday to Saturday. As a rough guide only, they open around 8 to 9 am, close for two hours in the middle of the day, and then re-open until 5 or 6 pm. Sunday is a public holiday. CITS offices, Friendship Stores and the foreign-exchange counters in the tourist hotels and some of the local branches of the Bank of China have similar opening hours, and are generally open on Sundays as well.

Many parks, zoos and monuments have similar opening hours, and are also open on Sundays and often at night. Shows at cinemas and theatres end at 9.30 to 10 pm.

Government restaurants are open for early morning breakfast (sometimes as early as 5.30) until about 7.30 am, then open for lunch and again for dinner around 5 to 8 or 9 pm. Chinese eat early and go home early – by 9 pm you'll probably find the chairs stacked and the cooks gone home. Privately run restaurants are usually open all day, and often late into the night.

Railway station and long-distance bus stations open their ticket offices around 5 or 5.30 am before the first trains and buses pull out. Apart from a one or two-hour break in the middle of the day, they often stay open until late at night – say 11 or 11.30 pm.

Admission Fees

Gardens, parks and tourist sights usually have an admission fee of a few fen. In some cases, fees for foreigners can be much higher, such as Y3 at the Longmen Caves outside Luoyang.

Toilets

Chinese toilets are the usual Asian-style holes in the ground over which you crouch and aim. Public toilets can often be found in the side streets of the cities and towns. Some have very low partitions (without doors) between the individual holes and some have none. The Chinese seem to crouch over these for ages reading books and newspapers. Toilet paper is not provided.

Some toilets don't look like they've been cleaned since the Han Dynasty. Often the problem is not the filth but the smell from the ground several feet below the floor of the toilet. Nothing is wasted; your shit is eventually shovelled up and sent to the countryside where it contributes to the Chinese economy as fertiliser.

Toilet paper is readily available in China from the big department stores, although it's a good idea to hang on to whatever's left in your hotel room. Dormitory rooms are not provided with toilet paper, probably because people steal it. The tourist hotels have western-style 'sit-down' toilets.

Remember:

men 男

women 女

Beggars

Yes, beggars do exist in China – but at least in the cities, towns and other tourist centres there are not as many as there are in countries like India. You may see as many beggars in a week in China as you would in an hour in India. There seem to be more in the north of China, particularly in Xian, Kashgar and Kaifeng. Some of them look no less wretched than their counterparts in other Asian countries. More common than beggars are the people who hang around in the public restaurants waiting to move in on the food scraps. The beggars don't tend to pounce on foreigners – the chief exceptions are the kids who practically have to be removed with a crowbar once they've seized your trouser leg. Some beggars squat on the pavement beside large posters which detail their sad story. Professional beggars are common – sometimes women clutching babies who regurgitate stories about having lost their train tickets and all their money.

Dope

One traveller found grass growing around the town of Dunhuang in Gansu Province: 'sad to say, I picked some, dried it in a plastic bag, smoked it and never got stoned. Some people in Beijing say Chinese dope is quite poor quality. Have seen it from the train near the Great Wall in Peking.'

Another traveller wrote of the Kunming area in Yunnan Province: 'if you walk around and explore the Stone Forest you might come across some marijuana. I had some with a Kiwi and we smoked it in one of the long bamboo bongs which one sees all over Kunming. You could say we were stoned in the Stone Forest!'

For centuries, Yunnan was connected with opium routes and we've recently heard of some mean dudes running *da yan* (the big smoke) over the Burmese border into China and across to Hong Kong. Several heroin smugglers from Hong Kong were recently caught in Kunming and within a week were scheduled for Public execution. The PSB issued a special invitation to the foreign press to attend the execution.

In Xinjiang Province, hashish and 'local tobacco' are available. The latter, a mixture of tobacco and marijuana, is very common in street markets and usually available in three blends.

We've no idea what the attitude of the Chinese police is towards foreigners using dope – it's too early to tell. If they *do* take an unfavourable view, we haven't heard what the penalties are. Discretion is strongly advised! Foreigners are mostly left to their own devices, as long as Chinese are not included, but turning the hotel yard into a drying factory is not likely to please the staff – so be considerate.

HOLIDAYS

The People's Republic has nine national holidays during the year:

New Year's Day
1January

Spring Festival
Usually February; also known as Chinese New Year, starts on the first day of the old lunar calendar. Warning: this is China's only three day holiday and, unless you've booked a month or two in advance, this is definately not the time to cross the borders (especially the Hong Kong one) or to look for transport or accomodation. Sit tight until the chaos is over!

International Working Women's day
8 March

International Labour Day
1 May

Youth Day
4 May Commemorates the Beijing student demonstrations of 4 May 1919, when the Versailles Conference gave Germany's 'rights' in the city of Tianjin to Japan.

Children's day
1 June

Anniversary of the founding of the Communist Party of China
1 July

Anniversary of the founding of the Chinese People's Liberation Army
1 August

National Day
1 October Celebrates the founding of the People's Republic of China in 1949.

MEDIA

News Agencies

China has two news agencies, the Xinhua News Agency and the China News Service. The national Xinhua (New China) Agency has its headquarters in Beijing and branches in each province and autonomous region as well as in the PLA and many foreign countries. It provides news for national, provincial and local papers and radio stations, transmits radio broadcasts abroad in foreign languages, and is responsible for making contact with and exchanging news with foreign agencies.

Xinhua serves not only as mouthpiece but also as the 'eyes and ears' of the political elite whose decisions rely heavily on *Neibu Cankao*, the most exclusive of all restricted-circulation information bulletins in China. Few, if any, foreigners have seen this Xinhua publication which appears twice daily, once in the morning and once in the afternoon, for an estimated readership of 2000, drawn from 'responsible comrades in the central leadership'. The elite readership derives a considerable proportion of its power from this 'real' news on everything from lapses in Party discipline, religious ferment or student unrest to crime, murder, porn or even the capitalist temptations of staff in joint-ventures. Another better-known restricted-circulation bulletin produced by Xinhua is *Cankao Ziliao*, which contains translations of international news from foreign sources.

The main function of the China News Service is to supply news to Overseas Chinese newspapers and journals, including those in Hong Kong and Macau. It also distributes Chinese documentary films abroad.

Newspapers and periodicals are distributed through the post office. The major distributor of books is the Xinhua Bookstore, which has around 5000 stores throughout China. There are also Foreign Language Bookstores in the major cities. Guoji Shudian (China Publications Centre) is the chief distributor of books and periodicals abroad.

Chinese-Language Publications

In 1986 there were 1777 national and provincial newspapers. The main one is *Renmin Ribao (People's Daily)*, with national circulation. It was founded in 1946 as the official publication of the Central Committee of the Communist Party. At the other end of the scale are several hundred 'unhealthy papers' hawked on street corners in major cities and severely criticised by the government for their obscene and racy content. There are also about 39 newspapers for the minority nationalities.

Almost 2200 periodicals were published in 1986, of which about half were technical or scientific; the rest were concerned with social sciences, literature, culture and education, or were general periodicals, pictorials or children's publications. One of the better-known periodicals is the monthly *Hongqi (Red Flag)*, the main Communist philosophical and theoretical journal.

In China the papers, radio and television are the last places to carry the news. Westerners tend to be numbed by endless accounts of heroic factory workers and stalwart peasants, and dismiss China's media as a huge propaganda machine. Flipping through journals like *China Reconstructs, Women of China* and *China Pictorial* only serves to confirm this view.

Nevertheless, the Chinese press does warrant serious attention since it provides clues to what is happening in China. When Deng Xiaoping returned to public view after being disposed of in the Cultural Revolution, the first mention was simply the inclusion of his name in a guest list at a reception for Prince Sihanouk of Kampuchea, printed in the *People's Daily* without elaboration or comment. Political struggles are described in articles in the Chinese newspapers as a means of warning off supporters of the opposing side and undermining its position rather than resorting to an all-out, dangerous conflict. 'Letters to the Editor' in *People's Daily* provides something of a measure of public opinion, and complaints are sometimes followed up by reporters.

Newspapers and journals are useful for following the 'official line' of the Chinese government – though in times of political struggle they tend to follow the line of whoever has control over the media. For example, in the immediate post-Mao days when the 'rightists' were making a comeback, the 'leftists' controlled the media.

Foreign-Language Publications

China publishes various newspapers, books and magazines in a number of European and Asian languages. The papers you're most likely to come across are: *China Daily*, the only English-language daily newspaper, which was first published in

June 1981 and now has overseas editions printed in Hong Kong, the USA and Europe; *Beijing Review*, a weekly magazine on political and current affairs; and *China Reconstructs*, a monthly magazine. They all suffer from an over-supply of political rhetoric, but there are usually some interesting articles on archaeological discoveries or travel. *China Daily* is notable for reporting crime, criminal executions and even stories about corrupt officials (a very popular theme in the papers at the moment).

Foreign Newspapers & Journals

Some western journals and newspapers are sold in a few of the major tourist hotels. The *Herald Tribune* and the Asian edition of the *Wall Street Journal* are sold in Beijing, Shanghai and Canton. *Time, Newsweek* and *Reader's Digest* have wide distribution; *Newsweek* is even sold in some foreign-language bookshops.

When the Communist Party committee of Beijing investigated the bustling black market for foreign books, magazines and newspapers they discovered that hotel staff and garbage collectors are well-placed intermediaries for this business. Foreign hotel guests regularly leave behind several tons of foreign publications every month, but resident foreign experts, journalists and diplomats throw out nearly 20 tons. The Beijing committee analysed printed matter left behind at the Xinqiao Hotel and was pleased to discover that nearly half of the publications had good or relatively good content. The remaining items contained 'partly erroneous' or 'problematic' material such as 'half-naked advertisements'. When the courageous committee delved into diplomatic dustbins, they discovered that 15% of their haul was 'anti-communist, anti-Chinese, obscene and pornographic' – definitely bottom of the barrel.

If you want to keep up with the world news, a short-wave radio receiver would be worth bringing. There are various compact and easy-to-carry units on the market.

Radio & Television

Domestic radio broadcasting is controlled by the Central People's Broadcasting Station (CPBS). Broadcasts are made in *putonghua*, the standard Chinese speech, as well as in local Chinese dialects and minority languages. There are also broadcasts to Taiwan in *putonghua* and Fukianese. Radio Beijing is China's overseas radio service and broadcasts in about 40 foreign languages, as well as in *putonghua* and several local dialects. It also exchanges programmes with radio stations in a number of countries and has correspondents in some.

The strangest radio story to emerge in 1986 was that of the 'backwards broadcasting policy'. From 1967 until very recently Beijing Radio had apparently been transmitting up to four of its daily Soviet news bulletins backwards – in other words, the last syllable spoken was the first to be transmitted. For years, learned China-watchers thought this was a subtle snub to the Soviets or a mistake which could not be corrected for fear of losing face. A more plausible explanation is that this was a scheme to circumvent Soviet jamming of Chinese broadcasts. Since the Soviets did not jam the 'backwards broadcasts', knowledgeable listeners in the Soviet Union could record them and listen to the 'correct' version by playing the tapes backwards. On 12 October 1986, the Soviets turned off the jamming and two weeks later the backwards broadcasts were off the air.

The other station, Chinese Central Television (CCTV), began broadcasting in 1958, and colour transmission began in 1973.

There are only something like eight million TV sets in the country, distributed among a billion people. Yet the Chinese seem to be addicted to TV, at least in the urban areas where sets are more common. Programming has bred a desire for more television sets and God knows how many get carried across the border every day by Hong Kong relatives! The most-watched shows are probably the English-language programmes; if you need a laugh watch the afternoon repeats of the English-language show 'Follow Me'. Private ownership of TVs is limited, but just about everyone has access to one: communes, factories and hotels usually buy a TV and put it in their recreation rooms or dining halls for collective viewing, or one set may serve a whole apartment block.

Noticeboards

Apart from the media, the public noticeboard retains its place as a means of educating the people or influencing public opinion. Other people who want to get a message across glue up big wall-posters in public places. This is a traditional form of communicating ideas in China and if the content catches the attention of even a few people then word-of-mouth can spread it very quickly. Deng Xiaoping stripped from China's constitution the right to put up wall-posters.

Public noticeboards abound in China. Two of the most common subjects are crime and road accidents. In China it's no holds barred. Before-and-after photos of executed criminals are plugged up on these boards along with a description of their heinous offences. Photos of people squashed by trucks are even more frequent. Industrial safety is another common theme.

BOOKS

There is enough literature on China to keep you reading for another 5000 years of their history. A few suggestions are given here.

History & Politics

The classic on the Chinese revolution is *Red Star Over China* (Pelican, 1972; first published in 1937) by Edgar Snow. Snow managed to get through the Kuomintang blockade of the Communists and spent four months with them in Yan'an in 1936. His was the first personal account by a western journalist of the Red Army and its leaders. Since the book was written before the Communists came to power, its information about the top Chinese leaders is undistorted by the power-struggles and propaganda of the post-Liberation period. It's been criticised as naive in that it glosses over some of the worst aspects of the Communist movement, but I think it conveys the hope and idealism of the time.

Snow's later books *The Other Side of the River, Red China Today* and *The Long Revolution* recount his visits to China in the 1960s, before and just after the Cultural Revolution. *Edgar Snow's China* (Orbis, 1981) is a compilation of his writings with photos taken by him, by his friends or from Chinese archives – graphic reminders of why the Communists carried on 22 years of war with the Kuomintang and the Japanese.

A first-hand account of China in the early 1950s is *China: an Uncensored Look* (Second Chance Press, 1979, first published in 1956 as *Assignment China*) by American journalist Julian Schuman. There's a lot of meaty argument in this book, particularly in regards to the way China is now viewed by the west. Schuman criticises the western consensus that the 'pragmatic' Deng Xiaoping is responsible for China's 'great leap outward'. He says that this was actually initiated by Mao and that 'the two hallmarks of the People's Republic, from its inception, were pragmatism and reasonableness'.

Chinese Shadows by Simon Leys is one of the most critical books on Mao and the Cultural Revolution. It was published in 1974, based on Leys' visits to China in 1972 and 1973. It's interesting to draw comparisons between the China of the post-Mao era and the one that Leys visited.

Roger Garside's *Coming Alive – China After Mao* describes the events which led to the downfall of the 'Gang of Four' and the rise of Deng Xiaoping. Garside served at the British Embassy in Beijing for two years at the end of the Cultural Revolution (1968 to '70) and was first secretary from 1976 to 1979.

A first-hand account of China during the Cultural Revolution is *Revolution: There and Back* (Faber & Faber, 1980) by Jan Bredsdorff, a Dane who lived in China from 1965 to 1967.

George Orwell's *1984* was ahead of its time in predicting the political trends in Communist China. *Animal Farm* is perhaps a closer approximation to post-1949 China and its bloated cadres.

The issue of human rights is covered in Amnesty International's *China: Violations of Human Rights* – a grim facet that should not be ignored.

Seeds of Fire: Chinese Voices of Conscience (Far Eastern Economic Review Ltd, 1986) is an anthology of blistering eloquence from authors such as Wei Jingsheng, Liu Qing, Wang Xizhe and Xu Wenli (all currently imprisoned for their roles in the Democracy Movement) and the poet Sun Jingxuan. Wei Jingsheng's description of Q1, China's top prison for political detainees, is utterly horrific.

Recent Accounts

Over the last few years, since foreign journalists were permitted to take up residence in China, there has been a spate of books delving into Chinese life, the universe and everything. Most are out of date, but if you read them in succession you can get an overview of the changes which have taken place in China since Mao died.

Fox Butterfield's *China – Alive in the Bitter Sea* (Coronet, 1983) is one of the biggest sellers. It tells you everything, from the location of Chinese labour camps to what the women use as substitutes for tampons.

Canadian John Fraser lived in China at the time of the 'Democracy Wall Movement' of 1978, and much of his book *The Chinese – Portrait of a People* (Fontana Paperbacks, 1982) centres on this event and its aftermath.

To Get Rich is Glorious (Pantheon Books, 1984) by American journalist and many-times China traveller Orville Schell is a concise and easy-to-read overview of the major changes in China's economic policies and political thinking over the last few years. If you want to get some idea of the path that China is now taking and what the country may be like in the 21st century, this is the book to get.

A dimmer view of China under Deng Xiaoping is Italian journalist Tiziano Terzani's *Behind the Forbidden Door* (Allen & Unwin, 1986). Terzani lived in China from 1980 to 1984, when he was booted out for his critical reporting.

A brilliant photographic record is *China After Mao: Seeking Truth From Facts* (Penguin) by photo-journalist Liu Heung Shing. Liu was born in Hong Kong, spent his childhood in Fujian Province, and is a fluent speaker of Mandarin and some dialects. He spent four years from 1979 photographing the changes in China under Deng Xiaoping. Capturing the rawer edge of reality, his book escapes the usual coffee-table picture-book clichés.

Travellers' Tales

Then there's the sort of stuff that fits more into the 'Mad Dogs & Englishmen' genre. You won't fail to be amused by two books by Englishman Peter Fleming, written in the mid 1930s. *One's Company* describes his travels across Siberia and eastern China meeting such notables as Pu Yi, the puppet-emperor of the Japanese-occupied Manchuria. *News from Tartary* describes his epic six-month trek on the backs of camels and donkeys across southern Xinjiang and into the north of Pakistan.

More recent is Vikram Seth's *From Heaven Lake* (Hogarth Press, London, 1983), an account by a young Indian student who hitched from northern China to his home in Delhi via Lhasa and Nepal in 1981. His battles with bureaucracy and the agonising discomfort of long-distance trucking are given in graphic detail.

A Peddlar in Beijing (Methuen, 1986) by Chris Hough is one young Englishman's often comical account of a would-be epic bicycle adventure from Europe to China.

A vivid account of life in the tourist-gullies of Asia with Lonely Planet guides, arrogant travellers and baffled Chinese. If you want to know what it felt like to travel in China in the early 1980s then this is the book to get.

An overview of western attitudes toward China is *To Change China: Western Advisers in China 1620-1960* (Penguin, 1980) by Jonathan Spence. A collection of 'cautionary histories for businessmen, diplomats, students, or any other foreigners who foolishly believe that they can transform this vast, enigmatic country'.

Living in China

If you intend to live in China, a couple of books are worth picking up:

The Administrative Divisions of the People's Republic of China (Cartographic Publishing House, Beijing, 1980) is a little booklet with extensive lists of Chinese cities and towns in both pinyin and Chinese characters – useful if you're going to travel to obscure places. It's sold in Hong Kong and in China.

The China Phone Book & Address Directory (published annually by the China Phone Book Company, Hong Kong) is available from major bookshops in Hong Kong. If you live in China or visit frequently it may be invaluable. It's in English and Chinese and contains the addresses and phone numbers of industrial firms, hospitals, government departments and the like in the major cities and towns.

Excellent background information can be had from *China Bound: A Handbook for American Students, Researchers and Teachers* published by the US-China education Clearing House. It's available from the National Association for Foreign Student Affairs, 1860 19th St NW, Washington, DC 20009, USA.

Living in Hong Kong (American Chamber of commerce in Hong Kong) has a very good section on living in Beijing. It's available on order from the Book Society, GPO Box 7804, Hong Kong.

Phrasebooks

If you don't speak Chinese these are essential. Lonely Planet's *China Phrasebook* includes common words, useful phrases and word lists in English, simplified Chinese characters and *putonghua*.

Some people use the *Speechless Translator*, which can be bought in Hong Kong; this has columns of Chinese characters and English translations that you string together to form sentences, with no speaking required.

Another useful book is *Instant Chinese* (Round Asia Publishing Company, 1985), which you can find in Hong Kong.

If you're visiting Tibet, you'll find Lonely Planet's *Tibet Phrasebook* useful.

Hong Kong Bookstores

A couple of bookstores in Hong Kong carry a good selection of books from or about China. The best is probably Swindon Books on 13-15 Lock Rd, Tsimshatsui, Kowloon.

Time Books, on Granville Rd near the corner with Nathan Rd, Kowloon, sells both English and Chinese books and has many travel books.

Chung Hwa Book Company, M/F 450-452 Nathan Rd, Kowloon, has books in Chinese and is also very good for maps of China and Chinese cities. The city maps here are worth forking out a bit more for since they are often unavailable, or can be very time-consuming to find in the relevant cities.

Joint Publishing Company, 6 Queen Victoria St, Central, Hong Kong Island, specialises in books published in China.

For glossy magazines and the like, try Hong Kong China Tourism Press, 1C Tsing Wan Building, 334-336 Kings Rd, North Point, Hong Kong Island.

General Thoughts

If you think it's hard deciding what to read on China, then spare a thought for the Chinese who don't have the right to choose. Books come and go in China; as the political winds change so does the availability of certain books and newspapers.

In a bookshop in Wuhan I came across a copy of a book printed in 1974 called *Criticise Lin Biao and Confucius*. It should have been removed long ago since that campaign was actually an attack on 'rightists' like Deng Xiaoping. The employees in the shop tried to take it from me when I picked it off the shelves, and despite a furious argument they refused to sell it to me. They claimed it was a damaged book (the front cover had been torn off) and they couldn't sell a damaged book. One bystander said it was an 'old' book and I couldn't learn anything from an old book. In utter frustration I left the shop. I returned the next day and all copies of the book had been taken off the shelves. So if you see something that looks interesting you'd better get it now, because in 10 years' time when the Chinese leadership is aiming in a different direction it won't be available.

The other problem with Chinese bookshops is that some books are *neibu* – restricted or forbidden except to those who have been granted access. Of course they won't tell you the book is neibu, but will make up some excuse like the book has no price on it. Books are neibu for various reasons. Sometimes it's because they're illegally printed copies of western books and the Chinese are sensitive about infringing international copyright. A more common reason – and this one afflicts university libraries throughout China – is that only certain people have permission to use certain books. Only law students can use law books, only economics students can use economics books, and so on. To use books outside your field requires permission from the unit in charge of the library which houses those books. The rules have been relaxed recently with the exception of classics with an erotic bent, such as *Jin Ping Mei (The Golden Lotus)*. Foreign students and teachers up to professorial level are not immune to the system – even they are restricted in their access to books, and this has become one of their most serious complaints.

MAPS

The most useful map of China is published by Cartographic Publishing House in Beijing. The detailed map is available in both pinyin and Chinese script, and is called the 'Map of the People's Republic of China (Zhonghua Renmin Gongheguo Ditu)'. You should be able to get it in your home country and it's readily available in Hong Kong and the large cities in China.

The *National Geographic* map of China has excellent coverage of minority areas. *Bartholomew's* maps are usually excellent, but not for China. Their China map is extremely detailed but uses the old Wade-Giles system of naming towns, which is a distinct nuisance. The map also leaves out Tibet and Xinjiang.

City maps, in Chinese, are often sold by hawkers outside railway and long-distance bus stations. They show bus routes and in most cases are very good. They're definitely worth buying and only cost about 25 to 40 fen. Maps in English are sometimes sold at the larger tourist hotels.

Large maps of 20 major cities in China have been made by the Cartographic Publishing House and are usually available from most tourist hotels. There are versions both in Chinese and in English, and they usually come complete with sub-maps of the area around the city, and of parks and sights within the city. They carry a lot of background info on the reverse side, and are cheap. They're excellent maps, although sometimes the sights are carelessly marked and it's hard to tell whether a building is on a main street or down some side alley. Getting these maps when you need them can be difficult – if you see one you think you'll need later, then buy it!

If you're after fine detail you can sometimes get booklets of maps (in Chinese) of the counties in the individual provinces, and these usually include maps of the main towns. Booklets of detailed maps of the individual Chinese provinces (in Chinese) are sold on the trains and at the railway stations.

If you arrive in a place where no map is available, take a look in the waiting room of the railway or long-distance bus-station; large maps of the town are often hung up on the wall. They're always in Chinese, but you may be able to orientate yourself from them, and they sometimes show the bus routes.

Chinese cities built or rebuilt under the Communists are laid out in neat grid patterns. Any curving or wandering streets on a map may indicate an old area where the houses have traditional architecture and courtyards, and are separated by narrow alleys and walkways. These small streets are often the location of interesting free markets.

Some of the most detailed maps of China available in the west are the aerial survey 'Operational Navigation Charts' (Series ONC, October 1979). These are prepared and published by the Defence Mapping Agency Aerospace Center, St Louis Air Force Station, Missouri 63118, USA. Cyclists have highly recommended these particular maps because of the extraordinary detail they provide. In Britain you can obtain them from Stanfords of London or from The Map Shop(tel 06 846 3146), A T Atkinson & Partner, 15 High St, Upton-on-Seven, Worcestershire, WR8 OHJ.

HEALTH

Vaccinations

Vaccinations against cholera are required if you arrive within five days of leaving an infected area. Yellow fever vaccinations are required if you arrive within six days of leaving an infected area. If you're coming from a 'clean' area then inoculations against cholera, yellow fever, typhoid and smallpox are not necessary.

Malaria

The parasite that causes malaria is spread by mosquitoes. The disease has a nasty habit of recurring in later years, even if you were 'cured' – and it can be fatal.

Malaria is a risk in the southern and south-eastern provinces of China, almost as far north as Beijing. Beijing itself and the provinces of Heilongjiang, Jilin, Inner Mongolia, Gansu, Xingjiang, Shanxi, Ningxia and Qinghai are considered to be free of malaria. Tibet is also considered free of malaria, except along the Zangbo River Valley in the extreme south-east. North of latitude 33°N the period of high malarial risk is July to November. Between 33°N and 25°N it's risky between May and December, and south of 25°N transmission can occur year round.

You can't be inoculated against malaria but protection is simple: either a daily or weekly tablet depending on which your doctor recommends. The tablets kill the parasites if they get into your bloodstream. You usually have to start taking the tablets about two weeks before entering the malarial zone and continue taking them for several weeks after you've left it. Resistance to two types of anti-malarial tablets, chloroquine and Fansidar, has been reported in China. There is little information on the extent of the resistance, but Guangdong (including Hainan Island), Guangxi and Yunnan provinces have been reported as chloroquine-resistant areas.

The best precaution is to avoid being bitten in the first place. A lot of Chinese hotels have mosquito-nets. Mosquito repellent is available but you may have trouble finding it, so bring your own. Mosquito coils are readily available.

Weighing the benefit of taking malaria tablets against the possible side-effects of long-term use is something you should do yourself.

Hepatitis

Hepatitis is a disease of the liver occurring in countries with poor sanitation – of which China is definitely one. The disease is spread by infected food and water or by contaminated cooking and eating utensils. Salads washed in infected water or fruit handled by an infected person might carry the disease. There are several varieties of hepatitis, of differing severity, but infectious hepatitis is the one you're most likely to pick up.

Symptoms appear 15 to 50 days after infection (generally around 25 days) and consist of fever, loss of appetite, nausea, depression, complete lack of energy, and pains around the bottom of your rib cage (the location of the liver). Your skin turns progressively yellow and the whites of your eyes turn yellow to orange. The best way to detect it is to keep watch on your eyes and also on your urine, which will turn a deep orange no matter how much liquid you drink. If you haven't drunk much liquid and/or you're sweating a lot, don't jump to conclusions! The severity of the disease varies. It may last less than two weeks and give you only a few bad days, or it may last for several months and give you a few bad weeks. You could feel depleted of energy for several months afterwards.

The usual protection against hepatitis is a gamma-globulin injection but its effectiveness is debatable – improved shots may provide protection for as much as six months, but some say it's not worth it at all.

The only way to guard against hepatitis is to avoid eating contaminated food or drinking contaminated water. Sharing eating utensils with other people can be a source of infection. It's easy to get paranoid about where to eat in China since most restaurants are incredibly scungy; some people even carry their own chopsticks.

Due to a lack of proper surveys it's hard to say how big a problem hepatitis is for China travellers. I personally think that it's not particularly common.

If you get hepatitis, rest and good food are the only cures. Don't use alcohol or tobacco since they only give your liver more work.

Diarrhoea

Diarrhoea (the 'Hong Kong dog' or 'Beijing Belly') is often caused simply by a change of diet or because your digestive system is unused to spicy or oily food, both features of Chinese cooking. A lot depends on what you're used to eating and whether or not you've got an iron gut. If you get diarrhoea, the first thing to do is nothing – it rarely lasts more than a few days. If it persists then the usual treatment is Lomotil tablets; in the west this is a prescription drug, so ask your doctor for a supply. If the condition persists for a week or more, it's probably not simple traveller's diarrhoea and you should see a doctor. If you get a severe bout of diarrhoea you'll get dehydrated, so keep up your fluid and salt intake.

Drinking Water

Getting sick from drinking the water is less of a problem in China than it is in other Asian countries. Even the cheap hotels have thermoses of boiled water in their rooms and dormitories. It's worth carrying a water-bottle with you and refilling it in the hotels. Many trains, railway stations and ferry terminals have boilers for passengers. If you don't have any boiled water with you then you can use water purification tablets, though many types are not meant for prolonged use. If you don't have either, you have to weigh the risks of drinking unboiled water against the risks of dehydrating – the first is possible, the second is definite.

Climate Problems

The climate is going to be one of the biggest strains on your health. The most usual affliction is not malaria, hepatitis or diarrhoea, but the common cold – usually in the form of a severe bronchial cough which can persist for several weeks.

It's wise to bring something to relieve the symptoms of flu and colds – respiratory ailments are prevalent in China and shouldn't be taken lightly! The fiercely cold winters and miserably wet spring and autumn are the worst times, while crowded living conditions and the Chinese habit of spitting help spread the germs.

Summer is fiercely hot. You can easily dehydrate if you don't keep up your fluid intake – which is why it's a good idea to carry a water-bottle with you. You are dehydrating if you urinate infrequently or if your urine turns a deep yellow or orange; you may also get headaches. The sun is bright, so good sunglasses are essential. Sunburn is a problem. Bring something to cover your head or buy one of the cheap straw hats for sale all over China.

Summer in the north is hot and dry. In the south it's hot and humid; places like Hong Kong and Canton are steam baths in July and August, and prickly heat can be a problem. This condition results when your sweat glands are blocked by your sweat. In humid climates your sweat can't evaporate because the air itself is already moist or because you're wearing clothes which prevent the sweat from evaporating or being absorbed. You become bathed in sweat and small red blisters appear on the skin where the sweat glands have been blocked. To prevent prickly heat, wear clothes which are light and leave an air space between the material and the skin. Don't wear synthetic materials like nylon since they can't absorb the sweat. Dry yourself well after bathing and use calamine lotion or a zinc-oxide based talcum powder. Anything that makes you sweat more – exercise, tea, coffee, alcohol – only makes the condition worse.

If you're sweating profusely you're going to lose a lot of salt, which leads to fatigue and muscle cramps. Make it up by putting extra salt in your food (a teaspoon a day is enough), but don't increase your salt intake unless you also increase your water intake.

High-Altitude Sickness

Tibet has a few problems all its own caused by high altitude and thin air. For full details see the Tibet chapter in this book.

Briefly, winter at high altitudes can be endless days and nights of incredibly piercing, dry cold that seems impossible to keep out. Summers are warm and dry, but because of the thin air the rays of the sun are much more penetrating and it's easy to get sunburnt. By the same token, a cloud across the sun will cause the temperature to drop suddenly and dramatically and you'll always have to carry a jacket.

Altitude sickness is the main problem. Rapid ascent from low altitudes, over-exertion, obesity, lack of physical fitness, dehydration, fatigue, advanced age or sickness can bring on symptoms which include headache, dizziness, lack of appetite, nausea and vomiting. Breathlessness and a pounding heart are normal at these altitudes and are not part of altitude sickness; your body will eventually start making more blood cells to carry extra oxygen. If you get altitude sickness, the best cure is to go to a lower altitude. A pain-killer for headache and an anti-emetic for vomiting will also help.

Medical Clinics & Hospitals

Don't get too worried about your health. By taking tablets you can generally avoid malaria (though some resistance has been reported), and by eating sensibly you can greatly reduce your chances of contracting hepatitis and diarrhoea.

As I said, the most usual affliction is the common cold, in various degrees of severity. Tour groups probably have a higher frequency of sickness than individual travellers, as their members are usually elderly and often find it difficult to cope with the long days and jam-packed schedules.

If you are going to get sick in Asia you have a certain advantage doing so in China; it's very unlikely you'll be left to rot. You may be dubious about the quality of the medical attention but at least you'll get it! If your sickness looks as if it's going to get worse then they'll probably pack you off to Hong Kong just so it doesn't get worse in China.

In Beijing, Canton and Shanghai there are medical clinics set aside to treat foreigners, and in some of the provincial towns there are clinics in the tourist hotels. In the three main cities, these clinics are at: Capital Hospital Clinic for Foreigners (tel 55-3731), Dongdan Beidajie, Beijing; Shanghai No 1 Hospital (tel 240100), 190 Suzhou Beilu, Shanghai; Guangzhou No 1 Hospital (tel 333090), 602 Renmin Beilu, Canton.

An unusual medical problem occurred when a fellow-traveller had piping-hot tea spilled over him, burning the skin off the top of his foot. Back in town a doctor pierced the blisters while the locals crowded into the room to watch. The hospital looked pretty dirty. Doctor's fees were Y6, including penicillin – the mainstay of Chinese antibiotics – and the foot healed up eventually.

Medical Supplies

There are lots of well-stocked pharmacies in China supplying both western and Chinese medicines, but you may have problems explaining what you want and then understanding what you've got and how to use it. Checking out pharmacies in China is an enjoyable pastime, but if you lack the time or really need something then bring it with you.

The good reputation of Chinese medicine is certainly justified and I have been helped out by many weird and wonderful medicines. But the following comments are definitely *not* intended to replace qualified medical opinion.

For coughs and respiratory ailments I've used 'Three Snake Gall & Fritillary Powder' (SheDan ChuanBei San) and 'Six Deity Pill' (Liu Shen Wan). For colds you can try Chai Hu Yin, Gan Cao Yao or Ban Lan Gen which is also meant to keep your immunity in shape. Ginger powder (Jiang Fen), used in small doses and dissolved in hot water, can act as a digestive or pick-me-up tea. Reportedly this powder can be sprinkled over bedclothes to keep the bugs at bay! There are many different types of sticky plasters (Luo Gao), both herbal and non-herbal, and they're great for sprains, backache, etc. The many types of essential balm such as Tian Liang You, Bai Hua You or Feng You are good for headaches. I also found them very useful to stave off nausea when, as was my usual fate, an entire bus started throwing up! For diarrhoea there's an amazingly effective medicine called Huang Lian Su Pian (berberine hydrochloride) which has also been used for bacillary dysentery and acute gastroenteritis.

And of course there are all those ginseng, royal jelly, deer antler and frog ovary potions which claim to put the ooomph back into life.

Herculean Potency Tablets

Vitamin C tablets and multi-vitamin tablets are worth bringing. Battered stomach flora seem to perk up with 'acidophilus' tablets which usually contain lactobacilli and pectin. Plain yoghurt often does the trick too. Some travellers carry a small bottle of pure alcohol with which to clean their personal chopsticks and mug.

Take a close look at the medicines when you buy them. A bottle of Wei C (Vitamin C) tablets bought in Shenyang proved, on later inspection, to contain the corpse of a giant bluebottle-fly on top of the tablets!

The good news for wearers of contact lenses is that a Chinese-American joint venture in Shanghai, Shanghai Hydron, now produces soft contact lenses and storage solution. These lenses are available at 594 Huaihua Lu, Shanghai. Foreign brands of lenses are available in most major cities.

Blood Supplies

If you're Rh negative, try not to bleed in China. The Chinese do not have Rh negative blood and their blood banks don't store it. Type O blood is also rare. If you're a Type O Rh negative, then you're in worse luck since you can only accept a transfusion of the same and nothing else – and there aren't many of us around.

WHAT TO TAKE & HOW TO TAKE IT

The usual traveller's rule applies: bring as little as possible. It is much better to buy things as you need them than to throw things away because you've got too much to carry. If you have to get something, there are large, well-stocked department stores in almost every town. Some people have all sorts of strange and wise ideas about what to take to China. You don't need to agonise over whether to bring a collapsible chair for the crowded trains; for Y11 you can now buy a combined trolley/collapsible seat at many railway stations!

Carrying Bags

For low-budget travellers the backpack is still the best form of luggage. It's a good idea to add some thief-deterrent (and there are thieves in China!) by sewing on a few tabs for a padlock.

On the other hand, packs can be cumbersome. Long-distance buses have very little space for stowing baggage, and city buses are so crowded that a large bag or pack will be almost impossible to lug around. Also, the opportunities for camping and hiking in China are limited in the extreme, so unless you're absolutely determined, a large pack with a frame is unnecessary. A soft pack, with no frame or with a semi-rigid frame, is much better all round.

A large, soft zip-bag with a wide shoulder strap is less prone to damage and a bit more thief-proof. Shoulder bags are easier to wield on crowded buses and trains, but they're hard to carry for any distance.

Whatever you bring, try and make it small. A day-pack is useful; you can dump your main luggage in a hotel or the left-luggage room at the train station and head off. It's good for hiking and for carrying extra food on long train rides.

Clothes

If you're travelling in the north of China at the height of winter, prepare yourself for incredible cold. A good down jacket, woollens, fur-lined boots, gloves and cap are what you need in this sort of weather. You can buy down jackets in some of the big cities, but not in large sizes and the supply is limited; they cost around Y85 to Y120.

Alternatively, you can buy one of the very functional, huge padded jackets which the Chinese wear. Fur-lined hats with Snoopy ear covers as well as fur-lined gloves and boots are sold in many department stores.

You shouldn't need a sleeping bag since sheets and blankets are provided even in the hard-sleeper carriages of the trains, and the hotels always provide warm bedding. However, a sheet sleeping bag is useful in scungy places off the beaten track. Umbrellas and plastic raincoats can be bought in China.

Jackets with silk wadding will be more than sufficient to guard against the cold, but not against the wind or rain. A silk T-shirt or other silkwear will also give good insulation. Silk is light and will pack small; it can absorb 30% of its weight in moisture and still feel dry.

In summer, the lightest of clothes will do for daytime wear: T-shirts, sandals and shorts. However, if you go up into the hills it can get very cold, and it can get cold on the trains at night. Wandering out of the summer heat into an air-con hotel room is a good way to catch a chill if you don't have some trousers and a jacket.

There is wide variation in weather conditions across the country, so the weather can be very fickle. Even daily temperatures are subject to wide variation; autumn in Beijing can be warm days and clear blue skies, but piercingly cold, frosty nights.

Generally speaking, the usual standards of Asian decorum apply. While shorts are less acceptable for women, plenty of Chinese women wear them and you shouldn't get any unpleasant reactions. Skirts and dresses are frequently worn in places like Beijing, Shanghai and Canton where the Chinese women are more fashion conscious, but wearing any dress of a revealing nature is considered risqué. Make-up and jewellery are becoming increasingly fashionable in the cities. The Chinese place little importance on what foreigners wear, as long as they remain within an acceptable level of modesty; casual clothes are always acceptable. Functional though baggy clothes (including the usual blue garb and surplus army uniforms) are available from department stores, small shops and street markets.

Style has made a comeback in China. Western dresses for women and suits with bell-bottom trousers for men are the standard apparel of the new breed of hip young Chinese urbanites. Forget those blue ant images from the '60s and early '70s. Most Chinese still dress like that, particularly the ordinary workers and peasants, but it no longer borders on the compulsory. There's now an extraordinary range of clothes sold in the shops in the larger cities, usually in styles that died out with the dinosaurs, but every so often you can pick up for a trifle some real gems that would cost a small fortune at home. The main problem with buying clothes in China, particularly shoes, is that big sizes are hard to come by.

A great variety of shoes is available: gym boots, sneakers, lace-ups, high-heels, sandals and plastic boots. In Hong Kong you can buy large-sized running shoes from 'Marathon Sports' (tel 3-674666) at Shop 6, Ambassador Hotel, Kowloon.

Accessories

Absolutely essential is a good pair of sunglasses, particularly in the Xinjiang desert or the high altitudes of Tibet where the sunlight can be extraordinarily bright. In summer the Chinese sun can be fierce. Good, wide-brimmed straw hats are very cheap and are sold everywhere in China. Sewing a map pocket to the inside of your jacket or vest is useful since you'll collect a lot of maps and it's a good idea to have something handy to hold them in.

Toiletries

Tampons are available in China but the supply is limited, so you would be wise to stock up in Hong Kong. Sanitary napkins are available but they're somewhat similar to the medieval concept of the chastity belt. The large tissues used to line this contraption, however, are useful since they're softer than local brands of toilet paper and cheaper; they can be found, after a search, in local dry-goods stores. Any medicines you use for menstrual cramp should be brought with you.

Condoms are freely available in China from the Family Planning Clinics at hospitals – they come in four sizes. It's a good idea to take a picture of the packet with you, to avoid confusion and embarrassment.

Shampoo, razor blades and make-up are also available in China but you may find them inferior to western brands. Suntan lotion (*fang shai lu*) and shaving cream are not widely available, and you should bring sunburn cream with you. Toilet paper (*wei sheng zhi*) is sold in flat and round forms at the department stores and some of the smaller shops.

Top: Sign of the times, Dali (RS)
Bottom Left: Cricket cages, Lanzhou (AS)
Bottom Right: Bamboo fish traps, Erhai Lake (RS)

Mosquito coils are readily available. The Chinese use a rub-on mosquito repellent, a camphor or menthol-based lotion that goes under the name *Shui Cho Yao* – but it will save you time hunting around if you bring your own.

Luxuries
Chinese tea is sold everywhere. Coffee can be found in some of the larger shops and department stores. If you're into endless cups of Chinese tea, a mug and teaspoon are useful for those long train trips where there's a continuous supply of hot water. Locally made cigarettes, beer and spirits are sold everywhere.

Many foreigners may consider Chinese cigarettes to have the gentle eastern aroma of old socks, but annual production of over 60 billion packs is a major source of tax revenue for the Chinese government. The latest additions to a vast array of Chinese cigarettes are some highly aromatic cigars.

Chinese beer is of fine quality providing you stick to top brands. *China Daily* recently called the quality of beer a 'problem nationwide'. The acute shortages of malt and hops have forced breweries to settle for second best in their bid to reach the next national production target – an incredible six billion litres or 5½ litres of beer for every person in the country.

Foreign-made cigarettes (and imitations) and alcohol are available from hawkers, small shops, hotel shops and Friendship Stores all over China. Top-grade foreign rocket fuel – like Morgan Rum, Napoleon Augier Cognac, even Manischewitz – can be bought at the larger tourist hotels and Friendship Stores.

Books
If you want to read, bring your own books. American and British paperbacks are available from shops in the tourist hotels in the big Chinese cities, but the supply and range are limited. Foreign-language bookshops cater for Chinese who are learning foreign languages, not for western reading interests – though they often stock classic foreign fiction. The Beijing Friendship Store has the best foreign bookshop in China. For information about foreign newspapers and journals available in China, see the section on Media.

Film, Cameras & Electronics
Agfa, Kodak, Fuji and Polaroid film are available in China from the Friendship Stores and tourist hotels, but they're usually about 50% more expensive than in Hong Kong. Nor can you rely on being able to get what you want when you want it. For details of film and camera equipment available in China, see the section on Photography. Many people bring Walkmans with them. Transistor radios will pick up music from local stations. A compact shortwave receiver is useful and easy to carry.

Gifts
If you must give the Chinese something, then give them an English book. If you have to teach them something then teach them English. It's the one element of western culture that's universally desired. Other than that, stick to simple things.

Stamps make good gifts; Chinese are avid stamp-collectors, congregating outside the philatelic sections of the post offices and dealing on the footpath. They seem to go for readily recognisable subject matter like people and scenery rather than abstract designs. Pictures of you and your family are very popular gifts.

Don't – as some people have done – insult them by trying to give away your old jacket. Don't turn every kid on the block into a scrounger by indiscriminately giving away stamps, pens and coins. Don't give away Walkmans, radios and the like unless you really have made a close friend – and make sure they're not listed on your Customs Declaration form.

PROBLEMS OF INDIVIDUAL TRAVEL

Just how long independent travel will last in China is a good question. It may go on for as long as the Chinese feel they're making enough money to justify the effort. They may stop it if they feel they are losing control over where individuals go, or if they feel that individuals are coming away with unfavourable impressions. Other people have suggested that individuals create too many problems for the Chinese, arguing for cheaper prices at hotels and getting angry when things don't go right – unlike the tour groups who are better-behaved. One Chinese even suggested to a foreign traveller that the People's Republic is letting individuals in because they give an unfavourable impression of the west.

Coping With China

In the first few years of individual travel to China many people came away with the impression that China was well worth the trip – but ask them if they liked it and the responses were too often negative. It was highly educational, it was different from other parts of the world, it had its moments, it was interesting, but it could also be immensely frustrating.

It still can be, but generally the problems have decreased greatly over the past few years. The Chinese are more used to foreign faces; hotel staff are more co-operative and it's generally no problem getting a cheap room or dormitory bed if there's one available; a number of railway stations have separate booking offices for foreigners; and the number and quality of restaurants have improved immensely. A few years ago most travellers were leaving the place probably never to return. These days most people actually seem to enjoy China, stay for considerably longer, and might well make a return trip.

The degree to which you cope with China depends on how long you stay there, where you want to go, what you want to do, how tolerant and even-tempered you are and how much money you're prepared to spend. The problems of travelling in China are usually the same as those in other Asian countries – generally they're all petty irritations, but they tend to get worse the longer you hang around.

One way to cope with China is to limit your time there. Leave with happy memories before the people and the country get irritating. Spend more time in the places you visit and less time tiring yourself out on buses and trains. The irritations of travel can make you oblivious to the good in the country. If you're in China for any length of time, then at some point you're going to explode. Sometimes this works, sometimes not. Chinese who are familiar with the eccentricities of foreigners often turn off if we get angry – the wall comes down and nothing is achieved.

Staring Squads

The programme is *Aliens*, you are the star, and cinema-sized audiences will gather to watch. You can get stared at in any Asian country, particularly when you go off the beaten track where the locals have seen few or no foreigners. But China is phenomenal for the size and enthusiasm of its staring squads. This is less of a problem in the major tourist centres where the Chinese are used to seeing foreigners, but take one step off the beaten track and you'll very quickly gather a small horde of curious onlookers.

Sometimes you don't even have to do anything to get a crowd. Stop for a minute or two on the street to look at something and several Chinese will also stop. Before long the number of onlookers swells until you're encircled by a solid wall of people. Travellers react differently to these crowds. Initially I found it amusing, but gradually the novelty wore off and I began to wave people away. Then it became tedious, and after a while it was outright aggravating to be unable to do the slightest thing without an audience. You'll even be stared at when you use a communal shower or toilet.

Some people get used to being stared at and some don't. There are a few things you can do to reduce the frequency of audiences. Don't wear fancy watches (particularly digitals), and keep the camera-case on when you're not taking a photo – western cargo tends to attract a lot of attention. If a Chinese comes up to talk to you on the street, then talk to him as you walk, since a conversation with a foreigner automatically attracts a crowd. If you stand on the street scribbling in a notebook someone is sure to poke their head right over the book to see what you're writing, and sometimes they'll lift it straight out of your hands for a closer inspection.

The other way to cope with staring squads is to limit your time in obscure places which have seen few foreigners, or alternate them with places more familiar with visitors. Travelling with someone else also helps; if you've got someone to talk to it's easier to ignore the crowd. Staring back never seems to help. Getting out your camera and taking a photo sometimes parts the waves but doesn't send people scurrying for cover. Hiring a bicycle is a good idea – you're zooming along so fast the crowds can't accumulate.

There are times when you've just had it. I got on a train after being stared at for an hour by a massive crowd in the waiting room, and was in no mood to deal with another crowd on the train. When the umpteenth Chinese came up and started the old English-lesson syndrome I retreated to a book. 'Where do you come from?' he asked. 'Moldavia', I said. 'Where's that?' he asked. 'Russia', I replied. I rather got the idea that Russia wasn't the most favoured nation at the time – the man was up like a rocket and back at the other end of the car, and I was left in peace and quiet for the rest of the trip. The solution to the waiting-room dilemma, by the way, is to find the 1st-class waiting room, which is where the cadres hide from the masses.

One of the reasons the Chinese crowd around and look at you is because westerners have things they don't have, like big eyes, beards, blonde hair, large noses, hairy arms and legs and big breasts. All these have an enduring fascination for the Chinese. The Chinese men can't grow anything resembling a beard until after 40 or 50 years of age. The only 'blondes' in the country are albinos and the occasional light-haired Uygur. Chinese skin is smooth and almost hairless or grows only very fine hair. The women are probably the most flat-chested on earth (difficult to determine under their baggy clothes). So don't be surprised if you begin to feel like a circus freak. Curious people may even rub their fingers up and down your arm or pull at the hairs.

Noise

Chinese is spoken at about 140 decibels and 120 km/hour. It is said to be the only language in the world that can't be whispered – Chinese speakers will tell you this is not true but you may decide it's a distinct possibility. Cheap Chinese hotels can be a dismal experience. The Chinese enjoy conversing with their friends at the other end of the corridor, practising Beijing Opera in the spacious concrete-walled echo chambers, and sitting up late at night amiably shouting at their acquaintances. In the last few years many cheap hotels have been installing television sets in every room. These are turned to full volume so the cacophony is like a battery of jackhammers. There are a couple of ways to avoid all this: pack a good set of earplugs, go to China with the tolerance of a saint, or spend more money and stay at the tourist hotels. A noisy hotel is not what you want after a long, tiring train or bus ride.

Spitting

If you thought the Indians were champion spitters, then go to China! Everyone does it, on the streets, on the floors of train carriages and on buses. Never walk too closely beside a stationary bus full of

passengers, and try not to get caught in the crossfire elsewhere!

Queues

Queues for tickets, particularly at larger railway stations, can be long. Sometimes it may be worth that extra money to have CITS get your tickets. Otherwise, be patient and accept the fact that this is China and there ain't nothing you can do about one billion people. Some large railway stations now have separate booking offices for foreigners; this means you'll always pay tourist price but at least you avoid the queues and have some hope of getting a sleeper on the crowded trains.

MAKING CONTACT

A Chinese travel guide had this to say about encountering foreign guests:

> In trains, boats, planes or tourist areas one frequently comes across foreign guests. Do not follow, encircle and stare at them when you meet. Refrain from pointing at their clothing in front of their faces or making frivolous remarks; do not vie with foreign guests, competing for a seat and do not make requests at will. If foreign guests take the initiative to make contact, be courteous and poised. Do not be flustered into ignoring them by walking off immediately, neither should you be reserved or arrogant. Do your best to answer relying on translation. When chatting with foreign guests be practical and realistic – remember there are differences between foreign and home life. Don't provide random answers if you yourself don't know or understand the subject matter. Refrain from asking foreign guests questions about age, salary, income, clothing costs and similar private matters. Do not do things discreditable to your country. Do not accept gifts at will from foreign guests. When parting you should peel off your gloves and then proffer your hand. If you are parting from a female foreign guest and she does not proffer her hand first, it is also adequate to nod your head as a farewell greeting.

Educating a billion Chinese to be courteous to foreigners is a formidable task. For many years few foreigners set foot in the country, let alone were seen in the flesh by the common people. Tourism was a dirty word and unauthorised contact with a foreigner was tantamount to asking to go to prison. Then came the Cultural Revolution and the xenophobia reached its greatest heights. Even before the communist takeover, foreigners could hardly expect to be viewed in a sympathetic light. Contact with westerners was largely in the form of policemen and soldiers who protected foreign settlements and business interests, established with gunboat diplomacy and the Opium Wars. Add the preceding 600 years of isolationism since the Ming Dynasty, and you start to wonder if it really is safe to walk down a Chinese street at night! Whether or not the Chinese actually like foreigners is open to debate – but they are curious about us and on the whole it is safe to walk the streets at any time.

Making contact with the Chinese can

be frustrating. Inevitably it begins with someone striking up a conversation with you on the street, in your hotel or on a train. Unfortunately many of these conversations have a habit of deteriorating into: 'You speak English very well' – 'Oh no, my English is very poor . . .'

You can hardly expect anyone to start revealing the intimate details of their private life, after all how would you feel if a foreigner in your country started asking you lots of personal questions!

Conversations with Chinese usually begin with 'What country are you from?' followed by 'How long have you been here?' or 'Is this your first time to China?' Then 'What is your name?' and 'Are you married?' 'How old are you?' If you're lucky the person will have advanced beyond the first few phrases that everyone learns in foreign-language classes; but conversations too often deteriorate into English lessons that become more and more tedious the longer you stay in China or the less patient you are. Even worse and far more boring, you end up talking about talking English.

Before long you may find yourself an unwilling teacher overwhelmed by limitless numbers of willing students. It's not uncommon for someone to knock on your room door at 10 pm, shyly ask to come in and practise their English with you, and then front up the following night with a couple of enthusiastic friends in tow. You spend the first six weeks in China trying to make contact with the people and the last six weeks trying to avoid them.

If a Chinese doesn't want to answer one of your questions he or she will suddenly become evasive; he may 'forget' how to speak English, fail to understand the question or how to translate the answer from Chinese to English, or he may tell you that the subject is complex and that he has forgotten the answer.

You should also remember that the Chinese are highly sensitive about political issues. Almost everyone you meet will criticise the Cultural Revolution – but that's official policy nowadays. You simply can't expect the Chinese to express their real views on the present government, though many will. At the same time, don't expect these 'real views' to be negative just because you think they should be. Many Chinese won't broach any political subject at all and may say that they have no interest in politics. Don't expect anyone to be too liberal with their views if they're in earshot of others, especially since a conversation with a foreigner on the street automatically attracts a crowd of onlookers.

The official policy on Chinese talking to foreigners tends to vary. During the Maoist era, it was absolutely forbidden. Presently it's encouraged. Modernisation of the country requires foreign technology, and if a foreign technical journal is going to be of any use you have to be able to read the thing. Fluency in English is a path to a better job, even a chance to travel overseas to work or study, and that helps explain the enthusiasm with which the Chinese are learning the language and seeking help from stray foreigners. Not all of them approach you out of pure curiosity or a desire to make friends. Some will approach you ostensibly to practise English but what they really want is to change your Foreign Exchange Certificates for Renminbi.

Interesting people to talk to are the elderly Chinese who learned English back in the 1920s and 1930s when there were large foreign communities in China. Then there are the middle-aged who were learning English just before the Cultural Revolution but were forced to stop and are only now starting to pick it up again. Next comes the younger generation of Chinese who went to school or university after the Cultural Revolution and have been able to take foreign-language courses. Even the level of proficiency attained by self-taught Chinese through English-language programmes on radio or television is quite remarkable. English is now being taught in high schools, and many young kids have a rudimentary knowledge of the language. Japanese is also popular at high school and university levels and you often come across French, German, Russian and Spanish speakers.

If you want to meet English-speaking Chinese then go to the 'English corners' which have developed in many large Chinese cities. Usually held on a Sunday morning in a convenient park, Chinese who speak or are learning English gather to practise the language. Also seek out the 'English Salons' – evening get-togethers at which the Chinese practise English, listen to lectures or hold debates in English. Don't expect to remain a member of the audience for very long; I went to an English Salon in Hangzhou and found myself giving the evening lecture and then struggling to answer questions about the outside world ranging from Star Wars to insurance policies!

If you make a Chinese friend and want to stay in contact through letters, then it's suggested that before you leave China you buy several stamps sufficient for letters from China to your home country. The first time you write to your Chinese friend enclose the stamps – say that you had them left over when you departed China, and that you're sending them to him because you have no use for them. One of these stamps could be half a day's wage to some Chinese – so for them to write to you really does involve a sacrifice! While you're in China you can arrange meetings by having the Chinese person phone your hotel or post a letter. If you get him to write down his address on several envelopes you can post them to him with messages. In the towns and cities a letter posted before 9 am should reach him that same afternoon. It *is* possible to visit people's homes – many Chinese feel greatly honoured by your visit, though others may feel embarrassed by their humble living conditions.

ITINERARIES

There's a lot of China, but planning a route around it isn't very difficult if you want to stick to the major towns and cities. The only problem is travelling time; on the whole, transport isn't bad, but distances are immense and if you can afford it you might find the odd plane trip well worth the money.

As a rule of thumb you should allow one day in three for 'logistics', which include obtaining information and tickets to or from places – be prepared to spend half a day or more chasing tickets. On long train and bus rides, some of my best moments have been when the Chinese share round cigarettes and peanuts and stoically accept hours of delay with the commiseration that travel is punishing work. Few Chinese would relish the sort of pace some foreign travellers set themselves. It is easy to become run down, so be kind to your nervous system and try to set aside a couple of days each month to do nothing but rest – have a total break. Avoid a surfeit of big cities.

Many provinces in China used to allow foreigners access to only a handful of cities, but have recently thrown open fascinating rural areas containing such diversity that they are worth considering in their own right for a trip of at least a month. Some provinces fall into natural pairs, such as Yunnan and Sichuan, Gansu and Xinjiang, Tibet and Qinghai. You have much more freedom now to choose your own itineraries, such as following the Yellow River, concentrating on border regions or minority areas, visiting Buddhist mountains or following the Silk Road. China is now linked with Pakistan and Nepal by the Karakoram and Friendship Highways respectively. Both routes are open to foreigners so it is possible to perform a massive loop through China using these highways as entry or exit points. In fact, this represents an Asian Overland Route Revival. Include the Trans-Siberian Railway on your routing and you could find yourself in endless orbit!

There is a fairly definite 'tourist route'

in China. Many people take the overnight ferry from Hong Kong to Canton, then the boat up the Pearl and Xi (West) rivers to Wuzhou. They bus to Yangshuo or Guilin, and from Guilin take the train to Kunming, Chengdu and Xian. From Xian they head west along the railway line to Turpan and Ürümqi, or north to Beijing via Datong. From Beijing many people go straight to Shanghai and take the boat to Hong Kong.

That's the basic route – a clockwise course starting and ending in Hong Kong. There are many popular variations and detours. One is to head from Chengdu by train to Chongqing and take the ferry down the Yangtse River; some go all the way to Wuhan but many get off at Yichang and take the train to Luoyang. From Luoyang they either take the train to Ürümqi or to Beijing.

Another popular route is to fly from Chengdu to Lhasa; or to take trains from Xian to Golmud, via Lanzhou and Xining, and then bus from Golmud to Lhasa. Others head from Beijing to Shanghai, stopping off along the way at interesting towns like Qufu (the birthplace of Confucius) and Qingdao.

Some places have become very popular, and others have lost out as people find they're not all they're cut out to be. The main tourist cities are Beijing, Shanghai, Canton, Guilin, Hangzhou, Suzhou, Kunming, Xian and Lhasa. Most people flit through Canton without giving it the time it deserves. Guilin has been replaced by the superior scenery of Yangshuo. In the north-west, Ürümqi and particularly Turpan and Kashgar remain the favourites of many travellers. Kunming and other popular destinations in the south-west, such as Dali, always get rave reviews. Datong and Luoyang with their Buddhist caves attract much attention. The towns of the south-east coast like Xiamen and Quanzhou deserve to become more popular. Unusual places like Qingdao and spectacular mountains like Huang Shan attract a steady stream of visitors.

One important thing to remember about planning a trip through China is timing. The weather ranges from furiously hot to bitterly cold – see the Climate section for details.

And a Warning

Many people go to China expecting a profound cultural experience. This has led to a lot of disappointment. While major attractions like the Forbidden City and the Dunhuang Buddhist caves still stand intact, many of China's other ancient monuments were ransacked or razed to the ground during the Cultural Revolution.

In the early 1970s, with the new turn in China's foreign policy towards rapprochement with the west, the Chinese government began a superficial revival of their ancient culture to present a more acceptable 'human face' towards the outside world. A very few of the ransacked temples and monasteries were restored as showpieces. Exhibitions were set up to display 'archaeological objects found during the Cultural Revolution' in some attempt to cover up the vandalism of that period. These early exhibits were open only to foreigners and Overseas Chinese, as were some antique and art-reproduction shops. A few hundred copies of Chinese classics were reprinted, but these were mainly for export.

While the Chinese government is still trying to eradicate 'feudal' ideas, it's generally accepted that wanton vandalism is no way to go about it. In the past few years there's been a determined effort to restore the sites destroyed during the Cultural Revolution, but many of the temples remain derelict or are used as schools, libraries, restaurants, offices, museums, parks, factories or warehouses. The amount of damage done both by deliberate vandalism on the part of the Red Guards and by years of neglect is evident. Some of the restored temples are attracting worshippers, but many are just mummified remains. Often restoration work has been poorly done and the buildings are shadows of their former selves.

China does have some marvellous cultural attractions, like the Beijing Opera, the acrobats of Beijing and Shanghai, travelling family circuses, magic shows and buskers. But culture in China is very much like exotic food – don't expect to find it on every street corner. The Cultural Revolution almost put an end to the old culture and the country is only now starting to recover.

'Recovery' often takes on bizarre forms, particularly where the Chinese experiment with western ideas or where Chinese ideas are tailored to suit the tastes of western tourists. Some two dozen Shakespearean plays have been adapted and performed in the style of Beijing Opera. Since many of Shakespeare's plays are set in royal courts during feudal times, they may be quite easy for Chinese to relate to since many of them lived through such times. Modern western plays, such as *Death of a Salesman* and *Equus*, have also been staged by Chinese actors. Chinese dance companies stage western-style classical and jazz ballet, and a school of Chinese surrealist art is influenced by western styles.

Real culture shock strikes when east meets west over the music score. Disco music is big with the hip young urban Chinese, and there are dance halls in all the major cities to cater for the craze – sometimes with taped music, often with live bands featuring batteries of horns and heavy-metal violins. Attempts to tailor Chinese classical music, song and dance to western tastes have resulted in a Frankenstein's monster of Broadway-style spectacular and Epic Theatre film score. There are even orchestras organised on western lines which substitute Chinese for western instruments. Exactly where all this is leading no one knows.

THEFT & OTHER CRIMES

There is crime in China, as anywhere else in the world, but it's unlikely to affect you if you take simple precautions. It's safer to travel through China than through other countries, and you're less likely to have stuff stolen. A level of prudence regarding both the safety of yourself and your property is worth maintaining, but the paranoia that may be justified in other countries is unnecessary in China.

Stories of exemplary honesty include the Beijing shop assistant who inadvertently shortchanged a foreign tourist and finally managed to track him down in Lhasa through an advertisement she inserted in *China Daily*. A foreign businessman on an extended tour round China decided to discard a pair of trousers in his hotel room before catching a taxi to the airport. Just as his flight was called, a breathless room-attendant came racing into the airport carrying the trousers. A second attempt to jettison the trousers in another hotel met with the same defeat.

The most common type of theft facing travellers is pickpocketing. Chinese are well aware of this, and places such as Xian, Beijing, Harbin, Lanzhou and Ürümqi are reportedly notorious for pickpocket schools whose 'graduates' ply specific bus routes or crowded places usually during peak hours. My own pocket was picked in a tightly-packed bus in Xining by a dinky lady who was part of a trio. Razoring of bags and pockets is also prevalent on buses in Chengdu and Xian. Since buses in China are usually so packed that passengers are virtually jammed into each other's pockets, there's plenty of scope for theft. If you want to avoid opening wallets or bags on the bus, keep a few coins or small notes ready in an accessible pocket before launching yourself onto the bus.

One traveller in Beijing had the whole kaboodle (passport, money, documents) ripped off him in a crowded bus – he was asking for it, wearing his money-belt on the outside! He lost US$2000 and it took two weeks to get the rest back. Another traveller had two attempts made on his pockets on one bus – the first by a child, judging from the size of the hand intercepted, and the second by a 'friendly drunk'. I was almost pickpocketed on a Shanghai bus on my first trip to China in 1981 – I reached down and found a hand in my pocket, ripped the hand out and flung it away. There's no way you'll get your message across to the other passengers on the bus, though.

Apart from buses, favorite venues for petty theft include bus stations, train stations and public toilets. Quite a few foreigners have laid aside their valuables, squatted down to business, and then straightened up again to discover that nifty fingers had scarpered with the lot!

Hotels are usually safe places to leave your stuff; each floor has an attendant watching who goes in and out of the hotel. If anything is missing from your room then they're going to be obvious suspects since they've got keys to the rooms. Don't expect them to watch over your room like a hawk – they don't. Dormitories could be a problem and there have been a few reports of thefts by staff. Some hotels have large storage rooms where you check your bags in; some insist that you do. In other hotels you may have to leave your stuff in the dormitory. This is sometimes locked so that all and sundry don't go wandering in and out. Unfortunately, your fellow travellers can be a problem – there are a few around who make the money go further by helping themselves to other people's. Don't leave your valuables (passport, travellers' cheques, money, health certificates, air tickets) lying around in dormitories.

One couple in Xian had the entire works stolen overnight from their locked hotel room – apparently the thief came through the window and ran off with two cameras, a wad of lenses, cheques, watches and luggage. Perhaps this was the work of Duan Xiaohua, a Japanese-speaking tour guide from Xian who was arrested in 1985 after five years of 'private enterprise'. Masquerading as a well-dressed Japanese tourist with a fluent Tokyo accent, he succeeded each time in persuading hotel personnel to hand over the keys to guests' rooms. While family members helped cache the stolen goods, Duan cleaned out flash hotels in Beijing and Xian and amassed a fortune.

Deterrents

A money-belt is the safest way to carry valuables, particularly when travelling on buses and trains. Against its possible loss, you could leave a small stash of money (say US$50) in your hotel room, with a record of the travellers' cheque serial numbers and your passport number. Other things of little or no apparent value to the thief – like film – should be safeguarded, since to lose them would be a real heartbreak to you. Make a copy of your address book before you leave home. And note down ticket numbers – a Swedish couple whose train tickets were stolen in Chengdu were told by the railway booking office that they would have received a refund had they done so.

Small padlocks are useful for back-packs and some dodgy hotel rooms. Bicycle chain locks come in handy not only for rented bikes but for attaching backpacks to railings or luggage racks. The trendy waist-pouches often used by

Hong Kong visitors are definitely *not* advisable for valuables. Street tailors are skilled at sewing inside pockets to trousers, jackets and shirts usually for a few mao. Small padlocks are useful on camera bags. Don't rely on swivel clips to attach a camera to your waist; I saw a German traveller lose a very expensive camera this way while getting onto a crowded bus in Lhasa.

The Chinese don't trust each other and there's no reason you should trust them. They run around with rings full of keys as if they were gaol keepers, everything is scrupulously locked, the walls of buildings have jagged glass concreted to the top and iron bars are fitted on 1st-floor windows. Announcements on trains (in Chinese) advise passengers neither to entrust baggage to the care of strangers nor to leave valuables unattended during stops or when going to the dining-car. You'll often see the Chinese secure their bags to the luggage racks with bicycle chains, and you can do the same. If you wander away from your bag in a crowded railway station don't expect it to be there when you come back.

Loss Reports & Other Hassles

If something of yours is stolen, you should report it immediately to the nearest Foreign Affairs Branch of the PSB. They will ask you to fill in a loss report before investigating the case and sometimes even recovering the stolen goods. In Dali I met a New Zealander who had lost all his camera gear at the bus station in Kunming. He had boarded the bus, left his camera bag on his seat and then hopped out to load his backpack into the side of the bus. When he reached his seat again a minute later, the camera bag was gone. After raising the alert, he was amazed to see squads of PSB officers surrounding the bus station and swarming onto the bus. The bus and all the passengers were given police escort to the PSB office where everyone and everything was searched. Nothing was found and the New Zealander was told to report back for further news on his return from Dali. When he did return, the PSB casually informed him that they had found camera equipment and asked him to check if it was his – it was! Judging by the lurid wall-posters outside the PSB, this New Zealander had found himself in the middle of a massive anti-crime campaign in Kunming, and the thieves turned out to be a professional gang from Canton.

There are at least two other good reasons for obtaining a loss report. When you enter China you declare on a form all your foreign currency and valuables such as watches, cameras and calculators. When you leave China you are expected to hand in your declaration and show your valuables again – as proof that they haven't been sold. The procedure is seldom strict but there'll be complications if you can't produce the items. If you lose any of the items listed on your declaration form through theft or negligence, obtaining a loss report can save possible exit hassles at the border.

If you have travel insurance (highly recommended), it is essential to obtain a loss report so you can claim compensation. Normally this is no problem for valuables (cameras, watches, calculators) and travellers' cheques, but some PSB offices in major cities absolutely refuse to provide a loss report for cash. One Chinese-speaking Austrian told an interesting tale about a visit to Chengdu PSB:

> I was told that this (no loss report for loss of cash) is a regulation and when I asked to see the regulation, was informed it was forbidden by regulation to show regulations – only oral transmission was allowed. When I requested this fact to be put into writing for my insurance company, back came the reply that this too was forbidden by regulation. There then followed a comment that they could not know whether I was telling the truth because no policemen had witnessed the theft. Stalemate was reached when I seriously doubted that theft would have taken place if the police had been there to watch and I apologised for not being able to

send prior invites for the occasion. When asked for their names so the insurance company could contact them, the PSB staff, including the office head, all refused. 'Regulation?' I asked. 'No, our personal rights!' they replied.

I've heard of western women being harassed by Chinese men in Beijing's parks or while cycling alone at night, but major crimes against foreigners are very rare and the perpetrators receive the severest punishment. In March 1986, two businessmen from Britain and Hong Kong were robbed at knife-point in Canton by a criminal trio from north-east China. All three were later sentenced to death and their appeal was rejected. The sentence for one member under 18 was suspended for two years.

Kill the Rooster to Frighten the Monkey

It's hard to say how China's crime rate compares with those in other countries, though it has its share of rapists and murderers. 'White collar' crime is also a big problem and the Chinese newspapers regularly report arrests and even the occasional execution of frauds and embezzlers.

The crackdown on corruption has been given extensive coverage in the official press. In 1986, the sons of three senior cadres were executed in Shanghai for attacks on women. Another Shanghai Party official was jailed for life for accepting over Y30,000 in bribes. Although such sentences were intended to show that all are equal before the law, the centuries-old practice of privilege for high officials and their relatives is unlikely to receive more than a dent.

A disciplinary inspection begun in 1986 within the Party has resulted in numerous warnings, dismissals and even imprisonment of Party members. The cases of accused Party members are not immediately handled by state law. The relevant Party organ must first determine the guilt of the accused before handing him or her over for conviction under state law. It's not hard to see the vested interests that could be involved when Party colleagues investigate one of their own members. The minister and vice minister of astronautics recently embezzled US$46 million in foreign exchange and were rebuked with 'serious disciplinary warnings within the Party'.

Intensive investigation of illegal detention has revealed some extraordinary stories about cadres or policemen with a 'special privilege' mentality who abused their power and violated legal procedures. In 1984, a village party secretary in Shaanxi Province put 72 villagers into custody under suspicion of stealing part of his bicycle bell. He then ordered torture for 17 of the villagers and forced 28 more to pay fines to cover the cost of the guards' wages during imprisonment, which in some cases lasted as long as eight days. In Baoshan, Yunnan Province, a group of policemen detained 201 people in 1986 for 'law-study class' which lasted as long as 80 days. Many of the detainees were forced to do manual labour, fined or tortured to confess to crimes they hadn't committed or to petty offences. As a result, two people committed suicide, one person died and many were wounded.

Juvenile crime is a growing problem in China's cities. The types of crime committed include murder, rape and theft of large sums of money. Criminal groups of youngsters are common and the official view is that they are influenced by images of foreign criminal cliques portrayed in mass media and by the persistent feudal idea of 'secret societies'. Contributory factors could also be unemployment and disillusionment.

Justice in China seems to be dispensed entirely by the police, who also decide the penalty. The ultimate penalty is execution, which serves the purpose of 'killing the rooster to frighten the monkey' or, to phrase this in official terms, 'It is good to have some people executed so as to educate others'. The standard manner of execution is a gunshot in the back of the head, often at a mass gathering in some sports stadium. This punishment is usually reserved for rapists and murderers. Afterwards a mugshot and maybe even a photo of the extinguished body gets plugged up on a public noticeboard. Criminals being paraded on the backs of trucks through the streets of Chinese towns are still a common sight.

A couple of years ago a tour group arriving in Xian were 'lucky' enough to witness one such event as they stepped out of the railway station. A protracted and embarrassed silence ensued. A public execution had just taken place and the dead bodies, with bullet holes in the backs of their necks, were lying on the pavement outside the station, surrounded by a large crowd. The police quickly dragged the corpses out of sight. China's last big purge of criminals started in 1983 with the rounding up of 100,000 suspects; estimates for the number of executions since then vary between 10,000 and 20,000. This campaign continues in tandem with a newer one to promote knowledge of the legal code amongst the masses.

PLACES TO STAY

One of the reasons tourism has suddenly expanded in China is that the Chinese need the foreign exchange. Hotel prices are steadily rising towards what you'd pay for a similar standard of accommodation in the west; there aren't too many bargains around, but at present the room prices in many of the middle-range hotels still compare very favourably.

On the whole the hotel situation is much better than it was a few years ago. Hotel staff are friendlier and more used to dealing with foreigners. Though room prices have gone up it's far easier now to get cheap dormitory accommodation without the interminable arguments that once characterised solo travel in China. The construction boom in top-class hotels means that high-budget travellers and tour groups will be much better catered for than they were just a few years ago.

外国人临时住宿登记表
REGISTRATION FORM OF TEMPORARY RESIDENCE FOR FOREIGNER

姓名 Name in full
中文 In Chinese
原文 In original language
性别 Sex
生年 Date of birth
来华身份或职业 Identity or occupation
国籍 Nationality
签证或旅行证号码及期限 Visa or travel document number and date of validity
抵达日期 Date of arrival
拟住日期 Duration of stay
停留事由 Object of stay
何处来何处去 Where from and to
房号或住址 Room number or address
旅馆或户主签章 Stamp of the hotel or signature of the householder
日期 Date

Hotels

The hotels are tourist attractions in themselves. The enormous, rambling structures in the major cities are like mini-states with post offices, banks, restaurants, arts & crafts shops, beauty parlours, taxi services, travel agents and staff trained not to bite tourists. The White Swan Hotel in Canton is so big it has its own waterfall in the lobby. The Jingling Hotel in Nanjing is a spectacular, gleaming white tower of 36 storeys capped with a revolving restaurant and a helipad! These hotels are the exception in China. You find them in the tourist centres like Xian, Shenzhen, Beijing and Shanghai, with each new building outdoing its predecessor in extravagance. Room prices in these extravaganzas start at about the 5th floor and skyrocket up the elevator shaft.

One down the ladder are the gigantic Soviet-built mammoths, constructed to house the Russian technicians and experts who came to China in the 1950s. Then there are the older European and British-built hotels – mainly in the coastal cities and a few of the inland river cities which were once foreign concessions – often with a faded touch of the colonial era about them. These usually provide simple but comfortable rooms of sufficient standard to accommodate foreign tour groups. Two favourites of mine are the Banna Hotel in Jinghong, Xishuangbanna and the Luhuitou Hotel in Sanya, Hainan Island – a last, drowsy taste of the exotic and colonial in China.

As you go down the scale the quality of the accommodation steadily decreases. An ordinary Chinese hotel is essentially a large concrete box, usually several floors high, and divided into numerous rooms of varying sizes. Each room might accommodate anything from four to a dozen or more people; single and double rooms are rare. Often there are only communal showers and toilets with partitions but no doors. The trend in China over the last few years has been to equip even these cheap hotels with a television in every room – which, reverberating through the vast concrete corridors, can produce the most incredible noise. Standards of repair and cleanliness vary greatly, but are usually OK.

The Chinese method of designating floors is the same as used in the USA, but different from, say, Australia's. What would be the 'ground floor' in Australia is the '1st floor' in China, the 1st is the 2nd, and so on.

Who Stays Where

Hotels in China fall into three main categories. In the first category are the expensive tourist hotels where high-budget westerners plus Hong Kong, Macau and Overseas Chinese (people of Chinese descent resident in foreign countries) are placed. In the next category are somewhat less expensive mid-range hotels which primarily cater for Hong Kong, Macau and Overseas Chinese. The third category includes the innumerable hotels and guest houses which cater solely to citizens of the People's Republic.

Segregation is not strictly applied, and depends on where you are. In small towns there may only be one or two decent hotels so westerners, Hong Kongers and high-ranking Chinese all get thrown into the same bag. In places which are primarily Hong Kong or Overseas Chinese destinations, stray westerners are housed in the local Overseas Chinese Hotel. If you're out in the sticks where tour groups never go, you stay at ordinary Chinese hotels because there's nothing else available.

If you front up at a Chinese-only hotel it's really a matter of luck if you get a room or a bed. Usually they're not supposed to take you and may be worried about breaking the rules which, incidentally, are under the supervision of the PSB. If you are really stuck for a place to stay, it sometimes helps to phone or visit the local PSB and explain your problem. Some towns seem to apply these rules more strictly than others. In Tianjin, for example, it's almost impossible to get a room or even a dormitory bed in a Chinese hotel even though the tourist hotels are nearly always full. There are no hard-and-fast rules; it just depends on where you are and who you're dealing with.

Prices

The cost of hotel rooms depends on what you are. People's Republic Chinese stay in the cheapest hotels; those who stay in the top hotels can do so because their rank entitles them to that privilege. The 'masses' are not permitted to tread the grounds of these hotels, let alone stay there.

If you have a white face and a big nose then you pay the most. The Chinese will often try to plug you into the most expensive hotels and rooms. They do this for two reasons: they want the money, and they think you're spectacularly wealthy and that you'll want to do things in spectacular style. Fortunately for the low-budget traveller this is not as big a problem as it was in the first few years of China travel. In most Chinese cities or tourist spots open to foreigners there is usually at least one hotel which will readily give you a cheap dormitory bed.

Accommodation charges also vary depending on where you are. Generally you can get a dormitory bed for around Y8 to Y10 even in a large city, sometimes for as little as Y3 in very small towns. Usually dormitories have lots of space, sheets, blankets, often mosquito nets and sometimes even air-conditioning; not your usual batch of bunk-beds and everyone falling over each other. Some dorms are segregated by sex, but mixed dorms (foreigners only) are becoming increasingly common. Many have an attached bathroom; if not, there'll be a shower-room down the hallway often with communal showers only.

If there are no dormitories in the hotel there will often be three-bed rooms and you may be able to pay for just one bed; anyone else who comes along will get thrown in with you. In less touristed areas, spartan hostels often charge just a couple of yuan for a bed in a four-bed room. The staff may ask if you want to 'occupy the whole room' (*bao fang*), which means you pay for the other beds. This can make a pleasant change after a long bus trip or if you want a little more privacy.

Smaller rooms are a problem. A bare concrete box with a hard bed in a Chinese hotel in Guilin can be had for around Y10. Cheapest double rooms in Beijing start from about Y32, and in Tianjin from about Y65. From there on the room charges go through the roof; rooms for hundreds of yuan per night are possible.

Getting Cheaper Prices Unless you're content to stay in Y10-per-night dormitories, it's almost impossible to say what you'll pay for hotel rooms because there is so much price variation and because so much relies on the hotel staff's willingness to give you cheap accommodation. Most Chinese hotels don't have single rooms, and if you're travelling on your own you usually have to pay the price of the double room. Sometimes they'll give you a reduction but usually not (this custom is not unique to China).

There are a few places where getting a dorm bed still involves a battle. In such a case you'll be told that there is no dormitory, or that the dormitory is full. If you keep your receipts for cheap rooms and dormitories you can show these – the fact that other hotels have given you cheap accommodation can weigh in your favour. Always ask for all the room prices if the first quote is too high for you. You'll often find that some of the staff don't know all the prices. Bargain!

A bit of vocabulary also helps in the search for cheaper accommodation; a *fandian* (hotel) is likely to have cheap rooms, but a *binguan* (guest house) generally won't. Watch for privately run hotels. There's been a boom in these in the last few years and you'll see Chinese standing outside railway stations trying to rake in customers off the trains. Some Chinese-speaking westerners have managed to find their way into these places, though for the moment it doesn't seem to be the done thing. By the time you get to China, who knows? There could be 20 flop-houses for foreigners on every main street in Beijing!

In 1986, hotels in most of the cities I visited in the north-east of China still hadn't got the message that foreigners aren't all millionaires travelling on expense accounts. During the peak summer season it helps to arrive early in the morning. It's important to point out that you are travelling at your own expense (*zi fei*) and do not require prices to be doubled for the sake of inflated receipts. Since most of the hotel receptionists assume foreigners require top-quality rooms, you will often be told that only the most expensive room is available and that the other rooms have 'inadequate conditions' (*tiaojian bu xing*). Try explaining that 'any condition will do' (*shenmo tiaojian dou keyi*). The existence of dormitories *(su she)* is often denied since they may not be designated as such in the hotel. But you can also ask for a 'multi-person room' (*duo ren fangjian*) and progress to an ordinary room (*putong fangjian*) or there might be an 'old building' (*jiu lou*).

Apart from paper credentials and previous hotel receipts, it helps to take along photocopies of old Lonely Planet newsletters or previous editions of guidebooks so you can point to the relevant prices or room categories. Sometimes you may pick the wrong time or person and it can help to come back later or try someone else. If there is zilch response or headway, you should ask them to phone a hotel with cheaper rooms. Since the staff often spot this as a great opportunity to be rid of you, they may well do this. Be appreciative and politely ask the person phoning to ascertain room price, name of hotel and exact address. Make careful note of these details before trudging off again. The final resort is a call to the PSB or preparations for a 'relaxing' night in the hotel lobby.

Student Discount If you're a foreign student in the People's Republic or in Taiwan (the PRC considers Taiwan to be part of China) then you can get a discount on room prices. Students usually have to show their student card, which is bound in bright red plastic. As for other travellers, the receptionist will sometimes accept your word that you're a student and will give you a discount. Other people have used forged made-in-Hong Kong student cards. Surprisingly enough a lot of these lies and tricks still work!

Room Service

Not good, but gradually getting better. Of course, you can't expect much in the cheap Chinese hotels, but in the tourist hotels the prices warrant some attention. The larger, foreign-built and sometimes foreign-managed hotels train their staff to handle the idiosyncrasies of foreign guests and usually provide service indistinguishable from that in a similar hotel in Hong Kong or the west. Sometimes it's rather rough around the edges but improvements made in the last few years are quite extraordinary. Lower down the price ladder, though, you can't really expect much.

In the cheaper Chinese hotels you'll just have to *tell* the attendants that you want the bedsheets and bath towels changed, the water mopped off the bathroom floor, the bathtub cleaned and the tea-cups washed. A lot of people don't complain because they're afraid of offending the Chinese, but unless you do, the Chinese won't learn how to treat western visitors.

Each floor of just about every hotel in China has a service desk, usually near the elevators. The attendant's job is to clean the rooms, make the beds, and collect and deliver laundry. Almost all tourist hotels have a laundry service, and if you hand in clothes one day you should get them back a day or two later.

The attendant also keeps an eye on the

hotel guests. This is partly to prevent theft and partly to stop you from bringing locals back for the night (I'm not joking!). Some hotels will turn away a local Chinese at the gate; others require that the Chinese person register name, address, work unit and purpose of visit at the reception desk. Since many Chinese are reluctant to draw attention to themselves like this, they may be reluctant to visit you at the hotel.

Something else to be prepared for is lack of privacy. Some visitors to China adamantly maintain that the Chinese lack the concept of privacy; others say that privacy is one of their highest values. Anyway, what happens is that you're sitting starkers in your hotel room, the key suddenly turns in the door and the roomperson casually wanders in . . . . This is becoming less of a problem as the Chinese gradually learn how to handle foreign visitors, but it's still a frequent occurrence. Don't expect anyone to knock before entering. You could try teaching them if you like, but you have to remember that in China people live in crowded rooms; the custom of knocking before entering is unnecessary and therefore hasn't developed. One suggestion is to tape a sign over the keyhole – it doesn't matter if it's in English because they get the idea.

It was pointed out to me that privacy is another privilege of rank; the high-ranking cadres live in large houses surrounded by high walls and are driven around in cars with drawn curtains. They stay in hotel rooms (not dormitories), and if they're sufficiently high in the ranks then they stay in government guest houses far from the milling proletariat.

FOOD

Many people who go to China expect a marvellous banquet to be available on every street corner. There is indeed some excellent food and some fascinating culinary exotica – but it's in limited supply, restricted to places like Canton, Shanghai, Beijing and Guilin.

Be warned that what's been dreamt up by Chinese chefs is not what's readily available for you to eat. Most of the time you're going to find yourself living on rice (steamed or fried), a few varieties of fried meat and vegetables, dumplings, bean curd, noodles and soup. Food in the south is generally better than in the north, and during the winter northern Chinese food can be perfectly dreadful.

On the whole though, you'll eat far better now in China than you would have a few years ago. Restaurants have proliferated in the last few years under the free enterprise system, and since they have to compete in order to survive, prices are low and the quality of the food has taken a turn for the better.

Traditional Fare

Chinese cooking is famine cooking. The Chinese will eat anything and everything that moves, and no part of an animal or plant is wasted. What we now regard as Chinese culinary exotica is really an effort to make the most of everything available; they salvage the least appetising ingredients which wealthy nations reject as waste, and make them into appetising food. This has led to some interesting dishes: fish heads, ducks' feet, dog and cat meat, bird saliva, fish lips and eyeballs, to name a few.

Even the cooking method reflects the

shortage of fuel; cutting the food into small pieces and stir-frying it in a wok is more fuel-efficient than baking or spit-roasting. Pigs and chickens have always been a feature of the cuisine because they have unchoosy eating habits and can be raised on very small areas of land.

Traditional Chinese food can be divided into four major categories: Beijing (sometimes called Mandarin) and Shandong; Cantonese; Shanghainese and Jiangzhenese; and Sichuan.

Beijing & Shandong Beijing and Shandong cuisine comes from one of the coldest parts of China and uses heaps of spices and chilli to warm the body up. Bread and noodles are often eaten instead of rice.

The chief speciality is Beijing duck, eaten with pancakes and plum sauce. Another speciality is beggar's chicken, supposedly created by a beggar who stole the emperor's chicken and had to bury it in the ground to cook it – the dish is wrapped in lotus leaves and baked all day in hot ashes.

Some good Beijing dishes: chicken or pork with soya-bean sauce; bean curd with pepper sauce; fried shredded beef with chilli sauce; stewed mixed vegetables; barbecued chicken; fried shrimp eggs and pork pancakes. Another speciality is Mongolian barbecue – assorted barbecued meats and vegetables cooked in a hotpot. Bird's nest soup is a speciality of Shandong cooking, as is sweet-and-sour Yellow River carp. The latter is served singed on the outside but tender inside.

Shanghainese & Jiangzhenese This cuisine is noted for its use of seafoods. It's heavier and oilier than either Beijing or Cantonese food, and uses lots of chilli and spices. Eels are popular, as is 'drunken chicken' cooked in *shaoshing*, a potent Chinese wine a bit like warm sherry. Other things to try are Tientsin cabbage, some of the cold meat-and-sauce dishes, ham-and-melon soup, bean curd and brown sauce, braised meat balls, deep-fried chicken, and pork ribs with salt and pepper.

Jiangzhe cooking specialises in poultry and seafood, and the dishes are cooked in their own juices to preserve their original flavour.

Sichuan This is the hottest of the four categories, and is characterised by heavy use of spices and peppers. Specialities include frogs' legs and smoked duck; the duck is cooked in peppercorns, marinated in wine for 24 hours, covered in tea leaves and cooked again over a charcoal fire. Other dishes to try are shrimps with salt and garlic; dried chilli beef; vegetables and bean curd; bear paws braised in brown sauce; fish in spicy bean sauce and aubergines in garlic.

Cantonese This is southern Chinese cooking – lots of steaming, boiling and stir-frying. It's the best of the bunch if you're worried about cholesterol and coronaries, as it uses the least amount of oil. It's lightly cooked and not as highly spiced as the other three. Lots of seafood, vegetables, roast pork, chicken, steamed fish and fried rice. Specialities are abalone, 1000-year-old-eggs (which are actually only a few months old), shark's fin soup, roast pig and a snake dish known as 'dragon's duel tiger', which combines wild cat and snake meat.

Culinary Exotica

Anteaters, pangolins (a sort of Chinese armadillo), cats, owls, monkeys and snakes are some of the more exotic creatures on the menu. Guilin and Canton are good places to find them; there's an old saying that if it's got four legs and isn't a table then the Cantonese will eat it. Even something without legs, like a snake, is regarded as a delicacy by the southerners.

Headless skinned and roasted dogs are a common sight in many of China's markets. Turtles, tortoises, toads and frogs can be found in abundance. If you like seafood then the coastal towns of Shantou, Xiamen and Quanzhou will stuff you full of prawns, squid, shellfish, octopus and other sea creatures.

One of the stranger Chinese delicacies is pig face. The meat is removed from the head and hot tar is poured over the pig's face. The dried tar is peeled off, removing the hair and leaving the skin intact, which is then used as an ingredient in soup.

Live rat embryos are supposedly a delicacy from Guizhou Province. The dish is nicknamed the 'three squeals' since the embryo squeals when you pick it up with your chopsticks, once again when you dip it in soya sauce, and finally when you put it in your mouth . . . or so the story goes.

Western Food

Western food is available in top-end hotels catering to large numbers of western visitors – anything from a croissant to a slab of cow can be found somewhere in this country. Western breakfasts are common, though they're usually only eggs with toast and jam, and the toast is sometimes more like chipboard than cooked bread!

In some places there's been a recent proliferation of restaurants catering to the idiosyncratic tastes of their backpacking clientele. Muesli and banana pancakes have found their way to China and restaurants have adopted western names like those along the travellers' trails of South-East Asia.

Vegetarianism

Difficult to cater for, though possible. Get someone to write a note in Chinese saying that you're a Buddhist/vegetarian and that you don't eat any meat, and hope that it finds its way to the responsible person in the kitchen. Sometimes this works, sometimes it doesn't. Many Chinese cooks will say that a dish without meat is not a proper dish. Most dishes in the dining-cars of the trains contain meat. Beijing has two good vegetarian restaurants; see that section for details.

Drinks

Tea is probably the most commonly served brew in the PRC; it didn't originate in China but in South-East Asia. Indian tea is not generally available but the Friendship Stores in Beijing and Shanghai should have it. Coffee is fairly common in the large cities. Cafés – remarkably similar in both style and atmosphere to western cafés – can be found in the larger cities and are popular with young Chinese.

Beer is probably the next most popular drink, and by any standards the top brands are great stuff. The best-known is Tsingtao, made with a mineral water which gives it its sparkling quality. It's really a German beer since the town of Qingdao (Tsingtao) where it's made was once a German concession and the Chinese inherited the brewery. Local brews are found in all the major cities of China and can prove insipid. Western liquor is sold in Friendship Stores and top-end hotels, but for a real taste of China try some of the innumerable local wines and spirits – the sort of stuff they run tanks on.

Many so-called Chinese wines are actually spirits, though China has probably cultivated vines and produced wine for over 4000 years. Chinese wine-producing techniques differ from those of westerners. Quality-conscious wine producers in western countries work on the idea that the lower the yield the higher the quality of the wine produced. But Chinese workers cultivate every possible square

centimetre of earth; they encourage their vines to yield heavily and also plant peanuts between the rows of vines as a cover crop for half the year. The peanuts sap much of the nutrient from the soil, and in cooler years the large grape crop fails to ripen sufficiently to produce a wine comparable to western ones.

There are also basic misunderstandings between the Chinese and the western growers brought in to advise on wine production. For example, an acre in Chinese terms is actually only one-fifth of what Europeans regard as an acre. Western producers try to prevent oxidation in the wines, but oxidation produces a flavour which the Chinese find desirable and go to great ends to achieve. The Chinese are also keen on wines with different herbs and other materials soaked in them, which they drink for their health and for restorative or even aphrodisiac qualities.

Dynasty white wine is produced near Tianjin in conjunction with the French company Remy Martin, but it's essentially an export wine – not designed for the local market. Tsingtao Chardonnay is another export brand produced in Shandong Province. Hejie Jiu, 'lizard wine', is produced in the southern province of Guangxi; each bottle contains one dead lizard suspended perpendicularly in the clear liquid.

Coca Cola, first introduced into China by American soldiers in 1927, is now produced in Beijing. Chinese attempts at making similar brews include TianFu Cola, which has a recipe based on the root of herbaceous peony. Fanta and Sprite are widely available. Foul Chinese soft drinks are cheap and sold everywhere. Many are manufactured in backyards by mixing artificial colour and flavour with sugar and bicarbonate of soda. Milk is rare but you can buy it in the Beijing Friendship Store. Bottles of sweet yoghurt are commonly sold in the larger cities. Avoid drinking too much soft drink or yoghurt drink because you'll get terrible sugar highs and will feel nauseous.

Tibetans have an interesting brew called *qingke*, a beer or spirit made from barley. Mongolians serve sour-tasting *koumiss*, made of fermented mare's milk. *Mao tai* is a favourite of the Chinese. It's a spirit made from sorghum (a type of millet) and is used for toasts at banquets –it tastes rather like methylated spirits and you can get drunk very quickly on the stuff.

With the exception of some of the older people, Chinese women don't drink or smoke but this behaviour is considered permissible for western women. As a rule Chinese men are not great drinkers; toasts are obligatory at banquets but drunkenness is frowned upon (refer to the section on Banquets).

Fruit

Canned and bottled fruit is readily available everywhere, in department and food stores as well as in dining cars on trains. Good quality fresh fruit, including oranges, mandarins and bananas, is commonly sold in the street markets, though you'll find that the supply and quality drop off severely in winter. Watermelons are common in the north; pineapples and lychees are common along the south-east coast. The lychee is an evergreen tree grown mainly in Guangdong, Fujian and Guangxi. The lychee nut has a reddish skin enclosing a jelly-like pulp with sweet, milky juice. It's in season around April to August.

Ration Coupons

The Chinese have to pay for rice and food grains with ration coupons, which are not issued to foreigners. Sometimes you get asked for them, but if you don't have any it usually doesn't matter. You may be charged a bit extra instead.

Chopsticks

An ancient Chinese text, *The Book of Wei*, contains this riddle: 'They go to bed together and get up at the same time. Wolfing down the food, they never get any 'booty' into their own stomach'. The answer is a pair of chopsticks. For over 3000 years the Chinese have been using chopsticks and are unlikely to change the habit despite encouragement to use knives and forks from reformers in the Party. Although most meals in China seem like a chopstick battlefield, there is, according to *China Daily*, such a thing as chopstick etiquette in which it is bad form to insert them vertically into one's rice bowl, stir the food with them to choose a tasty morsel, pick up food with them while looking at other dishes or use them as toothpicks. Well, the masses haven't heard the rules and are surviving well without them!

Most public restaurants and privately run restaurants use wooden chopsticks. Some people think wooden chopsticks are unhealthy because they harbour dirt in the cracks and may be a source of hepatitis, so they buy their own pair. Disposable wooden chopsticks are now catching on in trains and elsewhere. Plastic chopsticks are commonly sold in China. The best way to master chopsticks is to be hungry in a place where there are no knives and forks. The following diagrams may help:

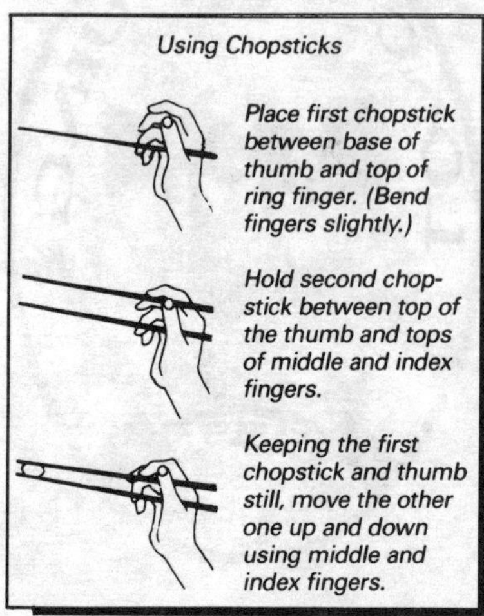

Don't worry about making a mess on the table – everyone does. If you want to, raise the bowl right up to your lips and shovel in the rice. This is how the Chinese eat so don't be embarrassed, though it does take practice to master the shovelling process.

Restaurants

In the towns the government-run restaurants are the size of canteens seating several hundred people at any one time. In Beijing, Shanghai and Canton, the older establishments have private rooms where small groups of people can eat away from the crowd but the Chinese don't go in for the western fashion of eating in dimly lit, intimate surroundings. In fact, the Chinese have a word, *renao*, which is the flip-side of privacy and intimacy; literally it means 'hot and noisy', suggesting the pleasure they find in getting together with a large group of friends and relatives for a meal in a noisy, brightly lit room, chopsticks clicking and everyone talking.

There's a multitude of privately run

restaurants in China, part of the boom in free enterprise since Mao died. As they do everywhere else, foreigners often end up paying more. Sometimes polite insistence will bring the price down, but at other times the Chinese can be frustratingly stubborn. Check prices before placing your order. Don't let the price arrive as a neat figure – ask firmly and politely for individual prices, preferably written on a receipt. You can also check the menu again, providing it has prices. In case of dispute, you can refer absolutely scandalous overcharging to the PSB or take your case to the local prices commission or office of commerce (Shang Ye Jü). On the positive side, you'll often find these privately run restaurants much more pleasant to eat in than the large, crowded canteens. The speed of the service and sometimes the quality of the food can also be substantially better.

Many restaurants have a habit of serving enormous helpings – a real problem if you're on your own because they'll often charge you appropriately. Try asking for small helpings – you can always order more if you're still hungry. Small street stalls are good for snacks. If you can't stand the staring any longer then flee to the restaurants in the tourist hotel; most are OK but you rarely find anything outstanding unless you're prepared to go up-market.

Most public restaurants have counters where you buy tickets for the food. Then you go to a window facing into the kitchen, hand in your tickets and get your food. Menus and prices are usually chalked up on a blackboard and scrubbed out as the restaurant runs out.

Unless you can speak Chinese, the best way to order a meal in a Chinese restaurant is to point at something that somebody else already has. Easy enough in the small, privately run restaurants, but more difficult in the large canteens where lines of people wait to be served. Sometimes somebody takes you in hand, leads you into the kitchen where you can point out what you want, and then buys the tickets for you. Some restaurants with a regular western clientele have menus in English; most don't. A phrasebook is a big help if you don't speak Chinese.

Tourist hotels almost always have menus in Chinese and English. If not, there's usually someone around who speaks some English. Sometimes they dispense with menus and you pay a flat rate for a bowl of steamed rice together with several small plates of fish and different types of vegetables and meat – not a bad way to eat.

In remote places or on long bus trips it helps to have a small bag of emergency rations such as instant noodles, dried fruit, soup extract, nuts, chocolate, etc. Some places have little food to offer, or you may choose to skip what is available and place your trust in something more appealing from the food bag.

Banquets

Visiting delegations, cultural groups, etc, are usually given a welcoming banquet by their host organisation. At the very highest levels there'll be formal invitations and a detailed seating plan based on rank and higher algebra. At lower levels it's a more simple affair, though the ritual and etiquette are much the same.

A formal dinner usually lasts about 1½ hours, and is preceded by 10 or 15 minutes of tea and polite conversation. The party is then seated with the host presiding at the head of the table and the high-ranking guests (that is, the leaders of the delegation) seated to his left or right. Dishes are served in sequence, beginning with cold appetisers and continuing through 10 or more courses. Soup is usually served after the main course and is used to wash the food down.

Sometimes the host will serve the guest, as is the Chinese custom. If not, use the small china spoon to take food from the large serving plates to your own bowl. The other small bowl is for tea, which will probably be constantly refilled. Small

dishes in the middle of the table contain soya sauce and chilli.

The usual rule is to serve everyone too much. Empty bowls imply that the host hasn't served a sufficient quantity of food, so if you see a bit left in a bowl then leave it there. Similarly, though rice may be the staple, at banquets it is used only as a filler; to consume great quantities at a banquet implies you are still hungry and is an insult to your host.

In a formal setting it is impolite to drink alcohol alone; toasts are usually offered to neighbours or to the whole table. It is appropriate for the leader of the guests to offer a toast to everyone at the table, and the Chinese host usually begins the toasts after the first course. Avoid excessive toasting since inebriation is frowned upon. There are usually three glasses per person on the table: one for soft drinks, one for beer and another for toasts. Toasts are often made using the fiery mao-tai with the expression *Gan bei!* which literally implies 'empty the cup'. In the course of a banquet there may be several gan bei toasts, but custom dictates that you need only drain your glass on the first one. Subsequent toasts require only a small sip – the Chinese are not great drinkers. The Han Chinese don't clink their classes when toasting.

Don't be late for a formal banquet; it's considered extremely rude. The banquet ends when the food and toasts end – the Chinese don't linger after the meal. You may find yourself being applauded when you enter a large banquet. This Chinese custom is used as a greeting or to indicate approval and the correct response it to applaud back!

FILM & PHOTOGRAPHY

Both Chinese and foreign film can be bought at the major tourist hotels, Friendship Stores and numerous photography shops which have sprouted all over the country. The range for foreign film is rarely complete and you may not be able to get the film type or speed you need even in a major city like Beijing or Shanghai.

Film

Prices for foreign film in China are high – about 40% to 50% more than what you'll pay in Hong Kong or in the west, so take as much of the stuff as you think you'll need. Black & white film is hard to buy in Hong Kong and China, as colour photos are now the big thing.

Kodak, Fujicolor and Agfacolor are commonly sold. Some Ektachrome and Fujichrome is sold but can be hard to come by when you want it. It's extremely difficult – even in Beijing and Shanghai – to find Kodachrome 64 KR135 film. When you do find it, it's very expensive; a roll of 36 exposures will cost about Y36, including processing. Various brands of colour 110 print film are also sold. Colour slide film is expensive and hard to find.

We all know the amazing effects of Polaroid photography on the natives – so you can easily set yourself up in the magic business in China. Some brands are sold in the country.

You're allowed to bring in 8 mm movie cameras; 16 mm or professional equipment is not permitted without the Kafkaesque red-tape and paperwork. Some brands of 8 mm movie film are sold in China.

Video cameras were once subject to

shaky regulations but there seems to be no problem now. One of the more amusing sights are the Japanese and Americans who, wearing porta-paks over their shoulders and Rambo-style battery-belts, tape everything in sight. The biggest problem is the power source and recharging your batteries off the strange mutations of plugs and voltages in China. You should be OK if you're staying in the five-star hotels where they cater for the idiosyncratic whims of foreign devils, but forget it if you're backpacking. How are you going to carry the stuff without a tour bus?

Processing

You can get your film processed in 24 hours in some of the major tourist cities like Beijing, Shanghai, Canton, Guilin – usually through the major tourist hotels and Friendship Stores and at the local photography stores.

Ektachrome and Fujichrome can be processed in Beijing and Shanghai but this can be incredibly expensive. Ektachrome processing can cost twice as much as what you'd pay in the west – though it may be worth it to make sure your camera's working OK.

Kodachrome film cannot be processed in China or in Hong Kong. The closest countries which process them are Japan and Australia. Undeveloped film can be sent out of China and, going by personal experience only, the dreaded X-ray machines do not appear to be a problem.

Technical Problems

These include dim interiors lit by 40-watt bulbs or low-voltage fluorescent lights. You should also be wary of X-rays at airports, which may fog your film. Dust is a major hazard; take your own cleaning devices along. Polarising filters are useful, and in places like Xinjiang a UV filter is good for reducing the haze. Photography from moving trains doesn't work unless you have high-speed film; if you have low-speed film then train-window shots tend to get blurred.

During summer, outdoor shots come out best if you shoot early before the sun is high overhead; otherwise you may get a bluish, washed-out look to your pictures. If you have to shoot at that time of day then a skylight filter will reduce the haze. Beware of sharp differences between sun and shade – if you can't get reasonably balanced overall light you may have to opt for exposing only one or other area correctly, or use a fill-in flash. Those lush, green rice paddies come up best if backlit by the sun.

Prohibited Subjects

Photography from planes and photographs of airports, military installations, harbour facilities and railroad terminals are prohibited; bridges may also be a touchy subject.

These rules do get enforced if the enforcers happen to be around. One traveller, bored at the airport, started photographing the X-ray procedure in clearance. PLA men promptly pounced on her and ripped the film out. In an age where satellites can zoom down on a number plate it all seems a bit ridiculous, but most countries have similar restrictions on photography.

Taking photos is not permitted in museums, archaeological sites and many temples, mainly to protect the postcard and slide industry. It prevents westerners from publishing their own books about these sites and taking business away from the Chinese-published books. It also prevents valuable works of art from being damaged by countless flash photos – but in most cases you're not allowed to take even harmless time exposures.

Be aware that these rules are generally enforced. If you want to snap a few photos in prohibited spots then start with a new roll of film – if that's ripped out of your camera at least you don't lose 20 other photos as well. In the Lama Temple in Beijing I couldn't resist one quick photo, but faster than me was an agile monk who bounded across the courtyard and slapped a hand over the lens – scared the daylights out of me. Must have had some special martial arts training.

People Photos

In China you'll get a fantastic run for your money; for starters there are one billion portraits to work your way through. Religious reasons for avoiding photographs are absent among the Han Chinese – some guy isn't going to stick a spear through you for taking a picture of his wife and stealing part of her soul – though the taboo may apply to some of the minority groups, and you probably won't be allowed to take photos of idols in Buddhist temples.

Some Chinese shy away from having their photo taken, even duck for cover. Others are proud to pose and will ham it up for the camera – and they're especially proud if you're taking a shot of their kid. Nobody expects any payment for photos – so don't give any or you'll set a precedent. What the Chinese would go for, though, is a copy of a colour photo, which you could mail to them. Black & white photography is a big thing in China but colour photos are still expensive. The Chinese also think that the negative belongs to the subject as well, and they'll ask for both the negative and the print – but through the post there's no argument.

There are three basic approaches to photographing people. One is the polite 'ask for permission and pose it' shot, which is often rejected. Another is the 'no-holds-barred and upset everyone' approach. The third is surreptitious, standing half a km away with a metre-long telephoto lens. Many Chinese will disagree with you on what constitutes good subject matter; they don't really see why anyone would want to take a street-scene, a picture of a beggar or a shot of an old man's bald head.

Another objection often brought up is that the subject is not 'dignified' – be it a labourer straining down the street with a massive load on his hand-cart, or a barrel of excrement on wheels. This seems a bit absurd in an age where poor peasants and

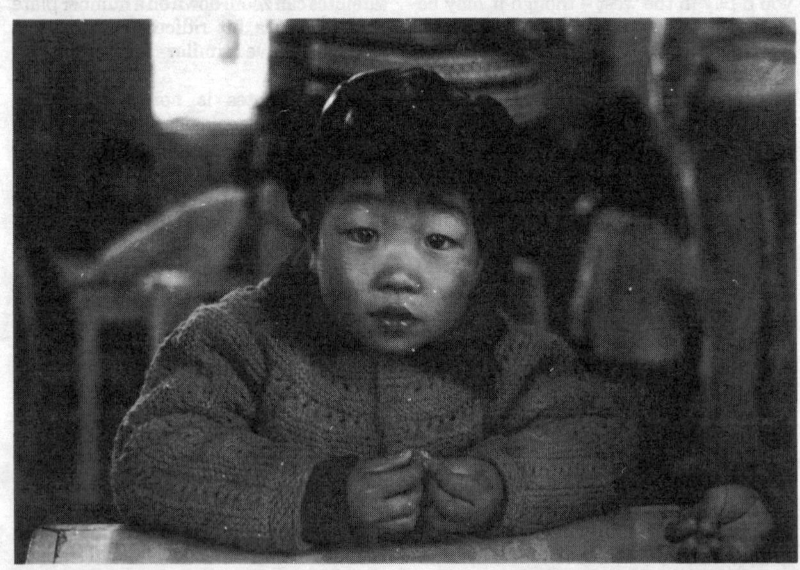

workers are glorified on huge billboards, but you'll have a tough time informing your subject of this.

During the Beijing winter I spotted a bicycle-hauler with a load of charcoal bricks headed my way, grimy face looking like something out of the Industrial Revolution. When I went 'click' the man shielded his face. My companion spoke Chinese and the coal-hauler said to 'come back when I've got my suit on'. Taking this as an invitation to try again, I raised the camera and the coal-hauler reached for a brick – end of photo session!

Chinese Photography

Shutterbugs abound in the PRC these days, although a good-quality camera is still the mark of a cadre or one of the nouveau-riche.

The common Chinese camera harks back to the age of the Box Brownie, or bellows-type twin-lens Rolleiflex with a top speed of 1/300th of a second using 120-size film. Top of the line is the Seagull Goeland DF, an SLR – it's a chunky-looking camera that does what most Japanese cameras can do. There is Seagull brand black & white film to go with it. Japanese cameras are sold in some photographic stores in China; these are expensive but a few Chinese come up with the money to buy them.

A lot of Chinese cannot afford a camera in the first place, and resort to photographers at tourist places. The photographers supply dress-up clothing for that extra touch. The subjects change from street clothing into spiffy gear and sometimes even bizarre costumes and make-up for the shot. Others use cardboard props such as opera stars or boats. In Beijing one prop is a real car – after all, the average Chinese has about as much hope of riding in a car as you've got of hitching on the space shuttle.

Some of the photo merchants hand-tint the black & white results. The tourist areas abound with places which develop black & white film in a few hours, and one of the stranger sights is the customer riding home on a bicycle with a roll of negatives flapping from the handlebars – a unique method of drying the results.

The standard shot is one or more Chinese standing in front of something significant. A temple, waterfall, heroic statue or important vintages of calligraphy are considered suitable backgrounds. The pose is usually stiff (the irony is that Chinese with expensive SLRs take exactly the same type of photo and achieve the same result as those with cheaper box cameras). If you hang around these places you can clip off some portrait shots for yourself – people expect photos to be taken and are more at ease with the cameras. The important thing for them is not the composition but what's in the photo; film is expensive, so a photo is a precious thing not to be wasted on a street-scene. They'll sometimes even drag you into the photo as an exotic backdrop.

TOURS

Tour groups are still considered the darlings of Chinese who have to deal with foreigners. It is much easier for the Chinese if you arrive in a tour group, if all your accommodation is pre-booked, and if everyone sits down at the same time to eat. If there's a CITS interpreter on hand someone doesn't have to struggle with a phrasebook or pidgin English. Groups don't make a nuisance of themselves by trying to go to closed places, and they usually channel complaints through the tour leader rather than hassle the desk clerk. Most importantly, tour groups spend more money!

Are tours worth it to you? Unless you simply cannot make your own way around, then probably not. Apart from the expense, they tend to screen you even more from some of the basic realities of China travel. Most people who come back with glowing reports of the People's Republic never had to travel bottom class on the trains or battle their way on board a local bus in the whole three weeks of their stay. On the other hand, if your time is limited and you just want to see the Forbidden City and the hills of Guilin, then the brief tours from Hong Kong, though expensive, are definitely worth considering.

One thing you will never be able to complain about on a tour is not being shown enough. Itineraries are jam-packed and the Chinese expect stamina from their guests. The tour may include an early-morning breakfast, a visit to a market, a morning's sightseeing, an afternoon visit to a school and a shopping session, and it may not finish until 10 pm after a visit to the local opera.

Stays in cities are, by necessity, short and in your few weeks in the country you'll be whisked from place to place at a furious and exhausting pace.

You are unlikely to complain about the quantity of food although you may complain about the quality or the degree of imagination involved in the cooking.

One advantage of being on a tour is that you may get into places that individuals often can't – such as factories.

On tours, just as at banquets, you may find yourself being applauded – simply return the compliment. For official functions the Chinese are exceedingly punctual and you should be too – to be late is considered very rude.

From Hong Kong & Macau

There are innumerable tours you can make into China from Hong Kong or Macau.

The best people to go to if you want to find out what's available are the Hong Kong travel agents, the Hong Kong Student Travel Bureau or the China Travel Service.

Also worth trying is the August Moon Tour & Travel Agency (tel 3-693151) at Shop 4, ground floor, Ambassador Hotel Shopping Arcade, 26 Nathan Rd, Kowloon. They keep a pretty good stock of leaflets and information on a whole range of tours to China. You usually have to book tours one or two days in advance.

I could go on endlessly regurgitating all the tours to China, but those to the border town of Shenzhen are probably the most popular. These are usually daily except Sundays and public holidays, and the price hovers around HK$300 to HK$350 for visa, transport and lunch. The tour normally includes visits to the Shenzhen Reservoir (from which Hong Kong gets most of its water), art gallery, kindergarten, commune and arts & crafts shop. Some trips also include the adjacent Shekou district just to the west of Shenzhen.

There are day trips from Hong Kong to Zhongshan, another Special Economic Zone north of Macau. You're taken by hydrofoil to Macau and then by bus over to Zhongshan. These tours include a visit to Cui Heng village, the birthplace and former residence of Sun Yatsen. Price is around HK$450.

There are one-day tours to Canton and tours of several days' length which include Canton, Zhongshan, Shiqi, Zhaoqing and Foshan. Many other combinations are possible.

Essentially the same tours can be booked in Macau. It's probably best to do so at the China Travel Service Office (Metropole Hotel, Rua de Praia Grande) or the travel agents in the large tourist hotels which have English-speaking staff.

Tours further afield are also available in Hong Kong. For instance, a six-day, five-night tour taking in Beijing and Xian will cost around HK$6900. A four-day, three-night tour to Canton and Guilin is around HK$2900.

An enthusiastic one-day visitor described her tour as follows:

> The tour starts in Macau at 9.30 am at the Mondial Hotel. Chinese Customs are no problem . . . Our whole bus group (about 20 people) crossed the border in just 15 minutes.
>
> The programme then was a 20-minute visit to the Dr Sun Yatsen Memorial Middle School followed by a half-hour visit (with a tea break) to the late founder of the Republic of China's residence. We then had an excellent 1½-hour lunch in Shaqi with prawns, fish soup, chicken, pork, duck and real beer . . . . We then had a half-hour walk around Shaqi, a short visit to a

farmer's house in a small village and tea back at the border before we crossed into Macau.

The guide would stop the bus while we were driving through the country if we wanted to take pictures. The Chinese guide was very well-informed, and to me he seemed very open. It was a well-organised, friendly and helpful tour – money well spent.

– Marian Yeuken

From Western Countries

These are handled by innumerable travel agents and any of them worth their commission will still tell you that you can't go to China except on a tour. They usually offer the standard tours that whip you round Beijing, Shanghai, Guilin, Xian, etc.

In an attempt to spice up the offerings the Chinese have come up with some new formulas. These include honeymoon tours (how many in the group?); acupuncture courses; special-interest tours for botanists, railway enthusiasts, lawyers and potters; trekking tours to Tibet and Qinghai; women's tours; bicycle tours, and Chinese-language courses. Check with your local travel agent.

Volunteer Expeditions

Some organisations need paying helpers to assist on projects. This is a contribution to the cost of the project and you have to pay your own air fares and living expenses to and on site.

Two organisations which have made such trips to China are Earthwatch, 10 Juniper Rd, Box 127, Belmont, Massachusetts 02178, USA; and the University Research Expeditions Program, University of California, Berkeley, California 94720, USA. You can send for a catalogue – they expect you to work hard when joining an expedition. Costs are tax-deductible for US citizens.

Mountaineering & Trekking

Mountaineering and trekking tours to China are organised by various agents in the west, but the prices are too high for low-budget travellers. Trekking is administered and arranged by the Chinese Mountaineering Association under the same rules that apply to mountaineering in China. The CMA makes all arrangements for a trek with the assistance of provincial mountaineering associations and local authorities.

The first few trekkers were allowed into China only in 1980 and the first groups were organised in 1981. Because trekking is under the mountaineering rules, all treks must be near one of the peaks open for mountaineering – these regions span the country and vary from the plains of Tibet to the lush bamboo forests of Sichuan Province and the open plains of Xinjiang.

Various travel agents will book you through to these operators. Scan their literature carefully – sometimes the tours can be done just as easily on your own. What you want are places that individuals have trouble getting into.

If you can afford it, a few mountaineering, trekking and cycling tour operators are:

USA Mountain Travel, 1398 Solano Avenue, Albany, California 94706; Wilderness Travel, 1760 Solano Avenue, Berkeley, California 94707; Ocean Voyages, 1709 Bridgeway, Sausalito, California 94965; China Passage, 302 Fifth Avenue, New York, New York 10001.

Australia World Expeditions, formerly Australian Himalayan Expeditions (tel 062 49 6634), 159 Cathedral St, Woolloomooloo, Sydney, 2011. Tail Winds Bicycle Touring, PO Box 32, O'Connor, ACT, 2601.

England Voyages Jules Verne (tel 01-486 8080) 10 Glentworth St, London NW1. Society for Anglo-Chinese Understanding (tel 01-267 9841) 152 Camden High St, London NW1. Both of these will provide individual travel arrangements (including visa) as well as tours. Voyages Jules Verne also has an office in Hong Kong at Room 214, 2nd floor, Lee Gardens Hotel, Hysan Avenue, Hong Kong Island.

Hong Kong In Hong Kong several operators organise interesting trips, cycling and commune living. Try the Hong Kong Student Travel Bureau, Room 1024, 10th floor, Star House, Salisbury Rd, Tsimshatsui, Kowloon; and the China Youth Travel Service, Room 904, Nanyang Commercial Bank Building, 151 des Voeux Rd, Hong Kong Island. CYTS is the younger arm of CITS and they liaise with many foreign student organisations and groups. Mera Travel Services Ltd, Room 1308, Argyle Centre, Phase 1, 688 Nathan Rd, Kowloon does trekking tours to Tibet, Nepal and India.

SHOPPING

Some people buy nothing in China and others come back loaded with souvenirs. Shopping and visits to arts & crafts 'factories' figure prominently on the itineraries of tour groups, and over the last few years there has been a boom in mass-produced Chinese arts & crafts. However, there are still many unique curios and beautiful pieces of art to be found.

Chinese Department Stores in Hong Kong

The Chinese government runs large department stores in Hong Kong which sell almost everything that China exports. Everything from antiques to chopsticks is available and you'll get a greater variety and often cheaper prices than you can in China itself!

There are two types of stores. The China Products store (Yue Hua) sells the domestic, down-market merchandise like cloth, garments, household goods and furniture, but also stocks silk kimonos, short 'happi' coats and negligees. The China Arts & Crafts store stocks the artsy/craftsy, curio/antiquity stuff.

The best of these stores is the one opposite Central Market in Queens Rd, Hong Kong Island. Another good store is at the corner of Percival St and Hennessy Rd in Causeway Bay. If you are going to buy stuff in China, get it in Hong Kong, where there is a better selection, and things are cheaper and easier to mail. At least use Hong Kong to check out prices.

Friendship Stores

These stores originally stocked goods either imported from the west or in short supply in the ordinary stores. They were primarily meant for foreigners, but since many stores now sell imported goods the whole concept of the Friendship Store is a rather archaic one. Only the large Friendship Stores – in Beijing, Shanghai and Canton – are really in a class by themselves for their extraordinary range of goods.

Some Friendship Stores will pack and ship your purchases for you. You usually have to pay for goods in these stores with FECs, which have become the subject of a black market since they enable ordinary Chinese to buy luxury goods which are otherwise unobtainable or would require a long wait. Ration coupons or approval from the work unit are not needed to buy stuff in the Friendship Stores; all that's needed is the right type of money, and that's why the Chinese are so anxious to get FECs.

Department Stores

If you need something, the big department stores are the places to go. With the rebirth of consumerism these stores are stocked with all types of goods, from daily needs to luxuries, locally made and imported. Most of the goods are very expensive based on Chinese wages, but cheap for westerners. Before you buy something in the Friendship Store, it's worth checking to see if it's available in the local department store, where it may be cheaper.

Hotel Shops

These shops, in the large tourist hotels, supply foreigners with western and Japanese film, western cigarettes and alcohol, Coca-Cola, biscuits, souvenirs, toothpaste, postcards, maps and books.

Free Markets

Free markets, which started around 1979-1980, are street markets where people sell produce and goods for their own profit. The goods include clothes, foodstuffs, cheap digital watches, and second-hand books and magazines.

Books & Posters

Chinese political books and magazines are interesting souvenirs, as are wall-posters. These are readily available in the bookshops and are very cheap. One delightful poster I bought showed Mao Zedong, Zhou Enlai, Zhu De and Liu Shaoqi amiably chatting in what looks like a Communist heaven, surrounded by trees and flowers with a beautiful waterfall behind them! Another shows Zhu, Mao and Liu welcoming Zhou at the airport on his return from a visit to the Soviet Union in the 1950s. Older versions of this poster have Liu scrubbed out, while newer ones include Deng Xiaoping and Peng Zhen.

All over China you'll see people on the footpath presiding over shelves of little books. These are the Chinese equivalent of comic books and are popular with both children and adults, who rent them from the stall-keeper and sit down on benches to read. The stories range from fantasies about animals to tales from classical China and episodes from the Communist revolution. They're all in Chinese but they make nice souvenirs – you can buy them in the shops for a few mao.

The fashion magazines printed in Beijing and Shanghai are interesting mementoes, with their western and Chinese beauties whose looks, hairstyles and dress are aeons away from the blue-garbed socialist women of the Maoist era. Racy front covers, often of semi-garbed western models, belie more austere interiors.

Arts & Crafts

Chinese musical instruments are sold in department stores and private shops. Some shops are devoted entirely to traditional Chinese opera costumes, so if you want something unique for the next masquerade party that's the place to go. Cassettes and records of traditional opera are also sold in these shops.

Brushes, paints and other art materials may be worth checking out – a lot of this stuff is imported by western countries and you should be able to pick them up cheaper at the source. Scroll paintings are sold everywhere and are invariably very expensive, partly because the material on which the painting is done is expensive. The many street artists in China sit out on the sidewalk drawing and painting and selling their products to passers-by.

Beautiful kites are sold in China and are worth getting, just to hang on your wall. Paper rubbings of stone inscriptions are cheap and make nice wall hangings when framed. Exquisite paper-cuts are sold everywhere.

Clothes & Jewellery

China is a hat-collector's paradise. The woven straw peasant hats vary from province to province. Peasant women near Xiamen lacquer their hats a bright yellow. In Hunan the peasants' hats have a distinctive squat, conical shape. In Xinjiang the Muslims wear attractive embroidered caps. Discarded PLA caps (or imitations) are available everywhere, as are the blue so-called 'Mao caps'.

In Xinjiang and in Hohhot in Inner Mongolia you can buy, or have made for you, decorative leather riding boots. Kashgar is the hat and knife-making centre of Xinjiang, and both are available in an extraordinary variety of designs.

Check out the cashmere jumpers, cardigans and skirts in the Beijing Friendship Store and its branch in the Beijing Hotel.

Jade and ivory jewellery are commonly sold in China – but remember that some countries like Australia and the USA prohibit the import of ivory.

Antiques

Many of the Friendship Stores have antique sections, and some cities have antique shops, but prices are high so don't expect to find a bargain. Only antiques which have been cleared for sale to foreigners may be taken out of the country. When you buy an item over 100 years old it will come with an official red wax seal attached. This seal does *not* necessarily indicate that the item is an antique though! A Canadian who bought 'real' jade for Y1500 at a Friendship Store in Guilin later discovered in Hong Kong that it was a plastic fake. After six months of copious correspondence and investigation, the Guilin Tourism Bureau refunded the money and closed down the offending store. You'll also get a receipt of sale which you must show to Customs when you leave the country; otherwise the antique will be confiscated. Imitation antiques are sold everywhere. Some museum shops sell replicas, usually at extravagant prices.

Stamps & Coins

China issues quite an array of beautiful stamps – generally sold at post offices in the hotels. Outside many of the post offices you'll find amateur philatelists with books full of stamps for sale; it can be extraordinarily hard bargaining with these guys! Stamps issued during the Cultural Revolution make interesting souvenirs. Old coins are often sold at major tourist sites; many are forgeries.

Oddities

If plaster statues are to your liking, the opportunities to stock up in China are abundant. Fat Buddhas appear everywhere, and 60-cm-high Venus de Milos and multi-armed gods with flashing lights are not uncommon. They're all incredibly crass, but the Chinese haven't had these things for 30 years so the market for them has really boomed.

Fireworks are sold all over China. You're not allowed to bring them into Hong Kong, so customs may ask you for them or inspect your bags. Fireworks are also prohibited on aircraft and some countries, like Australia, do not permit their import.

Lots of shops sell medicinal herbs and spices. Export tea is sold in extravagantly decorated tins; check the China Products stores in Hong Kong. In Kashgar you can buy wooden horse saddles. Hotan is the carpet-making centre of Xinjiang.

Advertising

Advertising for the foreign market is one area the Chinese are still stumbling around in. A French traveller reported seeing a television advertisement in Paris for Chinese furs. Viewers were treated to the bloody business of skinning and cadavers in the refrigerator rooms before the usual parade of fur-clad models down the catwalk. It would be fun to handle the advertising campaigns for their more charming brand names. There's Double-Bull Underwear and Pansy Underwear (for men), and Fang-Fang Lipstick and another anagrammatic brand called Maxam which sounds like a vaguely familiar factor. Pamper your stud with Horse Head facial tissues. While in Canton drop into the Checkmates Disco in the China Hotel. Wake up in the morning with a Golden Cock Alarm Clock (now called the Golden Rooster). For your trusty Walkman it may be best to stay away from White Elephant Batteries, but you might try the space-age Moon Rabbit variety. Flying Eagle Safety Razors don't sound too safe either. Out of the psychedelic '60s comes White Rabbit Candy. The rarer brand to look for is the Flying Baby series, which appears to have been discontinued, and there used to be some Flying Baby Toilet Paper around. The ideographs for Coca-Cola sound something like 'Kokuh-koluh' and translate as 'tastes good, tastes happy'. But the Chinese must have thought they were really on to something good when the 'Coke Adds Life' slogan got mistranslated and claimed to be able to resurrect the dead.

Getting There

There are all sorts of ways of entering and exiting China. The main entry and exit point is Hong Kong. Another popular route is the Trans-Siberian railway from Europe. Exotic routes include Tibet to Nepal and north-west China to Pakistan. There are direct flights from China to many Asian and western countries, and shipping connections to Japan. Many westerners will enter China via Hong Kong, which has air connections to Europe, Britain, the USA, Australia and many Asian countries.

AIR

The air ticket alone to Hong Kong can gouge a great slice out of anyone's budget, but you can reduce the cost by finding a discounted fare. However, a cheap ticket may (or may not) involve restrictions on route, advance purchase requirements, cancellation charges.

A common cheap ticket is the APEX (Advance Purchase Excursion) one, which usually has to be purchased two or three weeks ahead of departure, has a cancellation fee, does not permit stopovers and may have minimum and maximum stays as well as fixed departure and return dates.

Also useful is combined ticketing, in which a couple of tickets are issued at the same time to cover several projected trips, therefore guarding against fare increases.

Worth considering is a ticket which will take you from point A to point B with multiple stopovers. For example, such a ticket could fly you Sydney to London with stopovers in Denpasar, Jakarta, Hong Kong, Bangkok, Calcutta, Delhi and Istanbul.

If Hong Kong is just one stop on a round-the-world trip then consider getting a 'Round the World' (RTW) ticket. With these you get a limited period in which to circumnavigate the globe, and you can make a stopover anywhere the carrying airline goes as long as you don't backtrack. Some airlines have tickets which last for a year. Sometimes two or more airlines team up to provide the service. The best-known RTW ticket is Pan Am's 'Round the World in 180 Days' ticket.

Travel agents offer a host of other deals. Whatever you do, buy your air ticket from one of them because the airlines don't deal directly in discount tickets. And always check what conditions and restrictions apply to the tickets you intend to buy!

FROM AUSTRALIA

Australia is not a cheap place to fly out of, and air fares between Australia and South-East Asia are ridiculously expensive considering the distances flown. However, there are a few ways of cutting the cost.

Among the cheapest regular tickets available in Australia are the Advance Purchase Excursion (APEX) fares. The cost of the APEX tickets depends on your departure date from Australia. The year is divided into 'peak' and 'low' seasons; tickets bought in peak season (December to January) are more expensive.

It's possible to get reductions on the cost of APEX and other fares by going to the student travel offices and/or some of the travel agents in Australia that specialise in cheap air tickets.

If you book through such an agent, the APEX fares from Melbourne to Hong Kong are around A$495 one way and A$880 return, flying with Cathay Pacific. Discount fares from Melbourne to Beijing are around A$950 one way and A$1485 return, flying with Thai International.

Travel agents advertise in the travel sections of the Saturday papers, such as the Melbourne *Age* and *The Sydney Morning Herald*. Also look in *Student Traveller*, a free newspaper published by Student Travel Australia and distributed on campuses.

Well worth trying is The Flight Shop (tel 670 0477) at 386 Little Bourke St, Melbourne. They also have branches under the name of the Flight Centre in Sydney (tel (02) 233 2296) and Brisbane (tel (07) 229 9958). In Brisbane check out the Brisbane Flight Centre (tel (07) 229 9211).

Some good deals are available from Student Travel Australia and you don't have to be a student to use their services. In the major cities they're at:

Melbourne
  220 Faraday St, Carlton, tel (03) 347 6911
Hobart
  Union Building, University of Tasmania, tel (002) 34 1850
Sydney
  1A Lee St, Railway Square, tel (02) 212 1255
Adelaide
  Level 4, The Arcade, Union House, Adelaide University, tel (08) 223 6620
Perth
  Hackett Hall, University of WA, tel (09) 380 2302
Canberra
  Concessions Building, Australian National University, tel (062) 470 8005
Brisbane
  Shop 2, Societe General House, 40 Creek St, tel (07) 221 9629

For tours and package deals contact Martyn Paterson and Lucie Lolicato at Access Travel (tel (02) 241 1128), 5th floor, 58 Pitt St, Sydney. Apart from China tours they also organise tours on the Trans-Siberian railway from Beijing to Europe, including stopovers in Ulan Bator (Mongolia), Irkutsk, Lake Baikal, Leningrad and Moscow.

FROM NEW ZEALAND

Air New Zealand fly Auckland to Hong Kong. In 'peak' season a return excursion ticket costs NZ$1828, and in 'low' season NZ$1550. You have to pay for your ticket at least 21 days in advance and spend a minimum of six days overseas.

Cathay Pacific also fly Auckland to Hong Kong, using Air New Zealand carriers. In 'peak' season a one way excursion ticket from Auckland to Hong Kong is NZ$1426. An advance-purchase return excursion ticket is NZ$1828. As with the Air New Zealand excursion ticket, a minimum of six days must be spent overseas.

FROM BRITAIN

British Airways, British Caledonian and Cathay Pacific (the Hong Kong-based carrier partly owned by British Airways) fly London-Hong Kong.

Air-ticket discounting is a long-running business in the UK and it's wide open. The various agents advertise their fares and there's nothing under-the-counter about it at all. To find out what's going, there are a number of magazines in Britain which have good information about flights and agents. These include: *Trailfinder*, free from the Trailfinders Travel Centre, 48 Earls Court Rd, London W8 6EJ; *Time Out*, the London weekly entertainment guide widely available in London or from Tower House, Southampton St, London WC2E 7HD; *LAM*, a free weekly magazine for entertainment, travel and jobs; *The News & Travel Magazine (TNT)*, another free weekly magazine; and *Business Traveller*.

Discount tickets are almost exclusively available in London. You won't find your friendly travel agent out in the country offering cheap deals. The danger with discounted tickets in Britain is that some of the 'bucket shops' (as ticket-discounters are known) are shonky. Sometimes the backstairs over-the-shop travel agents fold up and disappear after you've handed over the money and before you've got the tickets. Get the tickets before you hand over the cash.

Two reliable London bucket shops are Trailfinders at 46 Earls Court Rd, London W8; and the Student Travel Association at 74 Old Brompton Rd, London SW7 or 117 Euston Rd, London NW1 (and other addresses).

You can expect a one-way London-Hong

Kong ticket to cost from around £250, and a return ticket around £480. London ticket discounters can also offer interesting one-way fares to Australia with a Hong Kong stopover from around £520.

FROM EUROPE

Fares similar to those from London are available from other European cities. In France try Point Air-Mulhouse, 4 Rue des Orphelins, 68200 Mulhouse (tel (89) 42 4461) or 54 Rue des Ecoles, 75006 Paris. Other agencies in Paris which deal in cheap fares are Le Point, 2 Place Wagram, and Uniclam-Voyages, 63 Rue Monsieur le Prince.

The Netherlands, Brussels and Antwerp are among other good places for buying discount air tickets. In Antwerp, WATS, de Keyserlei 44, Antwerp, has been recommended. In Zurich try SOF Travel (tel (01) 301 3333) and Sindbad, 3 Schoffelgasse. In Geneva try Stohl Travel (tel (022) 31 6560).

CAAC has flights from Beijing to Belgrade, Bucharest, Frankfurt, London, Moscow, Paris, Athens and Zurich. Other international airlines operate flights out of Beijing but there are very few, if any, cut-rate fares from the Chinese end. Try the Soviet airline Aeroflot and the Rumanian airline Tarrom. A standard-price one-way ticket from Beijing to London on CAAC will cost Y3284.

FROM THE USA

You can pick up some interesting tickets from North America to South-East Asia, particularly from the US west coast or Vancouver, Canada. In fact the intense competition between Asian airlines is resulting in ticket discounting operations very similar to the London bucket shops.

Canadian Pacific Air Lines sells tickets flying from San Francisco or Los Angeles to Hong Kong for US$315 (one way), US$599 return. This fare is offered all year. Maximum stay is six months, and if you have a return ticket you must set your return date before departure.

Cathay Pacific also fly from San Francisco or Los Angeles; US$599 return, US$699 high season. Maximum stay is one year.

Other airlines' return-ticket prices in US$, flying from San Francisco and Los Angeles are: Korean Air $629, Northwest $649, Japan Airlines $639, Singapore Airlines $615. All fares are low season, Monday to Thursday.

To find cheap tickets scan the travel sections of the Sunday newspapers for likely-looking agents; the *New York Times*, *San Francisco Chronicle-Examiner* and *Los Angeles Times* are particularly good.

The Student Travel Network (STN) and the American Student Council Travel (SCT) know a lot about cheap tickets and interesting routes. You don't have to be a student to use their services. Japan Air Lines also offers a student fare, US west coast to Hong Kong, US$380 one way, low season, with a stopover in Tokyo.

Major cities where you'll find Student Travel Network are:

Los Angeles
Suite 507, 2500 Wilshire Boulevard, tel (213) 380 2184

San Diego
6447 El Cajon Boulevard, tel (619) 286 1322

San Francisco
Suite 702, 166 Geary St, tel (415) 391 8407

Honolulu
Suite 202, 1831 South King St, tel (808) 942 7455

Dallas
6609 Hillcrest Avenue, tel (214) 360 0097

Addresses of Student Council Travel are:

New York
205 East 42nd St, tel (212) 661 1450; 356 West 34th St, tel (212) 23 4257; and 356 West 34th St, tel (212) 239 4257

Los Angeles
1093 Broxton Avenue, tel (213) 208 3551

San Diego
5500 Atherton St, Long Beach, tel (213) 598 3338; UCSD Student Center, B-023, La Jolla, tel (619) 452 0630; and 4429 Cass St, tel (619) 270 6401

San Francisco
312 Sutter St, tel (415) 421 3473; 2511 Channing Way, Berkeley, tel (415) 848 8604
Boston
729 Boylston St, Suite 201, tel (617) 266 1926
Seattle
1314 NE 43rd St, tel (206) 632 2448

For direct flights from the USA to China the general route is from San Francisco (with connections from New York, Los Angeles and Vancouver) to Tokyo, Shanghai and Beijing. So you could go through to Beijing and pick up the return flight in Shanghai. CAAC, Pan Am and Japan Airlines (JAL) fly the route. From Vancouver you can take a JAL flight direct to Tokyo and then on to China.

FROM CANADA

Travel Cuts is Canada's national student travel agency and has offices in Vancouver, Victoria, Edmonton, Saskatoon, Toronto, Ottawa, Montreal and Halifax. You don't have to be a student to use their services.

Getting discount tickets in Canada is much the same as in the USA. Go to the travel agents and shop around until you find a good deal. In Vancouver try Kowloon Travel, 425 Abbott St (Chinatown); Westcan Treks, 3415 West Broadway; and Travel Cuts, 1516 Duranleau St, Granville Markets.

Canadian Pacific Airlines are worth trying for cheap deals to Hong Kong although Korean Airlines, which is booked by some of the agents mentioned above, may still be able to undercut them.

FROM OTHER ASIAN COUNTRIES

There are direct flights between Singapore and Hong Kong. A good place for buying cheap air tickets in Singapore is Airmaster Travel Centre (tel 3383942), Room 1, 36-B Prinsep St, Singapore 7. Also try Student Travel Australia (tel 734 7091), mezzanine floor, Ming Court Hotel, Tanglin Rd. Other agents advertise in the *Straits Times* classified columns.

Garuda Airlines has direct flights from Jakarta to Hong Kong, and from Denpasar to Hong Kong via Jakarta. Cheap discount air tickets out of Indonesia can be bought from one of the numerous discount travel agents in Jakarta or Kuta Beach in Bali. There are several discounters along Jalan Legian, the main strip of Kuta Beach. You can also buy discount tickets in Kuta for departure from Jakarta.

In Jakarta, Kaliman Travel (tel 330101) in the President Hotel on Jalan Thamrin is a good place for cheap tickets. Other agents worth checking are Vayatour (tel 336640) next door to Kaliman, and Pacto Ltd (tel 320309) at Jalan Cikini Raya 24. The agent for AUS (Australian Union of Students) is Travair Buana (tel 371479) in the Hotel Sabang on Jalan H A Salim, close to Jalan Jaksa. Any student with an international student card is entitled to an AUS fare, which is usually cheaper than a normal student discount of 25%.

In Bangkok, Student Travel (tel 2815314-5, 2810731) in the Thai Hotel at 78 Prachatipatai Rd, Visutikasat, are both helpful and efficient. Other travel agents in Bangkok recommended for their service and prices are Asian Overland Adventures (tel 2810731, 2815314-5), also in the Thai Hotel; Bangkok Siam Travel in the Trocadero Hotel; and Onward Travel Service at 42-44 Khao San Rd, Banglumpoo, Phra Nakorn.

HONG KONG TO/FROM CANTON

From Hong Kong most people first make their way to Canton. You can get to Canton from Hong Kong by train, ferry, hydrofoil or plane. The one rule to remember is avoid going on weekends and even more so, holiday times like Easter and Chinese New Year! At those times everything is booked out and the crowds pour across the border from Hong Kong, trampling back-packers in their wake.

Overnight Ferry

The Pearl River Shipping Company runs

two ships between Hong Kong and Canton. They are the *Tianhu* and the *Xinghu*. One ship departs Hong Kong daily from the Tai Kok Tsui Wharf in Kowloon at 9 pm and arrives in Canton the following morning at 7 am. In Canton the other ship departs at 9 pm and arrives in Hong Kong at 7 am. The ferry is one of the best and most popular ways of getting to Canton. The vessels are large, clean and very comfortable – but bring a light jacket because the air-conditioning is fierce!

For ferries to Canton you can book tickets at the China Travel Service offices at 77 Queens Rd, Central, Hong Kong Island (tel 5-259121) or at the office on the 1st floor, 27-33 Nathan Rd, Kowloon (tel 3-667201) (entrance on the Beijing Rd side). Some of the agencies that issue China visas will also make bookings on this boat for you. There are no ferries on the 31st of each month. The fares per person are listed below, but you may find them a bit cheaper if you buy them from the wharf and not from an agent:

	Xinghu	*Tianhu*
2-person cabin	HK$210	HK$210
4-person cabin	HK$155	HK$135
dormitory bunk	HK$110	HK$110
seat only	HK$80	not available

If you can't get a cabin or a bunk then buy a seat ticket, and as soon as you get on board go to the purser's office. The purser distributes leftover bunks and cabins, but act quickly if you want one.

Ferries (and some of the hovercraft) to Hong Kong depart from Canton's Zhoutouzui Wharf. For details see the Canton section in the Guangdong chapter. Fares from Canton to Hong Kong are:

	Xinghu	*Tianhu*
2-person cabin	Y56	Y45
4-person cabin	Y44	Y35
dormitory bunk	Y28	Y28
seat only	Y18	not available

Express Train

The express train between Hong Kong and Canton is a comfortable and convenient way of entering China. The adult fare is around HK$190 one way.

Timetables change, so departure and arrival times are hardly worth mentioning here; check times when you're in Hong Kong. There's usually three or four express trains a day, and probably more will be put on during the holiday periods. For arrivals and departures there's usually one train early in the morning and two or more in the early afternoon. The whole trip takes a bit less than three hours.

In Hong Kong, tickets can be booked up to seven days before departure at the CTS office at 24-34 Hennessy Rd, Wanchai, and at 62-72 Sai Yee St, Tak Po Building, Mong Kok, Kowloon. Tickets for the day of departure can be bought from Kowloon Railway Station. Return tickets are also sold, but only seven to 30 days before departure. You're allowed to take bicycles on the express train, stowed in the freight car.

In Canton you must now buy tickets for all trains, including the Hong Kong-bound trains, at CITS – which means you will have to pay in FECs.

Local Train

A cheaper alternative to the express train is the electric train. The trains start running early in the morning, and the border stays open until 10 pm. Take it from Kowloon (Hunghom) Station to the Hong Kong/China border at Lo Wu Station, walk across the border bridge to Shenzhen and pick up the local train to Canton. The fare from Kowloon to Lo Wu is HK$14 ordinary class.

There are about a dozen local trains a day between Shenzhen and Canton. Tourist-price hard-seat is Y6.40, soft-seat Y9.90. Once you've been through Customs at Shenzhen train station you usually have to wait a while for the Canton-bound train. The waiting hall in Shenzhen station is always packed, but there are two large restaurants upstairs if you want to eat. It's also worthwhile to use the opportunity to wander around town. The trip from the border to Canton takes about 2½ to three hours. Extra trains may be put on during the holiday periods like Easter and Chinese New Year, when the Hong Kongers scramble across the border.

Hovercraft

The route taken by the hovercraft is the same as that used by the earliest navigators in these waters. At the mouth of the Pearl River (Zhu Jiang) is Lintin Island, where just over a century ago British merchant ships offloaded their cargoes of opium. The real gateway to Canton is Tiger Gate (Hu Men), popularly known to earlier generations of Europeans as The Bogue, only five km wide at its greatest point. From here the traffic on the river becomes noticeably busier.

The hovercraft depart from Tai Kok Tsui Wharf in Kowloon and dock at Canton's Zhoutouzui Wharf in the south-west of the city. There are several departures daily. The trip takes three hours and the fare is about HK$160.

Tickets can be bought at: the China Travel Service Offices in Hong Kong; the offices of the Hong Kong & Yaumati Ferry Company at the Jordan Road Ferry Pier (tel 3-305257) in Kowloon; or the Central Harbour Services Pier (tel 5-423428) on Hong Kong Island.

Hovercraft to Hong Kong depart from Canton's Zhoutouzui Wharf. The fare is about Y39. Tickets can be bought from the CTS office at Haizhu Square and at the Liu Hua Hotel service desk. You should also be able to buy them at the wharf, though it may be a good idea to book beforehand.

Bus

The Chinese have built a highway from Hong Kong to Canton and Zhuhai – so watch out for the opening up of bus services between Hong Kong and Canton. That will probably change the schedule and frequency of a lot of the other forms of transport currently used to get to Canton. The new highway also means that sometime in the future you may be able to bring your own car or motorcycle from Hong Kong to China.

HONG KONG TO/FROM CHINA BY AIR

The Civil Aviation Administration of China (CAAC) operates direct flights between Hong Kong and a number of Chinese cities, including Canton.

There are a couple of flights a day to Canton. The fare is around HK$297 (Y140 in the other direction), and the flight takes about 35 minutes.

There are daily flights to Beijing (HK$1446, Y685); flights six days a week to Shanghai (HK$1012, Y479); and flights twice a week to Kunming (HK$976, Y462).

In Hong Kong flights can be booked at the CAAC office on the ground floor of Gloucester Tower, des Voeux Rd, Central, Hong Kong Island (tel 5-216416).

There is another CAAC office on the ground floor, Hankow Centre, 4 Ashley Rd, Tsimshatsui, Kowloon (tel 3-7390022).

MACAU TO/FROM CHINA

On the other side of the border from Macau is the Chinese town of Gongbei, a sort of mini-Shenzhen. From Gongbei bus station, which is opposite the Customs building, you can catch buses to Canton and other parts of Guangdong Province. If you have fresh fruit with you then eat it before getting to the border, as you cannot take it into China.

There are several buses per day from Canton's long-distance bus station on Huanshi Xilu (a short walk west of the railway station) to Gongbei. The fare is around Y9 in an air-con minibus or about Y4 in the local bus. The ride to the border takes five hours. CTS air-con buses depart from the Overseas Chinese Hotel at Haizhu Square. The fare is about Y13.50.

A nightly ferry from Canton to Macau departs Canton's Zhoutouzui Wharf around 10 pm, and arrives in Macau around 7 am. Fares range from Y18 to Y44.

HONG KONG TO SHANGHAI BY FERRY

Two boats, the *Shanghai* and the *Haixing*, ply the south-east coast between Hong Kong and Shanghai. There are departures every five days. Many people take the boat when they leave China to return to Hong Kong – the trip gets rave reviews. Details of tickets and fares for the trip from Shanghai to Hong Kong are given in the Shanghai section. The fares for the trip from Hong Kong to Shanghai *per person* are:

Class	*The Shanghai*	*The Haixing*
Special A	2 people, HK$965	2 people, HK$894
1st class A	1-person cabin, HK$823	1-person cabin, HK$823
1st class B	3-person cabin, HK$751	3-person cabin, HK$751
2nd class A	2 or 3 people, HK$712	3 people, HK$712
2nd class B	3 people, HK$657	2 people, HK$657
3rd class A	2 people, HK$605	2, 3 or 4 people, HK$605
3rd class B	4 people, HK$554	2 people, HK$554
Economy class	dormitory HK$475	dormitory HK$475

In Hong Kong, tickets for the boat can be bought from the offices of China Travel Service and from the China Merchants Steam Navigation Company (tel 5-440558, 5-430945), 18th floor, 152-155 Connaught Rd, Central District, Hong Kong Island.

廣東省港澳航運公司
KWANGTUNG PROVINCE H.K./MACAU NAVIGATION CO.,
總代理：珠江船務有限公司
H.K. Agents: Chu Kong Shipping Co., Ltd.
廣州一香港客票 № 108530 BX
KWANGCHOW/HONG KONG SERVICE TICKET
持票人 Ticket Holder: 性別 Sex: 男/女 証件號碼 Travel Document No.
開航日期 Sailing Date:
開航時間 Sailing Time:
票價: FARE （七五折）兌換券 ¥ 47.00
座號 Cabin No. 1987年12月31日
7-G
注意: 1. 本票依照后列條件發出
IMPORTANT: (1) Issue subject to conditions overleaf.
2. 旅客須在開航前一小時到達碼頭（廣州河南洲頭咀港澳碼頭）
(2) Passengers should embark one hour before sailing.
售票章:

See the Shanghai chapter for details of tickets from Shanghai to Hong Kong.

OTHER FERRIES FROM HONG KONG

A couple of boats travel to Chinese ports on the south-east coast. These are worth investigating since the coast is one of the most attractive parts of China, and some of the most interesting towns are located here.

To Shantou & Xiamen

The *Dinghu* plies the water between Hong Kong and Shantou, and the *Jimei* and *Gulangyu* run between Hong Kong and Xiamen. Fares from Hong Kong to Xiamen start at HK$370 for a dorm bed.

To Hainan Island

There are direct boats from Hong Kong to Haikou and Sanya on Hainan Island. Hong Kong to Haikou takes about 18 hours; fares start at HK$176. Hong Kong to Sanya takes about 28 hours; fares start at HK$198 (Y53 in the other direction). There are about four departures a month to both these places.

To Wuzhou

There is a direct hovercraft from Hong Kong to Wuzhou. It departs Hong Kong on even-numbered dates from the Tai Kok Tsui Wharf at 7.20 am. The trip takes around 10 hours and the fare is HK$270. Tickets in Hong Kong can be bought at the China Travel Service and from some of the other agencies that issue China visas. Round-trip tickets can also be booked, but you must return within a month.

From Wuzhou you can get a bus to Guilin or Yangshuo, but you have to overnight in Wuzhou. Returning to Hong Kong, the hovercraft departs Wuzhou on odd-numbered dates at 7.30 am. The fare is Y56. Check departure time before leaving.

GETTING AWAY – FROM HONG KONG

Cheap Tickets

Hong Kong is also a good place to pick up a cheap air ticket, and again you have to go to the travel agents. Remember that prices of cheap tickets change and bargains come and go rapidly, and that some travel agents are more reliable than others. Travel agents advertise in the classified sections of the *South China Morning Post* and the *Hong Kong Standard* newspapers.

Oddly enough, some of them seem to have zero interest in actually selling you a ticket. You can do your shopping around by phone; a number of agents are listed below but check the newspapers for others. There's quite a cost variance among the Hong Kong bucket shops.

If you're travelling with kids you may be surprised to hear that the agents with the cheapest adult tickets may not necessarily have the cheapest children's tickets – even if you're all taking the same flight. Unless you've got the time to get adult tickets from one agent and children's from another, probably the simplest thing to do is go to the agent who offers the lowest total price for all tickets.

A popular place to buy cheap air tickets is the Hong Kong Student Travel Bureau or HKSTB (tel 3-7213269 or 3-693804), Room 1021, 10th floor, Star House, Tsimshatsui, Kowloon.

Another popular place is the Travellers Hostel (tel 3-7239993), 16th floor, Chungking Mansions, Nathan Rd, Tsimshatsui, Kowloon.

Well worth trying are Phoenix Services (tel 3-7227378 or 3-7233006) in Room 603, Hanford House, 221D Nathan Rd, Tsimshatsui, Kowloon. They are friendly and helpful and really deserve a plug from these guidebooks!

Also recommended is Travel World (tel 5-438876), Room 1403, Sam Cheong Building, 216 des Voeux Rd, Central.

Other places to try:

Overseas Travel (tel 5-246196), Room 603, Commercial House, 35 Queen's Rd, Central

A & J Travel (tel 5-222153), Room 906, United Overseas Bank Building, 48-54 des Voeux Rd, Central

Asian Express (tel 5-440263), Room M4, General Commercial Building, 158-162 des Voeux Rd, Central

Viking Travel (tel 3-699568), Room 1006, Mohan's Building, 14 Hankow Rd, Kowloon

Prestige Travel (tel 3-698271), 4th floor, Houston Centre, Mody Rd, Kowloon

Rip-Offs Be careful when you buy tickets. Rip-offs do happen. The territory has always been plagued by bogus travel agents and fly-by-night operations that appear shortly before peak holiday seasons and dupe customers into buying non-existent airline seats and holiday packages. Or you might pay a non-refundable deposit on an air ticket, and when you come to pay the balance they'll tell you the price of the ticket has risen. A popular trick is for an agent to accept a deposit for a booking, then, when you come to pick up the ticket, tell you that the flight is no longer available, and suggest you purchase a ticket on another flight for X dollars more.

If you think you have been ripped off, and the agent is a member of the HKTA (Hong Kong Tourist Association), the organisation can apply some pressure (and apparently has a fund to handle cases of outright fraud). Even if an agent is a member of the HKTA it still does not have to comply with any set of guidelines.

A law was passed in mid-1985 requiring all travel agencies offering outward-bound services to be licensed. The law also set up a fund to compensate cheated customers – could be worth enquiring about if you do get ripped off.

GETTING AWAY – FROM CHINA

Many travellers exit China on the Trans-Siberian or on the ship from Shanghai to Hong Kong. There are several other interesting options.

TO PAKISTAN

CAAC has direct flights from Beijing to Karachi and from Beijing to Karachi via

Islamabad. The Karakoram Highway leading from Kashgar in China's Xinjiang region into northern Pakistan is also open to foreigners. Exiting to Pakistan takes you through the dramatic snow-covered Karakoram mountain ranges. For details see the Xinjiang chapter.

TO NEPAL

The Lhasa-to-Kathmandu road is open to foreigners. For details of this route see the Tibet chapter. There may be a direct flight between the two cities by the time this book is out.

TO BURMA

An interesting possibility is the direct flight from Kunming to Rangoon on the once-weekly CAAC plane. You have to have a Burmese visa, and that's available in Beijing but not in Kunming. Your stay in Burma is limited to one week and you usually have to have an air ticket out of the country before they'll give you a visa.

TO JAPAN

CAAC has several flights a week from Beijing to Tokyo and Osaka, via Shanghai. Japan Airlines flies from Beijing and Shanghai to Tokyo, Osaka and Nagasaki. There is also a regular boat service between Shanghai and Osaka/Kobe. The fare is around US$100 (about Y320, or 22,000 Japanese yen). The ship departs once weekly, one week to Osaka and the next week to Kobe, and takes two days.

TO NORTH & SOUTH KOREA

China and South Korea have no direct transport links since the two have no diplomatic relations with each other. As for North Korea, *if* you can get a visa there are twice-weekly trains and a twice-weekly flights between Beijing and Pyongyang. At the time of writing there were rumours that the North Koreans may allow individual travellers to visit the country.

TO THE PHILIPPINES & THAILAND

CAAC has a once-weekly flight from Beijing to Manila via Canton. There may be direct flights from Xiamen in Fujian Province to Manila. There is a once-weekly flight from Beijing to Bangkok via Canton.

THE TRANS-SIBERIAN RAILWAY

A great way to start or finish your China trip is to travel on the Trans-Siberian Railway. Booking tickets or obtaining visas really isn't as mind-bending as people make out, providing you think ahead. Compared with the cost of a boring old flight, the train ride is competitively priced and provides much more scope for meetings and adventures of weird and wonderful dimensions. Mongolia and the Soviet Union are slowly relaxing their tight and expensive grip on tourism so perhaps the price of stopovers will soon drop within reach of budget travellers.

For the latest information, contact specialist agencies or national tourist agencies such as Intourist (USSR) or Ibusz (Hungary). For more depth, there's the *Trans-Siberian Rail Guide* (Bradt Publications, England, 1987) by Robert Strauss which is a comprehensive handbook and travelling companion with booking information, useful addresses, route and city maps, and strange tales for all three routes.

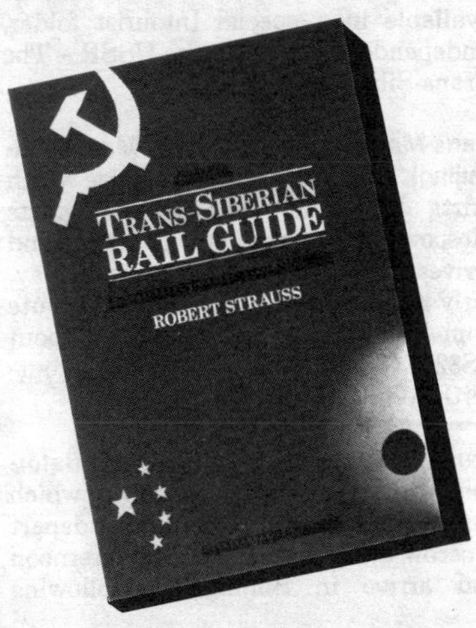

From Europe to China
There are three Trans-Siberian Railway routings, but travellers to China normally use only the Trans-Mongolian and Trans-Manchurian routes:

Trans-Siberian (Moscow-Khabarovsk-Nakhodka) This is the route for those heading for Japan; from the Soviet port of Nakhodka near Vladivostok there is a boat to Yokohama and there is also one to Hong Kong. You should probably allow about seven days for the Nakhodka-Hong Kong boat journey. Your Intourist rail ticket will be timed to connect with the specific sailing. The 'Rossia' express departs Moscow's Yaroslav Station daily in the morning and the trip to Nakhodka takes about 8½ days. It is also possible to travel part of the route by air, stopping at Irtutsk, Bratsk or Khabarovsk, where you usually stay overnight before picking up the train connection to Nakhodka and Japan. Prices for the complete rail/ship journey from Moscow to Yokohama start from 475.00 roubles (about US$731) for a 2nd-class sleeper on the train and a four-berth cabin on the ship. Intourist recommends a minimum of four weeks' notice to take care of visas, hotel bookings and train reservations. Further details are available in a special Intourist folder, 'Independent Travel to the USSR – The Trans-Siberian Railway'.

Trans-Manchurian (Moscow-Manzhouli-Beijing) This is the Russian service which skirts Mongolia. The train departs Moscow on Fridays late at night, and arrives in Beijing the following Friday, early in the morning. Prices on this route from Moscow to Beijing start at about US$210 for a 2nd-class sleeper in a four-berth compartment.

Trans-Mongolian (Moscow-Ulan Bator-Beijing) This is the Chinese service which passes through Mongolia. Trains depart Moscow every Tuesday in the afternoon and arrive in Beijing the following Monday in the afternoon. Prices on this route from Moscow to Beijing start at about US$200 for a 2nd-class sleeper in a four-berth compartment.

Visas The average time required to complete the visa and ticket hurdles is about two months. It is probably less for a simple route on a trip during winter and more for a complex routing on a trip taken in the summer peak period. Visas should be obtained in reverse order; so if you decide to do the Trans-Mongolian trip you should get Chinese, Mongolian, Soviet, Polish and East German visas in that order. A Mongolian visa is unnecessary if you take the Trans-Manchurian. East German transit visas cost five German marks and are available at the border on the train.

China Visa There are several ways to obtain a visa for individual travel to China. The first thing to do is try the CITS office or Chinese embassy in whatever country you happen to be in; the embassy in Sweden, for example, was readily handing out visas to Swedish citizens. It is much easier now to obtain one-month or three-month visas which can be extended in the usual way in China. Failing a full tourist visa, between 1 December and 31 March the Chinese embassies will give transit visas of seven days' duration (sometimes three-day extensions are possible) – this will allow you to cross China to Hong Kong, where you can pick up a tourist visa and re-enter the country. The Chinese embassy in Moscow has also been issuing visas to travellers on their way through to China, but don't rely on it.

You can also get a visa if you have an invitation from a diplomat or a foreign expert working in China (the invitation should include all the relevant details such as passport particulars, places to be visited, etc). Take the invitation to the Chinese embassy in your home country, who will then probably seek authorisation from China International Travel Service in Beijing. This usually gets you a tourist visa of 30 to 35 days' duration with extensions possible.

Soviet Visa If you apply for a visa through a Soviet embassy you must supply a confirmed Intourist itinerary and timetable. If you're applying through Intourist you must have an appropriate visa for your country of destination. Intourist will process visa and ticket applications together; they require four to five weeks. During summer, ticket reservations are essential because trains – especially the Trans-Mongolian which runs only once a week – are quickly booked out. For your Soviet visa you must supply three photos.

Other Visas Mongolian transit visas, Polish transit or tourist visas, and East German tourist visas are readily obtainable from the appropriate embassies. East German transit visas can only be obtained on the train at the border.

Tickets from London to Beijing via Berlin, Moscow and Ulan Bator, including one night's accommodation in Moscow, start from about US$440. Intourist provides an excellent timetable of the international passenger routes with rail prices. The most expensive section is usually the connection between Europe and Moscow, so you may want to save money by starting your trip close to Eastern Europe. You could also book an itinerary starting from Berlin or Helsinki, or you could fly to Moscow and continue from there by rail.

Other routes also exist; prices from Budapest are astoundingly low – between US$70 and US$100 for a ticket from Budapest to Beijing. However, the process of buying tickets is at the mercy of Soviet bureaucracy, and travelling during low season will improve your chances. Patience helps, although success is not guaranteed! You have to reserve a Moscow-Beijing ticket at least two months in advance at the Central Office of the Hungarian State Travel Company (IBUSZ), Tanacs Korut 3/c, Budapest V (office closes at 5 pm on weekdays and at noon on Saturdays) or at MAV-IRODA, Nepkoztarsasag utca, Budapest. Obtain your Chinese and Soviet visas as usual. The Soviet Consulate is at Nepkoztarsasag utca 104 (open Monday, Wednesday and Friday from 10 am to 1 pm). The Mongolian embassy is on the outskirts of Budapest and issues visas within the hour for US$3 cash – price hikes are frequent, so take more cash.

Daily train services from Budapest to Moscow depart Budapest at night – it's about a 33 to 35-hour trip to Moscow. Two trains depart each night, and the earlier one is usually certain to catch the connection to Beijing – reservations for this train should also be made well in advance. IBUSZ has offices in most countries through which some travellers have been able to obtain Trans-Siberian tickets without trekking off to Hungary. IBUSZ sometimes sells tickets, without reservations, for the journey from Beijing to Budapest. Since one-way tickets are valid for two months (possibly longer – check carefully), this means you can fly to Hong Kong, enter China and make your reservation with CITS in Beijing before obtaining relevant transit visas.

Pre-Departure Tips US dollars in small denominations are essential. Take food with you to supplement dining-car meals. Alcohol is not sold on the Trans-Siberian, so bring your own if you want to initiate Siberian train parties.

Several readers have recommended Scandinavian Student Travel Service (SSTS), 117 Hauchsvej, 1825 Copenhagen V, Denmark. This organisation has branch offices in Europe, Hong Kong and North America, and provides a range of basic tours for student or budget travellers (mostly in the summer). Prices start at US$1095 for a 20-day trip from Helsinki to Yokohama via Leningrad, Moscow, Novosibirsk, Irkutsk, Khabarovsk and Nakhodka.

From China to Europe

Travelling from China to Europe on the Trans-Siberian is easy to organise. All arrangements can be made in Beijing, but it's also possible to book (as far in advance as possible) through agencies in Hong Kong, which will add their fees to the cost of the ticket. Improve your chances by giving alternative dates, and make sure you specify which class you want to travel (deluxe, 1st or 2nd).

Wallem Travel Ltd (tel 5-221144), Suite 202, D'Aguilar Place 7, D'Aguilar St are Intourist booking agents and can obtain Soviet visas from the Soviet embassy in Bangkok. Hong Kong Student Travel Bureau or HKSTB (tel 5-414841), 8/F Tai Sang Bank Building, 130 Des Voeux Rd, Central also arrange Trans- Siberian travel and are agents for SSTS tours. Hong Kong is a good place to stock up on cash US dollars in small denominations, visa photos and any foods you crave for the Siberian crossing.

In Beijing, between seven to 10 days should be allowed for completing all visa and ticket arrangements, providing you're travelling during the quiet end of the season which lasts from December to May.

There are two train routes out of China into the Soviet Union. The Trans-Mongolian train takes about six days to reach Moscow from Beijing and the Trans-Manchurian takes about seven days.

The Trans-Mongolian train is the Chinese service which goes through Mongolia; it runs from Beijing, goes through Datong, crosses the China/Mongolia border at Erlian and carries on to the Soviet Union via Ulan Bator. In terms of overall comfort it is generally rated as preferable to the Russian train.

The Trans-Manchurian train is the Russian service which skirts Mongolia; from Beijing it crosses the China/Soviet border at Manzhouli.

Tickets These can be obtained from the China International Travel Service (CITS) Office in Beijing, which is in the Chongwenmen Hotel (see the section on Beijing for details). Some travellers have successfully made Trans-Siberian reservations at CITS offices in other major cities in China. Book your seat and sleeper on the train before you start getting your visas. Once you have the visas, return to CITS and pay for your ticket. If you intend to travel in the peak periods of June to September (summer) then you should reserve as soon as possible, preferably two months in advance. Provided your visas are in order, a ticket can be made out to virtually any destination served by the USSR railways.

Fares in FEC from Beijing to Moscow on the Trans-Mongolian railway are: deluxe-sleeper Y1017, soft-sleeper Y891, and hard-sleeper Y636. On the Trans-Manchurian railway the prices are as follows: deluxe-sleeper Y1056, soft-sleeper Y900, and hard-sleeper Y661.

Visas The basic rule when getting visas is to start with the final destination and work backwards. Make sure you are well supplied with FEC, cash US dollars in small denominations and passport photos. For details of locations of the foreign embassies, see the section on Beijing.

Most travellers will probably need a Mongolian, Soviet and Polish visa. If you are taking the Trans-Manchurian train (which skirts Mongolia) then you do not need a Mongolian visa. If you intend going to Finland from Moscow then you do not need a Polish visa – but the Soviet Embassy may not issue you a visa unless you have first obtained a Polish visa. If you are taking the Trans-Mongolian train then your Soviet visa can, if you wish, be issued for the day *after* departure from Beijing, thus giving you an extra day in the USSR since the train takes a day to go through Mongolia.

Mongolia The Mongolian Embassy is at 2 Xiushui Beijie, Jianguomenwai Compound. Hours are Monday, Tuesday and Friday from 8 to 10am. Transit visas take between 10 minutes to 24 hours to issue, require three photos, and cost US$18 – in cash. It is possible to break your journey in Ulan Bator for one or two days if you book a room in advance by telex – enquire at the embassy. If you're taking the Trans-Manchurian train then you do not require a Mongolian visa.

USSR The USSR Embassy is just off Dongzhimen, Beizhongjie 4, west of the Sanlitun Embassy Compound. Hours are Monday, Wednesday and Friday from 9 am to 1 pm (the embassy is closed on 7 and 8 November, New Year's Day, 8 March, 1, 2 and 9 May, and 7 October). Transit visas are valid for a maximum of 10 days and tourist visas are required if the journey is broken. Resumption of the journey will require purchase of a costlier Russian ticket. Transit visas are free if you apply over 10 days in advance; anything less than that costs Y20 FEC, possibly more for some nationalities. Transit visas take five days to issue but a cogent reason could speed things up. Three photos are required. The embassy does not keep your passport, so you are free to travel while your application is being processed.

All travel arrangements including overnight stays *have* to be arranged at the embassy and paid for in US dollars. Do not be deterred – theoretically the train should arrive in Moscow in time to catch the connection to Berlin, so it is not imperative to book a horribly expensive hotel room in Moscow – in fact you can sleep in transit in the waiting hall of Belaruski Station (not Yaroslav Station when you arrive), but lock up your bags in the luggage lockers near the hall.

Poland The embassy is at 1 Ritan Lu, Jianguomenwai Compound. Hours are Monday, Wednesday and Friday, 8.30 to 10.30 am in winter; 8 am to noon, and 2 to 5 pm in summer. Transit visas are available in two hours and are valid for two days, require two photos and cost Y26 FEC or Y20 FEC for students. Apparently the visa can also be obtained, more expensively, on the train at the Polish-Soviet border, but this is not certain and may be risky.

Finland The embassy is at 30 Guanghua Lu, Jianguomenwai Compound. Many western nationalities do not require Finnish visas – if in doubt, check.

East Germany The embassy is at 3 Sanlitun Dongsijie, Sanlitun Compound. Hours are Tuesday and Thursday, 9 am to noon. Transit visas are immediately available and cost Y4.50 FEC. It is not necessary to get an East German transit visa in Beijing as you can also obtain one for five German marks on the train when you cross the Polish-East German border.

Food En Route Provisioning on the train is better in summer than in winter. Once the restaurant car has been uncoupled at the Chinese border lean times are in store. Stock up in the car with whatever fuels your system. Reportedly, the brandy they sold for Y5 is readily swapped for 25 roubles by Soviet friends. Better still, the Friendship Store in Beijing is an excellent source of all sorts of goodies like coffee, tea, bread, sausage, cakes, sweets and fruit. Apparently the Russians are uneasy about the California fruit-fly and have been known to dissect incoming fruit at the border. Rolling through the Soviet Union, you'll find that the Russian dining car has an impressive menu but 90% of it is bluff. Station kiosks en route sell buns, stuffed rolls and other food.

Customs On reaching the Chinese border the train's bogies are changed from narrow gauge to broad gauge while passengers wander around the terminus building. A film theatre offers some distraction. You can change renminbi back into foreign currency here, but you'll have to be content with whatever foreign currency happens to be in the sack.

Photography is often tolerated here.

However, Mongolian Customs are very touchy about it and have a reputation for unpredictable reactions. Various stories include annoyance of females alone in compartments, film ripped out of cameras and requests for 'fees'.

At the Soviet border your baggage will be searched. Suspicious literature is usually confiscated. One Dutch guy brought a five-day hoard of reading matter. After a furious argument, two soldiers marched off with his papers, leaving the traveller pining for news – obviously an inability to read Dutch was at the root of the problem. You should be able to buy Russian roubles here. When you enter the Soviet Union you'll be required to produce your foreign currency and fill in a currency-declaration form. Make sure you retain all your bank receipts, as unused roubles can be exchanged for foreign currency at the border on leaving the USSR only if you produce the bank receipts. Check that your finances are in order, as body and baggage searches are rigorous.

Arrival in Moscow The train usually gets into Moscow's Yaroslav Station late – very late if you have encountered blizzards. For those who booked a hotel room the Intourist man will be waiting with a transfer taxi usually included in the hotel price. If you haven't booked, you could try sharing with someone who has. If you want to hire a taxi they are notoriously scarce (although foreign currency helps) and drivers are renowned for stinging the unwary with extravagant prices. Get the price straight first; US dollars work wonders. The metro (underground) is another choice, and providing you obtain some five-kopeck coins and reluctant advice from Intourist, you can find your way to Belaruski Station (for all trains to the west). There is an Intourist office at Belaruski Station (open 9 am to 8 pm) where you can buy tickets to the west. You can sleep on the seats in the huge waiting hall but do not forget to use the luggage lockers, as cameras and gear often disappear.

Stock up on food for the rest of the journey – the restaurant car sometimes disappears at the Polish border where the bogies are changed again. At the Polish border you will have your visas, currency forms and papers scrutinised and your baggage searched (there's a special interest in Russian correspondence intended for the outside world). For those staying a few days in Moscow you'll find students from developing countries very friendly and a mine of information regarding accommodation, food and currency if you're on a low budget.

Arrival in East Berlin Check with the train attendant whether your train goes to West Berlin (Bahnhof Zoo); some trains terminate in East Berlin where it's best to take the underground to Friedrichstrasse to cross into the west. This border crossing shuts late in the evening and if it is closed then you can trudge off to Checkpoint Charlie. In case you feel like waiting until early morning, just down the road from Friedrichstrasse there is a palatial, exorbitantly priced hotel with an all-night bar above a gleaming foyer serving, among other things, frankfurters and coffee. You may also witness the bouncer of unbelievable stature in action against an irritating, midget Glaswegian.

Arrival in West Berlin (Bahnhof Zoo) Whether you feel a sense of elation or deflation, West Berlin is definitely the west. At the station, there's a *bureau de change* with a 24-hour machine which takes a Eurocheque card and dispenses Deutschmarks. Amble down the Kuhdam (*the* shopping street) and observe the shops bulging with wares while stout ladies spoon double portions of cream into their coffee.

For a cheap place to stay, try the *Jugendgästehaus (Youth Hostel* (tel 2611097), Kluckstrasse 3, Tiergarten. The Mitfahrerzentrale (tel 6939101) at Willibald-Alexis Strasse 11 offers a cheap service for lifts all over Europe. From the Busbahnhof at Masurenallee (almost opposite the Kongresszentrum ICC) excellent buses run to most major German cities and offer reductions for student-card holders. Onward train connections are available from Bahnhof Zoo. For those under 26 the Transalpino tickets are recommended.

Unless you travel in a group, the selection of travelling companions for the journey is delightfully or excruciatingly random – a judgment upon which you have five or six days to ponder. A couple of years ago the 1st and 2nd-class carriages included a Dutch bargee returning from a stint as an au pair in Beijing; an all-American college boy who nonplussed all he met with his staggering naïvety; a know-all American college girl with innocent looks and a bulldozing intellect; a gracious Polish diplomatic couple; two Chinese students returning to Sweden to study Swedish; and a Chinese diplomat returning to Moscow. The Dutchman indulged in chain-smoking and a pungent style of clothing which was too much for the Chinese family in his compartment – they beat a hasty retreat before the train had even pulled out of Beijing station.

On the trip you can get stuck in the cross-fire of American Ivy League debates on baseball, or watch a bunch of earnest Germans solemnly catalogue, photograph and test everything for seminars in Frankfurt. The discussions rage or drag on past Naushki, Krasnojarsk – some retreat to chess games, epic novels or epic paralytic drinking bouts, or teach English to the train attendant – or they might just stare at mile after mile of melancholic birch trees as twilight descends.

At sub-zero temperatures you can exercise along the platform, start snowball fights or wonder about the destination of teenage recruits milling around a troop train; one recruit had a guitar with a Beatles sticker over one shoulder and a gun over the other. A chess set soon makes friends. The Russians produce not only talented players but also courteous ones – perhaps as a gesture of friendship they'll quickly cede the first game but the rest are won with monotonous regularity. Prodigious amounts of alcohol disappear down Russian throats, so expect a delighted interest in consuming your hoard of Chinese alcohol – for which there is plenty of time. On the other hand, if you want to repulse freeloaders you might try injecting them with a bottle of one of those ghastly Chinese liqueurs – the recipient is either going to stagger out in absolute revulsion or remain vaccinated and your stock is doomed.

For those interested in barter or fund-raising: tea, watches, jeans and Walkman cassette recorders are all sources of inspiration to passengers. Various sombre figures parade down the train corridors so use your discretion as to the extent and type of transaction. Import of roubles is forbidden, as is changing money on the black market (at rates of up to five times the official rate).

Getting Around

AIR

CAAC – Civil Aviation Administration of China – is China's domestic and international carrier. Its flights cover about 80 cities and towns throughout the country. For details of international flights, see the Getting There section.

Timetables

CAAC publishes a combined international and domestic timetable in both English and Chinese in April and November each year. It's almost impossible to get a copy in China, but they're readily available from the CAAC office in Hong Kong (ground floor, Gloucester Tower, des Voeux Rd, Central District, Hong Kong Island, tel 5-216416). The timetable also comes in useful as a phrasebook of Chinese place-names.

Fares

Foreigners pay a surcharge of 100 to 160% of the fare charged local Chinese. Unlike the situation with trains, there is no way past this CAAC regulation, except perhaps for foreign experts. If you do somehow happen to get Chinese price and it's discovered, your ticket will be confiscated and no refund given. Children over 12 are charged adult fare.

Cancellation fees depend on how long before departure you cancel. On domestic flights if you cancel 24 hours before departure you lose 10% of the fare; if you cancel between two and 24 hours before the flight you lose 20%; and if you cancel less than two hours before the flight you lose 50%. If you don't show up for a domestic flight, your ticket is cancelled and there is no refund.

Baggage

On domestic and international flights the free baggage allowance for an adult passenger is 20 kg in economy class and 30 kg in 1st class. You are also allowed five kg of hand luggage, though this is rarely weighed.

Stand-by

This does exist on CAAC flights. Some seats are always reserved in case a high-ranking cadre turns up at the last moment. If no one shows up it should be possible to get on board.

Airport Tax

There is no airport tax on domestic flights. On international flights there is an airport tax of Y15.

Service

Basically there is none. On international flights there is a concerted attempt to keep up appearances though, and the hostesses have spiffy uniforms and make-up and get their training in Japan – which makes for a pleasanter flight. On domestic flights you'll probably be given a little bag or two of sweets, or a key-ring as a souvenir – almost justifies the 100% tourist surcharge.

Other Airlines

At the time of writing the Chinese government had plans in the pipeline to establish a number of airlines independent of CAAC. These new airlines will fly both domestic and international routes, including services

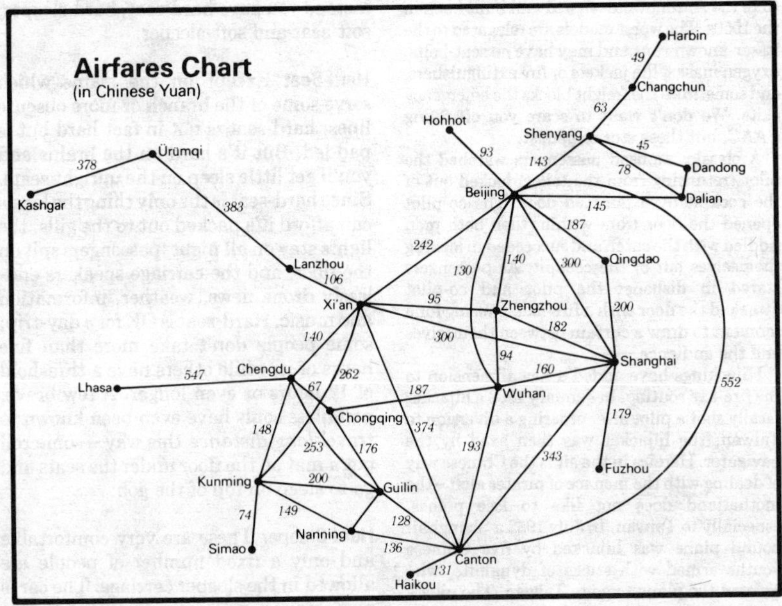

to Japan, Hong Kong and South-East Asia. Sometime in the life-span of this book you might find yourself flying around China on an airline other than CAAC. Whether this will also mean price competition is unknown, but it could improve the frequency of services on some under-catered routes.

Tales of the Unexpected

CAAC also stands for China Airlines Always Cancels (the usual excuse is bad weather), but more importantly, China Airlines Almost Crashes. The airline's safety record appears to be a poor one – but no information on crashes or incidents is released unless there are foreigners on board. Probably one of the worst accidents was a crash in April 1982 near Guilin which killed 112 people. CAAC profits in 1982 were estimated at about US$120 million but it seems little of that went into maintenance, equipment, upgrading the vintage planes or purchasing new aircraft. Things are improving on some runs. There are Boeing 737s out of Canton, and 707s and 747s out of Beijing and Shanghai. Yun-5, Yun-7 and Yun-10 jets (made-in-Xian copies of western aircraft) have come into service.

Riding through the clouds, I picked up CAAC's marvellous in-flight magazine, a glossy produced in Japan. It's full of heroic folk tales about air crews and their flawless safety records, doctored folk tales, how the attendant at a CAAC hostel in Beijing found a million yen and rushed after the passenger to whom it belonged. There are even some safety tips – if you put enough magazines together you could figure out where the exits were, since the stewardess did not dwell upon the ceremony. My attention was drawn by an unusual piece of airline photography – a passenger evacuating a meal into a paper bag held by a hostess. One of the passenger's testimonials read, 'Having travelled around the world twice, we have never heard of asking passengers to move from the front to the back because the plane was too heavy! If it is truly that risky the plane should not be flown!'

The basic problem with CAAC is old technology. For the international runs they use nice, relatively new Boeings. But on the domestic runs it's sometimes old Russian turbo-props (like the Antonovs) designed and built back in the 1950s. The worst models are relegated to the lesser-known runs and may have no seat-belts, oxygen masks, life jackets or fire extinguishers, and sometimes the freight blocks the emergency exits. We don't want to scare you off flying CAAC, but these stories persist.

A classic: amused passengers watched the pilot (returning from the toilet) locked out of the cockpit by a jammed door. The co-pilot opened the door from within, then both men fiddled with the catch and succeeded in locking themselves out of the cockpit. As passengers stared in disbelief the pilot and co-pilot attacked the door with a fire-axe, pausing for a moment to draw a curtain between themselves and the audience.

Hijackings have added a new dimension to the fire-axe routine. In January 1983 a hijacker fatally shot a pilot after ordering a diversion to Taiwan; the hijacker was then axed by the navigator. Heroics in the air is the Chinese way of dealing with the menace of pirates aloft – the motherland does not like to lose planes, especially to Taiwan. In July 1982 a Shanghai-bound plane was hijacked by five Chinese youths armed with sticks of dynamite, who ordered the plane to go to Taiwan. The pilot's response was to fly around in circles until the fuel was almost exhausted, whereupon the crew led passengers in an attack on the pirates with umbrellas and mop handles. The CAAC version of this near-calamity reads, 'The heroic deeds of the crew . . . showed the firm standpoint of their love for the Party and our socialist motherland . . . they feared no sacrifice . . . ' The captain of the flight was awarded a special title created by the State Council – 'anti-hijacking hero'. Similar honours were bestowed on the crew of a plane hijacked to South Korea on 5 May 1983.

RAIL

Trains are the best way to get around in reasonable speed and comfort. The network covers every province except Tibet, and that's next. There are an estimated 52,000 km of rail in China, most of them built since 1949 when the system had either been blown to bits or was non-existent in certain regions.

Classes

In socialist China there are no classes; instead you have hard-seat, hard-sleeper, soft-seat and soft-sleeper.

Hard-Seat Except on the trains which serve some of the branch or more obscure lines, hard-seat is not in fact hard but is padded. But it's hard on the brains and you'll get little sleep on the upright seats. Since hard-seat is the only thing the locals can afford it's packed out to the gills, the lights stay on all night, passengers spit on the floor, and the carriage speakers endlessly drone news, weather, information and music. Hard-seat is OK for a day-trip; some people don't take more than five hours of it, while others have a threshold of 12 hours or even longer. A few brave, penniless souls have even been known to travel *long-distance* this way – some roll out a mat on the floor under the seats and go to sleep on top of the gob.

Hard-Sleeper These are very comfortable and only a fixed number of people are allowed in the sleeper carriage. The car is made up of doorless compartments with a half dozen bunks in three tiers, and sheets, pillows and blankets are provided. It does very nicely as an overnight hotel. The best bunk to get is a middle one since the lower one is invaded by all and sundry who use it as a seat during the day, while the top one has little head-room. The worst possible bunks are the top ones at either end of the car or right in the middle; they're right up against the speakers and you'll get a rude shock in the morning about 6 am. Lights and speakers in hard-sleeper go out at around 9.30 to 10 pm. Few ordinary Chinese can afford hard-sleeper; those who use it are either the new class of nouveau-riche, or city folk on their way to one conference or other whose travel is being paid for by the state.

Soft-Seat On shorter journeys (such as Shenzhen to Canton) some trains have soft-seat carriages. The seats are a bit like reclining aeroplane seats and are used by higher-ranking cadres. They cost about the same as hard-sleeper and you may consider them if there are no hard-sleepers available or if you just want a break from everyone.

Soft-Sleeper Luxury. Softies get the works with four comfortable bunks in a closed compartment – complete with straps to stop the top fatso from falling off in the middle of the night. Wood panelling, potted plant, lace curtains, teacup set, clean washrooms, carpets (so no spitting), and many times air-conditioning. As for those speakers, not only do you have a volume control, you can turn the bloody things off! The carriages appear to be of East German origin. Soft-sleeper costs twice as much as hard-sleeper and is worth trying once to experience the height of bourgeois decadence in egalitarian China.

Train Types

Train composition varies from line to line and also from day to night, and largely depends on the demand for sleepers on that line. A typical high-frequency train line has about 13 carriages: six hard-seat, perhaps one soft-seat, three hard-sleeper, one soft-sleeper, one dining car and one guard/baggage car.

Half or even a whole car may be devoted to crew quarters on the longer trips. If the journey time is more than 12 hours then the train qualifies as a dining car. The dining car often separates the hard-seat cars from the hard-sleeper and soft-sleeper carriages.

The conductor is in a little booth in a hard-seat car at the middle of the train – usually car 7, 8 or 9 (all carriages are numbered on the outside). Coal-fired samovars are found in the ends of the hard-class sections, and from these you can draw a supply of hot water. The disc-jockey has a little booth at the end of one of the cars with a door marked *Boyinshi* which, apart from the reel-to-reel tape, radio and record-player, also contains the attendant's bed.

On some of the small branch lines there are various kinds of passenger carriages – some have long bench seats along the walls, others are just cattle cars without seats or windows.

Different types of train are usually recognised by the train number:

Nos 1 to 90 are special express and usually diesel-hauled. They have all classes and there is a surcharge for the speed and superior facilities. The international trains are included in this group.

Nos 100 to 350 Trains in this approximate number range make more stops than the special expresses. They have soft and hard-sleepers, but fewer of them. The speed surcharge is half that of the special expresses but the difference in overall price is minimal.

Nos 400 & 500 are slow, and stop at everything they can find. They may have hard wooden seats and no sleepers. They should have soft-seats, but these will be equivalent to the hard-seats on the fast trains. The trains have antique fittings, lamps and wood panelling, and are usually steam-pulled. There is no speed surcharge as there is no speed.

No 700 trains are suburban routes.

Apart from the speed breakdown, the numbers don't really tell you much else about the train. As a general rule, the outbound and inbound trains have matching numbers; thus train Nos 79/80 divide into No 79 leaving Shanghai and going to Kunming, and No 80 leaving Kunming and going to Shanghai. However, there are for example at least six different trains listed in the Chinese train timetable under 301/302, and the sequence-number match is not always the case. Trains also appear to shift numbers from one timetable to the following year's timetable, so train 175 becomes train 275. Simple.

The following is a tourist price rail ticket; the ticket is for a hard seat on train No. 143 from Wuhan to Yueyang. The train travels a total distance of 238 railway kilometres and the ticket is valid for two days. Total price is Y8.60, of which Y1.40 is the express train supplement. The triangular-bottomed stamp in the bottom right-hand corner of the ticket shows the train number and the time of departure.

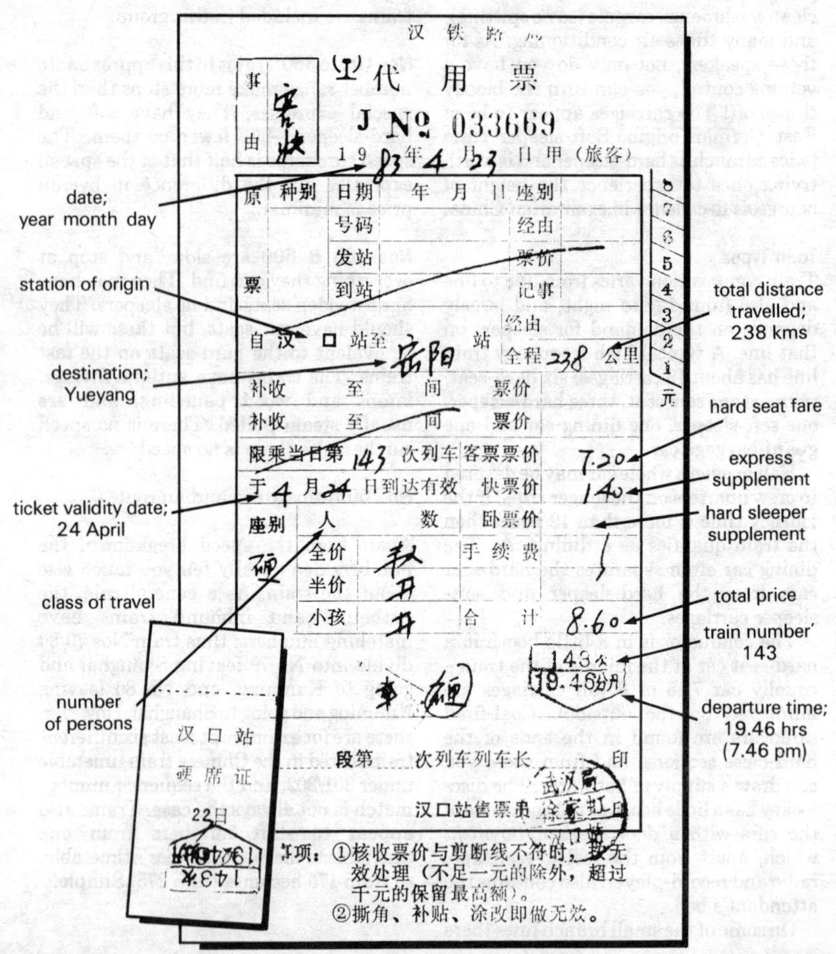

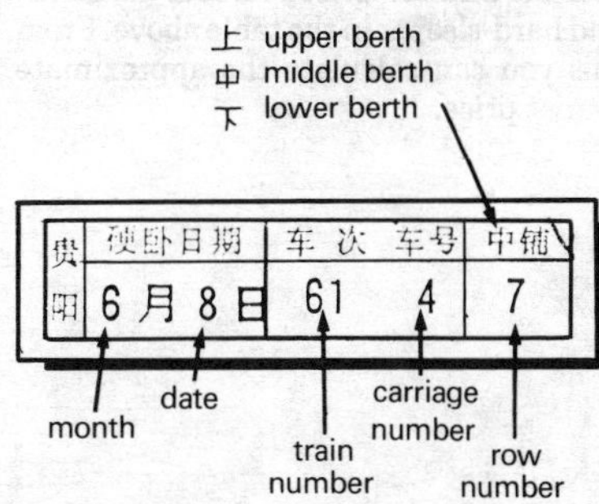

If a sleeper had been reserved at the time of booking, an additional sticker would have been attached to the ticket, showing date of travel, train number, carriage number and position of the sleeper.

Prices

Calculation of train prices is a complex affair based on the length of the journey, speed of the train and relative position of the sun and moon. There are a few variables such as air-con charges, whether a child occupies a berth or not – but nothing worth worrying about. The express surcharge is the same regardless of what class you use on the train.

The most important thing to remember is the double-pricing system on Chinese trains. Most foreigners are required to pay 75% more than People's Republic Chinese for their rail tickets. Other fares apply to Overseas Chinese, Chinese students, foreign students and foreign experts in China. (All train fares mentioned in this book are standard tourist-price.)

Trains are definitely cheaper than either long-distance buses or planes, but if you get a tourist-price soft-sleeper then the gap between train and air travel narrows considerably. Often the difference is so small that, given the savings in time and trouble, it's definitely worth considering flying.

Tourist price is the real crunch – it will clean your wallet out. Higher prices for foreign tourists in the hotels can be justified to some extent since the facilities and the quality of the accommodation are far better than in Chinese hotels. But on the trains and planes this doesn't apply, so the tourist pricing is purely a profit-making venture. In hard-seat there is absolutely no reason why you should pay more to ride in the same agony!

Calculating Ticket Prices The table below gives some typical Chinese prices. The hard-sleeper supplement is for a middle berth. The special express supplement applies to train Nos 1 to 90. The last column shows the total price of a hard-sleeper ticket for a journey, obtained by adding the first three columns.

rail km	*hard-seat*	*hard-sleeper supplement*	*special express charge*	*hard-sleeper total*
110	2.40	5.40	1.00	8.80
320	5.40	5.40	2.10	12.90
580	9.30	7.30	3.60	20.20
1020	14.70	11.50	5.80	32.00
1660	21.20	16.70	8.30	46.20
2020	24.50	19.20	9.60	53.30
3060	35.50	27.90	13.90	77.30
5100	57.30	103.19	22.50	125.60
6000	67.00	121.60	26.30	147.00

Train fares are related to distance travelled, so it's possible to calculate the fare you would expect to pay for any particular journey. An example of the calculation of a tourist-price fare is shown below:

Route: Beijing to Nanchang
Train: No 146
Distance: 2005 rail km

On the above table the rail distance closest to 2005 is 2020. Train No 146 is ordinary express, so halve the special express charge for 2020 km; the ordinary express charge is now Y4.80. So the hard-sleeper Chinese fare = Y24.50 + Y19.20 + Y4.80 = Y48.50 (middle berth). Tourist price of Y48.50 + 75% = about Y84.

The distances in km travelled by rail are shown in the tables below for some of China's major cities. To calculate the approximate cost of your rail ticket, look up the appropriate distance table, and then find the Chinese-priced fare for hard-seat and hard-sleeper in the table above. From this you can calculate the approximate tourist price.

Distances by rail (km) – Major Cities

Beijing	*Bei*										
Shanghai	1462	*Shan*									
Canton	2313	1811	*Can*								
Changsha	1587	1187	726	*Chan*							
Wuhan	1229	1534	1084	358	*Wuha*						
Nanjing	1157	305	2116	1492	1229	*Nanj*					
Qingdao	887	1361	2677	1951	1593	1056	*Qin*				
Xian	1165	1511	2129	1403	1045	1206	1570	*Xian*			
Kunming	3179	2677	2216	1592	1950	2982	3512	1942	*Kunm*		
Chengdu	2048	2353	2544	1920	1887	2048	2412	842	1100	*Chen*	
Chongqing	2552	2501	2040	1416	1774	2552	2916	1346	1102	504	*Chon*
Zhengzhou	695	1000	1618	892	534	695	1059	511	2453	1353	1857

Distances by rail (km) – Eastern Provinces

Hangzhou	*Han*									
Shanghai	189	*Shan*								
Suzhou	275	86	*Suz*							
Wuxi	317	128	42	*Wux*						
Nanjing	494	305	219	177	*Nanj*					
Shaoxing	60	249	335	377	554	*Shao*				
Nanchang	636	825	911	953	1130	59	*Nanc*			
Fuzhou	972	1161	1247	1289	1466	990	622	*Fuz*		
Xiamen	1187	1376	1462	1504	1681	1247	838	603	*Xia*	
Canton	1633	1811	1897	1936	2116	1640	1042	1608	1834	*Cant*
Beijing	1651	1462	1376	1334	1157	1711	2005	2623	2838	2313

Distances by rail (km) – South-West Provinces

Beijing	*Bei*										
Shanghai	1462	*Sha*									
Nanchang	2005	825	*Nan*								
Wuhan	1229	1545	776	*Wuh*							
Zhuzhou	1638	1136	367	409	*Zhu*						
Canton	2313	1811	1042	1084	675	*Can*					
Liuzhou	2310	1808	1039	1081	672	1079	*Liu*				
Nanning	2565	2063	1294	1336	927	1334	255	*Nann*			
Chengdu	2048	2353	2236	1887	1869	2544	1574	1829	*Che*		
Chongqing	2552	2501	1732	1774	1365	2040	1070	1325	504	*Cho*	
Guiyang	2540	2038	1269	1311	902	1577	607	862	967	463	*Guiy*
Kunming	3179	2677	1908	1950	1541	2216	1246	1501	1100	1102	639
Guilin	2134	–	–	–	–	903	176	–	–	–	–

Distances by rail (km) - North-Eastern Provinces

Beijing	*Bei*										
Tianjin	137	*Tia*									
Jinzhou	599	462	*Jinz*								
Shenyang	841	704	242	*Shen*							
Changchun	1146	1009	547	305	*Chan*						
Harbin	1388	1251	789	547	242	*Har*					
Qiqihar	1448	1311	849	760	530	288	*Qiq*				
Jilin	1287	1150	688	446	128	275	563	*Jil*			
Dandong	1118	981	519	277	582	824	1037	723	*Dan*		
Dalian	1238	1101	639	397	702	944	1157	84	674	*Dal*	
Jinan	494	357	819	1061	1366	1608	1668	1507	1338	1458	*Jin*
Jiamusi	1894	-	-	-	-	506	-	-	-	-	-
Mudanjiang	-	-	-	-	-	357	-	-	-	-	-

Distances by rail (km) - North-West Regions

Beijing	*Bei*						
Zhengzhou	695	*Zhen*					
Xian	1165	511	*Xian*				
Lanzhou	1813	1187	676	*Lan*			
Xining	2098	1403	892	216	*Xini*		
Ürümqi	3774	3079	2568	1892	2108	*Ürüm*	
Hohhot	668	1363	1292	1145	1361	3037	*Hoh*
Yinchuan	1346	1654	1143	467	683	2359	678

Getting Cheaper Tickets Getting a Chinese-priced ticket is possible but becoming more difficult. Officially the only foreigners entitled to local Chinese-priced tickets are foreign students studying in the People's Republic or in Taiwan (which is considered part of China), and probably foreign experts working in China.

In the past travellers have been using all sorts of impressive-looking 'student cards' or made-in-Hong Kong imitations to pass themselves off as students. Although more railway stations are catching on to these tricks, it's surprising how often they still work; many people report a high success rate.

Other people have asked Overseas Chinese, Hong Kongers or local Chinese to buy tickets for them, since these people also get the lower prices – but that method could get a local Chinese into trouble. Sometimes one railway station in a town will refuse to sell a Chinese-price ticket, but another one will. Or when CITS and CTS are located in the same place they can get their wires crossed and issue Chinese-priced tickets.

Some railway workers don't care if you get a Chinese-priced ticket. However, if you do get such a ticket the conductor on the train can still charge you the full fare, or you could be stopped at the railway station exit gate at your destination, have your tickets checked and be charged the full fare.

Hang on to your Chinese-priced tickets, as they'll count in your favour when you have to wrangle for another one at the next station. Another thing – before you argue at the railway station, ask yourself if it's really worth it. For short hauls it's hardly worth the hassle.

Some train stations have solved the problem by setting up separate booking

The following is a Chinese price rail ticket; the ticket is for a hard seat on train No. 304 from Shanghai to Nanjing. Total price is Y6.50. The sticker attached to the rear of the ticket shows the train number, departure time, date of travel, and the reserved seat number.

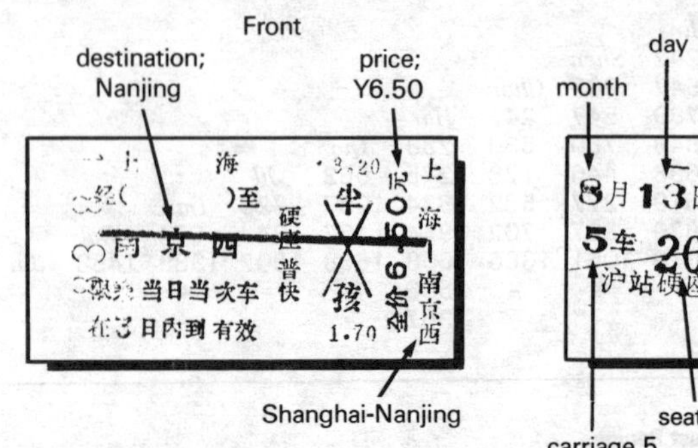

offices for foreigners. As a rule they'll charge you tourist price, though you can sometimes wrangle local price. On the credit side, you don't have to wait in formidable queues and you can often get a sleeper – so if you do have to pay tourist price stop bitching and consider your money well spent!

Tickets & Reservations

Tourist-price tickets are slips of paper with various details scribbled all over them. Chinese-price tickets are little stubs of cardboard. Getting either can be one of the most frustrating exercises you'll undertake in China.

Tickets can be bought in advance from CITS and CTS offices (usually attached to the major tourist hotels), from advance booking offices of which there may be several in a large city, and sometimes from separate booking offices for foreigners in the train stations. These places will usually issue tickets one to several days in advance.

You can buy tickets the night before departure or on the day of departure from the railway station. This involves queues – long queues – towards the tail they follow a traditional queue configuration, but at the front they can bulge with queue jumpers, people buying tickets for people 10 metres back, others unable to extricate themselves from the jumble. Some stations are better than others. When purchasing a hard-seat ticket for a train originating at the same station but the following day, insist on a numbered seat reservation. It often takes several requests to motivate the seller. Tickets bought on the same day will usually be unreserved – you get on board and try and find a place for your bum.

If you get on the train with an unreserved seating ticket, you can seek out the conductor and upgrade yourself to a hard-sleeper if there are any available. On some trains it's easy to get a sleeper but others are notoriously crowded (like the Shanghai-Kunming express). A lot of intermediary stations along the rail lines can't issue sleepers, so you just have to buy a hard-seat ticket, hop on the train and hope like everybody else. If the sleeper carriages are full then you may have to wait until someone gets off. That sleeper may only be available to you until the next major station which is allowed to issue sleepers, but you may be able to get several hours of sleep. The sleeper price will be calculated for the distance that you used it for.

Another possibility is not to bother with a ticket at all and simply walk on to the train. This is difficult – railway stations in China are well controlled, and you're not too likely to get on board without a ticket. Still, it could be worth a try . . . then go and see the conductor and get a ticket. One way of getting onto the platform is to buy a *zhantaipiao* (a platform ticket), available from the station's information kiosk for a few fen.

If you're buying a ticket from the railway station or an advance booking office, then you should write down clearly on a piece of paper what you want: train number, time, date, class of travel. The appropriate characters and phrases can be copied from a phrasebook. Learn a few key phrases like 'tomorrow' and 'hard-sleeper'. English-speaking Chinese are always willing to translate and there are usually one or two around in the larger places.

If you have a sleeper ticket the carriage attendant will take it from you and give you a metal or plastic chit – when your destination is close she will swap it back and give you the original ticket. Keep your ticket until you get through the barriers at the other end, as you'll need to show it there.

Ticket Validity Tickets are valid from one to seven days depending on the distance travelled. On a cardboard ticket the number of days is printed at the bottom left-hand corner. If you go 250 km it's valid for two days; 500 km, three days; 1000 km, three days; 2000 km, six days; about 2500 km, seven days.

Thus if you're travelling along a major line you could buy one ticket and break the journey where you feel like it. This will only work for unreserved seating though – that is, hard-seat. When you leave the train the station may be able to sell you a hard-sleeper ticket. If not you'll have to try and get one from the conductor when you reboard.

The advantage of this method is that you can keep away from railway ticket windows for a while. When you buy a ticket get one for special express so that you can take both special and ordinary express trains after that. They may quibble if you use an ordinary express ticket to ride a special-express train (though that would only be a case of paying a couple of yuan as a supplement).

An ideal route for trying such a ticket is the Shanghai-Nanjing line, a 305-km route, where you could get off at Wuxi, Suzhou and Changzhou, and continue on to Nanjing all on the one ticket. Because these places are very close together you needn't worry about sleepers – it takes only one or two hours to travel between each point.

There are a few more advantages to this system. If you miss a train you do not need to get a refund and book a new ticket (unless your ticket is only valid for one day and there is no other train within that period). If you're unable to get a sleeper and are sick of sitting hard-seat you can get off, find a refreshing hotel, and get back on board the next day on the same ticket. It also allows you to pass through cities or towns where it's difficult to get Chinese-price tickets. If you get sick – and can prove it – the ticket validity period is extendable.

Food

Cheapest meals are the 'rice boxes' brought down the carriages on trolleys and distributed to those who previously bought meal tickets. Tickets are sold by one of the train staff who walks through the train shortly before the trolley comes through. The boxes of rice, meat and vegetables cost around Y1 – filling, though some travellers have got the runs off them.

Trains on longer journeys have dining cars. Meals cost a couple of yuan. For breakfast you've got a choice of soup and maybe two plates of meat and/or vegetables, with cheap noodles for breakfast. There is a separate sitting for passengers in the soft-class carriages – as a foreigner you can join in even if you're in hard-class, and sometimes you can get a western breakfast. Some foreigners have been charged excessive prices for food ordered after the main sitting – check the price first.

After about 8 pm when meals are over you can probably wander back into the dining car. The staff may want to get rid of you, but if you just sit down and have a beer it may be OK. One Chinese-speaking traveller recalled getting drunk in the dining car with the train crew, one of whom stood up and loudly cursed the powers that be, saying they were all rotten to the core. He was threatened with ejection from the train at the next stop if he didn't sit down and shut up!

It's worth stocking up with your own supplies for long train trips – particularly if you're an obsessive nibbler. Jam, biscuits and fruit juice can be bought at department stores beforehand. If you like coffee or tea then bring your own – the trains have boilers at the end of the hard-class carriages. Sometimes the dining car will have canned fruit for sale, even whole chickens in plastic bags. At station stops you can buy food from the vendors.

Timetables
There are paperback rail timetables in both Chinese and English, but it's a drag working your way through them. Most people don't bother. Thinner versions listing the major trains can sometimes be bought from hawkers outside the railway stations. Hotel reception desks and CITS offices have copies of the timetable for trains out of their city or town. Thomas Cook publishes an overseas railway timetable, which includes China – single copies are expensive but you might get a xerox of the relevant pages from your friendly neighbourhood travel agent.

Train Stations
Once you have your ticket, you hang around in the railway station's waiting room, or in a designated area in the smaller stations outside. A sign is always put up with the train number and destination telling passengers where to line up. If you can't find the right line or the right waiting room, show your ticket to one of the railway staff.

If the horde of starers in the waiting room is annoying, you can usually head to the soft-class waiting rooms, which you'll often be able to use even if you've got a hard-class ticket. These soft-class waiting rooms can also serve as overnight hotels if you arrive at some disgusting hour of the morning; the staff may let you sleep there until 5 or 6 am, when you can get a bus to the hotel. You might also be able to shack up here if you arrive in or are in transit through a place closed to foreigners. Some soft-class waiting rooms require a 50 fen ticket which includes free tea.

Just about all railway stations have *xingli jicun chu* (left-luggage rooms) where you can safely dump your bags for a few mao.

Smile – It Helps
As far as foreigners are concerned many railway staff in China are exceedingly polite and can be very helpful – particularly if you look like a lost orphan. Sometimes they'll give you their own train seats – on one occasion I was allowed to

use the special car reserved for the rail staff sleepers until they found another place for me. So it helps to be nice.

In Jinan, two of us boarded a train with hard-seats to Qingdao – it was about 10 pm and the lights had gone out in the hard-sleeper section so the conductor took us into the soft compartment to write out an upgraded ticket for the hard-sleeper. Well, those soft bunks looked real nice at that hour. My friend stretched out on a bunk and indicated that it would do just fine – the conductor looked in amazement, motioning that the hard-sleepers were a few cars off – finally he gave up and let us have soft-class for Y5 each. Quite a bargain! It's China all over – one moment you're down in the dumps, the next you're up in the soft-department clouds.

BUS

Long-distance buses are one of the best means of getting around the country. Services are extensive and main roads are usually good though you'll get your fair share of rough rides. Nevertheless, since the buses stop every so often in small towns and villages you get to see bits of the countryside you wouldn't otherwise see if you only travelled on the trains. The symbol for a bus is:

Bus travel is not especially cheap when compared to hard-seats on trains. It will probably cost slightly more, too, but you have to take into account that there is no double-pricing system on buses. So if it's a choice between a tourist-price hard-seat ticket on the train and a bus ticket then the bus might come out slightly cheaper. As a rule of thumb, buses work out to around Y1 for every hour of travelling time.

It's a good idea to book a seat in advance. All seats are numbered. Buses depart from separate bus stations which are often large affairs with numerous ticket windows and waiting halls. The symbol for a bus station is:

汽车站

One disadvantage is the Chinese roads. Those that run along the railway lines are in better condition, but away from the rails a lot of them are just wide dirt tracks (one exception is Shandong Province, which has an extensive surfaced road network), although much road improvement seems to be going on.

If possible, try to avoid sitting at the rear of the bus since it's painful for the shock-absorbers in your back – and try to avoid the front since the noise from the engine and the multiple horns will drive you mad. Chinese law requires a driver to announce his presence to cyclists, and for this he uses a tweeter for preliminaries, a bugle or bullhorn if he gets annoyed and an ear-wrenching air-horn if he really gets stirred up.

Astronaut-type backpacks are a near-disaster to stow on buses – there's little space under the seats, no overhead racks, and sparse space in the aisles. If you intend doing a lot of bus travelling then travel light! In China, unlike other Asian countries, people do not ride on the roof – though luggage is sometimes stowed there.

Buses do not travel at night; about eight to 14 hours a day appears to be the

A local bus
China Daily, 13 November, 1986

maximum driving time. This includes a short lunch-break and assumes that there are no breakdowns; some of the geriatric models are prone to relapses on longer trips, but you'll be amazed how the old crates keep going. If the trip is a long one you'll overnight at a hotel en route and the bus will carry on the next morning.

BICYCLE

What the car is to the west, the bicycle is to China – the main mode of private transport. There are collective trucks, chauffeured cadre limos and private motorcycles, but the bicycle is still king of the road. There are over 220 million bikes in China, with some exported to Burma and India. Production can never keep up with demand because the Chinese will do anything to lay their hands on one rather than be at the mercy of the bus system. The bicycle is a workhorse, carrying anything up to a 100-kg slaughtered pig or a whole couch . . . you name it. Bikes are expensive – they're expected to last 15 years.

A bike licence is obligatory for Chinese but is not necessary for a foreigner. Some cities have bicycle licence plates, and in Beijing bikes owned by foreigners have special licence plates so they can't be sold to a Chinese. If a person has an accident or is drunk while riding a bike, a fine can be imposed and the bike impounded (there are posters to this effect in Chinese cities). Police also occasionally stop cyclists to do spot-checks on the brakes and other equipment. Bike-repair shops are everywhere and repairs are dirt cheap (say 50 fen per shot).

Useful Words

saddle	*zùo dīàn*	坐垫
brakes	*shā chē*	刹车
tyre	*wài tāi*	夕胎
inner tyre	*nèi tāi*	内胎
wheel	*lún*	轮
air	*qì*	气
pump	*dáqìtóng*	打气筒
broken	*huàilě*	坏了
flat (tyre)	*meí yōu qì*	没有气
mend	*xīulǐ*	修理
stolen	*toū diaò le*	偷掉了
lock	*sǔo*	锁
adjust	*gǎi*	改

Rental

Bicycles are definitely the best way of getting around Chinese cities, even to get away from them. The cities are built for bikes – long, wide avenues flat as pancakes (one exception is hilly Chongqing where there's hardly a bike in sight) so even those heavy gearless monsters ride OK. There are now established bicycle rentals dealing with foreigners in many tourist centres. Some bicycle rentals are attached to Chinese hotels or operate out of an independent rental shop, of which there are many.

Day rental, 24-hour rental or rental by the hour are the norm. It's possible to rent for a stretch of several days, so touring is possible if the bike is in good condition. Rates for westerners are creeping up to Y6 per day – some places are more expensive depending on the competition.

If you rent over a long period you should be able to reduce the rate. Most rental places will ask you to leave some sort of I.D. Sometimes they ask for your passport, which is asking a lot. Give them some other I.D. instead, like a student card or a driver's licence. Some rentals may require a deposit, but that should certainly not be more than the actual value of the bike.

Before taking a bike, check the brakes (are there any?) and get the tyres pumped up hard – and make sure that none of the moving parts are about to fall off. Get the saddle raised to maximum leg-power. It's also worth tying something on – a handkerchief for example – to identify your bicycle amidst the zillions at the bicycle parks.

Parking

In the cities bicycles are parked at designated places. Bicycle-park attendants will give you a token when you park; the charge is usually two or three fen.

In China bicycles can be 'towed' just as illegally parked cars can be in the west; one traveller who didn't use the parking lots finally found his bike at the police station – and was fined 30 fen!

Accidents

As for accidents, there are plenty of picture displays around Chinese cities showing what happened to cyclists who didn't look where they were going and got creamed – and I mean creamed! These displays also give tips on how to avoid accidents and show 're-education classes' for offenders who have had several accidents.

If you keep your eyes peeled and your head alert you shouldn't have an accident; after you get over the shock of seeing the old lady up front balancing a boxed TV set over her rear wheel and a couple of chickens off the front handlebars it shouldn't be too difficult. Many of the larger towns and cities have separate bicycle lanes on each side of the main streets.

Night riding is particularly hazardous

A Package Deal?
China Daily, 1 April, 1986

though – the only time buses and cars use their headlights is to flash them on and off to warn cyclists up ahead to get out of the way – so if you do ride at night watch out for the motorised monsters. On country roads look out for those Mad Max-style walking tractors; often they have no headlights.

One traffic hazard is the cyclists who spot you, glide by staring gape-mouthed, crash into something in front and cause the traffic behind to topple like ten-pins.

Theft

Bicycle theft does exist. The bicycle parks with their attendants help prevent this, but keep your bike off the streets at night, at least within the hotel gates. If the hotel has no grounds then take it up the elevator to your room. Most rented bicycles have a lock around the rear wheel which nimble fingers can pick in seconds. You can increase security by buying and using a cable lock, widely available from shops in China.

Touring

Probably the first time the Chinese saw a pneumatic-tyred bicycle was when a pair of globe-trotting Americans bumbled into Beijing around 1891 after a three-year journey from Istanbul. They wrote a book about it called *Across Asia on a Bicycle* by Allen & Sachtleben. The novelty was well-received by the Qing court, and the boy-emperor Puyi was given to tearing around the Forbidden City on a cycle.

Modern Chinese are great bicycle

tourists. An 85-year-old martial arts expert has spent three years pedalling over 16,000 km across China and plans to continue for another three years. A retired Chinese couple did 10,000 km from Gansu to Guangdong in two years; a 69-year-old retired worker set off on a self-made tricycle the back of which could be converted into a bed and kitchen!

Organised bicycle tours for groups have operated in China since the beginning of 1981. The range of tours has been extended to include the Silk Road, Inner Mongolia and Tibet.

For bike tours around Guangdong, Guangxi and Hainan try Bike China Tours (tel 5-9847208), GPO Box 9484 Hong Kong; very small groups, flexible and recommended by some travellers. Another company specialising in biking tours in different regions of China is Tail Winds Bicycle Touring (tel (062) 49 6634), PO Box 32, O'Connor, ACT 2601, Australia. One of the largest tour operators is China Passage Inc (tel (212) 564-4099), 302 Fifth Avenue, New York, New York 10001, USA.

Individual Freestyle

Prior to 1987, border guards and police officials in remote areas were often puzzled by the sudden appearance of muddy foreign bikers whizzing through from Canton to Kunming, Shanghai to Xian, Kathmandu to Lhasa, etc.

Officials in Beijing pondered this phenomenon and, reportedly, are now implementing legislation to prevent all foreigners except foreign students and experts from bringing in their own vehicles. At the same time, it's highly likely that there will be a tightening up on foreigners biking out of 'open' places within China.

Two Americans were recently intercepted at Kunming airport after flying in from Hong Kong with mountain bikes. The ensuing wrangle with Customs took several weeks before the officials, who had been coveting the bikes, graciously agreed to let the foreign couple sell them for a pittance to a local department store.

The legalities of cycling from town to town are open to conjecture; but until someone official (like the Public Security Bureau) tells you not to then you should assume you can. When choosing a route it's best to stick to 'stepping-stones' (places open with a visa) and steer clear of urban conglomerations which attract atrociously heavy traffic.

On a 22-kg standard Chinese bike, with a load of 10 kg, no gears, you could do about 10 km per hour on a flat sealed road. On an unweighted 10-speed you could do twice that. With amiable weather conditions on a flat sealed road you could cover 50 to 80 km a day on a Chinese bike – but 100 km would be possible. On the other hand, you could stick your bike on a train, plane or boat (buses may or may not let you take it) and travel from town to town that way.

Unfurl a topographic map of China and it should be easy to select the relatively flat areas. Include the climate in your calculations and certainly give the rainy season a miss! Bikes with plenty of gears are more suited for mountainous routes; or you could rely on lifts in trucks.

If you get hauled over, it is unlikely to be on the road. PSB keeps firm tabs on transients via hotels. If you're overnighting in closed places, try to arrive late and leave between 4 and 5 am. The worst that can happen is that you'll be told to put your bike on the train and asked to write a self-criticism and/or pay a fine. Foreigners repeating the offence sometimes lose their steeds. Apart from bargaining down the amount of the fine, it's interesting to see the reaction when you demand a formal receipt. With so many tour groups out on the road you might be considered a straggler!

Camping is possible if you can find a spare blade of grass. The trick is to select a couple of likely places about half an hour before sunset, keep pedalling and then backtrack so you can pull off the road at the chosen spot just after darkness falls.

Western Bicycles

Unless you have an impressive piece of paper, special authorisation or tour group status, you should expect problems when bringing a bicycle into China. If your bike is allowed through it's marked on your Customs declaration form to ensure that you leave with it.

One problem with western bikes is that they attract a lot of attention. Another problem is the unavailability of spare parts. One westerner brought a fold-up bicycle with him – but in most places it attracted so much attention that he had to give it to the locals to play with until the novelty wore off. One advantage of the fold-up bike is that you can stick it in a bag and stow it on the luggage racks of the trains; unfold it when you arrive at your destination and zip off, no hassles. They are, however, useless for long-distance travel and can be very expensive in the west.

It's essential to have a kick-stand for parking. A bell, headlight and reflector are good ideas. Make sure everything is bolted down, otherwise you'll invite theft. I added a cageless water bottle to my Chinese bike, but had to take it off in the cities because it attracted too much attention. Adhesive reflector strips also got ripped off.

Chinese Bicycles

There are four basic types of bike available in China: small wheel, light roadster (14 kg), black hulk (22 kg) and farmer's models (25-30 kg). An average bicycle costs around Y120 to Y275. The average price is around Y150 or three months' wages for a city worker.

Prestigious brands are the Fenghuang (Phoenix), Yongjiu (Forever) and Tianjin-built Fei Ge (Flying Pigeon). An interesting variation is the motorised bicycle; the better ones cost almost as much as a moped at Y300 to Y800. Like medicines and cigarettes, popular brands of bicycles have been part of a counterfeiting wave in China.

The standard Chinese bicycle is a copy of ye olde English Raleigh Roadster, complete to the last detail – even mimicking the crest. The Fenghuang is a heavy-duty bike, built to last with thick spokes, chaincase, upright bars, rear rack, heavy-duty tubing, wide wheelbase for heavy loads, rod-type brakes and no gears, headlights or reflectors. Dynamo sets are rare.

Then there are arrays of tricycles with spokes thicker than a motorcycle's, reinforced forks and double tubing – a sort of poor man's truck used to carry stupendous loads. Other bikes have little side-cars tacked on to carry children or invalids, or for use as makeshift pedicabs.

Depending on your motives, you could consider buying a bike in China from Friendship Stores, department stores or second-hand stores. Chinese bike manufacturers are beginning to produce a wider range of models. Some lighter Chinese bikes are now produced with gears. The new 10-speeds built in Shanghai would be great for roads in good condition, but too fragile for the rough stuff.

Providing you can get your wheels across the border with minimal bureaucratic hassles, you might want to look at the bikes in Hong Kong which are cheaper and better made than the ones across the border. There's a Raleigh agent, British Bicycle Company, and bike shops in the Mongkok area of Kowloon as well as over on Hong Kong Island. Hong Kong bikes are related to the Chinese versions, so Raleighs and Chinese-brand parts should be roughly compatible – or at least your Chinese bicycle repairman should know what he's looking at. You can also buy three-speed bikes in Hong Kong.

Transporting Your Bike

Train Bikes are not cheap to transport on trains; this can cost as much as a hard-seat fare (Chinese price). Boats are the cheapest means of transporting a bicycle; the cost is around a third of the 3rd-class passenger fare, which is not much. Trains have quotas for the number of bikes they may transport. As a foreigner you will get preferential treatment in the luggage compartment and the bike will go on the first available train. But your bike won't arrive at the same time as you unless you send it on a couple of days in advance. At the other end it is held in storage for three days free, and then incurs a small charge.

The procedure for putting a bike on a train and getting it at the other end is as follows:

1 Railway personnel would like to see a train ticket for yourself (not entirely essential).
2 Go to the baggage transport section of the station. Get a white slip and fill it out to get the two or three tags for registration. Then fill out a form (it's only in Chinese, so just fill it out in English) which reads: 'Number/to station x/send goods person/ receive goods person/total number of goods/from station y'.
3 Take the white slip to another counter, where you pay and are given a blue slip.
4 At the other end (delays of up to three days for transporting a bike) you present the blue slip, and get a white slip in return. This means your bike has arrived. The procedure could take 20 minutes to an hour depending on who's around. If you lose that blue slip you'll have real trouble reclaiming your bike.

Chinese cyclists spend ages at the stations mummifying their bicycles in cloth for transport. For the one scratch the bike will get it's hardly worth going through this elaborate procedure. Again, you can avoid all of this by taking a fold-up bicycle.

Transporting your bike by plane can be expensive, but it's often less complicated than by train. Some cyclists have not been charged by CAAC, others have had to pay 1% of their fare per kg of excess weight. For a bike and panniers weighing a total of 25 kg you'd have to pay Y136 on the flight between Chengdu and Lhasa; for the flight between Kunming and Chengdu, the cost would be Y27.30. These prices are approximate since airport staff juggle figures – bargaining sometimes helps.

DRIVING

With the building of the Hong Kong-to-Canton highway it is possible that by the time this book is out you'll be able to drive across the border, at least into the Shenzhen region.

Take heart for more widespread motoring. In March to July 1986, a 21-year-old Briton, Chris Reed, managed to motor his way through Tibet and China on a 500cc Honda trailbike. He entered from Nepal and spent most of his time dodging authorities. The authorities eventually caught up with him in northern China, but Chris realised his dream – he got to the Gobi, the Great Wall, and eventually to Shanghai.

HITCHING

Many people have hitch-hiked in China, and some have been amazingly successful. It's not officially sanctioned, so don't bother trying to get permission. The best way to get a lift is to find the outskirts of town. There are usually lots of trucks on the roads, and even army convoys are worth trying.

Much depends on where you are; in some parts the novelty of hitch-hikers has worn off among the locals. Otherwise, hitching is a good way of getting to closed or isolated areas, or to places where there is poor public transport.

As far as we know, there is no Chinese signal for hitching, so just try waving down the trucks. Unless you speak Chinese, you'll need to have where you want to go written down in Chinese – otherwise there's no hope of being understood.

BOAT

Apart from the ships which ply the coast of China (see the Getting There section for details), several inland shipping routes are worth considering. For details of each trip see the appropriate sections in this book. Boat travel is the slowest, but cheapest means of transport in China.

The best known is the three-day boat ride along the Yangtse River from Chongqing to Wuhan. Some people find this a dull trip but it's a good way to get from Chongqing to Wuhan, and it's a relief from the trains. You can also carry on down the Yangtse River and the Huangpu River to Shanghai. From Shanghai there is the boat to Qingdao.

Canton to Wuzhou along the West (Xi) River is popular with low-budget travellers as it is the cheapest way to get from Canton to Guilin and Yangshuo, disembarking at Wuzhou and then taking a bus to Guilin or Yangshuo the next morning. The Li River boat trip from Guilin to Yangshuo is a popular tourist ride which takes six hours.

You can also travel the Grand Canal from Hangzhou to Suzhou, and flit off on various other boats in this district. There are no passenger boats on the Yellow River.

LOCAL TRANSPORT

Long-distance transport in China is not really a problem – the dilemma occurs when you finally make it to your destination. As in American and Australian cities where the car is the key to movement, the bicycle is the key in China, and if you don't have one, life is more difficult. Walking is not usually recommended since Chinese cities tend to be very spread out.

One of a great many on the roads of China

Airport

Your plane ticket no longer includes the cost of transport between the CAAC office and the airport; expect to pay a couple of mao for short distances and several kuai for longer ones. The departure time of the bus will be noted on your ticket. You can also take a taxi to the airport.

Bus

Apart from bikes, buses are the most common means of getting around in the cities. Services are fairly extensive and the buses go to most places you want to go. The problem is that they are almost always packed. If an empty bus pulls in at a stop then the battle for seats ensues, and a passive crowd of Chinese suddenly turns into a stampeding herd. Even more aggravating is the slow traffic. You just have to be patient, never expect anything to move rapidly, and allow lots of time to get to the railway station to catch your train. One consolation is that buses are cheap, usually only five to 10 fen per trip.

Good maps of Chinese cities and bus routes are readily available and are often sold by hawkers outside the railway stations. When you get on a bus, point to where you want to go on the map, and the conductor (who is seated near the door) will sell you the right ticket. They usually tell you where to get off.

You may be offered a seat in a crowded bus, although this is becoming less common in the big cities. It's that peculiar Chinese politeness which occasionally manifests itself, and if you're offered a seat it's best to accept as refusal may offend.

Tour Bus

Most major cities have companies operating

short-range tour buses which carry both Chinese and foreigners to the local sights. Regular tours include Beijing (Ming Tombs and Great Wall), Kunming (Stone Forest) and Xian (terracotta soldiers).

Prices are low but sometimes the buses will whiz through interesting spots and make long stops at dull places. You might have difficulty getting a ticket if the destination is closed to foreigners, if the bus is booked out or if they think you're too much trouble.

In some places CITS organises tour buses for foreigners, and these are usually good value (Turpan for example). You can sometimes hitch up with a western tour group for which you'll be charged a fee; that may be the only way of getting a look at certain places (such as the steam locomotive factory in Datong).

Taxi

These do not cruise the streets in China, except in Canton and Beijing. They're available from the tourist hotels which sometimes have separate booking desks. You can hire them for a single trip or on a daily basis – the latter is definitely worth considering if you've got the money or if there's a group of people who can split the cost. Some of the tourist hotels also have minivans and even minibuses on hand. Beijing taxi-drivers have become notorious for ripping off foreigners (see Beijing chapter for details), and Canton taxi-drivers will often refuse to use their meters in order to jack up the price and keep the money themselves.

Pedicab

A pedicab is a pedal-powered tricycle with a seat to carry passengers. In most places it's like the pedicab you see in India, with the driver at the front and a seat for two behind him. In some places along the south-east coast it's improvised from an ordinary bicycle and a little wooden side-cart in which two people can sit. Beijing pedicabs don't have seats, but a flat tray at the rear on which the passenger squats. Motorised pedicabs are also common.

Pedicabs congregate outside railway and bus stations and sometimes outside the tourist hotels. Many drivers have become predatory and can be quite aggressive. Always bargain your fare! Asking-prices can be as much as 10 times the standard rate, and often the drivers will simply refuse to take foreigners unless you pay it. Agree on a price beforehand, otherwise you'll be in for a furious argument when you reach your destination. If there is more than one of you, make sure the agreed-on fare covers both people.

Pedicabs versus rickshaws: A rickshaw is a two-wheeled passenger cart pulled by a man on foot. It was invented in Japan, where the word *jin-rikisha* means 'human-powered vehicle'. It was introduced into China in the late 19th century, where it was called *yangche* (foreign vehicle). The rickshaw eventually became a symbol of human exploitation – one person pulling another in a cart – and disappeared from China in the 1950s. Its replacement, the pedicab – sometimes mistakenly called a rickshaw – is a vehicle pulled by a bicycle.

Auto-rickshaw (Auto-pedicab)

The auto-rickshaw – for want of a better name – is an enclosed three-wheeled vehicle with a driver at the front, a small motor-bike engine below and seats for two passengers behind. They congregate outside the train and bus stations in larger towns and cities. Some of these vehicles have trays at the rear with bench seats along the sides so that several people can be carried at once. Tempos are a large, ugly version of the auto-rickshaw and seat five or six passengers; they're not very common.

SOUTHERN AND CENTRAL CHINA

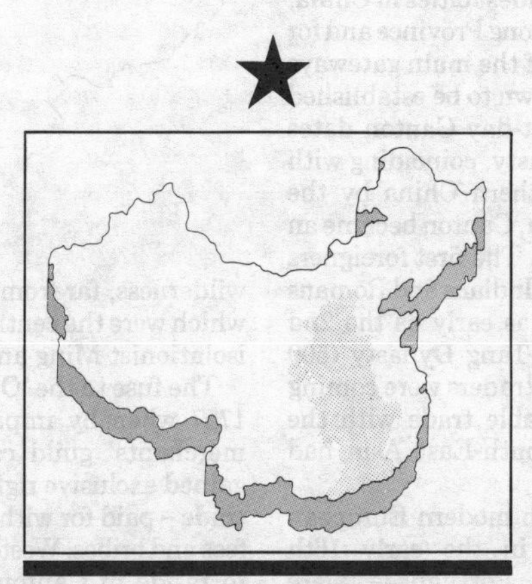

Canton 广州

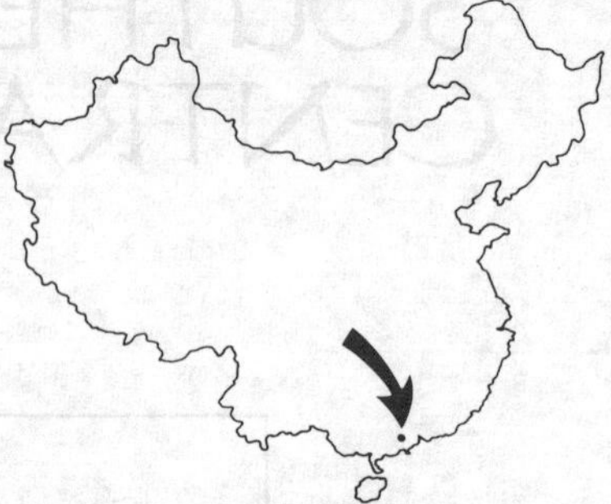

Known to the Chinese as 'Guangzhou', Canton is one of the oldest cities in China, the capital of Guangdong Province and for over 1000 years one of the main gateways to China. The first town to be established on the site of present-day Canton dates back to the Qin Dynasty, coinciding with the conquest of southern China by the north. Close to the sea, Canton became an outward-looking city. The first foreigners to come here were the Indians and Romans who visited the city as early as the 2nd century AD. By the Tang Dynasty (500 years later) the Arab traders were coming regularly and a sizeable trade with the Middle East and South-East Asia had arisen.

Initial contact with modern European nations was made in the early 16th century when the Portuguese were allowed to set up base downriver in Macau in 1557. Then the Jesuits came and in 1582 were allowed to establish themselves at Zhaoqing, a town north-west of Canton, and later in Beijing itself. The Jesuits impressed the court with their expertise in astronomy which permitted the all-important astrological charts to be produced more accurately. Others worked as makers of fountains and curios or as painters and architects, but otherwise the Jesuit influence on China was negligible. The first trade overtures from the British were rebuffed in 1625, but the imperial government finally opened Canton to foreign trade in 1685.

British ships began to arrive regularly from the East India Company bases on the Indian coast, and the traders were allowed to establish warehouses ('factories') near Canton as bases to ship out tea and silk. In 1757 a new imperial edict restricted all foreign trade to Canton, an indication of how little importance was placed on trade with the western barbarians. Canton was always considered on the edge of a wilderness, far from Nanjing and Beijing which were the centres of power under the isolationist Ming and Qing dynasties.

The fuse to the 'Opium Wars' was lit in 1757 when by imperial edict a Canton merchants' guild called the 'Co Hong' gained exclusive rights to China's foreign trade – paid for with royalties, kickbacks, fees and bribes. Westerners were permitted to reside in Canton from September to March only, and were restricted to Shamian Island where they had their factories. They had to leave their wives and families downriver in Macau (though not all found this a hardship) and were forbidden to learn Chinese or deal with anyone except the Co Hong. The traders complained of the restrictions and of trading regulations that changed from day to day. Nevertheless trade flourished – mainly in China's favour because the tea and silk had to be paid for in hard cash, normally silver.

Trade in China's favour was not what the western merchants had in mind. In 1773 the British unloaded 1000 chests at Canton, each containing 150 pounds of Bengal opium. The intention was to balance, and eventually more than balance, their purchases of Chinese goods. The Chinese taste for opium, or 'foreign mud' as it was called, amounted to 2000 chests a year by about 1800. Emperor Tao Kung, alarmed at the drain of silver from the country, issued an edict banning the drug trade. The foreigners had different ideas, and with the help of the Co Hong and corrupt Cantonese officials the trade expanded.

In 1839 opium was still the key to British trade in China. The emperor appointed Lin Zexu commissioner of Canton with orders to stamp out the opium trade once and for all. It took Lin just one week to surround the British in Canton, cut off their food supplies and demand that they surrender all the opium in their possession. The British stuck it out for six weeks until they were ordered by their own superintendent of trade to surrender 20,000 chests of opium. He tried negotiating with Kishen, Lin's representative, but when this failed he attacked Canton in the first 'Opium War'. The attack was ended by the Convention of Chuen Pi which ceded Hong Kong Island to the British. The convention was due to be signed on 20 January 1841 but never was. Nevertheless the British ran the flag up on Hong Kong Island. A later treaty ceded the island and a piece of Kowloon 'in perpetuity'.

In the 19th century the Cantonese sense of independence, aided by its distance from Beijing, allowed Guangdong to become a cradle of revolt. The leader of the anti-dynastic Taiping Rebellion, Hong Xiuquan (1814-1864), was born at Huaxian to the north-west of Canton, and the early activities of the Taipings centred around this area. Canton was also a stronghold of the republican forces after the fall of the Qing Dynasty in 1911. Sun Yatsen, the first president of the Republic of China, was born at Cuiheng Village south-west of Canton. Sun headed the Kuomintang (Nationalist) Party in Canton in the early 1920s, from which the republicans mounted their campaigns against the northern warlords. Canton was also the centre of activities of the fledgeling Communist Party.

These events were nothing new. Centuries before, the southerners had gained a reputation for thinking for themselves, and rebellions and uprisings were a feature of Canton from the time of its foundation. As early as the 10th century it became independent along with the rest of Guangdong Province. The assimilation of southern China was a slow process, reflected in the fact that the southerners refer to themselves as men of Tang (of the Tang Dynasty of 618 to 907 AD), while the northerners refer to themselves as men of Han (of the Han Dynasty of 206 BC to 220 AD). The northerners regarded their southern compatriots with disdain, or as one 19th-century northern account put it:

> The Cantonese . . . are a coarse set of people . . . Before the times of Han and Tang, this country was quite wild and waste, and these people have sprung forth from unconnected, unsettled vagabonds that wandered here from the north.

The traditional stereotype of the Cantonese – over five million of whom live in the city of Canton and its surrounding suburbs – is that of a proud people, frank in criticism, lacking restraint, oriented to defending their own interests, and hot tempered. They are regarded as shrewd business-people, quick, lively and clever in catching on to new skills.

Of all the Chinese the Cantonese have probably been influenced the most by the outside world. Part of this stems from Canton's geographical position – the Cantonese live a mere 110 km from Hong Kong and 2300 km from their national capital. Almost everyone in southern Guangdong has relatives in Hong Kong who for years have been storming across the border loaded down with the latest hair-styles and gifts of cooking oil, TV sets or Sony cassette recorders. Despite attempts by the authorities to tear down their tall TV antennas, many Cantonese can receive the latest shows from Hong Kong

A few years ago these shows would have been considered a ruinous influence on their moral and ideological uprightness. However, ideology is not what China is all about now. Economic progress, modern-isation and free enterprise – things which were anathema barely more than a decade

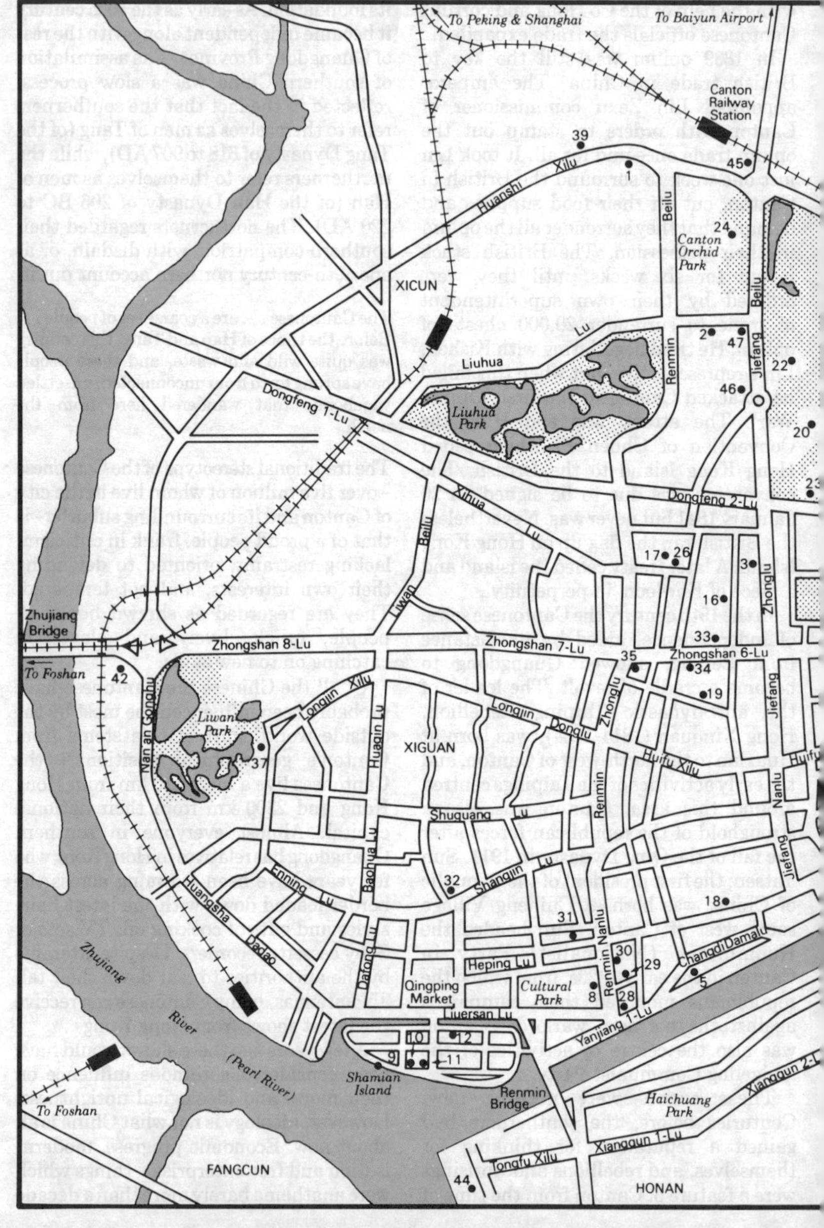
To Peking & Shanghai
To Baiyun Airport
Canton Railway Station
XICUN
Huanshi Xilu
Beilu
Canton Orchid Park
Liuhua Lu
Liuhua
Liuhua Park
Dongfeng 1-Lu
Dongfeng 2-Lu
Renmin
Jiefang
Xihua Lu
Beilu
Liwan
Zhongshan 8-Lu
Zhongshan 7-Lu
Zhongshan 6-Lu
Zhonglu
Zhujiang Bridge
To Foshan
Nan an Gonghu
Liwan Park
Longjin Xilu
Huagin
XIGUAN
Longjin Donglu
Huifu Xilu
Huifu
Renmin
Nanlu
Shuquang Lu
Shangjin Lu
Enning Lu
Baohua Lu
Datong Lu
Huangsha Dadao
Zhujiang River
(Pearl River)
Heping Lu
Qingping Market
Cultural Park
Renmin Nanlu
Changdi Damalu
Liuersan Lu
Yanjiang 1-Lu
Shamian Island
Renmin Bridge
Haichuang Park
Xianggun 1-Lu
Xianggun 2-Lu
Tongfu Xilu
To Foshan
FANGCUN
HONAN
1
2
3
5
8
9
10
11
12
16
17
18
19
20
22
23
24
26
28
29
30
31
32
33
34
35
37
39
42
44
45
46
47

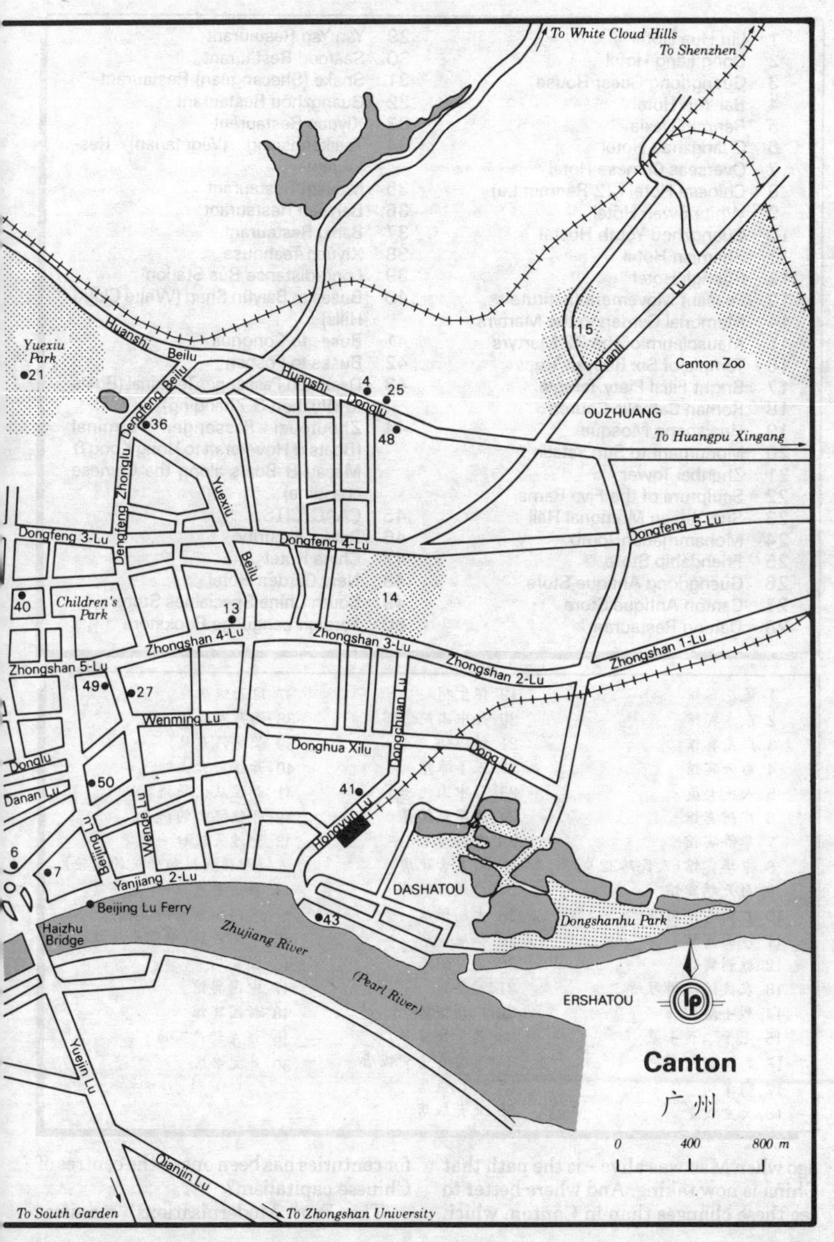

To White Cloud Hills
To Shenzhen
Yuexiu Park
21
Huanshi Beilu
Huanshi Donglu
Dengfeng Beilu
Dengfeng Zhonglu
4
25
48
36
15
Tianli Lu
Canton Zoo
OUZHUANG
To Huangpu Xingang
Yuexiu Beilu
Dongfeng 3-Lu
Dongfeng 4-Lu
Dongfeng 5-Lu
40
Children's Park
13
14
Zhongshan 4-Lu
Zhongshan 3-Lu
Zhongshan 2-Lu
Zhongshan 1-Lu
Zhongshan 5-Lu
49
27
Wenming Lu
Donghua Xilu
Dongchuan Lu
Dong Lu
Donglu
Danan Lu
50
41
Wende Lu
Beijing Lu
Hongyun Lu
6
7
Yanjiang 2-Lu
DASHATOU
Beijing Lu Ferry
43
Haizhu Bridge
Zhujiang River
(Pearl River)
Dongshanhu Park
ERSHATOU
Canton
广州
0
400
800 m
Yuejin Lu
Qianjin Lu
To South Garden
To Zhongshan University

1 Liu Hua Hotel
2 Dong Fang Hotel
3 Guangdong Guest House
4 Bai Yun Hotel
5 Renmin Daxia
6 Guangzhou Hotel
7 Overseas Chinese Hotel
8 Chinese Hotel (22 Renmin Lu)
9 White Swan Hotel
10 Guangzhou Youth Hostel
11 Shamian Hotel
12 Shengli Hotel
13 Peasant Movement Institute
14 Memorial Garden to the Martyrs
15 Mausoleum of the 72 Martyrs
16 Temple of Six Banyan Trees
17 Bright Filial Piety Temple
18 Roman Catholic Church
19 Huaisheng Mosque
20 Monument to Sun Yatsen
21 Zhenhai Tower
22 Sculpture of the Five Rams
23 Sun Yatsen Memorial Hall
24 Mohammedan Tomb
25 Friendship Store
26 Guangdong Antique Store
27 Canton Antique Store
28 Datong Restaurant
29 Yan Yan Restaurant
30 Seafood Restaurant
31 Snake (Shecanguan) Restaurant
32 Guangzhou Restaurant
33 Xiyuan Restaurant
34 Tsaikenhsiang (Vegetarian) Restaurant
35 Muslim Restaurant
36 Beiyuan Restaurant
37 Banxi Restaurant
38 Xiyuan Teahouse
39 Long-distance Bus Station
40 Buses to Baiyun Shan (White Cloud Hills)
41 Buses to Conghua
42 Buses to Foshan
43 Dashatou Passenger Terminal (Boats to Wuzhou & Zhaoqing)
44 Zhoutouzi Passenger Terminal (Boats & Hovercraft to Hong Kong & Macau & Boats along the Chinese coastline)
45 CAAC/CITS
46 Public Security
47 China Hotel
48 New Garden Hotel
49 South China Specialties Store
50 Foreign Language Bookstore

1 流花宾馆
2 东方宾馆
3 广东宾馆
4 白云宾馆
5 人民大厦
6 广州宾馆
7 华侨宾馆
8 中华宾馆(人民路22号)
9 白天鹅宾馆
10 广州青年招待所
11 沙面宾馆
12 胜利宾馆
13 农民运动讲习所
14 烈士陵园
15 七十二烈士墓
16 六榕树祠
17 明孝祠
18 天主教堂
19 怀生祠
20 孙中山纪念馆
21 镇海楼
22 五羊雕塑
23 孙中山纪念堂
24 穆罕默德墓
25 友谊商店
26 广东古玩店
27 广州古玩店
28 大同饭店
29 仁延饭店
30 海鲜饭店
31 蛇餐馆
32 广州饭店
33 西苑饭店
34 季肯香素食饭店
35 回民饭店
36 北苑饭店
37 班西饭店
38 西苑茶楼
39 长途汽车站
40 开往白云山的汽车
41 开往从化的汽车
42 开往佛山的汽车
43 大沙头渡口(开往武州和肇庆的渡轮)
44 肇头子渡口(开往香港、澳门和沿海的渡轮)
45 中国民航/中国旅行社
46 公安局
47 中国宾馆
48 新园宾馆
49 华东特产商店
50 外文书店

ago when Mao was alive – is the path that China is now taking. And where better to see these changes than in Canton, which for centuries has been one of the centres of Chinese capitalism?

'The Four Modernisations' manifest

themselves in great and small ways. Their most obvious mark in Canton are the giant hotels built in the last few years, including the China, New Garden and White Swan. Designed to rake in foreign exchange, they cater for every whim of the businessperson and up-market tourist, providing swimming pools, saunas, bowling alleys, discos, revolving restaurants, and armies of bow-tied waiters unobtrusively pampering dollar-bearing capitalists with duck terrine and white chocolate mousse.

At the other end of the economic ladder are the free markets and small private enterprises. Take a walk along Zhongshan Lu one night. A hawker squats on the footpath with a piece of cloth laid out before him covered with zips, tacky sunglasses and key-rings. Next to him a man with a scale and measuring stick determines for a fee the height and weight of passers-by. Up the road a group of women shoe-repairers can be found. The street peddlers may not seem so extraordinary – you see them all over Asia – but in China they're memorable because they simply did not exist during the Maoist era.

Today private enterprise goes under every form. Even cooks, maids and nannies are becoming commonplace in the homes of middle and upper-income Chinese families. Since mid-1984 at least one Canton company has been exporting cooks and cleaning women to Hong Kong. Whole street markets in Canton are devoted to the sale of Hong Kong goods or imitations. Smuggled Hong Kong pop records and porno video tapes fetch high prices in Canton.

Canton and neighbouring industrial zones like Shenzhen are hardly representative of the rest of China; most Chinese towns are much greyer and less prosperous. Canton is certainly an indication of the direction in which China is heading and a good place to catch a glimpse of some of the successes, pitfalls, fallacies and curious results of the new economic policies.

Information & Orientation

Canton is situated at the confluence of the Pearl and Zengbu rivers, much of the city lying on the north bank of the Pearl and bounded to the west by the Zengbu. As you look out from the upper storeys of the Zhenhai Tower, the city appears a nondescript jumble of drab buildings.

Canton was originally three cities. The inner city was enclosed behind sturdy walls and was divided into the new and old cities. The outer city was everything outside these walls. The building of the walls was begun during the 11th century and completed in the 16th. They were 15 km in circumference, eight metres high and five to eight metres thick.

Canton's main thoroughfares, now called Jiefang Lu (Liberation Rd) and Zhongshan Lu and running north-south and east-west respectively, divided up the old walled city. They met the walls at the main gates. The city began to take its present form in the early 1920s. The demolition of the walls was completed, the canals were filled in and several km of motorways were built.

Outside the city walls to the west lies the *xiguan* (western quarter). Wealthy Chinese merchants built their residences the same distance from the centre of the city as the foreign enclave of Shamian Island. The thoroughfare still known as Shibapu became the street of millionaires in the 19th century, and remained an exclusive residential district.

In the north-east of the city is the *xiaobei* (little north) area. During the late dynastic times it was inhabited mainly by out-of-town officials as it was close to the offices of the bureaucracy. It was later developed into a residential area for civil servants.

At the western end of Zhongshan Lu is a residential district built in the 1930s using modern town-planning methods. It's known as Dong Shan (East Mountain). Part of the Dong Shan residential area, Meihuacun (Plum Blossom Village), is a 'model village' laid out in the 1930s with beautiful residences for high-ranking officials.

Before the Communists came to power, the waterfront on the south side of the Pearl River was notorious for its gambling houses and opium dens. The area was increasingly integrated into the city with the completion of the first suspension bridge in 1932, and was then developed as a site for warehouses and factories.

Every year an Export Commodities Fair is held from 15 April to 15 May, and 15 October to 15 November. Most hotels are fully booked at this time, so it may be difficult to get a room.

CITS Once upon a time the only way you could get anything out of Canton CITS was to stick your fingers down their throats. Things have improved immensely over the last few years and there's now a large, well-staffed CITS office (tel 662447) at 179 Huanshi Lu next to the main train station. They have English-speaking staff. Foreigners must book all train tickets out of Canton at CITS. CITS also sells tickets for the plane, hovercraft and ship to Hong Kong. The office is open from 8.30 to 11.30 am and 2 to 5 pm.

Public Security (tel 331060) is at 863 Jiefang Beilu, opposite the road which leads up to the Zhenhai Tower – a 15-minute walk from the Dong Feng Hotel.

Consulates The USA Consulate (tel 669900) is in the Dong Feng Hotel, on the 11th floor of the old wing. It's open Monday to Friday, 8.30 am to 12.30 pm and 1.30 to 5.30 pm. For American citizens only, you can reach an after-hours emergency service by telephoning 669900 and asking for extension 1000.

Bank You can change money at branches of the Bank of China in most of the large tourist hotels, including the White Swan and Liu Hua.

Post & Communications Just about all the major tourist hotels have post offices where you can send letters and packets containing printed matter. The post office in the White Swan Hotel is convenient if you're staying on Shamian Island.

If you're posting parcels overseas you have to go to the post office by the side of the railway station; it's the large building with the SEIKO sign on top. You have to get the parcel contents checked and fill out a Customs form.

The tourist hotels have telex and long-distance telephone facilities. The Liu Hua Hotel, across the road from the railway station, has a cheap direct-dial service to Hong Kong. The International Telegraph & Telephone Office is at the north end of Renmin Beilu, opposite the train station.

CAAC (tel 662969) is at 181 Huanshi Lu, to your left as you come out of the train station.

Reading An interesting account of early western contact with China comes from the Jesuit missionary Matteo Ricci, who was permitted to take up residence at Zhaoqing near Canton in the late 16th century, and at Beijing in 1601. An English translation of his diaries has been published under the title *China in the 16th Century – the Journals of Matteo Ricci 1583-1610*.

Some poignant comments on the Jesuit influence in China are made by Jonathan Spence in his book *To Change China – Western Advisers in China 1620-1960* (Penguin, 1980).

Another old account is *Kwang Tung or Five Years in South China* (Oxford University Press, London, 1982) by the English Wesleyan minister Reverend John Arthur Turner, who worked as a missionary in China from 1886 to 1891. The book was originally published in 1894.

A personal account of Canton in the early days of China's Republican period is *Canton in Revolution – The Collected Papers of Earl Swisher, 1925-1928* (Westview Press, USA, 1977). Swisher was an an American academic and Sinologist.

Ezra F Vogel's *Canton Under Communism* (Harvard University Press, 1969) covers the history of the city from 1949 to 1968.

Maps Hawkers outside the railway station sell excellent bus maps in Chinese. Across the road in the Liu Hua Hotel you can get a good tourist map of Canton (in English) at the hotel bookshop.

Hospitals If you get sick you can go to one of the hospitals or to the medical clinic for foreigners – Guangzhou No 1 People's Hospital (tel 333090), 602 Renmin Beilu. The Foreign Guest Medical Room in the Dong Feng Hotel is open daily, 8 am to 10 pm.

Film Kodak, Fuji and some other foreign film can be bought; try the Friendship Store and the shops in the large tourist hotels. The Friendship Store's one-hour photo-processing service costs about 50 fen per colour print.

Things to See

Although Canton may first strike you as a congested city, you only have to side-step off the main streets and head down the alleyways to find the dimly lit houses of the Cantonese, where men play cards under a 40-watt light bulb, and Chinese pop songs waft across the evening air. Although it tends to pale in comparison with Hong Kong, Canton is one of the liveliest towns in China and it's not hard to imagine that Hong Kong looked like this before the skyscrapers sprouted. In summer the older areas make interesting walking and there are a number of sights worth checking out, including temples, churches, revolutionary pilgrimage spots, mosques and parks.

Peasant Movement Institute

Canton's Peasant Movement Institute was built on the site of a Ming Dynasty Confucian temple in 1924. In the early days of the Communist party, its members (from all over China) were trained at the Institute. It was set up by Peng Pai, a high-ranking Communist leader who believed that if a Communist revolution was to succeed in China then the peasants must be its main force. Mao Zedong – of the same opinion – took over as director of the institute in 1925 or 1926. Zhou Enlai lectured here and one of his students was Mao's brother, Mao Zemin. Peng was executed by the Kuomintang in 1929, and Mao Zemin was executed by a warlord in Xinjiang Province in 1942.

The buildings were restored in 1953 and they're now used as a revolutionary museum. There's not a great deal to see: a replica of Mao's room, the soldiers' barracks and rifles, and old photographs. The institute is at 42 Zhongshan Silu.

Memorial Garden to the Martyrs

This memorial is within walking distance of the Peasant Movement Institute, east along Zhongshan Silu to Zhongshan Sanlu. It was officially opened in 1957 on the 30th anniversary of the December 1927 Canton uprising.

In April 1927, Chiang Kaishek ordered his troops to massacre Communists in Shanghai and Nanjing. On 21 May the Communists led an uprising of peasants on the Hunan-Jiangxi border, and on 1 August they staged another in Nanchang. Both uprisings were defeated by Kuomintang troops.

On 11 December 1927 the Communists staged another uprising in Canton, but this was also bloodily suppressed by the Kuomintang. The Communists claim that over 5700 people were killed during or after the uprising. The memorial garden is laid out on Red Flower Hill (Honghuagang), which was one of the execution grounds.

There's nothing of particular interest here, though the gardens themselves are attractive. You'll also see the Pavilion of Blood-Cemented Friendship of the Sino-Soviet Peoples and the Pavilion of Blood-Cemented Friendship of the Sino-Korean Peoples.

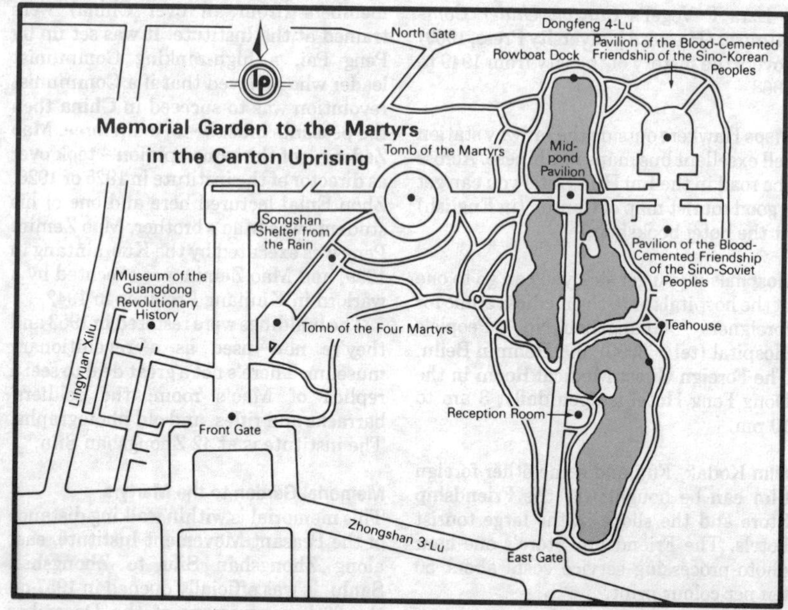

Mausoleum of the 72 Martyrs & Memorial of Yellow Flowers

This memorial was built in memory of the victims of the unsuccessful Canton insurrection of 27 April 1911. (It was not until October 1911 that the Qing Dynasty collapsed and a Republic of China was declared in the south of the country.) The uprising had been planned by a group of Chinese organisations which opposed the Qing and which had formally united at a meeting of representatives in Tokyo in August 1905, with Sun Yatsen as leader.

The memorial was built in 1918 with funds provided by Chinese from all over the world, and was the most famous revolutionary monument of pre-Communist China. It's a conglomeration of architectural symbols of freedom and democracy used worldwide, since the outstanding periods of history in the rest of the world were going to be used as guidelines for the new Republic of China.

What that really means is that it's an exercise in architectural bad taste. In front, a small Egyptian obelisk carved with the words 'Tomb of the 72 Martyrs' stands under a stone pavilion. Atop the pavilion is a replica of the Liberty Bell in stone. Behind stands a miniature imitation of the Trianon at Versailles, with the cross-section of a huge pyramid of stone on its roof. Topping things off is a miniature replica of the Statue of Liberty. The Chinese influence can be seen in the bronze urns and lions on each side.

The monument stands on Yellow Flower Hill (Huanghuagang) on Xianli Zhonglu, east of the Baiyun and New Garden hotels.

Sun Yatsen Memorial Hall

This hall on Dongfeng Lu was built in honour of Sun Yatsen, with donations from Overseas Chinese and from Canton citizens. Construction began in January

1929 and finished in November 1931. It stands on the site of the residence of the governor of Guangdong and Guangxi during the Qing Dynasty, later used by Sun Yatsen when he became president of the Republic of China. The Memorial Hall is an octagonal Chinese monolith some 47 metres high and 71 metres wide; seating capacity is about 4000.

Temples, Mosques & Churches
Canton has a number of temples and churches worth visiting. Some, by the way, are still active places of worship. One reader wrote:

I would like to suggest that you make a point of reminding readers that many of the temples listed are 'working', they're not there for tourists. At Liu Rong Si . . . some Americans and French were happily snapping shots of the kneeling worshippers; some even snuck up in front of the altar to do so. My Chinese friend said her blood was close to boiling . . . she did indeed seem awfully close to losing her temper.

Temple of the Six Banyan Trees (Liu Rong Si)
The temple's history is vague, but it seems that the first structure on this site, called the 'Precious Solemnity Temple', was built during the 6th century AD, and was ruined by fire in the 10th century. The temple was rebuilt at the end of the 10th century and renamed the 'Purificatory Wisdom Temple' since the monks worshipped Hui Neng, the sixth patriarch of the Zen Buddhist sect. Today it serves as the headquarters of the Guangzhou Buddhist Association.

The temple was given its name by Su Dongpo, a celebrated poet and calligrapher of the Northern Song Dynasty who visited the temple in the 11th or 12th century. He was so enchanted by the six banyan trees growing in the courtyard (no longer there) that he contributed two large characters for 'Six Banyans'.

Within the temple compound is the octagonal Flower Pagoda, the oldest and tallest in the city at 55 metres. Although it appears to have only nine storeys from the outside, inside it has 17. It is said that Bodhidharma, the Indian monk considered to be the founder of the Zen sect, once spent a night here, and owing to the virtue of his presence the pagoda was rid of mosquitoes forever.

The temple stands in central Canton, on Liurong Lu just to the west of Jiefang Beilu. Until a few years ago the three large Buddha statues stood in the open courtyard. The main hall was rebuilt in 1984. The Buddhas have been painted and several other shrines opened. One shrine houses a statue of Hui Neng. The temple complex is now a major tourist attraction.

Bright Filial Piety Temple (Guangxiao Si)
This temple is one of the oldest in Canton. The earliest Buddhist temple on this site possibly dates as far back as the 4th century AD. The place has particular significance for Buddhists because Hui Neng was a novice monk here in the 7th century. The temple buildings are of much more recent construction, the original buildings having been destroyed by fire in the mid-17th century. The temple is on Hongshu Lu, just west of the Temple of Six Banyan Trees. A section of the complex now houses the Guangdong Antique Store.

Five Genies Temple (Wuxian Guan) This Taoist temple is held to be the site of the appearance of the five rams and celestial beings in the myth of Canton's foundation – see the section on Yuexiu Park below for the story.

The stone tablets flanking the forecourt commemorate the various restorations that the temple has undergone. The present buildings are comparatively recent, as the earlier Ming Dynasty buildings were destroyed by fire in 1864.

The large hollow in the rock in the temple courtyard is said to be the impression of a celestial being's foot; the Chinese refer to it by the name of 'Rice-Ear Rock of Unique Beauty'. The great bell which weighs five tonnes was cast during the Ming Dynasty – it's three metres high, two metres in diameter and about 10 cm thick, probably the largest in Guangdong Province. It's known as the 'calamity bell', since the sound of the bell, which has no clapper, is a portent of calamity for the city.

At the rear of the main tower stand life-size statues with archaic Greek smiles; these appear to represent four of the five genies. In the temple forecourt are four statues of rams, and embedded in the temple walls are inscribed steles.

The temple is at the end of an alleyway whose entrance is on Huifu Xilu. Huifu Xilu runs westwards off Jiefang Zhonglu. Hours are daily from 8.30 to 11.30 am and 2.30 to 5.30 pm. Next door is 'Tom's Gym' with Stone Age equipment.

Roman Catholic Church This impressive edifice is known to the Chinese as the 'house of stone', as it is built entirely of granite. Designed by the French architect Guillemin, the church is an imitation of a European Gothic cathedral. Four bronze bells suspended in the building to the east of the church were cast in France; the original coloured glass was also made in France, but almost all of it is gone.

The site was originally the location of the office of the governor of Guangdong and Guangxi provinces during the Qing Dynasty, but the building was destroyed by British and French troops at the end of the Second Opium War in the 19th century. The area was leased to the French following the signing of the Sino-French 'Tianjin Treaty'. Construction of the church began in 1863 and was completed in 1888. It's on Yide Lu, not far from the riverfront, and is normally closed except on Sundays when masses are said. All are welcome.

Another church you may find interesting is the Zion Christian Church at 392 Renmin Zhonglu. The building is a hybrid with a traditional European Gothic outline and Chinese eaves. It's an active place of worship.

Huaisheng Mosque The original mosque on this site is said to have been established in 627 AD by the first Muslim missionary to China, possibly an uncle of Mohammed. The present buildings are of recent construction. The name of the mosque means 'Remember the Sage', in memory of the prophet. Inside the grounds of the mosque is a minaret, which because of its flat, even appearance is known as the 'Guangta' or 'Smooth Tower'. The mosque stands on Guangta Lu, which runs eastwards off Renmin Zhonglu.

Mohammedan Tomb & Burial Ground Situated in the Orchid Garden at the top of Jiefang Beilu, this is thought to be the tomb of the Muslim missionary who built the original Huaisheng Mosque. There are two other Muslim tombs outside the town of Quanzhou on the south-east coast of China, thought to be the tombs of missionaries sent by Mohammed with the one who is now buried in Canton.

The Canton tomb is in a secluded bamboo grove behind the Orchid Garden; continue past the entrance to the garden, walk through the narrow gateway ahead and take the narrow stone path on the right. Behind the tomb compound are Muslim graves and a monumental stone arch. The tomb came to be known as the 'Tomb of the Echo' or the 'Resounding Tomb' because of the noises that reverberate in the inner chamber.

The Riverfront

The northern bank of the Pearl River is one of the most interesting areas of Canton; filled with people, markets and dilapidated buildings, it's a stark contrast to the tidy greyness of the modern northern end of the city. A tourist boat-ride down the Pearl River runs daily from 3.30 to 5 pm and costs Y10. Boats leave from the pier just east of Renmin Bridge. They take you down the river as far as Ershatou and then turn around and head back to Renmin Bridge.

Liuersan Lu

Just before you reach the south end of Renmin Lu, Liuersan Lu heads west. 'Liu er san' means '6 2 3', referring to 23 June 1925, when British and French troops fired on striking Chinese workers during the Hong Kong-Canton Strike.

Qingping Market

A short walk down Liuersan Lu takes you to the second bridge which connects the city to the north side of Shamian Island. Directly opposite the bridge, on the city side, is Qingping Market on Qingping Lu – one of the best city markets in the whole country yet one of Canton's lesser-known attractions.

If you want to buy, kill or cook it yourself, this is the place to come since the market is more like a take-away zoo. Near the entrance you'll find the usual selection of medicinal herbs and spices, dried starfish, snakes, lizards, deer antlers, dried scorpions, leopard and tiger skins, bear paws, tree bark and unidentifiable herbs and plants.

Further up you'll find the live ones waiting to be butchered. Sad-eyed monkeys rattle at the bars of their wooden cages; tortoises crawl over each other in shallow tin trays; owls sit perched on boxes full of pigeons; fish paddle around in tubs aerated with jets of water. You can also get bundles of frogs, giant salamanders, pangolins, dogs and raccoons, alive or contorted by recent violent death – which may just swear you off meat for the next few weeks.

The market spills out into Tiyun Lu, which cuts east-west across Qingping Lu. Further north is another area supplying vegetables, flowers, potted plants and goldfish. There are small *dai pai dongs* (food stalls) in the streets on the perimeter of the market – very cheap.

Shamian Island

Liuersan Lu runs parallel to the north bank of Shamian Island. The island is separated from the rest of Canton by a narrow canal to the north and east, and by the Pearl River to the south and west. Two bridges connect the island to the city.

Shamian means 'sand flat', which is all

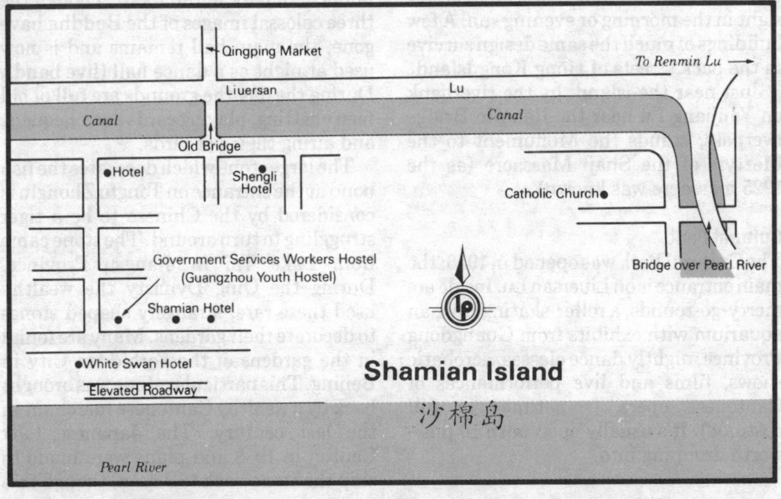

the island was until foreign traders were permitted to set up their warehouses (factories) here in the middle of the 18th century. Land reclamation has increased its area to its present size: 900 metres from east to west, and 300 metres from north to south. The island became a British and French concession after they defeated the Chinese in the Opium Wars, and is covered with decaying colonial buildings which housed trading offices and residences.

The French Catholic church has been restored and stands on the main boulevard. The old British church at the western end of the island has been turned into a workshop, but is betrayed by bricked-up gothic-style windows. Today most of the buildings are used as offices or apartment blocks and the area retains a quiet residential atmosphere detached from the bustle across the canals.

Another 30,000 square metres of land was added to the south bank of the island for the site of the 35-storey White Swan Hotel, which was built in the early 1980s. It's worth a walk along the north bank of Shamian Island to get a view of the houses on Liuersan across the canal – seedy three and four-storey terrace houses probably dating to the 1920s and 1930s, but a pretty sight in the morning or evening sun. A few buildings of much the same design survive in the back streets of Hong Kong Island.

Just near the island, by the riverbank on Yanjiang Lu near the Renmin Bridge overpass, stands the Monument to the Martyrs of the Shaji Massacre (as the 1925 massacre was known).

Cultural Park

The Cultural Park was opened in 1956; the main entrance is on Liuersan Lu. Inside are merry-go-rounds, a roller-skating rink, an aquarium with exhibits from Guangdong Province, nightly dance classes, acrobatic shows, films and live performances of Cantonese opera (sometimes in full costume). It's usually open until 10 pm – worth dropping into.

Shisanhang Lu

The Cultural Park backs on to Shisanhang Lu. *Shisanhang* means '13 Factories', a reminder that this is where the infamous opium warehouses were located. Nothing remains of the original buildings which were completely destroyed in 1857, following which the area was developed into a busy trading centre. By the 1930s it housed the leading banks and exchange houses, and so became known as Bankers Street. A shadow of the street's former importance remains in the many impressive, if faded, ornate buildings.

Haichuang Park & Ocean Banner Monastery

Renmin Bridge stands just east of Shamian Island and connects the north bank of the Pearl River to the area of Canton known as Honan, the site of Haichuang Park. This would be a nondescript park but for the remains of what was once Canton's largest monastery, the Ocean Banner Monastery. It was founded by a Buddhist monk in 1662, and in its heyday the monastery grounds covered 2½ hectares. After 1911 the monastery was used as a school and soldier's barracks. It was opened to the public as a park in the 1930s. Though the three colossal images of the Buddha have gone, the main hall remains and is now used at night as a dance hall (live band). During the day the grounds are full of old men chatting, playing cards and chequers, and airing their pet birds.

The large stone which decorates the fish pond at the entrance on Tongfu Zhonglu is considered by the Chinese to be a tiger struggling to turn around. The stone came from Lake Tai in Jiangsu Province. During the Qing Dynasty the wealthy used these rare, strangely shaped stones to decorate their gardens. Many are found in the gardens of the Forbidden City in Beijing. This particular stone was brought back by a wealthy Cantonese merchant in the last century. The Japanese took Canton in 1938 and plans were made to ship the stone back to Japan, though this did not happen. After the war the stone was sold to a private collector and disappeared from public view. It was finally returned to the park in 1951.

Other Parks & Gardens
Chinese make a great thing of their parks and neat gardens decorated with pavilions and bridges. Many of them can be quite disappointing as scenic attractions, but as places to see the Chinese at their most relaxed they're always worth a look. Along with films and restaurants, parks are a major source of leisure for the Chinese. It's worth getting up early (around 7 am) to see the young and old exercising; jogging, tai-chi and calisthenics are the usual activities, but you'll often find old women swinging from tree branches (no kidding) and old men running slower than they can walk. Others walk their pet birds, carrying them in wooden cages. The parks are sites for minor exhibitions of painting and photography or for flower shows (notably chrysanthemums in December).

Yuexiu Park This is the biggest park in Canton, covering 93 hectares, and includes the Zhenhai Tower, the Sun Yatsen Monument and the large Sculpture of the Five Rams.

The Sculpture of the Five Rams, erected in 1959, is the symbol of Canton. It is said that long ago five celestial beings wearing robes of five colours came to Canton riding through the air on rams. Each carried a stem of rice, which they presented to the people as an auspicious sign from heaven that the area would be free from famine forever. Guangzhou means Broad Region, but from this myth it takes its other name, City of Rams or just Goat City.

The Zhenhai Tower, also known as the Five Storey Pagoda, is the only part of the old city wall that remains. From the upper storeys it commands a view of the city to the south and the White Cloud Hills to the north. The present tower was built during the Ming Dynasty, on the site of a former structure. Because of its strategic location it was occupied by the British and French troops at the time of the Opium Wars. The 12 cannon in front of the tower date from this time (five of them are foreign, the rest were made in nearby Foshan). The tower now houses the City Museum with exhibits which describe the history of Canton from Neolithic times until the early part of this century.

The Sun Yatsen Monument is south of the Zhenhai Tower. This tall obelisk was constructed in 1929, four years after Sun's death, on the site of a temple to the goddess Kuan Yin (Guanyin). The obelisk is built of granite and marble blocks and there's nothing to see inside, though a staircase leads to the top where there's a good view of the city. On the south side of the obelisk the text of Dr Sun's last testament is engraved in stone tablets on the ground:

For 40 years I have devoted myself to the cause of national revolution, the object of which is to raise China to a position of independence and equality among nations. The experience of these 40 years has convinced me that to attain this goal, the people must be aroused, and that we must associate ourselves in a common struggle with all the people of the world who treat us as equals. The revolution has not yet been successfully completed. Let all our comrades follow the principles set forth in my writings 'Plans for National Renovation', 'Fundamentals of National Reconstruction', 'The Three Principles of the People' and the 'Manifesto of the First National Convention of the Kuomintang' and continue to make every effort to carry them into effect. Above all, my recent declaration in favour of holding a National Convention of the People of China and abolishing unequal treaties should be carried into effect as soon as possible.

This is my last will and testament.

(Signed) Sun Wen
11 March, 1925

West of the Zhenhai Tower is the Sculpture of the Five Rams. South of the tower is the large sports stadium with a seating capacity of 40,000. The park also has its

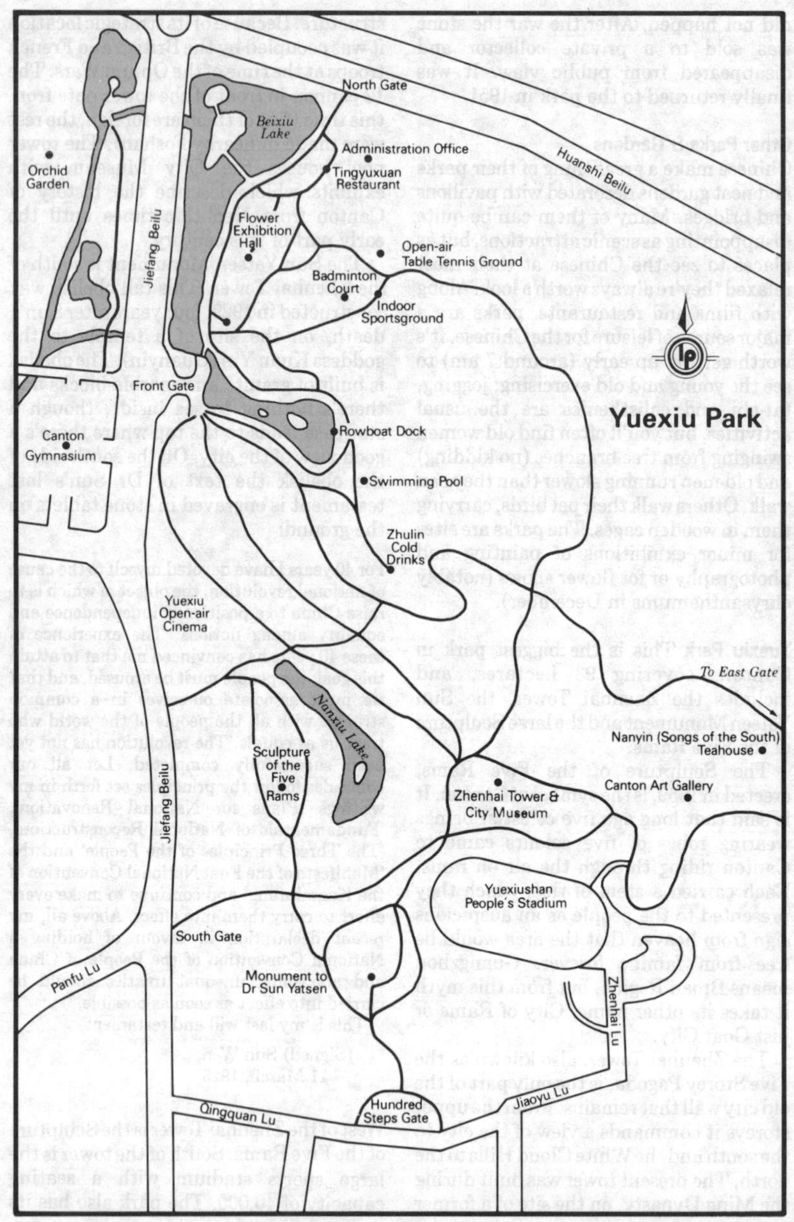
Yuexiu Park
North Gate
Beixiu Lake
Administration Office
Orchid Garden
Tingyuxuan Restaurant
Huanshi Beilu
Flower Exhibition Hall
Jiefang Beilu
Open-air Table Tennis Ground
Badminton Court
Indoor Sportsground
Front Gate
Canton Gymnasium
Rowboat Dock
Swimming Pool
Zhulin Cold Drinks
Yuexiu Open-air Cinema
To East Gate
Nanxiu Lake
Sculpture of the Five Rams
Nanyin (Songs of the South) Teahouse
Canton Art Gallery
Zhenhai Tower & City Museum
Jiefang Beilu
Yuexiushan People's Stadium
South Gate
Panfu Lu
Monument to Dr Sun Yatsen
Zhenhai Lu
Jiaoyu Lu
Qingquan Lu
Hundred Steps Gate

own roller-coaster. There are three artificial lakes: Dongxiu, Nanxiu and Beixiu – the last has rowboats which you can hire for 40 fen per hour, plus a Y5 deposit which is refunded when you cruise back into port.

Canton Orchid Park Originally laid out in 1957, this pleasant little park is devoted to orchids – over a hundred varieties. The Y1 admission fee includes tea by the small pond. The park is open daily from 7.30 to 11.30 am and 1.30 to 5 pm; closed on Wednesdays. It's at the northern end of Jiefang Beilu, not far from the main railway station.

And More The enormous Liuhua Park on Renmin Beilu contains the largest artificial lake in the city. It was built in 1958, a product of the ill-fated Great Leap Forward. The entrance to the park is on Renmin Beilu.

Just east of Beijing Lu, on the north side of Zhongshan Silu, is a Children's Park where parents bring their tiny tots.

The Canton Zoo on Xianli Donglu was built in 1958. It's one of the better zoos in China – which is the best that can be said for it.

Other Sights

Guangdong Provincial Museum is on Wenming Lu on the south side of the Pearl River, and houses exhibitions of archaeological finds from Guangdong Province.

In the same region is Zhongshan University, which houses the Lu Xun Museum. Lu Xun (1881-1936) was one of China's great modern writers; he was not a Communist though most of his books were banned by the Kuomintang. He taught at the university in 1927.

Down the road from Canton, the city's first commercial nuclear-power reactor is being built by foreign firms on the Leizhou Peninsula near Daya Bay. Daya Bay is just north-east of Mirs Bay, which borders Hong Kong's New Territories, and the plant will also provide power to Hong Kong.

Places to Stay – bottom end

Canton has quite a number of hotels to choose from, but only a few provide relatively cheap rooms and there's not much in the way of cheap dormitory accommodation.

Shamian Island is almost a happy hunting ground for cheapish hotels. To get to them, take bus No 5 from Huanshi Xilu; the stop is on the opposite side of the road and just to the west of the railway station. The bus runs along Liuersan Lu on the northern boundary of the canal which separates Shamian Island from the rest of Canton. Two footbridges connect Shamian Island to the city.

Near the massive White Swan Hotel is the *Government Services Workers' Hostel* (tel 884298) at 2 Shamian Silu. Also known as the *Guangzhou Youth Hostel*, it's the most popular hotel in Canton with low-budget travellers, reasonably clean and quiet, and easily the cheapest regular accommodation you'll find. Dormitory beds are Y8 and double rooms Y20. There are no single rooms. There are private bathrooms and hot water in the showers.

The *Shamian Binguan* (tel 888124) is next to the Guangzhou Youth Hostel. The new section is an uninspiring concrete block, but the old section is a red brick building with an ornate colonnaded front and iron railing, typical of the European colonial buildings on the island. Doubles are Y30. No single rooms.

One letter mentions a Chinese hotel a block from the long-distance bus station, with very comfortable air-con dorms for Y10. To get there, 'walk along Huanshi Xilu one block from the bus station and turn right. The hotel (which does not have a pinyin name) is on the left'.

Places to Stay – middle

A couple of hotels near the riverfront are worth trying:

The new *Aiqun Hotel*, at the corner of Yanjiang Xilu and Changdi Damalu, includes the old *People's Mansions* (*Renmin Daxia*) which was formerly

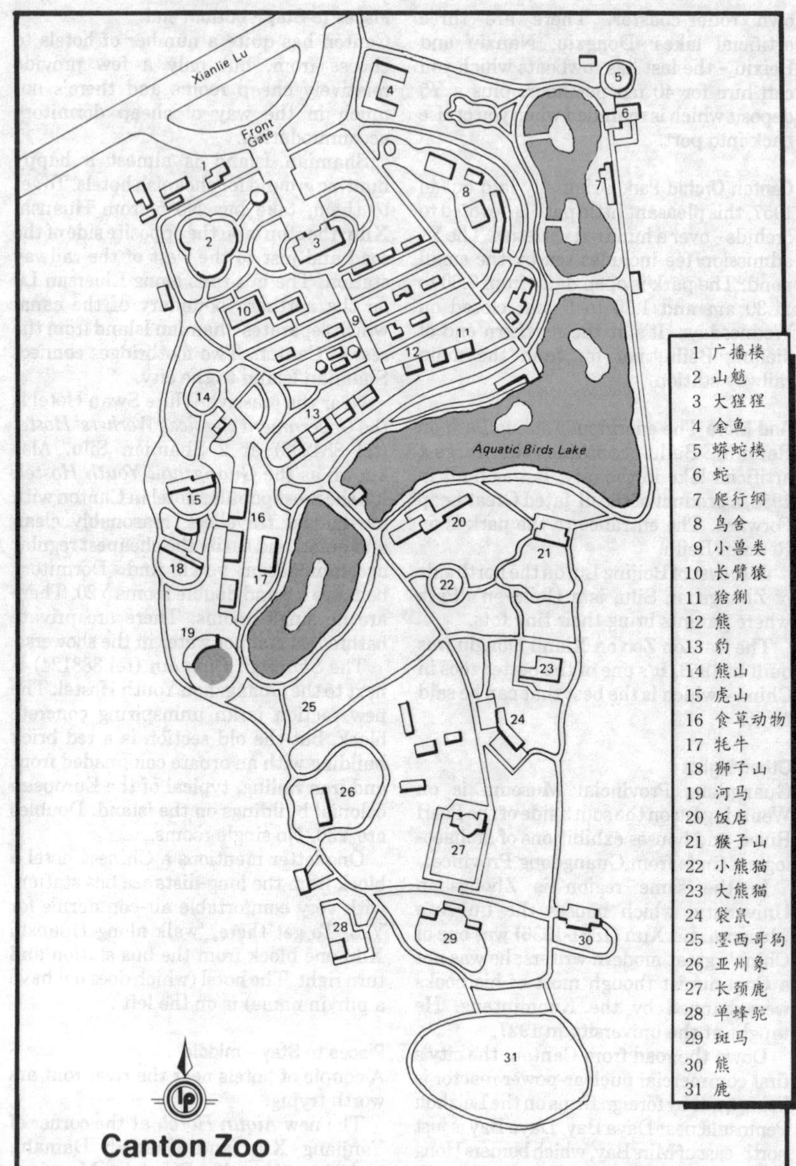
Xianlie Lu
Front Gate
Aquatic Birds Lake
1 广播楼
2 山魈
3 大猩猩
4 金鱼
5 蟒蛇楼
6 蛇
7 爬行纲
8 鸟舍
9 小兽类
10 长臂猿
11 猞猁
12 熊
13 豹
14 熊山
15 虎山
16 食草动物
17 牦牛
18 狮子山
19 河马
20 饭店
21 猴子山
22 小熊猫
23 大熊猫
24 袋鼠
25 墨西哥狗
26 亚州象
27 长颈鹿
28 单蜂驼
29 斑马
30 熊
31 鹿
lp
Canton Zoo

1	Broadcasting Room
2	Baboon, Mandrill
3	Gorilla
4	Goldfish
5	Boa House
6	Snakes
7	Reptiles
8	Birds
9	Smaller Animals
10	Gibbon
11	Lynx
12	Bear
13	Leopard
14	Bear Hill
15	Tiger Hill
16	Herbivores
17	Yak
18	Lion Hill
19	Hippopotamus
20	Restaurant
21	Monkey Hill
22	Lesser Panda
23	Panda
24	Kangaroo
25	Mexican Dog
26	Asian Elephant
27	Giraffe
28	Bactrian Camel
29	Zebra
30	Bear
31	Deer

known as the 'Love of the Masses'. If you can afford something upmarket then this is probably the best place to stay in Canton. It's in a fascinating part of town by the river; there are great views across the river and the city from the upper storeys. Rooms start at Y45 a single and Y65 a double. Take bus No 31 from the railway station; get off when you come to the river, turn left and walk up Yanjiang Lu for about 10 minutes.

The *Guangzhou Binguan* (tel 661556) is at Haizhu Square, east of the Aiqun Hotel. Singles start at Y65, doubles Y70. Bus No 29 from Huanshi Xilu near the train station goes past the hotel. Haizhu Square is a big roundabout with a giant statue in the middle - you can't miss it.

The *Overseas Chinese Mansion* (*Huaqiao Dasha*) (tel 661112) is on Haizhu Square. Single and double rooms start at around Y30 or Y40 but they're not particularly enthused about taking westerners. A few people have managed to get a dormitory bed; these cost about Y10.

Places to Stay - top end

The *Liu Hua Binguan* (tel 668800) is a large tourist hotel directly opposite the railway station. It's easily recognisable by the big 'Seagull Watch' sign on the roof. Double rooms range from Y80 to Y170 and are very comfortable, though the cheaper ground-floor rooms can be very noisy. Once rather plebeian (the ground floor even had its own dodgem car room), the south building now looks like a cross between a ballroom and a hair-dressing salon.

Named after the White Cloud Hills immediately to the north, the *White Cloud Guest House* (*Bai Yun Binguan*) (tel 667700) on Huanshi Donglu is a large tourist hotel east of the railway station. A lot of foreign tour groups get put up here. Singles cost from Y56 and doubles from Y82. The guest house is in an exceptionally dull part of town; it's convenient for the Friendship Store but that's about all. 'Bai' is pronounced 'bye' and the vowel in 'Yun' is a short 'o' as in 'book'. Bus No 30 from the railway station goes past the hotel.

The *Dong Fang Hotel* (tel 669900) at 120 Liuhua Lu is directly across from the Trade Fair building. The Dong Fang mainly caters to businesspeople and foreign tour groups. Singles cost from Y110 and doubles from Y160. 'Fang' is pronounced 'fung' to rhyme with 'hung'. It's about a 15-minute walk from the railway station, or take bus No 31.

Towering over the Dong Fang Hotel is the gleaming *China Hotel* (*Zhongguo Dajiudian*) (tel 66888) which boasts wall-to-wall marble, a disco and a bowling alley. Rooms start at Y205 singles and Y223 doubles. It's another Hong Kong venture, this time under the auspices of New World Hotels International.

Canton's most spectacular hotel is the

Garden Hotel (*Huayuan Jiudian*) (tel 773388) at 368 Huanshi Donglu, opposite the Bai Yun Hotel. It's a member of Hong Kong's Peninsula group of hotels and is built on a scale only possible with cheap socialist labour at hand. The hotel is topped by a revolving restaurant, and there's a snooker hall and a McDonald's-style fast-food joint on the ground floor. Singles cost from around Y190 and doubles from around Y200.

The *White Swan Guest House* (*Baitiane Binguan*) (tel 886968) is the huge white tower on the south-eastern shore of Shamian Island. It's got a first for China – a waterfall in the lobby! Doubles cost from Y222 (no singles). If you're staying across the road at the Youth Hostel you can use the post office, bank and other facilities in the White Swan. Very expensive shops in the hotel, but some goods are actually cheaper here than they are in the tourist shops attached to certain factories.

Another top-end place is the *Ocean Hotel* east of the New Garden Hotel. At the time of writing work had begun on a *Holiday Inn*.

Places to Eat

There is an old Chinese saying that to enjoy the best that life has to offer, one has to be 'born in Suzhou, live in Hangzhou, eat in Canton and die in Liuzhou'. Suzhou is renowned for its beautiful women, Hangzhou for its scenery, and Liuzhou for the finest wood for making coffins. Suzhou and Hangzhou are a bit overrated and I have no wish to die in China, but as Chinese food goes Canton ain't a bad place to stuff your face.

In this city there are dozens of famous old establishments along with heaps of smaller places, so eating out is not to be passed up. All the restaurants of any size have private rooms or partitioned-off areas if you want to get away from the hoi-polloi – and since restaurants tend to be crowded this is a distinct advantage.

Opening Hours Normal service hours in Canton's restaurants are usually around 5 to 9 am for breakfast, 10 am to 2 pm for lunch and 5 am to 8 pm for dinner. Several places have longer hours; many dai pai dongs and some small private restaurants stay open late into the night. However, China wakes up early and goes to sleep early; you can't wander into just any restaurant late at night and expect to be served. Some of the established restaurants are enormous places taking up several floors of one building: different floors, different prices.

Chinese Food There are a couple of good places close to the riverfront. Foremost is the *Datong Jiujia* (*Great Harmony Restaurant*) (tel 888988) at 63 Yanjiang Yilu, just around the corner from Renmin Lu. The restaurant occupies all of an eight-storey building overlooking the river. Specialities of the house are crisp fried chicken and roast suckling pig. The crisp-roasted pig skin is a favourite – eaten with sugar and salt, bean sauce and a spring onion in a steamed roll. This is a great place for morning dim sum, which should cost around Y5 per person.

Close to the Datong Restaurant is the *Yan Yan Restaurant* on a side street which runs east from Renmin Lu. Look for the pedestrian overpass on Renmin Lu near the intersection with Yanjiang Lu. The overpass leads down into a side street and the restaurant is opposite, easily recognisable by the fish tanks at the entrance; get your turtles, catfish and roast suckling pig here. It's also fantastically well air-conditioned. Nearby, you can tuck into a giant salamander at the *Seafood Restaurant* (sign in English) at 54 Renmin Lu.

One of the city's best-known restaurants is the *Guangzhou* (tel 887136) on Shangjin Lu at the corner with Wenchang Lu. It boasts a 70-year history and in the 1930s came to be known as the 'first house in Canton'. Its kitchens were staffed by the city's best chefs and the restaurant was frequented by the most important people of the day. The four storeys of dining halls and private rooms are built around a central garden courtyard, where potted shrubs, flowers and landscape paintings are intended to give the feeling (at least to the people in the dingy ground-floor rooms) of 'eating in a landscape'. Anyway, the food at this self-proclaimed illustrious restaurant ain't bad and ordinary dishes are quite cheap. Specialities of the house include shark fin soup with shredded chicken, chopped crabmeat balls and braised dove.

The *Huimin Fandian* (*Muslim Restaurant*) is at 326 Zhongshan Lu, on the corner with Renmin Lu. Look for the Arabic letters above the front entrance. It's an OK place, but go upstairs since the ground floor is dingy.

North of Zhongshan Lu is Dongfeng Lu, which runs east-west across the city. At 320 Dongfeng Beilu is the *Beiyuan Jiujia* (*North Garden Restaurant*) (tel 333365). This is another of Canton's 'famous houses' – a measure of its success being the number of cars and tourist buses parked outside. Inside is a courtyard and garden, from which the restaurant takes its name. Specialities of the house include barbecued chicken liver, steamed chicken in huadiao wine, stewed fish head with vegetables, fried boneless chicken (could be a first for China) and stewed duck legs in oyster sauce. Good value.

In the west of Canton, the *Banxi Jiujia* (tel 885655) on Longjin Xilu is the biggest restaurant in the city. It's noted for its dumplings, stewed turtle, roast pork, chicken in tea leaves and a crabmeat-sharkfin consommé. Its famed dim sum is served from about 5 to 9.30 am, at noon and again at night. Dim sum includes fried dumplings with shrimp, chicken gizzards, pork and mushrooms – even shark fin dumplings! You can try crispy fried egg rolls stuffed with chicken, shrimp, pork, bamboo shoots and mushrooms. Monkey brains are steamed with ginger, scallions and rice wine, and then steamed again with crab roe, eggs and lotus blossoms.

In the same general direction is the *Taotaoju* (*Abode of Tao Tao*) (tel 887501) on Dishifu Lu. Originally built as a private academy in the 17th century, it was turned into a restaurant in the late 19th century. Tao Tao was the name of the proprietor's wife. Dim sum is the speciality here; you choose sweet and savoury snacks from the selection on trolleys that are wheeled around the restaurant. Tea is the preferred beverage and is said to be made with Canton's best water – brought in from the Nine Dragon Well in the White Cloud Hills.

Not far from the Taotaoju is a mooncake bakery, the *Lianxiang Lou* (*Lotus Fragrance Pavilion*). Traditionally, mooncakes are eaten at the mid-autumn festival when the moon is brightest. The soft, golden crusts are stuffed with sweet and savoury fillings like fruits, nuts, lotus seeds and red beans. They're also used for weddings and receptions and are exported to Hong Kong.

Beijing Lu has two of Canton's 'famous' restaurants. The *Yeweixiang Fandian* (*Wild Animals Restaurant*) (tel 330997) at No 247 is where you can feast on dogs, cats, deer, bear paws and snake. Once upon a time they even served tiger. Highly recommended is the *Taipingguan Canting* (*Taiping Restaurant*) (tel 332938) at 344 Beijing Lu, which serves both western and Chinese food. The roast pigeon here is said to have been a popular choice with Zhou Enlai.

The *Nanyuan Jiujia* (*South Garden Restaurant*) (tel 448380) is at 120 Qianjin Lu. The specialities include pigeon in plum sauce and chicken in honey and oyster sauce. Qianjin Lu is on the south side of the Pearl River; to get to it you have to cross Haizhu Bridge and go down Yuejin Lu. Qianjin Lu branches off to the east.

Snake Restaurants Just to the west of Renmin Lu at 43 Jianglan Lu is the *Shecanguan* (*Snake Restaurant*) (tel 883811), with the snakes on display in the window. The restaurant was originally known as the 'Snake King Moon' and has a history of 80 years. To get to the restaurant you have to walk down Heping Lu which runs west from Renmin Lu. After a few minutes turn right into Jianglan Lu and follow it around to the restaurant on the left-hand side. Creative snake recipes include fricasseed assorted snake and cat meats, snake breast meat stuffed with shelled shrimp, stir-fried colourful shredded snakes, and braised snake slices with chicken liver.

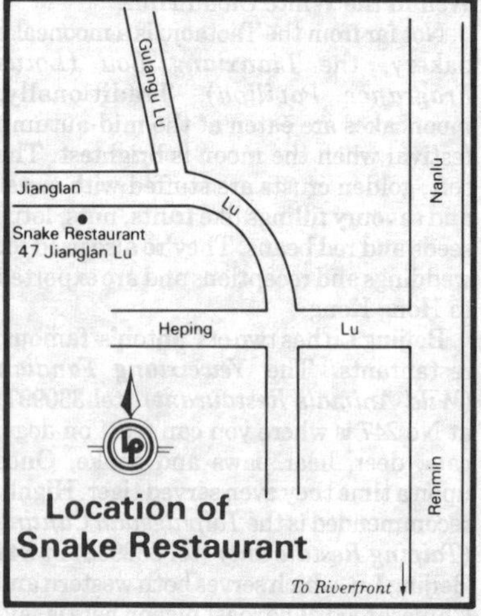

The Chinese believe that snake meat is effective in curing diseases. It is supposed to be good for dispelling wind and promoting blood circulation; and is believed to be useful in treating anaemia, rheumatism, arthritis and asthenia (abnormal loss of strength). Snake gall bladder is supposed to be effective in dispelling wind, promoting blood circulation, dissolving phlegm and soothing one's breathing. Way back in the 1320s the Franciscan friar Odoric visited China and commented on the snake-eating habits of the southern Chinese: 'There be monstrous great serpents likewise which are taken by the inhabitants and eaten. A solemn feast among them with serpents is thought nothing of'.

At 79 Haizhu Nanlu, a street behind the Aiqun Hotel, is a snake shop where hundreds of critters meet their demise daily. They get new shipments every Monday and do a brisk business in the morning; select your snake and stand back while they snip the head off, slit the belly open and skin it. Across the street is an alley with fish, frog and turtle stalls. It's next to an indoor market where you stock up on everything from vegies to pigeons and dogs.

Cheap Eats Innumerable dai pai dongs are open at night in the vicinity of the Renmin Daxia Hotel. If you walk around the streets, and particularly along Changdi Damalu on the north side of the hotel, you'll find sidewalk stalls dishing up frogs, toads and tortoises. At your merest whim these will be summarily executed, thrown in the wok and fried. It's a bit like eating in an abattoir, but at least there's no doubt about the freshness.

A couple of restaurants on Shamian Island are OK for a meal; they are popular with foreigners because of their proximity to the Guangzhou Youth Hostel.

Adequate but mundane food is served in the little restaurants in Zhanqian Lu, a lane which runs alongside the Liu Hua Hotel. A few of these places are marginally better than the others; look around until you see something you like. Some of the restaurateurs have an aggravating habit of trying to snatch you off the street and charge ridiculous prices, like Y1 for a small bowl of soupy noodles! In general, you should be able to get a sizeable helping of meat, rice, vegies and beer for a few yuan. Avoid the Double Happiness brand beer commonly sold here as it tastes like a sickly-sweet soft drink.

Fast Food Perhaps the most telling feature of the direction in which China is heading is the China Hotel's *Hasty Tasty Fast Food* shop which opens on to Jiefang Beilu. It looks and tastes exactly like any Hong Kong or American fast-food venue with banks of neon lights in the ceiling, laminex tables, and unremarkable food. A beef burger will knock you down Y1.80, a hot dog Y1.60 and a fruit jelly Y1.

As if to prove that the Chinese are no

less adverse to adopting the worst from the west as any other third-world country, there are several more fast-food venues in Canton and Beijing. None other than Donald Duck leads the hamburger and French fries revolution's advertising campaign. Be grateful for small mercies – it could have been Mickey Mouse.

Shopping

Canton's main shopping areas are Beijing Lu, Zhongshan Lu and the downtown section of Jiefang Lu. Beijing Lu is a most prestigious thoroughfare by Chinese standards. Names are sometimes misnomers; the Guangdong Products Exhibition Sales Centre, for example, seems to have more to do with the sale of Japanese ghetto-blasters and video units than with Chinese products. Some street markets specialise in Hong Kong-produced goods, including posters and brand-name jeans.

Department Stores Canton's main department store is the Nan Fang on Liuersan Lu, just to the east and opposite the main entrance to the Cultural Park.

Friendship Stores The Canton Friendship Store is next to the Bai Yun Hotel on Huanshi Donglu, and has two or three levels selling everything from Moskovskaya Osobaya Vodka to Foshan paper-cuts and life-size replicas of the terracotta soldiers at Xian. They'll take a number of credit cards, including American Express, Federal, Visa and Diners Club. Their packaging and shipping service will send stuff home for you, but they only handle goods bought from the store. You should be able to find a few bargains here. The store is open from 9 am to 9.30 pm in summer, probably shorter hours in winter. There are arts & crafts stores in the China and New Garden hotels.

Antiques For antiques try that major tourist trap, the Guangdong Antique Store, in the Guangxiao Temple at 575 Hongshu Beilu. At 146 Wende Lu (which runs off Zhongshan Lu) is the Canton Antique Store – not as large as the Guangdong Antique Store, but worth a look in.

Arts & Crafts The Jiangnan Native Product Store at 399 Zhongshan Lu has a good selection of bamboo and baskets. The Sanduoxuan on Beijing Lu, next door to the Foreign Languages Bookstore at No 326, is Canton's main art-supply shop.

Books, Posters & Magazines At 216 Beijing Lu there's a large Chinese-language book & poster store.

The Foreign Language Bookstore at 326 Beijing Lu has translations of Chinese books and magazines, as well as foreign magazines like *Time, Newsweek, Far Eastern Economic Review* and even *Readers Digest*.

The Classical Bookstore at 338 Beijing Lu specialises in pre-1949 Chinese string-bound editions.

The Xinhua Bookstore at 336 Beijing Lu is the main Chinese bookstore in the city. If you want to investigate the state of the pictorial arts in the country today, then this is a good place to come. There are lots of wall-posters as well as sets of reproductions of Chinese paintings. They also sell children's comic books, voraciously read by young and old alike.

The Ertong Shudian at 314 Beijing Lu is a children's bookshop.

Getting There & Away

Canton is a transport bottleneck; from here you can bus, train, fly or boat to numerous places in China. Even a few international flights pass through here (see the Getting There chapter at the start of this book for details).

Air Canton's Baiyun Airport is in the northern suburbs, 12 km from the city centre. Canton is connected by air to many parts of China, with daily flights to Beijing, Guilin, Kunming, Shanghai, Nanjing, Haikou (Hainan Island) and Xian. There are daily flights to Hong Kong (see the Getting There chapter for details).

Bus The long-distance bus station is on Huanshi Xilu, a 10-minute walk west of the railway station. From there you can get buses to many places in and beyond Guangdong Province.

One possibility is to head up the south-east coast of China. The first major town on the route is Shantou (Y15, two departures a day). There are also buses to Quanzhou (Y35), Xiamen (Y46) and Fuzhou (Y68).

Alternatively, head west to Zhanjiang. There are two buses daily. Air-con bus is Y27, non air-con Y15. The trip takes about 13½ hours. From Zhanjiang you can get a bus/boat combination to Haikou on Hainan Island.

There is a direct bus to Guilin which takes two days, overnighting in Wuzhou. Canton to Wuzhou is Y10. Canton to Guilin is Y26. There are one or two departures a day.

There are about eight or nine departures a day to Gongbei, the border town with Macau. The fare is about Y9 in an air-con bus and Y4 in a local bus. Other air-con buses to Gongbei leave from the Overseas Chinese Hotel in Haizhu Square, though these cost more; book with CTS at the hotel.

Rail Foreigners must now buy all train tickets out of Canton from the CITS office near the main train station. This means you'll have to pay tourist price, but at least you avoid the formidable queues!

There are two ways of getting to Hong Kong by train. Quickest is the express train to Kowloon. Slower but cheaper is the local train from Canton to the border town of Shenzhen, where you cross the border and pick up the electric train to Kowloon. For full details see the Getting There chapter at the start of this book.

The fastest express to Beijing takes about 33½ hours. The main line passes through Changsha, Wuhan, Zhengzhou and Shijiazhuang. Tourist-price fares from Canton to Beijing are Y70 hard-seat, Y110 hard-sleeper and Y210 soft-sleeper.

The express trip to Shanghai takes about 33 hours, and the line passes through Zhuzhou, Nanchang and Hangzhou. There is no direct train from Canton to Nanjing; you must first go to Shanghai and switch trains. An alternative would be to take the train as far as Hangzhou and then bus to Nanjing. Tourist-price tickets from Canton to Shanghai are Y56 hard-seat, Y87 hard-sleeper and Y154 soft-sleeper.

There is a direct train from Canton to Guilin. Alternatively, take a train to Hengyang and then change. The entire trip takes around 24 hours either way. Tourist-price tickets from Canton to Guilin are Y33 hard-seat, Y53 hard-sleeper and Y101 soft-sleeper.

Boat Canton has two main wharves, Zhoutouzui and Dashatou. There is another harbour, Whampoa (also known as Huangpu), 25 km east of Canton.

– Boats and hovercraft to Hong Kong, boats to Haikou (on Hainan Island) and boats to Macau leave from Zhoutouzui in the Honan area, on the south side of the Pearl River. For details of fares and departure times to Hong Kong and Macau see the Getting There chapter.

To get to Zhoutouzui you have to cross Renmin Bridge, continue down Hongde Lu and turn into Houde Lu. Look for the sign in English pointing the way to Zhoutouzui Pier. Bus No 31 not (trolley bus No 31) from the main train station will drop you off just near Houde Lu.

The ticket office for ferries and hovercraft to Hong Kong and Macau is at the gateway of the Guangzhou Zhoutouzui Liner Terminal. This ticket office may only sell tickets for same-day departure. Advance bookings can be made at the CTS office next to the Overseas Chinese Hotel in Haizhu Square.

– Boats to Wuzhou leave from Dashatou on Yanjiang Donglu, in eastern Canton.

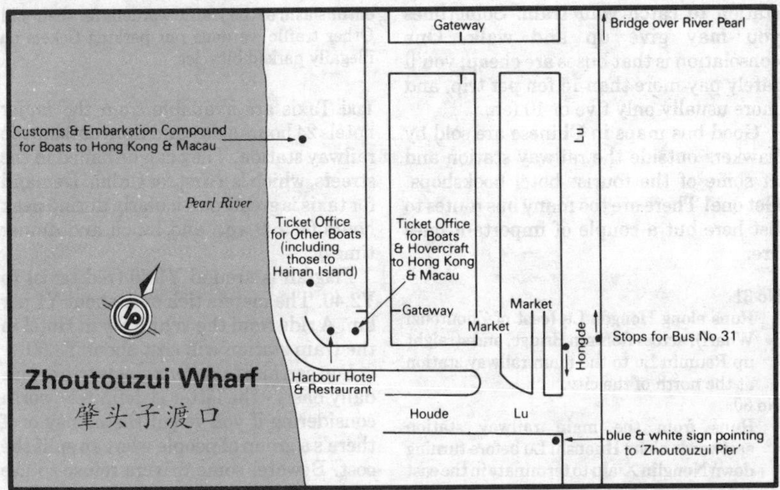

From Wuzhou you can continue by bus to Yangshuo or Guilin. This is a very popular route.

There are four boats a day from Canton to Wuzhou. The first boat departs Canton at around 12.30 pm. Fares are: 1st class Y17, 2nd class Y10.50, 3rd class Y9.50, 4th class Y8.

The lower classes have accommodation reminiscent of concentration-camp bunks. Passengers are laid out like sardines in two long rows; you get a thin mat to put on the hard wooden deck, and a small partition a few inches high between you and the next person. Food is dished up on the boat, and the aisle between the rows of people is filled by a rain of chicken bones. If it really does rain then the windows are closed and the cabin can be stifling.

You can also buy a combined boat/bus ticket from Canton to Yangshuo and Guilin. Canton to Yangshuo is Y22. Canton to Guilin is Y24, or Y29 with an air-con bus.

Getting Around

Canton proper extends for some 60 square km, with most of the interesting sights scattered throughout. Hence, seeing the place on foot is impractical. Just the walk from the railway station to the Pearl River is about six km.

Bus Canton has an extensive network of motor and electric trolley buses which will get you just about anywhere you want to go. The problem is that they're almost always packed, and if an empty bus pulls in at a stop then a battle for seats ensues.

Even more aggravating is the slowness with which Canton moves. Most of the streets are relatively narrow in comparison to those in other Chinese cities. They're also some of the most congested, a situation aggravated in the last few years by the import of hundreds of Toyota taxis and Japanese motorcycles (many of them driven by Chinese who seem to have picked up the kamikaze mentality as well). The end result is that even on a direct bus it can, for example, take up to 1½ hours to get from the zoo to Shamian Island in heavy traffic.

You just have to be patient, never expect anything to move rapidly and allow lots of time to get to the railway station to catch your train. Sometimes you may give up and walk. One consolation is that buses are cheap; you'll rarely pay more than 15 fen per trip, and more usually only five or 10 fen.

Good bus maps in Chinese are sold by hawkers outside the railway station and at some of the tourist hotel bookshops. Get one! There are too many bus routes to list here but a couple of important ones are:

No 31
: Runs along Hongde Lu (east of Zhoutouzi Wharf), across Renmin Bridge, and straight up Renmin Lu to the main railway station at the north of the city.

No 30
: Runs from the main railway station eastwards along Huanshi Lu before turning down Nonglin Xialu to terminate in the east of the city. This is a convenient bus to take from the railway station to the Baiyuan Hotel and New Garden Hotel.

No 5
: Takes a route similar to bus No 31, but instead of crossing Renmin Bridge it goes along Liurshan Lu on the north side of the canal which separates the city from Shamian Island. Get off here and walk across the small bridge to the island.

There is a shuttle bus from the White Swan Hotel to the main railway station, via Renmin Lu and the Canton Trade Fair Building. It runs daily, from early morning until 9.30pm, and costs Y1.

Bicycle Canton has at least one place to rent bicycles and no doubt other rental shops will follow. The Happy Bike Rental Station is on Shamian Island, across the road from the Guangzhou Youth Hostel. Cost is 90 fen per hour.

Check out Canton's unusual method of pedestrian and bicycle control. Old men and women, equipped with arm bands and small flags, stand on the streets apprehending jay-walkers and hauling them before a policeman who gives an on-the-spot fine; this is not taken lightly by many offenders, whose vehement arguments are matched only by the remarkable enthusiasm of the traffic wardens for their job! Other traffic wardens put parking tickets on illegally parked bicycles.

Taxi Taxis are available from the major hotels 24 hours a day and from outside the railway station. They can be hailed in the streets, which is a first for China. Demand for taxis is great, particularly during peak hours (8 to 9 am, and lunch and dinner times).

Flagfall is around Y1.80 (red taxis) to Y2.40. The meters tick over about Y1 per km. A ride from the White Swan Hotel to the train station will cost about Y3.60.

You can hire taxis for a single trip or on a daily basis – the latter is definitely worth considering if you've got the money or if there's a group of people who can split the cost. Beware, some drivers refuse to use their meters.

Minivan Minivans which seat about a dozen people ply the streets on set routes. If you can find out where they're going they're a good way to avoid the crowded buses.

AROUND CANTON

A couple of places around Canton make good full-day or half-day trips. Buses to some of these depart either from the long-distance bus station on Huanshi Xilu, or from the provincial bus station opposite the long-distance bus station. For some destinations you have to get buses from smaller bus stations around the city.

Baiyun Shan (White Cloud Hills)

These hills in the north-eastern suburbs of Canton are an offshoot of Dayu Ling, the chief mountain range of Guangdong Province. The White Cloud Hills were once dotted with temples and monasteries, though no buildings of historical significance remain today. The hills are popular with the local people who come here to admire the views and slurp cups of tea – the Cloudy Rock Teahouse on the hillside by a small waterfall is a pleasant place to do this.

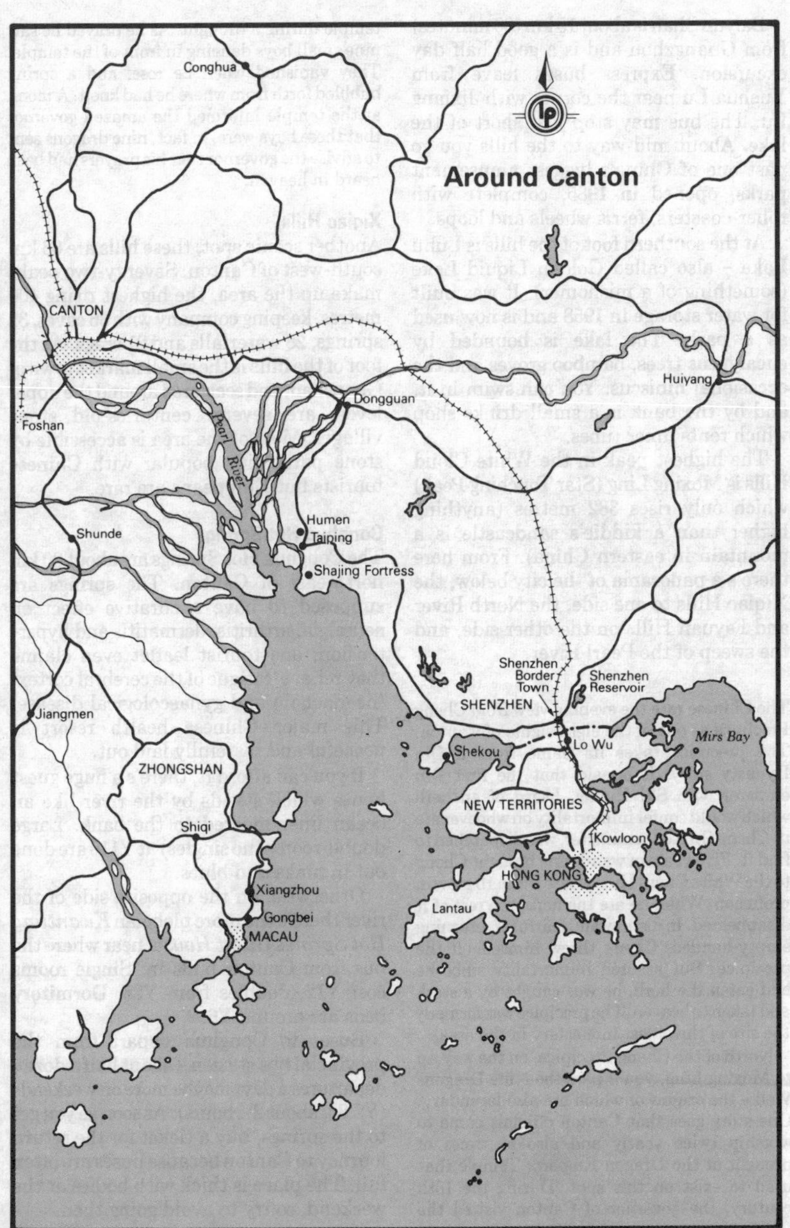
Around Canton
Conghua
CANTON
Foshan
Pearl River
Dongguan
Huiyang
Humen
Taiping
Shajing Fortress
Shunde
Shenzhen Border Town
Shenzhen Reservoir
SHENZHEN
Jiangmen
Shekou
Lo Wu
Mirs Bay
ZHONGSHAN
NEW TERRITORIES
Kowloon
Shiqi
HONG KONG
Lantau
Xiangzhou
Gongbei
MACAU

Baiyun Shan is about 15 km (30 minutes) from Guangzhou and is a good half-day excursion. Express buses leave from Yuehua Lu near the corner with Jixiang Lu. The bus may stop just short of the lake. About mid-way to the hills you go past one of China's biggest amusement parks, opened in 1985, complete with roller-coasters, ferris wheels and loops.

At the southern foot of the hills is Luhu Lake – also called Golden Liquid Lake (something of a misnomer). It was built for water storage in 1958 and is now used as a park. The lake is bounded by eucalyptus trees, bamboo groves and the occasional hibiscus. You can swim in it, and by the bank is a small drinks shop which rents inner tubes.

The highest peak in the White Cloud Hills is Moxing Ling (Star Touching Peak) which only rises 382 metres (anything higher than a kiddie's sandcastle is a mountain in eastern China). From here there's a panorama of the city below, the Xiqiao Hills to one side, the North River and Fayuan Hills on the other side, and the sweep of the Pearl River.

The Chinese rate the evening view from Cheng Precipice as one of the eight sights of Canton. The precipice takes its name from a Qin Dynasty story. It is said that the first Qin emperor, Qin Shi Huang, heard of an herb which would confer immortality on whoever ate it. Cheng On Kee, a minister, was dispatched to find it. Five years of wandering brought Cheng to the White Cloud Hills where the herb grew in profusion. When he ate the herb, the rest of it disappeared. In dismay and fearful of returning empty-handed, Cheng threw himself off the precipice. But assured immortality since he had eaten the herb, he was caught by a stork and taken to heaven. The precipice was formerly the site of the oldest monastery in the area.

North of the Cheng Precipice, on the way up to Moxing Ling, you'll pass the Nine Dragons Well – the origins of which are also legendary. One story goes that Canton officials came to worship twice yearly and also at times of drought at the Dragon Emperor Temple that used to exist on this spot. During the 18th century, the governor of Canton visited the temple during a drought. As he prayed he saw nine small boys dancing in front of the temple. They vanished when he rose, and a spring bubbled forth from where he had knelt. A monk at the temple informed the amazed governor that these boys were, in fact, nine dragons sent to advise the governor that his prayers had been heard in heaven.

Xiqiao Hills

Another scenic spot, these hills are 68 km south-west of Canton. Seventy-two peaks make up the area, the highest rising 400 metres, keeping company with 36 caves, 32 springs, 28 waterfalls and 21 crags. At the foot of the hills is the small market town of Guanshan, and scattered around the upper levels are several centuries-old stone villages. Most of the area is accessible by stone paths; it's popular with Chinese tourists but Europeans are rare.

Conghua Hot Springs

The Conghua Hot Springs are about 80 km north-east of Canton. The springs are supposed to have a curative effect on neuralgia, arthritis, dermatitis and hypertension; one tourist leaflet even claims they relieve 'fatigue of the cerebral cortex' (headache?) and gynaecological disease. This major Chinese health resort is peaceful and tastefully laid out.

If you can afford it, there's a huge guest house which stands by the river like an ocean liner moored to the bank. Large double rooms (no singles) at Y110 are done out in pinks and blues.

Otherwise, on the opposite side of the river there's the more plebeian *Kwantung Hot Springs Guest House*, near where the bus from Canton pulls in. Single rooms cost Y12, doubles from Y28. Dormitory beds are around Y6.

Buses to Conghua depart from the provincial bus station – about half a dozen departures a day, maybe more on weekends (Y2.85, about 2½ hours). As soon as you get to the springs, buy a ticket for the return journey to Canton because buses are often full. The place is thick with bodies at the weekend, so try to avoid going then.

Guangdong 广东

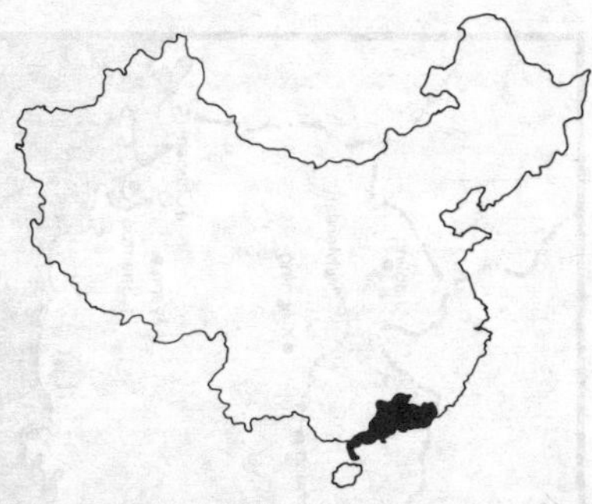

Over 2000 years ago when the Chinese were carving out a civilisation centred on the Yellow River, southern China remained a semi-independent tributary peopled by native tribes, the last survivors of which are found today as minority groups. It was not until the Qin Dynasty (221-207 BC), when the northern states were united for the first time under a single ruler, that the Chinese finally conquered the southern regions. Revolts and uprisings were frequent and the Chinese settlements remained small and dispersed amongst a predominantly aboriginal population.

Chinese emigration to the south began in earnest around the 12th century AD. The original native tribes were killed by Chinese armies, isolated in small pockets, or pushed further south (like the Li and Miao peoples who now inhabit the mountainous areas of Hainan Island). By the 17th century the Chinese had outgrown Guangdong, and population pressure forced them to move into adjoining Guangxi Province, and Sichuan which had been depopulated after rebellions in the mid-17th century.

Because of these migrations the people of Guangdong are not a homogeneous group. The term 'Cantonese' is sometimes applied to all people living in Guangdong Province. More commonly it refers to those who shared the language and culture of a grouping of counties during the last imperial dynasties. Other inhabitants of Guangdong are distinguished from the 'Cantonese' by their language and customs, like the Hakka people who started moving south from the northern plains around the 13th or 14th centuries.

What the migrants from the north found beyond the mountainous areas of northern and western Guangdong was the Pearl River Delta, a region richer than any in China except for the Yangtse and Yellow rivers. The Pearl River Delta lies at the south-east end of a broad plain which stretches over both Guangdong and Guangxi provinces. Because of their fertility the delta and river valleys could support very large populations. The abundant waterways, heavy rainfall and warm climate allowed wet rice cultivation, and two crops a year could be grown (although in the past century the growth of the population was more then Guangdong could sustain, so grain had to be imported).

The people of Guangdong Province were the first Chinese to make contact (often unhappy) with the merchants and armies of the modern European states. They spearheaded the Chinese emigration to America, Australia and South Africa in the mid-19th century, spurred on by the gold rushes in those countries and by the wars and growing poverty of their own country. The image which most westerners have today of a 'Chinatown' is based on Guangdong's chief city, Canton; it is Cantonese food which is eaten and the Cantonese dialect which is spoken among the Chinese populations from Melbourne to Toronto to London.

SHENZHEN SPECIAL ECONOMIC ZONE 深圳经济特区

The Shenzhen municipality stretches across the northern border of Hong Kong from Daya Bay in the east to the mouth of the Pearl River in the west. Though hardly a place to linger, Shenzhen town is worth

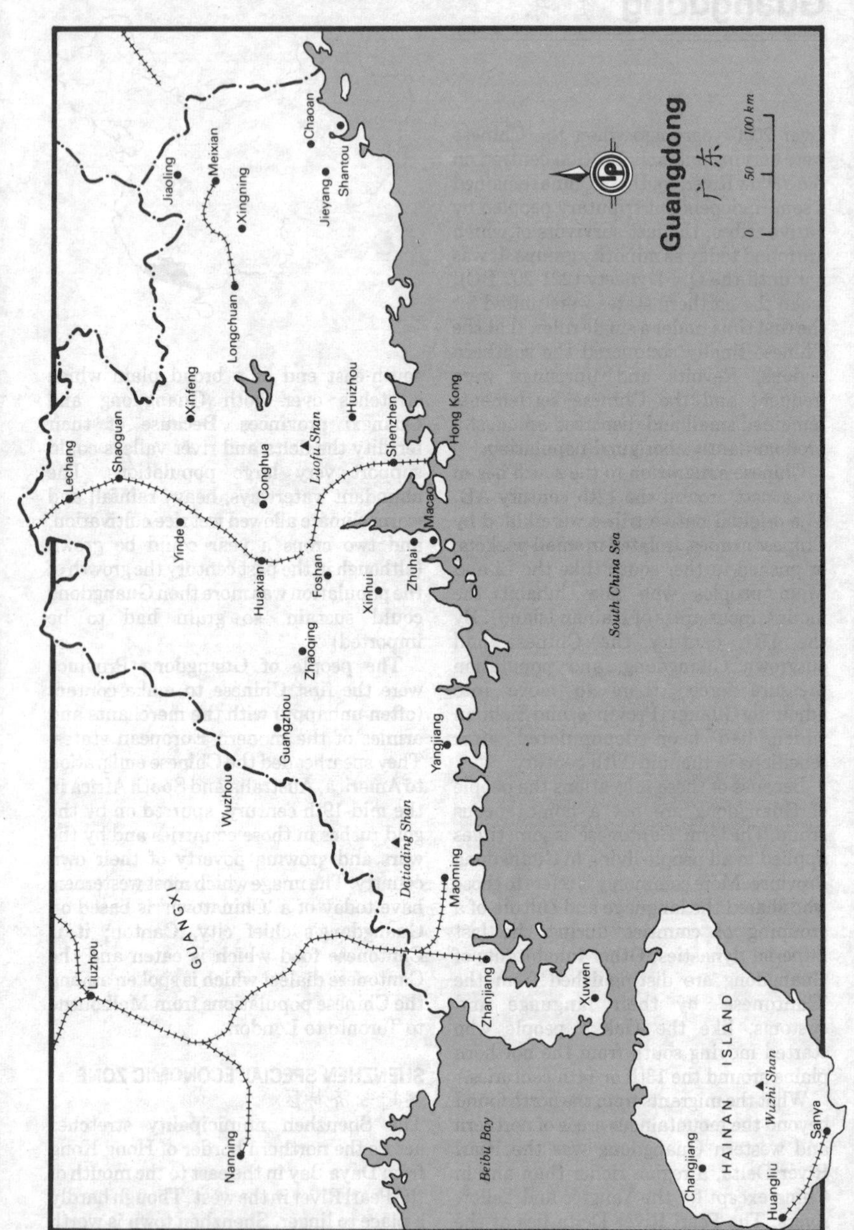
Guangdong
广东
0 50 100 km
South China Sea
Beibu Bay
HAINAN ISLAND
GUANGXI
Lechang
Shaoguan
Xinfeng
Longchuan
Jiaoling
Meixian
Xingning
Chaoan
Jieyang
Shantou
Yinde
Conghua
Luofu Shan
Huizhou
Shenzhen
Hong Kong
Huaxian
Foshan
Zhuhai
Macao
Xinhui
Zhaoqing
Guangzhou
Wuzhou
Yangjiang
Datiading Shan
Maoming
Zhanjiang
Xuwen
Liuzhou
Nanning
Changjiang
Wuzhi Shan
Huangliu
Sanya

looking around for a few hours since it is the centre of a major Special Economic Zone.

The Special Economic Zones were set up to promote foreign and Overseas Chinese investment in China using reduced taxation, low wages, abundant labour supply and low operating costs as encouragement. The theory behind this is that China can be modernised quicker and more easily if it imports foreign technology and expertise. The SEZs are a sort of geographical laboratory where western capitalist economic principles can be tested using cheap socialist labour. These zones are not a new idea, bearing some resemblance to the Export Processing Zones found in 30 other countries.

The SEZ was set up in a small part of the Shenzhen municipality in 1979. The area was chosen for several reasons: it is adjacent to Hong Kong, thus allowing easier access to the world market; most Hong Kong businessmen speak the same dialects and maintain kinship relations with people in Shenzhen and other parts of southern China; there is easy access to the port facilities of Hong Kong; and the level land is suitable for settlement and industrial plants, with a ready supply of raw materials for the construction industry.

In the SEZs foreigners can invest in anything which the state deems useful for the country, be it production of goods for export or construction of private-housing estates. These can be joint ventures, co-operative enterprises or wholly foreign-owned operations. A uniform income-tax rate of 15% is applied. Whether the SEZs actually benefit China is debatable. The zones were conceived of as a means of obtaining foreign technology and capital, and of producing exports with a minimum of disruption to the rest of the country's economy. The problem has been that these zones are importing equipment and raw materials but most of their output is ultimately sold in China, not exported. The amount of money they produce for China may be far less than the money the government puts into them to keep them running. What's more, most of the foreign industries set up in Shenzhen in the five years after it opened in 1979 have been relatively simple ones – like electronics assembly – which falls well short of the capital and technology-intensive investment that China seeks.

Other problems have been produced by unleashing this laissez-faire capitalism on Chinese territory, not least of which is the booming black market in just about everything. One of the main problems in Shenzhen has been that the Hong Kong Chinese 'compatriots' as well as PRC Chinese sell Hong Kong currency at a higher black-market rate than the official rate, then buy Chinese produce at the free markets, thus undercutting the official export prices and shipping the goods off to their markets in Hong Kong and Macau. It's said that one of the things that has upset many big-wigs in the Chinese government is that black-market dealing has been putting their own business enterprises in Shenzhen at a disadvantage.

Various plans have been conjured up to solve these problems. One is to introduce a whole new currency for use only in Shenzhen, and thus halt the black-market dealing in foreign currency. Once the new currency is in place all other currencies in the SEZ – Renminbi, Foreign Exchange Certificates and Hong Kong dollars – would be withdrawn. Whether this plan will go ahead is not known at the time of writing. However, partly in anticipation of this happening, the Chinese have fenced off the whole Zone from China and Hong Kong.

SHENZHEN TOWN 深圳

The showpiece of the SEZ is Shenzhen town, once a fishing village but transformed in just a few years into a small town of high-rise blocks. The centrepiece is the 600-bed, 33-storey Asia Hotel Complex topped by, you guessed it, a revolving restaurant. There are Friendship Stores and air-con restaurants (the locals pause in the doorways for a breath of cool air), and at

nearby Xili Reservoir there are holiday resorts and golf courses for Hong Kongers searching for more breathing space.

Places to Stay

The *Overseas Chinese Hotel* is across the tracks from the train station. Dormitory beds are HK$30, double rooms (no singles) HK$92.

For cheaper rooms try the *Shenzhen Hotel Co Ltd* (sign on doorway) four blocks up Jianshe Lu from the train station. Dorm beds are Y8.

Getting There & Away

For full details of transport between Hong Kong, Shenzhen and Canton see the Getting There chapter at the start of this book.

Bus By the time this book is out it may be possible to drive across the border from Hong Kong and all the way to Canton. Outside Shenzhen train station you can get minibuses to Canton; the fare is about Y3.40.

From Shenzhen there are CITS buses to Canton (Y11), and to towns on the south-east coast including Shantou (Y27) and Fuzhou, Xiamen, Zhangzhou and Quanzhou (Y50 to Y60). The buses leave from the CITS office in the Overseas Chinese Hotel.

Rail There are about a dozen local trains a day between Canton and Shenzhen. Tourist-price tickets are Y6.40 hard-seat, Y9.90 soft-seat. The trip takes 3½ hours.

At Shenzhen you pass through Customs and catch the electric train to Kowloon. The border closes at 10 pm (check this, it may vary throughout the year). The 2nd-class fare from the Hong Kong border station of Lo Wu to Kowloon Station is HK$14.50. The first train to Kowloon Station is at 6 am and the last is at 11.30 pm.

FOSHAN 佛山

Just 28 km south-west of Canton is the town of Foshan, the name means 'Buddha Hill'. The story goes that a visiting monk from India built a hilltop temple for three Buddha statues. In the following centuries the shrines and the statues were forgotten but hundreds of years later, during the Tang Dynasty (618-907 AD), the Buddha figurines were suddenly rediscovered, a new temple was built on the hill and the town renamed.

Whether the story is true or not, from around the 10th century Foshan has been an important religious centre. Because of its location in the north of the Pearl River Delta with the Fen River flowing through

Top: Piling on the poultry for market (RS)
Bottom Left: Bird market, Chengdu (RS)
Bottom Right: Pressed pork in bike pannier (RS)

Top: The Bund, Shanghai (AS)
Bottom: Rice paddies at Shaoshan (AS)

it, and its proximity to Canton, Foshan was ideally placed to take off as a market town and a trade centre as well.

From much the same time, around the 10th or 11th centuries, Foshan has also been noted as one of the four main handicraft centres of old China; the other three were Zhuxian in Henan Province, Jingdezhen in Jiangxi and Hankou in Hebei. Nearby towns, since swallowed up by the expansion of Foshan, also developed distinctive crafts. Shiwan became famous for its pottery and Nanpu for metal casting. Silk weaving and paper-cutting are other popular local crafts and today Foshan paper-cuts are one of the commonly sold tourist souvenirs in China.

Foshan has one other claim to fame: as Guangdong Province's top soya sauce producer it provides half of China's soya sauce exports to over 40 countries.

Orientation

The bus from Canton heads into Foshan from the north and pulls in outside Foshan train station. The train line starts in Canton, passes through Foshan and carries on west about 60 km to the town of Hekou.

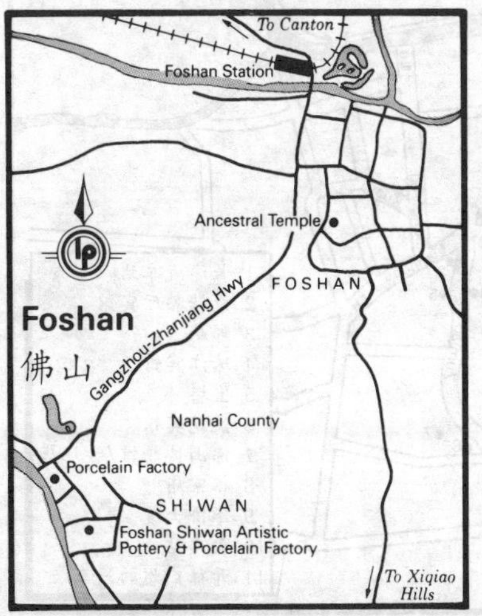

From the train station walk down the Canton-Zhanjiang Highway. Turn left down any side street. Walk for about 10 minutes and you'll come to one of Foshan's main streets, Song Feng Lu. A right turn onto Song Feng Lu will point you in the direction of the town centre and the market on Lianhua Lu.

Lianhua Market

The market can't compare to Qingping Market in Canton, but it's worth a wander if you're in Foshan. Stock up on half-dead fish, turtles, snakes, crabs or skinned and roasted dogs. Other stalls offer flowers, birds and goldfish. Pets are back in favour in the People's Republic; during the Cultural Revolution the keeping of goldfish and birds was regarded as a bourgeois pursuit and the Red Guards tried to wipe out the hobby.

Ancestors Temple

The Ancestors Temple is at the southern end of Zumiao Lu. The original temple was built during the Song Dynasty in the late 11th century, and was used by workers in the metal-smelting trade for worshipping their ancestors. It was destroyed by fire at the end of the Yuan Dynasty in the mid-1300s and was rebuilt during the reign of the first Ming emperor Hong Wu. The Ancestors Temple was converted into a Taoist temple since the emperor worshipped a Taoist god.

The temple was developed through renovations and additions in the Ming and Qing dynasties. The structure is built entirely of interlocking wooden beams, with no nails or other metal, and is roofed with coloured tiles made in Shiwan. The latest additions are a kiddie's amusement park in the forecourt, rows of souvenir hawkers outside, and plaster of Paris imitations to replace the original statues. Nonetheless, this temple/fairground is once again an active place of worship.

The main hall has an interesting collection of ornate weapons used on ceremonial occasions during the imperial days as well as a huge statue of Beidi or the Northern Emperor. Beidi is also known as the Black Emperor or Heidi, who rules over water creatures including fish, turtles and snakes.

To keep Beidi happy and to convince him not to cause floods, a frequent problem in Southern China, temples are frequently built in his honour. Carved figures of snakes and turtles are also offered to this god of the waters. In the courtyard is a pool containing a large statue of a turtle with a serpent slithering over it. The Chinese throw one, two and five-fen notes (plus the odd soft-drink can) onto the turtle.

1. Long-distance Bus Station
2. Rotating Palace Hotel
3. Post Office
4. Pearl River Hotel
5. Pagoda
6. Liu Hua Hotel
7. Foshan Museum/Antique Store
8. Ancestors Temple
9. Overseas Chinese Mansion
10. Railway Station
11. Buses to Canton

Places to Stay

Centrally located is the fairly inexpensive *Pearl River Hotel* (tel or 87512) in the centre of town. Doubles cost from Y16.

Across the road the *Rotating Palace Hotel* is Foshan's newest and is so-called because, yes, there's a revolving restaurant on top. Doubles in this glittering 16-storey tower are around Y85. Even if you don't stay here, take the elevator to the observation deck on the 16th floor and look across the sea of old, tiled roofs in the centre of town and the industrial smokestacks beyond; if Foshan began as a religious centre you'd hardly know it now.

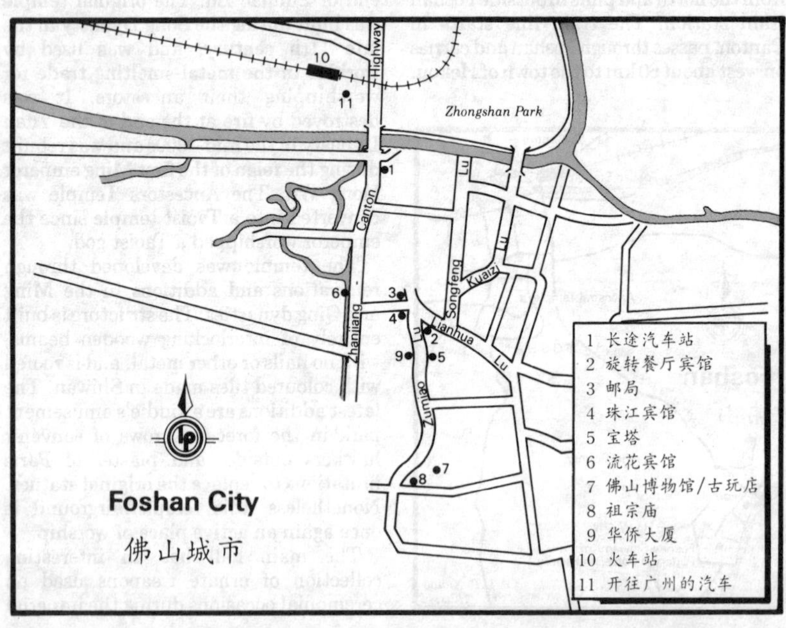

The *Overseas Chinese Mansion (Huaqiao Daxia)* (tel 86511) is on Zumiao Lu opposite the pagoda. Singles are Y40, doubles Y60. The *Liu Hua Hotel* on the Zhanjiang-Canton highway (see map) is similarly priced.

Places to Eat
Cheap eats are to be had at the bus station on the Zhanjiang-Canton Highway; squid, omelettes and chicken come in decent portions for a few yuan per person. Try the dai pai dongs along Songfeng Lu and Lianhua Lu; there are also several restaurants along here similar to the one at the bus station.

Getting There & Away
Buses to Foshan from Canton leave from the bus station in western Canton, on Huangsha Dadao just south of Zhujiang Bridge. The fare is around Y1.40; the trip takes 50 to 60 minutes. If you're only up from Hong Kong for a few days this will give you a glimpse of the countryside. In Foshan the bus drops you off at the square beside the Foshan train station; however, you can get buses back to Canton from the long-distance bus station just over the river. There are about 20 buses a day between Canton and Foshan.

Getting Around
Local bus Nos 1 and 10 will take you from the bus station on the Zhanjiang-Canton highway to the the Pearl River Hotel and the Overseas Chinese Hotel. Bus No 2 will take you as far as the Pearl River Hotel, and from there you can walk to the Overseas Chinese Hotel.

GONGBEI 拱北
Gongbei is the Chinese town bordering Macau. Like its big brother Shenzhen it's been built from the soles up in the past few years, with numerous office blocks and apartment buildings sprouting for a km or so back from the border. Yet for all this a bus ride from Gongbei to Canton still brings back the point that China is very much a rural society, where peasants water their fields with cans slung on poles over their shoulders, boatmen make their way up rivers standing as they push their oars, motorcyclists transport basket-loads of geese in panniers, and slaughtered pigs are slung over the pack-racks of bicycles. There's a surprising number of beggars in Gongbei, scraping a bit of their own off the Four Modernisations.

Places to Stay
The *Gongbei Palace Hotel* (tel 23831) comes complete with disco, billiard room, swimming pool, sauna and video games. They say it's modelled on a Qin Dynasty palace. Double rooms cost from Y200.

Across the road is the *CTS* – no singles but you may get a double for around Y36. Another hotel is the *Jiu Zhou* a few minutes' walk from the Customs Building; doubles cost from around Y50.

Getting There
Buses to Gongbei depart from Canton's long-distance bus station on Huanshi Xilu. Air-con bus is Y9, several departures a day. There are cheaper local buses for Y4.

THE PEARL RIVER DELTA 珠江三角州
The Pearl River Delta is the large, fertile and heavily populated territory immediately south of Canton. Apart from Canton the delta has several towns and places of interest.

Zhuhai
This area immediately to the north of Macau was set up as a Special Economic Zone in 1979. The principal town is Xiangzhou, nine km north of Macau. From Gongbei, the town bordering Macau, you can get buses to various places in Zhuhai.

Zhongshan County
Zhongshan County is immediately north of Zhuhai. The administrative centre is Shiqi. Zhongshan is the birthplace of Dr Sun Yatsen, who was born in the village of

Cuiheng, 29 km from Macau. His former house, which still stands in the village, was built in 1892 with money sent from Honolulu by his elder brother. There is also a Sun Yatsen Museum set up in 1966. South-west of Cuiheng are the Zhongshan Hot Springs, which have been turned into a tourist resort; three km away are the Yungmo Hot Springs. You should be able to reach all these places by bus from Gongbei. Jiangmen is an old town in the west of Zhongshan County; get there by bus from Canton's long-distance bus station on Huanshi Lu.

Humen

This small town about 100 km south-east of Canton was a centre of resistance during the Opium Wars. According to one Chinese leaflet:

> Humen was the place where the Chinese people captured and burned the opium dumped into China by the British and American merchants in the 1830s and it was also the outpost of the Chinese people to fight against the aggressive opium war. In 1839, Lin Zexu, the then imperial envoy of the Qing government, resolutely put a ban on opium smoking and the trade of opium. Supported by the broad masses of the people, Lin Zexu forced the British and American opium mongers to hand over 20,285 cases of opium . . . and burned all of them at Humen beach, Dongguang County. This just action showed the strong will of the Chinese people to resist against the imperialist aggression . . .

Today there is a 'Museum of the Humen People's Resistance Against the British in the Opium War', a monument and a memorial statue in the town.

Sanyuanli

Sanyuanli, on the outskirts of Canton, is also notable for its role in the first Opium War. A Chinese leaflet relates that:

> In 1840, the British imperialists launched the opium war against China. No sooner had the British invaders landed on the western outskirts of Guangzhou on 24 of May than they started to burn, slaughter, rape and loot the local people. All this aroused Guangzhou people's great indignation. Holding high the great banner of anti-invasion, the heroic people of Sanyuanli together with the people from the nearby 103 villages took an oath to fight against the enemy at Sanyuan Old Temple. On 30 May, they lured the British troops to the place called Niulangang where they used hoes, swords and spears as weapons and annihilated over 200 British invaders armed with rifles and cannons. Finally the British troops were forced to withdraw from the Guangzhou area.

A museum and a monument commemorate the struggle that took place at Sanyuanli.

Guanlubu

Forty km north of Canton is the village of Guanlubu where Hong Xiuquan, the leader of the Taiping Rebellion, was born in 1814 and lived in his early years. His house has been restored, and the Hong clan temple is now used as a museum.

ZHAOQING 肇庆

For almost 1000 years people have been coming to Zhaoqing to scribble graffiti on its cliffs or inside its caves – often poems or essays describing how much they liked the rock formations they were drawing on.

Zhaoqing is noted for the Seven Star Crags, a group of limestone towers – a peculiar geological formation abundant in the paddy fields of Guilin and Yangshuo. Legend has it that the crags were actually seven stars that fell from the sky to form a pattern resembling the Big Dipper. In keeping with their celestial origin each has been given an exotic name like 'Hill Slope' and 'Toad'. The artificial lakes were built in 1955, and the park is adorned with concrete pathways, arched bridges and little pavilions.

Among Zhaoqing's most famous visitors was the defunct Song Dynasty, the last of whom set up shop here on their flight from the Mongol invaders. Later, in 1583, foreign devils in the guise of the Jesuit priests Matteo Ricci and Michael Ruggieri came here and were allowed to establish a church. Marshal Ye Jianying passed through in 1966 and composed some inspired verse:

With water borrowed from the West Lake,
Seven hills transferred from Yangshuo,
Green willows lining the banks
This picturesque scenery will remain forever!

If you're going to Guilin or Yangshuo it's not worth coming here just to see the hills, but the ride to Zhaoqing from Canton and the town itself are interesting. Zhaoqing lies 110 km west of Canton on Xi (West) River.

Orientation

The town is bounded to the south by the West River and to the north by Duanzhou Lu. Zhaoqing is a small place and a good deal of it can be seen on foot.

The long-distance bus station is on Duanzhou Lu. Turn left out of the station and walk for a few minutes to the traffic circle where the multi-storey Zhaoqing Mansion and the entrance to Seven Star Crags Park are located. Tianming Lu is the main street with many shops, cheap restaurants and noisy canteens.

Streets to the right lead off into the older part of Zhaoqing. It's a 20-minute walk to Jiangbin Donglu, which hugs the north bank of the West River.

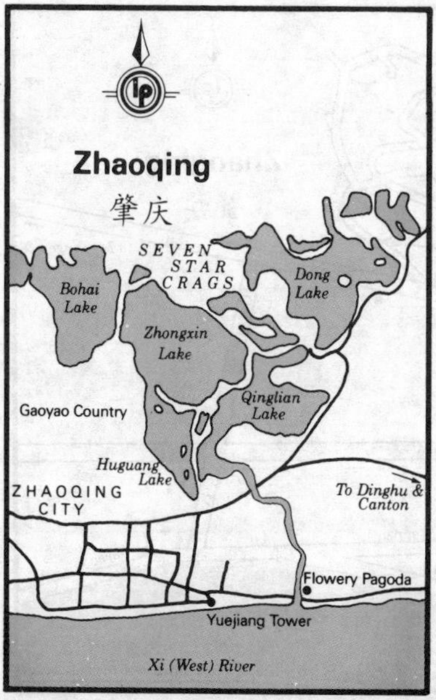

Things to See

Zhaoqing is a town for walking. It's a place where the peak-hour bicycle crush goes hand-in-hand with quiet side streets, and where dilapidated houses are equipped with colour TVs and outdoor communal toilets.

The nine-storey **Chongxi Pagoda**, in a sad state until a few years ago, has been restored and stands on Tajiao Lu in the south-east. On the opposite bank of the river are two similar pagodas. Tajiao Lu, a quiet riverside street, has interesting old houses. **Yuejiang Tower** is a restored temple about a 30-minute walk from the Chongxi Pagoda, just back from the waterfront at the eastern end of Zheng Donglu.

From the Yuejiang Tower, head down Zheng Donglu into the centre of town and past the intersection with Tianming Lu. Continue down Zheng Donglu for about 10 minutes; on your left you'll come to a busy street market where bicycles, people and hand-drawn carts compete for space. At the western end of town is **Plum Monastery**. To get there continue to the end of Zheng Donglu and turn right.

Mt Dinghu, 20 km east of Zhaoqing, is a summer resort for the Chinese. Apart from its streams, brooks, pools, hills and trees, the mountain is noted for the Qingyuan Temple, built towards the end of the Ming Dynasty.

Hire a bicycle and head off along the paths away from the lake. Old villages, duck ponds, door gods, buffalo swimming in ponds, strange pavilions and caves can all be found.

Places to Stay & Eat
There are a couple of places to stay in Zhaoqing, but the only convenient one is the *Zhaoqing Mansion* (the Overseas Chinese Hotel) on the corner of Duanzhou Lu and Tianming Lu. Big double rooms cost from Y25 on the ground floor (probably noisy) and Y30 upstairs. Very comfortable.

The *Bohailou Hotel* is on the north side of Zhong (Central) Lake in the Seven Star Crag Park. It's more attractive than other Chinese hotels but no less cold and dreary inside. If you're here in the off-season it's extremely quiet with farms to the rear and the lake to the front. Doubles cost from Y24. Nearby is the immaculate *Seven Star Crags Hotel*, with water-wheel in the foyer and doubles from Y78.

One can only hope that the Songs and the Jesuits ate somewhat better. There's nothing remarkable to be had here. The bus station has a cheap, tolerable restaurant, and there are cheap restaurants along Duanzhou Lu and Tianming Lu.

Getting There & Away
Bus There are buses to Zhaoqing from Canton's long-distance bus station on Huanshi Xilu. The fare is Y4. There are half a dozen buses a day and the trip takes about 2½ hours. Try to avoid returning to Canton on a weekend afternoon; traffic jams are common on this road.

Privately run minibuses operate between

1 Long-distance Bus Station
2 Local Bus Station
3 Zhaoqing Mansion
4 Bohailou Hotel
5 Post Office
6 Yuejiang Tower
7 Chongxi Pagoda
8 Furong Hotel
9 Bicycle Rental
10 Duanzhou Hotel

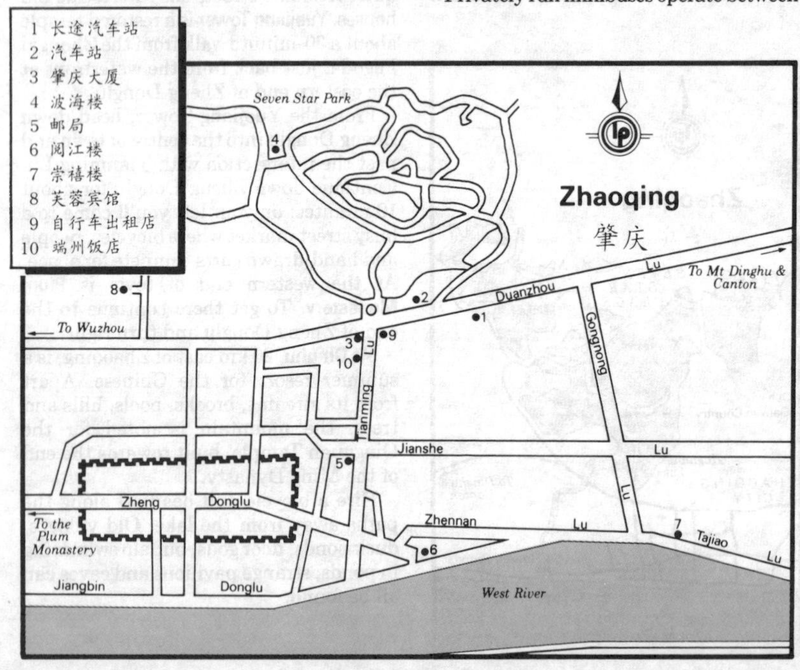

Zhaoqing and Canton. In Zhaoqing the minibus ticket office is inside the main gate to the Seven Star Crags Park. The fare to Canton is Y6.70 and there are several buses a day.

Boat The dock and ticket office for boats to Wuzhou and Canton is at 3 Jiangbin Donglu, just west of the intersection with Renmin Nanlu. It appears that only lower-class boat tickets can be bought here since Zhaoqing is an intermediate stop. Boats to Wuzhou and Canton depart in the early evening. Fares to both cities are Y5 in 3rd class and Y4 in 4th class. Zhaoqing to Wuzhou is an 11 to 12-hour trip. Zhaoqing to Canton is a 10-hour trip.

Getting Around

The local bus station is on Duanzhou Lu, a few minutes' walk east of the intersection with Tianming Lu. Bus No 1 runs to the ferry dock on the Xi River. Bus Nos 4 and 5 go to the Plum Monastery.

Auto-rickshaws may be hired from the rank opposite the long-distance bus station. If you catch one in the street beware of overcharging. Taxis are dispatched from an office at the rear of the bus station.

The best way to get around Zhaoqing is on bicycle. There is a hire place diagonally opposite the main entrance to the Seven Star Crags. They charge Y5 (!) per day.

ZHANJIANG 湛江

Zhanjiang is a major port on the southern coast of China, and the largest Chinese port west of Canton. It was leased to France in 1898 and remained under French control until WW II.

Today the French are back, but this time Zhanjiang is a base for their oil-exploration projects in the South China Sea. Perhaps more importantly, Zhanjiang is a naval base and part of China's southern defences against what is construed as a threat from the Vietnamese.

You're most likely to come to Zhanjiang if you're on your way from Canton or Nanning to Hainan Island. The bus ride from Canton is an interesting trip, although Zhanjiang itself is one of the greyest towns in China.

Zhanjiang is divided into two parts separated by a stretch of countryside several km long. The town is a good place to wander around at night when the crowds are out in the streets, but it's rather dusty and boring during the day – too many concrete blocks, drab streets and slums.

Perhaps to liven things up the Chinese have opened some coral reefs to snorkelling and scuba diving. One of the sites is off Naozhou on an island near the Zhanjiang Peninsula. The second is off Fangji Isle east of Zhanjiang. The third site is near Dongmao and Ximao islands in Hainan Island's Sanya Bay.

Places to Stay

There is a *Chinese Hotel* you can stay at in the northern part of town. Turn right out

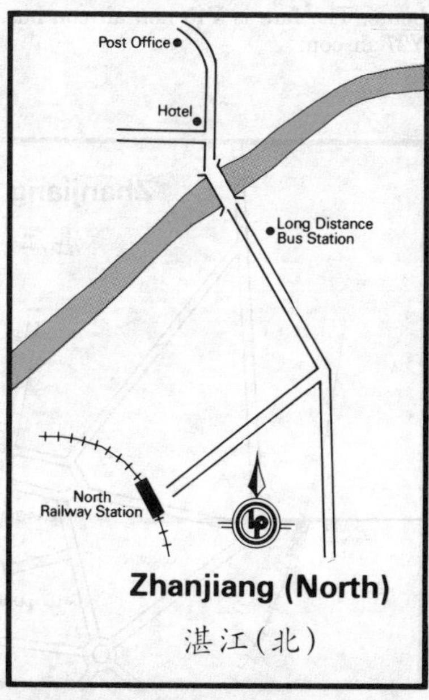

of the North Bus Station, and the hotel is 10 minutes up the road. It's very noisy – you won't want to hang around for too long – but otherwise it's OK. You should be able to get a bed or even a single room for a few yuan.

The *Overseas Chinese Hotel* is in the southern part of town and has dormitories. Double rooms start from Y18.

The *Hai Bin Hotel* (tel 23555) on Haibin Lu is a deluxe Hong Kong-China joint venture on the southern outskirts of Zhanjiang. Double rooms are Y80 in the new wing and Y35 in the old wing. The hotel boasts a Hong Kong-trained staff, Chinese restaurant, cocktail lounge, coffee shop, outdoor pool and sauna.

Getting There & Away

Air There are daily flights from Zhanjiang to Canton.

Bus You should be able to get buses to Canton from both the North and South bus stations. The trip takes about 13½ hours. The fare is Y15 non air-con bus, Y27 air-con.

Rail Trains to Guilin and Nanning leave from the South Train Station. Zhanjiang to Guilin takes about 13 hours. Zhanjiang to Nanning takes about 9½ hours. Tourist-price tickets from Zhanjiang to Nanning are Y19 hard-seat and Y29 hard-sleeper.

Boat You can take a bus/boat combination to Haikou on Hainan Island. A bus takes you from Zhanjiang to Hai'an on the Leizhou Peninsula (five hours), where you take a boat to Haikou (two hours). The bus station at Hai'an is about 100 metres uphill from the harbour. The harbour ticket office is a dingy place, but you can deposit baggage here or buy maps of Haikou.

Some travellers have reported persistent urchins here who dangle a slip of paper which says: 'I help you, you want to Haikou, you give me Y20, the boat leaves at . . . all aboard'. They'll try to hang on to the change and your baggage and generally create a nuisance until you're thankful to escape onto the boat.

Combined bus/boat tickets cost about Y12. You should be able to buy tickets at the Chinese hotel in the northern part of Zhanjiang. If not, there's a booking office

opposite the nearby post office. Or buy a separate bus ticket at the bus station and a boat ticket when you get to Leizhou Peninsula.

There's also a fast vessel (resembling a Hong Kong jetfoil) from Leizhou Peninsula to Hainan Island which takes 45 minutes; fare is Y5.50.

Getting Around

There are two train stations and two long-distance bus stations, one each in the northern and southern parts of town.

Bus No 1 runs between the two parts. This bus may be designated by a double-headed arrow (surrounded by calligraphy) rather than by a numeral.

If you arrive at the North Bus Station take bus No 1 to the southern part of town. This will drop you off in the vicinity of the Overseas Chinese Hotel. If you arrive at the South Train Station take bus No 10 to the hotel.

There are many motorcycles-and-sidecars cruising the streets; agree on a price beforehand or they'll charge you the earth.

SHANTOU 汕头

Considering the length of the southern and south-eastern coasts of China, they are remarkably deficient in sea-ports. The main problem is the constant accumulation of silt and mud rendering the natural harbours cramped and shallow. Only a few, like Xiamen and Hong Kong, are fortunate enough to have unlimited deep-water accommodation. On top of that, the mainland ports are handicapped by the mountainous country which surrounds many of them, making communication and transport of goods difficult. The predominance of Canton is partly due to the delta waterway system which gives it a better communication and transport system than any of its rivals.

Shantou is the chief port of eastern Guangdong. As early as the 18th century the East India Company had a station on an island outside the harbour, at a time when the town was little more than a fishing village on a mudflat. The port was officially opened up to foreign trade in 1860 with the Treaty of Tianjin, which ended another Opium War. The British were the first to establish themselves here, though their projected settlement had to relocate to a nearby island due to the locals' hostility. Before 1870 foreigners were living and trading in Shantou town itself.

Today Shantou is the first major stop on the long haul along the coast road from Canton to Fujian – well worth a visit.

Information & Orientation

Most of Shantou lies on a sort of peninsula, bounded in the south by the ocean and separated from the mainland in the west and the north by a river and canals. The bulk of the tourist facilities (CAAC, Friendship Store, Overseas Chinese Hotel) are in the western part of the peninsula along Jinsha Lu and Shanzhang Lu. From Shanzhang Lu two main arteries, Zhongshan Lu and Waima Lu, lead westwards to the town centre which is the area around Minzu Lu and Shengping Lu.

CTS is in the new wing of the Overseas Chinese Hotel. They sell bus tickets to Canton and Shenzhen, and boat tickets to Canton.

Public Security is on Yue Jin Lu, near the corner with Nanmai Lu.

Bank Black market change-money people are in plague proportions around the Overseas Chinese Hotel. The Bank of China has a branch on the ground floor of the new wing of the Overseas Chinese Hotel.

Post There's a post office at 415 Zhongshan Lu, near the intersection with Shanzhang Lu.

CAAC (tel 72355) is at 26 Shanzhang Lu, a few minutes' walk south of the intersection with Jinsha Lu.

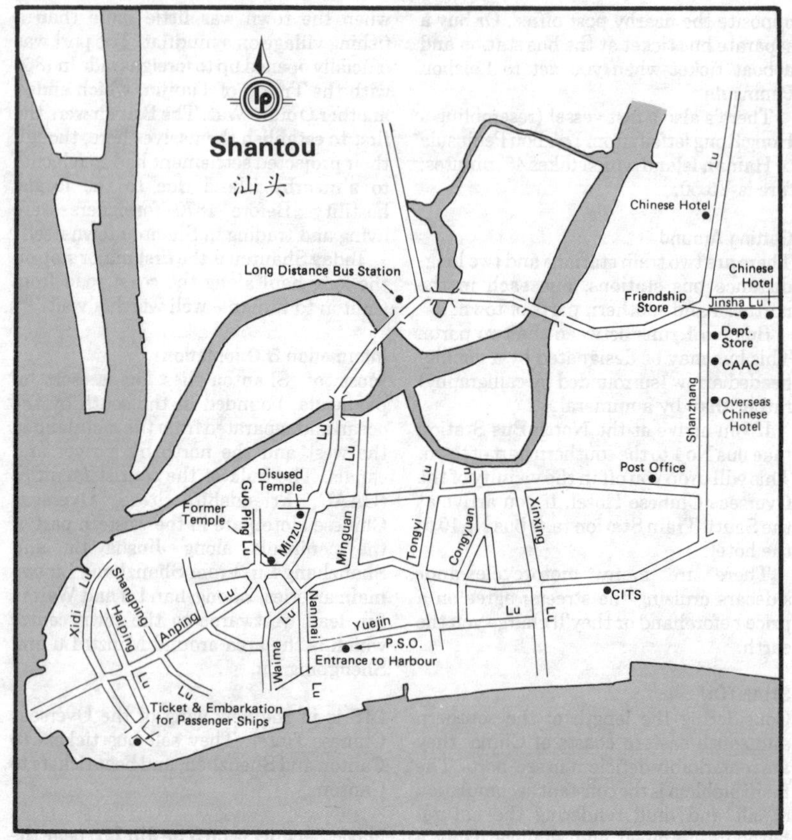

Maps Excellent bus maps of Shantou are available from the long-distance bus station and from hawkers outside.

Things to See

There's not much in Shantou 'to see' as such, but its intrinsic interest makes it worth a visit. The town is quite small and you could do a circuit of it in a day.

The best area to explore is the south-western section around Anping Lu, Xidi Lu and Shengping Lu. This is a dilapidated harbourside suburb – a slum by any other name. Many of the old buildings are making way for new apartment blocks, but much of the old area is still intact. Streets like Yuejin Lu are lined with ugly little mud-and-wood shacks.

Poking around the neighbourhood, you'll find the ruins of a temple at the corner of Minzu Lu and Zhongshan Lu. Further down Minzu Lu is a shop where you can stock up on cobras and lizards. Carry on to the eastern waterfront where there's a breakwater boat shelter, fishermen's hovels and lean-tos with statues of gods.

A good day trip is **Ma She (Ma Yi) Island.** A boat leaves from the waterfront at 9 am every day and returns at 2.30 pm. The hour-long ride takes you through the fishing area with close-ups of the fishermen and their equipment. On an ordinary weekday the boat is filled with people toting bags of food and sacrificial offerings. Follow the crowd from the landing to the **Temple of the Mother of the Heavenly Emperor**, built in 1985 with funds supplied by Overseas Chinese. The site has apparently always been holy to this deity. In the village there is another temple where the fishermen burn incense before they leave in the morning. It is called the **Temple of the Dragon of the Sea**, not as pretty but rather more authentic with discarded fishing gear strewn around the crumbling building.

Evidently the island has come in for some development to keep pace with the worshippers' enthusiasm; there is a new hotel and restaurant building and marked trails for getting around the island. There are no cars, and the beaches and views are refreshing after several months in large Chinese cities. According to the villagers the island was settled mainly during the Japanese occupation, although there were a few people living here before then.

Places to Stay

The *Overseas Chinese Hotel* is on Shanzhang Lu. Spacious doubles cost from Y24 with own bathroom; dorm beds are Y7. There are more expensive rooms in the new wing. Take bus No 3 from the traffic circle outside the long-distance bus station, and get off at the stop outside the CAAC office.

There's a *Chinese Hotel* on Shanzhang Lu, about 10 minutes' walk north of the Shanzhang/Jinsha intersection (see map). Spartan doubles are Y20 and dorm beds Y8. Take bus No 3 from the long-distance bus station; get off at the CAAC office and walk north.

The *Swatow Peninsula Hotel* (tel 76261) on Jinsha Lu is one of Shantou's newest and caters to a more up-market clientele. Doubles cost from Y46, triples from Y76. There's a Chinese and western restaurant attached, and you can dine to Chinese versions of Cliff Richard jingles.

Places to Eat

Forget the hotels, forget the restaurants – the best places to eat in Shantou are the street markets. 'Food St' is a small street near the Overseas Chinese Hotel, running west off Shanzhang Lu. There are many evening seafood stalls here – rather like Hong Kong's Temple St night market.

Shopping

There are several porcelain factories in the Shantou area, producing some interesting glazes and finishes not made elsewhere in southern China. They also produce the *gong fu cha* (tea) sets which are almost obligatory pieces of household ware in the Shantou area. After an introduction to this particular tea ritual you'll really know about Chinese hospitality. Embroidered cloth goods are produced in Shantou. The best place to look for these and other local products is the Arts & Crafts Services Store near the ferry docks.

Getting There & Away

From the long-distance bus station there are daily buses to Canton (Y15), Shenzhen (Y11.70), Chaozhou (Y2) and Xiamen (Y10.50).

Tickets for air-con coaches can be bought from the vendors outside the Overseas Chinese Hotel. There are daily coaches to Canton (Y26), Zhangzhou (Y10) and Shenzhen (Y21). Prices tend to vary so look around if you're on a tight budget.

There are boats from Shantou to Canton and to Hong Kong.

Getting Around

There are incredibly dilapidated pedicabs and auto-rickshaws outside the long-distance bus station and Overseas Chinese Hotel that charge about Y1 from the bus station to either of the hotels.

Tempos are also available. Other than that there are the local buses, although Shantou is small and a good deal of the town can be seen on foot.

CHAOZHOU 潮州

Chaozhou is an ancient commercial and trading city dating back 1700 years. It is situated on the Han River and surrounded by the Golden and Calabash hills.

One of the chief sights is the Kaiyuan temple, which was built during the Tang Dynasty to house a collection of Buddhist scriptures sent here by Emperor Qian Long. On the cliffs at the foot of the Calabash Mountains by the shores of the West Lake are the Moya Carvings depicting local landscapes and the customs of the people, as well as poems and calligraphy; they date back 1000 years. South-east of Chaozhou is the seven-storey Phoenix Pagoda built in 1585.

There are frequent buses from Shantou to Chaozhou (Y2). There is an Overseas Chinese Hotel in Chaozhou.

Hainan Island 海南岛

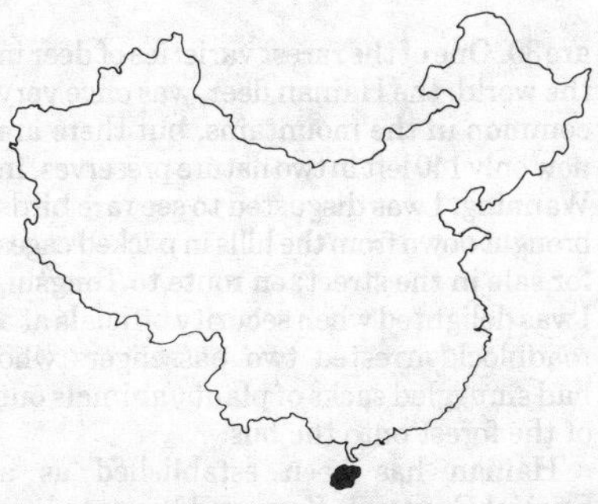

Hainan is a large tropical island off the south coast of China which is administered by the government of Guangdong Province. The island lies close to Vietnam and its military importance has increased over the past few years since China and Vietnam locked themselves into permanent war.

Consequently, the west coast of Hainan Island is dotted with naval bases, aircraft and missile bases, radio towers, radar stations and army bases. The bases are meant to defend Chinese shipping in the South China Sea and future Chinese-foreign joint ventures exploiting the oil and gas deposits in both the South China Sea and the Gulf of Tonkin (the body of water between Hainan and Vietnam). A naval force of 300,000 men is maintained on Hainan and in the mainland town of Zhanjiang, but Hainan's harbours are silted up and new ones need to be constructed to take larger warships and ocean-going cargo ships. It is planned to expand two of the existing 11 ports and to build one deep-water port.

The conflict with Vietnam started back in 1978, possibly initiated by the expulsion of as many as 250,000 ethnic Chinese from that country. In February of the following year the People's Republic invaded northern Vietnam – ostensibly to punish Vietnam for its treatment of the Chinese and for incursions on Chinese soil. When Foreign Minister Huang Hua announced on 16 March that the Chinese troops were being pulled back, the invasion was proclaimed a great success by the Chinese leadership, though clearly the PLA troops had been whipped by the Vietnamese with probably 20,000 Chinese troops killed or wounded in just two weeks of fighting. The Chinese fear that the Vietnamese alliance with the Soviet Union, their domination of Laos and occupation of Kampuchea are part of a Soviet plan to set up a hostile front on China's southern borders – a sort of Asian Cuba against which Hainan is being built up as a front-line defence.

Historically, Hainan has always been a backwater of the Chinese empire, a miserable place of exile and one of the poorest regions in the country. When Li Deyu, a prime minister of the Tang Dynasty, was exiled to Hainan he dubbed it 'the gate of hell'. It is, however, rich in mineral resources: the Japanese developed an open-cut iron-ore mine at Shi Lu in the west, and there are rich deposits of other important ores like copper and titanium. The island also exports large quantities of salt from the pans on the west coast to the mainland, and it's China's main rubber producer. Plans have been made to start up a new open-cut coal mine and to restore several oil wells to provide fuel for the island's industries. Back in 1955, Hu Yaobang (whose then rising star has now taken a tumble) toured the island and launched the concept of Hainan as a 'treasure island'.

Unfortunately, recent research shows that the most important treasure, the island's ecosystem, has been devastated. Between 1956 and 1978, random deforestation reduced the island's forest cover from 27.7% to 7.05%. This has caused climatic changes, acute water shortages and severe soil erosion. Animal and bird species have been decimated. For example, the black-headed gibbon population on Hainan once numbered 20,000 – now there are 30. One of the rarest varieties of deer in the world, the Hainan deer, was once very common in the mountains, but there are now only 140 left in two nature preserves. In Wanning, I was disgusted to see rare birds brought down from the hills in packed cages for sale in the street; en route to Tongshi, I was delighted when security officials at a roadblock arrested two passengers who had smuggled sacks of plants/animals out of the forest onto the bus.

Hainan has been established as a Special Economic Zone and hopes to lure foreign investment which will speed the island's development. More recently, the State Planning Commission gave Hainan province-level authority over economic management but not over financial affairs – and with good reason.

In 1985, mismanagement of the island's financial affairs caused some extremely red faces among Communist Party officials. Two years previously, Beijing had allocated Hainan massive sums of scarce foreign exchange to modernise the transport infrastructure. Officials on the island indulged at just about every conceivable level in a 14-month corruption bonanza. Over US$1.5 billion was used to buy 90,000 cars and trucks from Hong Kong which were then illegally 'funnelled' to the mainland where the rare goods sold like hot cakes to produce a massive profit. For good measure, the officials' shopping list included 2.9 million TV sets, 252,000 video recorders and 122,000 motorcycles.

Elsewhere in China lesser crimes are punished with a bullet in the back of the neck; on Hainan, the top three Communist Party officials in this pyramid of rake-offs were merely sacked and required to criticise their conduct.

The legacy of this absurd shopping spree is the island's unbelievable density of Japanese vehicles. Having imported more vehicles in one year than are imported annually in the whole of the rest of China, Hainan officials have been informed by Beijing that they have squandered Hainan's foreign exchange allocation for the next 10 years. Is it then purely coincidence that one of the best illicit exchange rates is now found on the streets of Haikou?

The original inhabitants of the island, the Li and Miao minority peoples, live in the dense tropical forests covering the Limu Ling Mountains that stretch down the centre of the island.

The Li probably settled on Hainan 3000 years ago after migrating from Guangdong and Guangxi provinces. Although there has been a long history of rebellion by the Li against the Chinese, they aided the Communist guerrillas on the island during the war with the Japanese. Perhaps for this reason the island's centre was made an 'autonomous' region after the Communists came to power.

Until recently the Li women had a custom of tattooing their bodies at the age of 12 or 13. The designs were first pricked out before a blend of oil and charcoal was applied. When the scabs fell off, blue tattoos appeared. The custom seems to have died out or been suppressed; it may have been done for beautification or to mar the girls and prevent their abduction by the Chinese rulers. *China Daily* recently produced an explanation which just happened to leave out the Chinese. According to the article, a pretty Li girl was once raped by the local headman who thus ruined the reputation of the girl and her family. From then on, all Li girls adopted tattooing to save themselves from a similar fate.

Today, almost all Li people wear standard Han dress except the elderly women. However, when a member of the Li dies, traditional Li costume is considered essential; otherwise the ancestors will not be able to recognise or accept the new arrival.

The Miao (Hmong) people spread from southern China across northern Vietnam, Laos and Thailand. In China they moved south into Hainan as a result of the Chinese emigrations from the north, and now occupy some of the most rugged

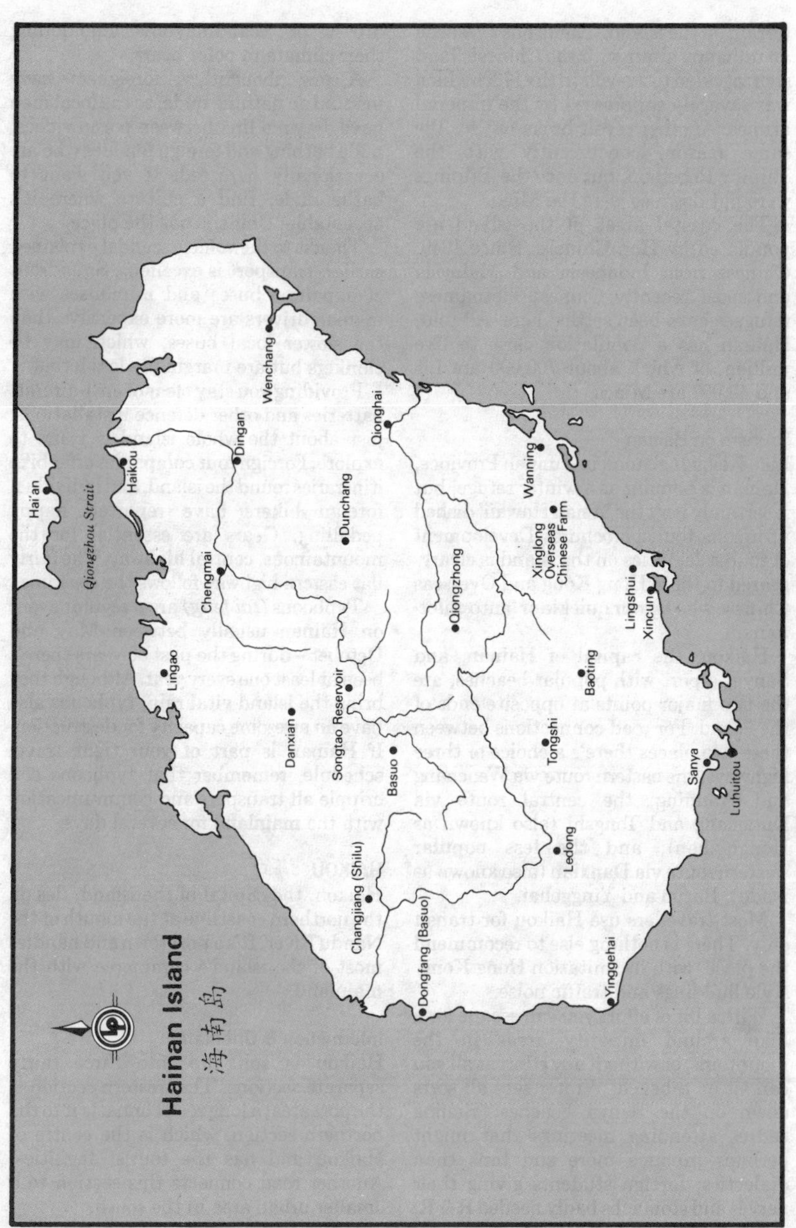
Hainan Island
海南島
Qiongzhou Strait
Hai'an
Haikou
Dingan
Wenchang
Qionghai
Chengmai
Dunchang
Lingao
Wanning
Xinglong Overseas Chinese Farm
Qiongzhong
Lingshui
Xincun
Songtao Reservoir
Danxian
Baoting
Tongshi
Basuo
Sanya
Luhuitou
Ledong
Changjiang (Shilu)
Dongfang (Basuo)
Yinggehai

terrain on the island. Theirs has also been an unhappy affair with the Chinese; land shortages led to a revolt in the 1780s which was savagely suppressed by the imperial armies. Another revolt broke out for the same reason, concurrently with the Taiping Rebellion, but once the Taipings were put down so were the Miao.

The coastal areas of the island are populated by Han Chinese. Since 1949, Chinese from Indonesia and Malaysia and most recently Chinese-Vietnamese refugees have been settled here. All told, Hainan has a population close to five million, of which about 700,000 are Lis and 40,000 are Miaos.

Tourism on Hainan

Like Xishuangbanna in Yunnan Province, Hainan is popular as a winter refuge, but it certainly isn't the 'Asian Hawaii' dished up in some tourist brochures. Development of tourist facilities on the island is clearly geared to those Hong Kong and Overseas Chinese who favour quickie or 'auto-pilot' tours.

Haikou, the capital of Hainan, and Sanya, a port with popular beaches, are the two major points at opposite ends of the island. For road connections between these two places there's a choice of three highways: the eastern route via Wenchang and Wanning; the central route via Dunchang and Tongshi (also known as Hongqizhen); and the less popular western route via Danxian (also known as Nada), Basuo and Yinggehai.

Most travellers use Haikou for transit only. There is nothing else to recommend the place, with its imitation Hong Kong-style buildings and traffic noise.

With a bit of effort you can escape for a hike around minority areas in the mountains, or without any effort at all you can sit on a beach. Winter sees all sorts down on the Sanya beaches: Beijing cadres attending meetings that might perhaps produce more sun tans than dialectics; foreign students giving their nerves and stomachs badly needed R & R; droves of Scandinavians abandoning their climate to polar bears.

A few thoughtless foreigners have insisted on bathing nude, so the local men have drawn a link between porno videos, nude bathing and foreign females who are occasionally harassed. If you want to bathe nude, find a culture where it's acceptable; China is *not* the place.

Thanks to the vehicle scandal explained earlier, transport is excellent. Squadrons of Japanese buses and minibuses with maniac drivers are more expensive than the slower local buses, which may be clonkers but are marginally less lethal.

Providing you stay clear of anti-aircraft batteries and other defence installations, just about the whole island is yours to explore. Foreign tour companies offer bike itineraries round the island, and individual foreign bikers have reported happy pedalling. Gears are essential for the mountainous, central highway. The fairly flat eastern highway follows the coastline.

Typhoons *(tai feng)* are a regular event on Hainan usually between May and October – during the past 50 years there's been at least one every year. Although they bring the island vital rain, typhoons also have an awesome capacity for destruction. If Hainan is part of your tight travel schedule, remember that typhoons can cripple all transport and communication with the mainland for several days.

HAIKOU 海口

Haikou, the capital of the island, lies on the northern coastline at the mouth of the Nandu River. It's a port town and handles most of the island's commerce with the mainland.

Information & Orientation

Haikou is split up into three fairly separate sections. The western section is the port area; a long road connects it to the northern section, which is the centre of Haikou and has the tourist facilities. Another road connects this section to a smaller urban area in the south.

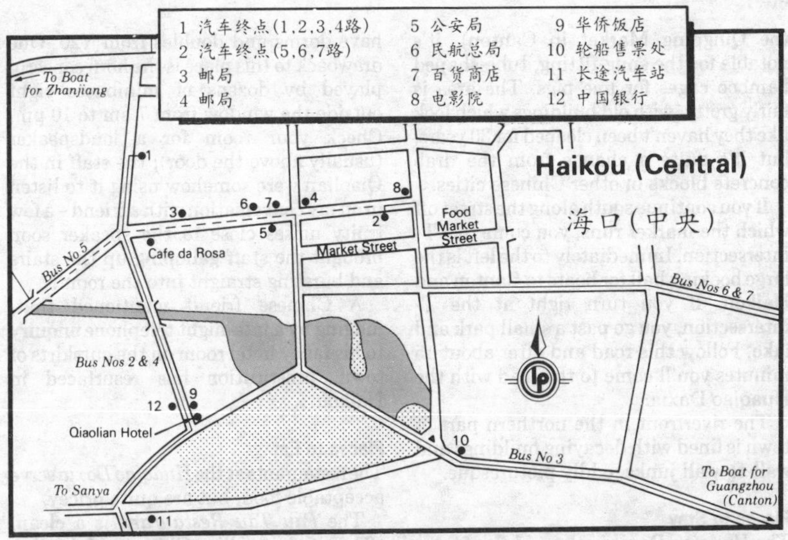

1 Terminus of Buses 1,2,3 & 4
2 Terminus of Buses 5,6 & 7
3 Post Office
4 Post Office
5 Public Security
6 CAAC
7 Department Store
8 Cinema
9 Overseas Chinese Hotel
10 Booking Office for Boats to Zhanjiang & Guangzhou (Canton)
11 Long-distance Bus Station
12 Bank of China

CITS All enquiries and tickets are handled at the offices on the ground floor of the Huaqiao Daxia (Overseas Chinese Hotel).

Public Security is a short walk from the Huaqiao Daxia. Turn right out of the hotel and walk until you come to a traffic circle with a small obelisk. Turn right again and the office is a short walk further on the right. They're a friendly lot here and they have an interpreter on call.

Bank The Bank of China is opposite the Huaqiao Daxia.

Post There is a post office in the foyer of the Huaqiao Daxia. There's another on the same street as the Public Security Office, but on the opposite side of the road and further west. A third is on the corner of the main intersection immediately east of the Public Security Office.

CAAC (tel 515) is at 50 Jiefang Lu.

Maps Maps of Haikou and Hainan Island, in Chinese, are available from the shop at the Huaqiao Daxia.

Things to See

There's not much to see in Haikou. The Huaqiao Daxia (Overseas Chinese Hotel) is a good starting point for a walk around the town. Turn right from the hotel and walk for about 15 minutes to the traffic circle marked by an obelisk. Turn hard right here and then right again at the second major intersection. A few minutes walk down is a jam-packed street market with the usual array of culinary delicacies that would normally end up in a zoo in other countries. One of the best markets you'll see in China (almost on a par with the Qingping Market in Canton), it's notable for the snug-fitting, tube-shaped bamboo cages for live pigs. The area is fairly grotty, with old buildings which look like they haven't been cleaned for 30 years, but it's quite a change from the drab concrete blocks in other Chinese cities.

If you continue south along the street off which the market runs, you come to a T-intersection. Immediately to the left is the large booking hall for boats to Canton and Haikou. If you turn right at the T-intersection, you go past a small park and lake. Follow this road and after about 15 minutes you'll come to the road with the Huaqiao Daxia.

The riverfront in the northern part of town is lined with decaying buildings and wall-to-wall junks, oddly picturesque.

Places to Stay

The *Huaqiao Daxia* in the middle of town is a vast structure renovated for the hordes of Hong Kong and Overseas Chinese. Double rooms are Y36, dorm beds Y10. The complex contains restaurants on the ground and 6th floors; the ground floor also houses shops, a currency-exchange counter and post office. Energetic grannies out front will glue themselves to you offering one of the best rates in China, but don't hand over your bills until you've counted theirs – having reached a fine old age, they are smooth operators.

To get to the hotel from the harbour where the boats from Zhanjiang pull in, take a motorcycle-and-sidecar for Y1 (although you'll probably end up paying Y2). A pedicab should only cost about Y1. Sometimes there's a minibus for about Y2 per person.

If you're coming in from Canton on the ship, take bus No 3 as far as the obelisk in the centre of town and then walk the last 15 minutes to the hotel. A taxi between the hotel and the harbour should cost about Y8 RMB.

The *Qiaolian Fandian* (Qiaolian Hotel) is on the corner, just up the street from the Huaqiao Daxia, and faces the park. They have dorms and doubles from Y20. One drawback to this place is the horn concerto played by dozens of minibuses right outside the window from 7 am to 10 pm. Check your room for a loudspeaker (usually above the door); the staff in the Qiaolian were somehow using it to listen in on my conversation with a friend – a few fruity noises close to the speaker soon brought the staff galloping up the stairs and bursting straight into the room!

A Chinese friend mentioned that, judging by a late-night telephone enquiry to his fancy hotel room on the outskirts of town, prostitution has resurfaced in Haikou.

Places to Eat

The restaurants at the *Huaqiao Daxia* serve acceptable food, but are quite pricey.

The *Pau Tau Restaurant* is a clean, efficient place selling Chinese, Malaysian and western food. To get there, turn left outside the gates of the Huaqiao Daxia and walk 50 metres towards the park. The Malay set dinner is excellent value for Y5.

The *Café de Rosa* is a slick fast-food restaurant which appears to be a Hong Kong joint venture. Turn right out of the Huaqiao Daxia and walk down the road until you come to the traffic circle with a small obelisk. Turn right again and it's the second building on the right-hand side. If you've been gasping for steak & chips, iced coffee, etc served on authentic plastic trays under fluorescent lighting, this is your chance.

There are a number of cheap places in the vicinity of the main market and along the road leading to the main post office. They serve the usual rice, meat and vegetable fare for Y2 or Y3. The seafood restaurants are good value. You buy your fish, prawns or whatever by the *jin* (kilo) or *ban jin* (half kilo); fish prices start at around Y6 per kilo and prawns should be about Y10 per kilo.

Getting There & Away

Air There are daily flights from Haikou to

Canton (Y101) and Sanya (Y62), but flights to Zhanjiang have been suspended. There are now three flights a week between Haikou and Hong Kong (HK$540). A new service has been introduced between Haikou and Singapore (Y950).

Bus The new bus station has departures to all major destinations on the island. Ticket prices are cheapest for the dinosaur buses; for a luxury bus or minibus the tickets cost more but you also get more speed and complimentary nervous stimulation. For example, a minibus direct to Sanya takes about seven hours and costs Y14. The standard buses take a couple of hours longer and cost Y8.25.

Tickets are also sold for deluxe buses running direct to Canton (Y46), Shenzhen (Y56) and Hong Kong (Y70). However, the combined boat/bus journey can be very tedious when it includes night travel at high speed with non-stop, pornographic kung-fu videos.

The Huaqiao Daxia sells tickets for luxury buses to Sanya. Minibuses to Wenchang leave from outside the Qiaolian Fandian – you can't miss the infernal tooting parade.

Boat Boats leave Haikou at 11.30 am, 12.30 pm and 1.30 pm for the 1½-hour trip to Hai'an on the Leizhou Peninsula, where you get connecting transport to Zhanjiang. The combined bus/boat ticket is available at the harbour after 11 am for Y11, but in this case your bus leaves at 3 pm. It's quicker to take a minibus from Hai'an to Zhanjiang for Y9. Tickets for a new hydrofoil service between Hainan and Leizhou Peninsula cost Y8.10 per person.

There are daily boats from Haikou direct to Canton; ticket prices vary between Y18.20 for 5th class to Y33.90 for 2nd class. It's worth paying a little extra to avoid the large dorm below deck, particularly if the boat is pitching and your bunk is next to the toilets. Third class will get you into an eight-bed dorm on deck. Watch out for petty thievery and take your own food – the food on board is poor. Buy tickets from the booking office in Huaqiao Daxia.

Two boats, the *Donghu* and *Malan*, run approximately once a week between Haikou and Hong Kong. Another boat, the *Shan Cha*, runs twice a month between Sanya and Hong Kong via Haikou. Prices vary from Y59 for 3rd class to Y110 for deluxe class. Buy tickets from the booking office in the Huaqiao Daxia.

There is reportedly a boat to Macao.

Getting Around

The central area of Haikou is small and easy to walk around, but the motorcycle-and-sidecars are cheap and the buses useful. The separate sections of Haikou are connected by bus.

THE EASTERN ROUTE

The eastern route is the most popular one. If you want to take it slow, it's easily divided into stages on a daily basis.

WENCHANG 文昌

Buses leave for Wenchang from Haikou's main bus station; or take a minibus from outside the Qiaolian Fandian. The 73 km could be done as a day-trip. The coconut plantations called Dong Jiao Ye Lin and Jian Hua Shan Ye Lin are a short ride out of town at Qing Lan Gang. Minibuses by the riverside in Wenchang will take you to Qing Lan Gang, where you can take a ferry to the stands of coconut palms and mile after mile of beach. Another way to get to the same plantation is to take the direct bus to Dong Jiao that leaves Haikou's main bus station daily at 12.30 pm.

XINGLONG 兴隆

Since 1952, over 20,000 refugee Chinese-Vietnamese and Overseas Chinese (mostly from Indonesia or Malaysia) have settled at the **Xinglong Overseas Chinese Farm.** The farm concentrates on tropical agriculture and related research. Many of the members speak excellent English and are a helpful source of information. They may be able to organise transport (about Y18) to Miao villages.

About three km from Xinglong bus station is the *Xinglong Wenchuan Binguan* (Xinglong Hot Spring Hotel). From the bus station to the hotel costs Y0.50 in a motorcycle-and-sidecar. The hotel is a peaceful spot for convalescence and well worth a stay. Prices start at Y10 per person for a double with a huge bed and a bath large enough for four people. The spring water is scalding hot – if there's no cold water available, you'll just have to let it cool in the bath.

In nearby Wanning, a local asked me where I came from and I sarcastically told him to guess. Without a moment's hesitation he said I could be nothing other than a Mongolian!

XINCUN 新村

Xincun is populated almost solely by Danjia (Tanha) minority people who are employed in fishing and pearl cultivation. In recent years, typhoons have repeatedly blown away the pearl and oyster cultivation farms, but the harbour area, fish market and nearby monkey island are worth an afternoon ramble.

Buses travelling the eastern route will drop you off at a fork in the road about three km from Xincun. It should then be easy to get a lift on a passing minibus and hitch or walk into Xincun. From Lingshui and Sanya frequent minibuses run directly to Xincun.

Houzi Dao (Monkey Island)

About 1000 Guangxi monkeys (Macaca mulatta) live on this narrow peninsula. The area is under state protection and a special wildlife research centre investigates all monkey business.

A shack on the beach at Xincun functions as a booking office selling return tickets on the ferry for Y0.80. They also sell a booklet put together in Chinese by the research centre. It includes exhaustive monkey data and an appendix which lists the monkeys' favourite plants like a menu.

The ferry put-puts from Xincun to Monkey Island in 10 minutes. At the island pier, motorcycle-and-sidecars will take you to the monkey enclosure (Houzi Yuan) for Y1.50. You can also get there on foot. Walk along the beach road to the left for about one km, then follow the road leading uphill to the right for another 1½ km.

At the entrance a stall sells tickets and peanuts which tasted pretty good as my emergency lunch, although they are meant for the monkeys. Apart from feeding times at 9 am and 4 pm, it's a case of the monkeys seeing you and not vice-versa. You can often hear them crashing around and chattering in the shrubs on the hillside; occasionally a wild, woolly head pops out of the top branches to see what's happening or to scream at you. This is one of the few places where they can run wild without being shot, trapped, tethered to table-legs, tortured in zoo cages or brutally mishandled in roadshows.

SANYA 三亚

Sanya is a busy port and tourist resort on the southern tip of Hainan island. The town lies on a strip of land parallel to the coast and is connected to the mainland on one side by two bridges.

The harbour area, which is mostly occupied by shabby wooden shanties, is protected to the east by the hilly Luhuitou Peninsula. On the western outskirts of Sanya there's a small community of Hui, the only Muslim inhabitants of Hainan.

The main part of town lacks any special features except perhaps for the local minority women who pester you to change money. A map of the area in Chinese is sold in the Luhuitou hotel shop.

Things to See

Most travellers head for Sanya for a few leisurely days at the beach. The popular beaches are at Dadonghai, Luhuitou Peninsula and Tianya Haijiao.

Dadonghai is a fine beach with a hotel and plenty of sand, surf and shade. It's about three km east of Sanya and easily

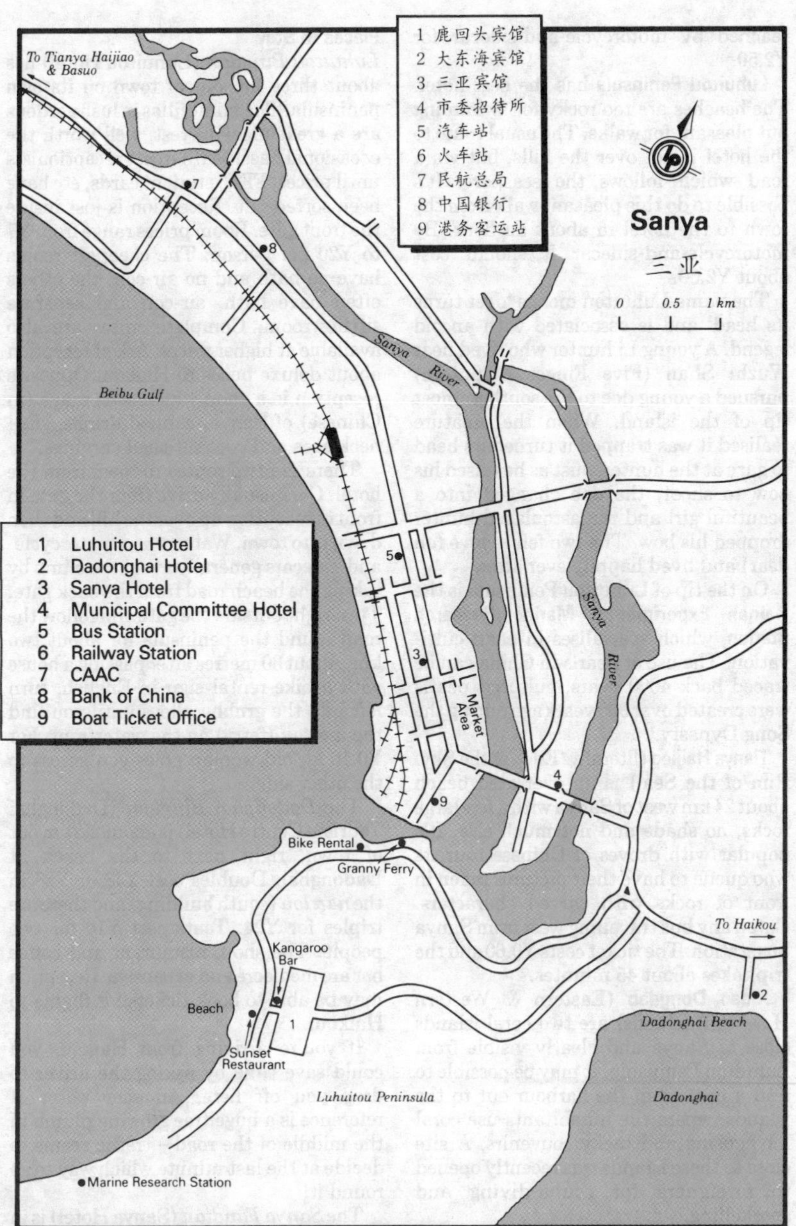
1 鹿回头宾馆
2 大东海宾馆
3 三亚宾馆
4 市委招待所
5 汽车站
6 火车站
7 民航总局
8 中国银行
9 港务客运站
Sanya
三亚
0
0.5
1 km
To Tianya Haijiao & Basuo
Sanya River
Beibu Gulf
Sanya River
Market Area
Bike Rental
Granny Ferry
Kangaroo Bar
Beach
Sunset Restaurant
Luhuitou Peninsula
Marine Research Station
To Haikou
Dadonghai Beach
Dadonghai
1 Luhuitou Hotel
2 Dadonghai Hotel
3 Sanya Hotel
4 Municipal Committee Hotel
5 Bus Station
6 Railway Station
7 CAAC
8 Bank of China
9 Boat Ticket Office

reached by motorcycle-and-sidecar for Y2.50.

Luhuitou Peninsula has the best hotel. The beaches are too rocky for swimming but pleasant for walks. The usual route to the hotel is not over the hills, but via a road which follows the seashore. It's possible to do this pleasant walk from the town to the hotel in about an hour. By motorcycle-and-sidecar it should cost about Y2.50.

The name Luhuitou means 'deer turns its head' and is associated with an old legend. A young Li hunter who lived near Wuzhi Shan (Five Finger Mountain) pursued a young doe to the southernmost tip of the island. When the creature realised it was trapped it turned its head to gaze at the hunter. Just as he raised his bow to shoot, the doe changed into a beautiful girl and the astonished hunter dropped his bow. The two fell in love (oh dear) and lived happily ever after.

On the tip of Luhuitou Peninsula is the **Hainan Experimental Marine Research Station**, which specialises in pearl cultivation. The use of pearls in China can be traced back 4000 years; cultured pearls were created over 900 years ago during the Song Dynasty.

Tianya Haijiao (literally 'Edge of the Sky, Rim of the Sea') is an overrated beach about 24 km west of Sanya with a few large rocks, no shade and not much else. It's popular with droves of Chinese tourists who queue to have their pictures taken in front of rocks with carved characters. Catch any bus travelling west from Sanya bus station. The ticket costs Y0.60 and the trip takes about 45 minutes.

Xidao Dongdao (Eastern & Western Hawksbill Islands) are two coral islands close to Sanya and clearly visible from Luhuitou Peninsula. It may be possible to find a boat from the harbour out to the islands, where the inhabitants use coral for housing and tacky souvenirs. A site close to these islands was recently opened to foreigners for scuba-diving and snorkelling.

Places to Stay

Luhuitou Binguan (Luhuitou Hotel) lies about three km out of town on its own peninsula. The mini-villas in lush gardens are a great place to rest, well worth the occasional hassle with frosty receptionists until prices, FEC, student cards, etc have been sorted out. Reception is just inside the front gate. Room prices range from Y7 to Y20 per person. The cheapest rooms have no bath and no air-con; the others often have bath, air-con and separate sitting room. Complete suites are also available at higher prices. Ask at reception about deluxe buses to Haikou. Opposite reception is a shop which sells maps (in Chinese) of Sanya, canned drinks, shell necklaces and coconut shell carvings.

There are two routes to town from the hotel. Cars usually drive from the gate in front of reception up over the hill and then down into town. Walkers and motorcycle-and-sidecars generally avoid the climb by taking the beach road from the back gate. Turn right outside the gate and follow the road round the peninsula for about two km. About 30 metres after passing a house with a bike-rental sign in English, turn left into the grubby alleys until you find the *ma tou* (ferry) on the waterfront. For Y0.10 an old woman poles you across to the other side.

The *Dadonghai Binguan* (Dadonghai Tourism Centre Hotel) is about 2½ km out of town, right next to the beach at Dadonghai. Doubles cost Y48 or Y28 in the *nan lou* (south building) and there are triples for Y24. Tents cost Y10 for two people. The shop, restaurant and coffee bar are mediocre and expensive. Reception may be able to book tickets for flights to Haikou.

If you're arriving from Haikou, you could save time by asking the driver to drop you off here. An easy point of reference is a huge tree growing plumb in the middle of the road – traffic seems to decide at the last minute which way to go round it!

The *Sanya Fandian* (Sanya Hotel) is in

the centre of town. If you want beach life, you'll have to commute from here. Single rooms cost Y24, doubles Y36.

The *Shi Wei Zhaodai Suo* (Municipal Committee Hotel) is just before the second bridge, on the left, if you're walking out of Sanya in the direction of Haikou. Rooms are spartan and as cheap as Y3 per bed.

Places to Eat

The *Luhuitou Binguan* restaurant is excellent. Various set meals are available at prices ranging from Y3 to Y5. Higher-priced set meals include fancy seafood.

Facing the sea, just outside the back entrance of the Luhuitou Binguan, are two private restaurants which offer disco music and cater for western tastes at higher prices. *Charlie's Kangaroo Club* beside the gate does Chinese and western food. The quality varies; lobster, crab, prawns and squid are best ordered in advance. Seafood is weighed in the kitchen and cooked as you wish; try the black bean sauce or the garlic one if you like the whiff. A decent meal with beer should cost around Y10 per person. Lobster costs about Y20 per kilo.

The *Sunset Restaurant* is on the beach, with a view across the bay to an oil rig that looks like a stranded spider. My breakfast of coffee and pancakes here was greasy and only just managed to stay in my stomach. I had to rush away from the meal because the owner started to slaughter a young goat close to my table. The early morning silence was shattered by five minutes of piercing screams from the dying goat.

In Sanya itself, there are plenty of restaurants and street stalls to try – nothing to be specially recommended yet.

Getting There & Away

Air There are four flights a week to Canton (Y166) via Haikou (Y52). Reception at the Dadonghai Binguan can book plane tickets; otherwise try the CAAC office, which is miles away at the western end of town.

Bus From Sanya bus station there are frequent buses and minibuses to most parts of Hainan. Deluxe buses for Haikou also depart from the Luhuitou and Dadonghai hotels.

Rail The sporadic passenger service between Sanya and Huangliu may soon be extended to Basuo.

Boat Boats leave Sanya twice a month (usually the 1st and 12th) for Hong Kong. Ticket prices range from Y65 in 5th class to Y148 in deluxe class.

There is a weekly boat connection between Sanya and Canton. Ticket prices range from Y19.80 for 5th class to Y60.20 for 1st class.

Buy tickets from the ticket office close to the harbour.

Getting Around

Apart from walking, the quickest way to get around is the motorcycle-and-sidecars which cruise the streets all day. Quite a blast, motoring around like WW II generals in a bathtub – especially if it's raining. One of the drivers told me the price for a new contraption is Y1000. Not too many new ones around in Sanya. Make sure you bargain with the drivers: the fare is per motorcycle, not per person, and is paid in RMB.

A motorcycle-and-sidecar from the centre of Sanya to Dadonghai costs about Y2.5. To Luhuitou Binguan should cost about the same.

Bikes can be hired for Y6 per day at the Sunset Restaurant outside the back entrance of the Luhuitou Binguan. Another bike-rental guy operates on the back road between Sanya and Luhuitou Binguan – look for the sign. He charges Y4 per day but wants it in FEC.

THE CENTRAL ROUTE

The central route is worth taking if you want to explore minority areas. The best mountain scenery is between Sanya and Qiongzhong – after that it's flat and plain.

TONGSHI 通什

Tongshi is the capital of the Li and Miao Autonomous Prefecture. The town obviously had the financial backing to transform all the major buildings into modern high-rises; there's even a supermarket.

There are several hotels in Tongshi. The flashiest is the *Tongzhi Resort Hotel* with double rooms for Y50. Minorities make the tourist cash register tinkle here – so the roof of the lobby is pyramid-shaped to give the feel of a straw hut, and minority women serve drinks or invite guests to dance and sing. A great chance for visitors to play the primitive in luxury.

The *Wuzhi Shan Binguan* charges Y25 for a double. A small hotel next to the bridge charges Y3.50 for a bed in a triple.

Minority Villages There are several Miao villages dotted around the edge of town. From Tongshi you could take local buses, for example, to Mao'an, Maodao or Maogan.

Mt Wuzhi (Mt Five Fingers), at 1867 metres Hainan's highest mountain, is close to Tongshi.

QIONGZHONG 琼中

The route between Tongshi and Qiongzhong passes through thick forest. Qiongzhong is a small hill-town with a lively market; the nearby waterfall at Mt Baihua drops over 300 metres.

THE WESTERN ROUTE

On the western route, it might be worth looking at the Institute of Tropical Plants near Danxian and the Nature Reserve for the Protection of the Hainan Deer at Datian. To the east of Datian is the town of Xiaodongfang, the site of the Li minority's 'Loving Festival' on the third day of the third lunar month (around April).

China's largest open-cast iron mine is at Shi Lu (also called Changjiang), which is linked by railway with Basuo, a shabby port.

There is reportedly a beautiful stretch of road between Basuo and Sanya which passes the saltworks at Yinggehai.

Hunan 湖南

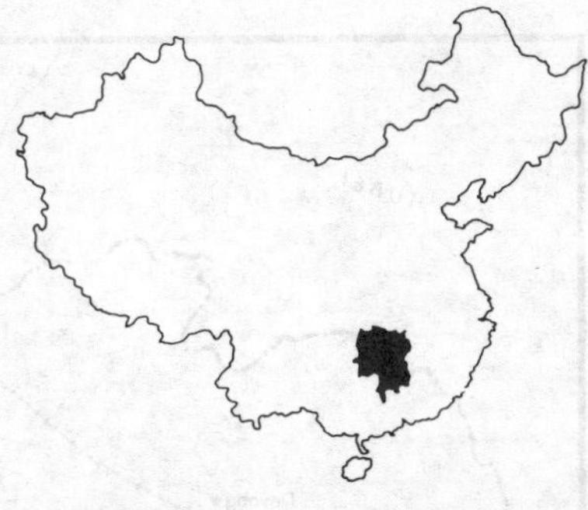

Hunan lies on some of the richest land in China. Its main period of growth occurred between the 8th and the 11th centuries when the population increased five-fold, spurred on by a prosperous agricultural industry and by migrations from the north. Under the Ming and the Qing it was one of the empire's granaries, and vast quantities of Hunan's rice surplus were shipped to the depleted regions to the north.

By the 19th century Hunan was beginning to suffer from the pressure of population. Land shortage and landlordism led to widespread unrest among the Chinese farmers and the hill-dwelling minority peoples. The result of this increasingly desperate economic situation was the massive Taiping Rebellion of the mid-19th century and the Communist movement of the 1920s.

The Communists found strong support amongst the poor peasants of Hunan, and a refuge on the mountainous Hunan-Jiangxi border in 1927. Some of the most prominent Communist leaders were born in Hunan, including Mao Zedong, Liu Shaoqi (both of whose villages can be visited), Peng Dehuai and Hu Yaobang. Hua Guofeng, a native of Shanxi, became an important provincial leader in Hunan.

Some 54 million people live in Hunan, most of them Han Chinese. Hill-dwelling minorities can be found in the border regions of the province. They include the Miao, Tujia, Dong (a Thai people) and Yao. In the far north of the province there is, oddly enough, a pocket of Uygurs.

Mao Zedong

Mao was Hunan's main export, a classic story of the poor peasant boy who makes good. Mao was born in the Hunanese village of Shaoshan, not far from Changsha, in 1893. His father was a poor peasant who had been forced to join the army because of heavy debts. After several years of service he returned to Shaoshan, and by careful saving through small trading and other enterprises managed to buy back his land.

As 'middle' peasants Mao's family owned enough land to produce a surplus of rice with which they were able to buy more land. This raised them to the status of 'rich' peasants. Mao's father began to deal in grain transport and sales, buying grain from the poor farmers and taking it to the city merchants where he could get a higher price for it. As Mao told American journalist Edgar Snow, 'My family ate frugally, but had enough always'.

Mao began studying in the local primary school when he was eight years old and remained at school until the age of 13, meanwhile working on the farm and keeping accounts for his father's business. His father continued to accumulate wealth (or what was considered a fortune in the little village) by buying mortgages on other people's land. Creditors of other peasants would be paid off in lump sums, and these peasants would then have to pay back their loans to Mao's father, who would profit from the interest rates.

Several incidents influenced Mao: a famine in Hunan and a subsequent uprising of starving people in Changsha ended in the execution of the leaders by the Manchu governor. This left a lasting impression on Mao, who 'felt that there with the rebels were ordinary people like my own family and I deeply resented the injustice in the treatment given to them'. He was also influenced by a band of rebels who had taken to the hills around Shaoshan to defy the landlords and the government, and by a radical teacher at the local primary school who opposed Buddhism and wanted people to convert their temples into schools.

At the age of 16, Mao left Shaoshan to enter middle school in Changsha, his first stop on the

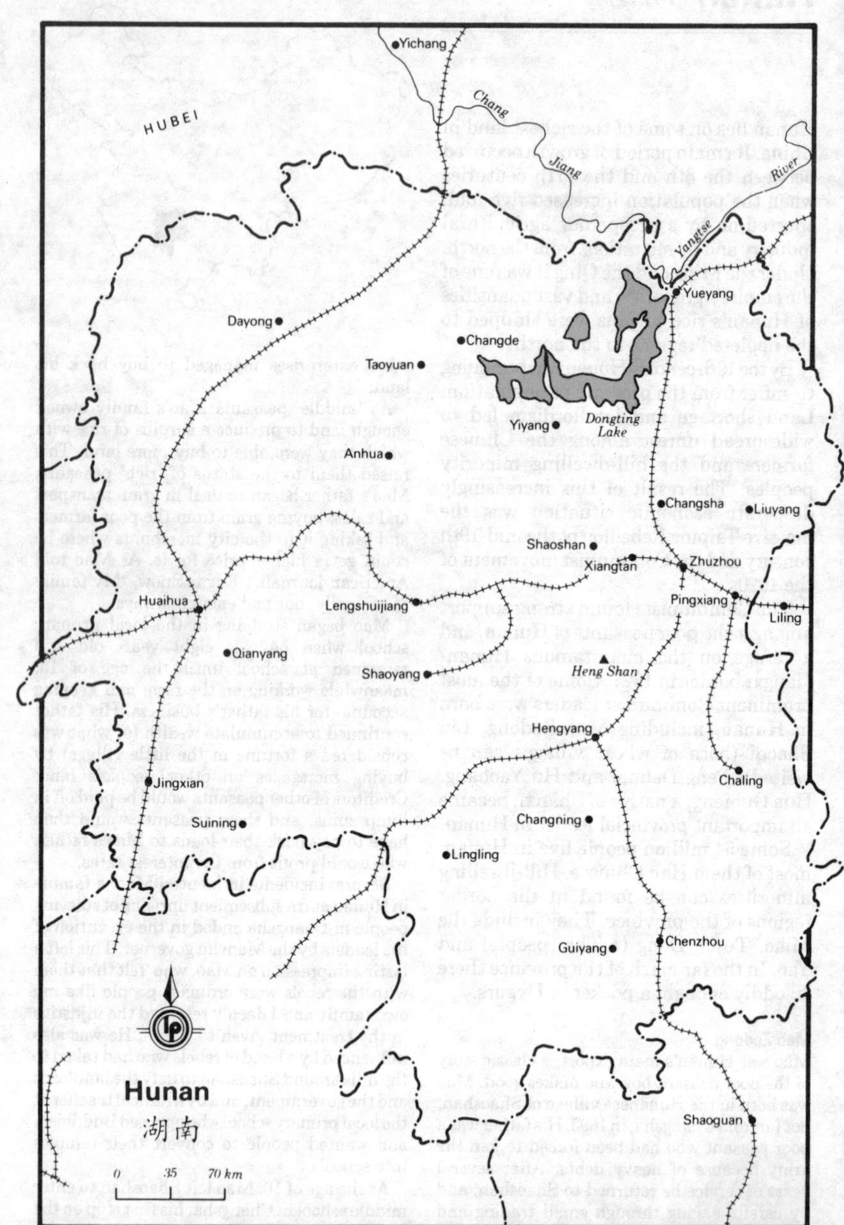

Yichang
Chang
Jiang
River
Yangtse
HUBEI
Yueyang
Dayong
Changde
Taoyuan
Yiyang
Dongting
Lake
Anhua
Changsha
Liuyang
Shaoshan
Xiangtan
Zhuzhou
Huaihua
Lengshuijiang
Pingxiang
Liling
Qianyang
Shaoyang
Heng Shan
Hengyang
Jingxian
Chaling
Suining
Changning
Lingling
Chenzhou
Guiyang
Shaoguan
Hunan
湖南
0
35
70 km

footpath to power. At this time he was not yet an anti monarchist:

'indeed, I considered the emperor as well as most officials to be honest, good and clever men'

He felt however that the country needed reform. He was fascinated by stories of the ancient rulers of China and learned something of foreign history and geography.

In Changsha Mao was first exposed to the ideas of revolutionaries and reformers active in China, heard of Sun Yatsen's revolutionary secret society, and read about the abortive Canton uprising of 1911. Later that year an army uprising in Wuhan quickly spread and the Qing Dynasty collapsed. Yuan Shikai made his grab for power and the country appeared to be slipping into civil war. Mao joined the regular army but resigned six months later, thinking the revolution was over when Sun handed the presidency to Yuan and the war between the north and south of China did not take place.

Mao became an avid reader of newspapers and from these was introduced to socialism. He decided to become a teacher and enrolled in the Hunan Provincial First Normal (Teachers' Training) School. During his time at the Teachers' Training School, he inserted an advertisement in a Changsha newspaper inviting young men interested in patriotic work to make contact with him. Among them was Liu Shaoqi, who later became president of the People's Republic, Xiao Chen who became a founding member of the Communist Party, and Li Lisan.

'At this time', says Mao, 'my mind was a curious mixture of ideas of liberalism, democratic reformism and utopian socialism . . . and I was definitely anti-militarist and anti-imperialist'.

Mao graduated from the Teachers' Training School in 1918, and went to Beijing where he worked as an assistant librarian at Beijing University. In Beijing he met future co-founders of the Chinese Communist Party: the student leader Zhang Guodao, Professor Chen Duxiu and university librarian Li Dazhao. Chen and Li are regarded as the founders of Chinese Communism. It was Li who gave Mao a job and first introduced him to the serious study of Marxism.

Mao was very much the perplexed convert, a Nationalist who found in Marxist theory a programme for reform and revolution in China. He did not found Chinese Communism but was introduced to it by Beijing intellectuals. On returning to Changsha Mao became increasingly active in Communist politics:

'I became more and more convinced that only mass political power, secured through mass action, could guarantee the realisation of dynamic reforms'.

He became editor of the *Xiang River Review*, a radical Hunan students' newspaper. He continued working in the New People's Study Society and also took up a post as a teacher. In 1920 he was organising workers for the first time and from that year onwards considered himself a Marxist. In 1921, Mao went to Shanghai to attend the founding meeting of the Chinese Communist Party. Later he helped organise the first provincial branch of the Party in Hunan, and by the middle of 1922 the Party had organised trade unions among the workers and students.

Orthodox Marxist philosophy saw revolution spreading from the cities as it had in the Soviet Union. The peasants, ignored through the ages by poets, scholars and political soothsayers, had likewise been ignored by the Communists. But Mao took a different stand and saw the peasants as the life-blood of the revolution. The Party had done very little work among them but in 1925 Mao began to organise peasant trade unions. This aroused the wrath of the landlords and Mao had to flee to Canton, where the Kuomintang and Communists held power in alliance with each other. Mao proposed a radical redistribution of the land to help the peasants, and supported

To Beijing
Liuyang River
Beizhan Lu
Xiangchun Lu
Xiang River Bridge
Bayi Lu
Wuyi Lu
Renmin Lu
Chenghan Lu
Jianxiang Lu
Daqing Lu
Laodong Lu
Shuyuan Lu
Shaoshan Lu
Xiang River
To Canton
To Airport
Changsha
长沙
1 新火车站
2 中国民用航空总局
3 中国共产党早期活动的地方
4 湖南宾馆
5 博物馆
6 烈士纪念碑
7 湘江宾馆
8 邮局
9 第一师范学校
10 桔子洲
11 烈士公园
12 公安局
13 长途汽车站
14 旅行社

(and probably initiated) the demands of the Hunan Peasants Union to confiscate large landholdings. Probably at this stage he foresaw the need to organise and arm them for a struggle against the landlords.

In April 1927, Chiang Kaishek launched his massacre of the Communists. The Party sent Mao to Changsha to organise what became known as the 'Autumn Harvest Uprising'. By September the first units of a peasant-worker army had been formed, with troops drawn from the peasantry, Hengyang miners and rebel Kuomintang soldiers. Mao's army moved south through Hunan and climbed up into the Jinggang Mountains to embark on a guerrilla war against the Kuomintang. The rest is history.

CHANGSHA 长沙

The site of Changsha has been inhabited for 3000 years. By the Warring States Period (770-221 BC) a large town had grown up here. The town owes its prosperity to its location on the fertile Hunan plains of central China and on the Xiang River, where it rapidly grew as a major trading centre of agricultural produce.

In 1904 the city was opened to foreign trade as the result of the 1903 Treaty of Shanghai between Japan and China. The 'most-favoured nation' principle allowed all and sundry foreigners to set themselves up in Changsha, and large numbers of Europeans and Americans came to build factories, churches and schools. The medical centre was originally a college established by Yale University.

Today Changsha is the capital of Hunan Province and has a population of around 2.6 million people.

1 New Railway Station
2 CAAC
3 Former Headquarters of Hunan Communist Party
4 Hunan Guest House
5 Hunan Provincial Museum
6 Monument to the Martyrs
7 Xiangjiang Hotel
8 Post Office
9 Hunan No 1 Teachers' Training School
10 Long Island
11 Martyrs' Park
12 Public Security
13 Long-distance Bus Station
14 CITS

Information & Orientation

Most of Changsha lies on the eastern bank of the Xiang River. The New Railway Station is at the far east of the city. From the station Wuyi Lu leads to the river, neatly separating the city's northern and southern sections. From Wuyi Lu you cross the Xiang Bridge to the western bank, passing over Long Island in the middle of the river. Most of the sights and tourist facilities are on the east side of the river.

CITS (tel 26448) has been made as hard to find as possible. It was last seen at 130 Sanxing Jie, which runs south from Wuyi Lu. There is no sign. Go through a gateway into a courtyard; the office is up the stairs through a doorway on your left.

Bank Change money at the bank in the Xiangjiang Guest House.

Post There is a post office in the Xiangjiang Guest House. There is a large post office at the corner of Wuji Xilu and Dazhai Lu in the centre of town.

CAAC (tel 23820) is at 5 Wuji Donglu.

Maps There's usually a hawker or two outside the New Railway Station selling good bus maps that cost 30 fen.

Hunan Provincial Museum

Most of Changsha's sights are related to Mao Zedong and the Communist Revolution, but don't miss the mummified remains of the Han Dynasty woman in the Hunan Provincial Museum. The preserved body was taken from a 2100-year-old Han tomb excavated a few km east of the museum at Mawangtui.

The only sign of the tombs above ground were two earthen mounds of similar size and height standing close together. The body was found in the eastern tomb, in a chamber 16 metres underground and approached from the north by a sloping passageway. The walls of the tomb were covered in a thick layer of charcoal surrounded by a layer of compact clay, which appears to have kept out moisture and prevented the decay of the body and other objects in the tomb.

At the bottom of the tomb was a chamber made of wooden planks, containing an outer, middle and inner coffin. In the coffin was the corpse of a woman about 50 years of age wrapped in more than 20 layers of silk and linen, with the outer layer bound in nine bands of silk ribbon.

Large quantities of silk garments and fabrics were found in the tomb as well as stockings, shoes, gloves and other pieces of clothing. One of the most interesting objects, now on display in the museum, is a painting on silk depicting the underworld, earth and heaven. The tomb also held lacquerware, pottery containing food, musical instruments (including a 25-stringed wooden instrument called a *se zither*, a set of reed pipes and a set of bamboo pitch-pipes) and a collection of wooden tomb figurines. Other finds included bamboo boxes containing vegetables and grain seeds, straw mats, medicinal herbs, seals and several hundred pieces of money made of unbaked clay with clear inscriptions. Numerous bamboo slips with writing on them listed the names, sizes and number of the objects.

The body is housed in the basement of the museum and is viewed from the floor above through perspex. Her organs have been removed and are laid out on display. Another building houses the enormous outer timber casks.

The museum is on Dongfeng Lu. Bus No 3 runs past it.

Maoist Pilgrimage Spots
Scattered about the city are a number of Maoist pilgrimage spots.

The **Hunan No 1 Teachers' Training School** is where Mao attended classes between 1913 and 1918, and where he returned as a teacher in 1920-21. The school was destroyed during the civil war, but has since been restored. Although of historical interest, there's not much to see; the main attraction is a sort of Mao 'shrine' with banners, photo, candles and attendants with black armbands. Bus No 1 from outside the Xiangjiang Guest House goes straight past the school, which is still open though the shrine may have been closed.

The **Former Office of the Hunan (Xiang District) Communist Party Committee** is now a museum that includes Mao's living quarters and an exhibition of photos and historical items from the 1920s. On the same grounds is a large museum containing a Mao exhibition and some archaeological relics – mainly pottery, tools, weapons and coins.

About 60 km from Changsha is the **Home & Tomb of Yang Kaihui**. Yang was Mao's first wife (discounting an unconsummated arranged childhood marriage) and is being pushed by the present government as his favourite, to counter the vilified Jiang Qing. Yang was the daughter of one of Mao's teachers at the First Teachers' Training School in Changsha, a member of a wealthy Hunanese land-owning family. Mao seems to have influenced Yang Kaihui towards radicalism, and also to marriage in 1920 when she was 25 years old. She was arrested by the Kuomintang in 1930 and executed after she refused to denounce the Communist Party and Mao. Yang had two children by Mao: Mao Anqing who escaped to the Soviet Union after his mother's arrest, and the elder son Mao Anying who was arrested with his mother but later released. Mao Anying was killed in the Korean War in 1950.

Other Attractions

The **Loving Dusk Pavilion** is on Yuelu Hill on the west bank of the Xiang River, from where you can get a good view of the town. **Long Island** or Long Sandbank, from which Changsha takes its name, lies in the middle of the Xiang River. The only remaining part of the old city walls is **Tianxin Tower** in the south of the city.

Places to Stay

The *Xiangjiang Guest House* (tel 26261) is at 267 Zhongshan Lu. It is an enormous, cold monolith of grey concrete. Take bus No 1 from the New Railway Station; it drops you off right outside the hotel. There are double rooms from Y46 and dormitory beds from Y9. The hotel restaurant isn't bad.

Within walking distance of the train station is the *Furong Binguan (Lotus Guest House)* on Wuyi Lu. It's a high-rise tourist hotel with singles for Y45 and doubles for Y60.

Places to Eat

Chilli peppers and hot spices are a strong feature of Hunanese food, just as with Sichuan food. There are many small restaurants in the vicinity of the Xiangjiang Hotel. The much-touted *Youyicun (Yu Yi Tsun) Restaurant* (tel 22797), at 116 Zhongshan Lu, is reportedly worth eating at if you know what to order.

Getting There & Away

Air Useful flights from Changsha include those to Beijing (four times a week), Canton (five times a week), and Zhengzhou, Xian and Shanghai (daily).

Bus There are three buses to Shaoshan, the birthplace of Mao Zedong, depart from the long-distance bus station just north of the New Railway Station. There is also a train to Shaoshan (see below).

Rail Changsha is on the main Canton-Beijing line. There are also direct trains to Guilin via the rail junction of Hengyang. Shanghai-Kunming trains pass through the railway junction of Zhuzhou just south of Changsha.

SHAOSHAN 韶山

The village of Shaoshan, about 130 km south-west of Changsha, has a significance to Chinese Communism which far overshadows its minute size for this is where Mao Zedong was born. During the height of the Cultural Revolution it was said to have been visited by three million pilgrims a year, and a railway line and a paved road were built from Changsha to transport them. Today it's foreign tourists who are the pilgrims!

The Great Helmsman revisited Shaoshan in June 1959, after an absence of 32 years. The visit inspired this poem:

Like a dream recalled, I curse the long-fled past,
My native soil and two and thirty years gone by.
The red flag roused the serf, halberd in hand,
While the despot's black talons held his whip aloft.
Bitter sacrifice strengthens bold resolve
Which dares to make sun and moon shine in new skies.
Happy, I see wave upon wave of paddy and beans,
And all around heroes homebound in the evening mist.

Orientation

There are two parts to Shaoshan, the railhead and the village several km away. Outside the station is a square where the bus to Shaoshan village meets the daily train from Changsha. Follow the road up the right-hand side of the park to the main street, where you'll find the long-distance bus station. At the junction of the main street and the road leading from the train station you can catch the irregular local buses to Shaoshan village.

Things to See

Shaoshan is hardly typical of Chinese villages, considering the number of tourists who have passed through since it

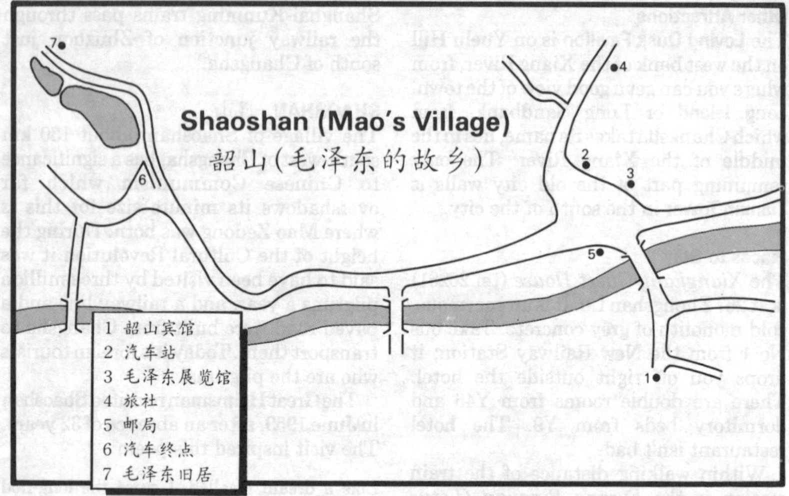

1 Shaoshan Guest House
2 Local Bus Station
3 Mao Exhibition Hall
4 Chinese Hotel
5 Post Office
6 Terminus of Buses from Shaoshan Railway Station
7 Mao's house

was established as a national shrine. It is, however, one opportunity to get a look at the Chinese countryside. The valley is beautiful and you could wander off for days exploring the little villages nearby. Apart from its historical significance, Shaoshan is a great place to get away from those grim, grey cities.

Mao Zedong's House

This is the principal shrine of Shaoshan. It's a fairly large building with mud walls and a thatched roof. There's not a great deal to see: a few utensils in the kitchen, the beds and some sparse furnishings, a photo of Mao's mother and father, but like the Chinese you can at least say you've been there. In front of the house is a pond, and on the other side a pavilion where the Chinese pose for photos with the house in the background.

Mao Zedong Exhibition Hall

Devoted to the life of Mao, this museum opened in 1967 during the Cultural Revolution. It originally had two wings, exact duplicates of each other, so that more visitors could be accommodated at the same time. Today there is only one set of exhibits. Lots of Maobilia for sale – plastic Mao heads and badges of the house – so buy up, as Shaoshan is the only place left in China where you can get it.

Places to Stay

The *Shaoshan Guest House* in Shaoshan Village is a pleasant, comfortable place surrounded by trees. The staff here are exceptionally friendly. The guest house is a 5-minute walk up from the bus stop. Doubles are Y30. Meals are Y6 each, beer Y1.30 a bottle. There is a large Chinese hotel in the village, but it's unlikely you'll be able to stay there. The guest house has pretty good meals.

Top: Yak hide coracle, Samye (RS)
Bottom Left: Chickens on wheels (RS)
Bottom Right: Steer-drawn basket (RS)

Top: The Terracotta soldiers, Xian (AS)
Bottom Left: Statue of Mao Zedong (AS)
Bottom Right: Yungang caves (AS)

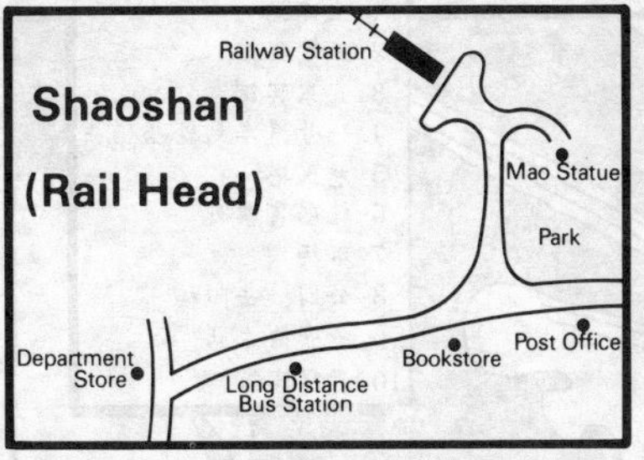

the river, and you might try some hitching and random exploration.

Information & Orientation
Yueyang lies on the southern bank of the Yangtse River. There are two sections: the southern section where you'll find the railway station, the hotel, etc, and the northern section several km away where the Yangtse ferries dock. CITS has its office at the Yunmeng Hotel. The hotel has a Chinese map of the town and Junshan Island that is worth getting.

Getting There
Bus There are three daily buses from Changsha's long-distance bus station (near the New Railway Station) to Shaoshan – they also return. The fare is Y2.30. In Shaoshan the long-distance bus station is on the main street at the Shaoshan railhead.

Rail There is a train from Changsha to Shaoshan each morning at about 8 am. On a sunny day it's a pleasant trip past numerous picturesque villages and attractive countryside. The train returns to Changsha in the afternoon so you can make Shaoshan a day trip if you like. Hard-seat fare (one way) is Y2.70 and the ride takes about three hours.

If you don't want to return to Changsha but want to get back on the railway lines, then you can take a bus first to Xiangtan and another bus to the rail junction town of Zhuzhou. There is no direct bus from Shaoshan to Zhuzhou.

YUEYANG 岳阳

Yueyang is a stop for the Yangtse ferries from Chongqing to Wuhan. The Wuhan-Canton railway passes through this small town; if you're heading to Canton you can get off the ferry here rather than go all the way to Wuhan. Yueyang is a neat little town, untrampled by tourists. The opposite bank of the river is a vast green plain punctuated by villages. A ferry regularly takes trucks and buses across

Things to See
Yueyang is a town for wandering and poking your nose down the laneways and street markets. The chief landmark is the leafy **Yueyang Tower (Cishi Pagoda)**, an old pagoda near the riverfront. To get there, walk down the street directly in front of the railway station and turn right at the end; the tower is up a laneway. Further north is the **Yueyang Pavilion**, an old temple complex now used as a park. The park is something of a mecca for Japanese tourists, apparently because of a famous poem written in its praise.

To the south-west of the town is enormous **Dongting Lake**, at 3900 square km the second largest body of fresh water in the country. There are several islands in the lake; the most famous is **Junshan**, where the Chinese grow 'silver needle tea'. When the tea is added to hot water it's supposed to remain on the surface, sticking up like tiny needles and emitting a fragrant odour.

Junshan Island can be reached by boat. To get to the boat dock walk north along the road past the Yueyang Tower. You'll come to a street market on your left. Walk to the end of the market, down the flight of steps and turn right for the ticket office and boat dock. Bus No 2 from the train station gets you in the general vicinity. There are two or three boats a day to Junshan – worth a visit not only for the tea plantations but for the other farming activity on the island.

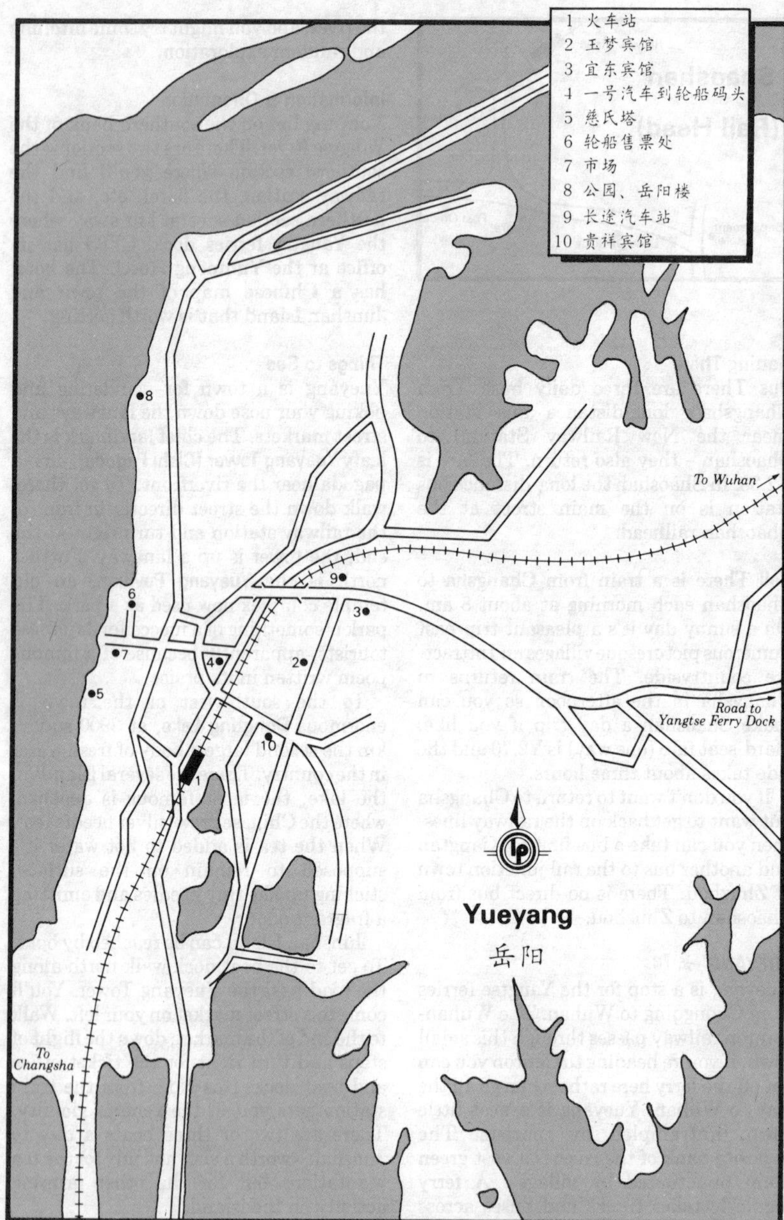
1 火车站
2 玉梦宾馆
3 宜东宾馆
4 一号汽车到轮船码头
5 慈氏塔
6 轮船售票处
7 市场
8 公园、岳阳楼
9 长途汽车站
10 贵祥宾馆
To Wuhan
Road to Yangtse Ferry Dock
To Changsha
Yueyang
岳阳

1 Railway Station
2 Yunmeng Hotel
3 Yue Dong Hotel
4 Bus No 1 to Yangtse Ferry Dock
5 Yueyang Tower
6 Ticket Office for Boats to Junshan
7 Street Market
8 Park & Temple
9 Long-distance Bus Station
10 Guangcheng Hotel

Places to Stay & Eat

The *Yunmeng Hotel* is a modest tourist hotel, readily identifiable by what looks like a concrete airliner tail at the front – imagination in architecture knows no bounds here. Doubles cost from Y40 for air-con, comfy double beds, private bathroom. You might manage a bed in a triple for Y12 or so but don't count on it. The hotel is about 20 minutes walk from the railway station. Or take bus No 4 from the railway station and get off at the second stop. The hotel is five minutes walk up the road on the left-hand side.

Yue Dong Fandian is a big concrete block with half of China inside. At Y7 a double it's as cheap as you'll get (also ask for dorm beds), but toilets and washing facilities are definitely sub-standard.

The Yunmeng Hotel has a fairly good restaurant. There are many other small restaurants around town, particularly near the train station and markets. Bring something to cool the Hunanese flames.

Getting There & Away

Yueyang is on the main Canton-Beijing railway line. There are trains to Wuhan (four hours), Changsha (two hours) and Canton (13 hours). There are daily buses to Changsha (Y8) from the long-distance bus station.

The Yangtse ferries dock at the pier in the northern section of the town. Bus No 1 takes you to the pier, a 20-minute ride. The ticket office (a largish building with an anchor and star over the entrance, five minutes walk around the corner from the bus terminus) should open about half an hour before the ferry docks. There are a number of small restaurants in the vicinity of the dock.

Upriver to Chongqing takes about four days and four nights. Fares are: 2nd class Y100; 3rd class Y42; 4th class Y30 (in egalitarian China there is no 1st class). The ferry is scheduled to depart Yueyang at about 9 pm.

Downriver to Wuhan takes about eight hours. Fares from Yueyang are: 2nd class Y16.60; 3rd class Y7; 4th class Y5. The ferry is scheduled to depart Yueyang about 7.30 am but expect delays.

ZHUZHOU 株州

Unlike nearby Changsha, Zhuzhou is an entirely modern town and owes its sudden development to the completion of the Canton-Wuhan railway line in 1937. Formerly a small market town, it became a river port for the shipment of coal. It later became an important rail junction town and a centre for the manufacture of railway equipment, locomotives and rolling stock. Today it harbours a diverse industry.

Places to Stay & Eat

There is at least one hotel in Zhuzhou where you can stay. Leaving the railway station, turn right along the small road in front of the station and right again at the first intersection. Cross the bridge – the hotel is a big grey concrete building a few minutes walk ahead on the right-hand side. You should be able to get a dorm bed here for a few yuan. Best places to eat are the small food stalls near the railway station.

Getting There

Zhuzhou is still a major rail junction; the Beijing-Canton and the Shanghai-Kunming rail lines intersect here. There's nothing of particular interest but you may come here to change trains.

If you're coming into Zhuzhou by bus from Xiangtan, the bus line terminates on Zhuzhou's main street. Continue straight

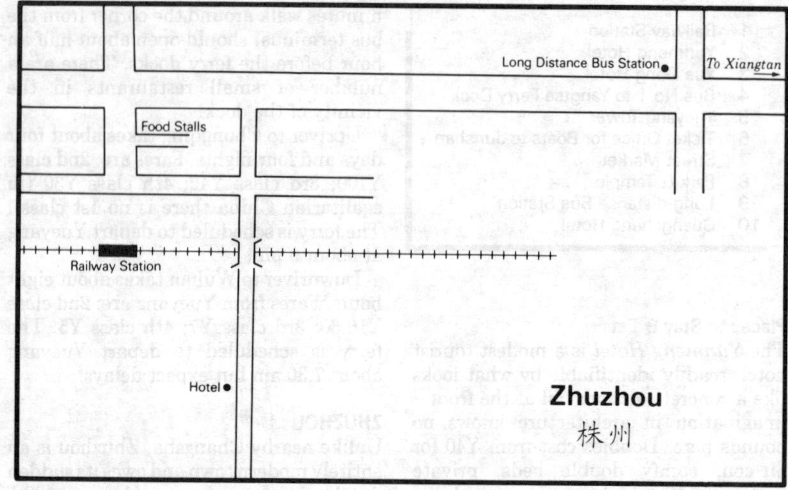

ahead to the railway station (a half-hour walk), or take the local bus.

HENGYANG 衡阳

Hengyang is the major town of southern Hunan, and like Zhuzhou grew rapidly after the construction of the Canton-Wuhan railway line in 1937. The town became a major lead and zinc-mining centre but its industry was badly damaged during the later stages of WW II. Though it was restored after 1949, the town was overshadowed by the growth of Zhuzhou and Changsha. Today it's a rather dull industrial town on the Beijing-Canton rail line. Travellers who take the train from Canton to Guilin have to wait a couple of hours here for a connection. It's not a bad stopover.

Places to Stay & Eat

The *Hengyang Guest House* is a 10-minute walk down the street in front of the train station. The CITS office is also here. Room prices may depend on who's at the desk, but spartan doubles for Y10 are possible. Comfy, air-con double rooms with private bathroom are Y44. The guest house has no sign-post so look for an ornate gateway. There is a Chinese hotel next door and one across the road, but it's unlikely you'll get in. There are many small restaurants in the vicinity of the train station.

Getting There & Away

Hengyang is a major rail junction with direct trains to Wuhan, Canton and Guilin among other places. Trains to Changsha take three hours, and tourist-price hard-seat is Y7.

XIANGTAN 湘潭

Once a river port and market centre, Xiangtan stagnated early this century when the railway took away much of its trade. The Kuomintang gave its industry a kick in the late 1930s and the Communists expanded it. Today Xiangtan is a rather flat, hot, drab town of 300,000 people on the Shanghai-Kunming rail line.

Getting There & Away

There are regular buses from Xiangtan to Zhuzhou (1¼ hours) and buses to Changsha. There are also buses to

Shaoshan which take 1½ hours to make the trip and pass several small villages on the way.

QINGYAN SHAN 青盐山

The Qingyan (Blue Rock) Mountains in north-west Hunan Province have been set aside as a national park. Visitors travel by train from Changsha to Dayong County, and then bus another 30 km to the Zhangjiajie Forest Farm within the mountainous area.

Jiangxi 江西

Jiangxi was incorporated into the Chinese empire at an early date, but it remained sparsely populated until the 8th century. Before this, the main expansion of the Han Chinese had been from the north into Hunan and then into Guangdong. When the building of the Grand Canal from the 7th century onwards opened up the south-eastern regions, Jiangxi became an important transit point on the trade and shipment route overland from Guangdong.

Before long the human traffic was diverted into Jiangxi, and between the 8th and 13th century the region was rapidly settled by Chinese peasants. The development of silver mining and tea growing allowed the formation of a wealthy Jiangxi merchant class. By the 19th century, however, its role as a major transport route from Canton was much reduced by the opening of coastal ports to foreign shipping – which forced the Chinese junk trade into a steady decline.

Jiangxi also bears the distinction of having been one of the most famous Communist guerrilla bases. It was only after several years of war that the Kuomintang were able to drive the Communists out on their 'Long March' to Shaanxi.

NANCHANG 南昌

The capital of Jiangxi Province, Nanchang is largely remembered in modern Chinese history for the Communist-led uprising of 1 August 1927.

After Chiang Kaishek staged his massacre of Communists and other opponents in March 1927, what was left of the Communist Party fled underground and a state of confusion reigned. At this time the Party was dominated by a policy of urban revolution, and the belief was that victory could only be won by organising insurrections in the cities. Units of the Kuomintang Army led by Communist officers happened to be concentrated around Nanchang at the time, and there appeared to be an opportunity for a successful insurrection.

On 1 August, a combined army of 30,000 under the leadership of Zhou Enlai and Zhu De seized the city and held it for several days until they were driven out by troops loyal to the Nanjing regime. The revolt was largely a fiasco, but it is marked in Chinese history as the beginning of the Red Army. The Army retreated from Nanchang south to Guangdong but part of it, led by Zhu De, circled back to Jiangxi to join forces with the rag-tag army that Mao Zedong had organised in Hunan and led into the Jinggang Mountains.

Not all of Nanchang's history has been so tumultuous – in fact, the name means 'southern prosperity'. It was founded back in the Eastern Han Dynasty and became a busy trading city, a major staging post on the trade route from Guangdong to Beijing, and a major distribution point for the gaolin pottery of nearby Jingdezhen. Since 1949 it has grown into another of China's multi-purpose, industrial-urban sprawls with something like 2½ million inhabitants.

Information & Orientation

Nanchang is bounded in the north by the Gan River and in the west by the Fu River, which branches off the Gan. The train station is in the south-east of the city. Bayi Lu is the main artery and cuts a circuitous route through the centre of

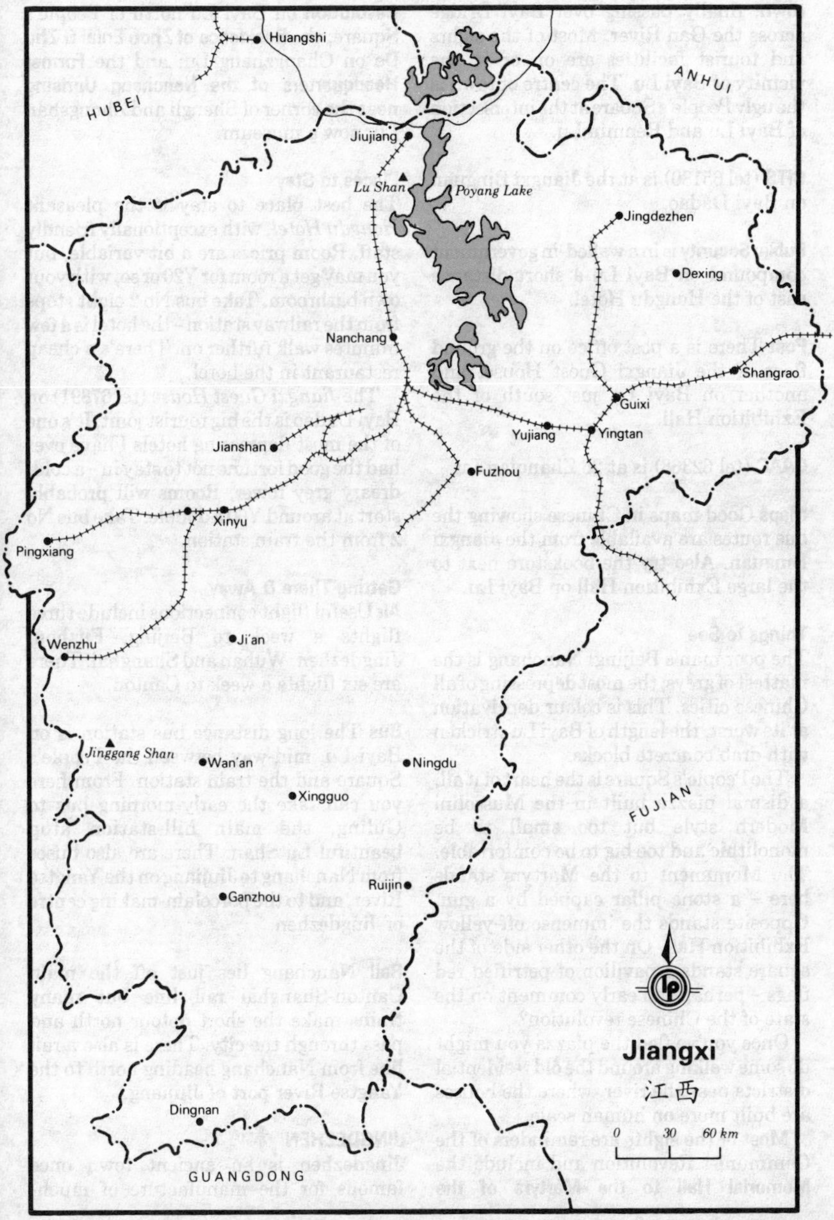
Huangshi
HUBEI
ANHUI
Jiujiang
Lu Shan
Poyang Lake
Jingdezhen
Dexing
Nanchang
Shangrao
Guixi
Yujiang
Yingtan
Jianshan
Fuzhou
Xinyu
Pingxiang
Wenzhu
Ji'an
Jinggang Shan
Wan'an
Ningdu
Xingguo
FUJIAN
Ruijin
Ganzhou
Jiangxi
江西
0
30
60 km
Dingnan
GUANGDONG

town, finally passing over Bayi Bridge across the Gan River. Most of the sights and tourist facilities are on or in the vicinity of Bayi Lu. The centre of town is the ugly People's Square at the intersection of Bayi Lu and Renmin Lu.

CITS (tel 65180) is at the Jiangxi Binguan on Bayi Dadao.

Public Security is in a walled-in government compound on Bayi Lu a short distance east of the Hongdu Hotel.

Post There is a post office on the ground floor of the Jiangxi Guest House, and another on Bayi Lu just south of the Exhibition Hall.

CAAC (tel 62368) is at 26 Zhanqian Lu.

Maps Good maps in Chinese showing the bus routes are available from the Jiangxi Binguan. Also try the bookstore next to the large Exhibition Hall on Bayi Lu.

Things to See

The poor man's Beijing: Nanchang is the mattest of greys, the most depressing of all Chinese cities. This is colour deprivation at its worst, the length of Bayi Lu stricken with drab concrete blocks.

The People's Square is the heart of it all, a dismal piazza built in the Mussolini Modern style but too small to be monolithic and too big to be comfortable. The Monument to the Martyrs stands here – a stone pillar capped by a gun. Opposite stands the immense off-yellow Exhibition Hall. On the other side of the square stands a pavilion of petrified red flags – perhaps an early comment on the state of the Chinese revolution?

Once you've fled the piazza you might do some walking around the old residential districts near the river, where the houses are built more on human scale.

Most of the sights are reminders of the Communist Revolution and include the **Memorial Hall to the Martyrs of the Revolution** on Bayi Lu north of People's Square; the **Residence of Zhou Enlai & Zhu De** on Changzhang Lu; and the **Former Headquarters of the Nanchang Uprising** near the corner of Shengli and Zhongshan Lu, now a museum.

Places to Stay

The best place to stay is the pleasant *Hongdu Hotel*, with exceptionally friendly staff. Room prices are a bit variable, but you may get a room for Y20 or so, with your own bathroom. Take bus No 2 eight stops from the railway station – the hotel is a few minutes walk further on. There's a cheap restaurant in the hotel.

The *Jiangxi Guest House* (tel 67891) on Bayi Dadao is the big tourist joint. It's one of the most depressing hotels I have ever had the good fortune not to stay in – a cold, dreary grey tower. Rooms will probably start at around Y60 a double. Take bus No 2 from the train station.

Getting There & Away

Air Useful flight connections include three flights a week to Beijing, Fuzhou, Jingdezhen, Wuhan and Shanghai. There are six flights a week to Canton.

Bus The long-distance bus station is on Bayi Lu, mid-way between the People's Square and the train station. From here you can take the early-morning bus to Guling, the main hill-station atop beautiful Lu Shan. There are also buses from Nanchang to Jiujiang on the Yangtse River, and to the porcelain-making centre of Jingdezhen.

Rail Nanchang lies just off the main Canton-Shanghai rail line but many trains make the short detour north and pass through the city. There is also a rail line from Nanchang heading north to the Yangtse River port of Jiujiang.

JINGDEZHEN 景德镇

Jingdezhen is an ancient town once famous for the manufacture of much-

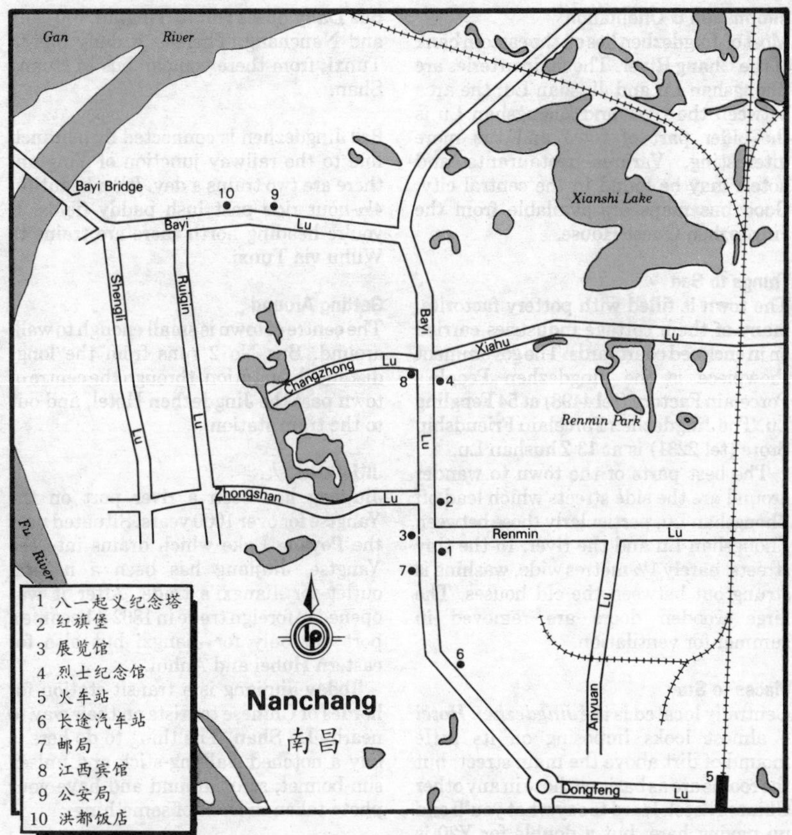

1 Monument to the Martyrs
2 Red Flag Pavilion
3 Exhibition Hall
4 Memorial Hall to the Martyrs of the Revolution
5 Railway Station
6 Long-distance Bus Station
7 Post Office
8 Jiangxi Guest House
9 Public Security
10 Hongdu Hotel

coveted porcelain. Today Jingdezhen still makes porcelain and other ceramics – smoke stacks sprout like giant weeds all over the town – but the quality is perhaps not what it once was.

In the 12th century the Song Dynasty fled south in the wake of an invasion from the north. The Song court moved to Hangzhou and the imperial potters moved to Jingdezhen, near Gaolin village and the rich supply of gaolin clay. Today 30,000 of Jingdezhen's 250,000 people are employed in the ceramics industry. For a run-down on the history of pottery in China see the Arts & Crafts section at the start of this book.

Information & Orientation
Most of Jingdezhen lies on the eastern bank of the Chang River. The main arteries are Zhongshan Lu and Jiushan Lu; the area between the river and Zhongshan Lu is the older part of town and the more interesting. Various restaurants and hotels may be found in the central city. Good bus maps are available from the Jingdezhen Guest House.

Things to See
The town is filled with pottery factories, many of them cottage industries carried on in enclosed courtyards. The government showpiece is the Jingdezhen People's Porcelain Factory (tel 4498) at 54 Fengling Lu. The Jingdezhen Porcelain Friendship Store (tel 2231) is at 13 Zhushan Lu.

The best parts of the town to wander around are the side streets which lead off Zhongshan Lu, particularly those between Zhongshan Lu and the river. In the tiny streets, barely 1½ metres wide, washing is strung out between the old houses. The large wooden doors are removed in summer for ventilation.

Places to Stay
Centrally located is the *Jingdezhen Hotel* – almost looks imposing on its little mound of dirt above the main street, but the rooms are as basic as those in any other Chinese hotel. Hard to say what you'll end up paying here, but a double for Y20 is possible. Take bus No 2 from either the long-distance bus station or the train station as it goes straight past the hotel. The hotel has an OK restaurant.

The *Jingdezhen Guest House* (tel 927) is the tourist joint, about a 15-minute walk from the Jingdezhen Hotel. The guest house is a pleasant building surrounded by trees and situated by a lake. Doubles cost around Y60.

Getting There & Away
Air Jingdezhen is connected by air to Nanchang; there are three flights a week.

Bus Daily buses run to Yingtan, Jiujiang and Nanchang. There is a daily bus to Tunxi; from there you can bus to Huang Shan.

Rail Jingdezhen is connected by a branch line to the railway junction of Yingtan; there are two trains a day. It's a beautiful 4½-hour ride past lush paddy fields. If you're heading north there are trains to Wuhu via Tunxi.

Getting Around
The centre of town is small enough to walk around. Bus No 2 runs from the long-distance bus station, through the centre of town past the Jingdezhen Hotel, and out to the train station.

JIUJIANG 九江
Jiujiang has been a river port on the Yangtse for over 1000 years. Situated near the Poyang Lake which drains into the Yangtse, Jiujiang has been a natural outlet for Jiangxi's trade. After it was opened to foreign trade in 1862 it became a port not only for Jiangxi but also for eastern Hubei and Anhui.

Today Jiujiang is a transit station for hordes of Chinese tourists on their way to nearby Lu Shan. The thing to do here is buy a notched walking-stick and unisex sun-bonnet, strut around and have your photo taken in front of something.

Information & Orientation
Jiujiang is stretched out along the south bank of the Yangtse River. The long-distance bus station is in the eastern part of town and the railway station is at the western end; the harbour is mid-way between the two in a narrow urban neck squashed between the river and the lake. In between the harbour and the lake are the hotels, restaurants, shops and other facilities.

Things to See
The seven-storey **pagoda** in the south-east of the town is worth a look. The local

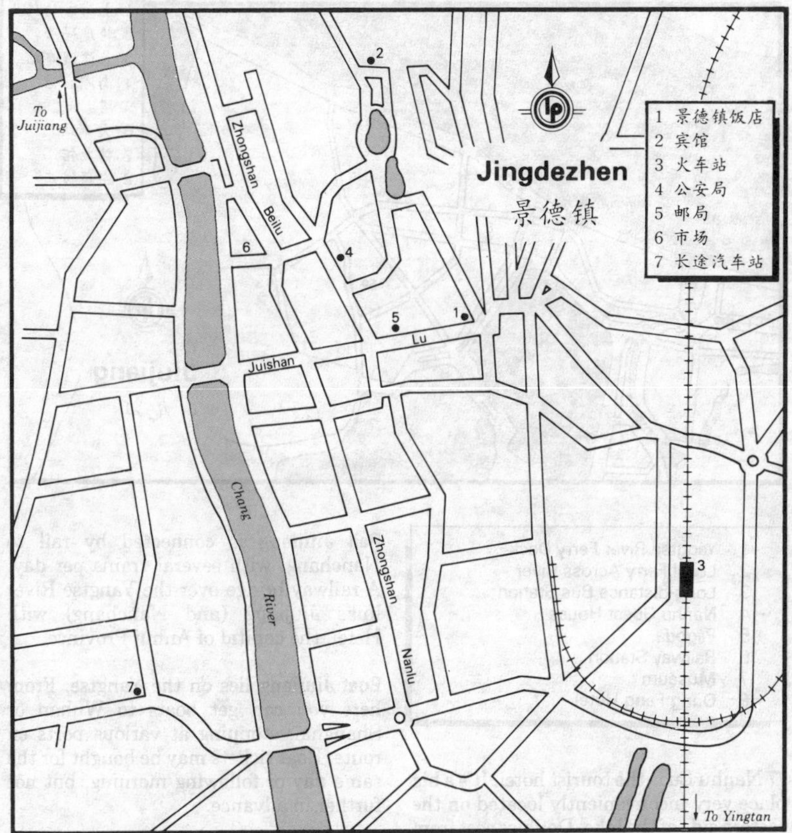

1 Jingdezhen Hotel
2 Jingdezhen Guest House
3 Railway Station
4 Public Security
5 Post Office
6 Street Market
7 Long-distance Bus Station

museum is in a quaint old building set in the lake near the centre of town, connected to shore by a zig-zag bridge. It's got an interesting collection of prehistoric tools and weapons but no English captions.

Places to Stay & Eat

The *Dong Fang Hotel* is on Xunyang Lu. They may try to send you to the Nanhu Hotel, but hold your ground since they are allowed to take foreigners. Not bad for a warehouse. A dorm bed should cost a few yuan, and a room less than Y20. Rooms facing the street are very noisy. The hotel is within walking distance of the boat dock. From the long-distance bus station or the train station, take bus No 1 and get off at the stop in front of the museum, then walk back.

The *Nanhu Guest House* (tel 2272) at

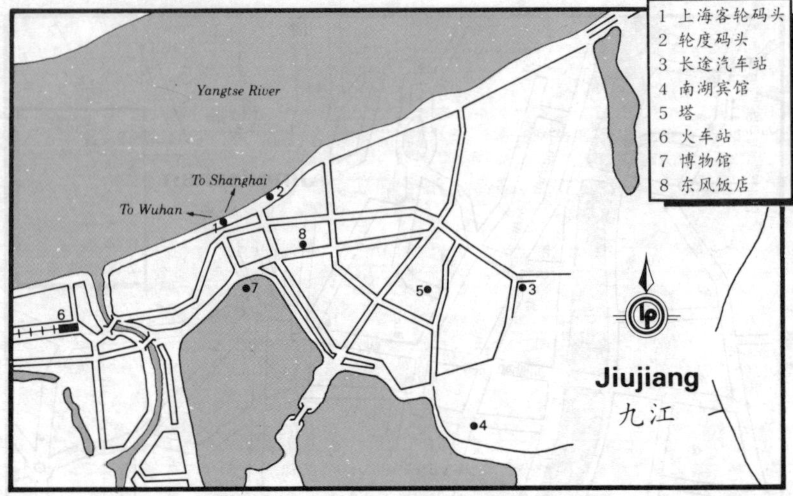

1. Yangtse River Ferry Dock
2. Local Ferry Across River
3. Long-distance Bus Station
4. Nanhu Guest House
5. Pagoda
6. Railway Station
7. Museum
8. Dong Feng Hotel

77 Nanhu Lu is the tourist hotel. It's a big place very inconveniently located on the eastern side of the lake. Doubles cost from Y30 or so (probably much more). There don't appear to be any buses to the hotel. It's a long walk from the train, so hop an auto-rickshaw.

There are a couple of restaurants around the dock and on the streets close to the Dong Feng Hotel – OK but not memorable.

Getting There & Away

Bus Daily buses run to Jingdezhen (about 5½ hours with many small villages on the way) and Lu Shan. The fare to Lu Shan is Y2.

Rail Jiujiang is connected by rail to Nanchang, with several trains per day. A railway bridge over the Yangtse River links Jiujiang (and Nanchang) with Hefei, the capital of Anhui Province.

Boat Jiujiang lies on the Yangtse. From here you can get boats to Wuhan or Shanghai, stopping at various ports en route. Boat tickets may be bought for the same day or following morning, but not further in advance.

Getting Around

Bus No 1 runs through Jiujiang from the long-distance bus station in the east, past the South Lake to the train station in the west. There are auto-rickshaws around the train and bus stations and the dock.

LU SHAN 庐山

Every so often China throws up something that takes you completely by surprise. A village lifted lock, stock and barrel out of Switzerland and grafted onto a Chinese mountaintop is the last thing you'd expect – but here's Lu Shan with its chunks of European architecture.

The mountain at the very north of Jiangxi Province is one of the most beautiful in China. Established as a hill resort by the foreign settlers in China in the 19th and 20th centuries, the top of the mountain is dotted with European-style stone cottages, churches and hotels. The bus ride from the plains of Jiangxi to the top of Lu Shan is dramatic as the road winds its way around the mountainside, looking down on sheer cliffs. Over the long drop below you can see immense stretches of terraced fields.

The mountain belies its significance in the destiny of a billion Chinese. It was here in 1959 that the Central Committee of the Communist Party held its fateful meeting which eventually ended in the dismissal of Peng Dehuai, sent Mao almost into a political wilderness and provided the seeds of the rise and fall of Liu Shaoqi and Deng Xiaoping.

In 1970, after Mao had regained power, another meeting was held in Lu Shan, this time of the Politburo. Exactly what happened is shrouded in as much mist as the mountain itself, but it seems that Lin Biao clashed with Mao, opposed his

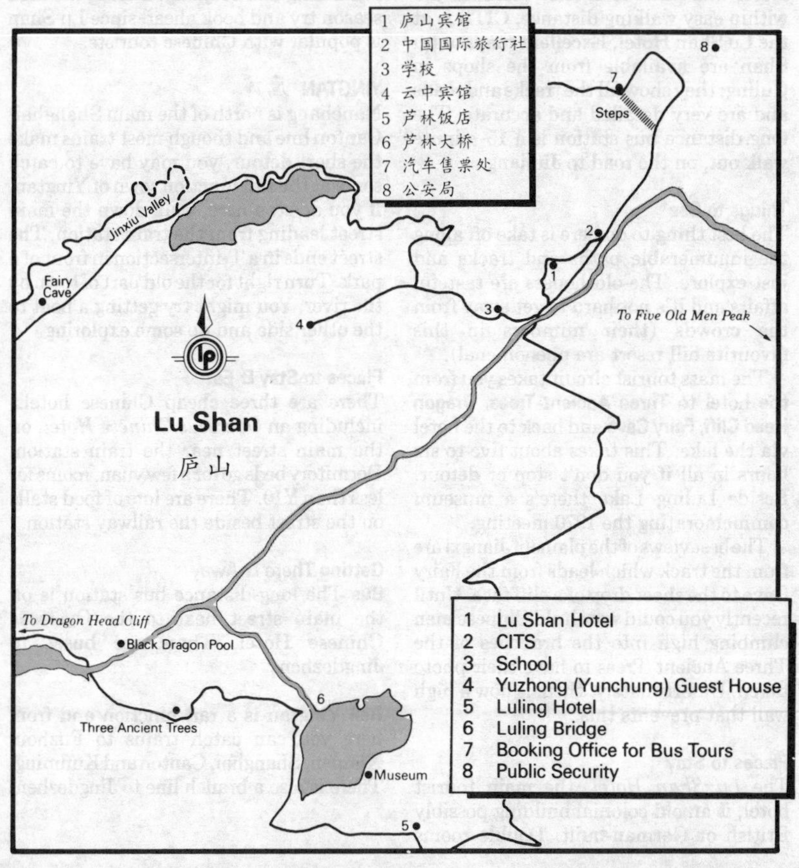

policies of rapprochement with the USA and probably proposed the continuation of the xenophobic policies of the Cultural Revolution. Whatever, Lin was dead the next year.

Information & Orientation
The bus puts you off at Guling, the main hill station, which is sprawled across the mountaintop. The 'centre' of Guling is the cluster of restaurants and shops near the long-distance bus station. There are food stalls in the large building overlooking the vegetable market in Guling. The Lu Shan Hotel and various tourist facilities are within easy walking distance. CITS is at the Lu Shan Hotel. Excellent maps of Lu Shan are available from the shops in Guling; they show all the tracks and roads and are very detailed and accurate. The long distance bus station is a 15-minute walk out, on the road to Jiujiang.

Things to See
The best thing to do here is take off along the innumerable paths and tracks and just explore. The old houses are tasteful affairs and it's not hard to get away from the crowds (their numbers in this favourite hill resort are phenomenal).

The mass tourist circuit takes you from the hotel to **Three Ancient Trees, Dragon Head Cliff, Fairy Cave** and back to the hotel via the lake. This takes about five to six hours in all if you don't stop or detour. Beside Luling Lake there's a museum commemorating the 1970 meeting.

The best views of the plains of Jiangxi are from the track which leads from the Fairy Cave to the sheer drop of a cliff face. Until recently you could watch old Chinese men climbing high into the branches of the Three Ancient Trees to have their photo taken. Unfortunately, there is now a high wall that prevents this.

Places to Stay
The *Lu Shan Hotel*, the main tourist hotel, is an old colonial building possibly British or German-built. Double rooms only, no singles. They also have dormitory beds but there's nowhere to wash. The hotel is a 30-minute walk from the bus terminus; go through the tunnel and down the hill.

Cheaper is the *Luling Binguan* which sits beside beautiful Luling Lake; the hotel is stunning though the rooms are spartan. The *Yuzhong Hotel* has recently been enlarged and upgraded. It's a tiring walk uphill from the Lu Shan Hotel.

Getting There
There are daily buses to Lu Shan from Nanchang and Jiujiang. During the high season try and book ahead since Lu Shan is popular with Chinese tourists.

YINGTAN 鹰潭

Nanchang is north of the main Shanghai-Canton line and though most trains make the short detour, you may have to catch some at the rail junction town of Yingtan. If you do stop here, walk down the main street leading from the train station. The street ends in a T-intersection in front of a park. Turn right for the old part of town by the river. You might try getting a boat to the other side and do some exploring.

Places to Stay & Eat
There are three cheap Chinese hotels, including an *Overseas Chinese Hotel*, on the main street near the train station. Dormitory beds go for a few yuan, rooms for less than Y10. There are lots of food stalls on the street beside the railway station.

Getting There & Away
Bus The long-distance bus station is on the main street next to the Overseas Chinese Hotel. There are buses to Jingdezhen.

Rail Yingtan is a rail junction and from here you can catch trains to Fuzhou, Xiamen, Shanghai, Canton and Kunming. There is also a branch line to Jingdezhen.

THE JINGGANG MOUNTAINS 井岗山

Located in the middle of the Luoxiao Range on the Hunan-Jiangxi border, the Jinggang Mountains are a remote region famed for their connection with the early Communist movement. The Communist leaders led their rag-tag armies into these hills to begin the struggle against the Kuomintang, and from here the Long March began. The main township is Ciping, surrounded on all sides by the hills, 320 km south-west of Nanchang. There are probably buses to Ciping from Nanchang.

Hubei 湖北

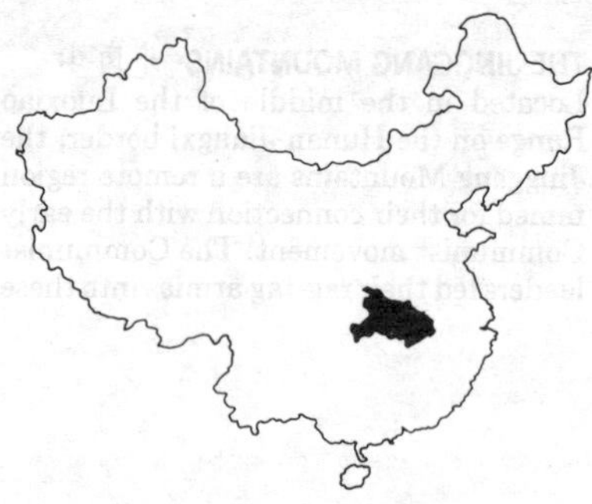

Hubei Province comprises two quite different areas. The eastern two-thirds is a low-lying plain drained by the Yangtse and its main northern tributary the Han Shui. The western third is an area of rugged highlands with small cultivated valleys and basins dividing Hubei from Sichuan. The plain has been settled by the Han Chinese since 1000 BC. Around the 7th century it was intensively settled and by the 11th it was producing a rice surplus. In the late 19th century it was the first area in the Chinese interior to undergo considerable industrialisation. Site of the great industrial city and river port of Wuhan, slashed through by the Yangtse River and its many tributaries, and supporting a population of almost 50 million, Hubei is still one of China's most important provinces.

WUHAN 武汉

With a population of three million, Wuhan is one of the largest cities in China. It's actually a conglomeration of what were once three independent cities: Hankou, Hanyang and Wuchang.

Wuchang was established during the Han Dynasty, became a regional capital under the Yuan and is now the seat of the provincial government. It used to be a walled city but the walls have long since gone.

Hankou, on the other hand, was barely more than a village until the Treaty of Nanjing opened it to foreign trade. Within a few years it was divided into British, French, German, Russian and Japanese concessions, all grouped around present-day Zhongshan Lu north of the Xuangong Hotel. With the building of the Beijing-Wuhan railway in the 1920s Hankou really began to expand and became the first major industrial centre in the interior of China.

Hanyang has been outstripped by neighbouring Hankou and today is the smallest municipality. It dates back to 600 AD, when a town first developed on the site. During the second half of the 19th century it was developed for heavy industry. The plant for the manufacture of iron and steel which was built at Hanyang in 1891 was the first modern one in China and it was followed during the early 1900s by a string of riverside factories. The 1930s depression and then the Japanese invasion totally ruined Hanyang's heavy industries and since the revolution light industry has been the main activity.

Not many people go out of their way to get to Wuhan, but a lot of people pass through the place since this is the terminus of the Yangtse ferries from Chongqing. Livelier, less grimy, more modern than Chongqing, it's a stepping-stone on the way to the comparatively sparkling, cosmopolitan citadels of Nanjing and Shanghai.

Like those cities, Wuhan has been a fortunate metropolis in unfortunate times. In Wuhan in 1911 an army revolt led to the downfall of the Qing Dynasty; in the fighting Hankou was almost totally burnt to the ground, except for the foreign concessions along the riverfront. The city was the centre of the bloodily suppressed 7 February 1923 strike of the workers building the Wuhan-Beijing railway line. The Kuomintang government first retreated from Nanjing to Wuhan in the wake of the

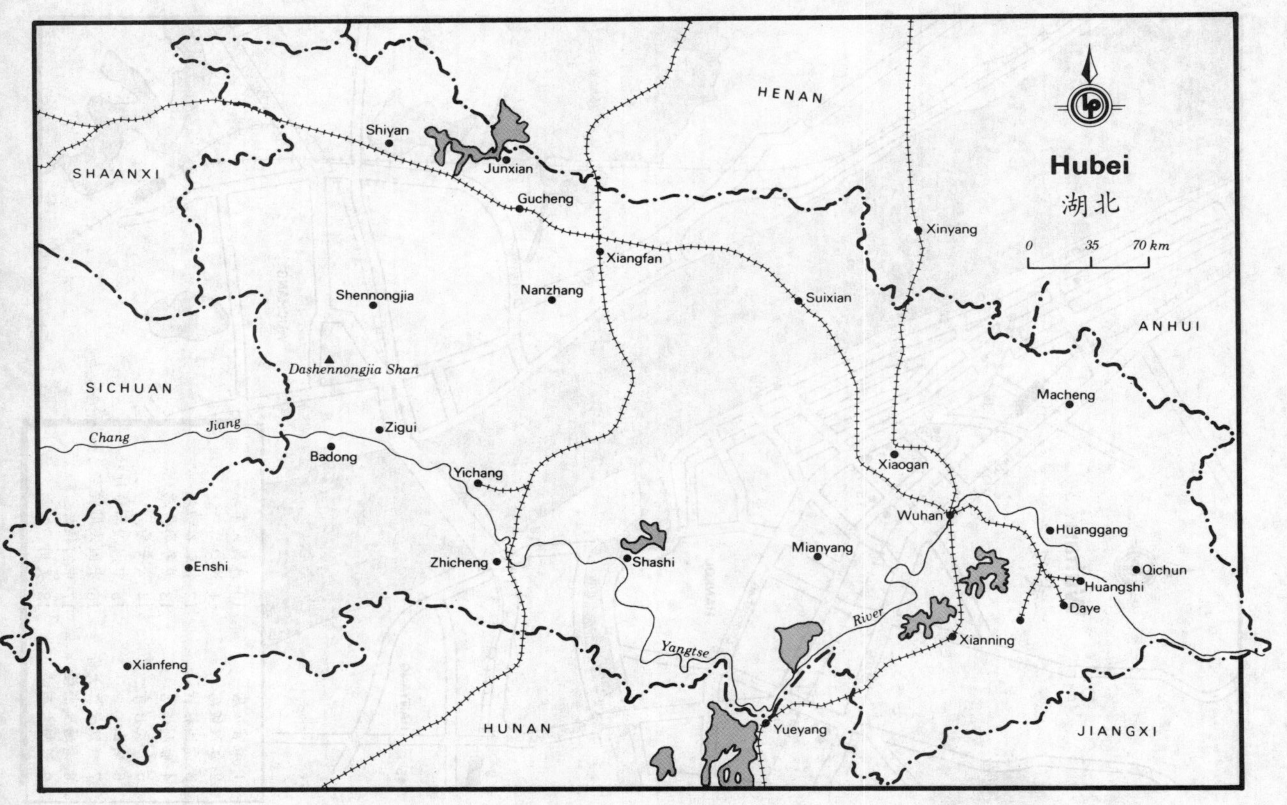
Hubei
湖北
0
35
70 km
HENAN
SHAANXI
ANHUI
SICHUAN
HUNAN
JIANGXI
Shiyan
Junxian
Gucheng
Xiangfan
Xinyang
Suixian
Shennongjia
Nanzhang
Dashennongjia Shan
Macheng
Chang
Jiang
Zigui
Badong
Yichang
Xiaogan
Wuhan
Huanggang
Zhicheng
Shashi
Mianyang
Enshi
Qichun
Huangshi
Daye
River
Xianning
Yangtse
Xianfeng
Yueyang

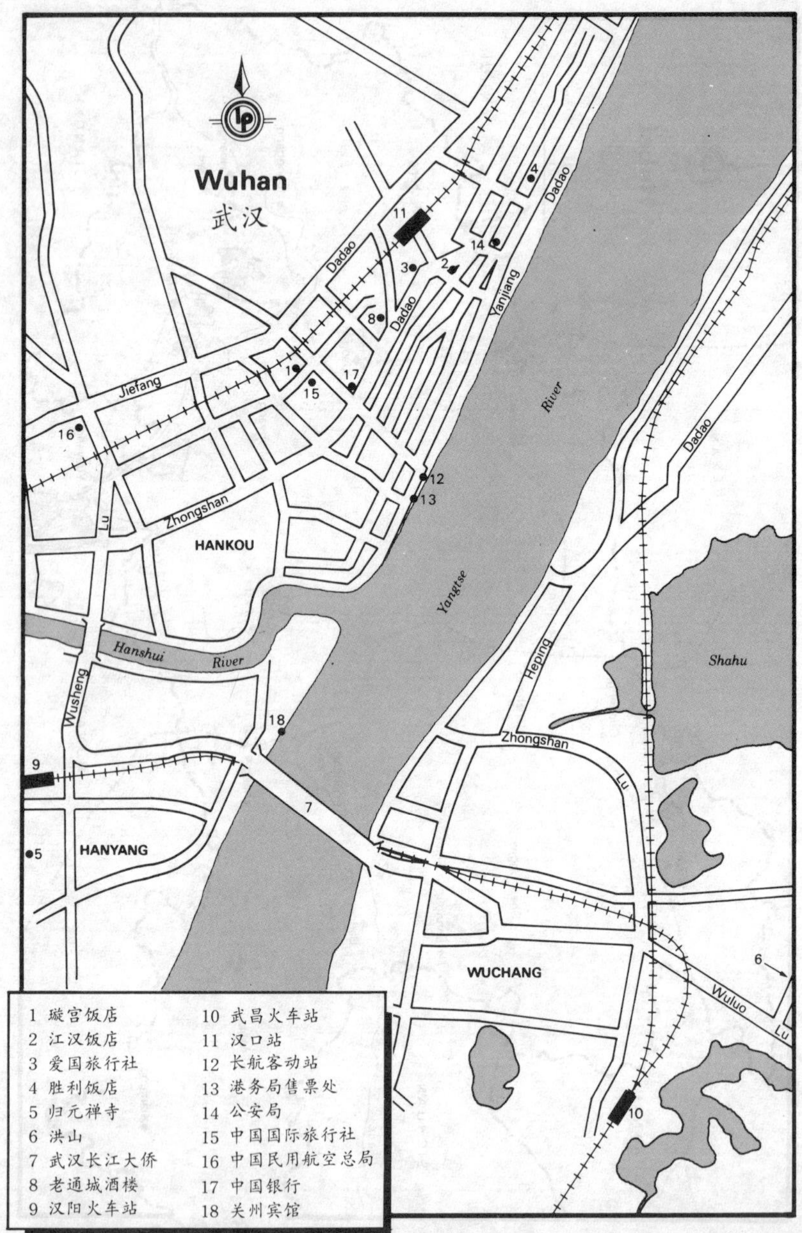
Wuhan
武汉
Dadao
Dadao
Dadao
Yanjiang
Dadao
Jiefang
Zhongshan
Lu
River
Yangtse
HANKOU
Hanshui
River
Wusheng
Heping
Shahu
Zhongshan
Lu
HANYANG
WUCHANG
Wuluo
Lu
1 璇宫饭店
2 江汉饭店
3 爱国旅行社
4 胜利饭店
5 归元禅寺
6 洪山
7 武汉长江大侨
8 老通城酒楼
9 汉阳火车站
10 武昌火车站
11 汉口站
12 长航客动站
13 港务局售票处
14 公安局
15 中国国际旅行社
16 中国民用航空总局
17 中国银行
18 关州宾馆

1. Xuangong Hotel
2. Jianghan Hotel
3. Aiguo Hotel
4. Shengli Hotel
5. Guiyuan Temple
6. Hong Shan
7. Wuchang Bridge
8. Laotongcheng Restaurant
9. Hangyang Railway Station
10. Wuchang Railway Station
11. Hankou Railway Station
12. Dock for Yangtse Ferries
13. Booking Office for Yangtse Ferries
14. Public Security
15. CITS
16. CAAC
17. Bank of China
18. Qing Chuan Hotel

Japanese invasion, until bombing and the advance of the Japanese army forced them further west to Chongqing.

Information & Orientation

Wuhan lies on both sides of the Yangtse River. Wuchang lies on the east bank. On the west bank lie Hankou and Hanyang, separated from each other by the Han River. Hankou is the centre of things where you'll find the dock for the Yangtse ferries, the hotels and other tourist life-support systems. The main artery is Zhongshan Dadao, which cuts through Hankou roughly parallel to the Yangtse River. Most of the trains into Wuhan stop at both Hankou and Wuchang but it's more convenient to get off at Hankou.

CITS is in the Hailu Hotel, opposite the Xuangong Hotel on Jianghan Yilu. Virtually useless for individuals.

Public Security (tel 25129) is at 206 Shengli Lu, a 10-minute walk north of the Jianghan Hotel. They're quite friendly and helpful.

Bank Change cash and travellers' cheques at the Bank of China, corner Zhongshan Dadao and Jianghan Lu.

CAAC (tel 51248, 52371) is at 209 Liji Beilu, Hankou.

Maps You should find hawkers selling bus maps of Wuhan near the Yangtse ferry dock and around Hankou train station. Otherwise, try the hotel shops.

Things to See

Hankou is the centre of Wuhan. Zhongshan Dadao is the main thoroughfare with the shops, department stores, restaurants and several market streets branching off it.

Jiefang Lu is a market street, but there's a better one selling food and live animals south of Jiefang Lu – it's a cobbled street lined with old houses.

The north of Hankou, around the Shengli Hotel, is a quiet residential area. Since Hankou was the foreign concession area, there are many European-style buildings, particularly along Yanjiang Lu in the north-east part of town. Government offices now occupy what were once the foreign banks, department stores and private residences. There were five foreign concession areas in Hankou; the British arrived in 1861, the Germans in 1895, the Russians in 1896, the French in 1896 and finally the Japanese in 1898.

Wuchang is a modern district with long, wide avenues lined with drab concrete blocks. The Hubei Provincial Museum is located here. The fine Guiyan Temple is across the river in Hanyang.

Guiyuan Temple

Doubling as a curiosity shop and active place of worship is this Buddhist temple with buildings dating from the late Ming and early Qing dynasties.

The main attraction is the statues of Buddha's disciples in an array of comical poses – like the guy sprouting a second head. Two heads are better than one? Behind the dusty glass showcases, it's difficult to tell. A few years ago the statues were out in the open, and the smoking incense and sunshine filtering through the skylights gave the temple a rare magic.

Other statues in the temple include the Maitreya Buddha and Sakyamuni. Lots of beggars outside the temple, and lots of professional photographers inside – the latter snapping souvenir shots of Chinese posing in front of rocks and puddles. Monks occasionally bang a gong or tap a bell for the amusement of the masses, but who cares?

It's hard to say what happened to this place during the Cultural Revolution. Different people tell different stories. One Chinese said, 'The people of Wuhan love this place so much. During the Cultural Revolution they protected it and would not let anyone in to harm it'. But 'Don't be silly', said another. 'It looks old – but in China we are very good at making things look old'. Your guess is as good as mine.

To get there take bus No 45 from the hotel district, down Zhongshan Dadao and over the bridge; there's a stop within walking distance of the temple. The temple is on Cuiweiheng Lu at the junction with Cuiwe Lu; a trinket market lines Cuiwe Lu.

Yangtse River Bridge

Before the Yangtse Bridge was built in 1957, ferries had to be used to take traffic across the river on the north-south route. Over 1100 metres long and 80 metres high, the road and rail bridge connects Wuchang to Hanyang. Both this bridge and the one in Nanjing are hailed as examples of the country's modern engineering achievements. A shorter bridge spans the Han River.

Hubei Provincial Museum

The museum is a must if you're interested in archaeology. Its large collection of artefacts came from the Zhenghouyi Tomb, which was unearthed in 1978 on the outskirts of Suizhou City. The tomb dates to the Warring States Period, around 433 BC. The male internee was buried with about 7000 of his favourite artefacts, including bronze ritual vessels, weapons, horse and chariot equipment, bamboo instruments and utensils, and gold and jade objects. Most impressive is the massive set of bronze bell chimes – enough to make Mike Oldfield's eyes water. Other musical instruments found in the tomb included a wooden drum, stringed instruments and a kind of flute similar to pan-pipes. The museum is beside Donghu (East Lake) in Wuchang. Take bus No 14 to the terminus.

Alternatively, see the museum as part of a day's activities. From Hankou, take a ferry across the river to Wuchang, then bus no. 36 to Moshan Hill. From here you take a ferry across the lake to East Lake Park, then walk to the museum, then take bus no. 14 to Yellow Crane Tower, and finally a ferry back to Hankou.

Wuhan University

Located in the northern part of Wuchang, the university was founded in 1913. Many of the rather charming traditional-style buildings date from that period. The campus was the site of the 1967 'Wuhan Incident' – a protracted battle during the Cultural Revolution with machine gun nests on top of the library and supply tunnels dug through the hill. For a bit of Cultural Revolution nostalgia take bus No 12 to the terminus.

Places to Stay

Apart from the *Xuangong Hotel* and the *Qing Chuan Hotel*, the tourist hotels are in the Hankou region, within walking distance of Hankou Railway Station. From the Yangtse ferry dock take bus No 30.

Places to Stay – bottom end

The *Aiguo Hotel* is on Zhongshan Dadao, a 10-minute walk from Hankou Railway Station. Rooms are around Y15 a single and Y30 a double. Dormitory beds are Y10. This used to be a nifty little hotel, until televisions were put in every thinly partitioned room. The noise is formidable! The showers and toilets are communal, though on the 2nd and 3rd floors there are a few private bathrooms with bathtub and toilet. Hot water at night.

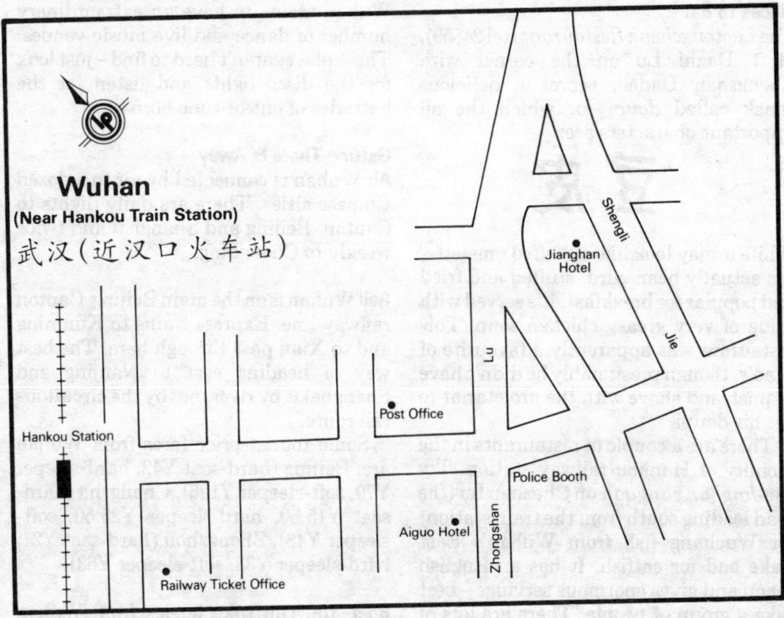

An article in the Wuhan newspaper *Changjiang Ribao (Yangtse River Daily)* records that over 1800 foreigners and over 700 Macau and Hong Kong Chinese stayed at the Aiguo in 1985. In the first six months of 1986 the hotel had already put up 600 foreign guests. The article explained that 'Here, the glass doors and windows, floors and walls are all kept very clean; the service is pleasant and thorough, and the price is reasonable. No wonder foreign travellers and many overseas compatriots, map in hand, come to find this hotel'. Unfortunately, with the television invasion it's hard to give the place an unconditional recommendation.

Places to Stay – middle

The *Jianghan Hotel* (tel 23998) at 245 Shengli Jie, a 15-minute walk from the Hankou Railway Station, is the place to stay if you can afford it. Only doubles are available, from Y50.

The *Shengli Hotel* (tel 22531) at 11 Siwei Lu is a dreary place a bit inconveniently located. On the other hand it's in a quiet part of town. Doubles cost from Y40 to Y60, including air-con.

The *Xuangong Hotel* (tel 24404) on Jianghan Yilu in a lively part of town has doubles from Y45. Doubles for Y55 include bathroom, television and air-con plus a gone-to-seed ambience. To get there from Hankou station you must first walk to Zhongshan Dadao, take trolley bus No 2 as far as Jianghan Lu then walk to the hotel. From the Yangtse ferry dock you may be best off taking a pedicab; alternatively, bus No 7 takes you part of the way.

Places to Stay – top end

Top of the range is the glittering *Qing Chuan Hotel* (tel 444361) on Qingchuan Jie by the riverbank. Singles are Y40 and doubles Y70, but expect prices to be higher by the time this book is out. You won't be hard done by the hotel restaurant – it's very good.

Places to Eat

The *Laotongcheng Restaurant* (tel 24559), at 1 Dazhi Lu on the corner with Zhongshan Dadao, serves a delicious snack called *doupi* for which the all important characters are:

While it may look like a stuffed omelette, it's actually bean curd, stuffed and fried and popular for breakfast. It's served with a jug of very greasy chicken soup. This restaurant was apparently a favourite of Mao's, though presumably he didn't have to push and shove with the proletariat to get his doupi.

There are a couple of restaurants in the vicinity of Hankou railway station. Try the *Jinghan canguan* on Chezhan Lu (the road leading south from the train station) for Wuchang fish from Wuhan's East Lake and for catfish. It has an English menu and gives enormous servings – best take a group of people. There are lots of noodle and dumpling shops, snack bars and ice cream places along Chezhan Lu.

Entertainment

One visitor reports finding a great evening entertainment establishment on Zhongshan Dadao in Hankou. The 'Fun Palace' or Min Zhong Le Yuan is in a vast three-storey building and re-opened in winter 1983-84. According to the letter:

> There are acrobats (excellent) in the central building, on top of which is a teahouse where young trendies slurp tea, spit melon seeds, and listen to Auld Lang Syne on the Hawaiian guitars. There are three or four different regional operas performed simultaneously, there are stand-up comic routines, slushy Engelbert Humperdinck-type love songs, a 'speak your weight' machine – and best of all, dancing on the very top floor (but westerners may find it hard to get in). All this, plus a wall-of-death woman motorcyclist in the courtyard, and the sight of thousands of ordinary Wuhan people enjoying themselves. To me that place alone makes Wuhan worth a visit.

Wuhan seems to have an extraordinary number of dance and live music venues. These places aren't hard to find – just look for the disco lights and listen for the batteries of out-of-tune horns.

Getting There & Away

Air Wuhan is connected by air to a dozen Chinese cities. There are daily flights to Canton, Beijing and Shanghai and twice weekly to Chongqing.

Rail Wuhan is on the main Beijing-Canton railway line. Express trains to Kunming and to Xian pass through here. The best way of heading east to Nanjing and Shanghai is by river, not by the circuitous rail route.

Some tourist-price fares from Wuhan are: Beijing (hard-seat Y42, hard-sleeper Y70, soft-sleeper Y126), Changsha (hard-seat Y15.50, hard-sleeper Y25.50, soft-sleeper Y48), Zhengzhou (hard-seat Y21, hard-sleeper Y33, soft-sleeper Y63).

Boat You can take ferries from Wuhan along the Yangtse River either west to Chongqing or east to Shanghai. See the section on the Yangtse below for details.

Getting Around

Wuhan has an extensive bus network but you may have to take two or even three to get where you want to go. There are ferries across the river from Hankou to Wuchang which you'll probably find more convenient than the buses.

Pedicabs can be taken from outside Wuchang Station and the ferry dock. Auto-rickshaws in Wuhan are decrepit blue-and-white machines which rattle and vibrate in the best traditions of Asian travel. They can also be found outside Wuchang Station and the ferry dock. Bargain hard.

UP & DOWN THE YANGTSE RIVER – WUHAN TO CHONGQING & SHANGHAI

Ferries continue from Wuhan to ports further east on the Yangtse River and

Ultimately as far as Shanghai on the Huangpu, which branches off the Yangtse. You can also take the ferry west from Wuhan to Chongqing, which is a five-day trip.

In Wuhan, you can buy tickets for the river ferries from CITS, from the booking office at the river port (near the Yangtse ferry dock), or through the tourist-hotel service desks. There are 2nd, 3rd and 4th-class tickets. Second class is a two-person cabin, 3rd class is an eight-person dormitory and 4th class is a 16-person dormitory.

Ticket prices in yuan are:

destination	*2nd class*	*3rd class*	*4th class*	*duration*
Jiujiang	17	8	6	1 night
Wuhu	37	16	12	30 hours
Nanjing	41	18	14	36 hours
Shanghai	59	27	20	48 hours
Chongqing	113	47	34	5 days

Heading downriver on leaving Wuhan, the steamer passes through the town of **Huangshi** in eastern Hubei Province. The town lies on the southern bank of the river and is being developed as a centre for heavy industry. Nearby is an ancient mining tunnel dating back to the Spring and Autumn Period; it contained numerous mining tools, including bronze axes. Near the border with Jiangxi on the north bank is the town of **Wuxue**, noted for the production of bamboo goods.

The first major town you come to in Jiangxi is **Jiujiang**, the jumping-off point for nearby **Lu Shan**. The mouth of **Lake Poyang** is situated on the Yangtse River and at this point on the southern bank of the river is **Stone Bell Mountain**, noted for its numerous Tang Dynasty stone carvings. This was also the place where Taiping troops were garrisoned for five years defending Jinling, their capital.

The first major town you approach in Anhui Province is **Anqing**, on the north bank, in the foothills of the Dabie Mountains. Next comes the town of **Guichi** from which you can get a bus to spectacular **Huang Shan** (Yellow Mountain). The town of **Tongling** lies in a mountainous area in central Anhui on the southern bank, west of Tongguan Shan. Tongling has been a copper-mining centre for 2000 years, and is a source of copper for the minting of coins. Still in Anhui Province, and at the confluence of the Yangtse and Qingyi rivers, is **Wuhu**, also a jumping-off point for Huang Shan. Just before Anhui Province ends is the city of **Mannshan**, the site of a large iron and steel complex.

The first large city you pass in Jiangsu Province is **Nanjing**, followed by **Zhenjiang**, then the port of **Nantong** at the confluence of the Tongyang and Tonglu canals. The ferry then proceeds along the Yangtse and turns down the Huangpu River to **Shanghai**. The Yangtse empties into the East China Sea.

WUDANG MOUNTAINS 武当山

The Wudang Mountains (otherwise known as the Canshang or the Taihe Shan) stretch for 400 km across north-western Hubei Province. The highest peak rises 1600 metres, and was known as the 'pillar propping up the sky' or 'Heavenly Pillar Peak'. The Wudang Mountains are a sacred range to the Taoists, and a number of Taoist temples were built here during the construction sprees of the Ming emperors Cheng Zu and Zhen Wu. Noted temples include the Golden Hall on Heavenly Pillar Peak, which was built entirely of gilded copper in 1416; the hall contains a bronze statue of Ming Emperor Zhen Wu, who became a Taoist deity. The Purple Cloud Temple stands on Zhanqifeng Peak, and the Nanyan Temple perches on the South Cliff.

SHENNONGJIA 神农架

This is an inaccessible mountain area in north-western Hubei, 160 km north of the Yangtse River gorges. The area is famous for the sightings of wild, ape-like creatures, a Chinese equivalent of the Himalayan Yeti or the North American Bigfoot. The stories are interesting, but the creatures seem to be able to distinguish between peasants and scientists – molesting the former and evading the latter. Graham Earnshaw's guidebook *On Your Own in China* gives a lengthy account of the creatures and some of the reported sightings. Apparently in Shanghai there is a club (with 3000 members) devoted to finding this thing.

YICHANG 宜昌

Yichang, regarded as the gateway to the Upper Yangtse, was once a walled city dating at least as far back as the Sui Dynasty. The town was opened to foreign trade in 1877 by a treaty between Britain and China, and a foreign concession area was set up along the riverfront south-east of the walled city.

Yichang is a port town and a stop for the Chongqing-Wuhan boats. There is a railway line from Yichang north to the town of Xiangfan, where you change trains and carry on to Luoyang. There are also direct trains from Yichang to Luoyang. Tourist-price hard-seat from Yichang to Luoyang is Y15. To get from the ferry dock to the train station in Yichang take bus No 3.

Henan 河南

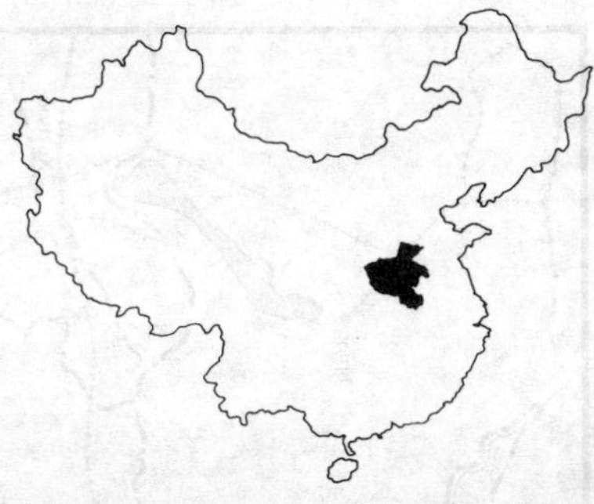

The Yellow River cuts its way across the north of Henan Province, where it all began. About 3500 years ago the Chinese were turning their primitive settlements into an urban-centred civilisation governed by the Shang Dynasty.

Excavations of Shang Dynasty towns have shown that these were built on the sites of even more ancient settlements. The Shang civilisation was not founded by people migrating from western Asia as was once thought, but was part of a continuous line which had been developing here since prehistoric times.

The Shang Dynasty ruled from the 16th to the 11th century BC. They controlled an area which included parts of what is today Shandong, Henan and Hebei provinces. To the west of their territory the powerful Zhou people arose and conquered the Shang; the last Shang emperor supposedly hurled himself into the flames of his burning palace.

The first Shang capital is believed to be the site of Yenshih, west of modern-day Zhengzhou, perhaps dating back 3800 years. Around the middle of the 16th century BC the capital was moved to Zhengzhou, where the walls of the ancient city are still visible. Later the capital moved to Yin, near the modern town of Anyang in the north of Henan.

The only clues as to what Shang society was like are found in the remnants of their cities, in divining bones inscribed with a primitive form of Chinese writing, and in ancient Chinese literary texts. Apart from the walls at Zhengzhou, all that has survived of their cities are the pounded earth foundations of the buildings, stone-lined trenches where wooden poles once supported thatched roofs, and pits used for storage or as underground houses.

Today Henan is one of the smaller Chinese provinces but also one of the most densely populated, with 74 million people squashed in. It was once the centre of Chinese civilisation, but lost political power when the Song Dynasty fled south from its capital at Kaifeng, in the wake of an invasion from the north in the 12th century. Nevertheless, with such a large population located on the fertile plains of the unruly Yellow River, Henan remained an important agricultural area.

Henan's urban centres rapidly diminished in size and population with the demise of the Song. It was not until the Communist takeover in 1949 that they once again expanded. Zhengzhou and Luoyang were transformed into great industrial cities making everything from tractors and diesel engines to towels and bedsheets. Other towns like Kaifeng and Anyang were also industrialised.

ZHENGZHOU 郑州

Zhengzhou is a 12-hour train ride and a couple of psychological decades from Shanghai and Beijing. Because of its importance as a railway junction, the city was made the capital of Henan Province after 1949. Since 1950 the population has increased ten-fold from around 100,000 people, and may even have passed the one-million mark. The city itself, not the individual sights, is the reason for coming here. In Zhengzhou the Communists had a chance to build an entire city from the ground up, in whatever style they saw as the ideal or whatever resources would allow, and this is what they came up with.

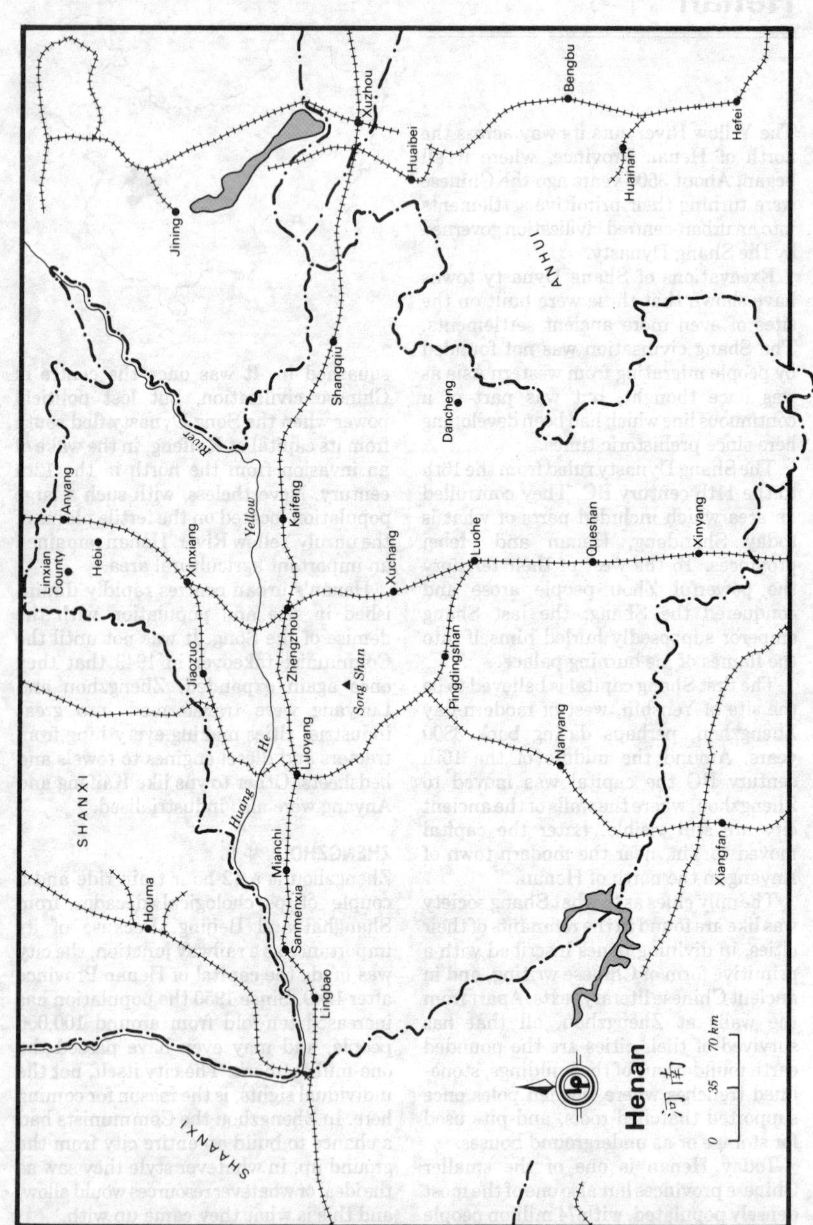
Henan
河南
0 35 70 km
Xuzhou
Bengbu
Hefei
Huaibei
Huainan
Jining
ANHUI
Shangqiu
Dancheng
Yellow River
Anyang
Linxian County
Hebi
Xinxiang
Kaifeng
Xuchang
Luohe
Queshan
Xinyang
Zhengzhou
Jiaozuo
Song Shan
Pingdingshan
Nanyang
Luoyang
Huang He
SHANXI
Mianchi
Xiangfan
Sanmenxia
Houma
Lingbao
SHANXI

Seen from the top floors of the Henan International Hotel, Zhengzhou's No 1 tourist joint, the city stretches into the distance, a sea of near-identical red-brick low-rise residential blocks interspersed with factories and smokestacks. These are plonked down like lego blocks on an orderly grid of tree-lined roads wide enough for hundreds of thousands of bicycles.

A typical group of apartment buildings consists of eight or 10 four-storey brick rectangles arranged in rows. The dirt courtyard in front of the complex is a play and gossip area, and the rear is divided among tenants and used for vegetable plots and makeshift chicken coops. Each complex, which might include a hospital and the factory or office block where the tenants work, is surrounded by a 12-foot wall, often topped with barbed wire or broken glass. There is only one entry gate per complex, two at most – sometimes with a gatekeeper.

In crowded China, happiness is having your own apartment. A four-person family would be privileged to have two rooms to themselves. Two families of four in a three-room apartment with shared kitchen and toilet would be the more common situation.

Information & Orientation

Most of the tourist facilities and sights are in the south-eastern and eastern sections of the city.

The city centre is a traffic circle on the intersection of Erqi Lu and Jiefang Lu, readily identifiable by the large February 7th Monument. South-east of the monument is the railway station. Directly opposite the railway station is Zhongyuan Mansions (one of Zhengzhou's major hotels) and the long-distance bus station. The area between the railway station and the February 7th Monument has many shops and restaurants.

Erqi Lu runs north from the monument; along it are the CAAC office, Public Security, post office and February 7th Hotel. Jinshui Lu runs east-west and intersects Erqi Lu; on it are the Provincial Museum and the Henan International Hotel.

CITS is on the ground floor of the Henan International Hotel. Some of the staff speak English.

Public Security is in a government compound at 70 Bei Erqi Lu.

Post There is a post office on the ground floor of the Henan International Hotel. The main post & telephone office is beside the square in front of the train station.

CAAC (tel 24339) is at 38 Bei Erqi Lu.

Shang City Ruins

On the eastern outskirts of Zhengzhou lie the remains of an ancient city from the Shang period: long, high mounds of earth indicate where the city walls used to be, now cut through by modern roads. This is one of the earliest relics of Chinese urban life. The first archaeological evidence of the Shang period was discovered near the town of Anyang in northern Henan.

The city at Zhengzhou is believed to have been the second Shang capital, and many Shang settlements have been found outside the walled area. Excavations here and at other Shang sites suggest that a 'typical' Shang city consisted of a central walled area containing large buildings (presumably government buildings or the residences of important people, used for ceremonial occasions) surrounded by a ring of villages. Each village specialised in such products as pottery, metalwork, wine or textiles. The village dwellings were mostly semi-underground pit houses, while the buildings in the centre were rectangular and above ground.

Excavations have also uncovered Shang tombs. These are rectangular pits, with ramps or steps leading down to a burial chamber in which the coffin was placed and surrounded with funeral objects such as bronze weapons, helmets, musical instruments, oracle bones and

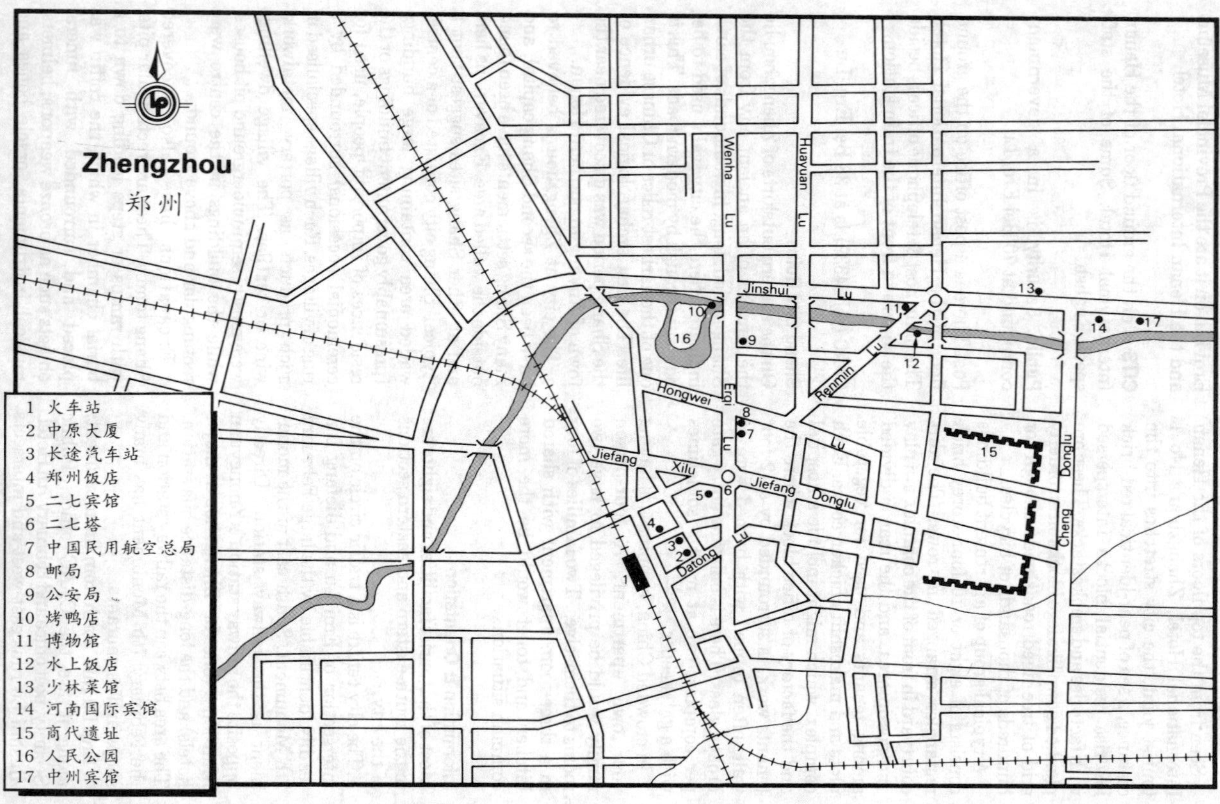
Zhengzhou
郑州
Huayuan Lu
Wenha Lu
Jinshui Lu
Renmin Lu
Erqi Lu
Hongwei
Jiefang Lu
Jiefang Donglu
Jiefang Xilu
Datong Lu
Chengdong Lu
1 火车站
2 中原大厦
3 长途汽车站
4 郑州饭店
5 二七宾馆
6 二七塔
7 中国民用航空总局
8 邮局
9 公安局
10 烤鸭店
11 博物馆
12 水上饭店
13 少林宾馆
14 河南国际宾馆
15 商代遗址
16 人民公园
17 中州宾馆

1 Railway Station
2 Zhongyuan Mansion
3 Long-distance Bus Station
4 Zhengzhou Hotel
5 February 7th Hotel
6 February 7th Monument
7 CAAC
8 Post Office
9 Public Security
10 'Restaurant Over the Water'
11 Henan Provincial Museum
12 'Restaurant Over the Water'
13 Restaurant
14 Henan International Hotel
15 Shang City Walls
16 People's Park
17 Zhongzhou Guest House

shells with inscriptions, silk fabrics, and ornaments of jade, bone and ivory. Among these, depending on the wealth and status of the deceased, have been found the skeletons of animals and other humans – sacrifices meant to accompany their masters to the next world. Study of the skeletons of the sacrificial victims suggests they were of a different ethnic origin from the Shang – possibly prisoners of war. This, and other evidence, has suggested that Shang society was not based on the slavery of its own people. Rather, it was a dictatorship of the aristocracy with the emperor/father-figure at the apex.

Henan Provincial Museum

The museum has an interesting collection of artefacts discovered in Henan Province, including some from the Shang period. There's also an exhibition on the February 7th revolt. Unfortunately, there are no English captions. The museum is on Renmin Lu, at the intersection with Jinshui Lu, readily identifiable by the large Mao statue. The February 7th Monument, in the centre of Zhengzhou, commemorates the 1923 strike organised by workers building the Wuhan-Beijing Railway. The strike was bloodily suppressed.

The Yellow River

The Yellow River is just 24 km north of Zhengzhou and the road passes near the village of Huaxuankou, where Kuomintang troops blew up the river dikes in April 1938. The ingenious tactic was ordered by Chiang Kaishek. The Japanese advance was halted for a few weeks at the cost of drowning maybe a million Chinese and making another 11 million homeless. The dike was repaired with American help in 1947 and today the point where it was breached has an irrigation sluice gate and Mao's instruction, 'Control the Yellow River', etched into the embankment.

The river has always been regarded as 'China's sorrow' because of its propensity to flood. It carries masses of silt from the loess plains and deposits them on the riverbed, causing the water to overflow the banks. Consequently the peasants along the riverbank have had to build the dikes higher and higher each century. As a result parts of the river flow along an elevated channel which is often as much as 1½ km wide and sometimes more than seven metres high!

Mang Shan is the site of Yellow River Park, on the south bank of the river. There should be buses to Mang Shan from the square in front of Zhengzhou train station or from the bus station.

People's Park

This is one of the few parks I'd recommend, not for scenic beauty but for the entranceway, which looks like someone's attempt to re-create either the Lunan Stone Forest or the Tiger Balm Gardens. Enough said. The park itself has little to offer but family circuses sometimes set up shop here, performing such feats as embalming their bodies in wire, or lying down with a concrete block on their stomach while dad takes to it with a sledge-hammer. You can play that venerated Chinese sport of ping-pong on the concrete tables in the park if you've got some paddles and a ball. The entrance to the park is on Erqi Lu.

Places to Stay
Accommodation prospects in Zhengzhou are pretty dreary. There are no firmly established places for low-budget traveller's to stay.

Opposite Zhengzhou Train Station and next to the long-distance bus station is *Zhongyuan Mansion*, a cavernous white tower with additions, wings, annexes and untold numbers of rooms all equipped with booming televisions. Outside, the street carnival rages into the early hours of the morning. If you can put up with the honkings and hootings and amplified disco muzak you might get a bed in a triple for Y9, or a single/double room for around Y30. Prices seem erratic.

Opposite the bus station is the *Zhengzhou Hotel*, which may be worth a try. Doubles go for around Y17, but cheap dormitory beds are possible.

The *February 7th Hotel* is adjacent to the February 7th Monument, a very convenient location within walking distance of the train station. Doubles cost from Y15, and dormitory beds are possible.

Top of the group is the *Henan International Hotel* (tel 23413) on Jinshui Lu. This is a big tourist joint but is inconveniently located in the distant eastern outskirts of the city on Jinshui Lu. Despite the hotel's great size the rooms are pleasantly small and have comfy beds, air-con, refrigerator and attached bathroom. Though rooms were once remarkably cheap, prices have now risen to Y69 a double. The restaurant is good.

Next door the *Zhongzhou Guest House* (tel 24255) has doubles from Y55 and should take foreigners. Bus No 2 from the train station (the stop is in front of Zhongyuan Mansions) takes you to these hotels.

Places to Eat
More dreary prospects. The only dish which seems distinctly 'Zhengzhou' is available from food stalls around the town centre – it looks like a slimy, wok-fried, gelatinised potato. It goes for a few mao per plate and is called *liang fen.* The characters for this dish are:

凉粉

There's a good restaurant on the corner of Jinshui Lu and Jingsi Lu, a 10-minute walk west of the Henan International Hotel. It's identifiable by a large painting of the Shaolin Monastery above the very ornate entrance. Friendly staff. Upstairs is pleasant. There have been some mixed reports about this place but give it a try.

There are two *Restaurants Over the Water* but don't expect tranquil pavilions on a pleasant lake. The first one, near the intersection of Erqi Lu and Jinshui Lu, is OK upstairs with moderate prices, but downstairs is just like any other Chinese canteen.

The extravagant three-storey *Regent Palace* on the grounds of the Henan International Hotel is a cross between a hotel, restaurant, disco and hair-dressing salon. On the 1st floor is a souvenir shop; upstairs are the Mandarin Chinese Restaurant, Napoleon French Restaurant (everything from filet le bouef Diane to screwdrivers) and Crystal Ballroom (disco, cover charge around Y7).

Getting There & Away
Air Some useful air connections include Beijing (three flights a week), Canton (once a week), Xian (twice a week) and Shanghai (twice a week).

Bus The long-distance bus station is opposite the train station. Buses also leave from the square in front of the train station.

There are frequent buses to Kaifeng (Y1.80, two hours) and Luoyang (Y4.50, 4½ to five hours). The road to Luoyang takes you past terraced grain fields, through dusty little towns, and past mud-brick houses and cave dwellings.

There are buses to the Shaolin Monastery from Zhengzhou. For details see the Shaolin section below.

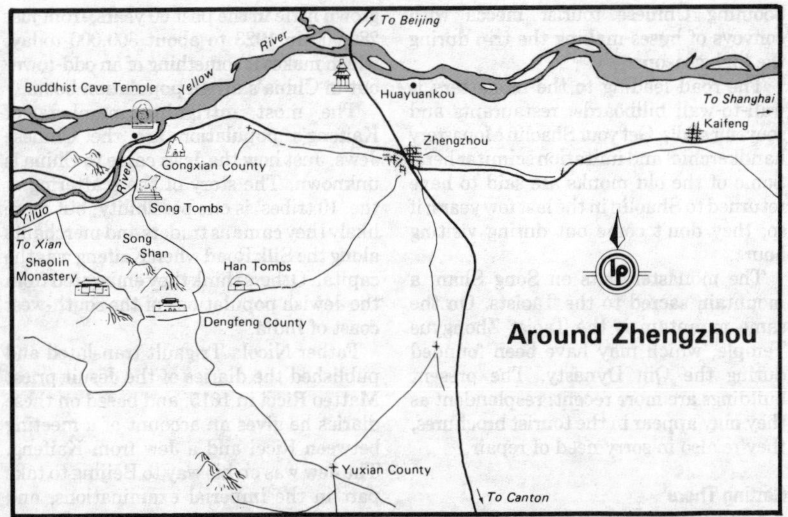

Rail Zhengzhou is on the main Beijing-Canton line. It's a major rail junction and you may have to stop here overnight to change trains. There are direct trains to Beijing, Shanghai, Xian, Canton, Taiyuan and Datong.

Tourist-price tickets to Beijing are. hard-seat Y26, hard-sleeper Y42 and soft-sleeper Y79. The trip takes 11½ hours. Tourist-price tickets to Xian are: Y26 hard-seat, Y50 hard-sleeper and Y81 soft-sleeper. The trip takes about 12 hours.

Zhengzhou station has a separate ticket window for foreigners. There is an advance booking office on Erqi Lu, just north of the crossing with Hongwei Lu.

Getting Around

Zhengzhou is very spread out and walking is only recommended for the relatively narrow confines of the central city area. Bus No 2 will take you from the train station to the Henan International Hotel. Bus No 3 runs through the old Shang City. There are many taxis, auto-rickshaws and touts in front of the train station – beware of ridiculous overcharging.

SHAOLIN MONASTERY 少林寺

David Carradine never actually trained here, but at Shaolin Monastery 80 km west of Zhengzhou a form of unarmed combat was indeed developed by Buddhist monks.

Separating myth from history is hard enough in China – Shaolin is no exception. It's said to have been founded by an Indian monk in the 5th century, and stories are told of how the monks fought invaders and led rebellions against foreign rulers. Perhaps as a result, their monastery was burned down several times – most recently in 1928 when a local warlord had a go. That was topped off with some more vandalism by the Red Guards.

Despite the fires and vandalism, many of the monastery buildings still stand. The most impressive and photogenic is the 'forest of stupas' outside the walls, each built in remembrance of a monk. The rest of the monastery is in a very sorry state.

The Chinese come here in droves – spurred on by a People's Republic movie which used the monastery as a set, and features high-flying unarmed gladiators doing their stuff. As a result Shaolin is a booming Chinese tourist mecca with convoys of buses making the trip during the high season.

The road leading to the monastery is wall-to-wall billboards, restaurants and souvenir stalls. Get your Shaolin Monastery handkerchief and imitation scimitar here. Some of the old monks are said to have returned to Shaolin in the last few years; if so, they don't come out during visiting hours.

The monastery sits on Song Shan, a mountain sacred to the Taoists. On the same mountain is the Taoist Zhongyue Temple, which may have been founded during the Qin Dynasty. The present buildings are more recent; resplendent as they may appear in the tourist brochures, they're also in sorry need of repair.

Getting There

A convenient way of getting to Shaolin is on one of the local Chinese tour buses from Zhengzhou; tickets can be bought from vendors outside Zhengzhou train station for around Y6 per person. Tour buses leave daily around 7.30 am and you get back to Zhengzhou around 6 pm. They stop off at the Zhongyue Temple and a set of underground Han Tombs. Alternatively, you could take a local bus from Zhengzhou to Dengfeng and walk or hitch to Shaolin. There may be tours available from Luoyang. Entry to Shaolin is Y2.

KAIFENG 开封

Kaifeng is a medium-sized city east of Zhengzhou. Its size belies the fact that this was once the prosperous imperial capital of China during the Northern Song Dynasty. With the invasion from the north in 1127 the Song fled south, where their poets wrote heart-wrenching verse as their beautiful capital was pillaged.

Kaifeng never recovered from the assault and was never restored. All that remains today of the imperial splendour is a scroll painting in Beijing's Forbidden City which depicts the bustling town centre as it once was. Kaifeng's population has grown little in the past 60 years, from just 280,000 in 1923 to about 300,000 today, which makes it something of an odd-town-out in China's urban population boom.

The most intriguing members of Kaifeng's population are the Chinese Jews. Just how the Jews came to China is unknown. The story of the scattering of the '10 tribes' is one possibility, but more likely they came as traders and merchants along the Silk Road when Kaifeng was the capital. Others think they emigrated from the Jewish populations of the south-west coast of India.

Father Nicola Trigault translated and published the diaries of the Jesuit priest Matteo Ricci in 1615, and based on these diaries he gives an account of a meeting between Ricci and a Jew from Kaifeng. The Jew was on his way to Beijing to take part in the imperial examinations, and Trigault writes:

> When he (Ricci) brought the visitor back to the house and began to question him as to his identity, it gradually dawned upon him that he was talking with a believer in the ancient Jewish law. The man admitted that he was an Israelite, but he knew no such word as 'Jew'.

Ricci found out from the visitor that there were 10 or 12 families of Israelites in Kaifeng. A 'magnificent' synagogue had been built there and the five books of Moses had been preserved in the synagogue in scroll form over 500 or 600 years. The visitor was familiar with the stories of the Old Testament, and some of the followers, he said, were expert in the Hebrew language. He also told Ricci that in a province which Trigault refers to as 'Cequian' at the capital of 'Hamcheu' there was a far greater number of Israelite families than at Kaifeng, and that there were others scattered about. Ricci sent one of his Chinese converts to Kaifeng, where he confirmed the visitor's story.

Today several hundred descendants of the original Jews live in Kaifeng, and though they still consider themselves Jewish, the religious beliefs and the customs associated with Judaism have almost completely died out. At the time of writing there were plans amongst Kaifeng's Jewish population to establish a synagogue and a Jewish museum in the town. The original synagogue was destroyed in a Yellow River flood in 1642. It was rebuilt but destroyed by flood again in the 1850s. This time there was no money to rebuild it. Christian missionaries rescued the temple's scrolls and prayer books in the late 19th century, and these are now in libraries in Israel, Canada and the USA. The Chinese government has recognised Jews as an official ethnic group.

A couple of other things make Kaifeng worth a visit. The old Maoist maxim 'Make one thing serve two purposes' has been given a pragmatic bent and Kaifeng's imperial relics double as temples, museums, exhibition centres, comedy venues, parks and monuments to bad taste. Speaking of Maoism, Kaifeng has the infamous notoriety of being the place where Liu Shaoqi is supposed to have ended his days in 1969.

Things to See

Chief sight is the **Xiangguo Monastery** in the centre of town, originally founded in 555 AD but frequently rebuilt over the next 1000 years. In was completely destroyed in 1644 when the Yellow River floodgates were opened in a disastrous attempt to halt a Manchu invasion. The current buildings date from 1766 and have had a thorough going-over since then. Try your hand at sharp-shooting; or check out the revolutionary history museums, mummies, tacky religious statues, funfair mirrors and, oh yes, bottled human embryos. At night there's stand-up comedy, dance lessons in the shadows, chess championships and lots of hip young Chinese.

Also on the tourist circuit is the 11th-century **Iron Pagoda**, actually made of normal bricks but covered in specially coloured tiles that look like iron. You can climb to the top of the impressive structure. The tiles on the lower levels have damaged Buddha images – possibly the result of Red Guard sledge-hammers.

The **Dragon Pavilion (Longting) Park** features the Dragon Pavilion itself and some peculiar displays. Worth visiting is the **Yanqing Taoist Temple** with its interesting architecture and strange 13-metre-high pagoda.

If you want to see the Yellow River then take local bus No 6 or a motorised pedicab to **Liuyuankou**. Ferries cross the river at this point.

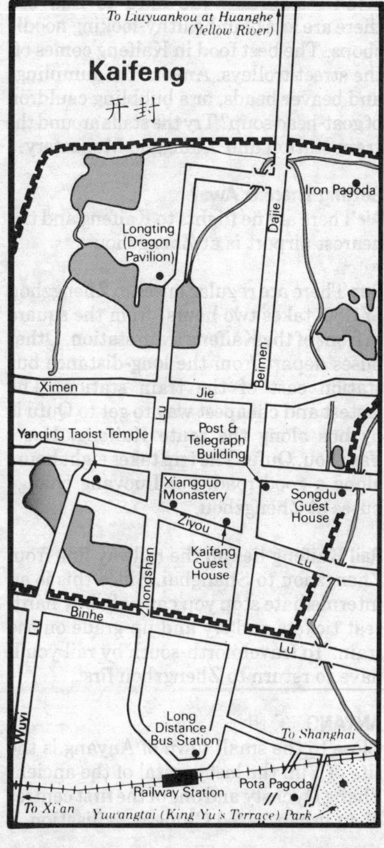

Places to Stay
The *Kaifeng Guest House* on Ziyou Lu was built by the Russians and appears to have had little maintenance since they left. The run-down concrete block has doubles for Y40. A bed in a triple is Y10. Dilapidated communal bathrooms. Take bus No 3 from the train station and get off at the third stop. Or you might try the *Songdu Guest House* near a Chinese hotel by Bianjing Park. Doubles are Y30 but cheaper accommodation may be possible. The Bianjing Hotel is FEC 32 a double.

Places to Eat
Good restaurants are hard to find but there are lots of unhealthy-looking noodle shops. The best food in Kaifeng comes off the street trolleys. Anyone for dumplings and beaver heads, or a bubbling cauldron of goat-head soup? Try the stalls around the train station and Xiangguo Monastery.

Getting There & Away
Air There are no flights to Kaifeng and the nearest airport is at Zhengzhou.

Bus There are regular buses to Zhengzhou (Y1.80, takes two hours) from the square in front of the Kaifeng train station. Other buses depart from the long-distance bus station east of the train station. The fastest and cheapest way to get to Qufu is by bus along the route Kaifeng, Heze, Yanzhou, Qufu. The trip takes eight hours along a good road. For Luoyang change buses at Zhengzhou.

Rail Kaifeng lies on the railway line from Zhengzhou to Shanghai. Since this is an intermediate stop you can only buy hard-seat tickets and try and up-grade on the train. To travel north-south by rail you'll have to return to Zhengzhou first.

ANYANG 安阳
Close to the small town of Anyang is the site of Yin, the last capital of the ancient Shang Dynasty and one of the first centres of an urban-based Chinese civilisation.

In the last few decades of the 19th century, peasants working near Anyang unearthed pieces of polished bone inscribed with an ancient form of Chinese writing – these turned out to be divining bones with questions addressed to the spirits and ancestors. Other inscriptions were found on the undershells of tortoises as well as on bronze objects, suggesting that the last capital of the Shang Dynasty once stood here.

The discoveries attracted the attention of both Chinese and western archaeologists, though it was not until the late 1920s that work began on excavating the site. These excavations uncovered ancient tombs, the ruins of a royal palace, workshops and houses – proof that the legendary Shang Dynasty had indeed existed.

Anyang is in the far north of Henan Province, near the border of Hebei Province. It lies on the main Zhengzhou-Beijing railway line.

LUOYANG 洛阳
Luoyang is one of the richest historical sites in China. Founded in 1200 BC, it was the capital of 10 dynasties before losing its rank in the 10th century AD when the Jin moved their capital to Kaifeng. In the 12th century Luoyang was stormed and sacked by Jurchen invaders from the north and never really recovered from the disaster. For centuries it remained a squalid little town vegetating on the edge of a vanished capital. By the 1920s it had only 20,000 inhabitants. It took the Communists to shake the lethargy from the area. They built a new industrial city similar to Zhengzhou at Luoyang, a vast expanse of wide avenues and endless brick and concrete apartment blocks now housing a million people.

Looking at it today, it's hard to imagine that Luoyang was once the centre of Buddhism in China. When the religion was introduced from India this was the site of the White Horse Temple (Baima Si), the first Buddhist temple built in China. At this temple Indian Sanskrit scriptures were first translated into Chinese. When the city was the imperial capital under the Northern Wei Dynasty there were supposed to be 1300 Buddhist temples operating in the area, and at the same time work was begun on the magnificent Longmen Buddhist Cave Temples outside the city.

Information & Orientation

Luoyang is spread across the northern bank of the Luo River. The main railway station is Luoyang West Station. The city centre is around Jinguyyuan Lu, which runs roughly south-east from the railway station and is criss-crossed by a couple of major arteries like Zhongzhou Lu. The old city is in the eastern part of Luoyang and some of the old walls can still be seen.

CITS, a bank where you can change money, and a post office are in the new wing of the Friendship Guest House at 6 Xiyuan Lu. Public Security is on Kaixuan Lu, near the town centre.

There's an indispensable map in Chinese showing all the bus routes, but it's hard to find – try the shop in the long-distance bus station.

Things to See

The only real reason to come to Luoyang is the Longmen Caves (see below). Around town the pickings are slim.

The Ming and Qing buildings of the **White Horse Temple (Baima Si)**, perhaps the most venerable Buddhist temple in China, are built on the site of the original temple. The story of the temple's origin is interesting. In 67 AD the second emperor of the Han Dynasty sent two envoys to India to collect Buddhist scriptures. Their journey preceded that of the Tang Dynasty monk Xuan Zhuang (whose story is told in the classic novel *Journey to the West*) by 500 years. When the envoys reached Afghanistan they met two Indian monks who gave them Buddhist scriptures and statues. The four then returned to Luoyang and had the temple built. The story goes that since the scriptures and statues were carried to Luoyang on the back of a white horse, the temple was named the White Horse Temple. In front of the temple are two Song Dynasty stone horses. To the east is a 13-storey pagoda built sometime between the 10th and 12th centuries. The two Indian monks lived in the temple, translating scriptures and lecturing on Buddhist teachings and Indian culture; they are buried there today.

The temple stands 13 km north-east of the city. To get there take bus Nos 5 or 9 to the turning circle at the edge of the old city walls. Walk east to the stop for bus No 56, which will take you to the temple. On weekdays the temple tends to be a quiet and relaxing place.

Wangcheng (Royal Town) Park is on Zhongzhou Lu and has two underground Han Dynasty tombs. Paintings and bas reliefs can still be seen on the stone doors but unfortunately the coffins have long gone. Other than that the park has a tiny and decidedly dismal zoo. Freak shows (stuffed and mounted animals and pickled human foetuses) occasionally set up in the park.

The **Luoyang Museum** is next to the park and houses a collection of early bronzes, Tang figurines and implements from the Stone Age. There are some eye-catching pieces but no English captions.

Once upon a time it was possible to tour the **East is Red Tractor Plant** (which I believe is now called the Luoyang No 1 Tractor Plant), on Changan Lu, a model factory which opened in 1959 and provides social services for its workers and families, including a hospital, schools and day-care centres. Enquire at CITS. These sorts of attractions don't get much attention on the standard tour circuit, and could prove a welcome relief.

Places to Stay & Eat

The *Friendship Guest House* (tel 22159) at 6 Xiyuan Lu is the only place taking foreigners. A bed in an air-con triple room in the old wing is Y11. Doubles in the new wing are Y60. To get there take bus No 2

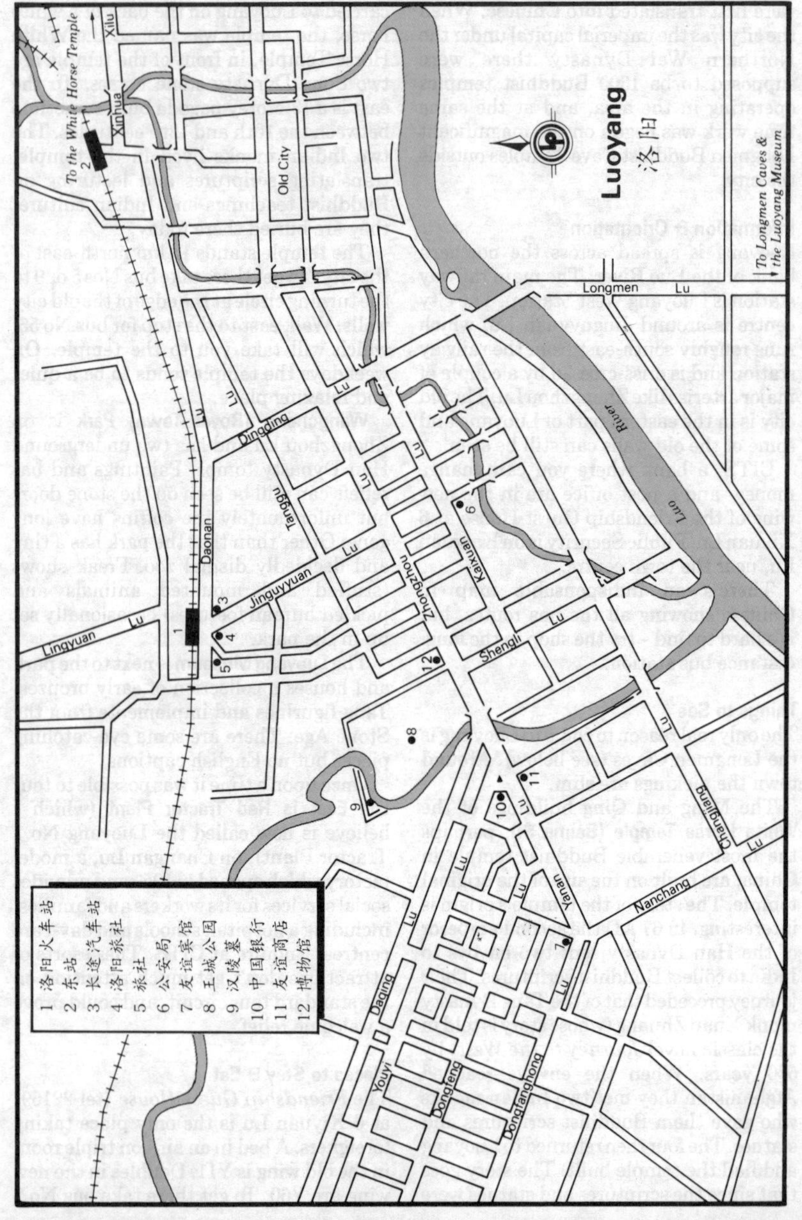
Luoyang
洛阳
To the White Horse Temple
To Longmen Caves & the Luoyang Museum
Old City
Luo River
Xilu
Xinhua
Longmen Lu
Dingding Lu
Tanggu Lu
Daonan
Jinguyuan Lu
Lingyuan Lu
Zhongzhou Lu
Kaixuan Lu
Shengli Lu
Changjiang Lu
Nanchang Lu
Yanan Lu
Daqing Lu
Youyi
Dongfeng
Dongfanghong
1 洛阳火车站
2 东站
3 长途汽车站
4 洛阳旅社
5 旅社
6 公安局
7 友谊宾馆
8 王城公园
9 汉陵墓
10 中国银行
11 友谊商店
12 博物馆

1 Luoyang West Railway Station
2 Luoyang East Railway Station
3 Long-distance Bus Station
4 Chinese Hotel
5 Chinese Hotel
6 Public Security
7 Friendship Guest House
8 Royal Town (Wangcheng) Park (also known as Working People's Park)
9 Han Dynasty Tombs
10 Bank of China
11 Friendship Store
12 Museum

from Luoyang West Train Station or from the long-distance bus station (opposite the train station). Stay on the bus until you see the enormous Friendship Store on your left, and get off at the next stop. The hotel is a 15-minute walk further, on the right-hand side. The hotel restaurant isn't bad, with Chinese meals for around Y7 per person. There's been a boom in food stalls over the last few years, and you'll find lots around the station.

Getting There & Away

Air The nearest airport is at Zhengzhou. At the time of writing there were plans to build an airport at Luoyang, so check when you get to China.

Bus The long-distance bus station is opposite Luoyang West Train Station. Regular buses run to Zhengzhou (Y4.50, 4½ to five hours). There's one bus daily from Luoyang to Xian at 6am (Y12).

Rail From Luoyang there are direct trains to Beijing via Zhengzhou; and to Xian, Taiyuan, and south to Xiangfan and Yichang. Yichang is a port on the Yangtse River, where you can pick up the Chongqing-Wuhan ferry.

Tourist-price tickets to Xian are: Y14 hard-seat, Y24 hard-sleeper and Y47 soft-sleeper. Tourist-price tickets to Beijing are: Y26 hard-seat, Y44 hard-sleeper and Y86 soft-sleeper.

THE LONGMEN CAVES 龙门石窑

In 494 AD the Northern Wei Dynasty moved its capital from Datong to Luoyang. At Datong the dynasty had built the impressive Yungang Caves where characteristic Buddhist art can be seen. A common form of display is a triad in which the Buddha is flanked by bodhisattvas, though sometimes the latter are replaced by Ananda and Kasyapa, Buddha's first disciples. Bodhisattvas generally have expressions of benign tranquillity; they are saints who have opted to return to earth instead of entering nirvana, so that they might help others to follow the path of righteousness. Flying apsaras (celestial beings similar to angels and often depicted as musicians or bearers of flowers and incense) can be found in abundance.

At Luoyang the dynasty began work on the Longmen Caves. Over the next 200 years, more than 100,000 images and statues of Buddha and his disciples were carved into the cliff walls on the banks of the Yi River, 16 km south of the city. The hard texture of the rock that was found here, like that at Datong, made it especially suitable for being carved. The caves of Luoyang, Dunhuang and Datong together represent the apogee of Buddhist cave art.

Apart from naturally occurring erosion at Luoyang, there has been a great deal of damage done to the sculptures since the 19th century by western souvenir hunters, who beheaded just about every figure they could lay their saws on. These pirated items now grace the museums and private paperweight collections of Europe and North America. These days, the Metropolitan Museum of Art, New York, and the Atkinson Museum, Kansas City, hold two murals showing religious processions which were entirely removed from this site.

Oddly enough, the caves appear to have been spared the ravages of the Cultural Revolution. Even during the most anarchic year of 1967 the caves were reported to be open, no one was watching over them and anybody could go in and have a look. Unfortunately, none of the captions at the caves are in English even though tourist price is charged.

The art of Buddhist cave sculpture largely came to an end around the middle of the 9th century as the Tang Dynasty declined. Persecution of foreign religions in China began, with Buddhism the prime target. Although Buddhist art and sculpture continued in China, it never reached the heights it had enjoyed previously.

Getting There

Take bus No 60 from the Friendship Guest House to the caves. It leaves from the far side of the small park opposite the hotel. Bus no. 53 from the old town west gate, also runs past the caves.

Entry to the caves is Y5. There's a good view of the Juxiansi Cave from the eastern bank of the river. Also on the east side of the river is a small group of caves dating from the Tang period.

Bingyang Caves

The main caves of the Longmen group are on the west bank of the Yi River. They stretch out along the cliff face on a north-south axis. The three Bingyang Caves are at the north end, closest to the entrance. All were begun under the Northern Wei, and though two were finished during the Sui and Tang dynasties the statues all display the benevolent saccharine expressions which characterised the Northern Wei style.

Ten Thousand Buddha Cave (Wanfo Dong)

Several minutes walk south of the Bingyang Caves is the Tang Dynasty Ten Thousand Buddha Cave, built in 680. In addition to the legions of tiny bas-relief Buddhas which give the cave its name, there is a fine big Buddha and images of celestial dancers. Other images include musicians playing the flute, *pipa* (a plucked stringed instrument), cymbals and *zheng* (a 13 to 14-stringed harp).

Lotus Flower Cave

This cave was carved in 527 AD during the Northern Wei and has a large standing Buddha, now faceless. On the ceiling are wispy apsaras (angels) drifting around a lotus flower at the centre. The lotus flower is a common symbol in Buddhist art and represents purity and serenity.

Ancestor Worshipping Cave (Fengxian)

This is the largest structure at Longmen and was built during the Tang Dynasty from 672 to 675 AD. The roof is gone and the figures lie exposed to the elements. The Tang figures tend to be more three-dimensional than the Northern Wei figures, standing out in high relief and rather freer from their stone backdrop. Their expressions and poses also appear to be more natural, but unlike the other-worldly figures of the Northern Wei the Tang figures are meant to be overpoweringly awesome.

The seated central Buddha statue is 17 metres high and is believed to be Vairocana, the supreme, omnipresent divinity. The face is thought to be modelled on that of the all-powerful Empress Wu Zetian of the Tang Dynasty.

As you face the Buddha, to the left are statues of the disciple Ananda and a bodhisattva wearing a crown, a tassel and a string of pearls. To the right are statues (or remains) of another disciple, a bodhisattva, a heavenly guardian trampling on a spirit, and a guardian of the Buddha.

Medical Prescription Cave

South of Fengxiansi is the tiny Medical Prescription Cave whose entrance is filled with 6th-century stone steles inscribed with remedies for common ailments.

Guyang Cave

Adjacent to the Medical Prescription Cave is the much larger Guyang Cave, cut between 495 and 575 AD. It's a narrow, high-roofed cave featuring a Buddha statue and a profusion of sculpture, particularly of flying apsaras. This is probably the first cave built at the Longmen Grottoes.

Shiku Cave

This cave is a Northern Wei construction. It's the last major cave and has carvings depicting religious processions.

LINXIAN COUNTY 林县

Linxian County is a rural area which rates with Dazhai and Shaoshan as one of the holy places of Maoism, since this is the location of the famous Red Flag Canal. To irrigate the district, a river was re-routed through a tunnel beneath a mountain and then along a new bed built on the side of steep cliffs. The Communists insist that this colossal work, carried out during the Cultural Revolution, was done entirely by the toiling masses without the help of engineers and machines.

The statistics are impressive: 1500 km of canal was dug, hills were levelled, 134 tunnels were pierced, 150 aqueducts were constructed and enough earth was displaced to build a road one metre high, six metres wide and 4000 km long. All this was supposedly done by hand and was a tribute to Mao's vision of a self-reliant China.

Critics have called it an achievement worthy of Qin Shi Huang, who pressed millions into building the Great Wall. They say that this sort of self-reliance only committed the peasants and workers to endless back-breaking toil. It would have made more sense to put the energy to some productive use, and with the profit buy a pump and lay a pipeline to bring the water straight over the hill.

Linxian County lies to the west of Anyang in the north-west corner of Henan Province, close to the border with Shanxi and Hebei.

GONGXIAN COUNTY 巩县

Gongxian County lies on the railway line which runs west from Zhengzhou to Luoyang. During the Northern Wei Dynasty a series of Buddhist caves were cut and a temple built on the bank of the Yiluo River. However, the main attractions of the area are the great tombs built by the Northern Song emperors.

The county is bounded in the south by Song Shan and in the north by the Huang (Yellow) River. The Yiluo River is a branch of the Yellow River and cuts through the centre of the county.

The **Buddhist Cave Temples** are at the foot of Dali Shan on the northern bank of the Yiluo River. Construction of the caves began in 517 AD and additions were made during the Eastern and Western Wei, Tang and Song dynasties. There are now 256 shrines containing over 7700 Buddhist figures.

The **Song Tombs** are scattered over an area of 30 square km. Seven of the nine Northern Song emperors were buried here; the other two were captured and taken away by the Jin armies who overthrew the Northern Song in the 12th century.

After the vicissitudes of more than 800 years of history and repeated wars, all that remains of the tombs are the ruined buildings, the burial mounds and the statues which line the sacred avenues leading up to the ruins. About 700 stone statues still stand, and these have a simple and unsophisticated but imposing manner about them.

Some of the earlier statues, such as those on the Yongan and Yongchang tombs, utilise very plain lines and are characteristic of late Tang Dynasty style. The statues of the intermediate period on the Yongding and Yongzhao tombs are carved with more exquisite, harmonious proportions. Later statues, such as those on the way to the Yongyu and Yongtai tombs, tend to be more realistic and lifelike. The statues of people include civil officials, foreign envoys and military leaders. There are also numerous statues of animals, including a *jiaoduan*, a mythical animal which symbolises luck.

Cave Dwellings

On the road from Zhengzhou to Luoyang you'll see some of China's interesting cave dwellings. These are not peculiar to Henan Province. Over 100 million Chinese people live in cave houses cut into dry embankments, or in houses where the hillside makes up one or more walls. A third of these are in the dry loess plateau.

Some communities use both caves and houses, since the former is warmer in winter and cooler in summer, but also tends to be darker and less ventilated than ordinary houses. Sometimes a large square pit is dug first and and then caves are dug into the four sides of the pit. A well is dug in the middle of the yard to prevent flooding during heavy rains. Other caves, such as those at Yanan, are dug into the side of a cliff face.

The floors, walls and ceilings of these cave dwellings are made of loess, a fine yellowish-brown soil which is soft and thick and makes good building material. The front wall may be made of loess, adobe (a mixture of mud and straw made into bricks and hardened in the sun or fired in kilns), concrete, bricks or wood depending on the availability of materials.

Ceilings are shaped according to the quality of the loess. If it is hard then the ceiling may be arched; if not the ceiling may rise to a point. Besides the doors and windows in the front wall, additional vents may let in light and air.

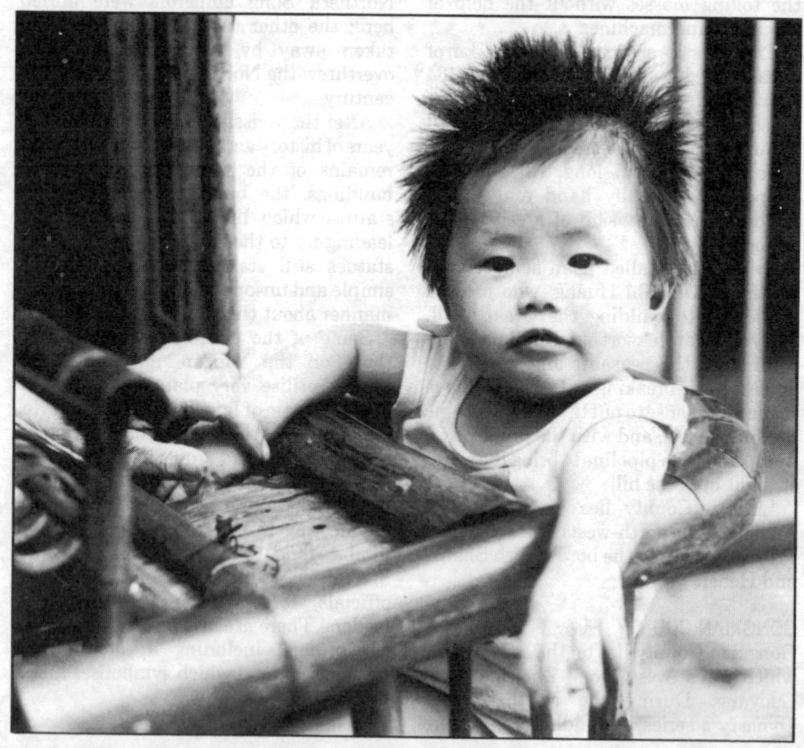

Shaanxi 陕西

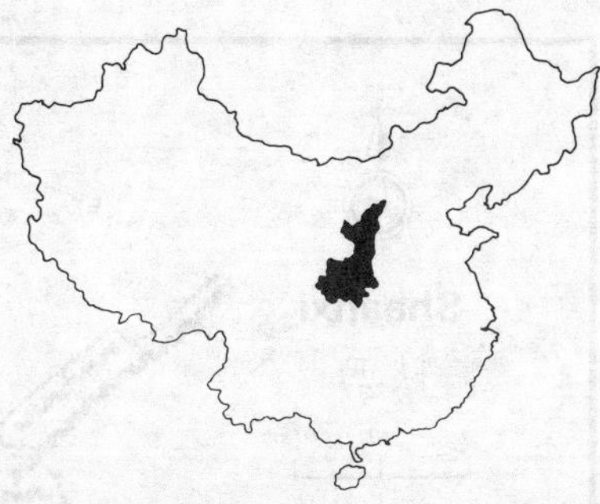

The northern part of Shaanxi is one of the oldest settled regions of China, with remains of human habitation dating back to prehistoric times. This was the homeland of the Zhou people, who eventually conquered the Shang and established their rule over much of northern China. It was also the homeland of the Qin, who ruled from their capital of Xianyang near modern-day Xian and was the first dynasty to rule over all of eastern China. Shaanxi remained the political heart of China until the 9th century. The great Sui and Tang capital of Xian was built there and the province was a crossroads on the trading routes from eastern China to Central Asia.

With the migration of the imperial court to pastures further east, Shaanxi became a less attractive piece of real estate. Rebellions afflicted the territory from 1340 to 1368, again from 1620 to 1644, and finally in the mid-19th century when the great Muslim rebellion left tens of thousands of the province's Muslims dead. Five million people died in the famine of 1876 to 1878 and another three million in the famines of 1915, 1921 and 1928. It was probably the dismal condition of the Shaanxi peasants that gave the Communists such willing support in the province in the late 1920s and during the ensuing civil war. From their base at Yanan the Communist leaders directed the war against the Kuomintang and later against the Japanese, before being forced to evacuate in the wake of a Kuomintang attack in 1947.

Some 29 million people live in Shaanxi, mostly in the central and southern regions. The north of the province is a plateau covered with a thick layer of wind-blown loess soil which masks the original landforms. Deeply eroded, the landscape has deep ravines and almost vertical cliff faces. The Great Wall in the far north of the province is something of a cultural barrier, beyond which agriculture and human existence were always precarious ventures.

Like so much of China, this region is rich in natural resources, particularly coal and oil. The Wei River, a branch of the Yellow River, cuts across the middle of the province. This fertile belt became a centre of Chinese civilisation. The south of the province is quite different from the north; it's a comparatively lush, mountainous area with a subtropical climate similar to that of Sichuan or the Yangtse Valley.

XIAN 西安

Once the focus of China, Xian vied with its contemporaries, Rome and later Constantinople, for the title of greatest city in the world. Over a period of 2000 years Xian has seen the rise and fall of numerous Chinese dynasties, and the monuments and archaeological sites in the city and the surrounding plain are a reminder that once upon a time Xian was a booming metropolis.

The earliest evidence of human habitation dates back 6000 years to Neolithic times, when the plain was lush and green and primitive Chinese tribes established their villages. The legendary Zhou established their capital on the banks of the Fen River near present-day Xian. Later, between the 5th and 3rd centuries BC, China split into five separate states locked in perpetual war, until the state of

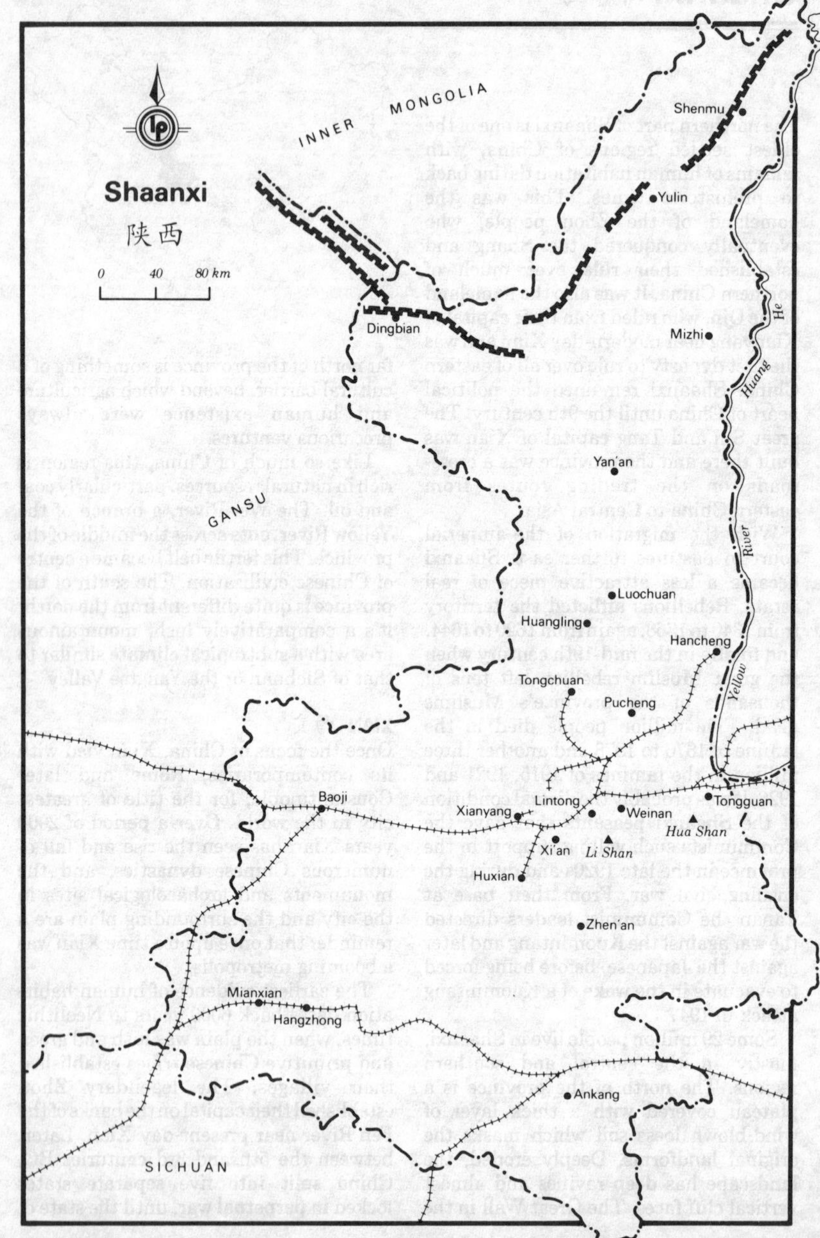
Shaanxi
陕西
0
40
80 km
INNER MONGOLIA
GANSU
SICHUAN
Shenmu
Yulin
Dingbian
Mizhi
Huang He
Yellow River
Yan'an
Luochuan
Huangling
Hancheng
Tongchuan
Pucheng
Baoji
Lintong
Tongguan
Xianyang
Weinan
Hua Shan
Xi'an
Li Shan
Huxian
Zhen'an
Mianxian
Hangzhong
Ankang

Qin conquered everyone and everything. Emperor Qin Shihuang became the first emperor of a unified China and established his capital at Xianyang near modern-day Xian. His longing for immortality gave posterity a remarkable legacy of those times – a tomb guarded by an army of thousands of terracotta soldiers.

The Qin Dynasty was unable to withstand the death of Qin Shihuang. In 206 BC it was overthrown by a revolt led by a commoner, Liu Pang. He established the Han Dynasty which lasted a phenomenal 400 years, during which time the boundaries of the empire were extended deep into central Asia. Despite its longevity, the dynasty was never really secure or unified. It collapsed in 220 AD, making way for more than three centuries of disunity and war. Nevertheless the Han empire had set the scene for later emperors' dreams of Chinese expansion, power and unity. This dream was taken up by the Sui and the Tang and encapsulated in their magnificent capital of Changan.

The new city was established in early 582 AD on the fertile plain where the capital of the Han Dynasty had once stood, and on which modern-day Xian now stands. After the collapse of the Han, the north of China was ruled by foreign invaders and the south by a series of weak and short-lived Chinese dynasties. When the Sui Dynasty united the country after a series of wars, the first emperor, Wen Ti, ordered the new capital of Changan to be built. It was a deliberate reference back to the glory of the Han period, a symbol of reunification.

The Sui were short-lived and in 618 AD they were replaced by the Tang. Under the Tang, Changan became the greatest city in Asia, if not the world. At the height of Tang power Changan was a cosmopolitan city of courtiers, merchants, foreign traders, soldiers, artists, entertainers, priests and bureaucrats, with a million people within the city walls and perhaps another million outside. The thriving metropolis of commerce, administration, religion and culture was the political hub of the empire and the centre of a brilliant period of creativity.

The city's design was based on traditional Chinese urban planning theories as well as on innovations introduced under the Sui. The outer walls of the new city formed a rectangle which ran almost 10 km east-west and just over eight km north-south, enclosing a neat grid system of streets and wide avenues. The walls were made of pounded earth faced with sun-dried bricks, and were probably about 5½ metres high and 5½ to nine metres thick at the base, penetrated by 11 gates. Within these walls the bureaucracy and imperial court were concentrated in a separate administrative city and a palace city which were also bounded by walls, a design probably based on the highly developed Northern Wei capital of Luoyang. Situated on a plain bounded by mountains, hills and the Wei River (which flowed eastward to join the Yellow River), the city was easy to defend against invaders.

The scale of Changan was unprecedented, perhaps an expression of the Sui and Tang rulers' vision of an expanded empire, but with power more centralised than anything their predecessors had imagined. With the final conquests in the south in 589 AD, Wen Ti was able to embark on an administrative reorganisation of the empire. A nationwide examination system enabled more people from the eastern plains and the increasingly populous southern regions to serve in the government bureaucracy in Changan, thus ensuring that the elite were drawn from all over the country, a system continued and developed by the Tang.

Communications between the capital and the rest of China were developed, mainly by the construction of canals which linked Changan to the Grand Canal and to other strategic places – another system also developed and improved by the Tang. Roads were built radiating from the capital, with inns for officials, travellers, merchants and pilgrims. These systems enabled Changan to draw in taxes and tribute and enforce its power. They extended to the sea ports and caravan routes which connected China to the rest of the world, allowing Changan to import the world's ideas and products. The city became a centre of international trade, and a large foreign community established itself there. Numerous foreign religions built temples and mosques, including Muslims, the Zoroastrians of Persia, and the Nestorian Christian sect of Syria. The growth of the government elite and the evolution of a more complex imperial court drew vast numbers of people to serve it: merchants, clerks, artisans, priests and labourers. By the 8th century the city had a phenomenal population of two million.

Towards the end of the 8th century the Tang Dynasty and its capital began to decline. From 775 onwards the central government suffered reverses at the hands of provincial warlords and Tibetan and Turkish invaders. The setbacks exposed weaknesses in the empire, and though the Tang still maintained overall supremacy they gradually began to lose control of the transport networks and the tax collection system on which their power depended. The dynasty fell in 907 AD and China once again broke up into a number of independent states. Changan was eventually relegated to the role of a regional centre, never to regain its former supremacy.

The modern-day city of Xian stands on the site of Changan. In the 19th century Xian was a rather isolated provincial town, a condition which persisted until the completion of a railway line from Zhengzhou in 1930. After 1949 the Communists started to industrialise the city and it now supports a population of 2½ million people. The capital of Shaanxi Province, Xian is an example of the government's efforts to create new inland industrial centres to counterbalance the traditional dominance of the large industrial cities on the coast. At first glance the city looks little different from other modern Chinese industrial cities, but scattered about are many reminders of its imperial past. Today, Xian is one of the biggest open-air museums in China.

Information & Orientation

Xian retains the same rectangular shape that characterised Changan, with streets and avenues laid out in a neat grid pattern.

The central block of the city is bounded by the old city walls. These were built during the Ming Dynasty on the foundations of the walls of the Tang Royal City. Caves were dug into the wall as air-raid shelters when the Japanese bombed the city. During the Cultural Revolution more caves were dug to store grain. Large sections of the wall have been restored in the last few years; some sections have completely disappeared, though they're still shown on the maps.

The centre of town is the enormous Bell Tower, and from here run Xian's four major streets: Bei, Nan, Xi and Dong Dajie. The railway station stands at the north-east edge of the central block. Jiefang Lu runs south from the station to intersect with Dong Dajie.

Many of the city's sights, as well as most of the restaurants, tourist hotels and facilities, can be found either along or in the vicinity of Jiefang Lu or Xi and Dong Dajie. There's a scattering of sights outside the central block, like the Big Goose and Small Goose pagodas. Other sights, like the terracotta soldiers at Xianyang and Qin Shihuang, and the remains of the Banpo Neolithic Village, can be found on the plain which surrounds Xian.

CITS (tel 21190) has its office on the ground floor of the rear building of the Renmin Hotel on Dongxin Jie. English is spoken. A wall chart lists trains out of Xian together with their departure and

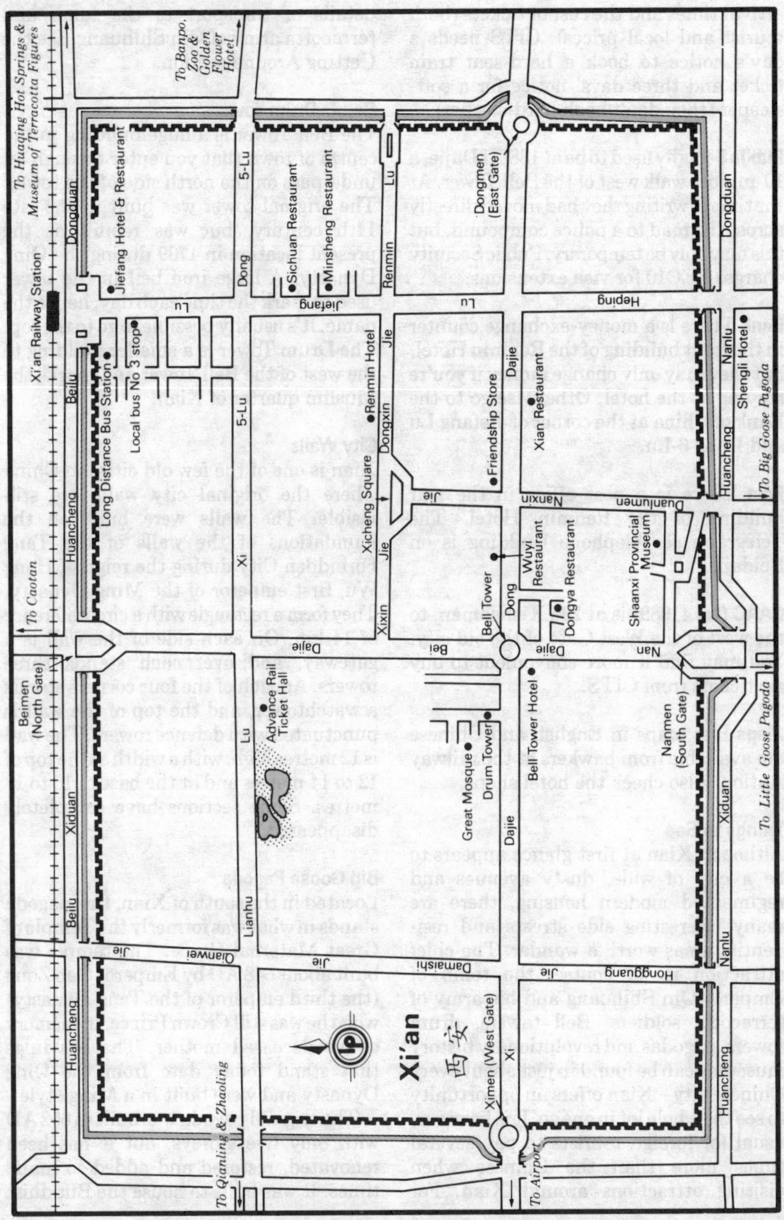
Xi'an
西安
To Huaqing Hot Springs & Museum of Terracotta Figures
To Banpo, Zoo & Golden Flower Hotel
Xi'an Railway Station
Dongduan
Jiefang Hotel & Restaurant
5-Lu
Sichuan Restaurant
Minsheng Restaurant
Renmin
Lu
Dongmen (East Gate)
Dongduan
Heping
Jiefang
Dong
Local bus No 3 stop
Long Distance Bus Station
Beilu
Huancheng
Xi
Xicheng Square
Renmin Hotel
Dongxin
Jie
Friendship Store
Dajie
Xian Restaurant
Shengli Hotel
Nanlu
Huancheng
To Big Goose Pagoda
Nanxin
Duanlumen
Shaanxi Provincial Museum
Wuyi Restaurant
Dongya Restaurant
Bell Tower
Bei
Xixin
Nan
To Caotan
Beimen (North Gate)
Advance Rail Ticket Hall
Bell Tower Hotel
Drum Tower
Great Mosque
Nanmen (South Gate)
Xiduan
To Little Goose Pagoda
Lianhu
Qianwei
Damaishi
Hongguang
Ximen (West Gate)
To Qianling & Zhaoling
To Airport

arrival times and the cost of tickets (both tourist and local prices). CITS needs a day's notice to book a hard-seat train ticket and three days' notice for a soft-sleeper (they don't book hard-sleeper).

Public Security used to be at 138 Xi Dajie, a 10-minute walk west of the Bell Tower. At the time of writing they had moved directly across the road to a police compound, but this may only be temporary. Public Security charges FEC10 for visa extensions.

Bank There is a money-exchange counter in the front building of the Renmin Hotel, but they may only change money if you're staying at the hotel. Otherwise go to the Bank of China at the corner of Jiefang Lu and Dong 6-Lu.

Post There is a post office in the rear building of the Renmin Hotel. The Telegraph & Telephone Building is on Beidajie.

CAAC (tel 41989) is at 296 Xishaomen, to the west of the West Gate of the old city. You may find it more convenient to buy air tickets from CITS.

Maps Bus maps in English and Chinese are available from hawkers at the railway station. Also check the hotel shops.

Things to See

Although Xian at first glance appears to be a city of wide, dusty avenues and regimented modern housing, there are many interesting side streets and residential areas worth a wander. The chief attraction is, of course, the tomb of Emperor Qin Shihuang and his army of terracotta soldiers. Bell towers, drum towers, pagodas and revolutionary history museums can be found in just about every Chinese city – Xian offers an opportunity to see the whole lot in one go. It is however, usual for foreign tourists to pay several times more than the Chinese when visiting attractions around Xian. For details of transport to the tomb and terracotta army of Qin Shihuang, see the Getting Around section.

Bell & Drum Towers

The Bell Tower is a huge building in the centre of town that you enter through an underpass on the north side of the tower. The original tower was built in the late 14th century, but was rebuilt at the present location in 1739 during the Qing Dynasty. A large iron bell in the tower used to mark the time each day, hence the name. It's usually possible to go to the top. The Drum Tower is a smaller building to the west of the Bell Tower and marks the Muslim quarter of Xian.

City Walls

Xian is one of the few old cities in China where the original city walls are still visible. The walls were built on the foundations of the walls of the Tang Forbidden City during the reign of Hong Wu, first emperor of the Ming Dynasty. They form a rectangle with a circumference of 14 km. On each side of the wall is a gateway, and over each stands three towers. At each of the four corners stands a watchtower, and the top of the wall is punctuated with defence towers. The wall is 12 metres high, with a width at the top of 12 to 14 metres and at the base of 15 to 18 metres. Some sections have completely disappeared.

Big Goose Pagoda

Located in the south of Xian, this pagoda stands in what was formerly the Temple of Great Maternal Grace. The temple was built about 648 AD by Emperor Gao Zong (the third emperor of the Tang Dynasty) when he was still Crown Prince, in memory of his deceased mother. The buildings that stand today date from the Qing Dynasty and were built in a Ming style.

The original pagoda was built in 652 AD with only five storeys, but it has been renovated, restored and added to many times. It was built to house the Buddhist scriptures brought back from India by the travelling monk Xuan Zhang, who then set about translating them into 1335 Chinese volumes. The impressive, fortress-like wood-and-brick building rises 64 metres. You can climb to the top for a view of the countryside and the city. Cost is 10 fen to visit the grounds, Y1.50 to climb the tower.

The pagoda is at the end of Yanta Lu, at the southern edge of Xian. Take bus No 5 down Jiefang Lu to the end of Yanta Lu and get off when it turns right into Xiaozhai Donglu. The entrance to the compound is on the southern side of the pagoda. On the western side is a former air-raid shelter now used as an amusement centre.

Little Goose Pagoda

The Little Goose Pagoda is in the grounds of the Jianfu Temple. The top of the pagoda was shaken off by an earthquake in the middle of the 16th century but the rest of the structure, 43 metres high, is intact. The Jianfu Temple was originally built in 684 AD as a site to hold prayers to bless the afterlife of the late Emperor Gao Zong. The pagoda, a rather delicate building of 15 tiers, was built in 707 to 709 AD and housed Buddhist scriptures brought back by another pilgrim to India.

You can get to the pagoda on bus No 3, which runs from the railway station through the south gate of the old city and down Nanguan Zhengjie. The pagoda is on Youyi Xilu just west of the intersection with Nanguan Zhengjie. Climb to the top of the pagoda for a panorama of Xian's apartment blocks and smokestacks. Entry to the grounds is Y1.20, plus Y1 to climb the pagoda or visit the museum.

Great Mosque

This is one of the largest Islamic mosques in China. The present buildings only date back to the middle of the 18th century, though the mosque might have been established several hundred years earlier. It stands north-west of the Drum Tower and is built in a Chinese architectural style with most of the grounds taken up by gardens. Still an active place of worship, the mosque holds several prayer services each day. The mosque is open 8am to 12pm, and 2 to 6pm. The courtyard of the mosque can be visited, but only Muslims may enter the prayer hall.

To get there, walk west along Xi Dajie and turn right at the Drum Tower. Go through the tunnel under the tower; at the second street on your left you'll see a small sign in English and Chinese pointing the direction to the mosque, which is down a small side street five minutes' walk away.

This is the large Muslim quarter of Xian where the narrow streets are lined with old mud-brick houses. There's some interesting shops in the vicinity of the mosque.

Shaanxi Provincial Museum

Once the Temple of Confucius, the museum houses a large collection of relics from the Zhou, Qin, Han, Sui and Tang dynasties, including a collection of rare relics unearthed in Shaanxi Province.

One of the more extraordinary exhibits is the Forest of Steles, the heaviest collection of books in the world. The earliest of these 2300 large engraved stone tablets dates from the Han Dynasty.

Most interesting is the Popular Stele of Daiqin Nestorianism. It's inscribed in Chinese and Syrian and stands just to the left of the entrance to the hall containing the collection; you'll recognise it by the small cross inscribed at the top. The Nestorians were a Syrian Christian sect whose disciples spread eastwards to China via the Silk Road. Marco Polo mentions making contact with members of the sect in Fuzhou in the 13th century.

The tablet was engraved in 781 AD to mark the opening of a Nestorian church. It describes how a Syrian named Raban came to the imperial court of Xian in 635 and presented Christian scriptures which were translated and then read by the emperor. The emperor, says the stone, was impressed and ordered that a monastery dedicated to the new religion be established in the city.

The Nestorians believed that Jesus had a human 'person' (that is, in the sense of having individual identity) as well as a divine person. This differs from the orthodox Christian view, which regards Jesus as one person (the 'Son' in the Father/Son/Holy Spirit trinity) but with two natures (human and divine).

Other tablets in the museum include the Ming De Shou Ji Stele which records the peasant uprising led by Li Zhicheng against the Ming, and the 114 Stone Classics of Kaichen from the Tang Dynasty inscribed with 13 ancient classics and historical records.

The rare relics exhibition is in another building. Among the artefacts is a tiger-shaped taliy from the Warring States Period, inscribed with ancient Chinese characters and probably used to convey messages or orders from one military commander to another. The rare relics section has captions in English.

The museum entrance is on a side street which runs off Baishulin Lu, close to the South Gate of the old city wall. It's open daily (except Mondays) from 8.30 am to 6 pm. Y2 admission, plus Y3 for the rare relics.

Old Xian

In the back streets of Xian are little-known but exceptionally fine temples, now converted into schools and warehouses or recently restored as tourist attractions. The good thing about temple hunting is that it changes your perspective of the city. Rather than seeing Xian as a city of wide avenues and large grey buildings, you find mud-brick houses, cobbled alleyways, old men playing chequers, market streets, and old women lugging buckets of water from the local water pump. Temple renovation is an interesting business still carried out mainly with manual tools.

The **Temple of the Eight Immortals (Ba Xian An)**, once Xian's largest Taoist establishment, has been renovated and is again an active place of worship. To get there walk east along Changle Xilu until you come to a street market on the south side identifiable by the large gateway. Walk down the market street, turn right at the end, then left to the temple complex.

The **East Peak Temple (Dong Yue Miao)** is about 50 metres to the north-west of the East Gate, and is now used as a primary school.

The **Dongmen (East Gate)** and parts of the wall have been restored. It may not be Jerusalem but for the meagre fee of Y1 you can walk or bicycle around the city walls. Entrance points are at **Nanmen (South Gate)** beside the Provincial Museum, and by some obscure steps at the eastern end of the south wall.

The **Town God's Temple (Cheng Huang Miao)** is being used as a warehouse. Its sadly dilapidated buildings feature some of the most beautiful and intricate woodcraft in China. The temple is within walking distance of the Bell Tower. Go to Xi Dajie 257, then take the small lane running north through the Muslim quarter and past an active mosque on the left. Turn right at the T-intersection, and right again down a cobbled alley cluttered with souvenir stalls. A right turn at the end of the alley leads you through the temple gates.

The **Temple of the Recumbent Dragon (Wolong Si)** was converted into a factory during the Cultural Revolution. The factory has since been removed and the temple was being renovated at the time of writing. To get there walk along Boshulin Lu. Between Nos 25 and 27 is a lane up to the temple. The entrance is on the left.

The 10th-century **Bao Qing Pagoda** pokes its head above the rooftops near the South Gate; you'll see it from Nan Dajie.

Banpo Neolithic Village

The earliest known agricultural villages in China were uncovered north of the Qinling Mountains, near the eastward bend of the

Yellow River where it's joined by the Fen and Wei rivers. The term 'Yangshao culture' is used because the first example was found near Yangshao Village. The oldest Yangshao-type village is Banpo, which appears to have been occupied from 4500 BC until around 3750 BC. The village was discovered in 1953 and is on the eastern bank of the Chan River in a suburb of Xian. A large hall has been built over what was part of the residential area of the village. Pottery found south of the Qinling Mountains has suggested that even earlier agricultural villages may have existed there, but this is speculation.

The Banpo ruins are divided into three areas: a residential area, a pottery-manufacturing area and a cemetery. These include the remains of 45 houses or other buildings, over 200 storage cellars, six pottery kilns and 250 graves (including 73 for dead children).

The earlier houses are half underground, in contrast to the later houses which stand on ground level and had a wooden framework. Some huts are round, others square, with doors facing south in both cases. There is a hearth or fire-pit in each house. The main building materials were wood for the framework and mud mixed with straw for the walls.

The residential part of the village is surrounded by a man-made moat, 300 metres long, about two metres deep and two metres wide. It protected the village from attacks by wild animals and from the effects of heavy rainfall in what was originally a hot and humid environment. Another trench, about two metres deep, runs through the middle of the village. To the east of the residential area is the pottery kiln centre. To the north of the village lies the cemetery where the adult dead were buried along with funerary objects like earthen pots. The children were buried in earthen pots close to the houses.

The villagers survived by hunting, fishing and gathering, but had begun to farm the surrounding land and keep domestic animals. Their stone tools included axes, knives, shovels, millstones, arrowheads and fishing-net sinkers. Bone objects included needles and fish hooks. Earthenware pots, bowls, basins and jars were used for storage and cooking; there was even a simple earthen vessel for steam cooking. Much of the pottery is coloured and illustrated with geometric patterns or animal figures like fish or galloping deer. The outside edges of some of the vessels are carved with what appears to be a primitive form of writing. Personal ornaments like hairpins, beads and rings were made of bone, shell, stone or animal teeth.

A museum at the site sells a book called *Neolithic Site at Banpo Near Xian*, which describes the objects on view. To get there take bus No 8 from the stop on Dong Dajie immediately to the east of the Bell Tower. This bus stops short of the village. About five minutes walk further up the road is the stop for trolley bus No 5, which will take you the last stretch to the village. Alternatively, take trolley bus No 5 from the stop on Bei Dajie just north of the Bell Tower. This bus goes past the village. Or take bus No 11 from the train station.

Places to Stay – bottom end

The *Jiefang Hotel* (tel 28946) is on Jiefang Lu, diagonally opposite the railway station. Once rated by this book as one of the grottiest hotels in China (with a staff who positively seemed to loathe foreigners), it's since undergone renovations and additions and can be recommended. A bed in a four-bed room is Y20. Rooms are very comfy with attached bathroom, carpet, air-con and television. Double rooms (no singles) from Y48. Staff are generally friendly and helpful; the nasties have been purged.

The *Shengli Hotel* (tel 23184) has become the main backpacker's haunt though it's inconveniently located just outside the city walls south of Heping Gate. Bus No 5 from the railway station will take you there. Rooms are OK though the bathrooms leave much to be desired. Dorm beds are Y7, double rooms Y20. The noise from the recently acquired televisions is likely to be overwhelming!

Places to Stay – middle

The *Renmin Daxia Hotel* (tel 25111) at 319 Dongxin Jie, one of the big tourist hotels, opened for business in 1953. Its central location has turned it into something of a meeting point for foreigners. The Soviet-style palace with Chinese architectural features has doubles (no singles) from Y55. At the time of writing there was a women's dormitory with beds for Y10, but no men's dorm. Ask other people you meet coming from Xian and check with the hotel once you get there. The hotel has at least three restaurants: a Chinese one which is not too good, a western one which is popular and quite cheap with ample portions, and a Muslim one. To get to the hotel take bus No 3 (not trolley bus No 3) from the train station. It goes down Jiefang Lu and turns right onto Dongxin Jie. Get off at the first stop on Dongxin Jie. In front of the hotel there once were decaying signs with quotations from Chairman Mao; now there are gaudy fountains.

The *Zhonglou (Bell Tower) Hotel* (tel 21000) is diagonally opposite the Bell Tower in the centre of town, and resembles an aircraft hangar. Take trolley bus No 1 from the train station and get off at the Bell Tower. Doubles (no singles) cost Y55. We've gotten mixed reports about this place.

The *Xian Double Dragon Hotel* is fairly new, but too out of the way to be worth staying at. It lies on the bus No 18 route several stops north of Xian's North Gate. A bed in a four-bed room is Y10, double rooms Y55.

Places to Stay – top end

The *Golden Flower Hotel* (tel 32981) resembles an enormous ice-block. American-built and Swedish-managed, this monument to mirrored walls stands at 8 Changle Xilu – unmistakable amidst standard grey concrete blocks. Singles cost US$100, doubles US$120. There are about 200 rooms, plus two restaurants, a bar and disco. Take bus No 11 from the train station.

Places to Eat

Some of the best places to eat are the food stalls down the side streets. Try the places near the train station, particularly along the lane by the Jiefang Hotel – anyone for roast pigs' feet? For Muslim food try the stalls along Sajinqiao Lu in the Muslim quarter – peppery stodge, made from crumbled bread heated in a wok with stocks, vegetables and a touch of meat, is something to be experienced at least once.

The *Wuji Restaurant* is on Dong Dajie, near the corner with Nanxin Jie and next to the Foreign Language Bookstore. Highly recommended. Although the ground floor looks none too impressive, the food is very good. The staff is helpful and friendly, and the menu is in both Chinese and English. Upstairs are the group-tour banquet rooms.

Dongya (East Asia) Restaurant used to be in Shanghai (founded in 1916) but moved to Xian in 1956. It serves possibly the best food in Xian. Try the ground floor's big trays of steaming dumplings. The restaurant is south-east of the Bell Tower on Luoma Shi, a small street which runs off Dong Dajie.

The *Xian Restaurant* is officially rated as one of the more illustrious eating houses, but the place gets very mixed reports from travellers. One person said it's 'living on past glory and should be struck off the list as a grotty, dirty dump'. Another wrote that 'several people in our hotel who had eaten there were quite ill'. There are four levels of dining halls in the huge grey building on Dong Dajie near Juhuayuan Lu.

Others worth trying include the *Sichuan Cuisine Restaurant* on Jiefang Lu (the cheap section at the back is very good), the *Heping Restaurant* at the corner of Jiefang Lu and Dong Dajie, and the *Misheng Restaurant* on Jiefang Lu.

Shopping

The Friendship Store is east of the Bell Tower, on Nanxin Jie just north of the intersection with Dong Dajie. Life-size Qin warriors go for Y15,000 apiece; if that blows your budget, try a kneeling figure for just Y5000 to Y10,000. Places like the terracotta soldier hangar are besieged by hawkers flogging everything from plastic pagodas to imitation mini-warriors. The cheapest warriors are about Y1 but the quality is not too good.

Getting There & Away

Train and plane are the usual means of leaving Xian. Centrally located and a major tourist city, it's a convenient jumping-off point for many destinations.

Air Xian is connected by air to many other cities and towns in China. Planes depart daily for Beijing, Canton and Shanghai; twice a week for Guilin; three days a week for Kunming; and once a week for Ürümqi.

There may be direct flights from Xian to Lhasa, but don't count on it. The CAAC timetable lists flights twice a week between these cities, but these are either pure fantasy, charter flights (group tours only) or for the future; check when you get to China. If you are heading to Tibet, consider the twice-weekly flights from Xian to Xining in Qinghai Province. From Xining you carry on to Golmud and Lhasa.

At the time of writing there were direct flights between Xian and Hong Kong (twice a week, fare Y450) but this may not be permanent; it's a great way to enter or exit central China quickly.

Rail There are direct trains from Xian to Ürümqi, Beijing, Shanghai, Chengdu, Taiyuan, Hefei, Qingdao and Wuhan. For Chongqing and Kunming change at Chengdu; for Guilin and Canton change at Wuhan.

A lot of people take the train from Xian to Ürümqi, which takes 2½ days. They either carry on from Ürümqi to Kashgar and Pakistan, or work their way back down the train line.

The booking office on Lianhu Lu is open 7 to 11.30 am, 12.30 to 2 pm, 2.30 to 8 pm. Tickets for same-day departure can be bought at the railway station, and there is also a special FEC advance booking office for foreigners .

Tourist-price tickets in yuan from Xian to some important destinations include:

destination	*hard-seat*	*hard-sleeper*	*soft-sleeper*
Beijing (22 hours)	47	72	127
Chengdu (19 hours)	32	50	98
Lanzhou (15 hours)	35	45	80
Shanghai (27 hours)	56	80	147
Taiyuan (12 hours)	34	56	81
Ürümqi (2½ days)	95	154	229
Xining (20 hours)	45	56	97
Zhengzhou (12 hours)	26	50	81

Bus

There's a daily bus from Xian to Lanzhou at 5.40am (Y18.50, 2 days) from the bus station near the railway station.

One frustrated Australian writes:

I don't believe Xian actually has an airport. It's certainly not worth trying to save time getting there by flying. Our flight was cancelled several times between Wednesday night and Friday night. It finally went on Saturday night, but we got in on the train some hours earlier. One other guidebook says that Xian airport has no radar. I reckon it's got no runway. Over three days of cancellations they got a bit bored with bad weather, and they came up with some beauties, like the plane having left Xian to fly to Beijing for us to fly back on it, but by mistake it had flown to Lengdu (or Nanso, depending on who you asked). Try to find those towns; I couldn't. Later we found it had left Lengdu (or Nanso) but they couldn't even estimate when it might arrive in Beijing. I thought I'd ask how long it usually takes to fly from Lengdu (or Nanso) to Beijing, to put an outside limit on the estimate of when we might actually do some flying ourselves, but it seems no one knows how long this flight lasts. The flight was cancelled about a half-hour after all luggage had been checked in. We'd already got a refund.

Getting Around

Transport around the city is almost entirely by bus. Taxis can be hired from the tourist hotels. Bicycles may be rented from the Renmin Hotel and from a bike shop opposite. There are local buses to the major sights around the city such as Banpo Village and the terracotta warriors of Qin Shihuang. To get to some of the more distant sites you may have to take a tour bus.

There are daily bus tours to the Neolithic village, the terracotta warriors and Huaqing Hot Springs. Tickets are available from the Jiefang Hotel for Y5 per person (not including entry fees to the sites). The buses spend several hours at incredibly boring Huaqing Springs, where you can watch Chinese having their photo taken in front of pavilions, rocks, lakes, bridges and trees. Entry to Banpo is Y0.70; to the Qin army Y3. Despite Huaqing, this is a good way to see everything at one time. Some tours either skip Huaqing or whiz through it, so shop around.

There are local buses from Xian to the entombed warriors at Xianyang. The bus terminus is on the eastern side of the train station. Ask for the bus to Lintong. At Lintong you get off and take another bus the rest of the way to the entombed army.

Tours for Y9 per person take in the Qian Tomb, Maoling Tomb, Xinyang Museum, Tomb of Prince Zhanghuai and Tomb of Princess Yongtai. Tickets are available from the Jiefang Hotel and other vendors; good value.

THE TOMB OF QIN SHIHUANG 秦始皇墓

When Qin Shihuang ascended the throne of Qin, construction of his final resting place began immediately. After he conquered the other states, work on the tomb was expanded on an unprecedented scale. Today the emperor's tomb and its accompanying army of terracotta soldiers is *the* reason to come to Xian. See the Getting Around section for Xian for details of transport to the tomb and terracotta soldiers, 30 km east of town.

The history of Xian is inextricably linked to this first emperor of a united Chinese people. In the 3rd century BC China was split into five independent and warring states. In the year 246 BC, at the age of 13, Ying Zheng ascended the throne of the state of Qin. One by one the Qin defeated the other states, until the last fell in 222 BC. The emperor is said to have become secretive and suspicious in his last days, fearing assassination and searching for an elixir of immortality. His tyrannical rule lasted until his death in 210 BC. His son held out for four years until he was overthrown by the revolt which established the Han Dynasty.

Qin Shihuang's tomb is covered by a huge mound of earth and has not been excavated. The *Historical Records* of Sima Qian, a famous historian of the 1st century BC, relate that the tomb contains palaces and pavilions filled with rare gems and other treasures, and is equipped with crossbows which automatically shoot intruders. The ceiling was inlaid with pearls to simulate the sun, stars and moon. Gold and silver cast in the form of wild geese and ducks were arranged on the floor, and precious stones were carved into pines. The walls of the tomb are said to be lined with plates of bronze to keep out underground water. Mercury was pumped in to create images of flowing rivers and surging oceans. At the end of the internment rites, the artisans who worked inside and the palace maids who had no children are said to have been forced to remain in the underground palace – buried alive so that none of its secrets could be revealed.

As to the size of the entire necropolis, a Ming Dynasty author in *Notes about Mount Lishan* states that the sanctuary of the mausoleum has four gates and a circumference of 2½ km, and that the outer wall has a perimeter of six km. Modern surveys of the site show that the necropolis is indeed divided into an inner sanctuary and an outer city, and measurements of the inner and outer walls closely match the figures of the Ming author. The southern part of the complex is marked by a large mound of rammed earth below which the emperor is buried. The mound is 40 metres high and at the bottom measures about 480 by 550 metres. It's now planted with trees and surrounded by agricultural fields.

Just how far the necropolis actually extends is anyone's guess. In 1974 peasants digging a well about 1500 metres east of the tomb uncovered one of the greatest archaeological sites in the world. Excavation of the underground vault of earth and timber revealed thousands of life-sized terracotta warriors and their horses in battle formation – a whole army which would follow its emperor into immortality. In 1976, two other vaults were discovered close to the first one, but each of these was refilled with soil after excavation. The first and largest pit has been covered with a roof to become a huge exhibition hall.

The underground vault measures about 210 metres east to west and 60 metres from north to south. The bottom of the pit varies from five to seven metres below ground level. Walls were built running east to west at intervals of three metres, forming corridors. In these corridors, on floors laid with grey brick, are arranged the terracotta figures. Pillars and beams once supported a roof.

The 6000 terracotta figures of soldiers and horses face east in a rectangular battle array. The vanguard appears to be three rows of 210 crossbow and longbow bearers who stand at the easternmost end of the army. Close behind is the main force of armoured soldiers holding spears, dagger-axes and other long-shaft weapons, accompanied by 35 horse-drawn chariots. Every figure differs in facial features and expressions. The horsemen are shown wearing tight-sleeved outer robes, short coats of chain mail and wind-proof caps. The archers have bodies and limbs positioned in strict accordance with an ancient book on the art of war.

Many of the figures originally held real weapons of the day, and over 10,000 pieces have been sorted out to date. Bronze swords were worn by the figures representing the generals and other senior officers. Surface treatment made the swords resistant to rust and corrosion so that after being buried for more than 2000 years they were still sharp. Arrowheads were made of a lethal metal alloy containing a high percentage of lead.

The second vault, excavated in 1976 but refilled, contained about 1000 figures. The third vault contained only 68 soldiers and one war chariot and appeared to be the command post for the soldiers in the other vaults. Presumably the soldiers represent the army which is meant to protect the necropolis. These are probably just a beginning, and excavation of the entire complex and the tomb itself could take decades.

It's not permitted to take photos at the site (partly to prevent damage to the figures from flashes, though they won't even let you take a time-exposure), and if you infringe that rule you can expect to have your film confiscated. A few people have sneaked some shots (including Michael Buckley who took about two dozen) but I wouldn't advise it unless you start with a blank roll of film . . . and if you do get caught try and remember that the attendants are just doing their job.

HUAQING POOL 华清池

At the foot of Li Shan, 30 km from Xian, is Huaqing Pool, where water from hot springs is funnelled into public bath-houses with 60 pools accommodating 4000 people. At Li Shan's summit are beacon towers built for defence during the Han Dynasty. A temple on the mountain is dedicated to the 'Old Mother' Nu Wa who created the human race and patched up cracks in the sky after a catastrophe. For details of transport to the pool, see the Getting Around section of Xian.

Li Shan is hardly worth the effort of going there as Chiang Kaishek would probably attest. His visit turned out to be most inauspicious. On 12 December 1936 he was arrested in Li Shan by his own generals, supposedly clad only in his pajamas and dressing gown, on the slopes of the snow-covered mountain up which he had fled. A pavilion marks the spot and there's a simple inscription, 'Chiang was caught here'.

In the early 1930s Kuomintang General Yang Huzheng was the undisputed monarch of those parts of Shaanxi not under Communist control. In 1935 he was forced to share power when General Zhang Xueliang arrived with his own troops from Manchuria in the wake of the Japanese occupation. Zhang assumed the office of 'Vice-Commander of the National Bandit Suppression Commission'.

In October and November 1935 the Kuomintang suffered severe defeats at the hands of the Communists and thousands of soldiers went over to the Red Army. Captured officers were given a period of 'anti-Japanese tutelage' and were then released. Returning to Xian, they brought Zhang reports of the Red Army's desire to stop the civil war and unite against the Japanese. Chiang Kaishek, however, stubbornly refused to turn his forces against the Japanese and continued his war against the Communists. On 7 December 1936 he flew to Xian to oversee another 'extermination' campaign against the Red Army.

Zhang Xueliang flew to Yanan, met Zhou Enlai and became convinced of the sincerity of the Red Army's anti-Japanese policies. A secret truce was established. On the night of 11 December Zhang met the divisional commanders of his Manchurian army and the army of General Yang. A decision was made to arrest Chiang Kaishek. The following night the commander of Zhang's bodyguard led the attack on Chiang Kaishek's residence at the foot of Li Shan and took him prisoner along with most of his general staff. In the city the 1500 'Blueshirts' (the police force controlled by Chiang's nephew and credited with numerous abductions, killings and imprisonments of Chiang's opponents) were disarmed and arrested.

A few days later, Zhang sent his plane to collect three representatives of the Red Army and bring them to Xian: Zhou Enlai, Ye Jianying and Bo Gu. Chiang Kaishek feared he was going to be put on trial and executed, but instead the Communists and the Manchurian leaders told him their opinions of his policies and described the changes they thought were necessary to save the country. Whatever Chiang did or did not promise to do, the practical result of the 'Xian Incident' was the end of the civil war.

Zhang released Chiang Kaishek on Christmas Day and flew back with him to Nanjing to await punishment. It was a face-saving gesture to Chiang. Zhang was sentenced by a tribunal to 10 years imprisonment and 'deprivation of civil rights for five years'. He was pardoned the next day. The extermination campaign against the Red Army was called off and the Kuomintang announced that their first task now was to recover the territory lost to Japanese.

Nevertheless, Chiang began organising what he hoped would be a quiet decimation of the Communist forces. By June 1937 Chiang had moved the sympathetic Manchurian army out of Shaanxi and replaced it with loyal Kuomintang troops. He planned to disperse the Communists by moving the Red Army piece-meal to other parts of the country supposedly in preparation for the war against the Japanese. The Communists were only extricated from their precarious position by Japan's sudden and all-out invasion of China in July 1937. Chiang was forced to leave the Red Army intact and in control of the north-west.

Chiang never forgave Zhang Xueliang and

never freed him. Thirty years later he was still held prisoner on Taiwan. General Yang was arrested in Chongqing and towards the end of WW II was secretly executed. Another reminder of this period is the office which the Communist Party set up in Xian to liaise with the Kuomintang. The office was disbanded in 1946, and after 1949 it was made into a memorial hall to the Eighth Route Army. It's on Beixin Lu, in the north of the city's central block.

XIANYANG 咸阳

This little town is a half-hour's bus ride from Xian. The chief attraction of Xianyang is the museum which houses a remarkable collection of 3000 miniature terracotta soldiers and horses, discovered in 1965. Each figure is about half a metre high. They were excavated from a Han Dynasty tomb. Admission to the Entombed Warriors is Y6, with an extra ticket needed for entry to the special exhibition hall.

To get to Xianyang from Xian, you take the No 1 trolley bus to the terminus and then get bus No 59. The fare is 55 fen. Get off at the terminus in Xianyang. Up ahead on the left-hand side of the road you'll see a clock tower. Turn right at this intersection and then left at Xining Jie. The museum is housed in a former Ming Dynasty Confucian temple on Zhongshan Jie, which is a continuation of Xining Jie. The entrance is flanked by two stone lions. It's about a 20-minute walk from the bus terminus.

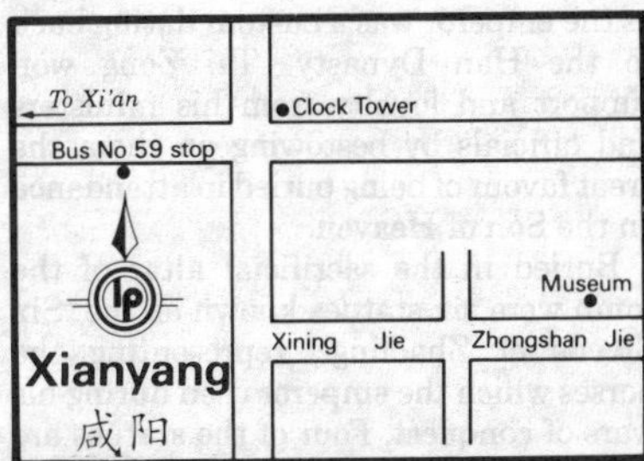

THE IMPERIAL TOMBS

Apart from the tomb of Qin Shihuang, a large number of other imperial tombs dot the Guanzhong Plain surrounding Xian. The easiest way to get to these tombs is with a tour from Xian; see the Getting Around section for Xian for details.

In these tombs are buried the emperors of numerous dynasties, as well as their empresses, concubines, government officials and high-ranking military leaders. Construction of an emperor's tomb often began within a few years of his ascension to the throne and didn't finish until he died.

The Tang tombs can be visited, and there's a touch of *I Claudius* in the stories behind them. The most famous is the Qian Tomb, the joint resting place of Tang Emperor Gao Zong and his wife Empress Wu Zetian. Gao Zong ascended the throne in 650 AD after the death of his father, Emperor Tai Zong. Empress Wu was actually a concubine of Tai Zong who also caught the fancy of his son, who made her his empress. Gao died in 683 AD, and the following year Empress Wu dethroned her husband's successor Emperor Zhong Zong. She reigned as an all-powerful monarch until her death around 705 AD. Nowadays it's fashionable to draw comparisons between Empress Wu and Jiang Qing.

Zhao Tomb (Zhaoling)

The Zhao Tomb set the custom of building imperial tombs on mountain slopes, breaking the tradition of building tombs on the plains with an artificial hill over them. This burial ground on Jiuzong Mountain, 70 km north-west of Xian, belongs to the second Tang emperor Tai Zong, who died in 649 AD.

Of the 18 imperial mausoleums on the Guanzhong Plain, this is probably the most representative. With the mountain at the centre, the tomb fans out to the south-east and south-west. Within its confines are 167 lesser tombs of the emperor's relatives and high-ranking military and government officials.

Burying other people in the same park

as the emperor was a custom dating back to the Han Dynasty. Tai Zong won support and loyalty from his ministers and officials by bestowing on them the great favour of being buried in attendance on the Son of Heaven.

Buried in the sacrificial altar of the tomb were six statues known as the 'Six Steeds of Zhaoling', representing the horses which the emperor used during his wars of conquest. Four of the statues are now in the Shaanxi Museum.

Qian Tomb (Qianling)

One of the most impressive tombs is the Qian Tomb, 85 km north-west of Xian on Liang Shan. This is the burial place of Emperor Gao Zong and Empress Wu.

The tomb consists of three peaks; the two on the south side are artificial, but the higher northern peak is natural and is the main part of the tomb. Walls used to surround the tomb but these are gone. South-west of the tomb are 17 smaller tombs of officials.

The grounds of the imperial tomb boast a number of large stone sculptures of animals and officers of the imperial guard. There are 61 (now headless) statues of the leaders of minority peoples of China and of the representatives of friendly nations who attended the emperor's funeral.

The two steles on the ground each stand over six metres high. 'The Wordless Stele' is a blank tablet; one story goes that it symbolises Empress Wu's absolute power, which she considered inexpressible in words.

Prince Zhang Huai's Tomb

Of the smaller tombs surrounding the Qian Tomb only five have been excavated. Zhang was the second son of Emperor Gao Zong and Empress Wu. For some reason the prince was exiled to Sichuan in 683 and died the following year at age 31 (a pillow across the face perhaps?). Empress Wu posthumously rehabilitated him. His remains were brought to Xian after Emperor Zhong Zong regained power. Tomb paintings show horsemen playing polo, but these and other paintings are in a terrible state.

Princess Yong Tai's Tomb

The nearby Tomb of Princess Yong Tai is in poor shape. Unless restoration is done, it seems unlikely that the exquisite tomb paintings, some showing palace serving-girls, will survive. The line engravings on the stone outer coffin are extraordinarily graceful. Yong Tai was a grand-daughter of the Tang emperor Gao Zong, and the seventh daughter of Emperor Zhong Zong. She was put to death by Empress Wu in 701 AD, but was rehabilitated posthumously by Emperor Zhong Zong after he regained power.

Mao Tomb

The Mao Tomb, 40 km from Xian, is the resting place of Emperor Wu, the most powerful ruler of the Han Dynasty. He died in 87 BC. The cone-shaped mound of rammed earth is almost 47 metres high, and is the largest of the Han imperial tombs. A wall used to enclose the mausoleum but now only the ruins of the gates on the east, west and north sides remain. It is recorded that the emperor was entombed with a jade cicada in his mouth and was clad in jade clothes sewn with gold thread, and that buried with him were live animals and an abundance of jewels.

HUA SHAN 华山

Hua Shan (Flower Mountain) is one of the sacred mountains of China, 2200 metres high. It lies 120 km east of Xian, just south of the Xian-Luoyang railway line. There is only one route to the top, a north-south path about 15 km long. You can hike from the base of the mountain to the summit in a day, and stay overnight at the hotel there. The trail to the top can be dangerously crowded.

Places to Stay & Eat
There are a couple of hotels at the base of the mountain. The *Shi Er Tong Lushe (Twelve Caves Travel Inn)* is good, and is run by monks from the adjacent Buddhist temple. To get there walk through the gate just behind the *Hua Shan Binguan (Hua Shan Guest House)*. The Twelve Caves Travel Inn has cool and clean rooms (former monks' cells) set around a peaceful courtyard for Y8 per person. Ideal to rest up in during the day. Food is available from nearby stalls. Be warned that the monks running the guest house and monastery definitely do not like travellers who dress as if they're off to a beach party; modesty rates highly. There is another hotel half-way up the mountain, and at least three on the summit – all in old monasteries.

Getting There
Xian is a good jumping-off point. There is a direct bus from the long-distance bus station to Hua Shan. Alternatively, take a train from Xian to Hua Shan station.

YANAN 延安
This town is on a deep valley of the Yan River, 270 km from Xian in the far north of Shaanxi Province. Although just a small town of around 30,000 people, it vies with Mao's birthplace at Shaoshan as the No 1 Communist pilgrimage spot. Between the years 1936 to 1947 this was the headquarters of the Chinese Communists. The 'Long March' from Jiangxi ended in 1936 when the Communists reached the northern Shaanxi town of Wuqi. The following year they moved their base to Yanan.

The numerous caves around the town were built by the Communists and the main sights are those in which the leaders lived and worked. Dominating the area is the Baota (Precious Pagoda), built during the Song Dynasty.

Places to Stay
The *Yanan Hotel* charges Y20 for a good, clean double room with television and bathroom. The hotel restaurant is cheap.

Getting There
There are flights twice a week from Xian to Yanan; the fare is Y51. There are once-weekly flights to Yanan from Beijing and Taiyuan.

Daily buses to Yanan from Xian depart from Xian's long-distance bus station just off Jiefang Lu, near the train station. The fare is Y9. It's a rough ride.

An interesting alternative is the bus from Yinchuan (in the Ningxia Autonomous Region) to Yanan. The fare on this route is about Y12. You see the Great Wall, lots of desert and cave houses on the way. Apparently this route is officially closed to foreigners.

HUANGLING 皇陵
Mid-way between Xian and Yanan is the town of Huangling. The tomb on nearby Qiao Shan is supposedly that of the Yellow Emperor Huang Di. Huang is said to be the father of the Chinese people, one of the 'Five Sovereigns' who reigned about 5000 years ago and by wars of conquest unified the Chinese clans. He is credited with numerous inventions and discoveries: silkworm cultivation, weaving, writing, the cart, the boat, the compass, building bricks and musical instruments. You can overnight in this town if you're taking the bus up from Xian to Yanan.

Shanxi 山西

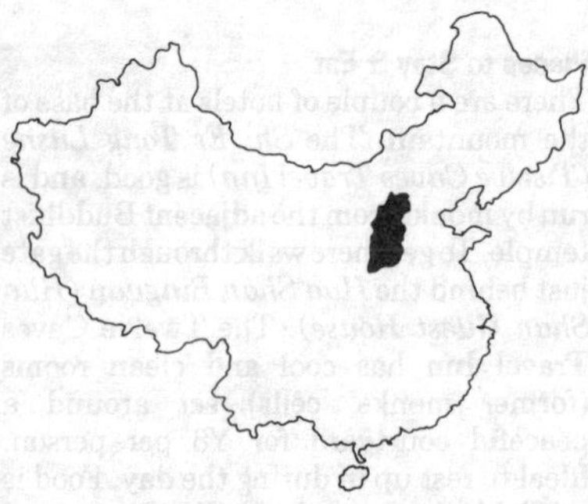

Shanxi Province, especially the southern half, was one of the earliest centres of Chinese civilisation and formed the territory of the state of Qin. After the first emperor, Qin Shihuang, unified the Chinese states, the northern part of Shanxi became the key defensive bulwark between the Chinese and the nomadic tribes to the north. Despite the Great Wall, the nomadic tribes still managed to break through and used Shanxi as a base for their conquest of the Middle Kingdom.

When the Tang Dynasty fell, the political centre of China moved away from the north-west. Shanxi went into a rapid economic decline, though its importance in the northern defence network remained paramount. Strategic importance coupled with isolation and economic backwardness was not an unusual situation for any of China's border regions, then or now.

It was not until the intrusion of the foreign powers into China that any industrialisation got under way. When the Japanese invaded China in the 1930s they carried out further development of industry and coal mining around the capital of Taiyuan. True to form, Shanxi was a bastion of resistance to this invasion from the north, this time through the Communist guerrillas who operated in the mountainous regions.

After 1949 the Communists began a serious exploitation of Shanxi's mineral and ore deposits, and the development of places like Datong and Taiyuan as major industrial centres. Some of the biggest coal mines can be found near these cities, and the province accounts for a third of China's known coal deposits.

Shanxi means 'west of the mountains' and is named after the Taihing range which forms its eastern border. To the west it is bordered by the Yellow River. The province has a population of about 25 million people, relatively light by Chinese standards unless you consider the fact that almost 70% of the province is mountains. The Taihing range, which also includes the Wutai Mountains, runs north-south, and separates the province from the great North China Plain to the east. The Central Shanxi Basin crosses the central part of the province from north to south in a series of valleys. This is the main farming and economic area. Most of the farmland is used to grow crops, though the north-west is the centre of the province's animal husbandry industry.

Despite its intended future as an industrial centre, Shanxi's wealth lies in its history. The province is literally a gold-mine of temples, monasteries and cave-temples, a reminder that this was once the political and cultural centre of China. The number-one attraction is the Yungang Buddhist Caves at Datong.

TAIYUAN 太原

The first settlements on the site of modern-day Taiyuan date back 2500 years. By the 13th century it had developed into what Marco Polo referred to as 'a prosperous city, a great centre of trade and industry'.

Like Datong, Taiyuan became an important frontier town, but despite its prosperity it has been the site of constant armed conflict. The trouble with Taiyuan was that it was always in somebody else's way, situated on the path by which

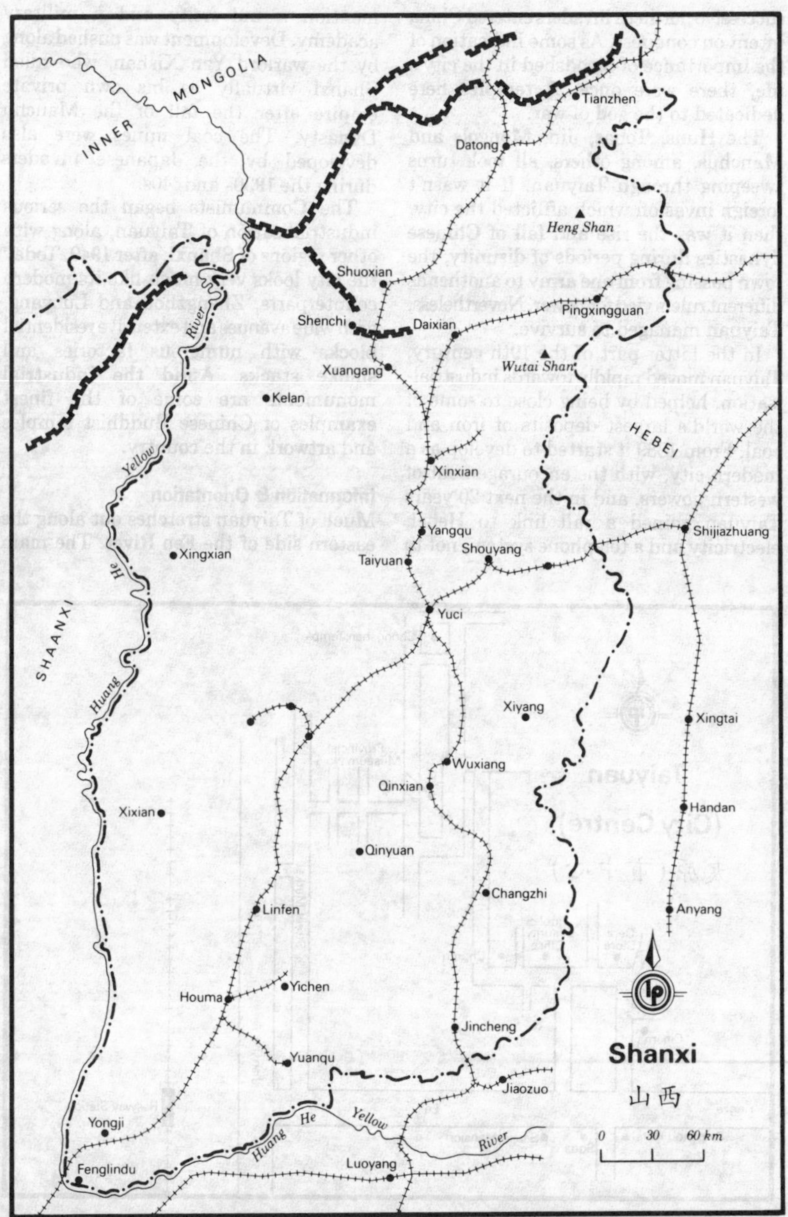
INNER MONGOLIA
Tianzhen
Datong
Heng Shan
Shuoxian
Pingxingguan
Shenchi
Daixian
River
Xuangang
Wutai Shan
Kelan
HEBEI
Yellow
Xinxian
Yangqu
Shijiazhuang
Xingxian
Taiyuan
Shouyang
Yuci
He
SHAANXI
Huang
Xiyang
Xingtai
Wuxiang
Qinxian
Xixian
Handan
Qinyuan
Changzhi
Linfen
Anyang
Yichen
Houma
Jincheng
Yuanqu
Shanxi
Jiaozuo
山西
Yongji
He
Yellow
Huang
River
0
30
60 km
Fenglindu
Luoyang

successive northern invaders entered China intent on conquest. As some indication of the importance of bloodshed in the city's life, there were once 27 temples here dedicated to the god of war.

The Huns, Tobas, Jin, Mongols and Manchus, among others, all took turns sweeping through Taiyuan. If it wasn't foreign invasion which afflicted the city, then it was the rise and fall of Chinese dynasties during periods of disunity, the town passing from one army to another as different rulers vied for power. Nevertheless, Taiyuan managed to survive.

In the latter part of the 19th century, Taiyuan moved rapidly towards industrialisation, helped by being close to some of the world's largest deposits of iron and coal. From 1889 it started to develop as a modern city, with the encouragement of western powers, and in the next 20 years Taiyuan gained a rail link to Hebei, electricity and a telephone system, not to mention a university and a military academy. Development was pushed along by the warlord Yan Xishan, who ruled Shanxi virtually as his own private empire after the fall of the Manchu Dynasty. The coal mines were also developed by the Japanese invaders during the 1930s and '40s.

The Communists began the serious industrialisation of Taiyuan, along with other regions of Shanxi, after 1949. Today the city looks very much like its modern counterparts, Zhengzhou and Luoyang, with wide avenues and extensive residential blocks with numerous factories and smoke stacks. Amid the industrial monuments are some of the finest examples of Chinese Buddhist temples and artwork in the country.

Information & Orientation

Much of Taiyuan stretches out along the eastern side of the Fen River. The main

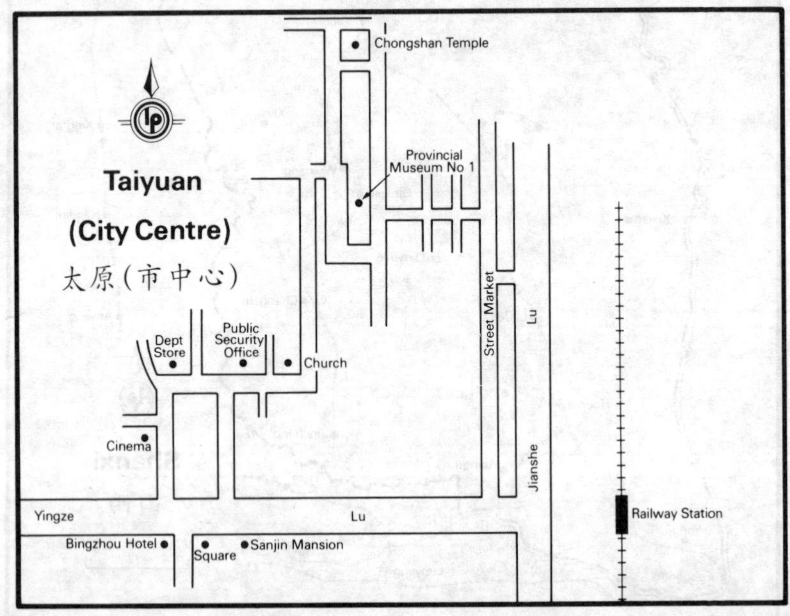

road is Yingze Dajie; from the railway station it cuts its way through the centre of the city in an east-west direction. Most of the tourist facilities and many of the sights are along this road or in the immediate vicinity. The centre of town is May 1st Square.

CITS (tel 29155) is on the ground floor of the Yingze Guest House.

Public Security is in a walled compound on a street running parallel to and just north of Yingze Lu. Refer to the map for directions.

Bank Money can be changed at the Yingze Guest House and possibly at the high-rise Friendship Store, both on Yingze Dajie.

Post & Communications There's a post office in the Yingze Guest House and a telephone office next door.

CAAC (tel 29903) is at 38 Yingze Dongdajie.

Maps Excellent bus maps of Taiyuan are available from hawkers around the train station.

Jinci Temple

This ancient Buddhist temple is located at the source of the Jin River by Xuanwang Hill, 25 km south-west of Taiyuan. It's not known for sure when the original buildings were constructed, but there have been numerous additions and restorations over the centuries right up to the Qing Dynasty. The temple probably dates back at least 1000 years.

Buses to the temple leave from the city centre. Walk one block east past May 1st Square, turn left and walk one block to the end of that street where there's a bus terminal. Take bus No 8 to the temple.

The gateway to the compound and a number of major buildings are situated on an east-west axis. As you enter the compound the first major structure is the Mirror Terrace, a Ming building used as an open-air theatre. The name is used in the figurative sense to denote the reflection of life in drama.

Zhibo's Canal cuts through the temple complex and lies west of the Mirror Terrace. Spanning this canal is the Huixian (Meet the Immortals) Bridge, which provides access to the Terrace for Iron Statues. At each corner of the terrace stands an iron figure cast in 1097 AD.

Immediately behind the statues is Duiyuefang Gate, fronted by two iron statues. The Offerings Hall behind the gate was built in 1168 to display temple offerings. To one side of the hall is a pavilion housing a large drum; the pavilion on the other side houses a large bell.

Behind the Offerings Hall is a quaintly named mediocrity, the Fish Pond with Flying Beams. The pond is one of the springs from the Jin River and is planted with 34 small octagonal stone pillars, on top of which are brackets and cross-beams supporting a bridge in the shape of a cross.

The bridge connects the Offerings Hall with the Goddess Mother Hall, otherwise known as the Sacred Lady Hall. It's the oldest wooden building in the city and one of the most interesting in the temple complex. The temple is fronted by large wooden pillars with carvings of fearsome dragons. Inside are 42 Song Dynasty clay figures of maid-servants standing around a large seated statue of the Sacred Lady herself. She is said to be the mother of Prince Shuyu of the ancient Zhou Dynasty, and the temple was built in her memory during the Northern Song period. It's suggested that the original building was constructed by the prince as a place to offer prayers and sacrifices to his mother. Today, people still throw money on the altar in front of the statue. Next to the Sacred Lady Hall is the Zhou Cypress, an unusual tree which has grown at an angle of about 30° for the last 900 years.

South of the Sacred Lady Hall is the Nanlao (Forever Young or Everlasting) Spring over which stands a pavilion. To the west of the spring is the two-storeyed Shuimou Lou (Water Goddess House, otherwise known as the Crystal Palace), originally built in 1563. On the ground floor is a statue of the goddess cast in bronze. On the upper storey is a shrine with a seated statue of the goddess surrounded by statues of her female servants.

In the north of the temple grounds is the Zhenguan Baohan Pavilion, which houses four stone steles inscribed with the handwriting of the Tang emperor Tai Zong. The Memorial Halls of Prince Shuyu include a shrine containing a seated figure of the prince surrounded by 12 Ming Dynasty female attendants, some holding bamboo flutes, pipes and stringed instruments. In the south of the temple grounds is the Sacred Relics Pagoda, a seven-storeyed, octagonal building constructed at the end of the 7th century.

Ming Library & Yingze Park

The Ming library is an ornate building in Yingze Park and is worth a look. The entrance to the park is on the opposite side of the road and to the west of the Yingze Guest House.

Chongshan Monastery

This Buddhist monastery was built towards the end of the 14th century on the site of an even older monastery, said to date back to the 6th or 7th centuries. The main hall contains three impressive statues; the central figure represents Guanyin, the Goddess of Mercy, with 1000 hands and eyes. Beautifully illustrated book covers show scenes from the life of Buddha. Also on display are Buddhist scriptures of the Song, Yuan, Ming and Qing dynasties.

Unfortunately the monastery only seems to be open when a tour group is visiting so you'll have to try and tag on to one. The monastery is on a side street to the west of Jianshe Beilu.

Yongzhuo Monastery

The Yongzhuo or 'Eternal Blessing' Monastery was built during the Ming Dynasty in the late 16th or early 17th century. It's usually referred to as the 'Twin Pagoda Monastery' because of its two identical pagodas, regarded as the symbol of Taiyuan. Each of these octagonal, 50-metre-high pagodas has 13 storeys and is built entirely of brick. In imitation of wooden pagodas, the bricks are carved with brackets and cornices. You'll have to walk to the pagodas – about 45 minutes from the train station.

Provincial Museums

The Shanxi Provincial Museum is housed in two separate complexes. The No 1 Museum is in an old Confucius Temple on Dilianggong Lu. The No 2 Museum is in Chunyang Palace, west of May 1st Square, and used to be a temple for offering sacrifices to the Taoist priest Lu Dongbin who lived during the Tang Dynasty. The temple was built during the Ming and Qing dynasties.

Shuanglin Monastery

This fine monastery contains exquisite painted-clay figurines and statues dating from the Song, Yuan, Ming and Qing dynasties. The monastery is about 97 km south of Taiyuan and is well worth the effort of getting there – you can do it as a day trip out of Taiyuan. Most of the present buildings date from the Ming and Qing dynasties, while the majority of

1 Railway Station
2 Provincial Museum No 1
3 Chongshan Monastery
4 Provincial Museum No 2
5 Sanjin Mansions
6 CAAC
7 Friendship Store
8 Yingze Guest House
9 Telephone Office
10 Ming Library
11 Hubing Hotel
12 Bingzhou Hotel
13 Yun Shan Hotel
14 Electric Hotel

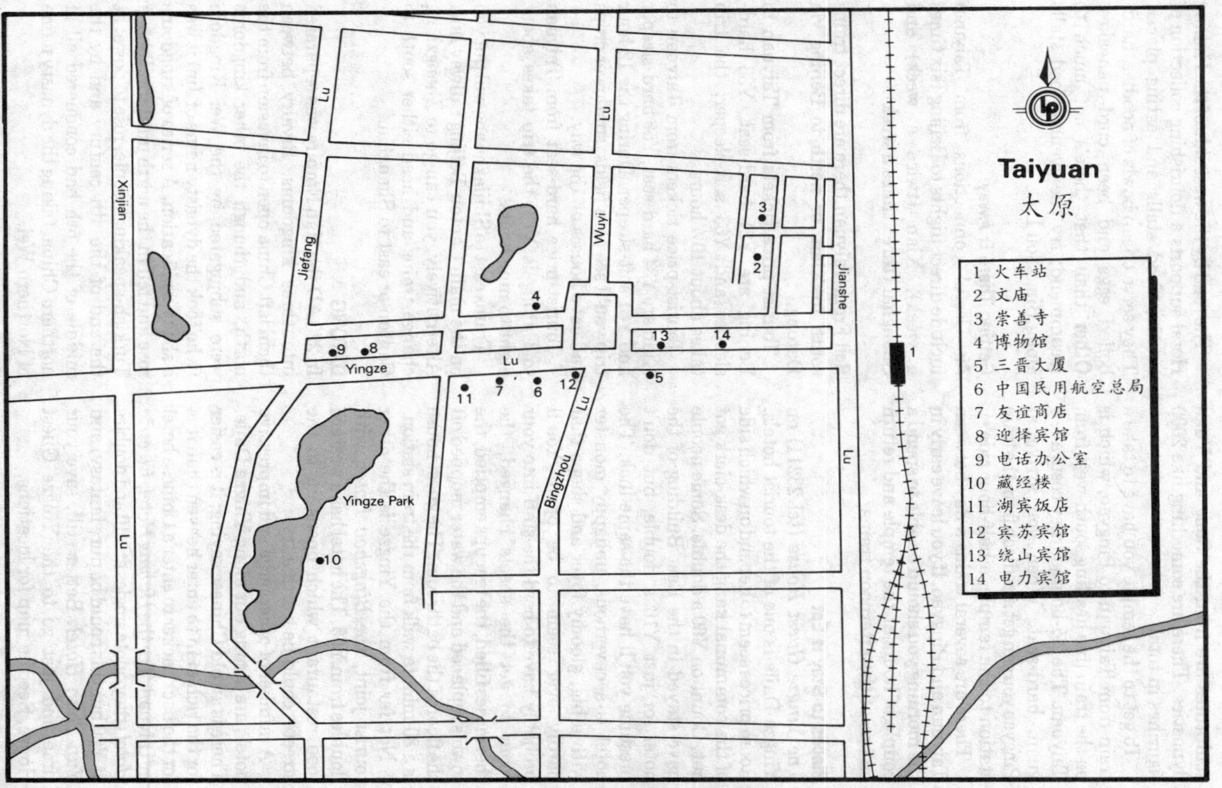
Taiyuan
太原
1 火车站
2 文庙
3 崇善寺
4 博物馆
5 三晋大厦
6 中国民用航空总局
7 友谊商店
8 迎泽宾馆
9 电话办公室
10 藏经楼
11 湖宾饭店
12 宾苏宾馆
13 绕山宾馆
14 电力宾馆
Jianshe
Lu
Wuyi
Lu
Yingze
Lu
Bingzhou
Lu
Jiefang
Lu
Xinjian
Lu
Yingze Park

sculptures are from the Song and Yuan dynasties. There are something like 2000 figurines in total.

To get to the temple you have to take a train from Taiyuan to Pingyao, which is on the train line heading south-west from Taiyuan. The 2½-hour journey costs a few yuan, hard-seat. When you arrive at Pingyao you can get a pedicab from the train station to the temple, a half-hour ride.

There are several trains a day between Taiyuan and Pingyao. If you leave early in the morning you should be able to spend a couple of hours at the temple and return on one of the afternoon trains.

Places to Stay & Eat

The *Yingze Guest House* (tel 23211) on Yingze Dajie is one of the tourist hotels. Room prices seem to depend on which side of the communal kang the desk-clerk got out. Count on Y60 a double. Some people have stayed in the East Building of the hotel for just Y16 a double, but don't presume you'll have the same luck. The hotel is a cavernous, unhappy monster with a big, gloomy foyer and shops that hardly ever seem to be open. You'll probably have to herd the staff into your room to get the sheets changed, the thermoses filled, the teacups emptied, the towels replaced and the water mopped off the floor of the bathroom. The guest house is a 30-minute walk from the train station.

Not far from the Yingze is the other tourist joint, the *Bingzhou Hotel*, with doubles from Y65. The hotel has a western food restaurant which opens on to the street – could be worth a try.

A number of other large and impressive hotels are strung out along Yingze Dajie. There is an old Chinese saying: it is easier for the rich man to enter heaven than it is for the backpacker to enter a Chinese hotel in Taiyuan. Try the *Hubing Hotel, Electric Hotel* (they quote singles at Y10 and doubles at Y20 but this could be pure fantasy) and *Yun Shan Hotel*. Better still, save your time and just go to the Yingze Guest House. See the map for locations.

The road by the west side of the Hubing Hotel supports a flourishing collection of evening food stalls and eating places. They serve cheap bowls of noodles, hard-boiled eggs and bean curd pancakes. Other than that there's not much to recommend; try the evening food stalls along Bingzhou Lu.

Getting There & Away

Air Useful connections from Taiyuan include direct flights to Beijing (six times a week), Xian (twice a week) and Shanghai (three times a week).

Rail From Taiyuan there are direct trains south to Xian, or north to Beijing via Datong.

Tourist-price tickets from Taiyuan to Beijing are Y21 hard-seat, Y33 hard-sleeper and Y63 soft-sleeper; the trip takes about 10½ hours.

Tourist-price tickets from Taiyuan to Xian are Y34 hard-seat, Y56 hard-sleeper and Y81 soft-sleeper. During the 12 hour trip you'll see corn fields, sunflower crops and cave houses on the way.

Tourist-price hard-seat from Taiyuan to Datong is Y12; the trip takes about eight to nine hours.

Trains east to Shijiazhuang will put you on the main Canton-Beijing railway line. Alternatively, you can go to Zhengzhou, change trains and head either south to Canton or east to Shanghai.

DATONG 大同

In 220 AD the Han Empire was separated into three kingdoms. Rivalry between them left China open to invasion from the north, and though the other kingdoms were subjugated by the Wei Kingdom (who took the dynasty name of Jin) it was a shaky unification. A series of kingdoms rose and fell in the north until the Toba, a Turkish-speaking people, rose to power at the end of the 4th century and by the middle of the 5th had conquered all of northern China, taking the dynasty name of Northern Wei.

Top: Pagoda in Black Dragon Park, Mt. Satseto in the background (RS)
Bottom: Interior roof of the Temple of Heaven, Beijing (AS)

Top: The Great Wall, Beijing (AS)
Bottom: Front Gate, Qianmen, Beijing (AS)

The success of the Tobas in ruling the northern Chinese was not due to their numbers, which were relatively small, but to their adoption of a Chinese style of administration and to intermarriage of Chinese gentry and Toba aristocracy. The dynasty appears to have been a very active period of development, particularly in agriculture, irrigation and trade, as well as a high point culturally, despite continuing wars and social instability. During this time Buddhist teachings of personal salvation and nirvana began taking root among the Chinese, and Buddhism was made a state religion.

The Northern Wei established their capital at Datong, an important centre because of its strategic location just south of the Great Wall and near the border with Inner Mongolia. The town had been fortified under the Han. When the Wei set up their capital here it became the political hub of the dynasty, until the court moved to Luoyang in 494 AD. Outside the modern-day city is the greatest legacy of the period, the Yungang Buddhist Caves.

Apart from the caves, there are few reminders today that Datong was once northern China's imperial city. The city of 700,000 people is a rather ugly version of the post-1949 Beijing prototype. However, it retains one of the largest and most intact old sections left in any Chinese city. It's one of the most interesting northern Chinese cities for walking – and one of the few places in the world still building steam engines. It's also Shanxi's leading coal producer.

Information & Orientation

Datong is divided into an old city and the modern post-1949 construction. In the north of town is the long-distance bus station and main train station. In the centre of town are the local bus station, Public Security office, main department store, post office and Exhibition Hall. In the south are the two tourist hotels. In the east are the old city, Huayuan Monastery and Dragon Screen. The Yungang Caves are just outside the city.

CITS (tel 23215) is in the Yungang Hotel on Yingbin Xilu.

Public Security is next to the large department store on Xinjian Beilu.

Bank To change money, try the exchange counter in the Yungang Hotel.

Post & Communications There is a post office in the Yungang Hotel. The main

post and telephone office is the large building with the clock tower facing the square in the city centre.

Maps Good maps of Datong are available from a booth on Xinjian Beilu near the train station.

Datong Steam Locomotive Factory

Opened in 1959, this factory builds steam engines based on a 1950s Soviet design – the 2-10-2 Qianjin (Forward) class, or 'QJ'. These were first produced in 1965. The factory is the only one in China making engines for the main train lines. Up until 1976, when the factory was destroyed by earthquake, the works at Tangshan were producing the Shangyang (Aiming at the Sun) or 'SY' class loco.

The factory is open to visitors on Tuesdays and Saturdays, but the only way you'll get to see it is to arrange a tour with CITS. You can only go if there's a spare seat on one of the tour buses or if you can get a group of at least eight people together.

The tour of the factory can best be described as educational. One American tourist said it reminded him of working in the American shipyards in the 1940s. You may be aghast at the safety conditions. After wandering through the factory you enjoy the ultimate experience of rail buffs – a ride in the cabin of one of the locomotives. Then it's off to the kindergarten where you're greeted by lines of applauding toddlers, topped off with a song-and-dance performance by some of the older children.

Dragon Screen

Situated in the old part of Datong on Dadong Jie, the Dragon Screen is said to have faced the mansion of the 13th son of the Ming Dynasty's first emperor, Hong Wu. The screen is eight metres high, over 45 metres long and two metres thick. On its main section, in relief, are nine stylised dragons. Unfortunately, it's in very bad condition.

Huayuan Monastery

The Huayuan Monastery is on the outskirts of the old city. The original monastery dates back to the reign of Emperor Tian Juan of the Jin Dynasty in 1140. Apparently about 50 monks and trainees now live there.

Mahavira Hall is the main building and one of the largest Buddhist halls still standing in China. In the centre of the hall are five gilded Ming Dynasty Buddhas seated on lotus thrones. The three statues in the middle are carved out of wood while the other two are clay. Around them stand bodhisattvas, soldiers and mandarins. The ceiling is decorated with colourful paintings – originally dating to the Ming and Qing dynasties but recently restored.

Bojiajiaocang Hall (Hall for the Conservation of Buddhist Scriptures of the Bojia Order) is smaller but more interesting than the main hall. It contains 29 coloured clay figures made during the Liao Dynasty (916-1125 AD) and representing the Buddha and bodhisattvas. The figures give the monastery a touch of magic lacking in other restored temples. Chinese artists come here for a bit of inspiration, and the clay replicas that are all the go.

Bus No 4 from the train station goes past the Dragon Screen and the Huayuan Monastery.

Shanhua Monastery

The Shanhua Monastery at the south end of Datong is commonly called the Southern Temple. Built during the Tang Dynasty, it was destroyed by fire during a war at the close of the Liao Dynasty. In 1128 more than 80 halls and pavilions were rebuilt, and further restoration was done during the Ming Dynasty in 1445.

Mass Graves Exhibition Hall

This is dedicated to the people executed here by the Japanese. A viewing hall has been built over a pit into which the bodies were thrown. Some have been exhumed and are on display in a nearby hall.

This is a difficult place to find if you don't speak Chinese, so get the name written down in Chinese by someone at CITS or the hotel. Take bus No 6 from the local bus station to the terminus. Then change to bus No 5. Ask the conductor where to get off, and ask people on the street for more directions. If you stay on bus No 5 and take it to the terminus you'll see what Datong is really all about.

Hanging Monastery

Dangling off Jinlong Canyon in the Heng Mountains (75 km from Datong), is the peculiar Hanging Monastery. It dates back more than 1400 years but has been rebuilt several times through the centuries and now has 40 halls and pavilions. They were built along the contours of the cliff face using the natural hollows and outcrops plus wooden beams for support. The buildings are connected by corridors, bridges and boardwalks and contain bronze, iron, clay and stone statues of gods and Buddhas.

Probably the best way to get there is with a Chinese tour bus from the long-distance bus station at the corner of Xinjian Beilu and Xinhua Jie. Tickets are Y8. Most people aren't all that impressed with the monastery itself (particularly its setting), but they usually enjoy the trip. The tour takes you to a second monastery, but you can skip that and climb Heng Shan instead for impressive views of the surrounding area.

Alternatively, take a bus from Datong to Hunyuan. The Hanging Monastery is a five-km walk from Hunyuan. You could stay overnight in Hunyuan and then bus back to Datong the following day. Another possibility is to take a bus from either Datong or Hunyuan to Yingxian and visit the Wooden Tower on the way to the Hanging Monastery. The tower dates from the 11th century and is one of the oldest large wooden buildings in the world. The bus ride to Yingxian takes 1½ hours from either Datong or Hunyuan.

Places to Stay & Eat

Cheap accommodation is available for foreigners at the *Datong Guest House*, a Chinese hotel which is undergoing renovation. Single rooms are Y54, and doubles Y60. Meals are Y11. Bus No 15 from the train station drops you off outside the front gate.

The tourist joint is the *Yungang Hotel* just down the road from the Datong Guest House, one stop beyond on the No 15 bus. Double rooms only are available from Y75.

There are several restaurants on the street between these two hotels that are worth checking out. Another place that may be worth trying is the big *Beijing Duck Restaurant* on Xinjian Beilu just north of the town centre. There are lots of small restaurants and food stalls around the town centre and train station.

Getting There

Datong is a major junction on the north-central China railway network. There are daily express trains to Taiyuan (seven to nine hours), Beijing (seven to 8½ hours, Y14 hard-seat, tourist-price), Hohhot (five to six hours), Lanzhou via Hohhot and Baotou, and Xian. If you arrive late in Datong take a motorised pedicab or auto-rickshaw from the train station to the hotel.

A Swiss traveller writes:

> (There's) a nice alternative to get from Datong to Beijing – unexplored and very interesting . . . . I took a bus at 6.40 am from the long-distance bus station in Datong to Lingqin (via Hunyuan), which is also in Shanxi. It's a five-hour bus ride through some stunning scenery, the whole area is very mountainous and the road winding and partly very narrow (after Hunyuan). The fare is Y4. I reached Lingqin at about noon. After a simple lunch in the midst of a horde of staring Chinese I went straight to the train station (by local bus) in time to catch the slow train at 2.20 pm to Beijing (Yongdingmen station). A hard-seat ticket Chinese-price only Y4.40 and the trip takes around 6½ hours. A fascinating and beautiful ride, particularly just before and after you reach the territory of Beijing municipality.

YUNGANG CAVES

The Yungang Buddhist Caves are cut into the southern cliffs of Wuzhou Mountain 16 km west of Datong, next to the pass leading to Inner Mongolia. The caves contain over 50,000 statues and stretch for about one km east to west. On top of the mountain ridge are the remains of a huge, mud-brick Qing Dynasty fortress from the 17th century. As you approach the caves you see the truncated pyramids which were once the watch towers.

History

Most of the Datong caves were carved during the Northern Wei Dynasty between 460 and 494 AD. 'Yungang' or 'Cloud Ridge' is the highest elevation of the sandstone range of Mt Wuzhou, on the north bank of the river of the same name. The Wei rulers once came here to pray to the gods for rain.

The Yungang Caves appear to have been modelled on the Dunhuang Caves of Gansu Province, which were dug in the 4th century AD and are some of the oldest in China. Recent studies suggest that the Kongwang grottoes at Lianyungang, a coastal city by the Yellow Sea, were dug 200 years earlier. Buddhism may have been brought to China not only overland along the Silk Road but by sea from Burma, India and Sri Lanka.

It was in India that methods of cutting out cave temples from solid rock first developed. At the Dunhuang Caves the statues are terracotta since the rock was too soft to be carved, but here at Datong are some of the oldest examples of stone sculpture to be seen in China. Various foreign influences can be seen in the Yungang Caves: there are Persian and Byzantine weapons, lions and beards; Greek tridents and the acanthus leaves of the Mediterranean; as well as images of the Indian Hindu gods Vishnu and Shiva. The Chinese style is reflected in the form of bodhisattvas, dragons and flying apsaras (celestial beings rather like angels).

Some think the gigantic Buddha statues at Bamiyan in Afghanistan may have inspired the Yungang statues. The first caves at Yungang had enormous Buddha images in the likenesses of five Northern Wei emperors. In fact, the first Northern Wei emperor Daiwu had been declared a 'living Buddha' in 416 AD because of his patronage of Buddhism.

Work on the Yungang Caves fizzled out when the Northern Wei moved their capital to Luoyang in 494. Datong declined in importance and the caves appear to have been deliberately abandoned. In the 11th and 12th centuries the Liao Dynasty founded by northern invaders saw to some repairs and restoration. Datong itself houses some gems of Liao architecture and sculpture. More repairs to the caves were carried out during the Qing Dynasty. In comparison with the caves at Luoyang, the Datong caves are probably the more impressive and have suffered less vandalism.

For additional background on the caves plus a comparison of Chinese Buddhist art with central Asian, European and other art, read Elfriede Regina Knauer's article 'The Fifth Century AD Buddhist Cave Temples at Yungang, North China' in the periodical *Expedition* (Summer, 1983).

The Caves

From east to west the caves fall into four major groups, though their numbering has nothing to do with the order in which they were constructed. The present appearance of the caves is also misleading. First, the whole front of the caves was formerly covered with multi-storey buildings. Secondly, the 14-metre-high seated Buddha in Cave 20 was not meant to be seen in the present manner; the front wall of the chamber collapsed, exposing the figure.

Caves 1 to 4 These early caves with their characteristic square floor plan are at the far eastern end, separated from the other caves. Caves 1 and 2 each contain carved pagodas. Cave 3 is the largest in this group, though it contains only a seated Buddha flanked by two bodhisattvas. Between this group of four caves and the others is a monastery dating back to 1652, with pavilions hugging the cliff face.

Caves 5 & 6 Yungang art is seen at its best in these two caves. The walls are wonderfully carved with illustrations of Buddhist tales and ornate processions.

Cave 5 contains an almost 17-metre-high colossal seated Buddha. The faded paint gives you some idea of the original colour schemes: bronze face, red lips and blue hair. Many of the smaller images in this cave have been beheaded, though on the whole the sculptures and paintings in Caves 5 and 6 are better preserved than those in other caves since they're protected from the elements by the wooden towers built over the entrances. Cave 5 also contains a five-storey pagoda perched on the back of an elephant, carved on the upper part of the south wall.

Cave 6 contains a richly carved pagoda covered with scenes from religious stories. The entrance is flanked by fierce guardians. In the centre of the rear chamber stands a two-storey pagoda-pillar about 15 metres high. On the lower part of the pagoda are four niches with carved images, including one of the Maitreya Buddha. The life story of Gautama Buddha from birth to his attainment of nirvana is carved in the east, south and west walls of the cave and on two sides of the pagoda. A relief on the east wall of the rear chamber of Cave 6 shows Prince Gautama's encounter with a sick man; the prince rides a horse while his servant protects him with an umbrella (a symbol of royalty) but cannot protect him from laying eyes on human suffering. Pilgrims walk around the chamber clockwise.

Cave 8 Cave 8 contains carvings with Hindu influences that found their way into Buddhist mythology. Shiva, with eight arms and four heads and seated on a bull, is on one side of the entrance. On the other side is the multi-armed, multi-faced Indra perched on an eagle.

Caves 9 & 10 These caves, fronted by pillars, are interesting for the smaller figures with their humorous faces. Some carry musical instruments. Cave 12 has apsaras with musical instruments.

Caves 16 to 20 These caves were carved in 460 AD and have oval floors. The roofs are dome-shaped to make room for huge Buddha statues – some standing, some sitting, all with saccharin-sweet expressions.

The cross-legged giant Buddha of Cave

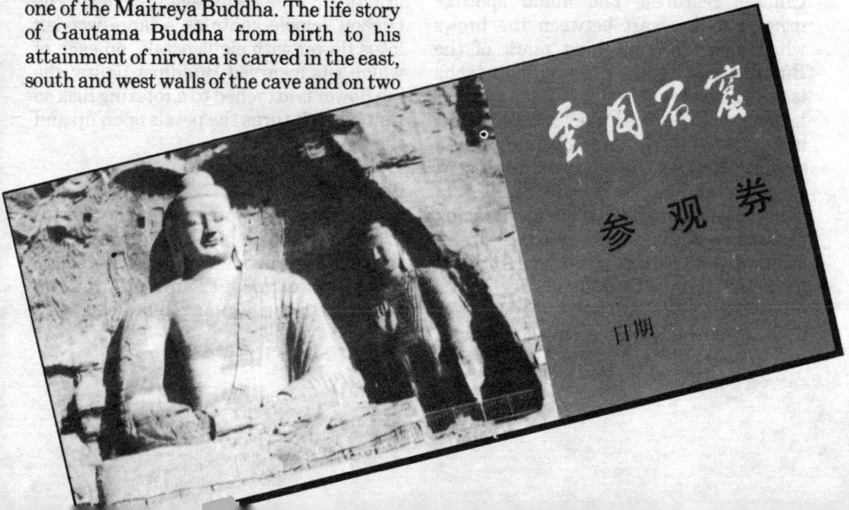

17 represents Maitreya, the future Buddha. The cave walls are covered with thousands of tiny Buddhas; carving them is considered a meritorious act.

The walls of Cave 18 are covered with sculptures of Buddha's disciples, including one near the Buddha's elbow who has a long nose and Caucasian features.

The seated Buddha of Cave 20 is almost 14 metres high. The front wall and the wooden structure which stood in front of it are believed to have crumbled away very early on, and the statue now stands exposed. It is thought to represent the son of Northern Wei Emperor Daiwu, who is said to have been a great patron of Buddhism, but later through the influence of a minister came to favour Taoism. Following a revolt which he blamed on the Buddhists, Daiwu ordered the destruction of their statues, monasteries and temples and the persecution of Buddhists. This lasted from 446 to 452 AD. Daiwu was murdered in 452 AD, though he had apparently repented of his cruel persecution. His son is said to have died of a broken heart, unable to prevent his father's atrocities, and was posthumously awarded the title of emperor. Daiwu's grandson (and successor) restored Buddhism. The statue in Cave 20 has distinctly non-Chinese features. The inlaid spotlike *urna*, a hairy wart between the brows which is a distinguishing mark of the Buddha, is missing. A carved moustache is faintly visible.

Next to Cave 20 is Cave 19, which is the largest cave and contains a 16-metre-high seated statue thought to represent Emperor Daiwu. It is possible he was deliberately carved with his palm facing forwards – the 'no fear' gesture – in an attempt to abate the painful memories of his persecution of Buddhism.

Cave 21 onwards These caves are small and in poor condition. Cave 51 contains a carved pagoda.

Getting There

To get to the caves take bus No 2-4 from the local bus station westward to the terminus on Xinkai Xilu. Then change to bus No 3 for the caves. Admission to the caves is 30 fen.

WUTAI SHAN

Wutai Shan is one of the sacred Buddhist mountains of China. It's actually a cluster of five peaks of which the northern peak, Yedongfeng, is just over 3000 metres high and is known as the roof of northern China.

The temples of Wutai Shan are concentrated at Taihuai. The **Tayuan Temple** is the most prominent, with its large white bottle-shaped pagoda, built during the Ming Dynasty. The **Xiantong Temple** has seven rows of halls totalling over 400 rooms. The **Nanshan Temple**, built during the Yuan Dynasty on the slopes of Nan Mountain to the south of Taihuai, contains frescoes of the fable 'Pilgrimage to the West'. Sixty km from the Nanshan Temple is the **Foguang Temple**, which was originally built during the Northern Wei Dynasty.

Other sights include the marble archway of the **Longquan Temple** and the 26-metre-high Buddha statue and carvings of 500 arhats in the **Shuxiang Temple**. The **Luohou Temple** contains a large wooden lotus flower with eight petals, on each of which sits a carved Buddhist figure; the big flower is attached to a rotating disk so that when it turns the petals open up and the figures appear.

Getting There

There are daily buses from Taiyuan to Wutai Shan. The fare is around Y6 and the trip takes nine hours. The bus stops at Wutai, 95 km away. From Wutai you can get a bus to the Foguang Temple.

THE EAST

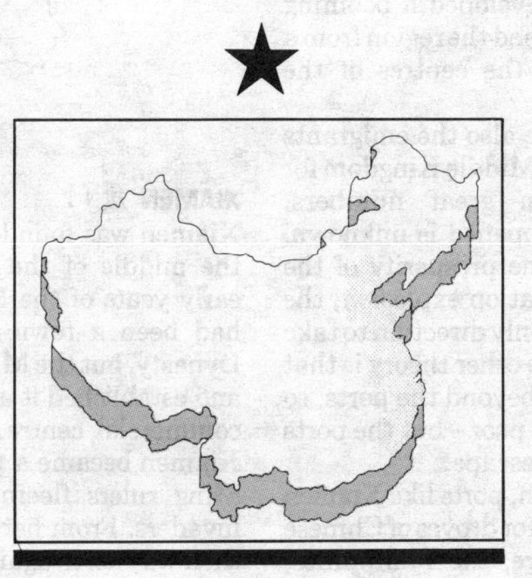

Fujian 福建

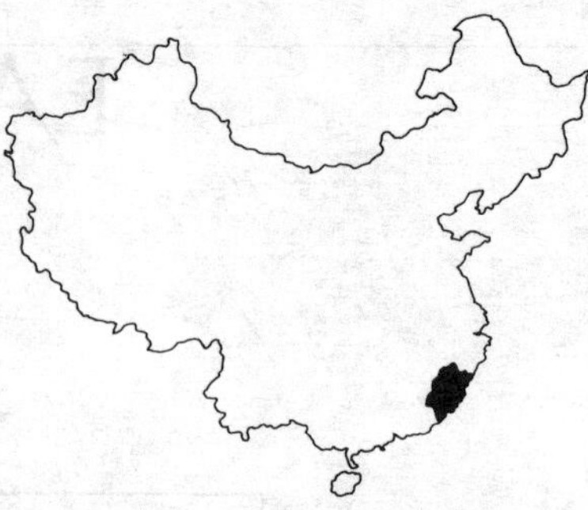

Fujian is an odd place. The coastal region has well-established trading ports which for centuries have enjoyed substantial contact with the outside world. Early on, the great seaports developed a booming trade which transformed the region from a frontier into one of the centres of the Chinese world.

The Fujianese were also the emigrants of China, leaving the Middle Kingdom for South-East Asia in great numbers. Exactly why this happened is unknown. One theory is that the prosperity of the ports caused a population explosion; the land ran out and the only direction to take was out of China. The other theory is that the money never got beyond the ports, so the interior remained poor – but the ports provided a means of escape.

Whatever the reason, ports like Xiamen were stepping-stones for droves of Chinese heading for Singapore, the Philippines, Malaysia and Indonesia. In 1718 the Manchus attempted to put a halt to Chinese emigration with an imperial edict that recalled all subjects from foreign lands. Finding this ineffectual, the court issued another proclamation in 1728 which declared that anyone who did not return to China would be banished and those captured would be executed. Chinese emigration was made lawful only by the Convention of Peking which ended the Fourth Opium War in 1860. Even now many of the original emigrants remit money to Fujian Province, and the Chinese government is campaigning to get them to invest more money in the motherland.

Fujian is a lush, attractive province inhabited by 26 million people. The rugged, mountainous interior of the province is closed to tourists and is said to be very poor, but the lively and prosperous port towns on the narrow coastal strip are open.

XIAMEN 厦门

Xiamen was founded some time around the middle of the 14th century, in the early years of the Ming Dynasty. There had been a town here since the Song Dynasty, but the Ming built the city walls and established it as a major seaport and commercial centre. In the 17th century Xiamen became a place of refuge for the Ming rulers fleeing from the Manchu invaders. From here Ming armies fought their way north again under the command of the pirate-general Koxinga.

The Portuguese, based on an island close to Xiamen, traded surreptitiously with the Chinese for 50 years from 1516 onwards. The Chinese government is supposed to have finally discouraged the Chinese traders by lopping off 90 heads. The Spanish arrived in 1575 and succeeded in building up a substantial trade in raw silk which was shipped to Manila and then to Mexico, but that also came to an end.

The Dutch arrived in 1604 but failed to gain a footing in Xiamen. After seizing Taiwan, they maintained a secret trade from the island Quemoy until Koxinga came into the picture and put an end to their aspirations. The British took the opportunity offered by the Dutch expulsion and opened up trade with the new regime on Taiwan, even establishing a base in Xiamen. However, by the early 1700s trade with westerners was carried on only intermittently and secretly.

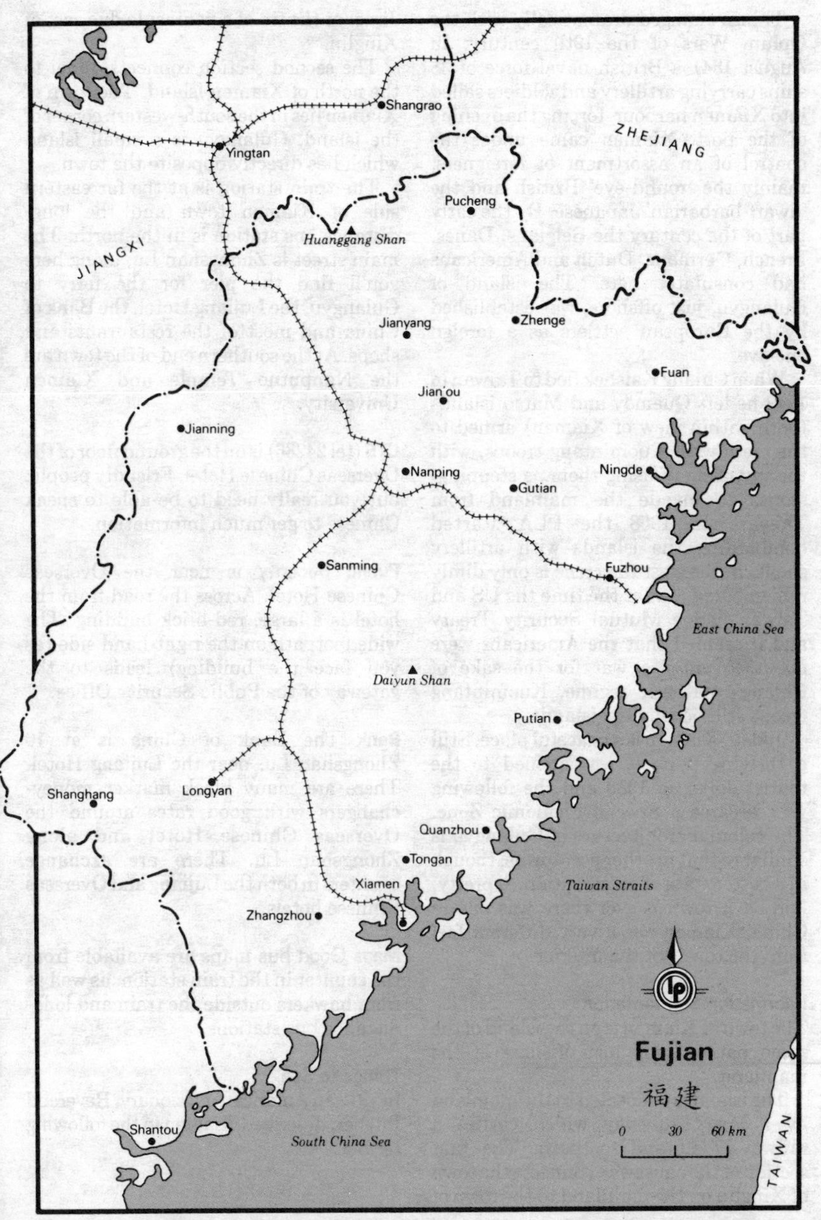
Fujian
福建
ZHEJIANG
JIANGXI
Shangrao
Yingtan
Pucheng
Huanggang Shan
Jianyang
Zhenge
Fuan
Jian'ou
Jianning
Ningde
Nanping
Gutian
Sanming
Fuzhou
East China Sea
Daiyun Shan
Putian
Shanghang
Longyan
Quanzhou
Tongan
Xiamen
Taiwan Straits
Zhangzhou
Shantou
South China Sea
0 30 60 km
TAIWAN

Things changed dramatically with the Opium Wars of the 19th century. In August 1841 a British naval force of 38 ships carrying artillery and soldiers sailed into Xiamen harbour, forcing the opening of the port. Xiamen came under the control of an assortment of foreigners, mainly the 'round-eye' British and the 'dwarf-barbarian' Japanese. By the early part of the century the Belgians, Danes, French, Germans, Dutch and Americans had consulates here. The island of Gulangyu, just offshore, was established by the European settlers as a foreign enclave.

When Chiang Kaishek fled to Taiwan in 1949 he left Quemoy and Matsu islands (both within view of Xiamen) armed to the teeth with Kuomintang troops, with the intention of using them as stepping-stones to invade the mainland from Taiwan. In 1958 the PLA started bombarding the islands with artillery shells. In the west the crisis is only dimly remembered, but at the time the US and Taiwan had a Mutual Security Treaty and it seemed that the Americans were about to enter a war for the sake of Chiang's pathetic regime. Kuomintang troops still occupy the islands.

Today, Xiamen is a peaceful place. Still a thriving port, it was opened to the tourist dollar in 1980 and the following year became a Special Economic Zone. The colonial architecture of Gulangyu is similar to that in other port towns, though in a better state of preservation. A pretty, laid-back town if ever there was one in China, Xiamen has a very different feel from the towns of the interior.

Information & Orientation

The town of Xiamen is on the island of the same name, lying just offshore of the mainland.

The island is connected to the mainland by a long causeway which carries a railway, road and footpath. The first section of the causeway connects the town of Xinglin on the mainland to the town of Jimei at the tip of a peninsula due east of Xinglin.

The second section connects Jimei to the north of Xiamen Island. The town of Xiamen lies in the south-western corner of the island. Gulangyu is a small island which lies directly opposite the town.

The train station is at the far eastern side of Xiamen town and the long-distance bus station is in the north. The main street is Zhongshan Lu; along here you'll find the pier for the ferry to Gulangyu, the Lujiang Hotel, the Bank of China and most of the restaurants and shops. At the southern end of the town are the Nanputuo Temple and Xiamen University.

CTS (tel 24286) is on the ground floor of the Overseas Chinese Hotel. Friendly people, but you really need to be able to speak Chinese to get much information.

Public Security is near the Overseas Chinese Hotel. Across the road from the hotel is a large, red-brick building. The wide footpath on the right-hand side (as you face the building) leads to the gateway of the Public Security Office.

Bank The Bank of China is at 10 Zhongshan Lu, near the Lujiang Hotel. There are many black market money-changers with good rates around the Overseas Chinese Hotel and along Zhongshan Lu. There are exchange counters in both the Lujiang and Overseas Chinese hotels.

Maps Good bus maps are available from the counter in the train station, as well as from hawkers outside the train and long-distance bus stations.

Things to See

In 1912 an American missionary, Reverend Pitcher, described Xiamen in the following terms:

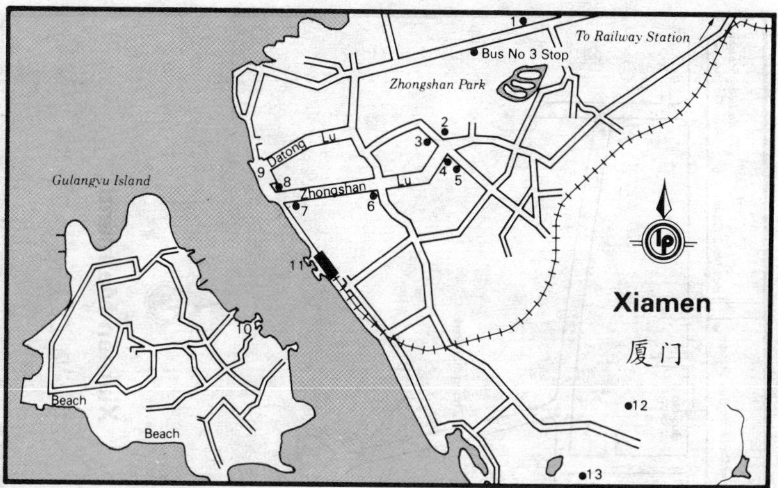

1	Long-distance Bus Station
2	Public Security
3	Post Office
4	Overseas Chinese Hotel (OCH)
5	New Wing of the OCH
6	Ludao Restaurant
7	Bank
8	Lujiang Hotel
9	Ferry Pier (Mainland-Gulangyu)
10	Ferry Pier (Gulangyu-Mainland)
11	Xiamen-Hong Kong Ferry Pier
12	Nanputuo Temple
13	Xiamen University

1	长途汽车站
2	公安局
3	邮局
4	华侨旅社
5	华侨旅社(新楼)
6	绿岛饭店
7	银行
8	鹭江大厦
9	渡船码头 (大陆→鼓浪屿)
10	渡船码头
11	渡船码头 (厦门→香港)
12	南普陀
13	大学

A city! But not the kind of city you have in mind. There are no wide avenues, beautiful residences, magnificent public and mercantile buildings. All is directly opposite to this condition of things. The streets are narrow and crooked . . . ever winding and twisting, descending and ascending, and finally ending in the great nowhere. The wayfaring man, tho' wise, is bound to err therein. There is no street either straight, or one even called 'Straight' in Amoy. Then in addition to the crookedness, they must add another aggravation by making some of them very narrow. There are streets in Amoy so narrow that you cannot carry an open umbrella, but there are others ten, twelve, and fifteen feet wide. Of course they are crowded . . . alive with a teeming throng . . . Here every aspect of Chinese life passes before you, presenting grotesque pictures. Here goes the motley crowd, from the wretched beggar clothed in filthy rags to the stately mandarin adorned in gorgeous array.

Today, the streets are wider. They still teem with people, but the beggars whom Pitcher described as 'spending idle hours picking out the vermin from their dirty and ragged garments' are conspicuous by their absence. The mandarins have been replaced by privileged cadres, or busloads of occidentals out from their tourist fortress for the day. Xiamen conveys an air of prosperity – it's a lively, colourful

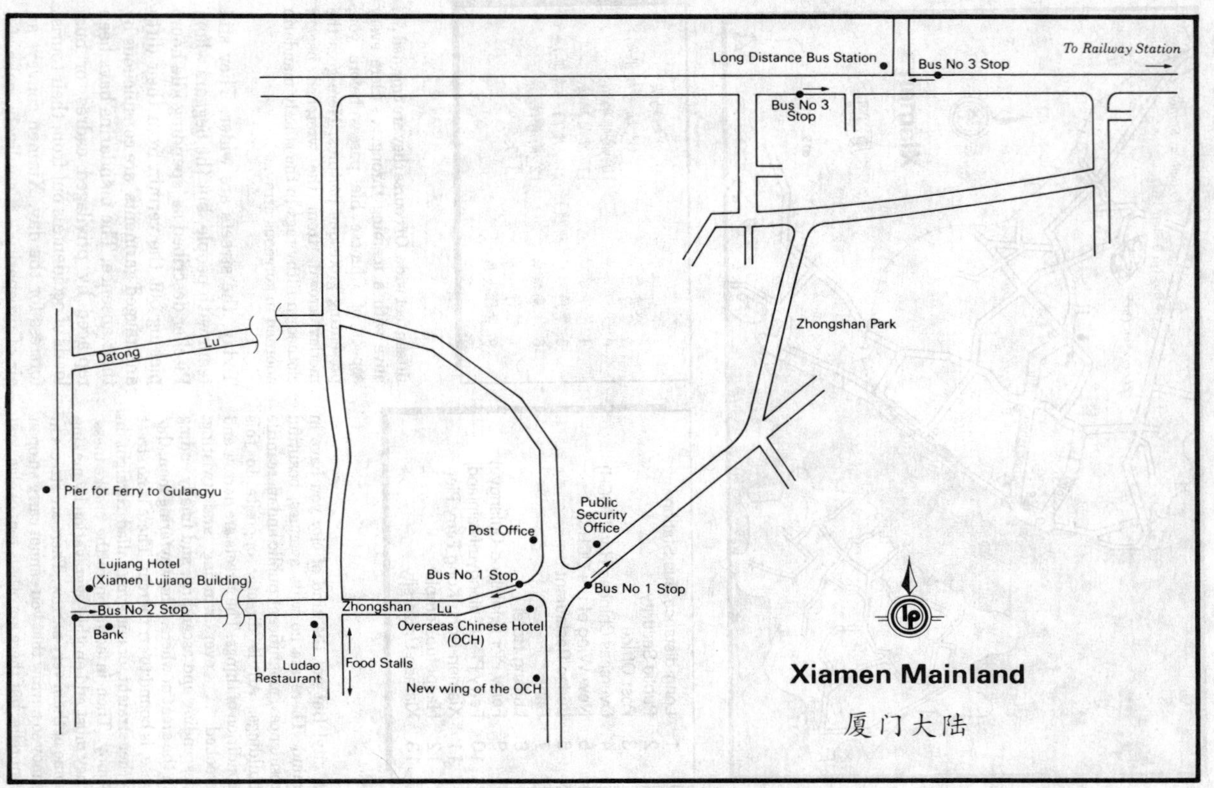
Xiamen Mainland
厦门大陆
To Railway Station
Long Distance Bus Station
Bus No 3 Stop
Bus No 3 Stop
Zhongshan Park
Datong Lu
Pier for Ferry to Gulangyu
Public Security Office
Post Office
Bus No 1 Stop
Bus No 1 Stop
Lujiang Hotel (Xiamen Lujiang Building)
Bus No 2 Stop
Bank
Zhongshan Lu
Overseas Chinese Hotel (OCH)
Ludao Restaurant
Food Stalls
New wing of the OCH

town of 300,000 people with many reminders of bygone turmoils.

Gulangyu Island

Neither Gulangyu nor Xiamen were considered paradise when the westerners landed here in the 1840s. However, by 1860 they had well-established residencies on Gulangyu, and as the years rolled by, they put up churches, hospitals, post and telegraph offices, libraries, hotels and consulates. The island was officially designated an International Foreign Settlement in 1903, and a municipal council was set up to govern it with a police force of Sikhs. Today the only reminders of the settlement are the charming colonial buildings which blanket the island – and the sound of classical piano wafting from the villa-style houses!

A ferry to Gulangyu leaves from the pier just north of Xiamen's Lujiang Hotel. You don't pay to go from the mainland to the island. On the way back you buy a counter at the pier on the Gulangyu side and drop it into a box at the barrier gate before boarding the ferry. Ferries run from about 5 am to midnight. Transport around Gulangyu is by foot; there are no buses, cars or pedicabs. It's a small island and the sights are within easy tramping of each other.

'In the past few years', says one of the tourist leaflets, 'many foreign visitors . . . plunged into the sea, indulging themselves in the waves, or lay on the golden sandy beach, being caressed by the sunshine, and made friends with the young people of Gulangyu. When the foreigners go away, they say: I am sure to come back again'. China is hardly a sun-worshipper's paradise but there are two beaches on Gulangyu, the East Beach and the West Beach. The first is overpopulated, with placid and scungy water; the second belongs to the Army and is off-limits, as I discovered when three PLA guards with machine-guns picked me up and escorted me back to base where my bag was checked. On the beaches are a number of old, disused concrete blockhouses which appear to have ringed the entire island at one time.

Sunlight Rock is the highest point on Gulangyu. It's an easy climb up the steps to the top of the rock where there's an observation platform and a great view across Gulangyu and the harbour. The Zheng Chenggong (Koxinga) Memorial Hall is at the foot of Sunlight Rock. It's a large colonial building, and the verandahs of the upper storeys afford a fine view across the island. Part of the exhibition is dedicated to the Dutch in Taiwan and the rest to Koxinga throwing them out. No English captions but still worth a look. The hall is open daily around 8 to 11 am and 2 to 5 pm.

Koxinga

When the Ming Dynasty collapsed in 1644, under the weight of the Manchu invasion, the court fled to the south of China. A melange of Ming princes assumed the title of emperor one after the other, in the hope of driving out the barbarians and ascending the Dragon Throne. One of the more successful attempts (which focused on the port of Xiamen) was by an army led by Zheng Chenggong, known to the west as Koxinga.

Koxinga's origins are a mystery. His father is said to have run away to Japan and married a Japanese woman, who gave birth to Koxinga. The father returned to China as a pirate, raiding the coasts of Guangdong and Fujian, even taking possession of Xiamen. Exactly how and why Koxinga came to be allied with the defunct Ming princes is unknown. One story goes that a prince took a liking to Koxinga when he was young and made him a noble. Another story goes that Koxinga was a pirate like his father, a local warlord who for some reason teamed up with one of the refugee princes.

Koxinga used Xiamen as a base for his attacks on the Manchus to the north. He is said to have had under his command a fleet of 8000 war junks, 240,000 fighting men, and all the pirates who infested the coast of southern China – a combined force of 800,000. He is supposed to have used a stone lion weighing 600 pounds to test the strength of his soldiers; those strong enough to lift and carry it were enlisted in the vanguard of the army. They wore iron

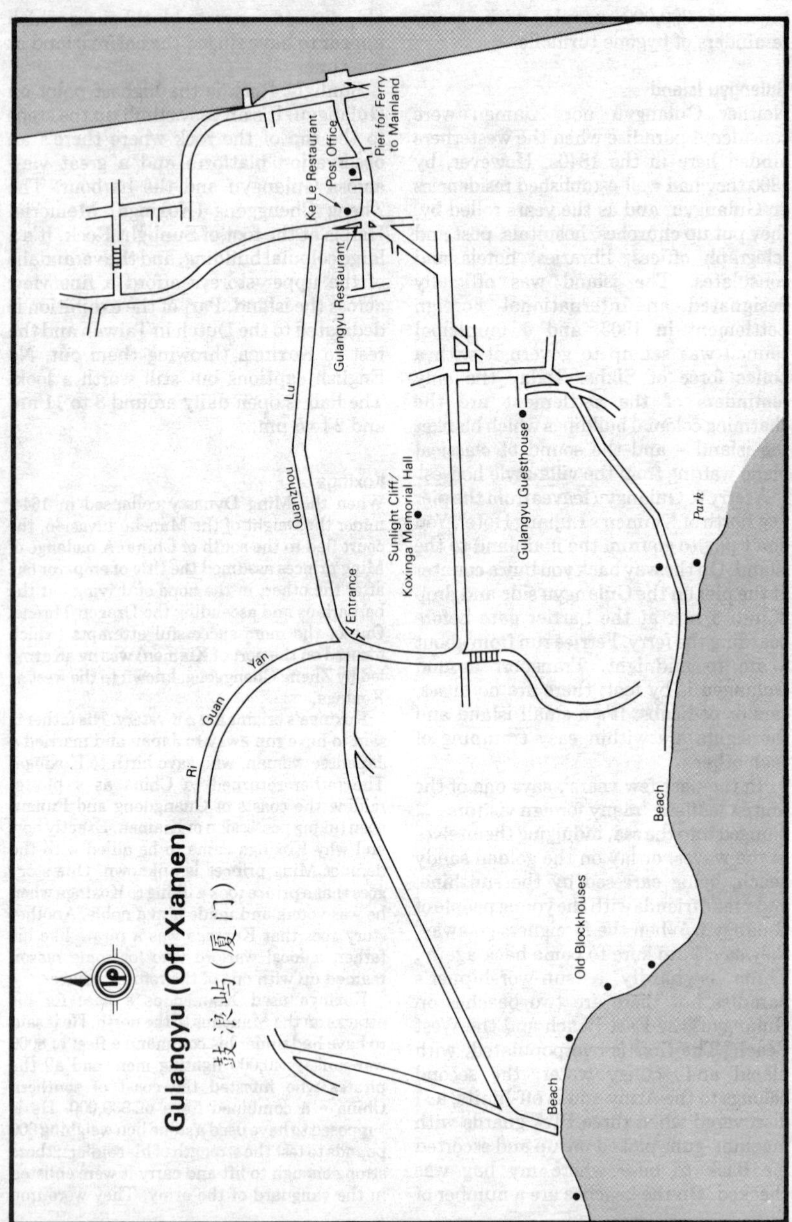
Gulangyu (Off Xiamen)
鼓浪屿(厦门)
Pier for Ferry to Mainland
Post Office
Ke Le Restaurant
Gulangyu Restaurant
Quanzhou
Lu
Entrance
Sunlight Cliff/
Koxinga Memorial Hall
Gulangyu Guesthouse
Park
Beach
Old Blockhouses
Beach
Ri
Guan
Yan

masks and armour, and carried long-handled swords with which to maim the legs of enemy cavalry horses.

Koxinga's army fought its way to the Grand Canal, but was forced to retreat to Xiamen. In 1661 he set sail with his army for Taiwan, then held by the Dutch. He attacked the Dutch settlement at Casteel Zeelandia, not far from present-day Taiwan on the west coast; after a six-month siege the Dutch surrendered. Koxinga hoped to use Taiwan as a stepping-stone from which to invade the mainland and restore the Ming Dynasty to power, but a year or two later he died. The Manchus finally conquered the island in the early 1680s.

While Koxinga may have been a pirate and a running-dog of the feudal Ming princes, he is regarded as a national hero because he recovered Taiwan from the Dutch – roughly analogous to the mainland's ambition to recover the island from the Kuomintang. Those in China who reinterpret (rewrite?) history seem to have forgotten that Koxinga was forced to retreat to Taiwan after his defeats on the mainland. The 'liberation' of Taiwan was superfluous to the story, which more closely parallels that of the Kuomintang, a regime which fled to Taiwan but awaits the day when it will invade and seize control of the mainland.

Nanputuo Temple

On the southern outskirts of Xiamen town, the Nanputuo Temple is a Buddhist temple built during the Tang Dynasty more than 1000 years ago. It was ruined in a battle during the Ming Dynasty but was rebuilt during the Qing.

You enter the temple through Tian Wang (Heavenly King) Hall, where the welcoming Maitreya, the fat Buddha, sits cross-legged exposing his protruding belly. On either side are a pair of guardians which protect the Buddha. Standing behind Maitreya is Wei Tuo, another Buddhist deity who safeguards the doctrine. He holds a stick which points to the ground – traditionally, this indicates that the temple is rich and can provide visiting monks with board and lodging (if the stick is held horizontally it means the temple is poor, a polite way of saying find somewhere else).

Behind Tian Wang Hall is a courtyard and on either side are the Drum and Bell towers. In front of the courtyard is Daxiongbao (Great Heroic Treasure) Hall, a two-storey building housing three buddhas representing Sakyamuni in his past, present and future lives. On the lotus-flower base of the buddha figure is carved the biography of Sakyamuni and the story of Xuan Zhuang, the monk who made the pilgrimage to India to bring back the Buddhist scriptures.

Inlaid in the buildings to the left and right of Daxiongbao Hall are eight stone tablets, inscribed in the handwriting of Emperor Qian Long of the Qing Dynasty. Four tablets are inscribed in Chinese and the others in the peculiar Manchu script. All record the Manchu government's suppression of the 'Tian Di Society' uprisings. The tablets were originally erected in front of the temple in 1789, but were inlaid in the walls when the temple was enlarged around 1920.

The Dabei (Great Compassion) Hall contains four bodhisattvas. Worshippers throw divining sticks at the feet of the statues in order to seek heavenly guidance.

At the rear of the temple complex is a pavilion built in 1936 which stores Buddhist scriptures, calligraphy, wood-carvings, ivory sculptures and other works of art – unfortunately it's closed to visitors. Behind the temple is a rocky outcrop gouged with poetic graffiti; the big red character carved on the large boulder simply means 'Buddha'.

To get to the temple, take bus No 1 from outside the Overseas Chinese Hotel, or bus No 2 from the intersection of Zhongshan Lu and Lujiang Lu.

Xiamen University

The university is next to the Nanputuo Temple, and was established with Overseas Chinese funds. The older buildings facing the shoreline are not without a certain charm, though most of the campus is a scattered collection of brick and concrete blocks. The entrance to the campus is next to the bus No 1 and bus No 2 terminus.

The Museum of Anthropology on the university grounds is worth a visit if you're down this way. It has a large collection of prehistoric stone implements and pottery from China, Taiwan and Malaya as well as human fossil remains. There are collections of porcelains, bronzes, jade and stone implements, coins, and inscribed Shang Dynasty bones and tortoise shells. You'll also see some fine calligraphy, exquisite paintings, glazed clay figurines, sculptures, clothing and ornaments from the Shang and Zhou through the Ming and Qing dynasties. After entering the campus, turn right at the first crossroads and walk until you come to a roundabout. The museum is the old stone building on the left with the cannon at the front.

Jimei School Village

This much-touted tourist attraction is across the causeway on the mainland north of Xiamen Island. The school is a conglomeration and expansion of a number of separate schools and colleges set up here by Tan Kahkee (1874-1961). Tan was a native of the area who migrated to Singapore when he was young and rose to become a rich industrialist. He set a fine example to other Overseas Chinese by returning some of that wealth to the mother country – the school now has around 20,000 students. The Chinese-style architecture has a certain appeal which may make a trip worthwhile.

Places to Stay

The *Overseas Chinese Hotel* is at the east end of Zhongshan Lu. The old building has triple rooms at Y9 per person; or you can have the room to yourself for Y27. Dorm beds are around Y3. The new wing, and the even more immaculate newer wing (a glossy Hong Kong transplant) have doubles from Y60. From the railway station take bus No 1. From the bus station it's probably better to walk – about 20 minutes – or take a pedicab.

The *Xiamen Lujiang Building* (tel 22212) is at 54 Lujiang Lu near the Gulangyu ferry pier. It once had the run-down charisma of an old colonial building gone to rack and ruin, but renovations have destroyed the atmosphere. Singles are Y75 and doubles Y110. There's a roof-top coffee garden which is very relaxing with views across the harbour. Bus No 3 from the train station and long-distance bus station terminates at the Gulangyu ferry pier outside the hotel.

The good news is that there is a *floating hotel*, converted from a Danish cruise ship, moored in the harbour between the mainland and Gulangyu. Double rooms start at Y12. More expensive rooms have windows and private bathrooms. An impressive cafeteria serves Chinese meals. A free launch connects the boat with the mainland, and operates three times per hour from 5 am to midnight. The ship has been highly recommended by travellers.

Places to Eat

Xiamen is Seafood City, with many seafood restaurants along Zhongshan Lu and its side streets. It's hardly worthwhile to recommend any one place in particular; just look around until you find something that looks good. Lots of fresh pineapples, frogs, peppers and the like.

On Gulangyu, try upstairs at the *Gulangyu Restaurant* for tasty seafood in generous servings – don't be put off by the grotty ground floor. There are many other places on Gulangyu serving lots of squid, crab, shrimp and sea-snails.

Getting There & Away

Air Some useful connections include flights from Xiamen to Shanghai, Beijing and Canton (Y126). There are four flights a week to Hong Kong (Y225). Book tickets at CTS in the Overseas Chinese Hotel.

Bus Buses to the towns on the south-east coast depart from the long distance bus station. Destinations include Fuzhou

(Y10.80, twice a day); Quanzhou (Y4, about a dozen buses a day); and Shantou (Y10.50, once daily). You can also get buses straight through to Canton and Shenzhen.

There are many privately run air-con buses with ticket offices in the vicinity of the bus station. Destinations include Quanzhou (Y5), Fuzhou (Y15) and Shantou (Y15). Air-con is a misnomer since the Chinese insist on opening all the windows. The addition of extra seats down the aisles makes the buses formidably crowded and they usually don't leave on time. The air-con buses are no more comfortable than the ordinary buses except, perhaps, on a rainy day.

Rail The train line from Xiamen heads north and connects with the main Shanghai-Canton line at the Yingtan junction. Another line runs from Yingtan to Fuzhou.

From Xiamen there are direct trains to Yingtan, Shanghai, Fuzhou and possibly Canton. The train to Fuzhou does a circuitous route, and unless you want to travel by night you're better off taking the bus.

Tourist-price fares from Xiamen to Shanghai are Y39 hard-seat, Y67 hard-sleeper and Y131 soft-sleeper.

Boat Ships to Hong Kong depart from the Passenger Station of Amoy Port Administration on Tongwen Lu, about 10 minutes walk from the Liujiang Hotel. There is a ticket office at the Passenger Station. There are two ships from Xiamen to Hong Kong: the *Jimei* which departs every Friday, and the *Gulangyu* which departs every Tuesday. Fares start at Y64.80 for a seat; Y76.80 3rd class; Y86.40 2nd class; Y96 1st class; and Y156 to Y180 special class. The trip takes 24 hours.

Getting Around

Much of the town can easily be seen on foot. The bus service is extensive but the buses are always extremely crowded. Pedicabs and auto-rickshaws congregate outside the train station, the long-distance bus station and the Gulangyu ferry pier on the mainland side. Taxis are available from the train station and from the tourist hotels. Bus No 1 will take you from the train station to the Overseas Chinese Hotel. Bus No 3 runs from the train station and long-distance bus station to the Lujiang Hotel. There are no buses, cars or pedicabs on Gulangyu – feet only.

QUANZHOU 泉州

Long before the large port of Xiamen became a centre for both domestic and foreign trade, there was another city in the vicinity known as Zaiton, which was a major port until the end of the 14th century. There is some debate as to the site of this port but it's generally accepted to be the present-day city of Quanzhou, to the north-east of Xiamen.

The port was probably one of the

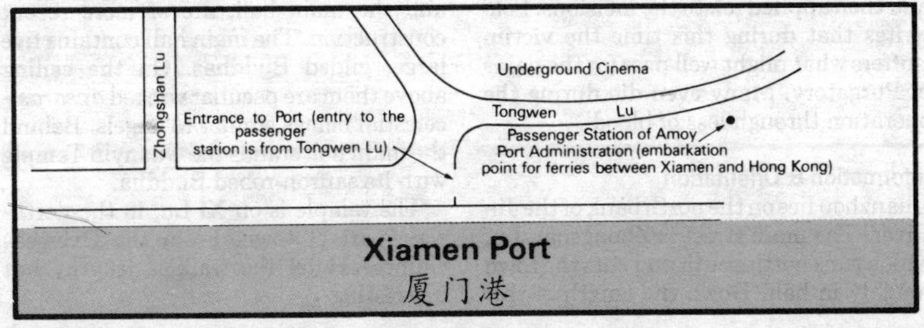

greatest commercial centres in the world; from it Chinese silks, satins, sugar and spices were exported to India, Arabia and western Asia. Kublai Khan's invasion fleets set sail from here for Japan and Java. Marco Polo visited the port and raved about it as:

> a great resort of ships and merchandise . . . for one spice ship that goes to Alexandria or elsewhere to pick up pepper for export to Christendom, Zaiton is visited by a hundred. For you must know that it is one of the two ports in the world with the biggest flow of merchandise.

With tariffs imposed on all imported goods, Zaiton was an important source of refills for the Great Khan's treasury. Zaiton's prosperity began to decline as a result of fierce fighting in the middle of the 14th century, towards the end of the Yuan Dynasty. When the first Ming emperor, Hong Wu, came to power his isolationist policies reduced foreign trade to a trickle. As if that wasn't enough, the fate of Quanzhou was finally sealed by the silting up of the harbour. Today there are few reminders of its former glory. Nevertheless, it's a lively little town of narrow streets, wooden houses, and numerous shops and restaurants.

Polo, by the way, remembers Zaiton as a place where many people came to have figures 'pricked out on their bodies with needles'. Marco had seen these tattooists at work elsewhere on his travels; the 13th-century method involved being tied hand and foot and held down by two assistants while the tattooist pricked out the images and then applied ink to the incisions. Polo writes that during this time the victim 'suffers what might well pass for the pains of Purgatory. Many even die during the operation through loss of blood'.

Information & Orientation

Quanzhou lies on the north bank of the Jin River. The main street is Zhongshan Lu, which runs north-south and cuts the town roughly in half. Down the length of this street or in the immediate vicinity you'll find most of the shops and restaurants, the long-distance bus station, the Overseas Chinese Hotel and the tourist facilities. The Kaiyuan Temple, which is the chief sight of Quanzhou, lies in the north-western part of the town. There's a scattering of sights in the hills to the north-east.

CTS (tel 2366) is on the ground floor of the Overseas Chinese Hotel. Friendly people, but they don't speak much English.

Public Security is at 334-336 Dong Jie, a few minutes walk east of the intersection with Zhongshan Lu.

Bank Change money at the Bank of China at the corner of Jiuyi Lu and Zhongshan Lu, just north of the Overseas Chinese Hotel.

Post There is a post office at 75 Xiamen Jie and the Overseas Chinese Hotel.

CAAC There are no flights from Quanzhou; the nearest airport is at Xiamen. Flight tickets can be booked at the CTS office in Quanzhou.

Kaiyuan Temple

This temple is the main attraction of Quanzhou and is distinguished by its pair of tall pagodas. The temple was founded in the 7th century during the Tang Dynasty and reached its peak under the Song when 1000 monks lived here. The present buildings, including the pagodas and the main hall, are of more recent construction. The main hall contains five large, gilded Buddhas. On the ceiling above them are peculiar winged *apsaras* – celestial beings similar to angels. Behind the main hall stands the Guanyin Temple with its saffron-robed Buddha.

The temple is on Xi Lu, in the north-west part of town. From the Overseas Chinese Hotel the walk is lengthy but interesting.

1 Mosque
2 Temple
3 Overseas Chinese Hotel (OCH)
4 Long-distance Bus Station
5 Seafood Restaurant
6 Bank
7 Clock Tower
8 Kaiyuan Temple & Museum of Overseas Communication History
9 Public Security
10 Post Office

Museum of Overseas Communications History

This museum is in the grounds of the Kaiyuan Temple behind the eastern pagoda. It contains one of *the* attractions of Quanzhou: the enormous hull of a Song Dynasty sea-going junk. The hull was excavated near Quanzhou.

On display are photos, coins and artefacts found in the wreck. A map shows the routes taken by Chinese junks and their points of contact with foreign countries, extending all the way from Japan to the east coast of Africa and as far south as Madagascar. The tombstones belong to Arab traders who lived in Quanzhou when it was a booming seaport.

The remains of the ship display the characteristic features of Chinese ship construction: square bow and stern and flat bottom (no keel), and the division by bulkheads into many watertight compartments. The Quanzhou wreck has at least 11 such compartments, an achievement unknown in Europe at the time. A highly efficient stern rudder had been developed several centuries before, and a mariner's compass was in widespread use by the 11th century. Both the compass and the rudder had a long period of development in China from the Han period onwards. In comparison the earliest western record of the rudder (northern Europe) and the compass (southern Europe) dates from the late 12th century.

The overseas trade of late Tang and Song China was closely tied to the river trade. Ocean-going ships brought goods to the great ports to be carried by inland river routes, which were slower but cheaper than the land routes and ideal for heavy loads like grain and salt. Canals were built and existing ones extended to link up the major river systems, which made possible the nationwide trade of the Song period. So much trade developed that some of the cities along the water routes (such as Yangzhou on the Grand Canal) developed into big consumer and commercial centres in their own right. Zaiton became the major seaport of the Song period.

Overseas trade revolved around the import and export of luxury goods. The chief imports were aromatics, spices, dyes, cotton fabrics, gold, swords, rhinoceros horn, ivory, ebony, precious stones, peacock and kingfisher feathers for use as insignia of rank – and slaves. Slaves were mainly Africans, who were usually employed as domestic servants in wealthy households. The central government encouraged the export of the highly prized Chinese silk and porcelain but was unsuccessful in halting the drain of precious metals, mainly gold, silver and copper. By the second decade of Southern Song rule a fifth of government revenue came from taxes on overseas trade. This encouraged them to continue and expand the trade. The Chinese began to take an active part in long-distance trade instead of depending on foreign traders to come to China. Chinese-built ships had been used on long-distance voyages for centuries but it was mainly Arabs, Persians and other foreigners who manned them.

The overseas trade replaced revenue which was no longer obtainable from the north, the Song having fled south from a northern invasion. The Southern Song government offered rewards for new inventions in ship-building, and used the tax on sea trade to develop a navy which would protect merchant shipping along the coast and at the entrance of the Yangtse – mainly against the northern invaders who had been halted at the river. China became a sea power, both in the sense of its ocean-going trade and its effective naval defence.

Chinese sea power effectively came to an end with the establishment of the Ming Dynasty under Emperor Hong Wu in the 14th century. Foreign trade was banned, possibly because the emperor feared conspiracies carried out under the guise of trade. Some trade did continue, but in an illicit form, and the government lost the customs revenue it might have had. The great exception to the isolationist policies of the Ming period occurred during the rule of the second Ming emperor Yong Le.

Between 1405 and 1433 Yong Le dispatched seven enormous maritime expeditions led by the palace eunuch Zheng He. The expeditions were court enterprises, not government ventures, and Zheng was the personal representative of the emperor. The purpose of the expeditions was complex: possibly to impress the southern Asian countries with Chinese power, to expand the maritime trade, and to extend Chinese knowledge of the outside world with the intention of founding colonies or a commercial empire. The fleets sailed to South-East Asia, Sumatra, Java, India and the Persian Gulf, and ventured up the Red Sea and the east coast of Africa.

These expeditions came to an end with the death of Yong Le – only 64 years before Vasco da Gama finally sailed around the tip of Africa in 1497 on his way to India. One reason may have been the expense, another the government bureaucrats who were jealous of the eunuchs' power in the imperial court – so much so that in the 1470s the official records of the voyages were

burnt. The restoration and improvement of the Grand Canal may also have contributed to the demise of the expeditions. With the inland trade route re-opened, coastal trade dropped off and a powerful naval escort was no longer needed. One by one the shipyards closed down and China's days as a maritime power came to a halt.

Qingjing Mosque

On Tonghuai Jie, just south of the Overseas Chinese Hotel, is the shell of a mosque originally built in 1009 during the Song Dynasty to serve Quanzhou's large Muslim population. This is the oldest mosque in eastern China. There's a small museum attached with explanations in Arabic, English and Chinese.

Temples

The town has its share of temples in various stages of repair. One is in the park opposite the Overseas Chinese Hotel; get up early to watch the tai chi workouts. Another temple is on Zhenfusi Lu, a side street which runs west off the square at the north end of Zhongshan Lu; it's now used as a middle-school library. More interesting is the active temple next to the mosque.

Places to Stay & Eat

The *Overseas Chinese Hotel* is close to Zhongshan Lu, a 15-minute walk from the long-distance bus station – see the map for directions. They'll give you a bed in a three-bed room for Y13.50 with television and own bathroom. Double rooms cost from Y72.

Two blocks to the west is the *Chen Chow Hotel*, which is mainly for Chinese but may take foreigners. They charge about Y5 for a bed in a triple room.

Quanzhou is a great place for seafood – perhaps better than Xiamen – with a couple of seafood restaurants in the vicinity of the Overseas Chinese Hotel. Just look around until you find something you like.

Getting There & Away

Air There may be regular CAAC flights between Quanzhou and Fuzhou by the time this book is out. If not, the nearest airport is at Xiamen. There is no CAAC office in Quanzhou but flights can be booked at CTS in the Overseas Chinese Hotel.

Bus The long-distance bus station is in the south-east part of town. Buses to Xiamen cost Y4 and take 2½ hours; there are about a dozen buses a day. The interesting ride takes you through villages with large colonnaded stone houses ostentatious enough to suggest that they're being built with Overseas Chinese money. Buses to Fuzhou cost Y7 and take six hours; there are several departures a day.

Ticket offices for air-con buses are in the vicinity of the Overseas Chinese Hotel. There are several departures daily to Xiamen (Y6), Fuzhou (Y12), Canton (Y65) and Shenzhen (Y65).

Rail The nearest railheads are at Xiamen and Fuzhou.

Getting Around

There are no city buses in Quanzhou. Buses to nearby places leave from the square at the north end of Zhongshan Lu. Transport within the city is by Quanzhou-style pedicab – a bicycle with a little wooden sidecart which seats two people. The drivers are predatory!

AROUND QUANZHOU

North of the town is an unusual stubby **statue of Lao Tzu**, the legendary founder of Taoism. The Chinese say that Kuomintang soldiers used the statue as target practice but there's no sign of bullet holes.

North of the statue is **Ling Mountain**. The Buddhist caves on the mountain were destroyed during the Cultural Revolution, though some people still pray in front of the empty spaces where the statues used to be. According to an old woman who lives on the mountain, two Red Guard factions fought each other here during the Cultural Revolution using mortars!

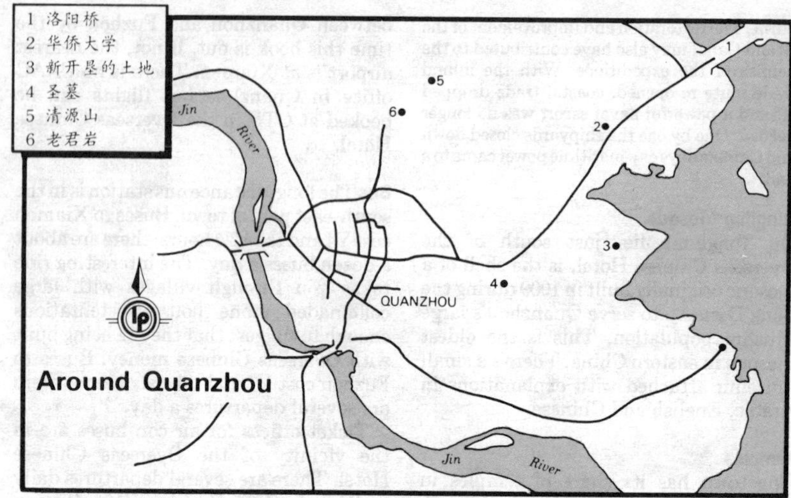

1 Ancient Bridges
2 Overseas Chinese Hotel
3 Land Reclaimed during the Cultural Revolution
4 Muslim Tombs
5 Ling Mountain
6 Lao Tzu Statue

The 'rock that moves' is situated on the mountain (there's a large painting of it hanging in the dining room of the Overseas Chinese Hotel). It's one of these nicely shaped and balanced rocks which wobbles when you give it a nudge – I'm told that to see it move you have to place a stick or a piece of straw lengthwise between the rock and the ground and watch it bend as someone pushes on the rock.

The Ling Shan **Muslim tomb** is thought to be the resting place of two Muslim missionaries who came to China during the Tang Dynasty. There are a number of Muslim burial sites on the north-east and south-east outskirts of Quanzhou containing the remains of thousands of Muslims who once lived at Quanzhou. The earliest dated tombstone belongs to a man who died in 1171. Many tombstone inscriptions are written in Chinese, Arabic and Persian giving names, dates of birth and quotations from the Koran.

East of Quanzhou is a peninsula built by hand during the Cultural Revolution. The 7000 mu (about 470 hectares) of land is now used for agriculture. A village on the northern side of the peninsula used to be a separate island before the land was reclaimed.

Due north of the peninsula is the **Overseas Chinese University**, originally built to attract Hong Kongers and Taiwanese (only the first group came) to study in China. Like universities elsewhere in China it was closed down during the Cultural Revolution. North-east of the university are two bridges built several hundred years ago and still intact.

FUZHOU 福州

In the 1320s the Franciscan friar Odoric spent three years in China on a missionary venture. He came via India and after landing in Canton travelled eastwards, where he:

came unto a city named Fuzo, which contains 30 miles in circuit, wherein are exceeding great and fair cocks, and all their hens are as white as the very snow, having wool instead of feathers, like unto sheep. It is a most stately and beautiful city and stands upon the sea.

Odoric's woolly hens are in fact what poultry-breeders call Fleecy Persians, though the Chinese call them Velvet-Hair Fowls. While the Chinese still breed chickens in makeshift pens in their backyards, Fuzhou seems to have lost both its fame as a poultry farm and as a stately and beautiful city.

Although the thriving port of Fuzhou is the capital of Fujian and exports much of the region's agricultural produce, the city is a letdown after colourful towns like Xiamen and Quanzhou. Fuzhou looks very much like the dull industrial towns of the north, with long avenues, concrete block buildings and expansive suburbs, yet surprisingly the economy is still based heavily on fishing and agriculture.

Fuzhou was founded in the 6th century AD and rapidly became a commercial port specializing in the export of tea. The name actually means 'wealthy town' and it was second only to Quanzhou. Marco Polo passed through Fuzhou towards the end of the 13th century, several years before Odoric's visit, and described the town as:

an important centre of commerce in pearls and other precious stones, because it is much frequented by ships from India bringing merchants who traffic in the Indies. Moreover it is not far from the port of Zaiton (Quanzhou) on the ocean, a great resort of ships and merchandise from India; and from Zaiton ships come . . . as far as the city of Fu-chau (Fuzhou). By this means many precious wares are imported from India. There is no lack here of anything that the human body requires to sustain life. There are gardens of great beauty and charm, full of excellent fruit. In short it is a good city and so well provided with every amenity that it is a veritable marvel.

Despite its prosperity, Fuzhou had a reputation for revolt. Marco noted that the city was garrisoned by a large number of soldiers, as there were frequent rebellions in the district. Nevertheless, Fuzhou's status as an important trading centre and port continued over the centuries and quickly drew the attention of the western traders who began to arrive in the area in the 16th century. They couldn't set up shop until 200 years later, when the Treaty of Nanking ended the Second Opium War and opened Fuzhou to foreign traders in 1842.

Oddly, Fuzhou had a long history as a centre of Chinese Christianity. Marco Polo describes a Christian sect that worshipped here and writes that his father and uncle:

enquired from what source they had received their faith and their rule, and their informants replied: 'From our forefathers'. It came out that they had in a certain temple of theirs three pictures representing three apostles of the 70 who went through the world preaching. And they declared that it was these three who had instructed their ancestors in the faith long ago, and that it had been preserved among them for 700 years.

The Christians who Polo met were probably Nestorians, descendants of a Syrian sect whose religion had been carried into China via the Silk Road. What eventually happened to the Nestorian Christians in Fuzhou is unknown, although Marco claims there were 700,000 such households in southern China – probably an exaggeration. A more recent addition to the Christian community were the converts made by the western missionaries during the 19th and 20th centuries, since Fuzhou was a centre of both Catholic and Protestant missionary activity.

Information & Orientation

Most of Fuzhou lies on the northern bank of the Min River, sprawling northwards in a roughly rectangular shape. The railway

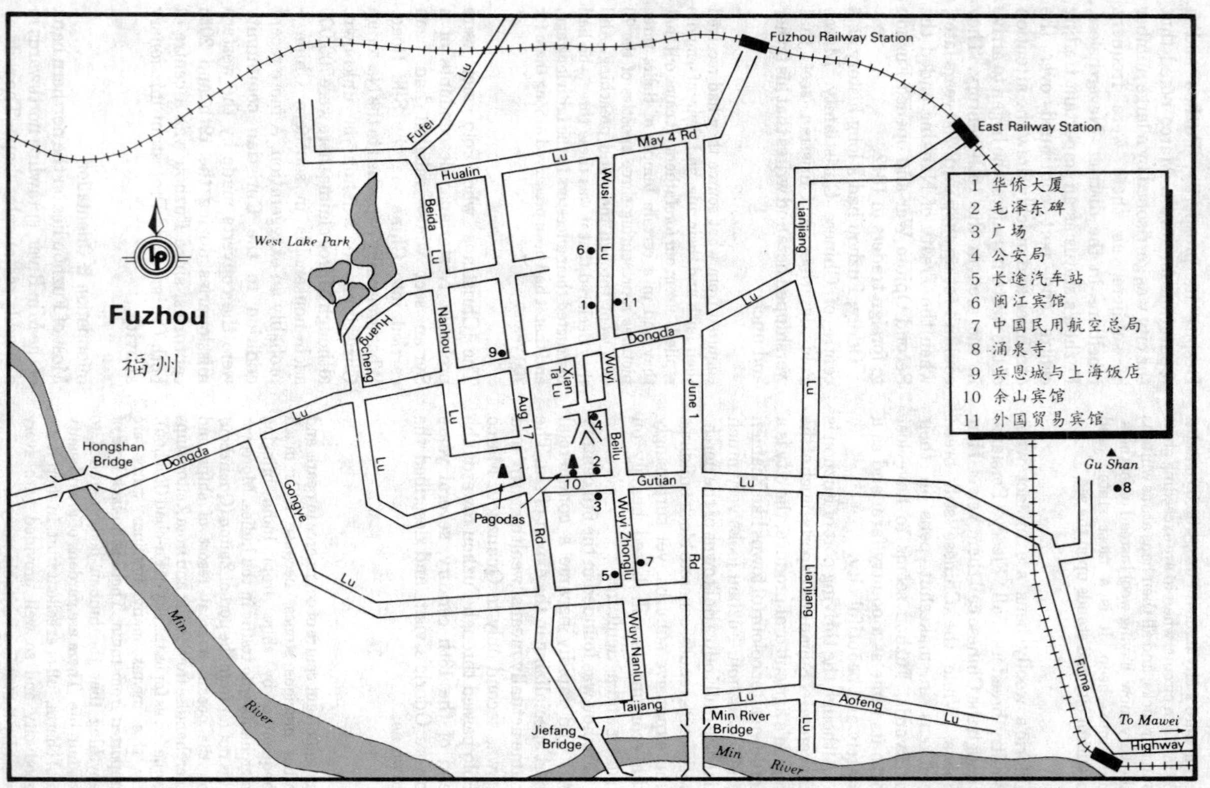
Fuzhou
福州
1 华侨大厦
2 毛泽东碑
3 广场
4 公安局
5 长途汽车站
6 闽江宾馆
7 中国民用航空总局
8 涌泉寺
9 兵恩城与上海饭店
10 余山宾馆
11 外国贸易宾馆
Fuzhou Railway Station
East Railway Station
Gu Shan
To Mawei
Highway
Fuma
Fufei
Lu
May 4 Rd
Lu
Hualin
Beida
Lu
West Lake Park
Wusi
Lu
Lianjiang
Lu
Dongda
Huangcheng
Nanhou
Wuyi
Xian
Ta Lu
June 1
Lu
Aug 17
Lu
Beilu
Hongshan Bridge
Dongda
Lu
Gongye
Gutian
Lu
Pagodas
Rd
Wuyi Zhonglu
Rd
Lianjiang
Lu
Wuyi Nanlu
Taijiang
Lu
Aofeng
Lu
Min River Bridge
Lu
Jiefang Bridge
Min River
Min River

1 Overseas Chinese Hotel
2 Mao Statue
3 Square
4 Public Security
5 Long-distance Bus Station
6 Min Jiang Hotel
7 CAAC
8 Yongquan Monastery
9 Banyan City & Shanghai Restaurant
10 Yu Shan Hotel
11 Foreign Trade Centre Hotel

station lies on the north-eastern outskirts of the city and the long-distance bus station is at the southern end. The few tourist attractions are scattered about. Most of the activity is in the central part of town, roughly between the bus and railway stations, and here you'll find the hotel and tourist facilities.

There are three main roads running north-south and approximately parallel to each other, two of which cross the Min River over old stone bridges. The main road between these two is divided into sections: Wusi Lu, Wuyi Beilu, Wuyi Zhonglu and Wuyi Nanlu. Along this stretch are the long-distance bus station, the CAAC office and the Overseas Chinese Hotel.

Running east-west and cutting across all three roads is Gutian Lu – here you'll find the large town square and a pair of ancient pagodas. Further north is Dongda Lu, which is the main shopping and restaurant street and the centre of activity at night.

CITS is on the ground floor of the Overseas Chinese Hotel on Wuyi Beilu. They speak some English and are friendly and efficient.

Public Security is on Xian Ta Lu which runs off Dongda Lu.

Bank There is a money-exchange counter on the ground floor of the Overseas Chinese Hotel.

Post There is a post office on the ground floor of the Overseas Chinese Hotel.

CAAC (tel 51988) is on Wuyi Zhonglu. Flight tickets can be bought here or at the CITS office.

Maps Good bus maps can be bought from hawkers around the train station.

Things to See

There's not a great deal to see. The northern and southern sections of the town are separated by the Min River. Two old stone bridges which link the halves have lost their former charm.

Much of the riverfront is a ramshackle collection of brick and wood houses hanging out for demolition. On a good day it can be interesting to watch the junks or the flotillas of sampans dredging the river-bottom for sand. Across the Min River is **Nantai Island**, where the foreigners set themselves up when Fuzhou became an unequal treaty port in the 19th century.

In the centre of town is a wind-swept square presided over by an enormous statue of Mao Zedong. The statue was erected to commemorate the Ninth National Congress of the Communist Party in which Maoism was enshrined as the new state religion and Lin Biao was officially declared Mao's successor.

In the north-western part of the town is **West Lake (Xi Hu) Park** on Hubin Lu, the site of the **Fujian Provincial Museum**.

Yongquan Monastery dates back 1000 years and is said to house a collection of 20,000 Buddhist scriptures – of which almost 700 are written in blood. The monastery is on **Drum Hill (Gu Shan)** immediately to the east of Fuzhou. The hill takes its name from a large, drum-shaped rock at the summit. There is a hot springs spa next to the monastery.

Places to Stay & Eat

The *Overseas Chinese Hotel* on Wuyi Beilu is the best place to stay. It has its act

together – shops are open, services actually service you, staff are friendly. One of the best hotels in China. No single rooms, but doubles with air-conditioning and own bathroom are Y40 and you may be able to knock the price down a bit. Take trolley-bus No 51 from the train station.

Opposite the Overseas Chinese Hotel is the luxurious *Foreign Trade Centre Hotel* (tel 50154) with singles for Y90, doubles for Y110. It includes Chinese and western-style restaurants.

In the town centre is the impressive *Yu Shan Hotel* on Gutian Lu, with singles for Y40 and doubles from Y55. From the train station take trolley bus No 51 to Gutian Lu; then walk or take bus No 8 eastwards.

Over the past few years there's been a proliferation of small street restaurants. Try the *Banyan City/Shanghai Restaurant* complex in the centre of town. The hotels have their own restaurants.

Getting There & Away

Air There may be flights from Quanzhou to Fuzhou by the time this book is out. Useful connections include flights from Fuzhou to Canton (five times a week), Nanchang (three times a week) and Shanghai (twice a week).

Bus The long-distance bus station is on Wuyi Zhonglu. Buses head south along the coast from Fuzhou to Quanzhou (Y7, several buses a day) and Xiamen (Y11, twice a day). Northbound buses go to Fuan (Y7, three buses a day) and Wenzhou (Y18, twice a day).

Just south of the Overseas Chinese Hotel are ticket offices for air-con buses. Daily buses run to Quanzhou (Y13), Xiamen (Y17), Shantou (Y45) and Canton (Y72). Air-con is something of a misnomer since the Chinese fling the windows open. These buses don't leave until they're very crowded ; depraved kung-fu movies are shown on the TV.

Rail The railway line from Fuzhou heads north and connects the city with the main Shanghai-Canton line at the Yingtan junction. A branch line splits from the Fuzhou-Yingtan line and goes to Xiamen. There are direct trains from Fuzhou to Beijing, Shanghai, Nanchang and Xiamen. The rail route to Xiamen is circuitous and you'd be better off taking the bus.

Boat Passenger ships from Fuzhou depart from the nearby port town of Mawei, south-east of Fuzhou. Don't go to Mawei expecting to find a bustling harbour full of ships and junks. The port is a boring sprawl of apartment blocks. There's a Friendship Store and International Seamen's Club. You can get to Mawei by train from Fuzhou Train Station. There may be buses to Mawei from the large square in front of the Mao statue, but check.

From Mawei you can take a ship to Shanghai. CITS does not handle tickets and you have to buy them either at the booking office on Dong Dajie in Fuzhou, or from the port at Mawei. Timetables vary but these boats usually go about every five days. Fares range from Y16 (5th class) to Y68 (1st class) and Y82 (special class).

Zhejiang 浙江

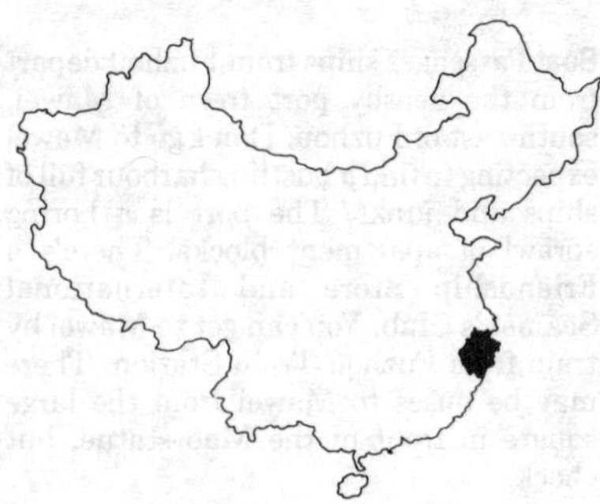

Almost 40 million people live in one of China's smallest provinces. Zhejiang, historically one of the most prosperous provinces, has always been more important than its size would indicate.

The region falls into two distinct parts. The area north of Hangzhou is part of the lush Yangtse River delta, similar to the southern region of Jiangsu Province. The south is mountainous, a continuation of the rugged terrain of Fujian Province. Intensely cultivated for 1000 years, northern Zhejiang has lost most of its natural vegetation cover and is a flat, featureless plain with a dense network of waterways, canals and irrigation channels. This is also the end of the Grand Canal; Zhejiang was part of the great southern granary from which food was shipped to the depleted areas of the north.

The growth of Zhejiang's towns was based on their proximity to the sea and their location in some of China's most productive farmland. Hangzhou, Ningbo and Shaoxing have all been important trading centres and ports since the 7th and 8th centuries. Their growth was accelerated when the Song Dynasty moved court to Hangzhou in the wake of an invasion from the north in the 12th century. Silk was one of the popular exports and today Zhejiang is known as the 'land of silk', producing one-third of China's raw silk, brocade and satin.

Hangzhou is the capital of the province. To the south-east of the city are several places you can visit without backtracking. A road-and-railway line runs east from Hangzhou to Shaoxing and Ningbo. From Ningbo you could take a bus to Tiantai Shan, and from there continue south to Wenzhou and down the coast road into Fujian Province. Jiaxing on the Hangzhou-Shanghai railway line is also open, as is Huzhou in the far north of Zhejiang Province on the shores of Lake Taihu.

HANGZHOU 杭州

When Marco Polo passed through Hangzhou in the 13th century he described it as one of the finest and most splendid cities in the world. Though Hangzhou had risen to prominence when the southern end of the Grand Canal reached here at the start of the 7th century, it really came into its own after the Song Dynasty was overthrown by the invading Jurchen.

The Jurchen were ancestors of the Manchus who conquered China five centuries later. The Song capital of Kaifeng, along with the emperor and the leaders of the imperial court, were captured by the Jurchen in 1126. The rest of the Song court fled south, finally settling at Hangzhou and founding the Southern Song Dynasty.

China had gone through an economic revolution in previous years, producing huge and prosperous cities, an advanced economy and a flourishing inter-regional trade. With the Jurchen invasion, the centre of this revolution was pushed south from the Yellow River Valley to the lower Yangtse Valley and the sea coast between the Yangtse and Canton.

While the north remained in the hands of the invaders – who rapidly became Sinicised – the hub of the Chinese state in the south was Hangzhou. The court, the military, the civil officials and merchants congregated here. The population rose from half a million to 1¾ million by 1275. The large population and its proximity to

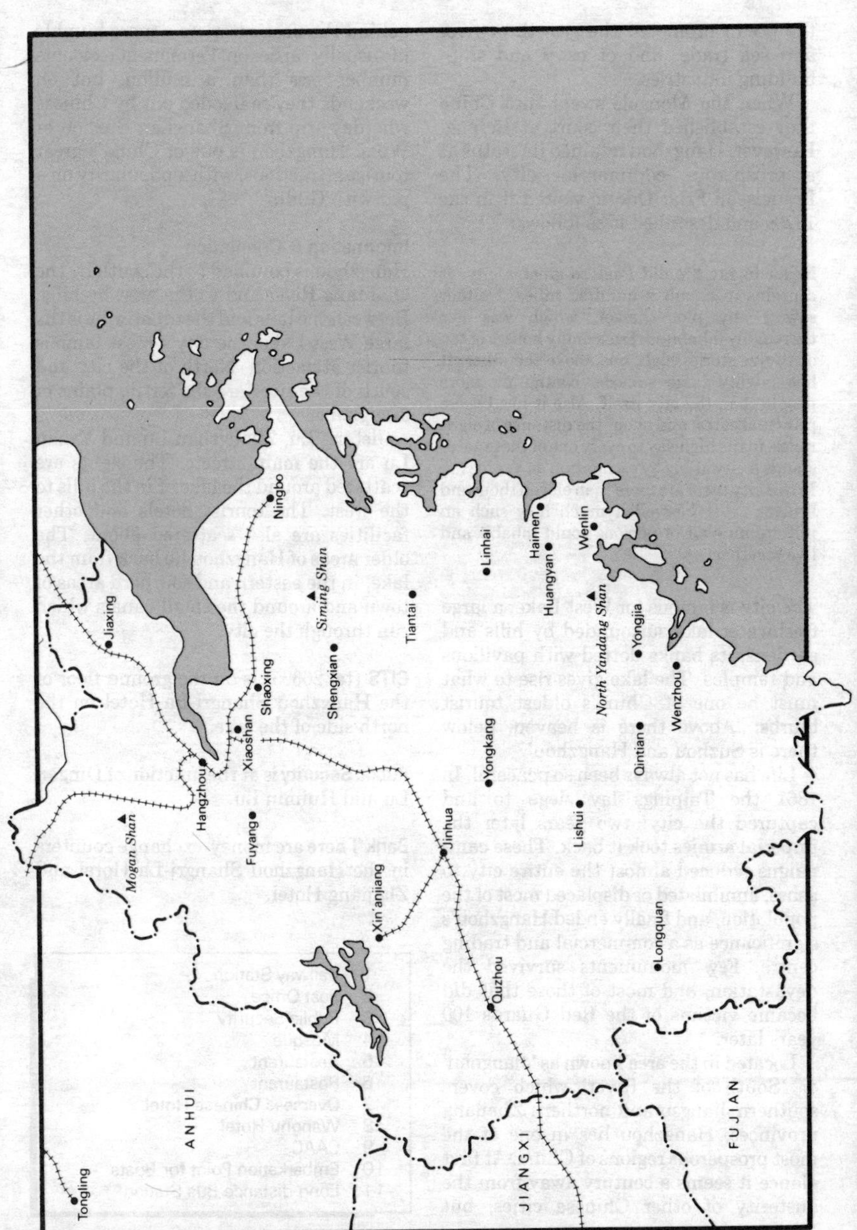
Jiaxing
Ningbo
Siming Shan
Shaoxing
Xiaoshan
Hangzhou
Mogan Shan
Fuyang
Shengxian
Tiantai
Linhai
Haimen
Huangyan
Wenlin
North Yandang Shan
Yongjia
Wenzhou
Qintian
Yongkang
Lishui
Jinhua
Xin'anjiang
Quzhou
Longquan
ANHUI
JIANGXI
FUJIAN
Tongling

the ocean promoted the growth of river and sea trade, and of navy and shipbuilding industries.

When the Mongols swept into China they established their court at Beijing. However, Hangzhou retained its status as a prosperous commercial city. The Franciscan Friar Odoric visited it in the 1320s and described it as follows:

> Never in my life did I see so great a city. It contains in circuit a hundred miles. Neither saw I any plot thereof, which was not thoroughly inhabited. I saw many houses of ten or twelve stories high, one above the other. It has mighty large suburbs containing more people than the city itself. Also it has twelve principal gates; and about the distance of eight miles, in the highway to every one of these gates stands a city as big by estimation as Venice . . . In this city there are more than eleven thousand bridges . . . I marvelled much how such an infinite number of persons could inhabit and live together.

The city is famous for West Lake, a large freshwater lake surrounded by hills and gardens, its banks dotted with pavilions and temples. The lake gives rise to what must be one of China's oldest tourist blurbs: 'Above there is heaven, below there is Suzhou and Hangzhou'.

Life has not always been so peaceful. In 1861 the Taipings lay siege to and captured the city; two years later the imperial armies took it back. These campaigns reduced almost the entire city to ashes, annihilated or displaced most of the population, and finally ended Hangzhou's significance as a commercial and trading centre. Few monuments survived the devastation, and most of those that did became victims of the Red Guards 100 years later.

Located in the area known as 'Jiangnan' or 'South of the River' which covers southern Jiangsu and northern Zhejiang provinces, Hangzhou lies in one of the most prosperous regions of China. At first glance it seems a century away from the austerity of other Chinese cities, but behind the neat exteriors a more humble life usually carries on. Permanent residents number less than a million, but on weekends they're flooded out by Chinese who day-trip from Shanghai, Suzhou or Wuxi. Hangzhou is one of China's great tourist attractions, with a popularity on a par with Guilin.

Information & Orientation

Hangzhou is bounded to the south by the Qiantang River and to the west by hills. Between the hills and the urban area is the large West Lake, the city's most famous tourist attraction. North of the city and south of the river are the fertile plains of Jiangnan.

Jiefang Lu, Zhongshan Lu and Yanan Lu are the main streets. The sights are scattered around the lake or in the hills to the west. The tourist hotels and other facilities are also scattered about. The older areas of Hangzhou lie back from the lake, in the eastern and southern areas of town and around the small canals which run through the city.

CITS (tel 26665) is on the ground floor of the Hangzhou Shangri-La Hotel on the north side of the lake.

Public Security is at the junction of Dingan Lu and Huimin Lu.

Bank There are money-exchange counters in the Hangzhou Shangri-La Hotel and Zhejiang Hotel.

1 Railway Station
2 Post Office
3 Public Security
4 Mosque
5 Restaurant
6 Restaurant
7 Overseas Chinese Hotel
8 Wanghu Hotel
9 CAAC
10 Embarkation Point for Boats
11 Long-distance Bus Station

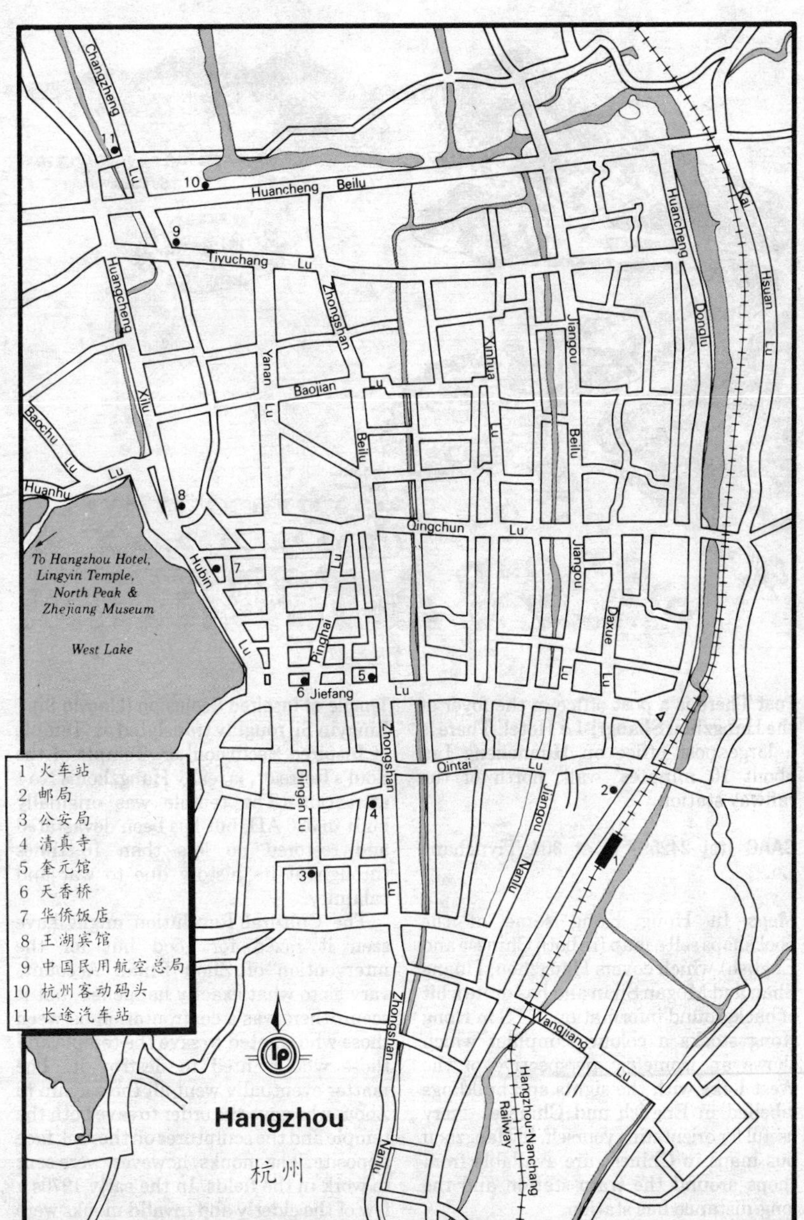
Changzheng Lu
Huancheng Beilu
Tiyuchang Lu
Huangcheng Xilu
Baochu Lu
Huanhu Lu
Zhongshan
Yanan Lu
Baojian Lu
Beilu
Xinhua Lu
Jiangou Beilu
Huancheng Donglu
Kai Hsuan Lu
Qingchun Lu
Jiangou
Hubin Lu
Pinghai Lu
Jiefang Lu
Daxue Lu
Qintai Lu
Dingan Lu
Zhongshan
Jiangou Nanlu
Zhongshan Nanlu
Wangjiang Lu
Hangzhou-Nanchang Railway
To Hangzhou Hotel, Lingyin Temple, North Peak & Zhejiang Museum
West Lake
1 火车站
2 邮局
3 公安局
4 清真寺
5 奎元馆
6 天香桥
7 华侨饭店
8 王湖宾馆
9 中国民用航空总局
10 杭州客动码头
11 长途汽车站
Hangzhou
杭州

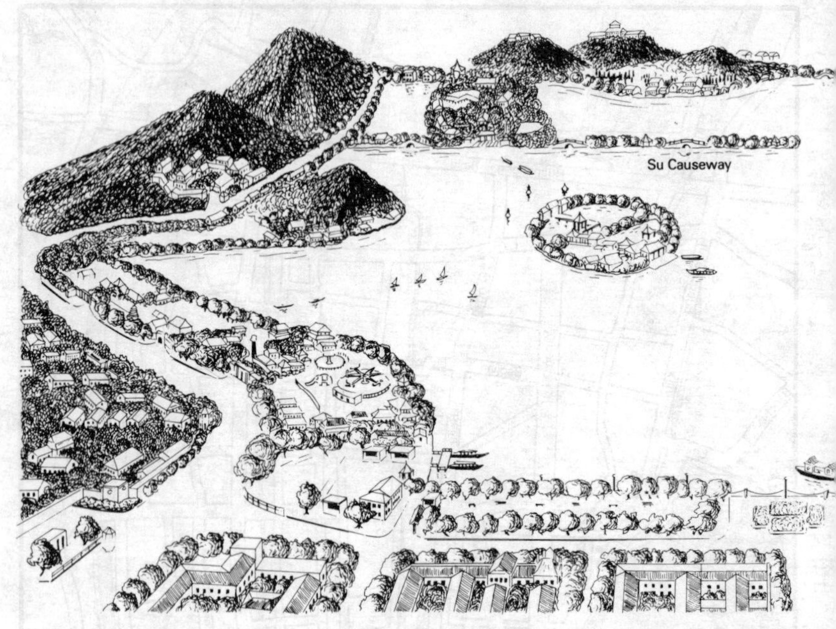

Post There is a post office in the foyer of the Hangzhou Shangri-La Hotel. There is a large post office on Huancheng Lu, about 10 minutes' walk north of the railway station.

CAAC (tel 24259) is at 304 Tiyuchang Lu.

Maps In Hong Kong some of the bookshops sell a map (in both Chinese and English) which covers Hangzhou, Huang Shan and Mogan Shan and has quite a bit of background information. CTS in Hong Kong stocks a colour pamphlet which shows an isometric perspective of the West Lake with the sights and buildings labelled in English and Chinese – very useful for orientating yourself. In Hangzhou bus maps in Chinese are available from shops around the train station and the long-distance bus station.

Temple of Inspired Seclusion (Lingyin Si)
Lingyin Si, roughly translated as 'Temple of Inspired Seclusion' or 'Temple of the Soul's Retreat', is really Hangzhou's No 1 attraction. The temple was originally built in 326 AD, but has been devastated and restored no less than 16 times throughout its history due to war and calamity.

The Cultural Revolution might have seen it razed for good but for the intervention of Zhou Enlai. Accounts vary as to what exactly happened, but it seems there was a confrontation between those who wanted to save the temple and those who wanted to destroy it. The matter eventually went all the way up to Zhou, who gave the order to save both the temple and the sculptures on the rock face opposite. The monks, however, were sent to work in the fields. In the early 1970s a few of the elderly and invalid monks were

Top: Labrang Monastery, Xiahe (RS)
Bottom Left: Riverside houses, Fuzhou (AS)
Bottom Right: West Pagoda, Yinchuan (RS)

Top: Sunrise over Huang Shan (AS)
Bottom Left: Lake of Heaven, Changbaishan (RS)
Bottom Right: Oasis at Dunhuang (AS)

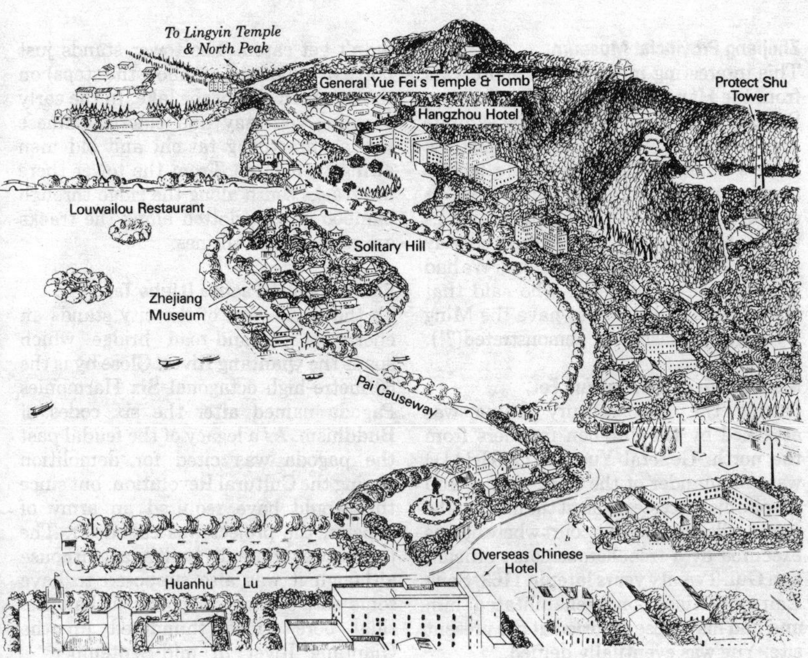

allowed to come back and live out their last few years in a small outbuilding on the hillside behind the temple.

The present buildings are restorations of Qing Dynasty structures. At the front of the temple is the Hall of the Four Heavenly Guardians. A statue of Maitreya, the future Buddha, sits on a platform in the middle of the hall flanked by two dragons. Behind the Hall of the Four Heavenly Guardians is the Great Hall, where sits the magnificent 20-metre-high statue of Siddhartha Gautama, sculpted from 24 blocks of camphorwood in 1956 and based on a Tang Dynasty original. Behind this giant statue is a startling montage of 150 small figures.

Facing the temple is Feilai Feng, the Peak That Flew From Afar. Some praise must go to the Chinese (or the Indians) for accomplishing the first successful solo flight of a mountain! The story goes that an Indian monk, who visited Hangzhou in the 3rd century, said the hill looked exactly like one in India and asked when it had flown to China. The rocky surface of the hill is chiselled with 330 sculptures and graffiti from the 10th to the 14th centuries. The earliest sculpture dates to 951 AD and comprises a group of three Buddhist deities at the right-hand entrance to the Qing Lin Cave. Droves of Chinese clamber over the sculptures and inscriptions to have their photo taken; the most popular backdrop is the laughing Maitreya, the fat buddha at the foot of the ridge. There is a vegetarian restaurant beside the Temple.

To get to the temple take bus No 7 to the terminus at the foot of the hills west of Hangzhou. Behind the Lingyin Temple is the Northern Peak. From the summit there are sweeping views across the lake and city.

Zhejiang Provincial Museum

This interesting museum is a short walk from the Hangzhou Shangri-La Hotel on Solitary Hill Island. Most of the exhibits are concerned with natural history; there's a large whale skeleton (a female *rhachianectos glaucus cope*) and a dinosaur skeleton. The museum buildings used to be part of the 18th-century holiday palace of Qing Emperor Qianlong. We had one letter from someone who said that visitors should be sure to have the Ming Dynasty eye-wash bowl demonstrated(?!).

Mausoleum of General Yue Fei

During the 12th century China was attacked by the Jurchen invaders from the north. General Yue Fei (1103-1141) was commander of the Song armies and despite his successes against the invaders he was recalled to the Song court where he was executed by a treacherous court official, Qin Gui. Twenty years later in 1163, Song Emperor Xiao Zong rehabilitated him and had his corpse reburied at the present site. Yue was eventually deified.

The mausoleum of this soldier/patriot is on Huanhu Lu, a few minutes' walk west of the Hangzhou Shangri-La Hotel in a compound bounded by a red-brick wall. It was ransacked during the Cultural Revolution but has been restored.

Inside is a glazed clay statue of the general and paintings of scenes from his life on the wall – including one of his back being tattooed with the words 'Loyal to the Last'.

Protect Shu Tower (Baoshu Ta)

The present tower is a 1933 reconstruction, 45.3 metres high and resembling a Stone Age rocket ship. The original Baoshu Ta was erected on Jewellery Hill in 938 during the Song Dynasty. It was built to ensure the safe return of Hangzhou's Prince Qian Shu from an audience with the emperor. In China there is an old saying something like 'Keeping company with the emperor is like keeping company with a tiger' – you had to make sure you didn't get eaten. The tower stands just north of Huanhu Lu (follow the steps) on the northern side of the lake. In the early morning you may find elderly Chinese women practising tai chi and old men airing their birds. From the tower there are tracks south along the ridge through bamboo groves; dotted along the tracks are temples and shrines.

Six Harmonies Pagoda (Liuhe Ta)

To the south-west of the city stands an enormous rail-and-road bridge which spans the Qiantang River. Close by is the 60-metre-high octagonal Six Harmonies Pagoda named after the six codes of Buddhism. As a legacy of the feudal past the pagoda was cited for demolition during the Cultural Revolution, but since this would have required an army of experts, the project was called off. The pagoda was originally built as a lighthouse although it was also supposed to have some sort of magical power to halt the tidal bore which thundered up the Qiantang River in mid-September.

The West Lake (Xi Hu)

There are 30 lakes in China called Xi Hu, but this one is by far the most famous. A pretty sight, but if you travel 1000 km just for the water you'll probably be disappointed. The lake was originally a lagoon off the Qiantang River. In the 8th century the governor of Hangzhou had it dredged; later a dike was built which cut it off from the river completely.

The lake is about three km long and a bit under three km wide. Two causeways, the Bai Ti and the Su Ti, split the lake into sections. The causeways each have a number of arched bridges, large enough for small boats and ferries to pass under. The sights are scattered around the lake, though most of them tend to be uninspiring pavilions or bridges with fanciful names. However, the whole being greater than the sum of the parts, it's still a pretty place to wander around and has a romantic feel on a fresh night.

The largest island in the lake is **Solitary Hill (Gu Shan)** – the location of the Provincial Museum, the Louwailou Restaurant and Zhongshan Park. Zhongshan Park was once part of an imperial palace during the 18th century, but was renamed after 1911 in honour of Sun Yatsen. The Bai causeway connects the island to the mainland.

Most of the other sights are connected with famous poets who once lived there, or perhaps an alchemist who bubbled up longevity pills; or they were once the private garden of some emperor who rolled around there with his palace whores. One such is the **Pavilion for Releasing Crane** on Solitary Hill Island, built in memory of the Song poet Lin Hejing, who it is said 'refused to serve the emperor and remained a bachelor his whole life. His only pastime was planting plum trees and fondling his crane'.

Hangzhou's botanical gardens even have a sequoia presented by Tricky Dickie on his 1972 visit. If you want to contemplate the moon in the privacy of your own boat there are a couple of places around the lake where you can hire paddle boats and go for a slow spin.

Santanyinyue is another island in the lake. Most guidebooks and maps refer to it as 'Three Pools Mirroring the Moon', but in fact the island is named after three poles which stick out of the water. The story is that in mid-August the moon is largest and roundest and is reflected in the water between the three poles. At this time the locals put lighted candles in the hollow tops of the poles. Hence the correct translation of the name should be something like 'Three Poles Fixing the Moon'.

Other

Some of the more interesting areas for walking are in the eastern part of town, around the scungy canals which cut through the urban areas. Lots of brick and wood doll-houses, and washing hung out to dry along the narrow lanes.

The Hangzhou Zoo has Manchurian tigers, though to my untrained eye they look no different from other tigers.

About 60 km north of Hangzhou is Mogan Shan. Pleasantly cool at the height of summer, Mogan Shan was developed as a resort for Europeans living in Shanghai and Hangzhou during the colonial era.

At the time of writing a couple of tourist attractions were planned for Hangzhou, including a centre for traditional Chinese medicine, a silk museum and a tea museum.

Places to Stay – bottom end

The *Zhejiang Hotel* (tel 25601) at San Tai Shan 68 is the best place to stay, though rather isolated on the outskirts of Hangzhou. Dorm beds cost Y10 and double rooms from Y85. To get to the hotel take bus No 28 from near the long-distance bus station; get off where the bus No 28 route intersects with the bus No 27 route and take bus No 27 to the hotel. The last No 27 bus is around 6.30 pm. From the train station take bus No 7 to the west side of the lake and then change to bus No 27. Coming back from the hotel, bus No 27 terminates on Pin Hai Lu, which is a street running off Yanan Lu close to the east shore of the lake. Reminiscent of a convalescent home, this quiet and relaxing hotel was (so the story goes) the personal HQ of all-purpose arch-villain and traitor Marshal Lin Biao. Underneath the grounds is a labyrinth of tunnels and rooms which appear to have been used as a military command post. These have been flung open to the general public, and Chinese tour groups are led through them – check out the massive indoor swimming pool. Building No 1 is supposed to have been Lin's private residence, and a dormitory for foreigners has been set up in the meeting room.

Places to Stay – middle

The *Overseas Chinese Hotel* (tel 23401) on Hubin Lu is conveniently located on the eastern shore of the lake. Doubles cost from Y76, dormitory beds Y20. A short distance to the north is the *Wanghu Hotel* (tel 71024), which charges Y90 a double – very comfortable. Take bus No 7 from the train station for both these hotels.

Places to Stay – top end

Up-market is the *Hangzhou Shangri-La Hotel* (tel 22921) on the north side of the lake. Rooms cost from US$40 a single and US$60 a double. Very expensive, but the facilities are great. Take bus No 7 from the train station; it goes past the hotel. Near the long-distance bus station it's probably easiest to take bus No 28; get off at the lake and walk back to the hotel.

Places to Eat

There's been a boom in places to eat in Hangzhou over the last few years. Probably the best way to find something is to walk around downtown on the east side of the lake.

At the corner of Jiefang Lu and Zhongshan Lu is a restaurant with oodles of noodles on the ground floor and more elaborate fare (shrimp, fish, eel) and friendly staff upstairs. Also try upstairs at the restaurant on the corner of Jiefang Lu and Hian Sha Lu. There's a vegetarian restaurant on You Dian Lu, just east of the intersection with Yanan Lu.

The *Louwailou* on Solitary Hill (Gu Shan) Island has good, cheap food; specialities are West Lake fish in vinegar sauce, and boneless fish in sauce.

Getting There & Away

Air Useful connections include daily flights from Hangzhou to Beijing and Canton; five flights a week to Hong Kong; and two flights a week to Xiamen.

Bus The long-distance bus station is on Changzheng Lu just north of the intersection with Huancheng Lu. There are several buses a day to Shanghai (Y5.40), Huang Shan (Y8.20), Tunxi (Y6.90), Hefei and Tiantai Shan. There may be buses to Shaoxing and Ningbo; if not, take the train.

Rail There are direct trains from Hangzhou to Fuzhou, Nanchang, Shanghai and Canton, and east to the small towns of Shaoxing and Ningbo. For trains to the north you must first go to Shanghai. Hangzhou Train Station has a separate ticket booking office for foreigners – through a doorway in the main booking hall.

Tourist-price tickets from Hangzhou to Shanghai are Y8 hard-seat and Y13 soft-seat. The trip takes about three hours with numerous trains daily.

Tourist-price tickets to Canton are Y51 hard-seat, Y85 hard-sleeper and Y171 soft-sleeper. The trip takes about 28 hours, but depends on the train.

Trains to Canton go via Nanchang, the capital of Jiangxi Province, or via the rail junction of Yingtan. Tourist-price tickets from Hangzhou to Nanchang are Y25 hard-seat, Y43 hard-sleeper and Y85 soft-sleeper.

From Yingtan a branch line extends to Fuzhou and Xiamen in Fujian Province on the south-east coast. There are direct trains from Hangzhou to Fuzhou. Tourist-price tickets are Y30 hard-seat, Y70 hard-sleeper and Y114 soft-sleeper. There is no direct train from Hangzhou to Xiamen; you must first go to Shanghai. However, you can catch a train to Fuzhou and then catch a bus to Xiamen.

Boat You can take a boat up the Grand Canal from Hangzhou to Suzhou. The boat leaves from the dock near the corner of Huancheng Lu and Changzheng Lu in the northern part of town. Tickets are available from the booking office at the dock. For details of fares, timetables and conditions on the boats see the section on Suzhou in the Jiangsu chapter.

SHAOXING 绍兴

Shaoxing is situated in the middle of the waterway system of the northern Zhejiang plain. It's been a major administrative town since early times and an agricultural market centre, though it never attained the same heights as neighbouring Hangzhou and Ningbo. Shaoxing is connected by train to Hangzhou (there may also be a bus connection). You can carry on by bus from Shaoxing to Tiantai Shan and Wenzhou.

NINGBO 宁波

Like Shaoxing, Ningbo rose to prominence in the 7th and 8th centuries as a trading port from which ships would sail to Japan and the Ryukyu Islands and along the Chinese coast, carrying the exports of Zhejiang Province.

By the 16th century the Portuguese had established themselves here, working as middlemen in the Japan-China trade since Chinese were forbidden to deal with the Japanese.

Although Ningbo was officially opened to western traders after the First Opium War, its once-flourishing trade gradually declined as Shanghai boomed. By that time the Ningbo traders had taken their money to Shanghai and formed the basis of its wealthy Chinese business community. Today Ningbo is a city of 250,000 people with fishing, salt production, textiles and food processing the primary industries.

About 60 km south of Ningbo is the small town of Qikou, the home of Chiang Kaishek. It has, surprisingly, become a Chinese tourist destination. Rumour has it that after Chiang's death, his body was secretly returned for burial at Qikou.

Ningbo is linked by train to Hangzhou (there may be also a bus connection) and by ship to Shanghai. There are daily buses from Ningbo to Tiantai Shan and Wenzhou, a small coastal town. From Wenzhou you can bus to Fuan in Fujian Province and on to Fuzhou and Xiamen.

TIANTAI SHAN 天台山

Tiantai Shan is noted for its many Buddhist monasteries which date back to the 6th century. While the mountain itself Buddhist monasteries which date back to the 6th century. While the mountain itself may not be considered sacred, it is very important as the home of the Tiantai Buddhist sect, which is heavily influenced by Taoism.

From Tiantai it's a 3½-km hike to the Gouqingsi Monastery at the foot of the mountain. You can stay overnight in the monastery. A motor road leads 25 km to Huadingfeng (over 1100 metres high) where a small village has been built. Public buses operate every second day. From Huadingfeng you can continue by foot one or two km to the Baijingtai Temple on the summit of the mountain. The other days the bus goes to other parts of the mountain, passing Shiliang Waterfall. From the waterfall it's a good walk along small paths five or six km to Huadingfeng.

Tiantai Shan is in the east of Zhejiang. Buses link it with Hangzhou, Shaoxing, Ningbo and Wenzhou.

WENZHOU 温州

Wenzhou is an ancient city, founded at the end of the 4th century. The ocean port was opened up to foreign trade in 1877 as the result of another treaty with Britain, though no foreign settlement developed. The few foreigners who did come here were missionaries and trade officials – the latter mainly concerned with the once-profitable tea trade.

The town lies on the south-east coast of Zhejiang Province. From Wenzhou you can continue by bus to Fuan in Fujian Province, and from there bus to the provincial capital of Fuzhou. There are also passenger ships between Wenzhou and Shanghai.

CHUNAN COUNTY 淳安县

Chunan County, in western Zhejiang, is known for its Lake of 1000 Islands. Worth investigating would be a route from Hangzhou – you'd cross the lake by boat, and perhaps pick up a bus for the last stretch to Huang Shan in Anhui Province.

Anhui 安徽

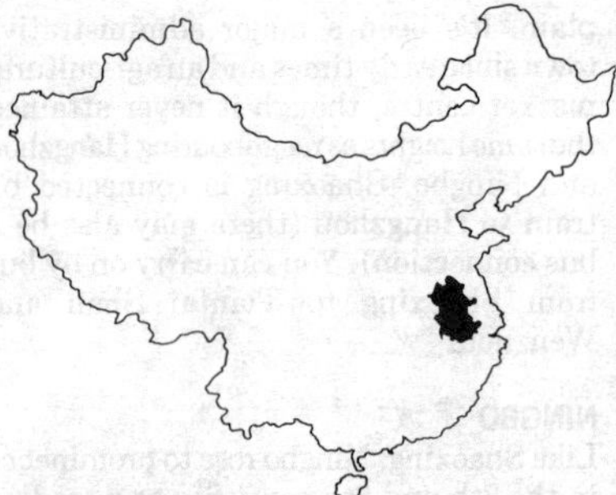

The provincial borders of Anhui were defined by the Qing government and except for a few changes to the boundary with Jiangsu have remained pretty much the same. The north of the province forms part of the North China Plain, and the Han Chinese settled here in large numbers during the Han Dynasty. The southern area below the Yangtse River was not settled until the 7th and 8th centuries. Today Anhui has a population of around 50 million.

The Yangtse cuts straight through the middle of this province. Most of Anhui's tourist attractions are in the southern part of the province, and you can get to them more easily from either Hangzhou or Shanghai than from the provincial capital of Hefei. There is a rail line from Hefei to Wuhu. Cross the river at Wuhu and take another train to Yingtan via Tunxi (the jumping-off point for Huang Shan) and Jingdezhen.

Most famous of the sights open to foreigners are the spectacular Yellow Mountains (Huang Shan) in the far south of the province, and the nearby Nine Flowers Mountains (Jiuhua Shan). On the eastern edge of the province, south of the Yangtse River, are the Maan Shan. The Yangtse River ports of Guichi and Wuhu are convenient jumping-off points for the Jiuhua and Huang Shan.

HUANG SHAN (YELLOW MOUNTAIN) 黄山

Li Bai, a Chinese poet of the Tang Dynasty, once took a trip to Huang Shan and wrote:

> Huang Shan is hundreds of thousands of feet high,
> With numerous soaring peaks lotus-like,
> Rock pillars shooting up to kiss empyrean roses,
> Like so many lilies grown amid a sea of gold.

Li got the altitude wrong since most people climb Huang Shan without oxygen masks. Don't expect the Himalayas, but by any standards the view from the top is worth the effort to get there. There's some rugged scenery, a spectacular sunrise, and the strange sight of hundreds of people scaling the endless stone staircases. This is not person-in-the-wilderness stuff; there are stone steps the whole way to the top of the mountain, concrete paths connecting the sights, and masses of Chinese.

Huang Shan is the name of the whole range of 72 peaks lying in the south of Anhui Province, 280 km west of Hangzhou. The highest is Lotus Flower Peak (Lianhua Feng), followed by Bright Summit Peak (Guangming Ding) and Heavenly Capital Peak (Tiandu Feng), all over 1800 metres. In all, 30 peaks rise above 1500 metres.

The area has been a famous scenic spot for at least 1200 years, since the Tang Dynasty emperor Tian Biao gave it its present name in the 8th century. Over the centuries the range has been an inspiration for Chinese poets and painters, attracted to the jagged peaks washed by a 'sea of clouds', the ancient pines clinging to the rock face and the nearby hot springs.

Information & Orientation

Buses pull into the Huang Shan 'base camp' at the foot of the range. The base camp is really an overgrown tourist resort

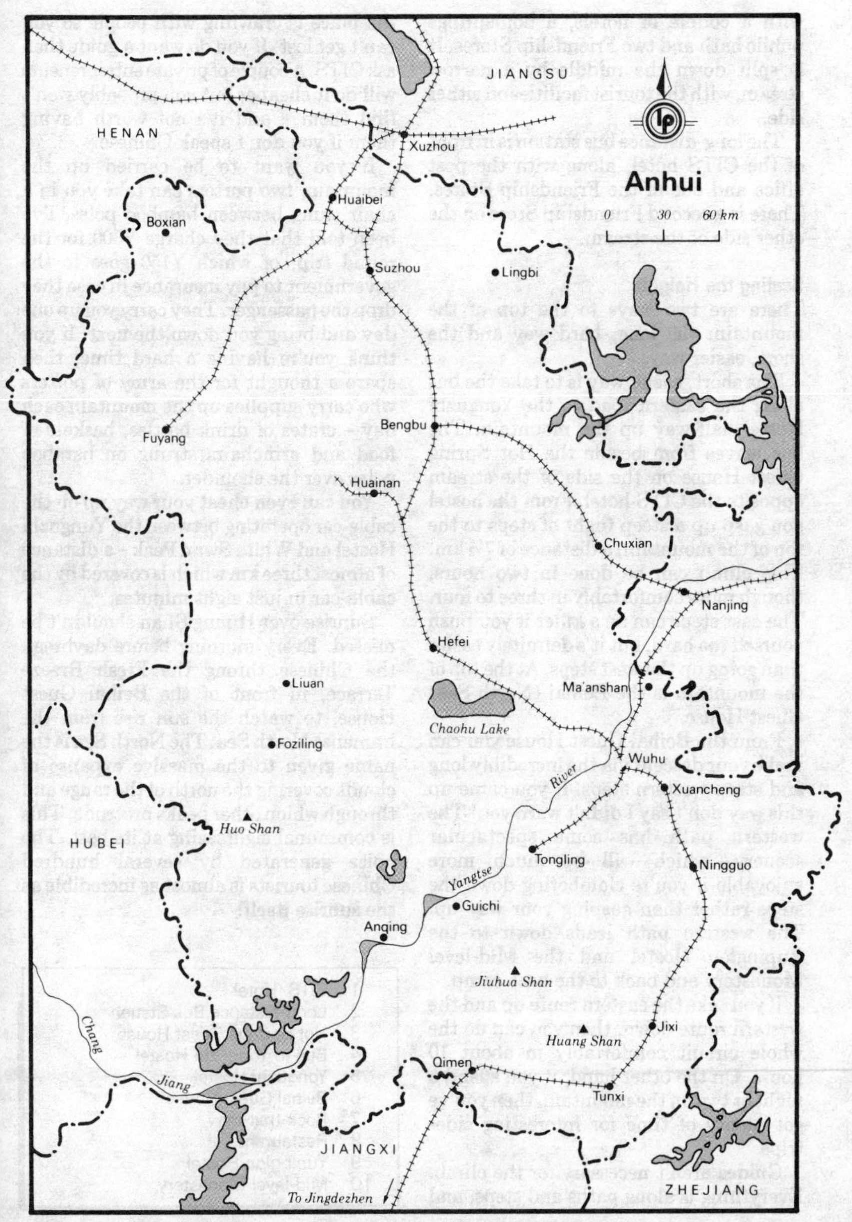
Anhui
0 30 60 km
JIANGSU
HENAN
HUBEI
JIANGXI
ZHEJIANG
Xuzhou
Huaibei
Boxian
Suzhou
Lingbi
Bengbu
Fuyang
Huainan
Chuxian
Nanjing
Hefei
Ma'anshan
Liuan
Chaohu Lake
Foziling
Wuhu
Xuancheng
River
Huo Shan
Tongling
Ningguo
Yangtse
Guichi
Anqing
Jiuhua Shan
Chang
Jiang
Jixi
Huang Shan
Qimen
Tunxi
To Jingdezhen

with a couple of hotels, a hot springs public bath and two Friendship Stores. It is split down the middle by a narrow stream, with the tourist facilities on either side.

The long-distance bus station is in front of the CITS hotel, along with the post office and one of the Friendship Stores. There is a second Friendship Store on the other side of the stream.

Scaling the Heights

There are two ways to the top of the mountain: the long, hard way and the short, easier way.

The short, easier way is to take the bus along the eastern road to the Yonguzhi Hostel half-way up the mountain. The bus leaves from beside the Hot Spring Guest House on the side of the stream opposite the CITS hotel. From the hostel you gasp up a steep flight of steps to the top of the mountain, a distance of 7½ km. This climb can be done in two hours, though more comfortably in three to four. The east steps can be a killer if you push yourself too hard, but it's definitely easier than going up the west steps. At the top of the mountain is the Beihai (North Sea) Guest House.

From the Beihai Guest House you can make your descent via the incredibly long and steep western steps. If you came up this way don't say I didn't warn you! The western path has some spectacular scenery, which will be much more enjoyable if you're clambering down the steps rather than gasping your way up. The western path leads down to the Yupinglou Hostel and the Mid-level Monastery and back to the base camp.

If you take the eastern route up and the western route down, then you can do the whole circuit comfortably in about 10 hours. On the other hand, if you spend a night or two on the mountain, then you've got plenty of time for interesting side-trips.

Guides aren't necessary for the climb. Everything is along paths and steps, and the place is crawling with people so you can't get lost. If you do want a guide then ask CITS. A couple of private entrepreneurs will do it cheaper but you probably won't find them – and it's not worth having them if you don't speak Chinese.

If you want to be carried up the mountain, two porters can take you in a chair slung between bamboo poles. I've been told that they charge Y300 for the round trip, of which Y150 goes to the government to pay insurance in case they drop the passenger. They carry you up one day and bring you down the next. If you think you're having a hard time, then spare a thought for the army of porters who carry supplies up the mountain each day – crates of drink bottles, baskets of food and armchairs strung on bamboo poles over the shoulder.

You can even cheat your way up on the cable-car operating between the Yunguzhi Hostel and White Swan Peak – a distance of almost three km which is covered by the cable-car in just eight minutes.

Sunrise over Huang Shan shouldn't be missed. Every morning before daybreak the Chinese throng the Fresh Breeze Terrace, in front of the Beihai Guest House, to watch the sun rise from the immense North Sea. The North Sea is the name given to the massive expanse of clouds covering the north of the range and through which other peaks protrude. This is communal sightseeing at its best. The noise generated by several hundred Chinese tourists is almost as incredible as the sunrise itself!

1 CITS/Hotel
2 Long-distance Bus Station
3 Hot Springs Guest House
4 Bus to Yonguzhi Hostel
5 Yonguzhi Hostel
6 Beihai Guest House
7 Rock-that-flew
8 Restaurant
9 Yupinglou Hostel
10 Mid-level Monastery

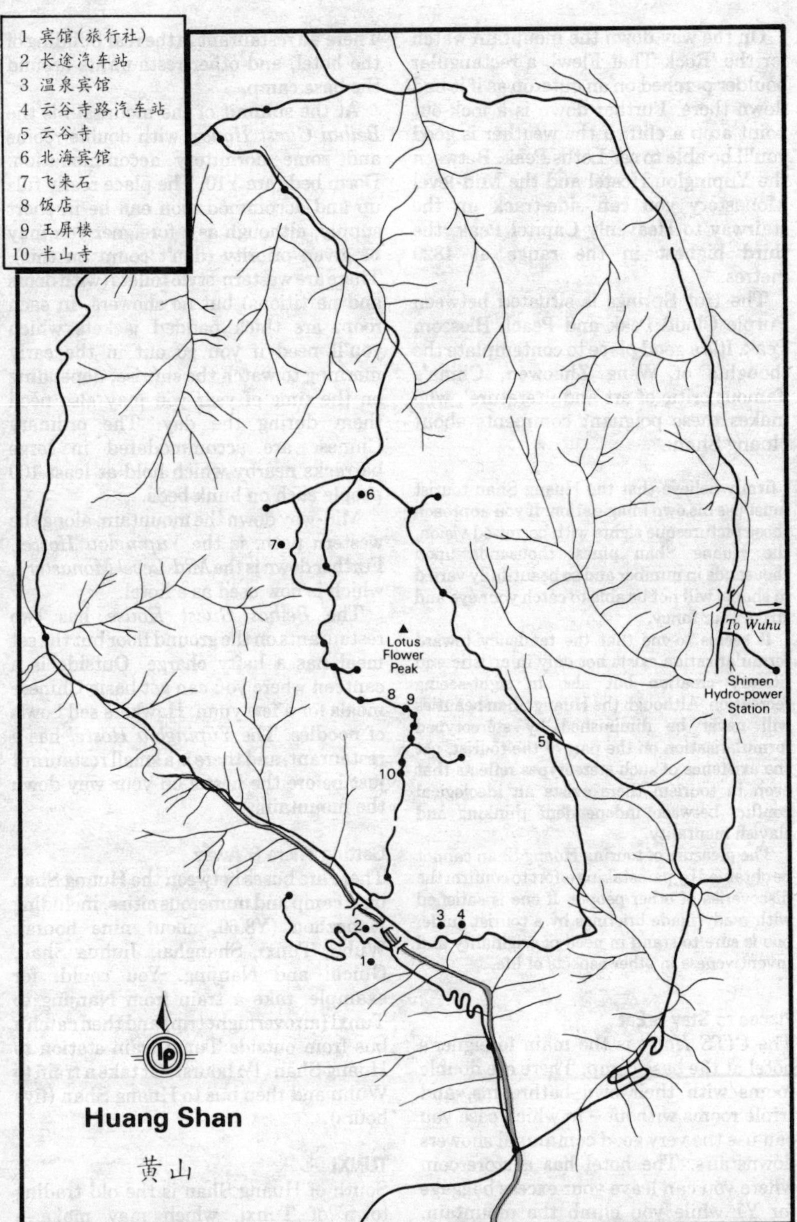
1 宾馆(旅行社)
2 长途汽车站
3 温泉宾馆
4 云谷寺路汽车站
5 云谷寺
6 北海宾馆
7 飞来石
8 饭店
9 玉屏楼
10 半山寺
Lotus Flower Peak
To Wuhu
Shimen Hydro-power Station
Huang Shan
黄山

On the way down the mountain watch for the 'Rock That Flew', a rectangular boulder perched on an outcrop as if it had flown there. Further down is a look-out point atop a cliff; if the weather is good you'll be able to see Lotus Peak. Between the Yupinglou Hostel and the Mid-level Monastery you can side-track up the stairway to Heavenly Capitol Peak, the third highest in the range at 1829 metres.

The Hot Springs is situated between Purple Cloud Peak and Peach Blossom Peak. It's a good place to contemplate the thoughts of Wang Zhaowen, China's 'famous critic of art and literature', who makes these poignant comments about Huang Shan:

> I firmly believe that the Huang Shan tourist must use his own imagination. If you approach those picturesque sights with borrowed vision, the Huang Shan pines, thousands upon thousands in number and so beautifully varied in shape, will not be able to catch your eye and strike your fancy.
>
> It seems to me that the tendency toward formularisation exists not only in artistic and literary creation but also in sight-seeing recreation. Although the Huang Shan beauties will never be diminished by stereotyped formularisation on the part of the tourist, yet the existence of such stereotypes reflects that even in tourism there exists an ideological conflict between independent thinking and slavish mentality.
>
> The pleasure of touring Huang Shan cannot be obtained by painstaking effort to confirm the discoveries of other people. If one is satisfied with ready-made briefings by a tourist guide, one is sure to stand in need of originality and inventiveness in other aspects of life.

Places to Stay & Eat

The *CITS Hotel* is the main foreigner's hotel at the base camp. There are double rooms with their own bathrooms, and triple rooms without – in which case you can use the very good communal showers downstairs. The hotel has a storeroom where you can leave your excess baggage for Y1 while you climb the mountain. There's a restaurant in the rear building of the hotel, and other restaurants around the base camp.

At the summit of the mountain is the *Beihai Guest House*, with double rooms and some dormitory accommodation. Dorm beds are Y10. The place really fills up and accommodation can be in short supply, although as a foreigner you may be given priority (don't count on this). There are western-style toilets (with doors and partitions) but no showers. In each room are thick padded jackets which you'll need if you go out in the early morning to watch the sunrise; depending on the time of year you may also need them during the day. The ordinary Chinese are accommodated in large barracks nearby which hold at least 100 people each on bunk beds.

Mid-way down the mountain, along the western path, is the *Yupinglou Hostel*. Further down is the *Mid-Level Monastery*, which is now used as a hotel.

The *Beihai Guest House* has two restaurants on the ground floor but the set meal has a hefty charge. Outside is a canteen where you can get basic Chinese meals for a few yuan. Hawkers sell bowls of noodles. The *Yupinglou Hostel* has a restaurant, and there is a small restaurant just before the hostel on your way down the mountain.

Getting There & Away

There are buses between the Huang Shan base camp and numerous cities, including Hangzhou (Y8.60, about nine hours), Wuhu, Tunxi, Shanghai, Jiuhua Shan, Guichi and Nanjing. You could, for example, take a train from Nanjing to Tunxi (an overnight trip) and then catch a bus from outside Tunxi train station to Huang Shan (1½ hours). Or take a train to Wuhu and then bus to Huang Shan (five hours).

TUNXI 屯溪

South of Huang Shan is the old trading town of Tunxi, which may make a worthwhile stopover. Tunxi is connected by bus to Huang Shan, Hangzhou and Jingdezhen. There are rail lines to Yingtan via Jingdezhen, and to Wuhu. At the time of writing there were plans to build an airport at Tunxi to make Huang Shan more accessible to foreign tourists.

JIUHUA SHAN 九华山

One way to escape the trampling hordes of Huang Shan is to head north-west to Jiuhua Shan, the Nine Flowers Mountains. The mountains take their name from the poet Li Bai, who wrote:

Looking far ahead from Jiujiang,
I saw the peaks of Mount Jiuhua
Emerging from the Heavenly River
Like nine beautiful lotus flowers.

Jiuhua Shan is regarded as one of the four sacred Buddhist mountains of China. Other mountains with this claim to fame are Pu Tuo in Zhejiang, Emei in Sichuan and Wutai in Shanxi. At least five other mountains (including Tai Shan in Shandong, which has a Taoist connection) are considered sacred or of some special significance to the Chinese.

Getting There

Jiuhuajie is the main centre of the Jiuhua Shan region and there are a couple of approaches to it. Easiest would be the daily bus from Huang Shan. There are buses from Wuhu and Guichi, ports on the Yangtse River. Another route is by train from Nanjing to Tonglingshi, and then by bus to Jiuhuajie.

WUHU & GUICHI 芜湖和贵池

Wuhu is a Yangtse River port. Rail lines branch off here south to Tunxi, and east to Shanghai via Nanjing. From the northern bank of the river another line heads north to Hefei, the provincial capital of Anhui. There are buses to Huang Shan and Jiuhua Shan from Wuhu. Further west from Wuhu is the Yangtse port of Guichi, with buses to Huang Shan and Jiuhua Shan.

HEFEI 合肥

This nondescript industrial city is the capital of Anhui but there's not much to recommend to tourists. It used to be a quiet market town but after 1949 was built up as an industrial centre and now has a population of about 500,000. The only real attraction is the local Provincial Museum with its wonderful 2000-year-old burial suit made of pieces of jade held together with silver thread.

Places to Stay

Try the *Jianghuai Hotel* on Changjiang Dadao; doubles cost around Y46. Further out is the expensive *Liujiang* at Y80 a single and Y190 a double. Near it is the *Daoxianglou*.

Getting There & Away

Hefei is connected by direct trains with Jinan, Beijing and Zhengzhou, southwards to the port of Wuhu on the Yangtse River, and westwards to Xian. Useful flights from Hefei include Beijing, Canton and Shanghai (all twice a week). There are direct buses between Hangzhou and Hefei ('Most pleasant, if your bladder can stand it', wrote one traveller), and buses from Hefei to Nanjing.

Shanghai 上海

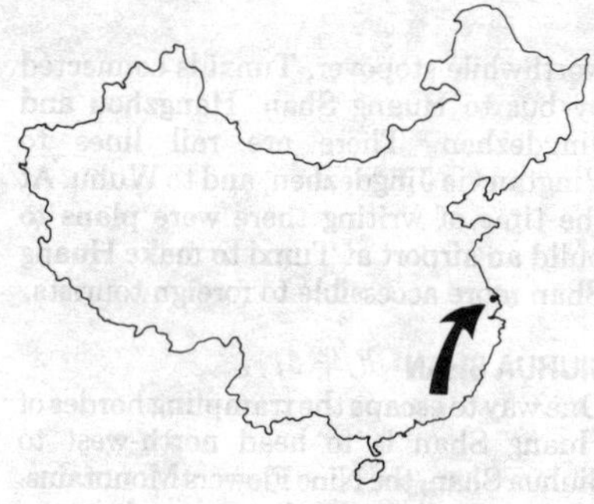

Shanghai, Paris of the East, Whore of China, Queen of the Orient; city of bums, adventurers, pimps, swindlers, gamblers, sailors, socialites, dandies, drugrunners. Humiliation, indignation, starvation, back-alley corpses, coolies, rickshaw drivers, deformed beggars, child prostitutes, scab-ridden infants, student activists, strikers, intellectuals, communist activists, rebels, foreign armies supporting foreign business interests. Trend-setter, snob, leader, industrial muscle, the name that keeps the Beijing bureaucrats awake at night . . . a hybrid of Paris and New York in the 1930s with millions trampling the streets where the millionaires once trod . . . one way or another Shanghai has permeated the western consciousness.

History

To seize the tail end of this leviathan you have to go back to the 1840s. At that time Shanghai was a prosperous weaving and fishing town – but not an important one – and was walled to keep out the Japanese pirates that roamed the China coast. Shanghai, at the gateway to the Yangtse, was in an ideal position to develop as a trading port and in 1842, after the first Opium War, the British forcibly opened up a concession here, and the French followed in 1847. An International Settlement was established in 1863 and a Japanese enclave in 1895, each completely autonomous and immune from Chinese law.

Spurred on by massive foreign investment, coupled with an inexhaustible supply of cheap Chinese labour, Shanghai quickly became a booming port and industrial city. In the mid-18th century it had a population of a mere 50,000 – by 1900 it had reached its first million, partly caused by the flood of refugees who came here when the Taipings took Nanjing in 1853. As for the foreign population, from a few thousand adventurers in the 1860s there were some 60,000 by the 1930s.

The International Settlement had the tallest buildings in Asia in the 1930s, the most spacious cinemas, more motor vehicles than any eastern metropolis or in all other Chinese cities combined. Powerful foreign financial houses had set up here: the Hong Kong & Shanghai Banking Corporation; the Chartered Bank of India, Australia & China; and the National City and Chase Manhattan Banks of New York. There were the blue-blood British firms of Jardine & Matheson, Sassoons and others that got their start with the opium trade, and newer but aggressive American firms that had *everything* for sale.

Guarding it all were the American, French and Italian marines, British Tommies and Japanese Bluejackets; foreign ships and submarines patrolled the Yangtse and Huangpu rivers and the coasts of China. They maintained the biggest single foreign investment anywhere in the world – the British alone had £400 million sunk into the place. After Chiang Kaishek's coup against the Communists in 1927, the Kuomintang closely co-operated with the foreign police and with Chinese and foreign factory owners to suppress the labour unrest. The Settlement police, run by the British, arrested Chinese labour leaders and handed them over to the Kuomintang for imprisonment or execution, and the Shanghai gangs were repeatedly called in to 'mediate' disputes inside the Settlement.

If you were rich you could get anything in the Shanghai of the 1920s and 1930s: dance halls, opium dens, gambling halls, flashing lights and great restaurants, plus the dimmed lights of the brothels and your choice of 30,000 prostitutes. Supporting it all were the Chinese who worked as beasts of burden and provided the muscle in Shanghai's port and factories. Shanghai was the largest manufacturing city in Asia, with more than 200,000 workers employed in the factories. American journalist Edgar Snow, who came to Shanghai in the late 1920s, wrote of the hundreds of factories where little boy and girl slave workers laboured 12 or 13 hours a day, and of little girls in silk filature factories – all of them, like most contract labour in Shanghai, literally sold into these jobs as virtual slaves for four or five years – unable to leave the heavily guarded, high-walled premises day or night, without special permission.

When the Communists came to power in 1949 one of the first things they wanted to do was turn Shanghai into a showcase of how Communism really worked. Today, while housing, sanitation, water supply and pollution are still serious problems in Shanghai, it should be remembered that the housing developments, the eradication of the slums, the rehabilitation of the city's hundreds of thousands of opium addicts, and the elimination of child and slave labour are staggering achievements.

Today, Shanghai has a population bordering on 12 million people – but that figure is deceptive since it takes into account the whole municipal area of 6100 square km. Nevertheless, the central core of some 220 square km has over 6.3 million people, which must rate as one of the highest population densities in China, if not in the world. In 1955 a plan was announced to reduce the city's population by one million. Some estimates put the number of people moved out of Shanghai at two million since 1949; perhaps three-quarters of these were young people 'sent down' to the countryside during the Cultural Revolution. Whatever the actual figure, Chinese officials will tell you that the professionals and technicians were 'persuaded' to go to the interior to start new schools, colleges and hospitals. Meanwhile, many of the 'exiled' young people who try to creep back into the city are nabbed and shipped back out again.

Population and unemployment are severe problems in Shanghai. Some economists claim that China's switch to light industry over the last five years or so is due to the fact that it can absorb up to three times the number of workers that heavy industry can – and at the same time increase the general standard of living. People are so numerous in Shanghai that the weekly day off is staggered – so shipyard workers don't rub shoulders with textile workers on the streets. Over-crowded as it is, Shanghai still enjoys a high living standard in comparison with the rest of China, at least in terms of wages, the availability of consumer goods and educational opportunities.

Shanghai continues to play an enormous role in the national economy. When the Communists came to power they set about downplaying this role, and priority of industrial development (under the first Five-Year Plan launched in 1953) was given to the strategically less vulnerable and poorer cities and towns of the interior. In 1956 the coastal regions were again reaffirmed as logical places for an industrial base, possibly because of the ease of import and export of goods by sea. That resulted in another boom for Shanghai, and in the late 1950s the city's limits were extended to encompass the surrounding counties, giving the city more control over its supply of food and raw materials. In 1963 Zhou Enlai put his personal seal of approval on the city, and output for certain facets of the city's

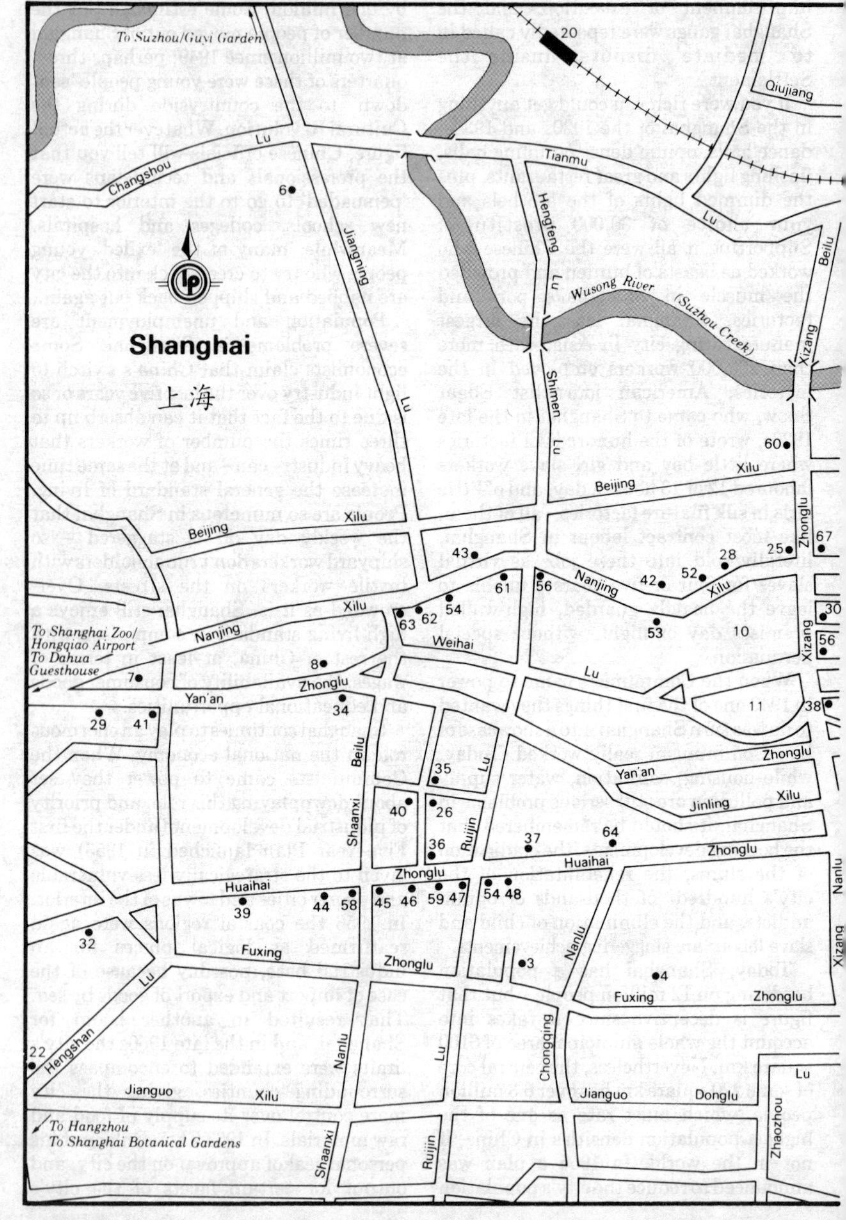
Shanghai
上海
To Suzhou/Guyi Garden
To Shanghai Zoo/
Hongqiao Airport
To Dahua
Guesthouse
To Hangzhou
To Shanghai Botanical Gardens
Wusong River (Suzhou Creek)
Changshou Lu
Jiangning Lu
Qiujiang
Tianmu Lu
Hengfeng Lu
Beilu
Xizang
Shimen Lu
Beijing Xilu
Nanjing Xilu
Weihai Lu
Zhonglu
Yan'an
Beilu
Shaanxi Nanlu
Ruijin Lu
Huaihai Zhonglu
Jinling
Xilu
Fuxing Zhonglu
Chongqing Nanlu
Hengshan Lu
Jianguo Xilu
Jianguo Donglu
Zhaozhou Lu
Xizang Nanlu
20
6
60
43
61
56
28
42
52
25
67
54
63
62
53
10
30
56
8
7
34
29
41
11
38
35
40
26
36
37
64
39
44
58
45
46
59
47
54
48
32
3
4
22

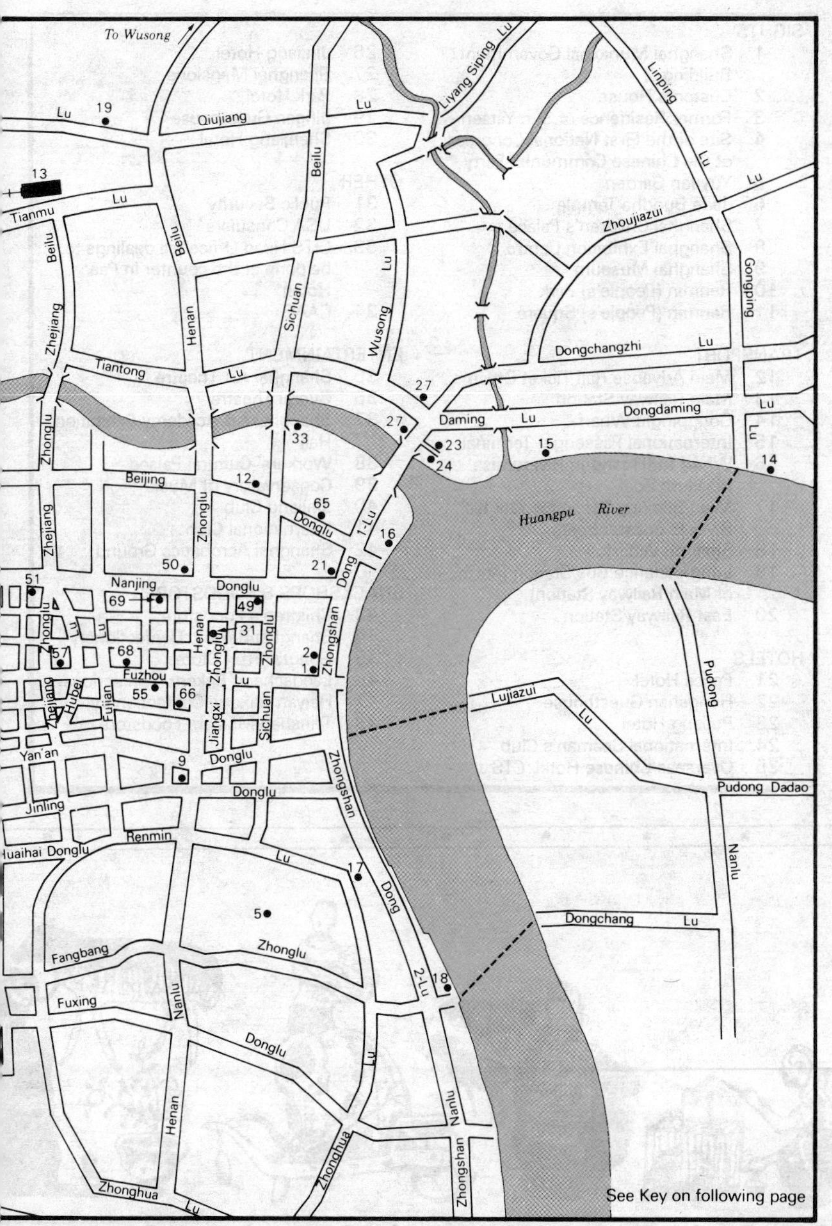
To Wusong
Liyang Siping Lu
Linping
Qiujiang
Lu
Tianmu Lu
Beilu
Zhoujiazui
Lu
Gongping
Zhejiang
Henan
Beilu
Sichuan
Wusong
Lu
Dongchangzhi
Lu
Tiantong
Lu
Daming
Lu
Dongdaming
Lu
Zhonglu
Beijing
Zhonglu
Donglu
1-Lu
Huangpu River
Zhejiang
Nanjing
Donglu
Dong
Zhongshan
Henan
Zhonglu
Zhonglu
Fuzhou
Jiangxi
Zhonglu
Lu
Hubei
Fujian
Sichuan
Lujiazui
Lu
Pudong
Yan'an
Donglu
Zhongshan
Jinling
Donglu
Pudong Dadao
Renmin
Huaihai Donglu
Lu
Dong
Nanlu
Dongchang
Lu
Zhonglu
Fangbang
2-Lu
Fuxing
Nanlu
Donglu
Lu
Henan
Nanlu
Zhonghua
Zhongshan
Zhonghua
Lu
See Key on following page

SIGHTS

1 Shanghai Municipal Government Building
2 Customs House
3 Former Residence of Sun Yatsen
4 Site of the First National Congress of the Chinese Communist Party
5 Yuyuan Garden
6 Jade Buddha Temple
7 Shanghai Children's Palace
8 Shanghai Exhibition Centre
9 Shanghai Museum
10 Renmin (People's) Park
11 Renmin (People's) Square

TRANSPORT

12 Main Advance Rail Ticket Office
13 Main Railway Station
14 Gongpinglu Wharf
15 International Passenger Terminal
16 Wharf for Huangpu Rivercruise Pleasure Boat
17 Main Booking Office for Yangtse River & Coastal Boats
18 Shiliupu Wharf
19 Long-distance Bus Station (north of Main Railway Station)
20 East Railway Station

HOTELS

21 Peace Hotel
22 Hengshan Guesthouse
23 Pujiang Hotel
24 International Seaman's Club
25 Overseas Chinese Hotel/CTS
26 Jinjiang Hotel
27 Shanghai Mansions
28 Park Hotel
29 Jingan Guesthouse
30 Shenjiang Hotel

OTHER

31 Public Security
32 USA Consulate
33 CITS Head Office (all dealings to be done at the counter in Peace Hotel)
34 CAAC

ENTERTAINMENT

35 Shanghai Art Theatre
36 Guotai Theatre
37 Shanghai Art Academy Exhibition Hall
38 Workers' Cultural Palace
39 Conservatory of Music
40 Jinjiang Club
41 International Club
42 Shanghai Acrobatics Ground

SNACKSHOPS & FOODSTORES

43 Children's Foodstore
44 Shanghai Bakery/Confectionery
45 Gongtai Fruit Store
46 Laodachang Bakery/Confectionery
47 Haiyan Bakery/Confectionery
48 Tainshan Moslem Foodstore

RESTAURANTS		SHOPPING	
49	Deda	60	24-Hour Department Store
50	Yangzhou	61	Chinese-Style Clothing Store
51	Xinya	62	Dongfang Furs & Leather Shop
52	Renmin	63	Jingdezhen Porcelain Shop
53	Luyangcun	64	Huaihai Secondhand Shop
54	Meilongzhen	65	Friendship Store
55	Xinghualou	66	Shanghai Antique & Curio Store
56	Muslim	67	Shanghai No 1 Department Store
57	Dahongyun	68	Foreign Languages Bookstore
58	Meixin	69	Xinhua Bookstore
59	Chengdu		

1	上海市人民政府	20	东火车站	39	音乐学校	58	美心饭店
2	海关	21	和平饭店	40	锦江俱乐部	59	成都饭店
3	孙中山故居	22	衡山宾馆	41	国际俱乐部	60	二十四百货商店
4	中共 — 大会址	23	浦江饭店	42	杂技场	61	龙凤中式服装厂
5	豫园	24	国际海员俱乐部	43	儿童食品店	62	东方毛服装厂
6	玉佛寺	25	华侨饭店	44	上海食品店	63	景德镇艺术瓷器服务部
7	少年宫	26	锦江饭店	45	公泰水果店	64	淮海旧货商店
8	展览馆	27	上海大厦	46	老大昌食品店	65	友谊商店
9	博物馆	28	国际饭店	47	海燕食物厂	66	文物商店
10	人民公园	29	静安宾馆	48	天山回民食品店	67	第一百货商店
11	人民广场	30	申江饭店	49	德西餐社	68	外文书店
12	火车售票处	31	公安局	50	杨州饭店	69	新华书店
13	火车站	32	美国领事馆	51	新雅饭店		
14	公平路码头	33	中国国际旅行社总局	52	人民饭店		
15	国际客运站	34	中国民用航空总局	53	绿阳春饭店		
16	浦江游船码头	35	艺术剧院	54	梅龙镇酒家		
17	轮船售票处(长江)	36	国泰剧院	55	杏花楼		
18	十六铺码头	37	画院美术馆	56	回民饭店		
19	长途汽车站	38	工人文化宫	57	大鸿运饭店		

economy was given priority. Today, the city accounts for 15% of China's total industrial output and 20% of its exports. Shanghai is now being looked upon as a source of technical expertise, the weak link in China's modernisation drive. Foreign business is also back in business in Shanghai with huge sums of money invested by foreign companies, like the massive Baoshan steelworks (aided by the Japanese) and a giant petro-chemical works.

Shanghai is also one of the most politically important centres in China – and one of the political hot spots. The meeting which founded the Chinese Communist Party was held here back in 1921. Shanghai was an important centre of early Communist activity when the Party was still concentrating on organising urban workers. Mao also cast the first stone of the Cultural Revolution in Shanghai, by publishing in the Shanghai newspapers a piece of political rhetoric he had been unable to get published in Beijing.

Most extraordinary, during the Cultural Revolution a People's Commune was set up in Shanghai, modelled on the Paris Commune of the 19th century. (The Paris Commune was set up in 1871 and controlled Paris for two months. It planned to introduce socialist reforms such as turning over management of factories to the workers' associations). The Shanghai Commune lasted just three weeks before Mao ordered the Army to put an end to it, and thus China was finished with this form of socialism for a long time.

The so-called 'Gang of Four' had their power base in Shanghai. The campaign to criticise Confucius and Mencius was started here in 1969, before it became nationwide in 1973 and was linked to Lin Biao. Shanghai's history as the most radical city in China, the supporter of dogmatic Maoism, one of the focuses of the Cultural Revolution, and the power base of Mao's wife is rather strange when you consider that the city is now, perhaps with the exception of Canton, the most capitalist and the most consumer-oriented in China. If you can work out how a whole city can change its loyalty from orthodox Maoism to laissez-faire capitalism then you have probably gone a long way to understanding what makes the Chinese world tick.

Climate

The best times to visit Shanghai are spring and autumn. Winters can drop well below freezing and are blanketed in drizzle. Summers are hot and humid with temperatures as high as 40°C. So, in short, silk longjohns and down jackets for winter, an iceblock for each armpit in summer – an umbrella won't go astray either.

Information & Orientation

Landmarks are a good way to navigate in Shanghai. The Peace Hotel at the intersection of the Bund and Nanjing Lu is just about the closest thing to a centre – it's the chief tourist crossroads. On the Bund the easy direction-finder is the Customs House (with its large red star and clock tower) and the Communist Party HQ – both of these are to the south of the Peace Hotel. To the north is the unmistakable looming slab known as Shanghai Mansions.

From the strip of the Bund near the Peace Hotel you can get a bus in almost any direction. Heading west along Nanjing Lu you'll come to the Park Hotel, which roughly marks the division between Nanjing Donglu and Nanjing Xilu. From here you can easily spot the TV Tower, which is a good intermediary point to aim for when heading to the area of the old French Concession (Frenchtown). The heart of Frenchtown is marked by the colossal wings of the Jinjiang Hotel.

Other destinations are a little awkward to get to on foot. Shanghai is a big place. Greater Shanghai covers an area of 6100 square km, with the city proper estimated at 220 square km. Some of the sights are right off the map – the zoo, for example, is near the airport.

Street names are in pinyin, which makes navigating easy, and many of the streets are named after cities and provinces. In the central district (around Nanjing Lu) the provincial names run north-south, and the city names run east-west. Some roads are split by compass points, such as Sichuan Nanlu which means Sichuan South Rd, and Sichuan Beilu which means Sichuan North Rd. Some of the monstrously long roads are split by sectors, such as Zhongshan Dong Erlu and Zhongshan Dong Yilu, which mean Zhongshan East 2nd Rd and Zhongshan East 1st Rd, respectively – simple!

There are four main areas of interest in the city: the Bund from the Friendship Store to the Dongfeng Hotel; Nanjing Donglu from the Peace to the Park Hotels, as well as the downtown sector to the south of this strip; Frenchtown, which is the strip of Huaihai Zhonglu from Shaanxi Nanlu to Chongqing Nanlu, plus the adjoining Jinjiang Hotel area; and the Jade Buddha Temple and the side trip along Suzhou Creek.

CITS does its dealings from the ground floor of the Peace Hotel. Trains, planes and boats can be booked here. They make the standard markups on planes and trains and a surcharge on boats out of Shanghai, but they give you a good chance of getting illusive sleepers without joining the phenomenal queues at the train stations. They will book tickets for the Trans-Siberian to Europe.

CITS has astronomically-priced excursions to Suzhou, Wuxi and the other wonders as far as Nanjing. There are two factories in Shanghai you may be able to get into by yourself – a jade carving factory and a carpet factory, next door to each other at 25 & 33 Caobao Lu in the Xuhui District on the south-western outskirts of Shanghai. Also try the Shanghai No 1 Silk Factory in the north of the city. CITS may be able to organise visits to various other industries – a toothpaste factory, a neon signs factory, a chocolate factory, a film studio. Their city tours for Y35 take in the carpet and jade-carving factories as well as the Children's Palace, Jade Buddha Temple and other interesting sights. They also handle tickets for the Huangpu River trip, but these will be cheaper at the source, which is virtually across the road.

Shanghai CITS is hopelessly overworked – you'll just have to be patient getting information from them. Some useful info, such as train timetables to Hangzhou, is laid out on the counter under glass and behind three ranks of customers.

Public Security (tel 215380) is at 210 Hankou Lu, near the corner with Henan Zhonglu.

Consulates There are a number of foreign consulates in Shanghai, including: USA (tel 379880) at 1469 Huaihai Zhonglu; France (tel 377414) at 1431 Huaihai Zhonglu; Japan (tel 372073) at 1517 Huaihai Zhonglu; Australia (tel 563050) at 17 Fuxing Xilu; West Germany (tel 379951) at 181 Yongfu Lu.

Bank There are money-exchange counters on the premises of the larger tourist hotels, such as the Peace, Pujiang and Jinjiang Hotels. Credit cards are more readily accepted in Shanghai than in other parts of China. Most tourist hotels will accept the main ones like Visa, Amex, Mastercharge, Diners, JCB, as will banks and Friendship Stores (and related tourist outlets like the Antique & Curio Store). The Bank of China branch right next to the Peace Hotel, on the Bund, will change foreign cash and travellers' cheques.

Post & Communications The larger tourist hotels have post offices from which you can mail letters and small packages.

The Express Mail Service and Poste Restante is at 276 Bei Suzhou Lu. Letters to London take just two days, or so they advertise.

The International Post & Communications Office is at the corner of Sichuan Beilu and Bei Suzhou Lu. The section for international parcels is in the same building but around the corner at 395 Tianting Lu.

To receive letters, address them c/o the Peace Hotel. There is a counter on the ground floor where incoming letters are held. Check the letter drop in both the north and south buildings.

Long-distance calls can be placed from hotel rooms and do not take long to get through. The International Telegraph Office, from which you can make long-distance phone calls and send international telexes and telegrams, is on Nanjing Donglu next to the Peace Hotel.

CAAC (tel 531960) is at 789 Yanan Zhonglu. The enquiry office at Hongqiao Airport can be reached by telephoning 537664.

Airline Offices Cathay Pacific (tel 582582) is in Room 123 of the Jinjiang Hotel; Japan Airlines (tel 378467) is at 1202 Huaihai Zhonglu; Pan Am (tel 563050) is in Room 103, Jingan Guest House, 370 Huashan Lu.

Maps There are quite a few variations around and lots of sources of them. For starters, get one from the hawkers outside the railway station. Other places to try are the bookstores in the tourist hotels, which are usually well stocked. Good English maps get snapped up fast – if you see a good map somewhere else on your travels and you're going to Shanghai, then it's wise to pick it up there and then.

The best Chinese-language map is a small foldup one with a picture of the Peace Hotel and the Bund on the cover, costing 40 fen. It's a masterpiece of map-making though the heap of detail squashed into it may well require a magnifying glass. Another good one has the pinyin *Shanghai – shiqu jiaotongtu* on the cover and is good for working out the bus routes; it's commonly sold in Shanghai.

Probably the best English map is *A Tourist Map of Shanghai* published by China Travel & Tourism Press. It's readily identifiable by the large advertisements for American Express, Remy Martin and Shanghai Arts & Crafts Jewellery. Another good map commonly sold in Shanghai is *A Map of Communication & Tour to Shanghai*, which also has the bus routes.

Reading There are numerous foreign-language outlets in Shanghai, if you take the tourist hotel bookshops into account. The main Foreign Language Bookstore is at 390 Fuzhou Lu. Next door is a stationery shop if you need writing supplies as well. Of special interest is the branch at 201 Shandong Zhonglu, which sells old books in foreign languages.

At 424 Fuzhou Lu is the Classics Bookshop. The books in the section serving foreigners are not as old as the books in the section serving Chinese customers – and the prices are higher. However, books from the foreigners' section can be exported, whereas books from the other section cannot.

There are other specialist bookshops around Shanghai, if you can read Chinese. Fuzhou Lu is the bookstore hunting ground – it always has been that way. Back in 1949 the bookshops removed the porn from the shelves and set up displays of Marx and company overnight.

If you're hungry for western reading material, worth checking out is the China National Publications Import & Export Corporation shop at 537 Yanan Lu, near the Jinjiang Hotel. The retail shop on the ground floor has a good stock of western magazines, including *Paris Match, L'Express, South* and many more.

A largish range of foreign newspapers and

magazines is available from the tourist hotels and some shops. They include the *Wall Street Journal, International Herald Tribune, Time* and *Newsweek*. The latter two make good gifts for Chinese friends.

The biggest selection of Chinese periodicals is found at 16 Sichuan Beilu – and while the lingo might not make these seem worth browsing through, there are oddities like the comic book rental section to dive into. The Xinhua Bookstore at 345 Nanjing Donglu has kids' books, lots of posters, some maps, and a foreigners' section on the 2nd floor.

Get a copy of Pan Ling's *In Search of Old Shanghai* (Joint Publishing Company, Hong Kong, 1982) for a run-down on who was who and what was what back in the bad old days.

Hospitals Shanghai is credited with the best medical facilities and most advanced medical knowledge in China. Western medicines are sold at the Shanghai No 8 Drugstore at 951 Huaihai Zhonglu. Foreigners are referred to Shanghai No 1 People's Hospital (tel 240100) at 190 Beisuzhou Lu.

Film Shanghai is a good place to stock up on film. Limited repairs to Japanese-brand cameras are available at Seagull Photo Supplies, 471 Nanjing Donglu (tel 221004). The shop also sells Japanese cameras. Another major photographic store is Guan Long, corner of Nanjing Donglu and Jiangxi Zhonglu.

Some brands of western film can be processed in Shanghai and quality seems to be on par with that in the west. Enquire at the photography stores or in the large hotels (the Peace Hotel has a photo-processing service).

Things to See

Shanghai's thrills and spills are found on the streets. If the world were to run out of gasoline tomorrow, it would make little difference to the noise level in Shanghai. The city has the most insane collections of hybrids on two, three and four-or-more wheels imaginable – parts cannibalised from breakdowns. Coming through the insectoid rush-hour is a legless rider using his hands to crank up the rear bike drive . . . and then, incredibly, a semitrailer-class tricycle with the rider pedalling backwards (using a rear sprocket and chain arrangement). The screech, squawk and jingle of the roads leading across Nanjing is offset by walls of pedestrians spilling into vacant bike lanes, while retired men with 'serve the people' armbands hurdle the railings to try and nail jaywalkers. As early as 5 am the city is alive: mass tai chi in the parks, while the younger set go for the more exotic martial arts, and there's the inevitable jogging and frisbee-playing. Covered food markets out in the neighbourhoods are readily identified by the mounds of fresh cabbage, or the halved pig carcasses thrown on the sidewalk nearby, or simply by the queues for eggs and slabs of bean curd. It's difficult to haul yourself out of bed at these hours, but Shanghai is a place for doing things and watching people – the sort of place where unobtainable Japanese products beckon from billboards, strips of pigs' innards dangle from a dim doorway that smells of herbs and incense, pedlars materialise on street corners with shady wares and cooks pound dough behind steamy windows, or a shoe repairer sets up shop on the sidewalk.

What Was What

Time to engage in the hobby of determining what building was what, when, how, and why. It's a bit like a giant game of Monopoly: Jimmy's Kitchen, St Petersburg Restaurant, Delmonte's Casino, the Lido, Roxy's, Kabul Rd, Oxford St, Luna Park, Singapore Park. Most of the taller structures are dead wood from the 1930s and the buildings rapidly changed function after the Japanese invasion of 1937. The westerners got a brief respite from 1945 to 1949, but then the game was up.

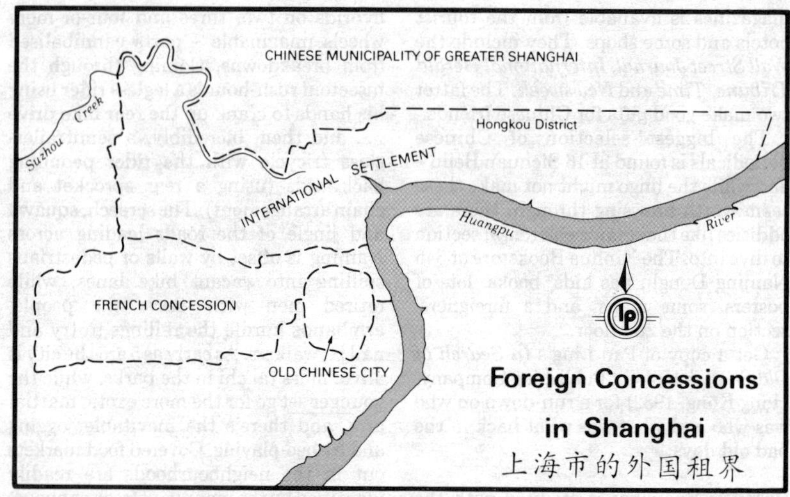

The old **Chinese city** is now identified by the Zhonghua-Renmin ring road, which encloses a shoddy maze of cobbled alleyways, with some newer buildings to the south. Old walls used to be surrounded by a moat, but these walls were torn down in 1912.

The **International Settlement** started off as small tracts of land on the banks of the Huangpu, north of the old Chinese city, and eventually snowballed to roughly the area shown by the map in this text. The British-dominated Settlement was a brave new world of co-operation by the British, Europeans and Americans (the Japanese were also included but were suspect). It's fairly easy to discern. If you draw a line directly north from the Jingan Guest House to Suzhou Creek, then the area is everything from Yanan Lu up to Suzhou Creek in the north, and to the Huangpu River in the east. The ritziest place to live was west of today's Xizang Lu – villas spread this way as far as the zoo (now the Jingan district). The foreign embassies were grouped on either side of the Waibaidu Bridge; the Friendship Store used to occupy the buildings of the old British Consulate, and the former Seaman's Club used to be the Soviet Consulate.

Throwing a pincer around the top of the Chinese city and lying on the southern flank of the International Settlement was the **French Concession**. The east-west dividing line between the French Concession and the International Settlement is the present-day Yanan Lu (previously known as Avenue Foch in the west, and Avenue Edward VII in the east). The French strip of the Bund (south of Yanan) was known as the Quai de France. Roughly, the boundaries of Frenchtown can be drawn by heading south from the Dahua Guest House on Yanan Lu to the Xujiahui Traffic Circle, east along Zhaojiabang Lu and Xujiahui Lu to the Hunan Stadium, then up alongside the western border of the Chinese city as far as Yanan Donglu – and then tack on the pincer between Yanan Donglu and the northern rim of the Chinese city. Not all of Frenchtown was densely inhabited back then, and in any case the name is a bit of a misnomer as there weren't too many French there to begin with – like the other concessions it was

90% Chinese, and in any case the most numerous foreign residents in Frenchtown were White Russians. Vietnamese troops were used by the French as a police force (just as the British used Sikhs in their concessions). For villa and mansion architecture the French concession holds the most surprises – there's a rather exclusive air to the elegant townhouses and apartment blocks. The core of things is around the present Jinjiang Hotel and Huaihai Lu.

The original **central district** was bounded by today's Xizang Lu, Yanan Lu, Suzhou Creek and the Huangpu River. If you bisect that with Nanjing Lu, then the key wining and dining, shopping and administrative/hotel area is the slab south of Nanjing Lu as far as Yanan Lu, with Nanjing Donglu being the chief culprit. This is today's Huangpu District.

The area north of the central district and up as far as Suzhou Creek used to be the **American Settlement**. The area on the other side of the creek, east of the Main Railway Station and along the banks of the Huangpu, used to be the **Japanese Concession**. These areas eventually became a Chinese industrial suburb, the **Hongkou District**, and are not of great interest, although the bridges above the polluted sections along Suzhou Creek are good for observing tugs and barges – there's a great deal of industry and warehouses along these banks. The major universities, Tongji and Fudan, are right up north. The main factory zones, shipyards, warehouses and new high-rise housing developments are in the sector north-east of here.

Over on the other side of the railway tracks to the west and the north of the city are rings of new industrial suburbs – **satellite towns** where the workers live in high-rises adjacent to their factories and plants – the Soviet model. This also includes the area due south of the old Chinese city and Frenchtown. The housing projects sprang up, as they did in other Chinese cities, in the 1950s, and were erected outside the original city limits. The initial building programme concentrated upon the construction of about 10,000 dwelling units in north-east Shanghai, and another 10,000 in southern, northern and western Shanghai. These satellite towns are about eight km from the centre of Shanghai, and they have their own schools, day-care centres, markets and hospitals.

Beyond the industrial zones are the **market gardens** that feed the Shanghai dynamo – a long way out there from downtown, but very close if you head due east. Directly east of the Bund, on the eastern banks of the Huangpu, is an area which was barely worked on by the western powers. There is now a mixed residential, industrial and warehousing strip running along the eastern bank, but immediately beyond it are farming areas. There are no bridges over the Huangpu, since it would disturb the heavy shipping, but lots of ferries do the job.

The Bund

The Bund is an Anglo-Indian term for the embankment of a muddy waterfront. In Chinese it's referred to as *Waitan* and on the map it's Zhongshan Donglu (Zhongshan Road East).

The Bund is an apt description. Between 1920 (when the problem was first noticed) and 1965 the city of Shanghai sank several metres. Correction of the problem involved pumping water back into the ground, but the Venetian threat is still there. Concrete rafts are used as foundations for high-rises in this spongy mass.

The Bund is a great meeting place for local Chinese and foreigners alike. People stroll up and down in search of vicarious excitement, often provided by street performers or free-marketeers. Pedlars sell anything from home-made underwear to naughty pictures. In the morning it's an exhibition of tai chi and martial arts; at night it's a lovers' lane.

Though startling to behold in a Chinese

city, the edifices that line the Bund are no special wonder. The exteriors are a solemn mix of neo-classical 1930s Chicago and New York with a bit of monumental Egyptian thrown in for good measure. To the Europeans, the Bund was Shanghai's Wall Street, and it saw a fever of trading as the city's fortunes rose and fell with each impending crisis. The buildings changed function several times as the crises got the better of traders, but originally they were banks, trading houses, hotels, residential buildings, commercial buildings and clubs.

One of the most famous traders was Jardine Matheson & Company. They registered in Canton in 1832, and dug into the China trade two years later when the British parliament abolished the East India Company's monopoly of the place. In 1848 Jardine's purchased the first land offered for sale to foreigners in Shanghai and set up shop shortly after, dealing in opium and tea. Today, Jardine Matheson just about owns half of Hong Kong and they're not finished with Shanghai either – they have an office across the way at Shanghai Mansions. James Matheson's nephew Donald, who inherited most of the Matheson side of the fortune, served in China from 1837 to 1849. By the age of 30 he'd had it, went to England, and later became the chairman of the Executive Committee for the Suppression of the Opium Trade.

At the north-west end of the Bund were, or are, the British Public Gardens (now Huangpu Park), off-limits to Chinese during the colonial era. A sign at the entrance listed regulations, which included the prohibition of Chinese and dogs from the park. A Sikh guard stood at the gateway; the British brought in an Indian force to protect themselves after the Boxer Uprising of 1900.

While the Bund may no longer be full of noisy hawkers, tramcars, Oldsmobiles, typists, blackmarketeers, sailors, taipans and rickshawmen, its function is still very much the same – only this time it's the foreigners who come to kowtow to the Chinese trading establishments now set up here. The Customs House (built in 1927) is still a customs house. A readily identifiable exterior by the dome on top is the Hong Kong & Shanghai Bank, completed in 1921 – one of the most impressive hunks of granite in colonial Asia. The rowdy RAF Club used to be up in the dome. Today the bank houses the Shanghai People's Municipal Government (City Hall, CCP and PLA HQ) so there's little chance of seeing the interior. As for the HK & Shanghai Bank, they have a more modest office further north.

The statues that lined the Bund were stripped away; the whereabouts of the pair of bronze lions that once stood outside the HK & Shanghai Bank remains a mystery. It was first thought that they were melted down for cannons by the Japanese, but later the Chinese claimed they had found them. Several western sources mention seeing the lions in the early 1970s – it's possible they were bought out for the making of a movie.

One interior that you can visit is the Dongfeng Hotel; as you sweep through the double doors, cross the marble paving and bump into what looks like a railway concourse, you get an idea of how the Dongfeng started life. This was the Shanghai Club, the snootiest little gang this side of Trafalgar Square. Membership was confined to highbrow Brits, men only. To the left of the entrance is a Suzhou-style restaurant where you'll find the Long Bar, a 33-metre span of thick wood now hacked into three separate pieces. Opposite was the smoking room, now a Cantonese-style restaurant, where the members, stomach replete, would doze with their copies of the *Times*, freshly ironed by the roomboys.

Nanjing Lu & the Downtown District

Nanjing Donglu (Nanjing Road East), from the Peace to the Park hotels, is the golden mile of China's commerce. Some display windows will even stop you in your

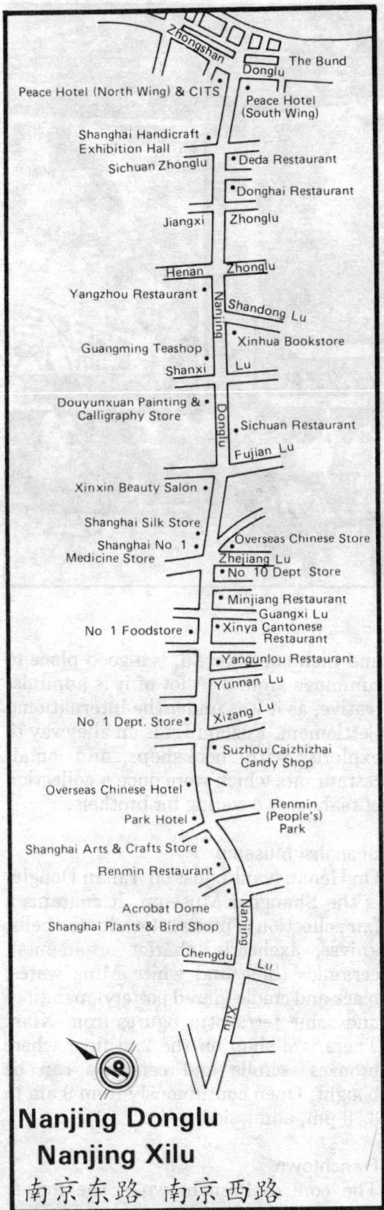

tracks! Just about everything can be found here, though back in Hong Kong it would be cheaper.

Before 1949 Nanjing Lu was a mixture of restaurants, nightclubs and coffinmakers. The most prestigious department stores were there – and still are, though now they are used by eager patrons clamouring for the latest things in short supply. Wing On's is now the No 10 Department Store, Sun Sun's is now the No 1 Food Store and The Sun is now the No 1 Department Store.

It's rather entertaining to drag yourself through these places where the escalators no longer function. The one practical souvenir that travellers like to get is a black vinyl carry bag, with 'Shanghai' embossed on it – proves you've been there.

A stroll down Nanjing Lu at night offers eye-catching window displays and neon signs. Shanghai has the best reputation in China for the art of hairdressing – considered yet another facet of decadence back in the '60s and early '70s.

By day, from 9 am to 6 pm, only buses are allowed on Nanjing Lu, which otherwise turns into a pedestrian thoroughfare. You'll see why there's such a keen one-child-only campaign in Shanghai; the human tide on Nanjing Lu has to be seen to be believed.

At the end of Nanjing Donglu you come to another shopping drag, Nanjing Xilu (called Bubbling Well Road before the well was sealed over). Dividing the sections for a bit of a breather are Renmin Square and Renmin Park, once the Shanghai Racecourse. The old Racecourse Clubhouse is now the Shanghai Municipal Library, and the building is among the oldest in the city.

The nondescript parkland and the desert-like expanses of paving at Renmin Square are where all those large meetings and rallies were held back in the '60s and '70s. In April 1969, 2.7 million people poured in here to demonstrate against the Soviet Union after clashes on the border (though even that figure didn't top the

peaceful 10 million who'd gathered for the May Day celebrations in Beijing in 1963). The area is also used for paramilitary training; under Renmin Square is a large air-raid shelter. Near Renmin Square is Jiangyin Lu, where you'll find Shanghai's chief goldfish market.

An interesting store at the dividing line of Nanjing Donglu and Nanjing Xilu is the *Shanghai Plants & Bird Shop*, at 364 Nanjing Xilu. It sells bonsai plants, pots, tools, birdcages, goldfish and funeral wreaths. Related to hobbies, such activities (with the possible exception of the last) were suppressed during the Cultural Revolution. This is possibly one of the few places in the city where you'll find fresh flowers for sale. Most Shanghainese will queue up to buy plastic flowers – they last longer and are cheaper than the real thing.

The downtown area, bounded by Yanan Donglu, Xizang Zhonglu, Jinling Donglu and Sichuan Zhonglu, is a good place to rummage around. A lot of it is administrative, as it was under the International Settlement. Fuzhou Lu is an alleyway to explore, with bookshops and small restaurants which were once a collection of teahouses covering for brothels.

Shanghai Museum

On Henan Nanlu, just off Yanan Donglu, is the Shanghai Museum. It contains a fair collection of bronzes (graduated bells, knives, axeheads, chariot ornaments), ceramics (blue and white Ming wares, black and cradle-glazed pottery), paintings and some terracotta figures from Xian. There is a shop on the 2nd floor where bronzes, scrolls and ceramics can be bought. Open continuously from 9 am to 3.30 pm, admission is Y1.

Frenchtown

The core of Frenchtown – the former

French concession – is the area around Huaihai Lu and the Jinjiang Hotel. The area was mainly inhabited by White Russian emigres who numbered up to a third of the foreign population in the 1920s and 1930s. They ran cafés and tailoring businesses along Huaihai, and took jobs as riding instructors, bodyguards – and prostitutes.

The cafés and tailoring outlets in today's Shanghai still centre around Huaihai Lu and the 1930s architecture is still standing. The area offers some good shopping (mainly shoe stores, household decorations and some secondhand shops) and excellent bakeries. The Parisian touch is about as chic as China will get. The street leading west off the north-western tip of the Jinjiang Hotel is intriguing for its squat, double-storied architecture where underwear flaps from the former residences of the rich, or a duck on a pole hangs out to dry.

Back in the bad old days the French Concession had a different set of laws from the International Settlement. The French licensed prostitution and opium smoking (while the Internationals just turned a blind eye). With such laws, and because of its proximity to the old Chinese city, a number of China's underworld figures were attracted to the French side of things. On Xinle Lu, a kind of cul-de-sac which is the first diagonal street to the west of Xiangyang Park, is the Donghu Guest House (at No 167). This used to be the headquarters of the Great Circle Gang. Chief mobster was Du Yuesheng, boss of the gang. After a career as a sweet-potato vendor, Du got his start in the police force of the French Concession, where he used his position to squeeze money out of the local opium merchants. In 10 years he had risen to a high position in the Chinese gangs that controlled the opium trade in the Yangtse Valley – they were said to contribute the equivalent of 20 million American dollars, annually, to the French authorities. In return the French allowed them to use the concession as a base for their operations. By the 1930s Du was on first-name terms with the Nanjing government leaders, and Chiang Kaishek even appointed him 'chief of the bureau of opium suppression'. In March 1927, as the Kuomintang troops approached Shanghai on their Northern Expedition, the Communist-led workers rose in revolt and took over the Chinese part of Shanghai as planned. But Chiang had different ideas. Financed by Chiang's supporters among the Chinese bankers in Shanghai, escorted by foreign police, and provided with rifles and armoured cars by the International Settlement, Du Yuesheng's gangs launched an attack on the workers, killing between 5000 and 10,000 people, many of them Communists and left-wing Kuomintang. The attack wiped out the Shanghai Communists in a single stroke, and was followed by further massacres in Canton, Changsha and Nanchang, forcing the Communists to move the focus of their movement to the countryside.

Site of the 1st National Congress of the Communist Party

One activity which the French, and later the Kuomintang, did not take to was political meetings – these were illegal. The Chinese Communist Party was founded in July 1921 in a French Concession building, at a meeting of delegates from the various Communist and Socialist organisations around China.

This building is usually recorded as being at 76 Xingye Lu – but according to the street signs in the area it stands at the corner of Huangpi and Ximen Lu, further south of Xingye Lu – see the map for directions. Captions are in English and the building is closed Mondays and Thursdays.

We don't really know if the 'First Supper' was as cool, calm or collected as the present museum makes out. We don't even know if this really was where the meeting took place, exactly who was there, how many were there, the actual date or what happened. Nevertheless, the museum has been organised here in what is supposed to be the house of one of the delegates, Li Hanjun. Two foreigners are also said to have been in attendance.

Simon Leys in his book *Chinese Shadows* drops 12 names in the attendance list. According to him, what happened to them afterwards doesn't reflect too well on Communist history. Only Mao Zedong and Tong Biwu, elder statesman of the Party and a remarkable political all-rounder, survived in good standing until their natural deaths in the 1970s.

As for the others, four were executed by the Kuomintang or provincial warlords; four defected to the Kuomintang and of these four, two went over to the Japanese. Another delegate, Li Da, remained loyal to the Party and eventually became president of Wuhan University after Liberation; he is supposed to have died of injuries inflicted on him by the Red Guards in 1966. The host, Li Hanjun, appears to have left or to have been excluded from the Party early on, but his execution by the Kuomintang in 1927 rehabilitated him.

The story continues that the delegates' meeting was disrupted by the intrusion of an outsider – presumably a spy – and fearing a raid by the French police, they left the premises and later continued their meeting on a houseboat in Jiaxing, half-way to Hangzhou. The Shanghai building is supposed to have been damaged during the massacre of 1927, again at the hands of the Japanese.

Sun Yatsen's Residence

At 7 Xianshan Lu, formerly the Rue Molière, is the former residence of Dr Sun Yatsen. He lived for six years in this house not far from Fuxing Park, supported by Overseas Chinese funds. After Sun's death, his wife, Soong Qingling, continued to live here until 1937, constantly watched by Kuomintang plain-clothes men and French police. Her sister had married Chiang Kaishek in 1927. Her brother, T V Soong, was on-and-off finance minister to Chiang and a wheeler and dealer in banking fortunes. Soong Qingling was a Communist, so it must have made for interesting dinner conversation. The house is set back from the street, furnished the way it used to be (it was looted by the Japanese). Gaining admission takes persistance as the staff usually tell you to come back another day to get rid of you. Fuxing Park is also worth a stroll if you're in the area; locals airing the kids off, playing chess, etc.

Arts & Crafts Research Institute

A French bourgeois villa is worth delving into; it's now the Arts & Crafts Research Institute at 79 Fenyang Lu. The mansion is magnifique, and the institute has something like 15 specialities including woollen embroidery, boxwood carving, lacquerware inlay, paper-cutting. The faculty here creates the prototypes for small factories and workshops around China, examines the traditional arts, and acts as technical adviser to the specialist factories in Shanghai. The first of its kind in the PRC, the institute was created in 1956. The Conservatory of Music is on the same street – for more details see the section on Nightlife.

Huangpu River Trip

There are three main perspectives of Shanghai – from the gutters, from the heights (aerial views from the battlements of the tourist fortresses), and from the waters. The Huangpu River offers some remarkable views of the Bund and the riverfront activity. There's something historical about doing this joy ride – the junks that cut in and out of the harbour bring back memories so old you probably last saw them in some pirate movie. Back in the 1920s you would have arrived in Shanghai by boat and today's touring vessels seem to ham it up, imitating the colonial style of that era.

Tour boats down the Huangpu depart from the dock on the Bund, slightly north of the Peace Hotel. There are several decks on the boat, but prices for foreigners are Y15 (special class A) and Y8 (special class B). Departure times are 8.30 am and 1.30 pm, with possible extra departures in the summer and on Sundays. The schedule may become more erratic in winter due to bad weather.

Tickets can be purchased in advance from CITS at the Peace Hotel, or at the boat dock – but there's no real need if you're taking upper deck since it is unlikely to be full. The boat takes you on a 3½-hour ride, 60 km round-trip, northward up the Huangpu to the junction with the Yangtse River, to Wusongkou and back again along the same route. On the return run they show videos on the lower deck – usually blood-thirsty kung-fu flicks.

Shanghai is one of the world's largest ports; 2000 ocean-going ships and about 15,000 river steamers load and unload here every year. Coolies used to have the backbreaking task of loading and unloading, but these days the ports are a forest of cranes, derricks, conveyor belts and forklifts. The tour boat passes an enormous variety of craft – freighters, bulk carriers, roll-on roll-off ships, sculling sampans, giant praying-mantis cranes, the occasional junk and Chinese navy vessels (which aren't supposed to be photographed).

Yuyuan Bazaar

At the north-eastern end of the old Chinese city, the bazaar area centres on what is known as Yuyuan or Mandarin Gardens, and includes the Temple of the Town Gods (Chenghuangmiao). The place gets some 200,000 visitors daily, so try and stay out of it on weekends! There's nothing of historical interest left – people just come here to gawk at each other, mix, buy, sell and eat (see the Places to Eat section), but it's all entertaining enough.

Yu Gardens were built for the Pan family, rich Ming Dynasty officials. The gardens took 18 years to throw together (from 1559 to 1577) and much less time to destroy. They were bombarded during the Opium War in 1842, which is somewhat ironic since the deity lurking in the Temple of the Town Gods is supposed to guarantee the peace of the region. In the mid-19th century the gardens became the home-base of the 'Society of Small Swords', who joined with the Taipings

and wreaked considerable casualties on the adjacent French Concession. The French responded promptly with thorough destruction. Within the gardens is a museum devoted to the uprising and the movement's demise. The area was again savaged during the Boxer Rebellion. The gardens close early for lunch.

The **Temple of the Town Gods (Cheng Huang Miao)** first appeared in the Song Dynasty, and disappeared somewhere in the last paragraph. The main hall was rebuilt in 1926 with reinforced concrete and has recently undergone renovation after being used as a warehouse.

Fanning out from the temple and the gardens is the Yuyuan shopping area – a Disneyland version of what the authorities think tourists might think is the real China. You enter the main action area via the **Wuxinting Teahouse**, a five-sided job set in a pond and looking as old as tea itself (it's pleasant to sit on the upper floor over a 60-fen pot of chai, but stay clear of the coffee and cocoa!). The zigzag bridges leading to the teahouse were once full of misshapen beggars at every turn, something to try and visualise as you take in the present scenery. The surrounding bazaar has something like 100 small shops selling the tiny, the curious and the touristy. Lots of places for Chinese snacks. You can get hankies emblazoned with Chinese landmarks – every time you blow your nose it will remind you of China. You can also get antiques, fans, scissors, bamboo articles, steamed ravioli, vegetarian buns, wine and meat dumplings, chicken and duck blood soup, radish-shred cakes, shell carvings, paintings, jigsaws, and so on.

The strangest thing about Yuyuan Bazaar is that if you get past the 'reception centre' and the stage shows and further into the cobbled alleyways, you strike near-poverty. The slums have been cleared, and newer housing blocks exist to the south, but the back alleys are certainly lower-end living. There's no sanitation – everything's done with buckets and public toilets. Notices in Chinese warn residents not to eat too much at the height of summer because disease spreads faster. Group tours that have requested a bit more of an in-depth visit have been somewhat misled – word goes out to the area to be visited ahead of time, and the sick and disabled are told to stay off the streets. A group of tourists remarked on the 'healthy' rouged cheeks of the children down this way – it was winter, and the red cheeks came from windchill. The maze of alleys is best explored early in the morning (5 to 8 am), when gutter teeth-cleaning and other ablutions are underway.

Jade Buddha Temple & Suzhou Creek

From the Yuyuan Bazaar you can hop on bus No 16 and ride all the way out to the Jade Buddha Temple (Yufosi). The ride takes in half of Shanghai en route, and most likely half the population will get off the bus with you.

The temple is an active one, with 70 resident monks at last count. It was built between 1911 and 1918. The exterior is readily identifiable by the bright saffron walls. Inside, the centrepiece is a 1.9-metre-high white jade buddha (some say it's alabaster), which was installed here after it had been brought by a monk from Burma to Zhejiang Province in 1882. This seated buddha, encrusted with jewels, is said to weigh 1000 kg. A smaller, reclining buddha from the same shipment lies on a redwood bed – the pose is suspiciously reminiscent of an opium smoker.

In the large hall are three gold-plated buddhas, and other halls house ferocious-looking deities. Artefacts abound, not all on display, and some 7000 Buddhist sutras line the walls. Should your timing coincide, a ceremony may be in progress. Also in the precincts is a branch of the Antique & Curio Store that sells miniature sandalwood drums and gongs, replicas of the larger ones used in ceremonies.

The temple was largely inactive from 1949 to 1980, as the monks were disbanded and the temple used for other functions. During the Cultural Revolution the place was only saved from destruction by a telegram (so the story goes) direct from the State Council. No doubt the recent picking up of activity is partly due to the tourist trade. The fact is that Shanghai, being so young, has few temples to show off. Yufosi is popular with Overseas Chinese. No photography is permitted. The temple closes for lunch between noon and 1 pm and is open daily except on some special occasions such as the Lunar New Year in February – that's when Chinese Buddhists, some 20,000 of them, descend on the place.

An interesting route to the Jade Buddha Temple is along Suzhou Creek. It's a long walk there, and you may prefer to bus part of the way. The creek (water and banks heavily polluted) is home to sampans, small craft and barges, with crews delivering goods from the Yangtse reaches. There are stacks of bridges along the route and from these you'll get a decent view of the river life. Warehouses occasionally block the paths along the banks. On the way is a former church with an interesting twist – it's now a research institute for the electric-light industry.

Kids

Chinese kids are the most baffling part of the population. Nappyless, never crying, never looking worried – who knows what goes on inside their heads? Around the city are Children's Palaces, where extra-curricular activities take place and special interests are pursued. In theory this supplements regular schooling – but it has overtones of an elitist educational system. The one most visited by group tours (you can get in by yourself if you push) is on Yanan Zhonglu, just west of Jingan Park. The building really is a palace that once belonged to the Kadoorie family, and was then known as Marble House. The children here make model aeroplanes, play video games, attend classes in drawing, drama, music – and practise how to love their country and impress tourists.

A stark contrast to the kids' palace is the Peiguang Middle School. Drop down here in the early morning when the kids are doing their exercises in the courtyard just off the street (to the sound of 'Oh Canada'). The school is along Xizang Lu, cornering Jiujiang Lu, which is one block south of Nanjing Donglu. The school used to be the notorious Laozhu Police Station in the concession days.

Children's stores are among the places where parents and their (usually one) offspring gather. Try the bookstore at 772 Nanjing Xilu, the Xiangyang at 993 Nanjing Xilu (toys, clothing and furniture), the foodstore at 980 Nanjing Xilu (cakes and cookies), the shoe and hat shop at 600 Nanjing Donglu, and the clothing stores at 939 and 765 Huaihai Zhonglu.

In the entertainment line, much-publicised child prodigies pop up at the Conservatory of Music (see the Nightlife section). Shanghai has its own film animation studio – China's equivalent of Disneyworld products. There's also a troupe called the Children's Art Theatre.

Tomb of Lu Xun (Hongkou Park)

Lu Xun (1881-1936) was a novelist and essayist, and was regarded as the founder of modern Chinese writing. He was also revered as a scholar and a teacher. Though he was not a Communist, most of his books were banned by the Kuomintang and he had to stay in hiding in the French Concession. His message to Chinese youth read, 'Think, and study the economic problems of society . . . travel through the hundreds of dead villages, visit the generals and then visit the victims, see the realities of your time with opened eyes and a clear mind, and work for an enlightened society, but always think and study'.

Lu Xun is best remembered for *The True Story of Ah Q*, the story of an illiterate coolie whose experiences through the first revolution of 1911 show the utter failure of that event to reach down to the ordinary people. Constantly baffled, seeing everything through a fog of ignorance and superstition, knowing words but not their meaning, he goes from one humiliation to the next, but each time rationalises his defeats into moral victories. Even when he is executed for a crime he did not commit, he goes cheerily to his death singing from a Chinese opera he does not understand: 'After 20 years I will be reborn again a hero'.

Lu Xun's tomb is within easy reach of the Bund, and is located in Hongkou Park. There's a pompous statue of the writer which would have horrified him. The statue was cast in 1961 and replaces an earlier concrete model, which would also have horrified him. His brother in Beijing wrote to another writer in Hong Kong, 'I have just seen a photograph of the statue they put up in front of Lu Xun's tomb in Shanghai; really, this is the supreme mockery! How could this personage sitting as on a throne be the effigy of someone who hated all solemn attitudes?' A museum in Hongkou Park tells the story of Lu Xun from the Communist point of view in Chinese.

Other Attractions

Plans for Shanghai include the erection of a 400-metre-high (!) television tower with observation deck on the east bank of the Huangpu, to provide tourists with satellite-views of the city below. If heights make you giddy then you might instead try searching out some of Shanghai's illicit gambling dens. Chinese newspapers report that illegal gambling dens are springing up in the city, with enormous stakes laid on the tables.

A further 20 km north of Hongkou Park, towards the banks of the Yangtse and requiring a longer bus ride, is Jiading County, with a ruined Confucian temple and a classical garden.

South-west of central Shanghai and nearing a bend in the Huangpu River (within reach of Frenchtown) is the **Longhua Pagoda**. This fell into disrepair, was used by the Red Guards as an advertising pole, and has since undergone renovation for the tourist trade. The pagoda is 40 metres high, octagonal with upturned eaves; it is said to date to the 10th century but was probably rebuilt a couple of times. The surrounding temple is largely restructured concrete, but the statuary of ferocious figures is impressive. The temple's once-famous peach blossoms have now disappeared.

The Xijiahui area bordering the western end of Frenchtown once had a Jesuit settlement, with an observatory (still in use). **St Ignatius Cathedral**, whose spires were lopped off by Red Guards, has been restored and is open once again for Catholic services. It's at 158 Puxi Lu, Xujiahui District.

Further south-west of the Longhua Pagoda are the **Shanghai Botanical Gardens**, with an exquisite collection of 9000 miniatures and 100 species.

On the way to the town of Jiaxing, by rail or road, is Sunjiang County, 20 km south-west of Shanghai. The place is older than Shanghai itself. On Tianma Shan, in Sunjiang County, is the **Huzhou Pagoda**, built in 1079 AD. It's the leaning tower of China, with an inclination now exceeding the tower at Pisa by 1.5 degrees. The 18.8-metre-high tower started tilting 200 years ago.

Heading in a westerly direction from the centre of Shanghai you'll encounter the **Industrial Exhibition Hall** – drop in here for a mammoth view of Soviet palace architecture. There are irregular displays of industrial wares and handicrafts from Shanghai.

Out near the airport is **Xijiao Park**, a zoo with a roller-skating rink, children's playground and other recreational facilities. To the west of that is the former **Sassoon Villas**.

At Qingpu County, 25 km west of Shanghai, they've made up for the dearth of real antiquities and temples by creating a new scenic area for tourists to visit.

Places to Stay

Shanghai hotels are sights in their own right, a trip back to the '20s and '30s when the city was the most sophisticated of travellers' destinations. Furnishings and art deco opulence have survived quite well, considering what has passed. Added to this is a strange armoury of electronic gadgets like closed-circuit TV, air-con, video games – all those creature comforts for today's visitor. A fair amount of renovation has been done on the buildings in the interest of tourism, though socialist plumbing is not always as successful as western.

Apart from being navigation landmarks, the lofty upper floors of the downtown hotels offer stupendous views, day or night. These can be combined with a trip to restaurants serving great Chinese and western food, the latter sometimes linked with pre-Liberation chefs and usually excellent. Shanghai's relatively decadent nightlife also happens within the walls of the hotels; those mainly guilty of this are the Peace Hotel, the Jinjiang Hotel, and to some extent, Shanghai Mansions.

Shanghai is a headache for the low-budget traveller. As in Beijing there is simply a chronic lack of space, and a lot of what's available is permanently occupied by businesspeople, foreign dignitaries or resident foreign experts. The one established dormitory in Shanghai is at the Pujiang Hotel, so head there first if you want the cheapest available accommodation.

Places to Stay – bottom end

The *Pujiang Hotel* (tel 246388) at 15 Huangpu Lu is near Shanghai Mansions, and caters to a mixed Chinese and western clientele. The dormitories are the main attraction and the hotel is now the established backpackers' hang-out of Shanghai. If the dorms are full they put you in a hallway with overhead walkways – rather like a cross between a military hospital and a prison. Dorm beds are Y17 a night, which includes a mediocre breakfast. Double rooms (no singles) cost from Y73. The communal showers are in need of renovation. The Pujiang used to be the Astor House Hotel, one of the most elegant in the early concession days, before it was dwarfed by Shanghai Mansions. Today the Pujiang is run down and can get cold and clammy in winter – otherwise it's nice enough. Take bus No 65 from near the Main (North) Railway Station.

Places to Stay – middle

The *Seagull Hotel* is on the waterfront and a minute's walk from the Pujiang Hotel. Doubles cost from Y88. A moderate-priced restaurant on the 2nd floor serves Chinese and European dishes. Generous helpings.

The *Park Hotel* (tel 225225) is at 170 Nanjing Xilu and overlooks Renmin Park. The rooms have some old-world furnishings (the place went up in 1934) and prices are a drop lower than most hotels. Single rooms cost Y66, doubles Y144. The best views of Shanghai are from the men's toilets on the 14th floor. Take bus No 18 from the railway station.

The *Shenjiang Hotel* (tel 225115) is at 740 Hankou Lu, down an alley facing south off Renmin Park, and is best approached from this direction. It's ostensibly for Chinese and Overseas Chinese only, but has been known to take foreigners. Doubles cost from Y50 (no single rooms). Beds are designed for short legs. The hotel was built back in 1934 and is an old American-style hotel. There are some dorm beds but for men only. Take bus No 18 from the railway station; or take bus No 65, which goes around the long way.

Places to Stay – top end

One thing worth thinking about – this is Shanghai, and the history and the character of the Bund is one of the reasons to come here. A number of modern hotels have been built in Shanghai in the last few years, but to get some feel for the place you really need a nice wood-panelled room in the Park or the upper storeys of the Peace Hotel.

Shanghai Mansions (tel 246260) is at 20 Suzhou Beilu, near the Pujiang Hotel on the same side of Huangpu River at the junction with Suzhou Creek. Double rooms (no singles) cost from Y127. For a suite toward the top of the hotel with a waterfront view and balcony and perhaps a grand piano – well, if you've got that sort of money then there's no need to ask the price. The Mansions are rather dull compared to other Shanghai hotels but try and make it to the rooftop because the views are stunning! The 20-storey brick building was constructed in 1934 as a posh British residential hotel. Since it was on the fringes of the International Settlement near the Japanese side of town, it was quickly taken over at the outset of the Sino-Japanese war in 1937. The Japanese stripped the fittings (like the radiators) for scrap metal, and the same fate befell other Shanghai hotels during the occupation. As for the billiard tables, these were sawn off at the legs to fit the smaller stature of Japanese enthusiasts. The place used to be known as Broadway Mansions; after the Japanese surrender and before 1949, the US Military Advisory Group to the Kuomintang set up shop on the lower floors, while the upper section was used by the foreign press and one floor was devoted to the Foreign Correspondents' Club.

The *Overseas Chinese Hotel (Huaqiao Fandian)* (tel 226226) is at 104 Nanjing Xilu – it's easily recognisable by the distinctive clock tower with the big Red Star on it, and by the fabulously ornate foyer. Doubles cost from Y120.

The *Jinjiang Hotel* (tel 534242) is at 59 Maoming Nanlu. It's so vast you need a map of the place to find your way around – a brochure with map is available in the north building. The colossus stretches north-south along an entire block with two gates on the western side. Nice old plumbing and excellent radiators; there are some doubles with shared bathrooms adjoining two rooms. Doubles cost from Y178. To get to the Jinjiang take bus No 41 from the railway station; bus No 26 goes there from the Bund area.

If you don't stay at the Jinjiang you should at least drop down and have a look at it; it's located in what used to be the old French Concession, an interesting alternative to the Bund, since the surrounding area is now entirely residential. The residents of the hotel, though, need never venture out since this fortress-like building has all you need to survive. Nixon stayed here in 1972 if that's any recommendation. Apart from his fingerprints, check out the North Building, a 14-storey block once called the Cathay Mansions and built as an exclusive French apartment block with amazing wood-panelling and iron chandelier period pieces. Additional attractions of the Jinjiang include the Jin Li Restaurant on the ground floor of the new South Building (with 24-hour service); a dance hall and western-style restaurant on the 11th floor of the North Building; and a Hong Kong-style disco called the *Club d'Elegance* on the ground floor of the West Building (with a Y35-per-person cover charge). Check out the expensive though rather elegant *Café Reve*.

The *Peace Hotel (Heping Fandian)* (tel 211244 for the northern high-rise wing, and 218050 for the south building) is on the corner of the Bund and Nanjing Donglu. Doubles cost from Y190. On the ground floor of the 12-storey edifice are the sumptuous lobby, shops, bookstore, bank, CITS office, video games parlour, snooker tables, café and barber. The scalp massage service at the latter has a good reputation.

To get to the hotel take bus No 65 from the railway station. The Peace is a highly-prized location for businesspeople since it is adjacent to the Chinese trading corporations along the Bund. During the winter months conferences are rife, large numbers of Chinese move in and it becomes a mite difficult to get in. Drop by and examine the decor: staggering! High ceilings, chandeliers, brass door-plates, ornate mirrors, art deco lamps and fixtures, and 1930s calligraphy. Go up to the Dragon & Phoenix Restaurant on the 8th floor for great views across the Bund and the Huangpu River. The south wing used to be the Palace Hotel and was built in 1906; the brass plumbing within is original.

The Peace is a ghostly reminder of the immense wealth of Victor Sassoon. From a Baghdad Jewish family, he made millions out of the opium trade and then ploughed it back into Shanghai real estate and horses. Sassoon's quote of the day was 'There is only one race greater than the Jews, and that's the Derby'. His office-cum-hotel was completed in 1930 and was known as Sassoon House, incorporating the Cathay Hotel. From the top floors Victor commanded his real estate – he is estimated to have owned 1900 buildings in Shanghai.

The Cathay Hotel fell into the same category as the Taj in Bombay, the Stanley Raffles in Singapore and the Peninsula in Hong Kong as *the* place to stay. Sassoon himself resided in what is now the VIP section below the green pyramidal tower, complete with Tudor panelling. He also maintained a Tudor-style villa out near Hongqiao Airport just west of the zoo. Anyone who was anyone could be seen dancing in the Tower Restaurant. The likes of Noel Coward (who wrote *Private Lives* in the Cathay) entertained themselves in this penthouse ballroom.

Back in 1949 the Kuomintang strayed into the place awaiting the arrival of the Communists. A western writer of the time records an incident in which 50 Kuomintang arrived carrying their pots and pans, vegetables and firewood, and one soldier was overheard asking where to billet the mules. After the Communists took over the city, the troops were billeted in places like the Picardie (now the Hengshen Hotel on the outskirts of the city), where they spent hours experimenting with the elevators, used bidets as face-showers, and washed rice in the toilets – which was all very well until someone pulled the chain. In 1953 foreigners tried to give the Cathay to the CCP in return for exit visas. The government refused but finally accepted after the payment of 'back taxes'.

Places to Eat

Shanghai has a couple of its own specialities and is noted for its seafood (such as the freshwater crab that appears around October to December). Eating in the major restaurants can be unpleasant as there is intense competition from the masses for tables and seats. Restaurants are forever packed in Shanghai and you really need some local help to overcome the language problems.

Lunch (around 11.30 am to 2 pm) is sometimes OK but dinner (5 to 7 pm) is a rat race. In these busy restaurants the waiters will try and get rid of you by either telling you that there are no tables, or by directing you to the cadre and foreigners' rooms – with their beefed-up prices. If it eases your digestion, back in the inflation-ridden China of 1947 a couple had dinner one evening in a hotel and found their bill came to 250 million yuan!

If you want to spend more time eating, and at local prices, then try restaurants a bit off the track, perhaps around the old French Concession area. You could also try the smaller places on Fuzhou Lu, where the greasy-spoon prices drop to a few yuan per head. On the other hand, if it's good food (either Chinese or western) you want, in surroundings that echo the days of the foreign concessions, then splash out on the restaurants in the old colonial hotels (details at the end of this section). It's one aspect of Shanghai not to be missed.

Also not to be missed in Shanghai is the ease and delight of snack-eating. You get waylaid for hours trying to make it along the length of Nanjing Lu, stumbling from pastry shops and wiping off the smudges of lemon meringue pie, chocolate and cream, only to fall immediately into the sweet store next door. The tourist hotels have a good range of cakes, chocolate eclairs and ice cream sundaes to get you started. The offerings for breakfast from the Chinese snack shops are so good you may be converted yet!

Common Chinese breakfast fare is the *youtiao*, a disgustingly greasy doughnut stick – but deep-fried variations in the dough line are smaller and much more palatable. Western snacks are a fad among the young of Shanghai; sandwiches are awful, coffee is terrible, cream cakes are fair to good, cocoa is disgusting, cold drinks are erk, but pastries are top notch. These snack hangouts have lots of character and there are lots of characters to be observed.

One thing worth noting – if you wander into a Nanjing Lu restaurant and see a couple in matching suits, a red rose in the lapel, and orange soft drinks on every table – then forget it, it's a wedding party. Around dinnertime all the Nanjing Lu restaurants seem to be occupied by them.

Nanjing Donglu The *Yangzhou* at 308 Nanjing Donglu has, as the name implies, Yangzhou-style food. No longer the greasy spoon it once was, it now caters to groups only. You'll need about eight people to fill a table.

The *Sichuan* (tel 221965) at No 457 has hot and spicy food, including camphor-tea duck and some rather strange-tasting chicken. Don't let them herd you into the private annexes. Stand your ground in the pleb section, where you'll get enough to fill three people for around Y12. Lively place at lunchtime; grab the back of someone's chair (everybody else does) and wait for them to go.

The *Minjiang* (tel 241009) at No 679 is a Fujianese-style establishment.

The *Xinya* (tel 224393) at No 719 has foreigners' cubicles on the 3rd floor with rail-car wood panelling and Cantonese food. Otherwise the lower floors are bare and bright like any self-respecting Chinese restaurant. Moderately priced dishes can be had for lunch and dinner, yum cha between 6.30 and 9.30 am. On the ground floor is a marvellous pastry shop featuring lemon and coconut tarts and cream-filled cones. Across the road is an enormous sweet and cake shop the size of a department store.

For snacks and pastries try the *Donghai Fandian* at No 145; it was once known as Chez Sullivan and is now full of bicycle punks.

Nanjing Xilu The *Luyangcun* (tel 539787) at No 763 has snacks downstairs; upstairs they serve Sichuan and Yangzhou-style chicken and seafood.

The *Meilongzhen* (tel 532561) at 22 Yilingbayi Long, Nanjing Xilu, also deals in Sichuan and Yangzhou styles (the upper floor is for banquets).

For snacks, try the *Wangjiasha Snack Bar* at No 805, off Shimen Lu: chicken, shrimp in soup, sweet and salty glutinous dumplings.

The *Shanghai Children's Foodstore* is at No 980 and is good for cakes, candies and cookies.

Fuzhou Lu This street provides the best chance of getting a feed at low prices. Try places other than those listed; there's enough around.

The *Xinghualou* (tel 282747) at No 343 has snacks, cakes and refreshments downstairs, including a kind of dim sum. Upstairs you'll get Cantonese food, including 'stewed wild cat' and snake.

The *Meiweishi* (tel 221705) at No 600 serves Suzhou and Wuxi styles, as does the *Dahongyun* (tel 223176) at No 556. The latter is somewhat gloomy.

For Chinese-style snacks there's no better than the Yuyuan Bazaar. Nanxiang dumplings (served in a bamboo steamer), pigeon-egg dumplings (shaped like a pigeon egg in summer), vegetarian buns, spicy cold noodles, etc.

Also in the Yuyuan Bazaar area the *Old Shanghai Restaurant* (tel 282782) at 242 Fuyou Lu is a major restaurant specialising in 'Shanghai cuisine' and has been around since day one – it's now housed in a new building. The 2nd floor is air-conditioned and used mainly for banquets, but you might try lunchtime. The *Green Wave Gallery (Lubolang)* serves main courses and more expensive snacks; a seafood dinner may consist of black carp raised in the Lotus Pond under the winding bridge. Snacks include crabmeat buns, lotus root and bamboo shoot shortbread, three-shred eyebrow crispcakes and phoenix-tail dumplings (whatever they are).

Old French Concession Area Try the *Shanghai Western Restaurant* (tel 374902) at 845 Huaihai Zhonglu, and the *Chengdu* (tel 376412) at No 795 – the latter is air-conditioned and has good Sichuan food.

The *Meixan* (tel 373991) at 314 Shaanxi Nanlu, near Huaihai Zhonglu, serves Cantonese crisp duck and chicken.

The *Red House* (tel 565748) at 37 Shaanxi Nanlu was formerly the Chez Louis and things haven't gone so well since Louis left; the food is generally terrible, but the snacks are better so long as they've got the right liqueur (baked Alaska and Grand Marnier soufflé); foreigners are expected to use the more expensive top floor but the ground floor is cheaper.

Along Huaihai Zhonglu is a string of confectioneries that will drive you bonkers! The *Canglangting* (tel 283876) at 9 Chongqing Nanlu south of Huaihai has glutinous rice cakes and Suzhou-style dumplings and noodles. The *Tianshan Moslem Foodstore* at 671 Huaihai has Muslim delicacies, sweets and cakes. The *Laodacheng Bakery & Confectionery* at 875 has a downstairs bakery with superb ice cream in season; upstairs is a café where they spray ice cream over everything, which also offers meringues and macaroons – open until 9.30 pm. The *Shanghai Bakery* at No 979 has French bread, wholemeal bread, cream cakes and chocolate.

Hotel Food The big tourist hotels have excellent Chinese and western food. Dining hours are around 7 to 9 am for breakfast, 11.30 am to 2 pm for lunch and 5.30 to 8 pm for dinner. While some of the offerings in the ritzier parts of the hotels are on the expensive side, a western breakfast is unbeatable and should cost no more than Y3.

The restaurant on the 11th floor of the north building of the *Jinjiang Hotel* serves great western breakfasts (including yoghurt) and has some of the most opulent surroundings and incredible views to be found in Shanghai.

The *Dragon & Phoenix Restaurant* on the 8th floor of the *Peace Hotel* has western, Shanghainese, Sichuan and Cantonese food (breakfasts are amazingly excellent but stay away from the T-bone steak at dinner!). If you examine the tableware closely you might find original Cathay crests. While the exotic seafood (like seaslug) is expensive, there are quite cheap vegetable and pork dishes – on the other hand, if you've never eaten a seaslug then this might be the time to spend some money and find out what it's like.

The *Overseas Chinese Hotel* has a few restaurants. Fujianese food is a speciality in the restaurant near the top of the nine-storey block; there's also a quaint little coffee bar to the left as you enter on the ground floor.

The *Park Hotel* has several restaurants. On the 14th floor (that's actually the 12th since two of the floors are below ground) is a restaurant that used to be called the Sky Terrace; a section of the roof could be rolled back to allow patrons to dine under the stars. Apparently the gizmo is still in place though we haven't heard of anyone getting the planetarium effect. Towards the top is the *Four Seasons Banquet Room* where extensive eight-course imperial banquets, including Beijing duck, can be ordered in advance.

The *Shenjiang Hotel* has some good, cheap restaurants – including places serving Sichuan, Cantonese and Yangzhou fare.

Vegetarian Food Vegetarianism became something of a snobbish fad in Shanghai

at one time; it was linked to Taoist and Buddhist groups, then to the underworld, and surfaced on the tables of restaurants as creations shaped like flowers or animals. Khi Vehdu, who ran the Jingan Temple in the 1930s, was one of the most celebrated exponents. The 1.9-metre-tall abbot had a large following – and each of his seven concubines had a house and car. The Jingan Temple was eventually divested of its Buddhist statues and turned into a factory.

Materials for vegetarian fare include bean products, dried mushrooms, fungus, bamboo shoots, noodles, seaweed – and vegetables. It should be possible to arrange for more elaborate presentation and quality by phoning in advance and booking a vegetarian banquet.

The *Gongdelin* (tel 580218) at 43 Huanghe Lu has mock crab, other mock seafood, mock duck and roasted bran-dough. Banquets can be arranged.

A couple of shops specialise in vegetarian food; these include the *Hongkouqu Grain Store* at 10 Bei Haining Lu, which is good for fresh peanut butter, tahini, grains, beans and vegetable oils. The *Sanjiaodi Vegetable Market* at 250 Tanggu Lu in the Hongkou District, north of the Bund, is a large indoor market selling fresh vegetables and bean curd products, and ready-to-cook dinners, fish and meat. The *Yuyuan Bazaar* area has snack bars serving vegetarian food.

Night Owl Food Food can be bought fairly late in Shanghai. There are a couple of established late-night venues (listed below) as well as numerous holes-in-the-wall serving drinks and noodles.

The *Kaifu Restaurant* (tel 244492) at 878 Sichuan Beilu has Beijing and other cuisines and is open until 10 pm.

The *Hongkouqu Moslem Restaurant* (tel 462233) at 2033 Sichuan Beilu has beef, lamb, baozi and jiaozi dumplings, and is open until 11 pm.

Cafés Shanghai's cafés are open until around 10 pm and sometimes until 10.30 pm – just follow the neon. These are meeting and gossip hangouts where coffee and cakes cost around Y2 for two people – dreadful coffee and lousy cakes, but if you've wondered what it must have been like in a Parisian café in the 1930s then the ambience is definitely there.

After they get booted out of all the shoe stores along Huaihai Zhonglu, young and old folk head for the upstairs section of the *Laodacheng Bakery* which is open until around 10 pm – you can choose cakes downstairs first if you want to. In case things get a bit out of hand there are little round coasters under the glass tops of the tables upstairs at the Laodacheng, reminding people of the one-child policy – with graphics of a lady feeding rabbits.

Nightlife & Entertainment

There's a bite-sized chunk of nightlife to be had here – like elsewhere in China it proceeds in fits and starts, and while it's tame by pre-1949 standards it's rewarding enough. Back in the bad old days the missionaries just didn't know where to start firing in this Sodom of the east; the acrid smell of opium hung in the streets, bevies of bar girls from the four corners draped themselves over the rich; there were casinos, greyhound- and horse-racing tracks, strings of nightclubs, thousands of brothels, lavish dinners, several hundred ballrooms.

The Kuomintang dampened the nightlife by imposing a curfew – the patrons just couldn't get it up in the daylight. When the Communists took over they wiped out in a year what the missionaries had failed to do in a hundred years. Since the average Chinese has to get up at the crack of dawn there's a self-imposed curfew of around 10 pm – nevertheless there are Chinese couples lolling about on the walkways and park benches of the Bund late into the night. Decadent foreign devils can rage on (as much as this place will allow) until around midnight.

Before the Communist takeover one of the major sources of diversion was the Great World Amusement Centre, offering girls, earwax extractors, magicians, mah-jong, jugglers, freak shows, dancing, slot machines, story-tellers, barbers, shooting galleries, pickpockets and a bureau for writing love letters. Today the place has been turned into the Shanghai Youth Palace and stands at the corner of Yanan and Xizang Lu. Since 1983 the place has been hosting 'Youth Evenings' where 30-year-olds come in the hope of finding a husband or wife. Match-making is back in vogue in the PRC.

Bars & Clubs The Peace Hotel Jazz Bar winds up the 1930s music machine from 8 to 11 pm nightly. The name is a misnomer – swing would be a more apt label, with the band pumping out polite renditions of 'Tea for Two', 'Gypsy Rag', 'When the Saints . . . ', 'I Wonder Who's Kissing her Now?' and a sprinkling of Hong Kong pop tunes – no singing but these old-timers do a splendid job with their piano, horns and drum smashes (it seems most of them are actually trained in western classical music). Elderly foreign guests are inspired to leap to the dance floor, but I couldn't tell if they do a foxtrot or a rhumba – before my time. It's time to clean out the eardrums too – what's this, they can't be playing Waltzing Matilda! It's a good place to meet the rest of the foreigners in the woodwork. In the background, waiters with starched napkins over their arms glide between the tables ready to dispense Hot Toddies, Manhattans, Russian Bears, Rusty Nails and Shanghai Cocktails (a mix of gin and Chinese white wine). Ice cream sundaes and other delectables can be procured. All this takes place on the ground floor of the Peace Hotel. The cover charge is Y5.

Alas, the Jinjiang Club is no more. Housed in a remarkable building opposite the main gates of the Jinjiang Hotel, this place had the most extraordinary nightlife museum in the PRC. The dazzling collection of interiors was thrown up in the 1920s and was then known as the Cercle Sportif Français – the French Sporting Club. It closed its doors in 1949, underwent a 30-year silence (when it was rumoured to be either a military training centre or Mao's Shanghai residence) and was re-opened in 1979 for foreigners and high-ranking Chinese. At the time of writing it was being renovated and was due to re-open as a hotel. Alternatively, try the Jinjiang Hotel across the road, which has a bar and (very expensive) disco.

Events There are three events of significance. The Mid-Autumn Festival is held in October when they lay on the mooncakes – the festival recalls an uprising against the Mongols in the 14th century when plans for the revolt were passed around in cakes. Mooncakes are usually filled with a mixture of ground lotus, sesame seed and dates, and sometimes duck egg. The Shanghai Music Festival is in May. The Shanghai Marathon Cup is in March and is one of the top sporting events in the country. The latter two, if not the first one, were suspended during the Cultural Revolution. Hotel space may be harder to come by at these times – also at Lunar New Year in February.

Performing Arts There are some 70 cinemas and theatres and 35 performing troupes in Greater Shanghai – with a little help from the numerous English-speakers in this place it should be possible to delve into the local listings, which may include top-notch travelling troupes. This is probably the best place in China to get a look at the local entertainment scene, acrobatics, ballet, music, burlesque, opera, drama, puppets, sporting events . . . a couple of venues are listed below to give you some idea of what's in stock here.

The Shanghai Art Theatre is just down the road from the Jinjiang Club, and is housed in what used to be the Lyceum Theatre. The theatre was completed in

1931 and was used by the Shanghai Amateur Dramatic Society – a favourite haunt of the Brits. The theatre company of the same name started up in 1929, the first drama troupe of the Communist Party. Nowadays there are all sorts of unexpected performances here – anyone for *Equus* in Mandarin?

The Shanghai Film Studio continues to produce some of the better material in China. The history of film-making in Shanghai extends back to the beginning of movie-making itself. One of the starlets of the B-grade set back in the 1930s was Jiang Qing. It's pot luck whether you'll find a good movie or not, but it won't cost much to find out. A good gauge of a film's popularity is the bike parking outside – if it spreads for two blocks then it must be a hit!

The Conservatory of Music (tel 370137) at 20 Fenyang Lu off Huaihai Zhonglu in Frenchtown is a treat not to be missed by classical music lovers. The conservatory was established in 1927 and its faculty members were mainly foreign – post WW I Shanghai was a meeting place for talented European musicians. The most enthralling aspect of the conservatory is the child prodigies. Back in 1979 Yehudi Menuhin was passing through here and picked 11-year-old violinist Jin Li for further instruction in England; the kid enthralled audiences in London in 1982 with his renditions of Beethoven. Other wonders, products of the special training classes set up in the 1950s, have gone to the west on cultural-exchange visits. The conservatory was closed during the Cultural Revolution, but Beethoven et al have now been rehabilitated along with the conservatory. Performances take place on Sunday evenings at 7 pm. Tickets are usually sold out a few days before, though. Also try the opera at the People's Opera Theatre on Jiu Jiang Lu.

There are several professional orchestras in Shanghai, including the Shanghai Philharmonic and the Shanghai National Orchestra. The latter specialises in native instruments.

The largest indoor sports venue in Shanghai is the Shanghai Gymnasium at the south-west corner of the city. It's air-conditioned, has computer-controlled score boards and seats 18,000.

Acrobatics Acrobats are pure fun and they're China's true ambassadors. Donating pandas may have soothed relations but it's the acrobats who capture the international imagination. The Shenyang Acrobatic Troupe toured the USA before the two countries established diplomatic relations, and Chinese troupes have gone to 30 countries with not a dud response.

The Shanghai Acrobatics Dome has shows most evenings. It's one of the best equipped in China for these acts. Sometimes performing tigers and pandas (not together) show up as an added bonus. Tickets for the regular shows are around Y1 but try and get them ahead of time from the office to the side of the Dome. CITS will also book seats. Or you could just try your luck and roll up when performances start, which is around 7 pm nightly – however, you may then be forced to buy the last tickets from scalpers at grossly inflated prices. Mixed reaction to the shows here; many people find the animal acts a bit sad.

The Dome is on Nanjing Xilu, a short walk west of the Park Hotel on the same side of the street.

Circus acts go back 2000 years in the Middle Kingdom; effects are obtained using simple props, sticks, plates, eggs, chairs, and apart from the acrobatics there's magic, vaudeville, drama, clowning, music, conjuring, dance and mime thrown into a complete performance. Happily it's an art which gained from the Communist takeover and which did not suffer during the Cultural Revolution. Performers used to have the status of gypsies, but now it's 'people's art'.

Most of the provinces have their own performing troupes, sponsored either by government agencies, industrial complexes, the army or rural administrations. About 80 troupes are active in China, and they're much

in demand with scalpers being able to get Y5 for a Y0.40 ticket. You'll also see more bare leg, star-spangled costumes and rouge in one acrobat show then you'll see anywhere else in China – something of a revelation to see dressed-up and made-up Chinese!

Acts vary from troupe to troupe. Some traditional acts haven't changed over the centuries, while others have incorporated roller skates and motorcycles. A couple of time-proven acts that are hard to follow include the 'balancing in pairs' with one man balanced upside down on the head of another mimicking every movement of the partner below, mirror image, even drinking a glass of water! Hoop-jumping is another. Four hoops are stacked on top of each other; the human chunk of rubber going through the very top hoop may attempt a backflip with a simultaneous body-twist.

The 'Peacock Displaying its Feathers' involves an array of people balanced on one bicycle. According to the Guinness Book of Records a Shanghai troupe holds the record at 13, though apparently a Wuhan troupe has done 14. The 'Pagoda of Bowls' is a balancing act where the performer, usually a woman, does everything with her torso except tie it in knots, all the while casually balancing a stack of porcelain bowls on foot, head or both – and perhaps also balancing on a partner.

Shopping

Good buys in Shanghai are clothing (silks, down jackets, traditional Chinese clothing, stencilled T-shirts, embroidered clothing), antiques, tea (chrysanthemum tea from Hangzhou), stationery . . . the list goes on and on, so just regard this place as one big department store. All consumer urges can be catered for here.

Major shopping areas in Shanghai besides crowded Nanjing Donglu are Huaihai Zhonglu, Sichuan Beilu, Jinling Donglu and Nanjing Xilu.

Some smaller streets offer specialities. Shimen Yilu has clothing and houseware stores. Over in Frenchtown – now we're getting specialised – is the Gujin Brassiere Store at 863 Huaihai Zhonglu.

You can shop around the clock in Shanghai should the urge take you. For example, the Caitongde Traditional Chinese Medicine Shop at 320 Nanjing Donglu is open 24 hours a day.

The Friendship Store, once housed in the former British consulate on the Bund, has moved around the corner to a multi-storey building on Beijing Donglu. It sells everything.

Getting There & Away

Shanghai has many rail and air connections to places all over China; ferries up the Yangtse River and many boats along the coast; and buses to destinations in adjoining provinces.

Air Shanghai is connected by air to many cities and towns in China. There are daily flights to Beijing, Canton, Wuhan, Guilin and Xian. Other useful flights include Kunming (four flights a week), Chengdu (six flights a week) and Qingdao (three flights a week).

Useful international flights include those to Hong Kong (Y479, daily), Tokyo (Y1172, daily), Osaka (Y914, daily) and Nagasaki (twice a week).

CAAC has a bus (the 'Friendship Taxi') to the airport which takes about half an hour and costs an additional Y3.50.

Bus The long-distance bus station is on Qiujiang Lu to the north of the North (Main) Railway Station. There are several buses a day to Hangzhou (Y6), Wuxi (Y3.70) and Changzhou (Y5).

There is another ticket office at Renmin Square, opposite the junction of Fuzhou Lu and Xizang Zhonglu, which has tickets for buses to Suzhou (Y2). The boarding points for the buses are marked on the ticket in Chinese (at the time of writing there were two boarding points for the Suzhou bus, one on Gongxing Lu near Renmin Square, and one on Huangpu Beilu Kou near the main station), so check where to board the bus when you buy a ticket.

Rail Shanghai is at the junction of the Beijing-Shanghai and the Beijing-Hangzhou lines. Since these branch off in various directions many parts of the country can be reached by direct train from Shanghai.

Not all trains originate in Shanghai. There is one, for example, which starts in Beijing and winds up in Fuzhou on the south-east coast. Others, like the train bound for Ürümqi, do start in Shanghai.

Tourist-price train tickets and journey times on some major routes out of Shanghai are listed at right.

destination	*duration (hours)*	*hard seat*	*hard sleeper*	*soft sleeper*
Beijing	17½	56	90	168
Xian	27	56	80	147
Canton	33	64	102	193
Nanjing	4	15		
Hangzhou	3½	9		

There are over a dozen trains a day on the Shanghai-Hangzhou line, and numerous trains on the Shanghai-Nanjing line, stopping at major towns like Zhenjiang and Wuxi on the way.

There are direct trains from Shanghai to Guilin and Kunming but these take 29 hours and 62 hours respectively. If you can't get a sleeper, forget it!

There are direct trains to Qingdao in Shandong Province. The trip takes 24 hours, but fortunately this can be conveniently broken at Qufu and Tainan/Tai Shan.

There are direct trains from Shanghai to Fuzhou (22½ hours) and Xiamen in Fujian Province. From Fuzhou and Xiamen you can continue by bus along the coast to Canton; or take the boat from Xiamen to Hong Kong.

Direct trains from Shanghai to Canton take about 33 hours. Tourist-price fares are Y56 hard-seat, Y87 hard-sleeper and Y154 soft-sleeper.

Getting Chinese-priced tickets is difficult in Shanghai. You could go as far as, say, Suzhou or Jiaxing, and try getting a Chinese-price ticket there. You might also try buying tickets from one of the smaller train stations, such as Xujiahui Station in the western suburbs of Shanghai, rather than from the main station.

There are five advance-ticket offices in Shanghai. The main one is at 230 Beijing Lu and handles all destinations north of the Yangtse and south of Jinhua (Jinhua is beyond Hangzhou to the south-west). Departures for these trains are from Shanghai North (Main) Station on Tianmu Donglu.

At the time of writing foreigners were

being sent to CITS to buy their train tickets. Although you'll have to pay tourist price, the advantage is that you avoid the enormous queues and you have a good chance of getting a sleeper.

Boat Boats are definitely one of the best ways of leaving Shanghai – they're also the cheapest. For destinations on the coast or inland on the Yangtse, they may even sometimes be faster than trains, which have to take rather circuitous routes. Smaller, grottier boats handle numerous inland shipping routes.

Tickets for larger boats (like the Hong Kong-Shanghai ferries) are handled by CITS, which charges a commission. Tickets for all domestic passenger shipping out of Shanghai can be bought from the ticket office at 1 Jinling Lu.

Considering how cheap boats are, you ought to consider taking a class or two above the crowd. It won't cost you that much more to do so.

Hong Kong This route was re-opened in 1980 after a gap of 28 years. Two passenger ships now ply the route: the *Shanghai* and the *Haixing*. A lot of travellers leave China this way and the trip gets rave reviews. The trip to Hong Kong takes 2½ days. There are departures every five days.

Ships depart from the International Passenger Terminal to the east of Shanghai Mansions. The address is Wai Hong Qiao Harbour, Taipin Lu No 1. Passengers are requested to be at the harbour three hours before departure.

The fares below are from CITS. Tickets can be bought from CITS or from the ticket office at 1 Jinling Lu.

Special class
Two-berth cabin, Y361 to Y391 per person.
1st class
One-berth cabin, Y301 to Y321 per person.
2nd class
Four-, three-, and two-berth cabins, Y261 to Y284 per person.
3rd class
Two- and four-berth cabins, Y218 to Y239 per person.
General class
Dormitory with upper and lower berths, and lights that stay on all night. Around Y184. Best to take at least 3rd class.

When you take into account the luxurious living, the boat is cheap. Both ships come complete with dance floor, library, swimming pool . . . just about the classiest things sailing regularly around Chinese waters. The *Haixing* sounds like it's the better of the two.

Yangtse River The main destinations of ferries up the Yangtse River from Shanghai are Nantong, Nanjing, Wuhu, Guichi, Jiujiang and Wuhan. From Wuhan you can change to another ferry which will take you to Chongqing. If you're only going as far west as Nanjing then take the train – much faster than the boat.

Tickets can be bought from the booking hall at 222 Renmin Lu (it's a large whitewashed building that looks like it was once a warehouse). There are daily departures from Shilipu Wharf. Tourist-price ferry tickets per person in yuan are:

destination	*1st class*	*2nd class*	*3rd class*	*4th class*
Nanjing	46	23	10	7
Wuhu	55	28	12	8
Jiujiang	88	44	18	13
Wuhan	111	55	23	17

Unless you can afford to fly, the most sensible way to head west from Shanghai is along the river. Wuhan, for example, is over 1500 km by rail from Shanghai. For just a quarter of the hard-sleeper train fare you can get a berth in 4th class on the boat. For a bit more than a tourist-priced hard-sleeper ticket on a train you'd probably be able to get a bed in a two-person cabin on the boat.

Coastal Boats Other inland shipping routes have hardly been explored by westerners. One possible route is a boat to Huzhou from Shanghai. Huzhou is on the southern shore of Lake Taihu. Worth checking out, though, are the coastal boats.

Frequency of coastal shipping varies according to destination. Some of the 5000-tonne liners have staterooms with private bath in 1st and special classes – wood panelling, red velvet curtains, the works. The ship should have a restaurant, bar, snack shops, but this depends on the boat. Fares in yuan are:

destination	*1st class*	*2nd class*	*3rd class*	*4th class*
Ningbo	37	19	10	8
Wenzhou	58	29	16	12
Fuzhou	68	55	27	20
Qingdao	68	34	19	15
Canton	93	62	53	40

Ships to Canton (six times a month), Qingdao (daily), Dalian and Fuzhou leave from Gongpinglu Wharf, to the east of Shanghai Mansions. Ships to Ningbo and Wenzhou leave daily from the Shilipu Dock. However, check the departure point when you buy your ticket!

The boat to Qingdao departs daily, with the exception of a few odd days of the month. It takes about 26 hours, while the train takes 24 hours. Second class on the liner is roughly equivalent to the price of a hard-seat on a train (if you get the Chinese price) and the boat would be incomparably more comfortable. Boat connections like Shanghai to Dalian, then Dalian to Tianjin, can be made, though you may find the huge number of passengers using the cheaper services a problem when getting tickets.

There may be other boats from Shanghai to points along the coast – possibly Haimen, Dinghai and Putuo Shan.

Getting Around

The sights in Shanghai are spaced a fair distance apart. Not only that, but vehicles swarm everywhere, with a host of noise generators to announce their oncoming right of way: buses and traffic police have megaphones, bells, buzzers, hooters, honkers, screechers, flashing lights; taxis may just as well have a permanent siren attached; pedestrians have no early warning system and rely on fast legs. If you've got the energy, then walking through Shanghai's various neighbourhoods is fascinating.

Bus Buses are often packed to the hilt and at times impossible to board. The closest thing to revolutionary fervour in Shanghai today is the rush-hour bus ambushes. Once on board, keep your valuables tucked away since pickpocketing is easy under such conditions, and foreigners are not exempt as targets.

Contrary to popular belief, buses are not colour coded. The bus map is. The bus map coding for trolley buses is prefixed by the following symbol, which roughly means 'electricity':

Routes 1 to 30 are trolley buses. Those numbered 31 to 99 are city buses. Routes 201 to 220 are peak-hour city buses, and 301 to 321 are all-night buses. Buses operate from 4 am to 10 pm. Suburban and long-distance buses don't carry numbers – the destination is in characters. Some useful buses include:

No 11
: Ring road around the old Chinese city.

No 16
: Jade Buddha Temple to Yuyuan Bazaar, then on to a ferry hop over the Huangpu River – a good linking bus for all those awkward destinations.

No 18
: Front of the Main Railway Station (it originates further north-east at Hongkou or Lu Xun Park) down Xizang Lu, and then south to the banks of the Huangpu.

No 26
: Starts downtown a few streets west of the Bund, drops to the Yuyuan Bazaar, then goes west along Huaihai Lu.

No 49
: Heads west along Yanan Lu from the Public Security terminus. Nos 48 and 42 follow similar routes from Huangpu Park, south along the Bund, west around the Donfeng Hotel, then link westbound along Yanan Lu.

No 65
: Starts behind the Main Railway Station, goes past Shanghai Mansions, across Waibaidu Bridge, then south along the Bund (Zhongshan Lu) to where it finishes.

Other Wheels Taxis operate out of the tourist hotels. Flagfall is around Y3 which is good for five km, and then it's about Y0.60 per km after that. For example, the Peace Hotel to the Jinjiang Hotel would cost about Y4. If you stray too far out of the metropolitan region then the rate goes up to around Y0.90 per km. All-day hire is possible. Rates are payable only in FECs.

The gun-metal grey Shanghai Saloons, resembling vintage Mercedes, are beautiful cars and worth a few rides but hang onto your wallet. Check the odometer; some of these things have been on the road since the 1950s! If you want to let go, then get one of those plush hearses, the Red Flags, and pretend you're the would-be president of Namibia for the day.

Jiangsu 江苏

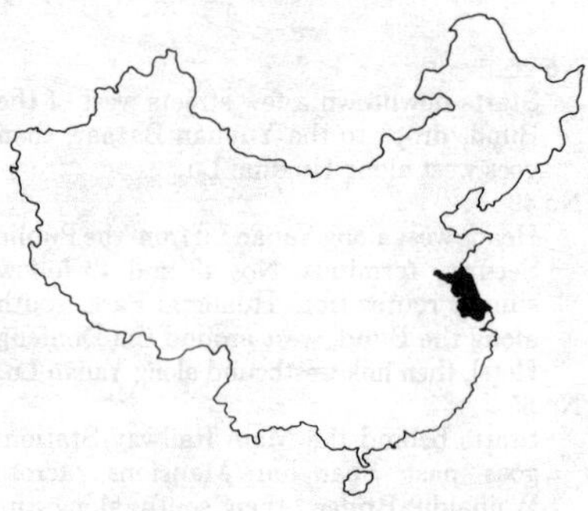

The southern part of Jiangsu lies in the rich Yangtse Basin, an incredibly beautiful tapestry of greens, yellows and blues, offset with whitewashed farm housing. Since the 12th century it's been the economic heart of China. It has the densest population of any province, the highest land productivity, an above average educational level, and mellow people. Woven into this land of 'fish and rice' is a concentration of towns and cities with the third highest industrial output in the land (After Shanghai and Liaoning).

As far back as the 16th century, the towns on the Grand Canal set up industrial bases for silk production and grain storage, and they still have the jump on the rest of the nation. Heavy industry is located in Nanjing and Wuxi. The other towns lean more to light industry, machinery and textiles; you might term them 'hi-tech canal towns'. They're major producers of electronics and computer components, and haven't been blotted out by the scourges of coal mining or steel works.

From Nanjing down to Hangzhou in Zhejiang Province the area is heavily touristed, full of Japanese Hino tour buses, and littered with luxury hotels. North of the Yangtse there's not really much to talk about; it's a complete contrast, decayed, backward and always lagging behind the rest of the province. In the north the major port is at Lianyungang and there's a big coal works in Xuzhou.

Climate

Hot and humid in summer, overcoat temperatures in winter (visibility can drop to zero in January). Rain or drizzle can be prevalent – but it's nice rain, adding a misty soft touch to the land, and the colourings in spring can be spectacular. Heavy rains come in spring and summer but there's not much rain in autumn.

NANJING 南京

Over Chungshan swept a storm, headlong
Our mighty army, a million strong, has crossed the Great River.
The city, a tiger crouching, a dragon curling, outshines its ancient glories;
In heroic triumph heaven and earth have been overturned.

Mao, from his poem 'The People's Liberation Army Captures Nanjing'.

The assault on Nanjing by the Communist army in April 1949 was not the first time that the heaven and earth of the city had been overturned. In fact, the city has been conquered many times by foreigners, rebels and imperial armies. It has been destroyed, rebuilt, destroyed again, emptied of inhabitants, repopulated and rebuilt, only to be decimated by the occasional natural disaster.

The area has been inhabited for about 5000 years, and a number of prehistoric sites have been discovered either in Nanjing or the vicinity. There are also sites which date back to to the Shang and Zhou dynasties.

The city's location is the source of both its prosperity and its troubles. Nanjing has a strategic position, guarded by the surrounding hills and rivers. The Yangtse narrows here and a bit further east it begins to form a delta, so the city is a focus of trade and communications along one of China's greatest water routes.

The city's recorded history dates back

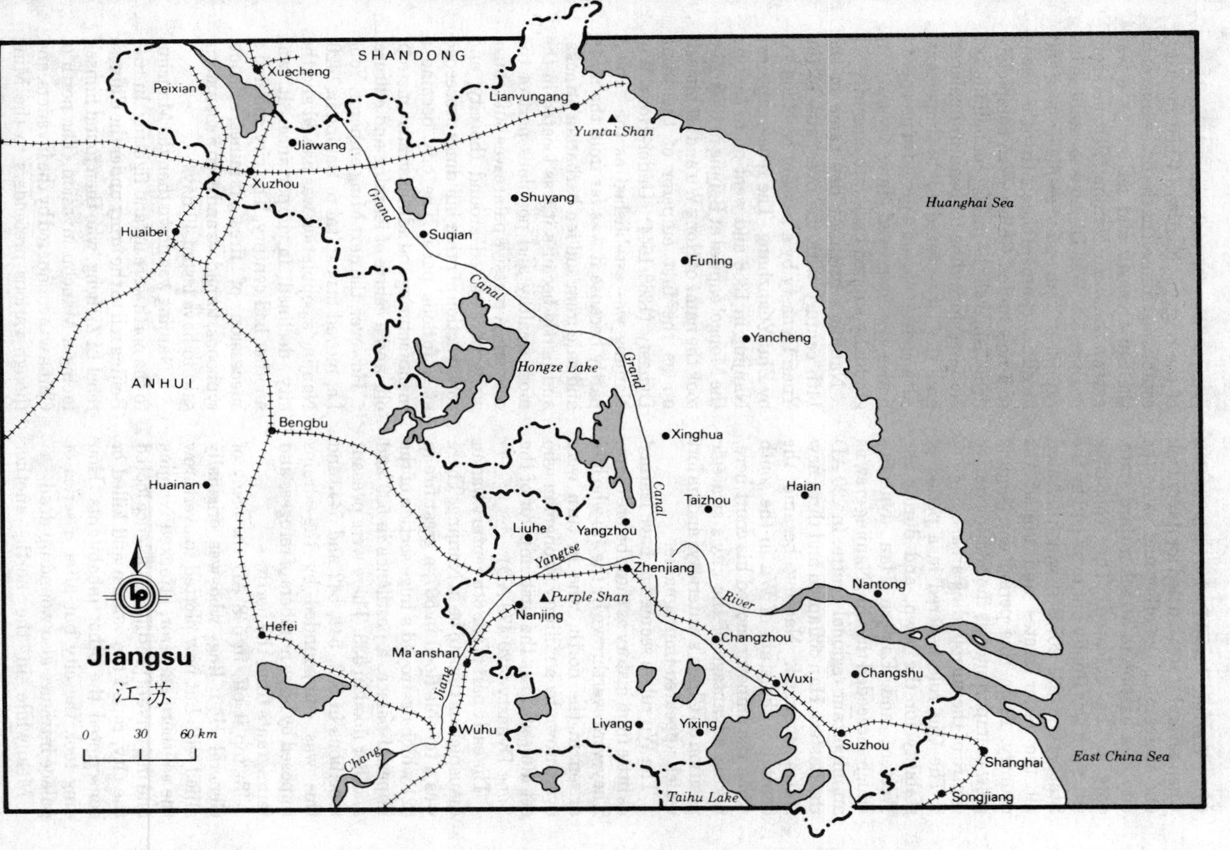

SHANDONG
Xuecheng
Peixian
Lianyungang
Yuntai Shan
Jiawang
Xuzhou
Grand Canal
Shuyang
Huanghai Sea
Huaibei
Suqian
Funing
Yancheng
Hongze Lake
ANHUI
Bengbu
Xinghua
Huainan
Haian
Taizhou
Liuhe
Yangzhou
Yangtse River
Zhenjiang
Nantong
Purple Shan
Nanjing
Hefei
Changzhou
Jiangsu
江苏
Ma'anshan
Wuxi
Changshu
Jiang
Wuhu
Liyang
Yixing
Suzhou
0 30 60 km
Chang
Shanghai
East China Sea
Songjiang
Taihu Lake

to the Warring States Period (475-221 BC) when several states battled for its control, one overcoming the other and using the city as a bastion to attack a third state, only to be defeated. This confusing situation was finally put to an end by the State of Qin (221-207 BC), which defeated all the other states and united the country. From this period on, Nanjing grew in importance as the administrative centre of the surrounding area.

The Qin rule ushered in a period of stability for the town, and during the Western and Eastern Han dynasties which succeeded the Qin, Nanjing grew as an important regional centre. In 220 AD the Eastern Han collapsed and three new states emerged. Nanjing became the capital of the state of Wu in the south when the emperor moved his court here, taking advantage of the city's strategic position on China's waterways and its fort which appeared impregnable.

The Wu rulers seemed to have learned as little from history as those before them. They were overthrown by the Jin who had arisen in the north, who in turn were overthrown by a military strongman who set himself up as the first emperor of the Song Dynasty (420-479 AD).

The early part of the 6th century was an inauspicious time to be in Nanjing. There was a terrible flood in 507, a great fire in 521 which destroyed a huge section of the imperial palace, a pestilence in 529 and another flood in 533. There were peasant rebellions in 533, 541, 542 and 544, and this was compounded by the strains imposed by large numbers of refugees and immigrants from the north.

To top it off, in 548 AD the army of General Hou Jing, who was originally allied with but now plotted to overthrow the southern emperor, attacked Nanjing and in a wave of gratuitous violence looted the city, raped the women and killed or conscripted the other inhabitants. Hou Jing took the city but after a series of palace intrigues also wound up dead.

Meanwhile in the north, another general, Wen Di, had usurped the throne of the reigning Northern Zhou dynasty, established himself as the first emperor of the Sui Dynasty and set out on a war against the south. Nanjing fell to his army in about 589. Wen Di chose to establish his capital at Xian and to eradicate once and for all any claims of the south to the throne of a now united China. Wen completely demolished all the important buildings of Nanjing, including its beautiful palaces, and the city ceased to be important. Although it enjoyed a period of prosperity under the long-lived Tang Dynasty, it gradually slipped back into obscurity.

Nanjing's brightest day came in the 14th century with the overthrow of the Yuan Dynasty by a peasant rebellion led by Zhu Yuanzhang. The rebels captured Nanjing in 1356 and went on to capture the Mongol capital at Beijing in 1368. Zhu took the name of Hong Wu and set himself up as the first emperor of the Ming Dynasty (1368-1644). Under Hong Wu, Nanjing was established as the capital partly because it was far from the north and safe from sudden barbarian attacks, and partly because it was located in the most wealthy and populous part of the country. A massive palace was built, huge walls were raised around the city, and construction of other buildings proceeded at a furious pace. The city became a manufacturing and administrative metropolis and a centre of learning and culture.

However, the next Ming emperor, Yong Le, moved his capital to Beijing in 1420. Nanjing's population was halved and the city declined in importance. It was another bad century. The city suffered a succession of fires, famines, floods, typhoons, tornadoes and even a snowstorm said to have lasted 40 days.

If Nanjing was down then the Manchus to the north were up and fighting. In 1644 Beijing fell to the army under the Chinese rebel Li Zicheng, who then found himself facing a Manchu invasion. The north of China was conquered by the invaders, and though various pretenders to the Ming throne tried to hold out in Nanjing and other places in the south, in time they were all overcome. Although Nanjing continued as a major centre under the Qing, nothing much of note happened until the 19th and 20th centuries.

The Opium Wars were waged right to Nanjing's doorstep in 1842 when a British naval task force of 80 ships sailed up the Yangtse River, took the city of Zhenjiang and arrived at Nanjing in August. Threats to bombard Nanjing forced the Chinese to sign the first of the 'unequal treaties' which opened several Chinese ports to foreign trade, and forced China to pay a huge war indemnity and officially cede the island of Hong Kong to Britain.

Just a few years later, one of the most dramatic periods in China's history focused attention on Nanjing – the Taiping Rebellion of 1851 to 1864 which succeeded in taking over most of southern China. This Chinese Christian army gained attention in the west but its success against the Qing worried the western powers, who preferred to deal with the corrupt and weak Qing than with the united and strong Taipings. After 1860 the western powers allied themselves with the Qing and the counter offensive began. By 1864 the Taipings had been encircled in their capital of Nanjing. A Qing army helped by British army regulars like General Charles Gordon (of Khartoum fame) and various European and American mercenaries besieged and bombarded the city for seven months, finally capturing it and slaughtering the Taiping defenders. Hong Xiuquan, the Taiping leader, committed suicide and the rebellion was ended.

The Manchus were overthrown in 1911 and Sun Yatsen established a republic, first with its capital at Beijing but later at Nanjing. In 1927 Chiang Kaishek ordered the extermination of the Communists, and Yuhuatai Hill to the south of the city was one of the main execution sites. In 1937 the Japanese captured the city and set about butchering the population. Just how many died in what became known as the 'Rape of Nanjing' is unknown, though the Chinese usually put the figure at around 300,000 dead. With the Japanese defeat in 1945 the Kuomintang government moved back to Nanjing, and between 1946 and 1947 peace talks were held here between the Kuomintang and the Communists. When these broke down the civil war resumed and Nanjing was captured in that great turning over of heaven and earth in 1949.

True to its past, the city has not remained outside conflicts. On 25 March 1976, 2½ months after the death of Zhou Enlai, the 'radicals' inflamed public opinion by publishing an article in two of Shanghai's mass-circulation newspapers stating that the late premier had been a 'capitalist-roader'. It was the time of the Qing Ming Festival when the Chinese traditionally honour their dead. The first reaction to the article was in Nanjing, where large crowds gathered to hear speeches and lay wreaths in honour of Zhou. Slogans and posters were put up, a protest march took place through the streets of the city and Zhang Chunqiao (later vilified as a member of the 'Gang of Four') was named and attacked. The story goes that the carriages of Beijing-bound trains were daubed with messages and slogans so that people in the capital would know what was happening in Nanjing, and that these contributed to the 'Tiananmen Incident' a week later.

Today, Nanjing is an industrialised city of around three million people, rebuilt by the Communist government. Its broad boulevards are lined with thousands of trees, alleviating the heat for which this city was justifiably known as one of the 'Three Furnaces' of China.

Information & Orientation

Nanjing lies on the eastern bank of the Yangtse River, bounded in the west by the Purple Hills. The centre of town is a traffic circle presided over by the Jingling Hotel tower. The long-distance bus station and

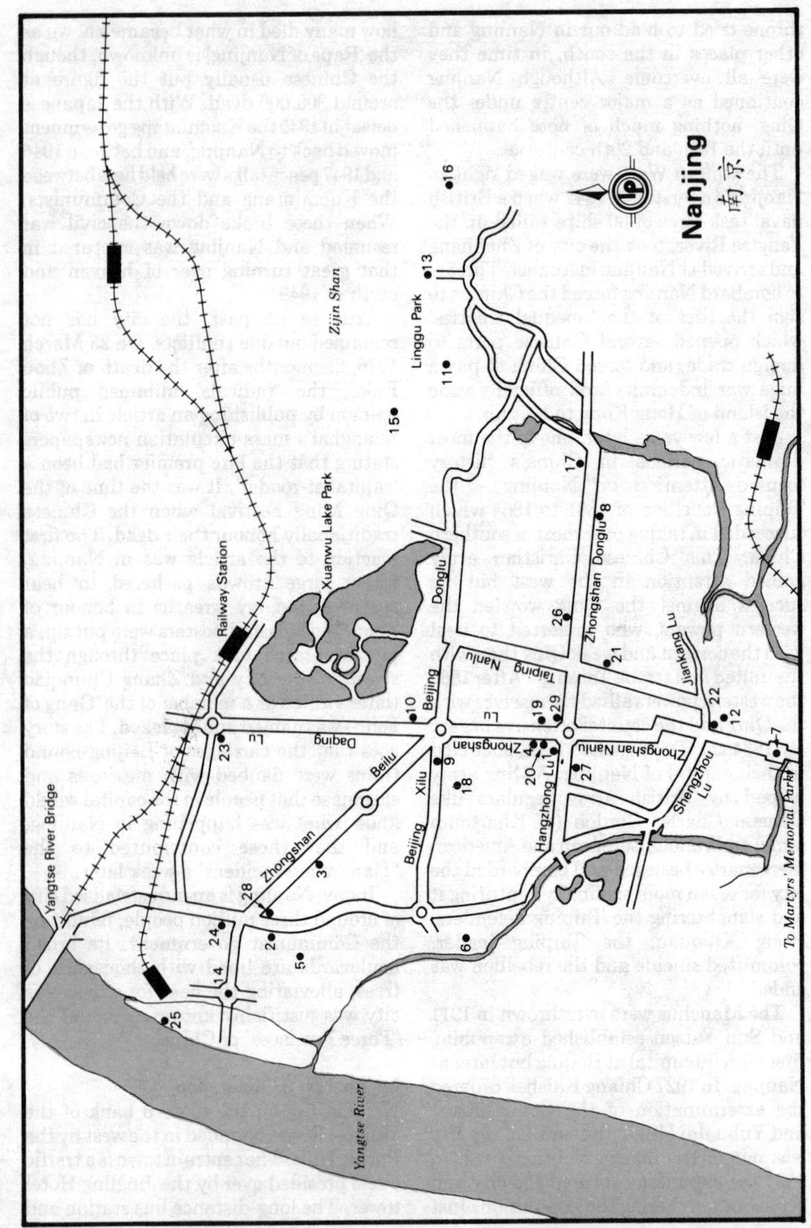

Nanjing
南京
Zijin Shan
Linggu Park
Xuanwu Lake Park
Railway Station
Yangtse River Bridge
Yangtse River
To Martyrs' Memorial Park
Zhongshan Donglu
Zhongshan Nanlu
Zhongshan Lu
Zhongshan Beilu
Taiping Nanlu
Jiankang Lu
Shengzhou Lu
Hangzhong Lu
Beijing Donglu
Beijing Xilu
Daqing Lu

1	Jingling Hotel
2	Shuangmenlou Guest House
3	Nanjing Hotel
4	Shengli Hotel
5	Dingshan Hotel
6	Han Dynasty Wall
7	Zhonghua Gate
8	Ruins of the Ming Palace
9	Drum Tower
10	Bell Tower
11	Tomb of Hong Wu
12	Taiping Museum
13	Sun Yatsen Memorial
14	Monument to Crossing the Yangtse River
15	Zijin Shan Observatory
16	Linggu Pagoda
17	Nanjing Museum
18	Nanjing University
19	Dasanyuan Restaurant
20	Laoguangdong Restaurant
21	Sichuan Restaurant
22	Jiangsu Restaurant
23	Long-distance Bus Station
24	Terminus for Local Buses across the Yangtse Bridge
25	Dock for Yangtse River Ferries (to Wuhan & Shanghai)
26	Buses to Qixia Mountain
27	Buses to Linggu Park
28	CITS
29	Bank

1 金陵饭店	16 灵谷塔
2 双门楼宾馆	17 博物馆
3 南京饭店	18 大学
4 胜利饭店	19 大三元酒家
5 丁山饭店	20 老广东菜馆
6 石头城	21 四川饭店
7 中华门	22 江苏酒家
8 午朝门	23 长途汽车站
9 鼓楼	24 汽车站(大桥南路)
10 钟楼	25 中山码头
11 明孝陵	26 汽车站(栖霞山)
12 太平天国历史博物馆	27 汽车站(灵谷)
13 中山陵	28 中国国际旅行社
14 渡江纪念碑	29 银行
15 天文台	

train station are in the far north of the city. Some of the hotels and most tourist facilities are in the centre of the city, in the vicinity of the Jingling Hotel. Most of the sights are to the east of Nanjing, in or around the Purple Mountains – including the Sun Yatsen Memorial, Linggu Park and the tomb of the first Ming emperor Hong Wu.

CITS is at No 1, 202 Zhongshan Beilu. They also have a ticket-booking office at the train station which sells soft-seat and soft-sleeper tickets (open daily, 7.30 to 11.30 am and 1.30 to 5 pm).

Bank The Bank of China is near the central traffic circle at 3 Zhongshan Donglu. There is also a money-exchange counter at the Jingling Hotel.

Post There are post offices in the Shuangmenlou Guest House, Jingling Hotel and Nanjing Hotel. The main post office is at 19 Zhongshan Lu, around the corner from the Jingling Hotel.

CAAC (tel 43378 - domestic flights, 45482 Ext 482 - international flights) is at 5 Rui Jin Lu.

Maps Good bus maps of Nanjing are available from hawkers outside the main train station. Also check the hotel shops.

Things to See

Before picking over the remnants of 3000 years of history, go and see Nanjing's prime tourist attraction, the Jingling Hotel. This 36 storey tower is one of the tallest buildings in China and was designed by a Japanese architect and built by a Singapore firm. The Chinese proletariat stand outside the fence gazing up at this thing and snapping friends' photos with the hotel as a backdrop. The Sky Palace revolving restaurant was the first of its type in China. You can dump yourself down in a comfy chair and spot the Yangtse Bridge, the observatory, the Linggu Pagoda and the Sun Yatsen Mausoleum in the distance. The Chinese receptionist wears a traditional *qipao*, the long Chinese gown split up the thigh. Drinks in the restaurant? Why not an East Meets West, Sky Lounge or Panda cocktail?

Once you've pulled yourself away from the gleaming hotel you can mull over Nanjing's extraordinary number of reminders of its splendid and not-so-splendid past. The city enjoyed long periods of prosperity, and this is evident in the numerous buildings which successive rulers built. There are a phenomenal quantity of tombs, steles, pagodas, temples and niches scattered around. For a complete run down get a copy of *In Search of Old Nanking* by Barry Till and Paula Swart (Joint Publishing Company, Hong Kong, 1982). Unfortunately, much of what was built has been destroyed or allowed to crumble into ruins.

Early Remains

Nanjing has been inhabited since prehistoric times. Remains of a prehistoric culture have been found at the site of today's Drum Tower in the centre of the city and in surrounding areas. About 200 sites of small clan communities dating back to the late Shang and Zhou dynasties have been found on both sides of the Yangtse, mainly represented by pottery and bronze artefacts.

In 212 AD, at the end of the Eastern Han period, the military commander in charge of the Nanjing region built a citadel on Qingling Mountain in the west of Nanjing. At that time the mountain was referred to as Shitou Shan (Stone Mountain) and so the citadel became known as the Stone City. The wall measured over 10 km in circumference. Today, some of the red sandstone foundations can still be seen.

The most interesting remains of the southern dynasties are the tombs of the Qi emperors (the dynasty which followed the Song) and the Qixia Shan Buddhist Grottoes. The tombs are near the town of Danyang, 70 km east of Nanjing. Danyang was the original home of the Qi royal family, so they chose to be buried here. The Buddhist grottoes lie about 20 km east of Nanjing. The earliest caves date from the Qi Dynasty (479-502 AD), though there are others from a number of succeeding dynasties right through to the Ming.

Ming City Wall

Since it was under the Ming that Nanjing enjoyed its golden years, there are numerous reminders of the period to be found. One of the most impressive remains is the Ming city wall. It is the longest city wall ever built in the world, measuring over 33 km. About two-thirds of it still stands. It took 20 years to build (1366-1386) and involved a labour force of over 200,000. The layout of the wall is irregular, an exception to the usual square walls of these times, because much of it is built on the foundations of earlier walls which took advantage of strategic hills. Averaging 12 metres high and seven metres wide at the top, the wall was built of bricks supplied from five Chinese provinces. Each brick had stamped on it the place it came from, the overseer's name and rank, the brickmaker's name and sometimes the date. This was to ensure that the bricks were well made, and if they broke they had to be replaced. Some stone bricks were used, but on the whole they were clay.

Ming City Gates

Some of the original 13 Ming city gates remain, including Heping Gate in the north and Zhonghua Gate in the south. The city gates were heavily fortified, and rather than being the usual weak points of the defences, they were defensive strongholds. Zhonghua Gate has four rows of gates, making it almost impregnable, and could be garrisoned by 3000 soldiers who lived in vaults in the front gate building. Today some of these vaults are used as souvenir shops and cafés, and are wonderfully cool in summer. Zhonghua Gate can be

visited, but Heping Gate is now used as a military barracks.

Ming Palace

Built by Hong Wu, the Ming Palace is said to have been a magnificent structure after which the Imperial Palace in Beijing was modelled. Almost nothing remains of the Ming Palace except five marble bridges lying side by side known as the Five Dragon Bridges, the old ruined gate called Wu Men, and the ping rebellion the bombardment of Nanjing by Qing and western troops almost completely destroyed the palace.

Drum Tower

Built in 1382, the Drum Tower lies roughly in Nanjing's centre, in the middle of a traffic circle on Beijing Xilu. Drums were usually beaten to give directions for the change of the night watches and in rare instances to warn the populace of impending danger. The Nanjing tower originally contained numerous drums and other instruments used on ceremonial occasions, though now only one large drum remains. The ground floor is used for exhibitions of paintings and calligraphy.

Bell Tower

North-east of the Drum Tower, the Bell Tower houses an enormous bell dating from 1388. The bell was originally in a pavilion on the west side of the Drum Tower. The present tower dates from 1889 and is a small two storey pavilion with a pointed roof and turned-up eaves.

Tomb of Hong Wu

This tomb lies east of the city on the southern slope of Zijin Mountain. Construction of the tomb began in 1381 and was finished in 1383; the emperor died at the age of 71 in 1398. The first section of the avenue leading up to the mausoleum is lined with stone statues of lions, camels, elephants and horses. There's also a mythical animal called a *xiezhi* which has a mane and a single horn on its head; and a *qilin* which has a scaly body, a cow's tail, deer's hooves and one horn. The second section of the tomb alley turns sharply northward and begins with two large hexagonal columns. Following the columns are pairs of stone military men wearing armour, and these are followed by pairs of stone civil officials. The pathway turns again, crosses some arched stone bridges and goes through a gateway in a wall which surrounds the site of the mausoleum. As you enter the first courtyard, a paved pathway leads to a pavilion housing several steles. The next gate leads to a large courtyard where you'll find the 'altar tower' or 'soul tower' – a mammoth rectangular stone structure. To get to the top of the tower you go through stairway leading upwards in the middle of the structure. Behind the tower is a wall, 350 metres in diameter, which surrounds a huge earth mound. Beneath this mound is the tomb vault of Hong Wu, which has not been excavated.

The Ming Quarry is located at Yanmen Shan (also known as Yang Shan) about 15 km east of Nanjing. It was from this quarry that most of the stone blocks for the Ming palace and statues of the Ming tombs were cut. The attraction here is a massive tablet partially hewn from the rock. Had the tablet been finished it would have been almost 15 metres wide, four metres thick and 45 metres high! The base stone was to be 6.5 metres high and 13 metres long. One story goes that Hong Wu wished to place the enormous tablet on the top of Zijin (Purple) Mountain. The gods had promised their assistance to move it, but when they saw the size of the tablet even they gave up and Hong Wu had to abandon the project. It seems, however, that Yong Le, the son of Hong Wu ordered the tablet to be carved; he planned to erect it at his father's tomb. When the tablet was almost finished he realised there was no way it could be moved.

Taiping Museum

Hong Xiquan, the leader of the Taipings, had a palace built in Nanjing, but the building was completely destroyed when Nanjing was taken in 1864. All that remains is a stone boat in an ornamental lake in the Western Garden, inside the old Kuomintang government buildings on Changjiang Lu, east of Taiping Lu.

The Taiping Museum is housed in the former mansion of the Hongs' 'Eastern Prince' Yang Xiuqing. The garden next to the mansion is called Zhan Yuan and originally belonged to the first Ming emperor.

The museum has an interesting collection of documents, books and artefacts relating to the rebellion. Most of the literature is copied, the originals being kept in Beijing. There are maps showing the northward progress of the Taiping army from Guangdong, Hong Xiuquan's seals, Taiping coins, cannon balls, rifles and other weapons, and texts which describe the Taiping laws on agrarian reform, social law and cultural policy. Other texts describe divisions in the Taiping leadership, the attacks by the Manchus and foreigners, and the fall of Nanjing in 1864.

Sun Yatsen Memorial

Some people admire the passive symmetry of Sun Yatsen's memorial; others say it lacks imagination and falls far short of the possibilities that the expenditure would have allowed.

The man regarded as the father of modern China (by both the Communists and the Kuomintang) died in Beijing in 1925, leaving behind an unstable Chinese republic. Sun wished to be buried in Nanjing, no doubt with greater simplicity than the Ming-style tomb which his successors built for him. Less than a year after his death construction of this immense mausoleum began.

The mausoleum lies at the southern foot of Zhongmao Peak in the eastern Purple Mountains which ring Nanjing.

The tomb itself lies on the mountain slope at the top of an enormous stone stairway, 323 metres long and 70 metres wide. At the start of the path stands a stone gateway built of Fujian marble, with a roof of blue glazed tiles. The blue and white of the mausoleum were meant to symbolise the white sun on the blue background of the Kuomintang flag.

At the top of the steps is a platform where you'll find the memorial ceremony chamber and the coffin chamber. Across the threshold of the memorial ceremony chamber hangs a tablet inscribed with the 'Three Principles of the People' as formulated by Dr Sun. The three principles are: nationalism, democracy and people's livelihood. Inside is a seated statue of Dr Sun. The walls are carved with the complete text of the 'Outline of Principles for the Establishment of the Nation' put forward by the Nationalist government.

Behind the hall is a crypt, in which a prostrate marble statue of Sun lies above his body. In fact, it's not known if Sun's body is still in the tomb; the story goes that it was carted off to Taiwan by the Kuomintang and has been there ever since.

Yangtse River Bridge

One of the great achievements of the Communists, and one of which they are justifiably proud, is the Yangtse River Bridge at Nanjing which was opened on 23 December 1968. One of the longest bridges in China, it's a double-decker with a 4500-metre-long roadway on top and a 6700-metre-long railway below. The story goes that the bridge was designed and built entirely by the Chinese after the Russians marched out and took the designs with them in 1960. Given the immensity of the construction it really is an impressive engineering feat, before which there was no direct rail link between Beijing and Shanghai.

Monument to the Crossing of the Yangtse River

This stands in the north-west of the city on Zhongshan Beilu. The monument, erected in April 1979, commemorates the crossing of the river on 23 April 1949 and the capture of Nanjing from the Kuomintang by the Communist Army. The characters on the monument are in the calligraphy of Deng Xiaoping.

Nanjing Museum

Just east of Zhongshan Gate on Zhongshan Lu, the Nanjing Museum houses an array of artefacts from Neolithic times through to the Communist period. The main building was constructed in 1933 with yellow-glazed tiles, red-lacquered gates and columns in the style of an ancient temple.

An interesting exhibit is the burial suit made of small rectangles of jade sewn together with silver thread, dating from the Eastern Han Dynasty (25-220 AD) and excavated from a tomb discovered in the city of Xuzhou in northern Jiangsu Province. Other exhibits include bricks with the inscriptions of their makers and overseers from the Ming city wall; drawings of old Nanjing; an early Qing mural of old Suzhou; and relics from the Taiping Rebellion.

Just east of the museum is a section of the Ming city wall. There are steps leading up from the road and you can walk along the top.

Linggu (Soul Valley) Park

To the east of the city is Linggu Park with an assortment of sights.

The **Beamless Hall** is one of the most interesting buildings in Nanjing. In 1381, when Hong Wu was building his tomb, he had a temple on the site torn down and rebuilt a few km to the east. Of this temple only the Beamless Hall remains, so called because it is built entirely of bricks. The structure has an interesting vaulted ceiling and a large stone platform where Buddhist statues used to be seated. In the

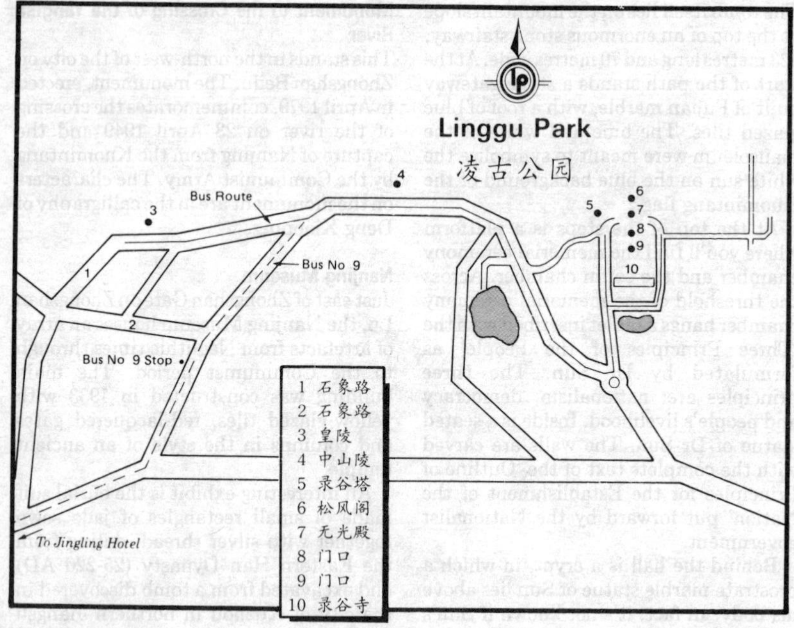

1 Avenue of Stone Figures
2 Avenue of Stone Animals
3 Tomb of Emperor Hong Wu
4 Mausoleum of Sun Yatsen
5 Linggu Pagoda
6 Pine Wind Pavilion
7 Beamless Hall
8 Gateway
9 Gateway & Surrounding Wall
10 Linggu Temple

1930s the hall was turned into a memorial to those who died in the 1926-28 revolution. One of the inscriptions on the inside wall is the old Kuomintang national anthem.

A road leads either side of the Beamless Hall and up two flights of steps to the **Pine Wind Pavilion**, originally dedicated to the Goddess of Mercy as part of the Linggu Temple. Today it houses a small shop and teahouse.

The **Linggu Temple** and its memorial hall to Xuan Zhang is close by; after you pass through the Beamless Hall, turn right and follow the pathway. Xuan Zhang was the Buddhist monk who travelled to India and brought back the Buddhist scriptures. Inside the memorial hall is a 13 storey wooden pagoda model which contains part of his skull, a sacrificial table and a portrait of the monk.

Close by is the **Linggu Pagoda**, which was built in the 1930s under the direction of an American architect. It's an octagonal building 60 metres high and has nine storeys. The pagoda was built as a memorial to Kuomintang members who died in the 1926-28 Revolution.

Places to Stay – bottom end

Most of the accommodation in Nanjing is expensive, and cheaper accommodation is in short supply. One consolation: the hotels in this city are excellent and you at least get your money's worth.

The *Shengli Hotel* (tel 43035) is the cheapest place to stay and is centrally located at 75 Zhongshan Lu, just near the Jingling Hotel. From the train station take trolley bus No 33. Double rooms are Y60 and triples Y68; dorm beds are readily dispensed for Y10 though they appear to be in short supply.

Places to Stay – middle

The *Shuangmenlou Guest House* (tel 85961) at 185 Huju Beilu mainly caters to tour groups. The hotel is in the north-west part of town and is rather isolated. Doubles cost from Y65. Dormitory beds for Y15 are possible. Take trolley bus No 32 from the train station. Take bus No 16 from near the Yangtse ferry pier.

The *Nanjing Hotel* (tel 34121) at 259 Zhongshan Beilu has excellent double rooms from Y65 with bathroom and TV. The hotel is situated in a large, well-kept garden setting, and even if you're not staying here it's worth visiting for a lounge around. Take trolley bus No 32 from the train station; bus No 16 from the Yangtse ferry pier. The hotel has a western restaurant and coffee shop.

The *Dingshan Hotel* (tel 85931) is at 90 Chahaer Lu – inconveniently located at the oblivion end of Nanjing on top of a hill. Once a fairly plebeian place, it's been jazzed up to accommodate elderly Japanese and Overseas Chinese tourists. Doubles cost from Y130. Take trolley bus No 32 from the long-distance bus station or train station; you have to walk the last km or two. Just look for the building with the fleet of Japanese tour buses parked outside.

Places to Stay – top end

The luxury, high-rise *Jingling Hotel* (tel 41121) stands at the centre of Nanjing. This place has everything, from revolving restaurant to sauna; from swimming pool to dual voltage shaver sockets. Double rooms start from US$55, presidential suites US$700. Take trolley bus No 33 from the train station. If you arrive by helicopter there's apparently a pad just metres above the revolving restaurant. The live band at night has a Y10 cover charge – keeps the riff-raff out. Piano bar on the ground floor is cheaper and very relaxing.

Places to Eat

Despite the size of this city the restaurants have short hours. Most of them stack their chairs on the tables by 8 pm, so eat early. The local speciality is Nanjing salted duck, which is slathered with roasted salt, steeped in clear brine, baked dry and then kept under cover for some time; the finished product should have a creamy-coloured skin and red, tender flesh.

The *Dasanyuan* (tel 41027) at 40 Zhongshan Lu looks like the best bet for a decent meal. Downstairs is a divey noodle canteen but upstairs is definitely worth a try.

Recommended is the *Jiangsu Restaurant* (tel 23698) at 26 Jiankang Lu, not far from the Taiping Museum. It has three floors of increasing excellence. Nanjing duck is the speciality – you can have it with a dish of pork and bamboo shoots, and vegetables with shrimp and rice, for a few yuan on the 3rd floor.

Others which may be worth trying are the *Laoguangdong* at 45 Zhongshan Lu across the road from the Dasanyuan; the *Sichuan Restaurant* (tel 43651) at 171 Taiping Lu; and the *Luliuju Vegetarian Restaurant* (tel 43644) at 248 Taiping Lu.

There are jiaozi (steamed dumpling) joints along Zhongshan Nanlu and a few odd Chinese coffee shops worth investigating.

Getting There & Away

Air There are lots of air connections, including Nanjing to Beijing (daily), Chongqing (three flights a week), Canton (daily), and Wuhan (three flights a week).

Bus The long-distance bus station is just west of the train station. There are buses to Yangzhou (Y2.30), Yixing (Y3.30), Zhenjiang (Y2.20), Changzhou (Y3.40), Wuxi (Y5.20) and Hangzhou (Y7.70). There are other buses departing from outside Nanjing train station which may be worth checking out.

Rail Nanjing is a major stop on the Beijing-Shanghai rail line and there are several trains a day in both directions. Heading eastwards from Nanjing, the railway line to Shanghai connects Zhenjiang, Changzhou, Wuxi and Suzhou.

There is no direct rail link to Hangzhou; you have to go to Shanghai first and then pick up a train or bus. Alternatively, there is a direct bus from Nanjing to Hangzhou. Likewise, to get to Canton by rail you must change trains at Shanghai.

Heading west there is a direct rail link to the port of Wuhu on the Yangtse River. If you want to go further west along the river then the most sensible thing to do is take the ferry.

Boat Ferries ply the Yangtse River from Nanjing eastward to Shanghai and westward to Wuhan; they leave from the dock at the western end of Zhongshan Beilu. There are about two boats a day to Shanghai (about 19 hours) and two a day to Wuhan (two days).

Getting Around

Taxis and pedicabs hang around the railway station. They are also available from the tourist hotels. A taxi from the train station to the Jingling Hotel will cost about Y7.

Buses and trolley buses are the main means of local transport. The network is confusing and bus maps rarely match up with what's going on in the streets.

A good way to combine Linggu Park with the Tomb of Hong Wu and the Sun Yatsen Memorial is to take bus No 9 from Hanzhong Lu (west and opposite the Jingling Hotel) as far as the avenue of stone animals and figures, then walk to the tomb. From outside the tomb there is a shuttle bus which goes to the Sun Yatsen memorial. Another shuttle bus leaves from opposite the gateway to the Sun Yatsen memorial and takes you to Linggu Park.

THE GRAND CANAL 大运河

The original Grand Canal (Da Yunhe), like the Great Wall, was not one but a series of interlocking projects from different eras. The earliest parts were dug 2400 years ago in the north to facilitate troop movements. During the Sui Dynasty (581-618 AD), the ruthless Emperor Yang Di conscripted a massive work force to link his new capital of Luoyang to the older capital of Changan (Xian). Then he extended the project down to Hangzhou in less than a decade, making it possible for junks to go along the Yangtse, up the Canal, and on to ports along the Yellow River – a trip that might take up to a year.

The canal at that time linked up four major rivers: the Huang (Yellow), Yangtse, Huai and Qiantang, which all run east-west. It thus gave China a major north-south transport route, and linked the compass points. It has been said that the canal, the longest artificial waterway in the world, was built by 'a million people with teaspoons'. In fact some estimate closer to five million people, but by even the crudest mathematics, the cost in lives must have been enormous.

The emperor was not so much interested in unification as subjugation. Grain from the rich fields of the south was appropriated to feed the hungry armies in the northern capitals. In the Tang Dynasty 100,000 tons of grain were transported annually to the north; long chains of imperial barges loaded with tax grain plied the waterways.

In the 13th century, Kublai Khan used the work of his predecessors for much the same purpose, and he did a bit of remodelling to bring the northern terminus up to Beijing, his capital. Marco Polo

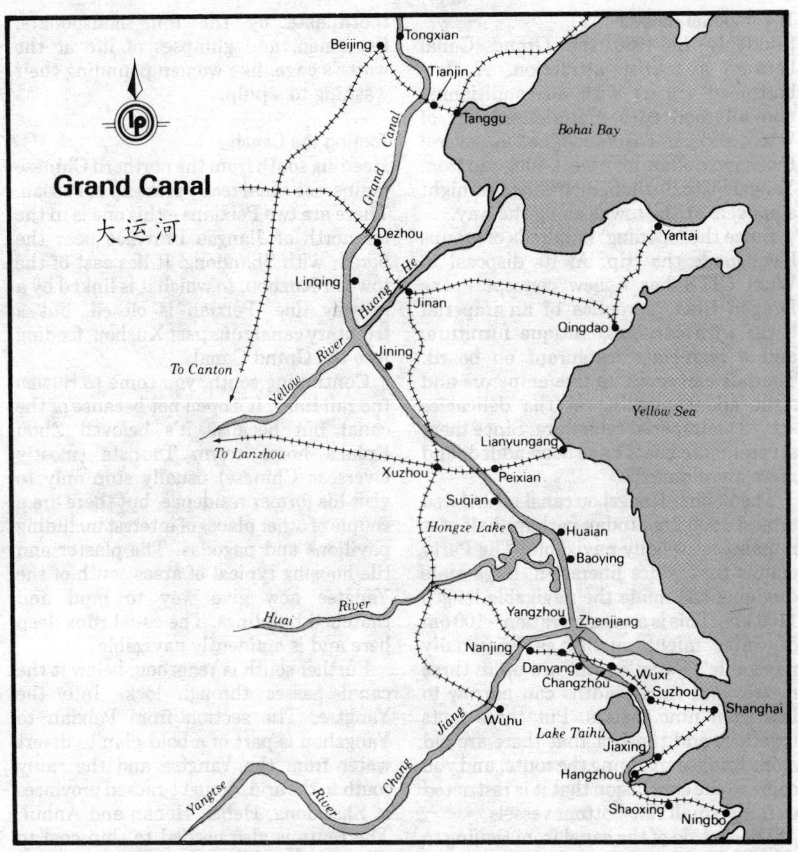

noted that boats were moved by horses, which walked along the banks of the canal pulling the boats with long harnesses; in this way large quantities of corn and rice were shipped northward. He wrote:

> This magnificent work (the canal) is deserving of admiration; and not so much from the manner in which it is conducted through the country, or its vast extent, as from its utility and the benefit it produces to those cities which lie in its course.

Apart from bringing prosperity to the towns along its course, the canal was also a means by which the sybaritic emperors travelled. In Emperor Qianglong's reign, it was suggested that the grain fleets be removed from the canal so as to allow the imperial pleasure-cruisers a freer passage.

As time went by, sections of the canal fell into disuse or were engulfed by Yellow River flooding. In this century the railways eclipsed the need for water transport. By 1980, silt, poorly planned dams, watergates and irrigation systems, or plain atrophy had reduced internal waterways mileage in China to one-third of that in the 1960s.

The Imperial Revival

Suddenly in 1980 the Grand Canal became a tourist attraction. A flat-bottomed cruiser with air-conditioning and all mod cons materialised out of Wuxi, and passengers coughed up several thousand dollars for a week-long run from Yangzhou to Suzhou, including overnight stopovers at the towns along the way.

Since the 'opening' hundreds of groups have made the trip. At its disposal in Wuxi CITS has a new concept – the Dragon Boat, a replica of an imperial barge with carvings, antique furniture, and a high-class restaurant on board. Tourists can dress up like emperors and strut about nibbling at the delicacies served on imperial tableware. Since then, several more boats have been added, and more are planned.

The Beijing-Hangzhou canal meandered almost 1800 km. Today perhaps half of it remains seasonally navigable. The Party claims that, since liberation, large-scale dredging has made the navigable length 1100 km. This is an exaggeration – 100 cm of water might qualify as 'seasonally navigable'. Canal depths are up to three metres and canal widths can narrow to less than nine metres. Put these facts together, add the fact that there are old stone bridges spanning the route, and you come to the conclusion that it is restricted to fairly small flat-bottom vessels.

The section of the canal from Beijing to Tianjin has been silted for centuries. A similar fate has befallen most sections from the Yellow River to Tianjin. The stretch from the Yellow River to Peixian (in northern Jiangsu Province) is highly dubious and is most likely silted from Yellow River flooding. Jining, which lies between those two points, was once a prosperous cloth producer; it now lies idle and is served by rail.

The canal itself is polluted with oil slicks and doubles as the local garbage bin, sewer and washing machine. There's still plenty to look at on the water: moss-stricken canal housing, barges laden with toothpaste by the ton, houseboats, fishermen, and glimpses of life at the water's edge, like women pounding their washing to a pulp.

Touring the Canal

Heading south from the northern Chinese plains, the canal really picks up at **Peixian**. There are two Peixians – this one is in the far north of Jiangsu Province near the border with Shandong. It lies east of the town of Xuzhou, to which it is linked by a railway line. Peixian is closed, but a tributary canal runs past Xuzhou, feeding into the Grand Canal.

Continuing south, you come to **Huaian** (no rail link). It's open not because of the canal but because it's beloved Zhou Enlai's home town. Tourists (mostly Overseas Chinese) usually stop only to visit his former residence, but there are a couple of other places of interest including pavilions and pagodas. The plaster and tile housing typical of areas south of the Yangtse now give way to mud and thatched buildings. The canal runs deep here and is eminently navigable.

Further south is **Yangzhou**; below it the canal passes through locks into the Yangtse. The section from Peixian to Yangzhou is part of a bold plan to divert water from the Yangtse and the rainy south to the arid, drought-racked provinces of Shandong, Hebei, Henan and Anhui. The route is also needed to ship coal to energy-hungry Shanghai from major coal producer Xuzhou. The plan, with a tentative completion date of 1990, calls for dredging the Yangzhou-Xuzhou section to a depth of four metres and a width of 70 metres at the bottom, so that 2000-ton vessels can pass. A double ship lock is being built at Huaian. So it seems the old canal still has its major uses. The water, it appears, will be provided for irrigation as far north as Jining in Shandong Province.

South of the Yangtse the picture is much brighter, with year-round navigation. The Jiangnan section of the canal

(Hangzhou, Wuxi, Suzhou, Changzhou, Danyang, Zhenjiang) is a skein of canals, rivers and branching lakes. Just as interesting as the Grand Canal are the feeder canals, many of them major thoroughfares in their own right, but sometimes it's difficult to tell which is the Grand Canal, since people may point to any canal and call it that.

Canal Ferries

Travellers have done the route from Hangzhou to Suzhou on overnight passenger boats (with sleeping berths) or on daytime 150-seater ferries. Some people regard this as the highlight of their China trip. Others have found the boats dirty, crowded and uncomfortable, with a fair percentage of the trip taken up by views of high canal banks. Some words of advice: you need a good bladder since the toilets are terrible; you need some food; and try and get a window seat, both to see the scenery and escape the many smokers on the boat. One reader wrote:

> The boat is terrible, dirty, cramped, its windows just above the waterline make it hard to see anything, but the 'toilet' won the prize as the worst in all China. It was a large bucket that was not emptied during our trip, which took 14 hours (including two hours when we were stopped by fog, which is very common in fall and winter).

Another wrote that the canal voyage was 'the highlight of our trip . . . a filthy but picturesque slice of life in China'.

Estimated times for the sections south of the Yangtse are:

Hangzhou to Suzhou
  14 hours, overnight berth or day boat
Suzhou to Wuxi
  five to six hours, early-morning day boat
Wuxi to Changzhou
  four to five hours
Changzhou to Zhenjiang
  eight to nine hours, with a possible break in Danyang

It's possible to break the Hangzhou-Suzhou journey at the fine canal town of **Jiaxing** around the half way mark. Jiaxing is also linked by rail to Shanghai or Hangzhou. It has textile and food-processing factories and deals in silk and rice. The pavilion to the south-east of the town, on an island lake, is reputed to be the site that gave shelter to founding members of the Chinese Communist Party disturbed by Shanghai police in 1921. There are other connections running through Lake Taihu.

BASIC RIVER TRANSPORTATION IN CHINA ...

YANGZHOU 杨州

Yangzhou, at the junction of the Grand Canal and the Yangtse, was once an economic and cultural centre of Southern China. It was home to scholars, painters, storytellers, poets and merchants in the Sui and Tang dynasties, but little remains of the greatness that Marco Polo witnessed. He served there as Kublai Khan's governor for three years and wrote that:

> Yangui has twenty-four towns under its jurisdiction, and must be considered a place of great consequence . . . the people are idolators, and subsist by trade and manual arts. They manufacture arms and other munitions: in consequence of which many troops are stationed in this part of the country.

Buried outside the town at Leitang, in a simple mound of earth, is Emperor Yang Di, the ruthless tyrant who completed the construction of the Grand Canal during the Sui Dynasty (518-618 AD). Yang Di is said to have levied exorbitant taxes, starved his subjects, and generally been very mean and nasty. The emperor's throne was usurped by a powerful noble family who were to found the Tang Dynasty, and Yang Di was strangled by his own generals at Yangzhou in 618.

To the north-west of Yangzhou once stood the Maze Palace, a labyrinth of bronze mirrors, couches and concubines. Yang Di is supposed to have torn about here in a leopard-skin outfit, turning one night into 10 before he finally emerged to deal with affairs of state – or maybe he just couldn't find his way out again? The building was burned down, and on the ruins was erected a structure called Jian (Warning) Building, a reminder for future generations. Still there, near Guanyin Hill, it is now used as a museum of Tang relics.

During the Qing Dynasty (1644-1911), Yangzhou got a new lease on life as a salt trading centre, and Emperor Qianlong set about remodelling the town in the 18th century. All the streets leading to the town gates were lined with platforms where story-tellers recited chapters from famous novels (the repertoire was reputed to be 30 novels). The period also saw a group of painters known as the 'Eight Eccentrics' break away from traditional methods, creating a style of natural painting that influenced the course of art in China. Merchants and scholars favoured Yangzhou as a retirement home.

The town was badly battered during the Taiping Rebellion in the 19th century. With old pavilions strangled by traffic, unkempt gardens, and amazing collections of kitsch in the downtown area, Yangzhou is well past its tourist prime – and you might do just as well exploring the downtown streets. The air of decay hangs heavy and Yangzhou's population has declined drastically from that of its glorious past. Nevertheless, there's some small town charm, a chance to escape the cities that crowd the traveller's route. It may appear presumptuous to dismiss so much history in so few words, but time has marched on!

Information

You should be able to make contact with CITS in the Yangzhou Hotel; the hotel also has a post office. Good bus maps of Yangzhou are available from the hawkers and booths around the bus station; also try the shop in the Yangzhou Hotel.

In Town

Ge Garden on Dongguan Lu was landscaped by the painter Shi Tao for an officer of the Qing court. Shi Tao was an expert at making artificial rocks; the composition here suggests the four seasons.

He Garden (alias Jixiao Mountain Villa), was built in the 19th century. It contains rockeries, ponds, pavilions and walls inscribed with classical poetry.

At the north-west end of town are a couple of pavilions and a small pagoda. The three-storey octagonal pavilion at the north is **Siwang**, more than 700 years old. The similar one to the south is **Wenchangge**,

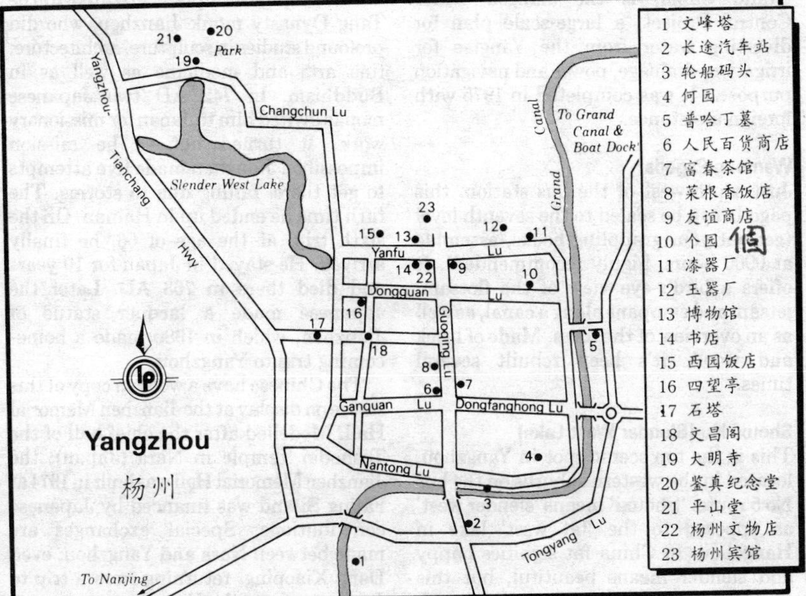

or 'Pavilion of Flourishing Culture', which is a reference to the time of its building 400 years ago.

To the west of that is the tiny **Stone Pagoda (Shita)**, which is 1100 years old and looks like someone's been at it with a sledge-hammer.

Canals

Yangzhou had, at one time, 24 stone bridges spanning its network of canals, and busy waterlife that attracted the attention of 18th-century travellers. It's now acquired an industrial fringe and noisy traffic.

You might like to investigate the environs a short way out of Yangzhou. The Grand Canal actually passes a little to the east of Yangzhou. The bus No 2 terminus in the north-east is a boat dock. Bus No 4 runs over a bridge on the canal. There are two ship locks to the south of Yangzhou.

North-east of the town, across the

1 Wen Feng Pagoda
2 Long-distance Bus Station
3 Boat Dock
4 He Garden
5 Tomb of Puhaddin
6 Renmin Department Store
7 Fuchun Teahouse (off Guoqing Lu)
8 Caigenxiang Restaurant (off Guoqing Lu)
9 Friendship Store
10 Ge Garden
11 Lacquer Factory
12 Jade Factory
13 Museum
14 Bookstore
15 Xiyuan Hotel
16 Siwang Pavilion
17 Stone Pagoda
18 Pavilion of Flourishing Culture (Wenchangge)
19 Daming Monastery (Fajingsi)
20 Jiazhen Memorial Hall
21 Pingshan Hall
22 Yangzhou Antique Store
23 Yangzhou Hotel

Grand Canal, is the Jiangsu Water Control Project, a large-scale plan for diverting water from the Yangtse for irrigation, drainage, power and navigation purposes. It was completed in 1975 with foreign assistance.

Wenfeng Pagoda
Just south-west of the bus station, this pagoda can be scaled to the seventh level (get out your grappling-hooks, assemble at 0900 hours, highly recommended). It offers a bird's-eye view of the flotsam, jetsam and sampans along a canal, as well as an overview of the town. Made of brick and wood, it's been rebuilt several times.

Shouxi Hu (Slender West Lake)
This is the top scenic spot in Yangzhou, located in the western suburbs on the bus No 5 route. 'Shouxi' means 'slender west' as opposed to the 'fat west' lake in Hangzhou. In China fat signifies happy and slender means beautiful, but this park verges toward the emaciated, desperately in need of rejuvenation.

It offers an imperial dragon boat ferry, a restaurant and a white dagoba modelled after the one in Beihai Park in Beijing. The highlight is the triple-arched, five-pavilion Wutang Qiao, a bridge built in 1757. For bridge connoisseurs it's rated one of the top 10 ancient Chinese bridges.

Emperor Qianlong's fishing platform is in the park. It is said that the local divers used to put fish on the poor man's hook so he'd think it was good luck and cough up some more funding for the town.

Fajing Si (Daming Monastery)
The temple complex was founded over 1000 years ago, subsequently destroyed and rebuilt. Then it was really destroyed during the Taiping Rebellion, and what you see today is a 1934 reconstruction. Nice architecture, even so, and if you time it right you'll find the shaven-headed monks engaged in mysterious ritual.

The original temple is credited to the Tang Dynasty monk Jianzhen, who did profound studies in sculpture, architecture, fine arts and medicine as well as in Buddhism. In 742 AD two Japanese monks invited him to Japan for missionary work. It turned out to be mission impossible. Jianzhen made five attempts to get there, failing due to storms. The fifth time he ended up in Hainan. On the sixth trip, at the age of 66, he finally arrived. He stayed in Japan for 10 years and died there in 763 AD. Later the Japanese made a lacquer statue of Jianzhen, which in 1980 made a home-coming trip to Yangzhou.

The Chinese have a wooden copy of this statue on display at the Jianzhen Memorial Hall. Modelled after the chief hall of the Toshodai Temple in Nara (Japan), the Jianzhen Memorial Hall was built in 1974 at Fajing Si and was financed by Japanese contributions. Special exchanges are made between Nara and Yangzhou; even Deng Xiaoping, returning from a trip to Japan, came to the Yangzhou monastery to add some cement to renewed links between the two countries.

West of Fajing Si is Pingshan Hall, the residence of the Song Dynasty writer Ouyang Xiu who served in Yangzhou. West of that, in the Western Gardens, is Number Five Lifespring Under Heaven. These spring waters were rated by Lu Yu, a Tang Dynasty tea expert.

Tomb of Puhaddin
This tomb contains documents regarding China's contacts with the Muslims. It's on the east bank of a canal on the bus No 2 route. Puhaddin came to China during the Yuan Dynasty (1261-1378) to spread the Muslim faith, spent 10 years in Yangzhou, and died here. There is a mosque in Yangzhou.

History Museum
The museum lies to the north of Guoqing Lu, in the vicinity of the Xiyuan Hotel. It's housed in a temple which was

originally dedicated to Shi Kefa, a Ming Dynasty official who refused to succumb to his new Qing masters and was executed. The museum contains items from Yangzhou's past. A small collection of calligraphy and paintings of the 'Eight Eccentrics' is displayed in another small museum just off Yanfu Lu near the Xiyuan Hotel.

Places to Stay

The *Yangzhou Hotel* is the prime tourist joint with doubles from Y65. If I was forking out the money, though, I'd opt for the nearby *Xiyuan Hotel* which is said to have been constructed over the site of Qianlong's imperial villa. Prices for this sprawling deluxe hotel range from Y60 a double and Y80 a triple. There are dorm beds for Y10. Doubles for Y50 are possible. The Xiyuan has a pretty garden setting complete with pond and gaggling geese. From the bus station take bus No 8 to the Friendship Store; the Yangzhou Hotel is the multi-storey building in front of you and the Xiyuan is in a compound next door. Both hotels have dining rooms.

Places to Eat

The big wining, dining (but no dancing) area is the crossroads of Guoqing Lu (which runs north from the bus station) and Ganquan. Yangzhou has its own cuisine, but bar a special banquet you might have trouble finding it. Try the *Caigenxiang Restaurant*, 115 Guoqing Lu. How about buns with crab-ovary stuffing? Along Guoqing Lu and Ganquan Lu are small bakeries and cafés which sell steamed dumplings, noodles, pastries and other goodies – you can see the stuff being kneaded right behind the counter.

Shopping

Downtown is full of shoe shops and housewares, but no sign of the lacquerware, jade, papercuts, woodcuts, embroidery or painting that Yangzhou is supposed to be famous for. So investigate the following if that's what you're after:

The Arts & Crafts Factory west of Xiyuan Hotel; the Friendship Store on Guoqing Lu; the Lacquer Factory which makes inlaid lacquer screens with translucent properties, due east of Xiyuan Hotel; the Jade Factory at 6 Guangchumenwai Jie; the Block Printing Co-op with handbound woodblock printed classics; the Yangzhou Antique Store opposite the Yangzhou Hotel; and possibly the Renmin Department Store.

Getting There & Away

The rail line gave Yangzhou a miss, one of the main reasons that this flower has wilted. Unless you're lucky enough to engineer a boat ride to Yangzhou from Nanjing or Zhenjiang, that leaves the buses.

From Yangzhou there are buses to Nanjing (Y2.40, 2½ hours); Zhenjiang (Y1.20, 1½ hours with amphibious crossing on the Yangtse); Wuxi (Y4.40); Suzhou (Y5.80); Changzhou and Shanghai.

A more comprehensive route would be Nanjing, Yangzhou, Zhenjiang, Nanjing. Or Changzhou, Zhenjiang, Yangzhou, Nanjing. On either of these you could also juggle with the trains. Allow an overnight stop for such a routing. The train station nearest Yangzhou is Zhenjiang.

Getting Around

The sights are at the edge of town. If you're in a hurry you might consider commandeering a 'turtle' (auto-rickshaw) – they can be found outside the bus station. The downtown area can easily be covered on foot.

Bus Nos 1, 2, 3, 5, 6, 7 terminate near the bus station. Bus No 1 runs from the bus station up Guoqing Lu and then loops around the perimeter of the inside canal, returning just north of the bus station. Bus No 4 is an east-west bus and cuts its way along Ganquan Lu.

ZHENJIANG 镇江

Zhenjiang takes its character not from the Grand Canal but from the Yangtse, which

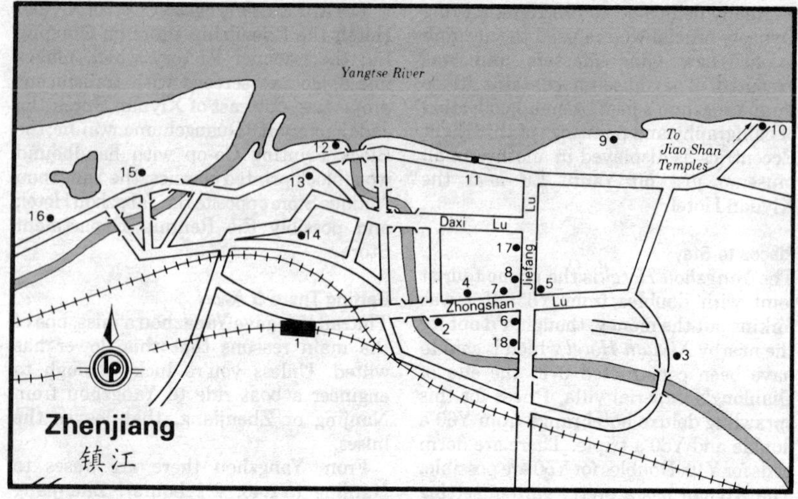

1 Railway Station & Buses to Yangzhou
2 Jingkou Hotel & CTS/CITS
3 Baota Shan
4 Hubin Restaurant
5 Department Store
6 Jingjiang Hotel/Restaurant
7 Tongxinglou Pastry Shop
8 Post Office
9 Ganlu Temple
10 Boat to Jiaoshan Temple
11 Boat Dock & Fish Factory
12 Ferry Dock for Yangzhou
13 Museum
14 Renmin (People's) Park
15 Jinshan Temple
16 Jinshan Hotel
17 Arts & Crafts Store
18 Long-distance Bus Station

1 火车站及汽车站
2 京口饭店
3 宝塔山
4 河宾饭店
5 百货商店
6 京江饭店
7 糕店
8 邮局
9 甘露寺
10 焦山船码头
11 镇江码头
12 轮渡码头
13 博物馆
14 人民公园
15 金山寺
16 金山宾馆
17 工艺品大楼
18 长途汽车站

it faces. In other words, it's large, murky and industrial. The old silk trade still exists, overshadowed by auto and ship-building and by textile and food processing plants. It's a medium-sized place, population well over 300,000 with 300 factories.

Attempts have been made to 'humanise' the city with tree-planting along the streets. The sights are pleasant enough since they're removed from the industrial eyesores. To the south are densely wooded areas, mountains and temples tucked away in bamboo groves but they are difficult to get to by local bus.

The city's history goes back some 2500 years. Its strategic and commercial importance, as the gateway to Nanjing, is underlined by the fact that the British and the French established concessions here. Don't be deterred by your first view of Zhenjiang from the train station; the older part of town is a picturesque area of busy streets, small enterprises, people, bicycles and timber houses.

Information
Bus maps are available from the booth outside the train station.

Things to See
The 'three mounts of Zhenjiang', vantage points strewn along the Yangtse, are the principal sights. The temple complexes on each are among the oldest gracing the river, dating back 1500 years.

Jiao Shan
Also known as 'Jade Hill' because of its dark green foliage (cypresses and bamboo), Jiao Shan is to the east on a small island. Good hiking here with a number of pavilions along the way to the top of the 150-metre-high mount, where Xijiang Tower gives a view of activity on the Yangtse. At the base of Jiao Shan is an active monastery with some 200 pieces of tablet engravings, gardens and bonsai displays. Take bus No 4 to the terminus, then a short walk and a boat ride.

Beigu Shan
Also on the No 4 bus route, this hill has a temple complex (Ganluo Si) featuring a Song Dynasty pagoda which offers expansive views of town. It was once six storeys high but is now four, having been vandalised by Red Guards.

Jin Shan
This hill has a temple arrayed tier by tier with connecting staircases on a hillside – a remarkable design. Right at the top is the seven-storey octagonal Cishou Pagoda, which gives an all-embracing view of the town, the fishponds immediately below and the Yangtse beyond. There are four caves at the mount: Fahai (Buddhist Sea), Bailong (White Dragon), Zhao Yang (Morning Sun) and Luohan (Arhat). Fahai and Bailong caves feature in the Chinese fairytale *The Story of the White Snake*. West of the base, within walking distance, is Number One Lifespring Under Heaven. The spring waters of Jiangsu were catalogued by Tang Dynasty tea expert Lu Yu (Number Two is Wuxi, Number Three is Hangzhou). Take bus No 2 to Jin Shan.

Museum
A fourth 'mount' of interest between Jin Shan and the downtown area is the old British Consulate, which is now a museum and gallery. It houses pottery, bronzes, gold, silver, paintings of the Chao and Tang dynasties, and a separate section with photographs and memorabilia of the anti-Japanese war. Its retail outlet sells calligraphy, rubbings and paintings. The museum is on the bus No 2 route, and is set high over a very old area of winding stone-laid alleys that go down to boat docks on the Yangtse. Well worth investigating on foot.

Places to Stay
For foreign devils the hotel is the *Jin Shan (Golden Hill)* (tel 24962) at 1 Jinshan Xilu, which more closely resembles a motel (an indication of its genesis as an Australian pre-fab). It's a 10-minute walk around the artificial lake near Jin Shan Temple, at the bus No 2 terminus. Doubles cost from Y66. If you're on your own you may be able to get a room for half that price.

Places to Eat
There's a pastry shop near the central town crossroads, and dumpling houses and noodle shops near the railway stations. The *Jingjiang Hotel* at 111 Jiefang Lu, city centre, is reputed to have the best food in town; the ground floor is mainly jiaozi and baozi, but upstairs you can get enormous main courses very cheaply.

Shopping
There's a very fine Arts & Crafts store at 191 Jiefang Lu which stocks embroidery, porcelain, jade and other artefacts. It may have some antiques.

Getting There & Away

Bus The long-distance bus station is in the south-east corner of the downtown area. There are buses from Zhenjiang to Nanjing and Changzhou, and a bus/ferry combination to Yangzhou. You can also get buses to Yangzhou from the front of the main train station.

Rail Zhenjiang is on the main Nanjing-Shanghai line, 3½ hours by fast train to Shanghai, and an hour to either Nanjing or Changzhou. Some of the special express trains don't stop at Zhenjiang. Otherwise, there is a grand choice of schedules so check the timetable in your hotel for a destination and time to suit.

Boat A more offbeat means of departure is via the ferries on the Grand Canal or the Yangtse River.

Getting Around

The city is ideal for day-tripping. Almost all the transport is conveniently close to the railway station, including local buses, buses to Yangzhou, taxis and auto-rickshaws.

Bus No 2 is a convenient tour bus. It goes east from the station along Zhongshan Lu to the downtown area where the Friendship Store, department stores, antique shop and post office are located. It then swings west into the older part of town where some speciality and second-hand stores are to be found, goes past the former British consulate, and continues on to Jin Shan, the terminus.

Bus No 4, which crosses No 2 downtown on Jiefang Lu, runs to Ganluo Temple and Jiao Shan in the east.

CHANGZHOU 常州

Changzhou is overlooked by the guidebooks, and the CITS offices in Wuxi and Suzhou will tell you it's not worth a visit. In the former case it is an oversight and in the latter it's regional jealousy – Changzhou has zero unemployment and is doing very well economically, thank you.

Changzhou is the largest textile producer in Jiangsu Province after Shanghai. The population is around half a million and the city's history is linked with the ancient canal. Industries include textiles, food-processing, machinery, chemicals, building materials, locomotives and diesel engines. Also produced are integrated circuits and electronic parts: large digital clocks around the place will tell you the time from Moscow to Canberra.

It's a delightful mix of old and new: Changzhou has managed to retain its timeless canal housing by placing new residential areas outside the old city core. If you look at the bus map, you'll see these dotted around the perimeter. It is very much a back-alley town, with some interesting sorties on foot. Tourism is only just getting off the ground, so at least for the moment the natives are very friendly. If you want to avoid the crush at Wuxi or Suzhou, Changzhou is a good place to go.

Information

Good bus maps of Changzhou are available from counters in the main train station. CITS (tel 24886), CTS and the Friendship Store are at 101 Dong Dajie, in a compound opposite the local bus terminus downtown (see map).

Things to See

Changzhou has a skein of canals and is an excellent place to observe canal life. There are quite a few archaic bridges which make good vantage points – these are easily found on the bus map. Some of the bridges shelter interconnected timeworn housing; if you took the older housing away the bridges would probably fall down or vice versa! Small markets occasionally take place along canal banks near bridges.

Mooring Pavilion

This is a small park in the south-east of Changzhou sited right on the Grand

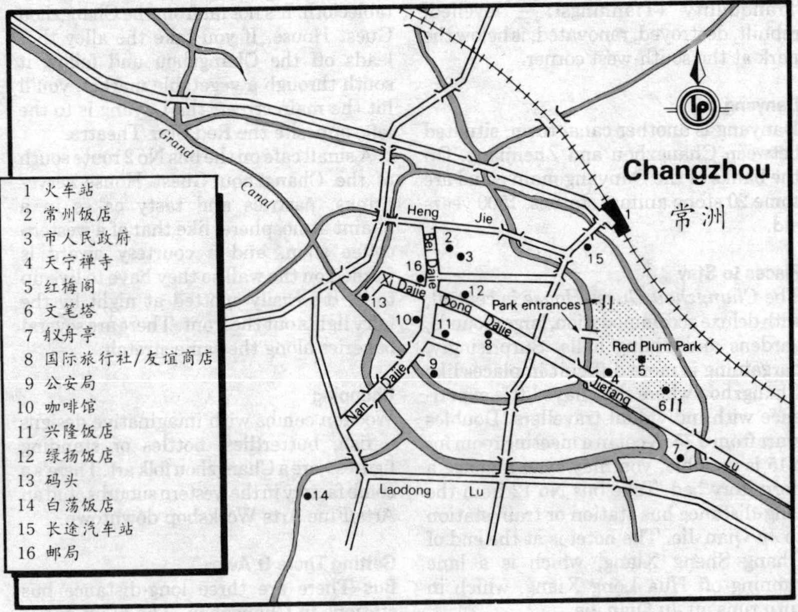

Canal. You can sit here and watch rusty hulks drift by and churn up the oil and pollution. There's a boat dock here, and much hooting and honking on the water. The park was set up in remembrance of Su Dongpo, a great poet. Take bus No 3 or bus No 7 to Mooring Pavilion. If you take bus No 7 further, it runs clear out of town south-eastwards along the banks of the canal past dry-dock repair zones. In the north-west bus No 4 does a similar job. No 4 and No 7 meet at a city centre terminus.

Red Plum Park

North of Mooring Pavilion is Red Plum Park. The very large park has a small pagoda, nicely sited teahouse and boating on the nearby lake. There are one or two structures of significance – Qu Qui Bai's house, now a museum, and Red Plum Pavilion. Qu was a literary man and an early member of the Chinese Communist

1 Railway Station
2 Changzhou Guest House
3 Municipal Government Building
4 Temple of Heavenly Tranquillity (Tianningsi)
5 Red Plum Residence
6 Literary Lion Tower
7 Mooring Pavilion & Boat Dock
8 CITS/CTS/Friendship Store
9 Public Security
10 Cafe
11 Xinglong Restaurant (down sidestreet)
12 Luyang Fandian (restaurant)
13 Boat Dock
14 Baidang Guest House
15 Long-distance Bus Station
16 Post Office

Party. The park itself is nondescript, and sits in an area that looks like the tail end of the Industrial Revolution. Around the park are shanties and other dark and gloomy housing. The Temple of Heavenly

Tranquillity (Tianningsi) – levelled, rebuilt, destroyed, renovated, is below the park at the south-west corner.

Danyang
Danyang is another canal town, situated between Changzhou and Zhenjiang. On the banks of the Danyang main canal are some 20 stone animal statues, 1500 years old.

Places to Stay
The *Changzhou Guest House* is central, with deluxe accommodation, large grounds, gardens and dining halls. Surprisingly, bargaining is more difficult in places like Changzhou where they have little experience with individual travellers. Doubles start from Y75. A cot in a meeting room for Y15 is possible; you may even manage a dormitory bed. Take bus No 12 from the long-distance bus station or train station to Ju Qian Jie. The hotel is at the end of Chang Sheng Xiang, which is a lane running off Hua Long Xiang, which in turn runs off Ju Qian Jie.

Baidung Guest House, on the southern edge of town, is more difficult to get to as some hiking is involved. This is a TV tour-bus hotel. Doubles start from Y94. Take bus No 14 from the train station, then hike.

Places to Eat
Xinglong Restaurant is on a lane off Nan Dajie. You'll know it by the noise level (80 decibels) and frozen pigs at the back near the kitchen. It's got gluey, gooey Jiangsu food – if you want to mail a letter, this is the place to seal it – just use the sauce. Check out the pastry shops on the same street; all sorts of pastries in 3-D animal, dragon and flower shapes.

The *Luyang Fandian* gets a Four Red Star rating. A full, tasty meal can be had for a few yuan per head. They'll probably try to shuffle you away from the noisy plebs and take you upstairs where it's quieter, the furniture is plusher, the food more expensive, and you get a white tablecloth. It's not far from the Changzhou Guest House. If you take the alley that leads off the Changzhou and follow it south through a vegetable market, you'll hit the main street; the Luyang is to the left, opposite the Red Star Theatre.

A small café on the bus No 2 route south of the Changzhou Guest House serves drinks, pastries and tasty cakes in a quaint atmosphere, like that of a western coffee shop, and a courtesy award is framed on the wall so they have to live up to it. It's easily spotted at night by the fairy lights out the front. There are several bakeries along the same stretch.

Shopping
Wooden combs with imaginative designs – fish, butterflies, bottles or standing figures – are a Changzhou folk art. There's a comb factory in the western suburbs, and an Arts/Fine Arts Workshop downtown.

Getting There & Away
Bus There are three long-distance bus stations in Changzhou. The main one is near the train station. Another is in the north-west sector, and the third is in the south-west sector near the Baidung Guest House.

There are buses from Changzhou to Wuxi, Zhenjiang, Suzhou and Nanjing, but they take longer than the fast trains. However, the trains on this line are incredibly crowded and you'd be wise to take a bus if you can!

There are several buses a day to Yixing (1½ hours, Y1.40). There are also direct buses from Changzhou to Dingshu, thus skipping Yixing town.

Rail Changzhou is on the Shanghai-Nanjing line. It is one hour from either Wuxi or Zhenjiang, two hours from Suzhou or Nanjing. If you're going by rail, you might consider doing some rail-hopping; buy a hard-seat ticket from, say, Suzhou to Nanjing, break the journey for a day in Changzhou, and continue with the same ticket.

Boat A more interesting route is along the Grand Canal; Wuxi, the closest major town, is five hours away by boat.

YIXING COUNTY 宜兴县

Yixing County, to the west of Lake Taihu, has enormous touring potential and is a chance to get out of the cities. There are fertile plains, tea and bamboo plantations, undulating mountains with large caves and grottoes. The spectacular potteries of Dingshu village are, however, the real prize. Though busloads of Chinese tourists descend daily on the county from Wuxi, Nanjing and Shanghai, along with the day-tripper western group tours, Yixing County has seen very few individuals.

The town of Yixing is *not* the place to go – you're likely to end up being the main attraction yourself. It's a small town of about 50,000 where the main business of selling noodles, zips, steamed bread, pigs' feet, pots and pans, tools and sunglasses, is all done out on the main street which terminates at the forbidding gates of the Yixing Guest House.

You'll probably end up in Yixing town one way or another since the only tourist hotel is there and the buses pass through the town. The attractions of Yixing County are all within a 30-km range of the town. The pottery town of Dingshu can be done as a day or half-day trip.

Things to See

If you have time, explore the north-east end of Yixing town with its heavy concentration of comic book rentals (and not just kids doing the reading) and all manner of strange transactions down side streets. This and more can be seen in Dingshu. The Confucius Temple at the north-west end of Yixing town was closed at the time of writing due to poor condition, though it's being renovated.

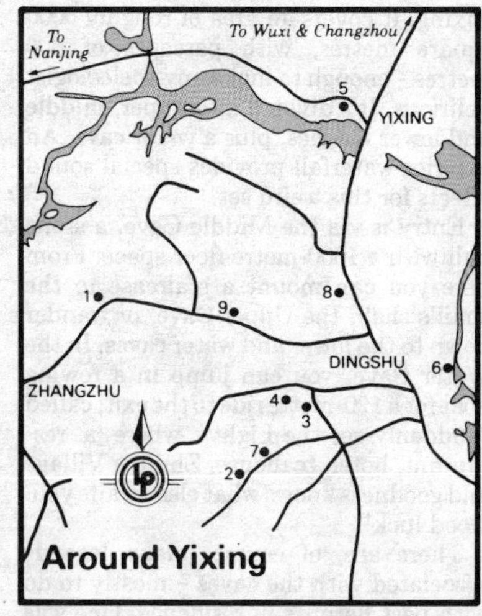

1 苔卷洞　4 玉女潭　7 茶场
2 录谷洞　5 养鱼场　8 川北茶场
3 张公洞　6 紫砂工艺厂　9 芙蓉寺茶场

1. Shanjuan Cave
2. Linggu Cave
3. Zhanggong Cave
4. Yunu Pool
5. Aquatic Breeding Farm
6. Purple Sandware Factory
7. Yangxian Tea Plantation
8. Chuanbu Tea Plantation
9. Furongsi Tea Plantation

Karst Caves

There are a number of these to the south-west of Yixing township, and they're a cut above average. The drab interiors are lit by the standard selection of coloured neon, but you may wish to supplement this with a torch for navigation. The caves are very wet, so take your raincoat, too. The countryside around the caves is attractive and actually worth more time than the underground.

Shanjuan Cave

This cave is embedded in Snail Shell Hill (Luoyan Shan), 27 km south-west of

Yixing. It covers an area of roughly 5000 square metres, with passages of 800 metres – enough to make any speleologist delirious. It's divided into upper, middle and lower reaches, plus a water cave. An exterior waterfall provides special sound effects for this weird set.

Entry is via the Middle Cave, a stone hall with a 1000-metre floor space. From here you can mount a staircase to the snail's shell, the Upper Cave, or wander down to the lower and water caves. In the Water Cave, you can jump in a rowing boat for a 120-metre ride to the exit, called 'Suddenly-see-the-Light', where a restaurant, hotel, teahouse, Zhuling Village and goodness knows what else awaits you. Good luck!

There are, of course, many legends associated with the caves – mostly to do with past hermits in residence. One was the hermit Zhu Yingtai. At the exit is a small pavilion which she used as her 'reading room'. Zhu, as the story goes, being a Jin Dynasty lass was not permitted to attend school, so she disguised herself as a male student and took up residence in the caves.

Every piece of stalagmite and stalactite in the cave is carefully catalogued – whether it be a moist sheep, a soggy plum, a cluster of bananas or an elephant. If the commentary is in Chinese, just exercise your imagination – that's what they did.

Buses run to Shanjuan from Yixing. The trip takes one hour and the fare is peanuts.

Zhanggong Cave

Nineteen km south of Yixing town are three-score-chambers-within caves, large and small, divided into upper and lower reaches. Their size is comparable to Shanjuan, but the layout is different. This is up-down caving. What you do is scale a small hill called Yufeng Shan from the inside, and you come out on the top with a splendid view of the surrounding countryside with hamlets stretching as far as Lake Taihu.

There are two large grottoes in this bunch of caverns. The more impressive is the Hall of the Dragon King, with a ceiling that definitely isn't sprayed-on stucco. The place would make a perfect disco! From the Hall of the Dragon King you make your way through the Dry Nostril Cave, pause to clear your sinuses, and work up to the aforementioned exit.

A little further south of Zhanggong is the Yunutan, or Jade Maiden Pond.

Buses to Zhanggong from Yixing take half an hour. From Zhanggong you can pick up a passing bus to Linggu – the terminus of the line. If you're stuck for transport, try to get to Dingshu Village, where bus connections are good.

Linggu Cave

Eight km down a dirt road from Zhanggong, Linggu is the largest and least explored of the three caves. You could easily get lost in this one and not because of the scenery either. The cave has six large halls arrayed roughly in a semicircle, and it's a long, deep forage.

Near the Linggu Cave is the Yanxian Tea Plantation, with bushels laid out like fat caterpillars stretching into the horizon, and the odd tea villa in the background. The trip is worth it for the tea fields alone.

There are buses to Linggu from Zhanggong; see the section on Zhanggong for details.

Dingshu

Dingshu is the pottery-making town of Yixing County and one of the highlights of Jiangsu Province. For details see the Dingshu section below.

Extraordinary Touring

For the adventurous, there are a number of unexplored routes once you're on the loose in Yixing County. A suggestion is to get there in the conventional manner, and try your luck on a different route out. Pottery is transported via canals and across Lake Taihu to Wuxi and it might be possible to transport yourself likewise. Highways skirt Lake Taihu, eventually running to Suzhou, Shanghai and Hangzhou. If you took a bus to Changxing, a slow branch line railway leads from there to Hangzhou. At the southern end of the lake is a cross-over point, Huzhou. A little way north of this, on Lake Taihu, is Xiaomeikou, where ferry routes are marked on the map as leading to Wuxi across the lake, and to Suzhou via Yuanshan and Xukou.

Place to Stay

The *Yixing Guest House* caters chiefly to cadres holding meetings. The guest house is at the end of Renmin Lu on the southern edge of Yixing town. If there's not a rash of meetings, or a rare tour bus assault, the hotel will be empty. It's a large building, with gardens and some luxury living.

Doubles cost from around Y45 but that depends on whoever's behind the reception desk. Figures tumble from their lips until you give up and go away, or give in and take what you get. The hotel does have dormitory rooms.

The hotel is a half-hour walk from Yixing bus station; turn right from the station, follow the main road south along the lakeside, cross three bridges and turn left, then right again to the hotel gates.

The long stretch across the bridges is the same road that runs to Dingshu, so if your bus goes to Dingshu, ask the driver to let you off closer to the hotel. If you don't mind the stroll, and want to see the main drag of Yixing town, another way of getting to the hotel is to walk three blocks straight ahead from the bus station, turn right onto Renmin Lu, and keep walking until you hit the hotel.

Places to Eat

The guest house has a dining room. If you don't mind 500 people at your table (staring at you, not their food), there are small restaurants opposite the bus station. Along Renmin Lu you'll find some baked food and dumplings.

Getting There & Away

There are buses from Yixing to: Wuxi (Y2, 2½ hours), Shanghai (Y4.80), Nanjing (Y3.80), Suzhou (Y2.90) and Changzhou (Y1.40, 1½ hours).

Getting Around

There are no local buses in Yixing. There are buses to the sights out of town and all of them end up in the bus stations of either Yixing town or Dingshu. There are frequent connections between the two stations. Hitch-hiking is a possibility.

DINGSHU (JIN SHAN) 丁蜀(金山)

In Yixing County they not only grow tea, they make plenty of pots to put it in. Small towns in China can be utterly engrossing if they specialise in some kind of product, and such is the case with Dingshuzhen.

The town has a history of bulk pottery output since the Qin and Han dynasties (221 BC to 220 AD), and some of the scenes you can witness here, especially at the loading dock that leads into Lake Taihu, are timeless. Almost every family is engaged in the manufacture of ceramics, and at the back end of town half the houses are made of the stuff. Dingshu is *the* pottery capital of China. There are also important porcelain-making plants in Jingdezhen, Handan, Zibo and parts of Guangzhou, but few that handle the wide range of ceramics Dingshu does.

Dingshu is about 25 km from Yixing town and has two dozen ceramics factories producing more than 2000 varieties of pottery – quite an output for a population of 100,000. Among the array of products are the ceramic tables and trash-cans that you find around China, huge jars used to store oil and grain, the famed Yixing teapots, and the glazed tiling and ceramic frescoes that are desperately needed as spare parts for tourist attractions – the Forbidden City in Beijing is one of the customers.

Dingshu is also known as Jin Shan. The characters for Jin Shan usually appear on

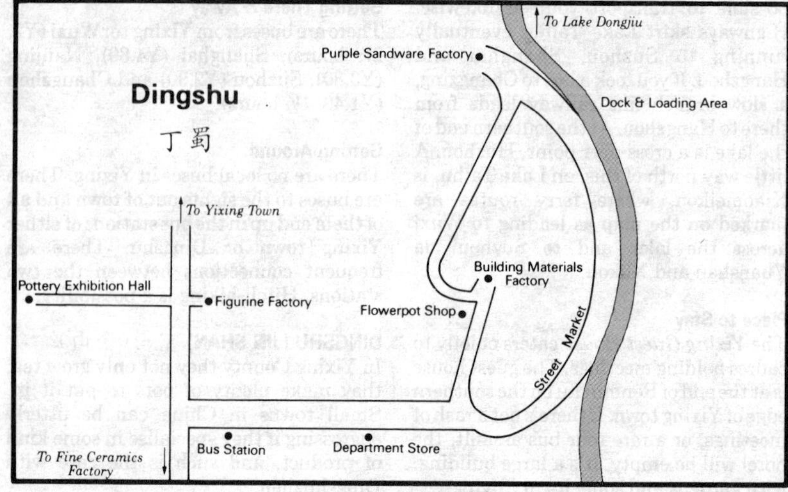

bus timetables, so ask for that place if Dingshu draws a blank.

Itineraries

The back end of Dingshu is a good 40 minutes from the bus station, but there's plenty to amuse you along the route. You can get into the factories if you persist. If you act like a bigshot buyer, all doors will automatically swing open, as far as the showrooms anyway. Each factory in theory has a retail outlet, so you can march in and say you're looking for the shop. Unfortunately, bigshots don't walk but arrive in big taxis. Perhaps an eccentric millionaire? If you have the bucks to sling around, CITS in Yixing town can get you into the factories of your choice at a price of their choice. Contact CITS at the Yixing Guest House. A suggested three-hour walking tour of Dingshu is described below.

The **Pottery Exhibition Hall** is the logical first step to get your bearings in Dingshu. Turn left from the bus station and veer right past a small corner store. The Exhibition Hall is the large solid building which looks rather like a palace, five minutes up the street on your left. You can view two floors and several wings of pottery and get a good idea of what might be a good purchase. The exhibits are well presented; they don't like photos. There are free markets nearby selling pottery.

Opposite the Hall is a **Figurine Factory** which produces kitsch lampstands and the like. Yet even this factory is experimenting with glazes like tigerskin and snowflake, which is the secret of Dingshu. Technology got off to a great start here when they introduced the new improved Dragon Kiln over 1000 years ago. Some distance north of the Exhibition Hall is the **Ceramics Research Institute**.

Backtrack to the bus station. By now you're an expert on Dingshu pots, so ignore the little retail shop on the corner! If you go straight down the street past the bus station, you'll get to the centre of town. En route, you pass two retail outlets. The second one has celadon-ware on the top floor, but you're better off loading up on the way back. Proceed about 10 minutes from here and you'll see a yellow police box, backed by a large billboard poster. Take the alley to the right and you stumble into a very strange market which runs along the banks of a small canal. If you follow the market up, you'll arrive at a boat-loading dock where you begin to get an idea of the scale of things. Concrete housing here is enlivened with broken ceramic tiling, and other lodgings are constructed entirely of large storage jars and pottery shards.

Further past the dock is the **Purple Sandware Factory** where they'll probably slam the door in your face. The dullish brown stoneware produced here, mostly teapots and flowerpots, is prized the world over and dates back 1000 years or so. Made from local clays, the unglazed teapots have a wide export market, which might have a lot to do with their remarkable properties and aesthetic shapes. They retain the flavour and fragrance of tea for a long time; it's said that after extended use with one type of tea, no further tea leaves are necessary. The teapots glaze themselves a darker, silkier tea-stain brown colour. It's claimed that the Purple Sands pots can be placed over a direct flame or shoved in boiling water without cracking (though it's a different story if you drop one on the floor).

From the Purple Sands you can return to town by a different route. Go back to the dock and take a right fork. This brings you to another road, and if you look left, you will spot the **Building Materials Factory**. This is a large operation which makes glazed tiles, garbage bins, ceramic tables and pottery pavilions. The production of pottery for civic and military use was what really got Dingshu off the ground, and is still the mainstay. Pottery is now produced for sanitation, construction, daily use and the tourist industry – throw together a pavilion here, re-tile a temple there.

Near the gates of the Building Materials Factory is a small retail outlet selling flowerpots and the bonsai arrangements in them. Some other factories around Dingshu are the **East Wind** (rubbish bins) and the **Red Star** (glazed vats, stools, tables).

Buying

Pottery in Dingshu is dirt cheap, and valued by the serious as *objets d'art*. Teapots go for Y0.50 and at that price you could afford one for your hotel room to keep the tea leaves out of your mouth. The same pots can be found around Yixing County, but not with the same variety, quality, or price.

Further down the line (Wuxi, Suzhou, Shanghai), the price doubles and the selection narrows. By the time it gets to Hong Kong, the same teapot could be worth Y30 or more, which is quite a jump but they did get it there in one piece.

You can get matching sets of cups to go with the teapot. The teapots, because of

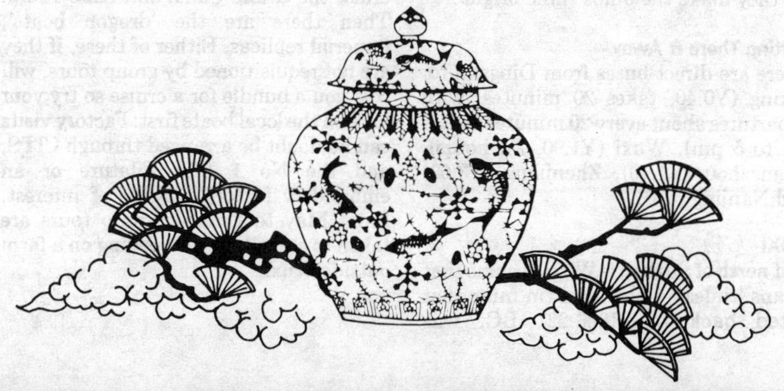

size and other considerations, are the best buy, and you can yarn on about all the tea in the PRC while you sip from one back home.

For starters there is the tomato-shaped dragon teapot, the lid of which has a free-rolling dragon's head embedded in it. This amazing pot costs Y1. Indeed, Dingshu is the home of the world's most surprising teapots, some with ingenious musical properties involving nipples of clay in the lid. Teapots start from Y0.50 to Y2.50 for a simple model and climb high into the yuans after that.

There is a complicated ritual that should be followed for breaking in a new teapot, depending on what kind of tea – oolong, black or green – is to be brewed. Check for tight lids when purchasing and test the pouring lip by transferring water from one pot to another. Also look for the small squarish teapots; they're lighter, pack better and travel easier.

The two retail outlets along the road from the bus station are the best places to stock up, but you may spot a better deal at a factory outlet. Anyway, at Y1 you're not about to lose on the deal. Some of the locals sell on the free market; they make the pots up, then get them fired at local factories.

Also on sale, and something that can be lugged out, are flowerpots, figurines and casseroles. The casseroles are supposed to make the meat tender. In the kitsch-enware department are ceramic lampshades. Do they make the bulbs shine brighter?

Getting There & Away

There are direct buses from Dingshu to: Yixing (Y0.40, takes 20 minutes, with departures about every 20 minutes from 6 am to 5 pm), Wuxi (Y1.90, 2½ hours), Changzhou (Y1.70), Zhenjiang (Y3.60) and Nanjing (Y4).

WUXI 无锡

Just north of Suzhou is Wuxi, a name that means 'tinless' – the local tin mine that dated back to c1066-221 BC, was exhausted during the Han Dynasty (206 BC-220 AD). Not that the locals especially cared. A stone tablet dug out of Xishan Hill is engraved, 'Where there is tin, there is fighting; where there is no tin, there is tranquillity'. And indeed there was tranquillity. Like Suzhou, Wuxi was an ancient silk producer, but it remained a sleepy backwater town barely altered by the intrusion of the Grand Canal (though it did once or twice come into the spotlight as a rice-marketing centre).

In this century Wuxi made up for the long sleep. In the 1930s Shanghai businessmen, backed by foreign technicians, set up textile and flour mills, oil-extracting plants, and a soap factory. After liberation, textile production was stepped up considerably and light and heavy industry boomed. Monstrous housing developments were flung up to accommodate a population that had surpassed Suzhou's and which today stands at 800,000. The town is now ranked among the top 15 or so economic centres in China, with hundreds of factories and an emphasis on electronics, textiles, machine building, chemicals, fishing, and agricultural crops serving the Shanghai market.

Wuxi is being promoted as a resort area, and if you have resort-type money the programme consists of cooking classes, fishing, 10-day acupuncture and massage courses, sanatorium treatments, and taijiquan lessons. At the command of CITS is a small fleet of power craft that cruise the Grand Canal and Lake Taihu. Then there are the 'dragon boats', imperial replicas. Either of these, if they are not requisitioned by group tours, will cost you a bundle for a cruise so try your luck on the local boats first. Factory visits can no doubt be arranged through CITS, and the No 1 Silk Filature or an embroidery factory may be of interest. From May to October group tours are taken to see silkworm breeding on a farm outside Wuxi.

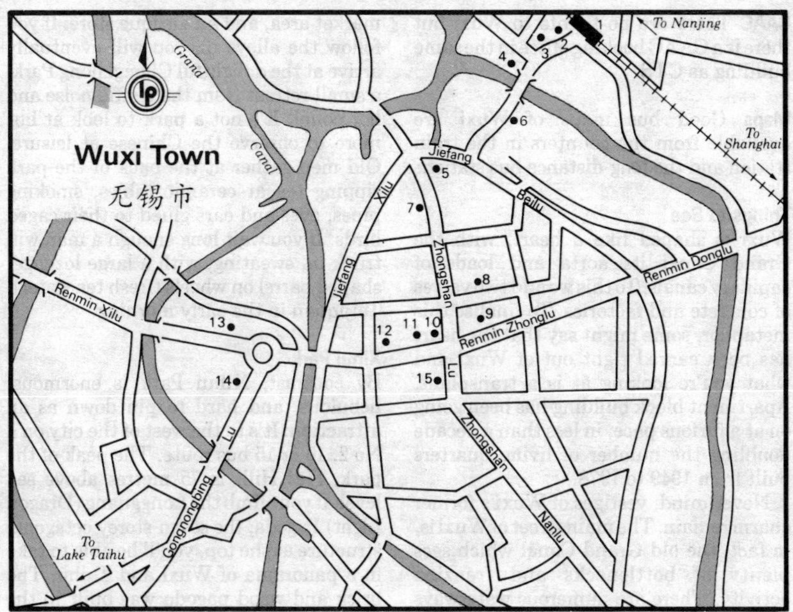

1	Wuxi Railway Station	1	无锡火车站
2	China Travel Service (CTS)/CAAC	2	中国旅行社
3	Long-distance Bus Station	3	长途汽车站
4	Canal Boat Dock	4	轮船码头
5	First Department Store	5	中百一店
6	Zhongguo Restaurant	6	中国饭店
7	Jiangnan Restaurant	7	江南菜馆
8	Chengzhong Park	8	城中公园
9	Free Markets (Chongansi People's Market)	9	崇安寺
10	Dongfanghong Emporium	10	东方红市场
11	Arts & Crafts Store	11	工艺美术服务部
12	Advance Bus, Rail & Boat Ticket Office	12	火车售票处
13	Bus No 2 Stop (To Xihui Park & Taihu starts at Station)	13	二路汽车站
14	Bus No 1 Stop (Goes to Hubin & Shuixiu Hotel)	14	一路汽车站
15	Dongfanghong Square	15	东方红市场

Information & Orientation

Wuxi is divided into two sections, five to 10 km apart, and the hotel situation is not good in either. Because of Wuxi's earlier stunted growth, there are few 'historical relics' and the main attraction is a natural one – Lake Taihu – which is clear out of town. Tourist land is out by the lakeside. If you want to observe the locals then the canal life around town holds interest.

CTS (not CITS) is conveniently located in a building facing the square in front of the main train station. Several people here speak English.

CAAC There are no flights to Wuxi but there is a CAAC booking office in the same building as CTS.

Maps Good bus maps of Wuxi are available from the counters in the train station and the long-distance bus station.

Things to See

Wuxi is shaped like a heart, with the Grand Canal its aorta and loads of capillary canals. To this we add two valves of concrete and factories. To finalise this metaphor, some might say that the heart has been carved right out of Wuxi and what you're looking at is a transplant. Apartment block building has been going on at a furious pace, in less than a decade doubling the number of living quarters built from 1949 to 1978.

Never mind, vestiges of Wuxi's former charm remain. The main street of Wuxi is, in fact, the old Grand Canal which sees plenty of bottlenecks and frenzied activity. There are numerous waterways cutting into the canal, and more than a fair share of bridges to observe from.

Just down from the train station is Gongyun Bridge with a passenger and loading dock close by – well worth your attention. In the north-west of the city is an older bridge, Wuqiao, which has a great view of canal traffic and overlooks an ancient pavilion stranded on tiny Huangbudun Isle. Traffic will, in fact, come at you from all directions. For an insider point of view, try zipping around in a small boat yourself – there are at least three boat stations within the city.

Free Markets

These are not far from the corner of Renmin and Zhongshan Lu. Go south on Zhongshan, turn left at Renmin, walk along a bit and you'll find the market entrance leading north again. This is about the most exciting thing in Wuxi. Be prepared to bargain for foodstuffs, as the prices suddenly rocket when they see your face. There's a restaurant in the food market area, and an antique store. If you follow the alleys in, you will eventually arrive at the delightful Chengzhong Park, a small retreat from the traffic noise and hoi polloi. It's not a park to look at but more to observe the Chinese at leisure. Old men gather at the back of the park sipping tea at ceramic tables, smoking pipes, eyes and ears glued to their caged birds. If you wait long enough a man will truck in, sweating, with a large lozenge-shaped barrel on wheels (fresh tea water). Taijiquan in the early morning.

Xihui Park

By contrast, Xihui Park is enormous, nebulous, and hard to pin down as an attraction. It's to the west of the city on a No 2, 10 or 15 bus route. The peak of the park, Hui Hill, is 75 metres above sea level. If you climb the Longguang (Dragon Light) Pagoda, the seven-storey octagonal structure at the top, you'll be able to take in a panorama of Wuxi and Taihu. The brick and wood pagoda was built in the Ming, burned down in the Qing, and rebuilt in the Spring many years later. For sunrises, try the Qingyun Pavilion, just to the east of the pagoda.

The park has a motley collection of pavilions, snack bars and teahouses, along with a small zoo, a large artificial lake, and a cave that burrows for half a km from the east side to the west. The western section of the park rambles off into Huishan Hill, where you'll find the famous Ming Dynasty Jichang Garden (Ming refers to the garden layout – the buildings are recent), and the remaining Huishan Temple nearby, once a Buddhist monastery.

What follows for this area is the standard catalogue of inscribed stones, halls, gates and crumbled villas from the Ming, Song, Qing and Tang. Sometimes you have to wonder who is pulling whose leg. There are so many copies, permutations and fakes in China it's hard to know exactly which year you're looking at. Still, the copies are nice.

Speaking of Tang, the Second Spring under Heaven is here so bring your tea mugs, or try the local teahouse brew. The Chinese patronise this watering hole to indulge in the ancient hobby of carp watching. From the Second Spring you can walk to vantage points and pavilions higher up. A major detour leads to the 329-metre peak in the north-west called Sanmao.

Lake Taihu

Lake Taihu is a freshwater lake with a total area of 2200 square km. Average depth of the lake is two metres. There are some 90 islands, large and small, within it. Junks with all sails set ply the waters – the winds of nostalgia make them a magnificent sight, gracefully clipping across the waters. The fishing industry is very active with over 30 varieties caught. There's fish breeding in the shoals, and women floating around in wooden tubs harvesting water-chestnuts. On the shores are plantations of rice, tea, mulberry trees and citrus fruits. Suitably grotesque rocks are submerged in the lake for decades and when they're sufficiently weathered they're prized for classical garden landscaping. To the north-west of the lake are hilly zones, to the south-east is a vast plain. The whole area is referred to as 'the land of fish and rice' because of its fertile soil, mild climate and abundant rainfall.

1 Taihu Hotel
2 Hubin Hotel
3 Shuixiu Hotel
4 Meiyuan (Plum Garden)
5 Yuantouzhu (Turtle Head Isle)
6 San Shan (Three Hills) Isles
7 Liyuan Garden
8 Xihui Park

Meiyuan (Plum Garden)

This was once a small *peach* garden built during the Qing Dynasty, since renovated or re-landscaped, and expanded. It is renowned for its thousands of red plum trees which blossom in the spring. Peach and cherry blossoms grow here too, and grotesque rockeries are arrayed at the centre of the garden. The highest point is Plum Pagoda, with views of Taihu. The garden is near the bus No 2 terminus.

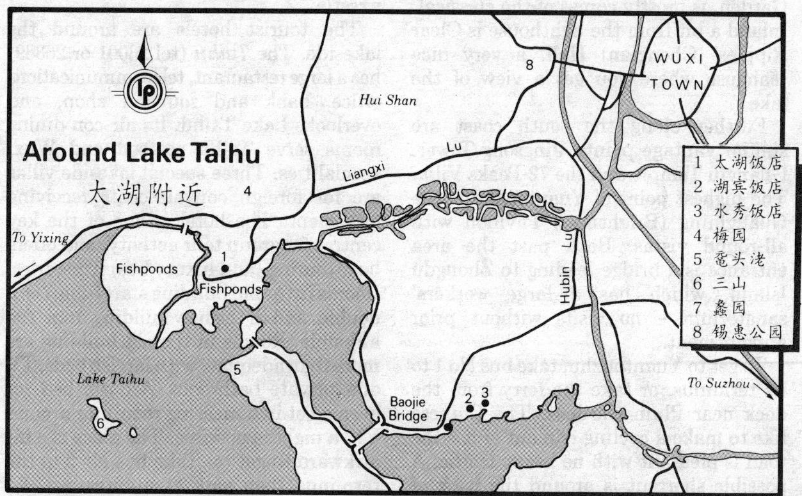

Liyuan Garden
This hideous circus is always packed out by the locals. As Chinese gardens go, this one is a goner. The whole tatty affair goes beyond bad taste – a concrete labyrinth of fishponds, walkways, mini-bridges, a mini-pagoda, and souvenir vendors hawking garish plaster and gilded figurines. Inside the garden on the shore of Taihu is a tour-boat dock for cruises to other points.

Yuantouzhu (Turtle-Head Isle)
So named because it appears to be shaped like the head of a turtle. (Elementary, my dear Watson). It is not actually an island, but being surrounded on three sides by water makes it appear so. This is the basic scenic strolling area where you can watch the junks on Lake Taihu.

You can make a round trip walk of the area. If you continue along the shore, you come to the ferry dock for the San Shan Isles, passing Taihujiajue Archway and Perpetual Spring (Changchun) Bridge. A walkway leads to a small lighthouse, near which is an inscribed stone referring to the island name and several pavilions. The architecture here, like that of Liyuan Garden, is mostly copies of the classical. Inland a bit from the lighthouse is Clear Ripples (Chenglan) Hall, a very nice teahouse where you get a view of the lake.

Further along the south coast are similar vantage points: Jingsong Tower, Guangfu Temple and the 72-Peaks Villa. The highest point of Yuantouzhu is the Guangming (Brightness) Pavilion with all-round vistas. Back past the area entrance is a bridge leading to Zhongdu Island, which has a large workers' sanatorium – no visits without prior appointment.

To get to Yuantouzhu, take bus No 1 to its terminus, or take the ferry from the dock near Plum Gardens. The Chinese like to make a cycling trip out of it – the road is pleasant with no heavy traffic. A possible shortcut is around the back of Zhongdu Island leading back towards Taihu Hotel.

San Shan (Three Hills) Isles
San Shan is an island park three km south-west of Yuantouzhu. If you haven't seen Wuxi and the lake from every possible angle by now, try this one as well. Vantage points at the top look back toward Yuantouzhu and you can work out if it really does look like a turtle-head or not. As one of the picture captions in a Chinese guide puts it: 'Sightseeing feeds chummies with more conversation-topics'. The Three-Hill Teahouse has outdoor tables and rattan chairs, and views. San Shan is a 20-minute ferry ride from Yuantouzhu.

Places to Stay
In the town itself is the *Liangxi Hotel* (tel 26812) on Zhongshan Nanlu. Take bus No 12 from the train station. The hotel is actually set back from Zhongshan Nanlu, on a small street which runs parallel to it; you'll have to watch out for it. They quote double rooms from Y67 but there's certainly cheaper stuff available. Getting a dormitory bed could require a good arm-wrestle.

The tourist hotels are around the lakeside. The *Taihu* (tel 23001 or 26389) has a large restaurant, telecommunications office, bank and souvenir shop, and overlooks Lake Taihu. Its air-con dining rooms serve Taihu seafood and Wuxi specialities. Three special lakeside villas are for foreign convalescents receiving treatment. The hotel is one of the key centres for group tour activity, and offers boat touring (and luxury bus) itineraries. Rooms in the old building start from Y66 a double, and in the new building from Y90 a double. Rooms in the old building are more than adequate with largish beds, TV and private bathroom. A dorm bed (or even a cot in a meeting room) for around Y12 a night is possible. The place is a bit awkward to get to: Take bus No 2 to the terminus, then walk 20 minutes.

The *Hubin Hotel* (tel 26712) on Liyuan Lu is a high-rise tour bus hotel. It charges from Y80 a double and stiff prices elsewhere in the building, for a dead and dull atmosphere. There are 356 beds, air-con, and a full range of facilities including a bar. Take bus No 1 from the train station.

The *Shuixiu Hotel* (tel 22985) is next to the Hubin Hotel. Doubles cost from around Y80. It's a squat Australian prefab with koalas and kangaroos crawling over the curtains, and rooms full of fridges, phones, digital devices – you get the picture. Yes, it's very expensive. There are rooms with views over the lake. Take bus No 1 from the train station.

The above three hotels (the Hubin was built in 1978, the Shuixiu was assembled in 1980) are designed for the group tours – there's nothing remotely close to them in the way of shops or anything else. Anglers can drop out of the hotels toting fishing licences, tackle and bait, cruise around Lake Taihu and have their catches cooked back at the hotel. A rubbing is made first as a memento so you can have your fish and eat it too! Amateurs are parcelled off to the fish ponds for an easy catch.

Places to Eat

The *China Restaurant* is recommended for its large servings and low prices. To get there, proceed directly from the train station and across the bridge; it's on your left, second block down, on the ground floor of the China Hotel which fronts on to Tong Yun Lu.

Other eating places can be found in the markets off Renmin Lu. The stretch along Zhongshan Lu (from the First Department Store to Renmin Lu) has lots of restaurants. Try the *Jiangnan Restaurant* at 435 Zhongshan Lu.

Out in the boondocks, around Taihu, it's the hotel dining rooms, or whatever you can scrounge from stalls or teahouses at the tourist attractions. One particularly fortifying discovery was a packet of Huishan shortcake cookies (delicious), continuing a tourist tradition that dates back to the 14th century when Buddhist monasteries from Huishan hillsides doled them out to vegetarians in transit. Seasonal seafood includes crab, shrimp, eel and fresh fish. Wuxi specialities include pork ribs in soy sauce, bean curd, a kind of pancake padded out with midget fish from Lake Taihu, and honey-peach in season.

Shopping

The Arts & Crafts Store is at 192 Renmin Lu. The Dongfanghong Emporium is nearby. The First Department Store is at the top end of Zhongshan Lu. The Huishan Clay Figurine Factory is near Xihui Park.

Silk products and embroidery are good buys. Apart from the places already mentioned, try the merchants in the side streets. Dongfanghong Square is the busiest shopping area.

There are some remarkably ugly clay figurines for sale around the place. A peasant folk art, they were usually models of opera stars, and after a little diversion into revolutionary heroes are back to opera and story figures again. (Wuxi has its own form of opera deriving from folk songs.) The 'Lucky Fatties' are obese babies – symbols of fortune and happiness and just the thing to fill up your mantelpiece with.

Getting There & Away

The advance ticket office for boat, bus and train in Wuxi is at 224 Renmin Lu. Some boats require one or two day's advance booking.

Bus The long-distance bus station is near the train station. There are buses to Shanghai (Y3.40), Suzhou (Y2), Dingshu (Y1.80), Yixing (Y2), Changzhou and Yangzhou.

Rail Wuxi is on the Beijing-Shanghai line, with frequent express and special-express trains. There are trains to Suzhou (40

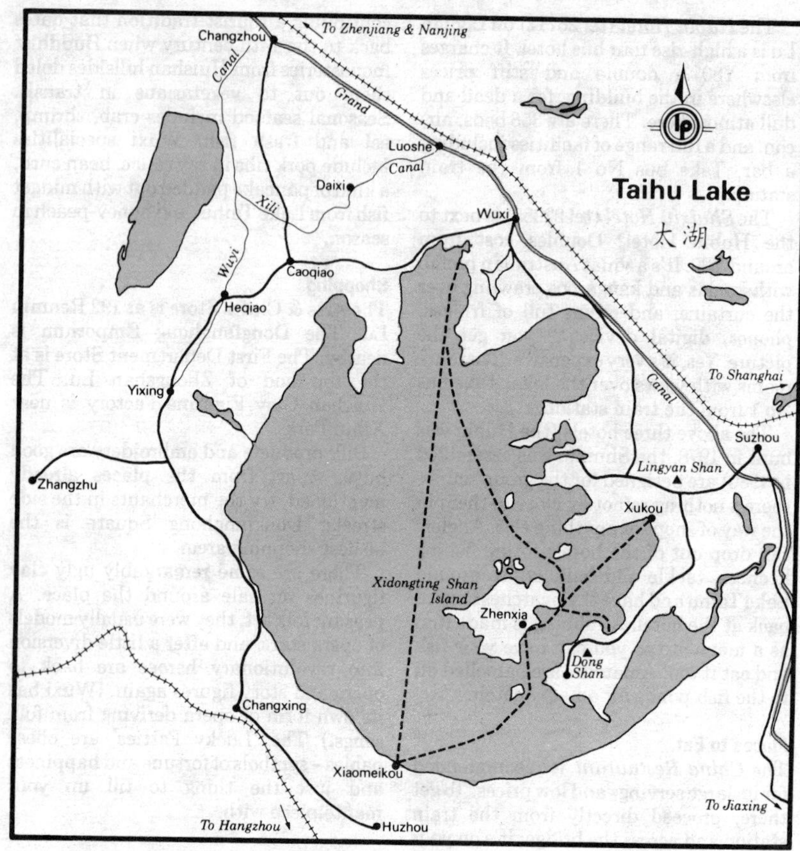

minutes), Shanghai (1¾ hours) and Nanjing (2¾ hours).

If you're day-tripping, get a through ticket from, say, Nanjing to Suzhou, alight at Wuxi and continue the same evening to Suzhou. Reserved seating is not necessary because of the short distances between cities, and in any case your chances of getting a seat on these impossibly crowded trains are nil. You can dump your bags at the railway station in Wuxi and look around town.

Boat With such a large lake there is a wealth of scenery and some fascinating routes out of the town. Yixing and Suzhou lie almost on the lake, Changzhou lies north-west of Wuxi on the Grand Canal, and Hangzhou lies inland but is accessible from Wuxi.

From Wuxi there are many boat routes running along smaller canals to outlying counties as well as boats across Lake Taihu and along the Grand Canal. There are many daily boats to Yixing and Changzhou. There is another route through the Wuxi canals, across Lake Taihu and down south through a series of canals to Hangzhou. Alternatively, you can take a boat across Lake Taihu to Huzhou on the southern side and then take a bus to Hangzhou.

Huzhou lies at the junction of routes to Shanghai, Hangzhou and Huang Shan (Yellow Mountain), and there is a tourist service in Huzhou. Just north of Huzhou is Xiaomeikou, the ferry dock. North-west of Huzhou is Changxing, a branch-line railway running to Hangzhou.

Another interchange point for boating is at Zhenxia on the east side of Xidongting Shan Isle. From Zhenxia there are connections to Wuxi, and to Xukou near Suzhou.

Since Wuxi itself covers an area of 400 square km, open without a permit, day-tripping along the canals is not technically out-of-bounds. There's no reason to stop you from travelling between Hangzhou, Yixing, Jiaxing, Huzhou, Wuxi and Suzhou on the canals. A variety of motor boats ply these routes, including two-deck motor barges with air-con, soft seats, restaurant and space for over 100 passengers. There may be some Chinese-designed passenger hovercraft.

Getting Around

There are about 15 local bus lines. An alternative for faster connections is to grab an auto-rickshaw – there are ranks at the main train station.

Bus No 2 runs from the railway station, along Jiefang Lu, across two bridges to Xihui Park, then way out to Plum Garden, short of the Taihu Hotel. Bus No 2 almost crosses the bus No 1 route at Gongnongbing Square.

Bus No 1 starts on Gongnongbing Lu, and runs to Liyuan Garden and the Hubin and Shuixiu hotels. The actual terminus of bus No 1 is further on across a bridge to the scenery on Turtle-Head Isle.

A good tour bus is No 10, which does a long loop around the northern part of the city area, taking in four bridges, Xihui Park and the shopping strip of Renmin Lu.

Enquire at CITS for a special tour boat which runs from the pier near the railway station. It cuts down the Liangxi River (through the city), under Ximen Bridge, and south to Liyuan Garden. The boat then continues to Turtle-Head Isle and finally the San Shan Isles.

A ferry runs from the south of Plum Garden to Turtle-Head Isle. Liyuan Garden is a major touring junction with a boat dock and motorboat cruises around Taihu; prices start from a few yuan, and cruises last from one hour to half the day.

SUZHOU 苏州

Suzhou's history goes back 2500 years, give or take 100 – it's one of the oldest towns in the Yangtse basin. With the completion of the Grand Canal in the Sui Dynasty (589-618 AD), Suzhou found itself strategically sited on a major trading route, and the city's fortunes and size rose rapidly.

Suzhou flourished as a centre of shipping and grain storage, bustling with merchants and artisans. By the 12th century the town had attained its present dimensions, and if you consult the map, the layout of the old town is distinct. The city walls, a rectangle enclosed by moats, were pierced by six gates (north, south, two in the east, two in the west). Crisscrossing the city were six north to south canals and 14 east to west canals. Although the walls have largely disappeared, and a fair proportion of the canals have been plugged, central Suzhou retains its 'Renaissance' character.

A legend was spun around Suzhou through tales of beautiful women with mellifluous voices, and through the famous proverb 'In Heaven there is Paradise, on earth Suzhou and Hangzhou'. The story picks up when Marco Polo arrived in 1276. He added the adjectives 'great' and 'noble', though he reserved his finer epithets for Hangzhou. The peripatetic's keen memory tells us that there were astonishing numbers of craftspeople and

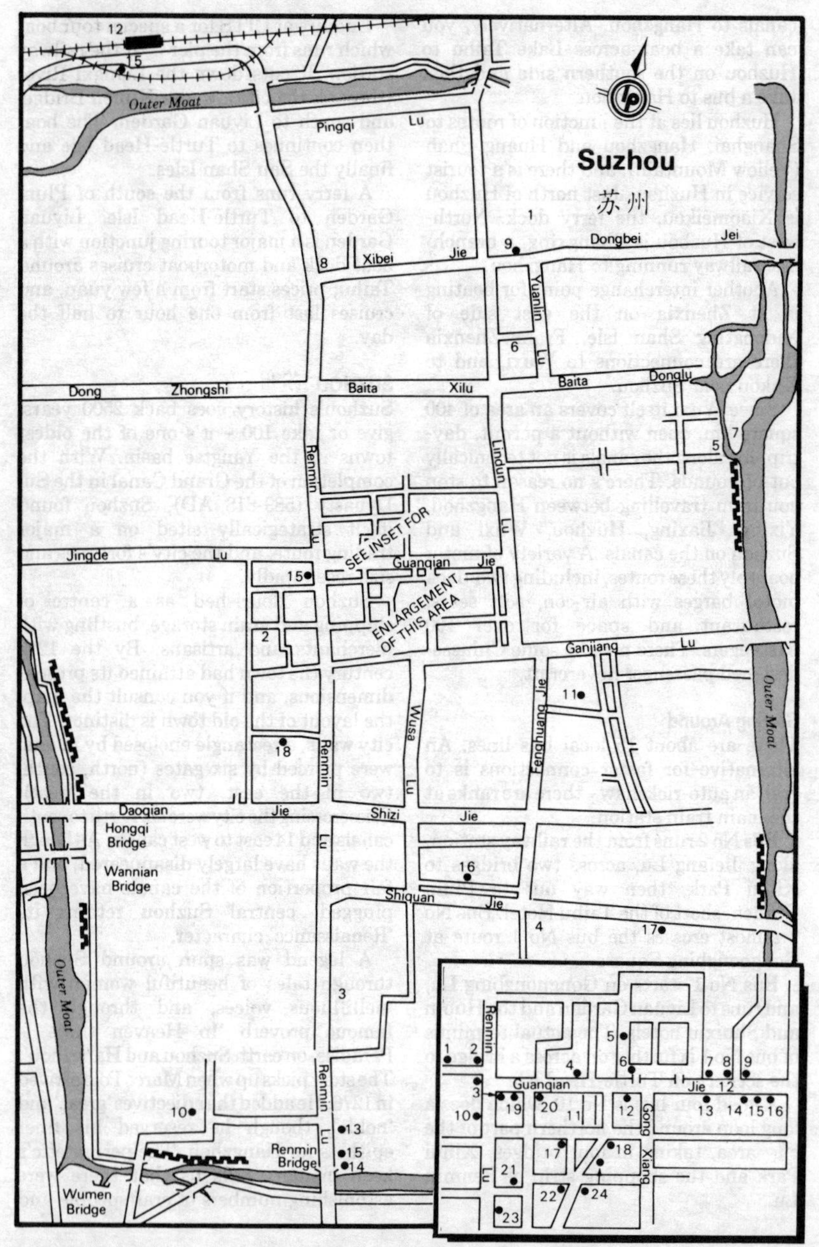
Suzhou
苏州
Outer Moat
Pingqi Lu
Dongbei Jei
Xibei Jie
Yuanlin Lu
Dong Zhongshi
Baita Xilu
Baita Donglu
Renmin Lu
Lindun
SEE INSET FOR ENLARGEMENT OF THIS AREA
Jingde Lu
Guanqian Jie
Ganjiang Lu
Fenghuang Jie
Wusa
Daoqian Jie
Shizi Jie
Hongqi Bridge
Wannian Bridge
Shiquan Jie
Renmin Bridge
Wumen Bridge
Outer Moat
Outer Moat
Renmin Lu
Guanqian Jie
Gong Xiang

1	Zhuozheng Garden	拙政园
2	Yiyuan Garden	怡园
3	Changlangting Garden	沧浪亭 滄
4	Wangshi Garden	网师园
5	Quyuan Garden	耦园
6	Shizilin Garden	狮子林
7	Dong Garden	东园
8	North Temple (Bei Si) Pagoda	北寺塔
9	Suzhou Museum	博物馆
10	Pan Gate Area/Ruiguang Pagoda	盅门/瑞光塔
11	Twin Pagoda Temple	双塔
12	Suzhou Railway Station	火车站
13	Long-distance Bus Station	长途汽车站
14	Grand Canal Boat Ticket Office & Dock	轮船运输公司
15	Taxi, Autorickshaw & Pedicab Stand	出租汽车站
16	Nanlin Hotel	南林饭店
17	Suzhou 1, Suzhou 2 & Gusu Hotels	苏州和姑苏饭店
18	Public Security (on Daishitou Xiang)	公安局

Suzhou (inset)

1	Arts & Crafts Store	工艺美服务部
2	Main Post Office	邮电大楼
3	Suzhou Underground Store Entrances	展销商店
4	Xinhua Bookstore	新华书店
5	Snack shops	玄外观点心店
6	Suzhou Speciality Shop	土特产商店
7	Huangtianyuan Cake Shop	黄天源糕团店
8	Ladies Clothing Shop	女用品商店
9	Seagull Photo Service	海鸥照相馆
10	Taxi, Pedicab & 3-Wheeler Station	出租汽车站
11	Songhelou Restaurant (front & back entrances)	松鹤照相馆
12	Oodles of Noodles	面店
13	Caizhizhai Confectionary	菜芝斋糖果店
14	Suzhou Pastry Shop	苏州糕店
15	Daoxiangcun Cake & Candy Store	稻香村糖果店
16	Xinle Noodles Restaurant	新乐面店
17	Renmin Department Store	人民商场
18	Shanghai Laozhenxin Restaurant	上海老正兴菜馆
19	Chunfeng Restaurant	春风饭店
20	Advance rail ticket office	火车售票处
21	Lexiang Hotel	乐乡饭店
22	Suzhou Story-Telling House	书场
23	Telecom Building	南门商业大楼
24	Theatres & Cinemas	电影院

rich merchants, as well as great sages, physicians and magicians. He writes:

> Moreover I tell you quite truly that there are six thousand bridges of stone in this city, below the greater part of which one galley or two could well pass.

He muses that if the inhabitants had turned their talents to the military arts, they would easily have overrun the whole province. But no, they were totally preoccupied with raising silkworms:

> They have vast quantities of raw silk, and manufacture it, not only for their own consumption, all of them being clothed in dresses of silk, but also for other markets.

Indeed, by the 14th century, Suzhou had established itself as the leading silk producer in the nation. Although Polo's estimate of 6000 bridges is a bit on the wild side, a map made 150 years before his visit shows 359 bridges, as well as 12 pagodas, more than 50 temples and numerous bathhouses. The town became a nesting spot for the Chinese aristocracy, pleasure-seekers, gentlemen of leisure, famous scholars, actors and painters who set about constructing villas and garden retreats for themselves.

At the height of Suzhou's development in the 16th century, the gardens, large and small, numbered over 100. If we mark time here, we arrive at Suzhou's tourist formula today – Garden City, Venice of the East – a medieval mix of woodblock guilds and embroidery societies, white-washed housing, cobbled streets, treelined avenues and canals.

This basically still holds true. Strangely enough Suzhou has managed to adapt itself to a modern era with old-world grace. Part of the reason is perhaps that the silk merchants in days of old succeeded, at the expense of commoners, in getting the maximum production figures. The wretched workers of the silk sweatshops, protesting against paltry wages and the injustices of the contract hire system, were staging violent strikes even in the 15th century, and the landlords shifted. In 1860 Taiping troops took the town without a blow. In 1896 Suzhou was opened to foreign trade, with Japanese and international concessions. During WW II, it was occupied by the Japanese and then by the Kuomintang.

Somehow Suzhou has slipped through the ravages of the Cultural Revolution and 'modernisation'. Though its reliance on the Grand Canal and water transport has shifted with the coming of rail and road, the common denominator – sericulture – is still the mainstay of the economy. The worms are now partially computer-assisted!

Some 600,000 people live here now, and around 500 enterprises have sprung up, including machine building, electronics, optical instruments, ferro-concrete boats and chemical industries. However, being relegated to the outskirts they've not greatly interfered with the central core. The artisans have regrouped and geared up for the export and tourist markets. Everything is absorbed – tourists, trains, silkworms, wheat, gardens, galleys, digital watches. They all melt into the calm rhythms of this ancient water-town.

Information

CITS has a separate building in the Suzhou Hotel compound.

Public Security is at 7 Dashitou Lane.

Bank The Bank of China is at 50 Guanqian Lu.

Things to See

Suzhou is one of those towns where walking becomes a pleasure, and where you get to do most of the staring. The solid French plane trees that canopy the avenues set the tone; for canal-side residents it's a two-way street, with boats gliding past their lounge rooms.

Once you discern the lines of the inner town canals, it's easy to work out walking routes to destinations, and you will probably find the canals themselves of more interest than the destination: a weary boatman sculls his sampan under a humpback bridge; an old woman nimbly bounces over the cobblestones with two laden baskets slung over a bamboo pole; a gentleman steps out of his rickety cottage to clean his teeth, his eye catching the lady opposite about to heave a nightsoil bucket into the canal; a street artist puts some final touches to a one-child-only mural.

For some lively action you really can't miss the bridges over the main moat, which offer great vantage points and are often host to impromptu markets. Because of their proximity to the Grand Canal, the six bridges to the west and south (Diaoqiao, Nanxin, Hongqi, Wannian, Wumen and Renmin) are especially rewarding. Two of these bridges face docks where barges from other villages come to unload produce. Wumen Bridge is the largest single-arched stone bridge in Suzhou. Next to it is the best-preserved city gate, Panmen, along with surviving fortifications. The dilapidated Ruigang Pagoda, once attached to a temple, adds a fitting dimension to the scene.

To get away from it all, the two parks bordering the moat at the north-east end (Dongyuan and Quyuan) are not noted for their layouts, but they are uncrowded and ideal for a quiet cup of tea. In the distance barges still patrol the waters.

North Temple (Bei Si)

The North Temple has the tallest pagoda south of the Yangtse – at nine storeys it dominates the north end of Renmin Lu. You can climb it for a fine aerial view of the town and the farmland beyond, used for growing tea, rice and wheat. The mere fact that you can see this in the first place means you're in a medium sized city. The factory chimneys, the new pagodas of Suzhou, loom on the outskirts, and so does the haze and smoke they create.

The temple complex goes back 1700 years and was originally a residence. The pagoda has been burned, built and rebuilt. Made of wood, it dates from the 17th century. Off to the side of it is Nanmu Hall, which was rebuilt in the Ming Dynasty with some of its features imported from elsewhere. There is a nice teahouse with a small garden out back.

Suzhou Museum

Situated some blocks east of the pagoda, near the 'humble administrator's garden', the museum was once the residence of a Taiping leader, Li Xiucheng. It's a good place to visit after you've seen something of Suzhou as it helps fill in the missing bits of the jigsaw as you retrace Suzhou's history. The museum offers some interesting old maps (Grand Canal, Suzhou, heaven & earth), a silk and embroidery exhibition room (Qing silk samples), Qing Dynasty steles forbidding workers' strikes, and relics unearthed or rescued from various sites around Suzhou (funerary objects, porcelain bowls, bronze swords).

Suzhou Bazaar

The area surrounding Guanqian Lu is riddled with restaurants, speciality shops, theatres, street vendors, hairdressing salons, noodle dispensaries, silk merchants and sweet shops. This maze of back alleys, the main shopping thoroughfare of Suzhou, is a strolling area with neither bicycles nor buses allowed on Guanqian by day. The bazaar is also the restaurant centre of the city.

Temple of Mystery (Xuanmiao Si)

The heart of Suzhou Bazaar is the Taoist Temple of Mystery. It was founded in the 3rd century (Jin Dynasty, laid out 275-279 AD) with additions from the Song. From the Qing Dynasty on, the bazaar fanned out from the temple with small tradespeople and travelling performers using the grounds. The enormous Sanqing Hall, supported by 60 pillars and capped by a double roof with upturned eaves, dates from 1181. It was burned and seriously damaged in the 19th century. During the Cultural Revolution the Red Guards squatted here before its transformation into a library. Today it's been engulfed by the souvenir shops; the square in front of it hosts all manner of outdoor industries including shoe repair, tailoring and bike parking.

Silk Factories

CITS tours are really your only option if you want to get into a silk reeling, silk weaving or silk printing mill – it's unlikely you'll get in there by yourself. The silkworms are hand fed on bamboo trays by peasants. When their cocoons are spun, these are sent off to the factories where the larva cases are boiled and the filament unwound in long strands. There is also an embroidery factory, a jade carving factory and a sandalwood fan factory – all within the central area.

The Gardens

Suzhou's gardens are looked upon as works of art – a fusion of nature, architecture, poetry and painting designed to ease the mind, move it, or assist it. Unlike the massive imperial gardens, the classical landscaping of Suzhou reflects the personal taste of officials and scholars south of the Yangtse. A rich official, his worldly duties performed, would find solace here in his kingdom of ponds and rockeries. The gardens were meant to be enjoyed in solitary contemplation or in the company of a close circle of friends, along with a glass of wine, a concert, reciting of poetry or a discussion about literature.

The key elements are rocks and water. There are surprisingly few flowers and no fountains – just as the Zen gardens of Japan give one an illusion of a natural scene with only moss, sand and rock. These microcosms were laid out by master craftspeople and changed hands many times over the centuries. The gardens suffered a set back during the Taiping Rebellion in the 1870s, and under subsequent foreign domination of Suzhou. Efforts were made to restore them in the 1950s but during the so-called Horticultural Revolution gardeners downed tools, as flowers were frowned upon. In 1979 the Suzhou Garden Society was formed, and an export company was set up to promote Suzhou-designed gardens. A handful of the gardens have been renovated and opened to the public.

It's best not to run around knocking off flowers from every garden on the list – this will swiftly turn Suzhou into weeds. Each garden is meant to be savoured at a snail's pace. The thing to do is take along a Sunday newspaper, a pot of tea, a deckchair, a sketch pad and a bath sponge. Having said that, let me add that it is very hard to wax contemplative when there are thousands of other visitors (mostly Chinese) examining every nook and cranny. The size of the crowds depends on the weather, which day of the week it is and which garden. They're an amiable enough lot – mostly taking photos of each other or sketching the foliage. Old-timers come to relax. The gardens are usually open early morning to dusk (7.30 am to 5 pm), and admission is a few mao.

A footnote on gardening in Suzhou: the common people, not having the resources for larger gardens, work at arranging miniatures (potted landscapes, courtyard cultivation). Suzhou, in fact, is the one place in China where you can count on real flowers instead of plastic. If there are any artificial ones, they will at least be silk. As you're strolling the streets it's worthwhile looking for plebeian miniatures. Potted landscapes are sold in various shops, so you can actually buy a piece of Suzhou – but what are you going to do with it?!

Zhuozheng (a humble administrator's garden)

Built in the early 1500s, this was a private garden belonging to Wang Xianchen, a censor with a chequered history. Some say he was demoted to Suzhou, some claim he extorted the money to have the garden constructed, others that the garden was lost to pay a gambling debt by his son.

The garden is also known as the 'Plain Man's Politics Garden' deriving from the quotation 'To cultivate one's garden to meet one's daily needs, that is what is known as the politics of the plain man'.

The garden contains a five-hectare water park, streams, ponds, bridges, islands of bamboo. You can sense the painter's hand in its design, meant to mimic parts of rural South China. Strong emphasis in Suzhou gardens is given to scenery not found locally. The garden is divided into East, Middle and West sections though there's nothing of great interest in the East Garden. The Middle Garden is the best. From the Ming Dynasty Distant Fragrance (Yuanxiang) Hall, you can get a view of the entire works through lattice windows.

In the same area is the Suzhou Museum, and several silk mills.

Lion Grove (Shizilin)

Just up the street from the humble administrator's garden, this grove was constructed in 1350 by the monk Tian Ru and other disciples as a memorial to their master Zhi Zheng. This guy, it appears, was some kind of cave dweller, and his last fixed address was c/o 'Lion Cliff', Tianmu Mountains, Zhejiang Province. The garden has rockeries that evoke leonine forms. The walls of the labyrinth of tunnels bear calligraphy from famous chisels. The grove encompasses one hectare; it's a bit on the dull side.

Garden of Harmony (Yiyuan)

A small Qing Dynasty garden owned by an official called Gu Wenbin, this one is quite young for a Suzhou garden. It's assimilated many of the features of other gardens and blended them into a style of its own. The garden is divided into eastern and western sections linked by a covered promenade with lattice windows. In the east are buildings and courtyards. The western section has pools with coloured pebbles, rockeries, hillocks and pavilions. The garden is off Renmin Lu, just south of Guanqian.

Surging Wave Pavilion (Changlangting)

A bit on the wild side with winding creeks and luxuriant trees. This is one of the oldest gardens in Suzhou, dating from the 11th century although it has been rebuilt following damage more than a few times. Originally the villa of a prince, it passed into the hands of the scholar, Su Zimei, who gave it its name. One hectare in size, the garden attempts to create optical illusions with outside and inside scenery by stealing scenes from the surroundings – from the pool immediately outside to the distant hills. Enlightened Way (Mingdao) Hall, the largest building, is said to have been a site for delivery of lectures in the Ming Dynasty. On the other side of Renmin Lu, close by, is the former Confucian Temple.

Master of the Nets (Wangshi)

This is the smallest garden in Suzhou – half the size of Changlangting, and one-tenth the size of Zhuozheng. In fact, it's so small, it's hard to find. But it's well worth the trouble since it outstrips the others combined. The garden was laid out in the 12th century, abandoned, then restored in the 18th century as the residence of a retired official. One story has it that he announced he'd had enough of bureaucracy and would rather be a fisherman. Another explanation of the name is that it was simply near Wangshi Lu.

The eastern part of the garden is the residential area – originally with side rooms for sedan chair lackeys, guest reception and living quarters. The central part is the main garden. The western part is an inner garden where a courtyard contains the Spring-Rear (Dianchun) Cottage, the master's study. This section and the study with its Ming-style furniture and palace lanterns was duplicated and

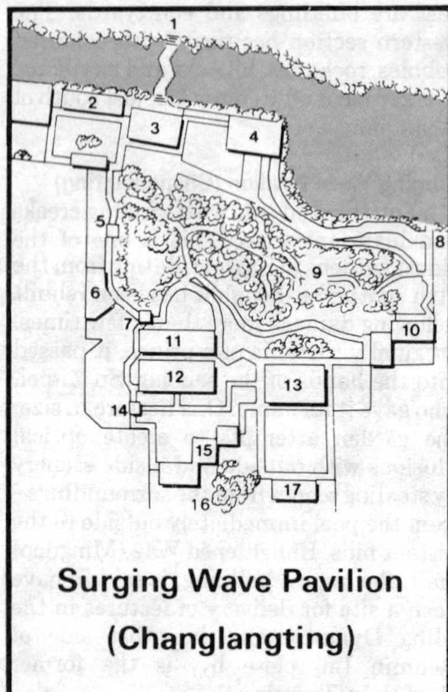

Surging Wave Pavilion (Changlangting)

1. Changlangshengji
2. Lotus Waterside Pavilion
3. Steles
4. Waterside House
5. Pavilion of Imperial Stele
6. Toilet
7. Buqi Pavilion
8. Pavilion for Admiring Fish
9. Changlangting Garden
10. Wenmiaoxiang House
11. Qingxiang Hall
12. Shrine of 500 Sages
13. Enlightened Way (Mingdao) Hall
14. Yangzhi Pavilion
15. Cuilinglong Houses
16. Kanshen Tower
17. Yaohuajingjie House

1	沧浪胜迹坊	10	闻妙香亭
2	面水莲亭	11	清香馆
3	碑纪	12	五百名贤祠
4	面水轩	13	明道堂
5	御碑纪	14	仰止亭
6	公厕	15	翠玲珑
7	步碕亭	16	看山楼
8	观鱼处	17	瑶华境界
9	沧浪亭		

unveiled at the Metropolitan Museum of Art in New York in 1981.

A miniature model of the whole garden, using Qingtian jade, Yingde rocks, Anhui paper, Suzhou silk and incorporating the halls, kiosks, ponds, blossoms and rare plants of the original design, was produced especially for a display at the Pompidou Centre in Paris in 1982.

The most striking feature of Wangshi is its use of space. Despite its size, the scale of the buildings is large, but nothing appears cramped. A section of the buildings is used by a co-operative of woodblock artists who find the peaceful atmosphere congenial to work. One should not spoil this garden's surprises any further. The entrance is a narrow alley just west of the Suzhou Hotel.

Garden for Lingering In (Liuyuan)

With an area of three hectares, Liuyuan is one of the largest Suzhou gardens, noted for its adroit partitioning with building complexes. It dates from the Ming Dynasty and managed to escape destruction in the Taiping Rebellion. A 700-metre covered walkway connects the major scenic spots, and the windows have carefully selected perspectives. The walkway is inlaid with calligraphy from celebrated masters. The garden has a wealth of potted plants. Outside Mandarin Duck (Yuanyang) Hall is a 6½-metre-high Lake Tai piece, the final word on rockeries. The garden is about one km west of the old city walls. The bus there will take you over bridges looking down on the busy water traffic.

West Garden Temple (Xiyuansi)

About 500 metres west of Liuyuan, this garden was built on the site of a garden laid out at the same time as Liuyuan and then donated to the Buddhist community. The temple was destroyed in the 19th century and entirely rebuilt; it contains some expressive Buddhist statues.

Cold Mountain Temple (Hanshan Si)

One km west of Liuyuan, this temple was named after the poet-monk Hanshan, who lived in the 7th century. It was repeatedly burnt down and rebuilt, and holds little of interest except for a stele by poet Zhang Ji immortalising nearby Maple Bridge and the temple bell (since removed to Japan). However, the fine walls and the humpback bridge are worth it. The temple was once the site for lively local trading in silk, wood and grain. Not far from its saffron walls lies the Grand Canal. To get to the temple take bus No 4 to the terminus, cross the bridge and walk to the No 6 bus route; or take bus No 5 and then connect with bus No 6.

Tiger Hill

At the Tiger Hill parking lot, the bus No 5 terminus, I counted 15 Chinese tour buses, six minibuses, five Toyotas, three Shanghai taxis and two Kingswoods (modified with drawn curtains), so it seemed good. Actually, Tiger Hill is below average to boring. It's an artificial hill, 36 metres high, set in a park of 20 hectares. Near the top of the hill is buried King He Lu, founding father of Suzhou, who died in the 6th century BC. A white tiger is said to have appeared to guard the tomb; hence the name.

Many Arthurian-type legends exist about Tiger Hill. There's a Sword-Testing Stone with a crack in it, split by He Lu. The old boy, according to legend, is buried with his 3000 swords. A thousand builders were reputedly bumped off after making the tomb so that its secrets would not be revealed. It's apparently booby-trapped with spring water and any attempt at digging would be bad news for the pagoda further up.

Tiger Hill Pagoda, which was finished in 961 AD, has been leaning for several centuries. This century the thing split, and had to be restabilised (it is, after all, the symbol of Suzhou!). Work has been done to reinforce the foundation now that the tilt has reached over two metres. Concrete piles have been driven into the ground around the base, rather like staking it in a flowerpot.

Places to Stay

The *Lexiang Hotel* (tel 22815) is central but lacking in ambience. It's at 18 Dajing Xiang, an alley which runs off Renmin Lu near the Guanqian markets. It's popular with travellers because of the dormitory, where beds go for Y12 per person. Double rooms cost from Y51. The Lexiang is a very habitable place and the staff quite friendly. To get there take bus No 1 from the railway station.

The *Gusu, Suzhou* and *Nanlin* hotels are grouped at the south-east end of town – further out but more spacious with more amenities, and preferable. The Nanlin has dormitory accommodation. To get to these hotels you can take bus No 1 straight down Renmin, alight at Shiquan and walk east. Or take bus No 1 to Baita Lu, change to No 4 and take it eastwards directly to the hotels. The third possibility is to take bus No 2, which passes close to the north side of the Nanlin Hotel.

The *Suzhou (Soochow) Hotel* (tel 24646) is at 115 Shiquan Jie. There are two wings, both air-con luxury, with a full range of services including Friendship Store branch, theatre and extensive gardens. Doubles in the old building cost from Y75. Doubles in the new building cost from Y110 including fridge and bath. The hotel has a rather weather-beaten appearance – on the inside! Shiquan Jie has wall-to-wall souvenir shops selling a mixed bag of trash and treasure.

The *Gusu Hotel* (tel 25126) is in the same enclosure as the Suzhou, and is an Australian prefab. Doubles cost around Y85. It is full of electronics and outback creature comforts, angled towards Overseas

Chinese. The hotel has a bar, café and dining rooms.

The *Nanlin Hotel* (tel 24641) is at 20 Gunxiufang off Shiquan Jie. Its very pleasant gardens include a small section with outdoor ceramic tables and chairs. Singles are Y70, doubles Y80, dormitory beds Y12. There's a full range of facilities and a dining hall. The hotel is conveniently located for the long-distance bus station and boat dock. The Nanlin is not to be confused with the *Nanyuan Guest House* across the way, where they'll chase you around the gardens till you find out where the Nanlin is. The mysterious Nanyuan is most likely a cadre/VIP hotel.

Places to Eat

Suzhou Bazaar is the restaurant centre of the city. If there's pleasure in anticipation, then westerners who are used to seeing items on the supermarket shelves all year round will perhaps not be too disappointed to learn that food in Suzhou is greatly dependent on the seasons. Towards autumn, the residents start salivating for a dish of a strange hairy crab, steamed with soy sauce and ginger. The crabs are caught at a freshwater lake seven km north-east of Suzhou in early autumn. The resulting feast is an annual event; Nanjingers and Shanghainese make the trip to Suzhou to sample it. There are prices around the area to suit all wallets. You can stuff your gills for 30 fen in a noodle shop, or blow your inheritance in the Songhelou Restaurant.

Main Courses The *Songhelou Caiguan* (tel 2066) at 141 Guanqian Jie is the most famous restaurant in Suzhou: Emperor Qianlong is supposed to have eaten there. The large variety of dishes includes squirrel fish, plain steamed prawns, braised eel, pork with pine nuts, butterfly-shaped sea cucumber, watermelon chicken and spicy duck. The waiter will insist that you be parcelled off to the special 'tour bus' cubicle at the back where an English menu awaits. The Songhelou runs from Guanqian to an alley behind, where tour minibuses pull up. There have been mixed reports about this place; you may find it something of a letdown.

In the same alley at the back of the Songhelou are two large, crowded prole restaurants. The *Shanghai Laozhenxin* is one and the other is at No 19 on a corner further east. The Shanghai Laozhenxin serves pot-stewed food, cold dishes and smoked fish.

There are lots of small places to explore. Pick the most crowded, wheel in and see what's cooking (unfortunately the most crowded will mean longer waits). Another indicator is the noise level. If it's over 100 decibels, it's a thumping good restaurant by Chinese standards – they like plenty of shouting, clatter and mayhem at the tables. The inner alley sections of Guanqian have a grand, almost homely feel to them with narrow doorways, ornamental windows and palace lanterns hung off some of the restaurants.

A pot of tea is the correct way to lubricate your repast. Suzhou has two native teas: Biluochun Green (Snail Spring Tea) and Jasmine Scented. Having consumed this, the correct thing to do next is belch heartily, march outside, spit into the gutter, and hang about with a toothpick.

A couple of other places worth trying are the *Xinjufeng Restaurant* at 615 Renmin Lu, which serves variations on duck and chicken and regional specialities. The restaurants in the *Suzhou* and *Nanlin* hotels serve local delicacies like Suzhou almond duck and phoenix shrimp (arisen from the ashes?)

Snacks For snacks there are loads of shops and vendors. On the corner of Renmin Lu and Guanqian Lu are night-time food stalls with sizzling tasty fare. In the soup line it's worth investigating a regional speciality made from Taihu aquatic plants – you might find it in a larger restaurant. In the late spring, fruit from the shores of Taihu comes to the

Guanqian markets, including loquats and strawberries.

Sweets Suzhou is famous for its sweets, candied fruits and pastries – some 170 varieties, depending on the stuffing. At the far end of Guanqian Lu is a concentration of the better known shops.

The *Huangtianyuan Cake-shop* at 88 Guanqian Lu has been in business for over a century. It serves steamed leaf-wrapped dumplings and savouries, and pastries with ingredients like cabbage juice, cocoa, walnuts and preserved fruits.

Almost opposite is the *Caizhizhai Confectionary*, equally as ancient and grubby. It sells pine-nut candy and sweetened flour cakes. A real treat here, in season, are the candied strawberries. Upstairs is a coffee shop – almost ambient despite the Hong Kong disco music.

Down the road is the *Suzhou Pastry Shop* and nearby is the *Daoxiangcun Cake & Candy Shop* at No 35 which, you must agree, is already a strain on the tooth enamel.

You may be asked in these cake shops for grain-flour coupons. Being a foreigner means never having to say 'sorry', but it allows the shopkeeper the discretion to jack up the prices of the 'ration'. Having been asked the question innumerable times, I got round to learning the Chinese for 'coupon' which is *liangpiao* – not only that, I managed to procure some of the correct ones. Just for kicks, I went into one of the candy stores, and when the dreary automatic question came, I produced my 'stamps' – the lady behind the counter almost died of fright. Well, bless me boots, don't the tourists come well equipped these days?

Entertainment
Try the barber shops and hairdressing salons on Guanqian Lu. I kid you not – these places have the brightest lights and the most action in the early evening. As you're walking along, peep over the curtains of the salons to discover China's great beauty secrets.

Suzhou has other nightlife, with over a dozen theatres and some storytelling houses. Suzhou Pingtan (ballad singing and storytelling) is where you can hear those sweet voices worked to their fullest. Most of the after hours activity takes place south of Guanqian. There's a theatre at the Suzhou Hotel which occasionally has live shows.

Shopping
Along Guanqian Lu and in the alleys behind it, you can find Suzhou-style embroidery, calligraphy, painting, sandal-wood fans, writing brushes and silk by the metre.

A curious store is Suzhou Y – no, not a dormitory, but a good place to spend WW III. This is an underground mini-department store that runs five blocks north to south on the west side of Renmin Lu, with Guanqian Lu at the northern end. It's about three metres wide (the store, not the silk) and has entrances that look like subway exits on the street. I thought they were WCs, but figured the place couldn't be *that* clean.

On Jingde Lu, which runs west from the Renmin/Guanqian Lu intersection, is the Arts & Crafts Store at No 274 which stocks, among other handicrafts, clay figurines, traditional painting, calligraphy, musical instruments and jade carving. Never tried embroidery myself, but the Suzhou pieces look nearly impossible to have been done with single filaments of silk. The double-sided hand embroidery, with its dazzling colours and striking patterns, is especially nifty.

It's worth tracking down the National Embroidery Institute display, which is in the same area as the Arts & Crafts Store. The institute specialised in hair-embroidery and the art is supposed to have been revived in Jiangsu Province since the Communists came to power. The technique uses human hair worked onto a silk backing. Suzhou embroidery is ranked among the top four needle-styles in China. Another Suzhou speciality is *Kesi*, which mixes raw and boiled-off silk in the weaving process, and is known as 'carved silk'. It was once reserved for imperial robing and can be bought in painting-scrolls, waistbands and other items.

A little further afield at 344 Renmin Lu is an Antique & Curio Store where a funny old man shuffles around after you to make sure you don't pocket anything. The shop has some antique hardwood furniture, and you might delve into sandalwood fans. Actually, sandalwood is scarce and the fans are now made of other kinds of wood, like oak.

Though not open to tourists, there is some fascinating activity going on at the Arts & Crafts Research Institute in Suzhou. In 1981 32-year-old Shen Weizhong carved the world's smallest Buddha – three mm tall, fingers as thin as hair, and a smiling face that can only be seen through a microscope. Another worker carved words onto the hair of a panda. (Now you know how they come up with those bus maps!)

Getting There & Away

Air There is no airport at Suzhou.

Bus The long-distance bus station is at the south end of Renmin Lu. There are bus connections between Suzhou and just about every major place in the region including Shanghai (Y2.40), Hangzhou (Y3.80), Wuxi (Y2), Yangzhou (Y5.80), Yixing and Changzhou.

Rail Suzhou is on the Nanjing-Shanghai line. To Shanghai is about 1¼ hours, Wuxi 40 minutes and Nanjing 3¼ hours. There are frequent expresses on this line.

If you're thinking of day-tripping then this line is ideal for rail hopping. Get a through ticket from, say, Nanjing to Shanghai, and break the journey in Suzhou and other towns along the way.

In Suzhou the advance booking office for the trains is at 203 Guanqian Lu.

Boat There are boats along the Grand Canal to Wuxi and to Hangzhou.

Boats from Suzhou to Hangzhou depart daily at 5.50 am and at 5.30 pm. The fare is Y2.70 for a seat on the day boat and Y6 for a sleeper on the night boat. The trip takes about 14 hours. Boats from Hangzhou to Suzhou depart at 5.50 am and 5.30 pm.

Boats to Wuxi depart Suzhou at 6.10 am and at noon. The trip takes around five hours. Boats to Suzhou depart Wuxi at 6.20 am and noon. The fare is Y0.80 for a seat.

Getting Around

The main thoroughfare is Renmin Lu with the railway station off the north end, and a large boat dock and long-distance bus station at the south end.

Bus No 1 runs the length of Renmin Lu. Bus No 2 is a kind of round-the-city bus. Bus No 5 is a good east to west bus. Bus No 4 runs from Changmen directly east along Baita, turns south and runs past the east end of Guanqian and then on to the Suzhou Hotel.

Taxis and auto-rickshaws can be found ranked at the Renmin and Guanqian intersection, outside the main railway station, down by the boat dock at the southern end of Renmin Lu, and at Jingmen (Nanxin Bridge) at the western end of Jingde Lu.

AROUND SUZHOU

While you may be right on track in Suzhou, go 20 km in any direction and you'll be off the record. The further out you go, of course, the less likely you should be there in the first place. Some of the local buses, it should be added, go for a considerable distance, such as bus No 11. You could hop on one for a ride to the terminus to see the enchanting countryside.

The Grand Canal

The canal proper cuts to the west and south of Suzhou, within a 10-km range of the town. Suburban bus route Nos 13, 14, 15 and 16 will get you there. Bus No 11 bus tracks the canal a fair distance in the north-west. Once you arrive, it's simply a matter of finding yourself a nice bridge, getting out your deckchair and watching the world go by.

Precious Belt Bridge (Baodai Qiao)
Welcome to the bridge club! This is one of China's best with 53 arches, the three central humpbacks being larger to allow boats through. It straddles the Grand Canal, and is a popular spot with fishermen. The bridge is not used for traffic – a modern one has been built alongside. The bridge is thought to be a Tang Dynasty construction named after Wang Zhongshu, a local prefect who sold his precious belt to pay for the bridge's construction for the benefit of his people. Precious Belt Bridge is about five km south-east of Suzhou. Bus No 13 will set you on the right track.

Taihu Hangouts
The following places can all be reached by long-distance buses from the station at the south end of Renmin Lu.

Lingyan Shan is 15 km south-west of Suzhou. Weirdly shaped rocks, a temple and pagoda (molested by Red Guards), and panoramas of mulberry trees, fertile fields and Taihu in the distance. A lovely place to cycle to.

Tianping Shan is 18 km south-west and has more of the same – plus some medicinal springwaters.

Guangfu is 25 km south-west, bordering the lake. It has an ancient seven storey pagoda and is dotted with plum trees.

Dong Shan is 40 km south-west and is noted for its gardens and the Purple Gold (Zijin) Nunnery, which contains 16 coloured clay arhats and is surrounded by Taihu on three sides.

Xidongting Shan Isle, also called Xi Shan, is a large island 60 km south-west of Suzhou. Getting there involves a 10-km ferry ride. Eroded Taihu rocks are 'harvested' here for landscaping. Take a bus from opposite Suzhou train station to Luxian, then catch a ferry across to Zhenxia.

Changshu is 50 km north-east of Suzhou. The town is noted for its lace making. To the north-west of the town is Yu Shan with historical/scenic spots, including a nine-storey Song pagoda.

Luzhi is a town on the water 25 km east of Suzhou. The canals are the main means of commuting – in concrete flat bottomed boats. The town has an old temple, Baosheng, with old arhats, although that is probably not why you should come here. You could try your luck getting to places like this via canals from small boat docks in Suzhou.

XUZHOU 徐州

Xuzhou does not fall into the category of a canal town, though a tributary of the Grand Canal passes by its north-east end. The history of the town has little to do with the canal. The colour brochure for Xuzhou shows the marshalling yard of the railway station as one of the sights and that, perhaps, is more to the point. If you're a rail buff there are plenty of lines to keep you happy since the town is at the intersection of China's two main railways: the Beijing to Shanghai line, and the Longhai line which runs from Kaifeng, Luoyang and Xian in the west to the coastal town of Lianyungang in the east. The place has lots of cinemas, bus lines and an airport, and also: the coal mines.

Orientation
The city centre is straight ahead of the main railway station, at the intersection of Huaihai and Zhongshan Lu. Note that there are two train stations, north and main. Take bus No 1 two stops west of the main station and you'll get to the main roundabout.

Things to See
The main railway station houses many beggars and vagrants. Meanwhile, there are a number of sights around town.

Yunlong Shan (Dragon in the Clouds Hill)
This hill has half the sights of Xuzhou: the Xinghua Temple, several pavilions, and a stone carving from the Northern Wei Dynasty. If you climb to the top of the hill, where the Xinghua Temple is located, there's a magnificent panorama of the concrete boxes that compose the Xuzhou valley and the mountains that ring it. There are even orchards out there somewhere. Set in a grotto off the mountainside is a giant gilded Buddha head, the statue of the Sakyamuni Buddha. The park itself is circus-land with an outdoor BB shooting gallery and peanuts and popsicles littering the slopes. The hill is a 10-minute walk west of the Nanjiao Hotel, or take bus No 2 or bus No 11.

Monument to Huaihai Campaign Martyrs
This is a revolutionary war memorial and obelisk opened in 1965, set in a huge wooded park at the southern edge of town. The Huaihai battle was a decisive one fought by the PLA from November 1948 to January 1949. The obelisk, 38½ metres high, has a gold inscription by Chairman Mao and a grand flight of stairs leading up to it. A Memorial Hall close by contains an extensive collection of weaponry, photos, maps, paintings and memorabilia – over 2000 items altogether – as well as inscriptions by important heads of state, from Zhou Enlai to Deng Xiaoping. The grounds, 100 acres of pines and cypresses, are meant to be 'symbolic of the evergreen spirit of the revolutionary martyrs'. The park lies on the bus No 11 route.

Places to Stay & Eat
The *Nanjiao (South Suburbs) Hotel* is the tourist joint on Heping Lu, three km from the main train station. This is a TV hotel: most of the staff are permanently glued to the box downstairs. Double rooms are Y55. Take bus No 2 from the main railway station. CITS is here and sells a Chinese/English map of the town.

There are no buses running in the evening, and the Nanjiao is quite a way from the train station. Try the *Xuzhou Hotel* on the right as you come out of the train station.

The Nanjiao has a dining room. Other places to try for a feed include the *Huaihaifandiancaiguanbu* (Huaihai Hotel) on Huaihai Donglu between the main station and the large roundabout, south side of the street. Also the *Pencheng Hotel* close by, on a corner after an overhead bridge. There are noodle shops on the right when you come out of the main railway station.

Getting There & Away
Xuzhou lies at the junction of the main Beijing to Shanghai and Longhai lines. The Longhai line runs from Xian, Luoyang, Zhengzhou and Kaifeng in the west to the town of Lianyungang in the east.

Getting Around
The local bus station is across the square in front of the main railway station. Auto-rickshaws are parked to the left as you leave the main railway station.

LIANYUNGANG 连云港
From Xuzhou, a branch line runs east to the major coastal port of Lianyungang (a six-hour ride). The town is divided into port and city sections. Yuntai Hill is the 'scenic spot' overlooking the ocean, and there are some salt mines along the shores, as well as a Taoist monastery. The mountain is reputed to be the inspiration for the Flowers and Fruit Mountain in the Ming Dynasty classic *Journey to the West* (but three other places in the PRC lay the same claim). Other sights include the 2000-year-old stone carvings at Kung Wang Mountain. There's an International Seamen's Club, Friendship Store, CITS

office and several hotels. It may be possible to get boat connections on the east coast.

NANTONG 南通

Nantong is an industrial city of over 200,000 people and an important textile and shipping centre for routes along the Yangtse and the canals running inland. The old walled city was on an island in the Hao River. There are no walls left, but the city administration is still on the island. There are three satellite towns outside the city core.

By boat would be the most sensible way of getting to Nantong – it's only six hours upriver from Shanghai. It's a long way round by road, but a possible land/boat route might be via Suzhou and Changshu, both of which are open to foreigners.

Shandong 山东

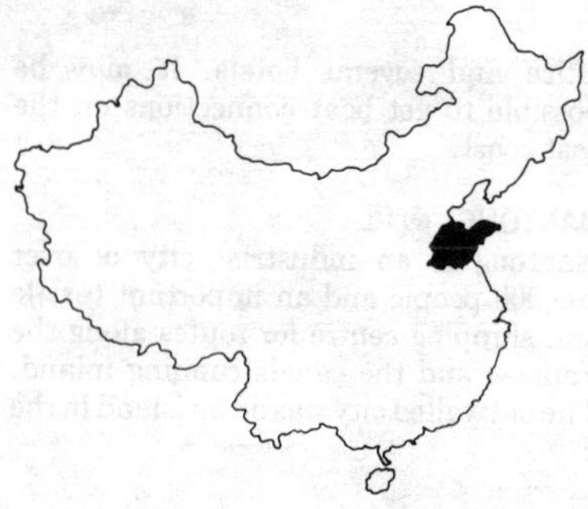

Shandong, the turtle-head bobbing into the Yellow Sea, is a slow starter. The province is relatively poor and beset with economic problems, not the least of which is the rotten Yellow River which can't decide where to void itself. The river has changed direction some 26 times in its history and flooded many more times. Six times it has swung its mouth from the Bohai Gulf (North Shandong) to the Yellow Sea (South Shandong), and wreaked havoc on the residents.

Back in 1899 the river flooded the entire Shandong plain, a sad irony in view of the two scorching droughts which swept the area that same year and the year before. Add to that a long period of economic depression, a sudden influx of demobilised troops in 1895 after China's humiliating defeat in the war with Japan, and droves of refugees from the south moving north to escape famines, floods and drought. Then top it off with an imperial government in Beijing either incapable or unwilling to help the local people, and foreigners whose missionaries and railroads had angered the gods and spirits. It created a perfect breeding ground for a rebellion, and in the last few years of the 19th century the 'Boxers' arose out of Shandong and set all of China ablaze.

Work on controlling the monstrous river that started it all is still going to take a fair bit of dikemanship. The other major problem is over-population. Shandong is third after Henan and Sichuan for the title of most populous province; at the 1982 census 74.4 million people were squashed into an area of just 150,000 square km. And just to make matters harder, about two-thirds of Shandong is hilly, with the Shandong massif (highest peak: Tai Shan) looming up in the south-west, and another mountain chain over the tip of the Shandong peninsula. The rest is fertile plains sprouting grain, potatoes, cotton, peanuts, soybeans, fruit and tobacco.

The Germans got their hands on the port of Qingdao in 1898 and set up a few factories. Shandong Province subsequently took a few quantum leaps towards industrialisation. The leading industrial town today is still Qingdao, with the capital Jinan in second place. Zibo is the major coal mining centre, and is also noted for its glassworks and porcelain output. The Shengli Oilfield in northern Shandong, which opened in 1965, is the second largest crude oil source in China. As for rail lines, you can count them on the fingers of one hand, but the Shandong peninsula has some first class harbours with good passenger links, and there is a dense road network.

Travellers tend to gloss over this province, which is unfortunate since it has quite a bit to offer. Lest it be forgotten, the Shandong tourist authorities are trying to tizz it up with special-interest group tours like martial arts, fishing, calligraphy and honeymooning. Curious entry that 'honey-mooning' – what would the special interest be in Shandong and how many in the group? Since 1979 Shandong has ploughed over 60 million yuan into building tourist hotels and in 1980 the road running up Tai Shan cost two million yuan. A new luxury hotel has been built in Qufu, the birthplace of Confucius. Other projects include pleasure-boat facilities in Qingdao.

A number of places are open, including

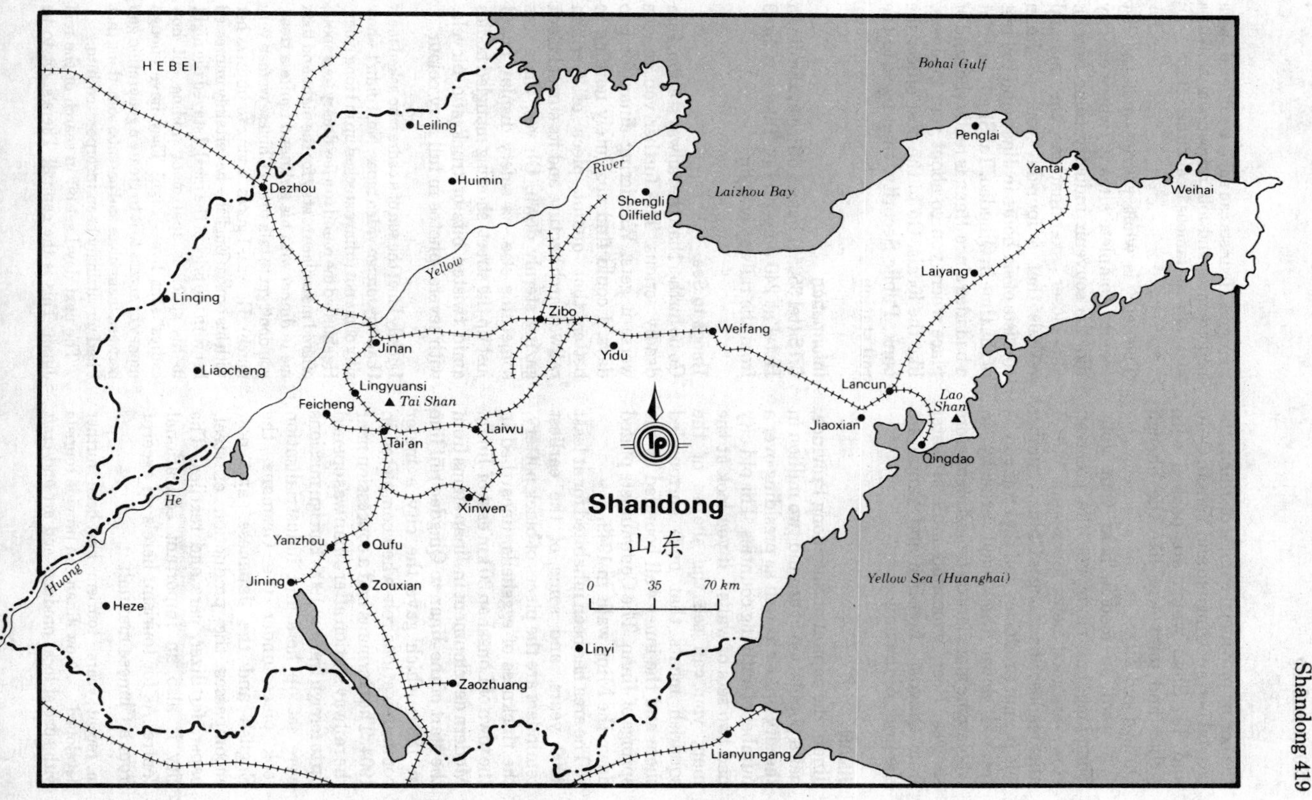
HEBEI
Bohai Gulf
Laizhou Bay
Yellow Sea (Huanghai)
Leiling
Dezhou
Huimin
Yellow River
Shengli Oilfield
Penglai
Yantai
Weihai
Laiyang
Linqing
Zibo
Weifang
Jinan
Yidu
Liaocheng
Lingyuansi
Tai Shan
Feicheng
Laiwu
Tai'an
Lancun
Lao Shan
Jiaoxian
Qingdao
Xinwen
Shandong
山东
He
Yanzhou
Qufu
Jining
Zouxian
Huang
Heze
0
35
70 km
Linyi
Zaozhuang
Lianyungang

the boring provincial capital of Jinan, the coastal ports of Qingdao and Yantai, Qufu and Tai Shan which are packed with sights, and unknowns like the Shengli Oilfield and Zibo.

A word on food – hold your guts. Shandong cuisine is not the greatest. However, good news for peanut butter aficionados: Shandong is China's number one peanut producer, and the stuff can be tracked down thick and crunchy in wholesome glass jars on department store shelves. Beer, wine and mineral water from Qingdao, Laoshan and Yantai are the pride of the nation.

JINAN 济南

Jinan, the capital of Shandong Province, has a population of around two million in the city proper as well as presiding over a number of outlying counties. The old city had two sets of walls – if you look at the map, you can see the shapes of the squarish moats that once surrounded them and the inner wall bounded by the springs of Jinan. The Communists pulled down the Ming walls in 1949.

The area has been inhabited for at least 4000 years, and some of the earliest reminders are the pieces of black pottery, the thickness of eggshells, unearthed in the town of Longshan 30 km east of Jinan. Modern development in Jinan stems from the start of the Jinan to Qingdao rail line in 1899, which gave the city a major communications role when completed in 1904. The Germans had a concession near the railway station after Jinan was opened up to foreign trade in 1906. Foreign missions were set up here and industrialisation took place under the Germans, the English and the Japanese, and now encompasses the production of steel, paper, fertilizer, cars and textiles. The city is also an important educational centre. As for tourism, here's an excerpt from a Chinese manual:

> In recent years, tourism has been further developed . . . Now Jinan can provide tourists with special local products and art and craft souvenirs. Tourists can enjoy traditional opera performances and folk recreational activities and taste the famous local dishes, etc.

The 'etc' is what worries me; the list seemed complete already (where exactly did the souvenir industry come from?). On closer examination, the manual reveals that a four-day tour to Jinan consists of six hours in Jinan and the rest of the time in Qingdao, Tai Shan, etc. Not a bad idea since Jinan is really the kind of place where you go about your business, like the locals. Go to the post office, the bank, Public Security, then back to the rail station.

Information

CITS (tel 35351) has an office at the Jinan Hotel at 240 Jingsan Lu. Take bus No 9 from the railway station.

Things to See

Go no further than the railway station. I am deadly serious. The further you go, the worse it gets. Wandering Jinan for two days, I could find absolutely nothing to better that quaint piece of German railway architecture and its surreal clock gazing sternly down. Oh yes, there was something else – a safety display board just up the street, showing mangled bodies amid twisted bits of truck and bicycle, with several photos in full gory colour.

> Luckily I met the son of a cadre who asked me if I had any foreign video tapes. No, I didn't – how silly of me not to have stocked up in Hong Kong. He shuffled me round to a few dreary tour spots, offered me a place to stay for the night and took me to dinner with his girlfriend (quite a treat, you don't get to talk to shy Chinese women very much). He was, I guess, trying to impress her with his broken English – he certainly impressed her with the price of the meal. I stayed the night in his spacious apartment finding out how cadres' sons live – high! They have enough money or access to it to create a generation gap between themselves and parents, something that I had unwittingly been incorporated into.
>
> The next day I set off in search of the real Jinan. This is the capital! There's got to be

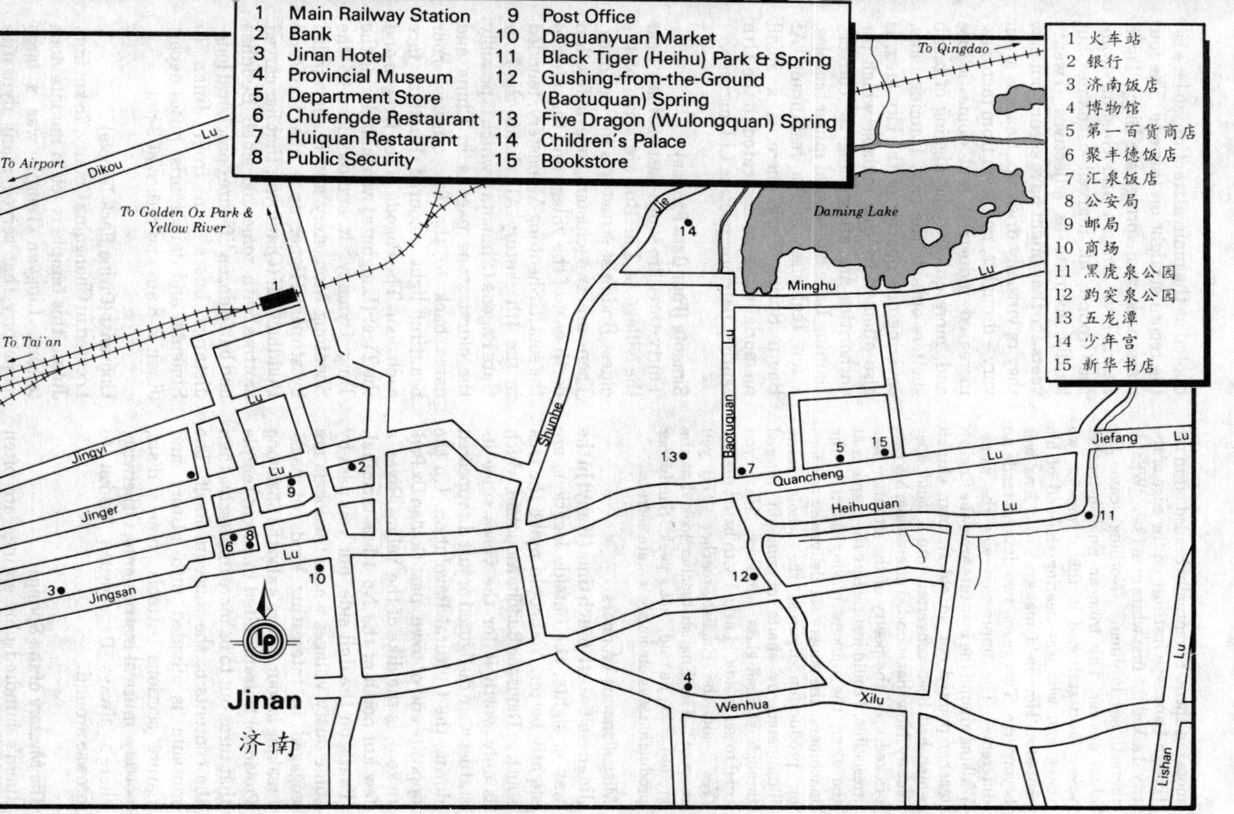
1 Main Railway Station
2 Bank
3 Jinan Hotel
4 Provincial Museum
5 Department Store
6 Chufengde Restaurant
7 Huiquan Restaurant
8 Public Security
9 Post Office
10 Daguanyuan Market
11 Black Tiger (Heihu) Park & Spring
12 Gushing-from-the-Ground (Baotuquan) Spring
13 Five Dragon (Wulongquan) Spring
14 Children's Palace
15 Bookstore
1 火车站
2 银行
3 济南饭店
4 博物馆
5 第一百货商店
6 聚丰德饭店
7 汇泉饭店
8 公安局
9 邮局
10 商场
11 黑虎泉公园
12 趵突泉公园
13 五龙潭
14 少年宫
15 新华书店
To Qingdao
To Airport
Dikou
Lu
To Golden Ox Park & Yellow River
To Tai'an
Daming Lake
Minghu
Lu
Jie
Shunhe
Baotuquan
Lu
Quancheng
Lu
Heihuquan
Lu
Jiefang
Lu
Jingyi
Jinger
Jingsan
Lu
Wenhua
Xilu
Lishan
Lu
Jinan
济南

more out there. I eventually headed off to the Foreign Language Institute on the edge of the city. I asked the first white man I saw, 'What is there to see in Jinan?' 'Nothing', came the blunt answer. This from an English teacher who'd been stationed in this dump for two years, and who was nearing the end of his sentence. How he'd managed that long was beyond me. Two years, two days, it made no difference. The impression was the same. Walking around the Institute area, the English teacher pointed out an old German church which had been converted into a sandpaper factory. Now that sounded interesting. My ears pricked up – the poetry of the situation was irresistible. I could just picture the manager at the altar, the workers bowing down to the machinery, the supervisor delivering sermons on production figures, the whole scene illuminated by shafts of sunlight filtered through stained-glass windows. 'Have you tried to get inside?' I asked with bated breath. 'Yes', said the English teacher. 'Did you succeed?' The English teacher looked at the ground. 'No', he said, 'not a peek'. Sandpaper production was obviously a state secret.

Miscellaneous Wonders

Jinan isn't worth much time (if any) in the way of sights; the outside locations are slightly better. You could make the trek south to **Thousand Buddha Mountain**, which is only worth it for the views since its statues were disfigured or just disappeared during the Cultural Revolution. Up the opposite end of town, past **Golden Ox Park** (a zoo), is the dike of the Yellow River, a few km north of the No 4 bus terminal. That's on the dull side, but you pass by some dusty villages where the locals are engaged in interesting kinds of back-breaking labour. There's also the **Shandong Provincial Museum** sited in an old temple that turns out to be more impressive than the contents of the museum itself. The museum is divided into history and nature sections – tools, objets d'art, pottery, musical instruments. Otherwise, there's always **Daguanyuan Market** to browse around.

The Mystery of the Springs

Jinan's hundred-plus springs are often quoted as the main attraction, so let's set the record straight on this one. The four main park-cum-springs are Black Tiger, Pearl, Five Dragon and Gushing-from-the-Ground, all marvellous names but hardly accurate as adjectives. Twenty years ago they might have sprung but now they're virtually dried up. Reasons given vary – droughts, pollution from factories, increased industrial and domestic use and, more quietly, the digging of bomb shelters outside the city. Daming Lake, covering one quarter of the city area, is also affected by this malaise which the authorities are attempting to 'correct'. Daming Lake has several minor temples, a few teahouses and a restaurant. At Baotu Spring Park there is a small memorial museum dedicated to the 11th century patriotic poetess Li Qingzhao.

Simenta (Four Gate Pagoda)

Thirty-three km south-east of Jinan, near the village of Liu Bu, are some of the oldest Buddhist structures in Shandong. There are two clusters, one a few km north-east of the village and the other to the south. Shentong Monastery, founded in the 4th century AD, holds the Four Gate Pagoda (Simenta), which is possibly the oldest stone pagoda in China and dates back to the 6th century. Four beautiful light coloured Buddhas face each door. The Pagoda of the Dragon and the Tiger (Longhuta) was built during the Tang Dynasty. It stands close to the Shentong Monastery and is surrounded by stupas. Higher up is the Thousand Buddha Cliff (Qianfoya), that has carved grottoes with some 200 small Buddhas and half a dozen life-size ones. Local long-distance buses run from Jinan to Simenta, and daily tourist buses depart Jinan at 8 am and return at 3 pm.

Lingyansi (Divine Rock Temple)

Located in Changqing County, 75 km from Jinan, this temple is set in mountainous terrain. Lingyan Temple was a large monastery that served many dynasties (the Tang, Song, Yuan, among others) and had 500 monks in its heyday. On view is a forest of 200 stupas, commemorating the priests who directed the institution. There's also a nine storey octagonal pagoda as well as **Thousand Buddha Temple (Qianfodian)**, which contains 40 fine, highly individualised clay arhats – the best Buddhist statues in Shandong. There are local long-distance buses from Jinan to Lingyansi, but these take about three hours to get there so it's better to approach the town from Wan De station (which is south of Jinan and 10 km from Lingyansi). Tourist buses from Jinan depart at 7.30 am and return at 4 pm.

Places to Stay

The sombre, Russian-style *Jinan Hotel* (tel 35351) at 240 Jingsan Lu has some sobering prices: you could be looking at around Y60 a double. Foreign experts and students may manage cheaper rates. Take bus No 9 from the railway station.

The *Nanjiao Guest House* (tel 23931) on Maanshan Lu is similar to the Jinan Hotel with similar prices. To get there requires more effort: a bus No 2 from the railway station and then a hike of one km. It was, so the story goes, flung up for an impending visit by Mao, who then decided to skip Jinan.

Places to Eat

A blank – there's nought really worth recommending. You can try the ones on the map – the *Chufengde*, etc – but the best thing is to get yourself a bottle of 16% proof Tsingtao Red and hope you'll be too far gone to notice the food. There's a sizeable Muslim population in Jinan, and a Muslim restaurant near the Provincial Museum (lamb and mutton, pancakes, sesame bread – not clean, but cheap). The *Yuji Paji*, at the corner of Jingsan and Weiyi Rds, serves boneless braised chicken.

Shopping

Shopping territory is mostly in the area of the Jinan Hotel, with another strip in the older town section along Quancheng Avenue. Indigenous artefacts for sale include feather paintings, inlaid mahogany boxes, gear from other parts of Shandong, and dough and wooden figurines. The Arts & Crafts Service Department is at 3 Nanmen Lu. There are a couple of antique stores, including the ones at 321 Quancheng and 28 Jingsan Lu.

Getting There

Air There are flights from Jinan to Beijing, Nanjing, Qingdao, Shanghai and Yantai.

Rail Jinan is a major link in the east China rail system, with over 30 trains passing through daily. From Jinan there are direct trains to Beijing (six hours) and Shanghai (13 hours). The Qingdao to Shenyang trains which pass through Jinan sidestep Beijing and go through Tianjin instead. There are direct trains from Jinan to Qingdao and Yantai in Shandong Province, and to Hefei in Anhui Province. There are also direct Qingdao-Jinan-Xian-Xining trains.

Getting Around

There are about 25 urban and suburban bus lines in Jinan, running from 5 am to 9 pm, and two late night lines (east-west, north-south) finishing at midnight. There are plenty of three-wheeler auto-rickshaws around the train station.

ZIBO 淄博

Zibo is a major coal mining centre on the railway line east of Jinan. The city has a population of two million, and is also noted for its glassworks and porcelain. Not far from Zibo, at Linzhi, a pit of horses dating back some 2500 years was excavated, older than those at Xian and with one big difference – the horses are real. So far, 600 horse skeletons have been discovered, probably linked to the state of Qi. Horses and chariots indicated the strength of the state, so it's not surprising that they were buried with their master when he died. About 90 horse skeletons are on display side by side in the pit.

QINGDAO 青岛

Qingdao is a remarkable replica of a Bavarian village plonked on the Bohai Gulf. Like Shanghai, it evokes an eerie feeling – have you passed this way before? A city of red tiled roofs and European angles, shapes and echoes, right down to the gardens. It was a simple fishing village until 1897 when German troops landed (the killing of two German missionaries having given them sufficient pretext). In 1898 China ceded Qingdao to Germany for a 99-year period, along with the right to build the Shandong railways and to work the mines for 15 km on either side of the tracks.

The Germans developed Qingdao as a coaling station and a naval base, and when the Jinan to Qingdao rail line was finished in 1904, harbour facilities blossomed, electric lighting appeared, the brewery (established 1903) belched beer, and a modern town arose. It was divided into European, Chinese and business sections. The Germans founded missions and a university, and before long Qingdao rivalled Tianjin as a trading centre, its independence from China maintained by a garrison of 2000 soldiers.

For a city with such a short history, Qingdao has seen a lot of ping pong. In 1914 the Japanese occupied it, in 1922 the Chinese wrested it back, it fell to the Japanese again in 1938 and was recaptured by the Kuomintang. The official history states that the people of Qingdao engaged in heroic struggles against the imperialists and the Kuomintang, and that industrial production has increased 10-fold since 1949.

The latter claim, it would seem, is not exaggerated. Behind the innocuous façade of a beach resort is a monstrous mess of factories. Not only does Qingdao brew up the nation's drinking supplies but it is also the largest industrial producer in Shandong, concentrating on diesel locomotives, automobiles, generators, machinery and light industry (watches, cameras, TVs, textiles). It has a population of 1.5 million, though its jurisdiction spreads over 5900 square km and another 3.5 million people.

If you ignore the megalopolis behind it – and most do – Qingdao has remarkable charm and is colourful for a Chinese city (irony intended). One can indulge in the guessing game of who once occupied its well preserved mansions, or how they functioned. The present function of the larger edifices is a combination of naval base, cadre playground and sanatorium. The town is a favourite for rest and recuperation, and for top-level meetings.

The German presence lingers strongly in Qingdao; in the famous beer, in the villas stretching along the beaches, in the rail station with the vintage clocks. At night you seem to travel further back in time to the pages of a Gothic novel. In the old German quarter you'll find low powered street lamps, dimly lit apartments, smoke rising from chimneys, chinks of light in a turret or attic window, the outlines of a cathedral, the hoot of a passing train; all you need is a heavy fog. Only the shapes of cyclists, hurtling out of the darkness,

1. Friendship Store, Youyi (Friendship) & Heping (Peace) Hotels
2. International Seamen's Club
3. Boat Station
4. Local Ferry
5. Chunhelou Restaurant
6. Xinhua Bookstore
7. Department Store
8. Overseas Chinese Hotel
9. Public Security
10. CAAC & Seafood Restaurant
11. Zhanqiao Guest House
12. Antique Store
13. Qingdao Department Store
14. Xinhao Hill Hotel
15. Trade Centre & Trade Exhibit Centre
16. Huiquan Dynasty Hotel
17. Badaguan Guest House
18. Seashell Carving Factory
19. Main Railway Station

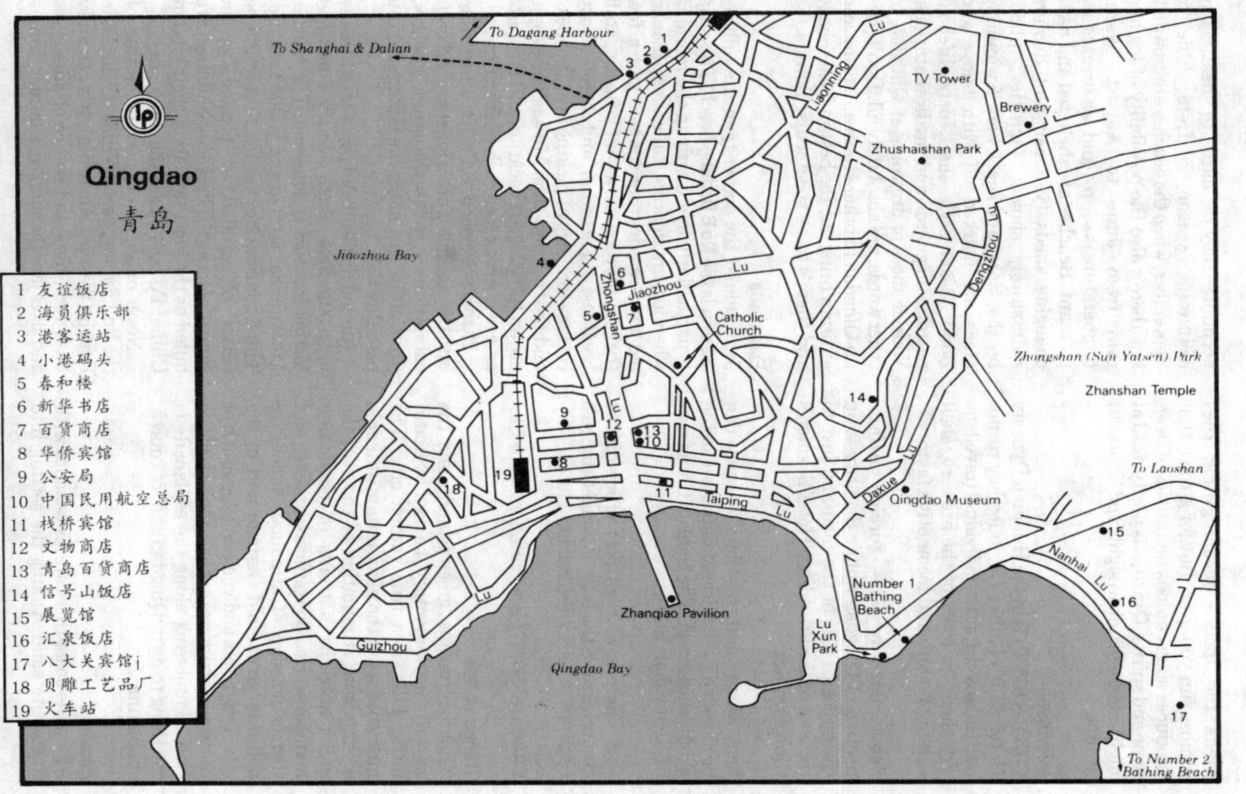
Qingdao
青岛
To Shanghai & Dalian
To Dagang Harbour
Jiaozhou Bay
Qingdao Bay
TV Tower
Brewery
Zhushaishan Park
Liaonning Lu
Dengzhou Lu
Jiaozhou Lu
Zhongshan Lu
Catholic Church
Zhongshan (Sun Yatsen) Park
Zhanshan Temple
To Laoshan
Qingdao Museum
Daxue Lu
Taiping Lu
Nanhai Lu
Zhanqiao Pavilion
Number 1 Bathing Beach
Lu Xun Park
Guizhou Lu
To Number 2 Bathing Beach
1 友谊饭店
2 海员俱乐部
3 港客运站
4 小港码头
5 春和楼
6 新华书店
7 百货商店
8 华侨宾馆
9 公安局
10 中国民用航空总局
11 栈桥宾馆
12 文物商店
13 青岛百货商店
14 信号山饭店
15 展览馆
16 汇泉饭店
17 八大关宾馆
18 贝雕工艺品厂
19 火车站

break the spell – meaning that they almost run you over. But for a town that produces such copious quantities of beer, wine and spirits, Qingdao is pretty dead at night – not a drunk in sight, and lights out at nine.

Information

CITS (tel 84830) is in the Huiquan Dynasty Hotel at 9 Nanhai Lu, but they're not particularly helpful to individual travellers. Try them for tours of the brewery, shell carving factory and locomotive factory.

Public Security The Foreign Affairs Section of Qingdao Public Security is on the opposite side of the road and just to the west of the Friendship Hotel/Seamen's Club complex.

Bank Money and travellers' cheques can be changed in the Friendship Store in the Friendship Hotel. The Bank of China is at 64 Zhongshan Lu.

Post There is a small post office on the ground floor of the International Seamen's Club, next to the Friendship Hotel.

CAAC (tel 86047) is at 29 Zhongshan Lu.

Things to See

'Qingdao' means 'green island', and the waterfront promontory, backed by undulating hills, is a true garden city. The misty beauty of the place is unmistakable – the visual stimulation of the sea, the parks and the patterns of boats and mansions. Heavy traffic is absent, and there's no sign of strenuous labour or pollution in the old German part of the city. Down this end you can't see much of the industrial zones so they don't spoil the view. Sauntering along the esplanade is the thing to do in Qingdao and, of course, sunbaking.

Beaches

Along the coast there are six beaches with fine white sand. Taking the setting into account, they're hard to beat. The swimming season is from June to September, when the beaches are crowded, but there's also the possibility of fog and rain from June to August. Water temperature is soupy, and sea breezes are pleasant. Beaches are sheltered and have changing sheds (you can rent demure swimsuits), shower facilities, photo booths, stores and snack bars. Swimming areas are marked off with buoys and Bondi Beach-style shark nets, lifeboat patrols, lifeguards and medical stations. Your chances of drowning at Qingdao, in other words, are absolutely nil. Don't pass up Qingdao in other seasons – spring and autumn bring out the best in local foliage and there's some spectacular flowers.

Esplanade

Just around the corner from the railway station is the **No 6 Bathing Beach**. This strip is particularly lively early in the morning when joggers, fencers, tai chi exponents, old men reading newspapers and a few frisbee players turn out. Street stall breakfast queues form, and there's a busy cottage industry of picking over the rocks and beach at low tide. Most of the people are on (privileged) vacation and it's quite an eye-opener to see such relaxed Chinese.

Zhanqiao Pavilion, on a jetty thrusting into the sea, holds occasional art and craft exhibitions – worth the stroll, anyhow. Continuing east along the esplanade, you pass **City Hall**.

Around the headland past the lighthouse is **Lu Xun Park** which has the combined **Marine Museum & Aquarium**. The Marine Museum has stuffed and pickled sea life. The Aquarium has sea life that would be better off stuffed or pickled, or in someone's soup. These tiny buildings are billed as the most famous of their kind in China; I'd hate to see the other ones.

Never mind, you're now at the start of the **No 1 Bathing Beach**. While it's no Cable Beach (Western Australia), it's certainly flash for China and bodies of all shapes and sizes jam the sands in summer. This is the largest beach in Qingdao, with a 580-metre stretch of fine sand, lots of facilities, multicoloured bathing sheds, restaurants (where you can munch prawns to 'Waltzing Matilda' on the muzak), ridiculous dolphin statues, and high-rise blocks rather like a Chinese version of Surfer's Paradise. Plonk yourself down on the sand and all sorts of odd people will come up to you. This is the hang-out of the Chinese 'winter swimmers' whose marvellous sun-bronzed physiques don't step into the water until winter; they are said to make bad husbands because they're always at the beach. The beach also has Public Security 'moral guardians' who ensure that indecent gymnastics between consenting couples don't get out of hand.

Past the Huiquan Dynasty Hotel and the Ocean Research Institute you come to the **Badaguan (Eight Passes Area)**, well known for its sanatoriums and exclusive guest houses. The spas are scattered in lush wooded zones off the coast, and the streets, named after passes, are each lined with a different tree or flower. On Jiayuguan Lu it's maples and on Zhengyangguan it's myrtles. The locals simply call them Peach St, Snowpine St or Crab-apple St. Gardens here are extremely well groomed.

As you head out of the Eight Passes Area **Bathing Beaches 2 and 3** are just east, and the villas lining the headlands are exquisite. No 2 Beach is smaller, quieter and more sheltered than No 1, and is preferred when No 1 is overloaded. Facing No 2 are sanatoriums – but at the western headland is a naval installation, so don't take short cuts.

At the eastern end of the No 2 beach is the former **German Governor's Residence**. This castle-like villa, made of stone, is a replica of a German palace. It is said to have cost 2,450,000 taels of silver. When Kaiser Wilhelm II got the bill, he immediately recalled the extravagant governor and sacked him.

Brewery

No guide to Qingdao would be complete without a mention of the brewery, tucked into the industrial part of town, east of the main harbour. The brewery was established early this century by the Germans who still supply the parts for 'modernisation' of the system. The flavour of the finest brew in Asia comes from the mineral waters of Laoshan close by. It was first exported in 1954 and in 1979 it received the national silver medal for quality in China (as judged by the National Committee on Wines & Liquors). Pilgrimages to the brewery are reserved for tour groups, but if you care to try then I suggest you approach CITS at the Huiquan Hotel and organise a guide and taxi (don't count on it though). Otherwise the drink is on tap in town, or cheap enough in the stores and in any case is sold all over China. Some people have simply fronted up at the factory and been shown around.

Other Sights

There are numerous parks in Qingdao. **Zhongshan (Sun Yatsen) Park** is north of the Huiquan Hotel, covers 80 hectares, has a teahouse and temple and is a heavily wooded profusion of flowering shrubs and plants in springtime.

Further west of the park at Daxue St, is the **Qingdao Museum** with a collection of Yuan, Ming and Qing paintings. Crossing the map north-west of that is an impressive piece of architecture, the **Xinhao Hill Hotel**, at the edge of a park.

Off Zhongshan Lu, up a steep hill, is a structure now simply known as the **Catholic Church** – its double spires can be spotted a long way off. The church is active and services are held on Sunday mornings.

You might try to arrange a tour with CITS to the Qingdao locomotive factory and shell carving factory.

Places to Stay – bottom end

The *Heping (Peace)* and *Youyi (Friendship)* hotels are both in the complex around the Friendship Store and the boat station on

Xinjiang Lu in the north-west end of town. The Friendship Hotel (tel 28865) has become the established hang-out for budget travellers, with dormitory beds for about Y5 to Y6, and double rooms from Y22 to Y24. Very relaxed place much in keeping with the general character of the town; friendly staff and some English spoken. Plumbing is very weird in this hotel. The Peace Hotel is behind the Seamen's Club and Friendship Store, through a small alley to the right of the boat station.

If you arrive in Qingdao by boat, these two hotels are just a step away. If you arrive by train then it's a bit complicated. First take bus No 6 along Zhongshan Lu to the northern terminus, where it turns around. Then walk back under an overhead bridge near the terminus, turn right, and – if you can find the stop – take the No 21 bus for one stop north. If you can't find the stop then just walk the last stretch. Qingdao buses are too horrendously crowded to even contemplate taking two in a row.

Places to Stay – middle

Opposite the No 1 Beach (and to the east of the Huiquan Dynasty Hotel) is a large, red brick guest house in colonial style with single rooms from Y30 and double rooms from Y77. A dormitory bed is Y20.

The *Yellow Sea Hotel* (tel 84215) at Yanan Yilu is a fairly new 19 storey building to the north of the Huiquan Dynasty Hotel. Some travellers have stayed in spacious four-bed dormitories here for Y15 per person.

Places to Stay – top end

The *Zhanqiao Guest House* (tel 83402) at 31 Taiping Lu is a marvellous old colonial villa facing the waterfront. Doubles only, from Y60 to Y110.

The high-rise *Huiquan Dynasty Hotel* (tel 85215), at 9 Nanhai Lu, presides over the No 1 Beach. Double rooms facing the sea go for around Y118, double rooms facing the rear for around Y107. No single rooms. The hotel serves a passable western breakfast. To get there take bus No 6 from near the railway station.

Places to Eat

The end of town with the boat station, Seamen's Club, Friendship Store, cinema and two hotels is supposed to have one of the best restaurants in town. The restaurant serves both the Friendship Store and the Seamen's Club, and is located between the two on the 2nd floor. They offer a large range of seafood (swordfish, red snapper, scallops, shellfish in season – more in autumn), all at very fishy prices, and higher for private booths. An attached bar serves cold dishes like jellyfish and cucumber for drinking with. The only problem is trying to pin down the opening hours.

If you want some cheaper fare and are staying at either the Peace or the Friendship hotels, there are a couple of decent little restaurants in the general vicinity dishing up jiaozi, beer and simple Chinese dishes.

Zhongshan Lu also has several restaurants. The top one is the *Chunhelou* towards the north end of Zhongshan at No 146. Pricey seafood, and 'Tsingtao' beer served in real pint beer mugs.

Further down Zhongshan, at the railway station end close to the CAAC office, is a cheap seafood restaurant – look for a glassed-in building with a corrugated green roof on the corner opposite an antique store. The restaurant sells ice cream, steamed buns, seafood, soup, duck eggs, various other dishes and dirt-cheap snacks.

For morning baozi and cakes go to the rather illustrious looking *Tian Fu Restaurant* at the north end of Zhongshan Lu. It's open from 6.30 am.

There are some cafés, sidewalk stalls and up-market canteens *(Happy Pub, White Spray)* in the vicinity of the Huiquan Dynasty Hotel serving large plates of prawns, dumplings, bean curd and the like, but none of them are particularly inspiring. Take potluck – that's what the signs say.

Alcohol in this town is plentiful and cheap. A bottle of Tsingtao Red is around Y3 and is a good addition to a meal. There's a huge stock in the department stores on Zhongshan Lu.

Shopping

The busiest shopping area is the length of Zhongshan Lu, which has an antique store at No 40, and the Arts & Crafts Service Department at the north end. Good buys are plaited straw wares (hats, mats), shell carvings (there's a small retail shop on a side street leading from Zhongshan Lu to the station) and for instant consumption, good cheap grog. Several market streets spill off the north end of Zhongshan Lu.

Getting There & Away

Air Qingdao is connected by air to Shanghai and Beijing (three flights a week); Canton, Nanjing and Dalian (two a week); and Jinan (three a week).

Rail All trains from Qingdao go through the provincial capital of Jinan, except for the direct Qingdao to Yantai trains. There are direct trains to Beijing (17 hours).

Direct trains to Shenyang (about 26 hours) pass through Jinan and Tianjin, sidestepping Beijing. There are direct trains to Xian (about 31 hours) which carry on to Lanzhou and Xining.

Trains to Dalian and to Shanghai (about 24 hours) will take almost the same time as the boats. The train is much more expensive and there's no foreigners' mark-up on boat fares as there is on train fares.

Tourist price tickets from Qingdao to Shanghai are: Y22 hard-seat, Y38 hard-sleeper and Y75 soft-sleeper.

Tourist price tickets from Qingdao to Beijing are: Y32 hard-seat, Y52 hard-sleeper and Y97 soft-sleeper.

Boat There are regular boats from Qingdao to Dalian and Shanghai. There are usually five classes on these boats, including four-, six-, and eight-berth cabins, plus a 'special class' which is about twice the price of 1st class.

The boat to Dalian on the Liaoning Peninsula, across the Bo Sea, is the best way to get there from Qingdao. It's a long way there by train. The boat takes 26 hours and leaves every four days, but sometimes there can be gaps of up to eight days. The boat is comfortable and fares range from Y10.50 in 5th class to Y59 in 1st class.

You could also take a train from Qingdao to Yantai and catch the Yantai to Dalian boat. Fares range from Y6.20 in 5th class to Y35 in 1st class.

The Qingdao to Shanghai boat departs Qingdao every day and the trip takes about 27 hours. Fares range from Y12.20 in 5th class to Y67.90 in 1st class. The ship is reportedly clean and comfortable, with friendly and helpful staff.

In Qingdao tickets can be bought in the large waiting hall at the boat dock near the Friendship Store.

Getting Around

Most transport needs can be catered for by the bus No 6 route, which starts at the north end of Zhongshan Lu, runs along Zhongshan Lu to within a few blocks of the main train station and then east to the area above No 3 beach. The location of the bus stops marked on maps of Qingdao appear to have no relation to reality. The No 6 bus stop closest to the main train station seems to be the one on Zhongshan Lu, just north of the street leading to the Catholic Church. If you're stuck for transport than an auto-rickshaw from outside the train station may help.

AROUND QINGDAO

Forty km east of Qingdao is Laoshan Mountain, covering some 400 square km. It's an excellent place to go hiking or climbing – the mountain reaches an elevation of 1133 metres. Historical sites and scenic spots dot the area and the local product is Laoshan mineral water. The

Song Dynasty Taiqing Palace (a Taoist monastery) is the central attraction; there are paths leading to the summit of Laoshan from there. With such a large area, there's plenty to explore. Due north of the Taiqing Palace is Jiushui, noted for its numerous streams and waterfalls.

An early morning bus runs from Qingdao rail station to Taiqing Palace and the fare is about Y6 for the round trip. Other travel agents around Qingdao have more extended itineraries, including an overnight stop in Laoshan, but it's probably hard to crash these tours unless you speak Chinese.

And a mystery tour. There's a local ferry to the west of the top end of Zhongshan Lu, shown on the bus map as running either to a large island off the coast or to a piece of mainland across the bay from Qingdao. Well, it won't cost you much to find out. Several new tourist boats have also been launched for harbour cruising in Qingdao.

TAI'AN

Tai'an is the gateway town to the sacred Tai Mountain. Apart from this it's the home town of Jiang Qing, Mao's fourth wife, ex-film actress, notorious spearhead of the all-purpose villains known as the 'Gang of Four' on whom all of China's ills are now blamed. She's since been airbrushed out of Chinese history and is now serving a life sentence.

Information

CITS is in the Tai Shan Guest House.

Places to Stay

The tourist HQ is the *Tai Shan Guest House*, a five storey complex with souvenir shops, telecommunication services, bank, dining halls, some deluxe suites, 250 beds, a roof garden snack bar in summer and several English-speaking staff. Dormitory beds are Y18. Double rooms only, from Y60.

The guest house is four km from the station and just a short walk from the start of the central route trail up Tai Shan. They will hold your bags for you while you climb the mountain.

To get to the guest house, take bus No 3 from the railway station to the second-to-last stop. Alternatively, get an auto-rickshaw or pedicab.

Places to Eat

Visitors generally keep to the set menus in the dining hall of the *Tai Shan Guest House*. The western breakfast leaves much to be desired, but enormous Chinese set dinners are only Y5 per person (I'd hate to see the size of their Y10 dinners!). There's no dearth of restaurants around town, but after Tai Shan your legs may not let you go hunting (if in need, there's a roaring trade in Tai'an selling walking sticks, many neatly crafted from gnarled pieces of wood). There are many restaurants along the street leading up to the mountain from the Daimiao Temple.

Getting There

Bus Tai'an can be approached by road from either Jinan or Qufu and is worth combining with a trip to the latter. There are buses from the long-distance bus station to Qufu (about four times a day, two hours, Y3) and to Jinan (twice a day).

There are also private bus companies, some of which operate from offices just south of the Tai Shan Guest House with early morning departures to Qufu (Y3.30) and to Jinan (Y2.20).

Rail There are more than 20 express trains daily running through Tai'an with links to Beijing, Harbin, Shenyang, Nanjing Shanghai, Xian, Zhengzhou, Qingdao and Jinan.

Trains go through Jinan and the station you want is Tai'an, about 1¼ hours from Jinan. Some special expresses don't stop at Tai'an. The town is a nine-hour ride from Beijing, 11 hours from Zhengzhou and nine from Nanjing. Arrival times in Tai'an are impossible, with trains pulling in during the early hours of the morning.

Tai'an and Tai Shan make good stopovers on the way south from Qingdao to Qufu and Shanghai. Tourist price train fares from Qingdao to Tai'an are Y9.60 hard-seat, Y16.30 hard-sleeper and Y64.60 soft-sleeper. The trip takes about 9½ hours.

Getting Around

Getting around is easy. The long-distance bus station is near the train station, so all local transport is directed toward these two termini. There are three main bus routes. Bus No 3 runs from the central route trailhead to the western route trailhead via the train station, so that just about covers everything. Bus Nos 1 and 2 also end up near the train station. Auto-rickshaws and pedicabs can be found outside the train station.

TAI SHAN 泰山

Tai Shan is the most revered of the five sacred mountains of China, adopted in turn by Taoists, Buddhists, Confucians and Maoists. From its summit imperial sacrifices to heaven and earth were offered. In China's long history , only five emperors dared to climb it – Emperor Qianlong scaled Tai Shan 11 times. From its heights Confucius uttered the dictum 'The world is small'; Mao lumbered up and commented on the sunrise: 'The East is Red'.

Poets, writers and painters have found Tai Shan a great source of inspiration and extolled its virtues, but one is left wondering now what natural beauty is left. A long string of worshippers has left its tributes on the slopes – calligraphy cut into rock faces, temples, shrines, stairs – to which modern history has added revolutionary memorials, guest houses, soft drink vendors, photo booths, a weather station and the final insult – a cable car.

No matter, the pull of the supernatural (legend, religion and history rolled into one) is enough. The Princess of the Azure Clouds, a Taoist deity whose presence permeates the temples dotted along the route, is a powerful cult figure for the peasant women of Shandong and beyond. Tribes of wiry grandmothers come each year for the ascent, a journey made difficult by bound feet. Their target is the main temples at the summit, where they can offer gifts and prayers for their progeny. It's said that if you climb Tai Shan you'll live to be 100, and some of the grandmothers look pretty close to that already. For the younger set, Tai Shan is a popular picnic destination. Tourists – foreign and Chinese – gather on the cold summit at daybreak in the hope of catching a perfect 747 sunrise. In ancient Chinese tradition, it was believed that the sun began its westward journey from Tai Shan.

As the adage goes: 'The journey of a thousand miles begins with a single step'. On Tai Shan there are some 6000 of them that you'll remember clearly. The mountain is relatively small, but the steps are the kind that get your blood pounding. You and 5000 other climbers, that is! After a while you realise that what you're looking at is not the mountain but the pilgrims toiling up it. The hackwork of China – the carting of concrete blocks, water, produce, goods – is a common sight on the streets, but nowhere does it appear more painful than on the sheer slopes of this mountain. Porters with weals on their shoulders and misshapen backs plod up the stairway to heaven with crates of drinks, bedding and construction for the hotels and dining halls further up. It's a time-honoured tradition, a job passed from father to son, and the cable car seems to have done little to alter it. The idea, as we understood it, was to use the cable car to transport passengers by day, and cargo by night. One wonders how many backs were broken in the building of the temples and stone stairs on Tai Shan over the centuries, a massive undertaking accomplished without mechanical aids.

All in all, as you may have surmised, Tai Shan is not the mountain climbing you might expect it to be, and it is not a particularly scenic beauty. But if you accept that, it's an engrossing experience

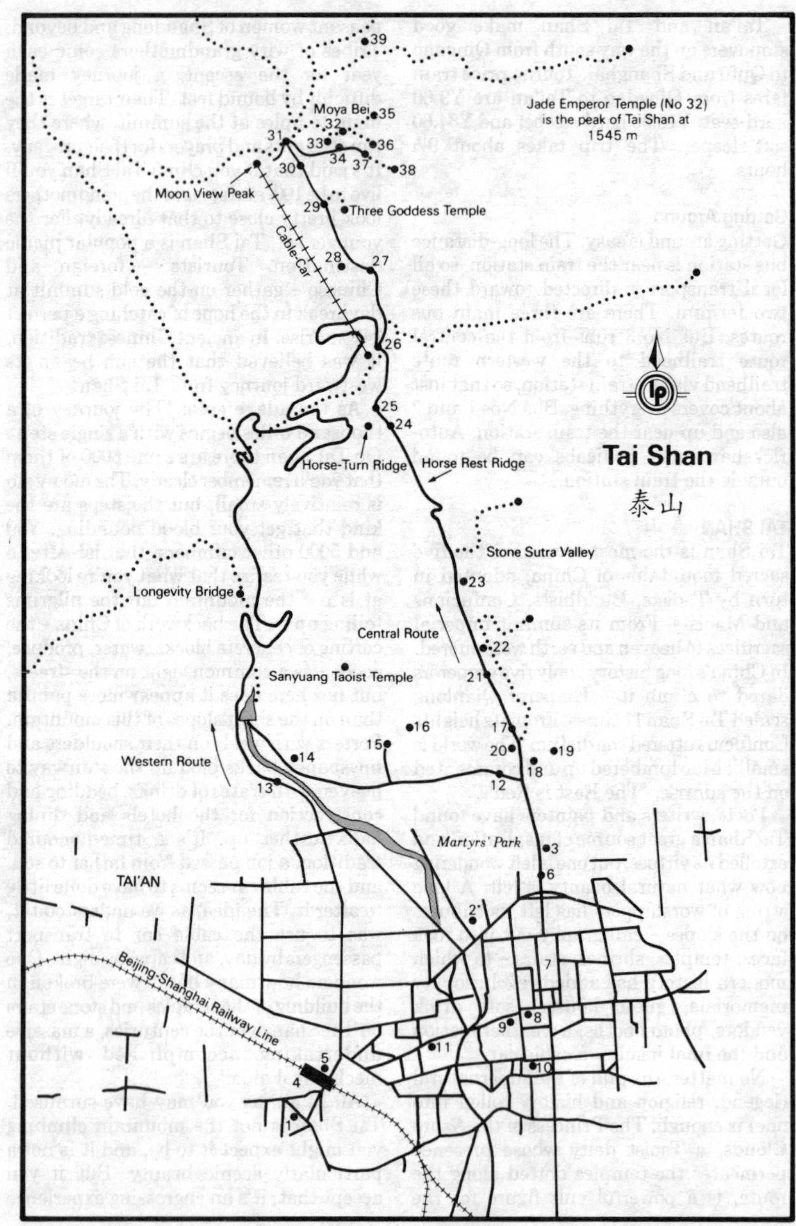

39
Moya Bei
35
32
31
33
36
34
37
30
38
Moon View Peak
29
Three Goddess Temple
Cable-Car
Jade Emperor Temple (No 32)
is the peak of Tai Shan at
1545 m
28
27
26
25
24
Horse-Turn Ridge
Horse Rest Ridge
Tai Shan
泰山
Stone Sutra Valley
23
Longevity Bridge
Central Route
22
21
Sanyuang Taoist Temple
16
17
15
20
19
14
18
Western Route
13
12
Martyrs' Park
3
6
TAI'AN
2
7
Beijing-Shanghai Railway Line
8
9
11
10
5
4
1

TAI'AN
1 Long-distance Bus Station
2 Taishan Restaurant
3 Taishan Guest House/CITS
4 Tai'an Railway Station
5 Taxi, Autorickshaw & Pedicab Rank
6 Daizong Archway
7 Daimiao (Temple Complex)
8 Dongfanghong Restaurant & Travel Agency
9 Post Office
10 Department Store & Arts & Crafts Centre
11 Restaurant
12 Trailhead for Central Route (No 3 Bus East Terminus)
13 Trailhead for Western Route (No 3 Bus West Terminus or No 2 Bus)

BASE OF MOUNTAIN
14 Everyman's Bridge (Dazhong Qiao) & Tomb of Feng Yuxiang
15 Puzhao Temple
16 Memorial Temple
17 Hongmen (Red Gate) Temple Complex
18 Cloud Empress Pool
19 Tiger Mountain Reservoir
20 Guandi Temple

CENTRAL ROUTE & ASCENDING
21 10,000 Immortals Pavilion
22 Monument to Revolutionary Heroes
23 Doumu Hall
24 Hutian Pavilion
25 Skywalk Bridge
26 Zhongtianmen (Midway Gate to Heaven) & Zhongtianmen Guest House & Cable Car
27 Cloud Bridge
28 Five Pine Pavilion
29 Pine Facing Pavilion

THE SUMMIT
30 Archway to Immortality
31 Nantianmen (South Gate to Heaven)
32 Jade Emperor Temple (Yuhuang Ding)
33 Summit Guest House
34 Bixia (Azure Cloud) Temple
35 Gongbei Rock
36 Sunview Peak
37 Bridge of the Gods
38 Zhanlu Terrace
39 Rear Temple (Huoshiwu)

1 长途汽车站
2 泰山饭店
3 宾馆
4 火车站
5 出租汽车站
6 岱宗坊
7 岱庙
8 东方红饭店
9 邮局
10 百货商店
11 饭店
12 三路汽车东终点
13 三路汽车西终点
14 大众桥
15 普照寺
16 记念寺
17 红门
18 王母池
19 龙山水库
20 关帝庙
21 万仙楼
22 革命烈士纪念碑
23 斗母宫
24 虚天阁
25 步天桥
26 中天门
27 云步桥
28 五松亭
29 对松亭
30 开仙坊
31 南天门
32 玉皇顶
33 岱顶宾馆
34 碧霞祠
35 拱石
36 日观峰
37 仙人桥
38 占鲁台
39 后石坞

and certainly worthwhile. If grandmother can make it up there, you should have no trouble, and it will exercise the other five walking muscles you haven't used in the streets already. The trip down, by the way, is more strenuous for the legs.

Weather

The peak tourist season is from May to October. But remember that conditions vary considerably on the mountain compared to sea-level Tai'an.

The mountain is frequently enveloped in clouds and haze, which are more prevalent in summer. The best times to visit are in spring and autumn when the humidity is low, though old-timers say that the clearest weather is from early October onwards. In winter the weather is often fine but very cold.

On average, there are 16 fine days in spring, eight in summer, 28 in autumn and 35 in winter. But take care – due to weather changes, you're best advised to take a small day-pack with you to carry warm clothing, no matter what the season. You can freeze your butt off on Tai Shan, though padded overcoats can be rented. The average seasonal temperatures in degrees Celsius are:

	winter	*spring*	*summer*	*autumn*
Tai'an	–3	20	24	20
Summit	–9	12	17	12

Scaling the Heights

The town of Tai'an lies at the foot of Tai Shan and is the gateway to the mountain. For details of Tai'an and how to get there, see the separate section in this book.

Upon arrival in Tai'an you have several options depending on your timing. There are three rest stops to bear in mind: *Tai Shan Guest House* at the base of the trail; *Zhongtianmen Guest House* midway up; and the *Summit Guest House* on top of Tai Shan.

You should allow at least two hours for climbing between each of these points – a total of eight hours up and down at the minimum. Allowing several more hours would make the climb less strenuous and give you more time to look around on top. If you want to see the sunrise, then dump your gear at the train station or the Tai Shan Guest House in Tai'an and time your ascent to reach the summit before sundown; stay overnight at one of the summit guest houses and get up early next morning for the famed sunrise (which, for technical reasons, may not be clearly forthcoming).

Chinese tourists without time or money at their disposal sometimes scale at night (with flashlights and walking sticks) to arrive at the peak in time for sunrise, descending shortly thereafter. Unless you have uncanny night vision or four hours of battery power, this particular option could lead to you getting lost, frozen, falling off a mountainside, or all three.

There are two main paths up the mountain: the central and the western, converging at the midway point of Zhongtianmen. Most people go up via the central path (which used to be the imperial route and hence has more cultural sites) and down by the western path. Other trails run through orchards and woods.

Tai Shan is 1545 metres above sea level, with a climbing distance of 7.5 km from base to summit on the central route. The elevation change from Zhongtianmen to the summit is approximately 600 metres.

Cheating Your Way to the Top

Minibuses run from the Tai'an train station to Zhongtianmen, halfway up Tai Shan, with several departures each morning. Occasional group tour minibuses run from the Tai Shan Guest House, if you care to try crashing one.

From Zhongtianmen there is a cable car to the top which holds 30 passengers. It takes eight minutes to travel from Zhongtianmen to Wangfu Peak near Nantianmen, and may be useful for bird's-eye view photos. The cable cars operate in both directions. This is China's first large cableway.

Buses come down the mountain hourly between 1 and 5 pm, but don't count on the schedule or the seats.

Central Route

On this route you'll see a bewildering catalogue of bridges, trees, towers, inscribed stones, caves, pavilions, temples complex and simplex (!). Half the trip, for the Chinese at least, is the colossal amount of calligraphy scoring the stones en route. Tai Shan in fact functions as an outdoor museum of calligraphic art, with the prize items being the Diamond Sutra (or Stone Valley Sutra) and the Moya Bei at the summit, which commemorates an imperial sacrifice.

The climb proper begins at **Number One Archway Under Heaven** at the mountain base. Behind that is a stone archway overgrown with wisteria and inscribed 'the place where Confucius began to climb'. **Red Gate Palace**, standing out with its wine-coloured walls, is the first of a series of temples dedicated to the Princess of the Azure Clouds (Bixia), who was the daughter of the god of Tai Shan. It was rebuilt in 1626. **Doumu Hall** was first constructed in 1542 and has the more poetic name of Dragon Spring Nunnery; there's a teahouse within.

Continuing through the tunnel of cypresses known as **Cypress Cave** is **Horse-Turn Ridge**, where Emperor Zhen Zong had to dismount and continue by sedan chair because his horse refused to go further. Smart move on the part of the horse; another emperor rode a white mule up and down the mountain and the beast died soon after the descent (it was posthumously given the title of general and its tomb is on the mountain).

Zhongtian Men is the second celestial gate. Beyond **Cloud Bridge** and to the right is the place where Emperor Zhen Zong pitched his overnight tents. A little way on is **Five Pine Pavilion**, where one day back in 219 BC, Emperor Qin Shihuang was overtaken by a violent storm and was sheltered by the kind pines. He promoted them to the 5th rank of minister; though the three you see are, understandably, not the same ministers!

On the slopes higher up is the **Welcoming Pine** with a branch extended as if to shake hands. Beyond that is the **Archway to Immortality**. The belief was that those passing through it would become celestial beings. From here to the summit, emperors were carried in sedan chairs – eatcha heart out!

The third celestial gate is **Nantian Men**. That, and the steep pathway leading up to it, are symbolic of Tai Shan and of Shandong itself; the picture pops up on covers of books and on Shandong maps.

On arrival at **Daiding (The Summit)** you will see the **Wavelength Pavilion** (a radio and weather station) and the **Journey to the Stars Gondola** (the cable car). If you continue along Paradise Rd, you'll come to **Sunset Statue** (where a frozen photographer sits slumped over a table with the view beyond dutifully recorded in sunrises and clipped in front of him).

Welcome to Tai Shan shopping centre. Here you'll see fascinating Chinese antics on the precarious rock lookouts – go and check out the **Bridge of the Gods**, which are a couple of giant rocks trapped between two precipices.

The grandmothers' Long March ends at the **Bixia (Azure Clouds) Temple** where small offerings of one sort or another are made to a bronze statue, once richly decorated. The iron tiling on the buildings is intended to prevent damage by strong wind currents, and on the bronze eaves are *chiwen*, ornaments meant to protect against fire. The temple is absolutely splendid, with its location in the clouds, but its guardians are a trifle touchy about you wandering around, and parts are inaccessible. Little is known of its history. What is known is that it cost a fortune to restore or make additions, as was done in the Ming and Qing dynasties. The bronze statuette of the Princess of Azure Clouds is in the main hall.

Perched on the highest point of the Tai Shan plateau is **Jade Emperor Temple**, with a bronze statue of a Taoist deity. In the courtyard is a rock inscribed with the elevation of the mountain. In front of the temple is the one piece of calligraphy that you can really appreciate – the **Wordless Monument**. This one will leave you speechless. One story goes that it was set up by Emperor Wu 2100 years ago – he wasn't satisfied with what his scribes came up with, so he left it to the viewers' imagination.

The main sunrise vantage point is a springboard-shaped thing called **Gongbei**

Rock; if you're lucky visibility could extend to over 200 km, as far as the coast. Sunset slides over the Yellow River side. On the backside of the mountain is **Rear Rocky Recess**, one of the better known spots for viewing pine trees; there are some ruins tangled in the foliage. It's a good place to ramble and lose the crowds for a while.

Western Route

On this route there's nothing of note in the way of structures, but there's considerable variation in scenery with orchards, pools and flowering plants. The major scenic attraction is **Black Dragon Pool** which is just below Longevity Bridge (between the bridge and West Brook Pavilion) and is fed by a small waterfall. Swimming in the waters are some rare, red-scaled carp which are occasionally cooked for the rich. Mythical tales revolve around this pool, said to be the site of underground carp palaces and of magic herbs that turn people into beasts. Worth looking into along the base of the mountain is the **Puzhao Monastery**, founded 1500 years ago.

Daimiao (Tai Shan Temple)

This temple is at the foot of the mountain, south of the Tai Shan Hotel. It was the pilgrims' first stopover and an ideal place to preview or recap the journey. It once functioned solely for that purpose, being a resting spot for the hiking emperors. The temple is a very large one of 96,000 square metres, enclosed by high walls. The main hall is the Temple of Heavenly Blessing (Tiankung) dating to 1009 AD. It towers some 22 metres and is constructed of wood with double-roof yellow tiling.

The Tiankung was the first built of the 'big three' (the others being Taihe Hall at the Forbidden City, and Dacheng Hall at Qufu). It was restored in 1956. Inside is a 62-metre-long fresco running from the west to east walls, depicting the god of Tai Shan on his outward and return journeys. In this case the god is Emperor Zhen Zong, who had the temple built. Zhen Zong raised the god of Tai Shan to the rank of emperor and there is a seven-metre-high stele to celebrate this in the western courtyard. The fresco has been painstakingly retouched by artisans of succeeding dynasties, and though recently restored, is in poor shape – but a majestic concept nonetheless.

The temple complex has been repeatedly restored; in the late 1920s, however, it was stripped of its statues and transmogrified into offices and shops. Later it suffered damage under the Kuomintang. It is gradually coming back together, not as a temple but as an open air museum with a forest of 200-odd steles. One inscribed stone, originally at the summit of Tai Shan, is believed to be over 2000 years old (Qin Dynasty). It can be seen at the Eastern Imperial Hall, along with a small collection of imperial sacrificial vessels. Out-of-towners flock to Tai Shan Temple to copy the styles of calligraphy and poetry, of which there is a masterly range. Also moved from the summit is a beautiful bronze pavilion.

Around the courtyards are ancient cypresses, gingkos and acacias. At the rear of the temple is a bonsai garden and rockery. By the cypress in front of Tiankung Hall locals and visitors can indulge in a game of luck. A person is blindfolded next to a rock, has to go around the rock three times counter-clockwise, then three times clockwise, and try and grope toward the cypress, which is 20 steps away. They miss every time. Outside the main temple gates, if it's the right season, street hawkers sell watermelons with the display pieces deftly cut into rose shapes.

Places to Stay & Eat

The *Zhongtianmen Guest House* is a halfway house at Zhongtianmen with little in the way of food, although there are food and drink stalls nearby. Doubles start at around Y12, and if you're on your own you may manage a room to yourself for Y6. A bed in a crowded dormitory is Y2.50. It's very quiet (provided no one brings their ghetto blaster) and very basic (outdoor troughs to wash in, open-pit toilets without doors), but if you're tired you probably won't notice.

The *Summit Guest House* is a basic Chinese-style hotel. If you get room in the right place then you get excellent views. The hotel provides extra blankets and rents out heavy padded cotton overcoats, PLA-type, in lieu of heating. There's even an alarm bell which tells you when to get up for sunrise. Rooms in the new wing have their own televisions (there's no escaping it) and no doubt the old wings will follow suit. Double rooms only from Y22. There are probably cheaper dormitory beds if you do a bit of arm-twisting with the staff.

If you wonder where all those amazing grannies go, it seems that there are lodgings tucked down side trails, possibly former monasteries. As for other sustenance, snacks and drinks and the like are sold on the mountain trail. Outside the Summit Guest House is a green shed masquerading as a restaurant.

YANTAI 烟台

Yantai, alias 'Chefoo', is a busy ice-free port on the northern coast of Shandong Peninsula. Like Qingdao it grew from a defence outpost and fishing village, but although opened for foreign trade in 1862, it had no foreign concessions. Several nations, the Japanese and the Americans among them, had trading establishments there and Yantai was something of a resort area at one time. About 60 km east of Yantai by road, the British had a concession at Weihaiwei around the turn of the century – it's now a major port. Since 1949, the port and naval base at Yantai have been expanded and apart from fishing and trading, the town is a major producer of wines, spirits and fruits.

Information

CITS has an office near the Overseas Chinese Hotel. They're set up to handle stray seamen and the tourist ships – as when a Scandinavian liner disgorges 500 passengers for five hours on their shores. CITS can be summoned over the phone and will arrive pronto in the lobby of the Overseas Chinese Hotel. That's when your problems begin – they're not terribly helpful.

Things to See & Do

Apart from getting drunk and building sand castles, there's very little. Group tours are corralled off to a fish-freezing factory, a brandy distillery or the orchards behind the town. Yantai's beaches are not the greatest – they're unsheltered and prone to heavy wind-lashing. The main one is hemmed in at the south-west side by an industrial complex and a naval establishment. Beach No 2, out by the Chefoo Guest House, is smaller and more likeable, but difficult to get to.

A convenient tour of the town can be done on local bus No 3, which leaves from the square near the train and boat stations – it takes half an hour to get to Yantai Hill. The bus cuts through Yantai, taking in the older parts of town (which are being eaten away by apartment blocks and chimney factories), and goes past the odd colonial edifice and newer sections. The bus turns around at the Yantai Hill terminus. If you get off at the terminus and follow a stone wall from there up to the headland, you get a nice view of the naval dockyards, heavy shipping and even navy manoeuvres.

Yantai means 'smoke-terrace': wolf-dung fires were lit on the headland to warn fishing fleets of approaching pirates, a practice that continued into the Opium Wars. If you continue round the headland, you hit the esplanade at No 1 Beach, where there is some distinctively European architecture – former foreign trading or resort housing. You can continue to the bus No 1 route, which will take you back into town.

Places to Stay

The bad news: the high-rise *Chefoo Guest House* has been built about eight km from the station. It's a nice place but a

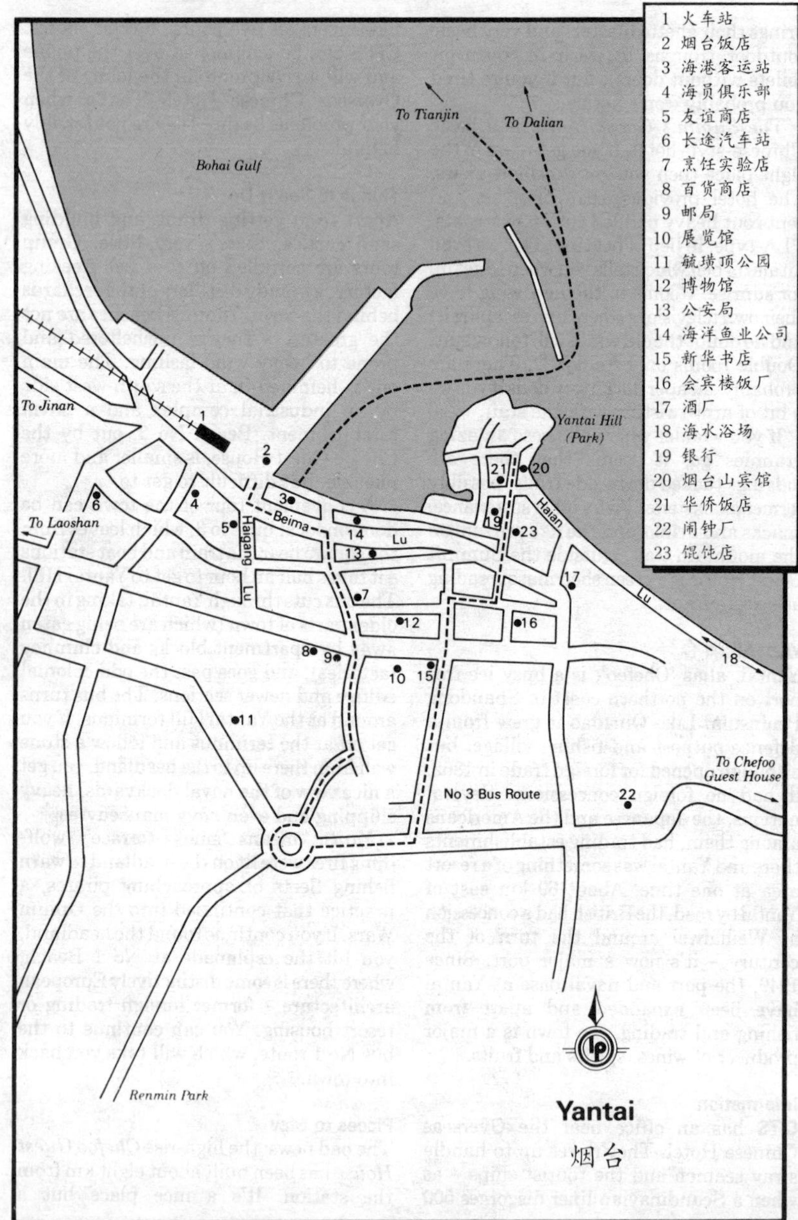
1 火车站
2 烟台饭店
3 海港客运站
4 海员俱乐部
5 友谊商店
6 长途汽车站
7 烹饪实验店
8 百货商店
9 邮局
10 展览馆
11 毓璜顶公园
12 博物馆
13 公安局
14 海洋鱼业公司
15 新华书店
16 会宾楼饭厂
17 酒厂
18 海水浴场
19 银行
20 烟台山宾馆
21 华侨饭店
22 闹钟厂
23 馄饨店
To Tianjin
To Dalian
Bohai Gulf
To Jinan
Yantai Hill
(Park)
To Laoshan
Beima
Haigang
Lu
Haian
No 3 Bus Route
To Chefoo
Guest House
Renmin Park
Yantai
烟台

1 Railway Station
2 Yantai Restaurant
3 Boat Ticket Office & Departures
4 Seamen's Club
5 Friendship Store
6 Long-distance Bus Station
7 Yantai Cooking School (Restaurant)
8 Department Store
9 Post Office
10 Exhibition Hall
11 Jade Emperor Taoist Temple
12 Museum
13 Public Security
14 Ocean Fishing Company
15 Bookstore
16 Huibin Restaurant
17 Wine Distillery
18 Beach & Esplanade
19 Bank
20 Yantai Hill Hotel
21 Overseas Chinese Hotel/ CITS/Bus No 3 Terminus
22 Alarm Clock Factory
23 Soup Dumpling Snackshop

transport disaster. You need three buses to get there (Nos 3, 4 and 5), and the last one is a rare species indeed. In other words you'll most likely end up commuting by taxi. Otherwise it's hitching or jumping the laundry bus which runs into town from the hotel every morning. Expensive rooms. There's nothing in the vicinity of the hotel except the No 2 Beach about 10 minutes' walk away, a set menu in the dining hall and a conference room for 200 which is set up for reclusive meetings (with participants ferried in by minibus).

The alternative is to try and worm your way into the *Yantai Hill Hotel*, a beautiful but expensive villa overlooking the sea. It used to be a tourist hotel but suddenly turned Chinese only. Some tactics: say you're only staying one night, leaving by train or boat next day and the Chefoo is too far out; or install yourself in the nearest Chinese hotel and wait for CITS to come and haul you off to the Yantai Hill Hotel after a good wrangle over hotel rates. Both the Yantai Hill Hotel and the Overseas Chinese Hotel are at the bus No 3 terminus.

Things to Eat
Cheap meals are available in the dining rooms of the *Yantai Hill* and the *Overseas Chinese Hotel*. Also try the *Yantai Cooking School* and the *Huibin*, both on the bus No 3 route.

The *Yantai Restaurant* is a large eatery between the rail station and the boat station. There are three rooms; the central one, the cheapest, has a mass of proletarian clientele with about four chairs between them; stand-up noodles, dumplings, beggars and bowls of hot water. The other two sections have beer, bigger and meatier dishes – and chairs.

As for alcohol, you can buy the stuff anywhere, including the train station. It's mostly under Y4 a bottle, and there's some evil-looking substance that retails for less than a yuan. Yantai is famous for rose-petal wine *(meiguijui)*, brandy *(bailandi)* and red and white wines. Renowned brands are Yantai Red, Weimeisi Wine and Jinjiang Brandy.

Getting There & Away
Rail There are two lines to Yantai, one from Jinan and one from Qingdao, joining at Lancun. There are express trains to Beijing (about 17½ hours) and a direct but slow train to Shanghai. There are direct trains to Jinan (about 12 hours).

Rail buffs should try to nail down the slow train from Qingdao which has hard wooden seats, steam, a magnificent dining car with genuine lamps, curtains and fittings, and beautiful woodwork. Last heard, this train was designated No 506 departing Qingdao and No 508 departing Yantai.

Boat The rail trip to Dalian on the Liaoning Peninsula cuts a circuitous route. Faster are the daily boats from Yantai. Yantai to Dalian is Y35 (1st class),

Y17.50 (2nd class, two-bed cabin), Y9.70 (3rd class, four-bed cabin), Y7.50 (4th class, eight to 10-bed cabin) and Y6.20 (5th class, which you'd rather not know about). The boat leaves Yantai at 8 pm and arrives in Dalian at 6 am the next day. There are other boats between Yantai and Tianjin (berthing at Tianjin's Tanggu Harbour) which run once every five days.

AROUND YANTAI

About 75 km north-west of Yantai by road is the coastal castle of Penglai, a place of the gods often referred to in Chinese mythology. The castle is perched on a clifftop overlooking the sea and is about 1000 years old. The last full mirage seen from this site was in July 1981 when two islands appeared, with roads, trees, buildings, people and vehicles. This phenomenon lasted about 40 minutes (had it lasted any longer, little red flags and factory chimneys would no doubt have appeared!). There are some pebbly beaches in the area and a seafood restaurant. Penglai is a two-hour bus ride from Yantai.

QUFU 曲阜

Qufu is the birth and death place of Confucius (551-479 BC). The sage's impact was not felt in his own lifetime. He spent his years in abject poverty and hardly put pen to paper. His teachings were recorded by dedicated followers (in the *Analects*), and his descendants, the Kong family, fared considerably better.

Confucian ethics were adopted by subsequent rulers to keep the populace in line, and Confucian temples were set up in numerous towns run by officials. Qufu acquired the status of a holy place, with the direct descendants as its guardian angels.

The original Confucian Temple at Qufu (dating from 478 BC) was enlarged, remodelled, added to, taken away from and rebuilt. The present buildings are from the Ming Dynasty. In 1513 armed bands sacked the temple and the Kong residence, and walls were built around the town to fortify it (1522-1567). The walls were recently removed, but vestiges of Ming town planning, like the Drum and Bell towers, remain.

More a code that defined hierarchical relationships than a religion, Confucianism has had great impact on Chinese culture. It teaches that son must respect father, wife must respect husband, commoner must respect official, officials must respect their ruler, and vice versa. The essence of its teachings are obedience, respect and selflessness, and working for the common good.

One would think that this code would have fit nicely into the new order of Communism. However, it was swept aside because of its connections with the past. Confucius was seen as a kind of misguided

feudal educator, and clan ties and ancestor-worship were viewed as a threat. In 1948 Confucius' direct heir, the first-born son of the 77th generation of the Kong family, fled to Taiwan, breaking a 2500-year tradition of Kong residence in Qufu.

During the Cultural Revolution the emphasis shifted to the youth of China (even if they were led by an old man). A popular anti-Confucian campaign was instigated and Confucius lost face. Many of the statues at Qufu also lost face (literally) amidst cries of 'Down with Confucius, down with his wife!' In the late '60s a contingent of Red Guards descended on the sleepy town of Qufu, burning, defacing and destroying. Other Confucian edifices around the country were also attacked. The leader of the Guards who ransacked Qufu was Tan Houlan. She was jailed for that in 1978 and was not tried until 1982. The Confucius family archives appear to have survived the assaults intact.

Confucian ethics have made something of a comeback, presumably to instil some civic-mindedness where the Party had failed. Confucianism is finding its way back into the Shandong school system, though not by that name. Students are encouraged once again to respect their teachers, elders, neighbours and family. If there's one thing you discover quickly travelling in China, it's that respect among the Chinese has fallen to pieces. With corruption at the top of the system, the cynical young find it difficult to reciprocate respect; the elderly remain suspicious of what has passed and afraid of the street fights and arguments.

In 1979 the Qufu temples were reopened and millions of yuan were allocated for renovations or Red Guard repairs. Tourism is now the name of the game; if a temple hasn't got a fresh coat of paint, new support pillars, replaced tiling or stonework, souvenir shop or photo merchant with a Great Sage cardboard cut-out, they'll get round to it soon. Some of the buildings even have electricity, with speakers hooked up to the eaves playing soothing flute music. Emanating from the eaves is some real music – you have to stop and listen twice to make sure – yes, real birds up there! Fully one-fifth of Qufu's 50,000 residents are again claiming to be descendants of the Great Sage, though incense burning, mound-burial and ancestor-worship are not consistent with the Party line.

Whether Confucianism can take fresh root in China is a matter for conjecture, but something is needed to fill the idealist void. A symposium a few years ago in Qufu by Chinese scholars resulted in careful statements reaffirming the significance of Confucius' historical role, and suggesting that the 'progressive' aspects of his work were a valuable legacy, which had been cited in the writings of Mao Zedong. It's simply a matter of picking Confucian hairs out of Marxist soup.

Information

CITS At the time of writing, CITS was at the reception desk of Confucius Mansions Hotel (tel 491), No 1 Dong Hua Men Dajie, but they may move to the new Queli Hotel. They're useful, speak English and are well organised. Help is not really needed as Qufu is a small place, but they have all the bus and train schedules written up in English and will buy bus tickets for you (there's no mark-up for bus travel). They also change money.

Things to See

With its marriage of stone, wood and fine imperial architecture, Qufu is a treasure house dripping with culture, second only to the Forbidden City. It's an excellent stopover worth one or two days – quiet, with real birds and grass. There's plenty to see, a Ming Dynasty manor for a hotel, no hassling with transport or big-city complications – a great place for traveller R & R.

There are two fairs a year in Qufu, in spring and autumn. The place comes alive with craftspeople, medicine men, acrobats,

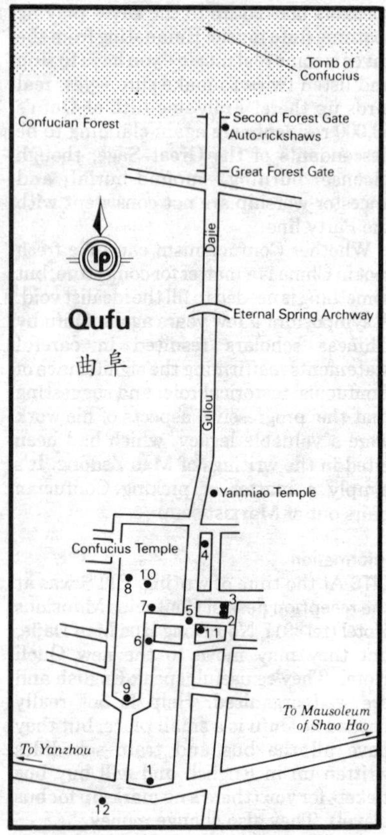

1 Long-distance Bus Station
2 Restaurant
3 Qufu Department Store
4 Arts & Crafts Factory
5 Drum Tower
6 Bell Tower
7 Ceremonial Gate
8 Dacheng Hall
9 Lingxingmen (Star Gate)
10 Confucius Mansions/ CITS/Bus Ticketing Office
11 Bookstore
12 Minibuses to Yanzhou

1 长途汽车站
2 饭店
3 曲阜百货商店
4 工艺工厂
5 鼓楼
6 钟楼
7 重光门
8 大成殿
9 棂星门
10 孔府/车售票处
11 书店
12 兖州汽车站

pedlars and poor peasants. The fair is a 2000-year-old tradition.

Kong Miao (Confucius Temple)

The temple started out as a simple memorial hall and mushroomed to a complex one-fifth the size of Qufu. It is laid on a north-south axis, over one km long. The main entrance is **Lingxingmen (Star Gate)** at the south, which leads through a series of portals emblazoned with calligraphy. The third entrance gateway, with four bluish characters, refers to the doctrines of Confucius as heavenly bodies which move in circles without end; it is known as the **Arch of the Spirit of the Universe**.

Throughout the courtyards of the Kong Miao, the dominant features are the clusters of twisted pines and cypresses, and row upon row of steles. The **tortoise tablets** record in archaic Chinese such events as temple reconstructions, great ceremonies or tree plantings. There are over 1000 steles in the temple grounds, with inscriptions from the Han to Qing dynasties – the largest such collection in China. The creatures bearing the tablets of praise are actually not tortoises but *bixi*, dragon offspring legendary for their strength. The tablets at Qufu are noted for their fine calligraphy; a rubbing once formed part of the dowry for a Kong lady.

At roughly the midway point along the north-south axis is the **Guiwenge (Great Pavilion of the Constellation of Scholars)**, a triple-roofed wooden structure (Jin Dynasty, 1190) of ceremonial importance. Further north through **Dacheng Gate** and to the right is a juniper planted by Confucius – or so claims the tablet in front of it. The small **Xingtan Pavilion** up from that commemorates the spot where Confucius is said to have taught under the shade of an apricot tree.

The core of the Confucian complex is **Dacheng Hall**, towering 31 metres on a white marble terrace. The reigning sovereign permitted the importation of glazed yellow tiling for the halls in the Kong Miao, and special stones were brought in from Xishan. The craftspeople did such a good job on the stone dragon-coiled columns that it is said they had to be covered with silk when the emperor came to Qufu lest he felt the Forbidden City's Taihe Hall paled in comparison. The present incarnation of Dacheng Hall dates to 1724. The hall was used for unusual rites in honour of Confucius. At the beginning of the seasons and on the great sage's birthday, booming drums, bronze bells and musical stones sounded from the hall as dozens of officials in silk robes engaged in 'dignified dancing' and chanting by torchlight. The rare collection of musical instruments is on view, but the massive stone statue of the bearded philosopher has disappeared – presumably a casualty of the Red Guards.

To the extreme north end of the Kong Miao is **Shengjidian**, a memorial hall containing a series of stones engraved with scenes from the life of Confucius and tales about him. They are copies of an older set which date to 1592. In the eastern compound of the Confucian Temple, behind the Hall of Poetry and Rites, is Confucius' well (a Song/Ming reconstruction) and the Lu Wall where the ninth descendant of Confucius hid the sacred texts during the anti-Confucian persecutions of Emperor Qin Shihuang. The books were discovered again in the Han Dynasty (206 BC-220 AD) and led to a lengthy scholastic dispute between the scholars who escaped and remembered the books, and those who supported the teachings in the rediscovered books.

Confucius Mansions (Kong Fu)

Built and rebuilt many times, the Mansions presently date from the Ming Dynasty (16th century), with recent patchwork. The place is a maze of 450 halls, rooms and buildings, and getting around it all requires a compass. There are all kinds of side passages to which servants were once restricted.

The Mansions are the most sumptuous aristocratic lodgings in China, indicative of the Kong family's great power at one time. From the Han through the Qing dynasties, Confucius' descendants were ennobled and granted privileges by the emperors. They lived like kings themselves, with 180-course meals, servants and consorts. Confucius even picked up some posthumous honours.

The town of Qufu, which grew around the Mansions, was an autonomous estate administered by the Kongs, who had powers of taxation and execution. Emperors could drop in to visit – the Ceremonial Gate near the south entrance was only opened for this event. Because of royal protection, copious quantities of furniture, ceramics, artefacts, costumery and personal effects survived and some may be viewed. The Kong family archives, a rich legacy, also seem to have survived, and extensive renovations of the complex have been made.

The Mansions are built on an 'interrupted' north-south axis. Grouped by the south gate are the former **administrative offices** (taxes, edicts, rites, registration, examination halls). To the north on the axis is a special gate **Neizhaimen** that seals off the residential quarters (used for weddings, banquets, private functions). East of Neizhaimen is the **Tower of Refuge** where the Kong clan could gather in case the peasants turned nasty. It has an iron-lined ceiling on the ground floor, and a staircase that is removable to the 1st floor. Grouped to the west of the main axis are former recreational facilities (studies, guest rooms, libraries, small temples). To the east is the odd kitchen, ancestral temple and the family branch apartments. Far north is a spacious garden with rockeries, ponds and bamboo groves. Kong Decheng, the last of the line, lived in the Mansions until the 1940s when he hightailed it to Taiwan.

Kong Lin (Confucian Forest)

North of Confucius Mansions, about 2½ km up Drum Tower Rd, is the Confucian Forest, the largest artificial park and best preserved cemetery in China. A timeworn route, it has a kind of 'spirit-way' lined with ancient cypresses.

The walk takes about 40 minutes, 10 minutes by auto-rickshaw. On the way, look into the **Yanmiao Temple** off to the right which has a spectacular dragon head embedded in the ceiling of the main hall, and a pottery collection. The route to the forest passes through the **Archway of Eternal Spring**, its stone lintels decorated with coiled dragons, flying phoenixes and galloping horses (Ming, 1594).

At the **Forest Gates** visitors had to dismount and permission was required to enter. The forest covers 200 hectares and is bounded by a wall 10 km long. Buried here is the Great Sage himself and all his descendants. The trees, numbering over 20,000, are pines and cypresses planted by followers of Confucius. Flanking the approach to **Confucius' Tomb** are a pair of stone panthers, griffins and larger-than-life guardians. The Confucian tumulus is a simple grass mound enclosed by a low wall, and faced with a Ming Dynasty stele. Nearby are buried his immediate sons. Scattered through the forest are dozens of temples and pavilions, and hundreds of sculptures, tablets and tombstones.

Places to Stay & Eat

Stay at the *Confucius Mansions Hotel* No 1, Dong Hua Men Dajie, in Confucius Mansions itself. Not often will you get to reside in such labyrinthine splendour. For genuine classical architecture, this is the finest hotel in China and all things considered, is reasonably cheap to boot. There are no TVs (not yet anyway!) and the rooms are comfortable and have bathrooms. Doubles are Y40, but if you're on your own they'll probably give you a room for Y20. Cheaper beds are possible; they seem to have some dormitory accommodation.

The Confucius Mansions dining hall, at the rear of the hotel, is reasonably cheap with largish servings. There are several restaurants along the main street with pretty good food.

The new up-market *Queli Hotel* No 1 Zhing Lu Jie, is now open but I'll still stick with Confucius Mansions.

Shopping

In the Confucius Temple there are some free-marketeers who do intricate personalised carving on chops and ballpoint pens while you wait. The ballpoint pen engraving, done with a kind of gold leaf, can be ordered in dragon designs; with the name of a friend added it makes an excellent gift. These vendors will do a chop with an English name that the top shops in Shanghai refuse to do (because it's not 'art'). The Friendship Store is also in the Confucius Temple and sells stele-rubbings for calligraphy lovers.

Getting There & Away

Bus There are about a dozen Qufu to Yanzhou buses a day. The first bus to Yanzhou departs Qufu at 6 am. The last bus to Yanzhou departs at 5.40 pm with a possible bus at 6.30 pm. The fare is around Y0.50 and the trip takes about 30 minutes. The last bus from Yanzhou to Qufu leaves at about 5 pm.

There are direct buses from Qufu to Tainan (two hours, Y3, about four departures a day) and direct buses from Qufu to Jinan (about two departures a day).

Privately run minibuses leave from just west of Qufu's long-distance bus station, and from outside Yanzhou railway station. You may be able to get from Yanzhou to Qufu on one of these even after the ordinary buses have stopped running. The fare is Y0.80 and they go when they're full.

Rail There's no direct railway to Qufu. When the question of a railway station project at Qufu was first brought up, the Kong family petitioned for a change of routes, claiming that the trains would disturb the Great Sage's tomb. They won in the end – the clan still had pull in those days – and the nearest the tracks go is Yanzhou, 13 km to the west of Qufu. The railway builders haven't given up and the next in line to disturb the sage's tomb is CAAC, with an airport planned at Qufu.

Yanzhou is on the Beijing to Shanghai line with a fair selection of trains, but note that some special express trains don't stop at Yanzhou and others arrive at inconvenient times (like midnight). Yanzhou is two hours by train from Tainan, three hours from Jinan, about seven hours from Nanjing, and about nine hours from Kaifeng.

If you get stuck in Yanzhou on your way to Qufu then this is your big chance to stay in a Chinese hotel. The *Yanzhou Hotel* is near the train station. They'll probably start off quoting prices around Y12 but you can get that down to Y5 or less per bed. Not even the mirrors work here – bare bulbs dangle from the ceiling, towels are all over the furniture, there's washing up and down the corridors, and no curtains. Follow your nose to the washroom. You can cook your own food downstairs out the back. There are one or two other Chinese hotels of about equal standard. Zero items of interest in Yanzhou, though perhaps that's reason enough for some to go there!

Leaving Qufu is less of a problem. Check the rail timetable at the CITS office in Qufu.

AROUND QUFU

Four km east of Qufu is the **Mausoleum of Shao Hao**, one of the five legendary emperors supposed to have ruled China 4000 years ago. The pyramidal tomb dates from the Song Dynasty and is made of large blocks of stone, 25 metres wide at the base, six metres high, with a small temple on top.

To the south of Qufu, a short hop on the rail line from Yanzhou, is **Zouxian**, the home town of Mencius. Mencius (372-289 BC) is regarded as the first great Confucian philosopher. He developed many of the ideas of 'Confucianism' as they were later understood.

Hebei 河北

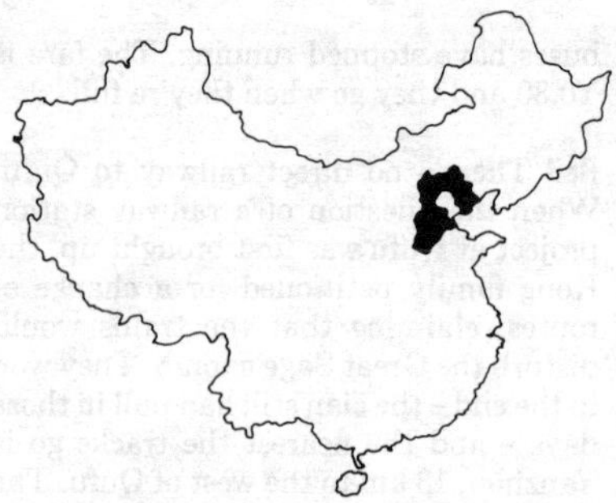

Wrapping itself around the centrally administered municipalities of Beijing and Tianjin is the province of Hebei. The province is often viewed as an extension of Beijing, the red tape maker or Tianjin, the industrial giant. This is not far off the mark since geographically speaking, they take up a fair piece of the pie anyway. In fact, Tianjin used to be Hebei's provincial capital, but when that came under central government administration the next largest city, Shijiazhuang, replaced it. The population of Hebei is over 53 million.

The relief map of Hebei falls into two distinct parts – the mountain tableland to the north, where the Great Wall runs (and also to the western fringes of the province), and the monotonous southern plain. Agriculture, mainly wheat and cotton, is hampered by dust storms, droughts (five years in a row from 1972-1977) and flooding – which will give you some idea of the weather. It's scorching and humid in summer, freezing in winter, there's dust fallout in spring and heavy rainfall in July and August. Coal is the main resource and most of it is shipped through Qinhuangdao, an ugly port town with iron and steel and machine industries secondary.

As far as tourist sights go the pickings in Hebei are slim, and if I were you, I'd make a wide detour around the capital, Shijiazhuang. Down that way also is Handan, an industrial city and one of the oldest in Hebei with an iron and steel plant, coal mining, textiles, a fair number of historical sites, production of imitation Song Dynasty glazed pottery and porcelain.

On the other hand, there's still Beidaihe, the weirdest summer resort you'll ever visit, and Chengde with its remaining palaces and temples. There's also Tangshan, the city that disappeared in a few minutes when an earthquake registering eight on the Richter scale struck it on 28 July 1976. The big attraction here is going to be the casting section of a rolling stock plant, with rusted equipment and rubble of walls and steel. Officials in Tangshan say there are no plans to clear it up – rather, it will be left for future generations to ponder.

Apart from all these, the greatest thing to see is the Wanli Changcheng, the Great Wall, which makes everything else look insignificant. While the rest of Hebei may not paint much of a pretty picture, the wall makes it all worthwhile.

CHENGDE 承德

Chengde is an 18th-century imperial resort area, also known as 'Jehol'. It's billed as an escape from the heat (and now the traffic) of summers in the capital and boasts the remnants of the largest regal gardens in China.

Chengde remained an obscure town until 1703, when Emperor Kangxi began building a summer palace here, with a throne room and the full range of court trappings. More than a home away from home, Chengde turned into a sort of government seat, since where the emperor went, his seat went too. Kangxi called his summer creation Bihushanzhuang (Fleeing-the-Heat Mountain Hamlet).

By 1790, in the reign of his grandson Qianlong, it had grown to the size of Beijing's Summer Palace and Forbidden City combined: a vast park bounded by a 10 km wall. Qianlong extended an idea started by Kangxi, to build replicas of

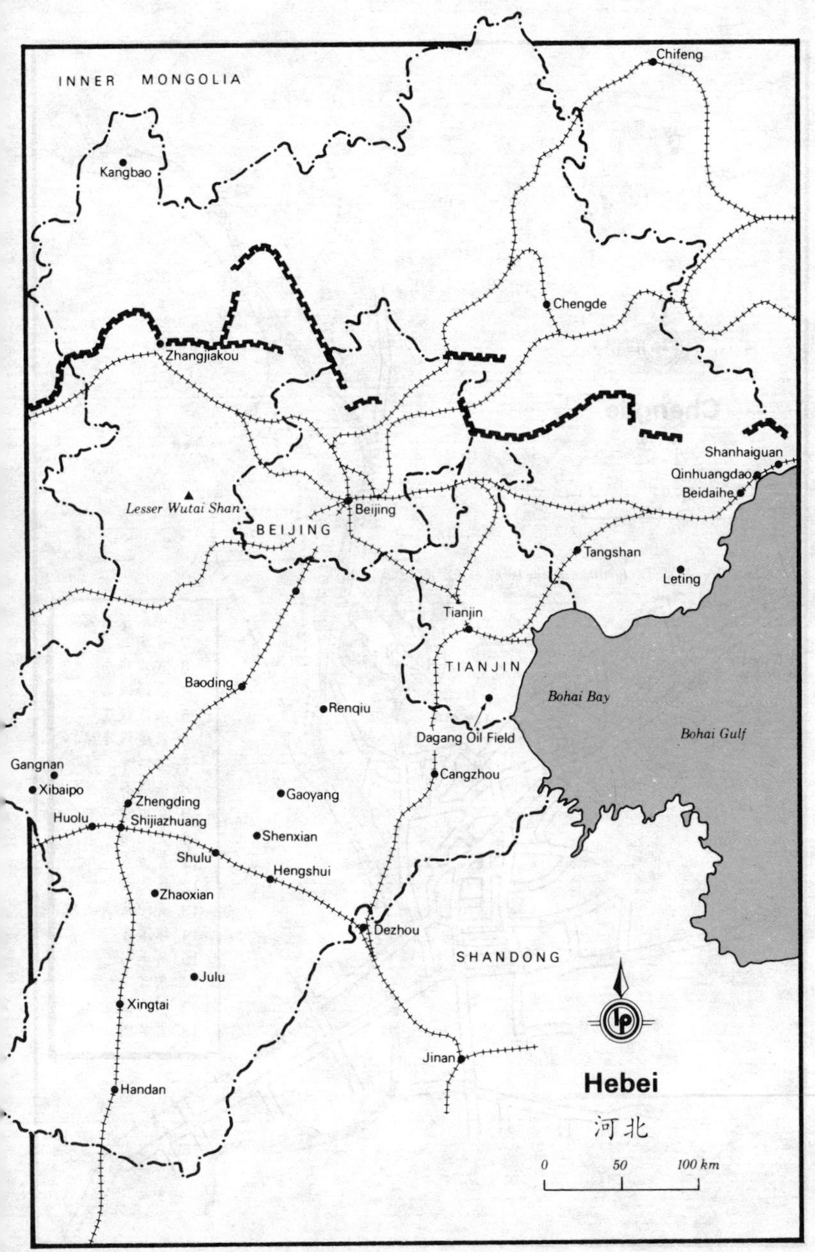

INNER MONGOLIA
Chifeng
Kangbao
Chengde
Zhangjiakou
Lesser Wutai Shan
Beijing
BEIJING
Shanhaiguan
Qinhuangdao
Beidaihe
Tangshan
Leting
Tianjin
TIANJIN
Bohai Bay
Bohai Gulf
Baoding
Renqiu
Dagang Oil Field
Gangnan
Xibaipo
Cangzhou
Zhengding
Gaoyang
Huolu
Shijiazhuang
Shenxian
Shulu
Hengshui
Zhaoxian
Dezhou
SHANDONG
Julu
Xingtai
Jinan
Handan
Hebei
河北
0
50
100 km

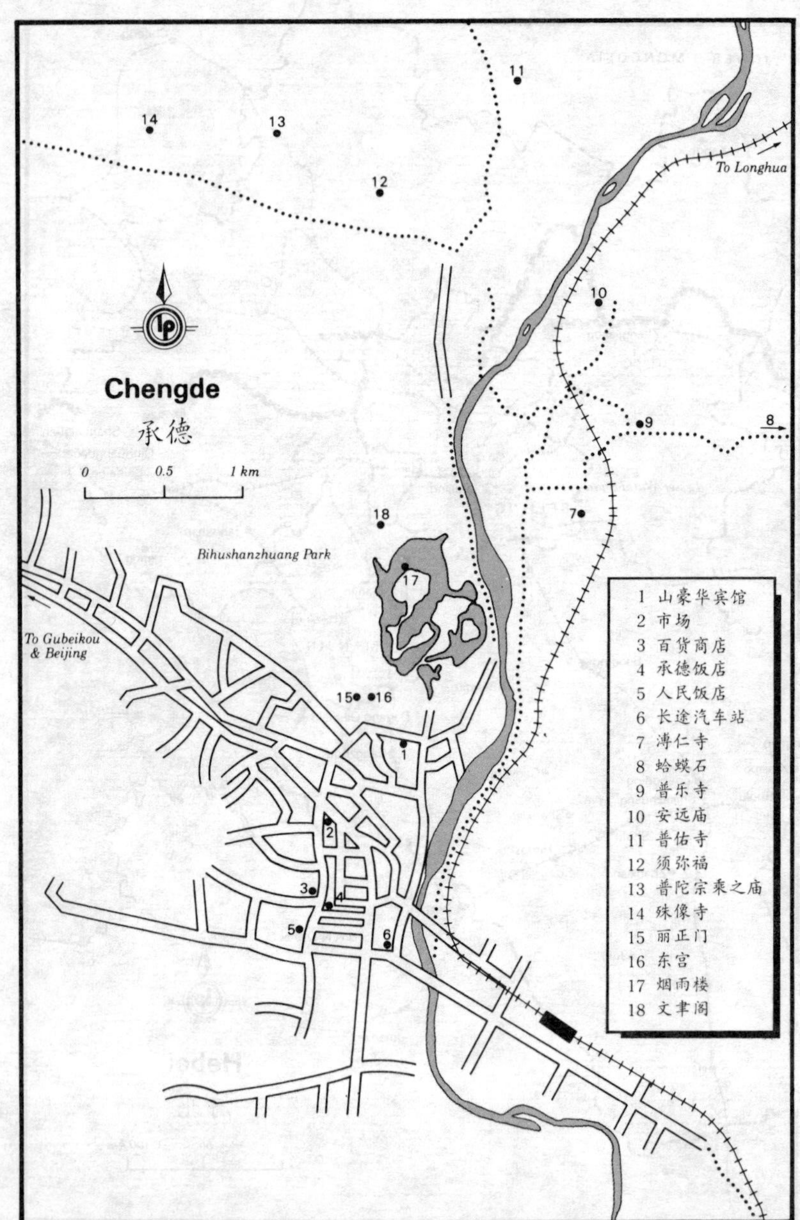
Chengde
承德
0
0.5
1 km
To Longhua
8
Bihushanzhuang Park
To Gubeikou & Beijing
1 山豪华宾馆
2 市场
3 百货商店
4 承德饭店
5 人民饭店
6 长途汽车站
7 溥仁寺
8 蛤蟆石
9 普乐寺
10 安远庙
11 普佑寺
12 须弥福
13 普陀宗乘之庙
14 殊像寺
15 丽正门
16 东宫
17 烟雨楼
18 文聿阁

1 Mountain Villa Hotel
2 Outdoor Markets
3 Chengde Department Store
4 Chengde Hotel
5 Renmin Restaurant
6 Long-distance Bus Station
7 Puren (Universal Love) Temple
8 Hammer Rock
9 Pule (Universal Joy) Temple
10 Anyuan (Distant Tranquillity) Temple
11 Puning (Universal Peace) Temple
12 Xumifushou (Mount Sumeru) Temple
13 Putuozhongsheng (Potala) Temple
14 Shuxiang (Wenshu Image) Temple
15 Lizhengmen (Main Gate)
16 Front Palace
17 Misty Rain Tower
18 Wenjin Chamber

minority architecture in order to make envoys feel comfortable. In particular he was keen on promoting Tibetan and Mongolian Lamaism, which had proved to be a useful way of debilitating the meddlesome Mongols. The Mongolian branch of Lamaism required one male in every family to become a monk – a convenient method of channelling manpower and ruining the Mongol economy. This serves to explain the Tibetan and Mongolian features of the monasteries north of the summer palace, one of them a replica of the Potala Palace in Lhasa.

So much for business – the rest was the emperor's pleasure: the usual bouts of hunting, consorts and feasting. Occasionally the outer world would make a rude intrusion into this dream-life. In 1793 British emissary Lord Macartney came along, seeking to open the China trade. Qianlong dismissed him with the statement that China possessed all things and had no need of trade.

Chengde has very much slipped back into the provincial town it once was, its grandeur long decayed, its monks and emperors long gone. The population, over 150,000, is engaged in mining, textiles, light industry, canned food and tourism. The Qing court has left them a little legacy, but one that needs working on. The palaces and monasteries are not what they're cracked up to be, or, alternatively, more cracked up than you'd expect them to be. The Buddhist statues are disfigured, on occasion beyond recognition, or else locked up in dark corners; windows are bricked up; columns are reduced to stumps and the temples are façades, impressive from the outside but shells inside.

All this is currently being restored, in some cases from the base up, in the interests of a projected increase in tourism. On the cards are the addition of Chinese and western restaurants, high-class shops, evenings of traditional music (with instruments rescued and copied from tombs around China) and horseback riding. Meanwhile there's absolutely nothing wrong with ruins – just a matter of changing your expectations. Chengde has nothing remotely approaching Beijing's temples in case you were expecting something along those lines. Chinese photography of the place is more a tribute to the skills of the photographers and lab technicians than anything else.

The dusty, small town ambience of Chengde is nice enough; there's some quiet hiking in the rolling countryside. Chinese-speakers are apparently delighted with the clarity of the local dialect (maybe because they can actually hear it in the absence of traffic).

Information

Good maps of Chengde are available from the counter in the waiting hall of the train station.

Bihushanzhuang

This park is 590 hectares, bounded by a 10 km wall. Emperor Kangxi decreed that there would be 36 'beauty spots' in Jehol; Qianlong delineated 36 more. That makes a total of 72, but where are they? At the north end of the gardens the pavilions were decimated by warlords and Japanese invaders, and even the forests have suffered cutbacks. The park is on the dull side, not much in the way of upkeep. With a good deal of imagination, you can perhaps detect traces of the original scheme of things with landscaping borrowed from the southern gardens of Suzhou, Hangzhou and Jiaxing, and from the Mongolian grasslands. There is even a feature for resurrecting the moon should it not be around – a pool shows a crescent moon created by reflection of a hole in surrounding rocks.

Passing through Lizhengmen, the main gate, you arrive at the Front Palace, a modest version of Beijing's palace. It contains the main throne hall, the Hall of Simplicity and Sincerity, built of an aromatic hardwood called *nanmu*. The hall now functions as a museum, with displays of royal memorabilia, arms, clothing and other accoutrements. The emperor's bedrooms are fully furnished. Around to the side is a door without an exterior handle, through which the lucky bed partner for the night was ushered and stripped and searched by eunuchs.

The double-storeyed Misty Rain Tower, on the north-west side of the main lake, was an imperial study. Further north of that is the Wenjin Chamber, built in 1773 to house a copy of the *Sikuquanshu*, a major anthology of classics, history, philosophy and literature commissioned by Qianlong. The anthology took 10 years to put together. Four copies were made but three have disappeared; the fourth is in Beijing.

Ninety per cent of the compound is taken up by lakes, hills, mini-forests and plains, with the odd vantage point pavilion. At the northern part of the park the emperors reviewed displays of archery, horsemanship and fireworks. Horses were also chosen and tested here before hunting sorties. Yurts were set up on the mock-Mongolian prairies (a throne, of course, installed in the emperor's yurt) and picnics were held for minority princes. So, a good idea is to pack a lunch, take your tent and head off for the day . . . the yurts are back again for the benefit of weary tourists.

Waibamiao (Outer Temples)

To the north and north-east of the imperial garden are former temples and monasteries. So how many are there? The count started off at 11 many years ago, plummeted to five (Japanese bombers, Cultural Revolution), and now the numbers given vary from five to nine. I make it five, after some heavy socialist reconstruction. The outer temples are about three to five km from the garden's front gate; a bus No 6 taken to the north-east corner will land you in the vicinity.

The surviving temples were built between 1750 and 1780. The Chinese-style Purensi and the vaguely Shanxi-style Shuxiangsi have undergone total rebuilding. Get out there in the early morning when the air is crisp and cool and the sun is shining on the front of the temples – that's the best time to take photos. Clockwise, these are the temples:

Putuozongsheng

The largest of the Chengde temples, this is a mini-facsimile of Lhasa's Potala. It was built for the chieftains from Xinjiang, Qinghai, Mongolia and Tibet to celebrate Qianlong's 60th birthday and was also a site for religious assemblies. It's a solid looking fortress, but has no guts and is in bad shape – parts are inaccessible or boarded up and gutted by fire. Notice the stone column in the courtyard inscribed in Chinese, Tibetan, Mongolian and Manchurian scripts.

Xumifushou

This was built in honour of the sixth Panchen Lama, who visited in 1781 and stayed here. It incorporates elements of Tibetan and Han architecture and is an imitation of a temple in Xigaze, Tibet. At the highest point is a hall with eight gilded copper dragons commanding the roof ridges, and behind that sits a glazed tile pagoda.

Puning
Puning is also modelled on a Tibetan temple. It was built to commemorate Qianlong's victory over Mongol tribes, when the subjugated leaders were invited to Chengde. A stele relating the victory is inscribed in Tibetan, Mongol, Chinese and Manchu. The main feature is an Avalokitesvara, towering 22 metres; this wooden Buddha has 42 arms with an eye on each palm. The temple appears to be used as an active place of worship.

Anyuan
Only the main hall is left. This copy of a Xinjiang temple contains Buddhist frescoes in a very sad state.

Pule
Pule is the most interesting temple, you can scramble along the banks of the nearby rivulet to a road that leads off near a pagoda at the garden wall. The temple was built in 1776 for visits of minority envoys (Kazaks among them). It's in much better shape than the other temples and has been retiled and repainted. At the rear of the temple is an unusual Round Pavilion, reminiscent of Beijing's Temple of Heaven, which has a magnificent ceiling.

Other Attractions
From Pule you can hike up to Hammer-Head. Nothing to do with sharks – the rock is meant to resemble an upside-down hammer. Commanding views of the area from here. Other scenic rocks to add to your collection include Toad Rock and Monk's Hat Hill. Hiking is good.

Places to Stay
The *Chengde Hotel* on Nanyingzi Dajie has comfortable double rooms for Y40 without bathroom, and Y60 with bathroom. A bed in a three-bed room in the Chinese wing is around Y7 – spartan but habitable. Bus No 7 from the train station drops you right outside the hotel. It's a half-hour walk if you arrive after the bus has stopped running. The hotel has two restaurants; the Chinese restaurant is likely to be cheaper than the foreigners' retreat.

Some travellers have stayed at the *Xinhua Hotel*, south of the Chengde Hotel, which has double rooms with bath for Y9.

Alternatively there's the *Mountain Villa Hotel* where some western tour groups are put up. Doubles are Y75. If you're on your own you may manage a room for half that price. The rooms are comfy with TV and private bathroom. Take bus No 7 from the train station and then a short walk; the hotel is opposite the entrance to Bihushanzhuang.

Places to Eat
There are small restaurants around town where you can get huge meals cheaply. The local speciality is food made from hawthorn fruit (wine, ice cream, sweets). An interesting early morning market by an old bridge on the main drag has side stalls dispensing Chinese breakfasts. Chengde Pule beer has an interesting flavour – perhaps it's the mountain water. Lots of trolleys around town dispensing baked turnip, very tasty.

Getting There & Away
The regular approach to Chengde is by train from Beijing. The slow trains from Beijing to Chengde take about seven hours and have two classes: hard-seat, which means wooden seats; and soft-seat, which means vinyl padded seats like you get in normal 'hard-seat' carriages. You're advised to choose soft-seat, particularly if you're taking a night train! The fastest trains to Beijing take about five hours.

An unexplored route to or from Chengde is the train from Jinzhou, which is in Liaoning Province on the way to Shenyang. There are also trains direct from Chengde to Dandong, via Jinzhou and Shenyang; sleepers are available though the train originates in Beijing.

From Longhua, about 40 km north of Chengde, there is an evening fast train to Datong (Shanxi Province) and Hohhot

(Inner Mongolia), with a brief stop at Xizhimen Station in Beijing. Sleepers are available. To get to Longhua from Chengde, there are several slow trains a day.

There are also long-distance buses between Chengde and Beijing. The airport at Chengde is used by CITS charter flights and there is no regular passenger service.

Getting Around
There are half a dozen bus lines but the only ones you'll need to use are the No 7 from the station to the Chengde Hotel, and No 6 to the outer temples grouped at the north-east end of town. The best way to get around town and to the outer temples is on a bicycle; there is a rental place opposite the Chengde Hotel which charges Y4 per day and asks you to leave some I.D. Motorised pedicabs and auto-rickshaws congregate outside the train station.

BEIDAIHE-QINHUANGDAO-SHANHAIGUAN

北戴河一秦皇岛一山海关

The Beidaihe-Qinhuangdao-Shanhaiguan district is a 35-km stretch of coastline on China's east coast, bordering the Bohai Gulf.

Getting There

Rail The three stations of Beidaihe, Qinhuangdao and Shanhaiguan are accessible by train from Beijing, Tianjin or Shenyang. The trains are frequent but don't always stop at all three stations, nor do they always arrive at convenient hours. The usual stop is Shanhaiguan; several skip Beidaihe.

The major factor to consider is that the hotel at Shanhaiguan is within walking distance of the train station, whereas at Beidaihe the nearest hotel is at least 10 km from the station – you can't count on a connecting bus after 6 pm, and a taxi could be quite expensive. So if you're going to arrive in the early hours of the morning it's better to do so at Shanhaiguan.

The fastest trains take five hours to make

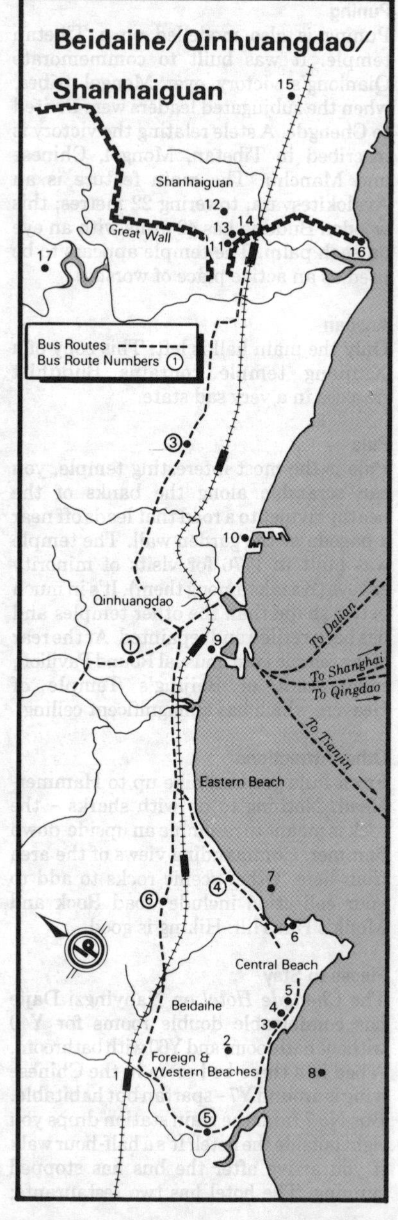

1 Beidaihe Railway Station
2 Liangfeng Park/ Sea Facing Pavilion
3 Central Beach (Zhonghaitau) Hotel
4 Bus Terminus/Free Market Area
5 Broadcasting Tower
6 Pigeon's Nest
7 Eagle Pavilion
8 Tiger Rocks
9 Seamen's Club & Hotel
10 Oil Wharf
11 Great Wall Museum
12 'First Pass Under Heaven'
13 Great Wall Souvenir Shops
14 Trade Service Hotel
15 Jiangnu Temple
16 Old Dragon Head (where the Great Wall meets the sea)
17 Yansai Lake

1	北戴河火车站	10	油码头
2	莲蓬山公园	11	文物保管所
3	中海滩宾馆	12	天下第一关
4	汽车终点	13	旅游纪念品服务部
5	广播楼	14	商业饭店
6	鸽子窝	15	孟姜庙
7	鹰角亭	16	老龙头
8	老虎石	17	燕塞湖
9	海员俱乐部		

it to Beidaihe from Beijing, and an extra 1½ hours to Shanhaiguan. From Shenyang (Liaoning Province) to Shanhaiguan is a five-hour trip.

Alternatively, you could get a train that stops at Qinhuangdao and then take a bus from there to Beidaihe. Or you could jump a midnight train from either Beijing or Shenyang, arrive early in the morning, day-trip, and go on to the next place.

One rail route to consider is the connection from the city of Jinzhou to Chengde. The resorts of Chengde and Beidaihe are usually considered separate round trips from Beijing. However, by going through Jinzhou, which lies between Shanhaiguan and Shenyang, it might be possible to do an all embracing round trip.

Boat There are some dubious maritime links between Qinhuangdao and Dalian, Shanghai, Qingdao and Tianjin, but it's unclear whether these are freight or passenger boats. If they are passenger then the journey will be cheaper than rail, and in the case of Dalian the trip could also be shorter.

Getting Around

Buses connect Beidaihe, Shanhaiguan and Qinhuangdao. These run from around 6 or 6.30 am to around 6.30 pm (not guaranteed after 6 pm), generally every 30 minutes. Some of the important routes are:

No 5
Beidaihe Train Station to Beidaihe Middle Beach, 30 minutes.

No 3-4
Beidaihe to Qinhuangdao, 45 minutes.

No 3-4
Beidaihe to Shanhaiguan via Qinhuangdao, one hour.

There are also minivans from Beidaihe train station to Beidaihe town and possibly to Qinhuangdao and Shanhaiguan. These may run later than the ordinary buses.

BEIDAIHE 北戴河

This seaside resort, opened to foreigners in 1979, was in fact originally built by westerners. The simple fishing village was transformed when English railway engineers stumbled across it in the 1890s. Diplomats, missionaries and businessmen from the Tianjin concessions and the Beijing Legations set about throwing up villas and cottages to indulge in the new fad of bathing.

The original golf courses, bars and cabarets have disappeared, though in the interests of the nouveau bourgeoisie, there are signs that these will be revived. An article a few years ago in the *People's Daily* suggested: 'It does much good to both body and mind to putt and walk under fresh air'.

What is more desperately needed than

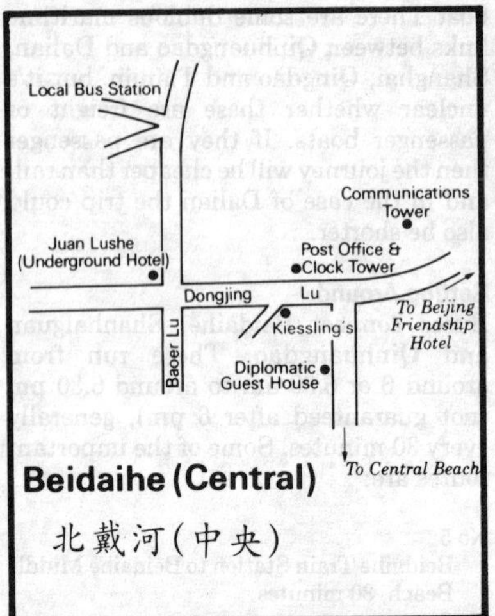

a golf course is a coat of paint since the architecture is monumentally drab. Something jars, though the setting is right enough – hills, rocks, beaches, pine forests, a sort of Mediterranean flavour. The buildings appear too heavy to the modern eye, and lacking in glass.

But really, who gives a damn about the architecture? Then, as now, Beidaihe is an escape from the hassles of Beijing or Tianjin. Kiesslings, the former Austrian restaurant, sells excellent pastries and seafood in the summer. The cream of China's leaders congregate at the summer villas, also continuing a tradition; Jiang Qing and Lin Biao had villas here, and Deng Xiaoping is said to have a heavily guarded residence.

Just to make sure nothing nasty comes by in the water, there are shark nets. It's questionable whether sharks live at this latitude – maybe they're submarine nets. Army members and working heroes are rewarded with two-week vacations at Beidaihe. There are large numbers of sanatoriums where patients can get away from the noise of the city, and, more importantly, can breathe some fresh air.

That's about all you need to know about Beidaihe. The Chinese have worked the place over trying to categorise the rocks and deciding whether they're shaped like camels or tigers or steamed bread, or immortalising the rocks where Mao sat and wrote lines about fishing boats disappearing. Nobody gives a hoot – they come for the beaches. For the Chinese that could mean indulging in the new fad of bathing all over again, and bare thighs are in style.

Climate

The village only comes to life in the summer (June to September) when it's warm and fanned by sea breezes; the beaches are jammed. Average June temperature is 21°C (70°F). In January, by contrast, temperatures rest at –5°C (23°F).

Beaches

There are three beaches at Beidaihe: the West Beach, Middle Beach and East Beach. Rank and ethnic divisions once applied to the use of these beaches, with the West Beach reserved for foreigners, the Middle Beach for Chinese cadres and the like, and the East Beach for sanatorium patients, but this system appears to have been abandoned.

Other Attractions

There's various hikes to vantage points with expansive views of villas or seaside, notably the pavilion at Lotus Rock Park. For early morning strollers the tide at the East Beach recedes dramatically and tribes of kelp collectors and shell-pickers descend upon it. In the high season you can even be photographed in amusing cardboard cut-out racing boats, with the sea as a backdrop. There may be some nightlife at the Diplomatic Guest House. The free market behind the bus terminus has the most amusing high kitsch collection of sculpted and glued shellwork this side of Dalian – go see. Handicrafts such as raffia and basketware are on sale in the stores. Some of these shops sell good maps of the Beidaihe/Shanhaiguan/Qinhuangdao area.

Places to Stay

The best place to stay is the *Diplomatic Guest House*. You don't need to be a diplomat to stay here, and the place caters for both up-market and budget visitors. Dormitory beds are Y10; double rooms start at Y30 (Y39 on weekends). The place has the appearance and the feel of an Indian Tourist Bungalow – all you'd need is the *dhobi* man to come knocking. It's situated in a very quiet compound with a pleasant garden. Hard-seat train tickets can be booked at the guest house; they need two days' notice. Their bus will take you to Beidaihe train station.

Up-market there's the spic-and-span *Jinshan Hotel* on the shorefront on Donghaitan Lu, which is a continuation of Zhonghaitan Lu. At the time of writing this place was still being built but it's going to be a glossy tourist joint.

Opposite the bus station (out the gate and turn right) is a relatively new Chinese hotel which may put you up. It asks only Y8 for a bed in a four-bed room. Very clean but lacks the ambience of the Diplomatic Guest House, which is one of the reasons for coming to Beidaihe in the first place.

At the corner of Baoer Lu and Dongjing Lu in the middle of Beidaihe is the *Juan Lushe*, an underground hotel – a bizarre pavilion marks the spot. Clean and tidy. Beds are Y4 per person. No ocean views.

Places to Eat

In season, seafood is dished up in the restaurants. There's the *Beihai Fandian* near the markets and the *Haibin Fandian* near the Bank of China (Broadcasting Tower area). Near the Haibin is *Kiesslings*, which is a relative of the Tianjin branch and only operates June to August. You can haggle for crabs in the markets, then take them over to Kiesslings for crab au gratin. There are other restaurants inside the hotels, as well as a couple of ice cream parlours scattered about. With so much seasonal variation in what's open and closed the best thing to do is just look around and see what's cooking.

Getting Around

There are a couple of short-run buses in Beidaihe, such as from the centre of town to Pigeon's Nest (summer only). Much of Beidaihe is small enough to walk around.

Unlike the buses in Shanhaiguan and Qinhuangdao, the buses in Beidaihe don't connect around the train station. Take bus No 5 from Beidaihe train station to Beidaihe beach. It's a half-hour trip and the bus puts you off within a short walk of the Middle Beach and the Diplomatic Guest House before carrying on to the bus terminal. There are minivans from outside the train station to Beidaihe; these may run later than the ordinary buses.

There are a couple of bicycle rentals around town; look for rows of bikes. They'll charge about Y2 per day, and you'll probably have to leave some identification.

QINHUANGDAO 秦皇岛

Qinhuangdao is an ugly port city that you'd have to squeeze pretty hard for signs of life, and even harder if you wanted to see something. It has an ice-free harbour, and petroleum is piped in from the Daqing oilfields to the wharves.

Pollution on both land and sea is incredible – like the chemical fumes from the glass factory. This is *not* the place to visit. The locals will be the first to suggest that you move along to Beidaihe or Shanhaiguan.

If you do get stuck here most needs are catered for on a bus No 2 route from the train station. This runs the short distance to the port area where the Seamen's Club has a hotel, restaurant (some seafood) and bar/store. The Seamen's Club is only a 15-minute walk from the station if you can't nail a bus No 2.

SHANHAIGUAN 山海关

Shanhaiguan is where the Great Wall

1 Bus Station
2 East Gate
3 Shanhaiguan Trade Service Hotel
4 Train Station
5 Beilu (North St) Hotel

meets the sea, or, should we say, crumbles into it. The wall, what's left of it, is in poor shape, but Shanhaiguan is well worth your time. It was a garrison town with a square fortress, four gates at the compass points, and two major avenues running between the gates. The present village is within the substantial remains of the old walled enclosure, making it a rather picturesque place to wander around. Shanhaiguan has a long and chequered history – nobody is quite sure how long or what kind of chequers. Plenty of pitched battles and blood, one imagines.

East Gate

The main attraction is the magnificent east gate, topped with a two storey, double-roofed tower (Ming Dynasty, rebuilt 1639). The calligraphy at the top (attributed to the scholar Xiao Xian) reads 'The First Pass Under Heaven'. The words reflect the Chinese custom of dividing the world into civilised China and the 'barbarians'. The barbarians got the better of civilised China when they stormed this gate in 1644. An intriguing mini-museum in the tower displays armour, dress, weaponry and pictures. A short section of the wall attached to the east gate has been rebricked; from this vantage point you can see decayed sections trailing off into the mountains. On top of the wall at the tower are souvenir shops selling First Pass Under Heaven handkerchiefs, and a parked horse waiting for photos. How about a pair of 'First Pass Under Heaven Wooden Chopsticks' or some 'Brave Lucky Jewellery'? Maps of Shanhaiguan are available from small shops in the vicinity of the East Gate.

Side Trips

A visit to the seaside to see Old Dragon Head (the legendary carved dragon head that once faced the sea) will end in disappointment. It's a four-km hike, and there's nothing much to see except a beach.

A more viable route is to follow the wall north (by road) to the first beacon tower. You can get part-way there by bicycle on a dirt road, and will pass a small village set in some pleasant countryside. Six km north-west of Shanhaiguan is Yansai Lake, an artificial reservoir 45 km long with tourist boating – give them a few years and they'll make a Guilin out of it yet.

Temple of Mengjiangnu

Six km east of Shanhaiguan (with regular bus service from the south gate) is the Temple of Mengjiangnu, a Song/Ming reconstruction. It has coloured sculptures of Lady Meng and her maids, and calligraphy on 'Looking for Husband Rock'. Meng's husband, Wan, was press-ganged into wall building because his views conflicted with those of Emperor Qin Shihuang. The beautiful Meng Jiang set off to take her husband warm clothing when winter came, only to discover that he had died from the backbreaking labour. Meng tearfully wandered the Great Wall, thinking only of finding the bones to give Wan a decent burial but the wall, obviously a sensitive soul, was so upset that it collapsed, revealing the skeleton entombed within. Overcome with grief, Meng hurled herself into the sea from a conveniently placed boulder.

Places to Stay & Eat

Near the train station is the *Shanhaiguan Trade Service Hotel*, a TV-type hotel. Your chances of getting a room here are slim; I found the staff mean and nasty.

The best place to stay is the *Beilu (North St) Hotel*, which has doubles for Y49, or a bed in a four-bed room for Y14. The spacious rooms come with fans and private bathroom. The hotel is built within the confines of what appears to have once been an old Chinese mansion; very quiet, pleasant courtyard gardens and friendly staff.

There are lots of small restaurants and snack places around the East Gate. Five people can feast on a large meal, including bottles of beer all round, for as little as Y14.

SHIJIAZHUANG 石家庄

The odd town out in Hebei, even though it is the capital of the province, Shijiazhuang is a rail junction town about 250 km south-west of Beijing. The population is approaching one million but at the turn of the century it was just a small village with a population of 500 and a handful of buildings. With the construction of the Beijing to Wuhan Line in 1905 (financed by a Belgian company) and the Shijiazhuang to Taiyuan Line which was finished in 1907 (a Russian/French project), the town rapidly expanded to a population of 10,000 in the 1920s.

Shijiazhuang serves as the centre of Hebei cotton production, and is a major producer of textiles, machinery (cars, diesel engines, mining equipment), petrochemicals and electronics equipment. It has the largest pharmaceutical plant in north China. The plains around it are used for the cultivation of wheat and cotton. To the west of the city, in the Taihang mountains, is a mining area for coal, iron ore and limestone.

Perhaps this is why this boring sprawl of railway lines and factories is euphemistically subtitled 'a developing city'. The tomb of Dr Norman Bethune is just about all there is to see in Shijiazhuang. Otherwise it's only useful as a transit point or a staging area to sights within the region.

Revolutionary Martyr's Mausoleum

The guerrilla doctor Norman Bethune (1890-1939) is interred here, together with a photo/drawing display depicting his life and works, and a white memorial. Bethune is the most famous *waigoren* in China since Marco Polo. Actually most Chinese don't know who Polo is, but they all know Bethune – or 'Baiqiuen' as pronounced in Chinese. He goes down in modern history as the man who fought alongside the Communists, serving as a surgeon with the Eighth Route Army in the war against

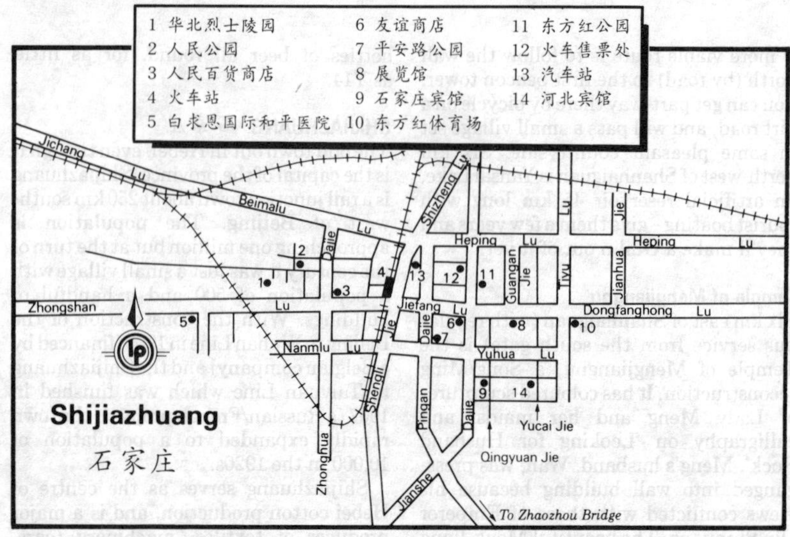

1 Cemetery of Revolutionary Martyrs
2 Renmin (People's) Park
3 Renmin Department Store
4 Railway Station
5 Bethune International Peace Hospital of the PLA
6 Friendship Store
7 Pingan Lu Park
8 Provincial Exhibition Hall
9 Shijiazhuang Guest House
10 Dongfanghong Stadium
11 Dongfanghong Park
12 Advance Railway Booking Office
13 Long-distance Bus Station
14 Hebei Guest House

Japan, having previously served with Communists in Spain against Franco and his Nazi allies. Bethune is eulogised in the reading of Mao Zedong thought: 'We must all learn the spirit of absolute selflessness from Dr Norman Bethune'.

'Bethune' is also synonymous with 'Canada' in China – it's about all they know about the country, and bringing up the name makes for instant friendship if you're Canadian.

There are more than 700 army cadres and heroes buried in the cemetery who died during the Resistance against Japan, the War of Liberation and the Korean War. The area is a large park and in the central alley of the cemetery is a pair of bronze lions from 1185 (Jin Dynasty). The Martyrs' Mausoleum is on Zhongshan Lu, west of the railway station. There is another Bethune statue in the courtyard of the Bethune International Peace Hospital of the PLA, a bit further west of the cemetery.

Zhengding

Ten km north of Shijiazhuang, the town of Zhengding has several temples and monasteries. Largest and oldest is the Longxing Monastery, noted for its huge, 20-metre-high bronze Buddha dating from the Song Dynasty almost 1000 years ago. The multi-armed statue is housed in the Temple of Great Mercy, an impressive structure with red and yellow galleries.

Zhaozhou Bridge

There's an old folk poem about the four wonders of Hebei which goes:

The Lion of Cangzhou
The Pagoda of Dingzhou
The Buddha of Zhengding
The Bridge of Zhaozhou

The bridge is in Zhaoxian County, about 40 km south-east of Shijiazhuang, two km south of Zhaoxian town. It has spanned the Jiao River for 1300 years and is possibly the oldest stone-arch bridge in China (another, believed older, has recently been unveiled in Linying County, Henan Province).

The Book of Records aside, the Zhaozhou Bridge is remarkable in that it still stands. It is 50 metres long and 9.6 metres wide, with a span of 37 metres; the balustrades are carved with dragons and mythical creatures. Credit for this daring piece of engineering is disputed. According to legend, the master mason Lu Ban constructed it overnight. The astounded immortals, refusing to believe this was possible, arrived to test the bridge. One immortal had a wagon, another a donkey, and they asked Lu Ban if it was possible for them both to cross at the same time. He nodded. Halfway across, the bridge started to shake and Lu Ban rushed into the water to stabilise it. This resulted in donkey-prints, wheel-prints and hand-prints being left on the bridge. Several more old stone bridges are to be found in Zhaoxian County.

Cangyan Shan

About 78 km south-west of Shijiazhuang is a scenic area of woods, valleys and steep cliffs dotted with pagodas and temples. The novelty here is a bizarre, double-roofed hall sitting on a stone arch bridge spanning a precipitous gorge. It is known as the Hanging Palace, and is reached by a 300-step stairway. The palace dates back to the Sui Dynasty. On the surrounding slopes are other ancient halls.

Xibaipo

In Pingshan County, 80 km north-west of Shijiazhuang, was the base from which Mao Zedong, Zhou Enlai and Zhu De directed the northern campaign against the Kuomintang from 1947 to 1948. The original site of Xibaipo Village was submerged by Gangnan Reservoir and the present village has been rebuilt close by. In 1977 a Revolutionary Memorial Museum was erected.

Places to Stay

The *Hebei Guest House* (tel 6351) is a modern eight storey block with a bar, restaurant and store. Bus No 6 will take you from the station to the south-east of the city – alight at Yucai Jie and walk five minutes south to the guest house. You can get any information you need there. A few blocks west of the Hebei Guest House on Qingyuan Jie is the *Shijiazhuang Guest House* (tel 45866), which is a possibility for lodgings.

Places to Eat

Shijiazhuang's main drag runs east-west just below the station. On the west side of the station it's Zhongshan Lu, on the east side it's Jiefang Lu, which merges into Dongfanghong Lu. There are some eateries along this strip – bland stuff. Bethune certainly had no effect on the level of hygiene in Shijiazhuang – the restaurants and snack bars in the station vicinity come straight from Dante's *Inferno* – thick layers of dirt on the tables, greasy disgusting food, and people filling the alleys waiting for train connections.

Getting There & Away

Shijiazhuang is a major rail hub with comprehensive connections: there are lines to Beijing (about four hours), Taiyuan (about five hours), Dezhou (about five hours) and Canton.

Getting Around

The long-distance bus station is within walking distance north-east of the rail station. From there you can get buses to sights outside Shijiazhuang. Within the city there are 10 bus lines.

Beijing 北京

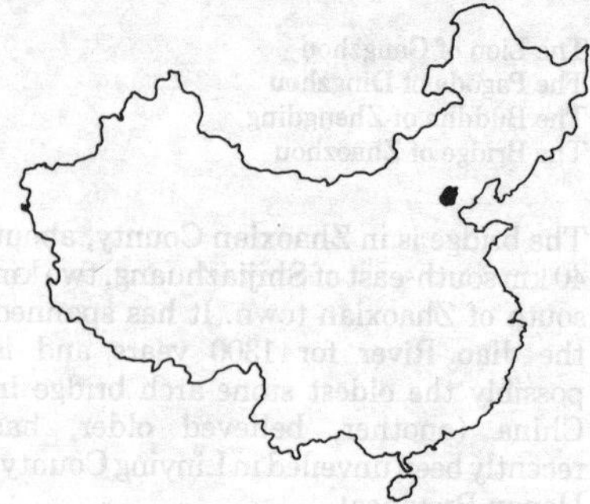

Beijing: home to stuffy museums and bureaucrats, puffy generals and backdoor elitists, host to disgruntled reporters and diplomats; a labyrinth of doors, walls, gates and entrances, marked and unmarked. As far away as Ürümqi they run on Beijing's clock; around the country they chortle in *putonghua*, the Beijing dialect; in the remote foothills of Tibet they struggle to interpret the latest directives from the capital. In 1983 the Chinese government announced that if the Dalai Lama were to return he'd be posted – where else? – to a desk job in Beijing. This is where they make the book and move the cogs and wheels of the Chinese universe, or try to slow them down if they're moving in the wrong direction.

Beijing is like a spoilt brat. It has the best of everything in China bar the weather: the best food, the best hotels, the best transport, the best temples. But its vast squares and boulevards, its cavernous monoliths and its huge numbers of tourists are likely to leave you cold. It's a weird city, one that has lost its energy and character, traces of which may be found down the back alleys where things are a bit more to human scale. Stepping off a train at Beijing Main Station and driving up to Tiananmen Square in a bulbous Russian Warszawa, you'd be forgiven if you were under the delusion that you'd strayed into the Red Square in Moscow.

In 1981 Beijingese were gazing at imported TV sets displayed behind plate glass at the Main Department Store on Wangfujing. In 1983 the same window sported a fashion display direct from Paris. Pierre Cardin has been and gone; Arthur Miller has drifted through; Elton John dropped in to pose for photos in a Sun Yatsen jacket; Jean Michel Jarre demonstrated his laser beams and synthesisers; Muhammed Ali traded mock punches with Chinese fans; Ronald Reagan and the Queen of England trod the Great Wall; Pavarotti sang his heart out.

Upstairs in the department store a western mannequin models a see-through top, nipples clearly visible, which sets passing Chinese (excuse the phrase) tittering. Outside the store a worker is stopped and fined for gobbing on the footpath, part of another cleanup campaign – more likely to prevent tourists being grossed out than to attack a health hazard. Further up Wangfujing, 6 pm and there's a parking problem: embassy cars and cadre limos have congregated at a restaurant for a banquet and there's nowhere to go except up on the footpath. For all its seeming liberalism, Beijing keeps an iron fist on its residents.

It's actually the foreigners who add the colour to dull, grey Beijing. The outskirts of town where the old walls used to stand are now ringed by four-lane highways with spaghetti-like flyovers devoid of the heavy traffic they were built for. Sprinkled around the perimeter are drab housing blocks. Is this it, is this the capital? Tourists are often disappointed with Beijing, seeing it as a third-rate European city divested of its energy. Others, having passed their time in the westernised parts of town, come away with the impression that everything is hunky dory in the PRC and that the Chinese are living high. The Chinese they encounter may, in truth, be doing so.

Group tourists are processed through

Beijing in much the same way the ducks are force-fed on the outlying farms. The two usually meet on the first night over the dinner table where the phenomenon known as the Jetlag Duck Attack overtakes the unwary traveller. Meanwhile, out in the embassy ghettoes long-term foreigners complain that they're losing their Chinese-language skills due to lack of contact. I asked a foreign journalist what she thought was the greatest sight in Beijing. Without hesitation, and in all seriousness, she replied, 'The sauna at the Finnish Embassy'.

Whatever impression you come away with, Beijing is not a realistic window on China. It's too much of a cosmetic showcase to qualify. It is, however, a large city, and with a bit of effort you can get out of the make-up department. Better still, try and get out of Beijing. At least once.

History

Beijing is a time-setter for China, but it actually has a short history as Chinese time spans go. Although the area south-west of the city was inhabited by cave dwellers some 500,000 years ago, the earliest records of settlements date from around 1000 BC. It developed as a frontier trading town for the Mongols, Koreans and the tribes from Shandong and Central China. By the Warring States Period (475-221 BC) it had grown to be the capital of the Yan Kingdom and was called Ji, a reference to the marshy features of the area. The town underwent a number of changes as it acquired new warlords, the Khitan Mongols and the Manchurian Jurchen tribes among them. What attracted the conquerors was the strategic position of the town on the edge of the North China Plain.

History really gets under way in 1215 AD, the year that Genghis Khan thoroughly set fire to the preceding paragraph and slaughtered everything in sight. From the ashes emerged Dadu the Great Capital, alias Khanbaliq, the Khan's town. By 1279 Genghis' grandson Kublai had made himself ruler of all China and Khanbaliq was his capital. Until this time attempts at unifying China had been centred around Luoyang and Changan (Xian). With a lull in the fighting from 1280 to 1300 foreigners managed to drop in along the Silk Road for tea with the Great Khan – Marco Polo even landed a job.

The Mongol emperor was informed by his astrologers that the old city site of Beijing was a breeding ground for rebels, so he shifted it slightly north. The great palace he built no longer remains, but here is Polo's description:

> Within these walls . . . stands the palace of the Great Khan, the most extensive that has ever yet been known . . . The sides of the great halls are adorned with dragons in carved work and gold, figures of warriors, of birds and of beasts . . . On each of the four sides of the palace there is a grand flight of marble steps . . . The new city is of a form perfectly square . . . each of its sides being six miles. It is enclosed with walls of earth . . . the wall of the city has twelve gates. The multitude of inhabitants, and the number of houses in the city of Kanbalu, as also in the suburbs outside the city, of which there are twelve, corresponding to the twelve gates, is greater than the mind can comprehend.

Oddly enough, Polo's description could well have been applied to the later Ming city; the lavish lifestyle of the great Khan set the trend for the Ming emperors. Polo goes on to recount what happened on Tartar New Year's Day:

> On this occasion, great numbers of beautiful white horses are presented to the Great Khan . . . all his elephants, amounting to five thousand, are exhibited in the procession, covered with housings of cloth, richly worked with gold and silk.

Polo was equally dazzled by the innovations of gunpowder and paper money. These were not without their drawbacks. In history's first case of paper-currency inflation the last Mongol emperor flooded the country with worthless bills. This, coupled with a large number of natural disasters, provoked an uprising led by the mercenary, Zhu Yanhang, who took Beijing in 1368 and ushered in the Ming Dynasty. The city was renamed Beiping (Northern Peace) and for the next 35 years the capital was shifted to Nanjing. To this day the Kuomintang regime on Taiwan refers to Beijing as 'Beiping' and recognises Nanjing as the capital.

In the early 1400s Zhu's son, Yong Le shuffled the court back to Beiping and renamed it Beijing (Northern Capital). Millions of taels of silver were spent on refurbishing the city. Many of the structures like the Forbidden City and the Temple of Heaven were first built in Yong Le's reign. In fact, he is credited with being the true architect of the modern city. The Inner City moved to the area around the Imperial City and a suburban zone was added to the south, a bustle of merchants and street life. The basic grid of present-day Beijing had been laid and history became a question of who ruled the turf.

The first change of government came with the Manchus, who invaded China and established the Qing Dynasty. Under them, and particularly during the reigns of the emperors Kangxi and Qianlong, Beijing was expanded and renovated and summer palaces, pagodas and temples were built. In the last 120 years of the Manchu Dynasty Beijing and subsequently China had been subjected to the afflictions of power struggles, invaders and the chaos created by those who held or sought power: the Anglo-French troops who in 1860 marched in and burnt the summer palace to the ground, the corrupt regime under Empress Dowager Cixi, the Boxers, General Yuan Shikai, the warlords, the Japanese who occupied the city in 1937 followed by the Kuomintang after the Japanese defeat. A century of turmoil finally ended in January 1949 when PLA troops entered the city. On 1 October of that year Mao proclaimed a 'People's Republic' to an audience of some 500,000 citizens in Tiananmen Square.

Post-1949 was a period of reconstruction. The centre of power has remained in the area around the Forbidden City, but the Communists have significantly altered the face of Beijing. Like the warlords of bygone eras they wanted to leave their mark. Under the old city-planning schemes high-rises were verboten – they would interfere with the emperor's view and lessen his sunlight. It was also a question of rank – the higher the building the more important the person within. The aristocrats got decorations and glazed tiling and the plebs got baked clay tiles and grey brick squats. This building code to some extent prevailed over the 'house that Mao built'. Premier Zhou suggested that nothing higher than 45 metres be built within the old city wall limits, and that nothing higher than Tiananmen Gate be erected in that area.

In the 1950s the urban planners got to work. Down came the commemorative arches, and blocks of buildings were reduced to rubble to widen Changan Avenue and Tiananmen Square. From 1950 to 1952 the outer walls were levelled in the interests of traffic circulation. Russian experts and technicians poured in, which may explain the Stalinesque features on the public structures that went up. Meanwhile industry, negligible in Beijing until this time, was rapidly expanded. Textiles, iron and steel, petrochemicals and machine-making plants were set up and Beijing became a major industrial city. Complicated by the fact that most of the city's greenery had been ripped up, this led to serious pollution problems. Five and six-storey housing blocks went up at a brisk pace but construction was of poor quality and it still didn't keep pace with the population boom. Communes were established on the city outskirts to feed the influx of people.

In 1982 the Central Committee of the Party adopted a new urban construction programme for Beijing, a revised version of the 1950s one. They faced tremendous challenges. On the one hand they wanted to continue the building of new roads and the widening of old streets; on the other hand they wanted to preserve the character of the old city and the historical sites. The population of the Beijing area, already well over nine million, is to be limited to 10 million by the year 2000, with four million in the metropolis, 2.5 million in satellite towns and 3.5 million in farming areas. Many new residential zones are being constructed in 12- to 16-storey blocks, but the workmanship is shoddy, facilities have to be bargained for (in some cases the water pressure does not go above the 3rd storey) and supply never meets demand.

The plan calls for a limitation on industrial construction, a halt to the growth of heavy industry and a shift to self-sufficient food production in the outlying counties. For the moment the self-sufficiency program appears to be working, with extended use of greenhouses for the winter months. Another major priority shift is environmental. A massive tree-planting campaign is underway which aims to turn some 50% of the metropolitan area into recreational zones. This, however, will mean less farmland and the mushrooming of buildings in satellite locations.

Small businesses, once the mainstay of Beijing's economy, have re-emerged after having been wiped out in the craze to nationalise. To solve a huge unemployment problem the government has offered incentives for the self-employed such as tax exemptions and loans. Those with initiative are faring better than average; some earn incomes above Y200 a month, and privately-run repair services such as those for bicycles, shoes and watches now outnumber state and collective-owned ones in Beijing.

Climate

The city is not blessed with congenial weather. Autumn (September to October) is the best time to visit; there's little rain, it's not dry or humid, and the city wears a pleasant cloak of foliage. Winter isn't bad if you're used to the cold; although the temperature can dip as far as -20°C and you can freeze your butt off, parts of the capital appear charming in this season. The subdued winter lighting makes the place very photogenic. Winter clothing is readily available – the locals wear about 15 layers. If the wind races down the wide boulevards like Changan there's a particularly nasty wind-chill factor. Spring is short, dry and dusty. In April to May a phenomenon known as 'yellow wind' plagues the capital – fine dust particles blown from the Gobi Desert in the north-west sandpaper everything in sight, including your face. The locals run around with mesh bags over their heads. In the 1950s the government ordered the extermination of the city's birds, which led to an insect uprising. They then ordered the insects' habitats (grass and other greens) to be dug up, which led to even more dust being set loose. In summer (June, July, August) the average temperature is 26°C – very hot, humid, semi-tropical weather, with mosquitoes and heavy rains in July.

Information & Orientation

Though it may not appear so on the shambles of arrival, Beijing is a place of very orderly design. Long, straight boulevards and avenues are criss-crossed by a network of lanes. Places of interest are either very easy to find if they're on the avenues, or impossible to find if they're buried down the narrow alleys *(hutongs)*.

This section refers to the chessboard of the downtown core, once a walled enclosure. The symmetry folds on an ancient north-south axis passing through Qianmen Gate. The major east-west road is Changan (Avenue of Eternal Tranquility).

As for the street names: Chongwenmenwai Dajie means the avenue (dajie) outside (wai) Chongwen Gate (Chongwenmen); whereas Chongwenmennai means the street inside Chongwen Gate (that is, inside the old wall). It's an academic exercise since the gate and the wall in question no longer exist.

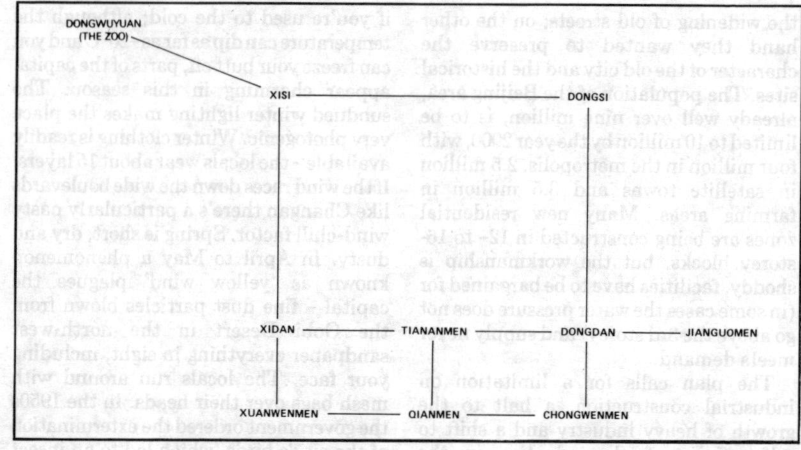

Streets are also split by compass points; Dongdajie (East Avenue), Xidajie (West Avenue), Beidajie (North Avenue) and Nandajie (South Avenue). These streets head off from an intersection, usually where a gate once stood.

A major boulevard can change names six or eight times along its length, so intersection points become important. The buses are also routed through these points. It therefore pays to study your gates and intersection points, and familiarise yourself with the high-rise buildings (often hotels) which serve as useful landmarks to gauge your progress along the chessboard. Other streets are named after bridges, also long gone, like the Bridge of Heaven (Tianqiao), and after old temple features or attractions which are still there.

The city limits of Beijing extend some 80 km, including the urban, the suburban, and the nine counties under its administration. With a total area of 16,800 square km, Beijing municipality is roughly the size of Belgium.

Evacuating the Railway Station Latitude 39°56'N, map-section 5E, elevation 44.8 metres you surface at Beijing Zhan, that is, Beijing Main Station. For most people, Beijing starts here. As you come out of the station there is a taxi depot straight ahead. If you keep going there are two subway entrances, the best and cheapest way of getting out of the area fast. Across the road from the station are various bus and minibus stops; see the Getting Around section for details.

CITS (tel 755017) is on the ground floor of the Chongwenmen Hotel at 2 Qianmen Dongdajie. It's within walking distance of the main railway station; alternatively, take the subway one stop west. CITS is open 8.30 to 11.20 am and 1 to 4.30 pm Monday to Saturday; and 9 to 11 am and 2 to 4.30 pm Sundays.

CITS come in very handy if you want tickets to the Beijing Opera, acrobatic shows or theatre. Costs are a bit higher than you'd pay at the door but at least you'll be sure of a seat. They also book the Trans-Siberian trains, but for domestic trains you have to go to the Foreigners' Booking Office in the main train station (see below). Bookings for the Shanghai-Hong Kong ferry cannot be made at

Beijing CITS; you have to telephone Shanghai to make the booking.

CITS runs tours of the Underground City every Wednesday for Y10 per person. They leave from the foyer of the Chongwenmen Hotel. Check out their other tours.

Public Security Bureau (tel 553102) is at 85 Beichizi Dajie, the street running north-south at the east side of the Forbidden City. It's open 8.30 to 11.30 am and 1 to 5 pm Monday to Friday; 8.30 to 11.30 am Saturday; closed on Sundays.

Bank There are money-exchange counters in many of the tourist hotels. The Beijing Hotel has an exchange counter on the ground floor and will change cash and travellers' cheques; you don't have to be staying at the hotel to use their service. The Qiao Yuan Hotel, where many low-budget travellers stay, also changes cash and travellers' cheques. The main branch of the Bank of China is at 32 Dengshikou Xilu.

There is a booming black market in FECs in Beijing, often fronted by sleazy Uygur mobsters. Beware that rip-offs have occurred frequently enough to warrant caution in dealing with the black-marketeers. Always count the RMB when they hand it over, and beware of tricks to short-change you.

Post & Communications The International Post & Telecommunications Building is on Jianguomen Beidajie, not far from the Friendship Store. Hours are 8 am to 7 pm. It has an efficient poste restante service for both letters and parcels. Overseas parcels must be posted here; a counter sells wrapping paper, string, tape and glue. There's also an international telegraph and telephone service – this is probably the best place to make international phone calls.

Most of the tourist hotels have post offices. You can send overseas packages from these as long as they contain printed matter only.

The Telegraph Building is on Xi Changan Jie, open 24 hours a day. Further west on Fuxingmennei Dajie is the International Telephone Office, open daily 7 am to midnight.

Long-distance calls can be made from your hotel room if it has a phone but patience is usually necessary as the exchanges are overworked and the lines can sometimes be bad.

CAAC (tel 558861 for enquiries) is at 155 Dongsi Xidajie. There is also a booking office in the Beijing Hotel.

Maps Until about 1978 there was no detailed English map of the capital. Now Beijing is thoroughly mapped out in excruciating detail.

A good sightseeing map is the *Beijing Tourist Map*, one of the series issued by the Cartographic Publishing House of Beijing and available in both Chinese and in English.

Another good one is the *Map of Beijing* (China Foreign Publishing Company), which shows the sights and is bilingual throughout; you can buy it in Hong Kong and it should be available in Beijing.

The main problem is showing transport routes on maps. *Transport Lines in Beijing City Area*, the regular English bus map, can be difficult to follow but is probably the best you'll ever get, given the sheer size of the city and the number of bus routes; a magnifying glass will help.

There are two maps in Chinese which can help if you follow some of the graphics and identify some landmarks. *Beijing Luyou Jiaotongtu* with a yellow cover is a small booklet with a foldout map in the middle showing buses, sights, taxis, etc.

The second map, *Beijingshi Chengqujiedaotu*, is the best bus map of the capital, with multi-coloured bus route lines and destinations outside Beijing. The large foldup map has a brown-and-blue cover.

Finally, for those staying longer, and aware of the lingo, there's a quarto-sized

1 天安门广场
2 毛主席纪念堂
3 中国历史博物馆
4 人民大会堂
5 前门
6 天安门
7 鼓楼
8 北京观象台
9 白塔寺
10 雍和宫
11 孔庙
12 白塔
13 牛街礼拜寺
14 广济寺
15 法源寺
16 天宁寺
17 天主教堂东堂
18 天主教堂南堂
19 鲁迅博物馆
20 中国美术馆
21 农业展览馆
22 北京展览馆
23 军事博物馆
24 北京图书馆
25 北京饭店
26 民族文化宫
27 崇文门饭店
28 鹿松园饭店
29 竹园饭店
30 光华饭店
31 天坛体育饭店
32 建国饭店
33 新华书店
34 前门饭店
35 民族饭店
36 燕京宾馆
37 和平饭店
38 华侨饭店
39 北纬饭店
40 宣武门饭店
41 全聚德烤鸭店
42 丰泽园
43 四川饭店
44 曲园酒楼
45 东来顺饭店
46 建国门外外交区
47 三里屯外交区
48 苏联使馆
To Friendship Hotel
Beijing University
Summer Palace
Baishiqiao Lu
To Badaling
Ming Tombs
Xinjiekouwai Dajie
Xizhimen Railway Station
Deshengmen Xidajie
Xinjiekou Beidajie
Xinjiekou Nandajie
Zizhuguan Park
Zoo
22
Xizhimenwai Dajie
Xizhimennei Dajie
Xizhimen Nandajie
Chegongzhuang Dajie
Di'anmen
Fuchengmen Beidajie
Xisi Beidajie
19
9
14
Fucheng Lu
Fuchengmenwai Dajie
Fuchengmennei Dajie
24
Wenjin
Yuetan Park
Fuchengmen Nandajie
Yuetan Dajie
Fuxingmen Beidajie
Xidan Beidajie
44
23
36
35
26
Telegraph Building
Fuxing Lu
Fuxingmenwai Dajie
Fuxingmennei Dajie
Xichang'an
43
Fuxingmen Nandajie
18
Xuanwumen Xidajie
Xuanwumen Dongdajie
40
Xuanwumenwai Dajie
16
Guang'anmenwai Dajie
Guang'anmennei Dajie
Luomashi Dajie
To Lugouqiao Zhoukoudian
13
15
Taoranting Park

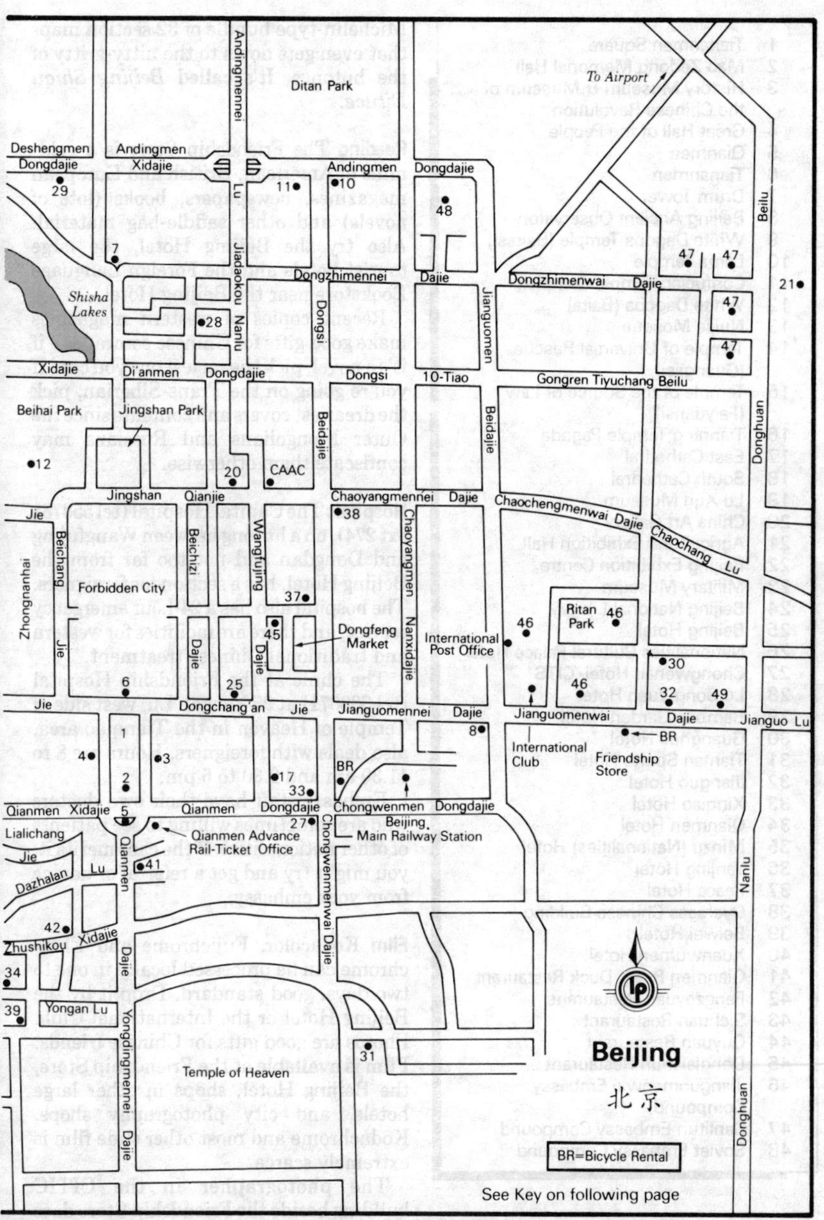
To Airport
Ditan Park
Andingmennei
Deshengmen Dongdajie
Andingmen Xidajie
Andingmen
Dongdajie
Jiaodaokou Nanlu
Dongzhimennei
Dajie
Dongzhimenwai
Dajie
Beilu
Shisha Lakes
Dongsi
Jianguomen
Xidajie
Di'anmen
Dongdajie
Dongsi
10-Tiao
Gongren Tiyuchang Beilu
Beihai Park
Jingshan Park
Beidajie
Beidajie
Donghuan
CAAC
Jingshan
Qianjie
Chaoyangmennei
Dajie
Chaochengmenwai Dajie
Chaochang Lu
Jie
Beichang
Beichizi
Wangfujing
Chaoyangmen Nanxiaojie
Zhongnanhai
Forbidden City
Ritan Park
Dongfeng Market
International Post Office
Jie
Dajie
Dajie
Jie
Dongchang'an
Jie
Jianguomennei
Dajie
Jianguomenwai
Dajie
Jianguo Lu
BR
International Club
Friendship Store
BR
Qianmen Xidajie
Qianmen
Dongdajie
Chongwenmen
Dongdajie
Beijing Main Railway Station
Lialichang
Jie
Qianmen Advance Rail-Ticket Office
Lu
Dazhalan
Chongwenmenwai Dajie
Nanlu
Zhushikou
Xidajie
Dajie
Yongan Lu
Yongdingmennei Dajie
Temple of Heaven
Beijing
北京
Donghuan
BR=Bicycle Rental
See Key on following page

1 Tiananmen Square
2 Mao Zedong Memorial Hall
3 History Museum & Museum of the Chinese Revolution
4 Great Hall of the People
5 Qianmen
6 Tiananmen
7 Drum Tower
8 Beijing Ancient Observatory
9 White Dagoba Temple (Baitasi)
10 Lama Temple
11 Confucian Temple Complex
12 White Dagoba (Baita)
13 Nuijie Mosque
14 Temple of Universal Rescue (Guangjisi)
15 Temple of the Source of Law (Faiyuansi)
16 Tianning Temple Pagoda
17 East Cathedral
18 South Cathedral
19 Lu Xun Museum
20 China Art Gallery
21 Agricultural Exhibition Hall
22 Beijing Exhibition Centre
23 Military Museum
24 Beijing National Library
25 Beijing Hotel
26 Nationalities Cultural Palace Hotel
27 Chongwenan Hotel/CITS
28 Lu Song Yuan Hotel
29 Bamboo Garden Hotel
30 Guanghua Hotel
31 Tiantan Sports Hotel
32 Jianguo Hotel
33 Xinqiao Hotel
34 Qianmen Hotel
35 Minzu (Nationalities) Hotel
36 Yanjing Hotel
37 Peace Hotel
38 Overseas Chinese Building
39 Beiwei Hotel
40 Xuanwumen Hotel
41 Qianmen Roast Duck Restaurant
42 Fengzeyuan Restaurant
43 Sichuan Restaurant
44 Quyuan Restaurant
45 Donglaishun Restaurant
46 Jianguomenwai Embassy Compound
47 Sanlitun Embassy Compound
48 Soviet Embassy Compound

Michelin-type bundle of 32 section maps that even gets down to the nitty-gritty of the hutongs. It's called *Beijing Shiqu Dituce*.

Reading The Friendship Store is a goldmine of American, British and European magazines, newspapers, books (lots of novels) and other saddle-bag material. Also try the Beijing Hotel, the large tourist hotels and the Foreign Language Bookstore near the Beijing Hotel.

Recent copies of western magazines make good gifts for Chinese comrades – if it's a novel, pick the raciest one you can! If you're going on the Trans-Siberian, pick the dreariest covers and contents since the Outer Mongolians and Russians may confiscate them otherwise.

Hospitals The Capital Hospital (tel 553731 ext 274), on a hutong between Wangfujing and Dongdan and not too far from the Beijing Hotel, has a section for foreigners. The hospital also has a 24-hour emergency service, and there are facilities for western and traditional Chinese treatment.

The clinic at the Friendship Hospital (tel 338671) at 95 Yongan Lu, west side of Temple of Heaven in the Tianqiao area, also deals with foreigners. Hours are 8 to 11.30 am and 2.30 to 5 pm.

Embassy staff have their own doctors who are sometimes willing to see patients of other nationalities. If the case merits it, you might try and get a referral or advice from your embassy.

Film Kodacolor, Fujichrome and Ektachrome can be processed locally in one to two days, good standard. Drop it by the Beijing Hotel or the International Club. Photos are good gifts for Chinese friends. Film is available at the Friendship Store, the Beijing Hotel, shops in other large hotels, and city photography shops. Kodachrome and most other slide film is extremely scarce.

The photographer in the CITIC building beside the Friendship Store does good passport photos in 12 minutes – RMB 7 for 4 photos. At 247 Wangfujing is another photo place. Although they usually take a few days to process them they will make you look 10 years younger!

A fun portrait can be had by posing in a cardboard cutout at various tourist spots around town. Capital Photographers at 25-29 Dazhalan allows you to dress up in theatre and minority costumes. It also produces a hand-painted product.

Airline Offices

Enquiries for all airlines can be made at Beijing International Airport (tel 552515). The individual offices are at:

Aeroflot
  5-53 Jianguomenwai (tel 523581)
Air France
  12-71 Jianguomenwai (tel 523894)
British Airways
  12-61 Jianguomenwai (tel 523768)
CAAC
  117 Dongsi Xidajie (tel 558861)
Japan Air Lines
  Beijing-Toronto Hotel, Jianguomenwai Dajie
Lufthansa
  Great Wall Sheraton Hotel, Dongsanhuan Beilu (tel 501616)
Pakistan International
  12-43 Jianguomenwai (tel 523274)
Pan Am
  Beijing-Toronto Hotel, Jianguomenwai Dajie (tel 501985)
Philippine Airlines
  12-53 Jianguomenwai (tel 523992)
Qantas
  1st floor, Beijing Toronto Hotel (tel 5002487)
Swissair
  12-33 Jianguomenwai (tel 523284)
Tarom Romanian Airlines
  Romanian Embassy Compound, Ritan Dongerjie, Jianguomenwai (tel 523552)
United Airlines
  Beijing-Toronto Hotel, Jianguomenwai Dajie

Embassies

Beijing has the greatest concentration of embassies in China and it's not a bad place to stock up on visas. There are Australian, US, Japanese, French and West German consulates in Shanghai also, as well as US and Japanese consulates in Canton. See the chapters on those cities for details.

In Beijing there are two main compounds: Jianguomenwai and Sanlitun. A trip to Embassy Land is a trip in itself – little sentry boxes with Chinese soldiers, posted not so much for the protection of staff as to scare the locals off.

The Jianguomenwai Compound is in the vicinity of the Friendship Store. The embassies located here are:

Austria
  5 Xiushui Nanjie (tel 522061)
East Germany
  3 Sanlitun Dongsijie (tel 521631)
Finland
  30 Guanghua Lu (tel 521817)
Ireland
  3 Ritan Donglu (tel 522691)
India
  l Ritan Donglu (tel 521908)
Japan
  7 Ritan Lu (tel 522361)
Mongolia
  2 Xiushui Beijie (tel 521203)
New Zealand
  1 Ritan Dongerjie (tel 522731)
Philippines
  23 Xiushui Beijie (tel 522794)
Poland
  1 Ritan Lu, Jianguomenwai (tel 521235)
Romania
  corner of Ritan Dongerjie and Ritan Donglu (tel 523315)
Thailand
  40 Guanghua Lu (tel 521903)
Sri Lanka
  3 Jianhua Lu (tel 521861)
UK
  11 Guanghua Lu (tel 521961)
USA
  Embassy: Xiushui Beijie (tel 523831). Consulate: 2 Xiushui Dongjie

The Sanlitun Compound is several km north-east of Jianguomenwai, near the Agricultural Exhibition Hall:

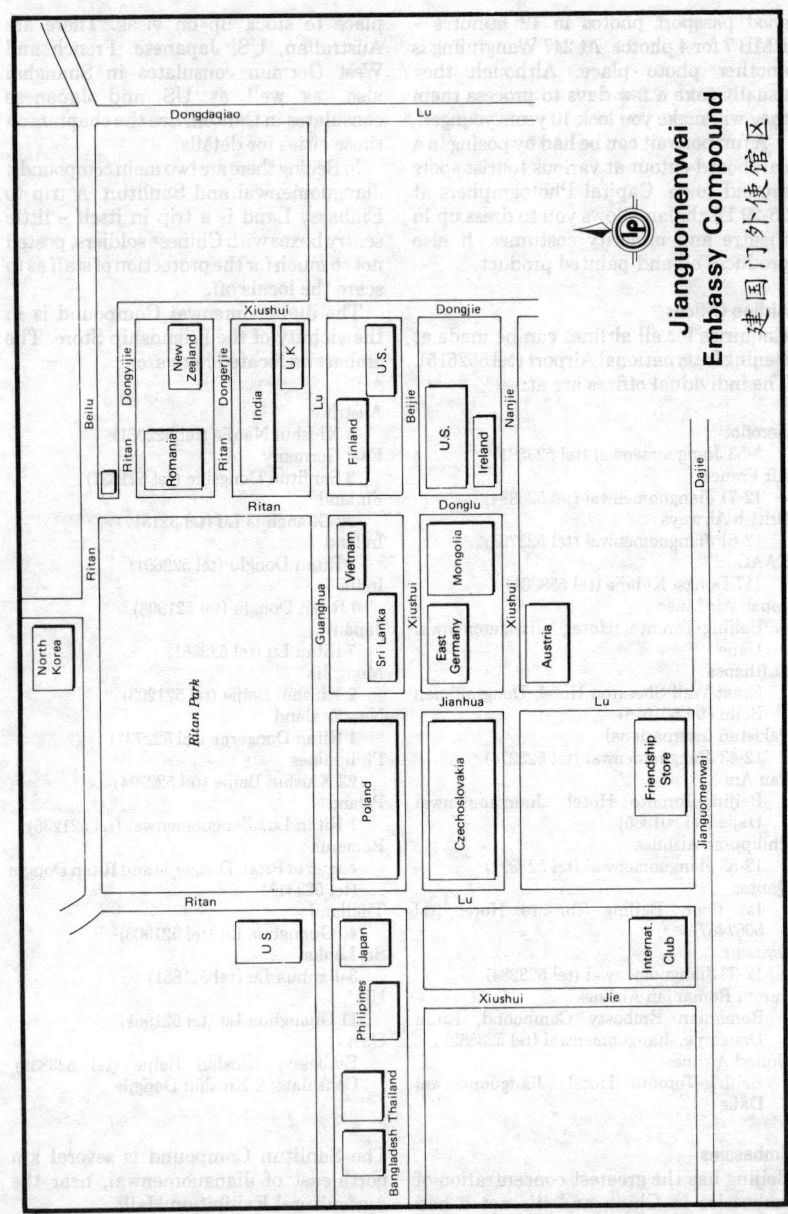
Jianguomenwai
Embassy Compound
建国门外使馆区
Dongdaqiao
Lu
Xiushui
Dongjie
Beilu
Dongyijie
Dongerjie
Ritan
New Zealand
UK
India
U.S.
Lu
Finland
Romania
Beijie
U.S.
Ireland
Nanjie
Dajie
Ritan
Donglu
Vietnam
Sri Lanka
Guanghua
Mongolia
East Germany
Xiushui
Austria
North Korea
Ritan Park
Jianhua
Lu
Poland
Czechoslovakia
Friendship Store
Jianguomenwai
Ritan
Lu
US
Japan
Internat. Club
Philipines
Xiushui
Jie
Bangladesh
Thailand

Australia
15 Dongzhimenwai Dajie (tel 522331)
Burma
6 Dongzhimenwai Dajie (tel 521302)
Canada
10 Sanlitun Lu (tel 521475)
France
3 Sanlitun Dongsanjie (tel 521331)
Hungary
10 Dongzhimenwai Dajie (tel 521683)
Italy
2 Sanlitun Dongerjie (tel 522131)
Malaysia
13 Dongzhimenwai Dajie (tel 522531)
Nepal
1 Sanlitun Xiliujie (tel 521795)
Netherlands
10 Sanlitun Dongsijie (tel 521731)
Norway
1 Sanlitun Dongyijie (tel 522261)
Pakistan
1 Dongzhimenwai Dajie (tel 522504)
Sweden
3 Dongzhimenwai Dajie (tel 523331)
Switzerland
3 Sanlitun Dongwujie (tel 522736)
USSR
4 Dongzhiman Beizhongjie, west of the Sanlitun Compound in a separate compound (tel 522051)
West Germany
5 Dongzhimenwai Dajie (tel 522161)
Yugoslavia
6 Sanlitun Dongsanjie

Things to See

Beijing has a glut of sights, both within and without the city limits. Try as you might you just can't knock off Beijing – it refuses to die. The Red Guards tried, after a fashion, to knock it down, but in the interests of tourism plenty of attractions have been restored or revived, so spruced-up sites are becoming available.

Tiananmen Square

Though it was a gathering place and the location of government offices in the imperial days, the square is Mao's creation, as is Changan Avenue leading onto it. This is the heart of Beijing, a vast desert of paving and photo-booths. The last major rallies took place here during the Cultural Revolution when Mao, wearing a Red Guard armband, reviewed parades of up to a million people. In 1976 another million people jammed the square to pay their last respects to him. Today the square is a place, if the weather is conducive, for people to lounge around in the evening, and a place to fly decorated kites – a striking sight. Surrounding or studding the square are a strange mish-mash of monuments past and present: Tiananmen Gate, the History Museum & Museum of the Revolution, the Great Hall of the People, Qianmen Gate, the Mao Mausoleum and the Monument to the People's Heroes. If you get up early you can watch the flag-raising ceremony at sunrise, performed by a troop of PLA soldiers drilled to march at precisely 108 paces per minute, 75 cm per pace.

Tiananmen Gate (Gate of Heavenly Peace)

A national symbol which pops up on everything from airline tickets to policemen's caps, the Gate of Heavenly Peace was built in the 15th century and restored in the 17th. From imperial days it functioned as a rostrum for dealing with or proclaiming to the assembled masses. There are five doors to the gate, and in front of it are seven bridges spanning a stream. Each of these bridges had restricted use, and only the emperor could use the central door and bridge.

It was from the gate that Mao proclaimed the People's Republic on 1 October 1949, and there have been a few alterations since then. The dominating feature is the gigantic portrait of Mao, the required backdrop for any photo the Chinese take of themselves at the gate (whether they like him or not). To the left of the portrait is a slogan 'Long Live the People's Republic of China' and to the right 'Long Live the Unity of the Peoples of the World'. Grandstands with a capacity of 20,000 dignitaries were added for reviewing purposes.

Photography is big at Tiananmen – the Chinese aspire to visit the heart of the nation almost like the Muslims aspire to

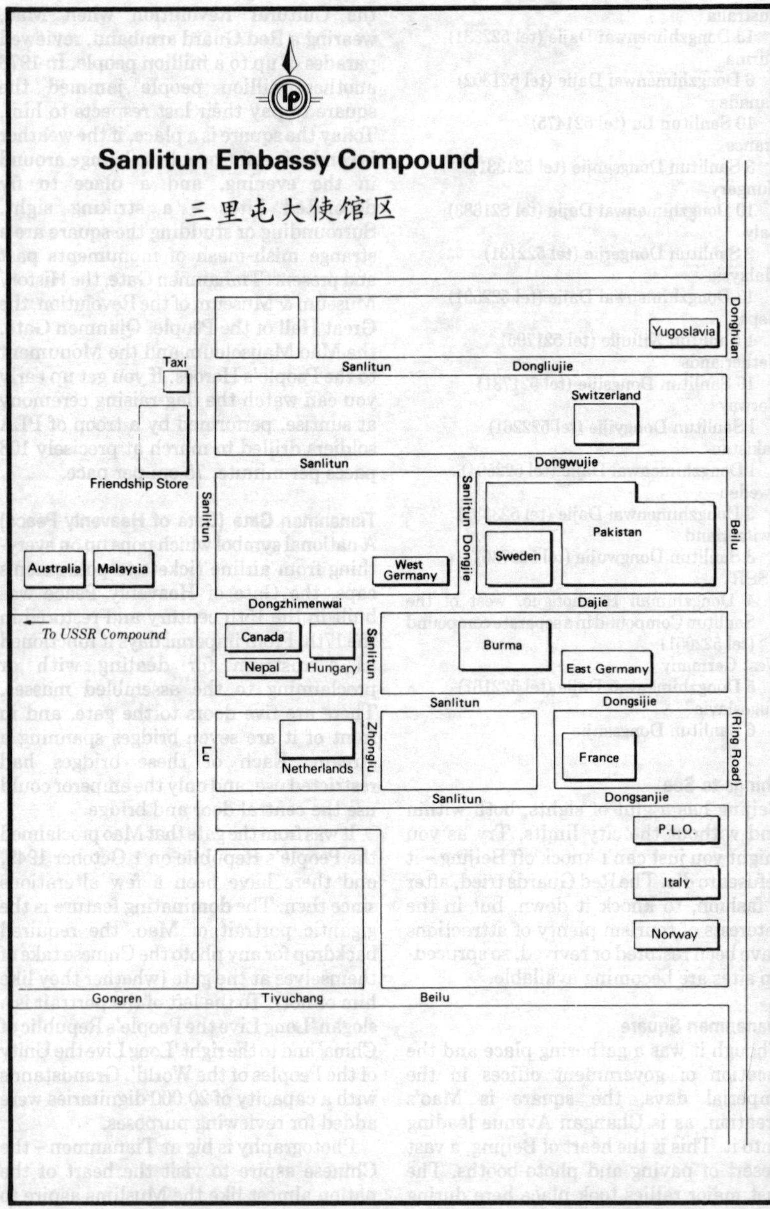
Sanlitun Embassy Compound
三里屯大使馆区
Taxi
Sanlitun
Dongliujie
Yugoslavia
Donghuan
Switzerland
Sanlitun
Friendship Store
Dongwujie
Sanlitun
Sanlitun Dongjie
Pakistan
Beilu
Sweden
Australia
Malaysia
West Germany
Dajie
Dongzhimenwai
To USSR Compound
Canada
Nepal
Hungary
Sanlitun
Burma
East Germany
Sanlitun
Dongsijie
(Ring Road)
Lu
Zhonglu
Netherlands
France
Sanlitun
Dongsanjie
P.L.O.
Italy
Norway
Gongren
Tiyuchang
Beilu

visit Mecca, and Chinese school kids grow up singing 'I Love Tiananmen'. If you venture a short distance into the Forbidden City through Tiananmen you'll find all kinds of bizarre cardboard cut-outs used as photo props.

History Museum & Museum of the Revolution Because both are housed in the same sombre building on the east side of Tiananmen Square, it's difficult to decide where one museum ends and the other begins. Access to both of these was long thwarted by special permission requirements. From 1966 to 1978 the Museum of the Revolution was closed so that history could be reassessed in the light of recent events.

The presentation of history poses quite a problem for the CCP. While the Maoist factions did their level best to destroy thousands of years of history and literature, they declined to publish anything of note on the history of their own party after it had gained power. This would have required reams of carefully-worded revision according to what tack politics (here synonymous with history) might take – so it was better left unwritten.

Explanations throughout most of the museums are, unfortunately, entirely in Chinese, so you won't get much out of this labyrinth unless you pick up an English-speaking student. An English text relating to the History Museum is available inside for Y5.

The History Museum contains artefacts and cultural relics (many of them copies) from Day 1 to 1919, subdivided into primitive communal groups, slavery, feudalism and capitalism/imperialism, laced with Marxist commentary. Without a guide you can discern ancient weapons, inventions and musical instruments.

The Museum of the Revolution is split into five sections: the founding of the CCP (1919-1921), the first civil war (1924-1927), the second civil war (1927-1937), resistance against Japan (1937-1945) and the third civil war (1945-1949).

In 1978 a permanent photo-pictorial exhibit of the life and works of Zhou Enlai became a star attraction, and in 1983 there was an exhibit tracing the life of Liu Shaoqi. PLA soldiers are occasionally taken through the museums on tours; they snap to attention, open portable chairs and sit down in unison for explanations of each section. Whatever spiel they're given would probably be engrossing if you had someone to translate for you.

Monument to the People's Heroes On the southern side of Tiananmen, this monument was completed in 1958 and stands on the site of the old Outer Palace Gate. The 36-metre obelisk, made of Qingdao granite, bears bas-relief carvings of key revolutionary events (one relief shows the Chinese destroying opium in the 19th century) as well as appropriate calligraphy from Mao Zedong and Zhou Enlai. In 1976 the obelisk was the focus of the 'Tiananmen Incident' when thousands gathered here to protest the tyranny of the Gang of Four and to mourn the death of Zhou Enlai.

Mao Zedong Mausoleum Behind the Monument to the People's Heroes stands this giant mausoleum built to house the body of Chairman Mao. Mao died in September 1976, and the mausoleum was constructed over a period of 10 months from 1976 to 1977. It occupies a prominent position on the powerful north-south axis of the city, but against all laws of geomancy this marble structure faces north. At the end of 1983 the mausoleum was re-opened as a museum with exhibitions on the lives of Zhou Enlai, Zhu De, Mao and the man he killed, Liu Shaoqi. Mao's body still remains in its place.

Whatever history will make of Mao, his impact on its course will remain unchanged: enormous. Easy as it now is to vilify his deeds and excesses, there is a good measure of respect when confronted with the 'physical' presence of the man. Shoving a couple of museums into the mausoleum was meant to knock Mao another rung down the divine ladder. Nevertheless the atmosphere in the inner sanctum is one of hushed reverence, with a thick red pile carpet muting any sound.

The mausoleum is open daily from 8.30 to 11.30 am (probably closed all winter). Join the enormous queue of Chinese sightseers, but don't expect more than a quick glimpse of the body as you file past the sarcophagus. The body is apparently lowered into the ground for the winter months, and not on view. The story goes that the Chinese had problems embalming Mao and had to call the Vietnamese to the rescue (Ho Chi Minh was also embalmed).

CITS guides freely quote the old 7:3 ratio on Mao that first surfaced in 1976. Mao was 70% right and 30% wrong (what, one wonders, are the figures for CITS itself?) and this is now the official Party line. His gross errors in the Cultural Revolution, it is said, are far outweighed by his contributions.

Don't forget, by the way, to buy some souvenirs of your visit. Mao Zedong Mausoleum keyrings, thermometers, face towels, handkerchiefs, sun visors, address books and cartons of cigarettes (a comment on the guy's chain-smoking?) are sold in souvenir bungalows outside the building.

Qianmen (Front Gate) Silent sentinel to the changing times, the Front Gate has had its context removed. It's one of the few old gates left, and a great landmark to get around by. It guarded the wall division between the ancient Inner City and the outer suburban zone, and dates back to the reign of Emperor Yong Le in the 15th century.

Great Hall of the People This is the venue of the National People's Congress, and is open to the public when the Congress is not sitting. You tramp through the halls of power, many of them named after provinces and regions of China and decorated appropriately. You can see the 5000-seat banquet room where Nixon dined in 1972 and the 10,000-seat auditorium with the familiar red star embedded in a galaxy of lights in the ceiling. There's a sort of museum-like atmosphere in the Great Hall, with objets d'art donated by the provinces, and a snack bar and restaurant. The hall was completed over a 10-month period, 1958 to 1959.

The Forbidden City

The Forbidden City, so-called because it was off-limits for 500 years, is the largest and best-preserved cluster of ancient buildings in China. It was home to two dynasties of emperors, the Ming and the Qing, who didn't stray from this pleasure-dome unless they absolutely had to.

The Forbidden City is open daily except Mondays, 8.30 am to 5 pm. Two hundred years ago the admission price would have been instant death, but this has dropped considerably to just Y5.

The basic layout was built between 1406 and 1420 by Emperor Yong Le, commanding battalions of labourers and craftspeople – some estimate up to a million of them. From this palace the emperors governed China, often rather erratically as they tended to become lost in this self-contained little world and allocated real power to the court eunuchs. One emperor devoted his entire career to carpentry – when an earthquake struck, an ominous sign for an emperor, he was delighted since it gave him a chance to renovate.

The buildings now seen are mostly post-18th century, as with a lot of restored or rebuilt structures around Beijing. The palace was constantly coming down in flames – a lantern festival combined with a sudden gust of Gobi wind would easily do the trick, as would a fireworks display. There were also deliberate fires lit by court eunuchs and officials who could get rich off the repair bills. The moat around the palace, now used for boating, came in handy since the local fire brigade was considered too common to quench the royal flames. Some of the emperors enjoyed the spectacle of fires, while Emperor Jiajing was so disturbed by them that he ordered a hall built in honour of the 'Fire-Pressing God'. Three fires caused by lightning broke out during his reign, including the biggest bonfire of the lot in 1557. A century later, in 1664, the Manchus stormed in and burned the palace to the ground.

It was not just the buildings that went up in smoke, but rare books, paintings, calligraphy, anything flammable. In this century there have been two major lootings of the palace: first by the Japanese forces, and second by the Kuomintang, who on the eve of the Communist takeover in 1949 removed thousands of crates of booty to Taiwan. The gaps have been filled by bringing treasures, old and newly discovered, from other parts of China.

The palace is so large (720,000 square metres, 800 buildings, 9000 rooms) that a permanent restoration squad moves around repainting and repairing. It's estimated to take about 10 years to do a full renovation, by which time the starting end is due for repairs again. The complex was opened to the public in 1949.

The palace was built on a monumental scale, one that should not be taken lightly. Allow yourself a full day for exploration, or perhaps several separate trips. The information given here can only be a skeleton guide; if you want more detail then tag along with a tour group for explanations of individual artefacts. There are plenty of western tour groups around, and overall the Forbidden City gets 10,000 visitors a day. Tour buses drop their groups off at Tiananmen and pick them up again at the north gate; you can also enter the palace from the east or west gates. Even if you had a separate guidebook on the Forbidden City, it would be rather time-consuming to match up and identify every individual object, building and so forth – a spoken guide has more immediacy.

On the north-south axis of the Forbidden City, from Tiananmen at the south to Shenwumen at the north, lie the palace's ceremonial buildings.

Meridian Gate (Wumen) Restored in the 17th century, this massive portal was reserved for the use of the emperor. Gongs and bells would be sounded upon royal comings and goings. Lesser mortals would use lesser gates – the military used the west gate, civilians used the east gate. The emperor also reviewed his armies from here, passed judgment on prisoners, announced the new year calendar and surveyed the flogging of cheeky ministers.

Supreme Harmony Gate (Taiheman) Across Golden Stream, which is shaped to resemble a Tartar bow and is spanned by five marble bridges, is Supreme Harmony Gate. It overlooks a massive courtyard that could hold an imperial audience of up to 100,000.

The Three Great Halls Raised on a marble terrace with balustrades are the Three Great Halls, the heart of the Forbidden City.

The Hall of Supreme Harmony (Taihedian) is the most important and the largest structure in the Forbidden City. Restored in the 15th century, it was used for ceremonial occasions such as the emperor's birthday, the nomination of military leaders, and coronations. Flanking the entrance to the hall are bronze incense burners. The large bronze turtle in the front is a symbol of longevity and stability – it has a removable lid and on special occasions incense was lit inside so that smoke billowed from the mouth. To the west side of the terrace is a small pavilion with a bronze grain-measure and to the east is a sundial; both are symbolic of imperial justice. On the corners of the roof, as with some other buildings in the city, you'll see a mounted figure with his retreat cut off by mythical and real animals, a story that relates to a cruel tyrant hung from one such eave. Inside

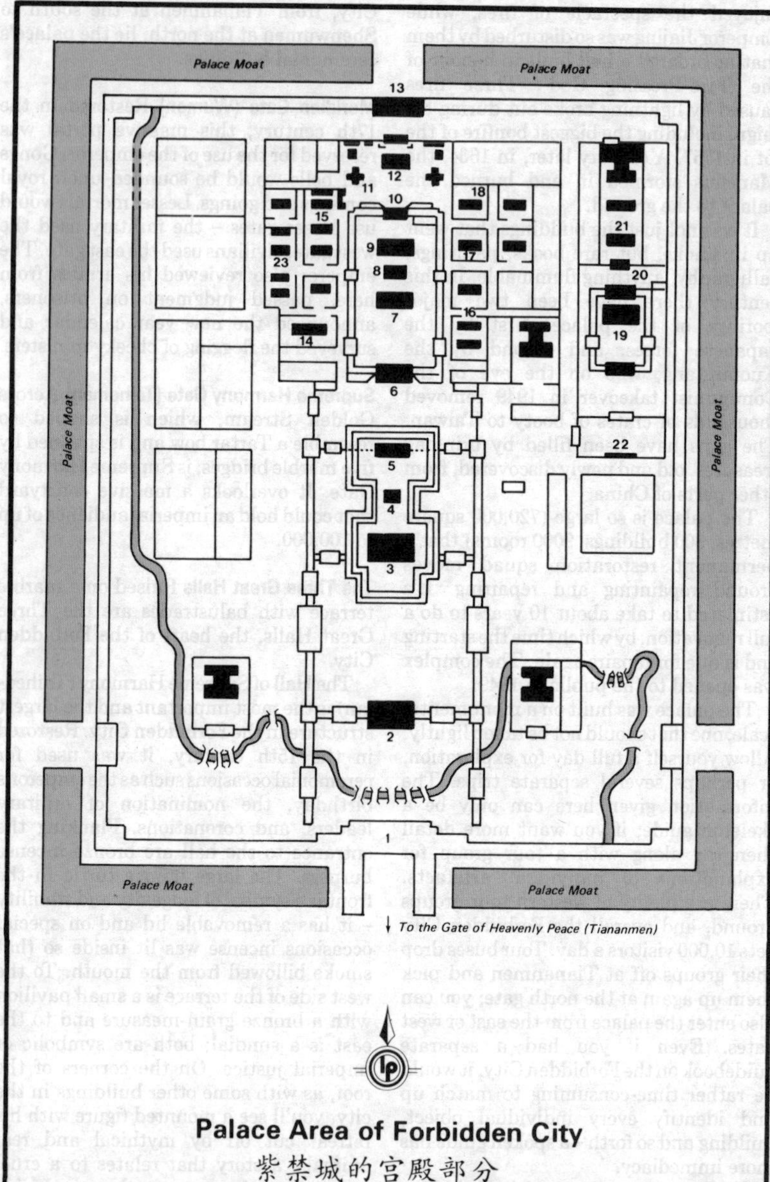

Palace Area of Forbidden City

紫禁城的宫殿部分

1 Meridian Gate (Wumen)
2 Gate of Supreme Harmony (Taihemen)
3 Hall of Supreme Harmony (Taihedian)
4 Hall of Middle Harmony (Zhonghedian)
5 Hall of Preserving Harmony (Baohedian)
6 Gate of Heavenly Purity (Qiangingmen)
7 Palace of Heavenly Purity (Qianginggong)
8 Hall of Union (Jiaotaidian)
9 Palace of Earthly Tranquillity (Kunningging)
10 Imperial Garden
11 Thousand Autumns Pavilion
12 Hall of Imperial Peace
13 Gate of Divine Military Genius (Shenwumen)
14 Hall of Mental Cultivation (Yangxindian)
15 Western Palaces Nos 16, 17 & 18 (residential palaces now used as museums)
16 Exhibition of Bronzes
17 Exhibition of Ceramics
18 Exhibition of Ming & Qing Dynasty Arts & Crafts
19 Exhibition of Paintings (Hall of Imperial Supremacy)
20 Palace of Peaceful Old Age
21 Exhibition of Jewellery (Hall of the Cultivation of Character)
22 Nine Dragon Screen
23 Palace of Eternal Spring (Changchungong)

1	午门	13	神武门
2	太和门	14	养心殿
3	太和殿	15	宫廷史迹陈列
4	中和殿	16	青铜器馆
5	保和殿	17	陶瓷馆
6	乾清门	18	明清工艺美术馆
7	乾清宫	19	绘画馆
8	交泰殿	20	养性殿
9	坤宁宫	21	珍馆
10	御花园	22	九龙壁
11	千秋亭	23	长春宫
12	钦安殿		

the hall is a richly decorated Dragon Throne where the emperor would preside (decisions final, no correspondence entered into) over trembling officials. The entire court had to hit the floor nine times with their foreheads; combine that with thick veils of incense and battering of gongs and it would be enough to make anyone dizzy. At the back of the throne is a carved Xumi Mountain, the Buddhist paradise, signifying the throne's supremacy.

Behind Taihedian is a smaller hall, the Hall of Middle Harmony (Zhonghedian) which was used as a transit lounge for the emperor. Here he would make last-minute preparations, rehearse speeches and receive close ministers. On display are two Qing Dynasty sedan chairs, the emperors' mode of transport around the Forbidden City. The last of the Qing emperors, Pu Yi, used a bicycle and altered a few features of the palace grounds to make it easier to get around.

The third hall is the Hall of Preserving Harmony (Baohedian) used for banquets and later for imperial examinations. It now houses archaeological finds. The Baohedian has no support pillars, and behind it is a 250-ton marble block carved with dragons and clouds which was moved from its location outside Beijing by sliding it over an ice path. The outer housing surrounding the Three Great Halls was used for storing gold, silver, silks, carpets and other treasures.

The Rear The basic configuration of the Three Great Halls is mimicked by the next group of buildings, smaller in scale but more important in terms of real power. In China, real power traditionally lies at the back door, or in this case, the back gate.

The first structure is the Palace of Heavenly Purity (Qianqinggong), a residence of Ming and early Qing emperors, and later an audience hall for receiving foreign envoys and high officials.

Immediately behind it is the Hall of Union, which contains a clepsydre – a water clock with five bronze vessels and a calibrated scale. Water clocks date back several thousand years but this one was made in 1745. There's also a mechanical clock on display, built in 1797, and a collection of imperial jade seals.

At the northern end of the Forbidden City is the Imperial Garden, a classical Chinese garden of 7000 square metres of fine landscaping, with rockeries, walkways and pavilions. A good place to take a breather, with snack bars, WCs and souvenir shops. Two more gates lead out through the large Gate of Divine Military Genius (Shenwumen).

Coal Hill Park (Jing Shan) North of Shenwumen and outside the present confines of the Forbidden City is Coal Hill Park (Jing Shan), an artificial mound made of earth excavated to create the palace moat. If you clamber to the top pavilions of this regal pleasure garden you get a magnificent panorama of the capital and a great overview of the russet roofing of the Forbidden City. On the east side of the park is a locust tree where the last of the Mings, Emperor Chongzhen, hanged himself (after slaying his family) rather than see the palace razed by the Manchus. The hill supposedly protects the palace from the evil spirits – or dust storms – from the north, but didn't quite work for Chongzhen.

The Western & Eastern Palaces Other sections of the palace are the former palatial living quarters, once containing libraries, temples, theatres, gardens, even the tennis court of the last emperor. These buildings now function as museums and often require separate but nominal admission fees. Opening hours are irregular and no photos are allowed without prior permission. Special exhibits sometimes appear in the palace museum halls – check *China Daily* for details.

On the western side of the Forbidden City, towards the north exit, are the six Western Palaces which were living quarters for the empress and the concubines. These are kept in pristine condition, displaying furniture, silk bedcovers, personal items, and fittings such as cloisonné charcoal burners.

Of particular interest is the Palace of Eternal Spring (Changchunggong), decorated with mural scenes from the Ming novel *A Dream of the Red Mansions*. This is where the Empress Dowager Cixi lived when she was still a concubine.

Nearby is the Hall of Mental Cultivation (Yangxindian), a private apartment for the emperors. It was divided into reception rooms, a study where important documents were signed and a bedchamber at the rear.

On the eastern side of the city, six more palaces duplicate the rhythms and layout of those on the west. There are museums here for bronzes, ceramics, and Ming Dynasty arts and crafts. Further east is a display of gold and jade artefacts and Ming and Qing paintings, sometimes augmented with Song and Yuan paintings. Just south, protecting the gateway to two of the palaces, is the polychrome Nine Dragon Screen built in 1773.

Other Features A few more interesting aspects of the Forbidden City include the watchtowers at the four corners of the city which stand atop the walls. Structural delights, they have three storeys, are double-roofed and measure 27.5 metres high.

Zhongshan Park, otherwise known as Sun Yatsen Park, is in the south-west of the city and was laid out at the same time as the palace. Here you'll find the Altar of Land and Grain, which is divided into five sections, each filled with earth of a different colour (red, green, black, yellow and white) to symbolise all the earth belonging to the emperor. There is also a concert hall and a 'modernisation' playground in the park.

The Workers' Cultural Palace in the south-east sector of the city is a park with halls dating from 1462 which were used as ancestral temples under the Ming and Qing; they come complete with marble balustrades, terraces and detailed gargoyles. The park is now used for movies, temporary exhibits, cultural performances and the odd mass wedding. There's boating at the north end and skating in winter on the frozen moat.

A Day in the Life . . .

Four hundred years ago the Jesuit priest Matteo Ricci spent 20 years in China, much of that time at the imperial court in Beijing. He recorded in his diary:

Just as this people is grossly subject to superstition, so, too, they have very little regard for the truth, acting always with great circumspection, and very cautious about trusting anyone. Subject to this same fear, the kings of modern times abandoned the custom of going out in public. Even formerly, when they did leave the royal enclosure, they would never dare to do so without a thousand preliminary precautions. On such occasions the whole court was placed under military guard. Secret servicemen were placed along the route over which the King was to travel and on all roads leading into it. He was not only hidden from view, but the public never knew in which of the palanquins of his cortège he was actually riding. One would think he was making a journey through enemy country rather than through multitudes of his own subjects and clients.

Behind the Wall

If ceremonial and administrative duties occupied much of the emperor's time, then behind the walls of the Forbidden City it was the pursuit of pleasure which occupied much of his attention. One of the imperial bedtime systems was to keep the names of royal wives and consorts on jade tablets near the emperor's chambers. By turning the tablet over the emperor made his request for the evening, and the eunuch on duty would rush off to find the lucky lady. Stripped naked and therefore 'weaponless' she was wrapped in a yellow cloth, and the little bound-footed creature was piggybacked over to the royal boudoir and dumped at the feet of the emperor; the eunuch recorded the date and time to verify legitimacy of a possible child.

Financing the pleasure-dome was an arduous affair that drew on the resources of the empire. During the Ming Dynasty there were an estimated 9000 maids of honour and 70,000 eunuchs serving the court. Apart from the servants and the prize whores there were also the royal elephants to upkeep. These were gifts from Burma and were stabled south-west of the Forbidden City. Accorded rank by the emperor, when one died a period of mourning was declared. Periodically the elephant keepers embezzled the funds intended for elephant chow. When this occurred, the ravenous pachyderms went on a rampage. While pocketing this cash was illegal, selling elephant dung for use as shampoo was not, and it was believed to give the hair that extra sheen. Back in the harem the cosmetic bills piled up to 400,000 taels of silver. Rather than cut back on expenditure, the emperor sent out eunuchs to collect emergency taxes whenever the money ran short.

As for the palace eunuchs, the royal chop was administered at the Eunuch Clinic near the Forbidden City, using a swift knife and a special chair with a hole in the seat. The candidates sought to better their lives in the service of the court but half of them died after the 'operation'. Mutilation of any kind was considered grounds for exclusion to the next life, so many eunuchs carried their appendages around in pouches, believing that at the time of death the spirits might be deceived into thinking of them as whole.

Museums & Libraries

The best museums are located in the Forbidden City, and the biggest are the combined History Museum & Museum of the Revolution in Tiananmen Square. The most interesting are the temporary exhibits held in parks or places like the Nationalities Cultural Palace. Museums in Beijing are poorly maintained and presented, and little research work is done.

Military Museum Perhaps more to the point than the Museum of the Revolution, this traces the genesis of the PLA from 1927 to the present and has some interesting exhibits: pictures of Mao in the early days, mind-boggling Socialist Realist artwork, captured American tanks and other tools of destruction. The 4th floor used to contain exhibits relating to China's war with Vietnam, but that's been cleared away and temporary exhibits are now housed here. Admission is 10 fen. Through a side-door is a shooting gallery where you can take pot-shots with dummy rifles at moving targets – rather like a carnival sideshow, but no prizes. The museum is on Fuxing Lu on the western side of the city; to get there take the subway to Junshibowuguan.

Lu Xun Museum Dedicated to China's No 1 Thinking Man's Revolutionary, this museum contains manuscripts, diaries, letters and inscriptions by the famous writer. To the west of the museum is a small Chinese walled compound where Lu Xun lived from 1924 to 1926. The museum is west of the Xisi intersection.

Beijing National Library This holds around five million books and four million periodicals and newspapers, over a third of which are in foreign languages. Access to books is limited and access to rare books is even rarer, though you might be shown a microfilm copy if you're lucky. The large collection of rare books includes surviving imperial works such as the *Yong Le Encyclopedia* and selections from the old Jesuit library. Of interest to Ming-Qing scholars is the special collection, the *Shanbenbu*. The library is near Beihai Park on the south side. Beijing University Library also has a large collection of rare books.

Capital Museum & Library Formerly a Confucian Temple, the museum houses steles, stone inscriptions, bronzes, vases and documents. It's near the Lama Temple.

China Art Gallery Back in the post-Liberation days one of the safest hobbies for an artist was to retouch classical-type landscapes with red flags, belching factory chimneys or bright red tractors. You can get some idea of the state of the arts in China at this gallery. At times very good exhibitions of current work including photo displays are held in an adjacent gallery. Check *China Daily* for listings. The arts & crafts shop inside has an excellent range of woodblock prints and papercuts. The gallery is west of the Dongsi intersection.

Xu Beihong Museum Here you'll find traditional Chinese paintings, oils, gouaches, sketches and memorabilia of the famous artist, noted for his galloping horse paintings. Painting albums are on sale, as well as reproductions and Chinese stationery. The museum is at 53 Xinjiekou Beidajie, Xicheng District.

Song Qingling Museum Madam Song was the wife of Sun Yatsen, the founder of the Republic of China. After 1981 her large residence was transformed into a museum dedicated to her memory and to that of Sun Yatsen. The original layout of the residence is unchanged and on display are personal items and pictures of historical interest. The museum is on the north side of Lake Shishahai.

Zhongnanhai

Just west of the Forbidden City is China's new forbidden city, Zhongnanhai. The name means 'the central and south seas' and takes its name from the two large lakes that are enclosed in the compound. The southern entrance is via Xinhuamen (The Gate of New China) which you'll see on Changan Avenue; it's guarded by two PLA soldiers and fronted by a flagpole with the Red Flag flying. The gate was built in 1758 and was then known as the Tower of the Treasured Moon.

The compound was first built between the 10th and 13th centuries as a sort of playground for the emperors and their retinue. It was expanded during the Ming but most of the present buildings only date from the Qing Dynasty. After the overthrow of the imperial government and the establishment of the republic it served as the site of the presidential palace.

Since the founding of the People's

Republic in 1949, Zhongnanhai has been the residence and offices of the highest-ranking members of the Communist Party. People like Mao Zedong, Zhou Enlai, Liu Shaoqi and Zhu De have all lived and worked in the area. The offices of the Central Committee of the Communist Party and of the State Council, the Central People's Government and the Military Commission of the Party Central Committee also have their offices here.

Prior to the arrival of the new batch of tenants Zhongnanhai had been the site of the emperor's ploughing of the first symbolic furrow of the farming season, and the venue for imperial banquets and the highest examinations in martial arts. Empress Dowager Cixi once lived here; after the failure of the 1898 reform movement she imprisoned Emperor Guangxu in the Hall of Impregnating Vitality where, ironically, he later died. Yuan Shikai used Zhongnanhai for ceremonial occasions during the few years of his presidency of the Chinese Republic; his vice-president moved into Guangxu's death-house.

Beihai Park

Approached by four gates, and just north-west of the Forbidden City, Beihai Park is the former playground of the emperors. It's rumoured to have been the private pleasure domain of the great dragon lady/white witch Jiang Qing, widow of Mao and now serving a life sentence as No 1 of the Gang of Four. The park covers an area of 68.2 hectares, half of which is a lake. The island in the lower middle is composed of the heaped earth dug to create the lake – some attribute this to the handiwork of Kublai Khan.

The site is associated with the Great Khan's Palace, the belly-button of Beijing before the creation of the Forbidden City. All that remains of the Khan's court is a large jar made of green jade, in the Round City near the south entrance. A present given in 1265, and said to contain the Khan's wine, it was later discovered in the hands of Taoist priests who used it to store pickles. In the Light Receiving Hall, the main structure nearby, is a 1½-metre-high white jade buddha inlaid with jewels – a gift from Burma to Empress Dowager Cixi.

From the 12th century on, Beihai Park was landscaped with artificial hills, pavilions, halls, temples and covered walkways. In the present era the structures have been massively restored and Beihai Park is now one of the best examples of a classical garden found in China.

Dominating Jade Islet on the lake, the White Dagoba is a 36 metre high pop-art 'Peppermint Bottle' originally dating from 1651. It was put up for a visit by the Dalai Lama and was rebuilt in 1741. It's believed that Lamaist scriptures, robes and other sacred objects are encased in this brick-and-stone landmark.

On the north-east shore of the islet is the handsome double-tiered Painted Gallery – with unusual architecture for a walkway. Near the boat-dock is the Fangshan Restaurant, dishing up recipes favoured by Empress Cixi. She liked 120-course dinners with about 30 kinds of desserts. The restaurant is expensive and high class, and takes reservations only (but check out the decor!). Off to one side, however, is a snack bar that dispenses royal pastries much cheaper.

From this point you can catch a barge to the north-west part of the park or, if energetic, double back and rent a rowboat (there's another rowboat on the north-west side). The attraction on the north side is the Nine Dragon Screen, five metres high and 27 metres long, made of coloured glazed tiles. It's one of the three famous ones in the PRC, and is in good shape. The screen's function was to scare off evil spirits; it stands at the entrance to a temple which has disappeared. To the south-west of the boat dock on this side is the Five Dragon Pavilion dating to 1651, where the emperors liked to fish or camp out at night to watch the moon.

On the east side of the park are the

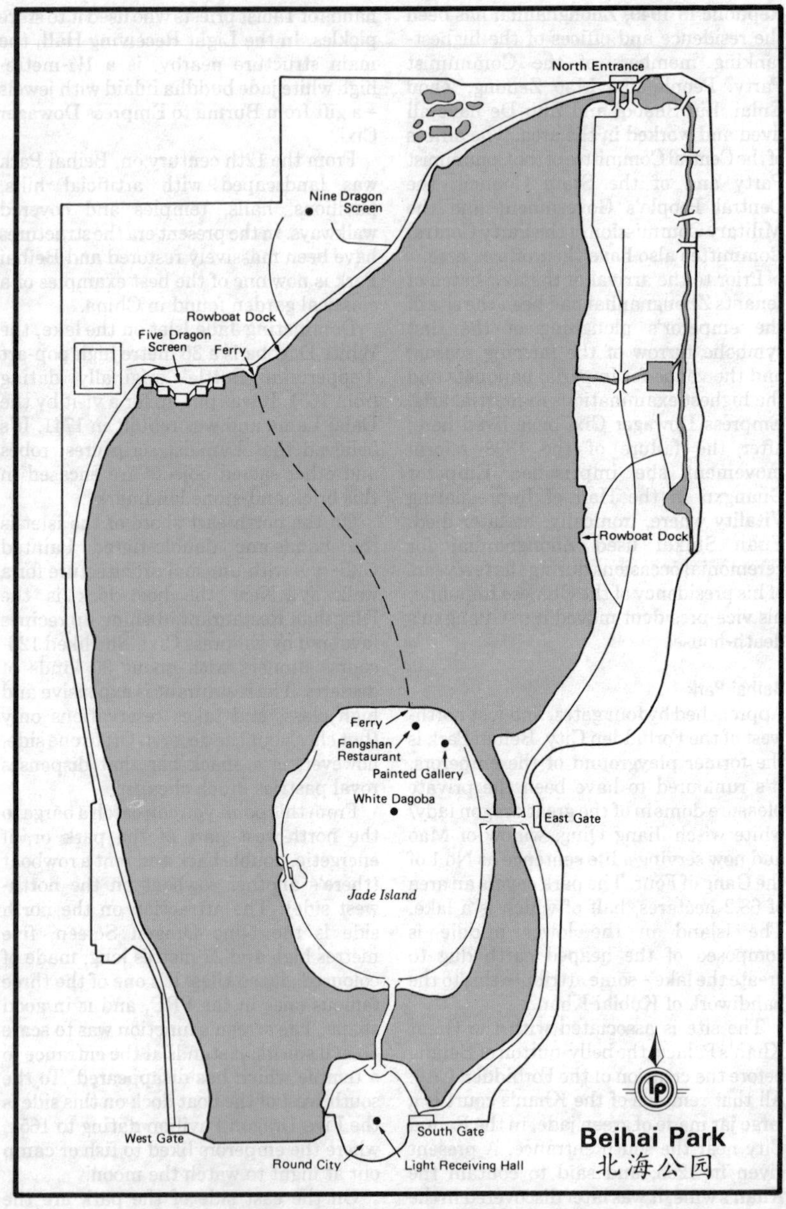
North Entrance
Nine Dragon Screen
Rowboat Dock
Five Dragon Screen
Ferry
Rowboat Dock
Ferry
Fangshan Restaurant
Painted Gallery
White Dagoba
East Gate
Jade Island
West Gate
South Gate
Round City
Light Receiving Hall
Beihai Park
北海公园

'gardens within gardens'. These waterside pavilions, winding corridors and rockeries were summer haunts of the imperial family, notably Emperor Qianlong and Empress Cixi. They date back some 200 years, with structures like the Painted Boat Studio and the Studio of Mental Calmness. Until 1980 the villas were used as government offices.

Beihai Park is a relaxing place to stroll around, grab a snack, sip a beer, rent a rowboat or, as the Chinese do, cuddle on a bench in the evening. Crowded on weekends. Some people dive into the lake when no-one's around – swimming is not permitted. In winter there's skating. Nothing is new in China; skating apparently goes back to the 18th century when Emperor Qianlong reviewed the imperial skating parties here. Admission is 5 fen and in summer the park stays open until late at night.

Other Parks

In imperial days the parks were laid out at the compass-points: to the west of the Forbidden City lies the Temple of the Moon (Yuetan) Park; to the north lies the Temple of the Earth (Ditan) Park; to the south lies the Agriculture (Taoranting) Park and to the east is the Temple of the Sun (Ritan) Park. To the south-east of the Forbidden City is the showpiece of them all, the Temple of Heaven (Tiantan).

All of these parks were venues for ritual sacrifice offered by the emperors. Not much remains of the shaman structures, bar those of Tiantan, but if you arrive early in the morning you can witness tai chi, fencing exercises, or perhaps opera-singers and musicians practising. It's well worth investigating the very different rhythms of the city at this time. Another park of note is Zizhuyuan, Purple Bamboo Park, west of the zoo.

Temporary exhibitions take place in the parks, including horticultural and cultural exhibitions, and there is even the odd bit of open-air theatre as well as some worthy eating establishments. Just to the north of Yuetan Park is the Emei Restaurant, which serves hot Sichuan food with no compromise for foreign palates, and is preferred by Sichuan food addicts to the Sichuan Restaurant itself. The Ritan Restaurant in Ritan Park serves jiaozi in an older-style pavilion and is very popular with westerners for snacks.

The Temple of Heaven (Tiantan)

The perfection of Ming architecture, the Temple of Heaven has come to symbolise Beijing. Its lines appear on countless pieces of tourist literature (including your 50 fen tourist bill), and as a brand name for a wide range of products from tiger balm to plumbing fixtures. In the 1970s the complex got a facelift and was freshly painted after pigment research. It is set in a 267-hectare park, with four gates at the compass points, and bounded by walls to the north and east. It originally functioned as a vast stage for solemn rites performed by the Son of Heaven who came here to pray for good harvests, seek divine clearance and atone for the sins of the people.

With this complicated mix in mind, the unique architectural features will delight numerologists, necromancers and the superstitious – not to mention acoustic engineers and carpenters. Shape, colour and sound take on symbolic significance. The temples, seen in aerial perspective, are round, and the bases are square, deriving from the ancient Chinese belief that heaven is round, and the earth is square. Thus the north end of the park is semicircular and the south end is square (remember that the layout of the Beijing parks places the Temple of Earth on the northern compass point and the Temple of Heaven on the southern compass point).

The Temple of Heaven was considered highly sacred ground and it was here that the emperor performed the major ceremonial rites of the year. Just before the winter solstice, the emperor and his enormous

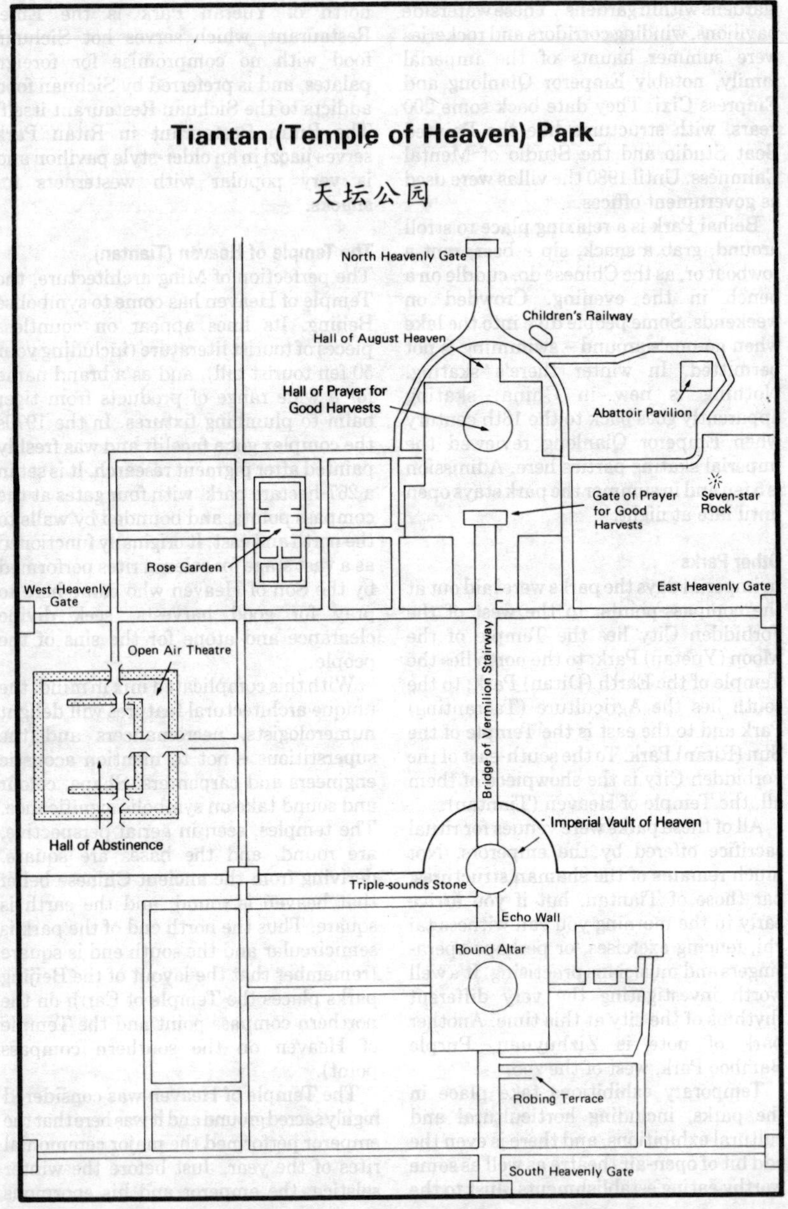
Tiantan (Temple of Heaven) Park
天坛公园
North Heavenly Gate
Children's Railway
Hall of August Heaven
Hall of Prayer for
Good Harvests
Abattoir Pavilion
Seven-star
Rock
Gate of Prayer
for Good
Harvests
Rose Garden
West Heavenly
Gate
East Heavenly Gate
Open Air Theatre
Bridge of Vermilion Stairway
Imperial Vault of Heaven
Hall of Abstinence
Triple-sounds Stone
Echo Wall
Round Altar
Robing Terrace
South Heavenly Gate

entourage passed down Qianmen Avenue to the Imperial Vault of Heaven in total silence – commoners were not permitted to view the ceremony and remained cloistered indoors. The procession included elephant chariots, horse chariots and long lines of lancers, nobles, officials and musicians, dressed in their finest. The next day the emperor waited in a yellow silk tent at the south gate while officials moved the sacred tablets to the Round Altar, where the prayers and sacrificial rituals took place. The least hitch was regarded as an ill omen, and it was thought that the nation's future was thus decided. This was the most important ceremony although other excursions to the Temple of the Earth (Ditan Park) also took place.

Round Altar The five-metre-high Round Altar was constructed in 1530 and rebuilt in 1740. It is composed of white marble arrayed in three tiers, and its geometry revolves around the imperial number nine. Odd numbers were considered heavenly, and nine is the largest single-digit odd number. The top tier, thought to symbolise heaven, has nine rings of stones, each ring composed of multiples of nine stones, so that the ninth ring has 81 stones. The middle tier – earth – has the 10th to 18th rings. The bottom tier – man – has the 19th to 27th rings, ending with a total of 243 stones in the largest ring, or 27 times nine. The number of stairs and balustrades are also multiples of nine. If you stand in the centre of the upper terrace and say something, the sound waves are bounced off the marble balustrades, making your voice appear louder (nine times?).

Echo Wall Just north of the altar, surrounding the entrance to the Imperial Vault of Heaven, is the Echo Wall, 65 metres in diameter. This enables a whisper to travel clearly from one end to your friend's ear at the other – that is, if there's not a group tour in the middle.

In the courtyard are the Triple Echo Stones. If you stand on number one and clap or shout, the sound is echoed once, on the second stone twice, and on the third, three times. Should it return four times, you will almost certainly not get a railway ticket that day, or any other day that is a multiple of three.

Imperial Vault of Heaven This octagonal vault was built at the same time as the Round Altar, and is structured along the lines of the older Hall of Prayer for Good Harvests, though it is smaller. It used to contain tablets of the emperor's ancestors, which were used in the winter solstice ceremony. Proceeding up from the Imperial Vault is a walkway: to the left is a molehill composed of excess dirt dumped from digging air-raid shelters and to the right is a rash of souvenir shops.

Hall of Prayer for Good Harvests The main structure of the whole complex is the Hall of Prayer for Good Harvests, a magnificent piece mounted on a three-tiered marble terrace. Built in 1420 it was burnt to cinders in 1889 and heads rolled in apportioning blame. The cause seems to have been lightning. A faithful reproduction based on Ming architectural methods was erected the following year, using Oregon fir as the support pillars.

The four pillars at the centre represent the seasons, the 12 ringing those denote the months of the year, and the 12 outer ones are symbolic of the day, broken into 12 'watches'. Embedded in the ceiling is a carved dragon, symbol of royalty. The patterning, carving and gilt decoration of this ceiling and its swirl of colour is a dizzy sight – enough to carry you into the Seventh Heaven.

In fact it looks peculiarly modern, like a graphic from a sci-fi movie of a spaceship about to blast into hyperspace. All this is made more amazing by the fact that the wooden pillars ingeniously support the ceiling without nails or cement – for a building 38 metres high and 30 metres in diameter, a stunning accomplishment of carpentry. Capping the structure is a deep blue umbrella of tiles with a golden knob and two complementary eaves.

Other Tiantan, it should not be forgotten, is also a park and a meeting place. Tai chi enthusiasts assemble at the gates in the morning and head off for their favourite spots, some practising snatches of opera en route. There are also nice floral exhibits; along the east wall is a poultry and food market.

Celestial Potpourri
There are heaps of temples and other divine edifices scattered around the capital, all in varying states of preservation, decay or renovation. These have now been put to various uses as warehouses, residences, schools, army barracks, factories and so on. They may even be open to visitors or quick peepers. Some are listed below.

Lama Temple (Yonghegong) By far the most pleasant temple in Beijing – beautiful gardens, stunning frescoes and tapestries, incredible carpentry. Get to this one before you're 'templed out' – it won't chew up your day.

Yonghegong is the most renowned Tibetan Buddhist temple within China outside Tibet itself (a carefully worded statement!). Located toward Andingmen, it became the official residence of Count Yin Zhen after extensive renovation. Nothing unusual in that – but in 1723 he was promoted to emperor, and moved to the Forbidden City. His name was changed to Yong Zheng, and his former residence became Yonghe Palace. The green tiles were changed to yellow, the imperial colour, and – as was the custom – the place could not be used except as a temple. In 1744 it was converted into a lamasery, and became a residence for large numbers of monks from Mongolia and Tibet.

In 1792, Qianlong, having quelled an uprising in Tibet, instituted a system whereby the government issued two gold vases. One was kept at the Jokhang Temple in Lhasa for determining the reincarnation of the Dalai Lama (under the supervision of the Minister for Tibetan Affairs), and the other was kept at Yonghegong for the lottery for the Mongolian Grand Living Buddha. The Lama Temple thus assumed a new administrative importance in minority control.

The lamasery has three richly worked archways and five main halls strung in a line down the middle, each taller than the preceding one. Styles are mixed – Mongolian, Tibetan and Han, with courtyard enclosures and galleries.

The first hall, Lokapala, houses a statue of the Maitreya (future) Buddha, flanked by celestial guardians. The statue facing the back door is Weituo, guardian of Buddhism, made of white sandalwood. Beyond, in the courtyard, is a pond with a bronze mandala depicting Xumi Mountain, the Buddhist paradise.

The second hall, Yonghedian, has three figures of Buddha – past, present and future.

The third hall, Yongyoudian, has statues of the Buddha of Longevity and the Buddha of Medicine (to the left). The courtyard following it has galleries with some nandikesvaras – joyful buddhas tangled up in multi-armed close encounters. These are coyly draped lest you be corrupted by the sight, and are to be found in other esoteric locations.

The Hall of the Wheel of Law, further north, contains a large bronze statue of Tsongkapa (1357-1419), founder of the Yellow Sect, and frescoes depicting his life. This Tibetan-style building is used for study and prayer.

The last hall, Wanfu Pavilion, has an 18-metre-high statue of the Maitreya Buddha in his Tibetan form, sculpted from a single piece of sandalwood and clothed in yellow satin. The smoke curling up from the yak-butter lamps transports you momentarily to Tibet, from where the log for this statue came.

In 1949 the Lama Temple was declared protected as a major historical relic. Miraculously it survived the Cultural Revolution without scars. In 1979 large amounts were spent on repairs and it was restocked with several dozen novices from Inner Mongolia, a token move on the part of the government to back up its claim that the Lama Temple is a 'symbol of religious freedom, national unity and stability in China'. The novices study Tibetan language and the secret practices of the Yellow Sect.

The temple is very much active again. Prayers take place early in the morning, not for public viewing, but if you enquire discreetly of the head lama you might be allowed to return the following morning. No photography is permitted inside the temple buildings, tempting as it is – in part due to the monkish sensitivity to the reproduction of buddha images, and partly perhaps to the postcard industry. The temple is open daily, except Mondays, from 9 am to 4.30 pm.

Confucian Temple Complex Just down the hutong opposite the gates of the Lama Temple is the former Confucian Temple (Kongmiao) and Imperial College (Guozijian). The Confucian Temple is the largest in the land after the one at Qufu. The temple was re-opened in 1981 after some mysterious use as a high-official residence and is now used as a museum – in sharp contrast to the Lama Temple.

The forest of steles in the temple courtyard look very forlorn. The steles record the names of those successful in the civil service examinations (possibly the world's first) of the imperial court. To see his name engraved here was the ambition of every scholar, but it wasn't made easy. Candidates were locked in cubicles (about 8000 of them) measuring roughly 1½ by 1½ metres for a period of three days. Many died or went insane.

The Imperial College was the place where the emperor expounded the Confucian classics to an audience of thousands of kneeling students, professors and court officials – an annual rite. Built by the grandson of Kublai Khan in 1306, the former college was the only institution of its kind in China; it's now the Capital Library. Part of the 'collection' are the stone tablets commissioned by Emperor Qianlong. These are engraved with 13 Confucian classics – 800,000 characters or 12 years' work for the scholar who did it. There is an ancient 'Scholar-Tree' in the courtyard.

Wutasi This is an Indian-style temple with five pagodas, first constructed in 1473 from a model presented to the court. North-west of the zoo, it's difficult to find but has been restored and re-opened. Take Bashiqiao Lu north for almost one km to a bridge, and turn east to the temple, which lies in the middle of a field.

Dazhongsi (Big Bell Temple) This temple is almost two km due east of the Friendship Hotel, and has an enormous 46-ton bell inscribed with Buddhist sutras. The bell was cast during the reign of Ming Emperor Yong Le in 1406 and the tower was built in 1733. This monastery is one of the most popular in Beijing and was re-opened in 1980.

Baitasi (White Dagoba Temple) The dagoba can be spotted from the top of Jing Shan, and is similar (and close to) the one in Beihai Park. It was used as a factory during the Cultural Revolution but re-opened after restoration in 1980. The dagoba dates back to Kublai Khan's days and was completed with the help of a Nepalese architect, though the halls date only from the Qing Dynasty. It lies off Fuchengmennai Dajie.

Guangjisi (Temple of Universal Rescue) This temple is on the north-west side of Xisi intersection, and east of the White Dagoba Temple. It's in good shape and is the headquarters of the Chinese Buddhist Association. It is said to contain some of the finest Buddhist statues in China and might be open to the public.

Huangsi (Yellow Temple) The Yellow Temple can be seen from Beihuan Donglu Ring Road (south side). It is north-west of the intersection of Andingmen and Andingmenwai Dajie. The temple has a distinctive gold-and-white dagoba and was used as the residence for visiting Panchen Lamas from Tibet in the 17th century.

Niujie District (Ox Street) In the south-west sector of Beijing, south of Guanganmennai Dajie, is a Muslim residential area with a handsome mosque facing Mecca. It's an area worth checking out with a feel all its own. In a lane further east of the mosque is the Fayuansi, the Temple of the Source of Law. The temple was originally constructed in the 7th century and is still going strong – it's now a Buddhist College, open to visitors.

Baiyunguan (White Cloud Temple) This is in a district directly south of Yanjing Hotel and west of the moat. It was once the Taoist centre of North China and the site of temple fairs. Check a map for directions. Walk south on Baiyun Lu and cross the moat. Continue south along Baiyun Lu and turn into a curving street on the left; follow it for 250 metres to the temple entrance.

Further south of the White Cloud Temple is the Tianningsi pagoda, looking pretty miserable in a virtual industrial junkyard. The temple once attached has disappeared.

Cathedrals Dongtang (East Cathedral) at 74 Wangfujing was built on the site of the Jesuit priest Adam Schall's house, founded 1666 and later used by the Portuguese Lazarists. It has been rebuilt several times and is now used as a primary school during the week; Catholic services are held early on Sunday mornings.

Nantang (Southern Cathedral) on Qianmen at the Xuanwumen intersection (north-east side) above the Metro station is built on the site of Matteo Ricci's house (first built 1703 and destroyed three times since then).

Beitang (North Cathedral, or the Cathedral of Our Saviour) was built in 1887. It was badly damaged during the Cultural Revolution and converted to a factory warehouse. It was re-opened at the end of 1985 after restoration work was completed. The cathedral is at Xishiku, in the West District.

Mahakala Miao The monastery here is dedicated to the Great Black Deva, a Mongolian patron saint. It's on the hutong running east from Beichizi Dajie (approximately in line with the south moat of the Forbidden City).

Zhihuasi (Black Temple) So nicknamed because of its deep blue tiling, this is a pretty example of Ming architecture (dating to 1443) but there's nothing else of note. If you strain at the bus map, looking north of the main railway station, you will find a hutong called Lumicang, which runs east off Chaoyangmen Nanxidajie (about 1½ km north of the station). The temple is at the east end of Lumicang. The coffered ceiling of the third hall of the 'Growth of Intellect Temple' is not at the east end of Lumicang – it's in the USA. Lumicang hutong had rice granaries in the Qing Dynasty.

The Underground City

With a Soviet invasion supposedly hanging over them in the late '60s, the Chinese built huge civil defence systems, especially in northern China. This hobby started before 1949 when the PLA used the tunnelling technique to surprise the enemy. Pressed for space, and trying to maximise the peacetime possibilities of the air-raid shelters (aside from the fact that the shelters are useless in the event of nuclear attack) Beijing has put them to use as warehouses, factories, shops, restaurants, hotels, roller-skating rinks, theatres and clinics.

CITS has tours to the Underground City, often combined with a visit to the Mao Mausoleum. The section you see on the brief tour is about 270 metres long with tunnels at the four, eight and 15-metre levels. It was constructed by volunteers and shop assistants living in the Qianmen area – about 2000 people and 10 years of spare-time work with simple tools – though the shelters were planned and construction was supervised by the Army. The people reap a few benefits now such as preferential treatment for relatives and friends who can stay in a 100-bed hotel, use of the warehouse space – and there's a few bucks to be made off tourists. Some features of the system you can see are the telecommunications room, first-aid room and ventilation system.

There are roughly 90 entrances to this particular complex. The guide claims that 10,000 shoppers in the Dazhalan area can be evacuated to the suburbs in five minutes (what about the other 70,000?!) in the event of an attack. Entrances are hidden in shops – the one you descend by is an ordinary-looking garment shop. It's got the flavour of a James Bond movie with a bit of Dr Strangelove thrown in. A terse lecture is given by a Civil Air Defence man at the end, complete with fluorescent wall map – oh, and a cup of tea before you surface.

If you want to give the CITS tour a miss then there are two bits of the underground city that are easy to get to yourself – the subway and the Dongtian Underground Restaurant.

Dongtian (Cave Heaven) Restaurant The Dongtian Restaurant is just north of Changan at 192 Xidan Beidajie, east side – look for a display of pictures of

subterranean scenes that mark the entrance. Descending 60 steps, you'll come to four small dining rooms, all served by the same restaurant. They have the decor of an American greasy-spoon truck-stop as interpreted by a crazed neoclassical Sino-Italian decorator. The chambers are the Plum Blossom, Orchid and Chrysanthemum rooms, and the Bamboo Chamber. Three of them serve spaghetti, pork cutlets, sausages, quasi-French and Italian dishes. The fourth, with Chinese-style decor featuring ceramic tables and stools, is an ice cream parlour. Eating western style with western utensils is chic among inhabitants of Beijing (leaving half of it on the plate is also chic), and good practice for that tiny, tiny possibility that one may end up in Paris on vacation. The customers are therefore amenable to the stray European face that wanders in.

Dongtian is one of about a dozen underground restaurants operating in Beijing. What better way to get there than by subway? Take the tube to Xuanwumen, then hop a bus north about two stops.

Changan Inn Next to the Dongtian, but not accessible to the public (you can try) is the Changan Inn with its 400 beds. There are some 100 underground hotels in Beijing with a total of 10,000 beds. While the views may not be great, the rooms are insulated by several metres of earth from traffic noise, dust, wind and pesky mosquitoes. Young Chinese honeymooners to the capital can rent one of the Changan Inn's special Double Happiness rooms, decorated with bright red calligraphy wishing them joys when they surface and re-enter the real world. As the Chinese saying goes, 'Make one thing serve two purposes.'

The Beijing Subway The Beijing Subway runs 15 to 20 metres underground and is a major link in the air-raid shelter system, providing fast evacuation of civilians to the suburbs. The East-West line, though opened in 1969, was for a time restricted to Chinese with special passes – and foreigners were not permitted to use it until 1980. Like most subways it loses money – several million yuan per year. One of the reasons given is that it employs a lot of people who give orders but do very little work. Unlike most other subways the crime rate is low (there is the odd pickpocket), graffiti is non-existent, it's very clean, and messy suicides are said to be rare (one every couple of years supposedly). The 'Underground Dragon' is mostly tiled, and has austere marble pillars. Some platforms are enlivened with brushwork paintings, illuminated ads – and, surprise, surprise, Hong Kong-based English-only advertising.

A good idea to familiarise yourself with urban and suburban Beijing is to hop off the subway at random, explore, and pop back down again. It's only 10 fen per ride and you can't get lost. Gives you some very fast first impressions of different sectors of Beijing, painlessly. The subway is open 5.30 am to 10.30 pm and trains run every few minutes. It can get very crowded but it sure beats the buses!

Hutong Hopping

A completely different side of Beijing emerges in the hutongs or back lanes. The original plan of the city allowed for enclosed courtyards buried down alleys and, though the politics have changed, many of the courtyards remain. Given the choice between a high-rise block and a traditional compound, most residents of Beijing would opt for the latter. The compounds have loads more character – and offer courtyards to grow vegetables in. Once occupied by a single family (with guest reception rooms near the front entrance), the compounds are now occupied by many, with courtyard space eaten away by newer structures.

The walled compounds mostly date from the Ming and Qing dynasties and come in three varieties – small, medium and large. The large ones, with two or more courtyards, are easily spotted by their elaborate gateways and outer-wall decorations. The Bamboo Garden Hotel and the Sichuan Restaurant are fine examples and were formerly residences of generals or high officials.

There are over 3000 hutongs in Beijing, so there's a lot out there to discover. The word derives from Mongolian and means a passageway between tents or yurts. Many of the hutongs are named after markets (fish, pig, rice, sheep) or trades (hats, bowstrings, trousers) once conducted along them. Others took their names as the seats of government offices, or specialised suppliers to the palace (granaries, red lacquer, armour). Yet others were named after dukes and officers. Each hutong has its own legends and history, and is its own little world.

Around the Forbidden City of yore there were some very odd industries: Wet-Nurse Lane was full of young mothers who breastfed the imperial offspring. They were selected from around China on scouting trips four times a year. Clothes-Washing Lane was where the old maids who did the imperial laundry lived. The maids, grown old in the service of the court, were packed off to far-away places for a few years so that their intimate knowledge of the royal undergarments would be out of date by the time they got round to gossiping.

Walking along the hutongs kind of destroys the advantage of a lightning visit, and may well lead to you accumulating a Chinese entourage. Charging off on a bicycle is the only way to go. If you see an interesting compound, you can stop and peer in – maybe even be invited in; the duller bits you can cruise by. There are two basic styles of this fine sport: the random tour and the semi-controlled tour. The random tour consists of ceremonially ripping up your bus map and, letting loose a loud roar, flinging yourself and bicycle down the nearest hutong (preferably together). An hour before sundown you start asking around for a big street, in order to find the bigger streets that might lead back to your hotel. The semi-controlled method is to pick larger hutongs running east-west between major streets (a lot of them do), so you know where you are at any given point, provided you have a magnifying glass for the bus map and a bit of luck navigating by a jumble of bus numbers.

Beijing Buster Bicycle Tour

Lama Temple – Confucian Temple – Bamboo Garden Hotel – Drum Tower – Northern Lakes – Jing Shan Park – Forbidden City – Beihai Park – Zhongnanhai – Tiananmen – Qianmen – Dazhalan

Obviously this is far too much to attempt in one day, and it's not recommended that you see everything unless you have only one whirlwind day to dive-bomb the capital. The Forbidden City alone is worth a full day's exploration. Attractions like this, however, can be visited several times rather than cased in one fell swoop. This bike tour takes in some of the many moods of Beijing – not, one hopes, just the temples. If the Lama Temple is closed then the Temple of Heaven would make a good substitute at the end of the tour.

Non-stop cycling time is about 80 minutes, Chinese bike, western legs, average pace. If you have trouble, there are two bike-repair shops on Dongdan (112 Dongdan Beidajie and 247b Dongsi Nandajie) and one at 107 Qianmen Jie.

Starting point is outside the CITS office at the Chongwenmen Hotel. What better place to start a self-guided tour that will cost you all of two yuan? Launch yourself into the sea of cyclists, and cycle the length of Dongdan north to the Lama Temple – about a 20-minute haul. Dongdan is a mildly busy shopping area, and this straight stretch is a good way to find your Beijing bicycle-legs and learn to watch for Chinese cyclists and buses cutting you off. The Lama Temple is the most refreshing, well-groomed temple you'll see in Beijing. Note that it's closed on Mondays.

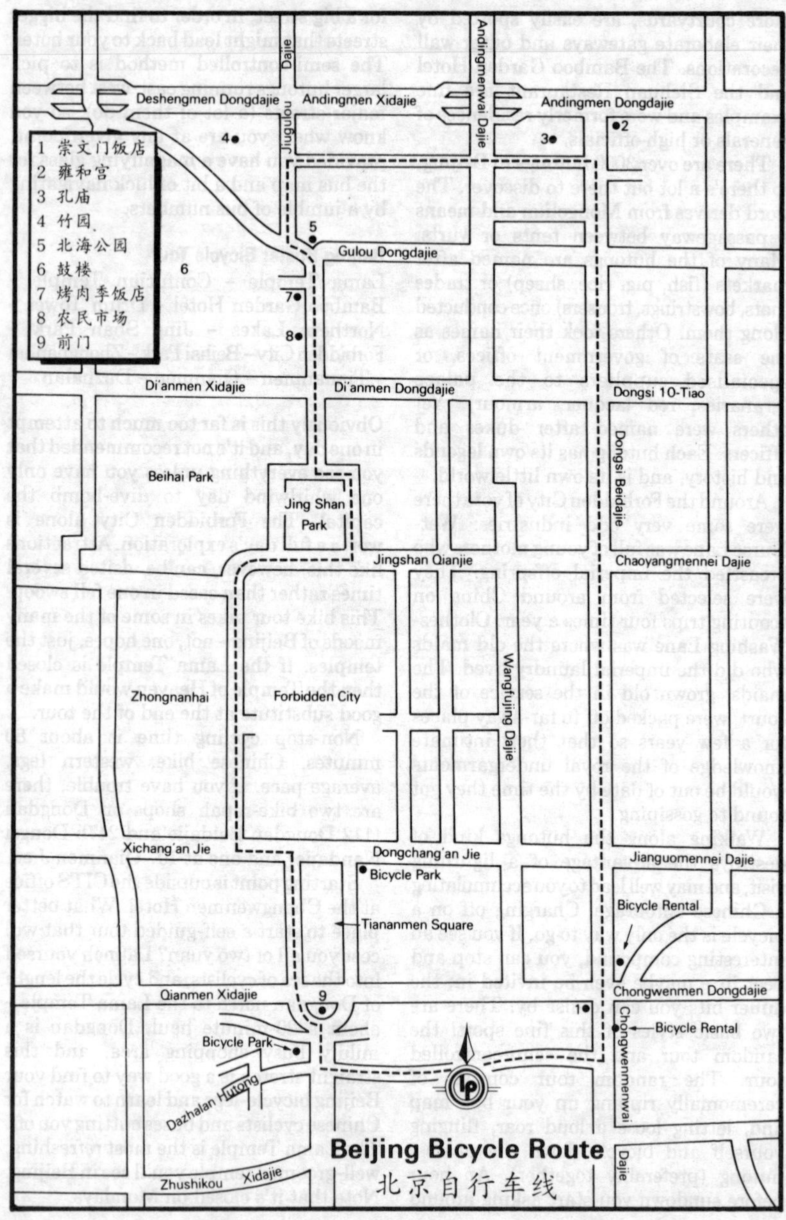
1 崇文门饭店
2 雍和宫
3 孔庙
4 竹园
5 北海公园
6 鼓楼
7 烤肉季饭店
8 农民市场
9 前门
Deshengmen Dongdajie
Jiugulou Dajie
Andingmen Xidajie
Andingmenwai Dajie
Andingmen Dongdajie
Gulou Dongdajie
Di'anmen Xidajie
Di'anmen Dongdajie
Dongsi 10-Tiao
Dongsi Beidajie
Beihai Park
Jing Shan Park
Jingshan Qianjie
Chaoyangmennei Dajie
Wangfujing Dajie
Zhongnanhai
Forbidden City
Xichang'an Jie
Dongchang'an Jie
Bicycle Park
Jianguomennei Dajie
Tiananmen Square
Bicycle Rental
Qianmen Xidajie
Chongwenmen Dongdajie
Bicycle Rental
Chongwenmenwai Dajie
Bicycle Park
Dazhalan Hutong
Zhushikou Xidajie
Beijing Bicycle Route
北京自行车线

1 Chongwenan Hotel/CITS
2 Yonghe Lama Temple
3 Confucius Complex
4 Bamboo Garden Hotel
5 Drum Tower (Gulou)
6 Northern Lakes
7 Kaorouji Restaurant
8 Farmers' Market
9 Qianmen

Take the hutong running west opposite the gates of the Lama Temple. You'll pass through several decorated lintels; these graceful *pailous* (triumphal archways), which commemorate mandarin officials or chaste widows, were ripped out of the thoroughfares of Beijing in the 1950s. The reason given was the facilitation of traffic movement. Some have been relocated in parks. The ones you see in this hutong are rarities.

On your right, a short way down the hutong, are the former Confucian Temple & Imperial College, now a museum/library complex. Unless you can read stele-calligraphy, it's not of great interest. A stele standing in the hutong ordered officials to dismount at this point but you can ignore that.

Continue west on this hutong, and to your right, further down, you will spot a charcoal briquette factory. If you peer in you will see – and hear – the grimy production of these noxious bricks, which are the major heating and cooking source for Beijing residents and the cause of incredible pollution in winter. In imperial days, Fuel-Saving Lane, down by the palace, supplied the court with charcoal and firewood. Some 400 years later it seems this factory is performing a similar task. Marco Polo marvelled at the black lumps that produced heat; you may feel otherwise.

The hutong eventually runs into a smaller one. Continue straight on until it ends at Jiugulou Dajie. Make a small detour here. If you go north on Jiugulou and take the first hutong to the left, you will arrive at the Zhuyuan (Bamboo Garden Hotel), which is a wonderful illustration of the surprises that hutongs hold. This was originally the personal garden of Sheng Xuanhuai, an important Qing official. Exquisite gardens, beautiful courtyards, renovated compound architecture, and expensive restaurant (English menu, al fresco in summer). A quiet place to sip a drink.

Go back to Jiugulou Dajie and head south following the bus No 8 route. Follow Jiugulou to a dead end, turn left and you will come to the Gulou (Drum Tower). It was built in 1420 and has several drums which were beaten to mark the hours of the day – in effect the Big Ben of Beijing. Time was kept with a water clock. It's in pretty sad shape, but an impressive structure nonetheless with a solid brick base. Occasional exhibitions take place here since the tower is connected with local artisans. Admission is Y2.

Behind the Drum Tower, down an alley directly north, is the Bell Tower (Zhong Lou). The Bell Tower was originally built at the same time as the Drum Tower, but it burnt down. The present structure is 18th century, and the gigantic bell which used to hang there has been moved to the Drum Tower. Legend has it that the bellmaker's daughter plunged into the molten iron before the bell was cast. Her father only managed to grab her shoe as she did so, and the bell's soft sound resembled that of the Chinese for 'shoe' *(xie). Xiuxi*, dingdong, time for lunch. The same story is told about a couple of other bells in China.

As you head due south of the Drum Tower, the first hutong to the right provides a very interesting excursion into the Northern Lakes area. This district is steeped in history; if you consult a Beijing map you will see that the set of lakes connects from north to south. In the Yuan Dynasty, barges would come through various canals to the top lake (Jishuitan), a sort of harbour for Beijing. Later the lakes were used for pleasure-boating, and were bordered by the residences of high officials.

The larger lake to the north-west is the Shisha Houhai (Lake of the Ten Back Monasteries). Below that is the Shisha Qianhai (Lake of the Ten Front Monasteries). Little evidence of the splendour left, but check out the Shoudu Karouji Restaurant which has balcony dining in summer; the restaurant is buried down a hutong. For those with some more time, it's possible to circumnavigate the lakes. It's a peaceful area and a good place to see what the locals are up to. You can't really get lost – just keep the lakes in sight.

Worth checking out is Prince Gong's Residence (Gongwangfu), which lies more or less at the centre of the arc created by the lakes running from north to south. It's reputed to be the model mansion for Cao Xueqin's 18th-century classic, *A Dream of Red Mansions* (translated as the *The Story of the Stone* by David Hawkes, Penguin, 1980). It's one of the largest private residential compounds in Beijing, with a nine-courtyard layout, high walls and elaborate gardens. Prince Gong was the son of a Qing emperor.

Back on track. Return to the Drum Tower. Looking south from it you can see the outlines of pavilions on Jing Shan (Coal Hill), which is where you're heading. From this point, you are tracing the historic north-south axis, travelling the ancient hour-glass that filters into Qianmen Jie. Continuing south of the Drum Tower, you come into a fairly busy shopping street. About half-way down you cross a small stone bridge (with buildings around it). If you turn right immediately after the bridge you'll arrive at a farmer's market on the shores of Shisha Front Lake – explore!

Continuing down Dianmen Dajie, you'll bump into the backside of Jing Shan Park. Proceed to the front, where there is bicycle parking. Jing Shan Park is a splendid place to survey the smog of Beijing, get your bearings with 360° views, and enjoy a good overview of the russet roofing of the Forbidden City opposite. There are snack bars in both the park and the north end of the Forbidden City.

Hop back on your trusty hulk and follow the moat west. Just beyond the traffic lights is the entrance to Beihai Park, where you can exercise your arms as well as your legs – rent a rowboat. There's a café near the south gate overlooking Beihai Lake, where you can get beer, coffee, tea or cold drinks.

Back-pedal a bit to the traffic lights, hang a right, and you're heading into the most sensitive part of the capital – the Zhongnanhai Compound. On the left, going down Beichang Jie, you pass some older housing that lines the moat. On the right is a high wall that shields from view the area where top Party members live and work (it was decided not to rip down this section of the old walls). In 1973, when the new wing of the Beijing Hotel shot up, the Public Security Bureau suddenly realised that guests with binoculars could observe activity in Zhongnanhai, so a fake building was erected along the western wall of the Forbidden City to short-circuit that possibility. Mysterious buildings, indeed, abound in this locale (also the strip back at the traffic lights along the way to Jing Shan Park), including private theatres for viewing foreign films and so on. On the flank of Zhongshan Park (that is, on your left) there's a rounded hole-in-the-wall entrance to the Tai Sam Yuen Restaurant which serves jet-set food and an incredible range of liquors – for cadre clientele.

At the end of the street is an archway that brings you into Changan Boulevard and Tiananmen Square. Traffic is one way for north/south avenues lining the square. If you want to go to Tiananmen Gate, dismount after the archway and wheel the bike to the parking areas along the sidewalk. Cycling across Tiananmen Square is a no-no, but you can walk the bike.

From Tiananmen it's a short ride to

Qianmen Gate, and if you continue down Qianmen St, you'll see a large bike parking lot on your right, open to 9 pm. It's right at the entrance to Beijing's most fascinating hutong, Dazhalan. Your bicycle is absolutely useless in the crowded streets so park it. From Dazhalan, you're within reach of good restaurants, and there's an acrobat theatre on Dazhalan itself.

The fast route back to the Chongwenmen Hotel is to go back to Qianmen Gate and take the wide avenue to the right. More interesting, but slower, is to take the eastern extension of Dazhalan. This hutong will run you right back to your starting point. You have to walk your bike for the first 50 metres or so, then the crowds thin out. Ride slowly since this is a market-type hutong and a shopping area (called Fishmouth Lane) and things can jump out at you.

Weary legs? Why not try the public baths? There's one at the Qianmen entrance side of the hutong. The baths are a bit like the Japanese communal tubs in concept, but split into men's and women's sections. There's a variety of services including massage, foot-treatment and hair cut. Tubs are at different temperatures including lukewarm, hot and searing. The locals are unabashed and a hairy, sweaty cyclist is bound to attract attention. The baths are nowhere near Japanese hygiene standards so try and get there early in the day before the water thickens. Private rooms may be possible and prices are low.

Jesuit Observatory

One of the newer perspectives on Beijing is the observatory mounted on the battlements of a watchtower, once part of the city walls. Dwarfed by embassy housing blocks, it lies in a no-man's land of traffic loops and highways just west of the Friendship Store. The views themselves are worth the visit. This is one of the sights that you can safely say you've seen – small in scope, interesting, some English explanation. The observatory dates back to Kublai Khan's days when it was north of the present site, and Marco Polo writes:

> There are in the city of Khanbalu . . . about five thousand astrologers and soothsayers . . . They have their astrolabes, upon which are described the planetary signs, the hours and their several aspects for the whole year . . . They write their predictions for the year upon certain small squares . . . and these they sell, for a groat apiece, to all persons who are desirous of peeping into the future.

Likewise, the Ming and Qing emperors relied heavily on astrologers before making a move. The present Beijing Observatory was built from 1437 to 1446, not only to facilitate astrological predictions but to aid seafaring navigators. Downstairs are displays of navigational equipment used by Chinese shipping. On the 1st floor are replicas of five 5000-year-old pottery jars, unearthed from Henan Province in 1972 and showing painted patterns of the sun. There are also four replicas of Han Dynasty eave tiles representing east, west, north and south. There is a map drawn on a wooden octagonal board with 1420 stars marked in gold foil or powder; it's a reproduction of the original, which is said to be Ming Dynasty but is based on an older Tang map. Busts of six prominent astronomers are also displayed.

On the 'roof' is a variety of astronomical instruments designed by the Jesuits. The Jesuits, scholars as well as proselytisers, found their way into the capital in 1601 when Matteo Ricci and company were permitted to work with Chinese scientists. The emperor was keen to find out about European firearms and cannons from them.

The Jesuits outdid the resident Muslim calendar-setters and were given control of the observatory, becoming the Chinese court's advisors. Of the eight bronze instruments on display (including an equatorial armilla, celestial globe and altazimuth) six were designed and constructed under the supervision of the Belgian priest Ferdinand Verbiest, who came to China in 1659 to work at the Qing court. The instruments were built between 1669 and 1673, and are embellished with sculpted bronze dragons and other Chinese craftwork, a unique mix of east and west. The azimuth theodolite was supervised by Bernard Stumpf, also a missionary. The eighth instrument, the new armilla, was completed in 1754. It's not known which of the instruments on display are the originals.

During the Boxer Rebellion, the instruments disappeared into the hands of the French and the Germans. Some were returned in 1902, while others came back under the provisions of the Treaty of Versailles (1919). Bertrand Russell commented that this was probably the most important benefit which the treaty secured to the world'. The observatory the Jesuits set up in Shanghai was used for meteorological predictions, and is still used for that purpose. The Jesuits even had some influence over architecture in Beijing, and designed the Italian rococo palaces at Yuanmingyuan (the Old Summer Palace, destroyed in 1860) using Versailles as a blueprint. The observatory is open daily, except Mondays, 9 to 11 am and 1 to 4 pm; admission is 20 fen.

Other Sights

The zoo is the pits – after you've been there you'll probably look as pissed off as the animals do. No attempt has been made to re-create their natural environments. It's all concrete and cages with little shade or water. The Panda House, right by the gates, has four dirty specimens that would be better off dead. Parents can buy their children miniature plastic rifles for only Y4.80 with which they can practise shooting the animals.

The zoo is in the north-west corner of the city; the former Ming Dynasty garden was converted to a zoo in 1908. It contains 400 species and is the largest in China. Some rare animals reside here, including golden monkeys from Sichuan, Yangtse alligators, wild Tibetan donkeys, the snow leopard and the black-necked crane.

Nearby are the Beijing Planetarium and the bizarre Soviet-style Beijing Exhibition Hall (irregular industrial displays, theatre, Russian restaurant) which looks like some crazed Communist architect's wedding-cake decoration.

Places to Stay

Beijing has chronically overbooked hotel space, a situation that is aggravated in peak seasons. New hotels are going up to alleviate the problem, but if you want a bed for the night it is likely you will encounter problems for some time to come. Hotels in Beijing fall into different categories: those permanently occupied by foreign businesspeople, diplomats and visiting dignitaries; those used by foreign experts; the group-tour hotels; the Overseas Chinese hotels; the 'cadre' hotels; and the scarcer low-budget hotels.

Hotels perform a number of functions other than lodging and this listing provides a guide to what those functions might be. The listing is by no means complete, nor are your chances of getting into these hotels. Even if you have the money and you look like the kind of person the hotel deems acceptable, you could be turned away for any number of reasons or whims. Those who have the correct I.D. (like foreign experts) can usually get much cheaper prices.

Places to Stay – bottom end

There is now one established low-budget, backpacker's hotel in Beijing regularly dispensing cheap dormitory beds and relatively cheap rooms. This is the *Qiao Yuan Hotel* (tel 338861) on Dongbinhe Lu near the Yongdingmen Railway Station. Dorm beds are Y8, double rooms Y36 with shower, triples Y32. To get there take bus No 20 from Beijing Main Station to the terminus; walk for about 10 minutes along the canal (there's a sign in English) to the hotel. Or from just north of the Chongwenmen Hotel take trolley bus No 106 to the terminus. There are also minibuses for Yongdingmen which leave from the bus No 20 stop opposite the main train station; these cost Y1 and run all night. The hotel has a money-exchange service, restaurant and bicycle hire.

A number of travellers have stayed at the *Long Tan Hotel*, which has beds for Y10 in three-bed rooms. Friendly staff and a good, cheap restaurant. The hotel is opposite Long Tan Park, close to a hospital. From Chongwenmen take bus No 41.

Tiantan Sports Hotel (tel 752831), 10 Tiyuguan Rd, derives its name from its position between the Temple of Heaven and the gymnasium. It hosts sports-minded group tours but will take whoever else turns up. The hotel has a YMCA tinge to it but is a bright, airy place in a good location with friendly staff. It even boasts the *Shanghai Jakarta Restaurant*, which dishes up decent Indonesian-style food like *gado-gado*. To get there take the subway one stop from Beijing Main Station to Chongwenmen, then bus Nos 39, 41 or 43. Singles are Y45 and doubles Y68, which makes it one of the best value places in Beijing.

Beiwei (tel 338631) is on the west side of the Temple of Heaven at 13 Xijing Rd on the corner with Beiwei Lu. It caters for a similar clientele to the Sports Hotel but will also take whoever fronts up. Take the subway two stops from Beijing Main Station, then bus No 5 south. Or you can take bus No 20 direct from Beijing Main Station. Double rooms only (no singles) range from Y63 to Y84.

The *Lu Song Yuan* (tel 442352), one of the best low-budget hotels, is at 22 Jiao Dou Kou Lu (South Eight Lane). It's difficult to find – directly north of China Art Gallery, second hutong north of Dianmen, turn left. This is a very pleasant place with courtyard-style architecture, no high-rise and plenty of sunlight. There are about three dozen double rooms at Y55 each, as well as a bar and dining hall with basic food. The hotel has connections with China Youth Travel Service. Take bus No 104 from the train station.

Places to Stay – middle

Middle-range hotels in Beijing usually offer air-con rooms with colour TV, phone, bath and desk.

The *Xinqiao* (tel 557731) at Chongwenmen intersection, north-west side, was built in the '50s, Soviet-style, and used to be a favourite hangout for foreign journos and businesspeople until the Beijing Hotel drew them away. These days it seems to cater for a Pakistani and Japanese clientele. The main attraction of the place is its international-cuisine restaurant (ground floor, orders taken until 11 pm) which serves curries, pasta, fillet mignon, borsch, chocolate sundaes, kebabs . . . I could go on. Mind you, it's not cheap; even a simple spaghetti carbonara will set you back about Y10, but the setting is most relaxing. There's also a Japanese restaurant and noodle bar. The Chinese restaurant on the 6th floor is a bright, airy place. Double rooms only, from Y130.

The *Friendship Hotel (Youyi Fandian)* (tel 890621) on Baishiqiao Lu, north of the zoo, was also built in the '50s to house Soviet experts, and is now primarily used by western experts and their families, though it does have some tourist accommodation. Double rooms cost from Y144. Decor and fittings are Sino-Russo, facilities are legendary, including full-size swimming pool (open to all), theatre, tennis courts and a foreign experts' club. It's a long way out – up past the zoo in the Haidian area, but it runs its own bus service to the downtown area. The nightlife here is worth checking out, with movies, dances and multi-national congregations of party-goers. The hotel has a staggering 2600 rooms and you practically need a map of the grounds to find your way around. Bus No 332 runs past the hotel.

The *Minzu* (tel 668541) is west of Xidan intersection on Fuxingmennei. It's an 11-storey Russian monolith with doubles from Y172. The ground-floor restaurant is pleasant.

The *Yanjing* (tel 868721) is near the Muxudi subway on Fuxingmenwai. The 20-storey hotel which opened in 1981 was formerly called the 'Fuxing', which came across rather strongly when pronounced with a thick Scottish accent. Inside are some impressive modern murals; the one on the 1st floor is a glazed ceramic fresco with a Silk Road theme. Singles are Y114 and doubles Y196.

Qianmen (tel 338731) at the corner of Yongan Lu and Hufang Lu, south-west of Qianmen Gate, is an eight-storey mid-50s block with fountains in the snazzy foyer. Singles start from Y135 and doubles from Y350.

The *Ritan Hotel* on Ritan Lu, near the corner with Ritan Beilu, has doubles from Y120.

Huadu (tel 501166) is at 8 Xinyuan Nanlu, in the eastern suburbs near Dongzhimen Gate. The six and five-storey blocks are managed by CITS and opened in 1982.

Huaqiao Daxia (Overseas Chinese Building) (tel 558851) at the corner of Wangfujing and Chaoyangmennei caters for overseas Chinese as the name suggests, and is housed in an eight-storey block.

Xiyuan (tel 890721) in the Erligou area near the zoo is very big and modern, with a revolving disco atop the 26-storey block, coffee shop, bar and fitness centre. The restaurants serve Muslim, Chinese and western food. A bit far from the centre of town, but if money is no object then that's no problem.

Places to Stay – top end

Keeping up with the top-end hotels in Beijing is an exasperating task. No sooner does one extravaganza open its doors then the foundations for an even more voluptuous building are laid.

The *Beijing Hotel* (tel 507766), Dong Changan Jie, has the most central location of any hotel in the capital and is therefore prized by businesspeople, embassy staff and dignitaries. Prices start from Y238 single and Y500 double! Rooms are also used on a long-term basis. The roof of the west wing commands a great view of Tiananmen Square and the Forbidden City. There's a money-exchange service (which you can use even if you're not staying at the hotel), post office and telegram/telex service. The hotel is riddled with restaurants and banquet rooms (styles include Sichuan, Beijing duck and Japanese) and some of the specials are worth chasing. Japanese men come here at night to wax lyrically about the Land of the Rising Sun in the Karaoke Bar. The main attraction of the Beijing, however, is that it has great temperature control and is a meeting place for a great cross-section of foreigners, not just tourists. The café in the east wing is nicknamed 'The Zoo' – a reference to the selection of stuffed animals on a souvenir-shop shelf surveying the exotic humans stuffed into easy-chairs opposite. The café serves all kinds of drinks, liquors, ice cream sundaes and apple pie, and is open throughout the day to 11.30 pm. You can get yourself some excellent postcards (made in Japan) and copies of *China Daily*, and forget you're in the capital for a while.

The *Xiangshan (Fragrant Hills Hotel)* (tel 284943) is in north-west Beijing, in the forested grounds where Emperor Kangxi had his summer villas. It's a joint-investment project financed with US loans and designed by Guangdong-born American architect I M Pei. Pei travelled the length and breadth of China in his search for architectural forms and this 'palace' has its fair share of them: northern-style courtyards, Suzhou-style gardens and landscapes (including a mini stone-forest imported from Yunnan) and a layer of electronics and 'modernisation'. The western facilities include paging and security systems, gym, sauna, swimming pool, restaurants and main lobby-courtyard crowned with a glass roof. The hotel opened in 1983 and has 300 rooms. If you want to see what a well-behaved, well-dressed Chinese hotel-staffer looks like, visit this place. The locals stand at the gate and have their picture taken against this wonder of the western world.

The *Great Wall Sheraton Hotel* (tel 505566) is on Donghuan Beilu, near the Agricultural Exhibition Centre in embassy-land, north-east Beijing. It's got 22 floors, over 1000 rooms, a staff of 1300 and a foreign management team of 14. Rooms start from Y370 a double plus 10% service charge; presidential suite around Y3100. There's restaurants, lounges (Le France, Silk Road, Cosmos Club), an indoor swimming pool, tennis courts, a beauty salon.

The *Jianguo* (tel 502233) on Jianguomenwai Dajie is just east of the Friendship Store. The hotel was opened in 1982 and has the distinction of being China's first joint-venture hotel. San Francisco architect Clement Chen, who fled Shanghai in 1949, came back for his magic 49% share of the Jianguo. The place is managed by the Hong Kong-based Peninsula group, which has a 10-year contract and is responsible for the spiffy-green uniforms worn by the Chinese maids. The Chinese staff of about 600 have no spittoons and are thoroughly trained not to bite the tourists. They're not allowed newspapers, cigarettes, naps or even chairs. As a compensation prize they can rake in as much as three times an ordinary Beijinger's salary. Facilities include three restaurants, heated indoor swimming pool, disco, queen and king-size beds, cocktail lounge, late-night coffee-bar, health club and other facets of bourgeois decadence. This place could be anywhere – which is part of the idea. Single and double rooms start from Y315.

Next door to the Jianguo Hotel is the equally extravagant *Toronto-Beijing Hotel* (tel 502266) with single and double rooms from Y335. Buffet lunches are Y32 per person, but a few shoe-string travellers who have footed the bill say it's worth every fen!

The Temple of Heaven Crashpad

Getting a cheap bed in Beijing wasn't always as easy as stumbling into the Qiao Yuan Hotel and smiling at the bleary-eyed receptionist. Back in 1983, when we were researching the first edition of this book, dormitory accommodation was hard to come by and to get it often required some aggressive arm-wrestles with un-cooperative hotel managers. Michael Buckley witnessed the creation of such a dormitory:

Scene 1 The meeting room, ground floor, Tiantan Sports Hotel. I roll in at 11 pm – good timing – the next hotel is miles off, and the manager knows even before he picks up the phone that everything else in town is chockablock. After a laborious wait, he allows me a couch in the meeting room. Two more travellers, I discover, are already snoozing on the couches within. Cost is Y3 per night per couchette. Three days later, travellers discover there is another meeting room on the 4th floor – the word spreads.

Scene 2 A traveller strides straight past the manager, backpack on. 'Where are you going?' he demands. 'To the meeting room', she answers, taking the stairs three at a time, not looking back, unrolls sleeping bag on arrival. Manager scratches head – she didn't even bother to ask if there were any rooms free. Manager, driven crazy by travellers' preference for the low-priced meeting rooms, transforms the one on the 4th floor into a dorm with camp beds, Y8, men only. Female travellers quickly point out the injustice – a conference is held, where else, in the ground-floor meeting room and, amazingly enough, a third meeting room is found (2nd floor) and designated a women's dorm. Both of these former meeting rooms, now established dorms, are large and filled with campbeds entirely surrounded by facing armchairs, a somewhat surreal decor.

Scene 3 Word has spread along the travellers' grapevine as far as Hong Kong, but CITS has received neither news nor reservations. A fresh group of travellers steps into the Tiantan off the Trans-Siberian and heads straight for the dorms – later they set up a disco near the restaurant. The manager has given up denying that the dorms exist: the campbeds are given a shakedown, spruced up, and the price jumps to Y10.

Scene 4 Much later. The dorms are full, *really* full. I am sharing a room with two people, one sleeping on the floor. I pass the desk as two travellers argue with the manager, refusing to believe the dorms are really really full, otherwise known as 'aw-full'. The room I'm in is large – space for two more on the floor, so I offer the travellers the option if they get stuck and tell them the room number. When I return in the evening, there are about seven travellers in the room arguing with the manager about floor space, and I quietly slip back out again. Ah yes, time to leave Beijing before another crashpad is created.

Places to Eat – Pigging Out in Beijing

In 1949 Beijing had an incredible 10,000 snack bars and restaurants; by 1976 that number had dwindled to less than 700. Restaurants, a nasty bourgeois concept, were all to have been phased out and replaced by revolutionary dispensaries dishing out rice. We could hazard some wild guesses about what happened to some of the chefs – they were allocated jobs as bus drivers while the bus drivers were given jobs as chefs. Anyhow the number of eateries is well on the rise again. While there are still not enough to cater for the million-odd Chinese customers, they certainly present ample variety for the average gastronome and there's no way you'll get through them all. Most of the regional and minority styles are represented in the capital.

When & Where Location and timing have a lot to do with whether you get your meal. At around 5 pm, a strange eating hour for westerners, the internal alarm clock hasn't got the message yet. Dinner is under way, and the panic is on. Where's the nearest hotpot? Which bus? Listed below are some favourite restaurants and a brief rundown of some others. It's the tip of the epicurean iceberg. Go and hunt for more. Eating out in the capital is a true adventure, one that should be seized with both chopsticks. Dining hours are 5 to 7 pm sharp but try and get there by 6 pm. Lunch is 11 am to 1 pm and is less crowded. If you miss out, there's always, of course, predictable hotel food.

Table Manners Forget those! We speak here of the popular prole section of a restaurant – waiters are in the nasty habit of intercepting foreigners and detouring them to private cubicles where the furniture is plusher, crowds are non-existent, prices sky-rocket and the kitchen is exactly the same. Any number of tactics will be employed to steer you away from the popular section. Never mind, throw yourself in anyway. Fighting for your supper increases the appetite, and your table company will be congenial enough once you manage to land a seat.

Order by pointing to your neighbour's dishes. Make sure your finger gets within an inch of the food and that you didn't order three of that dish. Beer is usually obtained with tickets at a separate counter, but you can solve this by arriving with your own beer from a nearby store. At the established restaurants you can reserve tables by phoning ahead. This will mean cubicles, banquet-style and more expensive food, although some dishes can only be obtained by phoning ahead with a group order. Food, like the trains, comes in different classes; if you want to get more you'll have to pay more.

Specialities Northern cuisine specialities are Beijing duck, Mongolian hot pot,

Muslim barbecue and Imperial food. Imperial cuisine is served up in the restaurants of Beihai Park, the Summer Palace and the Western Hills – very expensive, but go for the cheaper snacks. Mongolian hot pot is a winter dish – a brass pot with charcoal inside it is placed at the centre of the table and you cook thick strips of mutton and vegetables yourself, fondue fashion, spicing as you like. Muslim barbecues use lamb, a Chinese Muslim influence; shish kebabs are called *shashlik*.

Beijing duck is the capital's famous invention, now a production-line of sorts. Your meal starts at one of the agricultural communes around Beijing where the duck is pumped full of grain and soya bean paste to fatten it up. The ripe duck is lacquered with molasses, pumped with air, filled with boiling water, dried, and then roasted over a fruitwood fire. The result, force-fed or not, is delicious.

I forgot to mention that the poor duck is killed somewhere along the line. In fact, the story goes that the original roast duck was not killed. In Changan, where the dish is said to have been devised 1200 years ago, two nobles placed live geese and ducks in an iron cage over a charcoal fire. As the heat increased the thirsty birds would drink from a bowl filled with vinegar, honey, malt, ginger and salt until they passed away.

Beijing Duck Otherwise known as the 'Big Duck', the *Qianmen Roast Duck* (tel 751379) is at 32 Qianmen, east side, near Qianmen subway. This is one of the oldest in the capital, dating back to 1864. Prices for foreigners range from Y20 and up per head, but there's a cheaper section through the right-hand doorway. Same duck, same kitchen. The cheap section is very crowded – if you don't get there by 6 pm, forget it. Beer is brewed on the premises for around Y1.50 a jug. The duck is served in stages. First come boneless meat and crispy skin with a side dish of shallots, plum sauce and crêpes, followed by duck soup made of bones and all the other parts except the quack. Language is not really a problem; you just have to negotiate half or whole ducks. The locals will show you the correct etiquette, like when to spit on the floor.

The *Beijing Hotel* has a number of top-class restaurants. Of interest is the genial west-wing dining room on the 7th floor, where you can get painless Beijing duck. Some think the food's not up to scratch, but perhaps their taste buds are more finely tuned than most. Other gourmet novelties like bear paws are served if you've got the bucks.

The *Small Duck (Bianyifang)* (tel 750505) at 2 Chongwenmenwai Dajie is just east of CITS and has been in business for donkey's years. It uses a slightly different method of preparation – closed oven.

The *Sick Duck Restaurant* (tel 338031) is nicknamed such because of its location close to the Capital Hospital. The restaurant is on Shuaifuyuan Hutong.

Sichuan The place to go is the *Sichuan* (tel 336356) at No 51 Rongxian Hutong. To get there go south from Xidan intersection (where Xidan meets Changan), turn left into a hutong marked by traffic lights and a police-box, and continue along the hutong till you find the grey wall entrance. In contrast to the bland interiors and peeling paint of most of the capital's restaurants, this one is housed in the sumptuous former residence of Yuan Shikai (the general who tried to set himself up as an emperor in 1914). The compound decor is spectacular, and the several dining rooms will clean out your wallet very fast. For cheaper food continue to the back of the courtyard, veer right, and there's a dining room with good meals for a few yuan per head if you're sharing dishes. You'll need some drinks for this one! It's a good idea to bring your own in case they've run out (or better still, a flask of yoghurt to cool the flames). The food is out of this world: fiery pork, explosive prawns, bamboo shoots, bean curd, beef dishes, some seafood, and side dishes of cucumber and bakchoi. In the more expensive parts of the restaurant variety is greater, but the back dining room will sate the appetite.

Another favourite haunt is the *Emei Restaurant* (tel 863068) on Yuetan Beilu, with very cheap, hot Sichuan food. Three dishes plus rice and beer cost around Y15 between two people. Friendly staff.

Next to the *Qianmen Roast Duck* you'll find the *Lili* (tel 752310) at 30 Qianmen. The Sichuan-style spicy chicken and hot noodles with peanuts and chillies are very good. They serve some of the best dumplings in Beijing too.

Also try the *Shuxiang Canguan* (tel 551715) at 40 Chongwenmennei near the Xinqiao Hotel.

Shandong *Fengzeyuan* (tel 332828) at 83 Zhushikou Xidajie serves Shandong-style cuisine. It's highly rated by gourmets and is famous for seafood and soups. Specialities include sea cucumber braised with scallion, snowflake prawns and chicken puffs with shark skin. They also serve duck, crisp chicken, duck-marrow soup and turtle soup with egg. For dessert there's silver-thread rolls, toffee apples and almond curd with pineapple. Despite the restaurant's grubby appearance the food is very good.

This 'cornucopia' is famous for another reason. In 1980 a young cook, Chen Aiwu, announced that Minister of Commerce, Wang Lei had often dined here on the best food at low prices. As a result the minister wrote a self-criticism. Then in 1983 a municipal delegation inspected the restaurant and later dined there at much reduced prices. Up shot Chen, dashed a letter off to *China Youth* newspaper, and the delegation had to pay up and make a personal critique. Well, if you can't have a sex scandal you may as well have a food scandal. There doesn't seem to be a way round the high prices, unless you're a minister – or if you stay away from the seafood.

Tongheju near the Xisi intersection on Xidan Beidajie serves Shandong-style crispy spiced duck, seafood and a renowned pudding, *san bu zhan*, made of eggs, lard and flour.

The crowded *Cuihualou* at 60 Wangfujing, north of Dongfeng Market, has Shandong-style seafood, velvet chicken and toffee apples.

Hunanese The *Quyuan* (tel 662196) is at 133 Xidan Beilu north of Changan, west side, in a red-fronted building by an overhead bridge. The Hunan food served here is hot and spicy like Sichuan cuisine. If the French can do it with frogs, how often do you get a chance to digest dog? Anyone for hot dog? On the menu is onion dog, dog soup (reputed to be an aphrodisiac) and dog stew. For those with canine sensibilities, perhaps a switch to Hunan-style duck spiced with hot pepper, or some seafood, and several styles of noodles. The desserts with lychee nuts are good; they can be varied or custom-made if you phone in advance. The food is cheap and the management nice.

Xiangshu Canting is on the Wangfujing side of Dongfeng Market. The food is a combination of Sichuan and Hunan, highly recommended. Try the Xiangshu for the 'silver-thread rolls' which are Beijing's best pastry.

Mongolian Hotpot & Muslim Barbecue *Jianchun* at 6 Liangshidian is in an alley off the beginning of Dazhalan. It's a very small place and serves Mongolian hotpot, but in winter only.

Kaorouwan at 102 Xuanwumennei, south of Xidan intersection, east side of the street, serves Muslim barbeques and you can do your own skewers if the wind is blowing in the right direction.

Hongbinlou at 82 Xi Changan Jie, just east of Xidan intersection, serves shashlik (kebabs), Beijing duck and Mongolian hotpot. Lamb banquets can be ordered in advance.

Shoudu Karouji (tel 445921) at 37

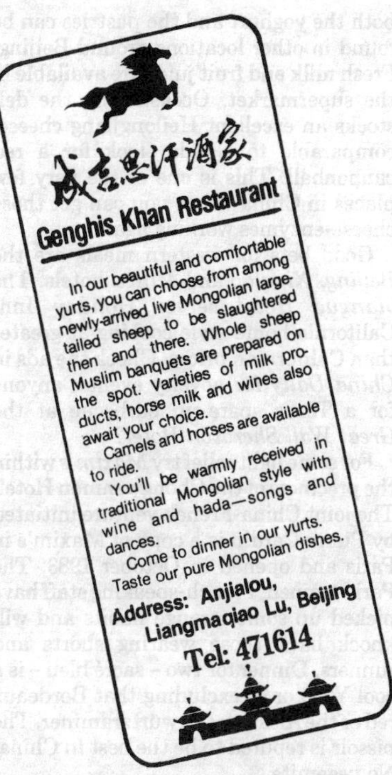

China Daily, 18 October 1986

Shichahai is difficult to find but worth it in summer. Go to the Drum Tower (Gulou) area, turn into a hutong to the left immediately before the Drum Tower as you go north, and follow it down to the lakeside. The dowdy interiors of most Chinese restaurants make you feel boxed in – no windows – but here you've got a view of the lake, the alleys and activity in the area. In summer tables are moved onto the balcony. This is a place for potless hotpot and Muslim barbecue.

Donglaishun (tel 550069) is at 16 Donghuamen, north entrance to Dongfeng Market. This is a minorities restaurant, with a variety of Xinjiang Muslim and other foods. On the ground floor is the masses section serving dumplings. On the 2nd floor you might be able to get Mongolian hotpot – or else it's greasy and gluey fare for a few yuan a head. Top floor is duck with pancakes or shashlik with sesame bread.

Xijiao Huimin Canting is in the Xijiao market area opposite the zoo, south side. They serve Beijing duck, shashlik and, in winter, hotpot.

Shanxi *Jinyang* is at 241 Zhushikou Xidajie, in a red-fronted building west of the Fengzeyuan. You can dine on Shanxi-style salty duck, squirrel fish, noodles and onion cakes in a pleasant atmosphere.

Shanghai *Laozhengxing* at 46 Qianmen is Shanghai-style with a range of seafood, fish, eel, and hairy crabs when in season.

Cantonese *Guangdong Canting* in the Xijiao market serves up Beijing duck and Cantonese-style cuisine, including turtle and snake.

Vegetarian The *Beijing Sucai Canting (Beijing Vegetarian Restaurant)* (tel 654296) is at 74 Xuanwumennei, just around the corner from the Sichuan (north of the Xuanwumen intersection). Downstairs you'll find cold dishes, beer, jiaozi and baozi. Upstairs there's a wider selection, including fungus, bean curd, nuts, fresh vegetables and cauliflower soup. Things come shaped like fish, chicken and duck, except that they're made of soya meat or tofu. Get there early for fresh stuff. They turn out better fare for pre-ordered banquets.

Perhaps better is the Yangzhou-style *Gong De Lin Vegetarian Restaurant* at 158 Qianmen Lu. It gets rave reviews and serves up wonderful veggie food with names to match. How about the 'peacock in pride' or 'the fire is singeing the snow-capped mountains'? The helpings are generous, the prices low and the staff friendly. Probably one of the best restaurants in Beijing.

Other Chinese Restaurants *Huaiyang Fanzhuang* at 217 Xidan Beidajie has a Jiangsu cuisine section serving hairy crab in season.

Shagouju in a tacky building at 60 Xisi Nandajie is further north toward the Xisi intersection. Pork is served in many forms, some dishes in earthenware pots; the food is cheap.

Kangle at 259 Andingmennei is further east of the Drum Tower near the Jiaodaokou intersection. This place serves up Fujian and Yunnan styles. Expensive 'across-the-bridge noodles' must be ordered in advance, minimum four people. Also try Yunnan-style steamed chicken, seafood and *san bu zhan* (sweet sticky pudding).

Russian The *Moscow Restaurant* (tel 894454) is on the west side of the Soviet-designed Exhibition Centre in the zoo district. The vast interior has chandeliers, a high ceiling, fluted columns. Foreigners are shuffled to a side room overlooking the zoo (which has, by the way, no connection with the menu). What you could do is grab the English menu from the side room and run back to the central section, which has the cavernous decor. Ukrainian borsch, cream prawns au gratin, pork a la Kiev, beef stroganoff, black bread, soups and black caviar all come at moderate prices. They also have good vegetable dishes and coffee with ice cream.

Western All the large tourist hotels serve western food of varying quality and price. As for petit déjeuner, travellers pining for a croissant or strong coffee will be pleased to know that Beijing is the best place in China to find such delicacies.

The *Friendship Store* is the best place to assemble breakfast, though a mite on the expensive side. The deli adjacent to the supermarket has sliced ham, bread rolls, scotch eggs and sausage. It also offers a range of pastries and croissants that can be heated up in a microwave. You can get yoghurt in ceramic flasks – though both the yoghurt and the pastries can be found in other locations around Beijing. Fresh milk and fruit juice are available in the supermarket. Occasionally the deli stocks an excellent Heilongjiang cheese, comparable to Gouda: look for a red cannonball. This is one of the very few places in China where you can get those cheese-enzymes working again.

Good bets for western meals are the *Beijing, Xinqiao* and *Minzu* hotels. The *Jianguo Hotel* serves Holiday Inn, California home-style cooking at greater than Californian prices. Check the ads in *China Daily* for novelty events; anyone for a Texas spare-rib barbecue at the *Great Wall Sheraton Hotel*?

For some light relief try *Maxim's* within the precincts of the Chongwenmen Hotel. The joint China-French venture initiated by Pierre Cardin is a copy of Maxim's in Paris and opened in October 1983. The Paris-trained, French-speaking staff have picked up some strange habits and will knock back those wearing shorts and runners. Dinner for two – sacré bleu – is a cool Y200 or so excluding that Bordeaux red or the Alsatian Gerwürtzraminer. The pissoir is reputed to be the best in China. No vegemite.

The *Huadu Restaurant* at 76 Dongdan Beidajie is a small place that serves pizzas! The dish was first introduced by tourists.

Snacks Off Da Trax Beijing has a fair number of snack bars, noodle bars, dumpling shops and cake shops – nowhere near the number it used to have, but sufficient to sate the curiosity. A Beijing newspaper suggested there weren't nearly enough snack bars and that the locals should resort to selling hot dogs!

Snacks can be found at roadside stalls, especially around breakfast time. Also try the market areas, and the ground floor of restaurants (the masses section). Small vendors are making a comeback, ever since the return of the ice cream soda in 1980 after an absence of 14 years. In fact a health problem exists with the random production of popsicles by home entrepreneurs.

Historically, the different varieties of snack (some 200 survive) were trotted out with the changing of the seasons or at temple fairs. In winter it was *wonton* or quick-boiled tripe, in summer jellied cheese or almond curd. In spring it was *aiwowo*, a glutinous rice stuffed with sesame and sugar, of Mongolian origins. This still holds true to some extent. At Chinese New Year moon-shaped *jiaozi* (meat-filled ravioli) are consumed for five days solid.

A few suggestions for snack-trackers are given, but you're better off thinking of it as 'chance food', to jump at when you see it. You've got nothing to lose but your taste buds. The street market behind the Beijing Hotel is a good, cheap source.

The Qianmen area in bygone Beijing had the largest concentration of snack bars, and is a good place to go hunting. Down Qianmen Lu is the *Zhengmingzhai Cakeshop*. The *Jinfeng* at 157 Qianmenwai sells Beijing-style baozi dumplings.

The *Duyichu* at No 36 Qianmen and close to Dazhalan is an ancient restaurant serving *shaomai* (steamed dumplings).

Off the beginning of Dazhalan on Liangshidian alley is *Zhimielou*, which sells dragon-whisker noodles. Strands as fine as silk, an old Qing recipe.

For *baozi* and *jiaozi* try the *Hongxinglou* at 1 Beiwei Lu on the west side of the Temple of Heaven. It also serves shaomai and noodles. Twenty different kinds of jiaozi (in season) can be ordered and there's even frozen take-away. The crowded ground floor has two kinds of jiaozi, beer and cold cuts. The next floor has jiaozi and Shandong-style seafood and pork dishes. The seafood is not cheap, but if you stick to jiaozi this can be a very inexpensive place to eat.

The *Ritan Park Restaurant* to the north of the Friendship Store has classy jiaozi and western snacks. It's patronised by westerners and housed in a classical-style building.

Near Xisi, on Xianmen Dajie, is a genuine coffee and tea house, a private business called the *Daoshanzhuang*. Refreshments are served to music by Chopin, Mozart and Schubert, or to light foreign and Chinese music. Art on the walls is by the manager-owner, Su Daoshan.

In 1982 a group of Beijing chefs set about reviving the imperial pastry recipes. They even went so far as to dig up the last emperor's brother to try their products out on. The same year, an Overseas Chinese outfit was permitted to start up a snack bar specialising in South-East Asian snacks. Snacking is where you can experience the free market. Jobless youths have carved out small businesses for themselves, and there are licensed family-owned restaurants. The other person you'll meet is the snacker, someone who can't afford a full-course meal. In winter I hit a bakery to get out of the cold for a moment. I gathered 99% of the clientele was in there for the same reason. A group of people huddled round a woodburner clutching bowls of hot water – good way to warm up the hands! It will cost you next to nothing to sample these places, all highly educational.

Fast Food For a taste of China's gastronomic future try *Minim's*, the poor person's Maxim's. I kid you not; it's one door down from its famous big sister in the Chongwenmen Hotel. Lots of tin-foil and surly staff. Mediocre coffee, OK chocolate mousse, and the tomato soup is said to be good. Otherwise, it has few redeeming features.

Across the road is *Rosenbac's* which has a fine bakery dispensing real bread, croissants and pastries. Behind it is a glossy fast-food joint indistinguishable from a university cafeteria. I have no idea why the Chinese would want to eat here.

Nightlife & Entertainment

La Dolce Vita is almost non-existent in Beijing, but in a city of museums, red tape and paperwork hacks what did you expect? The town goes to bed early – most cultural events start around 7 pm and are finished by 9.30 pm, when transport becomes infrequent. The Chinese mostly stick to restauranting or playing chess in the gutters at midnight; young people go to the Chinese-only discos.

Discos Back in the late '70s, Saturday Night Fever (1940s style) hit Beijing. Discos popped up in various hotels and notably in the Nationalities Cultural Palace on Changan Avenue, where dancing was punctuated by a floor show with minority groups. The authorities reasoned that the high admission price of Y10 would keep the locals out, but they misjudged the craze for the joys of dancing. Due to problems of mixing and drinking, the music died, and even the *Life Disco* at the Jianguo Hotel had trouble getting started. Many of the large tourist hotels have discos; best way to check which dance floor is still operating (and how much it will cost) is to phone ahead.

Fun with the Foreign Community Embassy staff and journalists, bored with Peking's 'nightlife', have created their own. At one time in the '70s the sole source of decadence in Beijing was the 'Down Under Club' in the basement of the Australian Embassy, which got such a reputation that taxi drivers refused to collect passengers late at night (this problem was overcome by summoning a taxi to the Malaysian Embassy next door). They started something of a precedent, which has evolved into a Friday night get-together at varying embassies or residences – the news sometimes hits the lobby of the Beijing Hotel. The Brits have imported their nightlife – there's a British pub called *The Bell* inside the grounds of the UK Embassy, but the last time we heard, the place was not exactly open to the public.

Clubbing Sporting, recreational and club facilities are to be found in the Friendship Hotel, the International Club and the Minority Nationalities Cultural Palace. The International Club is pretty lifeless, patronised by dozy diplomats, and has signs around the place telling you what not to do. There are dusty tennis courts, billiard tables, a full-sized swimming pool, a bowling alley (a bummer – you have to set up your own pins) and a bar/restaurant (it's debatable whether the chef isn't in fact a can opener).

The Nationalities Cultural Palace is a toffee-nosed Chinese and foreign hangout with a large range of amenities including bowling alley, ping-pong, bar, restaurant and ballroom and banquet rooms. Of interest here might be minority singing and dancing events by night (or shows which have nothing to do with minorities) and occasional exhibitions featuring minority wares by day. If you get to the upper floors of this massive group of buildings there are some very nice views.

What's On *China Daily* carries a listing of cultural evenings recommended for foreigners. Offerings include concerts, theatre, minority dancing and some cinema. There are about 35 theatres and 50 cinemas in the capital. You can reserve ahead by phoning the box office via your hotel, or pick up tickets at CITS for a surcharge – or take a risk and just roll up at the theatre.

Entertainment is dirt cheap, Y1 to Y2 at the most. Beijing is on the touring circuit for foreign troupes, and these are also listed in *China Daily*. They're somewhat screened for content, but lately they've been beefing up what's available. In 1983 Arthur Miller's *Death of a Salesman* was acted out by Chinese at the Capital Theatre, and held over for two months by popular demand.

The same theatre staged some avant-garde Chinese theatre. It put on two plays by Gao Zingjian, incorporating theatre of the absurd and traditional Chinese theatrical techniques. One of the plays,

Bus-stop, is based on eight characters who spend 10 years at the bus stop to discover that the service was cancelled long ago. That's either a vicious comment on the Beijing bus service, or a sly reference to Gao's stint in re-education camp during the Cultural Revolution – or else it's a direct steal from Samuel Beckett or Luigi Pirandello.

In the concert department they've presented Beethoven's Ninth played on Chinese palace instruments, such as tuned bells found and copied from an ancient tomb. Other classical instruments are being revived for dance-drama backings. Bizarre performances are often staged for foreign tour groups and some of these have to be seen to be believed. Perhaps trial runs before touring overseas with cultural shows tailored to western tastes? Some of this stuff would go down great in Las Vegas!

Film is out of the boring stage and starting to delve into some contemporary issues, even verging on Cultural Revolution after-shock in a mild manner. The International Club near the Friendship Store shows Chinese films with English subtitles or simultaneous translation into English, every Saturday night at 7 pm. The Friendship Hotel shows old foreign and Chinese films (with simultaneous translation) every Friday night.

Television, if you're that kind of addict, brings a lot of different types of Chinese entertainment directly into your hotel room, if you have that kind of room. There are a couple of channels, and if you have the right kind of electronic hookups perhaps some naughty Hong Kong video. Programmes are listed in *China Daily*. TV is actually a good way of studying Chinese, especially the kids' programmes with fascinating forms of Chinese animation.

As for other events, you might like to delve into items listed in the local newspapers. If you can read Chinese or get a translation you can find out about sporting events, puppet theatre, story-telling and local cinema. These may be sold out, but scalpers do a roaring trade.

You can even set yourself up as an English teacher at the Beijing 'English corner' in Purple Bamboo Park, near the Capital Stadium in the Haidian District.

A Night at the Opera It used to be the Marx Brothers, the Gang of Four and the Red Ballet – but it's back to the classics again these days. Beijing Opera is one of the many forms of the art and the most famous, but it's only got a short history. The year 1790 is the key date given; in that year a provincial troupe performed before Emperor Qianlong on his 80th birthday. The form was popularised in the west by the actor Mei Lanfang (1894-1961) who played *dan* or female roles, and is said to have influenced Charlie Chaplin. There is a museum devoted to Mei Lanfang at 9 Huuguosi Lu, in western Beijing.

Earlier in the century, teahouses, wine shops and opera were the main nightlife in Beijing; of these, only the opera has survived (just). The opera bears little resemblance to its European counterpart. The mixture of singing, dancing, speaking, mime, acrobatics and dancing can go on for five or six hours; an hour is usually long enough for a westerner. Plots are fairly basic so the language barrier is not really a problem – the problems are the music, which is searing to western ears, and the acting, which is heavy and stylised.

When you get bored after the first hour or so, and are sick of the high-pitched whining, the local audience is with you all the way – spitting, eating apples, breast-feeding an urchin on the balcony, or plugging into a transistor radio (important sports match?). It's a lively prole audience viewing entertainment fit for kings.

Another problem is trying to find a performance that really is Beijing Opera. All you can do is patiently troop around the theatre circuit until you hit the one that's still dishing up the real thing. Most performances start around 7 or 7.30 pm.

The best bet is the *Changan* theatre at 126 Xi Changan Jie, just east of the intersection with Xuanwumennei Dajie. The audience is mainly elderly Chinese and the performances are definitely not for mass tourist consumption.

Major Beijing opera theatres include the *Capital* at 22 Wangfujing, though I fronted up there one Saturday night and the place had been taken over for a Chinese-only disco.

Also try the *Erqi* on Fuxingmenwai Dajie; the *Tianqiao* at 30 Beiwei Lu near the Temple of Heaven; the *Renmin* on Huguosi Dajie; and the *Jixiang* at 14 Jinyu Hutong, off Wangfujing.

The oldest in Beijing is the *Guanghe* at 24-26 Qianmen Lu – it's actually down an alleyway leading off Qianmen.

Beijing opera is usually regarded as the *crème de la crème* of all the opera styles prevalent in China. Traditionally it's been the opera of the masses. In some ways it's very similar to the ancient Greek theatre, with its combination of singing, dialogue, acrobatics and pantomime, the actors wearing masks and the performance accompanied by loud and monotonous rhythms produced with percussion instruments. The themes are usually inspired by disasters, natural calamities, intrigues or rebellions. Many have their source in the fairy tales and stock characters and legends of classical literature. Titles like *The Monkey King, A Drunken Beauty* and *A Fisherman's Revenge* are typical.

The music, singing and costumes are products of the opera's origins. Formerly, Beijing opera was performed mostly on open-air stages in markets, streets, teahouses or temple courtyards. The orchestra had to play loudly and the performers had to develop a piercing style of singing which could be heard over the throng. The costumes are a garish collection of sharply contrasting colours because the stages were originally lit by oil lamps.

The movements and techniques of the dance styles of the Tang Dynasty are similar to those of today's Beijing opera. Provincial opera companies were characterised by their dialect and style of singing, but when these companies converged on Beijing they started a style of musical drama called *kunqu*. This developed during the Ming Dynasty, along with a more popular variety of play-acting with pieces based on legends, historical events and popular novels. These styles gradually merged by the late 18th and early 19th centuries into the Beijing opera we see today.

The musicians usually sit on the stage in plain clothes and play without written scores. The *erhu* is a two-stringed fiddle which is tuned to a low register, has a soft tone and generally supports the *huqin*, another two-stringed fiddle tuned to a high register. The *yueqin*, a sort of moon-shaped four-stringed guitar, has a soft tone and is used to support the *erhu*. Other instruments are the *sheng* (reed pipes) and the *pipa* (lute), as well as drums, bells and cymbals. Last but not least is the *ban*, a time-clapper which virtually directs the band, beats time for the actors and gives them their cues.

There are four types of actor's roles: the *sheng, dan, jing* and *chou*. The *sheng* are the leading male actors and they play scholars, officials, warriors, etc. They are divided into the *laosheng* who wear beards and represent old men, and the *xiaosheng* who represent young men. The *wensheng* are the scholars and the civil servants. The *wu sheng* play soldiers and other fighters, and because of this are specially trained in acrobatics.

The *dan* are the female roles. The *laodan* are the elderly, dignified ladies such as mothers, aunts and widows. The *qingyi* are aristocratic ladies in elegant costumes. The *huadan* are the ladies' maids, usually in brightly coloured costumes. The *daomadan* are the warrior women. The *caidan* are the female comediennes. Traditionally, female roles were played by male actors.

The *jing* are the painted-face roles, and they represent warriors, heroes, statesmen, adventurers and demons. Their counterpart is the *fu jing*, ridiculous figures who are anything but heroic. The *chou* is basically the clown. The *caidan* is sometimes the female counterpart of this male role.

Apart from the singing and music, the opera also uses acrobatics and mime. Few props are used, so each move, gesture or facial expression is symbolic. A whip with silk tassels indicates an actor riding a horse. Lifting a foot means going through a doorway. Language is often archaic Chinese, music is ear-splitting (bring some cotton wool), but the costumery and make-up are magnificent. The only action that really catches the western eye is a swift battle sequence – the women warriors involved are trained acrobats who leap, twirl, twist and somersault into attack.

There are numerous other forms of opera. The Cantonese variety is more 'music hall', often with 'boy meets girl' themes. Gaojia opera is one of the five local opera forms from Fujian Province and is also popular in Taiwan, with songs in the Fujian dialect but influenced by the Beijing opera style.

Strange as it may sound, Chinese music is actually quite closely related to western music. The 12 notes worked out by the ancient Chinese correspond exactly to those of the ancient Greeks (on which western music is based). Although most Chinese musical instruments were introduced from India and central Asia, Chinese music is tonally closer to western music. Western music, however, uses groupings (scales) of eight notes whereas Chinese music uses groupings of five notes. The five-note scale is one of the main reasons Chinese music sounds different from western music. The other important difference (shared with Indian music) is a lack of harmony, usually considered an important component of western music.

Acrobatics Two thousand years old, and one of the few art forms condoned by Mao, acrobatics is the best deal in town. For Y1.50 or so you can forget CITS, forget train stations, forget hotels, forget language problems. Magic!

Acts take place in various locations. For authentic atmosphere, try the Acrobat Rehearsal Hall on Dazhalan, once the major theatre location in Beijing. CITS also sells tickets for around Y3 but you can usually roll up, roll in and get a seat. The show starts at 7.15 pm and acts change nightly. Closed on Saturdays. Dazhalan is a hutong off the subway end of Qianmen Dajie. For a rundown on some popular acrobatic stunts see the Shanghai chapter.

And the Unusual A golfing club in China? Try the Beijing International Golf Club, a Chinese-Japanese joint venture opened in mid-1986, 35 km north of Beijing near the Ming Tombs. Visitor fees are Y120 weekdays, Y200 weekends and public holidays, and Y25 for a caddie.

If hitting balls isn't quite your style then try hitting targets. At the time of writing there were reports of plans to open a firing range near Beijing where red-neck foreigners, presumably with a copy of *Soldier of Fortune* tucked under one arm, will be able to play with weapons and live ammo. Rambo goes to China.

Shopping

Once upon a time in China you got what you paid for. A double-edged pun; if the man said it was top-quality jade then it was top-quality jade and you'd pay through the nose for it. These days there are all sorts of forgeries and imitations about, from Tibetan jewellery to Qing coins and even phony packets of western cigarettes. This doesn't apply in Friendship Stores and other government-run emporiums, so there's no need for paranoia about being ripped off by fakes in these places. Beware that out in the streets and free markets it's a different story.

Bargains can still be had on certain goods. Prices are sometimes higher than in other Asian countries but lower than in the west. How about a blouson-style leather jacket to beat around in for just US$50? For heftier goods you have to take into account the sometimes outrageous tariffs for shipping. It therefore makes sense to go for smaller or lighter items that you can carry yourself. Some Chinese emporiums are like Aladdin's Caves – tourist attractions in themselves.

Shopping Districts Fast shopping can be done at the Friendship Store, which stocks most things that you'd want, and also carries luxury items not available elsewhere.

More fun and a bit cheaper for hard-to-find items is to rummage around with the Chinese. Shopping is concentrated in three busy areas: Wangfujing, Qianmen (in the Dazhalan hutong) and Liulichang (antiques). Other mildly interesting shopping streets are Xidan and Dongdan, north of Changan.

Tourist attractions like the Temple of Heaven, as well as major hotels, have garish souvenir shops stocking arts and crafts. Otherwise, speciality shops are scattered around the city core. Stores are generally open 9 am to 7 pm seven days a week; some are open 8 am to 8 pm. Bargaining is not a way of life in the stores, but on the free market it certainly is.

Good buys are stationery (chops, brushes, inks), prints, handicrafts, clothing (fur, silk, down jackets, sometimes leather but styles are usually primeval) and antiques. Small or light items to buy are silk scarves, T-shirts, embroidered purses, papercuts, wooden and bronze buddhas, fold-up paper lanterns and kites.

Friendship Store The Friendship Store at 21 Jianguomenwai (tel 593531) is the largest in the land, with guards posted near the entrance to keep the Chinese out.

The top floor carries furniture, carpets, arts & crafts (stones, paintings, carvings, cloisonné). On the middle floor are clothing items, fabrics, cosmetics, toys and 'daily necessities'. The ground floor has tinned and dried imported/local foods, tobacco, wines, spirits, Chinese medicines, film, foreign books and magazines. To the right are a supermarket, deli and florist.

If they're out of the food you want, try the branch at 5 Sanlitun Lu. The Friendship Store also has tailors (alterations and made-to-measure), taxi service, money exchange, and a packing and shipping service.

Wangfujing This street just east of the Beijing Hotel is lined with a number of specialty stores, and has Beijing's largest department store. Opposite the department store is the Dongfeng, a covered market with a similar selection of dry goods.

This is the classiest shopping area in the capital, with largest-of-the-kind stores and appropriately sized crowds on weekends and holidays. In pre-49 days it was known as Morrison Street, catering largely for foreigners.

Swiss and Seiko have moved in – among the first foreign businesses to set up shop in Beijing. The name Wangfujing derives from a 15th-century well, the site of which is now occupied by offices of *The People's Daily*.

Qianmen Area If Wangfujing is too sterile for you, the place to go and rub shoulders is Dazhalan, a hutong running west from the top end of Qianmen. It's a heady jumble of silk shops, department stores, theatres, herbal medicines, food and clothing specialists and some unusual architecture. The hutong is really more of a sight than a place to shop, but you might find something that catches your eye.

Dazhalan has a definite medieval flavour to it, a hangover from the days when hutongs sold specialised products – one would sell lace, another lanterns, another jade. This one used to be called Silk Street. The name Dazhalan refers to a wicker-gate that was closed at night to keep undesirable prowlers out.

In imperial Beijing, shops and theatres were not permitted near the city centre, and the Qianmen-Dazhalan district was outside the gates. Many of the city's oldest shops can be found along or near this crowded hutong.

Just off the beginning of Dazhalan at 3 Liangshidian Jie is Liubiju, a 400-year-old pickle-and-sauce emporium patronised by discriminating housewives. Nearby is the Zhimielou Restaurant, which serves imperial snacks. On your right as you go down Dazhalan is a green concave archway with columns at No 5; this is the entrance to Riufuxiang, one of the better-known material and silk stores and a century old.

Next door to that is the entrance to the Acrobat Rehearsal Hall. Dazhalan at one time had five opera theatres. The place used to be thronged with theatre-goers both day (cheap rehearsals) and night (professionals). The nightlife lingers on with two performing theatres, and pedicab men wait for the post-theatre crowds as the rickshaw drivers did many years ago. No 1 Dazhalan was once a theatre.

Another famous shop is the Tongrengtang at No 24, selling Chinese herbal medicines. It's been in business since 1669, though it doesn't appear that way from the renovations. It was a royal dispensary in the Qing Dynasty, and derives its pills and potions from secret prescriptions used by royalty. All kinds of weird ingredients – tiger bone, rhino horn, snake wine – will cure you of anything from fright to encephalitis, or so they claim. Traditional doctors are available on the spot for consultation; perhaps ask them about fear of railway stations (patience pills?).

Dazhalan runs about 300 metres deep off Qianmen. At the far end where the hubbub dies down is a bunch of Chinese hotels, and if you sense something here . . . yes, you're right, Dazhalan was the gateway to Beijing's red-light district. The brothels were shut down in 1949 and the women packed off to factories to make wares instead of plying them.

Qianmen Dajie, and Zhushikou Xidajie leading off to the west, are interesting places to meander. On Qianmen Dajie there are pottery stores at Nos 99 and 149, minorities musical instruments at Nos 18 and 104, and a nice second-hand shop at No 117.

Second-hand Shopping Second-hand shopping is one of the favourite pastimes of embassy staff in Beijing. This is reputedly worked on a rote-system so that anything of real value can be snapped up the moment it hits the shelf. Most of the second-hand or commission shops sell recycled radios, TVs and household goods, but some are specialised and are unmarked and hard to find. Here are a few:

Arts & Crafts Trust Company, 12

Chongwenmennei, just north of Xinqiao Hotel and CITS, has a very pleasant atmosphere. It sells theatrical costumes, used furs and clothing, jewellery and a large selection of antiques including a wonderful array of clocks. The antiques and clocks aren't necessarily Chinese – some are European or Japanese. A separate section next door sells furniture, carpets and embroidery.

Beixinqiao, 30 Dongsi Bei Dajie, has old chests of all shapes and sizes, some made of camphor and mahogany. Other second-hand furniture can be found in the shops at 32 Chongwenmenwai and 56 Wangfujing. It's all expensive stuff.

Possibly the best antique furniture shop in town is at 38 Dongsi Nandajie. They will also repair furniture for you, although the last we heard, mailing goes through the Friendship Store, which will identify antiques.

Qianmen Trade Commission House, 117 Qianmen, has furs and fur-lined coats and jackets. The older style of wealth was all about having it, not displaying it, so long coats look cheap from the outside but have a 'silver lining' and expensive skin such as fox. This is one of Beijing's largest second-hand goods stores, with all sorts of other goods for sale.

Markets With the resurgence of individual trading, going to a market is a good way of observing some lively interaction between locals. Markets are a bit difficult to locate. 'Market' on a bus map basically means department store.

The lower end of Qianmen Dajie, west Zhushikou Lu and the Tianqiao area are pretty brisk. Along the north-east wall of the Temple of Heaven is a very busy market with poultry and gardening supplies.

The Dongsi People's Market in a hutong near the CAAC building may be worth a visit for another reason – the newer store is in an old area once occupied by the Longfusi Temple, the remains of which are still visible.

There's a bird-and-fish market west of Pinganli intersection, in the vicinity of the zoo. There's a large fruit-and-vegetable market near the Beitaipingzhuang intersection north-west of Deshengmen – follow Xinjiekouwai Dajie.

Pigeon racing is coming back into style in China; there is a pigeon market on Changping Lu, about three km north of Deshengmen on the way to the Ming Tombs.

Getting There & Away

Getting to Beijing is no problem – one of those rail or air lines will lead you to the capital sooner or later. The real problem is getting away, and your exodus is best planned well in advance. There are planes from Beijing to numerous destinations but most people will probably depart by train – book early to get a sleeper.

Air Beijing Capital Airport, operational since 1980, was built as part of the 'Four Modernisations' drive, and is modelled on Paris's Orly Airport. It's 29 km north-east of the city.

To get to the airport you can take the CAAC bus which leaves the downtown office at irregular times – likewise coming from the airport to Beijing. It's not a free bus as in most cities.

Alternatively take a taxi. Split between a maximum of four passengers, the fare is not too bad; plus the taxi leaves from your hotel – an important consideration if your plane leaves at 6 am. The journey takes half an hour. Local bus No 359 runs to the airport from Dongzhimen.

The partially computerised CAAC ticket office is at 117 Dongsi Xidajie. Telephone 553072 for domestic reservations; 552945 for international reservations; and 558861 and 552515 for enquiries.

The CAAC aerial spider web spreads out in every conceivable direction, including daily flights to major cities like Canton, Shanghai, Chongqing, Wuhan and Kunming. For a complete list get a CAAC timetable.

Top: Hawkers at Terracotta Army, Xian (AS)
Bottom Left: Scaling Tai Shan (AS)
Bottom Right: Street scene, Datong (RS)

Top: River life, Wuzhou (AS)
Bottom: The blues and greys of a Canton winter (JH)

United China Airlines (run by the Army) has a number of flights from Beijing; there is a booking office in the Beijing Hotel. By the time this book is out several other airlines, independent of CAAC, should have been established.

For international flights out of Beijing see the Getting There chapter in this book.

Bus Beijing is approachable by bus from outlying locations – the roads are bumpy except for the highway from Tianjin, which is in good nick.

Long-distance bus lines within Beijing are located on the perimeter: at Dongzhimen (north-east), Guangqumen (south-east) and Tianqiao (near the theatre on the west side of Temple of Heaven).

There are two bus stations near Yongdingmen Station, another at the Ganjiakou intersection south of the zoo, and one off Deshengmenwai Dajie. They are usually located part-way along the direction you want to travel.

These bus stations also have cheaper alternatives to tour buses, such as cheap, local buses to out-of-town locations like the Ming Tombs.

Rail There is a Foreigners' Ticketing Office at Beijing Main Station, through a door inside the main entrance hall. Look for the sign saying 'International Passenger Booking Office'. It's open daily, 5.30 to 7.30 am, 8 to 11.30 am, 1 to 5.30 pm and 7 pm to 12.30 am. There's a waiting room and a left-luggage room (charges Y2). Tickets can be booked several days in advance. Your chances of getting a sleeper (hard or soft) are good so long as you book ahead.

Some travellers have managed to get Chinese prices at the regular ticket windows, usually using a student I.D. The problem is that these ticket windows, two dozen of them, can't be seen half the time for the crowds! Also, they may direct you back to the Foreigners' Ticketing Office, where you will be charged tourist price.

The booking office for international rail tickets is on the third floor of the Chongwenmen Hotel; you get there via a flight of stairs accessible from the southern gate of the hotel – there should be a sign at the front entrance pointing the way. It's open 9 am to 12 noon and 2 to 5 pm.

For departures allow plenty of time to get to your train. If you're early then there are plenty of 1st-class and foreign waiting rooms.

Train Fares The following is a table of approximate train fares out of Beijing for hard-seat, hard-sleeper and soft-sleeper. For journey times under eight hours only hard-seat is quoted. All fares given below are tourist price, and express charges are included.

Variations in fares and travel times may arise because of different routings of different trains. For example, the journey to Shanghai can take between 17 to 25 hours depending on the train.

Train numbers also change from year to year. When booking tickets, keep in mind that fast trains have one or two-digit numbers. Trains with three-digit numbers are slower though tickets cost a bit less.

Advance Train Ticket Offices

These are scattered around Beijing. The offices listed below sell hard-seat and hard-sleeper for one, two or three days in advance of intended departure. These offices may refuse to sell you a ticket and direct you back to the Foreigners' Ticket Office in Beijing Main Station. With such heavy demand for tickets it's likely that the Foreigners' Ticket Office is your only chance of getting a ticket anyway, particularly if you want a sleeper.

Qianmen ticket office East side of loop at top end of Qianmen Lu but set back from the street by the cinema. Tickets to Kunming, Chongqing, Ürümqi, Canton, Baotou, Chengde, Shijiazhuang, Taiyuan, Chengdu, Lanzhou.

Xizhimen ticket office On the approach to Xizhimen Station. Tickets to Nanchang, Qingdao, Suzhou, Shanghai, Xiamen, Hohhot.

destination	*rail distance (km)*	*approx travel time (hours)*	*hard seat Y*	*hard sleeper Y*	*soft sleeper Y*
Baotou	–	16½	29	47	91
Beidaihe	–	6	16	–	–
Canton	2313	35	68	108	205
Changchun	1043	16½	39	63	118
Changsha	1587	22½	51	81	153
Chengde	–	5	9	–	–
Chengdu	2048	34	61	98	185
Chongqing	2552	39½	75	120	227
Dandong	1118	15½	39	63	118
Dalian	1238	19	36	61	120
Datong	382	7	16	26	49
Fuzhou	2623	43	77	123	232
Guilin	2134	31	63	100	189
Guiyang	2540	48½	74	117	221
Hangzhou	1651	24	52	83	156
Harbin	1285	17	46	73	138
Hefei	1107	18½	34	57	113
Hohhot	668	12	25	41	76
Jinan	494	8½	21	33	63
Kunming	3179	59	91	145	274
Lanzhou	1882	35	57	91	172
Luoyang	–	–	26	44	86
Nanchang	2005	36	51	87	171
Nanjing	1157	19½	–	–	–
Nanning	2565	39	75	120	227
Qingdao	887	16½	32	52	97
Shanghai	1462	17	56	90	168
Shenyang	738	10½	31	50	93
Shijiazhuang	283	3	13	23	43
Suzhou	–	24½	39	67	131
Taiyuan	514	10½	21	33	63
Tianjin	137	1¾	7	–	–
Ürümqi	3774	75	106	169	318
Wuhan	1229	20½	42	67	126
Xian	1206	22	42	67	126
Xining	2098	44	–	–	–
Yantai	1343	17½	31	53	103
Yinchuan	1343	25	–	–	–
Zhengzhou	695	11½	26	42	79

Also non-express to Baotou and regular Chinese trains to the Great Wall.

Dongdan ticket office On Dongdan Beidajie, third block north of Changan up Dongdan, on the left-hand side. Tickets to all of the north-east lines such as Shenyang, Harbin, etc.

Beixinqiao ticket office On Dongsi Beidajie, north of Dianmen Lu. Tickets for any destination leaving from Beijing Main or

Yongdingmen ticket office Near Yongdingmen Station. Tickets for the suburban lines and for available. It also sells tickets to some boats such as the Tanggu-Dalian one.

Yongdingmen ticket office Near Yongdingmen Station. Tickets for the suburban lines and for very slow trains heading out of Beijing for the southern part of the country. Not very useful.

Getting Around

Bus Sharpen your elbows, chain your money to your underwear and muster all the patience you can – you'll need it. Overstuffed buses are in vogue in Beijing, and can be particularly nauseating at the height of summer when passengers drip with perspiration. Cosy in winter if you haven't frozen to the bus stop by the time the trolley arrives.

There are about 140 bus and trolley routes, which makes navigation rather confusing, especially if you can't see out the window in the first place. Bus maps are listed in the Information & Orientation section of this chapter.

Buses run from around 5 am to 11 pm. A minor compensation for the crowding is that the conductor rarely gets through to you. Bus stops are long and far between. It's important to work out how many stops to go before boarding. Avoid these torture-chambers like the plague at rush hours or on holidays.

Buses are routed through landmarks and key intersections, and if you can pick out the head and tail of the route, you can get a good idea of where the monster will travel. Major terminals occur near long-distance junctions: Beijing Main Station, Dongzhimen, Tianqiao, Yongdingmen, Qianmen. The zoo (Dongwuyan) has the biggest pile-up with about 15 lines, since it's where inner and outer Beijing get together.

One or two-digit bus numbers are city core, 100-series buses are trolleys, and 300-series are suburban lines. If you can work out how to combine bus and subway connections, the subway will speed up part of the trip. Some useful buses are:

No 1
: travels east-west across the city along Changan, from Jianguo Lu to Fuxing Lu.

No 5
: travels the north-south axis, from Desheng-men/Gulou and down the west side of the Forbidden City to Qianmen/Tianqiao; ends at Youanmen.

No 44
: follows the Circle Line subway in a square on the ring road.

No 15
: zigzags from the Tianqiao area to the zoo and passes several subway stops.

No 7
: runs from the west side of Qianmen Gate to the zoo.

No 20
: zigzags from Beijing Main Station to Yongdingmen Station via Changan and Qianmen Dajie.

No 103
: trolley runs from the Main Station to the zoo via Chongwenmen, Wangfujing, Art Gallery, Jing Shan and Beihai parks.

No 106
: runs from Dongzhimenwai via Chong-wenmen Dajie to Yongdingmen Station.

No 116
: travels from the south entrance of the Temple of Heaven up Qianmen Dajie to Tiananmen, east along Changan to Dongdan and directly north on Dongdan to Lama Temple. A good sightseeing bus.

No 332
: Dongwuyan (zoo), Minzuxueyuan (Institute for Nationalities), Weigongcun, Renmin-daxue (People's University), Zhongguancun, Haidian, Beijingdaxue (Beijing University) and Yiheyuan (Summer Palace). There are actually two Nos 332: regular and express – both make good sightseeing buses. The express bus has fewer stops and is at the head of the queue near the zoo.

Subway The Underground Dragon is definitely the best way of doing it. Trains can move at up to 70 km/hour – a jaguar compared to the lumbering buses. The subway is also less crowded per square cm than the buses, and trains run at a frequency of one every few minutes during peak times. The carriages have seats for 60 and standing room for 200. Platform signs are in Chinese and pinyin. The fare is a flat 10 fen regardless of distance. The subway is open 5 am to 11 pm. At the time

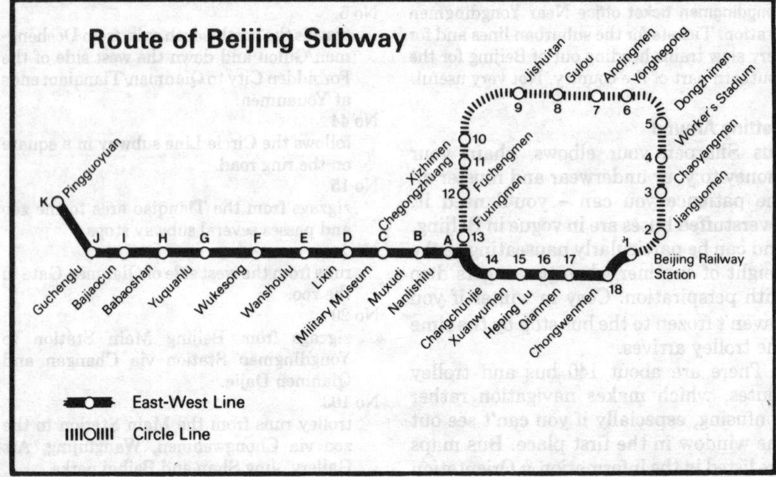

of writing there was no connection between the Circle Line and the East-West line; you have to walk between the two.

East-West Line The 24-km line has 17 stops and runs from the main station to Pingguoyan which is, no, not the capital of North Korea, but a western suburb of Beijing. It takes 40 minutes to traverse the length of the line. The stops are Beijing Zhan (main station), Chongwenmen, Qianmen, Heping Lu, Xuanwumen, Changchunjie, Lishilu, Muxudi, Junshibowuguan (Military Museum), Lixinzhan, Wanshoulu, Wukesong, Yuquanlu, Babaoshan, Bajiaocun, Guchenglu and Pingguoyan. It takes 40 minutes to traverse the length of the line. It's a five minute walk between station A on the East West Line and station 13 on the Circle Line and there is no direct connection between them.

Circle Line This 16-km line presently has 13 stations: Beijing Zhan, Jianguomen, Chaoyangmen, Dongsi 10, Dongzhimen (the subway here tunnels right around the USSR Embassy), Yonghegong (Lama Temple), Andingmen, Gulou, Jishuitaan, Xizhimen (North Station and zoo), Chegongzhuang, Fuchengmen and Fuxingmen.

Bicycle The scale of Beijing is suddenly much reduced on a bike, which can also give you a great deal of freedom. Beijing is as flat as a chappati. An added advantage is that Beijingers will ride up alongside you to chat. You can check your bearings with them, but it's not claustrophobic like being on the sidewalk, and you can break off at any time. Just push those pedals!

Bicycles can be hired at the Qiao Yuan Hotel for about Y3 per day. Another good place is the bike shop near the Chongwenmen intersection, on the north side at No 94; cost is about Y2 per day. Bikes can be rented for longer periods, say three days continuous. The renter may demand you leave your passport, but a deposit of about Y100 will usually do.

Make sure the tyres are pumped up, the saddle is adjusted to the correct height (fully extended leg from saddle to pedal) and, most important, that the brakes work. Brakes are your only defence – and the roller-lever type on Chinese bikes are none too effective to begin with. What you get in the way of a bike is pot-luck. It could be so new that all the screws are loose, or it could be a lethal rustbin. If you have problems later on, adjustments can be made at any bike shop, dirt cheap.

Traffic rules for bikes: there are none. Cyclists pile through red lights, buses sound warning horns and scatter a slew of bikers over a bus stop, taxis zip past the mess and policemen look the other way. Traffic policemen have no power to fine cyclists, and if they stop one, everybody will gather to jeer the cop. In the absence of any law and order, it's best not to adopt a 10-speed mentality in Beijing. Cruise slower and keep your eyes peeled. A constant thumb on a clear bell is good fun, but nobody takes any notice. You're better off screaming in a foreign language. Insurance – what's that?

Several shopping areas are closed to cyclists from 6 am to 6 pm; Wangfujing is one. Parking is provided everywhere for peanuts – compulsory peanuts since your velo can be towed away. Beijingese peak hours can be rather astounding – a roving population of three million-plus bicycles, a fact explained by the agony of bus rides. This makes turning at roundabouts a rather skilled cycling procedure. If nervous, dismount at the side of the road, wait for the clusters to unthicken, try again. Beijing in winter presents other problems, like slippery roads (black ice) and frost-bite. You need to rug up and be extra careful.

Car Resident foreigners such as embassy staff and journos are allowed to drive their own cars in the capital, and to drive the Beijing-Tianjin highway. Cars and mini-buses can be rented from some of the major hotels. All vehicles are chauffeur-driven. Try Beijing Car Company (tel 594441) and Capital Car Company (tel 867084).

Taxi Taxi rates are Y0.50 to Y0.80 per km with a four-km minimum. They usually have a sticker on the window indicating their per-km charge. There are few meters so pricing depends on size, make, age of car, backway subsidy, air-con, heating, waiting time – I could go on. In general, if you want a cheap ride, search for the oldest, smallest, most decrepit-looking bomb you can. The light-brown Russian Warszawas (known as Huashache) are not only half the price of regular cabs but you're riding an antique. Taxis can be summoned to a location of your choosing or hailed in the streets. They're scarce at certain hours such as drivers' dinnertime (6 to 8 pm) or the sacred lunchtime siesta.

Award for the most memorable taxi ride: stuck out at the Summer Palace on a public holiday with 5000 people clawing at the buses, four of us hijacked a Shanghai, the Chinese Mercedes. Boy could that driver drive! She shot down those hutongs and boulevards like a champion – chickens, cyclists, jaywalkers, policemen flying past – we arrived with mouths open and hands riveted to the seats. Taxis have a reputation for driving cautiously as they don't carry insurance, but after that ride, I dunno.

Beware of the tyrannical ways of some Beijing taxi-drivers. A letter to *China Daily* relates:

It has happened several times now that we had bad experiences in trying to get a taxi . . . to return to Beijing University. If one has to return in the evening, the drivers seem to find it normal to set their own tariff . . . Drivers wanted to take us to the university only after we agreed to pay a fixed amount of money beforehand, refusing to use their meters. This was Y30. One driver who agreed to take us for Y25 was sneered at by his colleagues who found he was 'too cheap'. One driver who charged us Y35 after arrival at the university agreed suddenly to accept Y20 when we threatened to contact his company. Arguing about rules with these drivers was quite useless since as far as they were concerned it was a matter of 'Take it or walk to Beijing University'.

Beijing taxi-drivers, incidentally, pull in between Y200 to Y400 a month. In the non-profit public sector, bus-drivers average just Y120 per month and conductors Y80 per month.

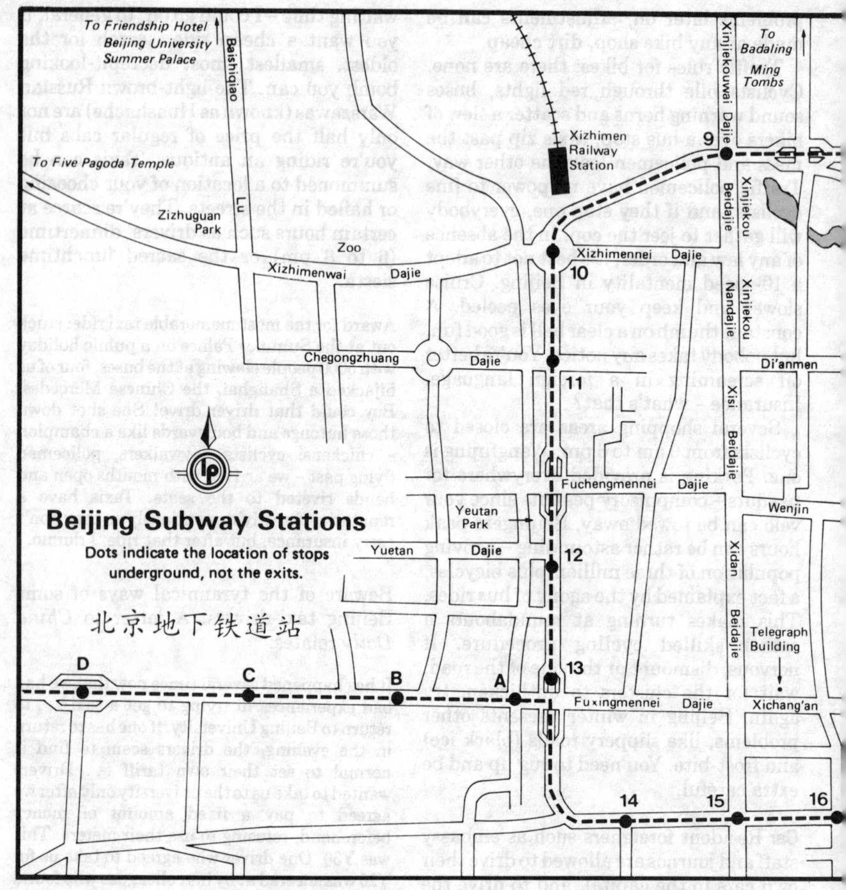

Auto-rickshaw Far cheaper than cars and good to get your adrenalin up. They can be summoned by phone. Some of their congregation points can be discerned from the bus map; a few rough locations are the main train station (tel 555661), Qianmen Gate, and half-way up Wangfujing Jie on the right. They can take ages to arrive, though.

Tours Northern China is blotted with the huge municipal areas of Beijing and Tianjin, each of which contains some of China's prime tourist attractions.

CITS operates a number of high-priced tours to destinations outside Beijing (Great Wall and Ming Tombs, Y50, including guide and lunch). You can dispense with the guides and food and go for the Chinese tour-bus operators who offer much cheaper tours to the same places.

The tours operated out of the Qiao Yuan Hotel are popular. An alternative is

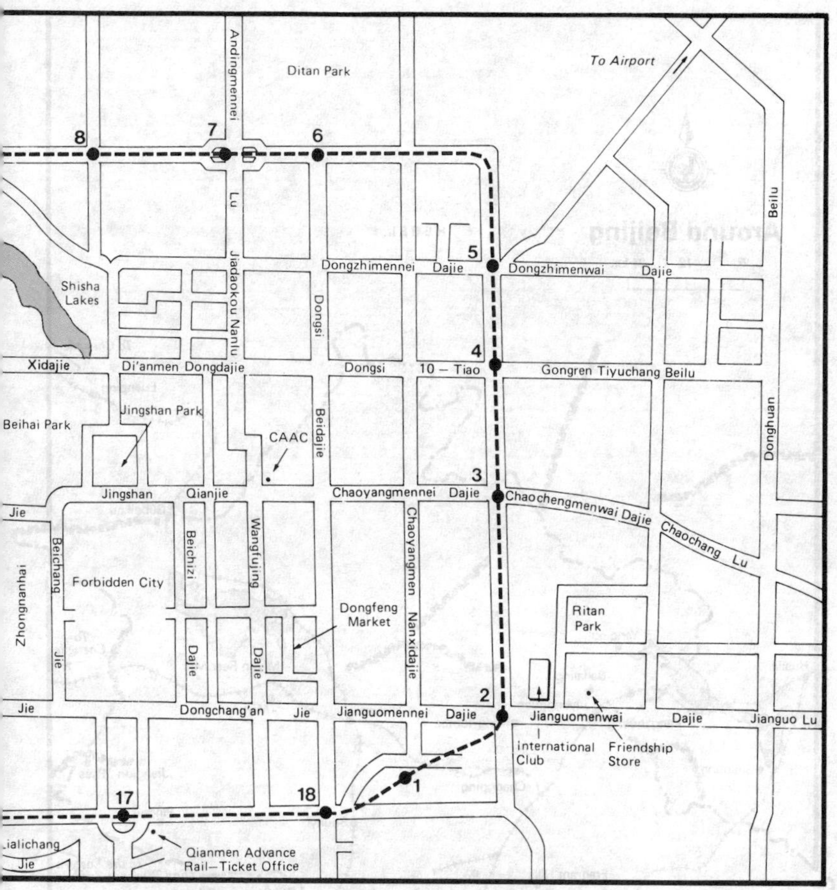

the tour buses which leave from the northwest side of the Chongwenmen intersection, across the road from the Chongwenmen Hotel. Tickets for these tours can be bought at the same place, from the parked minibus labelled 'booking office',

Typical tours take in the Great Wall and Ming Tombs; Western Hills and Summer Palace; Western Hills and Sleeping Buddha Temple; Tanzhe Temple; Yunshui Caves; Zhoukoudian; and Zunhua (Eastern Qing Tombs). Tours further afield to Chengde (three days) and Beidaihe (five days) are possible.

THE GREAT WALL AT BADALING

八达岭长城

Known to the Chinese as the '10,000 li Wall' (5000 km), the Wall stretches from Shanhaiguan Pass on the east coast to Jiayuguan Pass in the Gobi Desert, crossing five provinces and two autonomous regions.

The undertaking was begun 2000 years ago during the Qin Dynasty (221-207 BC),

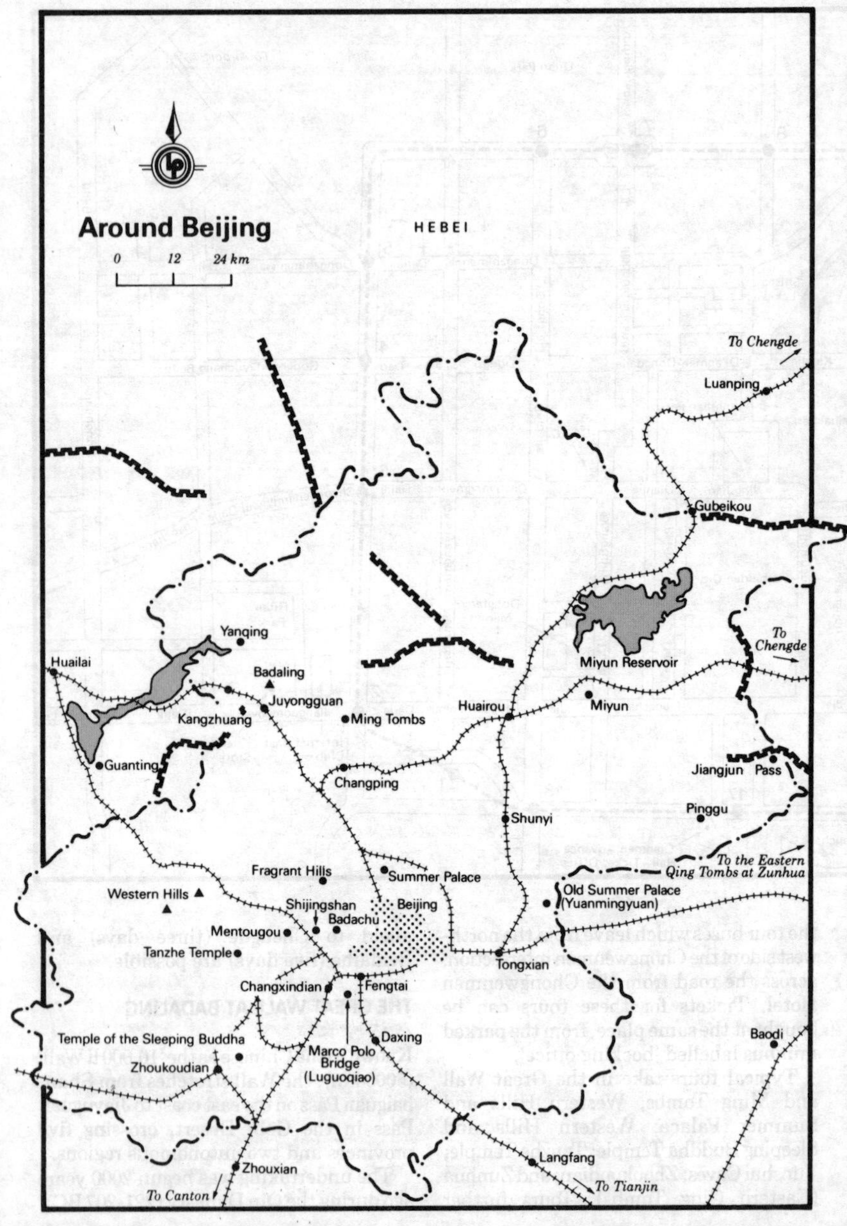
Around Beijing
0
12
24 km
HEBEI
To Chengde
Luanping
Gubeikou
To Chengde
Miyun Reservoir
Yanqing
Huailai
Badaling
Juyongguan
Kangzhuang
Ming Tombs
Huairou
Miyun
Guanting
Changping
Jiangjun Pass
Pinggu
Shunyi
To the Eastern Qing Tombs at Zunhua
Fragrant Hills
Summer Palace
Western Hills
Old Summer Palace (Yuanmingyuan)
Shijingshan
Beijing
Badachu
Mentougou
Tanzhe Temple
Tongxian
Changxindian
Fengtai
Temple of the Sleeping Buddha
Daxing
Marco Polo Bridge (Luguoqiao)
Baodi
Zhoukoudian
Zhouxian
Langfang
To Tianjin
To Canton

when China was unified under Emperor Qin Shihuang. Separate walls, constructed by independent kingdoms to keep out marauding nomads, were linked up. The effort required hundreds of thousands of workers, many of them political prisoners, and 10 years of hard labour under General Meng Tian. An estimated 180 million cubic metres of rammed earth was used to form the core of the original wall, and legend has it that one of the building materials used was the bodies of deceased workers.

The wall never really did perform its function as a defence line to keep invaders out. As Genghis Khan supposedly said, 'The strength of a wall depends on the courage of those who defend it'. Sentries could be bribed. However, it did work very well as a kind of elevated highway, transporting men and equipment across mountainous terrain. Its beacon tower system, using smoke signals generated by burning wolves' dung, transmitted news of enemy movements quickly back to the capital. To the west was Jiayuguan Pass, an important link on the Silk Road where there was a customs post of sorts, and where unwanted Chinese were ejected through the gates to face the terrifying wild west.

Marco Polo makes no mention of China's greatest tourist attraction. Both sides of the wall were under the same government at the time of his visit, but the Ming Great Wall had not been built. During the Ming Dynasty (1368-1644) a determined effort was made to rehash the whole project, this time facing it with bricks and stone slabs – some 60 million cubic metres of them. They created double-walling running in an elliptical shape to the west of Beijing, and did not necessarily follow the older earthen wall. This Ming project took over 100 years, and costs in manpower and resources were phenomenal.

The wall was largely forgotten after that, but now it's reached its greatest heights as a tourist attraction. Lengthy sections of it have been swallowed up by the sands, claimed by the mountains, intersected by road or rail, or simply returned to dust. Other bits were carted off by local peasants to construct their own four walls – a hobby that no-one objected to in the Cultural Revolution. The depiction of the wall as an object of great beauty is a bizarre one. Like the hated Berlin Wall, it's really a symbol of tyranny.

Badaling

Most travellers see the wall at Badaling, 70 km north-west of Beijing at an elevation of 1000 metres. It was restored in 1957 with the addition of guard rails. The section is almost eight metres high with a base of 6½ metres and a width at the top of almost six metres. It runs for several hundred metres, after which are the unrestored sections where the crowds peter out. Originally the wall here could hold five horsemen riding abreast – nowadays it's about 15 tourists walking abreast.

Unfortunately, if you take a tour bus or train from Beijing you hit peak hour, and you only get a touch over an hour at the wall. Many are dissatisfied with such paltry time at far and away one of the most spectacular sights in the PRC. The solution is to take one-way tours or public transport, spend the time you want, and then figure out a way to get back. Many people take their sleeping bags and picnic baskets, head off from the crowds and camp out overnight.

The Badaling section of the wall has a train station, lots of shops and a few restaurants. Once the convoys of buses take off back to Beijing with their human cargo Badaling is almost a ghost town. For Y5 or so you can get your snapshot taken aboard a camel and pretend to be Marco Polo – though he wasn't tethered to a wall. There's a story attached to the camel. In 1981 when director Labella was filming the travels of Polo, the commune that owned the camel refused to move it from the camera's field of view unless they were paid the day's lost earnings. The bill came to Y2000!

Getting There

Tours Many travellers get to the Great Wall via the tour buses operated out of the Qiao Yuan Hotel. These also take you to the Ming Tombs on the way. The tour costs Y15 per person; entrance to the underground vault of the Ming Tomb is an additional Y3. You're left to your own devices at the wall, and get about two hours, which is adequate.

There are other tours available from ticket offices opposite or in the vicinity of the Chongwenmen Hotel. These are a bit cheaper than the Qiao Yuan tours, but they often spend much less time at the wall. Some have nice air-con buses; others have older, more uncomfortable buses.

Bus Local buses ply the route to the wall; take bus Nos 5 or 44 to Deshengmen, then No 345 to the terminus (Changping), then a no-numbered bus to the wall (alternatively, bus No 357 goes part-way along the route and you then hitch). The cost is less than Y1 in fares. Another route is bus No 14 to Beijiao Market, which is north of Deshengmen, then a no-numbered bus to the wall.

Rail There is a local train from Xizhimen (north railway station) in Beijing which stops at Badaling and continues to Kangzhuang. Check departure times with CITS. Roughly, the train leaves Xizhimen around 8.10 am and arrives at Badaling at 11.15 am. It departs Badaling around 2.11 pm and arrives at Beijing at 5 pm. The return fare is about Y5. At Xizhimen Station there is a special booking office for this train. Badaling Station is one km from the wall. The Badaling line is quite a feat of engineering; built in 1909, it tunnels under the wall.

You can reach the wall by express train

from Beijing, getting off at Qinglongqiao, which is the station before Badaling. Several express trains from Beijing Main Station stop at Qinglongqiao, but not at Badaling. There are actually two stations called Qinglongqiao. One has a statue of Chian Tianyu, the engineer in charge of building the Beijing-Baotou line; trains to Beijing leave from this station. Trains from Beijing arrive at the other station, where it's an easy one-km walk to the wall. If you're coming from the direction of Hohhot or Datong you could get out at Qinglongqiao, look around the wall and then continue the same day to Beijing. Your ticket will still be valid for the last stretch to Beijing and you can dump your bags in the left-luggage room at Qinglongqiao station while you look around.

Taxi A taxi to the wall and back will cost at least Y75 for an eight-hour hire with a maximum of four passengers.

OTHER PARTS OF THE WALL

About 10 km south-east of Badaling, Juyong Pass was a garrison town dating back to the Mongol period. There remains a solid stone and marble gateway, Cloud Terrace, built in 1345 and now entirely rebuilt. The vault of the archway bears superb bas-reliefs of the Four Heavenly Guardians, and inscribed on the walls are incantations in six different languages – Sanskrit, Tibetan, Mongolian (Phagspa script), Uygur, Chinese and Tangut (a rare language from a 13th-century Gansu kingdom) – all of which drive philologists crazy!

Other parts of the wall open to foreigners are those stretches at Jiayuguan in Gansu Province and Shanhaiguan in Hebei Province. More bits and pieces are scattered around. To ease the squeeze on Badaling, another section has been renovated at Jinshanling (Shalinkou), 130 km north-east of Beijing on the bus route to Chengde. It's 10 km east of Gubeikou Pass and with a combined package to Chengde it should be a real money-raker.

This section of the wall dates from the Ming Dynasty and has some unusual features like 'obstacle-walls', which are walls-within-walls used for defending against enemies who'd already scaled the Great Wall. Small cannon have been discovered here, as well as evidence of rocket-type weapons such as flying knives and flying swords.

An early western visitor was Lord Macartney, who crossed Gubei Pass on his way to Chengde in 1793. His party made a wild guess that the wall contained almost as much material as all the houses in England and Scotland.

In the early 1970s a Gubeikou PLA unit destroyed about three km of the wall to build barracks, setting an example for the locals, who did likewise. The story goes that in 1979 the same unit was ordered to rebuild the section torn down.

Along the route to Jinshanling, another plus is the Miyun Reservoir, a huge artificial lake slated to become a holiday resort for foreigners. It already has touring vessels but they're limited to group tours. Trains running to Chengde stop at Miyun, which is 90 km from Beijing. Gubeikou is on the Beijing-Tongliao Line.

THE MING TOMBS 明陵

The general travellers' consensus on the tombs is that you'd be better off looking at a bank vault, which is, roughly, what the tombs are. Each held the body of an emperor, his wives and girlfriends, and funerary treasures. The scenery along the way is charming though, and the approach through a valley is rewarding.

The seven-km 'spirit way' starts with a triumphal arch, then goes through the Red Gate, where officials had to dismount, and passes a giant tortoise (made in 1425) bearing the largest stele in China. This is followed by a guard of 12 sets of stone animals. Every second one is in a reclining position, legend has it, to allow for a 'changing of the guard' at midnight. If your tour bus driver whips past them, insist on stopping to look – they're far more interesting than the tombs – because the drivers like to spend half an hour at the Ming Tombs Reservoir, which is dead boring. Beyond the stone animals are 12 stone-faced human statues of generals, ministers and officials, each distinguishable by headgear. The avenue culminates at the Dragon and Phoenix Gate.

Dingling is the only tomb excavated at Shisanling although 13 of the 16 Ming emperors are buried in this 40-square-km area. The other tombs, such as Changling, can be viewed from the exterior. Changling, which was started in 1409 and took 18 years to complete, is the tomb of Emperor Yong Le and, so the story goes, of 16 of his concubines who were buried alive with his corpse.

Dingling, the tomb of Emperor Wan Li (1573-1620), is the second-largest tomb. Over six years the emperor used a half-million workers and a heap of silver to build his necropolis and then held a wild party inside the completed chambers. It was excavated between 1956 and 1958 and for Y3 you can now visit the underground passageways and caverns. The underground construction covers 1195 square metres, is built entirely of stone, and is sealed with an unusual lock stone. The tomb yielded up 26 lacquered trunks of funerary objects, some of which are displayed on-site; others have been removed to Beijing museums and replaced with copies.

Wan Li and his royal spouses were buried in double coffins surrounded by chunks of uncut jade. The jade was thought to have the power to preserve the dead (or could have bought millions of bowls of rice for starving peasants), so the Chinese tour literature relates. Meanwhile cultural relics experts as well as chefs are studying the ancient cookbooks unearthed from Dingling with a view to serving Wan Li's favourite dishes to visitors, using replicas of imperial banquet tableware. Until they figure that one out, you might have to be content with the amusing cardboard cut-outs and other props used by Chinese photographers at the site.

The tombs lie 50 km north-west of Beijing and four km from Changping. The tour buses usually combine them with a visit to the Great Wall. You can also get there on the local buses. Take bus Nos 5 or 44 to Deshengmen terminus. West of the flyover is the terminus of bus No 345 which you take to Changping, a one-hour ride. Then take bus No 314 to the tombs (or hitch the last stretch).

It's only fair to mention that many people find the Ming Tomb a wipeoff. 'What a monumental disappointment!' said one letter. 'There isn't anything down there, and you pay Y3 just to walk into a four-storey deep hole and back out again.' Another letter complained that 'other than seeing that they knew how to make deep excavations in China several centuries ago, there is nothing to justify the trip'. I think that's a bit like saying that all the Great Wall proves is that Chinese were capable of putting one brick on top of another for a very long distance. True, there may not be anything inside the tombs, but like the Wall and the Mao Zedong Mausoleum, I find it interesting to see the product of an incredible amount of misspent human labour.

THE NORTH-WEST SUBURBS 西北交区

About five to 15 km from downtown, the north-west suburbs have a number of attractions: the Summer Palaces, Western Hills, Azure Clouds Temple and Sleeping Buddha Temple. You can easily get there on the local buses or by bicycle.

Some round-trip suggestions: Take bus No 332 from the zoo to the Old Summer Palace and to the Summer Palace; change to bus No 333 for the Western Hills; change to bus No 360 to go directly back to the zoo.

Another round-trip route is to take the subway to Pingguoyan (the last stop in the west) and then take bus No 318 to the Western Hills; change to No 333 for the Summer Palace, and then to No 332 for the zoo.

Beijing University (Beida Daxue)

Beijing has about 50 colleges and universities. A curious one is the Minorities Institute (Minzuxueyan), just north of the zoo. The institute trains cadres for the minority regions.

Beijing University (Beida) and Qinghua University are the most prestigious institutes in China. Beida was founded at the turn of the century; it was then called Yanjing University and was administered by the Americans. Its students figured prominently in the 4 May 1919 demonstrations and the later resistance against the Japanese. In 1953 the university moved from Coal Hill to its present location. In the 1960s the Red Guards first appeared here and the place witnessed some scenes of utter mayhem as the persecutions of the Cultural Revolution took place. Today there are hundreds of foreign students at Beida, studying a range of subjects.

The shopping district for Beida is the Haidian area to the south, where students congregate in the small restaurants and where locals come from surrounding communes to stock up on provisions.

Beida is on the bus No 332 route from the zoo, or about a 45-minute cycle from downtown. Further east, past Qinghua University, is the Beijing Languages Institute (BLI) with its own contingent of foreign students. The institute is on the No 331 bus route.

Old Summer Palace (Yuanmingyuan)

The original Yuanmingyuan was laid out in the 12th century. By the reign of Emperor Qianlong, it developed into a set of interlocking gardens. Qianlong set the Jesuits to work as architects for European palaces for the gardens – elaborate fountains, baroque statuary, kiosks included.

In the second Opium War (1860), foreign troops destroyed the place and sent the booty abroad. Since the Chinese pavilions and temples were made of wood they did not survive fires, but a marble facade, some broken columns and traces of the fountains stick out of the rice-paddies.

The ruins are a favourite picnic spot for foreigners living in the capital and for Chinese twosomes seeking a bit of privacy. The ruins can be reached on foot (about half an hour) or by bike from Beida. They aren't signposted so they're easy to miss. Go north from Beida, turn right along the road to Qinghua University, detour left into the rice fields – and then ask whoever happens to be wandering by.

Summer Palace (Yiheyuan)

This is an immense park containing some newish Qing architecture. The site had long been a royal garden and was considerably enlarged and embellished by Emperor Qianlong in the 18th century. He deepened and expanded Kunming Lake with the help of 100,000 labourers – and reputedly surveyed imperial Navy drills from a hilltop perch.

In 1860 Anglo-French troops gutted and looted the place during the Opium War. Empress Dowager Cixi began rebuilding in 1888 using money that was supposedly reserved for the construction of a modern navy – but she did restore a marble boat that sits immobile at the edge of the lake. She had this ugly thing fitted out with several large mirrors and used to dine at the lakeside.

In 1900 foreign troops, annoyed by the

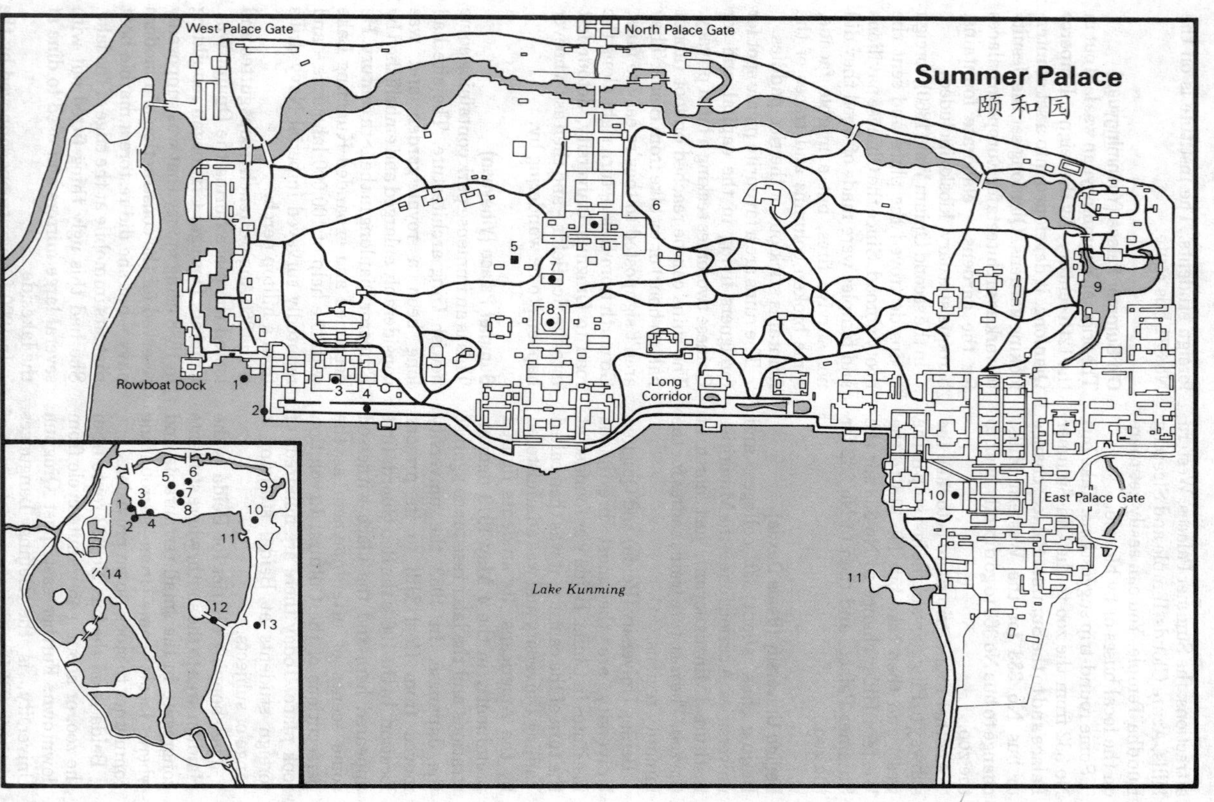
Summer Palace
颐和园
West Palace Gate
North Palace Gate
Rowboat Dock
Long Corridor
East Palace Gate
Lake Kunming

1 Marble Boat
2 Ferry Dock
3 Pavilion for Listening to the Orioles
4 Long Corridor
5 Pavilion of Precious Clouds
6 Hall of Buddhist Tenants
7 Temple of the Sea of Wisdom
8 Temple of Buddhist Virtue
9 Garden of Harmonious Interest
10 Hall of Benevolence & Longevity
11 Rowboat Dock
12 Pavilion of Knowing in the Spring
13 Bronze Oxen
14 Jade Belt Bridge

1	清晏船	8	佛香阁
2	码头	9	偕趣园
3	饭店	10	仁寿殿
4	长廊	11	划船码头
5	云会寺	12	知春阁
6	香崇宗印之阁	13	铜牛
7	智慧海	14	玉带桥

Boxer Rebellion, had another go at roasting the Summer Palace. Restorations took place a few years later and a major renovation occurred after 1949, by which time the palace had once more fallen into disrepair.

The original palace was used as a summer residence, an escape from the ferocious heat. The Forbidden City packed up and decamped here for their holidays, so the emphasis is on cool features – water, gardens, mounts. It was divided into four sections: court reception, residences, temples and strolling or sightseeing areas. Three-quarters of the park is occupied by Lake Kunming, and most items of structural interest are located toward the east or north gates.

The main building is the **Hall of Benevolence & Longevity**, just off the lake toward the east gate. It houses a hardwood throne, and has a courtyard with bronze animals. In it the emperor-in-residence handled state affairs and received envoys.

Along the north shore of the lake is the **Long Corridor**, over 700 metres long, which is decorated with mythical scenes. If the paint looks new it's because a lot of pictures were white-washed during the Cultural Revolution.

On man-made **Longevity Hill** are a number of temples. The **Pavilion of Precious Clouds** on the western slopes is one of the few structures to escape destruction by the Anglo-French forces. It contains some elaborate bronzes. At the top of the hill sits the Buddhist **Temple of the Sea of Wisdom**, made of glazed tiles; good views of the lake can be had from this spot.

Other sights are largely associated with Empress Cixi, like the place where she kept Emperor Guangxu under house-arrest, the place where she celebrated her birthdays, and exhibitions of her furniture and memorabilia. A very Disneylandish atmosphere pervades this 'museum'; tourists can have their photos taken, imperial dress-up fashion.

The **Tingliguan Restaurant** serves imperial banquet food – fish from Lake Kunming, velvet chicken, dumplings – on regal tableware look-alikes. It has a splendid al fresco location and exorbitant prices, and is housed in what was once an imperial theatre, with attached souvenir shops.

Another noteworthy feature of the Summer Palace is the 17-arch bridge spanning 150 metres to South Lake Island; on the mainland side is a beautiful bronze ox. Also note the **Jade Belt Bridge** on the mid-west side of the lake; and the **Garden of Harmonious Interest** at the north-east end which is a copy of a Wuxi garden.

You can get around the lake to the bridges by rowboat. Boating and swimming are popular pastimes for the locals (windsurfing for the richer) and in winter you can skate on the lakes. As with the Forbidden City Moat, slabs of ice are cut out of the lake in winter and stored for summer use.

The park is about 12 km north-west of the centre of Beijing. Take bus No 332 from the zoo. You can can also get there by bicycle – it takes about 1½ to two hours from downtown. If you consult a bus map, you'll see the Beijing-Miyun Irrigation Canal feeding from Yuyuan Lake to Kunming Lake. The route is good for biking although it's a dirt road. The bus map will show which side of various sections of the canal is bikeable. Entry to the park is 10 fen, but there are additional charges to certain sections.

THE WESTERN HILLS 西山

Within striking distance of the Summer Palace, and often combined with it on a tour, are the Western Hills, another former villa-resort area.

Temple of the Sleeping Buddha (Wofo Si)

On the approach to the hills is the Temple of the Sleeping Buddha. During the Cultural Revolution the buddhas in one of the halls were replaced by a statue of Mao (since removed). The draw card is the huge reclining buddha, 5.2 metres long, cast in copper. The history books place it in the year 1331 but it's most likely a copy. Its weight is unknown but could be up to 50 tons. Pilgrims used to make offerings of shoes to the barefoot statue.

Azure Clouds Temple (Biyun Si)

A short distance from the North Gate of Western Hills Park is the Azure Clouds Temple, whose landmark is the Diamond Throne Pagoda. Of Indian design, it consists of a raised platform with a central pagoda and stupas around it. The temple was first built in 1366, and was expanded in the 18th century with the addition of the Hall of Arhats, containing 500 statues representing disciples of Buddha. Dr Sun Yatsen's coffin was placed in the temple in 1925 before being moved to Nanjing. In 1954 the government renovated Sun's memorial hall, which has a picture display of his revolutionary activities.

Other Attractions

Like the Summer Palace, the Western Hills area was razed by foreign troops in 1860 and 1900 but a few bits still poke out. A glazed tile pagoda and the remains of the **Zhaomiao**, a mock-Tibetan temple built in 1780, are both in the same area. The surrounding, heavily wooded **Xiangshan Park** was a hunting ground for the emperors, and once contained a slew of pavilions and shrines. It's a favourite strolling spot for Beijingers, many of whom go to gaze through the gates of the Xiangshan Hotel. You can scramble up the slopes to the top of **Incense-Burner Peak**, or for Y3 you can take the crowded cable-car. From the peak you get an all-embracing view of the countryside. You might also like to hunt for a restaurant, called the Xiangshan but not linked with the hotel, which serves excellent spring rolls, fried duck liver, spiced pork and fried noodles – service is said to be slow so some people place their orders, ramble off around the 150 hectares of parkland, and come back to the table.

Badachu

Directly south of the Western Hills is Badachu, the 'Eight Great Sites'. It has eight monasteries or temples scattered in wooded valleys. The 'Second Site' has the Buddha's Tooth Pagoda, built to house the sacred fang and accidentally discovered when the Allied army demolished the place in 1900. Unfortunately, Badachu seems to be part of a military zone and foreigners are not allowed in. This may change in the future as the demand for more tourist sites increases, so check out the situation when you get there.

Getting There

There are a couple of ways of getting to the Western Hills: bus No 333 from the Summer Palace, bus No 360 from the zoo, and bus No 318 from Pingguoyan (the last stop in the west on the subway).

You might end up at Badachu on a magical mystery tour from the Qianmen ticket/tour office. Otherwise take bus No 347, which runs there from the zoo (it crosses the No 318 route).

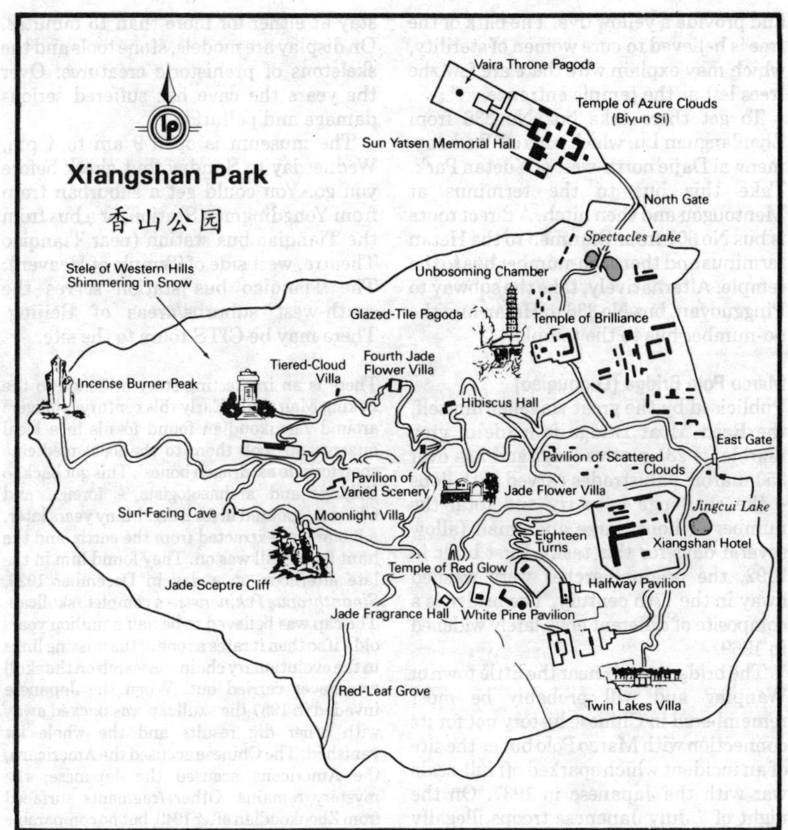

THE OUTLYING AREAS 外围

Try as you might to cover it, Beijing refuses to end. Apart from the Great Wall, Ming Tombs, Summer Palace and a host of other imperial monuments, there are more temples, caves, bridges and Stone-Age relics beyond the city limits.

Tanzhe Temple

South-west of Badachu, or 45 km directly west of Beijing, is Tanzhesi, the largest of all the Beijing temples, occupying an area 260 metres by 160 metres. The Buddhist complex has a long history dating as early as the 3rd century (Jin Dynasty); structural modifications date from the Liao, Tang, Ming and Qing dynasties. It therefore has a number of features – dragon decorations, mythical animal sculptures and grimacing gods – no longer found in temples in the capital.

The temple takes its name from its proximity to the Dragon Pool *(Longtan)* and some *zhe* trees. Locals come to the Dragon Pool to pray for rain during droughts. The zhe trees nourish silkworms and provide a yellow dye. The bark of the tree is believed to cure women of sterility, which may explain why there are few zhe trees left at the temple entrance.

To get there take bus No 336 from Zhanlanguan Lu, which runs off Fuchengmenwai Dajie north-west of Yuetan Park. Take this bus to the terminus at Mentougou and then hitch. A direct route is bus No 307 from Qianmen to the Hetan terminus and then a no-number bus to the temple. Alternatively, take the subway to Pingguoyan, bus No 336 to Hetan and the no-number bus to the temple.

Marco Polo Bridge (Lugouqiao)

Publicised by the great traveller himself, the Reed Moat Bridge is made of grey marble, is 231 metres long, and has over 250 marble balustrades carved with lions – the challenge is to try and total the number of lions, large and small (allow several days for this task). First built in 1192, the original arches were washed away in the 17th century. The bridge is a composite of different eras, lately widened in 1969.

The bridge stands near the little town of Wanping and will probably be most remembered in Chinese history not for its connection with Marco Polo but as the site of an incident which sparked off full-scale war with the Japanese in 1937. On the night of 7 July Japanese troops illegally occupied a railway junction outside Wanping – Japanese and Chinese soldiers started shooting at each other and that gave Japan enough of an excuse (as if they really needed one!) to attack and occupy Beijing.

You can get to the bridge by taking bus No 109 to Guanganmen and then catching bus No 339. By bicycle it's about a 16-km trip.

Zhoukoudian

Site of those primeval Chinese, the Peking Men, Zhoukoudian is 48 km south-west of Beijing. There's a dig-site here and a fossil exhibition hall – you'd have to be a fossil to stay at either for more than 15 minutes. On display are models, stone tools and the skeletons of prehistoric creatures. Over the years the cave has suffered serious damage and pollution.

The museum is open 9 am to 4 pm, Wednesday to Sunday, but check before you go. You could get a suburban train from Yongdingmen Station, or a bus from the Tianqiao bus station (near Tianqiao Theatre, west side of Temple of Heaven). The Tianqiao bus station serves the south-west suburbs/areas of Beijing. There may be CITS tours to the site.

There is an interesting story attached to the Peking Man skull. Early this century, villagers around Zhoukoudian found fossils in a local quarry and took them to the local medicine shop for sale as 'dragon bones'. This got back to Beijing, and archaeologists – foreign and Chinese – poured in for a dig. Many years later, a molar was extracted from the earth, and the hunt for a skull was on. They found him in the late afternoon on a day in December 1929, *Sinanthropus Pekinensis* – a complete skullcap. The cap was believed to be half a million years old – if so then it rates as one of the missing links in the evolutionary chain. Research on the skull was never carried out. When the Japanese invaded in 1937 the skullcap was packed away with other dig results and the whole lot vanished. The Chinese accused the Americans, the Americans accused the Japanese, the mystery remains. Other fragments surfaced from Zhoukoudian after 1949, but no comparable treasure was found.

Yunshui Caves

In the direction of Zhoukoudian in Fangshan County are the more pedestrian Yunshui Caves, with coloured lights, passageways and snack bar. There are some recently discovered caves in the same area, too.

Western Qing Tombs (Qing Xiling)

These tombs are in Yixian County, 110 km south-west of Beijing. If you didn't see enough of the Dingling, Yuling, Yongling and Deling, well, there's always Tailing, Changling, Chongling and Muling.

The tomb area is vast and houses the corpses of the emperors, empresses and other members and hangers-on of the royal family. The tomb of Emperor Guangxu (Chongling) has been excavated – his was the last imperial tomb and was constructed between 1905 and 1915.

Eastern Qing Tombs (Qing Dongling)

Qingdongling is Death Valley – five emperors, 14 empresses and 136 imperial consorts. In the mountains ringing the valley are buried princes, dukes, imperial nurses, and so on.

The approach to the tomb area is a common 'spirit way', similar to that of the Ming Tombs but with the addition of marble-arch bridges. The materials for the tombs come from all over China, including 20-ton logs pulled over iced roads, and giant stone slabs.

Two of the tombs are open. Emperor Qianlong (1711-1799) started preparations when he was 30, and by the time he was 88 the old boy had used up 90 tons of his silver. His resting place covers half a square km. Some of the beamless stone chambers are decorated with Tibetan and Sanskrit sutras; the doors bear bas-relief bodhisattvas.

Empress Dowager Cixi also got a head start. Her tomb, Dingdong, was completed some three decades before her death. The phoenix, symbol of the empress, appears above that of the dragon (the emperor's symbol) in the artwork at the front of the tomb – not side by side as on other tombs. Both tombs were plundered in the 1920s.

Located in Zunhua County, 125 km east of Beijing, the Eastern Qing Tombs have more to see in them than the Ming Tombs – but after the Forbidden City, who cares? Again, the scenery may make the visit worthwhile.

The only way to get there is by bus and it's a rough ride. Tour buses are considerably more comfortable and take three or four hours to get there; you have about three hours on site. It may be possible to make a one-way trip to Zunhua and then take off somewhere else rather than go back to Beijing. A little way north along the road to Chengde is a piece of the Great Wall.

Jixian

Half-way to Zunhua the tour bus makes a lunch stop at Jixian, more interesting than Zunhua. One way of getting to Jixian is to hop a regular long-distance bus from Guangqumenwai bus station, south-east of Beijing Main Station. Jixian is also connected by a direct rail link to Tianjin.

The Jixian area is about 90 km due east of Beijing and is little explored by individuals. In the west gate is the Temple of Solitary Joy (Dule Si). The main multi-storey wooden structure, the Avalokitesvara Pavilion, qualifies for the oldest such structure in China at 1000 years vintage. It houses a 16-metre-high statue of a bodhisattva with 10 heads which rates as one of China's largest terracotta statues. The buddha is Liao Dynasty and the murals inside are Ming Dynasty. The complex has been recently restored.

To the north-west of Jixian is **Pan Shan**, ranked among the 15 famous mountains of China – wooded hills, springs, streams.

Tianjin 天津

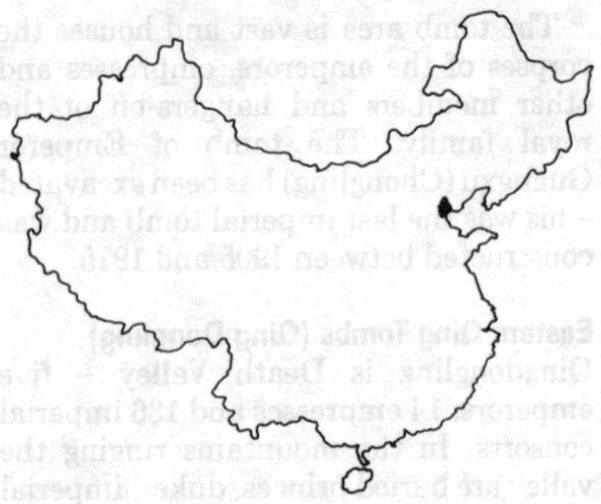

Tianjin is the 'Shanghai of the North' – a reference to its common concession background, heavy industrial output, large port, and direct administration by the central government. In terms of energy and character, however, Tianjin is more like a mongrel cross between Beijing and Shanghai – dowdier than Shanghai, more stimulating than Beijing.

The city's fortunes are, and always have been, linked to those of Beijing. When the Mongols established Beijing as the capital in the 13th century, Tianjin first rose to prominence as a grain storage point. Pending remodelling of the Grand Canal by Kublai Khan, the tax-grain was routed along the Yangtse River, out into the open sea, up to Tianjin, and then through to Beijing. With the Grand Canal fully functional as far as Beijing, Tianjin was at the intersection of both inland and port navigation routes. By the 15th century, the town was a walled garrison. In the 17th century Dutch envoys described the city thus:

> The town has many temples; it is thickly populated and trade is very brisk – it would be hard to find another town as busy as this in China – because all the boats which go to Beijing, whatever their port of origin, call here, and traffic is astonishingly heavy.

For the sea-dog western nations, Tianjin was a trading bottleneck too good to be passed up. In 1856 Chinese soldiers boarded the *Arrow*, a boat flying the British flag, ostensibly in search of pirates. This was as much of an excuse as the British and the French needed. Their gunboats attacked the forts outside Tianjin, forcing the Chinese to sign the Treaty of Tianjin (1858), which opened the port up to foreign trade and also legalised the sale of opium. Chinese reluctance to take part in a treaty they had been forced into led the British and French to start a new campaign to open the port to Western trade. In 1860 British troops bombarded Tianjin in an attempt to coerce another treaty.

The English and French settled in. Between 1895 and 1900 they were joined by the Japanese, Germans, Austro-Hungarians, Italians and Belgians. Each of the concessions was a self-contained world with its own prison, school, barracks and hospital. Because they were so close together, it was possible to traverse the national styles of architecture in the course of a few hours, from Via Vittorio Emanuele to Cambridge Road. One could cross from the flat roofs and white housing of the Italian concession, pass the Corinthian columns of the banks along the Rue de France, proceed down to the manicured lawns of Victorian mansions, and while away the wee hours of the morning dancing at the German Club (now a library).

The palatial life was broken only in 1870 when the locals attacked the French-run orphanage and killed, among others, 10 of the nuns – apparently the Chinese thought the children were being kidnapped. Thirty years later, during the Boxer Rebellion, the foreign powers levelled the walls of the old Chinese city. Other than that, the European presence stimulated trade and industry including salt, textiles and glass manufacture. Heavy silting of the Hai River forced a new port to be built at Tanggu, 50 km downstream, and

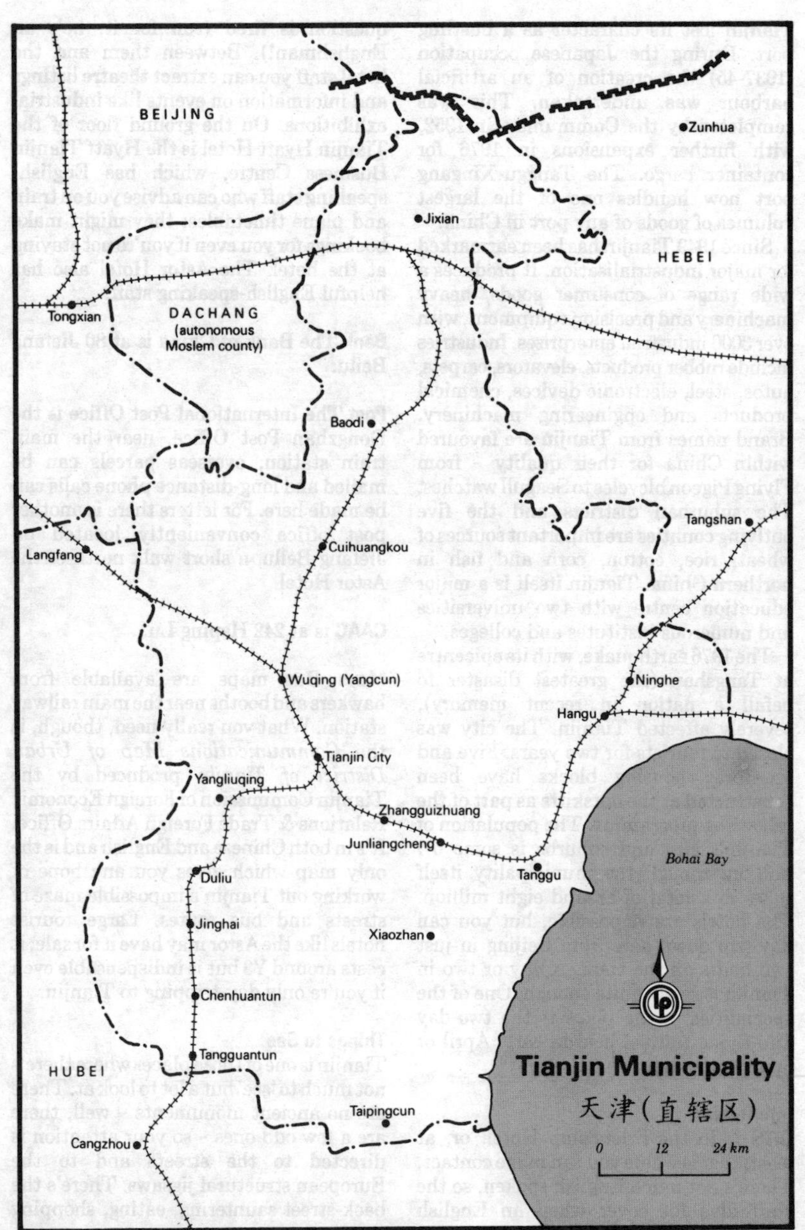
BEIJING
Zunhua
Jixian
HEBEI
Tongxian
DACHANG
(autonomous
Moslem county)
Baodi
Tangshan
Langfang
Cuihuangkou
Wuqing (Yangcun)
Ninghe
Hangu
Tianjin City
Yangliuqing
Zhangguizhuang
Junliangcheng
Bohai Bay
Tanggu
Duliu
Jinghai
Xiaozhan
Chenhuantun
Tangguantun
HUBEI
Tianjin Municipality
天津(直辖区)
Taipingcun
Cangzhou
0
12
24 km

Tianjin lost its character as a bustling port. During the Japanese occupation (1937-45) the creation of an artificial harbour was undertaken. This was completed by the Communists in 1952, with further expansions in 1976 for container cargo. The Tanggu-Xingang port now handles one of the largest volumes of goods of any port in China.

Since 1949 Tianjin has been earmarked for major industrialisation. It produces a wide range of consumer goods, heavy machinery and precision equipment, with over 3000 industrial enterprises. Industries include rubber products, elevators, carpets, autos, steel, electronic devices, chemical products and engineering machinery. Brand names from Tianjin are favoured within China for their quality – from Flying Pigeon bicycles to Seagull watches. The suburban districts and the five outlying counties are important sources of wheat, rice, cotton, corn and fish in northern China. Tianjin itself is a major education centre with two universities and numerous institutes and colleges.

The 1976 earthquake, with its epicentre at Tangshan (the greatest disaster to befall a nation in recent memory), severely affected Tianjin. The city was closed to tourists for two years. Five and six-storey housing blocks have been constructed at the outskirts as part of the rehousing programme. The population of Tianjin's city and suburbs is some 5½ million, though the municipality itself takes in a total of around eight million. The hotels are impossible, but you can day-trip down here from Beijing in just two hours on the train. A day or two in Tianjin is really quite enough. One of the specialities of the place is the two-day kite-flying festival held in early April or late September.

Information

CITS is in the Friendship Hotel, or, at least, that is where you can make contact. There's not much English spoken, so the staff dive for cover when an English question is fired (run for it, he's an Englishman!). Between them and the hotel staff you can extract theatre listings and information on events like industrial exhibitions. On the ground floor of the Tianjin Hyatt Hotel is the Hyatt Tianjin Business Centre, which has English-speaking staff who can advise you on train and plane timetables; they might make bookings for you even if you're not staying at the hotel. The Astor Hotel also has helpful English-speaking staff.

Bank The Bank of China is at 80 Jiefang Beilu.

Post The International Post Office is the Dongzhan Post Office, near the main train station; overseas parcels can be mailed and long-distance phone calls can be made here. For letters there is another post office conveniently located on Jiefang Beilu, a short walk north of the Astor Hotel.

CAAC is at 242 Heping Lu.

Maps Bus maps are available from hawkers and booths near the main railway station. What you really need, though, is the *Communications Map of Urban District of Tianjin* produced by the Tianjin Commission of Foreign Economic Relations & Trade Foreign Affairs Office. It's in both Chinese and English and is the only map which gives you any hope of working out Tianjin's impossible maze of streets and bus routes. Large tourist hotels like the Astor may have it for sale; it costs around Y3 but is indispensable even if you're only day-tripping to Tianjin.

Things to See

Tianjin is one of those places where there's not much to 'see' but a lot to look at. There are no ancient monuments – well, there are a few odd ones – so your attention is directed to the streets and to the European structural jigsaws. There's the back-street sauntering, eating, shopping

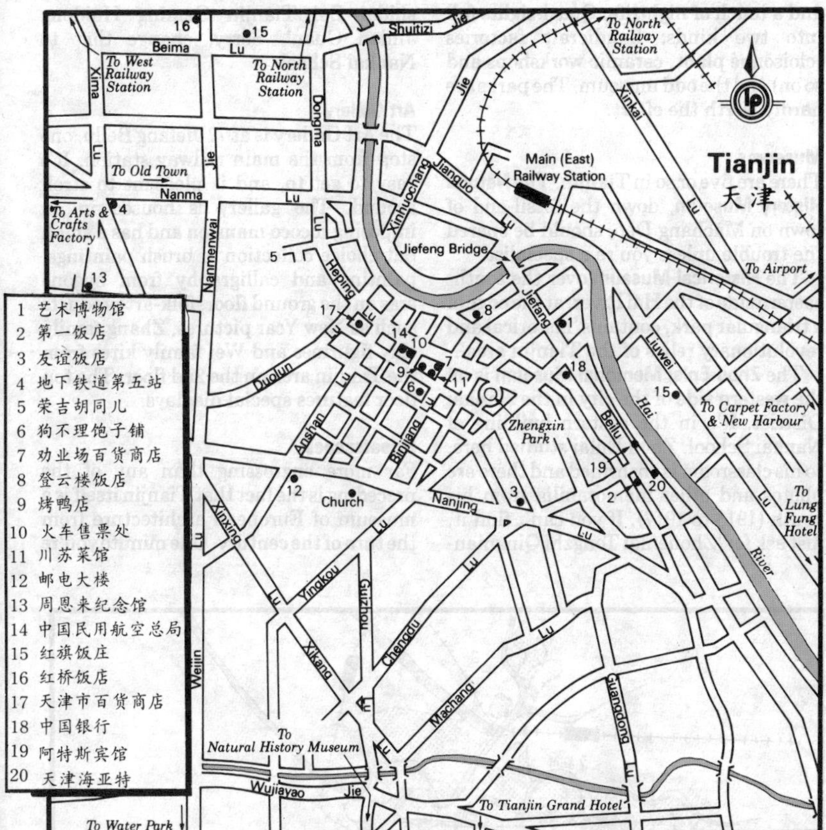

1 Art Gallery
2 Tianjin No 1 Hotel
3 Friendship Hotel/CITS
4 5th Subway Exit
5 Rongji Hutong (location of restaurants in small alley)
6 Goubuli Baozi Shop (in alley not marked on map)
7 Quanyechang Department Store
8 Dengyinglou Restaurant
9 Tianjin Roast Duck (Tianjin Kaoya) Restaurant
10 Advance Rail Ticket Office
11 Chuansu Sichuan Restaurant
12 Post & Telephone Building
13 Zhou Enlai Memorial Museum
14 CAAC
15 Red Flag Restaurant
16 Red Bridge Restaurant
17 Tianjin Department Store
18 Bank of China
19 Astor Hotel
20 Tianjin Hyatt

and a touch of nightlife. Quasi-sights fall into two kinds: handicraft factories (cloisonné plant, ceramic workshops and so on) and the odd museum. The parks are hardly worth the effort.

Museums

There are five or so in Tianjin. The **Natural History Museum**, down the fossil-end of town on Machang Dao, should be spared the trouble unless you're a specialist.

The **Historical Museum** over the south-eastern side of the Hai River, at the edge of a triangular park, contains 'historical and revolutionary relics of the Tianjin area'.

The **Zhou Enlai Memorial Museum** is on the western side of the city in the Nankai District. It's in the eastern building of Nankai School. Zhou Enlai studied here, so his classroom is enshrined and there are photos and other memorabilia from his youth (1913 to 1917). If you can't find it, just ask for 'Zhouenlai Tongzhi Qingnian-shidai Zai Tianjin Geming Huidong Jinian Guan'. Sorry, change that to Nankai School.

Art Gallery

The Art Gallery is at 77 Jiefang Beilu, one stop from the main railway station. It's easy to get to, and is pleasant to stroll around. The gallery is housed in an imposing rococo mansion and has a small but choice collection of brush paintings, painting and calligraphy from bygone eras on the ground floor, folk-art products such as New Year pictures, Zhang family clay figurines and Wei family kites from the Tianjin area on the 2nd floor. The top floor features special displays.

Streetscapes

Far more engrossing than any of the preceding is the fact that Tianjin itself is a museum of European architecture from the turn of the century. One minute you're

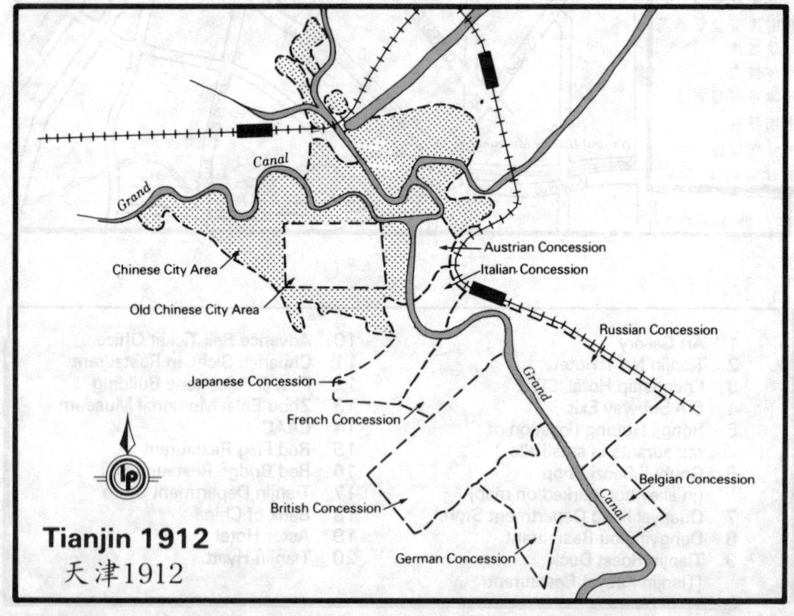

Tianjin 1912
天津1912

in little Vienna, turn a corner and you could be in a London street, hop off a bus and you're looking at some vintage French wrought-iron gates or a neo-Gothic cathedral.

If you're an architecture student, go no further – Tianjin is a textbook of just about every style imaginable, a draftsman's nightmare or a historian's delight, depending on which way you look at it. Poking out of the post-earthquake shanty rubble could be a high-rise castle of glass and steel; and anyone with a sense of humour will be well-satisfied with some of the uses that the bastions of the European well-to-do have been put to.

Tianjin traffic is equally as mixed: horse carts, cyclists with heavy loads struggling to make it across an intersection before an ambush from a changing light cuts them off, a parent with a kid in a bicycle sidecar. Judiciously selected buses will take you through as many former concessions as you want – and presuming that you have a window seat, this kind of random touring will be quite rewarding, architecturally speaking.

There's enough action on the main shopping drags of Tianjin and around the former Chinese city to keep even the most hardened of alley-cats interested. Some of these features are described in the touring section further on, but should one have the time, there's much more than this to see.

Touring Tianjin

The following is a combined bus, subway and foot tour which will whip you round the streets, the eating holes and the buy-and-sell stretches – allow at least three hours. The route follows an elliptical shape in a clockwise direction, starting at the main railway station and taking in the Art Gallery, Kiesslings, the old Chinese sector, Heping Lu and the downtown district. Because opening and closing hours for places mentioned may not fit your own schedule, you might skip some places, or return to them later, or do the route in reverse, or just scrap the whole thing and use the information as you see fit. If you have a bit more time, then more walking is preferable at the beginning and end of the tour.

Step One – Main Railway Station Turn right out of the main railway station; you'll find the 24-hour baggage room with its windows facing onto the street – dump your bags here. Get a bus map – they're available from booths near the station and also from the post office near the station. To catch the elusive bus No 13, continue past the baggage offices to the end of the street, turn left, walk 1½ blocks south and you'll find the terminus queue (bus No 13 actually goes back towards the station first before heading over Jiefang Bridge into town).

Step Two – Bus No 13 Route First stop is the former French concession and the Art Gallery. If you're interested in Tianjin folk art in the buying sense, this would be a logical stop-over, as the best examples are to be found within.

Second stop – you are now entering the former British concession.

Third stop is the park near the Tianjin No 1 Hotel and the Astor Hotel.

Fourth stop, get off. This lands you between the Friendship Hotel and Kiesslings. Just ahead of the bus stop is Kiesslings Restaurant on Zhejiang Lu. It's an excellent place to knock off those long-overdue postcards.

Step Three – The Subway Walk south to Nanjing Lu and then west to the first subway station. Tianjin's subway opened in 1982; the cars shuttle back and forth on a single track. There's nothing to see down in the depths except the subterranean bathroom tiling, but it saves a lot of paperwork with buses. Ride it to the fifth stop. When you surface you're within walking distance of the old Chinese town.

Step Four – Chinatown My apologies in advance for this misnomer – couldn't resist it. The old Chinese sector can easily be identified on the bus map as a rectangle with buses running around the perimeter. Roughly, the bounding roads are Beima (north horse), Nanma (south horse), Xima (west horse) and Dongma (east horse). Originally there was one main north-south street, crossing an east-west one within that (walled) rectangle.

Within this area you can spend time fruitfully exploring the lanes and side streets where traditional architecture remains, and perhaps even find a dilapidated temple or two. Basically, though, this is a people-watching place, where you can get snatches of daily life through doorways. There's a good run of shops on Nanma, Dongma and Beima Lu.

Step Five – Heping Lu A massive shopping drag extends from the West Station down via Beima Lu, where it meets another shopping drag coming from the North Station along Zhongshan Lu. Both of these snake down the length of Heping Lu as far as Zhongxin Park.

If you make your way on foot along Nanma Lu, the southern fringe of 'Chinatown', you'll arrive at the top end of Heping Lu. Going south on Heping, you will find a busy alley, Rongji Jie, leading off to the right – plenty more food, but try to save some space in the lower intestines for the Goubuli dumpling shop which is a little way off yet.

From Rongji Jie you can walk south, or jump a bus several stops down Heping to the heart of the shopping district – downtown.

Step Six – Downtown This area buzzes with activity till late in the evening, crammed with theatres, speciality shops, restaurants, large department stores, ice cream parlours. The street to walk on is Binjiang Dao, with alleyways and other shopping streets gathered around it – eight whole blocks of shopping!

You can find just about anything – from silk flowers to a hot bath – in the many boutiques, curio stores and emporiums. The area is particularly lively between 5 and 8 pm, when the streets are thronged with excited shoppers and in-going theatre fans.

Quanyechang (Encouraging Industrial Development Emporium) is Tianjin's largest department store and is at the corner of Heping Lu and Binjiang Lu. Besides selling a large variety of consumer goods, the emporium has two theatres and some electronic amusement facilities. The original smaller Quanyechang has a fascinating balcony interior. If you follow the galleries around they will eventually lead into the main seven-storey block. The older section was founded in 1926.

Some western trends in the downtown district include public phone boxes (a rare item on the streets of China) and an eyewear shop (next to the second-hand store on Binjiang). At the south-eastern fringes of the downtown district are some street markets, mostly selling food.

Step Seven – The Home Run A bus No 24 will get you back to the main station – you can pick it up opposite the Dengyinglou Restaurant on the north section of Binjiang.

Alternatively, stroll back along the banks of the Hai River (a popular pastime with the locals) and see photo booths, fishing, early-morning tai chi, opera-singer practice and old men toting bird cages. The Hai River esplanades have a peculiarly Parisian touch, in part due to the fact that some of the railing and bridge work is French.

At the north end of town are half a dozen canals that branch off the Hai River. One vantage point is Xigu Park. Take bus No 5 running from near the main station and passing by West Station.

Places to Stay

Rates at Tianjin's hotels start from around Y60 double and they don't bargain. In any case most of Tianjin's hotels are full of foreign businesspeople who stay for one or two months or longer. Tianjin can be a hard place to find a room, let alone a cheap room. You have no hope of getting into the Chinese hotels.

Unless you've got the money, or can work your way into a Chinese hotel, or ingratiate yourself into one of the university residences or the Foreign Language Institute (or a church or bath house?), you may end up back at the station. A smart move is to dump your luggage at the station (there's a 24-hour left luggage) so if the worst comes to worst, you can stay up late somewhere without having to cart your gear around. Ideally, make Tianjin a day-trip from Beijing.

Strung along Jiefang Beilu (on the bus No 13 route from the Main Railway Station, or the trolley bus No 96 route leaving from Jiefang Bridge) are six or seven Chinese and western hotels – some of them fortresses when it comes to fighting your way past the front desk, who will yank the drawbridge from under you.

The *Astor Hotel* (tel 311112) at 199 Jiefang Beilu dates from early this century. Once considered sub-standard by foreign businesspeople with its rather dead, old wooden fittings and dusty couches in the lobby, it's now been given a going-over to bring it up to scratch. Rooms start at Y100 plus 10% service charge. It has several restaurants, a cocktail and snack lounge, bakery, in-house videos, laundry, beauty salon, the works. The hotel is near what was once Victoria Park. Take bus No 13 three stops from the main railway station.

The *Tianjin Di Yi Fandian (Tianjin No 1)* (tel 36438) is at 198 Jiefang Beilu. This is probably your best bet in Tianjin; doubles cost from Y64 with a bit of old world charm into the bargain. The No 1 is an old colonial building diagonally opposite the *Tianjin Hyatt Towers*. Spacious rooms have their own bathroom, and the staff is fairly amiable. Take bus No 13 three stops from the main railway station and walk south. The hotel phone number is also the number of the CTS service counter.

The *Friendship Hotel (Youyi Fandian)* (tel 35663) is on Nanjing Lu. It's a nine-storey Holiday Inn-type place, built in 1975 in air-con deluxe style and permanently stocked with foreign businessmen. Doubles cost from Y78. Take bus No 13 four stops from the main railway station and then walk west on Nanjing Lu for about 10 minutes.

The *Tianjin Grand* (tel 39613) is on Youyi Lu, Hexi District. And grand it is: 1000 beds in two high-rise blocks built in 1960 in the air-con deluxe style, complete with a four-storey conference building, 1500-seat dining room, and 1000-seat auditorium. Doubles cost from Y90. The hotel is set in the gone-to-seed end of town and is deadly quiet. Take bus No 13 from the main train station.

One of Tianjin's newer hotels is the *Long Feng*, also set in a rather dreary, distant part of town on the east side of the Hai River, off Liuwei Lu. Doubles cost from Y65. Take trolley bus No 92 from the main train station.

Top of the range is the peculiar-looking *Hyatt Tianjin* (tel 318888) on Jiefang Beilu overlooking the Hai River. Singles and doubles cost from US$80 plus 10% tax. The presidential suite is US$500.

Places to Eat

There's some wonderful digestibles in Tianjin, which is more than you can say for most places in China. If you're staying longer, you can get a small group together, phone ahead, and negotiate gourmet delights. 'Tianjin flavour' specialties are mostly in the seasonal seafood line and include crab, prawns, cuttlefish soup and fried carp.

Downtown District The *Tianjin Kaoya (Tianjin Roast Duck Restaurant)* (tel 23335) is at 146 Liaoning Lu. You can get Beijing duck here – either the full works or a cheaper basic duck. This place has Mao Zedong's seal of approval (one doesn't really know if that's positive or positively embarrassing advertising these days) and on the rèstaurant walls are a couple of black & white photos of a relaxed-looking Mao talking to the chefs and autographing the visitors' book.

The *Chuansu Caiguan* (tel 25142) is on Changchun Dao, between Xinhua Lu and Liaoning Lu, very close to the Tianjin Roast Duck. It serves hot Sichuan food and other styles.

Rongji Jie This is an alley running west off the north end of Heping Lu, and has a fair share of restaurants. The *Quanjude* (tel 20046) is at 53 Rongji Jie. Upstairs are banquet rooms – moderate to expensive prices. Seafood is expensive (like sea-cucumber, a delicacy that chefs love to foist on foreigners). Beijing duck and Shandong food are also served.

Directly opposite the Quanjude is the *Yanchunlou* (tel 22761) at 46 Rongji Jie. It serves Muslim food, lamb dishes and hotpot in winter.

Finger Food A permanent cake box clipped to a bicycle rack is one of the eccentricities of Tianjin residents – and a prerequisite for a visit to friends.

Yangcun rice-flour cake is a pastry produced in Wuqing County suburbs since the Ming Dynasty, so they say. It's made from rice and white sugar.

Eardrum Fried Spongecake, made from rice powder, sugar and bean paste, and fried in sesame oil, is so named from the proximity of the shop that makes it to Eardrum Lane (Erduoyan). Another specialty that takes its name from the shop location is 18th Street Sough-Twists. They sell bars made of sugar, sesame, nuts and vanilla.

The best area to go snack-hunting is the downtown zone, where you can find both the Chinese and the western varieties – well, mock western. The 'coolest' places to be are the ice cream parlours or the sandwich and refreshment hangouts in this district.

King of the dumpling shops is *Goubuli* (tel 23277) on Shandong Lu, between Changchun Lu and Binjiang Lu. Very crowded, this place serves some of the finest dumplings in the nation – so you might as well dine in style, and it won't cost you an arm or a leg to do so. You can back up the dumplings with tea, soup or beer, and you get upper-crust lacquered chopsticks with which to spear the slippery little devils on your plate. The shop has a century-old history. The staple of the maison is a dough bun, filled with high-grade pork, spices and gravy, that disintegrates on contact with the palate. Watch for the baozi with the red dot since this indicates a special filling like chicken or shrimp. Baozi can be ordered by the *jin* (1 *jin* = 10 *leung* = 1/2 kilo = 30 baozi approximately). 'Goubuli' has the alarming translation of 'dogs won't touch them' or 'dog doesn't care'. The most satisfying explanation of this seems to be that Goubuli was the nickname of the shop's founder, a man with an extraordinarily ugly face – so ugly that even dogs were turned off by him. The shop turns out tens of thousands of buns a day; baozi and jiaozi are Tianjin specialties which are frozen and exported to Japan.

Should you wish to fortify a main meal, an ice cream or a coffee, Tianjin produces a variety of liquid substances. There's Kafeijui, which approximates to Kahlua, and Sekijiu, which is half-way between vodka and aviation fuel.

Shopping

The four traditional arts and crafts in Tianjin are New Year posters, clay figurines, kites and carpets. You can also go hunting for antiques and second-hand goods – Tianjin is less picked-over than Beijing.

The Quanyechang Department Store, the Overseas Chinese store and the other department stores are mainly directed toward consumer goods and the craft stocks are low or non-existent, so it's a matter of finding the specialty shops or going to the factory source.

For a taste of things to come check out the Tianjin International Market at the junction of Binjiang Lu and Nanjing Lu. It stocks anything from Japanese felt-tipped pens to Sanyo medical freezers and dental chairs. Foreign goods, Chinese systems – just try purchasing something and you'll see what I mean!

Rugs & Carpets If you're serious about carpets (that's serious money!), the best bet is to get to a factory outlet. There are eight carpet factories in the Tianjin municipality. Making the carpets by hand is a long and tedious process – some of the larger ones can take a proficient weaver over a year to complete. Patterns range from traditional to modern. The Number Three Carpet Factory (tel 81712) is in the Hexi District. Small tapestries are a side line.

Kites Kites are not easily found. Again it's better to go directly to the source, which is the Arts & Crafts Factory (tel 72855) at the western end of Huanghe Dao, in the Nankai district. The Wei kites were created by master craftsman Wei Yuan Tai at the beginning of the century, although the kite has been a traditional toy in China for thousands of years. One story has it that Mr Wei's crow kite was so good that a flock of crows joined it aloft. The body of this line is made of brocade and silk, the skeleton made of bamboo sticks. Wings can be folded or disassembled, and will pack into boxes (the smaller ones into envelopes). Different kite varieties are made in Beijing, where there is a Kite Arts Company and a Kite Society. One member, Ha Kuiming, made a kite with an eight-metre diameter which took two men to hold back once it got going.

Clay Figurines The terracotta figures originated in the 19th century with the work of Zhang Ming Shan: his fifth-generation descendants train new craftspeople. The small figures take themes from human or deity sources and the emphasis is on realistic emotional expressions. Master Zhang was reputedly so skilful that he carried clay up his sleeves on visits to the theatre and came away with clay opera stars in his pockets. In 1900, during the Boxer Rebellion, western troops came across satirical versions of themselves correct down to the last detail in uniforms. These voodoo dolls were ordered removed from the marketplace immediately! Painted figurines are now much watered down from that particular output; the workshop is at 270 Machang Dao, Hexi District (south end of Tianjin). The Art Gallery on Jiefang Lu has a collection of earlier Zhang family figurines.

New Year Posters A batch of these is also on display at the Art Gallery. They first appeared in the 17th century in the town of Yangliuqing, 15 km west of Tianjin proper. Woodblock prints are hand-coloured, and are considered to bring good luck and happiness when posted on the front door on Lunar New Year – OK if you like pictures of fat babies done in dayglo colour schemes. Rarer are the varieties that have historical, deity or folk-tale representations. There's a salesroom and workshop on Changchun Jie, between Xinhua Lu and Liaoning Lu.

Other There are second-hand stores selling mostly chintz, though some older fur clothing can be found. A few of these stores are downtown; also try Dongma Lu. The Yilinge Antique Store at 161 Liaoning Lu has bronzes, ceramics, carvings, paintings and calligraphy, and will engrave seals or arrange artist-commission work. The Wenyuange at 191 Heping Lu is another curio store, mainly dealing in hardwood furniture, and will arrange packing, customs and delivery.

Getting There & Away

Air Some useful flights include Tianjin to Canton (daily), Hong Kong (four flights a week), Nanjing and Shanghai (both twice a week).

Bus For buses to Beijing look around Tianjin Main Train Station. Many buses depart from this area for the capital. The trip takes about three hours and costs about Y5. Buses don't leave until they're full, so in this regard they're less reliable than the trains. They drop you off near Beijing Main Train Station.

There are three long-distance bus stations, with buses running to places that are not in the lexicon of the average traveller's catalogue.

Bus stations are usually located part-way along the direction of travel. Nanzhan (Balitai) is on the north-east edge of the Water Park south-west of the city centre. Xizhan (Xinqingdao) is at 2 Xiqing Jie near Tianjin West Railway Station.

The bus station of interest is Tianjin Zhan (Dongbei), which has the most destinations and the largest ticket office. It's just west of the Hai River, in the north end of Tianjin. Bus No 24 from downtown will land you in the general vicinity. From the Dongbei station you can get buses to Beijing, Jixian, Zunhua and Tangshan. A road route worth considering (also served by rail) is Tianjin to Beijing via Jixian.

The bus station in Beijing for buses to Tianjin is Yongdingmen.

Rail Tianjin is a major north-south rail junction with frequent trains to Beijing, extensive links with the north-eastern provinces, and lines southwards to Jinan, Nanjing, Shanghai, Fuzhou, Hefei, Yantai, Qingdao and Shijiazhuang.

There are three rail stations in Tianjin: Main, North and West. Ascertain the correct station. For most trains you'll want the Main Station. Some trains stop at both Main and West, and some go only through the West Station (particularly those originating in Beijing and heading south). Through trains to North-East China seem to stop only at the North Station.

If you have to alight at the West Station, bus No 24 connects the West Station to the Main Station, passing through the downtown shopping district.

The advance rail ticket office in Tianjin is at 236 Heping Lu. After 8 pm you can purchase next-day sleeper tickets at one of the windows at the Main Station.

Express trains take just under two hours for the trip between Tianjin and Beijing. Normal trains take about 2½ hours. The last train to Beijing leaves Tianjin around 4 pm, so your time in the city is rather limited if you're only day-tripping. Tourist-price hard-seat from Beijing to Tianjin is Y7.

Since Tianjin is only two hours from Beijing and three to four hours from Beidaihe/Shanhaiguan, it may be worth buying a through ticket from Beijing to Beidaihe and making Tianjin a stopover. You can then continue on to Beidaihe on the same day using the same ticket. You'll probably have to stand, but if you only want to wander around Tianjin for a few hours then it'll be cheaper than buying two tickets.

Other rail routes worth considering (also served by road) are Tianjin to Beijing via Jixian, and Tianjin to Qingdao in Shandong Province (direct trains).

Boat Tianjin's port is Tanggu, which was renamed Xingang (New Harbour), so just refer to Tanggu Xingang and everyone will know what you're talking about. The port is 50 km from the centre of Tianjin.

Boats to Dalian depart 12 times a month. The trip takes about 20 hours. Tickets range from Y7.40 in 6th class to Y50.10 in 1st class.

Boats to Yantai depart about four times a month. The trip takes about 30 hours. Tickets range from Y7.30 in 6th class to Y48.90 in 1st class. Due to the high volume of passengers on the boats, it's recommended that the traveller stick to 4th class (Y10.40) and higher. The liners are comfortable, can take up to 1000 passengers, and are equipped with a bar, restaurant and movies.

In Tianjin tickets can be bought at 5 Pukou Jie. This tiny street runs west off Taierzhuang Lu and is difficult to find.

Pukou Jie is roughly on the same latitude as the enormous smokestack which stands on the opposite side of the river.

Tickets can also be purchased at Tanggu port opposite the Tanggu Theatre, but you'll be best off buying in Tianjin. The embarkation/disembarkation point in Tanggu is opposite Tanggu South Railway Station.

To get to Tanggu from Tianjin, take a train from Tianjin South Railway Station. There are also buses. There are direct trains between Beijing and Tanggu, and between Tanggu and Tangshan.

Car Foreigners with their own cars, i.e. diplomatic corps or similar, are permitted to drive the Beijing-Tianjin highway.

Getting Around

A pox on local transport in this city! Tianjin is one of the most confusing places you can take on in China, compounded by the fact that your visit there may turn, by necessity, into a very short one. If your time is indeed limited, refer to the touring section and save yourself the trouble – it's a real mess out there trying to find bus stops. Your chances of getting on a bus at rush-hour are about 2% – and you'll get a unique chance to find out what it feels like to be buried alive in a pile of people. If you must use a bus then try and ambush it at the point of origin.

Key local transport junctions are the areas around the three rail stations. The Main (that is, the East) Station has the biggest collection: bus Nos 24, 27 and 13, and further out toward the river are Nos 2, 5, 25, 28, 96. At the West Station are bus Nos 24, 10 and 31 (Nos 11 and 37 run past West Station); at the North Station are bus Nos 1, 7 and 12.

Another major bus terminus point is located around Zhongxin Park, at the edge of the downtown shopping district. From here you'll get bus Nos 11 and 94, and close by are bus Nos 9, 20 and 37. To the north of Zhongxin Park are bus Nos 1, 91, 92, 93.

A useful bus to know is the No 24, running between Main Station and West Station 24 hours a day. Other bus services run from 5 am to 11 pm.

A few alternatives to the buses are the auto-rickshaws or the taxis from the railway stations. The subway can be useful – it runs all the way from Nanjing Lu to the West Train Station. Unfortunately, there doesn't seem to be a bicycle rental. The downtown shopping area can be covered on foot – in fact, some streets are closed to motor traffic.

AROUND TIANJIN

Were it not for the abysmal hotel situation, Tianjin would make a fine staging point for trips directly north (to Jixian, Zunhua, Tangshan, Beidaihe), and a launching pad for roaring into the north-east (Manchuria). Preliminary bus tours have been set up for some northern routes, but it's expensive stuff.

Jixian

Jixian is rated as one of the 'northern suburbs' of Tianjin, though it's actually 125 km from Tianjin City proper. For more details see the section on Beijing. The **Pan Hills**, 12 km north-west of Jixian, and **Zunhua (East Qing Tombs)** are about 40 km due east of Jixian. A suburban-type train runs to Jixian from Tianjin; you can also get there by bus from the Dongbei bus station.

Tangshan

Tangshan was devastated in the earthquake of July 1976 and since rebuilt. Over 240,000 people (almost a fifth of Tangshan's population) were killed in the quake and over 160,000 seriously injured; with casualties from Beijing and Tianjin added the figures could be considerably higher. A new Tangshan has arisen from the rubble. As early as 1978 it was claimed that industrial output (steel, cement, engineering) was back to 1976 levels. The present population of the city is around 1.4 million. Oddly, it wasn't until 1978 that the *People's Daily* finally got around to reporting the catastrophe – in a small article that didn't even make the front page. You could drop off in Tangshan for a few hours en route by train from Beijing to Beidaihe.

Yangcun & Dagang

The town of Yangcun (famous for its rice-flour cakes) is in Wuqing County, about 30 km north-west of Tianjin proper. You can get there either by rail or road. The Dagang Oilfield is to the south-east of Tianjin, and is approachable by road.

Tanggu

There are three harbours on the Tianjin municipality stretch of coastline: Hangu (north), Tanggu-Xingang (centre) and Dagang (south). Tanggu is about 50 km from Tianjin proper. The road and rail route from Tianjin to Tanggu passes by salt-works which furnish roughly a quarter of the nation's salt. There's a Friendship Store and International Seamen's Club in Tanggu. The harbour is where 'friends from all over the world' come to drop anchor, so Tanggu is used foreign faces. The port is kept open by ice-breakers in winter.

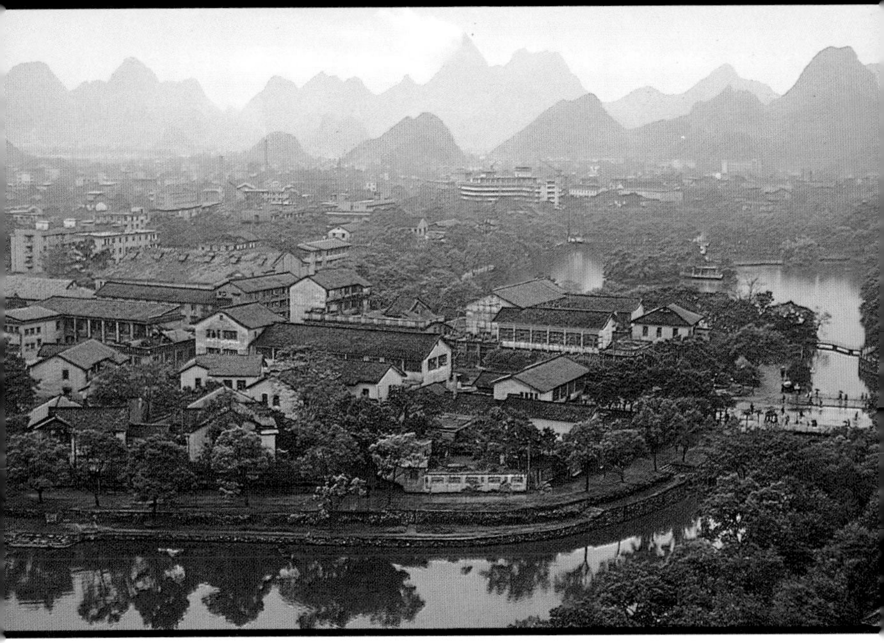

Top: The Pearl River, Canton (AS)
Bottom: View from Lijiang Hotel, Guilin (AS)

Top: Keeping an eye on the masses, Dali (RS)
Bottom Left: Upright official declining foreign enticement, Xiahe (RS)
Bottom Right: Apprehended criminals, Guilin (AS)

THE NORTH-EAST

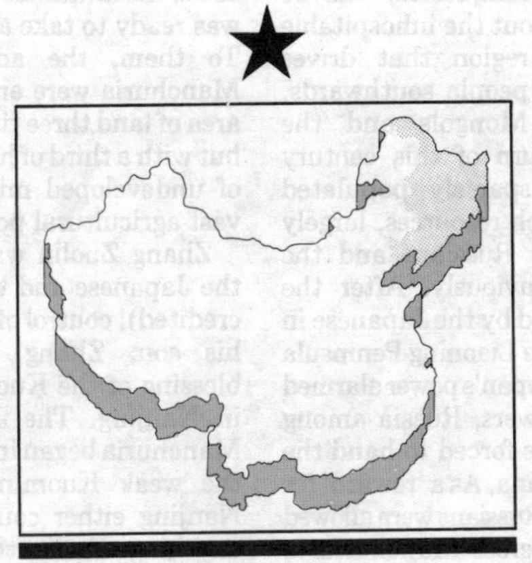

INTRODUCTION

Steam trains, mud houses, Mao statues, chimney stacks, logging towns, Soviet-clone hotels, red maples . . . Manchuria is a bleak area that's played more than its fair share in the tumultuous events of 20th-century China.

Historically, Manchuria has been the birthplace of the conquerors; maybe there's something about the inhospitable geography of this region that drives successive waves of people southwards, among them the Mongols and the Manchus. At the turn of this century Manchuria was a sparsely populated region, but it had rich resources, largely untapped. Both the Russians and the Japanese eyed it enviously. After the Chinese were defeated by the Japanese in the war of 1894-95, the Liaoning Peninsula was ceded to Japan. Japan's power alarmed the other foreign powers, Russia among them, and Japan was forced to hand the peninsula back to China. As a 'reward' for this intervention, the Russians were allowed to build a railway across Manchuria to their treaty port of Port Arthur (Lushun). The Russians moved troops in with the railway, and for the next 10 years effectively controlled north-east China.

The Japanese-Russian war of 1904-05 put an end to Russia's domination of Manchuria. The land battles were fought on Chinese soil and when the Russians surrendered Japan gained control of the trans-Manchurian railway and Port Arthur. Meanwhile, the overall control of Manchuria moved into the hands of Zhang Zuolin. Zhang had been a bandit-leader at the time the Russian-Japanese War broke out, in control of a large and well-organised private army. Lured by promises of reward, he threw his lot in with the Japanese and emerged from the war with the strongest Chinese army in Manchuria. By the time the Qing Dynasty fell he held the power of life and death in southern Manchuria, and between 1926 and 1928 ran a regional government which was recognised by the foreign powers. He was ousted by the 'Northern Expedition' of the Kuomintang which unified southern and northern China, and was forced to retire.

Zhang's policy in Manchuria had been to limit Japan's economic and political expansion, and eventually to break Japan's influence entirely. But by the 1920s the militarist Japanese government was ready to take a 'hard line' on China. To them, the advantages of seizing Manchuria were enormous; here was an area of land three times as large as Japan, but with a third of her population; an area of undeveloped mines and timber, and vast agricultural possibilities.

Zhang Zuolin was assassinated (both the Japanese and the Kuomintang were credited); control of Manchuria passed to his son, Zhang Xueliang, with the blessing of the Kuomintang government in Nanjing. The Japanese invasion of Manchuria began in September 1931, and the weak Kuomintang government in Nanjing either couldn't or wouldn't do anything about the invasion. Chiang Kaishek urged 'reliance' (whatever that meant) on the League of Nations and continued to organise his annihilation campaigns against the Communists. Manchuria was lost to the Japanese, who renamed it the independent state of 'Manchukuo' – a Japanese puppet state. The exploitation of the region began in earnest, with heavy industry established and extensive railway lines laid.

The Japanese occupation of Manchuria was a fateful move for the Chinese Communist forces locked up in Shaanxi. The invasion forced Zhang Xueliang and his 'Dongbei' (North-Eastern) army out of Manchuria; these troops were eventually moved into Central China to fight the Communists. Up until the mid-1930s Zhang's loyalty to Chiang Kaishek never wavered, but he gradually became convinced that Chiang's promises to cede no more territory to Japan and to recover the Manchurian homeland were empty ones. Zhang made a secret truce with the

Communists, and when Chiang Kaishek flew to Xian in December 1936 to organise yet another extermination campaign against the Communists, Zhang had Chiang arrested. This forced Chiang to call off the extermination campaign and to form an alliance with the Communists to resist the Japanese.

When WW II ended the north-east suddenly became the focus of a renewed confrontation between the Communist and Kuomintang troops. In February 1945 the meeting of Allied leaders at Yalta discussed the invasion of Japan; Roosevelt was anxious that the Russians should take part, but in return for Soviet support Stalin demanded that Mongolia (part of the Chinese empire until 1911) should be regarded as independent (in fact, a Soviet satellite) and that Russian rights in Manchuria, lost to Japan, should be restored – that meant the restoration of Russian control over trans-Manchurian railways, the commercial port of Dalian and the naval base of Port Arthur (Lushun). Chiang Kaishek wished to keep the Russians favourably disposed and began negotiations for a treaty with the USSR on the basis of the Yalta agreements. A treaty was eventually signed which pledged each side to 'work together in close and friendly collaboration' and to 'render each other every possible economic assistance in the post-war period' – Stalin had sold out the Communists and thrown Russian support behind the Kuomintang. At the Potsdam conference of July 1945 it was decided that the Russians would take the surrender of all Japanese forces in Manchuria and North Korea, and that the Kuomintang would take it elsewhere.

After the A-bombs obliterated Hiroshima and Nagasaki in August 1945 and forced the Japanese to surrender, the Russian armies moved into Manchuria, engaging the Japanese in a brief but bloody conflict before the Japanese surrendered. The Americans started transporting Kuomintang troops by air and sea to the north where they could take the surrender of Japanese forces and regain control of north and central China. The American Navy moved in to Qingdao and landed 53,000 marines to protect the railways leading to Beijing and Tianjin and the coal mines which supplied those railways.

The Communists, still in a shaky peace with the Kuomintang, also joined the rush for position; although Chiang Kaishek told them to remain where they were, the Communist troops marched to Manchuria on foot, picking up arms from abandoned Japanese depots as they went. Other Communist forces went north by sea from Shandong. In November 1945 the Kuomintang attacked the Communists even while American-organised peace negotiations were taking place between the two. That attack put an end to the negotiations.

All these moves came within days of the Japanese surrender. The Russian troops established themselves along the railways and the main cities of Manchuria – Harbin, Changchun, Dalian and the like – and since the Kuomintang troops could not move in to replace them by the agreed date of mid-November, Chiang asked the Russians to stay in the cities and prevent the Chinese Communist forces from entering the Russian-controlled zones. The Russians met those requests and did not withdraw until March 1946 when the Kuomintang troops were finally installed. In the meantime the Russians stripped the Manchurian cities of all the Japanese military and industrial equipment; whole factories, machinery, machine tools, even office furniture, were dispatched by train to the USSR; even the railway tracks were taken up and shipped out, and gold in the Manchurian banks was taken away. The Russians remained in Port Arthur and Dalian, and the last of the American troops were not withdrawn until March 1947, though Qingdao (in Shandong Province) continued to be used by the American navy.

The Communists, meanwhile, occupied the countryside, and set in motion their land-reform policies which quickly built up their support among the peasants. There was a tremendous growth of mass support for the Communists, and the force of 100,000 regulars who had marched into Manchuria rapidly grew to 300,000 as soldiers of the old Manchurian armies that had been forcibly incorporated into the Japanese armies flocked to join them. Within two years the Red Army had grown to 1½ million combat troops and four million support personnel. On the other side, though the Kuomintang troops numbered three million and had Russian and American arms and support, its soldiers had nothing to fight for and either deserted or went over to the Communists – who took them in by the thousands. The Kuomintang armies were led by generals whom Chiang had chosen for their personal loyalty to himself rather than military competence, and Chiang ignored the advice of the American military advisers whom he himself had requested.

In 1948 the Communists took the initiative in Manchuria. Strengthened by the recruitment of Kuomintang soldiers and the capture of American equipment, the Communists were both the numerical and material equals of the Kuomintang. Three great battles in Manchuria, led by Lin Biao, decided the outcome; in the first battle of August 1948, the Kuomintang lost 500,000 men. In the second battle of November 1948 to January 1949 whole Kuomintang divisions went over to the Communists, who took 327,000 prisoners. The Kuomintang lost seven generals, dead, captured or deserted, and seven divisional commanders crossed sides. The third decisive battle was fought in the Beijing-Tianjin area; Tianjin fell on 23 January and another 500,000 troops came into the Communist camp. It was these victories which sealed the fate of the Kuomintang and allowed the Communists to drive southwards.

With almost a century of perpetual turmoil behind them, the north-eastern regions are being developed into the backbone of China's industries, and attempts are being made to turn them into a bread-basket with state-run farms out on the prairies – it's the same sort of economic possibility which the Japanese sought to exploit and which the Russians stripped bare. To preserve the ailing forests, the last great timber reserves in the land, zones have been placed off-limits to hunters and lumberjacks, albeit a small area (at the end of 1982, 0.4% of China's total land area had been set aside for nature reserves). A vigorous tree-planting campaign is also in progress.

Of the three provinces making up the north-east, Liaoning is China's richest in natural resources. It has large deposits of coal and iron ore, as well as magnesium and petroleum. The heaviest industry and the densest rail network are here. While there is much hoopla about this year's production of knitted underwear exceeding that of last year by x per cent, and exceeding that of 1949 by xxx per cent, the PRC has kept very quiet on the subject of industrial pollution. But from every direction it glares at you in the cities of the north-east and particularly in Liaoning. This may sound like a sweeping generalisation, but the situation may be more sweeping and more general than at first imagined. A rare snippet on the topic comes from *Beijing Review* in a 1983 article which says: 'Then in 1949, with the liberation, progress arrived, and with it chimneys belching coal smoke into blue skies, factory sluices emptying into once-clear rivers, and an ever-growing and hungry populace indiscriminately clearing ancient forests in their search for arable land'. Those keen on delving into heavy industry and the accompanying soot, grime and fallout, can find no better place than Liaoning. Seeing this aspect of China is probably as valid as visiting its temples, but success at getting into the factories is not guaranteed. In lieu of an expensive CITS liaison it pays to befriend a ranking factory worker.

The population of the north-east has increased dramatically over the last 35 years: 1982 figures put Heilongjiang at 32.6 million people, Jilin at 22.5 million and Liaoning at 35.7 million. Most are Han Chinese immigrants or their progeny. Of the local minority groups, the Manchus have sunk without a trace, the Koreans are over a million strong (mostly in the south-east of Jilin Province), and in the freezing far north of Heilongjiang are pockets of Oroqens, few in number, hunters who have only recently been persuaded to give up their nomadic ways.

Climate

The weather tends to extremes in the north-east – mostly cold. Up in Harbin, come January, they'll all be huddled round their Russian stoves drinking vodka – and so would you be if it was minus 20 outside, with howling Siberian gales. Activity slows to a crunch in this snowflake-spitting weather, while the animals pass the season over totally and sensibly hibernate. At the higher latitude along the Sino-Soviet border there's a nine-month snow period (September to May); moving south to Harbin it lessens to a November to March cold snap; by the time you get to Dalian, it's about December to February. High points for rain are June to August.

Minimum temperatures (°C):

	Jan	*Apr*	*Jul*	*Oct*
Harbin	–38	–13	11	–12
Changchun	–37	–8	11	–11
Shenyang	–30	–5	16	–8
Dalian	–20	–4	15	–2

Maximum temperatures (°C):

	Jan	*Apr*	*Jul*	*Oct*
Harbin	4.2	28	36	27
Changchun	–1	25	38	26
Shenyang	3	25	35	25
Dalian	7	28	33	28

This is not to say that you should avoid winter, merely to suggest that it would be a damn good idea! If, however, you know how to deal with the cold, and have a good pair of earmuffs, you may be attracted by the winter-sporting activities. At least all that muck will be covered in snow. In terms of being able to get around freely, May to September is the best time. Mohe, in northern Heilongjiang, has the record for the coldest temperature recorded in China, a mere –52.3° Celsius.

Getting There

Air There are flights to several cities and towns in the north-east, including a new connection between Dalian and Hong Kong; for details, see the individual sections.

Bus Bus travel in the north-east is on poor dirt roads and is best avoided when possible. Apart from rail, the other major approach to the north-east is by boat to Dalian. Some boating information is given in the Dalian section.

Rail Far flung as the north-east might be, the rail connections on the main lines are very good. Shenyang is the hub of all lines in the north-east. Plans have been announced to build a new railway line from Shenyang to Jining in Inner Mongolia. This will eventually provide an easier circuit to travel round the north-east without backtracking to Beijing. Harbin is also a possible starting or finishing gate for a Trans-Siberian trip on the Trans-Manchurian.

There are high-frequency trains on the Beijing-Tianjin-Shenyang-Changchun-Harbin line and good connections from Beijing to Qiqihar, Dalian, Dandong and Jilin. All other lines are slow and trains are of low frequency. In Harbin there may be departures from Sankeshu Station, while in Shenyang, the slower trains to Jilin may leave from Shenyang North Station.

Some examples of travel time (in hours) by express train: Beijing to Harbin 18 hours, Beijing to Shenyang nine hours, Jilin to Harbin eight hours, Changchun to Harbin three hours, Changchun to Jilin two hours, Shenyang to Anshan one hour, Shenyang to Dandong five hours, Harbin to Jiamusi 15 hours, Harbin to Yichun 12 hours.

A couple of sample fares: Beijing to Shenyang is Y91.40 hard-sleeper (tourist price), Shenyang to Dalian is Y8.20 hard-seat (local price), Mudanjiang to Harbin is Y7.35 hard-seat (local price).

Tourism

Tourism in the north-east is the proverbial 'good news, bad news'. The good news: the open-site listing jumped from 18 in late 1982 to 46 in late 1986, with offerings dangled for well-heeled visitors ranging from backpacking, fishing and hunting in Heilongjiang, to skiing in Jilin. The bad news: in a word, monotonous! The industrial city landscapes are supposed to look (starkly) beautiful in winter with photogenic blacks and whites, and some extra-sooty greys. To break up the boredom, a few nature reserves have appeared, accessible in the summer. This is very much a fledgeling tourist operation and there are signs that more places will be opened up. Deep in the woods north-east of Harbin, a hunting and winter sport range is being set up, centred around Taoshan Manor, and log cabins are under construction. In Bei'an (Dedu County), way, way up there north of Harbin, a set of volcano crater lakes and a volcano museum have recently opened. Sino-Soviet tourism has re-emerged and there's talk of running boat trips down the Heilongjiang (Amur). CITS in Shenyang has started to organise trips to North Korea. All in all, the north-east remains a place of specialised interests; pharmacology, ornithology and metallurgy are among the disciplines that can be catered for.

As a result, most visitors to the north-east are with tours or on business. Backpackers are few and far between, and my hunch is that the only reason they'll consider the northward trek worthwhile despite the immense distance and time involved is the rugged border regions. It's also worth remembering to stock up on RMB in Beijing – the black market in the north-east is elusive. Hotels in the uninspiring, major cities charge astronomical prices and, judging by my last trip, their staff consider all foreigners to be gold-plated. In summer domestic tourism and giant 'conventions' give the overloaded hotel system the final chop in places such as Harbin, Changchun and Dalian. The PSB certainly hasn't helped by placing many perfectly acceptable hotels off-limits to foreigners . . . unless you pull out every imaginable stop. The most enjoyable parts are out in the backwoods where you get the opposite treatment – very spartan places to stay but really friendly, helpful locals.

Skifields

We have to fuel our travelling fantasies – are there any skiers out there? Some foreign skiers have been granted the ultimate sanction to ski the Chinese slopes, and if an individual gets one, we'd like to know about it! There are a number of skifields; locals consider Jilin more suited for beginners while Heilongjiang could cater for the more advanced. You're well advised to bring your own equipment. The Chinese make wood and fibreglass skis, and there is a possibility of rental, but the quality or size of boots and so on cannot be vouched for.

Twenty km from Jilin town (in Jilin Province, east of the capital Changchun) are the Songhua Lake Skifields of Daqing Mountain, with a 1700-metre cableway, lounge, drying rooms and restaurant. Another skifield is at Tonghua, where championships have been held. In Heilongjiang there's the Qingyun skifield, in Shangzhi County, south-east of Harbin; it has a cableway, guest house rooming 350 and stone cottages. North of Shangzhi, and approachable by bus, is the Yanzhou County skifield. The snow period is long; the main season is late November to early April.

Tigers

China has three subspecies of tiger: the Bengal, the South China and the North-eastern or Manchurian. All told there are no more than 400 tigers left in China, of which the South China subspecies is the most endangered and numbers only about 50 in the wild and about 30 in zoos both in China and abroad. (Even when India launched its Project Tiger in 1973 there were 1800 Royal Bengal tigers left in its territory and that was considered perilously low.) Unlike the Bengal and Manchurian tigers which are found in several countries, the South China tiger is peculiar to China only. Its plight began in the 1950s, with indiscriminate hunting and deforestation. At that time the tiger was still fairly numerous in many southern provinces, especially in Hunan, Fujian, Guizhou and Jiangxi. Throughout the '50s and early '60s there were 'anti-pest' campaigns and many areas had their entire tiger populations wiped out. Today the subspecies only exists in the mountainous regions of south-west and south-east Hunan, and in northern Guangdong. The Manchurian tiger seems doomed since it now numbers only 30 in the wilds of Jilin and Heilongjiang; zoos account for about 100 more and some are still found in the Soviet Union and North Korea. The exact number of Bengal tigers in China is not known; they live in the Xishuangbanna Autonomous Region and southern Yunnan near Burma and Laos, in a few counties in western Yunnan bordering Burma, and in the subtropical mountainous region of south-eastern Tibet and the neighbouring Assam.

Meanwhile, off in Mengxian County on the Yellow River, Henan Province, lives a 74-year-old gent, He Guangwei, who makes a living catching the big cats *barehanded* – with a bit of help from the martial arts. Over the past 50 years he's captured 230 leopards and seven tigers, as well as killed 700 wild boars and 800 wolves. If you do happen to come across one of the beasties his advice is to go for the muzzle: 'The most sensitive part of a leopard or tiger is on the muzzle between the eyes and the nose. A quick hard blow there will make its eyes water, and it stops to rub them. But the blow must be sharp and accurate. If several blows aren't effective, you're in trouble. You have to kick the animal quickly and hard in vulnerable places like the ears or the belly. But this usually kills the animal. So I don't do it unless my life is at stake'. Good luck.

The East is Steam

The following article was sent to us by Patrick Whitehouse.

The first railway in China was the line from Shanghai to Woosung, built by foreign capital. Negotiations for its construction began in 1865 and, after fierce opposition, the first eight km out of Shanghai were completed in 1876. The line was pushed on until a Chinese was knocked down and killed, and the resulting riots caused the whole line to close. Subsequently the Chinese government bought and re-opened it but, after completing payments in 1878, they closed the line, took up the permanent way, and sank it in the sea with all the rolling stock and equipment!

A few lines were built within the next decade but it was not until after the Japanese War in 1894 that railway building really got going. With the formation of the Chinese Republic in 1912 came nationalisation, and considerable construction took place in the next two decades. The Japanese made their mark on the Manchurian railways after 1931; their influence extended into China as the country was overrun during WW II, and a high proportion of locomotives and rolling stock in operation after the war was of Japanese manufacture or design. During this period a large number of American-built locomotives were sent to China to help rehabilitate the railways, and many of these survive as Class 'KD' 2-8-0s. At the time of liberation China's railways lay in ruins after 15 years of war. Before 1935 the country had approximately 20,000 km of railway, but by 1949 less than half of it was in working order.

The new government was faced with the gigantic task of reconstructing its war-torn network. The first five-year plan envisaged the building of 55 new railways and the reconstruction or double-tracking of 29 existing lines. In the first 15 years, to 1964, the length of operating railways was estimated to have reached 35,000 km; today the total length is close to 40,000 km and still expanding – only Tibet is without at least some railway facility. There was hardly any signalling 15 years ago; today, China Railways have some of the most modern and sophisticated signalling. Before WW II China imported practically all its rolling stock, equipment and supplies; now it manufactures its own. About 500 locomotives of all types are built each year; imported diesels to date have come from France and Romania.

The major development plan calls for main line electrification. Today a small proportion of lines have wire (Baoji to Chengdu; Yangpingquan to Xiangfan). Also being electrified are the Beijing-Baotou and the Guiyang-Kunming lines. Diesel will be kept to a minimum since fuel is deemed too precious for railway combustion; the jump is direct from steam to electricity. The system employed is 25,000V AC single-phase 50Hz, with overhead conductor. The French electrical industry has assisted in the initial development of electrification, although the Chinese are becoming increasingly self-reliant in this work.

Three grateful Brits joined a small party of Australians in an official 'rail visit' to Manchuria. As always in China, we were treated as honoured guests – and if our dedication to railways was deemed to be slightly unusual, this was never made known. On this trip everything really begins at Shenyang, the capital of Liaoning Province, and both the largest industrial centre and the communications hub of north-east China. From the rail-fan's point of view, Shenyang is one of the most important rail centres in the country. Six lines converge on the city, and with the coal traffic from Fushun and other mines in the area, with the inbound iron ore and outbound steel to and from nearby Anshan, and with the chemical and manufacturing goods flowing from and through Shenyang itself, freight traffic is plentiful.

Space forbids a detailed description of the Fushun mine complex with its attendant steam and electrified railway system – except to say that it's immense. The highlight of the visit to Shenyang was Sugintun steam depot, which is all freight and consequently almost 100% 'QJ' class 2-10-2s, and 'JS' class 2-8-2s. Like most Chinese depots, Sugintun shed is fully equipped to carry out heavy repair work, but not boiler fitting. The 'two-star' attractions were found hidden away. These were two Japanese Pacifics sitting at the back of the shed – a class 'SL8' No 296 (in steam) and a class 'SL7' (very dead). Both were pre-war Manchurian express classes of note, the former being used on the Port Arthur (Luda, near Dalian) to Harbin overnight service on the South Manchurian Railway, and the latter between Port Arthur and Shenyang. The 'SL7s' made their trip with fully air-conditioned trains (some of the first in the world) and ran at an average speed of 110 km per hour (68.75 miles per hour).

From Shenyang we journeyed to Jilin, behind steam 'SL' class Pacifics hauling 12 bogies of about 518 tonnes, which is a good load for these engines over a steeply graded route. At least eight sizeable rivers are bridged during the trip. As foreign guests we travelled extremely comfortably in a soft-class coach with tea on hand at any time from the blue-uniformed coach attendant. Jilin provided an opportunity for that most relaxing of railway pursuits – railway sauntering, at a place called Dragon Pond Hill station. Locomotive variety here was classes 'QJ' 2-10-2, 'JF' 2-8-2 and, on the passenger runs, 'RM' Pacifics.

At Changchun, further along the line, there are two railway factories: a Locomotive Works and a Passenger Coach Works. The Locomotive Works built the first of the big 'Heping' (Peace) steam locomotives, as well as the power cars for the Peking Metro. The Passenger Coach Works was built in 1957 to help overcome the shortage of passenger stock and today builds lightweight coaches for 160 km-per-hour operation, deluxe coaches and sleeping cars. The plant has been modernised and expanded since 1978; technological aid comes from Japan's largest railway vehicle builders, Nippon Sharyo Seizo Kaisha. The Locomotive Works and the Carriage Works have been visited by foreigners, as have the social complex with its schools, housing and hospital. Other Changchun joys included lineside photography and an early-morning visit to the steam shed. The latter was so fantastic – clean engines, variety and hospitality – that I just stood there in the sunshine for a moment and said out loud, 'I just don't believe it!' In addition to the usual tender engines, the depot sported two different classes of 2-6-4T Class 'DB2' No 89, a Japanese-built locomotive dating from 1934-36, and 'DB1' No 28, an Alco of 1907. The main classes based here are the 'QJ' 2-10-2, 'RM' 4-6-2 and 'SL' 4-6-2, with a shed allocation for around 100. As with Sugintun depot, Changchun was equipped for overhauls at 100,000-km intervals. A heavy general overhaul is carried out on steam locomotives at the main works after 300,000 km.

Our last stop northwards was Harbin, some 500 km north of Vladivostok and at one time on the Trans-Siberian railway; the Manzhouli-to-Harbin and Harbin-to-Mudanjiang lines form most of the original route. Harbin itself is the junction of two major and three secondary lines. Winter comes to Harbin early and lineside photography included snow scenes, albeit dull ones from the weather point of view. Even so, it was impossible not to be thrilled by the sight of heavy double-headed freights hauled by thundering 'QJs', headlights on in the gloom, pounding up the bank at Wang Guang on their way south. Of particular interest was one of China's three named engines – *General Zhu De*, No 2470. Passenger trains were 'RM' hauled.

At a further shed there was another gem hiding in the yard – a Tangshan-built 2-6-2T of 1949-50, No PL275. Harbin is the area freight depot containing the usual high quota of 'QJs' (still being built at Datong). The shed itself dates from 1899 and has a working staff of some 2600 for the 100% steam allocation of approximately 100 locomotives. Winter is the busy season as the roads become impassable, and 70 locomotives from the shed are in daily service, with an equal number coming in for servicing.

Suffice it to say that our visit covered only a small section of China's rail network, but along the way we saw a great deal of Manchuria. Help was always at hand, and we were fortunate enough to find interpreters and guides who showed a positive interest in our hobby – purchasing technical books and crawling over engines for special identification points. One guide had worked his service out on the installation of the Tan Zam Railway ('Uhuru' or 'Freedom' Railway). The Tan Zam Railway was completed in 1975, linking Zambia's copper mines with Tanzania's ports, thus enabling the two countries to bypass the usual South African export routes. Twenty thousand Chinese worked on the project alongside 36,000 Africans. That particular guide had some fascinating stories to tell.

Patrick Whitehouse Millbrook House Ltd
England

Liaoning 辽宁

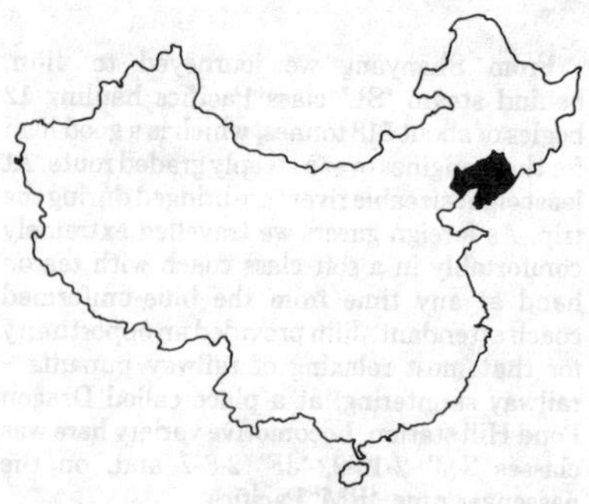

SHENYANG 沈阳

The first grey city on the north-east route, Shenyang has the distinction of being the only one to hold historical interest. It is the cradle of the Manchus, starting as a nomad trading centre as far back as the 11th century, and becoming established as the capital in the 17th century. With the Manchu conquest of Beijing in 1644, Shenyang became a secondary capital under the Manchu name of Mukden, and a centre of the ginseng trade.

The city was occupied by the Russians around the turn of the century as part of their 'railway colonialism', and it was a key battleground during the Russian-Japanese War (1904-05). The city rapidly changed hands – dominated by warlords, the Japanese (1931), the Russians (1945), the Kuomintang (1946) and the CCP (1948). The present population is around five million (for a jurisdiction area of 8500 square km – the urban population is 2.7 million), which represents something like a 900% increase in population since 1949.

Shenyang's latest claim to fame is its role as a guinea-pig for new bankruptcy laws. Another astoundingly capitalist arrival is the new stock exchange, which is booming.

Shenyang is the centre of the Liaoning Province Industrial Effort; six major rail lines converge on the city, including those freight lines from Anshan, the steel giant, and Fushun, the coal capital. Industrial output of Shenyang rivals that of Shanghai and includes machinery, aircraft, tramcars, textiles, pharmaceuticals, rubber products, you name it. The latest products can be viewed at the Liaoning Industrial Exhibition Hall, and factory visits are on the group-tour agenda.

Information

CITS (tel 66037 or 66953) is at Huanghe Lu, which is close to Liaoning Mansions (see the Places to Stay section for details). Shenyang CITS is now organising trips to North Korea for foreign tour agencies. One traveller who tried to organise a tour from here on an individual basis was given the 'come back next year' routine. Even if you do surmount this hurdle, you'll have to first obtain the visa from the North Korean embassy in Beijing. Holders of US, Japanese and Israeli passports cannot go.

CAAC (tel 33705) is at 31 Zhonghua Lu Sanduan.

Things to See

Before thundering off to the sights, it might be worth noting that consumerism is alive and rife in Shenyang. The Lianying Corporation, opened in 1983, is an enormous (clean) four floors of glassed-in counters and muzak that is superior to any department store in Beijing. It stocks arts and crafts. Shenyang seems to be one long bout of buy and sell, with a high density of department stores. The main arteries are Taiyuan Lu and Zhongshan Lu. Taiyuan Lu has a poster shop, arts and crafts store and antique shop. The Overseas Chinese come to raid the medicine shops of Shenyang. On the streets there is a rampant population of *binggun* (popsicle) vendors who inexplicably patrol the streets at the height of the bitter winters. The Shenyang Acrobatic

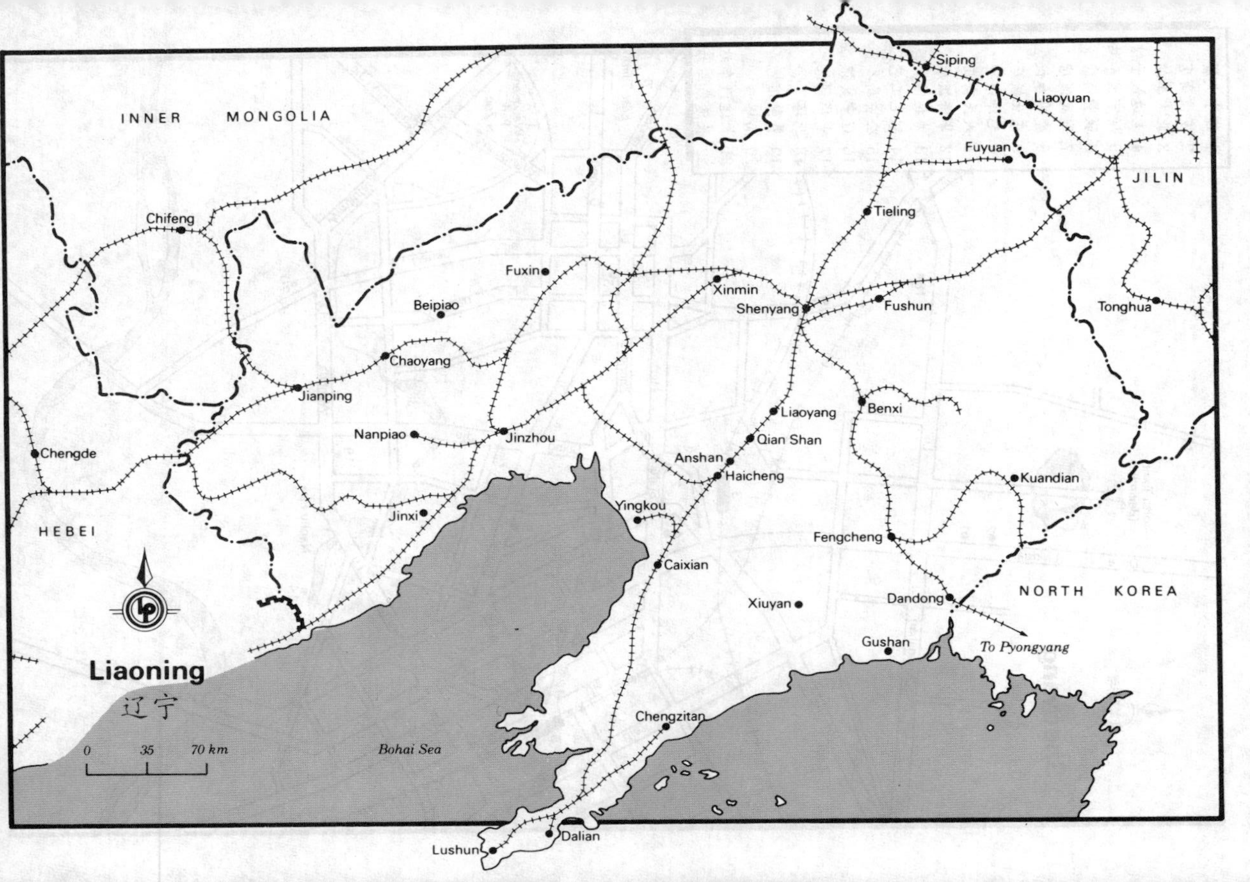
INNER MONGOLIA
JILIN
NORTH KOREA
HEBEI
Siping
Liaoyuan
Fuyuan
Tieling
Chifeng
Fuxin
Xinmin
Shenyang
Fushun
Tonghua
Beipiao
Chaoyang
Jianping
Benxi
Liaoyang
Nanpiao
Jinzhou
Qian Shan
Chengde
Anshan
Haicheng
Kuandian
Jinxi
Yingkou
Fengcheng
Caixian
Dandong
Xiuyan
Gushan
To Pyongyang
Liaoning
辽宁
Chengzitan
0
35
70 km
Bohai Sea
Dalian
Lushun

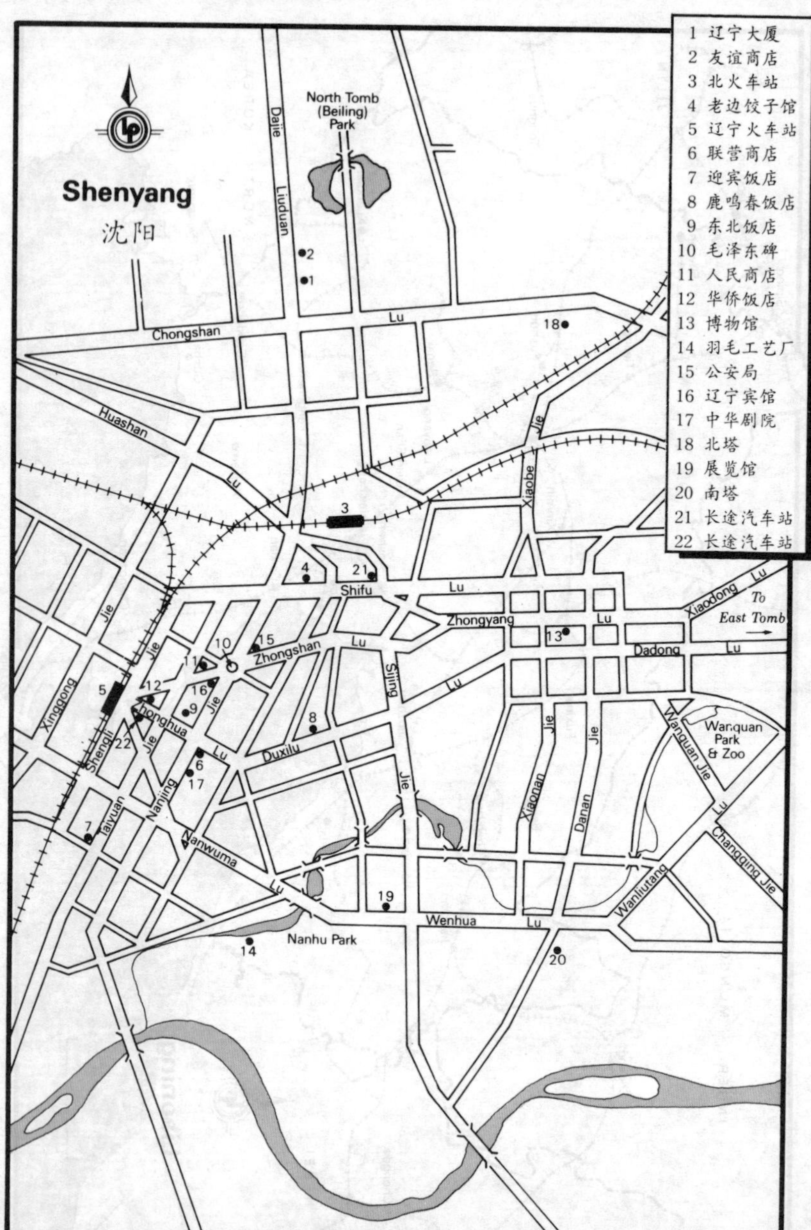
Shenyang
沈阳
North Tomb
(Beiling)
Park
Dajie
Liuduan
Chongshan
Lu
Huashan
Lu
Xiaobe
Jie
Shifu
Lu
Zhongyang
Lu
Xiaodong
Lu
To
East Tomb
Dadong
Lu
Zhongshan
Lu
Sijing
Lu
Jie
Xinggong
Shengli
Zhonghua
Jie
Jie
Jie
Lu
Duxilu
Taiyuan
Nanjing
Nanwuma
Lu
Jie
Xiaonan
Jie
Danan
Jie
Wanquan Jie
Wanquan
Park
& Zoo
Lu
Changqing Jie
Wanliutang
Wenhua
Lu
Nanhu Park
1 辽宁大厦
2 友谊商店
3 北火车站
4 老边饺子馆
5 辽宁火车站
6 联营商店
7 迎宾饭店
8 鹿鸣春饭店
9 东北饭店
10 毛泽东碑
11 人民商店
12 华侨饭店
13 博物馆
14 羽毛工艺厂
15 公安局
16 辽宁宾馆
17 中华剧院
18 北塔
19 展览馆
20 南塔
21 长途汽车站
22 长途汽车站

1 Liaoning Mansions/CITS
2 Friendship Hotel
3 North Railway Station
4 Lao Bian Dumpling Restaurant
5 Main Railway Station
6 Lianying Corporation Department Store
7 Yinbin Restaurant
8 Lu Ming Chun Restaurant
9 Liaoning Dongbei Hotel
10 Mao Statue
11 Renmin Store/Friendship Store
12 Overseas Chinese Hotel/CITS
13 Imperial Palace Museum
14 Feather-picture Factory
15 Public Security
16 Liaoning Guest House
17 Zhonghua Theatre
18 North Pagoda
19 Industrial Exhibition Hall
20 South Pagoda
21 Long-distance Bus Station
22 Long-distance Bus Station

Troupe is one of China's best and definitely worth chasing up.

The Imperial Palace
This is a mini-Beijing model in layout, though the features are Manchu. The main structures were started by Nurhachi, leader of the Manchus, and completed in 1636 by his son, Huang Taiji.

Straight through the main gate, at the far end of the courtyard, is the main structure, the octagonal Dazheng Hall with its caisson ceiling and an elaborate throne. It was here that Emperor Shunzhi was crowned before setting off to cross the Great Wall in 1644. In the courtyard in front of the hall are the Banner Pavilions, formerly administrative offices used by tribal chieftains. They now house displays of 17th and 18th-century military equipment – armour, swords, bows. The central courtyard, west of Dazheng Hall, contains a conference hall, some living quarters, and some shamanist structures (one of the customs of the Manchus was to pour boiling wine into a sacrificial pig's ear, so that its cries would attract the devotees' ancestors). The courtyard to the western fringe is a residential area added on by Emperor Qianlong in the 18th century, and the Wenshu Gallery to the rear housed a copy of the Qianlong anthology.

Like the Forbidden City, the Shenyang imperial palace functions as a museum, with exhibitions of ivory and jade artefacts, musical instruments, furniture, and Ming and Qing paintings. Admission is Y2 and there are extra charges to visit some of the pavilions. Unfortunately the captions to exhibits are all in Chinese. The palace is in the oldest section of the city; bus No 10 will get you there.

North Tomb (Beiling or Zhaoling)
This is the burial place of Huang Taiji (1592-1643), who founded the Qing Dynasty (although he did not live to see the conquest of China). The tomb took eight years to build, and the impressive animal statues on the approach to it are reminiscent of the Ming Tombs. The larger buildings, used as barracks by various warlords, are in a state of disrepair, though some attempt has been made to restore them. The tumulus of the tomb is a grassy mound at the rear. To get to the North Tomb take bus No 220 from the railway station, bus 213 from the Imperial Palaces or bus No 6.

East Tomb (Dongling or Fuling)
This tomb is set in a forested area eight km from Shenyang. Entombed here is Nurhachi, grandfather of Emperor Shunzhi who launched the invasion of China in 1644. Nurhachi is entombed with his mistress. Construction of the tomb started in 1626 and took several years to complete, with subsequent additions and renovations. It's similar in layout to the North Tomb, but smaller, and is perched on a wooded hilltop looking over a river. To get to the East Tomb take bus No 18 from the imperial palace and then walk.

Steam Engine Museum
This was set up recently and includes steam locos from the USA, Japan, Eastern Europe and China. Check with CITS for location and opening hours.

Mao Statue
Of all the bizarre statues in north-east China (Russian war heroes, mini-tanks atop pillars . . .), this Mao statue takes the cake. Like some kind of strange machine, it zooms out of Red Flag Square, a giant epoxy-resin Mao at the helm, flanked by vociferous peasants, soldiers and workers. The last word on the personality cult and the follies of the Cultural Revolution, this is a rare item, erected in 1969.

Places to Stay
All the provinces in the north-east have attempted to 'standardise' prices for foreigners. Liaoning pitches in with Y60 FEC for a single or Y120 FEC for a double. You may be able to improve on this.

The *Liaoning Guest House* facing Red Flag Square was constructed in 1927 by the Japanese; it's got 77 suites, a billiard room with slate tables and art nouveau windows.

The *Liaoning Dasha (Liaoning Mansions)* (tel 62536) is at No 2, Sector 6, Huanghe Lu in the direction of the North Tomb. This is an enormous Soviet-style place complete with chandeliers. It's used for meetings and group tours.

The *Friendship Hotel* (tel 62822) just north of Liaoning Mansions is a villa-type place used for state guests.

The *Overseas Chinese Hotel* (tel 34214) is near the railway station at No 3, Sector 1, Zhongshan Lu. China Travel Service (CTS) is located here.

The *Liaoning Dongbei Hotel* (tel 32031) is at No 1, 7 Li 3 Duan, Taiyuan Lu. It's a difficult place to find: veer left from the station, take Zhongshan Jie toward the Mao statue, turn right into Taiyuan Lu and take the first street left – you'll find the hotel further down that alley.

The *North-East University* (Dongbei Daxue) near Nanhu Park has doubles for Y30. Take trolley bus No 11.

Places to Eat
Can't really say there is anything to recommend. Mouth-watering banquet fare will undoubtedly surface in the classier hotels for a hefty (advance order) price, but on the streets the level of sanitation will quickly cure your hunger pangs without you having to eat anything! The local solution to the problem of germs seems to be plenty of firewater, served up in saké-like cups placed in a can of hot water, with a side dish of raw garlic. The *Lao Bian* dumpling restaurant, up in an alley lined with market stalls, has the vodka side drinks, as well as cold cuts (sausage) and trays of jiaozi. North of the imperial palace, near the Drum Tower, is the *Li Liangui* smoke-cured meat and flat-bread shop, over a century old. Ice cream outlets abound, particularly on Taiyuan Lu – a shovel is used to put the stuff in containers.

The *Overseas Chinese Hotel* and the *Liaoning Dongbei Hotel* both have reasonably clean dining rooms. The *Yingbin* restaurant and the *Lu Ming Chun* are passable, serving northern food, and will dish up regional specialties if there is an advance order and you are willing to fork out. Shenyang's winter speciality is hotpot.

Getting There & Away
Air Shenyang has numerous air connections. Some sample prices are: Beijing (Y110), Canton (Y483), Changchun (Y49), Dalian (Y60), Harbin (Y85), Dandong (Y35), Yanji (Y101), Mudanjiang (Y115).

Rail Shenyang is the hub of the north-eastern rail network; for details see the introduction to the north-eastern provinces.

Getting Around
There is a bicycle rental to one side of the Liaoning Dongbei Hotel – look for a shed.

DALIAN 大连

Dalian is known under a jumble of names – Dalny, Dairen, Lushun, and Luda. Lushun is the part further south (formerly Port Arthur, now a naval base), and Lushun and Dalian comprise Luda. In the late 19th century the western powers were busy carving up pieces of China for themselves, and to the outrage of Tsar Nicholas II, Japan gained the Liaoning Peninsula under an 1895 treaty (after creaming Chinese battleships off Port Arthur in 1894). Nicholas II gained the support of the French and Germans and managed to get the Japanese to withdraw from Dalian; the Russians got the place as a concession in 1898 and set about constructing the port of their dreams – as opposed to the only partially ice-free port of Vladivostok.

To Russia's further dismay, however, the Japanese made a comeback, sinking the Russian East Asia naval squadron in 1902, and decimating the Soviet Baltic squadron off Korea in 1905. The same year, Dalian passed back into Japanese hands, and the Japanese completed the port facilities in 1930. In 1945, Russia reoccupied Dalian and did not definitively withdraw until 10 years later.

Dalian is a major port, on par with Tianjin; Dalian's harbour facilities have been expanded and deepened, with a new harbour completed in 1976 for oil tankers (with a pipeline coming in from Daqing). The city is also an industrial producer in its own right – shipbuilding, glassware, textiles, petroleum refinery, food-processing, diesel engines and chemical industries. These developments have polluted Dalian Bay and affected the fishing enterprises, but efforts are being made to clean it up with waste treatment and oil-reclaiming ships.

Dalian recently hit the headlines as the first of the 14 open coastal cities to offer a package of attractive terms to foreign investors who had expressed great dissatisfaction with previous discriminatory practices.

Dalian has also become China's 'first rat-free city'. With military precision, local residents planned an intensive eradication campaign and chose April 1986 (when the rats were celebrating peak powers of performance and pregnancy) as the day of assault. A team of rodent specialists from Liaoning Province was called in for an official inspection of the city. *China Daily* reported that the inspection method involved the spreading of talcum powder in favourite rat haunts such as grain depots, shops, factories, schools, ports, etc. After 21 days of powdering, only 0.353 per cent of the total powdered space showed paw prints. The inspection showed that the density rate of rats in key areas of the city met the 2% requirement of the country: 0.46% at the harbour; 0.16% at the railway station and 0.83% at the airport. Sounds like the rats had packed their bags and were hastily emigrating by boat, train or plane!

The city of Dalian itself is remarkably clean and orderly – wide avenues, well designed, quiet and atypically uncrowded. Urban and suburban population amounts to 1.3 million over an area of 1000 square km – the Dalian jurisdiction area extends to 12,000 square km with a population of 4.4 million, including five counties. It's also a prime apple-growing region.

Information

CITS (tel 44057) Municipal Government (Shi Zhengfu) No 1, Stalin Square, has some helpful English speakers. Unfortunately, the office seems to change location monthly.

CAAC (tel 35884) is at 12 Dagong Jie.

Things to See

Access to the port facilities, probably one of the top sights of Dalian, is limited for the individual traveller. You'll have to be content with the large **Natural History Museum** with its stuffed sea-life behind the station. It's open Tuesday, Thursday, Saturday and Sunday, 8 am to 4 pm. **Laodong Park** at the centre of town offers

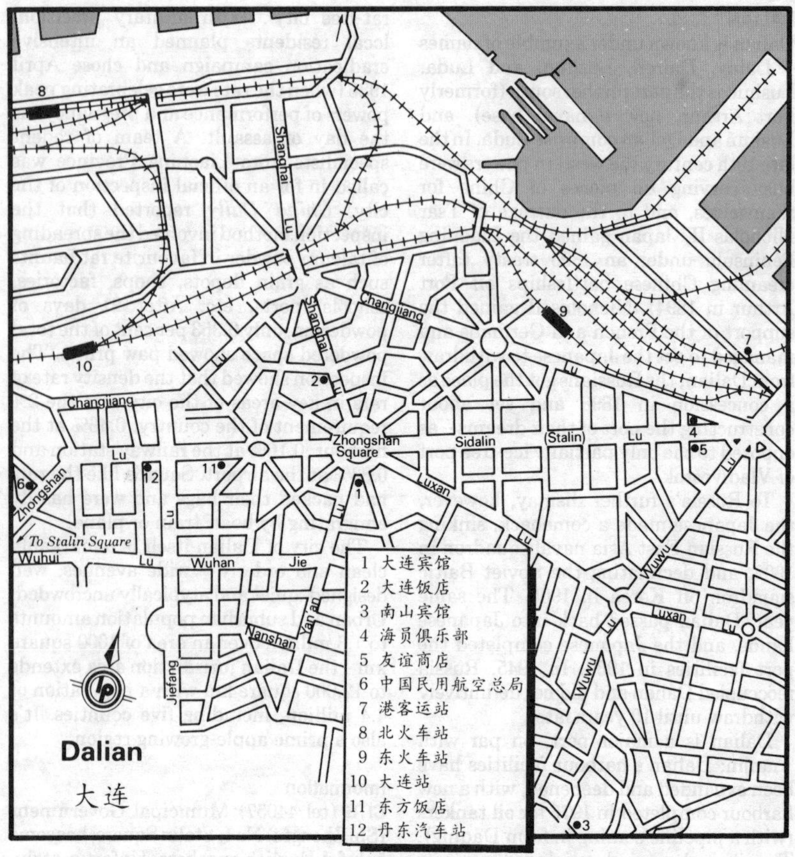

1 Dalian Guest House
2 Dalian Hotel
3 Nanshan Guest House
4 International Seamen's Club
5 Friendship Store/Hotel
6 CAAC
7 Harbour Passenger Terminal
8 North Railway Station
9 East Railway Station
10 Dalian Railway Station
11 Dong Fang Hotel
12 Bus to Dandong

good city views. There's also an assortment of handicraft factories, whose products include glasswork and shell mosaic.

Dalian is actually a health resort of a kind, so beaches with their attached parks are the attraction. The beach five km to the south-east is for western VIPs and is bordered by the exclusive Bangchuidao Guest House. **Tiger Beach (Laohutan)** is rocky and poor for swimming (you can get there on bus No 102 from the city centre). **Fujiazhuang Beach** is the best – it's small, has fine sand and surreal rock outcrops in the deep bay, is excellent for swimming but has few facilities. Like the other beaches, this one has a sanatorium nearby, and the patients sometimes venture out in their pyjamas to assist rubber-booted fishermen hauling in their catch. The beach is a fair way out of town – take bus No 102 and then change to bus No 5. **Xinghai Park & Beach** is five km to the south-west – it's crowded and a little on the slimy side, but it's got a good seafood restaurant (take bus No 2, or else take tramcar No 201 and then change to tramcar No 202). There is another shallow beach called **Xiajiahezi**, to the north-west of Dalian. July and August are the hottest months.

Places to Stay

Dalian sees few individual travellers – mostly cruise-ship passengers or seamen. Here's a quick summary of the hotel battlefield:

The seven-storey *Dalian Hotel* (tel 23171) is at 6 Shanghai Lu. Double rooms go for Y100 – it's an Overseas Chinese hangout with renovation in progress, so expect renovated prices.

The *Dalian Guest House* (tel 23111) at 7 Zhongshan Square is of similar size. Singles cost from Y45, doubles from Y55.

The *Dalian Friendship Hotel* (tel 23890) is above the Friendship Store at 137 Stalin Lu. It's got 27 rooms and prices start at Y50 for a double. The Dalian Guest House, the Dalian Friendship Hotel and the Seamen's Club are used by local businesspeople and incoming sailors, and will supply a rousing round of rejection when called upon to provide accommodation.

The *Nanshan Guest House* (tel 28751) is at 56 Fenglin Lu, and has a dozen villas tucked into very pleasant gardens. It once had the atmosphere of a country club, but has now been renovated and resembles a battleship. It's on the expensive side at Y60 for a single or Y110 for a double. There's a brand-new indoor drinks patio with concrete bridges and a slimy pond. To get there take the round-the-city unnumbered bus; or take tramcar No 201 and then change to bus No 12 or walk uphill.

Another possibility is the *Bangchuidao Guest House* (tel 25744) to the east of the town on the coast. It's next to an exclusive beach.

The *Dong Fang Hotel* (tel 23261) is at 28 Zhongshan Lu and has doubles for Y58. It sometimes provides male travellers with a bed for Y10 in a four-bed room. No sooner had I checked into my room than I had a bird's-eye view of yet another public sentencing. An execution cavalcade complete with sirens, PSB Landcruisers, motorbike escorts and execution squads with rifles, reflective sunglasses and immaculate white gloves drove a chilling circuit round the town. The criminals rode in the back of trucks with placards round their necks showing their names and crimes. Loudspeakers blasted messages to the sky: 'Crush the criminal elements' or 'The enemies of socialism receive their rewards'.

Reportedly, there is now a new place with dorm beds for Y10 just off Tianjin Jie – CITS should be able to provide the name.

Places to Eat

People make the trip to Dalian to gorge themselves on seafood, and let's face it, you could use a change of diet. The *Haiwei Seafood Restaurant* (tel 27067), near the railway station at 85 Zhongshan Lu, will begrudgingly serve up prawns and sea urchins once you demonstrate that not all foreigners are imbeciles.

Tianjin Jie is the wining-dining-shopping street. It's within walking range of the station, and boasts a number of restaurants and snack bars. Opposite the Tianjin Department Store (No 199), nearing the east end of Tianjin Jie, is the *Shanshui Restaurant* which serves Jiangsu-style seafood. Half-way down the street is an open-air *cafeteria* serving coffee and cakes. The hotels around town dish up more expensive clams and scallops – the dining rooms of the *Dalian Guest House* are noted for this. The *Seamen's Club* has

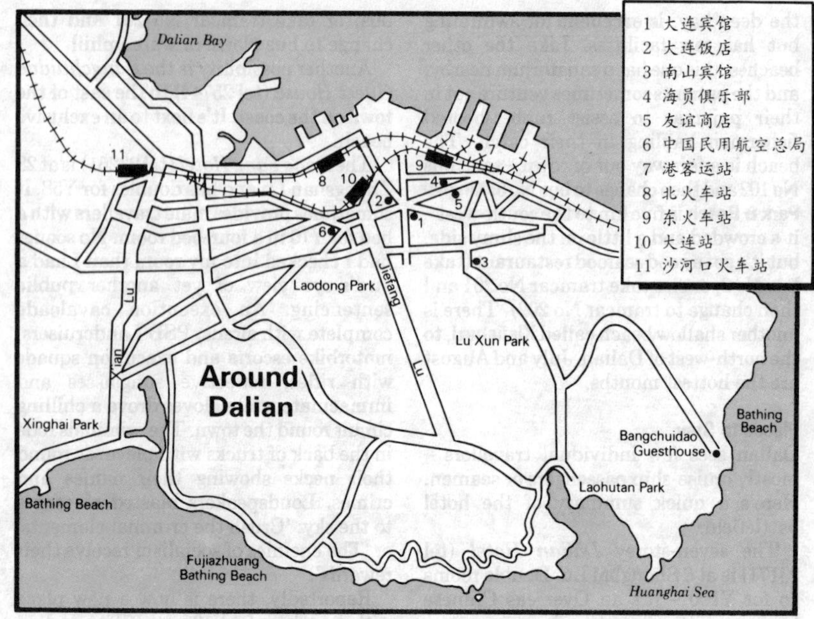

1 Dalian Guest House
2 Dalian Hotel
3 Nanshan Guest House
4 International Seaman's Club
5 Friendship Store/Hotel
6 CAAC
7 Harbour Passenger Terminal
8 North Railway Station
9 East Railway Station
10 Dalian Railway Station
11 Shahekou Railway Station

several dining sections on the 2nd floor, not cheap, but you can get plates of *guotie* (dumplings) in peace and quiet. Xinghai Park, out by the beachfront, has a kind of elevated club house with beach umbrellas – you'll be charged about Y15 a head for giant prawns, fish and beer, which is not bad for an al fresco location overlooking windsurfers and sunbathers.

Entertainment
The Copacabana of Dalian is the International Seamen's Club, open until 10.30 pm, with dining and banquet rooms, a bar where sailors doze with their stale beers to the chirp of video-game machines, and a disco. It has a full-size theatre with weekend offerings – Beijing Opera or perhaps a film or an acrobat show. One of the innovations at the acrobat show is half a dozen Chinese grinding away to the strains of 'YMCA', followed by 'Hawaii Five-0'.

Shopping
The Friendship Store has stock that rivals Beijing's. Handicrafts such as glassware, feather paintings and shell mosaics can also be found in the Tianjin Department Store at 199 Tianjin Jie. There's an antique store at 229 Tianjin Jie.

Getting There & Away

Air Dalian has numerous air connections. Sample fares are: Beijing (Y112), Qingdao (Y85), Shanghai (Y239) and Shenyang (Y60). Weekly flights have just started between Dalian and Hong Kong.

Bus Buses to Dandong, Fushun and Jinzhou leave from the bus station which is on the corner of the first street west of the intersection of Jiefang Lu and Zhongshan Lu (about 100 metres down the street from the Dongfang Hotel). Book your ticket peacefully the day before or arrive at the last minute and fight for it. Several buses leave daily for Dandong between 6 am and 8 am. The trip takes nine hours and costs Y13 in a Polish Autosan complete with maniac driver, air-con, tinted windows, soft seats and the fragrance of seaweed carried by fellow passengers. Alternatively, you could have the pleasure of riding in a 'Dalian' bus, made in Dalian.

Rail There are direct trains from Dalian to Shenyang, Beijing, Harbin and Jiamusi. For more details, see the introduction to the north-eastern provinces.

Boat The booking office is at the boat terminal, east of the Seamen's Club, and has a left-luggage office (modern facilities, too). Providing you have a ticket, you can sleep in the comfy building beside the booking office. Since the rail lines from Dalian have to go all the way round the peninsula before proceeding south, boats can actually save you time as well as money.

There are boats to Yantai or Shanghai daily; to Qingdao every other day; to Canton every four to six days; to Tanggu (the port of Tianjin) every four to six days. There are other departures to Weihai, Longkou, Shidao and Yingkou. Boat rides are very cheap (for example, 3rd class to Shanghai is Y23, takes about 40 hours; 3rd class to Qingdao is Y16, takes about 28 hours; 3rd class to Yantai is Y9.70, takes about eight hours) and comfortable, but avoid cargo class. Meals cost Y2 to Y3 and the seasickness pills are free.

Getting Around

Bus No 13 runs from the railway station area, along behind the Friendship Store, and to the boat terminal. Tramcar No 201 starts from the railway station, heads in the same direction as bus No 13, but turns south before the Friendship Store and proceeds east (it's good for getting part-way to the Nanshan Guest House). There is a round-the-city bus with no number, but the characters for *huan lu* (circle route) appear on the destination sign. This bus is useful for a tour through Dalian.

ANSHAN 鞍山

South of Shenyang is Anshan, another huge industrial city, producing about 25% of the nation's iron and steel. It is a massive vista of factories, blast furnaces, converters, rolling mills, metallurgy labs, refractories and chemical plants. The plant started under the Japanese, was taken apart by the Russians, was revived by the Chinese, and now employs over 130,000 workers. Outside the town are five iron-ore mines, and to the south is a bunch of scenery and sanatoriums. My most vivid memories of Anshan are gangs of kids with butterfly nets chasing dragon-flies; trams grinding through dust and pollution; a western-style restaurant where a woman had skewered a club sandwich with her fork and was eating it like a kebab.

If you really want to stay here, the only hotel that takes foreigners is the *Anshan Binguan* which charges Y58 for a double and is a short walk from the station. There's a large city map in front of the station. The Chinese duo with whom I shared a taxi were 'taken for a ride' all round town and charged Y12!

QIAN SHAN 千山

About 25 km south-east of Anshan, Qian Shan is a preferable place to stay or visit.

To get there from Anshan, take bus No 8 which leaves from a side street about 50 metres in front of Anshan station. If you just want to make a day trip, luggage can be left at the station. The trip takes 1½ hours and costs Y0.55. The last bus in either direction is at 6.30 pm.

The bus drops you off at the entrance to Qian Shan. Food, drink, Qian Shan T-shirts, locally made clickers and knobbly walking sticks are available from hawkers. The entrance fee is Y0.30 and maps can be bought for Y0.25 from hawkers or at the ticket office.

Here you can escape Anshan's pollution and hike around the hills, which have a motley scattering of Tang, Ming and Qing temples. At the southern foot of the mountain is the Tanggangzi Hot Spring. The last Qing emperor, Pu Yi, used to bathe here with his empresses. Tanggangzi has hot springs piped into ordinary baths, and a sanatorium for chronic diseases – there is some hotel accommodation. Day trippers can provide raucous accompaniment to the peaceful surroundings; when my companion slipped off into the bushes to throw up after one bottle too many of sickly qishui, a small crowd instantly materialised to appreciate the ceremony.

Qian Shan is an abbreviation for Qianlian Shan (1000 lotuses mountain). According to legend (do you really want to hear another one?), there was once a fairy who wanted to bring spring to the world by embroidering pretty clouds on lotuses. Just as she was making the 999th lotus, the gods found it, accused her of stealing the clouds and had her arrested. The fairy put up a fight and during the struggle all the lotuses dropped to earth, where they immediately turned into green hills. In memory of the fairy, people began to call the mountain '1000 lotuses mountain' or just Qian Shan. Later, when a monk arrived and actually counted the peaks he discovered there were only 999, so he built an artificial one to make a round number.

There are several places to stay at Qian Shan: to the right of the park entrance is the *Qian Shan Binguan*. The *Lu Cui Binguan* is in a pleasant spot about 100 metres into the park on the right. Taoist temples on the hills also take in people overnight. Prices for a double vary between Y14 and Y30 depending on the standard of the room.

LIAOYANG 辽阳

South of Shenyang and just north of Anshan is Liaoyang – the scene of lighter industry, such as textiles, food-processing and machine tools. The only sights here are the White Pagoda from the Liao Dynasty, the Tanghe Hot Spring (it's a rare radon spring, in case you feel like a therapeutic dip) and China's largest Petrochemical Fibre Complex.

BENXI 本溪

About two hours drive south-east of Shenyang is Benxi, an iron, steel and coal-mining town, with a cement works. Liaoning Province accounts for some 10% of national coal production, with eight large-scale mining areas.

The main reason tourists traipse out to Benxi is to see the Xiejiaweizi Water Cavern 27 km east of town. A boat trip costs Y3 per person or Y40 if you rent the whole boat (maximum 10 people). The cave is chilly and there are overcoats for hire. The Chinese have given the stalactites and stalagmites in the cave weird names and associated stories which may require an almighty shove from your imagination.

FUSHUN 抚顺

Fushun, on the railway line to the east of Shenyang, was the birthplace of the Qing court and is presently the largest open-cut coal mine in China; the city also has a sideline in specialised steel, heavy machinery, cement and petrochemicals. In the souvenir line, products from Fushun include cigarette holders, coal sculptures and amber ornaments (especially valued are the pieces with imprisoned insects). Better examples of these art forms are displayed in the city's Exhibition Hall.

YINGKOU 营口

Yingkou is a port city recently opened to the foreign touring public. It is south-east of Shenyang at the end of a railway line which branches off the main Shenyang-Dalian line.

TIELING 铁岭

Tieling, north of Shenyang on the railway line, was recently opened to tourism. A British couple I met were probably among the first individual tourists to arrive there. The local tourism committee, after recovering from the shock of actually receiving a tourist, decided to solve the problem by chauffeuring the couple around in a sedan and providing two blow-out banquets in a row. Zhou Enlai spent his youth in Tieling so one of the 'highlights' is a model replica of the town as he knew it – complete with fairy lights to show the route he used to take to school.

DANDONG 丹东

Dandong lies at the border of Liaoning Province and North Korea. Along with Dalian and Yingkou, this is one of the three key trading and communication ports for the whole north-eastern area. The city has been designated one of Liaoning Province's major export production centres and is being revamped for greater light industry production, like wristwatches, knitwear, printing and foodstuffs. This is the home of 'Ganoderma', wrinkle-killer face cream. You can buy tussah silk at the local silk factory.

Dandong isn't a cultural mecca, but it's clean, leafy, easy to cover and doesn't suffer from over-crowding. The people are friendly and it was one of the places I enjoyed most in the north-east.

Information

CITS (tel 27721) is inside the Dandong Guest House and will supply a brochure with sketchy map. Not much English spoken here, but they will arrange visits to factories, a Korean family and school; or with destinations out of town.

Things to See

Dandong has few sights, but its chief attraction is its location on the North Korean border. Information on crossing to North Korea was hazy. All questions concerning visas, etc have to be sorted out in Beijing – not in Dandong. There is a bus four times a week for Y1 from Dandong to the Korean town of Sinuiju on the other side of the bridge. A train ticket from Dandong to Pyongyang, the capital of North Korea, costs Y36 one way. If you want to get close to North Korea, an amusing boat ride will take you down the middle of the Yalu River, which is the boundary line. Boats leave every half hour from a pier at the Yalu River Park. Tickets cost Y1 for the upper deck and Y0.60 for the lower deck. Photography is not allowed. The boat passes under the bridge, runs close to the Korean side and then makes a long loop back down the Chinese side to the pier. There's nothing stunning about what you see: rusty tubs being welded, antiquated tubs being loaded, cheerful schoolkids waving, a steam engine chuffing across the bridge.

There are, in fact, two bridges – well, one and a half. The original steel-span bridge was 'accidentally' strafed in 1950 by the Americans, who also succeeded in accidentally bombing the airstrip at Dandong. The Koreans have dismantled this bridge as far as the mid-river boundary line. All that's left is a row of piers on the Korean side and half a bridge (still showing shrapnel pockmarks) on the Chinese side.

Yalu River Park (admission Y0.10) is a favourite picnic site, full of photographers trying to squeeze Mum, Dad, kids, Gran and Granpa into the standard 'I visited the Sino-Korean border' shot which has to include the bridge as a backdrop. You can even get your portrait taken in the cockpit of a Chinese MIG fighter.

Jinjiang Shan Park is close to the Dandong Binguan. From the top of the park there's a panoramic view of the city and North Korea across the Yalu River.

1 Dandong Guest House & CITS
2 Yalu River Hotel (Yalu Jiang Binguan)
3 International Post Office (Guoji Youjü)
4 CAAC (Min Hang Ban Gong Shi)
5 No 1 Government Hostel (Di Yi Zhaodai Suo)
6 Bank of China (Zhong Guo Yin Hang)
7 Si Hai Restaurant (Si Hai Canting)
8 Bike Shop (Hire) (Chu Zu Zi Xing Che)
9 No 1 Department Store (Di Yi Bai Huo Shang Dian)
10 Jinjiang Park (Jinjiang Gong Yuan)
11 Domestic Post Office (Guo Nei You Jü)
12 Railway Station (Huo Che Zhan)
13 Bus Station (Qi Che Zhan)
14 Cultural Palace (Wen Hua Gong)
15 Boat Trip Pier (Lü You Matou)
16 Yalu River Park (Yalu Jiang Gong Yuan)

The local crimeboard in Dandong had a sad picture story about a bus driver who ran over a chicken. When the teenage girl who owned the chicken pressed the driver for compensation, he engaged second gear and promptly ran over the girl too!

Places to Stay

The *Yalu River Hotel (Yalu Jiang Binguan)*, opened in 1986, is a shiny, Sino-Japanese joint-venture with 300 rooms in the centre of town. Prices are steep: Y80 to Y160 for doubles. There are dorms with beds for Y6 but for Chinese only. A profusely apologetic manager personally arranged a cheaper room for me in another hotel.

The *Dandong Binguan* (tel 27312 or 27313) is at No 2 Shan Shang Jie, about two km or a half hour's walk uphill from the train station. Apart from its inconvenient location, the mixture of main buildings and villas set in a park is pleasant to stay in. Doubles start at Y40, singles at Y20; the equivalent student rates are Y28 and Y14 respectively. The rooms all have TV and you can kill time stone dead by watching North Korean TV, which seems to function as a portrait studio for 'the great leader, Kim Il Sung'. Turn off the telly and it's just serenading crickets and the lonesome whistling of steam locos shunting outside.

Foreigners have also stayed at the *No 1 Government Hostel (Di Yi Zhaodai Suo)* a few metres uphill from the Yalu River Hotel. There are several Chinese hotels *(lüshe)* along the main street.

Places to Eat

The Dandong Binguan offers pricey (FEC only) and unexciting food, including western breakfasts. The food scene is more lively downtown, where the free-enterprise merchants have set up red lanterns and neon lights to attract passers-by. Many of these restaurants are clean and serve *hun dun* (a delicious type of ravioli soup) or seafood. The *Si Hai Canting*, just off the main street (see map), has excellent seafood and foreigners are well received. The western-style paintings on the walls were done by the owner's husband.

Getting There & Away

Air There are regular flights to Beijing (Y156), Dalian (Y56) and Shenyang (Y35).

Bus The bus station is a five-minute walk from the railway station. Helpful staff try hard to get foreigners on the right bus.

A bus leaves daily for Tonghua at 6.30 am. The trip takes 10 hours and costs Y10.60.

My bus appeared to have been overbooked, but the inventive staff placated irate travellers by producing collapsible chairs! The route follows mostly dirt roads through villages with the typical thatched houses of the Korean minority. At the lunch stop, the drivers invited the foreigners to eat with them – a delicious meal of egg and onions, aubergines and sliced cucumber with garlic. Shortly after passing a bus that had plunged off the road and almost landed in a reservoir, the bus ground to a halt again. In the middle of the road was a large, mobile office which had embedded itself in an overhanging branch and slipped off its trailer.

The bus from Dandong will drop you off in Tonghua about three km from the station. To continue to the station, cross to the opposite side of the road outside the bus station and take a city bus from the next bus stop – ask for *huo che zhan* (railway station).

Several buses leave daily between 5.10 and 6.40 for the nine-hour trip to Dalian. Tickets for the express bus cost Y13; the ordinary bus is cheaper.

The express bus trip from Dalian to Dandong was some ride. About 10 minutes after departure, considering the speed – perhaps I should say take-off – the lovely Korean girl sitting in front of me was already looking green and fumbling for the window catch. Her well-meaning companions were insistent that the best solution for her problem was to eat more tomatoes.

Meanwhile the driver decided to improve his banshee act by using not only his double air-horns but also the outside loudspeaker to harangue traffic in front. His tactic was to move up within three inches of the back bumper of the vehicle in front and then scream in Chinese, 'Move it, move it, let the vehicle behind overtake'. Donkey-carts, walking tractors, jeeps scattered like buckshot.

The Korean girl succumbed to motion sickness and threw up out of the window. Since the window was very small, the girl had quite a struggle before she finally managed to get her head outside. Traffic coming from the other direction came within a hair's breadth of knocking her block off. The driver kept flying along, turned the internal loudspeaker on and blasted the girl: 'Hey you behind, get your head in, get it in, observe safety, observe safety'. While his voice rose to a frenzy, he turned in his seat to look back and the bus swayed violently.

The scenery along this route is meant to be beautiful, but I can't give an honest opinion because this girl gave my window a nauseating landscape.

Rail There are direct trains to Dandong from Shenyang and Changchun; the trip from Shenyang takes five hours. The combined Pyongyang-Moscow and Pyongyang-Beijing train passes through Dandong on Saturdays at about 3 pm. Buy a platform ticket and watch the international crowds of passengers (mostly Russians, North Koreans and Chinese) buying luxury items.

Boat At present, there are no boat connections for foreigners.

AROUND DANDONG

About 52 km north-west of Dandong is the town of **Fengcheng**. The nearby mountain, Fengkuang Shan, is dotted with temples, monasteries and pagodas from the Tang, Ming and Qing dynasties. The Fengkuang Mountain Temple Fair takes place in April and reportedly attracts thousands of people.

Wulongbei Hot Springs (Wulongbei Wenchuan) are at **Wulongbei**, about 20 km north of Dandong on the road to Fengcheng. There's a guest house here and you could try the springs, which average 73°F.

Dagu Shan lies close to the town of Gushan, about 90 km south-west of Dandong. There are several groups of Taoist temples dating from the Tang Dynasty.

Jilin 吉林

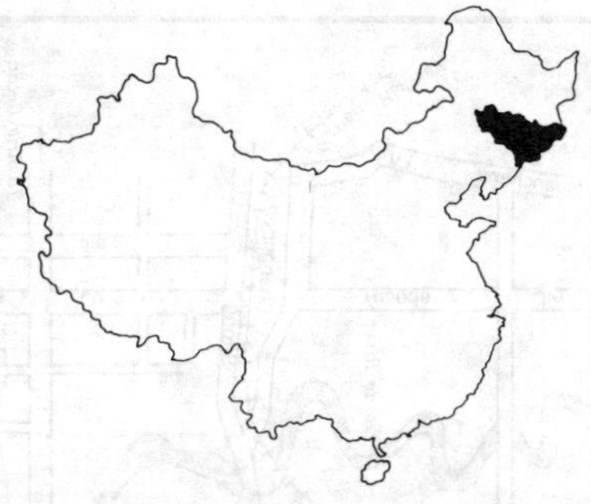

CHANGCHUN 长春

Changchun, with its broad leafy avenues, is a well laid-out city, and an exceedingly dull one. Those responsible for the uninspiring militaristic structures are the Japanese who developed it as the capital of 'Manchukuo' from 1933 to 1945. In 1945 the Russians arrived in Changchun on a looting spree; when they departed in 1946, the Kuomintang moved in to occupy the cities of the north-east, only to find themselves surrounded by the Communists in the countryside (roving around blowing up railway lines). The Communists had assembled a formidable array of scrounged and captured weaponry, from ex-Japanese tanks to US jeeps, and Changchun saw more than a few of them in action. The city was taken over by the Communists in 1948.

China's first auto plant was set up here in the 1950s with Soviet assistance, starting with 95 hp Jiefang (Liberation) Trucks, and moving on to bigger and better things like the Red Flag limousines. Changchun's other claim to fame – the Film Studios – got their start in the civil war, making documentaries. You might try and arrange a visit via CITS to the Film Studios or the Number One Auto Plant (both are on the tramcar No 2 route). Lesser factories (tractor, rail-car, carpet, fur, wood-carving) may be accessible. Otherwise, there are numerous wooded parks in the city, a reservoir 20 km to the south, and perhaps a chance to see a deer farm or ginseng garden. The former administrative buildings of the Japanese are now used by the university.

One building with an interesting background is the Provincial Museum, located in the former palace of Pu Yi. Henry Pu Yi was the last person to ascend the dragon throne. He was two years old at the time and was forced to abdicate just six years later when the 1911 revolution swept the country. He lived in exile in Tianjin and in 1935 was spirited away to Changchun by the Japanese invaders and set up as the puppet emperor of Manchukuo. Pu Yi was captured by the Russians in 1945 and was only returned to China sometime in the late 1950s, where he was allowed to work as a gardener at one of the colleges in Beijing. He died of cancer in 1967, thus ending a life which had largely been governed by others.

Information

CITS (tel 52401, 52419) is in the Changbai Shan Binguan. They have a useful bilingual bus map of Changchun plus other literature.

CAAC (tel 39772) is at 2 Liaoning Lu.

Places to Stay

The *Chunyi* (tel 38495) is at 2 Stalin Boulevard, just across from the railway station. It's got Stalin-period decor, old-world opulence and double rooms at Y70. When I asked about cheaper rooms, an eavesdropping waiter promptly offered me the use of his dorm bed at half the rate, but only from 11 pm to 5 am when he was on duty! In a similar class of exclusivity are the *Nanhu Guest House* (tel 53571) and the *Changchun Guest House* (tel 26771) at 128 Changchun Lu.

The *Changbai Shan* (tel 53679) at 12 Ximen Lu is a new high-rise with topnotch plumbing, luxury accommodation and

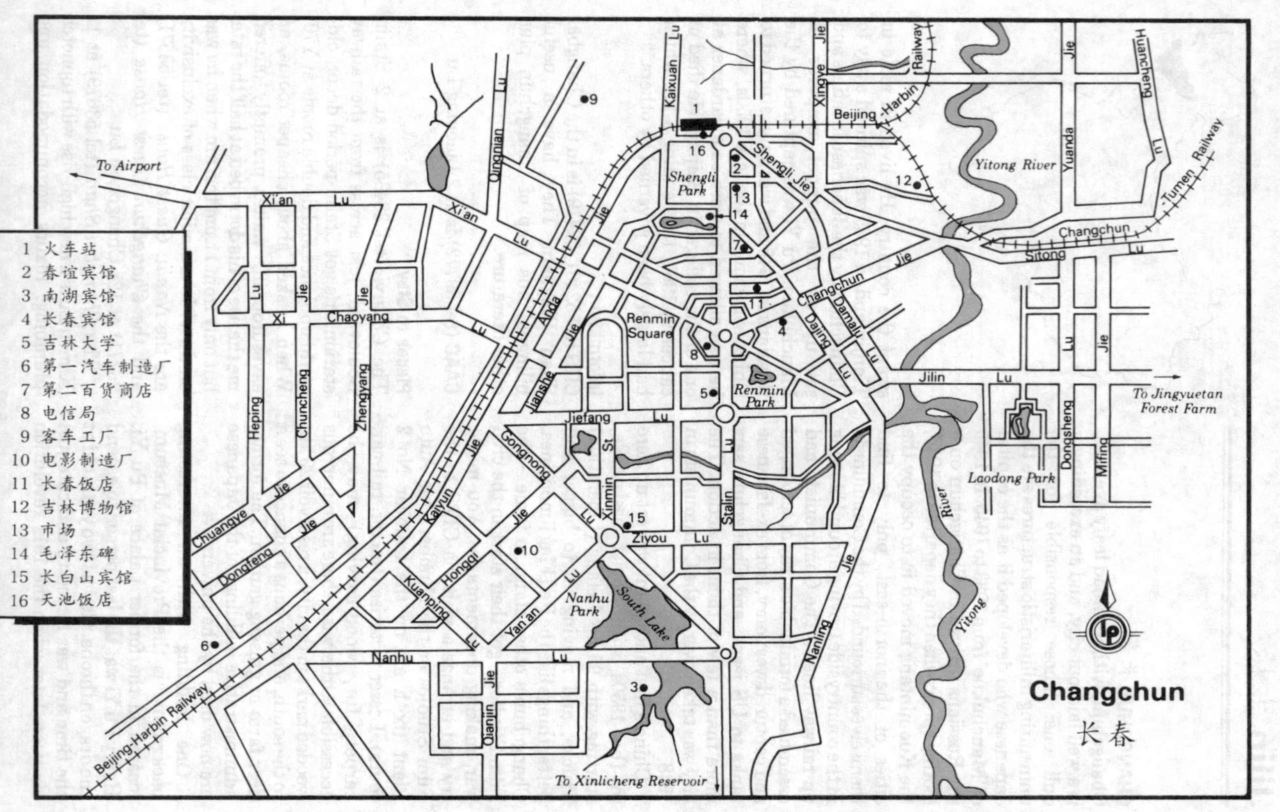
Changchun
长春
To Airport
To Jingyuetan Forest Farm
To Xinlicheng Reservoir
Tumen Railway
Beijing-Harbin Railway
Yitong River
Huancheng Lu
Yuanda Jie
Changchun Jie
Sitong Lu
Jilin Lu
Mifing Jie
Dongsheng Lu
Laodong Park
Nanling Jie
Stalin Lu
Renmin Park
Renmin Square
Shengli Park
Shengli Jie
Xingye Jie
Changchun Damalu
Dajing Lu
Kaixuan Lu
Anda Jie
Jianshe Jie
Jiefang Lu
Xinmin St
Ziyou Lu
South Lake
Nanhu Park
Nanhu Lu
Yan'an Lu
Gongnong Jie
Honggi Jie
Kuanping Lu
Qianjin Jie
Qingnian Lu
Xi'an Lu
Xi Jie
Chaoyang Jie
Zhengyang Jie
Chuncheng Jie
Heping Lu
Kaiyun Jie
Chuangye Jie
Dongfeng Jie
1 火车站
2 春谊宾馆
3 南湖宾馆
4 长春宾馆
5 吉林大学
6 第一汽车制造厂
7 第二百货商店
8 电信局
9 客车工厂
10 电影制造厂
11 长春饭店
12 吉林博物馆
13 市场
14 毛泽东碑
15 长白山宾馆
16 天池饭店

1 Changchun Railway Station
2 Chunyi Hotel
3 Nanhu Guest House
4 Changchun Municipal Guest House
5 Jilin University
6 Changchun No 1 Automobile Plant
7 No 2 Department Store (Friendship Store on the top floor)
8 Telecommunication Bureau & Public Security
9 Railway Carriage Factory
10 Film Studio
11 Restaurant
12 Jilin Provincial Museum
13 Shopping/Market Street
14 Mao Statue
15 Changbai Shan Guest House
16 Tianchi Fandian

prices to match. Doubles start at Y102, although this dropped to Y68 after a midnight bargaining session. For those who want to peg out for a rest from bargaining, there's plenty of furniture. Take trolley bus No 62 from the railway station.

The *Tianchi Fandian* is 20 metres to the left as you come out of the railway station. A big sign near the reception desk says, 'Foreigners welcome to put up at our hotel'. The staff are helpful, providing you persevere. Doubles vary between Y22 and Y33; triples are Y44; a four-bed room is Y50.

Outside the station, women with bicycle carts seem to be operating a hotel racket. I didn't use their services, but it seems that they line up a bed or room beforehand and then charge you Y4 to take you there. There is, of course, no guarantee that the hotel will suddenly decide not to take a foreigner.

Getting There & Away

For details on trains, see the introduction to the north-eastern provinces. Changchun is connected by air with Beijing (Y151), Harbin (Y38) and Shenyang (Y49).

JILIN 吉林

East of Changchun is the city of Jilin. A Chinese pamphlet puts it in a nutshell: 'Under the guidance of Chairman Mao's revolutionary line, it has made rapid progress in industrial and agricultural production . . . From a desolate consumer city, Kirin (Jilin) has become a rising industrial city with emphasis on chemical and power industries'.

Three large chemical plants were built after 1949. The Fengman Hydroelectric Station, built by the Japanese, disassembled by the Russians and put back together by the Chinese, fuels these enterprises, and provides Jilin with an unusual tourist attraction: water passing from artificial Songhua Lake through the power plant becomes a warm, steamy current that merges with the Songhua River and prevents it from freezing. Overnight, vapour rising from the river meets the minus 20 Celsius weather, causing condensation on the branches of pines and willows on a 20-km stretch of bank. During the Spring Festival (25 January), hordes of Japanese and Overseas Chinese come for the resulting icicle and spraypaint show. To reach this hydroelectric station, take bus No 9 from the roundabout north of the Xiguan Hotel.

If you want to try some elementary ski slopes, there's the Songhuahu ski-ground at Daqing Shan which is 16 km from Jilin, and just west of Fengman. CITS can provide further details about snow conditions, lift operation, transport and hire of equipment.

Jilin, like Harbin, has an ice-lantern festival, held at Beishan Park. In 1976, the Jilin area received a heavy meteorite shower and the largest bit, weighing 1770 kg, is on view in the meteorite exhibition hall (take bus No 3 from outside the Dongguan Hotel). It's also possible to visit the Jilin Special Products Research Centre, where there is a deer park, ginseng garden and a collection of sables. Take bus No 12 from the station and get off on the other side of the bridge over the Songhua River. Walk south for half an hour and ask for 'Longtan Shan Luchang'.

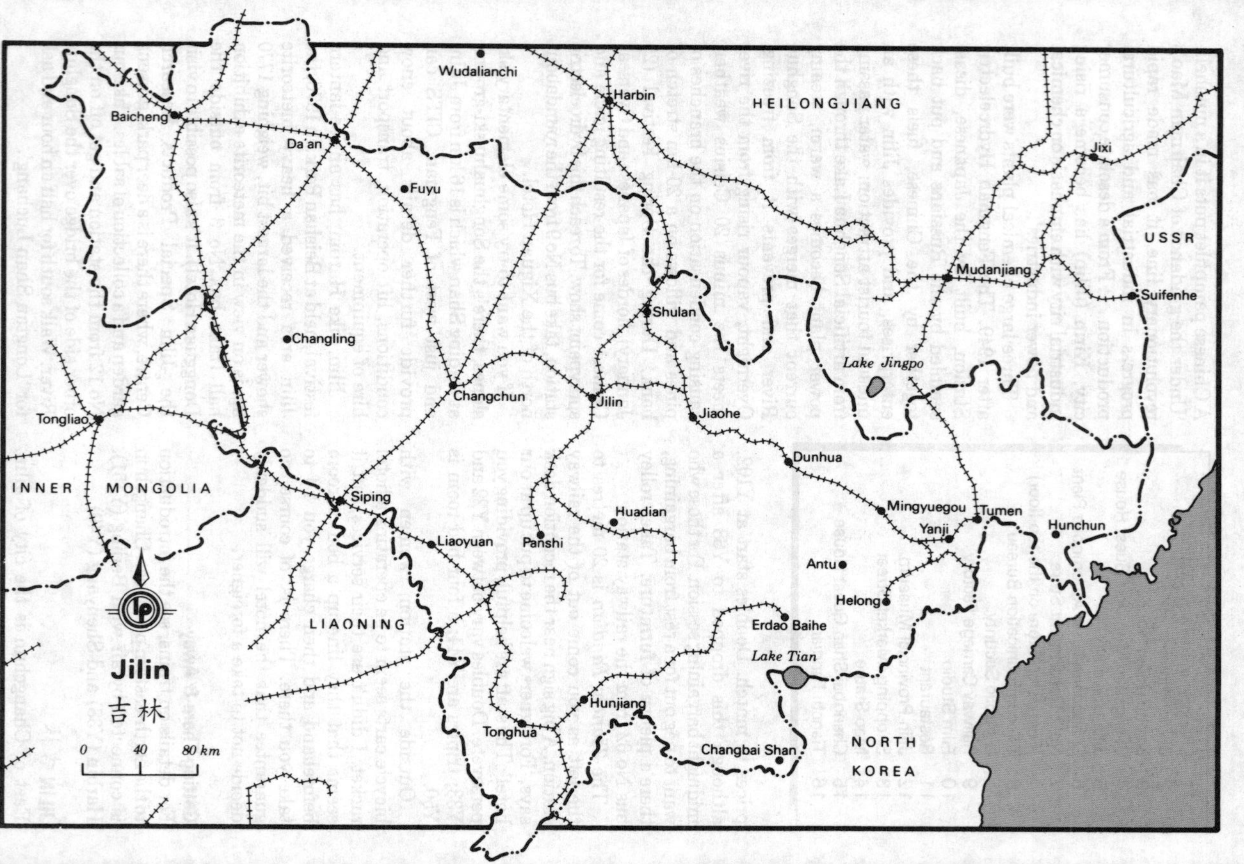
Wudalianchi
Harbin
HEILONGJIANG
Baicheng
Da'an
Jixi
Fuyu
USSR
Mudanjiang
Suifenhe
Shulan
Changling
Lake Jingpo
Changchun
Jilin
Tongliao
Jiaohe
Dunhua
INNER MONGOLIA
Siping
Mingyuegou
Tumen
Huadian
Hunchun
Yanji
Liaoyuan
Panshi
Antu
Helong
LIAONING
Erdao Baihe
Lake Tian
Jilin
吉林
Hunjiang
Tonghua
NORTH KOREA
Changbai Shan
0 40 80 km

Information

CITS is in the Xiguan Binguan at 661 Songjiang Lu.

Places to Stay

The *Xiguan Binguan* (tel 3545) at 661 Songjiang Lu is about seven km from the station. Take bus No 1 from the station to its terminus beside a roundabout; from there it's about a two-km walk along the riverside. This place is not only inconvenient to reach, it's also expensive and, when I was there, had an incredibly xenophobic receptionist. Doubles start at Y66.

The *Dongguan Binguan* (tel 3555) at 223 Songjiang Lu is about three km from the station and has doubles for Y55. Take trolley bus No 3 from the station. A small group of Italians took a taxi late at night to this hotel. The hotel refused them entry and the taxi driver promptly demanded Y50 for the short drive. The Italians refused to pay and demanded to be driven to the PSB where they explained their predicament. One phone call from the PSB was enough to make rooms magically become vacant at the same hotel which had just refused them; the driver was ordered to drive them back and charge half the original price.

CHANGBAI NATURE RESERVE
长白自然保护区

The Changbai (Ever-White) Nature Reserve is China's largest, covering 210,000 hectares of dense virgin forest. The forest is divided into a semi-protected area where limited lumbering and hunting are permitted, and a protected area where neither is allowed. Because of elevation changes, there is wide variation in animal and plant life. From 700 to 1000 metres above sea level there are mixed coniferous and broad-leaf trees (including white birch and Korean pines); from 1000 to 1800 metres are cold-resistant coniferous trees such as dragon spruce and fir; from 1800 to 2000 metres is another forest belt; above 2000

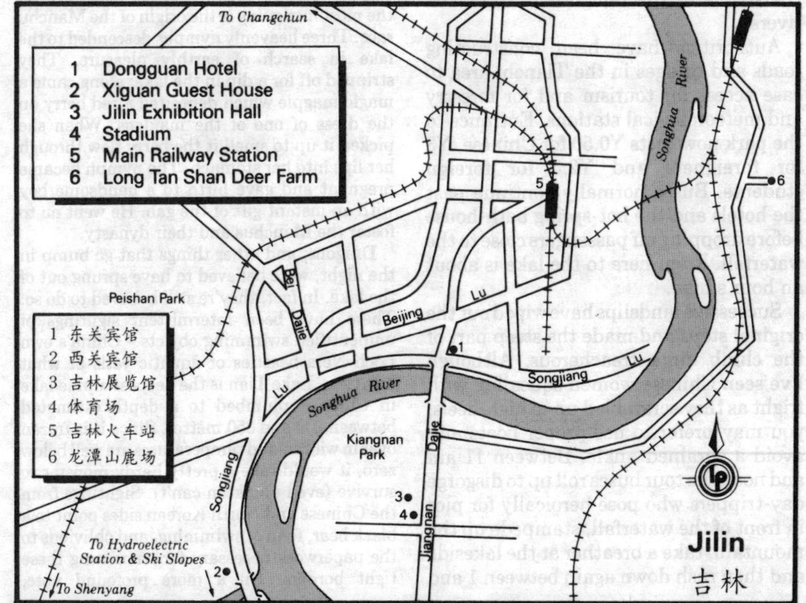

metres is alpine tundra, treeless and windy. For the budding natural scientist there's plenty to investigate. Some 300 medicinal plants grow within the reserve (including winter daphne, asiabell and wild ginseng); and some very shy animal species make their home in the mountain range (the rarer ones being the protected cranes, deer and Manchurian tiger).

The reserve itself is a recent creation, first designated in 1960. During the Cultural Revolution all forest and conservation work was suspended, and technical and scientific personnel were dispersed to menial jobs. Locals had a free-for-all season on the plant and animal life during this period.

Lake Tian, the Lake of Heaven, is the prime scenic spot. It's a volcanic crater-lake, five km from north to south, 3½ km from east to west, 13 km in circumference, and sits at an elevation of 2194 metres. It's surrounded by jagged rock outcrops and peaks; three rivers run off the lake, with a rumbling 68-metre waterfall identified as the source of the Songhua and Tumen rivers.

Authorities have been constructing roads and bridges in the Tianchi area to ease access for tourism and for forestry and meteorological stations. Entrance to the park now costs Y0.50 for Chinese, Y3 for foreigners and Y2.5 for foreign students. Buses normally continue past the hotels and the hot-spring bath-house before dropping off passengers close to the waterfall. From here to the lake is about an hour's hike.

Successive landslips have wiped out the original steps and made the steep part of the climb quite treacherous. Although I've seen Chinese women squealing with fright as they scrambled up in high-heels, you may prefer to use proper boots and avoid a sprained ankle. Between 11 am and noon the tour buses roll up to disgorge day-trippers who pose heroically for pics in front of the waterfall, stampede up the mountain, take a breather at the lakeside and then rush down again between 1 and 2 pm. The beauty of the place is badly marred by picnic detritus, smashed glass and discarded film wrappers. Some of these day-trippers display amazing tenacity. On my way down, I met a small group consisting of a semi-paralysed old man being propelled upwards by two pullers and three pushers!

Apart from mid-day when the day-trippers take over, this is a peaceful spot at which to stay for a couple of days and hike around. A vehicle route also runs to a meteorological station on top of one of the peaks overlooking the lake. Hiking at the lake itself is limited by the sharp peaks and their rock-strewn debris, and by the fact that the lake overlaps the Chinese/North Korean border – there's no tourist build-up yet on the Korean side. Cloud cover starts at 1000 metres and can be prevalent. The highest peak in the Changbai Shan range is 2700 metres.

Enchanting scenery like this would not be complete in the Chinese world without a legend or mystique of some sort. Of the many myths, the most intriguing is the origin of the Manchu race. Three heavenly nymphs descended to the lake in search of earthly pleasure. They stripped off for a dip in the lake; along came a magic magpie which deposited a red berry on the dress of one of the maidens. When she picked it up to smell it the berry flew through her lips into her stomach. The nymph became pregnant and gave birth to a handsome boy with an instant gift of the gab. He went on to foster the Manchus and their dynasty.

Dragons, and other things that go bump in the night, were believed to have sprung out of the lake. In fact, they're still believed to do so. There have been intermittent sightings of unidentified swimming objects – China's own Loch Ness beasties or aquatic yetis or what have you. Lake Tian is the deepest alpine lake in China – plumbed to a depth estimated between 200 and 350 metres. Since it is frozen over in winter, and temperatures are well below zero, it would take a pretty hardy monster to survive (even plankton can't). Sightings from the Chinese and North Korean sides point to a black bear, fond of swimming, and oblivious to the paperwork necessary for transitting these tight borders. On a more profound note,

Chinese couples throw coins into the lake, pledging that their love will remain as deep as Tianchi, and as long lived.

The local post office, next to the guest houses, has scenic first-day covers. The hot-spring bath-house, where water from lake and underground sources is mixed, is close to the hotels; Y0.5 for a communal dip, Y3 for a private cubicle. If you cross the nearby river via either the tree-trunk or the bridge lower down, there's a forest path which leads to the dark, brooding, Lesser Tianchi Lake.

Places to Stay

There are two guest houses: the *Baishan Zhaodai Suo* and the *Changbai Shan Binguan*. Both of these are small (less than 100 beds) and rudimentary, and prices are low (Y8 to Y12 starting price for a double). If no rooms are available, the Binguan has huts with 15 beds, dirt floors and the occasional rat – Y3 per bed. At 7 pm, an infernal din and cloud of diesel smoke announce the return to power of the generator. Meals at the guest house cost Y4; or bring your own food to supplement the meagre supplies in the tourist stalls. The local delicacies are *mogu* (mushrooms) and a type of dried fish which, for lack of a better name, I'll call 'gearstick fish' since that's where bus drivers dangle them.

Getting There

The Changbai area is remote, and a journey there is somewhat expeditionary: you're advised to bring loads of ginseng, frog-tonic oil and other supplies and refreshments with you, plus good hiking gear (due to high elevations, flash thunderstorms are not uncommon).

The *only* season in terms of transport access is late June to September, when snow and ice-cover drop. The road from Erdao Baihe to Changbai is open only for this period. Autumn colourings are the goal of Chinese hikers – so the peak season is mid-July to mid-August with a high local turnover. Although Changbai was only opened to foreigners in 1982, it has been on the Chinese tour map for some time, with something like 30,000 visitors from north-eastern provinces over the July to September period.

There are two 'transit points' to Changbai: Mingyuegou (occasionally referred to as Lao Antu or Old Antu) and Erdao Baihe (sometimes abbreviated to Baihe). Before you go, get a weather forecast from someone in Jilin, Changchun or Shenyang (July/August will be no problem). Allow about five days for the round trip from, say, Shenyang. Tour buses go up the mountain in the July/August period, but in other periods you may have trouble finding a bus from Erdao Baihe. The only other local transport is logging trucks and official jeeps – the latter are expensive to rent, the former are very reluctant to give rides.

Mingyuegou Route There are trains to Mingyuegou from Shenyang North Railway Station; the trip takes about 16 hours. If you arrive in Mingyuegou at night you can sleep in the station waiting room. There is also a small hotel in Mingyuegou which charges Y5 per person. Buses for Erdao Baihe depart from 7.20 to 10.30 am. The one-way trip costs Y4.30; it takes five hours to travel the 125 km. Unless you arrive early in Erdao Baihe, you may find yourself waiting till the next morning for transport to Changbai, a further 40 km. Special tourist buses run from Mingyuegou to the Changbai Hot Springs area in July and August; these cost Y20 return for a three-day package. There are also trains from Changchun to Mingyuegou.

Erdao Baihe Route Erdao Baihe is the end of the line as far as trains go – a scrapyard for locos. To get to Erdao Baihe from Jilin, Changchun or Shenyang, you must take a train to Tonghua and then change to a train for Erdao Baihe. The two daily trains between Erdao Baihe and Tonghua have two steam locos (one pushing, the other pulling); there are no sleepers, only cars

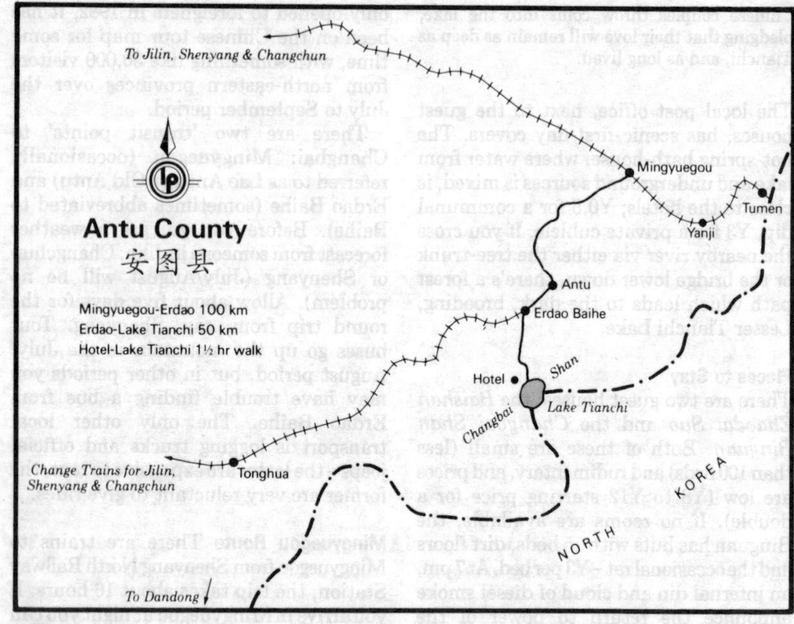

with soft seats (green velvet) and hard wooden benches (ouch!). The 500-series trains take 10 hours to cover the 277 km between Tonghua and Erdao Baihe. If you're overnighting, it's worth paying Y9.70 for soft-seat in lieu of sleeper. The soft-seat waiting-room at Tonghua Station is the lap of anti-macassared luxury. Look for the sign saying 'soft-seat waiting-room' beside the packed hard-seat waiting-room, and ring the red bell.

The feeling of entering a time-warp while travelling on this train was reinforced by the behaviour of the *che zhang* (head of the train). Shortly after leaving Tonghua, all Chinese were asked to leave our soft-seat compartment, which was then taken over by train staff. Several passengers put up a spirited resistance and refused to budge. A librarian from Beijing struck up a conversation with me and borrowed my companion's book, which was an English translation of a Taoist text. A few minutes later, a train attendant asked the man to go to the end of the carriage for a chat with the *che zhang*, who then ordered him to return the book and desist from communicating with foreigners since it was forbidden. A heated discussion followed before he returned, sat down opposite me and started reading again from the borrowed book.

The *che zhang* then strode down the compartment and insisted on breaking the contact. During the ensuing argument, the train staff defended the decision of their leader and put concerted pressure on the raging librarian, who backed down on the advice of his elderly parents. This was the sort of behaviour I'd have expected during the Cultural Revolution; for the man from Beijing it was, as he said, proof of the isolation of the north-east and the simple fact that, propaganda notwithstanding, it takes decades to change patterns of thought.

The early-morning train arrives in Erdao Baihe at 5.20 am and is met by an excursion bus *(youlan che)*, which takes you about three km into the grubby shackery of the town for breakfast before a change of buses for the two-hour trip to the mountain. Buses usually return from the mountain at 2 pm. A one-way ticket costs Y3 plus Y0.70 compulsory accident insurance. There are several cheap places at which to stay in town, all within a few minutes of the bus station.

Buses leave between 5.30 and 6.40 am for Mingyuegou and Yanji. The bus bounces past tobacco fields, villages with thatched roofs and log chimneys, stockaded gardens, pigs on mud heaps and howling dogs. Allow five hours to Mingyuegou or seven hours to Yanji. Close to Yanji, watch out for an air field with low-flying, antique MIG-fighters (Chinese copies) practising scrambles – the Soviet Union is just a few minutes' flying time away.

BACKWOODS

The Changbai Shan region presents some possibilities for shaking off the cities and traipsing through the wastelands – and gives you some good reasons for doing so. Rough travel, rough places, rough toilets – if you can find one.

The whole zone is the Yanbian (Chaoxian) Korean Autonomous Prefecture, which is populated by people of Korean descent – often indistinguishable in dress from their Chinese counterparts. If you visit this area around 15 August, you can join in the 'Old People Festival'. The Koreans are a fairly lively lot, given to spiced cold noodles, dog meat, song and dance – and hospitality. They can also drink you under the table. Yanbian has the greatest concentration of Korean and Korean-Han groups in China, who mostly inhabit the border areas north and north-east of Erdao Baihe, extending up to Yanji.

Transport is faster by rail, as opposed to spine-jangling dirt roads. Apart from public buses the only other means of transport is jeeps or logging trucks. Off the main track, the trains are puffing black dragons, possibly of Japanese vintage. The fittings are old and the uncrowded trains have no sleepers.

Food in general leaves a lot to be desired – in the Korean places you can get by on cold noodles topped with a pile of hot spices or some meat and egg. In a Tonghua restaurant I was rather relieved when two beggars fought it out and wolfed down the remaining grey dumplings on my plate. A bus lunch-stop along the way yielded a hell's kitchen, with pig's heads bloodying the floor, fires going in corners, and concoctions bubbling away in cauldrons.

Yanji is the capital of the autonomous zone – both Korean and Chinese languages are spoken here, and some semblance of traditional costume and custom is maintained. The surrounding countryside is sprinkled with clusters of thatched cottages. Since Yanji lies on the rail line between Mingyuegou and Tumen (and thence to Mudanjiang in the south-east of Heilongjiang Province) it should not be too difficult to drop in for a visit. However, rail frequencies are low along this route and there's nothing to see in Yanji. CITS (tel 5018) arranges day trips for Y70 to see a genuine Korean family and a Korean museum. The *Yanji Binguan* charges Y62.4 for doubles between June and August and Y38 during the other months. Reception at the door includes a fancy female flunky who whirls you inside with a flourish; reception at the desk then ignores you. A better bet is the *Minzu Fandian*, which has helpful staff and charges a down to earth Y19.60 a double. Both hotels are about 40 minutes from the station on foot, or ask the bus driver to drop you nearby if you're coming from Erdao Baihe. There's a train from Yanji to Tumen at 5.49 am (Y1.8, hard-seat).

Tumen is a small city on the North Korean border. You could spend a few hours there, strolling along the riverside or climbing the hill for a view of the border area. The *Dongfang Fandian*, close to the station, charges Y4 for a dorm bed. The *Tumen Binguan* charges Y22 to Y26 for doubles or Y18 for triples. The most convenient train departure from Tumen is the 8.23 am to Mudanjiang; it takes 6½ hours and costs Y7.70 soft-seat.

Heilongjiang 黑龙江

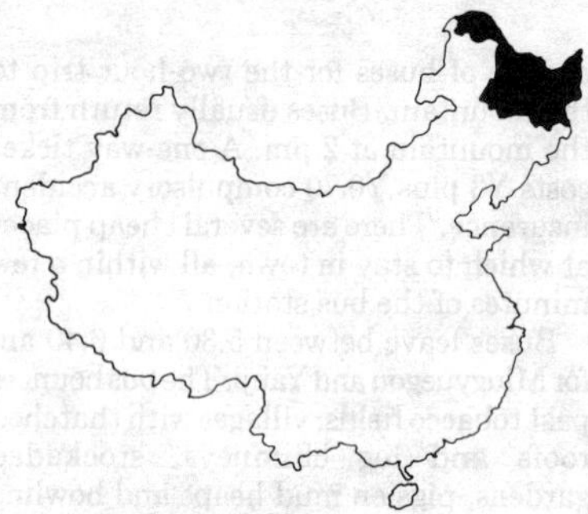

HARBIN 哈尔滨

Harbin was a fishing village until 1896, when the Russians negotiated a contract for shoving a rail line through it to Vladivostok (and Dalian). The Russian imprint on the town remained until the end of WW II in one way or another; by 1904 the 'rail concession' was in place, and with it came other Russian demands on Manchuria. These were stalled by the Russo-Japanese war of 1904 to 1905, and with the Russian defeat the Japanese gained control of the railway. In 1917 large numbers of White Russian refugees flocked to Harbin, fleeing the Bolsheviks; in 1932 the Japanese occupied the city; in 1945 the Russian Army wrested it back for a year and held it until 1946 when the Kuomintang troops were finally installed, as agreed by Chiang Kaishek and Stalin.

As the largest former Russian settlement outside the USSR, Harbin has been acutely aware of Soviet colonial eyes, and the outward manifestation is the large-scale air-raid tunnelling in the city. On the ethnic score, there is nothing to fear as there are hardly any Russian settlers left (the total population of Harbin is 2.3 million, including the outlying areas. Perhaps the Chinese have more to fear from each other – during the Cultural Revolution, according to one source, rival factions took to the air to drop bombs on one another). Heilongjiang Province has recently started to develop cross-border trade and tourism with the Soviet Union; a Soviet consulate is planned in Harbin. For travellers on the Trans-Siberian Railway, Harbin is a possible start or finish to the trip.

Harbin's industry grew with its role as a transport hub. Predominant production includes food-processing, machinery, tools, cement, paper, pharmaceuticals, electric motors and steam turbines. Output has taken its toll on the Songhua River, where the fish population has been decimated (there are reports of mercury poisoning) and the water level has dropped. As the provincial capital, Harbin is the educational, cultural and political centre of Heilongjiang.

In 1985 an American businessman was convicted by a Harbin court for setting fire to the Swan Hotel through negligence. His late-night smoke turned into a full-scale blaze which resulted in 10 deaths. The court sentenced him to 18 months' imprisonment and payment of Y150,000 compensation.

In the same year one of China's worst ferry accidents took place in Harbin. An official investigation subsequently revealed that the ferry operating between Harbin and Taiyang Island was carrying 234 passengers or nearly twice its admissible capacity. Two drunken crew members became involved in a brawl at the prow of the ferry and were soon joined by the equally inebriated boat's engineer, who left the controls. As all the passengers rushed to one side for a good view of the fight, the boat immediately started to list. The engineer staggered away from the brawl and pulled the rudder full to the right, which caused the boat to capsize; 174 lives were lost.

If you don't mind the cold then try not to miss Harbin's No 1 drawcard, the Ice Lantern Festival held from 1 January to early March (Lunar New Year) in Zhaolin Park. Fanciful sculptures are made in the

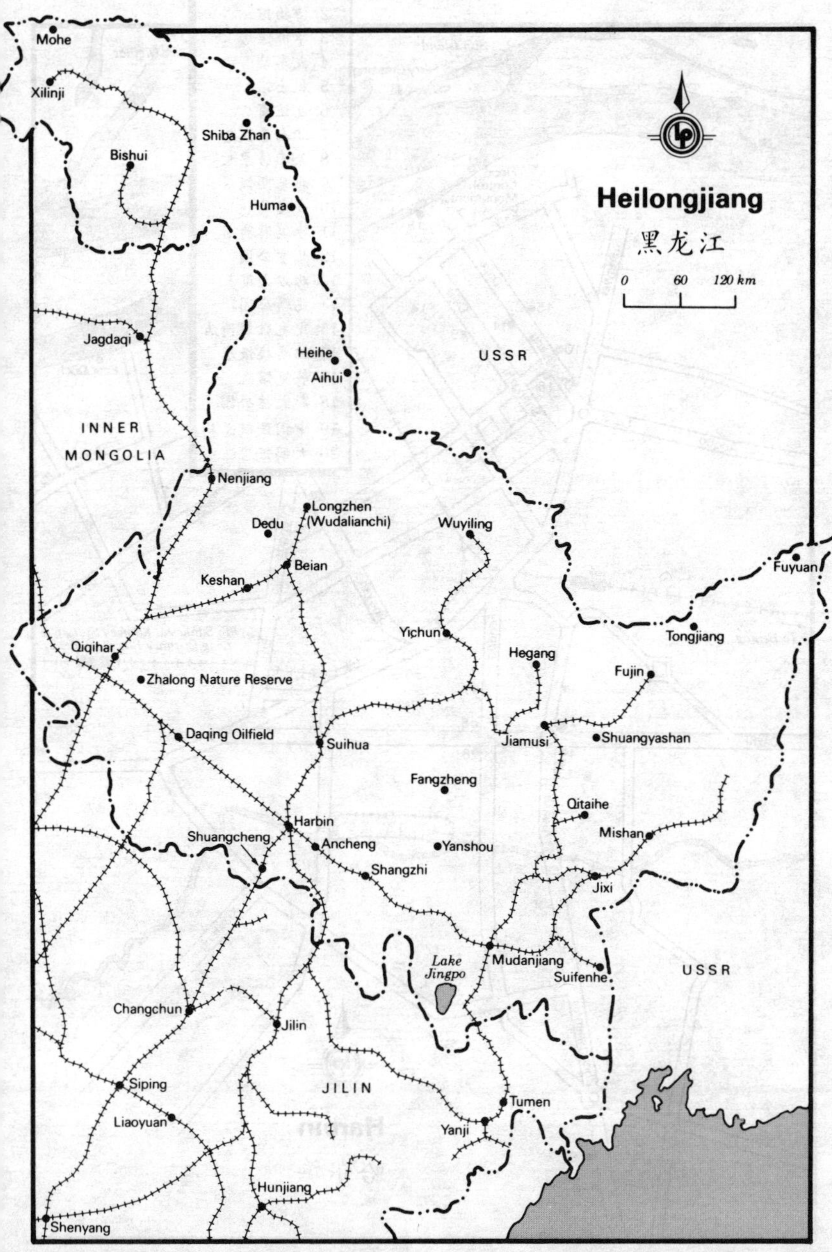
Heilongjiang
黑龙江
0 60 120 km
Mohe
Xilinji
Shiba Zhan
Bishui
Huma
Jagdaqi
Heihe
Aihui
USSR
INNER
MONGOLIA
Nenjiang
Longzhen
(Wudalianchi)
Dedu
Wuyiling
Beian
Keshan
Fuyuan
Yichun
Tongjiang
Qiqihar
Hegang
Fujin
Zhalong Nature Reserve
Jiamusi
Shuangyashan
Daqing Oilfield
Suihua
Fangzheng
Qitaihe
Harbin
Mishan
Shuangcheng
Ancheng
Yanshou
Shangzhi
Jixi
Lake
Jingpo
Mudanjiang
Suifenhe
USSR
Changchun
Jilin
Siping
JILIN
Tumen
Liaoyuan
Yanji
Hunjiang
Shenyang

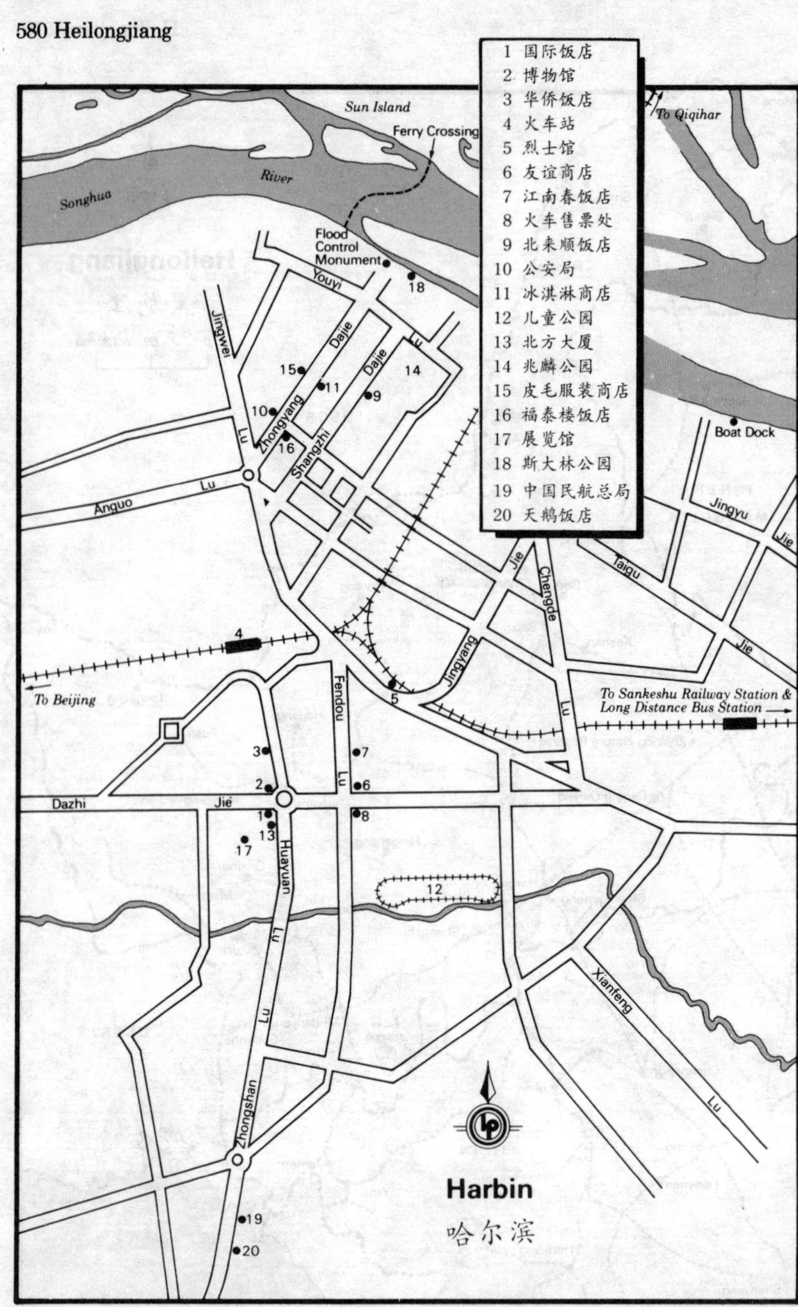
1 国际饭店
2 博物馆
3 华侨饭店
4 火车站
5 烈士馆
6 友谊商店
7 江南春饭店
8 火车售票处
9 北来顺饭店
10 公安局
11 冰淇淋商店
12 儿童公园
13 北方大厦
14 兆麟公园
15 皮毛服装商店
16 福泰楼饭店
17 展览馆
18 斯大林公园
19 中国民航总局
20 天鹅饭店
Sun Island
To Qiqihar
Ferry Crossing
Songhua
River
Flood Control Monument
Youyi
Jingwei
Dajie
Zhongyang
Lu
Shangzhi
Anguo
Boat Dock
Jingyu
Jie
Taigu
Chengde
Jingyang
To Beijing
To Sankeshu Railway Station &
Long Distance Bus Station
Fendou
Dazhi
Huayuan
Xianfeng
Zhongshan
Harbin
哈尔滨

1 International Hotel (Guoji Fandian)
2 Natural History & Science Museum
3 Overseas Chinese Hotel
4 Main Railway Station
5 Martyr's Museum
6 Friendship Store/Department Store
7 Jiangnanchun Restaurant
8 Advance Rail Ticket Office
9 Beilaishun Moslem Restaurant
10 Public Security Bureau
11 Ice-Cream Shop (Run by Harbin Hotel)
12 Children's Railway Park
13 Beifang Mansions
14 Zhaolin Park
15 Fur Shop
16 Futailou Restaurant
17 Industrial Exhibition Hall
18 Stalin Park
19 CAAC
20 Swan Hotel (Tian E Fandian)

shapes of animals, plants, buildings or motifs taken from legends. Some of the larger ones have included a crystalline ice bridge and an ice elephant that children could mount from the tail in order to slide down the trunk. At night the sculptures are illuminated from the inside, turning the place into a temporary fantasyland. Skiers can head for Shangzhi close to Harbin, but it's best to bring your own equipment and check first with CITS whether the lift is operating. In warmer times there's the Harbin Music Festival, a 12-day event that takes place in July (it was suspended during the Cultural Revolution).

Information

CITS (tel 31088) is in a separate building on the grounds of the Swan Hotel (Tian E Fandian), which is on the bus No 3 route. Several excellent English-speakers do their best to help, but independent backpackers may receive only standard information geared to the expensive group mentality. CITS can arrange specific tours for every conceivable taste, including elderly health build-up, bicycling, Chinese law, trade unions, steam locos, hunting, welding technology, honey production, abacus twiddling, etc. There are reportedly plans to promote Sino-Soviet and Sino-Japanese tourism through air connections between Harbin, Niigata, Khabarovsk and Irkutsk.

Public Security is on Zhongyang Dajie; see the map for directions.

CAAC (tel 52334) has its office at 87 Zhongshan Lu.

Things to See

Put wandering around the market areas and the streets high on your list. There's a very different kind of architectural presence in Harbin, with Soviet spires, cupolas and scalloped turreting; Zhongyang Lu and Sun Island are good to investigate.

Harbin has several dozen Orthodox churches, but most were sacked during the Cultural Revolution and have since been boarded up or converted to other uses. A few stray onion-domes punctuate the skyline in the Daoliqu district, which is the rectangle bounded by the Flood Control Monument, Zhaolin Park, the Public Security Bureau and the railway line.

The Daoliqu district, in the section toward the banks of the Songhua River, has the best specialty-type shops and some market activity, and is worth your time on foot. Another shopping and market area is to be found north-east of the Guoji Hotel, a short walk away at Dazhi Dajie.

Children's Railway

Located in the Children's Park, this railway was built in 1956. It has two km of track and is plied by a miniature diesel pulling seven cars with seating for 190; the round trip (Beijing-Moscow?) takes 20 minutes. The crew and administrators are kids under the age of 13.

Stalin Park

Down by the river, this is a tacky strip

stacked with statues, and it's the No 1 perambulating zone, with recreation clubs for Chinese. A 42-km embankment was constructed along the edge to curb the unruly Songhua River – hence the Flood Control Monument which was built in 1958. The sandy banks of the Songhua take on something of a beach atmosphere in summer, with boating, ice cream stands, photo booths. Tour boats arranged through CITS are possible but you might like to investigate local boat docks for a quick sortie down the Songhua.

During winter the Songhua River becomes a road of ice (when it's one metre thick it can support a truck) and the Stalin Park/Sun Island area is the venue for hockey, skating, ice-sailing, sledding and sleighing – equipment can be rented.

Sun Island

Opposite Stalin Park, and reached by a ferry hop, is Sun Island, a combo sanatorium/recreational zone still under construction. The island covers 3800 hectares and has a number of artificial features – a lake, hunting range, parks, gardens, forested areas – all being worked on to turn this into Harbin's biggest touring attraction. In summer there's swimming and picnics; in winter it's skating and other sports. There are a number of restaurants on Sun Island, and more facilities are planned.

Other Attractions/Non-Attractions

The **Retirement Home for Foreigners** (Waiqiao Yanglao Yuan) at No 1 Wenjing Jie is unique in China. Koreans, Americans, Japanese, Russians or stateless persons spend their last years here. Many of them have interesting tales to tell. On the street I met an old White Russian with streaked beard, blue eyes and gold teeth. This spritely resident of the home explained in broken Russian and Chinese how he had crossed Siberia in 1928 and reached Harbin with his father, who was shot soon after.

If you have not visited concentration camps such as Belsen or Auschwitz, a similar lesson in the horrors of extermination can be learnt at the **Japanese Germ Warfare Experimental Base – 731 Division** (Riben Xijun Shiyan Jidi – Qi San Yi Budui). Take bus No 38 from the main railway station to the terminus, which is close to Pingfang Qu. It may be necessary to apply for admission to the site from the nearby Foreign Affairs Department of the People's Government (Renmin Zhengfu Wai Shi Ke).

In 1939 the Japanese army set up a top-secret, germ warfare research centre here. Japanese medical experts experimented to their heart's content on Chinese, Soviet, Korean, British and other prisoners. Over four thousand were exterminated in bestial fashion: some were frozen or infected with bubonic plague, others were injected with syphilis and many were roasted alive in furnaces. When the Soviets took back Harbin in 1945, the Japanese hid all trace of the base. The secret would probably have remained buried forever, but a tenacious Japanese journalist dragged out the truth only recently. Japan's medical profession was rocked by the news that some of its leading members had a criminal past which had hitherto escaped detection. Another disturbing angle to the story was the claim that the Americans granted freedom to the perpetrators of these crimes in return for their research data.

The **Provincial Museum** is opposite the Guoji Hotel and has some boring historical and natural history sections; the **Industrial Exhibition Hall** is dead boring; the **zoo** is lukewarm but does have some Manchurian tigers and red-crowned cranes. The **Martyr's Museum** in the centre of town has relics from the anti-Japanese campaign.

Places to Stay

There are three hotels grouped in the same area, and you can take any bus (or even a rickety tram) on the road leading from the railway station to get there – alternatively, they're about a one-km walk.

The *Guoji Fandian (International*

Hotel) (tel 31441) is at 124 Dazhi Jie, Nangang District. It's got two wings, a new nine-storey high-rise and an old wing, but the latter has been renovated. The classy place charges Y60 to Y90 a double. For seekers of dormitories, abandon hope all ye who enter here – or bring out your boxing gloves because it's a guaranteed two-hour wrangle.

The *Overseas Chinese Hotel (Huaqiao Fandian)* is down the street from the International, and will take foreigners. Comfortable double rooms (without TVs) are Y36.

The *Beifang Dasha (Beifang Mansions)* (tel 33061) looks like the Kremlin – you can't miss it! Ten floors harbour 350 rooms, but the staff is not at all interested in foreigners; double rooms are Y36 if you can get one. The Beifang is at 115 Huayuan Lu, Nangang District.

The *Tian E Fandian (Swan Hotel)* (tel 54041) at 73 Zhongshan Lu is yet another glossy structure. Doubles cost a cool Y75. CITS is installed in the same compound. It's a long way from the station, so you'll probably need to take a taxi or ride five stops on bus No 2, which you can catch from the street (Hong Jun Jie) just past the International Hotel. My Italian friends who had survived a hotel skirmish in Jilin took an evening train to Harbin which was delayed a mere five hours. They took a taxi to this hotel and were turned away at 3 am by a porter who could hardly have known that he was facing experts in hotel combat. The Italians instantly regrouped, stormed the door with a flanking movement and raised both hell and the manager with the news that the PSB had sent them. The manager graciously offered them a luxury suite for Y120, but the exhausted foreigners finally settled on the couches in the lobby.

There are also several exclusive villa-style hotels in Harbin with billiards and all mod cons, but they're meant for foreign heads of government and the like. The Chinese Air Force has entered business here with the appropriately named Blue Sky Hotel (Lan Tian Binguan). Some additional tourist accommodation is proposed for Sun Island, and another proposal is a floating hotel – a converted 3000-ton liner.

Places to Eat

Within easy walking distance of the hotel locations on Dazhi Jie is a large back-street market with lots of snacks – it's big on sausage, bread and noodles. Also in this area is a large dinery, the *Jiangnanchun* (tel 34398), with dumplings downstairs and main fare upstairs, including roast duck and braised dishes. It's at 316 Fendou Jie, Nangang District.

There are a couple of places around Stalin Park; on the edge of Zhaolin Park at 113 Shangzhi Lu is the *Beilaishun Restaurant* (tel 45673) serving Muslim beef and mutton dishes upstairs and also hotpot in winter. The *Futailou Restaurant* (tel 47598) at 19 Xi Shisandao serves Beijing roast duck and other dishes, but you need to order two days in advance for regional specialties. The *Huamei Restaurant* (tel 47368) at 142 Zhongyang Lu serves western-style food.

For snacks, head to Zhongyang Lu, leading south off the Flood Control Monument. This is a quieter shopping area with pink, cream, mustard and grey Euro-style buildings. It's a quiet street – that is, until you reach *Hongxia Lengshibu*, a few blocks down from the monument on the west side. Candles, beer, sausage, bread and crates of bottles are stacked to the ceiling here – aye, matey, it's a Chinese pub! Well, about as close as you'll get to one this side of the Elephant & Castle. There are also several ice cream, keke and kafei places along Zhongyang, including a quaint greenhouse-type café that abuts the Harbin Hotel (the Harbin is a Chinese-only hotel). The glacé variety of ice cream is quite good.

As for the hotels, the *International* is riddled with dining rooms of all shapes, sizes and prices; anyone for grilled bear paws? Or some stewed moose nose with monkey-leg mushrooms? These and other elaborate delicacies are served up only in the banquet rooms. The front-section ground-floor dining room of the new wing serves western breakfasts for Y5. The *Beifang Mansion* has several restaurants and banquet rooms within.

Shopping

The Friendship Store is on the top floor of the Department Store on Dazhi Jie, but it has a measly selection. The Fur Product Shop on Zhongyang Lu has slightly lower prices and a larger fur selection than the Friendship Store (coats, vests, hats, gloves). Fur overcoats run from Y200 up (fox, squirrel, sable, some otter collars, sheepskin cushions). Harbin is the best place to buy furs.

Getting There & Away

Air From Harbin there are numerous flight connections, including Beijing (Y188), Canton (Y543), Mudanjiang (Y53), Jiamusi (Y55), Heihe (Y90), Changchun (Y38), Shanghai (Y379) and Shenyang (Y85). The airport is 35 km outside Harbin.

Bus There is a long-distance bus station near Sankeshu Railway Station which takes care of a large proportion of bus departures.

Rail For details of trains, see the introduction to the north-eastern provinces.

Boat Boat services operate from mid-April to late November. A regular service between Harbin and Jiamusi takes 27 hours and costs Y23.80 (1st class) or Y6.10 (5th class). Buy tickets from the boat dock on Bei Qidao Jie.

Getting Around

There are over 20 bus routes in Harbin; buses start running at 5 am and finish at 10 pm (9.30 pm in winter). Bus No 1 or trolley bus No 3 will take you from the hotel area to Stalin Park. CITS has a boat tour along the Songhua River which lasts 2½ hours and costs Y10 per head.

MUDANJIANG & LAKE JINGPO
牡丹江和镜泊湖

Mudanjiang is an industrial city of 700,000 to the south-east of Harbin. The main reason for coming here is Jingpo (Mirror) Lake, 110 km south-west of Mudanjiang. If you have to spend a night in Mudanjiang, turn left outside the station and walk for 15 minutes to the *Mudanjiang Binguan*, opposite a large park with a lake. Doubles start here at Y65, but an hour's bargaining achieved a reduction to Y42.

During the summer (June to September) buses to the lake leave between 6 and 7 am from the square in front of Mudanjiang station. Tickets cost Y6 one way or Y8 return. You can buy them a day in advance from a booth at the far side of the square or roll up early the same day to get the unsold seats. The bus trip provides more interest than the lake. Geese, donkeys, ducks, sheep, goats; just about everything with wings or hooves seemed hell-bent on suicide beneath the wheels of the bus. Later we passed an accident where a bus had wiped out a jeep which had then rammed a tree. The next horrific apparitions were two monstrous lumber trucks, travelling at top speed, which were losing their loads of giant tree trunks and side-swiping everything else on the road. Our brilliant driver took violent evasive action and the tree-trunks missed by an inch. Ten minutes later we stopped to aid a bus full of locals in bright Korean dress which had evaded the lumber monsters by diving nose-first into the mud.

The lake itself covers an area of 90 square km; it's 45 km long from north to south, with a minimum width of 600 metres and a maximum of six km, and is dotted with islets. The nature reserve encompasses a strip of forest, hills, pools and cliffs around the lake and there is a lava cave in the area. The main pastime is fishing (the season is June to August), and tackle and boats can be rented for Y30 to Y40 a day; different varieties of carp (silver, black, red-tailed, crucian) are the trophies. Wandering through the jostling mob of photo posers, litter-collectors and knick-knack sellers, I heartily agreed with a Mudanjiang resident's candid opinion that Jingpo Lake is extremely puny compared to the splendour of Qinghai Lake.

The name 'Mirror Lake' comes from a legend related to a wicked king who sent his minister out every week to find a beautiful girl – if the girl wasn't the right material, he'd have her killed. A passing monk gave the king a mirror to aid in the selection, saying that this mirror would retain the reflection of a true beauty, even after she turned away. The minister duly trotted off, found a beautiful girl at the lake, and discovered that the mirror test worked. The king immediately asked for the lady's hand. 'What is the most precious thing in the world?' asked the girl. The king thought for some time; 'Power' he replied. Upon hearing this, the girl threw the mirror into the lake, a storm broke out, and she vanished.

Places to Stay

The centre of operations is *Jingpo Villa*, at the north end of the lake. Double rooms start from Y30. Boat cruises cost Y2 round trip and there is a small beach nearby. The smallish Mansion Falls (20 metres high, 40 metres wide) is north of Jingpo Villa and within easy hiking distance of it.

Getting There & Away

Mudanjiang is linked by rail to Tianjin and Beijing (via Harbin), with two or three trains a day. There are also slower connections by rail to Tumen (about six hours, one train a day), Suifenhe (over five hours, one train a day) and Jiamusi (about 10 hours, two trains a day).

While I was hunting for train tickets at Mudanjiang station, a friendly drunk offered to help. He said he was a truck driver who often delivered lumber into the Soviet Union at Suifenhe. Just as he was joyfully getting the wrong end of the stick and assuming he'd found a drinking partner from the Soviet side, two railway policemen (one uniformed, the other plain-clothes) shoved us both into a side-room. After inspecting my passport, they allowed me to go, but the poor drunk was detained while his wife and young daughter stood outside the door wondering what had happened to him in the space of a minute's conversation with a barbarian.

SUIFENHE 绥芬河

This town achieved commercial importance in 1903 with the opening of the South Manchurian Railway, which was a vital link in the original Trans-Siberian route running from Vladivostok to Moscow via Manchuria. The railway was later re-routed via Khabarovsk to Vladivostok and Nakhodka. In recent years, cross-border trade has livened up here again with even a trickle of Soviet tourism. The grandiose nickname of 'Little Moscow of the East' is certainly appropriate for the Russian atmosphere in Suifenhe, but there's little else to do unless you like a lusty Sino-Soviet friendship evening when, according to a local tourist brochure, Soviet visitors sing 'Evening in Suburban Moscow'. Although the whole place is Chinese, most of the buildings are Russian left-overs in the elegant, gingerbread style from the turn of the century – a place for pre-revolutionary memories. There's one train daily at 6.45 am from Mudanjiang to Suifenhe; the trip takes about six hours and returns from Suifenhe at 1.12 pm.

WUDALIANCHI 五大连池

Wudalianchi ('the five large connected lakes') is a nature reserve and health spot which has also been turned into a 'volcano museum'. To get there, take a six-hour train ride northwards from Harbin to Bei'an, where there are regular buses covering the 60 km to the lakes.

This area has a long history of volcanic activity. The most recent eruptions were during 1719 to 1720, when lava from craters blocked the nearby Beihe River and formed this series of five barrier lakes. The malodorous mineral springs are the source of legendary cures and thus the No 1 attraction for hordes of chronically sick who slurp the waters or slap mud onto themselves. To increase blood pressure, immerse your feet in a basin of the water; to decrease blood pressure, immerse your head. Baldness, cerebral haemorrhages, skin diseases and gastric ulcers are a few of the ailments helped by drinking the water or applying mud packs.

HEILONGJIANG RIVER BORDERLANDS
黑龙江边境

Much of the north-eastern border between China and the Soviet Union follows the course of the Heilongjiang (Black Dragon) River, also known to the Soviets as the Amur River. Several places along this river have recently been opened to foreigners, so it should now be possible to see some Siberian forest and the dwindling settlements of Siberian tribes such as the Oroqen, Ewenki, Hezhen and Daur. In Harbin the CITS office confirmed that they will be running boat tours between Huma, Heihe and Tongjiang. Telescopes on the boats will let you take a closer look at Soviet settlements or even Blagoveshchensk, a large Soviet port opposite Heihe.

Assuming you have at least two weeks to spare and are flexible about transport, an independent trip should also be viable during the summer – take some iron rations and insect repellent. Connections between Harbin and this region include the fast option of a flight to Heihe, the much slower option of a train at least as far as Jagdaqi, possibly further, and, of course, buses – God bless the old bangers! – to the ends of the wilderness. Remember, this is a border region where it's best to tread softly since Caucasian features can easily be mistaken for those of a visitor from the other side.

Jagdaqi

This is the administrative centre of the Oroqen Autonomous Banner in the region of the Greater Hinggan Mountain Range. From this reportedly unexciting rail junction, now open to foreigners, it may be possible to make side trips. An express train runs once daily from Harbin via Qiqihar to Jagdaqi, in about 14 hours.

Mohe

Natural wonders are the attraction at Mohe, China's northernmost town, sometimes known as the 'Arctic of China'. In mid-June, the sun is visible in the sky for as long as 22 hours. The Northern Lights (aurora borealis) are another colourful phenomenon seen in the sky at Mohe. China's lowest absolute temperature of -52°C was recorded here in 1965; on normal winter days temperatures of -40°C are common.

The PSB in Jagdaqi could be worth a try for a permit. To reach Mohe would require a rail trip north from Jagdaqi to Gulian, followed by a 34-km bus ride.

During May 1987, the Greater Hinggan Mountain Range was devastated by China's worst forest fire in living memory. The towns of Mohe and Xilinji were completely gutted, more than 200 people died and over one million hectares of forest were destroyed.

Shiba Zhan

In 1887 news of a fabulous gold strike at Laojingou ('old gold gully') close to Shiba Zhan prompted the empress dowager to order the regional governor to exploit the find immediately. The governor sailed off by boat and transferred to sedan chair on land. The sequence of his nightly stops was given numbers which are still used (Shiba Zhan translates as Post No 18). This is also a settlement centre for the Oroqens.

Huma

Mineral deposits around Huma recently attracted interest when a local gold miner found China's largest single piece of gold, weighing 50 grams. Huma can be reached by continuing north from Jagdaqi to Tahe by train and then taking a bus for 60 km to Shiba Zhan. From Shiba Zhan it's 91 km to Huma by bus or boat.

Heihe

Heihe is now open to foreigners. The quickest access between Harbin and Heihe is the plane (Y90) on Mondays and Fridays. It's a small Antonov, so seats should be booked in advance. Boats also connect Heihe with Mohe and Tongjiang.

The Oroqen minority lived, until recently, the nomadic life of forest hunters. Present estimates put their numbers at about 4000, although they are scattered over a vast area. The traditional tent, called a *xianrenzhu*, is covered with birch-bark in the summer and deerskin in the winter. Hunting and the raising of reindeer are still their main activities. A major source of income is deer hunting since the deer's embryo, antlers, penis and tail are highly prized in Chinese medicine. Lifestyle is changing rapidly for the Oroqens, although they retain self-sufficiency: boots, clothes and sleeping bags are made from deerskins; baskets, eating utensils and canoes are made from birch-bark; horses or reindeer provide transport. Their food consists mostly of meat, fish and wild plants. Oroqens are particularly fond of raw deer liver washed down with fermented mare's milk. Meat is often preserved by drying and smoking.

Interesting facets of their religion included (and probably still do to a lesser degree) a belief in spirits and the consulting of shamans. It was once taboo to kill bears. If this happened, perhaps in self-defence, a complicated rite was performed to ask the bear's 'forgiveness' and its bones were spread in the open on a tall frame of willow branches. This 'wind burial' was also the standard funeral for an Oroqen. 'Shaman' is a word meaning an 'agitated or frenzied person' in the Manchu-Tungus language. Such persons could enter a trance, become 'possessed' by a spirit and then officiate at religious ceremonies.

It's hard to determine how much of their culture the Oroqens have kept. Official publications trumpet stories of a wondrous change from primitive nomadism to settled consumerism. The following extract from a *China Daily* article about sedentary Oroqen at Shiba Zhan in 1986 clearly demonstrates the Han assumption that they know what's best for a minority:

'Meng Pinggu, a venerable senior citizen in the community, started hunting at age 12. At his home, bear skins and a hunting rifle hang on the walls, and a birch canoe is under the eaves. But a colour TV set and washing machine overshadow the old furniture.

Meng has shifted from hunting to forestry. In the evening, the family watches TV. "Now we Oroqens can see movies at home", he said.'

The Oroqens – China's Nomadic Hunters by Qiu Pu (Foreign Languages Press, Beijing, 1983) is a surprisingly informative publication, providing you skip the political salad dressing.

Tongjiang

Tongjiang lies at the junction of the Songhuajiang and Heilongjiang rivers and was recently opened to foreigners. The rivers meet and swell to a combined width of 10 km but the respective colours of the rivers, black for the Heilong and yellow for the Songhua, don't mix until later.

The Hezhen minority, numbering a mere 1300, lives almost entirely from fishing in this region. A local delicacy is sliced, raw fish with a spicy vinegar sauce. Apart from carp and salmon, the real whopper here is the huso sturgeon *(huang yu)* which can grow as long as three metres and weigh up to 500 kg!

Tongjiang has boat and bus connections with Jiamusi; boats also connect with Heihe.

Fuyuan

The earliest sunrise in China starts at 2 am in Fuyuan; at the same time, the locals in Kashgar (China's westernmost city) in Xinjiang Province are tucking into their kebabs for dinner. Close to Fuyuan is the junction of the Heilongjiang and Ussuri rivers. On the Soviet side is the city of Khabarovsk; on the Chinese side, there's the tiny outpost of Wusu which has 20 inhabitants who see visitors only during the salmon season in September.

JIAMUSI 佳木斯

North-west of Harbin is Jiamusi. Once a fishing village, it mushroomed into a city of half a million, and now deals in aluminium smelting, farm equipment manufacture and sugar refining, and has a paper mill, plastics factory and electrical appliances factory.

Among the sights are **Sumuhe Farm**, located in the suburbs of Jiamusi. This farm grows ginseng and raises over 700 head of sika and red deer for the antlers. Martens, close kin to the weasel family, are also raised. It's not really such a strange combination – in fact the 'three treasures' of the north-east are ginseng, deer antlers and sable pelts. Each of these are also well represented further south in Jilin Province, where production is largely domesticated. The magic properties of ginseng are peddled in a wide range of Jilin products, from cosmetics to wines. Use of the ginseng root dates back to the Han Dynasty, 1700 years ago. It's a general pep-tonic and life-lengthener, and is thought to be helpful in dealing with 'women's problems'. Deer pilose antler, cut into wafers or powdered, is claimed to benefit internal organs, and improve horniness and performance. If ginseng and deer antler are combined in tablet form the earth is yours, and it will take care of bladder disorders and nightmares (is there a relation between the two?). Wild ginseng from the Changbai Shan area fetches astronomical sums on the Hong Kong market.

Other curious items in the north-eastern pharmacopoeia include frog oil, taken from a substance in the frog's ovary. These and other entries will arrive in soups or with stewed chicken if a banquet is ordered at a ritzy hotel. (Non-banquet food, on grease-laden dining tables, is abysmal in the north-east region, so a visit to the local medicine shop is obligatory for stays of more than a week's duration).

The **New Friendship Farm** is about 110 km east of Jiamusi on the rail line, a state-run frontier enterprise that is the pride of Heilongjiang – the pioneers who built it arrived in the 1950s and now number around 100,000, organised into numerous agricultural brigades.

The **Village of Fools** is not the pride of Heilongjiang; it's in Huachuan County to the east and north-east of Jiamusi. The cretins and bearers of bulbous goitre are being studied at Jiamusi Medical College – the cause of their problems is suspected to be dietary deficiencies.

Getting There & Away

Jiamusi is connected by rail to Harbin (15 hours), Dalian and Mudanjiang. Steamers ply the Songhua River so it may be possible to travel between Harbin and Jiamusi by water. There are also flights between Harbin and Jiamusi.

DAQING 大庆

Daqing is an oil boom town which appeared on the swamplands in 1960. This is one of those triumph of the spirit towns, and a demonstration of China's awesome ability to mobilise manpower for the cause. The first drilling began in the 1950s with Soviet technical assistance; when the Russians withdrew in 1959, the Chinese decided to carry on alone. Shortly after, the first well gushed, and a community of tents, wooden shanties and mud housing erupted in the sub-zero wilderness. By 1975, Daqing was supplying 80% of the PRC's crude oil; production has since tapered off to less than 50%. Most of the oil is piped to the coast near Dalian.

Daqing is an industrial model – 'In industry, learn from Daqing' being one of the oft-repeated slogans – but whether much is being done to alleviate the harsh conditions of the Daqing workers is another question. In the late 1970s large sums of money were pumped into this vast sprawl of refineries, petrochemical plants and agricultural centres for the construction of apartment blocks. The figure given is 20,000 families accommodated – a drop in the bucket for a population of 760,000. The rest wait out the Manchurian winter in their mud or wood sheds.

There's no downtown in Daqing as such – there are some 8000 oil wells scattered throughout the 5000-square-km area with small communities attached. Saertu, however, serves as the administrative, economic and cultural sector, with residential and office buildings, library, stores, modernisation playground, exhibition halls and greenhouses. There's a spartan hotel in Saertu, and you may be allowed to view model bits of the Daqing area such as medical facilities, school or recreational props.

YICHUN 伊春

Towns in the north-east are either built of mud, or in transition to brick buildings (minus the plumbing). Yichun falls into the former category, a real frontier town hacked out of the forest in the 1950s, and still in progress, with adobe housing, horse carts, mud, pigs and slime. It's a logging town (pine, maple, oak and birch in the surrounding forest tracts) with a timber-processing plant; some of the timber tracts are protected from logging. Yichun's population is about 100,000 – the place is actually a number of isolated settlements with Yichun as the focal point.

Yichun is linked by rail to Jiamusi and to Harbin (two trains a day between April and September, and the trip to Harbin takes about 12 hours).

QIQIHAR & THE ZHALONG NATURE RESERVE 齐齐哈尔与札龙自然保护站

Qiqihar is one of the oldest settlements in the north-east. It's another industrial town, with a population of over a million, dealing with locomotives, mining equipment, steel, machine tools and motor vehicles. There's not much to see here: a zoo, a stretch of riverside and the ice-carving festival from January to March. The *Hubin Hotel* is close to the railway station and double rooms start from Y42. CITS (tel 72016) is at 2 Wenhua Lu. The town is linked by direct rail to Beijing (about 22 hours) via Harbin (about four hours).

Qiqihar is the gateway to the Zhalong Nature Reserve, 35 km to the south-east, linked by a brand-new road – though there's not much traffic along it and you may have to resort to hitching or getting a taxi. The modest *Zhalong Hotel* has double rooms for Y42, and offers touring through the freshwater marshes of the reserve for Y40 per day, in flat-bottom boats.

The Zhalong Reserve is at the north-west tip of a giant marshland, made up of about 210,000 hectares of reeds, moss and ponds. It lies strategically on a bird migration path which extends from the Soviet Arctic, around the Gobi Desert, and down into South-East Asia and some 180 different species of bird are found there including storks, swans, geese, ducks, herons, grebes and egrets. The tens of thousands of winged migrants arrive in April to May, rear their young June to August, and depart September to October. Birds will be birds – they value their privacy. While some of the cranes are over 1.5 metres tall, the reed cover is taller. The area is mainly of interest to the patient binoculared and rubber-booted ornithologist.

The nature reserve, one of China's first, was set up in 1979. In 1981 the Chinese Ministry of Forestry invited Dr George Archibald (director of the ICF, the International Crane Foundation) and Wolf Brehm (director of Vogelpark Walsrode, West Germany) to help set up a

crane centre at Zhalong. Of the 15 species of cranes in the world, eight are found in China, and six are found at Zhalong. Four of the species that migrate here are on the endangered list: the red-crowned crane, the white-naped crane, the Siberian crane and the hooded crane. Both the red-crowned and white-naped cranes breed at Zhalong (as do the common and demoiselle cranes), while hooded and Siberian cranes use Zhalong as a stopover.

The centre of attention is the red-crowned crane, a fragile creature whose numbers at Zhalong (estimated to be 100 in 1979) were threatened by drainage of the wetlands for farming. The near-extinct bird is, ironically, the ancient symbol of immortality and has long been a symbol of longevity and good luck in the Chinese, Korean and Japanese cultures. With some help from overseas experts, the eco-system at Zhalong has been studied and improved, and the number of these rare birds has risen. A small number of hand-reared (domesticated) red-crowned and white-naped cranes are kept in a pen at the sanctuary for viewing and study. On the eve of their 'long march' southwards in October, large numbers of cranes can be seen wheeling around, as if in farewell. The birds have been banded to unlock the mystery of their winter migration grounds (thought to be either Korea or southern China).

Since the establishment of the International Crane Foundation George Archibald and Ron Sauey have managed to create a 'crane bank' in Wisconsin, USA, stocking 14 of the 15 known species. They've even convinced the North Koreans to set up bird preserves in the mine-studded demilitarised zone between North and South Korea, and the travel baggage of these two includes suitcases full of Siberian crane-eggs picked up in Moscow (on one trip a chick hatched en route was nicknamed 'Aeroflot'). Last on the egg-list for the ICF is the black-necked crane, whose home is in remote Tibet and for whom captive breeding may be the final hope.

THE SOUTH-WEST

★

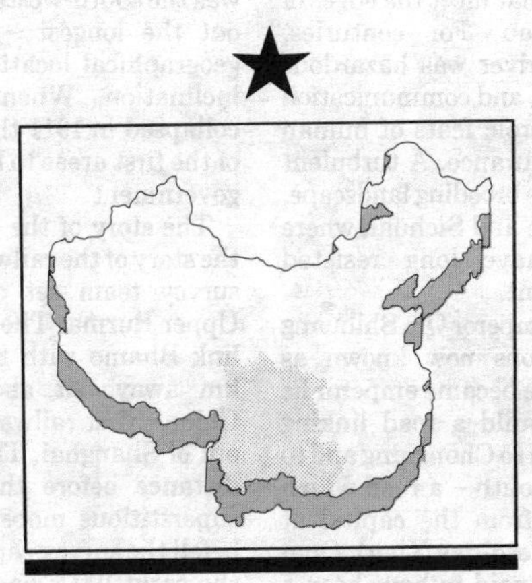

Introduction

The south-west of China is a region of immense mountains and precipitous cliffs covered by dense sub-tropical forests, and cut through by mountain rivers fed by melting snows. This is China's backyard jungle, with fertile basins, exotic flora and fauna, rapids, jagged limestone pinnacles, caverns, and peaks that meet the edges of the Tibetan Plateau. For centuries, communication by river was hazardous because of the rapids, and communication by road assumed heroic feats of human engineering and endurance. A turbulent history lies behind the brooding landscape, especially in Yunnan and Sichuan where tribal kingdoms have long resisted colonial encroachment.

The ancestors of Emperor Qin Shihuang conquered the regions now known as Sichuan, and after he became emperor he had his engineers build a road linking what is now Chengdu to Chongqing and to the regions further south – a road which stretched 1600 km from the capital at Xianyang (near modern-day Xian). One-third of its length is said to have been a 1.5-metre-wide wooden balcony cantilevered out from the sheer cliff, supported by wooden brackets driven into the rock face. Despite this new means of communication, and the creation (on paper) of new administrative divisions, the chiefs of the people south of Sichuan in the areas now known as Guizhou and Yunnan continued to rule the region themselves. In the later Han period these chiefs were given titles and ranks as tribute bearers to the imperial court, and gifts of silk in return for 'protecting' the southern borders of the Chinese empire – but their loyalty to the empire was mainly an invention of the Han and later Chinese historians.

After the fall of the Han Dynasty another 1000 years was to pass before much of the south-west could be effectively integrated into the empire, and even then it continued to revert to independence at every opportunity. In the mid-13th century the region was almost pounded into final submission – this time by the Mongol armies of Mangu Khan. When the Mongol rule collapsed in 1368 the south-western regions once again broke with the north; Sichuan was won back by a Ming military expedition in 1371 and Yunnan the following year. Again, when the Manchus invaded in the 17th century it was the south-western regions which held out the longest – partly due to their geographical location and partly due to inclination. When the Qing Dynasty collapsed in 1911 the south-west was one of the first areas to break with the central government.

The story of the modern south-west is the story of the railways. In 1875, a British survey team set out from Bhamo, in Upper Burma. The British dream was to link Bhamo with Shanghai, easily 3000 km away. At about the same time, China's first railway tracks were coming out of Shanghai. They proceeded a short distance before they were torn up by superstitious mobs; an even worse fate befell the survey captain from Bhamo. By the early 1900s various foreign gauges – Russian, Japanese, Anglo-American, German, Belgian-French – were running from the treaty ports as far as was necessary to trade and to exploit raw materials, but the south-west was almost forgotten. The only spur was a narrow-gauge French line, completed in 1910, linking Hanoi with Kunming. During WW II another spur was added in Guangxi, trailing off toward Guizhou. The first major link was the Baoji-Chengdu line (1956), which connected with the Chengdu-Chongqing line (1952), and thus with what for centuries was the south-west's lifeline, the Yangtse River.

The railway lines that today's travellers take for granted were completed with great difficulty and loss of life over the past two decades. More than 5000 km of added track have sliced literally months off travel time in the south-west. The crowning achievement is the Kunming-Chengdu line, some 12 years in the making (finished 1970), boring through solid rock, bridging deep ravines and treacherous rivers.

Apart from Sichuan, the south-west region is relatively underpopulated, and since its (substantial) natural resources remain largely untapped, the mainstay is agriculture. Its industrial contribution to China as a whole is therefore negligible. The opening of the Chengdu-Kunming line has boosted various industries (including iron, steel, farm machinery and chemical fertilisers) in the cities along the way. It has also caused a gravitation of population to the railway havens. This railway line can be added to China's list of impossible projects that have become fact.

TRAVEL IN THE SOUTH-WEST

Trains – the Horrors of Hard-Seat Travel

Trains in the south-west are a pain in the arse. The problems arise, as they always do, with hard-class seating. No person in his or her right mind would want to endure hard-seat for more than 12 hours – although some masochistic travellers have survived 48-hour ordeals and arrived somewhat dazed, to put it mildly. Hard-sleeper is very comfortable (no crowding permitted), but the tickets may require as much as four days of waiting to get. In a place like Kunming, where you're likely to spend several days anyway, this is OK – just book a ticket out of the place immediately upon arrival.

If you wish to speed things up and carry on regardless, there are very low chances of upgrading your hard-seat to a hard-sleeper once on the train – this is eminently possible in northern China but not in the south-west. Soft-class sleepers will be available, but most low-budget travellers find them prohibitively expensive. You could try for a soft-seat, which is about the same price as a hard-sleeper ticket, but the trains in the south-west don't seem to carry this class very much.

Apart from lack of sleepers, crowding is another big problem. Sichuan has the highest population of any province in China, and Yunnan has the fewest rail lines, so at times it seems that the whole quarter of humankind is hurtling down those tracks. Often the train is packed out before it even gets to the south-west, having loaded up in Shanghai (the No 79 Shanghai-Kunming express is a good example – if you get on board at Guilin you have about zero hope of getting a hard-sleeper, and you may not even get a soft-sleeper).

On some trains hard-seat carriages have people hanging from the rafters, watering their turtles in the wash basins, spitting everywhere. On one train two westerners almost came to fisticuffs with locals over musical chairs (unreserved section). If a foreigner got up to go to the toilet, a local would take the seat and refuse to budge; if the same displaced foreigner tried to pull the same stunt, all hell would break loose. At night, people are toe to toe in the aisles, or curled in foetal positions on the furniture. Hong Kongers refer to a phenomenon known as 'fishing' – which is when your head bobs up and down all night, with intermittent jerks. A jerk of a ruder nature – an Australian, supine under a hard seat, woke up in the middle of the night and discovered to his horror that some Yellow River was coming his way from the child above.

One has to retain one's sense of humour in such situations – it pays to distract yourself. Compensation can be found in the scenery, which is sheer magnificence for much of the route – you should try and travel by day as much as possible to downplay the discomfort of night. The Chengdu-Baoji train, for my money, was one of the most scenic rides. The Kunming-Chengdu route I found to be a disappointment: engineering marvel that it is, it has tunnels every few metres (427 tunnels and 653 bridges to be exact, 40% of the route) – and these plunge one into a darkness that precludes any attempt to talk, read or view the landscape. I made good use of the tunnels, however. I had gained some facility at Chinese chess on my travels, and had ingratiated myself into a window seat. My opponent had the largest tea mug I'd ever seen – it must've held a gallon – and he kept foisting food on me at an alarming rate. It's rude to say no – but the peanuts were the kind that break on your teeth, and the grey dumplings had fingerprints all over them. Each time we hit a tunnel, I simply hurled the dumplings over my shoulder and out the window – and spilled the peanuts to the floor.

Since the actual act of travelling in the south-west eats up so much of your time there, some strategy is called for. It's better to stop in fewer places, get to know people and leave time for decent train reservations (intermediary stations are not empowered to issue hard-sleeper tickets). If you're really in a bind in hard-class seating, and you've had all you can take, consider getting off at some intermediary station; tickets can be valid for up to seven days, and no re-purchase is necessary – you just use the same ticket to hop back on the next train heading in your direction. You'll be back in the same situation on the next train, but at least you'll get a refreshing night's sleep out of the stop (the 1st-class waiting room at the station can be wonderfully comfortable upon a midnight arrival). Another booster is to hang out in the dining-car after the rabble has been through – the staff may let you stay or they may kick you out, but it's worth a try – regale the staff with English lessons on food terminology.

Provisioning on south-west trains is not the greatest – you should stock up like a squirrel for the long journey ahead where possible (coffee, fruit, bread, chocolate?).

Itineraries

Distances are stretched in the south-west (Guangzhou to Kunming is 2216 km by rail) and the only way to speed it up is to shove an airplane in there somewhere or cut out destinations. The well-worn (and proven) route is to take a boat from Canton to Wuzhou, then a bus to Guilin, and then to travel by train Guiyang-Kunming-Emei-Chengdu-Chongqing. From Chongqing people usually take the Yangtse ferry to Yichang or further. You can also proceed directly from Guiyang to Chongqing, and another option is to bypass the Yangtse trip and head directly to Xian from Chengdu.

Approximate rail prices can be calculated using the distance tables in the Getting Around section of this book.

A favourite plane trip is Canton to Guilin; it costs only Y99 (the cost can be made up anyway by changing money on the black market in Guilin), and gives you an amazing view of the landscape as you fly in. The view is virtually guaranteed since CAAC will not take off if there is a rain cloud in the sky (though that can lead to lengthy delays). One of the newer services for tourists in Guilin is a flight over the karst formations – but you can get an aerial tour by flying there in the first place. You should also remember that the train ride from Canton to Guilin takes 20 hours(!) while flying takes 1½. The other useful flight is Guilin-Kunming, which costs Y154 and takes 1½ hours as compared with 33 hours on the railways. A hard-sleeper ticket will cost you around Y40 (Chinese price) – if you can get Chinese price, and if any hard-sleepers are available.

An unexplored option is boating. The hovercraft from Hong Kong considerably speeds up the trip to Wuzhou, and from Wuzhou it should be possible to navigate to Nanning (this would be a very slow trip, but possibly a scenic one – larger boats anchor in midstream due to difficulties with rapids). An exit to consider is the flight from Kunming to Bangkok or Rangoon.

Guangxi 广西

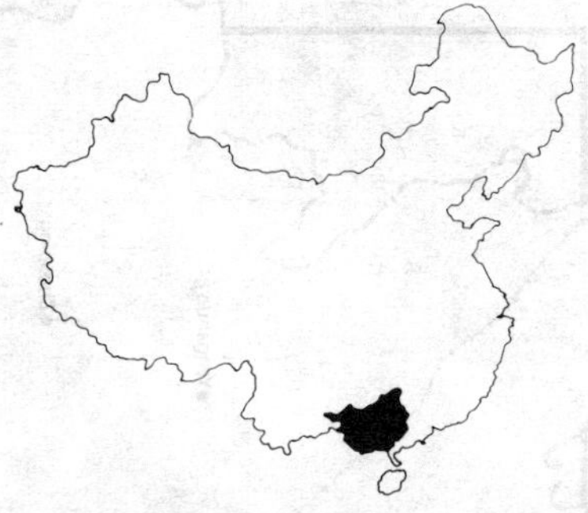

Guangxi first came under Chinese sovereignty when a Qin army was sent southwards in 214 BC to conquer what is now Guangdong Province and eastern Guangxi. Like the rest of the south-west the region was never firmly under the Chinese foot; the eastern and southern parts of Guangxi were occupied by the Chinese, while a system of indirect rule through chieftains of the aboriginal Zhuang people prevailed in the west.

The situation was complicated in the northern regions by the Yao and Miao tribespeople, who had been driven there from their homelands in Hunan and Jiangxi by the advance of the Han Chinese settlers. Unlike the Zhuang who easily assimilated Chinese customs, the Yao and Miao remained in the hill regions, often cruelly oppressed by the Han. There was continuous trouble with the tribes, with major uprisings in the 1830s and another coinciding with the Taiping Rebellion.

Today China's largest minority, the Zhuang, well over 13 million people, is concentrated in Guangxi. They're virtually indistinguishable from the Han Chinese. The last outward vestige of their original identity is their linguistic links with the Thai. Back in 1955 Guangxi Province was reconstituted as the Guangxi Zhuang Autonomous Region; the total population numbers about 40 million people.

The province remained a comparatively poor one until the present century. The first attempts at some modernisation of Guangxi were made during 1926-27 when the 'Guangxi Clique' (the main opposition to Chiang Kaishek within the Kuomintang) controlled much of Guangdong, Hunan, Guangxi and Hubei. After the outbreak of war with Japan the province was the scene of major battles and substantial destruction.

On a more pleasant note Guangxi also has Guilin, one of China's great drawcards and the jumping-off point for exploring the bizarre landscape for which the region is famous. If Guilin seems too congested there's always the backpackers' mecca of Yangshuo, a couple of hours down the Li River.

WUZHOU 梧州

Situated at major and minor river junctions, Wuzhou was an important trading town in the 18th century. In 1897 the British dived in there, setting up steamer services to Canton, Hong Kong and later Nanning. A British consulate was established – which gives some idea of the town's importance as a trading centre at the time – and the town was also used by British and American missionaries as a launching pad to convert the heathen Chinese.

Post-1949 saw some industrial development with the establishment of a paper mill, food-processing factories, and machinery and plastics manufacturing among other industries. During the Cultural Revolution, Guilin and the nearby towns appear to have become battlegrounds for rivals, both claiming loyalty to Mao. In what must have been more like a civil war half the town was reportedly destroyed.

Today, Wuzhou has large snake depositories, probably the one thing of interest, but it's unknown if you can see these. More than one million snakes are transported annually to Wuzhou (from places like Nanning, Liuzhou and Yulin)

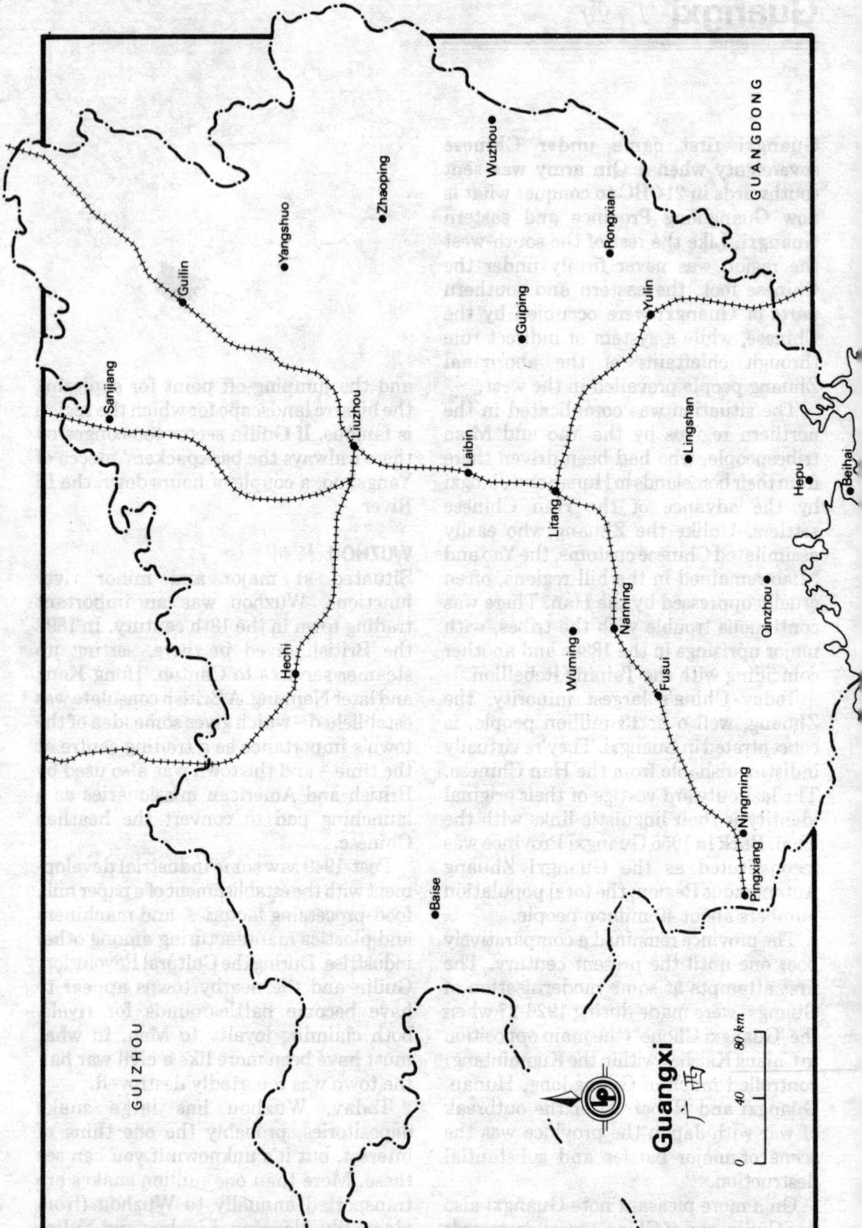

Guangxi 广西
0 40 80 km
GUANGDONG
GUIZHOU
Wuzhou
Zhaoping
Yangshuo
Guilin
Rongxian
Guiping
Yulin
Sanjiang
Liuzhou
Laibin
Lingshan
Litang
Hepu
Beihai
Nanning
Qinzhou
Wuming
Hechi
Fusui
Ningming
Pingxiang
Baise

for export to the palates of Hong Kong, Macau and other countries. Wuzhou also has some fine street markets, tailors, tobacco, herbs, roast duck and riverlife to explore. If you need a corn or wart removed then this is the place to come. Sidewalk beauticians armed with blades, needles and solutions will whip the nasties out in a jiffy, much to the interest of the crowd of onlookers.

For the most part travellers use Wuzhou as a stopover on the popular trip from Canton to Guilin/Yangshuo – boat from Canton to Wuzhou and then bus to Yangshuo or Guilin. A walk in Wuzhou turns up some unusual sights. Check out the industrial and residential areas on the west bank if you've got the time. The river level rises as much as 20 metres during the summer monsoon rains, which is why the town is perched high up on the banks.

Information

The post office is on Nanhuan Lu, just before the bridge. Good maps of the city, with bus routes, are available from shops in the town centre.

Places to Stay

The *He Bin Hotel* (also written *Ho Bin*) is a 20-minute walk from the long-distance bus station or the boat dock (if arriving by bus, check with the driver if the hotel is on his route – he could drop you off there). To get to the hotel walk north up the main road by the bus station and turn left at Nanhuan Lu; the hotel is over the bridge. It's a big concrete block, on the sleazy side. A bed in a four-bed hole in the dungeon is Y5.50 but overhead fans make it half-bearable. Better rooms are available upstairs from Y22 a double, but every corridor has a thundering television.

If you're going to spend more than a night in Wuzhou, I'd seriously suggest you look around town for another hotel. Some possibilities are the *Yuan Jiang Hotel* on Xijiang Yilu by the waterfront (see map) which has triple rooms with bathroom for Y40. Triples without bathroom are Y27. This hotel has been known to take foreigners. The same work unit runs the *Guo Ying Hotel* nearby.

Places to Eat

There's no shortage of small restaurants. Try the cheap places opposite the Ho Bin Hotel; the people are friendly and the servings generous. The illuminated mirages by the riverbank are floating restaurants a la Aberdeen (Hong Kong) with extravagant names such as *Water City Paradise*. If that doesn't appeal to you, there are other small restaurants along the east bank of the Gui River on Guijiang Erlu.

Getting There & Away

Bus From Wuzhou's long-distance bus station there are two buses a day to Yangshuo (Y11) and Guilin (Y13). There are daily departures to Nanning (Y17) and Canton (Y11).

Alternatively, take an air-con bus to Nanning or Yangshuo. Tickets can be bought from the booth outside the Ho Bin Hotel, or from vendors near the long-distance bus station. Fares are about Y3 more than for the ordinary buses. It's really only worth it if the passengers keep the windows of the bus closed (which is unlikely unless the weather is bad).

All buses leave early in the morning. The trip from Wuzhou to Yangshuo takes seven hours, with another two hours to Guilin. The scenically impressive marathon from Wuzhou to Nanning takes 15 hours. A tolerance of Bony M, bad '60s pop and other muzak is advised on the air-con buses.

Boat There are daily hovercraft between Wuzhou and Hong Kong; for details see the Getting There chapter at the start of this book. Tickets can be bought from the booking office just east of Wuzhou's long-distance bus station. This office also sells tickets for the ferries to Canton and Zhaoqing.

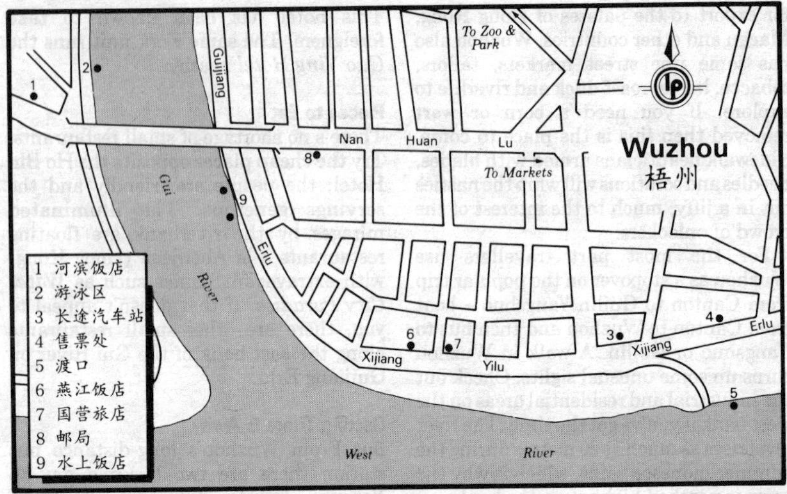

1 Ho Bin Hotel
2 Swimming Enclosure
3 Long-distance Bus Station
4 Booking Office
5 Ferry Dock
6 Yuan Jiang Hotel
7 Guo Ying Hotel
8 Post Office
9 Floating Restaurants

GUILIN 桂林

Guilin has always been famous in China for its scenery and has been eulogised in innumerable literary works, paintings and inscriptions since its founding. For many western visitors Guilin *is* the landscape of China. For the Chinese it's the most beautiful spot in the world – the world of course meaning China.

The town sits in the midst of huge limestone peaks which jut haphazardly out of the plains. Except for these, Guilin looks like other modern Chinese towns, with its long wide streets lined with concrete blocks and factories. The place bursts with Chinese and western tourists.

The tourist scene is actually what makes Guilin so interesting. Despite 35 years of Communism and the brutal Cultural Revolution, the Chinese didn't forget the meaning of private enterprise. Very early on in the tourist boom there was a proliferation of privately-run shops with souvenirs and exorbitant prices catering for the foreign horde. Travellers' coffee-shops, bicycle rentals, a substantial black market and one or two shonky discount-tour-ticket operators got off to an early start. Guilin was, and still is, a great place to learn about capitalism!

The city, by the way, was founded during the Qin Dynasty and developed as a transport centre with the building of the Ling Canal which linked the important Pearl and Yangtse river systems. Under the Ming it was a provincial capital, a status it retained until 1914 when Nanning became the capital. During the 1930s and throughout WW II Guilin was a Communist stronghold and its population expanded from about 100,000 to over a million as people sought refuge here. Today it's the home of over 300,000.

All that said, it's not the place to see

those magnificent peaks. A combination of heat, hazy skies, industry, congested streets, enormous crowds and over-development has sent the backpackers packing south to the smaller town and finer scenery of Yangshuo. Summer is the worst time to be in Guilin – but Yangshuo does not pale.

Information & Orientation

Most of Guilin lies on the west bank of the Li River. The main artery is Zhongshan Lu, which runs roughly parallel to the river on its western side. At the southern end of this street – that is, Zhongshan Nanlu – is Guilin South Railway Station where most trains pull in. The length of Zhongshan Lu is a hodge-podge of shops and tourist hotels and a gourmet's delight of restaurants.

Closer to the centre of town is Banyan Lake on the western side of Zhongshan Lu, and Fur Lake on the eastern side. Further up is the main Zhongshan Lu/Jiefang Lu intersection. In this area you'll find the CITS office, Public Security and places to rent bicycles, as well as one of Guilin's up-market crash-pads and orienteering posts, the large Li River Hotel.

Jiefang Lu runs east-west across Zhongshan Lu. Heading east, it runs over Jiefang (Liberation) Bridge to the large Seven Star Park, one of the town's chief attractions. Most of the limestone pinnacles form a circle around the town, though a few pop up within the city limits.

CITS (tel 2648) is at 14 Ronghu Beilu, fronting Banyan Lake. They are friendly and reasonably helpful.

Public Security (tel 3202) is on Sanduo Lu, a side-road running west off Zhongshan Lu, in between Banyan Lake and Jiefang Lu.

Bank The Bank of China is on Jiefang Lu. Several hotels, including the Hidden Hill and Li River, have money-exchange services which you can usually use even if you're not staying at the hotel. There's a substantial black market in the town for Foreign Exchange Certificates.

Post & Communications The Post & Telecommunications Building is on Zhongshan Lu. There is a second post office by the large square in front of the train station; you can also make long-distance phone calls there. Some of the large hotels, such as the Li River Hotel, have post offices.

CAAC (tel 3063) is at 144 Zhongshan Lu, just to the south of the intersection of Zhongshan Lu and Shahu Beilu.

Things to See

For the best views of the surrounding karst formations you either have to climb to the top of the hills or get out of the town altogether. The peaks are not very high and are often obscured by the buildings – the best views are from the top of the Li River Hotel.

Solitary Beauty (Duxiu) Peak

The 152-metre pinnacle is at the centre of the town. The climb to the top is steep but there are good views of the town, the Li River and surrounding hills. The nephew of a Ming emperor built a palace at the foot of the peak in the 14th century, though only the gate remains. The site of the palace is now occupied by a teacher's college.

Bus No 1 goes up Zhongshan Lu past the western side of the peak. Or take bus No 2, which goes past the eastern side along the river. Both buses leave from Guilin South Railway Station.

Whirlpool (Fubo) Hill

Close to Solitary Beauty and standing beside the west bank of the Li River, this peak offers a fine view of the town. There is an odd story about how the hill gets its name – something to do with torrents of water plunging into the Li River and forming whirlpools. Try not to get caught in the rush.

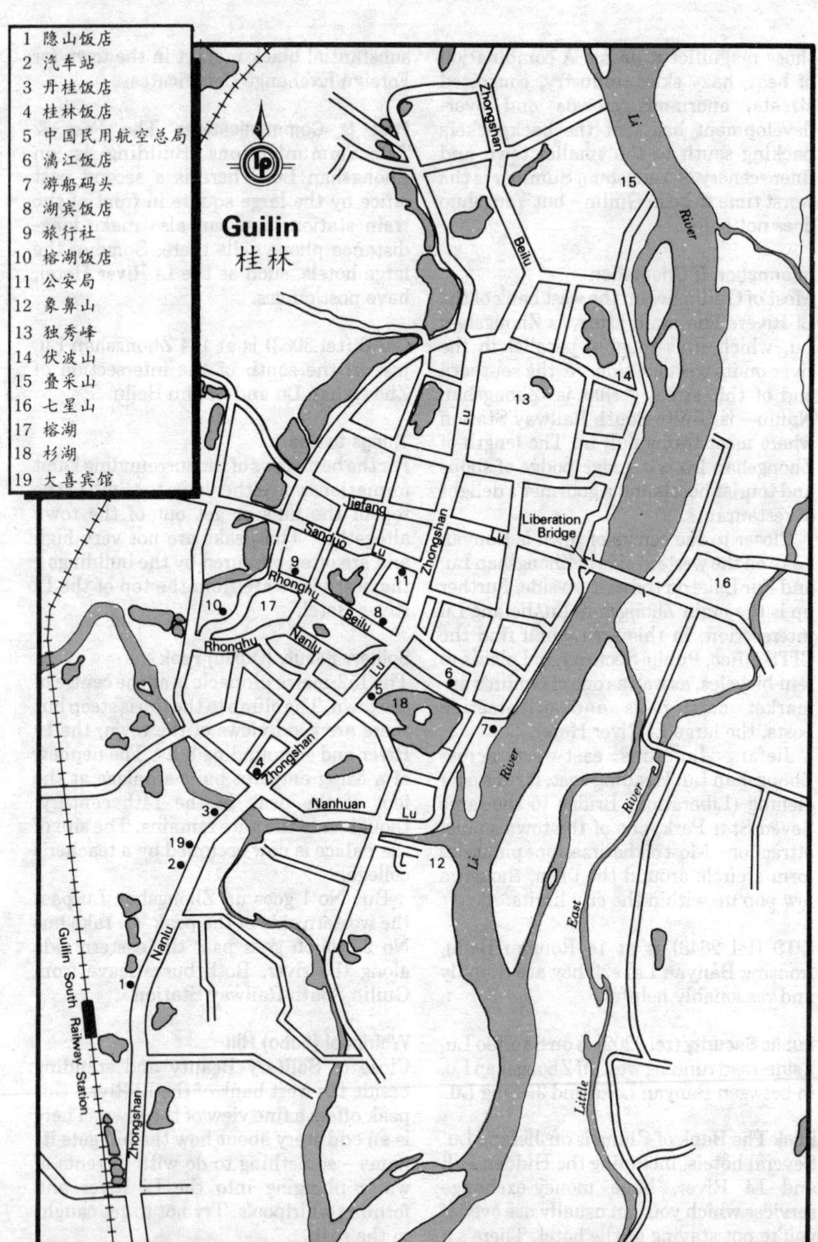
1 隐山饭店
2 汽车站
3 丹桂饭店
4 桂林饭店
5 中国民用航空总局
6 漓江饭店
7 游船码头
8 湖宾饭店
9 旅行社
10 榕湖饭店
11 公安局
12 象鼻山
13 独秀峰
14 伏波山
15 叠采山
16 七星山
17 榕湖
18 杉湖
19 大喜宾馆
Guilin
桂林
Zhongshan Beilu
Li River
Jiefang Lu
Sanduo Lu
Rhonghu Beilu
Rhonghu Nanlu
Zhongshan Lu
Liberation Bridge
Zhongshan
Nanhuan Lu
Nanlu
Guilin South Railway Station
Zhongshan
Li River
East River
Little East River

1 Hidden Hill Hotel
2 Buses to Yangshuo
3 Osmanthus Hotel
4 Guilin Hotel
5 CAAC
6 Lijiang Hotel
7 Pier for Tour-Boats down the Li River
8 Hubin Hotel
9 CITS
10 Banyan Lake Hotel
11 Public Security
12 Elephant Trunk Hill
13 Solitary Beauty
14 Fubo Hill
15 Decai Hill
16 Seven Star Park
17 Banyan Lake
18 Fur Lake
19 Taihe Hotel

On the southern slope of the hill is Returned Pearl (Huanzhu) Cave. The story goes that the cave was illuminated by a single pearl and inhabited by a dragon; one day a fisherman stole the pearl but he was overcome by shame and returned it.

Near this cave is Thousand Buddhas (Qianfo) Cave – a misnomer since there seem to be a couple of dozen statues at most, dating from the Tang and Song dynasties. Admission to the hill is 10 fen, and there's a bicycle park at the entrance. Bus No 2 runs past the hill.

Seven Star (Qixing) Park

Seven Star Park is on the eastern side of the Li River. Cross Liberation (Jiefang) Bridge and the Ming Dynasty Flower Bridge to the park.

The park takes its name from its seven peaks, which are supposed to resemble the star pattern of the Ursa Major (Big Dipper) constellation. There are several caves in the peaks, where visitors have inscribed graffiti for centuries – including a recent one which says, 'The Chinese Communist Party is the core of the leadership of all the Chinese People'. It takes a lot of imagination to see the 'Monkey Picking Peaches' and 'Two Dragons Playing Ball' in the stalagmites and stalactites. Otherwise, try the pitiful zoo.

To get to the park take bus Nos 9, 10 or 11 from the railway station. From the park, bus No 13 runs back across the Li River, past Fubo Hill and down to Reed Flute Cave.

Reed Flute (Ludi) Cave

Ironically, the most extraordinary scenery Guilin has to offer is underground. If you see nothing else then try not to miss the Reed Flute Cave – rather like a set from *Journey to the Centre of the Earth*. At one time the entrance to the cave was distinguished by clumps of reeds used by the locals to make musical instruments, hence the name.

One grotto, the Crystal Palace of the Dragon King, can comfortably hold about 1000 people, though many more crammed in here during the war when the cave was used as an air-raid shelter. The dominant feature of the cave is a great slab of white rock hanging from a ledge like a cataract, while opposite stands a huge stalactite said to resemble an old scholar. The story goes that a visiting scholar wished to write a poem worthy of the cave's beauty. After a long time he had composed only two sentences and, lamenting his inability to find the right words, turned to stone.

The other story is that the slab is the Dragon King's needle, used as a weapon by his opponent the Monkey King. The Monkey King used the needle to destroy the dragon's army of snails and jellyfish, leaving their petrified remains scattered around the floor of the cave. You can no doubt invent your own stories.

The cave is on the north-western outskirts of town. Take bus No 3 from the train station to the last stop. Bus No 13 will take you to the cave from Seven Star Park. Otherwise, it's an easy bicycle ride. For a guided tour try tagging on to one of the western tour groups. Try to avoid the cave in the tourist (carnival) season.

Ling Canal

The Ling Canal is in Xingan County, about 70 km north of Guilin. It was built during the 2nd century BC in the reign of the first Qing emperor, Qin Shihuang, to transport supplies to his army. The canal links the Xiang River (which flows into the Yangtse) and the Tan River (which flows into the Pearl River), thus connecting two of China's major waterways.

You can see the Ling Canal at Xingan, a market town of about 30,000 people, two hours by bus from Guilin. The town is also connected to Guilin by train. Two branches of the canal flow through the town, one at the north end and one at the south. The total length of the Ling Canal is 34 km.

Other Hills

Time to knock off a few more peaks. North of Solitary Beauty is **Folded Brocade (Decai) Hill**. Climb the stone pathway which takes you through the Wind Cave, with walls decked with inscriptions and Buddhist sculptures. Some of the smashed faces on the sculptures are a legacy of the Cultural Revolution. Great views from the top of the hill. Bus No 1 runs past the hill.

Old Man Hill is a curiously shaped hill to the north-east. There's a good view of it from Fubo Hill. The best way to get there is by bicycle as buses don't go near it. At the southern end of town, one of Guilin's best-known sights is **Elephant Trunk (Xiang Bi) Hill** which stands next to the Li River and is a lump of rock with a large hole in it.

South Park is a pretty place at the southern end of Guilin. You can contemplate on the mythological immortal who is said to have lived in one of the caves here; look for the carving of him. Admission to the park is 10 fen.

There are two lakes near the city centre, **Banyan Lake (Rong Hu)** on the west side and **Fur Lake (Shan Hu)** on the east side. Banyan Lake is named after an 800-year-old banyan tree on its shore. The tree stands by the restored South City Gate (Nan Men) originally built during the Tang Dynasty.

Places to Stay – bottom end

The *Kweilin (Guilin) Hotel* (tel 2249) is on Zhongshan Zhonglu, a 15-minute walk from the train station. Once upon a time it was only for use of Overseas, Hong Kong and Macau Chinese, and frantic guards at the gate kept big-noses out. Nowadays it's an established backpackers' refuge, with mixed dormitories on all four or five floors. Beds are around Y5 or Y6, but the dormitories face the main street, which can be incredibly noisy. Worse still are the televisions in the hallway outside each dormitory which do not go off until late at night. Spartan single rooms are Y11 and doubles Y28. The staff tends to be quite disorganised, with no idea how many beds or rooms are available.

The *Hubin Hotel*, on Shahu Beilu facing Banyan Lake, has double rooms from Y18. It is possible to get dorm beds for Y6. Could be worth investigating.

Places to Stay – middle

Most of Guilin's major hotels are laid out along Zhongshan Lu. A few minutes walk from Guilin South Railway Station is the *Hidden Hill Hotel* on Zhongshan Nanlu, with a money-exchange service and restaurant. Doubles cost from about Y33; the rooms are comfortable and have private bathrooms.

The relatively new *Taihe Hotel* is next to the long-distance bus station on Zhongshan Nanlu. They only have double rooms, which start at Y66.

The *Osmanthus Hotel* is just before the first bridge on Zhongshan Lu. Double rooms start at Y64 on the noisy ground floor, and Y65 upstairs.

The *Ronghu (Banyan Lake) Hotel)* (tel 3811) at 17 Ronghu Lu once catered for Overseas Chinese. Indeed, you practically needed a map of the hotel grounds and a fluent command of the local dialect to find the reception desk! Since then a new wing has been added, the range of

ART PAGE

Traditional Chinese Painting by Zhou Zhilong

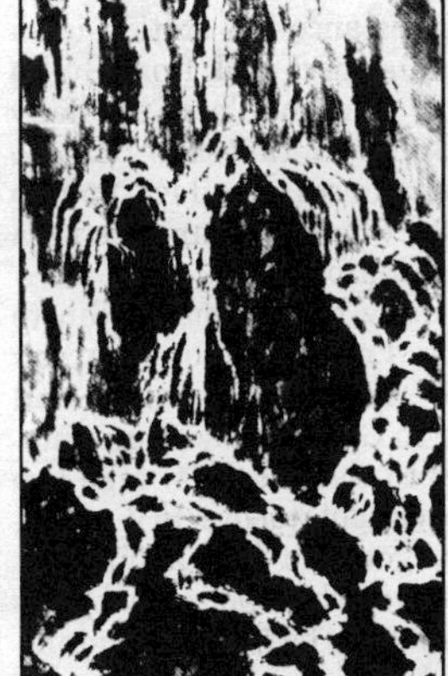

Zhou Zhilong, born in Guangxi in 1940, now teaches painting at the Chinese Institute of Traditional Opera in Beijing.

Zhou's landscapes are realistic and as fresh as nature itself.

clientele expanded and room prices have shot through the roof. Doubles start at Y121 in the new wing and rise into the hundreds of yuan per night. The old wing has doubles for Y30 (without air-con) and Y50 (with air-con). It's a bit inconveniently located unless you have a bicycle.

Places to Stay – top end

The *Lijiang Hotel* (tel 2881) at 1 Shahu Beilu is the main tourist hotel in Guilin. It's right in the middle of town and the roof provides a panoramic view of the encircling hills. Double rooms are Y92, no singles. Once a fairly plebeian hotel, it's now got the full works: post office, barber, bank, restaurants, tour groups and bell-boys in monkey suits. Take bus Nos 1 or 11 from Guilin South Railway Station. Get off when you cross Banyan Lake Bridge, the second bridge on Zhongshan Lu. Then walk for about 15 minutes up Shahu Beilu beside Fur Lake.

Places to Eat

Guilin food is basically Cantonese. Traditionally the town is noted for its snake soup, wild cat or bamboo rat, washed down with snake-bile wine. You could be devouring some of these animals into extinction. The pangolin (a sort of Chinese armadillo) is a protected species but still crops up on restaurant menus. Other protected species include the muntjac horned pheasant, mini-turtle, short-tailed monkey and gem-faced civet. Generally the most exotic stuff you should come across is eels, catfish, pigeons and dog.

Many small, cheapish eateries have sprung up along Zhongshan Lu in the last few years. It's really not worth mentioning any one in particular, but try the *Li River Café* at 142 Zhongshan Lu. A small seasoned pangolin will cost about Y30, stewed hedgehog Y30, fried snake with chicken and mushrooms Y30, snake soup Y20 and fried eel Y6.

Getting There & Away

Guilin is connected to many places by bus, train, boat and plane. Give serious thought to flying in or out of this place, as train connections are not good.

Air Worth considering is the flight from Guilin to Kunming. The fare is Y154 or just slightly more than a tourist-price soft-sleeper on the train. There are flights three days a week, but getting even one of these can involve a long wait due to heavy demand.

Other useful connections include Canton (daily), Chengdu (five days a week), Chongqing (five days a week) and Shanghai (six days a week).

Bus The long-distance bus station is on Zhongshan Lu, a short walk from Guilin South Railway Station. There are daily buses from Guilin to Yangshuo (Y2, 1½ hours, a dozen buses per day) and to Wuzhou (Y13), where you can pick up a boat or bus to Canton.

There are daily buses from Guilin to Liuzhou (Y7). From Liuzhou you can carry on by rail to Nanning and Zhanjiang, or to Guiyang and Kunming.

Daily buses to Canton (Y24) take two days with an overnight stopover in Wuzhou. Alternatively, you can buy a bus/boat combination ticket which takes you by bus to Wuzhou and then by boat to Canton.

Rail There are useful train connections to Guilin, but some of these (like the Kunming-Guiyang-Guilin-Shanghai route) tend to involve hauls on unbelievably crowded carriages. Guilin train station has a separate ticket office for foreigners; this means you'll have to pay tourist price but at least you avoid the impossible queues.

Direct trains out of Guilin include those to Kunming (about 33 hours), Guiyang (18 hours), Zhanjiang (about 13 hours), Liuzhou (three hours) and Nanning. For Chongqing change trains at Guiyang.

The train to Kunming via Guiyang comes through from Shanghai and is impossibly crowded. It's virtually impossible to get a seat, let alone a sleeper, if you pick it up mid-way. You may manage a soft-sleeper but for much the same price you could fly, which is what many people are now doing. To book a sleeper from Guilin to Kunming, you have to line up at the FEC counter in the station no later than 7 am. Only six hard-sleepers a day are sold for this train and you must book three days in advance. Tourist-price tickets from Guilin to Kunming are Y47 hard-seat, Y75 hard-sleeper and Y142 soft-sleeper.

There is a direct train to Canton. Tourist-price fares are Y33 hard-seat, Y53 hard-sleeper and Y101 soft-sleeper. Otherwise you have to stop at Hengyang and change trains. The non-direct route will take about 24 hours and fares are a few yuan cheaper.

If you're heading east on the train, consider breaking your journey at the rail junction of Hengyang. Tourist-price hard-seat from Guilin to Hengyang is only Y13, and from there you can continue your trip east to Shanghai, north to Changsha and Beijing, or south to Canton. In any case, by the time the train reaches Hengyang you might get off whether you planned to or not!

Getting Around

Bicycle Bicycles are definitely the best way to get around Guilin. There's been a proliferation of bicycle rentals over the last few years – just look along Zhongshan Lu for the signs. Most charge about Y0.50 to Y0.60 per hour, but you may be able to negotiate a cheaper day rate.

Taxi & Bus Taxis are available from the major tourist hotels. Most of the town buses leave from the terminus at Guilin South Railway Station and will get you to many major sights, but a bicycle is definitely better.

Boat A popular tourist trip is the boat ride from Guilin down the Li River to Yangshuo. Although this is still popular with tour groups (whole fleets of boats do the run every day in the high season), low-budget travellers have been put off by the exorbitant ticket prices. Standard prices for foreigners are around Y35 one way and Y50 return. Look along Zhongshan Lu for the ticket offices. The boats leave from a dock on the Li River about 100 metres north of Elephant Trunk Hill.

YANGSHUO 阳朔

The place to escape the congestion of Guilin is Yangshuo, 80 km and 1½ hours by bus to the south. Yangshuo is a tiny country town set amidst the limestone pinnacles, and from here you can explore the small villages in the countryside. In fact, the scenery around Yangshuo makes giving Guilin a complete miss no hardship at all. As the Chinese tourist leaflets say:

> The peaks surrounding the country town are steep and delicate, rising one higher than another like piled-up petals. Their inverted images mirrored in the river are just like green lotuses shooting up from the water, elegant and graceful. The scenery of Yangshuo will make you enjoy the beauty of the natural world whenever you come. On fine days they bathe in the sunlight; in the rainy season they are in the misty rain; in the morning the glory casts upon them; at dusk the mountain haze enwraps them – all in all, they are colourful and in different postures, and make you feel intoxicant.

Information

CITS (tel 2256) has an office on the grounds of the Yangshuo Hotel. Their useful maps of Yangshuo and the surrounding area show villages, paths and roads. They advertise visits to local factories, schools and villages; fishing trips; and acupuncture and massage services. They were planning to provide guides for local hiking and caving; could be worth enquiring about.

Bank The Bank of China at 38 Xilu will change cash and travellers' cheques. There are quite a few black-market money-changers around.

Things to See

Yangshuo is a laid-back town if ever there

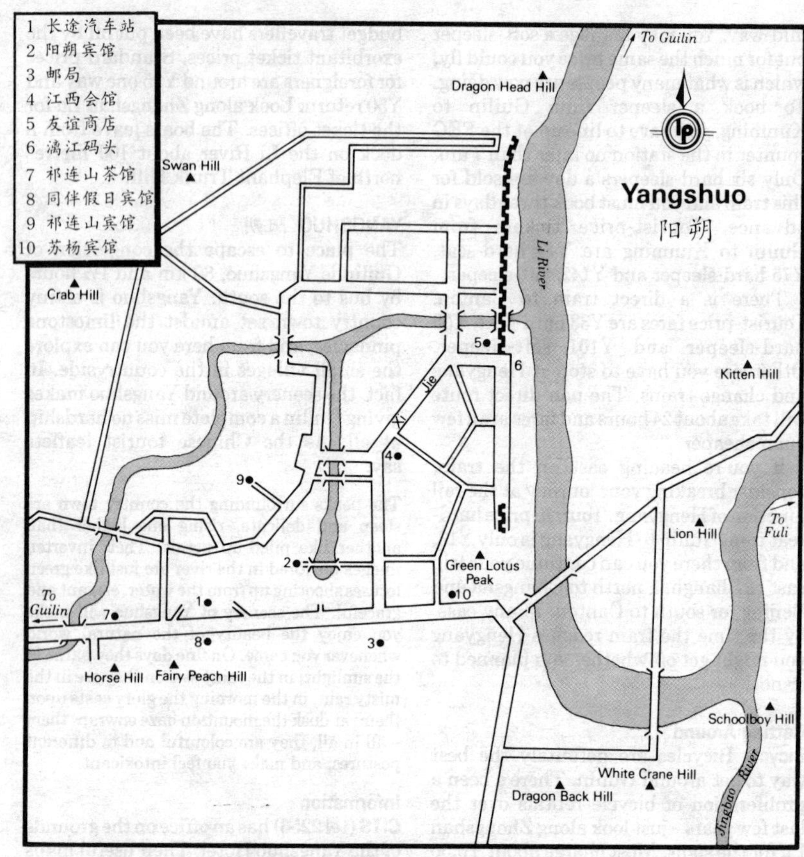

1. Long-distance Bus Station
2. Yangshuo Hotel
3. Post Office
4. Temple
5. Friendship Store
6. Pier for Li River Tour Boats
7. Xilang Shan Tea House
8. Good Companion Holiday Inn
9. Xi Lang Hill Hotel
10. Zhu Yang Hotel

was one in China, and offers a rare opportunity to relax and explore the villages and countryside. Hire a bicycle and take off along the tracks which lead to old settlements. A lot of people have stayed overnight in the villages, and if you want to go camping on the mountains you shouldn't have any problem. It's probably not permitted to camp out, but who's going to climb a 200-metre peak to bring you down? There are caves in the peaks, unlit by fairy lights, many no doubt untrod by human feet.

In 1983, when the first edition of this book was being researched, there wasn't much in Yangshuo. The tourist market by the dock catered to the flotilla of tour boats bearing Chinese, Japanese and westerners who swept through like a plague of locusts before being bundled on buses and whisked back to Guilin. Three hotels (one of which they wouldn't let you stay at, and another which didn't have toilets) and a couple of soupy noodle dispensaries catered to the meagre number of backpackers who found their way here. Today you can munch on banana pancakes and muesli, slurp coffee and hang out in half a dozen or more travellers' cafés with Midnight Oil and Dire Straits tapes playing in the background.

Peaks

Green Lotus Peak is the main peak in Yangshuo and stands next to the Li River in the south-east corner of the town. It's also called Bronze Mirror Peak because it's got a flat northern face which is supposed to look like an ancient bronze mirror. **Yangshuo Park** is in the west of the town, and here you'll find **Man Hill**, which is supposed to resemble a young man bowing and scraping to a shy young girl represented by **Lady Hill**. The other hills are named after animals: **Crab Hill, Swan Hill, Dragon Head Hill** and the like. Sights along the Li River in the vicinity of Yangshuo include **Green Frog Watching & Enjoying the Moon**.

Moon Hill

The highway from Guilin turns southward at Yangshuo and after a couple of km crosses the Jingbao River. South of this river and just to the west of the highway is Moon Hill, a limestone pinnacle with a moon-shaped hole in its peak. To get to Moon Hill by bicycle, take the main road out of town towards the river and turn right on the road about 200 metres before the bridge. Cycle for about 50 minutes – Moon Hill is on your right and the views from the top are incredible!

River Excursions

There are many villages close to Yangshuo which are worth checking out. A popular riverboat trip is to the picturesque village of **Fuli** a short distance down the Li River, where you'll see stone houses and cobbled laneways. There are a couple of boats a day to Fuli from Yangshuo (foreigners are usually charged Y5, but you might try looking around for local boats); you can bring a bicycle and pedal back. Friday is market day and the main street is packed with people from the outlying villages buying and selling everything from herbal medicines to piglets in bamboo cages. **Pinglo** is a small, industrialised river town 35 km from Yangshuo, at the junction of the Li and Gui rivers.

Places to Stay

Hawks (usually women or kids) dive-bomb the buses as they pull into the bus terminal. They have no more idea which hotels have vacancies then you do, and Yangshuo is so small you don't need a guide anyway!

One of the most popular places is the *Good Companion Holiday Inn* (which bears no relation to the famous chain), roughly opposite the bus station. Clean and reasonably quiet, it offers dormitory beds for Y3, single rooms for Y6 and doubles for Y10.

The *Xi Lang Hill Hotel* is set back from the street and is very quiet at night. Simple but comfortable double rooms with own bathroom go for Y20 (no singles but you may manage a reduction if you're on your own). Dormitory beds go for Y4.

The *Zu Yang Hotel* has dormitory beds from Y4, single rooms from Y16 and doubles from Y24. This is one of Yangshuo's newer hotels and could be worth checking out.

The *Yangshuo Hotel* is up-market, offering air-con doubles with attached bathroom from Y44. There seem to be some cheaper rooms and possibly dormitory accommodation. Beds for Y10 per person in a triple are possible. This place gets mixed reports from travellers; some like it while others find it dingy and the staff unfriendly. Could depend on what level of accommodation you take. CITS has its office on the hotel grounds.

Places to Eat

My personal favourite is the *Green Lotus Peak Wine House*, which has more to do with beer than wine and serves up a fine banana pancake and banana muesli. Pidgin English signs appear in the windows and you'll find some wacky Chinese and westerners within.

Up the road by the ferry pier, *Susanna's Café* could be another stayer. Or try *Joanna's Place, Hilton Restaurant, Cocktail Restaurant, Happy Restaurant*.

Fresh fruit is sold down at the wharf where the tour boats dock. Avoid Guilin Beer (deep blue label with white characters), which tastes much like a pancake looks.

Getting There & Away

There are over a dozen buses a day from Yangshuo to Guilin, the first departing Yangshuo about 8 am and the last about 6.30 pm. The fare is around Y2, and the trip takes 1½ to two hours.

The Li River tour boats from Guilin to Yangshuo are expensive, but you can do it cheaper in the other direction. Daily boats to Guilin leave Yangshuo around 8.30 am. The fare is about Y20 per person, and you can pay on the boat.

If you're heading to Canton you can take a bus/boat combination from Yangshuo; you bus to Wuzhou and then take a boat from Wuzhou to Canton. Get tickets from Yangshuo's long-distance bus station, where an unfathomable confusion reigns regarding departure times and availability of seats.

There are also daily buses from Yangshuo to Liuzhou; the fare is Y5. From Liuzhou you can carry on by train to Nanning, Zhanjiang, or Guiyang and Kunming.

Getting Around

The town itself is small enough to walk around easily, but if you want to get further afield then hire a bicycle. Just look for rows of bikes and signs. The charge is about Y2 per day.

CITS organises half-day river trips for around Y5 per person, and full-day trips for around Y12 per person. Check the signs near the boat dock for what's available.

THE LI RIVER 漓江

The Li River is the connecting waterway between Guilin and Yangshuo and is one of the main tourist attractions of the area. A thousand years ago a poet wrote of the scenery around Yangshuo: 'The river forms a green gauze belt, the mountains are like blue jade hairpins'. The 83-km stretch between the towns is hardly that but you do see some extraordinary peaks, sprays of bamboo lining the river banks, fishermen in small boats and picturesque villages.

As is the Chinese habit, every feature along the route has been named. **Paint Brush Hill** juts straight up from the ground with a pointed tip like a Chinese writing brush. **Cock-fighting Hills** stand face to face like two cocks about to engage in battle. **Mural Hill** just past the small town of Yangti is a sheer cliff rising abruptly out of the water; there are supposed to be the images of nine horses in the weathered patterns on the cliff face. Further on is the old town of **Xingping**, where the river widens and meanders around to Yangshuo.

Tour boats depart Guilin from a jetty about 100 metres north of Elephant Trunk Hill each morning around 7.30 am. The trip takes about six hours. Many people find that the time drags by the end. It's probably not worth it if you're going to be spending any length of time in Yangshuo. Buses meet the incoming boats to take passengers back to Guilin, pausing at a tourist market and photo stop near Moon Hill.

NANNING 南宁

By way of introduction, a few statistics to dwell upon about Nanning. According to Chinese sources, the number of factories in the city shot from four in 1949 to 400 by 1979.

Top: Bikes travelling piggy-bike! (RS)
Bottom Left: Junk under sail (RS)
Bottom Right: Sheep-hide raft, Binglingsi (AS)

Top: View from Moon Hill, Yangshuo (AS)
Bottom Left: Fastest fish-trap on two legs, Shapin market (RS)
Bottom Right: Mt. Maijishan (RS)

From 1949 to 1981 the area of Nanning city increased twelve-fold. From 1976 to 1983 it appears that the population doubled (from 1949 to 1979 it quadrupled) and now stands at over 650,000. A prestigious list of light and heavy industry could be rattled off here, but perhaps you already have a picture in mind.

At the turn of the century Nanning was a mere market town; now it's the capital of Guangxi. Apart from the urban expansion that the post-1949 railway induced in the south-west, Nanning became important as a staging ground for shipping arms to Vietnam. The rail line to the border town of Pingxian was built in 1952, and was extended to Hanoi, giving Vietnam a lifeline to China. In 1979, with the Chinese invasion of Vietnam, the train services were suspended indefinitely. The border with Vietnam in Guangxi and Yunnan is a hot one these days, and (ridiculous as it is) the Vietnamese are considered a threat to Chinese oil exploration in the Gulf of Tonkin.

At street level, the town of Nanning is a poor one, with a promise of progress in the solid-looking department stores. Elsewhere the city is a motley collection of cracked, peeling, stained, crumbled, worn, seedy, ramshackle walls, facades and fittings. The population in the Nanning region is mostly a Zhuang-Han mix, though the rest of the Zhuang are scattered over Guangxi's rural areas.

Nanning is also a jumping-off place for visits to Wuming, Yiling, Binyang, Guixian, Guiping and Beihai.

Information

CITS (tel 22986) is in the Mingyuan Hotel. Quite helpful.

CAAC (tel 23333) is at 64 Chaoyang Lu.

Things to See

There's a plethora of free markets in Nanning. You can follow a series of different outdoor markets (spices, medicinal herbs and potions, clothing, sunglasses, housewares, eating stalls . . .) by taking the route marked on the map in this book. There are food stalls at the northern and southern sections of the route. Check out the unusual street commerce in progress – strips of car tyre, dead rats, desiccated cockroaches, dried snake skins. For the rice-weary there's an abundance of subtropical fruit in season. Another market strip is Fandi Lu, the road leading diagonally to the north-east toward Renmin Park. If you happen to be a smoker there are shaggy mounds of tobacco lying around the markets, and you can order it rolled in filter packs on the spot. To the south and west of the Yongjiang Hotel, along the riverbanks on the same side, is the older section of town. Check out the underground bomb-shelter disco/amusement hall in Renmin Park.

Dragon Boat Races

As in other parts of the south-west (and Guangdong and Macao), Nanning has Dragon Boat races on the fifth day of the fifth lunar month (June) in which large numbers of sightseers urge the decorated rowing vessels along the Yong River. The oarsmen are coordinated by a gong-player on board.

Guangxi Provincial Museum

The museum is in Nanhu Park, and has a collection of tribal, archaeological and Taiping relics. Take bus No 3 to the terminus. The museum's opening hours are variable, and lunchtime is definitely not one of them.

Yiling Caves & Wuming

Twenty-five km to the north-north-west of Nanning are these caves with their stalagmites and galactic lights; 15 minutes is enough for the caves, but the surrounding countryside is worth exploring.

Wuming is 45 km from Nanning, on the same road that leads to the Yiling Caves. There are CITS-organised visits to the local Two-Bridge Production Brigade which you probably won't get on. A few

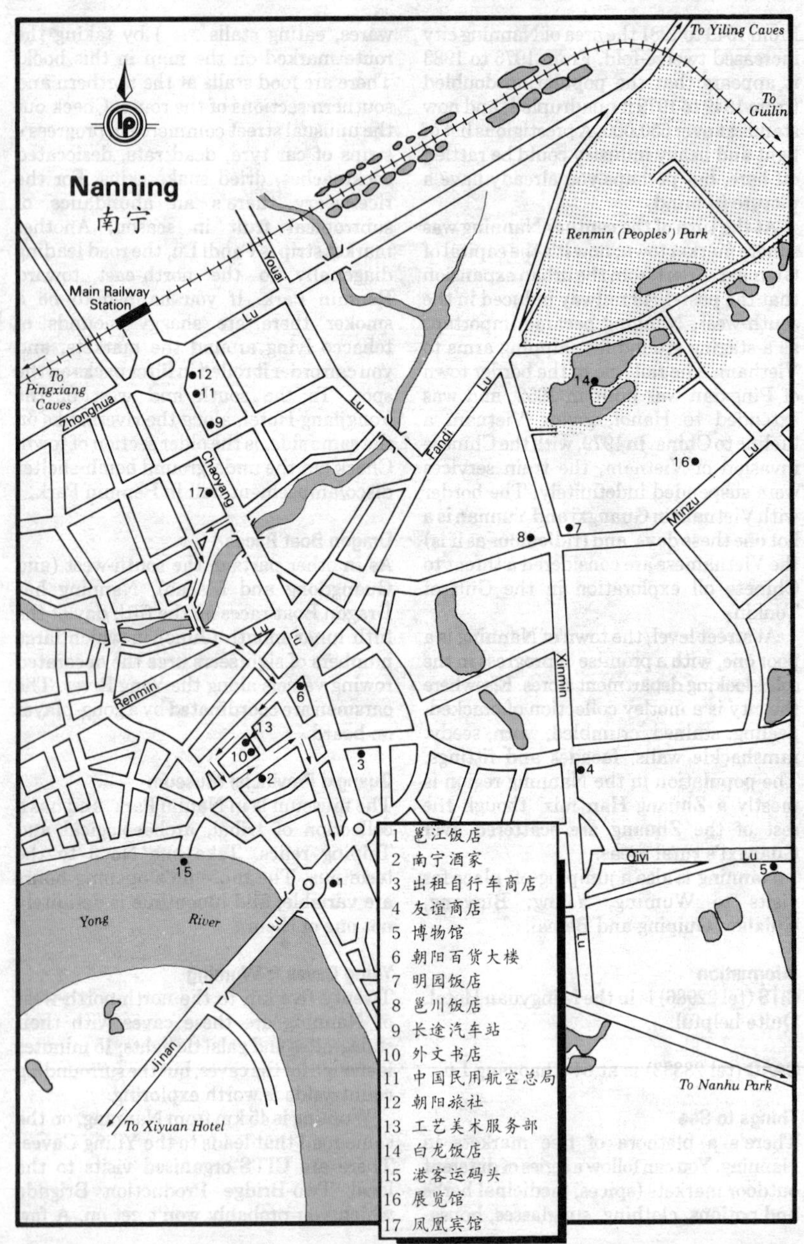
Nanning
南宁
To Yiling Caves
To Guilin
Renmin (Peoples') Park
Main Railway Station
To Pingxiang Caves
Zhonghua
Youai
Lu
Chaoyang
Lu
Fandi
Lu
Minzu
Lu
Xinmin
Lu
Renmin
Lu
Lu
Qiyi
Lu
Yong
River
Jinan
Lu
To Xiyuan Hotel
To Nanhu Park
1 邕江饭店
2 南宁酒家
3 出租自行车商店
4 友谊商店
5 博物馆
6 朝阳百货大楼
7 明园饭店
8 邕川饭店
9 长途汽车站
10 外文书店
11 中国民用航空总局
12 朝阳旅社
13 工艺美术服务部
14 白龙饭店
15 港客运码头
16 展览馆
17 凤凰宾馆

1 Yongjiang Hotel
2 Nanning Restaurant
3 Bike Rental
4 Friendship Store
5 Guangxi Museum
6 Chaoyang Department Store
7 Mingyuan Hotel (CITS)
8 Yongzhou Hotel
9 Long-distance Bus Station
10 Foreign Language Bookstore
11 CAAC Office
12 Chaoyang (Chinese) Hotel & Travel Agency
13 Arts & Crafts Service Department
14 Bailongdong Restaurant
15 Boat Dock
16 Exhibition Hall
17 Phoenix Hotel

km further up the line is Lingshui Springs, which is a big swimming pool.

To get to either Wuming or the Yiling Caves, take a bus from Nanning's long-distance bus station. Also try the Nanning Tourist Company which operates out of the Chaoyang Hotel near the train station – they cover short round trips.

Places to Stay

The *Yongjiang Hotel* (tel 23951) on Jinan Lu has two wings: a high-rise for foreigners and for Hong Kong and Macau citizens, and a squat building for People's Republic Chinese. Rooms in the high-rise are luxurious and start from Y46 a single and Y65 a double. Dorm beds are Y6. Local buses running to the Yongjiang from the train station are Nos 2 and 5. There are great views of the city from the restaurant on the 8th floor.

The *Yongzhou* (tel 28323) on Xinmin Lu is of a similar standard to the Yongjiang. Single rooms with hard beds and own bathroom start at Y21, and doubles at Y40. Once the television in the corridor goes off it's rather quiet. Not a bad place, if a bit tattered round the edges. It's rather awkward to get to – you take bus No 2 one stop from the railway station, alight and walk left to the next big intersection, and then take bus No 1 for two stops.

Close to the Yongzhou is the CITS *Mingyuan Hotel* (tel 22986) on Xinmin Lu. Foreigners are sent off to the new wing, which is a snazzy building with singles from around Y40 and doubles from Y60. Comfy rooms, soft beds, own bathroom, television and enough lights per room to illuminate a rock concert.

You may or may not be able to get into the *Xiyuan Hotel* (tel 29923) by the riverside, but take bus No 5 from the railway station. As for the *Nanning Hotel*, they will take only those who meet their unspecified requirements.

Places to Eat

Market-stall food is good – snakes and snails and puppy dogs' tails, glazed chicken, roast duck, and fruit all part of the menu. Opposite the Foreign Language Bookstore is a large restaurant where the specialities include turtle, snake, ants and fruit-eating fox.

In *Nanhu Park* there's a fish-speciality restaurant where the creatures are taken from tanks – not too expensive. Take bus No 2 to the terminus.

The penthouse dining room in the high-rise block of the *Yongjiang Hotel* is a bit pricey, but has nice views.

Renmin Park, with a market run leading up to it (Fandi Lu), has a tea house and restaurant, the *Bailongdong*.

Getting There & Away

Air There are flights three times a week from Nanning to Beijing, Canton, Guilin and Kunming.

Bus There are daily buses to Wuzhou from Nanning's long-distance bus station. The fare is Y17. Tickets for air-con buses to Wuzhou can be bought from the tourist hotels.

Rail Plan your rail trips ahead of time, as the choice of departures is not great.

There are direct trains from Nanning to

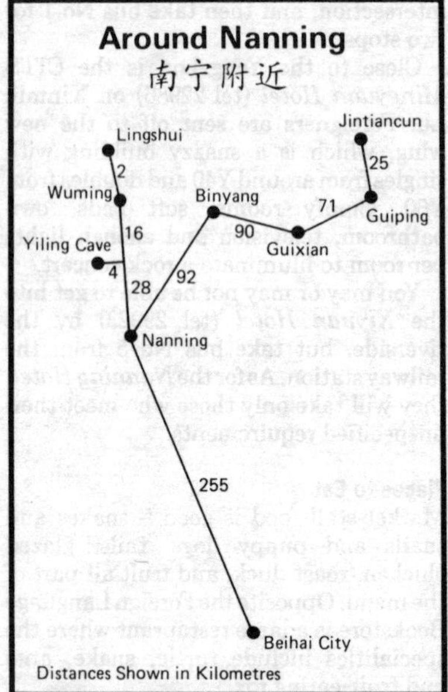

Guilin. Tourist-price tickets are Y19 hard-seat, Y30 hard-sleeper and Y56 soft-sleeper. The trip takes about nine hours.

The trains to Guilin travel via Liuzhou. Tourist-price tickets from Nanning to Liuzhou are Y11 hard-seat, Y21 hard-sleeper and Y41 soft-sleeper.

If you're continuing from Nanning to Guiyang you have to change at Liuzhou. There are also special express trains direct from Nanning to Beijing.

There are direct trains from Nanning to Zhanjiang on the coast of Guangdong Province. From Zhanjiang you can get a ferry to Haikou on Hainan Island, a direct bus to Canton, or a direct overnight boat to Hong Kong. Tourist-price tickets from Nanning to Zhanjiang are Y19 hard-seat and Y29 hard-sleeper. The trip takes about 9½ hours.

Boat Boating out of Nanning is unexplored. There are links downstream to Wuzhou via Guixian and Guiping that would be worth checking out. Guixian can be reached by rail or bus in four hours. There *may* be a boat from Guixian to Wuzhou, taking about 12 hours and leaving Guixian in the early afternoon.

The Binyang-Guixian-Guiping route, going north-east from Nanning, is useful for getting to Wuzhou cross-country. The roads are rough, the areas backward, and it's a sugar cane/grain basin. It's 90 km by road from Nanning to Binyang; 90 km by road from Binyang to Guixian; and 70 km by boat from Guixian to Guiping. From Guiping there are boats to Wuzhou, a 10-hour trip. Guixian can also be reached by rail from Nanning, and the line continues to Zhanjiang.

There are a couple of cultural sights along the way, but nothing of note. Just 25 km north-west of Guiping is Jintiancun, with one of the weirdest chapters in Chinese history. A schoolmaster, supposedly suffering from hallucinations generated by an illness, declared himself the brother of Jesus Christ and took upon himself the mission of liberating China from the Manchus. These were the seeds of the Taiping Rebellion (1850-64).

Another approach to Hainan Island is via Beihai, which is 255 km from Nanning. Beihai is a port town and a very sensitive naval base. The bus trip from Nanning takes eight hours. From Beihai you can continue to Zhanjiang and get a bus/boat combination to Haikou on Hainan Island.

Getting Around

There are at least two bicycle-rental places, but they're difficult to find. The one marked on the map in this book is hidden by a (crowded) bus stop. Look for a batch of numbered bikes near the bus stop. The owner will want to know at which hotel you're staying.

Pedicabs and auto-rickshaws can be found at the town centre and outside the major hotels. Taxis are available from the hotels.

LIUZHOU 柳州

Liuzhou, with a population of over 500,000, is the largest city on the Liu River. The place dates back to the Tang

Dynasty, at which time it was a dumping ground for disgraced court officials. The town was largely left to its mountain wilds until 1949, when it was transformed into a major industrial city. Both light and heavy industry are engaged in (and the city is also known for) medicinal herbs, fruit and coffins. Liuzhou is the only place in China where you can buy an exquisitely wrought ashtray-sized wooden coffin.

Liuzhou is Guilin's poor cousin with similar but less impressive karst scenery on the outskirts. Try some cave-lake-park sightseeing. River transport is the best way of viewing the karst landscape.

Places to Stay & Eat

A few minutes' walk from the main train station down Yanan Lu is a large Chinese hotel which will take foreigners (there's no English or pinyin sign – see the map for directions). Singles cost Y28, doubles Y32 with hard beds and your own television and mouldy bathroom. You may manage a cheaper room with a bit of effort. Dormitory beds are Y8. Not a bad place all told with friendly staff.

The *Liuzhou Hotel* is the centre of tourist operations. The hotel is quite remote. From the train station get an articulated bus No 2. This takes you most of the way, followed by a short walk – ask the conductor where to get off. Double rooms cost from Y43. They deny the existence of dormitories but try wrangling something cheaper. Some people have managed to get fairly cheap rooms.

Apparently women of the Dong minority are known to serve *youcha* or oil-tea (actually a kind of soup) within the confines of the Liuzhou Hotel. The women seem a bit far from home, since the heartland of the Dongs is 200 km or more north of Liuzhou in Songjiang County. Songjiang is the area where the borders of Guizhou, Guangxi and Hunan meet.

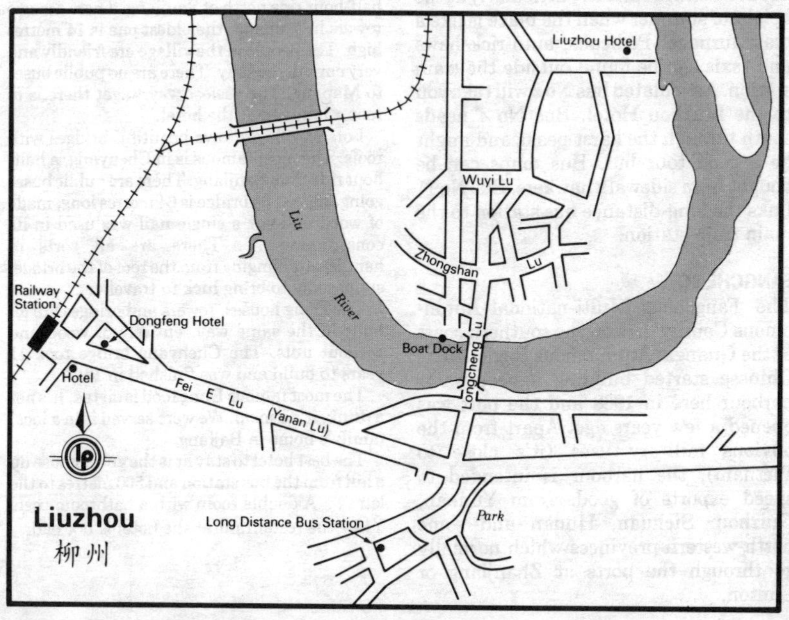

On the streets there's not much to recommend – more noodles, boiled eggs, jiaozi and baozi.

Getting There & Away

Bus There are daily buses from Liuzhou's long-distance bus station to Guilin (Y7) and Yangshuo (Y5).

Rail Liuzhou is a railway junction which connects Nanning to Guilin. Guilin-to-Kunming trains pass through Liuzhou. If you're coming up from Nanning you'll probably have to change trains in Liuzhou to get to Kunming.

Tourist-price hard-seat fare from Liuzhou to Guilin is around Y7, and the trip takes just under three hours. Tourist-price tickets from Nanning to Liuzhou are Y11 hard-seat, Y21 hard-sleeper and Y41 soft-sleeper.

Getting Around

Liuzhou is uncomfortably large – forget about walking round it, particularly at the height of summer when the place is like a blast furnace! Pedicabs, auto-rickshaws and taxis can be found outside the train station. Articulated bus No 2 will take you to the Liuzhou Hotel. Bus No 4 heads south through the karst peaks and might be a good tour bus. Bus maps can be bought from sidewalk hawkers. Bus No 11 links the long-distance bus station to the main train station.

FANGCHENG 防城

The 'Fangcheng Multi-national Autonomous County' lies on the southern coast of the Guangxi Autonomous Region. The Chinese started building a deep-water harbour here in 1968 and the port was opened a few years ago. Apart from the obvious military uses (it's close to Vietnam), the harbour is intended to speed exports of goods from Yunnan, Guizhou, Sichuan, Hunan and some north-western provinces which normally go through the ports at Zhanjiang or Canton.

RONGSHUI & SANJIANG 融水 三江

Two Swedish travellers write to recommend the towns of Rongshui and Sanjiang:

> (Rongshui) . . . is on the railway line which heads north from Liuzhou. It's connected to Sanjiang by train and bus. Sanjiang is about 110 km from Rongshui.
>
> Rongshui is surrounded by 'sugartop' mountains – there are even some in the middle of town. Climb a mountain, walk around amongst the curious people, or you can cross the river and walk.
>
> The best place to stay is at the *Yiyuan Hotel*, 15 minutes walk from the bus station. The staff are very friendly. A double room costs Y12 and that includes private bathroom . . . The restaurant at the back is excellent. Try their sweet & sour fish or deep-fried tofu with meat and mushrooms.
>
> (Sanjiang) . . . is on a river and a lot of new development is in progress. There's a Drum Tower in nearly every Dong County in the province. When something happened the headman used to beat the drum in the tower. The biggest tower is in a place called Mapang, a half-hour ride north of Sanjiang. There are two towers in Mapang; the oldest one is 14 metres high. The people in the village are friendly and very curious, but shy. There are no public buses to Mapang. The easiest way to get there is to rent a minivan at the hotel.
>
> Lots of villages have beautiful bridges with roofs. The most famous is in Chenyang, a half-hour ride from Sanjiang. There are public buses going there. The bridge is 64 metres long, made of wood and not a single nail was used in its construction . . . There are all sorts of handicrafts hanging from the roof of the bridge, supposedly to bring luck to travellers.
>
> The Dong houses, towers and bridges are all built in the same way, entirely of wood and without nuts. The Chenyang bridge took 11 years to build and was finished in 1917.
>
> The most famous Dong food is oil tea. It's not a drink, it's a meal. We were served it in a local family's home in Bajiang.
>
> The best hotel to stay at is the guest house up a hill from the bus station and 500 metres to the left . . . A double room with a bathroom costs Y15 – the restaurant at the hotel is not bad.

Guizhou 贵州

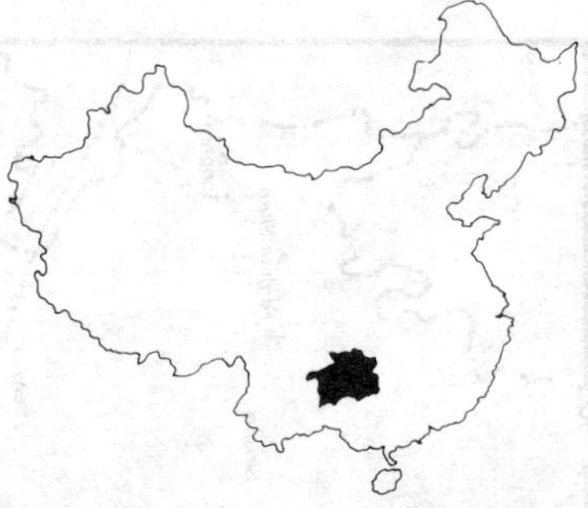

Until recent times Guizhou was one of the most backward and sparsely populated areas in China. Although the Han Dynasty set up an administration in the area, the Chinese merely attempted to maintain some measure of control over the non-Chinese tribes who lived here, and Chinese settlement was confined to the north and east of the province. The eastern areas were not settled until the 16th century, when the native minorities were forced out of the most fertile areas. Another wave of Chinese immigration in the late 19th century brought many settlers in from overpopulated Hunan and Sichuan. But Guizhou remained impoverished and backward, with poor communications and transport.

When the Japanese invasion forced the Kuomintang to retreat to the south-west, the development of Guizhou began; roads to the neighbouring provinces were constructed, a rail link was built to Guangxi, and some industries were set up in Guiyang and Zunyi. Most of the activity ceased with the end of WW II, and it was not until the construction of the railways in the south-west under Communist rule that some industrialisation was revived.

Recent analyses in the Chinese press have provided grim warnings about backwardness and poverty. Eight million of the province's population are living below the national poverty line – an annual per capita income of Y120 and 200 kg of grain. Between 60 and 70% of the population are illiterate and nearly 50% of the villages are not accessible by road.

However, in typical Han fashion the blame was laid at the door of the minorities who were castigated for 'poor educational quality'; more self-righteous arguments were levelled at cave-dwellers because 'the temptations of modern life have failed to lure these Miao out of their dark, unhealthy cave'. These self-sufficient minorities living without TV, radio, electricity, etc are certainly poor, but they show few signs of embracing consumer life and throwing away their cultural identity as a reward for assimilation with the Han.

Today the population of Guizhou is 28.5 million, of which about 75% is Han and the rest a flamboyant mixture of minorities such as Miao, Bouyei, Dong, Yi, Shui and Gelao. Between them these minorities celebrate nearly 1000 festivals each year which preserve fascinating customs and elaborate skills in architecture, dress and handicrafts. A recent drive to increase income from tourism should see more remote regions of Guizhou opening for foreigners to explore caves, waterfalls and minority areas. The star attraction close to Guiyang is the Huangguoshu Waterfalls, China's biggest. The neighbourhood also presents opportunities for hiking and stumbling around some of China's all-too-little visited villages.

GUIYANG 贵阳

Guiyang, the capital of Guizhou Province, is a dump. Stronger words could be used; one would not want to inflict this unfortunate place on the rail-weary traveller, or any traveller for that matter. It is incredibly poor, and has always been that way. Even the weather has turned against it – the drizzle gives it the name of Guiyang, which translates as 'Precious

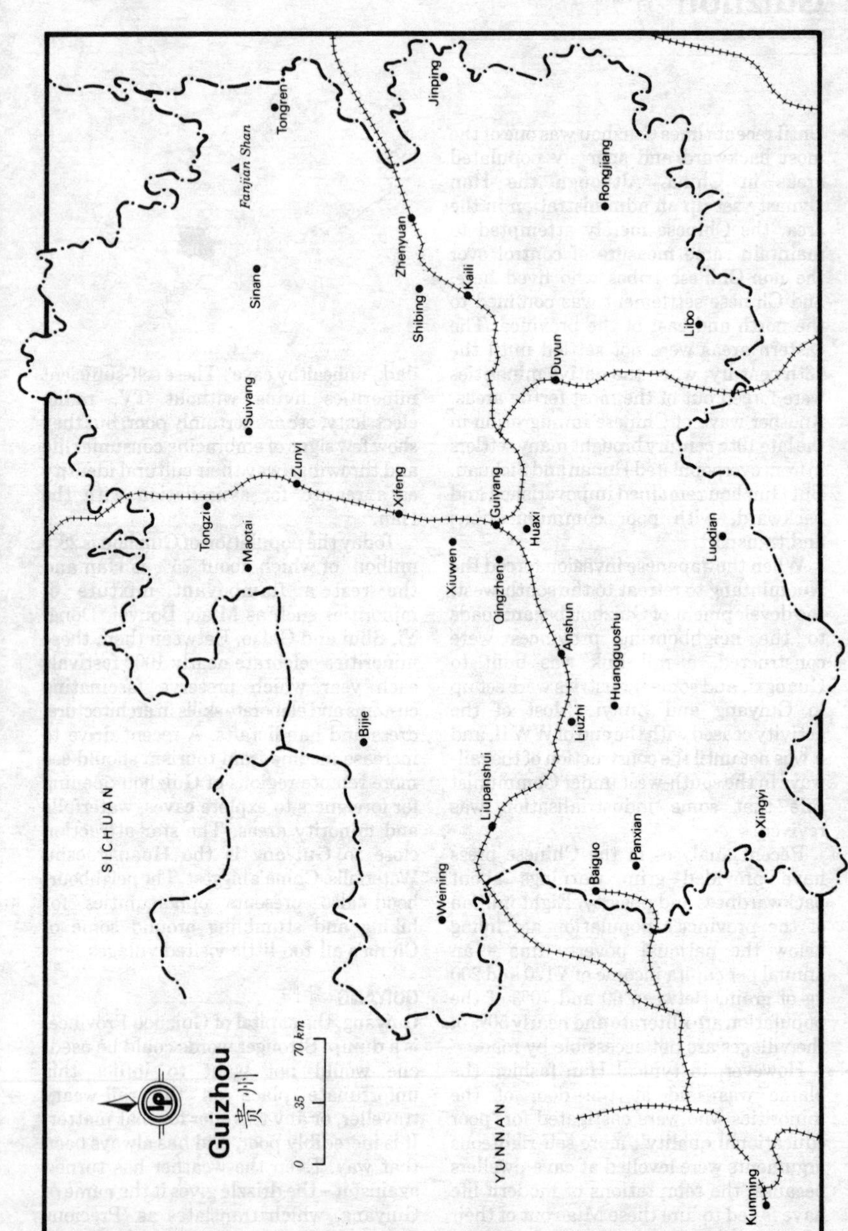
Guizhou
贵州
0
35
70 km
SICHUAN
YUNNAN
Fanjian Shan
Tongren
Jinping
Rongjiang
Zhenyuan
Sinan
Shibing
Kaili
Libo
Duyun
Suiyang
Zunyi
Tongzi
Xifeng
Guiyang
Huaxi
Luodian
Maotai
Xiuwen
Qingzhen
Anshun
Huangguoshu
Liuzhi
Bijie
Liupanshui
Xingyi
Panxian
Baiguo
Weining
Kunming

Sun'. A rush of post-liberation factories, including manufacturers of diesel engines, machinery, textiles and the like, has added a polluting dimension, and rapid population expansion has created nightmares in concrete and brick over the top of what was formerly little more than a village. Down dark streets lie some grimy markets in the vestiges of the older town, and along the murky river that threads through the city are one or two dilapidated temple structures. On paper, Guiyang bristles with societies and educational and military institutes – in reality it's backward to the extreme.

The only reason you'd want to come here is to go somewhere else (if you're on your way to Chongqing from Guilin, for example, you'll have to change trains at Guiyang) or to use it as a jumping-off point for the Huangguoshu Waterfalls or other places rapidly opening to foreigners in the province.

Information

CITS (tel 25121) is staffed by two extremely friendly and helpful gentlemen; one speaks good English and the other speaks French – exactly why their talents have been placed in Guiyang, where there's really nothing to see, is one of the ironies of the China International Travel Syndrome. Bus Nos 2 or 1 from the railway station will get you to the office. It's in a government compound of colonnaded buildings, in the building to the right of the compound's main gateway.

CAAC (tel 23000) is at 170 Zunyi Lu.

Things to See

The distinctive architectural characteristic of Guiyang's handful of Mussolini-modern buildings is the columns – like the ones at the Provincial Exhibition Hall. The main street leading down from the railway station harbours one of the largest glistening white statues of Mao Zedong in China. For details on the scenic bus loop around the city, see the Getting Around section.

Sights on the edges of the city are of the dreary cave-lake-park type, but the **Huaxi Caves** in Huaxi Park did yield a surprise – photocells along the underground path are activated by the guide's flashlight, triggering strings of coloured bulbs and neon signs as well as musical effects. This electronic wizardry will cost Y1.40 entrance fee for a foreigner, and Y0.10 for a local. Other sights that may (or may not) be worth checking out are the late Ming Dynasty **Hongfu Monastery** in Qianling Shan Park to the north-west of the city; and the **Kanzhu Pavilion** atop the mountain, which is the vantage point overlooking the city. Five km to the south-west of Guiyang is **Nanjiao Park**, noted for its caves.

Out at the Huaxi Hotel, I was approached by a woman (not sure of her credentials – PSB? CITS? maid?) who tried to rope me into a minibus tour of Guiyang at Y100 for four passengers for the day, including a transfer to the railway station – having given up on that she proceeded to tell me I was not to wander around Guiyang on foot, and not to use the local buses. I suppose there might have been a connection between the offering and the warning, since I had looped around the city on the buses for Y0.15, a substantial saving. What a load of rubbish some of these tourist authorities come up with!

One thing we were in agreement on, though for different reasons, was that one should gloss over the town and stick to the countryside periphery. I headed straight for the rice paddies near the Huaxi Hotel, where mud can only look like mud. The Huaxi's one saving grace is that right outside the front gates is a Bouyei village, with tattered New Year posters plastering the wooden doors. Nothing to get excited about, but a bit of rural living (the Bouyei are one of China's minority peoples – they number about 2.1 million and appear to live exclusively in Guizhou). Further away, across the rice paddies at the edge

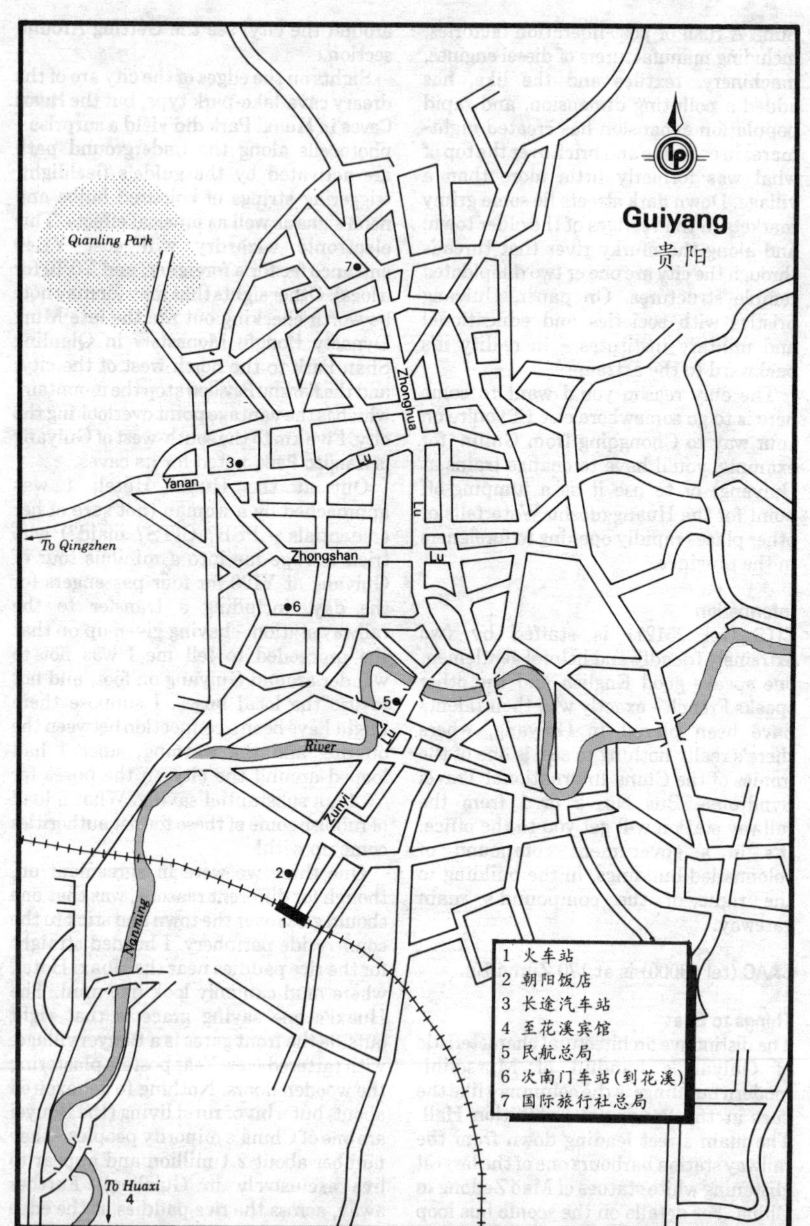
Guiyang
贵阳
Qianling Park
Zhonghua
Lu
Yanan
Lu
To Qingzhen
Zhongshan
Lu
River
Lu
Zunyi
Nanming
To Huaxi
1 火车站
2 朝阳饭店
3 长途汽车站
4 至花溪宾馆
5 民航总局
6 次南门车站(到花溪)
7 国际旅行社总局

1 Railway Station
2 Chao Yang Lushe Hotel
3 Long-distance Bus Station
4 To Huaxi Guest House
5 CAAC
6 Cinanmen Bus Depot (Buses to Huaxi)
7 CITS

of Huaxi Park, is another village with TV antennae poking through stone-slate roofing. The rural aspects are better viewed at Huangguoshu, although if you were to continue further south of the Huaxi Hotel, you would be right in the hamlet zones.

Places to Stay

If you're changing trains and stranded (going to Chongqing, for example), or attempting to get to the Huangguoshu Falls and in need of overnight lodgings, then try and use the 1st-class waiting room at the rail station. It's on the upper floor; on the ground floor there's a 24-hour baggage cage. Some students hang around the railway station waiting to catch a glimpse of the outside world, and you're a prize catch.

There are two hotels open to foreigners in Guiyang. The *Chao Yang Lushe* is a large building on Zunyi Lu, the main street leading down from the railway station. Walk across the square in front of the station; the hotel is just after the square on the left-hand side of the main street. It's actually a Chinese hotel and is super-filthy; you can probably get a bed here for Y4, single room for Y5, double room for Y5.70, four-person room for Y7.40, five-person room for Y7.75. If you have trouble getting in then phone CITS (tel 25121) and tell them that you only intend to overnight for a train connection.

Further into town on the bus No 1 route is the *Jinqiao Hotel* – it's Y9 a double but hard to get into.

The official tourist hotel is the *Huaxi Binguan* (tel 25973), which is 20 km south-west of the city, half-way to the airport. The dun-coloured buildings are on a hill in a landscaped and mini-forest area. Single rooms go for Y10, doubles Y17, and there are dormitory beds for Y7 (although Y5 is possible). The problem is that this hotel is a logistical disaster for transport; from the railway station it requires bus No 2 to Cinanmen (south-west bus depot), then a no-number bus (it's sometimes identified as No 16) to Huaxi Park, then a two-km walk – by this time you're almost in the countryside so it's not a bad two-km walk. But the last bus connection to Huaxi Park is around 6 pm. A taxi from the railway station would cost at least Y15. Taxis and minibuses are available for hire at the Huaxi Binguan, and if you're in town CITS should be able to get you one. The other problem is that there's little chance of an early-morning bus connection from the Huaxi Binguan to the Guiyang long-distance bus station to catch an early-morning bus to Huangguoshu – that would require a taxi also.

Places to Eat

Food in the local restaurants is abominable – one attempt to get into the cleaner-looking *Jinqiao Hotel Restaurant* was summarily rejected by the doorman, who appeared to be under the impression that Guiyang was still closed. (Guiyang opened in late 1982.) For munchies try the one or two restaurants on the perimeter of the square around the railway station. The *Huaxi Hotel* has a dining room, not too bad, and at least it's clean.

Some food stalls in Guiyang sell traditional snacks such as *kao doufu* (roasted bean curd), *liangfen* (bean jelly), *bijie tangyuan* (sweet dumpling) and *kao baogu* (roast corn).

In 1986, drinkers in Guiyang (home of the famous Maotai spirit) received a very raw deal when local bootleggers laced liquor with methanol to cut costs and add more kick before selling it to local merchants. Within days, 20 people had died and teams of medical workers were treating hundreds of seriously sick boozers. The mayor of Guiyang went on TV to warn the public about the evil brew which contained 300 times the permitted level of methanol.

Getting There & Away

Air Guiyang is connected by air to Beijing (Y332), Canton (Y153), Kunming (Y68), Guilin (Y74), Shanghai Y288), Chongqing (Y62), Chengdu (Y112) and Changsha (Y128).

Bus Buses to the Huangguoshu Falls depart from the long-distance bus station in the north-west of the city. The bus station is a distinctive building, an old temple-like structure. For details, see the section on Huangguoshu.

Rail Direct trains run to Kunming, Guilin, Chongqing and Nanning. For Zhanjiang you may have to change trains at Liuzhou. Some sample fares, *Chinese price*, hard-sleeper, are: to Guilin, 18 hours, Y26; to Liuzhou, 15 hours, Y20.50; to Kunming, 15 hours, Y20; to Chongqing, 11 hours, Y14.70.

Getting Around

If you want to do a city-loop tour, then across the square from the railway station are two round-the-city buses, Nos 1 and 2. They follow the same route but No 2 goes clockwise while No 1 goes anti-clockwise. These will get you to most places (bar the Huaxi Binguan) – the round trip from the station takes about 45 minutes for the grand sum of Y0.15. You can get a good window seat since you get on at the terminus; the same cannot be said if you choose to alight at random for a foot-sortie. The main shopping street is on the bus No 1 route heading north.

AROUND GUIYANG

Hong Feng Hu (Red Maple Lake) lies close to Qingzhen, which is 33 km west of Guiyang. This complex of four lake districts covers over 74 square km. The main attractions seem to be boating to some of the hundreds of small islands and exploring caves.

HUANGGUOSHU FALLS 黄果树瀑布

Located 155 km south-west of Guiyang, China's premier cataract is about 50 metres wide, with a drop of 70 metres into the 'Rhinoceros Pool'. For a preview, there is a drawing of the falls on the 10-fen Foreign Exchange Certificate. Huangguoshu is an excellent chance to go rambling through the superb rural minority areas on foot. Once you're there, no transport problems as everything you need is within walking range, or if you wish to go further, hiking range. Take a raincoat if you're off to waterfalls and a warm jacket or sweater if you're descending into caves, which can be chilly.

The thunder of Huangguoshu Falls can be heard for some distance, and the mist from the falls carries to the local villages during the rainy season, which lasts from May to October. The falls are at their most spectacular about four days after heavy rains. The dry season lasts from November to April, so during March and April the flow of water can become a less impressive trickle.

The main falls are the central piece of a huge waterfall, cave and karst area, covering some 450 square km. It was only explored by the Chinese in the 1980s as preliminaries to harnessing the hydro-electric potential. They discovered about 18 falls, four subterranean rivers, and 100 caves, many of which are now being gradually opened up to visitors.

Water Curtain Cave is a niche in the cliffs at the edge of the falls, which is approached by a slippery (and dangerous) sortie wading across rocks in the Rhino Pool – from the cave you'll get an interior view of the gushing waters through six 'windows'.

Doupo (Steep Slope Falls) is one km above the main falls and easy to reach.

Steep Slope Falls is 105 metres wide and 23 metres high, and gets its name from the criss-cross patterning of sloping waters. Eight km below Huangguoshu Falls are the **Star Bridge Falls**.

Ten km north-west of the Huangguoshu area (there may be a bus) are the **Gaotan Falls**, which lie on another river system. The falls here have a graduated drop of 120 metres. About 30 km from the Gaotan Falls is a newly-discovered underground cavern, reputedly quite large, which must be toured by boat. The cavern lies in Anshun County, at the Bouyei settlement of Longtan (Dragon Pool).

Huangguoshu (Yellow Fruit Tree) is in the Zhenning Bouyei and Miao Autonomous County. The Miao are not in evidence around the falls, but for the Bouyei, who favour river valleys, this is prime water country. The Bouyei are the 'aboriginals' of Guizhou. The people are of Thai origin and related to the Zhuangs in Guangxi. They number 2.1 million, mostly spread over the south-west sector of Guizhou Province. Bouyei dress is dark and sombre, with colourful trimmings; 'best' clothes come out on festival or market days. The Bouyei marry early, usually at 16, but sometimes as young as 12. Married women are distinguished by headgear symbols.

The Bouyei are very poor, showing signs of malnutrition and wearing clothes that are grubby and tattered. The contrast with the postcard minority image of starched and ironed costumes, or ring-of-confidence sparkling teeth is obvious. The Bouyei tribespeople are also shy and suspicious of foreigners. In Huangguoshu, in a concrete-floored hut, you might see a mother picking lice from a child's hair, while pigs, chickens, and rabid dogs have the run of the house and town.

Cloth wax-dyeing is one of the skills of the Bouyei. The masonry at Huangguoshu is also intriguing – stone blocks comprise the housing, but no plaster is used; the roofs are finished in stone slates. There is a Bouyei festival in Huangguoshu lasting 10 days during the first lunar month (usually February or early March).

Places to Stay & Eat

At the bus park near the Huangguoshu Falls are some food stalls. Below them, down the cliff, is a teahouse and souvenir shop. The viewing area for the falls is a short downhill walk from the bus park. Further away from the bus park is *Huangguoshu Guest House*, which is only for foreigners. Clean rooms with bathroom start at Y12 per person. Its decent restaurant charges Y4 for set meals; buy tickets at the reception desk. Other doss houses in the village with no facilities charge Y2 per night, but the authorities require foreigners to stay in the guest house.

Getting There

You can get to Huangguoshu Falls from either Guiyang or Anshun – both have logistical obstacles but Anshun is preferable.

The falls are 150 km by road from Guiyang. A bus (usually No 103) leaves Guiyang's long-distance bus station at 7 am; the fare is around Y4 or Y5, and the trip takes four to five hours. Tour buses depart the falls for Guiyang at around 3 or 4 pm.

Guiyang CITS offers minibus tours to the falls, departing from the Huaxi Hotel in Guiyang. Prices are in the region of Y0.50 to Y0.80 per km, dependent on the size of the group and vehicle. For a same-day return trip to the falls you'd be looking at, say, Y230 – no food, no guide. The same deal, but considerably cheaper, can be got in Anshun.

Anshun lies on the Guiyang-Kunming railway line, about two hours from Guiyang. Anshun is 50 km from the falls, so a local bus takes about 1½ hours to get there; the fare is Y1.30. If you arrive in Anshun by train you may have problems with a bus connection to Huangguoshu, so you may have to overnight in Anshun and take a bus out the next morning. Bus service between Anshun and the falls is sporadic; on weekdays buses depart Anshun at 7.40 am and noon, and there may be one as late as 2.30 pm. Bus frequencies on weekends are higher than on weekdays.

Alternatively, you could go from Anshun to Zhenning, near the falls. The trip takes an hour and costs Y0.80. There are five morning buses from Anshun to Zhenning and five afternoon buses.

There's a local bus from Huangguoshu to Guiyang at 12.30 pm; other buses depart Huangguoshu for Anshun at 10.30 am, 2 pm, 3 pm, 4 pm and 4.30 pm. These will probably connect with trains departing Anshun for Guiyang or Kunming.

As a rule of thumb, you have a better chance of getting a hard-sleeper on the section between Kunming and Anshun if you start out from Kunming and buy your ticket in advance there. There's usually little chance of buying a hard-sleeper ticket from Anshun to Kunming.

You could bus between Kunming and Huangguoshu. Some travellers spurn the trains between Guizhou and Yunnan provinces and simply take buses via Panxian and Qujing.

The bus to Panxian passes through Huangguoshu daily at about 9 am and will stop outside the ticket office if you flag it down. The trip costs Y5.3 and takes 10 hours. Panxian has a hostel at the bus station. The bus from Panxian to Qujing leaves at 7.30 am, takes six hours and costs Y4.3. The hotel in Qujing is about 20 minutes walk from the bus station. Follow the road which runs from the other side of the roundabout directly opposite the front of the bus station. After passing a modern house (pagoda style) on your left, take the first road on the right. The hotel is about 200 metres down this road on the left. The bus from Qujing to Kunming departs at 7.30 am, takes four hours and costs Y4.

ANSHUN 安顺

Anshun, once an opium-trading centre, remains the commercial hub of western Guizhou but is now known for its wax-dyed fabrics. At the north-east end of town is a large Confucian temple. The town lies on the Guiyang-Kunming railway line, a two-hour ride from Guiyang.

You can make Anshun a jumping-off point for the Huangguoshu Falls. The bus from the Hongshan Hotel is sent to the station if they receive word that foreigners are looking lost there. You'll then be charged Y4 for the ride to the hotel. If you avoid being intercepted at the train station, you may be able to get down to Huangguoshu on the same day. Walk straight ahead from the railway station for about 1½ km, and the bus station is on your left – ask for 'Huang Guo Shu, Duan Tu Qi Che Zhan' (Huangguoshu, short-distance bus station). If you intend to come back on the same day, dump your bags at the left-luggage room in Anshun Train Station.

Places to Stay

There are a couple of convenient places close to the bus station. The high-storeyed hotel beside the station has dorm beds for Y3 (student price). Across the road is a tourist hotel with dorm beds for Y10 FEC (student price).

The main tourist joint, inconveniently located on the outskirts of Anshun, is the *Hongshan Binguan*, definately lacking in the electricity and plumbing departments, but solid. The hotel gardens overlook an artificial lake, leaving the mud of Anshun town behind. Double rooms cost Y18. The hotel is completely isolated but the dinner-bell of the hotel dining-room is loud enough to warn of impending food shortages should you miss the occasion. CITS (tel 3173) has an office here which organises trips to Huangguoshu and the surrounding area. The bus station is four km away and the train station three km. The hotel minibus charges about Y4 per person for transfer to the train station.

Festivals

Festivities amongst the minorities in Guizhou offer plenty of scope for exploration. Festivals take place throughout the lunar calendar at specific sites and are technicolour spectaculars which can feature bull fighting, horse racing, pipe playing, comic opera, singing contests and gigantic courting parties.

Guiyang has several festivals during the first lunar month (usually February or March), fourth lunar month (around May) and sixth lunar month (around July). Some of these take place in Huaxi.

Kaili, a town on the railway line east of Guiyang, is open to foreigners. A profusion of festivals is held in nearby minority areas such as Lei Gong Shan, Xijiang, Danxi, Qingman and Panghai. The town of Zhijiang, about 50 km from Kaili, is also a festival centre.

Zhenyuan, recently opened to foreigners, lies further east on the railway line and is renowned for its festivals between April and July. This town was once an important staging point on the ancient post road from central China to south-east Asia.

Sichuan 四川

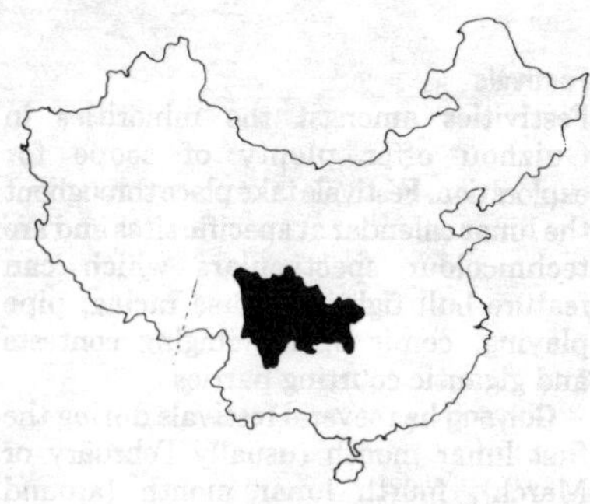

There is a Chinese saying that the real riches in life are not jade or pearls, but the five grains (rice, soybeans, wheat, barley and millet). These are well represented in the fertile Sichuan Basin, under irrigation since the 3rd century BC, and the PRC's greatest rice producer.

Sichuan is the largest province in China but also the most heavily populated, with almost 100 million people. It is the eastern region of Sichuan, the great Chengdu plain, that supports one of the densest rural populations in the world, while the regions to the west are mountainous and sparsely populated, mainly by Tibetans.

Back in the Maoist era birth control was a pair of dirty words, a capitalist plot to make China weak. Mao believed in strength in numbers – much the mentality of a peasant who needs many children to work the fields – and anyone who opposed him was put out to pasture. Today, Sichuan has a determined birth control campaign which is attempting to reduce the birth rate to less than half – a huge billboard spells it out (inexplicably in English) in the centre of Chengdu, the provincial capital. That's not the only Maoist policy being debunked in Sichuan.

Possibly because this is the home of Deng Xiaoping (who was born here in 1904), Sichuan has become a testing ground for the debunking of the commune system; he has called the commune a utopian dream of 'reaching heaven in one step'. The efforts now are towards decentralisation of agriculture, greater autonomy of decision making, establishment of free markets at which peasants can sell their produce, and greater individual incentives. Xindu County, outside Chengdu, is one of the first experimental stations; farms are state-owned, but if a peasant meets the required quota, any surplus is his. He also decides what to plant and when. If the streets of Chengdu are any indication, the 'responsibility system' is a howling success.

Roughly the size of France, give or take Luxembourg, Sichuan has rich natural resources. Wild mountainous terrain and fast rivers blocked access until the present era, and much of the western fringe is still remote. The capital is Chengdu; the largest city is Chongqing, which is also the stepping-stone for the ferry ride down the Yangtse River.

The remote mountains of Sichuan, Gansu and Shaanxi provinces are the natural habitat of the giant panda. Of China's 1174 species of birds, 420 species of mammals and 500 species of reptiles and amphibians, the one animal which westerners automatically associate with China is the giant panda. This is probably due to the Chinese fondness several years ago for giving them away as presents to foreign governments.

CHENGDU 成都

Chengdu is Sichuan's capital and the administrative, educational and cultural centre, as well as a major industrial base. It boasts a 2500-year history, linked closely with the art and craft trades. During the Eastern Han Dynasty (25-220 AD) the city was named Jinjiang Cheng (Brocade City), due to its thriving silk manufacturing. Like other major Chinese cities, the place has had its share of turmoil. First it was devastated by the Mongols in retaliation for fierce fighting

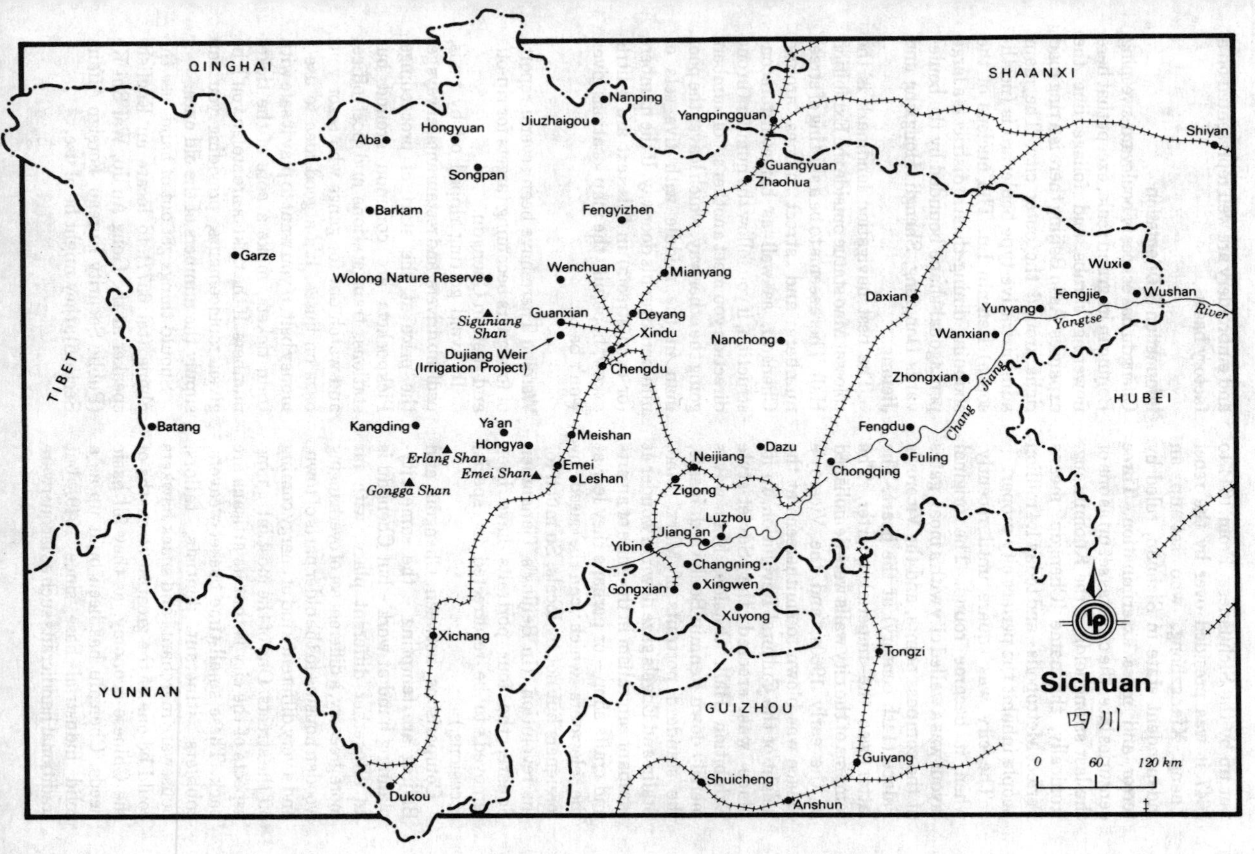
QINGHAI
SHAANXI
TIBET
HUBEI
YUNNAN
GUIZHOU
Nanping
Yangpingguan
Shiyan
Jiuzhaigou
Aba
Hongyuan
Songpan
Guangyuan
Zhaohua
Barkam
Fengyizhen
Garze
Wenchuan
Mianyang
Wolong Nature Reserve
Wuxi
Daxian
Fengjie
Wushan
Siguniang Shan
Guanxian
Deyang
Yunyang
Yangtse
River
Xindu
Wanxian
Dujiang Weir (Irrigation Project)
Nanchong
Chengdu
Zhongxian
Chang Jiang
Batang
Kangding
Ya'an
Fengdu
Hongya
Meishan
Dazu
Erlang Shan
Fuling
Neijiang
Emei
Chongqing
Emei Shan
Leshan
Gongga Shan
Zigong
Luzhou
Jiang'an
Yibin
Changning
Gongxian
Xingwen
Xuyong
Xichang
Tongzi
Sichuan
四川
Guiyang
Shuicheng
0 60 120 km
Dukou
Anshun

put up by the Sichuanese. From 1644 to 1647 it was presided over by the rebel Zhang Xiangzhong, who set up an independent state in Sichuan, ruled by terror and mass extermination. Three centuries later the city was set up as one of the last strongholds of the Kuomintang. Ironically, the name 'Chengdu' means Perfect Metropolis – and today 1.4 million people inhabit the perfect city proper.

The city was square until recently, when it became round. The original layout was a walled city with a moat, gates at the compass points, and the Viceroy's Palace (14th century) at the heart. The latter was the imperial quarter. The remains of the city walls were demolished in the early 1960s, and the Viceroy's Palace was blown to smithereens at the height of the Cultural Revolution. In its place was erected the Soviet-style Exhibition Hall. Outside, Mao waves merrily down Renmin Boulevard; inside, the standard portraits of Marx, Mao, Stalin and Engels gaze down in wonder at rampant capitalism in the guise of an arts and crafts shop – or perhaps they leer at the elevators which can be used by foreigners but not by locals. So much for the revolution. (In Beijing's Tiananmen Square, the four portraits have been removed, to be resurrected for special occasions.)

Comparisons between Chengdu and Beijing are tempting – the same city-planning hand at work – but Chengdu is an altogether different place, with far more greenery, a different set of overhanging wooden housing in the older parts of town, and a very different kind of energy coming off the streets. One of the most intriguing aspects of the city is that its artisans are back. These small-time basket-weavers, cobblers, itinerant dentists, tailors, houseware merchants and snack hawkers could be one of the greatest strengths of the Chinese economy, as they fill basic needs. Chengdu has been built up as a solid industrial base since 1949, but traditional handicrafts such as lacquerware and embroidery are well represented on a factory basis.

Information & Orientation

Chengdu has echoes of boulevard-sweeping Beijing in its grand scale, except that here flowering shrubs and foliage line the expanses. As in Beijing there is a ring road right around the outer city. The main administrative-type boulevard is (north-south) Renmin Lu. The nucleus of the shopping-dining-theatre district is a large pentagonal shape bounded by the boulevards Dongfeng, Shengli, Hongxing and Jiefang.

The best navigation landmark is the colossal Mao statue outside the Exhibition Hall. There seems to be a shifting of street numbers and street names around Chengdu, as well as boulevard reconstruction, if you follow the numbers in one direction you meet another set of numbers going the other way, which leaves the poor man in the middle with five sets of numbers over his doorway. If the numbers (or even streets) in this text are a little askew, hopefully the map locations given won't be.

Warning There have been several reports of foreigners becoming targets for rip-offs and theft in Chengdu.

To avoid getting ripped off by taxis, pedicab drivers, and restaurants, always get the price at the start of proceedings. Pickpockets are common around bus stations, train stations and post offices and watch out for gangs who razor your bags on buses. It's a good idea to use a money belt. If you want to play it safe with train tickets, make a note of the ticket numbers. If the tickets are stolen you'll be given replacements, providing you can supply the numbers of the old ones.

Should things get out of hand, use the phone (tel 6577) to locate an English-speaker at the Gong An Ju, Wai Shi Ke (Public Security Bureau, Foreign Affairs Section); they might be of use.

CITS (tel 28731) is next to hopeless. They're in the Jinjiang Hotel and mainly interested in raking up group-tour money. Their information is almost useless. Try the front-desk staff as they make a lot more sense, and their English is superior.

Public Security (tel 6577) has two staff members who speak English. They are unable or unwilling to do much more than extend a visa and are, reportedly, most unhelpful in the event of theft, loss reports, etc. In the Theft & Other Crimes section of the Facts for the Visitor chapter is an Austrian traveller's story about this PSB and its handling of a loss report. They're on Xinhua Donglu, east of the intersection with Renmin Zhonglu.

Consulates The US Consulate General has an office in Chengdu in the Jinjiang Hotel. Telephone direct on 51912 or 52791, or dial 24481 and ask for extension 138.

CAAC is diagonally across the street from the Jinjiang Hotel.

Maps City bus maps can be found at train stations, the Jinjiang Hotel and Xinhua bookstores. Three different maps in Chinese provide excellent detail for Sichuan Province, Chengdu city or its surrounding areas.

Reading & Music The Foreign Language Bookstore has mildly captivating tourist literature and general data. And while you're here, there's a counter selling watery versions of western music and traditional Chinese music in cassette form (the store shares the same corner as a Xinhua Bookstore).

Things to See

Free markets, flea markets, black markets, pedlar markets – whatever they are, Chengdu is cooking with them. Each twist and turn down the back alleys seems to reveal a new specialty. Around the corner comes a florist shop on wheels – a bicycle laden with gladioli – or you chance upon a butcher market, a vegetable market, spice market, or side street devoted to a species of repairman. Add to this the indoor food markets, and you're looking at a thriving small business economy.

There is a busy poultry market a short walk from the Jinjiang Hotel, amusing for reasons that will quickly become apparent (not amusing for the animals). To get there cross the bridge to the south and turn left. If you go north to the Furong Restaurant and then take an alley to the left, off Renmin, you'll find an outdoor factory of sorts, where the street is lined with women at their sewing machines. Further west, bordering the south-east edge of Renmin Park, is a small strip devoted entirely to the sale of eggs.

Engrossing to stroll through is the tinker-and-tailor free market (for lack of better terminology) which runs north from near Chengdu Restaurant, and then turns east along another alley leading to Chunxi Lu – this one is a local mecca for clothing and on-the-spot tailoring. It appears that the market is not affected by cotton-ration coupons, and it also appears that those with fast scissors can earn double what a factory worker gets.

In 1986, a local student told me the hottest and most bizarre story in town (which he swore was true) about a market woman who had an argument with a customer. The squabble became so vicious that the woman had a fit of rage, grabbed her opponent's testicles and twisted them so hard that he fell into a coma and died. At the woman's trial, the judiciary concluded that she had used specially acquired kung-fu skills and gave her the death sentence.

Renmin Park

I am not a fan of Chinese parklands – but this one I will recommend. The teahouse here is excellent (see the Places to Eat section), and just near the entrance is the candyman. Works of art in toffee: China's back-street merchants can be truly

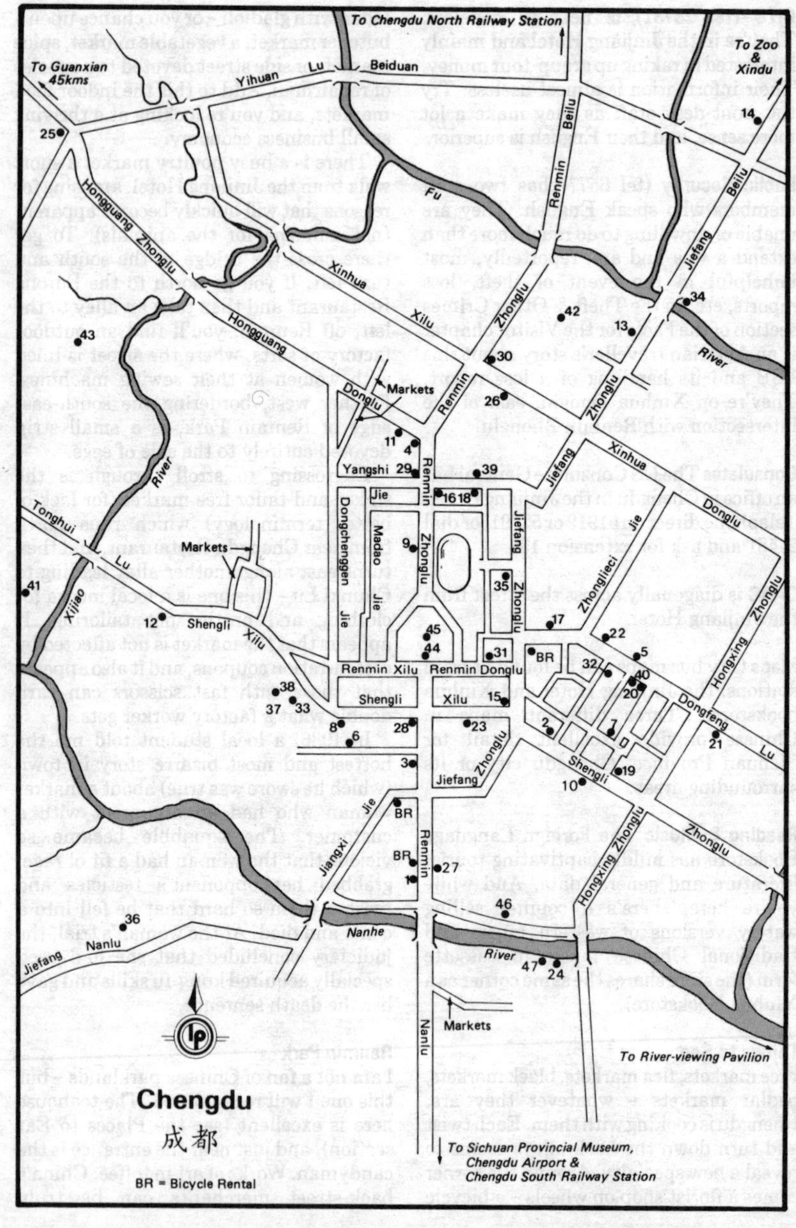
To Chengdu North Railway Station
To Guanxian 45kms
To Zoo & Xindu
Yihuan Lu
Beiduan
Renmin Beilu
Jiefang Beilu
Fu River
Hongguang Zhonglu
Xinhua Xilu
Hongguang Donglu
Markets
Renmin Zhonglu
Zhonglu
Jiefang Zhonglu
Xinhua Donglu
Yangshi Jie
Dongchenggen Jie
Madao Jie
Renmin Zhonglu
Jiefang Zhonglu
Zhonglieci Jie
Tonghui Lu
Xijiao River
Shengli Xilu
Renmin Xilu
Renmin Donglu
Shengli
Xilu
Hongxing Zhonglu
Dongfeng Lu
Shengli
Jiefang Zhonglu
Jiangxi Jie
BR
Renmin Nanlu
Hongxing Zhonglu
Nanhe River
Jiefang Nanlu
Markets
To River-viewing Pavilion
To Sichuan Provincial Museum, Chengdu Airport & Chengdu South Railway Station
Chengdu
成都
BR = Bicycle Rental

1 Jinjiang Hotel/CITS
2 Chengdu Restaurant
3 Furong Restaurant
4 Rong Le Yuan Restaurant
5 Dongfeng Restaurant
6 Rongcheng Restaurant
7 Yao Chua Restaurant
8 Wang Pang Duck Restaurant
9 Waisolo Cold Duck Restaurant
10 Friendship Store
11 Drum & Cymbal Shop
12 Lacquer Ware Factory
13 Sichuan Embroidery Factory
14 Bamboo Weaving Factory
15 Renmin Market
16 Soda Bar
17 Fuqi Feipian (Husband & Wife Lungs) Snackshop
18 Chen Mapo (Granny's Beancurd) Snackshop
19 Long Chaoshou Soup Dumplings
20 Lai Tangyuan Rice-Ball Restaurant
21 Snackshops (Sweets)
22 Zhong Shuijiao Ravioli Restaurant
23 Advance Rail Ticket Office
24 Chengdu Bus Terminal (Xinanmen Station)
25 Ximen Bus Station (Buses for Guanxian)
26 Public Security
27 CAAC
28 Xinhua Bookstore
29 Foreign Languages Bookstore
30 Chengdu Theatre
31 Telecommunications Building
32 Bank of China
33 Renmin Teahouse
34 Teahouse
35 Xiao Yuan Teahouse & Bar
36 Temple of Wuhou
37 Renmin Park
38 Monument to the Martyrs of the Railway-Protecting Movement 1911
39 Blind People's Massage Parlour
40 Acrobat Theatre
41 Cultural Park & Qingyang Palace
42 Wenshu Monastery
43 Tomb of Wang Jiang
44 Mao Statue
45 Sichuan Exhibition Centre
46 Black Coffee Hotel
47 Jiaotong Hotel

1 锦江宾馆
2 成都餐厅
3 芙蓉饭店
4 荣乐饭店
5 东风饭店
6 容城饭店
7 耀华饭店
8 王胖鸭店
9 烤鸭店
10 友谊商店
11 鼓店
12 漆器厂
13 蜀绣厂
14 竹编工艺厂
15 人民市场
16 冷饮柜台
17 夫妻肺片
18 陈麻婆豆腐
19 龙抄手饭店
20 赖汤元饭店
21 小吃(东风路)
22 钟水饺饭店
23 火车售票处
24 成都汽车站
25 西门汽车站
26 公安局
27 中国民用航空总局
28 新华书店
29 外文书店
30 成都剧院
31 电讯大楼
32 银行
33 人民茶馆
34 解放北路茶馆
35 晓园茶馆
36 武侯祠
37 人民公园
38 烈士纪念碑
39 按摩院
40 杂技场
41 文化公园
42 文殊院
43 王建墓
44 毛泽东碑
45 展览馆
46 黑咖啡饭店
47 交通饭店

amazing. While most of the action, or relaxation, is around the entrance to Renmin Park, the rest of it is not too shabby – a bonsai rockery, a kids' playground, a few swimming pools (for locals), and the Monument to the Martyrs of the Railway Protecting Movement (1911). Apparently this obelisk, decorated with shunting and tracks, marks an uprising of the people against officers who pocketed cash raised for the construction of the Chengdu-Chongqing Line. Since Renmin Park was also at the time a private officer's garden, it was a fitting place to erect the structure.

The English-speaking Club meets outside in the Jinjiang Park on Tuesdays, Fridays and Sundays at 7.30 pm. A good opportunity to meet some interesting locals.

Temple Parks

Of perhaps more middling interest are the

temple parks of Chengdu. These are all a fair distance from the Jinjiang Hotel, although a cycle out to them would be a rewarding exercise in itself.

Du Fu Caotang is the thatched cottage of celebrated Tang poet Du Fu (712-770 AD). Something of a rover, Du Fu was born in Henan and left his home turf to see China at the tender age of 20. He was an official in Changan (the ancient capital on the site of modern-day Xian) for 10 years, was later captured by rebels after an uprising, and fled to Chengdu, where he stayed for four years. He built himself a humble cottage and penned over 200 poems on the sufferings of the people.

The present grounds – 20 hectares of leafy bamboo and luxuriant vegetation – are an expansion over time of the original cottage area. It's also the centre of the Chengdu Du Fu Study Society, and houses Chinese and western editions of the poet's works, a Du Fu statue and miniature calligraphy (a miniaturist might be on hand to engrave rings). From the time of his death in exile (in Hunan), Du Fu acquired a cult status, with the poems themselves being great inspiration for painting (which is displayed on site).

Praise for Du Fu comes from the highest source, Chairman Mao. The Great Helmsman seems to have overdone it a bit – the right-hand section of the park is largely devoted to commemorating his visit in 1958. The park offers tranquil strolling in tea gardens and is about five km west of the city centre.

The **Temple of Wuhou** is in Nanjiao (south suburb) Park. Wuhou or Zhu Geliang was a famous military strategist of the Three Kingdoms Period (220-265 AD). He was the prime minister of the state of Shu, and shares the tomb space and shrine with his emperor, Liu Bei. Chengdu was the capital of Shu state. Structures at the site date to the Tang Dynasty, with renovations and enlargements from the 17th and 20th centuries. There's some fine stele calligraphy, and statues of military and civic officers. To the west of the temple is a large park with a lake, picnicking, a nice teahouse, and a small antique store at the north end.

Wanjian Lou (River Viewing Pavilion) is as the name suggests. It is to the south-east of Chengdu, near Sichuan University. The pavilion is a four-storey Qing wooden structure with a teahouse and restaurant. Lush bamboo forests with over 100 types, surround the building. The bamboos range from skyscrapers to bonsai-sized potted plants, so this might be a good place to escape the summer heat. The pavilion was built to the memory of Xue Tao, a Tang Dynasty poet. Nearby is a well, said to be the place where she drew water to dye her writing paper.

These three temple parks are open from 7.30 am to 6 pm.

Qingyang Gong (Cultural Park), where an ancient Taoist temple once stood, is the site of the Lantern Festival at Chinese New Year.

Tomb of Wang Jian

To the north-west of Chengdu, the tomb's exhibition hall features a display of relics, including jade belt, mourning books, imperial seals, warrior and musician sculptures. Wang Jian (847-918 AD) was emperor of Shu in the 10th century. The hall is open daily except Monday, 9 am to noon and 2 to 5.30 pm.

Sichuan University Museum

The museum is on the 1st and 3rd floors of Sichuan University's Liberal Arts building. Recently re-opened, it is reputed to have imaginative displays in four exhibition rooms devoted to Sichuan's four major minorities – the Tibetans, Qiang, Yi and Miao. Description tags in English are a welcome innovation. The museum is open Monday to Saturday, 9 am to noon and 2.30 to 5.30 pm. If you want to make sure you'll be allowed inside, phone the Foreign Affairs Office (tel 54111, extension 235) or the museum (tel 54111, extension 313) – they can also give directions for getting there.

As you start to leave town, still within easy range is the **Temple of Divine Light** at Xindu, the **Wenshu Monastery** and the **zoo** – the three together are a guaranteed A-1 excursion. A suggested route: Get to Xindu first in the early morning, proceed to the zoo and then visit Wenshu.

Baoguangsi (Monastery of Divine Light)
This monastery in the north of Xindu County is an active Buddhist temple. It comprises five halls and 16 courtyards, surrounded by bamboo. Pilgrims, monks and tourists head for Xindu, which makes for lively proceedings and attracts a fine array of hawkers. The temple was founded in the 9th century, was subsequently destroyed, and was reconstructed in the 17th century.

Among the monastery treasures are a white jade Buddha from Burma, Ming and Qing paintings and calligraphy, a stone tablet engraved with 1000 Buddhist figurines (540 AD), and ceremonial musical instruments. The temple is rich in artefacts, but most of the more valuable items are locked away, and require special permission to view them – you may be able to if you can find whoever's in charge around here.

The Arhat Hall, built in the 19th century, contains 500 two-metre-high clay figurines representing Buddhist saints and disciples. Well, not all of them: in among this spaced-out lot are two earthlings – emperors Kangxi and Qianlong. They're distinguishable by their royal costumes, beards, boots and capes. One of the impostors, Kangxi, is shown with a pockmarked face, perhaps a whim of the sculptor.

The temple has an excellent vegetarian restaurant where a huge array of dishes is prepared by monastic chefs (special requests can be catered for). Be punctual if you want to make certain of lunch, which is served between 11 am and noon. The temple is open daily, 8 am to 6 pm. The countryside around Xindu is fertile, with bracing farm scenery. About a km from Baoguangsi is Osmanthus Lake and its bamboo groves, lotuses, and osmanthus trees. In the middle of the lake is a small memorial hall for Ming scholar Yang Shengan.

Xindu is 18 km north of Chengdu: a round trip on a bicycle would be 40 km, or at least four hours' cycling time on a Chinese bike. Otherwise, buses leave from the traffic circle south of the Chengdu North Railway Station; the bus trip takes about 40 minutes. Hitching is another possibility, but better done returning from Xindu.

Zoo
For the humans there are lush, beautiful grounds (the animals get concrete, but at least some attempt has been made to make them feel at home). Since Sichuan is the largest panda habitat, Chengdu Zoo is the best place to see them in China. There are about eight on hand for observation.

The zoo is about six km from Chengdu centre, and is open 8 am to 6 pm daily.

Take bus No 1 to the terminus and then change to bus No 9, or drop off the Xindu bus. It's a half-hour by bicycle from Chengdu.

Wenshu Monastery

Whatever its background, Wenshu (God of Wisdom) Monastery offers a spectacle that few PRC temples do: it's so crowded with worshippers that you may have trouble getting in there on weekends. The object of veneration drawing the burners of incense appears to be a Buddhist statue made in Tibet. Wenshu dates back as far as the Tang Dynasty, with reconstruction in the 17th century. Various halls contain Buddhist artefacts, but you may not be permitted to view all of these. There is also a teahouse, and a gallery displaying paintings and calligraphy. It is open daily, 8 am to 8 pm. The alley on which Wenshu is located is a curiosity in itself, with joss-stick vendors, foot-callus removers, blind fortune-tellers with bamboo spills, and flower and fireworks salesmen. The alley runs eastwards off Renmin Zhonglu.

Places to Stay

The *Jinjiang Guest House* (tel 24481) at 180 Renmin Nan Lu has just undergone a partial facelift. The acres of reflective surfaces now require the full-time ministrations of polishers and, presumably, are also the justification for rocketing room prices.

This is a 1000-bed mini-state deluxe block with high walls around it and all facilities. At peak hours the elevators are jammed with an odd mix of touring French, resident foreign experts, businesspeople, chirpy Hong Kongers, even a stray Tibetan dignitary in flowing robes. Everyone seems to use the facilities, but it's hard to tell who's actually staying here.

If you want to leap in at the top, there's a deluxe suite for Y1500 or the simple version for Y160. Doubles range between Y75 and Y99, depending on the facilities. The cheapest option is a bed in a triple, which costs Y21.

On the 1st floor is an immense dining-room which doubles as an occasional theatre. A student-priced dinner is Y2.50 as opposed to Y6 for a regular, but it's not the same meal because the scale is smaller and there's no trimmings or dessert (though you could try pinching it from other tables). The cuisine here hardly matches the quality of spicing in Chengdu's restaurants.

The Jinjiang Garden Restaurant on the 9th floor has a sign: 'sloppy dressers is not welcome'. The indoor dining area which serves western and Chinese dishes is not good value. The western breakfast costs Y12 for skimpy portions. The outdoor terrace with a view across the city haze is a pleasant place for a drink. Watch out for blatant short-changing by surly staff – a quick word with the manager helps iron this out.

On the same floor, the billiards room and disco should now be operating again after renovation. Expect to pay around Y10 FEC to enter the disco. The ballroom disco held on Saturdays (possibly more frequently now) on the ground floor is for Chinese only – no dogs or foreigners.

In the lobby there's a taxi counter which can also arrange minibuses or Landcruisers for trips further afield. At the open-plan coffee shop there's a minimum charge of Y3 but it's useful as a meeting point or rest-stop – pick up your copy of *China Daily* from the reception desk.

To find the CITS office, walk through the lobby and past the bank, and it's just before the rear exit on your left.

The bank is on the ground floor; go through the lobby in the direction of the rear exit. Efficient staff change most currencies and you can use credit cards to draw up to Y500 daily. Unorthodox money-changing takes place outside the hotel gates, or try the Friendship Store downtown for a less obtrusive change.

The telephone office, next to the bank, operates until 11 pm. Overseas connections are erratic as one operator is helpful, the other stroppy. The World Trade Centre

Club has an office next to the telephone office.

Opposite the bank and the telephone office are two shops. One sells export quality food and drink; the other sells handicrafts and tourist paraphernalia. Between the two you should be able to stock up on Kodachrome, Johnny Walker, Nescafe and other items close to your heart.

The corridor to the right as you enter the lobby houses the post office and telex rooms, a photo-processing and photocopying centre and a shop right at the end.

Since the Jinjiang Hotel has become a centre for foreigners, all Poste Restante mail sent to Chengdu tends to land up here. It helps if your surname is clearly written on the envelope in block capitals and underlined. Even if your mail makes it through the system, you then have to find it. The search & find operation should include at least the following three places:

1. The reception desk where the latest mail (which usually arrives at 5 pm) is kept in several boxes – ask if they have any other boxes.
2. The Jinjiang Hotel Post Office which is down the corridor to your right when entering the lobby. The mail kept here for a maximum of three months is literally a mixed bag or bags. There's a small charge for any letters you receive.
3. The Zong You Ju (Central Post Office) in town where names of foreigners whose mail has arrived there are written up on large blackboards hanging on the wall behind the counter. It took me hours to find; it's in the vicinity of Xing Long Jie – ask someone at reception to write the full name in Chinese.

There's a bicycle-rental conveniently located on the wall along Renmin Lu (see the Getting Around section). If you park your bike in the Jinjiang's bike parking lot just before the bike-rental, take a look at the signs in English and Chinese. For the same amount of time, foreigners pay Y0.30 while Chinese pay Y0.03. Of course it's peanuts, but when I casually asked the attendant if there was any special reason for the price difference, she said the Chinese sign was not intended for me – I was meant to read the foreigners' sign!

If you're arriving in Chengdu from Leshan or Emei by bus, ask the driver to let you off at the hotel en route to the Chengdu South Bus Station (Xinanmen) – otherwise you'll have to walk back (about 15 minutes). If arriving by train, take bus No 16 (from either North Station or South Station) – it will deposit you on the hotel doorstep. Everybody knows where the Jinjiang is, so it's no trouble asking for directions to the hotel (ask for the *Jinjiang Binguan*).

The *Jiaotong Fandian* (Transport Hotel), next to Ximen Bus Station, has now become the backpacker's palace. There are two types of single for Y10 or Y15; doubles cost Y8 per person; a bed in a four-bed dorm costs Y4. The staff at reception are friendly and there's a noticeboard with travel info next to the counter. Another useful service here is a baggage room where you can leave heavy backpacks for a few days while you head off to Emei Shan, Jiuzhaigou or wherever.

The hotel restaurant has reasonable food, but may still be implementing a 30% surcharge for foreigners on the Chinese menu price. If foreigners and Chinese are eating the same food, I can't see the justification for this. Anyway, judge for yourself and vote with your feet.

The *Hei Kafei Fandian* (Black Coffee Hotel), a few minutes' walk east of the Jinjiang Hotel, is a bomb-shelter which has been converted into an underground hotel. Unless you like living in a rat-hole, this place won't appeal. Doubles cost Y16; a bed in a four-bed room costs Y5. In the dank maze of rooms, all sorts of things go on: disco dancing, snogging, furtive fumbling and even prostitution.

The *Rongcheng Fandian* (tel 22687) is

at 130 Shaanxi Jie, about 20 minutes on foot from the Jinjiang Hotel. It's currently being renovated and has sometimes taken foreigners. Doubles and triples cost Y27.

The *Minshan Fandian* is a high-rise hotel scheduled to open in 1988 opposite the Jinjiang Hotel.

Places to Eat

Sichuan cuisine is a class unto itself. It emphasises extremities of the tastebuds, with an armoury of spicing designed, it seems, to permanently damage them. The art in Chengdu is better represented in the snack line (these are not necessarily tongue-searing – could be sweet or salty). Dishes that won't make your forehead drip or your eyeballs pop out are Sichuan duck (smoked with camellia and camphor leaves), stuffed fish and certain chicken dishes. If you head for the Jinjiang dining-halls, of course, you are simply asking for western meals, or else over-priced parodies of local fare, minus the heavy-handed spicing (and minus the table-manner displays). Special dishes may require an advance phone order, so get the hotel to ring for you.

Main Courses The *Chengdu Restaurant* (tel 7301) at 642 Shengli Zhong Lu is one of the largest and best in the city, a favourite with travellers. Good atmosphere, decent food, reasonable prices – downstairs is adequate. Try to assemble a party of vagabonds from the hotel before sallying forth, since tables are large and you get to sample more with a bigger group. It's about a 20-minute walk along a side alley opposite the Jinjiang Hotel. Arrive early.

The *Furong* (tel 4004) is at 124 Renmin Nanlu. Despite the claim at the front ('Gods will you be if you take meals here'), more than a few travellers have found this place not to their liking. Well, with items on the English menu such as 'pig's large intestines head fried in lard' what does one expect. The Furong is an easy walk from the Jinjiang.

The *Rong Le Yuan* (tel 24201) is at 48 Renmin Zhonglu. It's hard to find – look for a small, red-fronted doorway that leads to a larger courtyard. It's open for lunch and dinner, and the servings are more than honest here – order dishes one by one. Mapo dofu is Y1, large soups Y0.50, main courses Y1 to Y2. A nice setting with outdoor breezes that pass under the high roof. The two back rooms are for weddings or special occasions. Examine dishes of other diners carefully because they may not be to your liking if duplicated.

A misunderstanding that turned out for the better: I spotted a mouth-watering mirage at a neighbouring table, dragged the waitress over, almost stuck my finger in the dish in a delirium of anticipation and, mission accomplished, returned to my seat with a silly grin. Two other foreign devils at the table – we were horrified when the waitress, after the standard time lag, returned with what appeared to be a mere stack of rice bubbles. Once again, we surmised, China had got the better of the salivary glands. We were about to let loose a string of bad words when the lady proceeded to baptise the rice with piping hot soup. The dish erupted in fireworks – when the steam and sizzle had cleared, she had vanished, leaving the mirage on the table. Delicious! The base is a kind of hardened rice-cake, scraped off the bottom of the barrel – crisp and fried. Soupy additions are meat and vegetables, which soften the rice to a crunchy texture. The magic characters for this dish (called *huo ba rou pian*) are:

锅粑肉片

Another main-course restaurant in the core of downtown is the *Yaohua* (tel 6665) at 22 Chunxi Lu. On the edge of Renmin Park, to the south side of Shengli Xilu, is *Nuli Canting*, which translates as 'Make the Great Effort'. May not be worth doing that, but if you happen to be in the vicinity, drop by and check it out – this small place bears the numbering (or renumbering) 55 57 59 61 63 65 67.

Two Chinese hotel dining-rooms with unpredictable fare, are the *Dongfeng Fandian* (tel 7012) at 147 Dongfeng Lu, and the *Rongcheng Fandian* (tel 22687) at 130 Shaanxi Jie.

A special treat for ailing vegetarians is to ride out to *Xindu Monastery*, 18 km north of Chengdu, in time for lunch (11 am to noon). You can also get a good, cheap, vegetarian lunch at Wenshu Monastery. For details of the bus service see the Things to See section.

Duck Platters Chengdu has lots of cold duck places. Some are nondescript, and serve duck in a disappointing fashion. Care should be taken because these are not snacks – you are moving out of the pittance price bracket. The next trick is getting that duck heated up!

On a corner, at the foot of Dongchenggen Jie (and south-east of Renmin Park) is *Wang Pang (Fat Mr Wang's Duckshop)* – it is one of the better-known places. The nicest duck shop sighted is *Weiyuelou* at No 46 Renmin Zhonglu. It's friendly and clean. Outside it has a brown-tiled frontage under an apartment block; inside are marble table-tops, paintings, calligraphy and real windows. American beer is served in bowls. Half a chopped stone-cold duck goes for Y3. The restaurant's name translates to 'tasty and delicious chamber', and the place does not fall short of it.

Snacks Many of Chengdu's specialities originated from *xiao chi* or finger food. The snack bars are great fun and will cost you next to nothing. It's not quite clear why there are so few main-course restaurants in Chengdu – there are better Sichuan restaurants in Beijing. However, in the snack line, the offerings can be outdone in no other Chinese city – and if you line up several of these places, you will get yourself a banquet in stages. The offerings run through the whole vocabulary – Chengdu won ton, dandan noodles (hot spiced noodles in soup), beef fried in thin pancakes, pearl dumplings, steamed buns, leaf cakes (wrapped in banana leaves), flower cakes (made to resemble a white chrysanthemum), water dumplings in hot chilli oil. A few of the more renowned snack outlets are listed here:

Pock-marked Grandma's Bean Curd serves mapo dofu with a vengeance. Small squares of bean curd are accompanied by a fiery meat sauce (laced with garlic, minced beef, salted soybean, chilli oil – enough to make you shut up for a few days). As the story goes, the madame with the pock-marked face set up shop here (reputed to be the same shop as today's) a century ago, providing food and lodging for itinerant pedlars (the clientele look to be roughly the same today too, as does the decor). Bean curd is made on the premises and costs Y0.30 a bowl. A bottle of beer to cool it off is Y0.70 – making Y1 for the right ratio of heater and cooler. The restaurant has grotty, greasy decor – but those spices will kill any lurking bugs, as well as take care of your sinus problems. Also served are spicy chicken and duck, and plates of tripe. Situated at 113 Xi Yulong Jie, the small white shop has a green front.

Almost directly opposite (No 90) is the Blind People's Massage Parlour (English sign) where you can rest up after a bean curd – don't expect a massage, all you'll get is a feeble feel-around. Best if you come attired in a minimum of clothing since none is removed. A session lasting 20 minutes costs Y4.10; if you have come to help China's socialist reconstruction as a foreign expert, then it costs Y1.30 (also student rate). The third logical step in the bean curd-massage route is to plunge into a soda bar for an ice cream or soft drink – there's one nearby on the corner of Renmin and Xi Yulong.

Ming Xiao Chi Dian (Chengdu Snack Bar) serves noodles, baozi and a kind of jaffle. *Fuqi Feipian (Husband & Wife Lungs)*, at 51 Dongfeng Lu Yi Duan, serves spiced and sliced cow lungs (hot!). *Zhong Shuijiao (Chef Zhong's Ravioli)*, at 107 Dongfeng Lu Yi Duan, is renowned for its boiled dumplings. At the south end of Chunxi Lu, Nos 6 and 8 are two of the better-known noodle shops – they will also make up sugar jaffles. No 8 is *Cook Long's Soup-Dumpling Restaurant (Long Chaoshou)*.

Off the north end of Chunxi Lu, and situated on Dongfeng, is *Lai's Rice-balls*. Lai started off as a street-stall vendor, and has moved up in the world. You get four dumplings in a soup, and a side dish of sesame sauce. Each dumpling has a different sweet stuffing – preserved rose petals or mandarin oranges, for example – and they should be dipped in the sugar-sesame sauce before devouring. This exercise will cost you no more than 30 fen. Further east on Dongfeng, past the intersection with Hongxing Zhonglu, is a sweet-tooth snack shop, at No 75 – elaborate decor, jaffles, sweet and sticky concoctions.

The *Tongrentang Dinetotherapy Restaurant* (tel 24519) at 111 Shengli Lu, is run by a Chinese medicine practitioner. All dishes are prepared according to traditional Chinese diet therapy. On the ground floor a blackboard lists inexpensive daily specials such as snow pear soup, ox penis soup, ginseng flour dumplings and cardamom on steamed bread. Arrive early for lunch; dinner has to be reserved in advance. On the 1st floor you can put in an order a day in advance for excellent dinner banquets costing from Y10 per person.

Teahouses The teahouse, or *chadian*, has always been the equivalent of the French café or the British pub in China – or at least this was true of the pre-49 era. Activity ranged from haggling over the bride's dowry to fierce political debate. The latter was true of Sichuan, which historically has been one of the first to rebel and one of the last to come to heel.

Chengdu's teahouses are thus somewhat special – as in other Chinese cities, they were closed down during the Cultural Revolution because they were thought to be dangerous assembly places for 'counter-revolutionaries'. With faction battles raging in Sichuan as late as 1975, re-emergence of this part of daily life has been slow – but you can't keep an old tea addict down! Teahouses sprawl over Chengdu sidewalks (in back-alley sections), with bamboo armchairs that permit ventilation of one's back. In the past, Chengdu teahouses also functioned as venues for Sichuan opera – the plain-clothes variety, performed by amateurs or retired workers. There's been a revival of the teahouse opera, but such places (and the times of performances) are difficult to locate, so it's best to find a local to take you there. Other kinds of entertainment include story-telling and musicians, while one teahouse caters entirely for chess players.

Most Chinese teahouses cater for the menfolk, young and old (mostly old), who come to meet, stoke their pipes or thump cards on the table. Chengdu, however, offers some family-type teahouses. More in the old-man teahouse variety, with a nice balcony view, is a chadian parked by a bridge (see map for location). Downtown is a pleasant interior teahouse, the *Xiao Yuan*. It's very popular and has a certain sophistication.

A more comfortable setting is the *Renmin Teahouse* in Renmin Park, which is a leisurely tangle of bamboo armchairs, sooty kettles and ceramics, with a great outdoor location by a lake. It's co-ed, a family-type chadian – crowded on weekends. In the late afternoon workers roll up to soothe shattered factory-nerves – and some just doze off in their armchairs. You can do the same. A most pleasant afternoon can be passed here in relative anonymity over a bottomless cup of stone-flower tea at a cost so ridiculous it's not worth quoting. When enough tea-freaks appear on the terrace, the stray earpicker, with Q-tips at the ready, roves through (advertising to improve the quality of conversation?), and paper profile-cutters with deft scissors also make the rounds.

Another charming indoor co-ed teahouse is to be found in Wenshu Monastery, with crowded and steamy ambience. Other major Chengdu sights have chadians attached to them – and the back lanes hold plenty more.

Nightlife & Entertainment

Nightlife can be fruitful hunting in Chengdu, and you will have to hunt. Delve into local newspaper listings via desk liaison at the Jinjiang. If something strikes your fancy, get it written down in Chinese, and get a good map location – these places are often hard to find, especially at night. If you have more time, try and get advance tickets. Offerings include teahouse entertainment, acrobatics, cinema, Sichuan opera, Beijing opera, drama, art exhibits, traditional music, story-telling, shadow plays, sporting events and visiting troupes.

A rented bicycle is a useful adjunct to nightlife since bus services are low frequency or unreliable after 9 pm (also packed to the hilt). Chengdu is Sichuan's cultural centre, home of Sichuan opera which has a 200-year tradition, and which features slapstick dress-up, eyeglass-shattering songs and old men dressed as old women. You can see Chinese opera at the Xinsheng Theatre. Cinemas abound – there's the Sichuan Cinema a block north of the Jinjiang Hotel (same side of street) – pot luck, but at 30 fen a seat it's not about to break the piggy-bank.

Shopping

Chengdu has a large range of handicrafts of excellent quality. If you want to see an even larger range of a particular output, try and get to the factory source (the brocade and filigree factories are to the west, towards Du Fu Cottage).

Chunxi Lu is the main shopping artery, a walking street lined with department stores, art dealers, secondhand bookstores, stationers, eyeglass shops and photo stores. At No 10 is the Arts & Crafts Service Department Store, dealing in most of the Sichuan specialties (lacquerware, silverwork, bamboo products). This place also has branches in the Jinjiang Hotel, the airport and the Exhibition Centre. At No 13 Chunxi Lu is a musical instrument shop selling hand-tempered brass gongs and cymbals. At No 14 is a cavernous teahouse for resting weary shopping legs. At No 51 is Shi Bi Jia, specialising in mounting artwork and in calligraphy and Chinese stationery. Right at the north end of Chunxi Lu is the Sichuan Antique Store (on Shangyechang Jie), also a largest-of-the-kind, with branches in the Jinjiang and Exhibition Centre; it deals in porcelain, jewellery, embroidery, bamboo wares, ivory and jadeite.

At No 22 Chunxi Lu is the Derentang Pharmacy, largest of its kind in Chengdu, a century old. It offers, among other elixirs, caterpillar fungus (a mix of the fungus and larva of a moth species – good for TB, coughs, restoring the kidneys, Y250 for 500 grams) and the rhizome of chuanxiong (pain reliever, blood purifier).

The Exhibition Hall, which actually does have industrial exhibitions, has Friendship wares with a capital F scattered on the ground floor, 3rd floor and 5th floor. Antiques are sold on the 5th floor. These expanses of counters are staffed by mild-mannered clerks who put in strenuous hours of newspaper-reading in between tour-bus assaults. The largest section is the 5th floor, where you can find anything from a sword to an antique bird cage to your aunt's lost wedding ring. There's double-sided embroidery (Sichuan Shu embroidery is famous in China), stage costumes, palmwood walking sticks, lacquerware screens, bamboo-thread-covered tea-sets – a list as long as your arm.

The Friendship Store is disappointing for foreigners on a shopping spree, but its stocks are popular with Chinese who may hang around outside to exchange their lucre for yours. Of the Chinese shopping variety are the specialty stores – but they're difficult to locate. There's a very nice place selling drums, cymbals and brass gongs at the eastern end of Hongguang Donglu (near Renmin Zhonglu). At 154 Renmin Nanlu Sanduan is a household goods store selling cane furniture, baskets, bamboo and porcelain.

Renmin Market is a maze of daily necessity stuff – worth poking your nose into but not of great interest for purchases. Further north of that, along Jiefang Zhonglu, are small shops selling fur-lined and sheepskin coats and jackets (as well as heavy PLA-type overcoats) – a good selection, not found in too many other places. Although a few Tibetans drift into Chengdu, there's little sign of minority wares from the high plateau, and what there is may be of dubious authenticity.

Getting There & Away

Transport connections in Chengdu are more comprehensive than in other parts of the south-west.

Air Chengdu has plenty of air connections, including Beijing (Y316), Canton (Y272), Changsha (Y169), Chongqing (Y52), Guilin (Y195), Guiyang (Y112), Kunming (Y114), Lanzhou (Y138), Lhasa (Y421), Nanjing (Y274), Shanghai (Y327), Wuhan (Y192), Xian (Y108), Xichang (Y61).

Direct charter flights have recently been introduced between Chengdu and Hong Kong. Flights depart Hong Kong and Chengdu weekly on Saturdays; economy tickets are HK$870 one way or HK$1380 return.

Bus The main bus station is Xinanmen Che Zhan (Xinanmen bus station), conveniently next to the Jiaotong Hotel. It handles departures for Emei, Baoguo, Leshan, Dazu, Zigong, Ya'an, Kangding.

The Ximen Che Zhan (Ximen bus station), in the north-east of the city, runs buses to Guanxian (irrigation project and vicinity) and to places on the Jiuzhaigou route such as Nanping, Songpan and Barkam. The best way to get there from the Jinjiang or Jiaotong hotels is to take bus No 35 west to the terminus at Qingyang Gong bus station and then change to bus No 5 – ask to get off at Ximen Che Zhan.

Rail Most rail traffic proceeds from Chengdu North (main) Railway Station. Ticket offices in Chengdu may try to sell foreigners soft-sleepers and deny that hard-sleepers are available. The advance rail ticket office, a smaller building on Shengli Xilu, works OK for the right prices, but go early in the day. CITS has also been known to dish out Chinese-priced tickets (especially for soft-sleepers) to foreigners. Perhaps this is because they're mixed in with CTS. Their top speed for obtaining tickets seems to be four days. For more information on trains in the south-west, see the introductory section.

From Chengdu there are direct trains to Emei (three hours, Y3.40 hard-seat, Chinese price), Leshan (four hours, Y4.70 hard-seat, Chinese price), Kunming (25 hours, Y31 hard-sleeper, Chinese price), Chongqing (11 hours, Y17 hard-sleeper, Y10.20 hard-seat, Chinese price) and Xian (about 20 hours, around Y25.80 hard-sleeper, Chinese price).

For the routing to Kunming via Lijiang and Dali, travel to Jinjiang (railhead for Dukou) on the Chengdu-Kunming line and then take buses. For some reason, the timetables don't include train No 91 which leaves Chengdu at 7.53 pm and arrives in Jinjiang at 10.40 am – Y25.50 hard-sleeper, Chinese price.

There are also direct trains to Lanzhou, Hefei and Beijing. For more information, see the introduction in the chapter on the south-west region.

Combination Tickets Combination rail/bus/boat tickets are sold at the North Rail Station, window No 14. You may have trouble trying to get one of these – I can't even locate half the places these tickets take you to on my map! There are at least 15 combinations, and some brief details are given here for the sake of interest. Rail/bus tickets are sold for the route from Chengdu via Jiajiang to Leshan, Wutong Qiao and Mabian. There is a combined rail/bus ticket from Chengdu via Longchuan to Luzhou, Fushun, Naxi, Xuyong, Gusong, Guilin, etc. Another option is a rail/boat/bus ticket from Chengdu via Jiajiang, Leshan and then along the Min River to wherever. Also on sale is a combined ticket which will take you by rail to Chongqing, and then by ferry to Shanghai. There is a similar combination ticket service in Chongqing.

Getting Around

Bus The most useful bus is No 16, which runs from the North Railway Station to the South Railway Station, passing by Public Security, the Foreign Language Bookstore and the Jinjiang Hotel. Bus maps carry colour coding for trolleys and ordinary buses – bus Nos 1, 2, 3, 4 and 5 can also be trolleys bearing the same number. Trolleys have wires; it's easy to work out which colour is the wiring – it can only go so far around the city. Trolley bus No 1 runs from Chengdu main bus station (Xinanmen) to Chengdu North Railway Station. Ordinary bus No 4 runs from the Ximen bus depot (north-west end of town) to the south-east sector, and continues service until 1 am (most others cease around 9.30 to 10.30 pm).

Bicycle There are three rental locations (see the map). The one near the Jinjiang Guest House is open from 8 am to 10 pm, and charges 40 fen per hour. Longer rentals are possible. Get there early if you want to choose something half-way roadworthy from the fleet of decrepit crates. This place is expensive, but conveniently located – you can whip down there at suppertime, bike to a restaurant and return by 10 pm. Do not park the bike outside the hotel gates overnight, as it may be towed away. One traveller had a rental towed from outside a storefront and, after a complex inquiry, found the bike in what turned out to be the local police station.

Around the corner from the Jinjiang, Nos 31-33 on Jiefang Lu, is a rental with an English sign, open 7 am to 6 pm. They charge Y1.80 for a half-day, Y2.40 for 24 hours, Y3.60 for 48 hours. In the downtown district at No 105 Jiefang Zhong Lu (a bit difficult to find) there is an even cheaper rental place, designed for Chinese – they charge Y1.40 for 24 hours.

Buses are very crowded in Chengdu, and bike rentals come as a relief. More than this, however, they give access to back alleys where thriving markets and strange industries are in progress (comic-book rentals, teahouses, small shops, weathered housing). Some areas are walking streets by day (Chunxi Lu), but otherwise you can use back streets to get to your destination. You may get lost, so it's best to have the destination written in Chinese.

The north-west sector of Chengdu is an interesting area – Tudor-style housing, a Mao statue almost hidden from view inside a military institution (visible from the alley that Wenshu Monastery is on, looking north-west), street stalls and markets tucked down the byways.

If you have good reflexes, good night vision and a strong sense of compass points, night-riding is a dangerous sport that yields a different side of Chengdu. Headlights are only used to warn cyclists that something large is speeding through; no Chinese bikes carry lamps (the cost is too high), very few carry reflectors. Add to this the complete disdain of red lights (manually operated, the police box nearby may be empty), and some accidents are bound to occur.

The back alleys are a little safer in terms of the number of large random objects coming towards you, but more hazardous in terms of the small random objects. With reduced visibility, it is advisable to ride slower. Although Beijing is soundly snoring by 9.30 pm, Chengdu hangs in there for a bit longer – the glow of TV tubes visible from dark house doorways, the occasional cluster of night-markets, theatre crowds spilling onto the streets, and the brilliant blues, greens and reds of the ice cream parlours and soda bars.

AROUND CHENGDU

Guanxian

The **Dujiangyan Irrigation Project**, some 60 km north-west of Chengdu, was undertaken in the 3rd century BC to divert the fast-flowing Min River and rechannel it into irrigation canals. The Min was subject to flooding at this point, yet when it subsided, droughts could ensue. A weir system was built to split the force of the river, and a trunk canal (Mouth of Precious Jar) was cut through a mountain to irrigate the Chengdu Plain. Thus the mighty Min was tamed, and a temple (Fulong) was erected to commemorate the occasion during the Jin Dynasty (265-420 AD).

The project is ongoing – it originally irrigated some 1.2 million hectares of land, and since liberation this has expanded to 3.2 million hectares. Most of the present dams, reservoirs, pumping stations, hydroelectric works, bridgework and features are modern; a good overall view of the outlay can be gained from **Two Kings Temple (Er Wang Si)**. The two kings are Li Bing, governor of the Kingdom of Shu and father of the irrigation project, and his son, Er Lang, who were given the titles posthumously – this makes for a rather unusual and dilapidated engineering temple. Inside is a statue of Li Bing, shockingly lifelike; in the rear hall is a standing figure of his son holding a dam tool. There's also a Qing Dynasty project map, and behind the temple there is a terrace saying in effect, 'Mao was here' (1958).

Although Guanxian is of immense importance to specialists interested in the progress of agriculture in China, other visitors may find that dams and irrigation offer less scope for enthusiasm. Of local flavour, there is precious little. A nice teahouse is sited on **South Bridge**, near

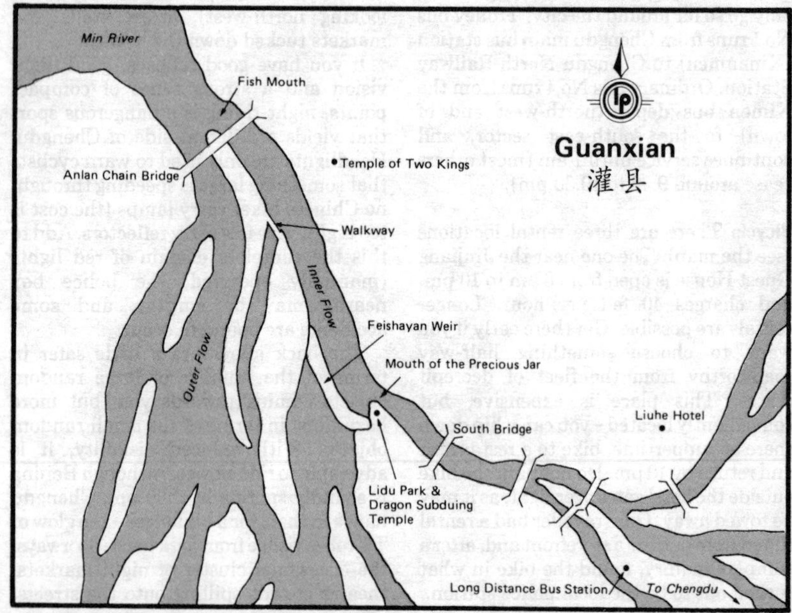

Top: Shepherds and flock approaching Sunday market, Kashgar (RS)
Bottom Left: Uyghur crowds, Kashgar (RS)
Bottom Right: Mosque at Ürümqi (AS)

Top: Genghis Khan's mausoleum, Dongsheng (RS)
Bottom Left: Kebab arcade, Ürümqi (RS)
Bottom Right: Disturbed camel (RS)

Lidu Park entrance. The main hotel, about 15 minutes' walk from the Guanxian bus station, has beds from Y3.

Buses run to Guanxian from Ximen bus depot in Chengdu every half hour from 7 to 11.30 am, and hourly from 1 to 6 pm. They cost Y1 and the trip takes 1½ hours over bumpy roads. You'd do better to take a bus directly to the Temple of Two Kings (a further half hour beyond the Guanxian bus station), and work your way back to Guanxian township. If you can't get a direct bus from Chengdu to the temple, change buses at Guanxian bus depot.

Wolong Nature Reserve

Wolong Nature Reserve lies 40 km north-west of Chengdu, about nine hours of rough roads by bus (via Guanxian). It was set up in the late 1970s and is the largest of the 10 reserves set aside by the Chinese government for panda conservation. Other animals protected here are the golden monkey, golden langur, musk deer and snow leopard. The reserve is estimated to have some 3000 kinds of plants and covers an area of 200,000 hectares. To the north-west is Mt Siguniang (6240 metres) and to the east it drops as low as 155 metres. Pandas like to dine in the 2300 to 3200-metre zone, ranging lower in winter.

The panda inhabits the remote mountains of the provinces of Sichuan, Gansu and Shaanxi. The earliest remains of the animal date back 600,000 years. It's stoutly built, rather clumsy, and has a thick pelt of fine hair, a short tail, and a round white face with eyeballs set in black-rimmed sockets. Though it staggers when it walks, the panda is a good climber, and lives on a vegetarian diet of bamboo and sugar-cane leaves. Mating season has proved a great disappointment to observers at the Wolong Reserve, since pandas are rather particular. Related to the bear and the raccoon, pandas – despite their human-looking shades – can be vicious in self-defence. In captivity they establish remarkable ties with their keepers after a period of time, and can be trained to do a repertoire of tricks.

Estimates place the total number of giant pandas at a round figure of 1000, most of which are distributed in north and north-western Sichuan (with further ranges in Gansu and Shaanxi). The giant panda was first discovered in 1896 in Sichuan, and is headed for extinction. Part of the problem is the gradual diminution of their food supply; in the mid-70s more than 130 pandas starved to death when one of the bamboo species on which they feed flowered and withered in the Minshan Mountains of Sichuan. Pandas consume enormous amounts of bamboo, although their digestive tracts get little value from the plant (consumption is up to 20 kg of bamboo a day in captivity). They are carnivorous, but they're slow to catch animals. Other problems are genetic defects, internal parasites and a slow reproductive rate (artificial insemination has been used at Beijing Zoo).

The Chinese invited the World Wildlife Fund (whose emblem is the lovable panda) to assist in research, itself a rare move. In 1978 a research centre was set up at Wolong. Eminent animal behaviourist Dr George Schaller has paid several visits to the area to work with Chinese biologist Professor Hu Jinchu. There are signs that Wolong will establish observation facilities for tourists – half a dozen pandas are kept at the commune for research. At present, access to this small community is limited to trek-type tours since the road in is a treacherous one. There is little chance of seeing a panda in the wild; Dr Schaller spent two months trekking in the mountains before he got to see one.

One of Schaller's research tasks was to fit wild pandas with radio-monitoring devices. In early 1983, the *People's Daily* reported that Hanhan, one of the very few pandas tagged, was caught in a steel wire trap by a Wolong local. The man strangled the panda, cut off its monitoring ring, skinned it, took it home and ate it. I'm not quite sure what the moral of the story is –

but the meal earned the man two years in jail. On a brighter note, directives have been issued forbidding locals to hunt, fell trees or make charcoal in the mountainous habitats of the panda. Peasants in the areas are being offered rewards equivalent to double their annual salary if they save a starving panda. In late 1983 more pandas were found dead, but several starving pandas have been rounded up for nursing on special farms.

EMEI SHAN 峨眉山

Emei, locked in a medieval time warp, receives a steady stream of happy pilgrims with their straw hats, makeshift baggage, walking canes and fans. The monasteries hold sombre Buddhist monks, the tinkle of bells, clouds of incense, and firewood and coal lumped in the courtyards for the winter months.

It is more or less a straight mountain climb, with your attention directed to the luxuriant scenery – and, as in *The Canterbury Tales*, to fellow pilgrims. Admirable are the hardened affiliates of Grannies Alpine Club, who slog it up there with the best of them, walking sticks at the ready lest a brazen monkey dare think them easy prey for a food-mugging. They come yearly for the assault, and burn paper money as a Buddhist offering for longevity. The climb no doubt adds to their longevity, so the two factors may be related. For the traveller itching to do something, the Mt Emei climb is a good opportunity to air the respiratory organs, as well as to observe post-76 religious freedoms in action from the inside, since you are obliged to stay in the rickety monasteries along the route. Admission to the mountain is only Y1, and no alien's permit is needed.

One of the Middle Kingdom's four famous Buddhist mountains (the others are Putuo, Wutai and Jiuhua), Emei Shan has little of its original temple-work left. The glittering Golden Summit Temple, with its brass tiling engraved with Tibetan script, was completely gutted by fire. A similar fate befell numerous other temples and monasteries on the mount – war with the Japanese and Red Guard looting have taken their toll.

The original temple structures dated back as far as the advent of Buddhism itself in China; by the 14th century, the estimated 100 or so holy structures housed several thousand monks. The present temple count is around 20 active after a Cultural Revolution hiatus, bearing traces of original splendour. Since 1976 the remnants have been renovated, access to the mountain has been improved, hiking paths widened, lodgings added, and tourists permitted to climb to the sacred summit.

Hiking is spectacular enough. Fir trees, pines and cedars clothe the slopes; lofty crags, cloud-kissing precipices, butterflies, and azaleas together form a nature reserve of sorts. The major scenic goal of Chinese hikers is to witness a sunrise or sunset over the sea of clouds at the summit. On the rare afternoon there is a phenomenon known as Buddha's Aureole – rainbow rings, produced by refraction of water particles, attach themselves to a person's shadow in a cloud bank below the summit. Devout Buddhists, thinking this was a call from yonder, used to jump off the Cliff of Self-Sacrifice in ecstasy, so during the Ming and Qing dynasties, officials set up iron poles and chain railing to prevent suicides. These days your head can be stuck in a cardboard cut-out on the site, and you can be photographed in that same act of attaining Nirvana.

Weather

The best season to visit is May to October. Winter is not impossible, but will present some trekking problems – iron soles with spikes can be rented to deal with encrusted ice and snow on the trails. At the height of summer, which is scorching elsewhere in Sichuan, Emei presents cool majesty. Temperate zones start at 1000 metres.

Cloud cover and mist are prevalent, and will most likely interfere with the sunrise.

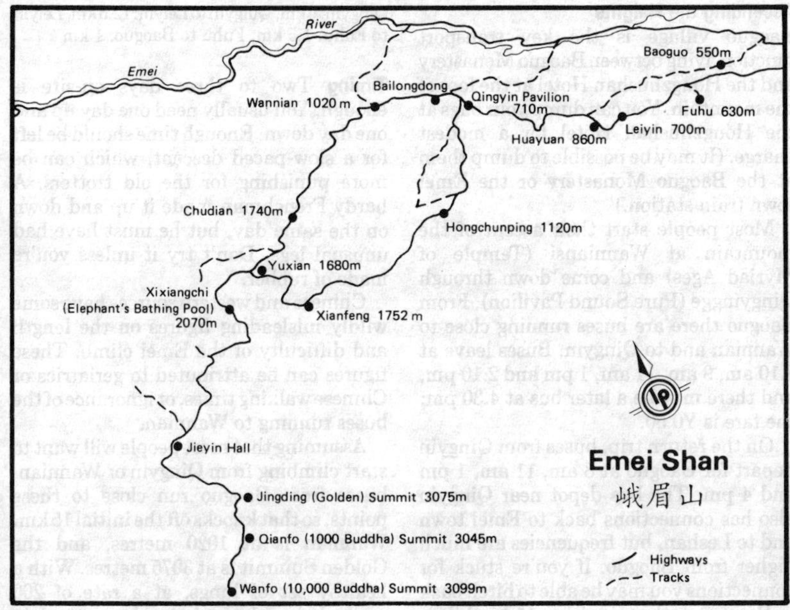

If lucky, you'll see Mt Gongga to the west; if not, you'll have to settle for the telecom tower 'temple' and the meteorological station. Monthly average temperatures in degrees Celsius are:

	Jan	*Apr*	*Jul*	*Oct*
Emei town	7	21	26	17
Summit	–6	3	12	–1

Gear

Emei is a tall one at 3099 metres, so the weather is uncertain and you'd be best advised to prepare for sudden changes without weighing yourself down with a huge pack (steps can be steep). There is no heating or insulation in the monasteries, but blankets are provided, and you can rent heavy overcoats at the top. Heavy rain is a problem, calling for a good pair of rough-soled shoes or boots, so you don't go head over heels on the smooth stone steps further up. Flimsy plastic macs are sold by enterprising vendors on the slopes – these will last about 10 minutes before you get wet.

Strange hiking equipment as it may sound, a fixed-length umbrella would be most useful – for the rain, and as a walking stick (scare the hell out of those monkeys by pressing auto-release!). These kinds of umbrellas are not cheap in China, though they may have some resale value. If you want to look more authentic you can get yourself a hand-crafted walking stick, very cheap – and while you're at it, get a fan and a straw hat too. A flashlight would be handy. Food supplies are not necessary, but a pocket of munchies wouldn't hurt. Bring toilet paper with you. Luggage can be left at Emei train station, at the Hongzhushan Hotel, or at one of the monasteries.

Recent reports indicate that some travellers have been getting sick from contaminated water supplies on the mountain.

Ascending the Heights

Baoguo village is the key transport junction, lying between Baoguo Monastery and the Hongzhushan Hotel at the foot of the mountain. You can dump your bags at the Hongzhushan Hotel for a modest charge. (It may be possible to dump them at the Baoguo Monastery or the Emei town train station.)

Most people start their ascent of the mountain at Wanniansi (Temple of Myriad Ages) and come down through Qingyingge (Pure Sound Pavilion). From Baoguo there are buses running close to Wannian and to Qingyin. Buses leave at 7.10 am, 9 am, 11 am, 1 pm and 2.10 pm, and there may be a later bus at 4.30 pm; the fare is Y0.50.

On the return trip, buses from Qingyin depart for Baoguo at 8 am, 11 am, 1 pm and 4 pm. The bus depot near Qingyin also has connections back to Emei town and to Leshan, but frequencies are much higher from Baoguo. If you're stuck for connections you may be able to hitch back to Baoguo – otherwise it's a 15-km hike.

For a 'softer' combination, take the bus to Qingyin and then walk along the more scenic route via Hongchunping and Yuxian to the Golden Summit. From there you can descend the six km to Jieyin Hall to take a bus back down. If you want to 'cheat' in earnest, see below for the separate section on cheating or wait until installation of an imported Japanese cable car is complete.

Routes Most people ascend Emei Shan by the Wanniansi-Chudian-Xixiangchi-Summit route, and descend from the summit via Xixiangchi-Xianfeng-Hongchunping-Qingyingge. The paths converge just below Xixiangchi, where there are three small restaurants at a fork. A common route is:

Wannian to Xixiangchi: 15 km, Xixiangchi to Jinding: 15 km, Jingding to Wanfo: 3.5 km, Wanfo to Jingding: 3.5 km, Jingding to Xixiangchi: 15 km, Xixiangchi to Xianfeng: 12.5 km, Xianfeng to Hongchunping: 15 km, Hongchunping to Qingyin: 6 km, Qingyin to Leiyin: 12.5 km, Leiyin to Fuhu: 1.5 km, Fuhu to Baoguo: 1 km

Timing Two to three days on-site is enough. You usually need one day up and one day down. Enough time should be left for a slow-paced descent, which can be more punishing for the old trotters. A hardy Frenchman made it up and down on the same day, but he must have had unusual legs. Don't try it unless you're made of rubber.

Chinese and western sources have some wildly misleading figures on the length and difficulty of the Emei climb. These figures can be attributed to geriatrics or Chinese walking times, or ignorance of the buses running to Wannian.

Assuming that most people will want to start climbing from Qingyin or Wannian, buses from Baoguo run close to these points, so that knocks off the initial 15 km. Wannian is at 1020 metres, and the Golden Summit is at 3075 metres. With a healthy set of lungs, at a rate of 200 metres' elevation gain per hour, the trip up from Wanniansi could be done in 10 hours if foul weather does not start.

Starting off early in the morning from Wannian, you should be able to get to a point below the Jingding summit by nightfall, then continue to the Jingding and Wanfo summits the next day, and descend to Baoguo the same day. If you have more time to spare, you could meander over the slopes to villages hugging the mountainsides.

On the main routes described above, in climbing time you'd be looking at:

Ascent Qingyin to Wannian: one hour, Wannian to Xixiangchi: four hours, Xixiangchi to Jieyin: three hours, Jieyin to Golden Summit: one hour, Golden Summit to Wanfo Summit: one hour

Descent Wanfo Summit to Golden Summit: 45 minutes, Golden Summit to Jieyin: 45 minutes, Jieyin to Xixiangchi: 2½ hours, Xixiangchi to Xianfeng: two hours, Xianfeng to Qingyin: 3½ hours

Cheating Several minibuses and buses leave from the square in front of Baoguo Monastery between 7 and 8 am, and run along a recently made dirt road round the back of the mountain up to the Jieyin Summit (2640 metres). From there, it's only 1½ hours to the top. Minibuses (Y7 to Y9 one way) and buses (Y4.50) take about three hours to get up the mountain. Minibuses are usually chartered by prior arrangement.

Cheating is a popular pastime on Emei (the name Emei means 'moth-eyebrow mountain' – raised or lowered these days?). Grannies are portered up on the sturdy backs of young men (likewise healthy-looking young women are carried up).

Talking of cheating, another traveller has reported that he was recently up on the mountain watching a three-card trickster raking in money when a police patrol suddenly appeared on the scene. As the startled trickster packed his cards, the police opened fire and pursued the man into the undergrowth!

The most spectacular brawl I witnessed in China took place at 2640 metres:

> The bus was waiting for passengers to go down – well, not exactly waiting ... What had happened was that a group of Hong Kong visitors, easily discernible by their clothing and cameras, had set up a deal with the driver to charter the whole bus back down the mountain, leaving no space for locals. The driver, in his wisdom, did not open the main bus door, but his driver's cabin door – to let the Hong Kongers squeeze onto the vehicle. Pandemonium broke out in the crowd of Chinese onlookers – they burst through the main bus door, and old women piled through the windows . . . Some very nasty scenes ensued as conductor and driver rushed to boot them out again and re-seal the bus.
>
> The remaining Hong Kongers, the ones still on terra firma, regrouped. The Charge of the Light Brigade followed as they smashed through the ranks of the locals and were pulled up by the scruffs of their necks through the driver's cabin. Meanwhile, old and young alike, the locals bashed at the bus with their walking sticks and screamed abuse – finally the bus pulled out, horns blaring, with Chinese running after it, kicking the paintwork for all they were worth, and almost doing in the rear lights with walking sticks.

Places to Stay & Eat

The old monasteries are food, shelter and sights all rolled into one, and, while spartan, are a delightful change from the regular tourist hotels. They've got maybe as much as 1000 years of character.

You'll probably be asked to pay some ridiculous prices. Bargaining is definitely necessary. Prices range from Y0.80 in a very large dormitory (10 beds or more) to Y10 for a single room. In between are other options like a four-bed room at Y4 per person. Plumbing and electricity are primitive; candles are supplied. Rats can be a nuisance, particularly if you leave food lying around your room.

There are eight monastery guest houses – at Baoguo, Qingyin, Wannian, Xixiangchi, Xianfeng, Hongchunping, Fuhu and Leiyin. There's also a host of smaller lodgings at Chudian, Jieyin, Yuxian, Bailongdong, the Jinding Summit and Huayan, for instance. The smaller places will accept you if the main monasteries are overloaded. Failing those, you can virtually kip out anywhere – a teahouse, a wayside restaurant – if night is descending.

Be prepared to backtrack or advance under cover of darkness, as key points are often full of pilgrims – old women two to a bed, camped down the corridors, or camping out in the hallowed temple itself, on the floor. Monasteries usually have half-way hygienic restaurants with monk-chefs serving up the vegetarian fare; Y1 to Y2 should cover a meal. There is often a small retail outlet selling peanuts, biscuits and canned fruit within the monastery precincts. Along the route are small restaurants and food stalls where you can replenish the guts and the tea mug. Food gets more expensive and comes in less variety the higher you mount, due to cartage surcharges and difficulties.

An exception to the monasteries is the *Hongzhushan Hotel*, at the foot of Emei

Shan. It's got dreary brick and plaster dorm accommodation at Y4 per person. Better villa-type rooms are available, Y5 per person and up. This hotel has a very pleasant dining section which is a 10-minute walk back into the forest. There you can dine on a 2nd-floor balcony. Copious servings of good food (set menu) cost Y2.5 a head. It's open 6 to 6.30 pm only.

Some notes on the monasteries follow. Most of the ones mentioned are sited at key walking junctions and tend to be packed out. If you don't get in, do check out the restaurant and its patrons.

Baoguosi (Monastery of Country Rewards) was built in the 16th century, enlarged in the 17th by Emperor Kangxi, and recently renovated. Its 3.4-metre porcelain Buddha, made in 1415, is housed near the Sutra Library. To the left of the gate is a rockery for potted miniature trees and rare plants. A grubby bed costs Y3.50. There's a nice vegetarian restaurant and tearoom with solid wood tables.

Fuhusi (Crouching Tiger Monastery) is sunk in the forest. Inside the monastery is a seven-metre-high copper pagoda inscribed with Buddhist images and texts. The monastery was completely renovated recently, with the addition of bedding for 400 and restaurant seating for 200. A stay costs a bit more (Y4/Y5 a head) but is well worth it if you can get in.

Wanniansi (Temple of 10,000 Years) is the oldest surviving Emei monastery (reconstructed in the 9th century). It's dedicated to the man on the white elephant, the Bodhisattva Puxian, who is the protector of the mountain. This statue, 8½ metres high, cast in copper and bronze, weighing an estimated 62,000 kg, is found in Brick Hall, a domed building with small stupas on it. The statue was made in 980 AD. Accommodation in the Wanniansi area is Y4 per person, with good vegetarian food. If it's full, go back towards Qingyingge to Bailongdong, a small guest house.

Qingyingge (Pure Sound Pavilion) is so named because of the sound effects produced by rapid waters coursing around rock formations in the area. It has a nice temple perched on a hillside, and small pavilions from which to observe the waterworks and appreciate the natural music. A bed is Y3.

Xixiangchi (Elephant Bathing Pool) is, according to legend, the spot where the monk Puxian flew his elephant in for the big scrub, but now there's not much of a pool to speak of. Being almost at the crossroads of both major trails, this is something of a hangout and beds are scarce. New extensions are in progress for handling human overload on the trail. A dorm bed is Y1.20, double Y6, single Y5.

The monkeys have got it all figured out – this is the place to be. If you come across a monkey 'toll-gate', the standard procedure is to thrust open palms toward the outlaw to show you have no food. The Chinese find the monkeys an integral part of the Emei trip, and like to tease them. As an aside, monkeys form an important part of Chinese mythology – and there is a saying in Chinese, 'With one monkey in the way, not even 10,000 men can pass' – which may be deeper than you think!

Wo Yun An (Cloud-Reposing Hermitage), at 3075 metres, is just below the summit. It was built in 1974, a dark, gloomy, primitive wooden structure. A bed in a six-person dorm costs Y1.20, a two-bed room Y2.90 and a single Y3.90 (another innovation in these 'advanced' hotels – singles!). The hotel will rent padded cotton overcoats for 40 fen a day. Another shop nearby offers the same deal. These are mostly intended for patrons of the sunrise – on a very clear day (rare) the most spectacular sight is not the sunrise but the Mt Gongga range rising up like a phantom to the west.

Xianfeng (Magic Peak) Monastery has a wonderful location backed into rugged cliffs, and has loads of character. Try and get a room at the rear of the monastery, where the floors give pleasant views. It's off the main track so it's not crowded. Rates are Y2.50 a person in a four-bed room, Y1.20 dorm, Y4 to Y6 single. Upstairs there are doubles for Y20. Nearby is **Jiulao Cave**, inhabited by big bats.

Getting There & Away

The hubs of the transport links to Emei Shan are Baoguo village and Emei town. Emei town itself is best skipped, though it has markets, a cheap dormitory at the Emei Hotel, a good restaurant, and a long-distance bus station. One traveller saw a bizarre sight in town:

> While going by bus to the station we saw a Chinese sitting on a bridge. He was totally naked and actively masturbating with a happy grin on his face – when he saw us he laughed. All the Chinese on the bus seemed not to register the event!

Emei town lies 3½ km from the railway station. Baoguo is another 6½ km from Emei town. At Emei Station, buses will be waiting for train arrivals – the short trip to Baoguo is Y1 in a mini-bus, and Y0.30 in a local bus. From Baoguo there are 11 buses a day to Emei town, the first at 7 am and the last at 6 pm – no service during lunch hour.

There are also direct buses running from Baoguo to Leshan and Chengdu. There are eight buses a day from Baoguo to Leshan, the first at 7 am and the last at 5.30 pm. The trip takes one hour and the fare is Y1.30. There are good bus connections between Leshan and Chengdu. The bus from Baoguo to Chengdu costs Y5.50 and takes four hours.

Emei Railway Station is on the Chengdu-Kunming railway line, and the three-hour trip to Chengdu costs Y3.40 hard-seat (Chinese price). The train from Emei town is actually cheaper than the bus, but does not offer the convenience of leaving Baoguo (trains are also less frequent and timing may be off). You can purchase one-day advance train tickets at two little booths by the pavilion in Baoguo square.

LESHAN 乐山

The opportunity to delve into small-town life in the PRC should always be followed up. While Leshan is no village, it's on a scale that you can be comfortable with. It's an old town where parts have that lived-in-forever look, while the trendiest addition from this century is the odd soda-bar with garish fluorescent tubes, disco music, and patrons huddled over sickly-sweet fizzy orange drinks. The hotel situation is good, decent food can be unearthed and it's a good resting spot for those Emei-weary legs – and there is a major site, the Grand Buddha.

The **Dafu (Grand Buddha)** is 71 metres high, carved into a cliff-face overlooking the confluence of the Dadu and Min rivers. It qualifies as the largest Buddha in the world, with the one at Bamian, Afghanistan, as runner-up (besides, the Leshan model is sitting down!). Dafu's ears are seven metres long, insteps 8½ metres broad, and a picnic could be conducted on the nail of his big toe, which is 1.6 metres long – the toe itself is 8.3 metres long.

This lunatic project was begun in the year 713 AD, engineered by a Buddhist monk called Haitong who organised fund-raising and hired workers; it was completed 90 years later. Below the Buddha was a hollow where boatmen used to vanish – Haitong hoped that the Buddha's presence would subdue the swift currents and protect the boatmen, and Dafu did do a lot of good, as the surplus rocks from the sculpting filled the river hollow. Haitong gouged out his own eyes in an effort to protect funding from disappearing into the hands of officers, but he died before the completion of his life's work. A building used to shelter the giant statue, but it was destroyed during a Ming Dynasty war.

Inside the body, hidden from view, is a

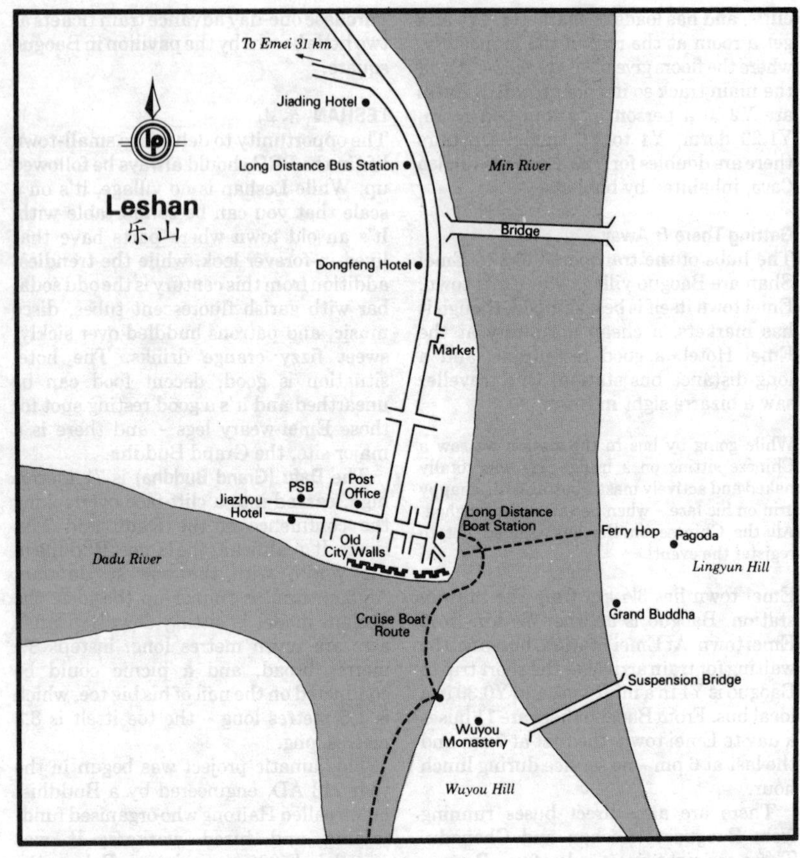

water-drainage system to prevent weathering, although the stone statue has seen its fair share. Dafu is so old that foliage is trying to reclaim him – flowers growing on the giant hands, a bushy chest, ferns in his topknots, and weeds winding out of his earholes. He gazes down, perhaps in alarm, at the drifting pollutants in the river that presumably come from the paper mill at the industrial end of town (which started large-scale operation in 1979).

Officials are now worried about the possibility of a collapse due to soil erosion; one suggestion that has not met with an enthusiastic response is to cover Buddha with a huge transparent shell.

It's worth making several passes at big Buddha, as there are all kinds of angles on him. You can go to the top, opposite the head, and then descend a short stairway to the feet for a Lilliputian perspective. A local boat passes by for a frontal view, which reveals two guardians in the cliffside, not visible from land.

To make a round-tour that encompasses these possibilities, take the passenger vessel from the Leshan pier. It leaves from the pier every 40 minutes or so until 5.30 pm; sit on the upper deck facing the dock, since the boat turns around when leaving. You pass in close by the Grand Buddha and the first stop is at the **Wuyou Temple**. The temple dates, like the Grand Buddha, from the Tang Dynasty with Ming and Qing renovations; it's a museum piece containing calligraphy, painting and artefacts, and commands panoramic views. You can get off the boat here if you want and cross-country over the top of Wuyou Hill, continue on to the suspension bridge linking it to Lingyun Hill, and reach the semi-active **Grand Buddha Temple** which sits near Dafu's head. To get back to Leshan walk south to the small ferry going direct across the Min River. This whole exercise can be done in less than 1½ hours from the Leshan dock.

It would be a mistake to think of Leshan as one big Buddha, for the area is steeped in history. Over 1000 rock-tombs were built here in the Eastern Han Dynasty (25-220 AD). By the remains of the town ramparts is an older section of town with cobbled streets and green, blue and red-shuttered buildings; the area around the ferry docks and the old town buzzes with market activity. In season, the markets yield a surprising array of fresh fruit and vegetables, so you can do more than look at them. Further out, by the Jiazhou Hotel, are teahouses with bamboo chairs spilling onto the street.

If you happen to be in town on a Sunday evening, you might like to visit the English Corner which takes place in the riverside park close to the Jiazhou Hotel.

Places to Stay & Eat

Top of the line is the *Jiazhou Hotel* which has deluxe, super-clean rooms with attached bathroom for Y34; Y5 for a dorm bed. Amazing dinners cost Y7 per head – they're only for hotel guests with advance orders, but friends can creep in (service is in a separate foreigner enclave, but with food like that, who cares!). Dinner is 6 to 7 pm. Avoid breakfast though – it's murky Chinese fare for Y2 per head. The hotel is in a pleasant area; to get there take the town's sole bus line to the terminus.

There are two small guest houses in the area above the head of the Grand Buddha. Perhaps due to the Buddha's drainage system, the cliff around here is wet, and the dampness can extend to the rooms. The guest houses are nice; one has 30 rooms at Y10 a head, and lower rates are possible. There is an excellent restaurant in this vicinity, in a building to the right of the Buddha as you look towards the river.

You could try the two Chinese hotels, which are sleazy but conveniently located. The *Dongfeng* has doubles and triples from Y3 per person. At the dull end of town near the bus station is the *Jiading Hotel*, which will accept stray foreign faces. The overflow of patrons is stuffed down the hallways, and the washrooms are hard to find (you might throw up when you see them anyway). Rooms have simple beds and seem to cost Y3.90 regardless of whether two, three or four people occupy one. A single person pays Y1.35. Whatever the price, it's a pittance, at least for foreign wallets. Make sure you lock your room when you leave it. Down the main street from here are sidewalk stalls dispensing victuals.

Getting There & Away

Bus From the Leshan long-distance bus station there are five daily buses running to Chengdu (the first at 7.20 am and the last at 1 pm). The 165-km trip takes over five hours; fares are Y4.70 in an ordinary bus and Y6.30 in a soft-seat coach. Get the driver to drop you at the Jinjiang Hotel in Chengdu.

Emei Shan to Leshan is 30 km; buses run to Emei town, Baguosi, or Pure Sound Pavilion. The highest bus frequency is to Baguosi, and there are only two buses a day to Pure Sound.

There's a soft-seat coach daily at 7 am to Chongqing. The trip takes 15 hours and costs Y15.

Boat There is a boat to Chongqing, departing Leshan at 5.30 and 7.30 am every few days, but it's difficult to get aboard. The trip takes 36 hours and costs Y23 in 3rd class. A shorter run to Yibin departs at 7 am, and costs Y10.20 in 3rd class. Yibin is part-way to Chongqing and has a train station.

Getting Around

Bus There is one bus line in Leshan, running from the bus station to the Jiazhou Hotel. The schedule is posted at the Jiazhou bus stop; The bus runs from 6 am to 6 pm, at roughly 20-minute intervals with no service at lunchtime (about 11.20 am to 1.20 pm). On foot, it's a half-hour walk from one end of town to the other.

Bicycle You can rent a bike just near the bridge across the Min River. The price is Y0.50 an hour, which is expensive (for China), and watch out if you rent overnight as charges continue while you snore, unless otherwise negotiated. Bikes are of limited use if visiting the Grand Buddha since uphill work is required, and the track to Wuyou Hill is a dirt one. However, if you wish to explore the surrounding countryside, the bike will be useful – a suggested route is to continue out of town past the Jiazhou Hotel.

MEISHAN 眉山

Meishan, 90 km south-west of Chengdu by road or rail (it's on the Kunming-Chengdu railway line) is largely of interest to those with a knowledge of Chinese language, literature and calligraphy. It was the residence of Su Xun and his two sons, Su Shi and Su Zhe, the three noted literati of the Northern Song Dynasty (960-1127). Their residence was converted into a temple in the early Ming Dynasty, with renovations under the Qing emperor Hongwu (1875-1909). The mansion and pavilions now operate as a museum for the study of the writings of the Northern Song period. Historical documents, relics of the Su family, writings, calligraphy – some 4500 items all told are on display at the Sansu shrine.

CHONGQING 重庆

Chongqing was opened as a treaty port in 1890, but not very many foreigners made it up the river to this isolated outpost, and those that did had little impact. A programme of industrialisation got underway in 1928, but it was in the wake of the Japanese invasion that Chongqing really took off as a major centre; the city was the war-time capital of the Kuomintang from 1938 onwards and refugees from all over China flooded in, swelling the population to over two million. The irony of this overpopulated, overstrained city with its bomb-shattered houses is that the name means something like 'double jubilation' or 'repeated good luck'. Emperor Zhao Dun of the Song Dynasty succeeded to the throne in 1190, having previously been made the prince of the city of Gongzhou; as a celebration of these two happy events, he renamed Gongzhou as Chongqing.

Edgar Snow arrived in the city in 1939 and found it a:

> place of moist heat, dirt and wide confusion, into which, between air raids, the imported central government . . . made an effort to introduce some technique of order and construction. Acres of buildings had been destroyed in the barbaric raids of May and June. The Japanese preferred moonlit nights for their calls, when from their base in Hankow they could follow the silver banner of the Yangtze up to its confluence with the Kialing, which identified the capital in a way no blackout could obscure. The city had no defending air force and only a few anti-aircraft guns . . . . Spacious public shelters were being dug, but it was estimated that a third of the population still had no protection. Government officials, given advance warning, sped outside the city in their motor cars – cabinet ministers first, then vice-ministers, then minor bureaucrats. The populace soon caught on; when they saw a string of official cars racing to the west, they dropped everything and ran. A mad scramble of rickshaws, carts, animals and humanity blew

up the main streets like a great wind, carrying all before it.

The war is over, and today the city is hardly a backwater; six million people live here and it's a heavily industrialised port – as all those belching chimneys along the riverfront testify. Chongqing sets itself apart from other Chinese cities by the curious absence of bicycles! There's barely a cyclist to be found, as the steep hills on which the city is built make it coronary country for any would-be pedaller.

Despite the modern apartment and industrial blocks there's enough of old Chongqing left to give the city an oddly ramshackle, picturesque quality. Other Chinese cities such as Beijing have been rebuilt almost in their entirety in the post-1949 urban development programmes, but Chongqing still conveys something of what an old Chinese city looked like: neighbourhoods with stone steps meandering down narrow streets and alleys, and unkempt, grotty wooden houses.

Information & Orientation

The heart of Chongqing spreads across a hilly peninsula of land wedged between the Jialing River to the north and the Yangtse River to the south. The rivers meet at the tip of the peninsula at the eastern end of the city.

The city centre is the main shopping and cinema district around the intersection of Minsheng, Minguan and Minzu Lu in the eastern part of the town; the large Chaotianmen Dock is at the tip of the peninsula. The hotels, tourist facilities, railway and long-distance bus stations and most of the sights are scattered about the city, and there are a number of sights outside the city limits.

Chongqing's railway station is built on low ground, at the foot of one of the city's innumerable hills in the south-eastern part of town. When you go out of the gates of the station, walk straight ahead along the concrete path – on your left is a long row of noticeboards, followed by a left-luggage room, and on the right and further up are the ticket windows. Go through the concrete archway at the end of the pathway. On your right is Gaiyuanbazheng Jie. In front of you is Nanqu Lu and on the left is Shahoqingsi Lu.

Over on the left, on the other side of Shahoqingsi Lu, is the beginning of a long flight of steps. About 340 of these will take you up to Changjiang Lu, which runs into Zhongshan Lu where you can get buses to the tourist hotels. If you don't feel like walking then beside the steps is a building with the ticket office and cable-car up to Zhongshan Lu – a three-fen, 45-degree, one-minute ride to the top. Taking the cable-car to the top, you exit from a subway; turn right to go to the other side of Zhongshan Lu, or turn left and up the short flight of steps to Changjian Lu. For details of the buses to the tourist hotels, see the section on Places to Stay.

CITS (tel 51449) has its office in a building in the Renmin Hotel compound. They're a friendly mob but hopelessly disorganised. They have been known to charge 100% extra on the price of train tickets (as against the usual 75%), and they never seem to know what tickets are available on the Yangtse boats. Hopefully that situation will change.

Public Security (tel 43973) is on Linjiang Lu. A bus No 13 from the front of the Renmin Hotel will take you there. They're a friendly lot, but don't expect any permits for strange places.

Bank There is a money-exchange office in the Renmin Hotel.

Post There is a post office in the Renmin Hotel.

CAAC (tel 52970 or 52643) is at 190 Zhongshansan Lu.

Maps Good maps in Chinese – one with the bus routes and another without – are

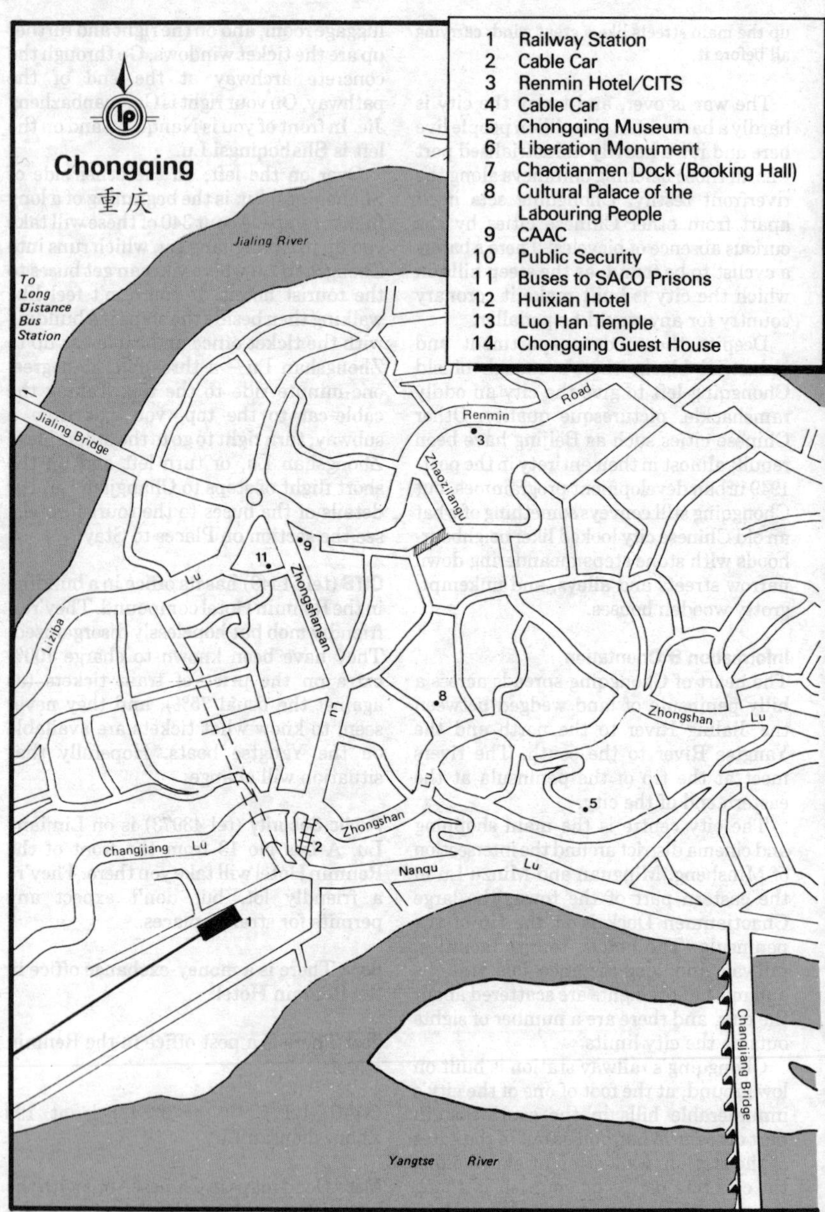

Chongqing
重庆
1 Railway Station
2 Cable Car
3 Renmin Hotel/CITS
4 Cable Car
5 Chongqing Museum
6 Liberation Monument
7 Chaotianmen Dock (Booking Hall)
8 Cultural Palace of the Labouring People
9 CAAC
10 Public Security
11 Buses to SACO Prisons
12 Huixian Hotel
13 Luo Han Temple
14 Chongqing Guest House
Jialing River
To Long Distance Bus Station
Jialing Bridge
Renmin Road
Zhaozilangu
Zhongshansan Lu
Liziba
Lu
Zhongshan Lu
Changjiang Lu
Zhongshan Nanqu Lu
Changjiang Bridge
Yangtse River

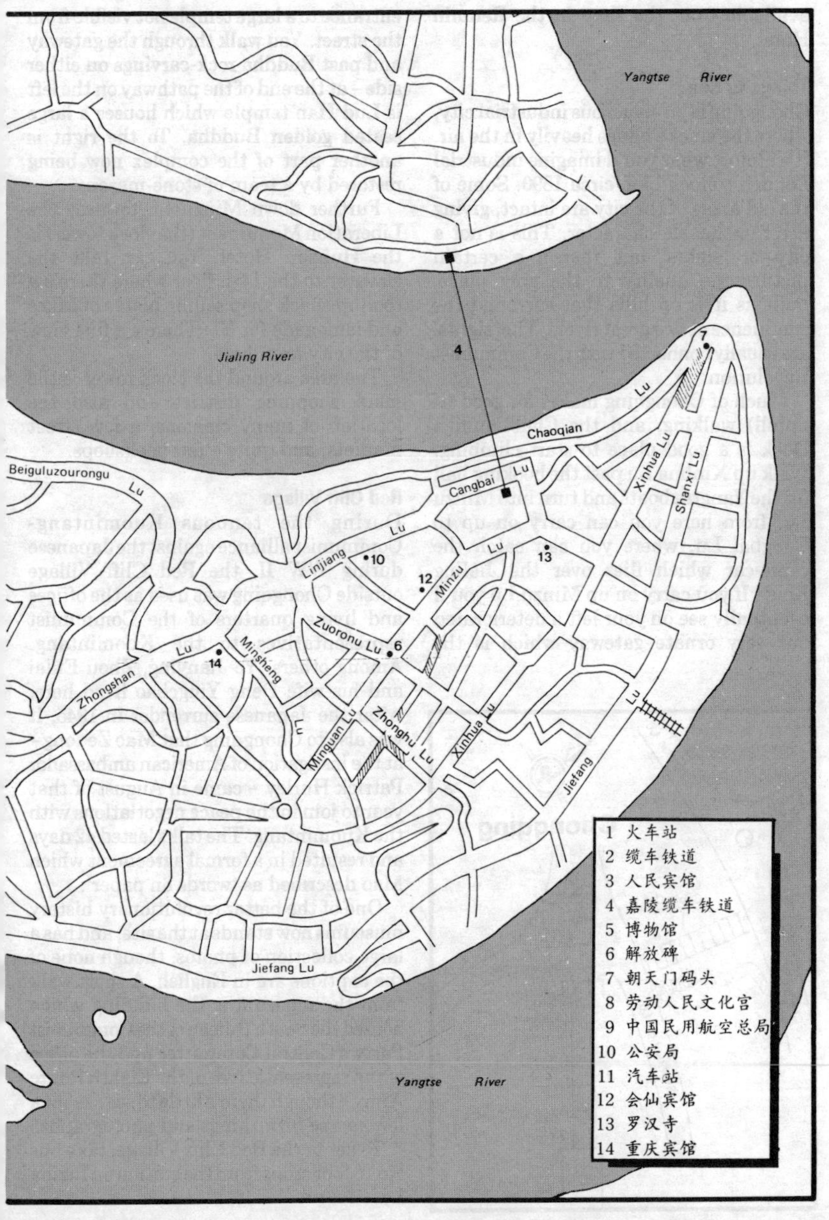
Yangtse River
Jialing River
4
7
Chaoqian Lu
Cangbai Lu
Xinhua Lu
Shanxi Lu
Beiguluzourongu Lu
Linjiang Lu
10
12
Minzu Lu
13
Zuoronu Lu
6
14
Minsheng Lu
Zhongshan Lu
Minquan Lu
Zhonghu Lu
Xinhua Lu
Jiefang Lu
Jiefang Lu
Yangtse River
1 火车站
2 缆车铁道
3 人民宾馆
4 嘉陵缆车铁道
5 博物馆
6 解放碑
7 朝天门码头
8 劳动人民文化宫
9 中国民用航空总局
10 公安局
11 汽车站
12 会仙宾馆
13 罗汉寺
14 重庆宾馆

available fron the shop in the Renmin Hotel.

Things to See

Chongqing is an enormous industrial city, where the smoke hangs heavily in the air. It's almost what you'd imagine industrial London to look like, circa 1890. Some of the old areas of the city are intact, giving it a ramshackle character. This is not a city of 'sights' but there's a certain picturesque quality to the grey place, built as it is on hills that surround the confluence of two great rivers. The 'sights' are usually connected with the Communist Revolution.

Much of Chongqing makes for good (if uphill) walking, and the Chaotianmen Dock is a good place to start climbing. Walk up Xinhua Lu past the booking hall for the Yangtse boats and turn into Minzu Lu; from here you can carry on up to Cangbai Lu, where you can catch the cable-car which flies over the Jialing River. If you carry on up Minzu Lu you'll eventually see on your left a deteriorated but very ornate gateway which is the entrance to a large temple not visible from the street. You walk through the gateway and past Buddha rock-carvings on either side – at the end of the pathway on the left is Lud Han temple which houses a large seated golden Buddha. To the right is another part of the complex now being restored by a team of stone-masons.

Further down Minzu Lu towards the Liberation Monument (the clock tower) is the Huixian Hotel. You can take the elevator to the 14th floor where there's a rooftop snack shop selling plates of cakes and lemonade for Y1. There's a fine view of the city from here.

The area around the clock tower is the main shopping district and also the location of many cinemas, a few street markets, and quite a few bookshops.

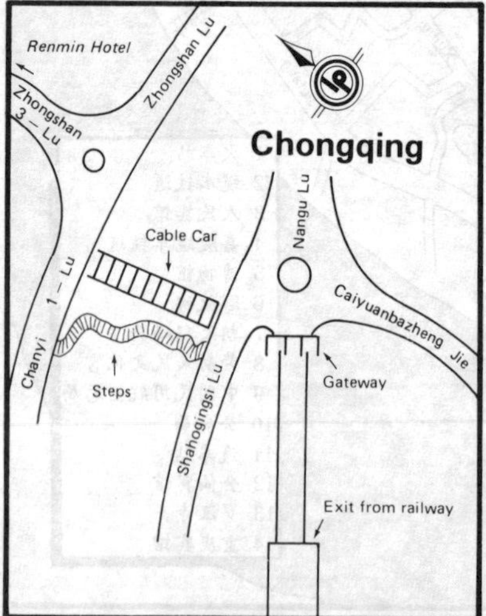

Red Cliff Village

During the tenuous Kuomintang-Communist alliance against the Japanese during WW II, the Red Cliff Village outside Chongqing was used as the offices and living quarters of the Communist representatives to the Kuomintang. Among others, Ye Jianying, Zhou Enlai and his wife Deng Yingchao lived here. After the Japanese surrender in 1945, it was also to Chongqing that Mao Zedong – at the instigation of American ambassador Patrick Hurley – came in August of that year to join in the peace negotiations with the Kuomintang. The talks lasted 42 days and resulted in a formal agreement which Mao described as 'words on paper'.

One of the better revolutionary history museums now stands at the site, and has a large collection of photos, though none of the captions are in English. A short walk from the museum is the building which housed the South Bureau of the Communist Party's Central Committee and the office of the representatives of the Eighth Route Army – though there's little to see except a few sparse furnishings and photographs.

To get to the Red Cliff Village, take bus No 16 four stops from the station on Liziba Lu.

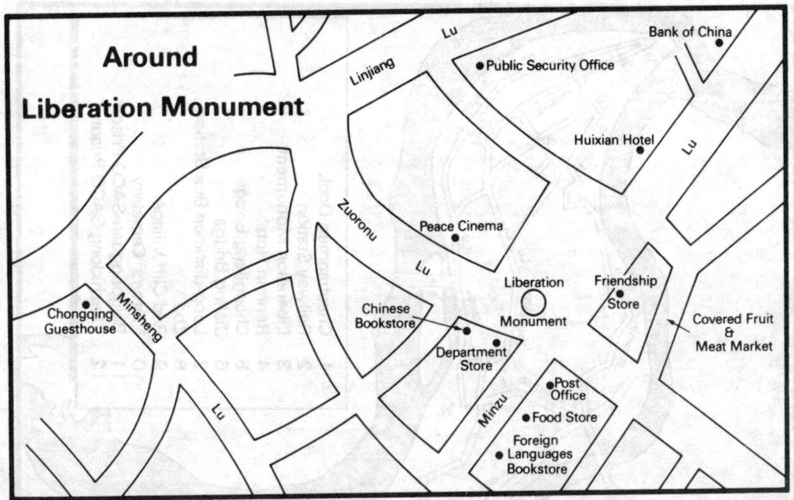

US-Chiang Kaishek Criminal Acts Exhibition Hall & SACO Prisons

In 1941 the United States and Chiang Kaishek signed a secret agreement to set up the Sino-American Cooperation Organisation (SACO), under which the United States helped to train and dispatch secret agents for the Kuomintang government. The chief of SACO was Tai Li, head of the Kuomintang military secret service; its deputy chief was a US Navy officer, Commodore M E Miles.

The SACO prisons were set up outside Chongqing during WW II. The Kuomintang never recognised the Communist Party as a legal political entity, only the Army. Civilian Communists remained subject to the same repressive laws, and though these were not enforced at the time, they were not actually rescinded. Hundreds of political prisoners were still kept captive by the Kuomintang in these prisons and others, and according to the Communists many were executed.

One of the prisoners held in the Chongqing SACO prisons for five years was General Ye Ding, a Whampoa Military Academy cadet, commander of a Nationalist division during the Northern Expedition of 1926-27 and one of the principal leaders of the Nanchang uprising of 1 August 1927. After the failure of the insurrection Ye retreated to Shantou with some of the Red Army and then took part in the disastrous Canton uprising of December 1927. He escaped to Hong Kong and withdrew from politics for a decade.

In 1937, with the anti-Japanese alliance between the Kuomintang and the Communists established, he was authorised by Chiang Kaishek to reorganise the surviving Red partisans on the Jiangxi-Fujian-Hunan borders, and to create the New Fourth Army – these were soldiers who had been left behind as a rearguard when the main part of the army began its Long March to Shaanxi in 1934. In 1941, Chiang Kaishek's troops ambushed the rear detachment of the New Fourth Army while it was moving in an area entirely behind Japanese lines to which it had been assigned by Chiang. This non-combat detachment was annihilated and Ye Ding was imprisoned in Chongqing.

Chiang ruled that the massacre was caused by the New Fourth's 'insubordination' and henceforth all aid was withdrawn from that army and also from the Communists' Eighth Route Army; from this time on the Communists received no pay and no ammunition and a

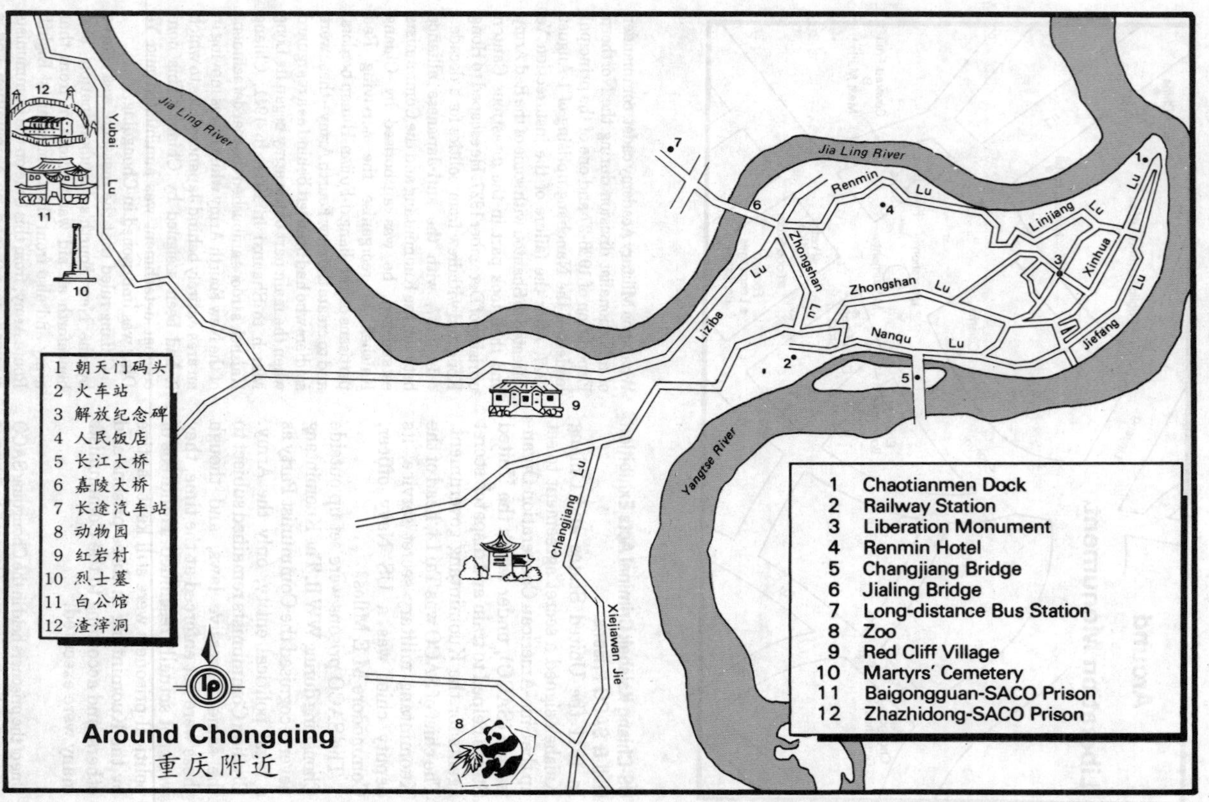
Around Chongqing
重庆附近
1 Chaotianmen Dock
2 Railway Station
3 Liberation Monument
4 Renmin Hotel
5 Changjiang Bridge
6 Jialing Bridge
7 Long-distance Bus Station
8 Zoo
9 Red Cliff Village
10 Martyrs' Cemetery
11 Baigongguan-SACO Prison
12 Zhazhidong-SACO Prison
1 朝天门码头
2 火车站
3 解放纪念碑
4 人民饭店
5 长江大桥
6 嘉陵大桥
7 长途汽车站
8 动物园
9 红岩村
10 烈士墓
11 白公馆
12 渣滓洞
Jia Ling River
Jia Ling River
Yangtse River
Renmin Lu
Zhongshan Lu
Zhongshan Lu
Nanqu Lu
Linjiang Lu
Xinhua Lu
Jiefang
Liziba Lu
Changjiang Lu
Xiejiawan Jie
Yubai Lu

blockade was thrown up around their areas to prevent access to supplies. Although the Communists did not retaliate against the Kuomintang – which would have made Japan's task much simpler – clashes between Kuomintang and Communist were continuous, at times amounting to major civil war.

After Ye's release in 1946 he died en route to Yanan, in a plane crash which also killed among others Deng Fa (chief of the Red Army's Security Police) and Bo Gu (general secretary of the Communist Party from 1932 to 1935 and a supporter of urban-insurrection policies which had cost the Communists dearly in the 1930s).

While the events that surround them are fairly dramatic, the prisons and the exhibition hall are not and you'll probably find them fairly boring unless you're an enthusiast. The exhibition hall has lots of photos on display but no English captions. There are manacles and chains but nothing to ghoul over. The hall is open 8.30 am to 5 pm and admission is 20 fen. To get there take bus No 17 from the station on Liziba Lu. It's about a 20-minute ride and make sure that the driver knows where you want to get off, as the place is not obvious. The SACO Prisons are a long hour's walk from the hall (there appears to be no transport, though you could try waving down a truck or jeep), and there's really nothing to see here.

The Bridges

Worth checking out are the enormous Jialing and Yangtse bridges. The Jialing Bridge, which crosses the river north of central Chongqing, was built between 1963 and 1966. It is 150 metres long and 60 metres high and for 15 years was one of the few means of access to the rest of China. The Yangtse Bridge to the south was finished in 1981.

Chongqing Museum

The museum is a reasonably interesting place, though nothing outstanding. They usually have some dinosaur skeletons on display, unearthed between 1974 and 1977 at Zigong, Yangchuan and elsewhere in Sichuan Province. Hours are 9 to 11.30 am and 2 to 5.30 pm.

The museum is at the foot of Pipa Shan in the southern part of town, a short walk from the Renmin Hotel. Walk up Zaozilanyu along the eastern side of the hotel compound; on the right you'll come to a little street market. Walk down this street and turn left where it branches into two smaller streets. Follow the street up to the entrance of a park (admission four fen); head through the park, past the 'Cultural Palace of the Laboring People' and at the other end you'll come out on Zhongshan Lu. Directly opposite the entrance to the park, on the other side of the road, is a small street which leads uphill to the Chongqing Museum.

The Zoo

The zoo is little more than the hideous sight of badly kept animals in bare concrete cages. There are a couple of slumbering, dirty pandas here. Whatever you do, don't come on a Sunday, because you'll be the main attraction. From near the entrance to the cable-car on Zhongshan Lu, take bus No 3 up Changjiang Lu to its terminus. From the terminus walk along the road directly in front of you for about 10 minutes and this will get you to the zoo.

Northern Hot Springs

North-east of the city, overlooking the Jialing River, the Northern Hot Springs are in a large park which is the site of a 5th-century Buddhist temple. The springs have an Olympic-size swimming pool where you can bathe to an audience. There are also private rooms with hot baths – big tubs where the water comes up to your neck if you sit and up to your waist if you stand. Swim suits can be rented here – they're coloured red, symbolising happiness. There's another group of springs 20 km south of Chongqing but the northern group is said to be better.

Places to Stay

The *Renmin Hotel* is one of the most incredible hotels in China, and if you don't stay here you have got to at least visit the place. It's quite literally a palace, with a design that seems inspired by the Temple of Heaven and the Forbidden City in Beijing. Two wings make up the hotel, and these are separated by an enormous circular concert hall that is 65 metres high and seats 4000 people. The hotel was constructed in 1953.

For all the grandeur of the facade, the rooms themselves are as basic as in any other Chinese hotel. The floor of the concert hall is concrete and the seats are bare wood and metal. The concrete railings on the balconies are sloppily painted, air-conditioners are tacked on here and there and the backyard is a hodge-podge of tacky little buildings. Nevertheless, there's a certain something about being able to come home to half a palace at the end of the day.

Prices at the hotel suit every pocket. Cheapest accommodation is Y5 for a dormitory bed, with common bathroom. A bed in a double room goes for Y6 or Y7 with common bathroom. A bed in a dormitory with attached bathroom is Y8. Various other double rooms go for Y22, Y24, Y30 and Y32. A 'double twin room' is Y55. Most of the staff speak adequate to excellent English, and they're quite friendly.

Travellers report that the hotel has been closed for many months of renovation so it should resurface soon in refurbished splendour.

To get there, take bus No 1 from above the railway station up Zhongshansan Lu as far as the first traffic circle. Then change to bus Nos 13 or 15, which will take you down past the hotel. It may be just as easy to walk from the traffic circle.

The *Huixian Hotel*, close to the Liberation Monument, has a dorm (Y10 per bed) on the 11th floor with a panoramic view and roof garden. The hotel restaurant is on the 2nd floor.

The *Chongqing Guest House* on Minsheng Lu is a cold, dreary hotel. The cheapest bed is Y8. The hotel does have the advantage of being more centrally located than the Renmin Hotel. Take bus No 1 from Zhongshan Lu, above the railway station.

Places to Eat

Eating in Chongqing is something of a joke. You've got the restaurants at the Renmin and Huixian hotels and not much else if you want a decent meal. For Mongolian hotpot (*huo guo*) or snacks you might try the area near the centre of town, around the corner from Minquan Lu on Zhonghu Lu. On Zhonghu Lu are a number of street stalls where you can get little plates of vegetable, duck, pork, peanuts and rice for maybe 60 fen to Y1.

Getting There & Away

Air Chongqing is connected by air to Beijing (Y281), Canton (Y122), Changsha (Y125), Chengdu (Y52), Guiyang (Y62), Guilin (Y136), Kunming (Y113), Nanjing (Y226), Shanghai (Y298), Wuhan (Y144) and Xian (Y110).

Bus The long-distance bus station is on the northern side of the Jialing River, across the Jialing Bridge. Getting to the station isn't so straightforward. Take bus No 5 from the intersection of Zhongshan Lu and Renmin Lu, cross the Jialing Bridge, and get off at the terminus. The bus station is further up ahead and you can walk if you're not carrying too much, or take bus No 10 the last stretch.

Buses from here to Dazu depart at 7.20 and 8 am; the fare is Y4.50 and the trip takes about eight hours.

A company called Kang Fu Lai (KFL), about a 10-minute walk from the Renmin Hotel (ask reception for directions), runs modern buses to Dazu. Tickets cost Y10 and buses depart at 8 am.

Rail From Chongqing there are direct trains to Beijing, Chengdu (11 hours, Y17 hard-sleeper, Chinese price) and Guiyang

(11 hours, Y14.70 hard-sleeper, Chinese price). For Kunming you must change trains at Chengdu and for Guilin you must change trains at Guiyang.

Boat There are boats from Chongqing down the Yangtse River to Wuhan. The ride is a popular tourist trip, a good way of getting away from the trains and an excellent way to get to Wuhan. For details, see the following section on the Yangtse River as well as the sections on Wuhan, Shanghai and Yueyang.

Getting Around
Buses in Chongqing are tediously slow, and since there are no bicycles they're even more crowded than in other Chinese cities. Taxis can be hired from CITS or the reception desk of the Renmin Hotel.

Chongqing has announced plans for an overhead transport system which is to run on an east-west axis, between Shapingba and Linjiangmen. Once funding has been secured, the first phase of the aerobus project should take 2½ years before the inhabitants of Chongqing can be jiggled through the air courtesy of Swiss technology.

DOWNRIVER ON THE YANGTSE: CHONGQING TO WUHAN

The dramatic scenery and rushing waters of China's greatest river have been a great artistic inspiration but to those forced to navigate the tricky waters the reality has been far harsher. Tackling the Yangtse can mean hard work as well as danger, a large boat pushing upstream often needed hundreds of coolies ('trackers') who lined the banks of the river and hauled the boat with long ropes against the surging waters. Today smaller boats can still be seen being pulled up the river by their crews.

The Yangtse is China's longest river and the third longest in the world at 6300 km, emanating from the snow-covered Tanggula Mountains in south-west Qinghai and cutting its way through Tibet and seven Chinese provinces before emptying into the East China Sea just north of Shanghai. Between the towns of Fengjie in Sichuan and Yichang in Hubei lie three great gorges, regarded as one of the great scenic attractions of China. The steamer ride from Chongqing to Wuhan is one of the popular tourist trips. It's a nice way to get from Chongqing to Wuhan, a relief from the trains and the scenery is pleasant, but don't expect to be dwarfed by mile-high cliffs! A lot of people find the trip quite boring, possibly because of over-anticipation.

The ride downriver from Chongqing to Wuhan takes three days and two nights. Upriver the ride takes five days. One possibility is to take the boat as far as Yichang, which will let you see the gorges and the huge Gezhouba Dam. At Yichang you can take a train north to Xiangfan and another to Luoyang. If you continue the boat ride you can get off at Yueyang and take the train to Canton, or you can carry on to Wuhan.

Tickets You can buy tickets for the boats from CITS in Chongqing or from the booking office at Chaotianmen Dock. You'll generally have to book two or three days ahead of your intended date of departure, but some people have arrived, got their tickets and left the same day. CITS adds a service charge of Y5 to the price of the tickets, but you may wonder where the service went since they're hopelessly disorganised and never seem to know just what tickets are available. The booking office at Chaotianmen Dock is open daily 9 to 11 am and 2.30 to 5 pm; it's worth trying if CITS doesn't have tickets for the day you want. You can take the boat upriver – see the Wuhan section for details.

Second-class cabins get hopelessly overbooked in the middle of the year when the tour groups are piling into the country, and even they sometimes end up being relegated to 3rd-class cabins, so don't be surprised if you can't get a ticket at this time of year.

Classes In egalitarian China there is no 1st

class on the boat. Second class is a comfortable two-berth cabin, with soft beds, a small desk and chair, and a wash-basin. Showers and toilets are private cubicles shared by the passengers. Adjoining the 2nd-class deck and at the front of the boat is a large lounge where you can while the time away.

Third class has either four or eight beds depending on what boat you're on. Fourth class is a 24-bed cabin. Toilets and showers are communal, though you should be able to use the toilets and showers in 2nd class. If they don't let you into the 2nd-class area then have a look around the boat; the one I was on had some toilet cubicles on the lower deck with doors and partitions. There doesn't seem to be any problem just wandering into the lounge and plonking yourself down.

The boat I was on also had a couple of large cabins the entire width of the boat accommodating about 40 people on triple-tiered bunks. In addition, there's deck-class where you camp out in the corridors, but it's highly unlikely you'll be sold tickets for these classes. If you take one of the large dormitories, remember that this part of China is very cold in winter and very hot in summer. Petty thieves have been reported in the dorms, so keep valuable items safe – particularly at night.

Fares CITS in Chongqing charges the following fares in yuan per person:

	2nd class	*3rd class*	*4th class*
Wanxian	35.70	25.50	8.50
Yichang	64.70	36.30	20.90
Shashi	74.70	39.40	17.90
Wuhan	102.00	52.90	32.80

If you want to go further down the Yangtse to places like Jiujiang, Wuhu, Nanjing or Shanghai, then you have to change boats at Wuhan. CITS in Chongqing can only sell you tickets as far as Wuhan. The luxury *M/S Yangzijiang* sails the river, though it appears to be primarily for tour groups and high-ranking Chinese – prices range between Y600 and Y1050, depending on the season. Between Nanjing and Wuhan a hydrofoil service cuts travelling time down from 40 hours to just 10 – see the Wuhan section for details.

Departure Times The boat departs Chongqing at 7 am from Chaotianmen. A special bus from the Renmin Hotel at 6 am will take you straight to the dock. Book a seat on the bus beforehand at the hotel reception desk – it's only Y1.20 per person. Or you can take a taxi. There are probably local buses running at that time, but it's hardly worth the effort.

You're supposed to be able to sleep on the boat the night before departure for Y6 – it's worth asking, but don't be surprised if you're turned away. Perhaps if you have a 2nd-class cabin you'll be allowed to.

Food There are two restaurants on the boat. The one on the lower deck caters for the masses and is pretty terrible. The restaurant on the upper deck is quite good, but how much you're charged seems to vary from boat to boat. One person was charged Y6 per meal (expensive but worth it, considering the alternative) and another Y12. Second-class passengers usually get charged either Y10, Y12 or Y15 for three meals each day. It's a good idea to bring some of your own food with you.

First Day The boat departs Chongqing at around 7 am. For the first few hours the river is lined with factories, though this gives way to some pretty, green terraced countryside with the occasional small town.

Around 11.30 am you arrive at the town of **Fuling.** The town overlooks the mouth of the Wu River which runs southwards into Guizhou; it controls the river traffic between Guizhou and eastern Sichuan. Near Fuling in the middle of the Yangtse River is a huge rock called Baihe Ridge. On one side of the rock are three carvings known as 'stone fish' which date back to ancient times and are thought to have served as watermarks – the rock can be seen only when the river is at its very lowest. In addition to the carvings, there are a large number of inscriptions describing the culture, art and technology of these ancient times.

Fengdu is the next major town. Nearby Pingdu Mountain is said to be the abode of devils. The story goes that during the Han Dynasty two men, Yin Changsheng and Wang Fangping, lived on the mountain, and when their family names were joined together they were mistakenly thought to be the Yinwang, the King of Hell. Numerous temples containing sculptures of demons and devils have been built on the mountain since the Tang Dynasty, with heartening names like 'Between the Living and the Dead', 'Bridge of Helplessness' and 'Palace of the King of Hell'.

The boat then passes through **Zhongxian County**. North-east of the county seat of Zhongzhou is the **Qian Jinggou** site where primitive stone artefacts including axes, hoes and stone weights attached to fishing nets were unearthed.

In the afternoon the boat passes by **Shibaozhai (Stone Treasure Stronghold)** on the northern bank of the river. Shibaozhai is a 30-metre-high rock which is supposed to look something like a stone seal. During the early years of Emperor Qianlong's reign (1736-1797) an impressive red wooden temple, the Landruodian, shaped like a pagoda and 11 storeys high, was built on the rock. It houses a statue of Buddha and inscriptions which commemorate its construction.

Around 7 pm the boat arrives in the large town of **Wanxian** where it ties up for the night. Wanxian is the hub of transportation and communications along the river between eastern Sichuan and western Hubei and has traditionally been known as the gateway to Sichuan. It was opened to foreign trade in 1917. It's a neat, hilly town and a great place to wander around for a few hours while the boat is in port. There's a pleasant park around the tower in the centre of town. A long flight of steps leads from the pier up the riverbank to a bustling night market where you can get something to eat or buy very cheap wickerwork baskets, chairs and stools.

Second Day The boat departs Wanxian at 4 am. Before entering the gorges the boat passes by (and may stop at) the town of **Fengjie**. This ancient town was the capital of the state of Kui during the Spring and Autumn and Warring States Period (770 BC-221 BC). The town overlooks the Qutang Gorge, the first of the three Yangtse gorges. Just east of Fengjie is a km-long shoal where the remains of stone piles could be seen when the water level was low. These piles were erected in the Stone and Bronze ages, possibly for commemorative and sacrificial purposes, but their remains were removed in 1964 since they were considered a danger to navigation. Another set of similar structures can be found east of Fengjie outside a place called Baidicheng.

Baidicheng or White King Town is on the river's north bank at the entrance to the Qutang Gorge, 7½ km from Fengjie. The story goes that a high official proclaimed himself king during the Western Han Dynasty, and moved his capital to this town. A well was discovered which emitted a fragrant white vapour; this struck him as such an auspicious omen that he renamed himself The White King and his capital 'White King Town'.

Sanxia The 'Three Gorges', Qutang, Wuxia and Xiling, start just after Fengjie and end near Yichang, a stretch of about 200 km. The gorges vary from 300 metres at their widest to less than 100 metres at their narrowest. The seasonal difference in water level can be as much as 50 metres.

Qutang Gorge is the smallest and shortest gorge (only eight km long), though the water flows most rapidly here. High on the north bank, at a place called Fengxiang (Bellows) Gorge, are a series of crevices. There is said to have been an ancient tribe in this area whose custom was to place the coffins of their dead in high mountain caves. Nine coffins were discovered in these crevices, some containing bronze swords, armour and other artefacts, but are believed to date back only as far as the Warring States Period.

Wuxia Gorge is about 40 km in length and the cliffs on either side rise to just over 900 metres. The gorge is noted for the Kong Ming tablet, a large slab of rock at the foot of the Peak of the Immortals. Kong Ming was prime minister of the state of Shu during the period of the Three Kingdoms (220-280 AD). On the tablet is a description of his stance upholding the alliance between the states of Shu and Wu against the state of Wei. **Badong** is a town on the southern bank of the river within the gorge. The town is a communications centre from which roads span out into western Hubei Province. The boat usually stops here.

Xiling Gorge is the longest of the three gorges at 80 km. At the end of the gorge everyone crowds out onto the deck to watch the boat pass through the locks of the huge **Gezhouba Dam**.

The next stop is the industrial town of **Yichang**, at about 3 pm if the boat is on time. From here you can take a train north to Xiangfan, where you can catch a train to Luoyang. Yichang is regarded as the gateway to the Upper Yangtse and was once a walled city dating back at least as far as the Sui Dynasty. The town was opened to foreign trade in 1877 by a treaty between Britain and China, and a foreign concession area was set up along the riverfront to the south-east of the walled city. After leaving Yichang, the boat passes under the immense **Chanjiang Bridge** at the town of **Zhicheng**. The bridge is 1700 metres long and supports a double-track railway with roads for trucks and cars on either side. It came into operation in 1971.

The next major town is **Shashi**, a light-industrial town. As early as the Tang Dynasty Shashi was a trading centre of some importance, enjoying great prosperity during the Taiping Rebellion when trade lower down the Yangtse was largely at a standstill. It was opened up to foreign trade in 1896 by the Treaty of Shimonoseki between China and Japan, and though an area outside the town was assigned as a Japanese concession it was never developed. About 7½ km from Shashi is the ancient town of **Jingzhou**, which you can bus to.

Third Day There is absolutely nothing to see on the third day; you're out on the flat plains of eastern China, the river widens immensely and you can see little of the shore. The boat continues downriver during the night and passes by the town of **Chenglingji**, which lies at the confluence of Lake Dongting and the Yangtse River. East of Lake Dongting is the town of **Yueyang**, which you'll reach at around about 6 am. If the boat is on time then you'll get into **Wuhan** late that afternoon, around 5 pm. (For details on Yueyang and Wuhan and the Yangtse River between Wuhan and Shanghai, see the separate sections in this book.)

DAZU 大足

The grotto art of Dazu County, 160 km north-west of Chongqing, is rated alongside China's other great Buddhist cave sculpture at Dunhuang, Luoyang and Datong. Historical records for Dazu are sketchy; the cliff carving and statues (with Buddhist, Taoist and Confucian influences) amount to thousands of pieces, large and small, scattered over the county in some 40-odd places. The main groupings are at Bei Shan (North Hill) and the more interesting Baoding. They date from the Tang Dynasty (9th century) to the Song (13th century).

The town of Dazu is a small, unhurried place. It's also been relatively unvisited by westerners, and the surrounding countryside is superb.

Bei Shan

Bei Shan is about a 30-minute hike from Dazu town – aim straight for the pagoda

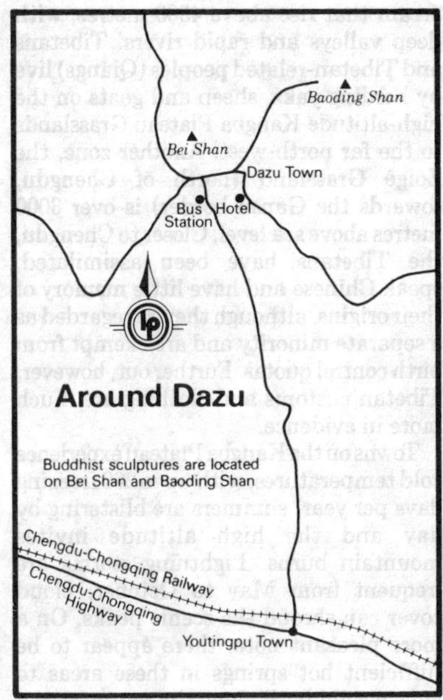

visible from the bus station. There are good overall views from the top of the hill. The dark niches hold small statues, many in poor condition; only one or two are of interest.

Niche No 136 depicts Puxian the patron saint (a male) of Emei Shan, riding a white elephant. The same niche has the androgynous Sun and Moon Guanyin. Niche 155 holds a bit more talent, the Peacock King. According to inscriptions, the Bei Shan site was originally a military camp, with the earliest carvings commissioned by a general.

Baoding

Fifteen km north-east of Dazu town, the Baoding sculptures are definitely more interesting than those at Bei Shan. The founding work is attributed to Zhao Zhifeng, a monk from an obscure Yoga sect of Tantric Buddhism. There's a monastery in the throes of renovation with nice woodwork and throngs of pilgrims. On the lower section of the hill on which the monastery sits is a horseshoe-shaped cliff sculpted with coloured figures, some of them up to eight metres high. The centrepiece is a 31-metre-long, five-metre-high reclining Buddha, depicted in the state of entering Nirvana, the torso sunk into the cliff face – most peaceful.

Statues around the rest of the 125-metre horseshoe vary considerably: Buddhist preachers and sages, historical figures, realistic scenes (on the rear of a postcard one is described as 'Pastureland – Cowboy at Rest'), and delicate sculptures a few cm in height. Some of them have been eroded by wind and rain, some have lost layers of paint, but generally there is a remarkable survival rate (fanatical Red Guards did descend on the Dazu area bent on defacing the sculptures, but were stopped – so the story goes – by an urgent order from Zhou Enlai).

Baoding differs from other grottoes in that it was based on a preconceived plan which incorporated some of the area's natural features – a sculpture next to the Reclining Buddha, for example, makes use of an underground spring. Completion of the sculptures in 1249 AD is believed to have taken 70 years. Especially vivid are the demonic pieces: an emblem shows the six ways to transmigrate (look for a large dartboard held by the fangs of a Mr Hyde), and a one-storey section contains sobering sculptures on the evils of alcohol and other misdemeanours. Inside a small temple on the carved cliff is the Goddess of Mercy, with a spectacular gilt forest of fingers (1007 hands if you care to check). Each hand has an eye, the symbol of wisdom.

Buses to Baoding leave Dazu town every half hour from 7 am to 3 pm; the fare is 40 fen. The last bus departs Baoding for Dazu at around 5 pm. The sites are open from 8 am to 6 pm. As you pass by in the bus, keep an eye on the cliff-faces for solo sculptures that may occasionally pop up.

CITS (inside the Dazu Binguan) can arrange a four-hour trip by taxi (Y30) or minibus (Y40).

Places to Stay & Eat

The *Dazu Binguan* charges Y12 per person for a room with bath, rudimentary but comfortable. The hotel is a major hike from the bus station. Turn left from the station, cross a bridge to a place which bears a sign 'Cold Drinks/Dining-room', turn right after it and walk for about 10 minutes – the hotel is on your left.

The *Cold Drink* place has the best fare in town. Next door is a Chinese hotel which charges Y10.

Getting There

Bus There are several options by bus. The first is the direct bus from Chongqing to Dazu which leaves at 7.20 am from Chongqing's north-west bus station; there are seven buses a day, the fare is Y4.50, and the trip takes five to seven hours depending on whether there is a lunch break. The second is the Kang Fu Lai (KFL) bus company, which is a 10-minute walk from the Renmin Hotel (ask reception for directions), and runs modern buses to Dazu. Tickets cost Y10 and buses depart at 8 am. There is also the daily bus from Chengdu to Dazu; departs 6.50am, takes 10 hours, fare Y10.

Rail To get to Dazu by rail, you should drop off the Chengdu-Chongqing rail line at Youtingpu town (five hours from Chongqing, seven hours from Chengdu). The 7 am train from Chengdu arrives at 2.20 pm in time for a connecting 2.30 pm bus outside the station. It's a 30-km ride and the fare is Y1. Buses for Youtingpu depart Dazu irregularly on the hour or half-hour from 11.30 am to 3.30 pm. There are six buses a day.

WESTERN SICHUAN & THE ROAD TO TIBET

Literally the next best thing to Tibet are the Sichuan mountains to the north and west of Chengdu – heaps of whipping cream that rise above 4500 metres, with deep valleys and rapid rivers. Tibetans and Tibetan-related peoples (Qiangs) live by herding yaks, sheep and goats on the high-altitude Kangba Plateau Grasslands to the far north-west. Another zone, the Zoigê Grassland (north of Chengdu, towards the Gansu border) is over 3000 metres above sea level. Closer to Chengdu, the Tibetans have been assimilated, speak Chinese and have little memory of their origins, although they're regarded as a separate minority and are exempt from birth control quotas. Further out, however, Tibetan customs and clothing are much more in evidence.

Towns on the Kangba Plateau experience cold temperatures, with up to 200 freezing days per year; summers are blistering by day and the high altitude invites mountain burns. Lightning storms are frequent from May to October; cloud cover can shroud the scenic peaks. On a more pleasant note, there appear to be sufficient hot springs in these areas to have a solid bath along the route.

A theme often echoed by ancient Chinese poets is that the road to Sichuan is harder to travel than the road to heaven. In the present era, with the province more accessible by road, we can shift the poetry to Tibet and the highway connecting it with western Sichuan.

The Sichuan-Tibet Highway, begun in 1950 and finished in 1954, is one of the world's highest, roughest, most dangerous and most beautiful roads. The highway has been split into northern and southern routes. The northern route runs via Kangding, Garzê and Dêgê before crossing the boundary into Tibet. The southern route runs via Kangding, Litang and Batang before entering Tibet.

The Public Security Bureau in Chengdu directs all foreigners to take the plane to Lhasa; the land route between Chengdu and Lhasa is closed to foreigners for safety reasons. Some palefaces have succeeded and arrived intact in Lhasa. Less fortunate were some Americans and Australians on the back of a truck which overturned close to Dêgê; one member of the group lost half an arm and another member sustained multiple injuries to her back. It took several days for medical help to be sent and even longer before the injured could be brought back to Chengdu.

At present, the bus service on the Sichuan-Tibet highway only seems to function well as far as Kangding. A couple of years ago there was a legendary crate, the Chengdu-to-Lhasa bus, which suffered countless breakdowns and took weeks to arrive. In 1985, a monumental mudslip on the southern route took out the road for dozens of km and the service has been discontinued.

Trucks are the only transport travelling consistently long hauls on this highway. The major truck depots are in Chengdu, Chamdo and Lhasa. Trucks usually run from Lhasa or from Chengdu only as far as Chamdo, where you have to find another lift. The police have now clamped down on truckers giving lifts to foreigners; there is rumoured to be a sign in Chinese near Dêgê which warns drivers not to take foreigners. Certainly at Dêgê itself, there is a checkpoint on the bridge where guards turn back foreigners. If a driver is caught, he could lose his licence or receive a massive fine. Foreigners caught arriving from Chengdu are often fined and always sent back. If you're arriving from Tibet nobody gives a damn.

In sum, the odds are stacked much higher against you when travelling into, rather than out of, Tibet. Whatever you do, bear in mind the risk and equip yourself properly with food and warm clothing. For information on Tibet and Qinghai see the separate section in this book. More information about the Sichuan-Tibet Highway is given in Lonely Planet's *Tibet – a Travel Survival Kit*.

Some travellers have followed the highway across the Kangba Plateau to the following places:

Kangding (Dardo)

Kangding (2620 metres) is a small town nestled in majestic scenery. Swift currents from rapids give Kangding hydro-power, the source of heating and electricity for the town. There is a daily bus service from Chengdu main bus station to Kangding via Ya'an and Luding.

Towering above Kangding is the mighty peak of Gongga Shan (7556 metres) – to behold it is worth 10 years of meditation, says an inscription in a ruined monastery by the base. The mountain is apparently often covered with cloud so patience is required for the beholding. It sits in a mountain range, with a sister peak just below it towering to 5200 metres. Pilgrims used to circle the two for several hundred km to pay homage.

Gongga Shan is on the open list for foreign mountaineers – in 1981 it buried eight Japanese climbers in an avalanche. Known conquests of this awesome 'goddess' are those by two Americans in 1939, and by six Chinese in 1957.

Dêgê

This town lies in the Chola Shan at the north-west corner of Sichuan, and has an extensive Scripture Printing Lamasery with a 250-year tradition. Its vast collection of ancient Tibetan scriptures of the five Lamaist sects is revered by followers the world over. Under the direction of the abbot are some 300 workers; housed within the monastery are over 200,000 hardwood printing plates. Texts include ancient works on astronomy, geography, music, medicine and Buddhist classics. A history of Indian Buddhism, comprising 555 plates, is the only surviving copy in the world (written in Hindi, Sanskrit and Tibetan). Protecting the monastery from fire and earthquake is a guardian goddess, a green Avalokitesvara.

Litang

Further west of Kangding is Litang, which at 4700 metres is 1000 metres higher than Lhasa and a few hundred metres short of the world record for high towns (Wenchuan, on the Qinghai-Tibet Plateau). Litang rests at the edge of a vast grassland. A trading fair and festival lasting 10 days is held here annually; it's sponsored by the Grand Living Buddha of the Kangba Plateau.

NORTHERN SICHUAN 四川北郊

Jiuzhaigou

In northern Sichuan, close to the Gansu border, is Jiuzhaigou (literally: nine stockade gully), which was 'discovered' in the '70s and is now being groomed for an annual influx of 300,000 visitors. In 1984, Zhao Ziyang made the famous comment which all Sichuanese tourism officials love to quote: 'Guilin's scenery ranks top in the world, but Jiuzhaigou's scenery even tops Guilin's'.

Jiuzhaigou, which has several Tibetan settlements, offers a number of dazzling features – it is a nature reserve area (some panda conservation zones) with North American-type alpine scenes (peaks, clear lakes, forests). The remoteness of the region and the chaotic transport connections have kept it clean and relatively untouristed.

Despite the good intentions of the authorities, all this looks certain to change fast. A helicopter landing pad is under construction even though the mountain ranges between Chengdu and Jiuzhaigou are not ideal terrain for helicopters. Tourism officials are already going one step further and planning an airport for small jets.

You should calculate between a week and 10 days for the round trip by road. It takes two to three days to get there and you can easily spend three or four days doing superb hikes along trails which cross a spectacular scenery of waterfalls, ponds, lakes and forests – just the place to rejuvenate polluted urban senses.

The admission fee of Y3 FEC is collected at the entrance to the reserve, close to the Yangtong Hotel. From there a dirt road runs as far as the Nuorilang Waterfall where the road splits: branch left for Swan Lake; branch right for Long Lake. From Yangtong to Nuorilang is 13.8 km, Nuorilang to Long Lake is 17.8 km, Nuorilang to Rize is nine km, Rize to Swan Lake is eight km.

Jiuzhaigou and Huanglong Si are both around 3000 metres in altitude. Between October and April snow often cuts off access for weeks on end. Make sure you take warm clothing; food can be abysmal so take iron rations with you. The rainy season lasts between June and August.

Roads in these regions are dangerous so don't expect more than minimum standards of vehicle, driver or road maintenance. Shock horror stories circulating last year about Jiuzhaigou included a minibus-load of Hong Kongers which reported sighting a UFO; another bus-load plunged over a precipice with the loss of all 20 passengers. An outbreak of plague in the area caught two more Hong Kongers, who were immediately cremated.

Transport is not plentiful and unless you catch a bus at its originating point, be prepared when boarding en route for some tough competition for any seats. To maximise your chances of a seat on a bus out of Jiuzhaigou, it's best to book your ticket three days in advance at the entrance to the reserve. Hitching has worked.

Huanglong Si (Yellow Dragon Temple)

This valley studded with terraced ponds and waterfalls is about 56 km from Songpan, on the main road to Jiuzhaigou. Admission costs Y1.5 FEC. The most spectacular terraced ponds are behind the Yellow Dragon Temple, about a two-hour walk from the main road. Huanglong Si is almost always included on the itinerary for a Jiuzhaigou tour, but some people find it disappointing and think an extra day at Jiuzhaigou is preferable. An annual Miao Hui (Temple Fair) held here around the middle of the sixth lunar month (roughly mid-August) attracts large numbers of traders from the Qiang minority.

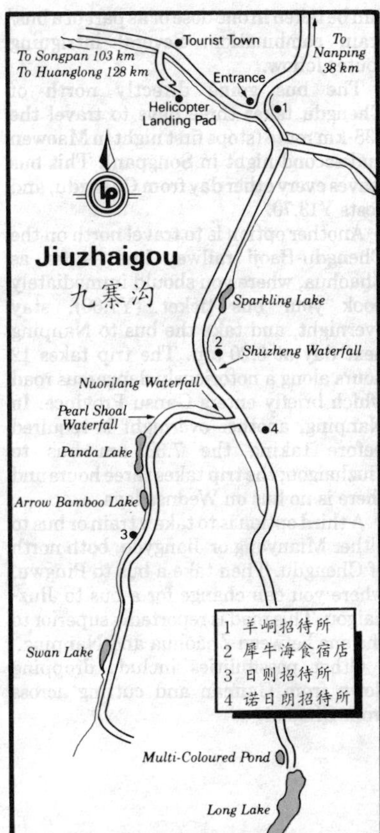

1 Yangtong Zhaodaisuo
2 Xiniu Haishi Sushe
3 Rizi Zhaodaisuo
4 Nuorilang Zhaodaisuo

Places to Stay

In Songpan, the *Songpan Zhaodaisuo* has doubles, triples and five-bed rooms; prices average Y5 per bed.

In Jiuzhaigou, the state-run *Zhaodaisuo* hotel and the privately-run *Sushe Hostel* compete happily for FEC. At places like the *Yangtong Zhaodaisuo, Nuorilang Zhaodaisuo* and *Rizi Zhaodaisuo* prices range between Y28 and Y10 double, Y14.50 and Y10 triple.

The hostels charge an average of Y3 per person for a room with no frills. The *Xiniu Haishi Sushe* has been recommended.

Nobody has a decent word for food in this region. Chengdu would be a good place to stock up.

Getting There & Away

Tours During the summer, various companies in Chengdu operate tours to Jiuzhaigou. Some include side-trips in the region. The most welcome customers are Hong Kongers, who tend to travel in miniature armies and book out a whole bus. Most of the trips are advertised for a certain day, but the bus will only go if full. If you are unlucky you may spend days waiting. Find out exactly how many days the trip lasts and which places are to be visited. If you're not sure about the tour company, avoid paying in advance. If there's a booking list, have a look and see how many people are on it. You can register first and pay before departure.

A standard tour includes Huanglong Si and Jiuzhaigou, lasts seven days and costs Y75 to Y100 per person. There are longer tours which include visits to the Tibetan grassland areas of Barkam and Zoigê. Prices vary according to the colour of your skin, availability of FEC and scruples of the companies involved.

I mention scruples because I spent several days investigating the Jiuzhaigou 'business' before foreigners were allowed to go there. Judging by the hankypanky that came to light before the opening, it will be interesting to see what happens now.

The following places have been known to offer tours:

Ximen bus station offered an eight-day tour for Y80 (soft-seat) or Y70 (hard-seat). After a great deal of backstage whispering, the office clerk asked for half the price in RMB and the rest in FEC.

In the front courtyard of Xinanmen bus station (next to Jiaotong Hotel) is Tianfu Luxingshe (Tianfu Travel Service), reputedly one of the best and most reliable tour operators. They offer tours from Y59 per person.

The taxi desk in the lobby of the Jinjiang Hotel can organise minibus tours. I was offered a seven-day tour at Y175 FEC per person in a minibus (maximum 15 persons).

Caoyuan Luxingshe (Grasslands Travel Service) have a ticket outlet on Renmin Nanlu close to Shaanxi Jie. They offer nine-day trips to the grasslands, Jiuzhaigou and Huanglong Si for Y75 per person.

A word of warning: Several tour operators in Chengdu have been blacklisted by Hong Kong travellers for lousy service, rip-offs and rudeness. Be especially careful when dealing with Qingnian Luxingshe (Youth Travel Service), which operates out of the shop opposite the Jinjiang Hotel, or with Shenzhou Minzu Luxingshe, which operates out of the Rongcheng Hotel.

Bus Until helicopters and jets send shock waves over Jiuzhaigou, the local bus remains the best means of transport. It can be taken in one dose or as part of a bus/train combination. Several intriguing routes follow.

The bus going directly north of Chengdu takes three days to travel the 438-km route (stops first night in Maowen and second night in Songpan). This bus leaves every other day from Chengdu, and costs Y13.70.

Another option is to travel north on the Chengdu-Baoji railway line as far as Zhaohua, where you should immediately book your bus ticket (Y7.30), stay overnight, and take the bus to Nanping next day at 6.20 am. The trip takes 12 hours along a notoriously dangerous road which briefly enters Gansu Province. In Nanping, another overnight is required before taking the 7.30 am bus to Jiuzhaigou; the trip takes three hours and there is no bus on Wednesdays.

A third option is to take a train or bus to either Mianyang or Jiangyou, both north of Chengdu. Then take a bus to Pingwu, where you can change for a bus to Jiuzhaigou. This road is reportedly superior to the one between Zhaohua and Nanping.

Other possibilities include dropping down from Gannan and cutting across from Qinghai.

Yunnan 云南

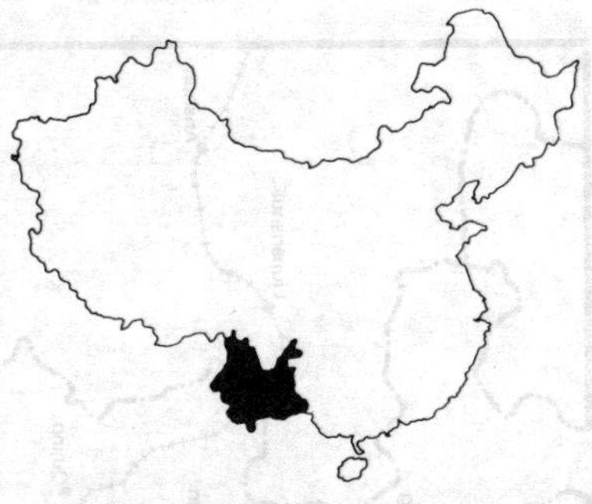

When Qin Shihuang and the Han emperors first held tentative sway over the south-west, Yunnan was occupied by a large number of non-Chinese aboriginal peoples without any strong political organisation. But by the 7th century AD the Bai people had established a powerful kingdom, the Nanzhao (Southern Princedom) south of Dali. Initially allying its power with the Chinese against the Tibetans, this kingdom extended its power until, in the middle of the 8th century, it was able to challenge and defeat the Tang armies. It took control of a large slice of the south-west and established itself as a fully independent entity, dominating the trade routes from China to India and Burma. The Nanzhao kingdom fell in the 10th century and was replaced by the Kingdom of Dali, an independent state which lasted until it was overrun by the Mongols in the mid-13th century. After 15 centuries of resistance to northern rule, this part of the south-west was finally integrated into the empire as the province of Yunnan.

Even so it remained an isolated frontier region, with scattered Chinese garrisons and settlements in the valleys and basins, and a mixed aboriginal population occupying the uplands. Like the rest of the south-west, it was always one of the first regions to break with the northern government. Today, however, Yunnan Province looks firmly back in the Chinese fold; it's a province of 32½ million people, including a veritable constellation of minorities: the Zhuang, Hui, Yi, Miao, Tibetans, Mongols, Yao, Bai, Hani, Dai, Lisu, Lahu, Va, Naxi, Jingpo, Bulang, Pumi, Nu, Achang, Benglong, Jinuo and Drung. Its chief attraction is the provincial capital of Kunming, one of the favourites of many travellers and a delightful city with the flavour of old-fashioned, back-street China.

KUNMING 昆明

The region of Kunming has been inhabited for the last 2000 years. Tomb excavations around Lake Dian to the south of the city have unearthed thousands of artefacts from that period – weapons, drums, paintings, silver, jade and turquoise jewellery – that suggest a well-developed culture and provide clues to a very sketchy early history of the city. Until the 8th century the town was a remote Chinese outpost, when the kingdom of Nanzhao, centred to the north-west of Kunming at Dali, captured it and made it a secondary capital. In 1274 the Mongols came through sweeping all and sundry before them. Marco Polo, who put his big feet and top hat in everywhere, gives us a fascinating picture of Kunming's commerce in the late 13th century:

> At the end of these five days journeys you arrive at the capital city, which is named Yachi, and is very great and noble. In it are found merchants and artisans, with a mixed population, consisting of idolaters, Nestorian Christians and Saracens or Mohametans . . . The land is fertile in rice and wheat . . . For money they employ the white porcelain shell, found in the sea, and which they also wear as ornaments about their necks. Eighty of the shells are equal in value to . . . two Venetian groats. In this country also there are salt springs . . . the duty levied on this salt produces large revenues to the Emperor. The natives do not consider it an injury done to them when others have connexion with their wives, provided the act is voluntary on the woman's part. Here there is a

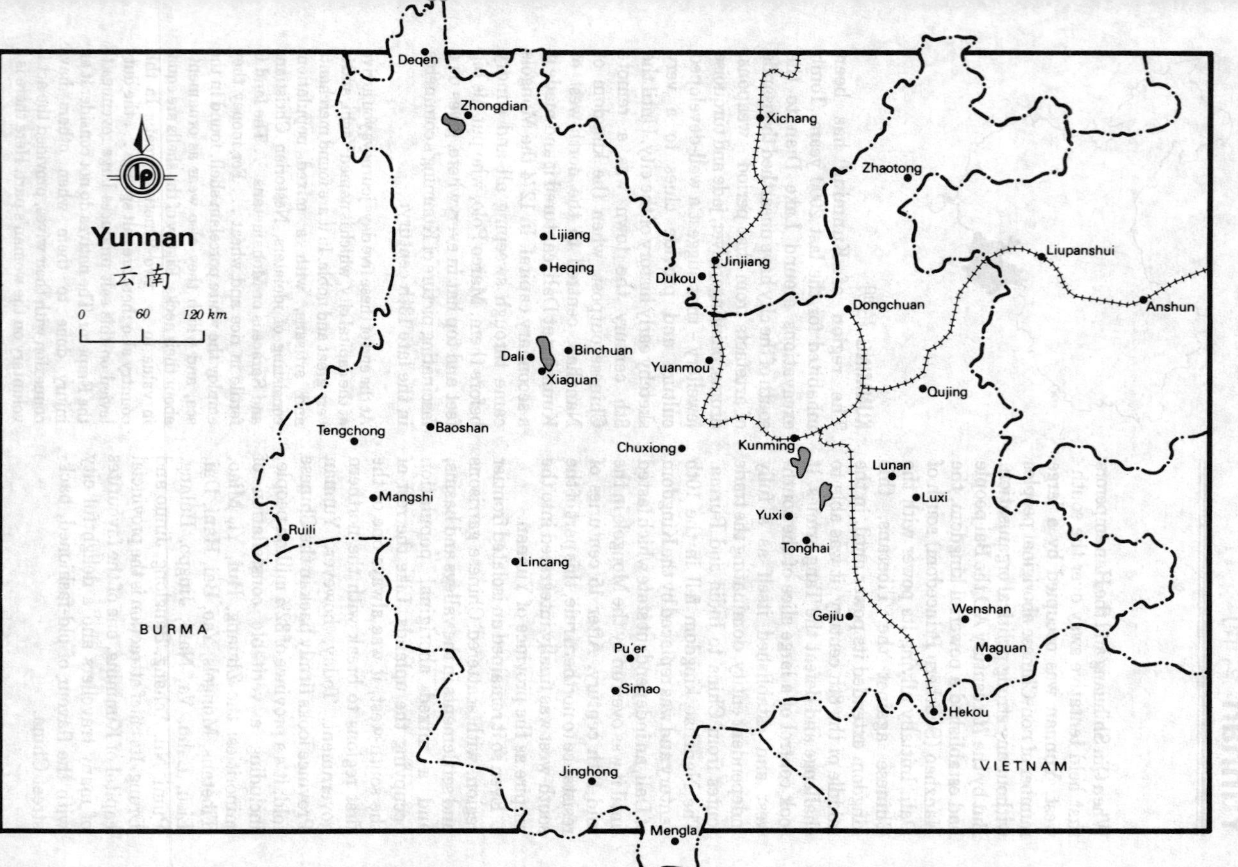
Yunnan
云南
0 60 120 km
Deqen
Zhongdian
Xichang
Zhaotong
Liupanshui
Anshun
Lijiang
Heqing
Jinjiang
Dukou
Dongchuan
Dali
Binchuan
Xiaguan
Yuanmou
Qujing
Tengchong
Baoshan
Chuxiong
Kunming
Lunan
Luxi
Mangshi
Yuxi
Ruili
Tonghai
Lincang
Gejiu
Wenshan
BURMA
Maguan
Pu'er
Simao
Hekou
VIETNAM
Jinghong
Mengla

lake almost a hundred miles in circuit, in which great quantities of fish are caught. The people are accustomed to eat the raw flesh of fowls, sheep, oxen and buffalo . . . the poorer sorts only dip it in a sauce of garlic . . . they eat it as well we do the cooked.

In the 14th century the Ming set up shop in Yunnanfu, as Kunming was then known, building a walled town on the present site. From the 17th century onwards the history of this city becomes rather grisly; under the local warlord Wu Sangui the city broke away from Qing control and was not brought to heel until 1681. In the 19th century, the city suffered several bloodbaths as the rebel Muslim leader Du Wenxiu, the Sultan of Dali, attacked and besieged the city several times between 1858 and 1868. A large number of buildings were destroyed and it was not until 1873 that the rebellion was finally and bloodily crushed. The intrusion of the west into Kunming began in the middle of the 19th century when Britain took control of Burma and France took control of Indo-China, providing access to the city from the south. By 1900 Kunming, Hekou, Simao and Mengzi were opened to foreign trade. The French were keen on exploiting the region's copper, tin and lumber resources and in 1910 their Indo-China railroad, started in 1898, reached the city.

Kunming's expansion began with WW II, when factories were established here and refugees fleeing the Japanese poured in from eastern China. To keep the Japanese tied up in China, Anglo-American forces sent supplies to Nationalist troops entrenched in Sichuan and Yunnan. Supplies came overland on a dirt road carved out of the mountains in 1937-38 by 160,000 Chinese with virtually no equipment. This was the famous Burma Road, a 1000-km haul from Lashio to Kunming (today, the western extension of Kunming's Renmin Lu, leading in the direction of Heilinpu, is the tail end of the Road). Then in early 1942 the Japanese captured Lashio, cutting the line. Kunming continued to handle most of the incoming aid from 1942-45 when American planes flew the dangerous mission of crossing the 'Hump', the towering 5000-metre mountain ranges between India and Yunnan. A black market sprang up and a fair proportion of the medicines, canned food, petrol and other goods intended for the military were siphoned off into other hands.

The face of Kunming has been radically altered since then – streets widened, office buildings and housing projects flung up. With the coming of the railways, industry has expanded rapidly, and a surprising range of goods and machinery available in China now bears the 'made in Yunnan' stamp. Kunming also has its own steel plant. The city's production includes foodstuffs, trucks, machine tools, electrical equipment, textiles, chemicals, building materials and plastics. The population hovers around the two million mark; minority groups have drifted toward the big lights in search of work, and some have made their home there. At most the minorities account for 6% of Kunming's population, although the farming areas in the outlying counties have some Yi, Hui and Miao groups native to the area. Also calling Kunming home are some 150,000 Vietnamese refugees from the Chinese-Vietnamese wars and border clashes that started in 1977.

Climate

At an elevation of 1890 metres, Kunming has a mild climate, and can be visited at any time of year without need of great clothing adjustments. There's a fairly even spread of temperatures from April till September. Winters are short, sunny and dry. In summer (June to August) Kunming offers cool respite, although rain is more prevalent then.

Information & Orientation

The jurisdiction of Kunming covers 6200 square km, including four city districts and four rural counties (which supply the

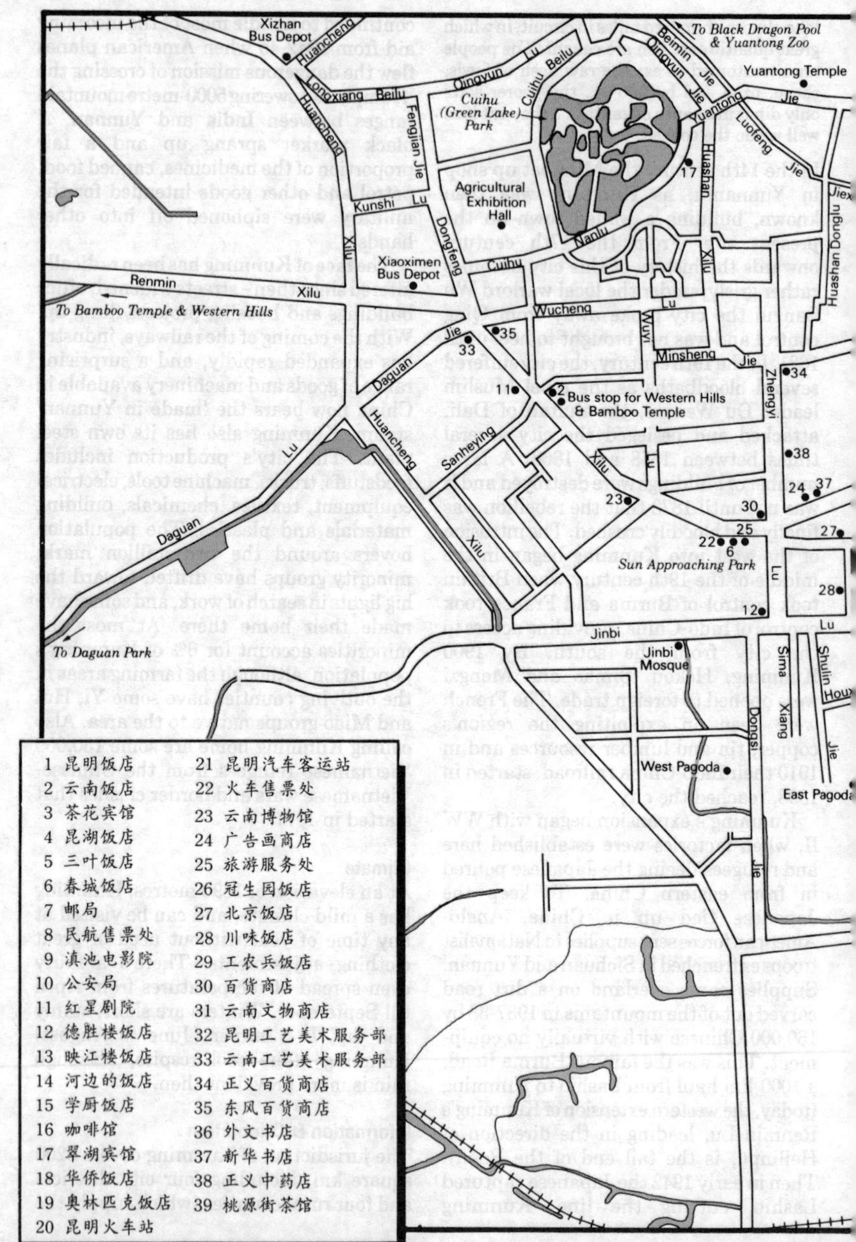

Xizhan
Bus Depot
Huancheng
Longxiang Beilu
Fengjian Jie
Kunshi Lu
Xilu
Dongfeng
Qingyun Lu
Cuihu Beilu
Cuihu
(Green Lake)
Park
To Black Dragon Pool
& Yuantong Zoo
Beimin Jie
Qingyun Jie
Yuantong Temple
Yuantong Jie
Luofeng Jie
Huashan
Agricultural
Exhibition
Hall
Nanlu
Cuihu
Xiaoximen
Bus Depot
Renmin Xilu
To Bamboo Temple & Western Hills
Wucheng Lu
Wuyi
Minsheng Jie
Zhengyi
Huashan Donglu
Daguan Jie
Bus stop for Western Hills
& Bamboo Temple
Sanheying
Xilu
Daguan Lu
Huancheng
Xilu
Sun Approaching Park
Lu
Jinbi
Jinbi
Mosque
Sima
Shulin
Xiang
Jie
Dongsi
Jie
West Pagoda
East Pagoda
To Daguan Park
1 昆明饭店
2 云南饭店
3 茶花宾馆
4 昆湖饭店
5 三叶饭店
6 春城饭店
7 邮局
8 民航售票处
9 滇池电影院
10 公安局
11 红星剧院
12 德胜楼饭店
13 映江楼饭店
14 河边的饭店
15 学厨饭店
16 咖啡馆
17 翠湖宾馆
18 华侨饭店
19 奥林匹克饭店
20 昆明火车站
21 昆明汽车客运站
22 火车售票处
23 云南博物馆
24 广告画商店
25 旅游服务处
26 冠生园饭店
27 北京饭店
28 川味饭店
29 工农兵饭店
30 百货商店
31 云南文物商店
32 昆明工艺美术服务部
33 云南工艺美术服务部
34 正义百货商店
35 东风百货商店
36 外文书店
37 新华书店
38 正义中药店
39 桃源街茶馆

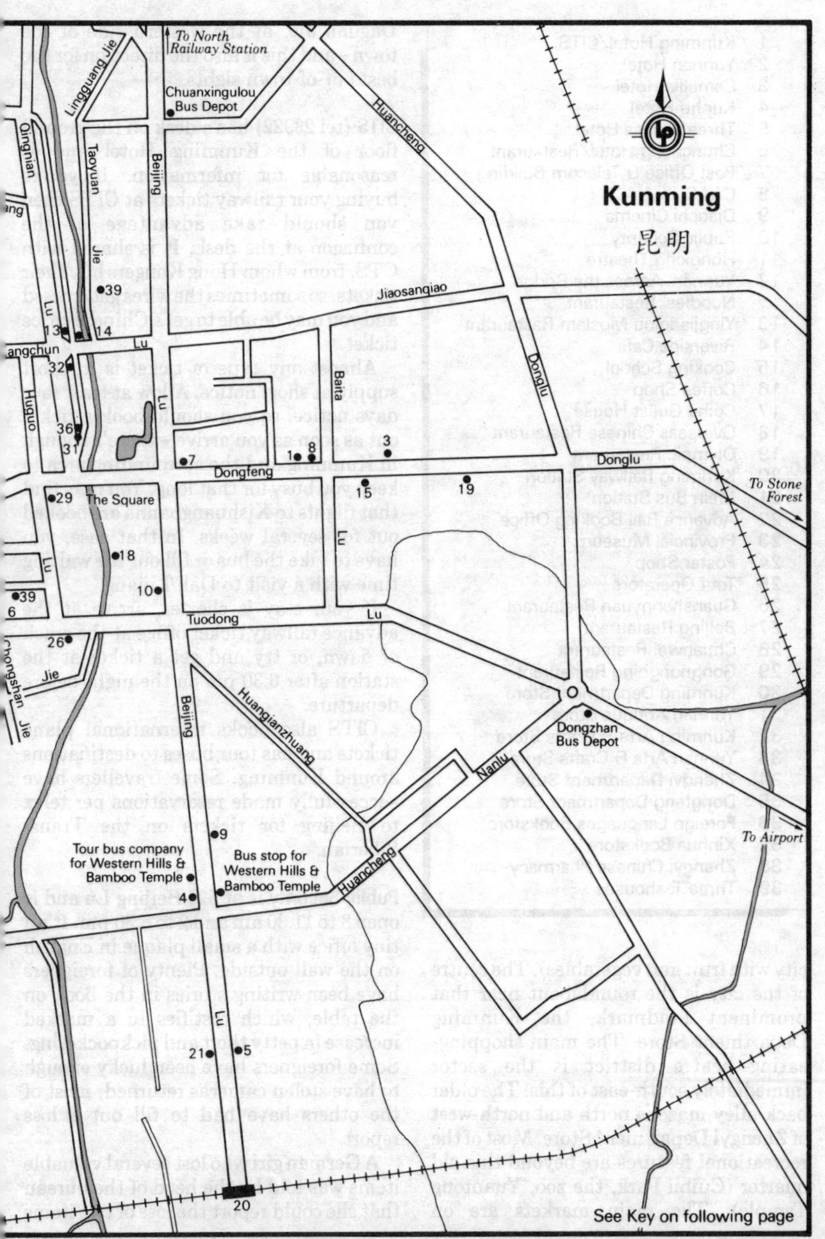
Kunming
昆明
To North Railway Station
Chuanxingulou Bus Depot
Lingguang Jie
Qingnian
Taoyuan
Beijing
Jie
Huancheng
Jiaosanqiao
Lu
39
13
14
32
Huguo
Lu
Baita
Donglu
36
31
3
1
8
7
Dongfeng
Donglu
To Stone Forest
15
19
29
The Square
Lu
Lu
18
10
39
6
Tuodong
Lu
26
Jie
Jie
Beijing
Huangianzhuang
Dongzhan Bus Depot
Nanlu
To Airport
9
Tour bus company for Western Hills & Bamboo Temple
4
Bus stop for Western Hills & Bamboo Temple
Huancheng
Lu
21
5
20
See Key on following page

1 Kunming Hotel/CITS
2 Yunnan Hotel
3 Camellia Hotel
4 Kunhu Hotel
5 Three Leaves Hotel
6 Chuncheng Hotel/Restaurant
7 Post Office & Telecom Building
8 CAAC
9 Dianchi Cinema
10 Public Security
11 Hongxing Theatre
12 Yunnan 'Across the Bridge Noodles' Restaurant
13 Yingjianglou Moslem Restaurant
14 Riverside Cafe
15 Cooking School
16 Coffee Shop
17 Cuihu Guest House
18 Overseas Chinese Restaurant
19 Olympic Restaurant
20 Kunming Railway Station
21 Main Bus Station
22 Advance Rail Booking Office
23 Provincial Museum
24 Poster Shop
25 Tour Operators
26 Guanshengyuan Restaurant
27 Beijing Restaurant
28 Chuanwei Restaurant
29 Gongnongbing Restaurant
30 Kunming Department Store
31 Yunnan Antique Store
32 Kunming Arts & Crafts Store
33 Yunnan Arts & Crafts Store
34 Zhengyi Department Store
35 Dongfeng Department Store
36 Foreign Languages Bookstore
37 Xinhua Bookstore
38 Zhengyi Chinese Pharmacy
39 Three Teahouses

city with fruit and vegetables). The centre of the city is the roundabout near that prominent landmark, the Kunming Department Store. The main shopping-eating-theatre district is the sector immediately south-east of this. The older back-alley maze is north and north-west of Zhengyi Department Store. Most of the recreational features are beyond this old quarter (Cuihu Park, the zoo, Yuantong Temple). The main markets are on Daguan Jie, at the western side of the town – and this is also the direction for the best out-of-town sights.

CITS (tel 23922) has a desk on the ground floor of the Kunming Hotel and is reasonable for information. If you're buying your railway tickets at CITS then you should take advantage of the confusion at the desk. It is shared with CTS, from whom Hong Kongers buy their tickets, so sometimes the wires get crossed and you may be able to get a Chinese-price ticket.

Almost any type of ticket is in short supply at short notice. Allow at least four days notice, so you should book a ticket out as soon as you arrive – there's enough in Kunming and the surrounding area to keep you busy for that long. You may find that flights to Xishuangbanna are booked out for several weeks. In that case, you have to take the bus or fill out the waiting time with a visit to Dali/Lijiang.

If your stay is shorter, arrive at the advance railway ticket office at the crack of dawn, or try and get a ticket at the station after 6.30 pm on the night before departure.

CITS also books international plane tickets and has tour buses to destinations around Kunming. Some travellers have successfully made reservations per telex to Beijing for tickets on the Trans-Siberian.

Public Security is at 525 Beijing Lu and is open 8 to 11.30 am and 2 to 5.30 pm. It's a tiny office with a small plaque in English on the wall outside. Plenty of foreigners have been writing stories in the book on the table, which testifies to a marked increase in petty theft and pickpocketing. Some foreigners have been lucky enough to have stolen cameras returned; most of the others have had to fill out a loss report.

A German girl who lost several valuable items was told by the head of the bureau that she could report the loss of two items

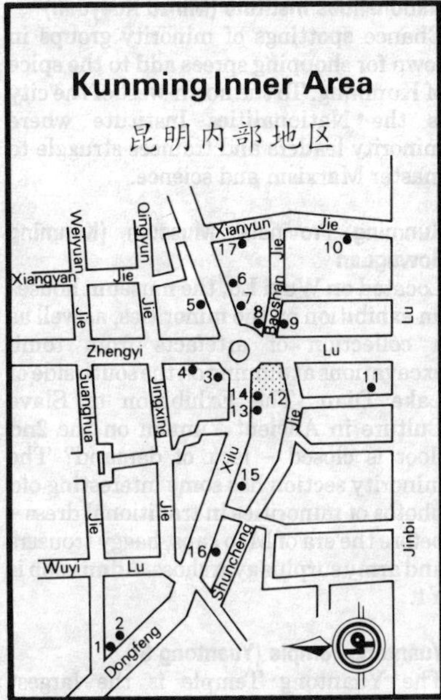

1 Bus Stop for Western Hills & Bamboo Temple
2 Yunnan Hotel
3 Department Store
4 Ice-cream & Bakeshop
5 Poster Shop
6 Minority Trade Store
7 Antique Shop
8 Foreign Language Bookstore
9 Noodle Shop
10 Sichuan Restaurant
11 Yunnan Restaurant
12 Sun Approaching Park
13 Tour Operators
14 Chuncheng Hotel/Restaurant
15 Bakery
16 Museum
17 Beijing Restaurant

1 汽车站
2 云南饭店
3 百货商店
4 冰淇淋店
5 广告画商店
6 民族贸商店
7 文物商店
8 外文书店
9 面条店
10 四川饭店
11 云南过桥米线
12 近日公园
13 旅游服务处
14 春城饭店
15 面包店
16 博物馆
17 北京饭店

only. When she objected, he replied that only he could decide. The girl insisted on including all the items in her report; the official took one look at what she had written, spat in front of her, crammed the loss report into his pocket and stormed out.

Poste Restante has turned up in several post offices in Kunming. The Kunming Hotel has a cardboard box on the CITS desk for mail addressed c/o Kunming Hotel: this has worked fine for some travellers and not at all for others – don't rely on it.

CAAC (tel 24270) is at 146 Dongfeng Donglu.

Maps There are at least five varieties of map, some with a smattering of English names, available from hotels and the Foreign Language Bookstore.

Hospital The Yanan Hospital (Yanan Yiyuan) is on Jiaosanqiao Lu, about a km north-east of the Kunming Hotel – there's a foreigners' clinic (tel 2184) on the 1st floor of the outpatients' building.

Things to See

There's very little to see in the way of temples and such in Kunming. The city is a great place to wander around on foot, once you get off the wide boulevards and away from the Kunming Hotel end of town.

A suggested walking tour is to go north on Huguo Lu up to the busy Changchun shopping area, turn left on Changchun and head west to the teahouse marked on the map (set in a derelict temple and devoted to bong-smoking chess players). From here you select your own route through the cobbled back alleys in the general direction of the Cuihu (Green Lake) Guest House – if you get lost, that's the whole point.

Opposite the Green Lake Guest House is the Green Lake Park. Pleasantly decked out with foliage and waterways, it offers several rollerskating rinks and the possibility of art exhibitions, floral displays or special shows. The walking distance so far is about two km. From the park you could head up to Yuantong Temple or cross down to Daguan Jie (south), which has an extensive free market (from the southern end of Daguan you can pick up a bus No 4 direct to Yuantong Temple).

In both the north-west sector of Kunming (in the Green Lake vicinity) and along Daguan Jie are green-shuttered, double-storey shop fronts – a rarer glimpse of that elusive traditional wooden architecture that Hollywood would have us believe is all over the country. The stretch of Daguan Jie between Dongfeng Xilu and Huancheng is lined with a large range of produce coming from out-of-town farms, along with cobblers and strange merchants.

Another section to perambulate is the shopping bit south of Dongfeng (east of Zhengyi), around Jinbi Lu – plenty of back-alleys there too.

Keep an eye out for street performers – I am still puzzling over an artiste who stuck knives in his stomach and pulled skewers through his cheeks – he seemed quite well enough to pass around the hat as he plugged the wounds with a blood-soaked towel.

Tang Dynasty Pagodas

To the south of Jinbi Lu are a couple of crumbled Tang pagodas. The East Pagoda was, according to Chinese sources, destroyed by an earthquake; western sources say it was destroyed by the Muslim revolt. It was rebuilt in the 19th century, though the temples are no longer attached.

Nationalities Institute (Minzu Xueyuan)

Chance spottings of minority groups in town for shopping sprees add to the spice of Kunming. To the north-west of the city is the Nationalities Institute where minority leaders and trainees struggle to master Marxism and science.

Kunming Provincial Museum (Kunming Bowuguan

Located on Wuyi Lu, the museum houses an exhibition on the minorities, as well as a collection of artefacts from tomb excavations at Jinning on the south side of Lake Dian. The Exhibition of Slave Culture in Ancient Yunnan on the 2nd floor is closed – lack of demand? The minority section has some interesting old photos of minorities in traditional dress – before the era of Mao caps, baggy trousers and army surplus gym shoes. Admission is Y1.

Yuantong Temple (Yuantong Si)

The Yuantong Temple is the largest Buddhist complex in Kunming, and is a target for pilgrims. Located to the north-west of the Green Lake Hotel, the temple is over 1000 years old, and has seen many renovations. Leading up to the main hall from the entrance is an extensive display of flowers and potted landscapes. The central courtyard holds a large square pond intersected by walkways and bridges, and has an octagonal pavilion at the centre. Art exhibitions and potted landscape miniatures are often to be seen at the temple.

Zoo (Dongwu Yuan)

Behind Yuantong Temple is the zoo, and as Chinese zoos go it's not too shabby. It's pleasantly leafy, high up, and gives a bird's-eye vista of the city. The zoo and the temple are not linked, and you have to exit the temple and go around it to get to the zoo.

Ancient Mosque (Qingzhen Si)

Today, while Kunming's Buddhist shrines,

desecrated during the Cultural Revolution, are humming with renovations for the tourist trade, the local Muslim population seems to have been left out of the action. The 400-year-old Ancient Mosque, a ramshackle building at the city centre, was turned into a factory during the Cultural Revolution. In 1977, the machinery was removed and the mosque re-opened, but a dozen households remained living in its courtyard. Three other mosques have also been re-opened, and the one on Jinbi Lu has had some restoration work done on it. To repair the Ancient Mosque would cost an estimated 350,000 yuan – which would have to be raised by the Muslims themselves. Ten million yuan has been allocated for renovation projects of a historical nature, but the mosque is certainly not on the priority list.

Yunnan's Muslim population seem to be largely forgotten, despite the Muslim Rebellion of the last century, a period when China was being torn end to end by one rebellion or another.

The one best known to the west was the Taiping Rebellion, mainly because it affected areas which were accessible to western observers and because the Christian beliefs of the Taipings attracted western interest. But there were several other major rebellions: the Nien Rebellion which afflicted the Hunan-Hubei-Shaanxi region from 1850 to 1868, the Muslim Rebellion in the north-west from 1862 to 1873, and the rebellion of the Miao minority in the south coinciding with the Taiping Rebellion.

In Yunnan the Muslims rose up in 1855. Their revolt was put down by the imperial armies after years of destruction; untold numbers fled or were massacred, reducing Yunnan's total population from eight million to half or even less.

The Cultural Revolution was the next major assault on the Yunnan minorities, whose rights were severely curtailed. There was a clampdown on religious activity of any nature. Kunming's Muslims came under much pressure during the Cultural Revolution to change their beliefs and fall in line with the new orders from Beijing; one story goes that a delegation of young Muslims went to Beijing to lodge a protest – they were promptly imprisoned, some for up to 10 years, and accused of being anti-revolutionary and anti-socialist. Punishments included being bound and gagged for up to two days at a time.

Once again the mosques are open, but Kunming's Muslim community is a struggling one, with little access to educational resources by which to spread their faith – or, in this case, hang onto it – though apparently they have their own underground press.

The Golden Temple (Jindian)

The Golden Temple is seven km north-east of Kunming. The original model was carted off to Dali; the present one, with bronze pillars and ornate door frames, fittings and roofs, laid on a white marble foundation, dates from the Ming Dynasty. It was enlarged by General Wu Sangui, who was dispatched by the Manchus in 1659 to quell the uprisings in the region. Wu Sangui turned against the Manchus and set himself up as a rebel war lord, with the Golden Temple as his summer residence. The temple is 6.5 metres high and estimated to weigh more than 200 tons. The roof tiles are covered in copper. In the courtyard are ancient camellia trees. At the back is a 14-ton bronze bell, cast in 1423.

To get to the temple take bus Nos 3 or 23 to the Chuanxingulou bus terminal, and then take bus No 10 to the temple.

Black Dragon Pool (Heilongtan)

Eleven km north of Kunming is this uninspiring garden, with old cypresses, dull pavilions and no bubble in the springs. Within walking distance is the **Kunming Botanical Institute**, where the collection of flora is of interest to specialists.

From the Chuanxingulou bus terminal take bus No 9. The Golden Temple and the Black Dragon Pool require separate trips from Chuanxingulou bus terminal.

Bamboo Temple (Qiongzhu)

Twelve km north-west of Kunming, this temple dates back to the Tang Dynasty. Burned down and rebuilt in the 15th century, it was restored from 1883 to 1890 when the abbot employed the master Sichuan sculptor Li Guangxiu and his apprentices to fashion 500 arhats.

These life-size clay figures are stunning – either very realistic or very surrealistic – a sculptural tour de force that will blow your mind. Down one huge wall come the incredible surfing Buddhas, some 70 odd, riding the waves on a variety of mounts – blue dogs, giant crabs, shrimp, turtles, unicorns. One gentleman has metre-long eyebrows; another has an arm that shoots clear across the hall to the ceiling.

In the main section are housed row upon row of standing figures. The statues have been done with the precision of a split-second photograph – a monk about to chomp into a large peach (the face contorted into almost a scream), a figure caught turning around to emphasise a discussion point, another about to clap two cymbals together or cursing a pet monster. The old, the sick, the emaciated – nothing is spared – the expressions of joy, anger, grief or boredom are extremely vivid.

So accurate are the sculptures that they can be read as an anthropological documentation of the times. The sculptor's work was considered in bad taste by his contemporaries (some of whom no doubt appeared in caricature), and upon the project's completion Li Guangxiu disappeared into thin air. The temple actually had no bamboo on the grounds until the present, when bamboo was transplanted from Chengdu. The main halls were restored in 1958 and again, extensively, in 1981.

By far the easiest way to get there is to take an express bus from the Yunnan Hotel, directly to the temple. To get there from the Kunming Hotel, take bus No 5 to Xizhan (West Bus Station), where there's a direct bus to the temple.

Anning Hot Springs

Forty km south-west of Kunming, this is basically a hotel where the waters are piped into baths. Large, private bathrooms are Y5 per person, or Y3 per person if you're sharing – but no mixed couples allowed! The springs themselves are hidden from view. Anning is a bore; it's a sanatorium for privileged Chinese vacationers and there's also a military hospital here.

One km south of the springs is Caoxi Temple, a wooden structure from the Song Dynasty, and within the region are muddy Miao villages, but they're not overly interesting. If you miss the last bus back to Kunming you might be able to coerce the hotel staff into letting you stay (Y8 double, or Y4 per person in a four-bed dorm).

Several buses run to Anning from Xiaoximen bus terminal. The best one to take is bus No 18, which departs Kunming at 8 am, 11.30 am, 2 pm and 2.30 pm. It departs Anning for Kunming at 10.30 am, 2 pm and 4.30 pm. Other possible buses (involving a bit of hiking in) are bus Nos 35, 16, 17 – also departing from Xiaoximen.

Lake Dian

Lake Dian, to the south of Kunming, is dotted with settlements, farms and fishing enterprises around the shores; the western side is hilly, while the eastern side is flat country. The southern end of the lake, particularly the south-east, is industrial, but other than that there are lots of possibilities for extended touring and village-crashing. The lake is an elongated one, about 150 km in circumference, about 40 km from north to south, and covering 300 square km. Plying the waters are *fanchuan*, pirate-sized junks with bamboo-battened canvas sails. It's mainly an area for scenic touring and hiking, and there are some fabulous aerial views from the ridges up at Dragon Gate in the Western Hills.

Daguan Park (Grand View) Located at the northernmost tip of Lake Dian and three km south-west of the city centre, this park was redesigned by the governor of Yunnan in 1866. It covers 60 hectares and includes a nursery with potted plants, children's playground, rowboats and pavilions. The Daguan Tower is a vantage point for Lake Dian. Its facades are inscribed with a long poem by Qing poet Sun Ranweng. Bus No 4 runs to Daguan Park from Yuantong Temple via the downtown area.

At the north-east end of the park is a boat dock where an 8 am departure takes you from Daguan to Haikou on Lake Dian, passing by Dragon Gate Village. The boat departs Haikou for Daguan at 2 pm and the one-way trip takes four hours. One hour boat trips on the lake are possible from Daguan Park. Pay the Y1 aboard. From Haikou you can pick up a bus No 15 which runs back to the Xiaoximen terminal in Kunming. On the way back the bus comes close to the Anning Hot Springs. Bus No 15 departs Xiaoximen for Haikou at 8 am, 10 am, 12.30 pm and 4 pm; it returns from Haikou at 10.30 am, 12.30 pm, 3 pm and 7.30 pm.

Xi Shan (Western Hills) The Western Hills spread out across a long wedge of parkland on the western side of Lake Dian; they're also known as the 'Sleeping Beauty Hills' – a reference to the undulating contours resembling a reclining woman with tresses of hair flowing into the sea. The path up to the summit passes a series of famous temples – it's a steep approach from the north side. The hike from Gaoyao bus depot at the foot of the Western Hills to Dragon Gate takes 2½

hours. If you're pushed for time, there's a connecting bus from Gaoyao to the top section.

At the foot of the climb, about 15 km from Kunming, is the **Huatingsi Temple**, a country villa of the Nan Zhao kingdom believed to have been first constructed in the 11th century, rebuilt in the 14th century, and extended in the Ming and Qing dynasties. The temple has some fine statues and excellent gardens.

The road from the Huatingsi Temple winds up from here to the Ming Dynasty **Taihua Temple**, again housing a fine collection of flowering trees in the courtyards including magnolias and camellias .

Between the Taihua Temple and Sanqingge Taoist Temple near the summit is the **Tomb of Nie Er** (1912-36), a talented Yunnan musician. Nie composed the national anthem of the PRC before drowning in Japan en route for further training in the Soviet Union.

The **Sanqingge Temple** near the top of the mountain was a country villa for a prince of the Yuan Dynasty, and was later turned into a temple dedicated to the three main Taoist deities.

Further up is **Longmen (Dragon Gate)**, a group of grottoes, sculptures, corridors and pavilions hacked from the cliff between 1781 and 1835 by a Taoist monk and co-workers, who must have been hanging up there by their fingertips. That's what the locals do when they visit – seek the most precarious perches for views of Lake Dian. The tunnelling along the outer cliff edge is so narrow that only one or two people can squeeze by at a time, so avoid public holidays! One of the last grottoes is dedicated to the deity who assisted those preparing for imperial exams – there is graffiti on the walls from grateful graduates, but nowadays the Chinese use it as a urinal.

From Kunming to the Western Hills the most convenient connection is the express bus which runs direct to the Sanqingge temple at the top, though you could get off at, say, the Taihua Temple and do the rest on foot.

Alternatively, there's a regular bus combination: take bus No 5 from the

Kunming Hotel to Xiaoximen bus depot, and then change to bus No 6, which will take you to the Gaoyao bus (terminus) at the foot of the hills.

From the Western Hills to Kunming you can either take the bus or scramble down from the Dragon Gate area directly to the lakeside along a zigzag dirt path and steps that lead to Dragon Gate Village. A narrow spit of land leads from here across the lake. At the western side of the 'spit' is a nice fish restaurant with simple food, wooden hut, fish from the lake – just go into the kitchen to organise some tasty food. Continuing across the land spit, you arrive at a narrow stretch of water which is negotiated by a tiny ferry. It's worthwhile hanging around here to see what passes by as this is the bottleneck of the lake, and junks, fishing vessels and other craft must come through.

Having made the short ferry crossing, you proceed by foot through a village area to Haigeng Beach, where you can pick up bus No 24 for the run back to Kunming main bus terminal (Kunming Zhan).

The tour can easily be done in reverse; start with bus No 24 to Haigeng Beach, walk to Dragon Gate Village, climb straight up to Dragon Gate, then make your way down through the temples to the Gaoyao bus depot, where you can get bus No 6 back to the Xiaoximen depot. Alternatively, bus No 33 runs along the coast through Dragon Gate Village, or you can take the early-morning boat from Daguan Park.

In 1986, I met an American in Xishuangbanna who told me he'd been doing a little bushwalking around the Western Hills when he was suddenly confronted by a 'large puma'. The American froze and the 'puma' blended swiftly into the undergrowth. At the time, I assumed this was an exaggerated story since no puma in its right mind would leave the virgin forest for a lungful of Kunming's polluted air. However, I believed the story when, a couple of months later, I came across the article reproduced at the top of the next column.

2 killed, 3 injured by tiger in Kunming

A tiger killed two people and injured three others on Wednesday morning in the city of Kunming, Yunnan Province, then was shot to death by police after it roamed the city for more than six hours, the Shanghai Evening News reported yesterday.

The tiger was first spotted, about 6:30 in the morning by Li Deming, a worker at the Yunnan Tyre Repair Factory, who was doing morning exercises.

He was knocked to the ground by the tiger, which sprang from behind tall grass.

After a fierce scuffle with the tiger, Li got free. Li's face and both shoulders were badly cut by the animal's paws. He was able to get to his factory, where he reported the attack. Police immediately started a search of the city.

But it wasn't until well after noon that the tiger was reported attacking another victim. It bit to death a farmer cutting grass in the fields and another farmer transporting manure to the field, the paper reported. The tiger also injured two people walking on the streets.

According to the paper, the tiger jumped onto a highway and ran toward a crowd of people as police rushed to the scene. They surrounded the tiger, in an attempt to catch it alive, but were forced to open fire as the tiger pounced toward them.

According to the paper, the tiger did not come from any of the city's zoos or animal research institutes. Investigation is under way to find out where the animal came from.

China Daily, 6 December 1986

Baiyukou, on the south-western side of Lake Dian, is a sanatorium and scenic spot. Bus No 33 from the Xiaoximen depot runs via Dragon Gate Village to the sanatorium, departing Xiaoximen at 8 am, 2 pm and 4 pm and returning at 10 am, 4 pm and 7.30 pm.

Zheng He Park at the south-east corner of the lake commemorates the Ming Dynasty navigator Zheng He. A mausoleum here holds tablets describing his life and works. Zheng He, a Muslim, made seven voyages to over 30 Asian and African countries in the 15th century in command of a huge imperial fleet (for details, see the section on the town of Quanzhou in Fujian Province).

Bus No 21 from the Xiaoximen depot terminates at the Phosphate Fertiliser Factory near Gucheng at the south-west side of the lake, and north-west of Zheng He Park. From here it may be possible to hike along the hills to the bus No 15 terminus at Haikou; bus No 15 will take you back to Xiaoximen.

Jinning County at the southern end of the lake is the site of archaeological discoveries from early Kunming. Bronze vessels, a gold seal and other artefacts were unearthed at Stone Village Hill, and some items are displayed at the Provincial Museum in Kunming. Bus No 14 runs to Jinning from Xiaoximen depot, via Chenggong and Jincheng.

Chenggong County on the eastern side of the lake is an orchard region. Climate has a lot to do with Kunming's reputation as the florist of China. Flowers bloom year round, with the 'flower tide' in January, February and March – which is the best time to visit. Camellias, azaleas, magnolias, orchids are not usually associated with China by westerners although many of the western varieties derive from south-west China varieties. They were introduced to the west by adventuring botanists who carted off samples in the 19th and 20th centuries. Azaleas are native to China – of the 800 varieties in the world, 650 are found in Yunnan. During the Spring Festival (February/March) a profusion of blooming species can be found at temple sites around Kunming – notably Taihua, Huating and Golden temples, as well as Black Dragon Pool and Yuantong Hill.

To get to Chenggong County, take bus No 12 from Juhua Cun bus terminus, which is also the western terminus for bus No 5. Bus No 13 from Kunming's Xiaoximen depot runs to Chenggong via Jincheng; departures from Xiaoximen are at 7.30 am, 8 am, 2 pm, 2.30 pm, 4.30 pm and 5 pm. The bus departs Chenggong for Xiaoximen at 9.30 am, 10 am, 4 pm and 4.30 pm.

Haigeng Beach on the north-eastern side of the lake has adequate swimming frontage and a mini-resort area (rollerskating, restaurants, snacks, and you can rent airbeds for swimming). Take bus No 24 from Kunming main bus station. Haigeng Beach is a useful approach to the Western Hills from the eastern side of the lake.

Places to Stay

The *Kunming Hotel* (tel 25268) at 145 Dongfeng Donglu is split into two wings, a squat older building and a 15-storey newer high-rise.

The old wing had (and probably still has) some excellent dormitories (4th floor) in old-fashioned comfort complete with writing desk, mahogany furniture and mosquito nets. The staff are snooty or comatose – sometimes they admit the dorm exists, sometimes they couldn't give a cuss. There's little reason to bother with them for long since there are dorms in other hotels such as the Camellia, Kunhu and Three Leaves. Doubles in the old wing cost Y48.

The new wing also has a dorm (50-bed room on the 14th floor) – same problem with desk staff pretending to be blind. Doubles cost Y60; dorm beds are Y10 each, if you can get them.

The Kunming Hotel has some useful facilities: CITS/Poste Restante, post office, photocopying, bike hire and lobby shop. To get there from the main station, take bus No 23 to the intersection of Dongfeng Lu and Beijing Lu, and then take a bus east or walk. From the west bus station (Xizhan) take bus No 5.

The *Cuihu Binguan (Green Lake Guest House)* (tel 23514) is at 16 Cuihu Nanlu. It's at the edge of an older section of Kunming and is quiet and pleasant. It's more in the deluxe category with closed-circuit TV, heating, air-con and fridges in special-class suites – and some of the staff wear minority dress. Double rooms are Y52; triples are Y60. Dorm beds are Y5 in the three-bed rooms in the old wooden building at the back. Bus No 1 runs between Xizhan (west bus station) and the centre of town via the Cuihu.

The *Chahua Binguan (Camellia Hotel)* is about 100 metres east of the Kunming Hotel and just past the Yunnan TV factory. The hotel is on the left of a square entered under a red banner; it's as good as the Kunming Hotel but cheaper. Doubles are around Y40. The billiards room has been converted into a dormitory which is comfy but seldom cleaned; Y8 per bed. It's on the bus No 5 route.

The *Sanye Fandian (Three Leaves Hotel)* is a short walk from Kunming main rail station and right opposite Kunming main bus station. Doubles cost Y26; a bed in a triple costs Y10. The dorm costs Y5 per bed but feels like a sardine can. Showers are at 8 pm sharp – as the hot water pressure drops quickly, hotel residents leap down from floor to floor to finish their showers. Try the 2nd floor if you want to know where the hot water stays for the rest of the day. The noisy, grubby hotel is in a very handy location for transport. A bookshop just a few metres to the right of the entrance sells maps; to the left is a window for tour-bus tickets. The adjacent luggage check will keep your gear for a week or more – useful if you're going on a round trip to Lijiang, Dali or Xishuangbanna. Just below the steps in front of the hotel is a tin shack whose owner hires out bikes at Y0.60 per hour.

The *Kunhu Hotel* (tel 27732) is on Beijing Lu close to Kunming south railway station. The place has improved although one Swedish girl who stayed in the dorm found an unwelcome bedfellow – a rat. Doubles are Y22. Dorm beds are Y4 each. Tickets for the bus to Dali (Y13.75) are sold at reception; the bus leaves from behind the hotel. The hotel is two stops from the station on bus Nos 3, 23 or 25.

The *Xiyuan (West Garden) Hotel* (tel 9969) is a villa-style hotel. The inner section has rooms with private baths, and the outer section has rooms with a communal bathroom. The hotel is at the western edge of Lake Dian, on the shores below Taihua Temple. It seems to serve a dual purpose – group tours in the inner section, and convalescing Chinese in the outer section. The hotel is worth keeping in mind if you're doing an extended tour of Lake Dian, but also keep in mind the low frequency of transport back to Kunming. The outer section is said to have cheap rates. To get to the hotel, take bus No 33 from the Xiaoximen bus depot in Kunming; it departs around 8 am, 2 pm and 4 pm.

Places to Eat

Kunming has some great food, especially in the snack line. Regional specialities are ginger chicken in an earthenware pot, Yunnan duck and ham, across-the-bridge noodles, Muslim beef and mutton dishes; and there's good western fare to be had. One of the nicest side dishes in the restaurants is toasted goat cheese (*zhishi*) – very tasty.

For gourmets with money to burn, perhaps a whole banquet based on Jizhong fungus (mushrooms) or 30 courses of cold mutton, not to mention fried grasshoppers or elephant nose braised in soy sauce. Gourmets, or anyone else for that matter, are advised to steer clear of Kunming beer – it's disgusting.

There are two places near the Kunming Hotel. The overrated *Cooking School* on Dongfeng Lu has an English menu, seafood and vegetable dishes. Across-the-bridge noodles must be ordered one day in advance, cost Y5 and come with lots of side dishes.

The *Olympic Bar* (east of the Cooking School and so named because of its proximity to the gym) is a popular spot for foreigners and locals. The staff can be surly. The English menu includes chicken steampot, toasted goat cheese, French toast and French salad.

Near the Foreign Language Bookstore is the *Gongnongbing (Worker-Peasant-Soldier Restaurant)* (tel 5679) at 262 Huguo Lu. It's got ratty decor but there are foreigner cubicles on the 2nd floor, and here you'll get northern Chinese food with a touch of south-western spicing. On the ground floor is a lunch counter where you can buy tickets and select from cauldrons immediately in front of you. You can also get whole chicken or duck.

North of this is the *Yingjianglou Muslim Restaurant* (tel 25198) at 360 Changchun Jie. It serves what is considered the best Hui food in Kunming – mutton and beef.

South of Dongfeng Lu is the *Overseas Chinese Restaurant*. It's on the expensive side but you get large servings of seafood and vegetable dishes.

Guangshengyuan (tel 22970) on Jinbi Lu has Cantonese-style food including dim sum, fried chicken, sweet & sour pork, fried beef curry. The restaurant has a special section for foreigners.

There is a string of eateries on Xiangyun Jie between Jinbi Lu and Dongfeng Lu. At the Dongfeng end at No 77 is the *Beijing Restaurant* (tel 3214) with northern-style seafood, chicken and duck. The service can be annoying here and the restaurant has foreigner cubicles. At the Jinbi end of Xiangyun Jie is the *Chuanwei Restaurant* (tel 23171), which serves Sichuan-style chicken, spicy bean curd, hot pork, duck and seafood.

Also along this alley (close to Jinbi Lu) is a private restaurant operated by a wily gentleman of Burmese descent who speaks good English – don't worry about finding it, he'll find you. Mr Tong's has main courses, Budweiser beer (Y2.20), Coca Cola (Y1.40) and rock music.

Pick of the pleb restaurants is the *Shanghai* (tel 22987) at 73 Dongfeng Xilu, in a yellow-fronted building. To the left side you'll get cheap noodles, to the right are chicken steampot, cold cuts and dumplings.

Two of the better-known places for chicken steampot are the *Chuncheng Hotel* (tel 23962) and the *Dongfeng Hotel* (tel 24808), around the corner of Wuyi and Wucheng Sts, in the direction of the Cuihu Hotel. Try the 2nd floor of the Chuncheng Hotel, though service can be bad. Chicken steampot is served in dark brown Jianshui County casserole pots, and is imbued with medicinal properties depending on the spicing – caterpillar fungus (*chongcao*), pseudo-ginseng (*sanqi*) or gastrodia.

Across-the-Bridge Noodles is Yunnan's best-known dish. You are provided with a bowl of oily soup (stewed with chicken, duck and spare ribs), a side dish of raw pork slivers (in classier places this might be chicken or fish) and vegetables, and a bowl of rice noodles. There is a story to the dish:

> Once upon a time there was a scholar at the South Lake in Mengzi (Southern Yunnan) who was attracted by the peace and quiet of an island there. He settled into a cottage on the island, in preparation for official examinations. His wife, meanwhile, had to cross a long wooden bridge over the lake to bring the bookworm his meals. The fodder was always cold in winter by the time she got to the study bower. Oversleeping one day, she made a curious discovery – she'd stewed a fat chicken and was puzzled to find the soup still hot, though it gave off no steam – the oil layer on the surface had preserved the food temperature. Subsequent experiments enabled her to triumphantly carry food to her husband – with hot results.

You can get hold of the same downtown for less than Y2, at two restaurants which serve only the noodles. Language is therefore no problem, and all you have to do is get your meal tickets and let the company at the table give you all the necessary instructions for etiquette.

The *Guoqiao Mixian (Yunnan Restaurant)* on Nantong Jie asks Y1.20 for a huge helping. Decor is, shall we say, basic – the predominant noise is a chorus of hissing and slurping; tattered beggars circulate among the stainless-steel-topped tables pursued by management. Never mind the beggars or the decor – the food is absolutely delicious! Atmosphere, as can be imagined, is very different from the Kunming or Cuihu hotels, where this fare will cost you exponentially more.

A second across-the-bridge noodles establishment is as cheap as the Yunnan but has less space to play around in (try the 2nd floor) – it's at 99 Baoshan Jie.

Continental Breakfast Filtered through the cultures of France, Vietnam and Yunnan is this unlikely combination of French bread and Yunnan coffee. Seek out the wooden benches of the *Coffee Shop* at No 289 where you pay Y0.50 for a mug of *real* coffee. Three types of bread, including brown rolls, are sold at the front. Some foreign devotees of the western breakfast cult can be seen bringing their own butter and jam. On the 2nd floor you may also meet interesting English-speakers and devotees of the foreign-exchange cult.

Snack Tracking There are some good bakeries in Kunming – flatbreads, shortbreads and highly edible cakes make a change from those biscuits sold on store shelves. For on-the-premises baking go to the *Hsing He Yuan*, near the Provincial Museum on Dongfeng Xilu. Just north of the Kunming Department Store on Zhengyi Lu is a bakery and ice cream parlour. A similar but larger concept (nicknamed *The Neon*) is on Dongfeng Xilu near Kunming Bookstore – it's the 'in' place for Kunming nights and stocks cakes, ice cream, fruit sundaes (may be canned) and other gooey desserts.

Another place to go snack-hunting is Huguo Lu, north of Nantaiqiao, for simmering noodle bars and a tea shop. The intersection of Changchun and Huguo yields lots of small eateries. Along the canal near the Arts & Crafts Shop is a pleasant riverside café with beach umbrellas – for a split second it looks like you got lost and ended up in the wrong country. Also try Baoshan Jie, an east-west street running between Zhengyi Lu and Huguo Lu – Baoshan is known as Number One Food Street because of the retail shops, but it also has noodle bars and eateries.

The whole area around here is a hub of restaurant activity. The stretch of Daguan Jie from Dongfeng to Huancheng is a busy free market, and in season you'll get fruit – mangoes, pineapples, 'ox-belly' fruit from Xishuangbanna, and pears from the Chenggong orchards or from Dali.

Hotel Food The *Kunming Hotel* has a restaurant on the ground floor of the old wing which is patronised by Overseas Chinese, so prices will probably be a bit lower. There are other restaurants scattered on various floors. Breakfast is Y3.50; across-the-bridge noodles in the Yunnan-style restaurant is expensive and must be pre-ordered – forget it. At the *Green Lake Guest House* there is a bar and café on the 3rd floor, a western restaurant on the 5th floor and a Chinese restaurant on the 2nd floor. The food in these has a good reputation.

Nightlife & Entertainment

The Shi Gongren Wenhuagong (Municipal Worker's Cultural Palace) is the gigantic steel-and-concrete building towering to the west of the Kunming Hotel. Very popular with local photographers as a 'modern' backdrop, the rabbit warren of entertainment and hobbies on at least 14 floors is worth ascending (entrance Y0.10). Keep climbing the floors, each of which offers something different: a gallery with sheepish portraits of valiant workers; video and computer games which cost a few mao; English-language lessons (skip that floor quick); hair-cutting class; body-building class (very trendy for young Chinese, male and female); stuffed Yunnan fauna; table-tennis. There's an open-air teahouse on the roof of a side-building.

You might be able to chase up minority dancing displays (more often held for the benefit of group tours), travelling troupes or Yunnan opera (Hongxing Theatre on Dongfeng Xilu is one of the performing arts venues).

The teahouse to the right-hand side of the canal (off Taoyuan Jie), north of Changchun Jie, has plain-clothes Yunnan opera in an old temple structure with fluorescent tubes. It is, however, extremely difficult to recognise from the front – there's a side entrance.

Recovery

The Yunnan Comprehensive Quick Recovery Qigong Sanatorium is one of the four main *qigong* research bases in China. Their recent advertisement in *China Daily* concluded, 'We give preferential treatment to model workers, heroes, scientific and technical cadres, teachers and patients seeking treatment at their own expense'.

If you think you might qualify for treatment, their contact address is: Shenzhen Yunxing Kunming Touring Company (tel 24318, cable 5150), Chuanjin Lukou, Kunming.

Shopping

You have to do a fair bit of digging to come up with inspiring purchases in Kunming. Yunnan specialities are jade (related to Burmese), marble (from the Dali area), batik, minority embroidery (also musical instruments and dress accessories) and spotted brass utensils.

One of the main shopping drags is Zhengyi Lu, which has the Zhengyi Department Store, Overseas Chinese Department Store and Kunming Department Store, but these mainly sell consumer goods. The Friendship Store is on the 3rd floor of the Kunming Department Store. Other shopping areas are Jinbi Lu by the Zhengyi Lu intersection, and Dongfeng Donglu, between Zhengyi Lu and Huguo Lu.

The Kunming Arts & Crafts Shop, on Qingnian Lu, has some batik, pottery, porcelain and handicrafts, but it's pretty dull. The counters at the Kunming Hotel, and particularly the Cuihu Hotel, look more interesting. Outside the Kunming Hotel you will probably be ambushed by minority 'bag' ladies flogging their handiwork – bargain if you want a sane price. Both the Green Lake and the Cuihu hotels sell batik which you can also find in Dali. Delve into the smaller shops around Jinbi Lu if you're into embroidery. Yunnan is also known for its medicines, and there's a large pharmacy on Zhengyi Lu (on the east side, several blocks up from the Kunming Department Store).

Kunming is a fairly good place to stock up on film. Fuji and other film can be bought at the Green Lake Hotel, and the Kunming Hotel's stock includes Ektachrome.

Getting There & Away

Air Kunming's most useful air connections are those to Beijing (Y471), Canton (Y251), Changsha (Y196), Chengdu (Y114), Chongqing (Y113), Guilin (Y154), Guiyang (Y68), Nanning (Y115), Shanghai (Y398), Simao (Y57) and Xian (Y202).

There are also international flights to Hong Kong (Y462 FEC, Tuesday and Saturday), to Bangkok (Y595 FEC, Wednesday) and to Rangoon (Y810 FEC, every second Wednesday). There's a CAAC charter flight Kunming-Bangkok every Wednesday, Y595 oneway. CITS was vague about details for the flights to Burma , and gave a sort of 'the plane flies when it's full' comment. Don't put too much faith in punctuality for this exit.

During April (Water-Splashing Festival) and summer, the Simao air connection for Xishuangbanna can be booked rock solid for two to three weeks. The CAAC office is jammed with maniacs pushing, shoving and trying to pull rank. Make your plans for Xishuangbanna as flexible as possible: consider the bus option or book your flight several weeks ahead and spend the intervening time in Dali or elsewhere.

Bus The two most useful bus stations are the main bus station (Kunming Chezhan) close to the main railway station and the west bus station (Xizhan).

For details on Shilin (Stone Forest), see the Getting There section under Shilin.

For Dali there are minibuses and buses (mostly soft-seat) travelling by day or night to Xiaguan; from Xiaguan to Dali is then a short minibus ride for Y0.40. The journey takes a minimum of 10 hours, sometimes 14. Tickets cost between Y15 and Y22; the more expensive tickets are for luxury buses and may even include meals. It's up to you whether you want to do the trip by day or by night – the driving is just as crazy.

Tickets to Xiaguan (some departures direct to Dali) are sold at the main bus station, west bus station and Kunhu Hotel, and by tour operators.

There are direct buses to Lijiang from the main bus station and the west bus station. They take two days, usually overnight in Xiaguan and cost Y19.90.

Some people have travelled for four or five days on different buses between Kunming and Guiyang (Guizhou Province), on a routing via Qujing and Zhenning (Huangguoshu waterfalls).

Rail There are only two rail approaches to Kunming, via Guiyang or Chengdu (a new line is under construction from Nanning to Kunming).

During peak season Kunming can become a real trap for rail travellers. Make a point of booking your tickets at least four days in advance. The advance booking office close to the Chuncheng Hotel is only worth a try if you queue there at 6.30 am. The ticket office in the main station sells tickets from 6.30 pm for trains departing the next day, but these are probably rare returns. CITS and the railway ticket offices often muddle their prices, so it's worth enquiring about soft-sleepers for which you might be given a Chinese price.

If you are heading for Guilin, it's sometimes possible to escape the railway congestion by flying to Nanning and then taking a train to Guilin.

There are direct trains from Kunming to Shanghai, via Guiyang, Guilin, Zhuzhou, Nanchang and Hangzhou. There are direct trains from Kunming to Beijing. For Chongqing you must change at Guiyang, and for Canton you must change at Hengyang. For hard-sleeper train travel from Kunming to Guiyang it is 15 hours, Y20; to Anshun, 13 hours, Y19.80; to Emei, 21 hours, Y28; Chengdu, 25 hours, Y31; (Chinese prices).

Getting Around

Most of the major sights are within a 15-km radius of Kunming. Local transport to these places is awkward, crowded and time-consuming; it tends to be an out-and-back job, with few cross-overs for combined touring. If you wish to take in everything, you'd be looking at something like five return trips, which would consume about three days. You can simplify this by pushing Black Dragon Pool, Anning Hot Springs and the Golden Temple to the background, and concentrating on the trips of high interest – the Bamboo Temple and Western Hills, both of which have decent transport connections with special express buses in the mornings. Lake Dian presents some engrossing circular-tour possibilities on its own.

Bus The relevant bus terminals and depots in Kunming for catching buses to various sites around the city and around the lake are:

Chuanxingulou on the north end of Beijing Lu. Take bus No 9 to the Black Dragon Pool (Hei Long Tan); bus No 10 to the Golden Temple (Jindian).

Xiaoximen on Renmin Lu, just west of Dongfeng Lu. Take bus No 6 to the Gaoyao terminal at the foot of the Western Hills, where you can connect with another bus which travels up the mountain. Bus No 19 goes to Fumin via the Bamboo Temple. Bus No 18 goes to Anning Hot Springs. The following buses run to spots around Lake Dian: Bus No 33 to Baiyukou (western side of Lake Dian); bus No 13 to Chenggong and Jincheng (eastern side); bus No 14 to Jinning (southern side).

Xizhan The west bus terminal is near the Yunnan Hotel. A direct bus runs from here to the Bamboo Temple.

Nantaiqiao bus terminal, previously west of the Kunming Hotel, appears to have ceased functioning. The Xiaoximen terminal now handles the relevant bus services.

Zhuantang terminus appears to have been phased out for buses, including bus No 24 to

Haigeng Beach. Kunming Main Bus station is now the terminus for bus No 24.

Express buses are the best option; they cost only a fraction more than local transport and will save considerable mucking around.

There are two routes – to the Bamboo Temple and to the Western Hills. The starting point is the south end of Beijing Lu, where there are specially posted bus stops near Dianchi Cinema (the tour company that operates the buses has an office across the street from the bus stop). No advance booking is necessary. The buses make a few stops along the route – the first one is to the left of the Yunnan Hotel in the downtown core, where there are two more special bus stops; the bus will wait here till it fills up before proceeding, so there is little point in trying to board the bus any further down the line than this hotel. Returning buses may not go back to the Dianchi Cinema; they could stop at the Yunnan Hotel, turn around with a fresh load of passengers and head back out again.

Buses from the Dianchi Cinema via the Yunnan Hotel to the Bamboo Temple depart at 8 am, 8.30 am and 9 am. More buses leave from the Yunnan Hotel only at 11 am, noon, 1 pm and 2 pm. Return buses usually go to the Yunnan Hotel only, leaving the Bamboo Temple from 10.30 am to 3 pm at hourly or half-hourly intervals. The one-way fare is 40 fen.

Buses from the Dianchi Cinema, via the Yunnan Hotel, to the Dragon Gate (with stops at the temples on the mountainside along the way if you want to get off before the top) depart at 7.30 am, 8 am, and 8.30 am (with possible extra departures at 9 am and 9.30 am, probably from the Yunnan Hotel). The bus leaves the Dragon Gate from 2 to 4 pm at hourly or half-hourly intervals. The fare is 60 fen.

Bicycle Bikes are a fast way to get around town. The Kunming Hotel offers a rip-off rental rate of Y10 per day. The bike rental in front of the Three Leaves Hotel charges Y0.60 per hour.

Tours Several outfits cover the ground faster than the express buses, but certainly not cheaper. They include downright boring sights like the Black Dragon Pool, and downtown sights like Yuantong Temple (which is not difficult to get to).

The Kunming Bus Service Company at Sun-Approaching Tower (booths opposite main Department Store) caters mainly for locals and Overseas Chinese, and they speak little if any English. They organise a Golden Temple, Black Dragon Pool, Bamboo Temple, Daguan Park tour, Monday, Wednesday or Friday, departing at 8.30 am and returning at 5 pm. The cost is Y7 per person. They also do a Western Hills-Anning Hot Springs tour (stops at Huating and Taihua temples and Dragon Gate), leaving Tuesday, Thursday or Saturday. The cost is Y7 per person.

The Yunnan Tourist Bus Company with departures and bookings from the Kunming Hotel offers a Western Hills, Bamboo Temple, Daguan Park, Yuantong Temple tour. The Kunming Hotel also has taxi-trips to the Stone Forest – enquire at the counter on the ground floor.

The Xiyuan Hotel, at the western shores of Lake Dian, has tour boats which you can most likely crash. Some tours are operated out of the Kunhu Hotel, such as buses to the Stone Forest (you should at least be able to get tickets for the buses there).

THE STONE FOREST 石林

The Stone Forest (Shilin) is a collection of grey limestone pillars, split by rain water and eroded to their present fanciful forms, the tallest model standing 30 metres. Marine fossils found in the area suggest that it was once under the sea. Legend has it that the immortals smashed a mountain into a labyrinth for lovers seeking some privacy – and picnicking Chinese couples take heed of this myth (it can get busy in there!).

The maze of grey pinnacles and peaks, with the odd pool, is treated as an oversized rockery, with a walkway here, a pavilion there, some railings along paths and, if you look more closely, some mind-bending weeds. The larger formations have titles like Baby Elephant, The Everlasting Fungus, Baby Buffalo, Moon-Gazing Rhino, Sword Pond. The maze is cooler and quieter by moonlight, which is the kind of viewing that would enthrall a surrealist painter.

There are actually several stone forests in the region – the section open to foreign tourists covers 80 hectares. Twelve km to the north-east is a larger (300-hectare) rock series called Lingzhi (Fungi Forest), with karst caves and a large waterfall.

The Stone Forest is basically a Chinese tour attraction and is grossly overrated on the scale of geographical wonders. Considering that so many other 'ethnic' areas of Yunnan are now open, you could be disappointed if you make the trip just to see the Sani branch of the Yi tribespeople who live in this area (Lunan County). Their craftwork (embroidery, purses, footwear) is sold at stalls by the entrance to the forest, and comely Sani maidens act as tour guides for groups. Off to the side is Five-Tree Village, which is an easy walk and has the flavour of a Mexican pueblo, but the tribespeople have been somewhat influenced by commercialism.

For those keen on genuine village and farming life, well, the Stone Forest is a big place – and you can easily get lost. Just take your butterfly net and a lunch-box along and keep walking – you'll get somewhere eventually.

Things to Do

The Shilin Hotel puts on a Sani song-and-dance evening – usually when there are enough tourists around. Surprisingly, these events turn into good-natured exchanges between Homo Ektachromo and Sani Dollari, and neither comes off the worse for wear. Performances are short-lived – costumery, ethnic musical instruments. Cost is Y1 a ticket; performances start around 8.30 pm with tickets on sale from 7 pm. The Torch Festival (wrestling, bull fighting, singing and dancing) takes place on 24 June at a natural outdoor amphitheatre by Hidden Lake.

Places to Stay

The *Shilin Hotel* is a villa-type place with souvenir shop and dining hall. A double room costs Y50 but you may be able to bargain down to Y36; a triple costs Y18 per person. There are large dorms to the rear; a bed in an eight-bed room (building No 6) costs Y10. There are no showers, but you can use the public ones in building No 5, or nip into a vacant suite.

There's another hotel, a yellow building, on the hill behind the bus station (a 15-minute walk from the Forest). A double costs Y13, dorm bed Y5.

Places to Eat

The *Shilin Hotel* has a western breakfast for Y3, but their other fare (set dinner Y6) is under par. Try the outdoor tables just inside the entrance to the Forest. Hours are 11 am to 4.30 pm. You could also eat at the Chinese hotel.

Getting There & Away

There is a variety of tour options for getting to the Stone Forest. In all cases the trip takes around 3½ hours one way. If you know exactly how long you intend to stay, book return transport in advance in Kunming. It's best to take an overnight stop in the Forest for further exploration – though if you're just looking at the Forest itself then a day trip will do. Departures leave Kunming between 7 and 8 am. Options are same-day return, next-day return, or one-way tickets.

The regular long-distance bus costs Y3.50 one way. In theory this bus leaves Kunming west bus station (Xizhan) at 7.30 am and 1.30 pm, and passes by the

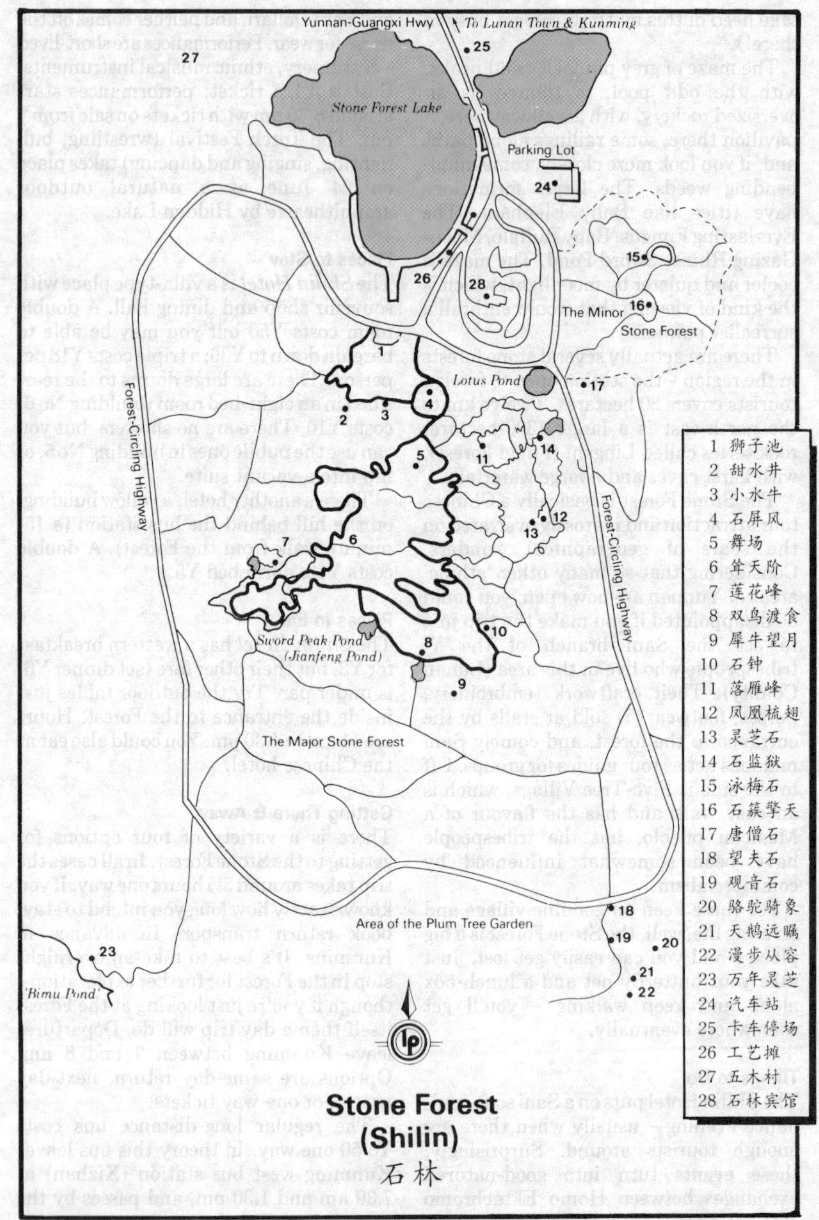
Yunnan-Guangxi Hwy
To Lunan Town & Kunming
Stone Forest Lake
Parking Lot
The Minor Stone Forest
Lotus Pond
Forest-Circling Highway
Forest-Circling Highway
Sword Peak Pond (Jianfeng Pond)
The Major Stone Forest
Area of the Plum Tree Garden
'Bimu Pond'
1 狮子池
2 甜水井
3 小水牛
4 石屏风
5 舞场
6 耸天阶
7 莲花峰
8 双鸟渡食
9 犀牛望月
10 石钟
11 落雁峰
12 凤凰梳翅
13 灵芝石
14 石监狱
15 泳梅石
16 石簇擎天
17 唐僧石
18 望夫石
19 观音石
20 骆驼骑象
21 天鹅远瞩
22 漫步从容
23 万年灵芝
24 汽车站
25 卡车停场
26 工艺摊
27 五木村
28 石林宾馆
Stone Forest
(Shilin)
石林

1 Lion Pond
2 Sweet Water Well
3 Stone Buffalo
4 Stone Screen
5 Open Stage
6 Steps to the Sky
7 Lotus Peak
8 Two Birds Feeding Each Other
9 Rhinoceros Looking at the Moon
10 Stone Bell
11 Resting Peak for Wild Geese
12 Phoenix Combing its Wings
13 Stone Mushroom
14 Stone Prison
15 Inscription of Mao Zedong's Poem 'Ode to the Plum Blossom'
16 Rock Arrowhead Pointing to the Sky
17 The Figure of Monk Tanseng
18 Wife Waiting for Her Husband
19 Goddess of Mercy
20 A Camel Riding on an Elephant
21 Swan Gazing Afar
22 Old Man Taking a Stroll
23 Stone Mushroom
24 Bus Departures
25 Truck Stop
26 Local Handicraft Stalls
27 Five-Tree Village
28 Shilin Hotel/CITS

stop outside the Kunming Hotel. In practice some travellers have been left high and dry at the bus stop near the Kunming, so double-check arrangements. Y7 return is also possible. Tickets can be bought at the bus stations in Kunming.

Opposite the department store at the centre of Kunming, two booths sell tickets for tour buses to the Forest, but these are mainly for Chinese. The cost is Y9.30 return for bus (leaves 7 am, returns 3 pm), or Y12 for minibus. Getting picked up outside the Kunming Hotel could be a problem, so sort out the situation when you buy a ticket. Other agents operate out of hotels such as the Kunhu and the Kunming. The Kunming Hotel has a minibus at Y7 for a one-way ticket, or Y14 return. The minibus leaves at 8 am and returns at either 3.30 or 5 pm.

CITS and CTS, operating out of the Kunming Hotel, have a three-day trip to the Western Hills, Bamboo Temple and Stone Forest for Y35 per person, reducible for larger groups.

To get from the Stone Forest to Kunming, take one of the local buses leaving at 7 am and 3 pm from the bus parking lot. They make another departure at 1 pm from the Shilin Hotel. These may be pre-booked, but empty seats can be found due to passengers overnighting. You could also try hitching back to Kunming from the Stone Forest.

The railway line you see on your trip between Kunming and the Stone Forest is the old French narrow-gauge line on which trains used to run all the way to Hanoi from Kunming.

LUNAN 路南

Lunan is a small market town about 10 km from the Stone Forest. It's not worth making a special effort to visit, but if you do go, try and catch a market day (Wednesday or Saturday), when Lunan becomes a colossal jam of donkeys, horse carts and bicycles. The streets are packed with produce, poultry and wares, and Sani women are dressed in their finest.

To get to Lunan from the Stone Forest, head back towards Kunming and take the first major crossroads left, then the second crossroads straight on but veering to the right. You'll have to hitch a truck or hire a three-wheeler (Y1.50 for a 20-minute ride). Plenty of trucks head that way on market day, some from the truck stop near the Forest.

XIAGUAN 下关

Xiaguan lies at the southern tip of Erhai Lake about 400 km west of Kunming. It was once an important staging-post on the Burma Road and is still a key centre for transport. Xiaguan is the capital of Dali Prefecture and was previously known as Dali; if your destination is Dali, you can avoid misunderstanding by asking for *Dali Gu Cheng* (Dali Old City).

Things to See
Xiaguan has developed into an industrial city specialising in tea processing, cigarette making and the production of textiles and chemicals. There is little to keep you here other than transport connections.

Erhai Lake Park (Er Hai Gong Yuan) has good views of the lake and mountains. You can reach the park by boat. A larger boat runs round the lake; get details at Xinqiao Matou, the pier beside the new bridge.

Places to Stay
The official tourist abode is *Erhai Binguan (Erhai Guest House)*, which has doubles for Y40 and dorm beds for Y8. Outside the bus station a sign pointing in the right direction informs foreigners that they should only stay at the hotel. Other hotels with lower prices (Y12 for a double) can be found if you walk in the opposite direction and ask around.

Getting There & Away
There are frequent buses running between Xiaguan and Kunming. You have the choice of hard or soft-seat on a day or night bus. Depending on your bus, tickets cost between Y13 and Y20.

Minibuses provide a shuttle service for the 15 km between Xiaguan and Dali. The fare varies between Y0.50 and Y1, depending on the vehicle.

Some foreigners have been fined for taking the direct route from Xiaguan to Simao and thence to Jīnghong in Xishuangbanna. Until this route is opened to foreigners, there doesn't seem much point in using it since it's almost as quick to take the bus from Kunming to Xishuangbanna.

Xiaguan also has bus connections for Lijiang, Binchuan (Mt Jizu), Weishan and Yongping.

AROUND XIAGUAN
There are several places around Xiaguan which are already on the Chinese tour circuit so perhaps even a big-nose can investigate them on a day trip or overnight basis. They involve just a little trial and error, with no satisfaction guaranteed.

Jizu Shan (Mt Jizu) is one of China's sacred mountains and attracts Buddhist pilgrims, including Tibetans. Kasyapa, one of Sakyamuni's 10 disciples, is said to have booted out the mountain's resident deity and settled down here in 833 BC. The mountain is called Jizu Shan (Chicken-Foot Mountain) because the three slopes resemble the claws of a chicken. The Cultural Revolution damaged many of the temples, which have been gradually renovated from 1979 onwards. Over 150,000 tourists and pilgrims clamber up the mountain every year to watch the dawn. Tianzhufeng, the main peak, is a cool 3240 metres high, so you will need some warm clothing.

To reach Jizu Shan from Xiaguan you should first take a bus to Binchuan, which is 70 km east of Xiaguan. Then take another bus from Binchuan for the 33-km ride to Shazhi, a village at the foot of Jizu Shan. During peak tourist season there may be a direct bus between Xiaguan and Shazhi.

Weishan is famous for the Taoist temples on nearby Wei Bao Shan (Mt Weibao). There are reportedly some fine Taoist murals here. It's 61 km due south of Xiaguan so it could be done as a day trip. You might have to convince the ticket clerk at Xiaguan bus station that you are not taking this route to Xishuangbanna.

Yongping is 55 km south-west of Xiaguan on the old Burma Road. The Jinguang Si (Jinguang Temple) is the attraction here.

DALI 大理
Dali lies on the western edge of Erhai Lake, with the imposing Cangshan mountain range behind it. The main inhabitants of the region are the Bai, who number about 1.1 million in Yunnan.

Dali has a long history. In 126 BC a Han ambassador to Afghanistan was amazed

1 No 2 Guest House
2 Public Security
3 Bus Station (Kunming)
4 Post Office
5 Bank of China
6 Bus Stop (Shapin)
7 Minibus Stop (Xiaguan)
8 Bus Stop (Lijiang)
9 To Xiaguan
10 To Lijiang
11 Three Pagodas
12 Coca Cola Restaurant
13 Pancake Restaurant
14 Happy Bike
15 Bath House
16 Coffee & Croquette Bar

1	第二招待所	9	至下关
2	公安局	10	至丽江
3	汽车站(昆明)	11	三塔
4	邮局	12	可口可乐饭店
5	中国银行	13	薄饼饭店
6	汽车站(沙平)	14	快乐自行车
7	面包车站(下关)	15	浴室
8	汽车站(丽江)	16	炸肉丸酒吧

to see bamboo wares and bolts of cloth from Sichuan here; the traders were ahead of him and had found a corridor through to India and Burma from Sichuan and Yunnan. Dali lies just off the Burma road and was a centre of the Bai Nanzhao kingdom. After that the kingdom of Dali held sway in south-western China up until the 13th century, when it was overrun by the Mongols and then by the Chinese. Dali has long been famous for its marble, which has been used in temples and palaces around China. A major drive is now being made to gain income from tourism.

Chinese indulge their fantasies by acclaiming this region as China's Switzerland; foreigners blow rings of sweet-smelling smoke and hazily discuss a 'new Kathmandu'. Dali is unlikely to match the sophistication of such places, but it's already a haven for foreigners who want to slow the pace, and tune out for a while.

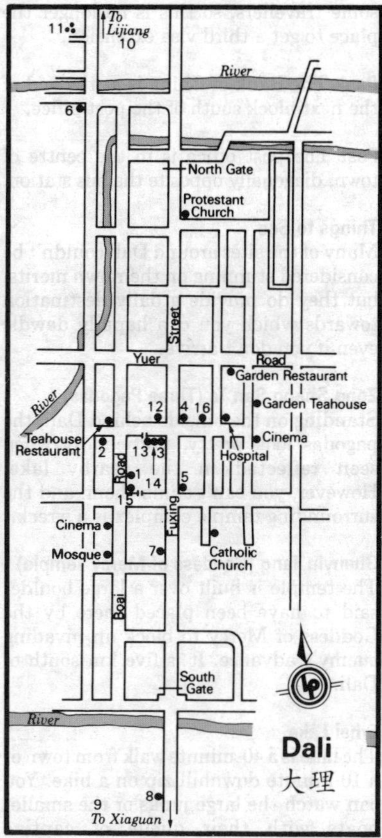

Information & Orientation

Dali is a midget-sized city which has preserved some cobbled streets and traditional stone architecture within its old walls. Unless you are in a mad hurry (in which case use a bike), you can get your bearings just by taking a walk for an hour or so. It takes about half an hour to walk from the southern gate across town to the northern gate.

Public Security is at the northern end of the block behind the No 2 Guest House. Previous goodwill has been overtaxed by some travellers, so this is no longer the place to get a third visa extension.

Bank The Bank of China is at the end of the next block south of the post office.

Post The post office is in the centre of town, diagonally opposite the bus station.

Things to See

Many of the sites around Dali couldn't be considered stunning on their own merits, but they do provide a daily destination towards which you can happily dawdle even if you don't arrive.

Zong Sheng San Ta (Three Pagodas)

Standing on the hillside behind Dali, the pagodas look pretty, particularly when seen reflected in the nearby lake. However, you can't climb them, and the surrounding temple complex is a wreck.

Guanyin Tang (Goddess of Mercy Temple)

The temple is built over a large boulder said to have been placed there by the Goddess of Mercy to block an invading enemy's advance. It is five km south of Dali.

Erhai Lake

The lake is a 40-minute walk from town or a 10-minute downhill zip on a bike. You can watch the large junks or the smaller boats with their queue of captive cormorants waiting on the edge of the boat for their turn to do the fishing. A ring placed round their necks stops them from guzzling the catch.

From Caicun, the lakeside village due east of Dali, there's a ferry at 4 pm to Wase on the other side of the lake. You can stay overnight and catch a ferry back at 5.30 am. Plenty of locals take their bikes over. Since ferries criss-cross the lake at various points, there could be some scope for extended touring. Close to Wase is Putuo Dao (Putuo Island) with the Xiao Putuo Si (Lesser Putuo Temple). Other ferries run between Longkan and Haidong, and between Xiaguan and Jinsuo Island. Ferries appear to leave early in the morning (for market) and return around 4 pm; timetables are flexible.

Zhonghe Si (Zhonghe Temple)

The temple is a long, steep hike up the mountainside behind Dali. When you finally get there, you may be received with a cup of tea and a smile.

Gantong Si (Gantong Temple)

This temple is close to the town of Guanyin, which is about six km from Dali in the direction of Xiaguan. In Guanyin you should follow the path uphill for three km. Ask friendly locals in the tea bushes for directions.

Qin Bi Xi (Qinbi Stream)

This scenic picnic spot near the village of Qiliqiao is three km from Dali in the direction of Xiaguan. After hiking four km up a path running close to the river, you'll reach three ponds.

Hudie Quan (Butterfly Spring)

Hudie Quan is a pleasant spot about 26 km north of Dali. The inevitable legend associated with the spring is that two lovers committed suicide here to escape a cruel king. After jumping into the bottomless pond, they turned into two of the butterflies which gather here en masse during May.

If you're energetic you could bike to the spring. Since it is only four km from Shapin, you could combine it with a visit to the Shapin market.

Shapin Market

The market happens every Monday at Shapin, which is 30 km north of Dali. An extraordinary mixture of livestock, handicrafts and farm produce changes hands here. The colourful costumes of the local Bai minority and the antics of the fair-goers make it all seem like a film set for *The Hobbit*. What looks like a fishing basket with two legs turns out to be a

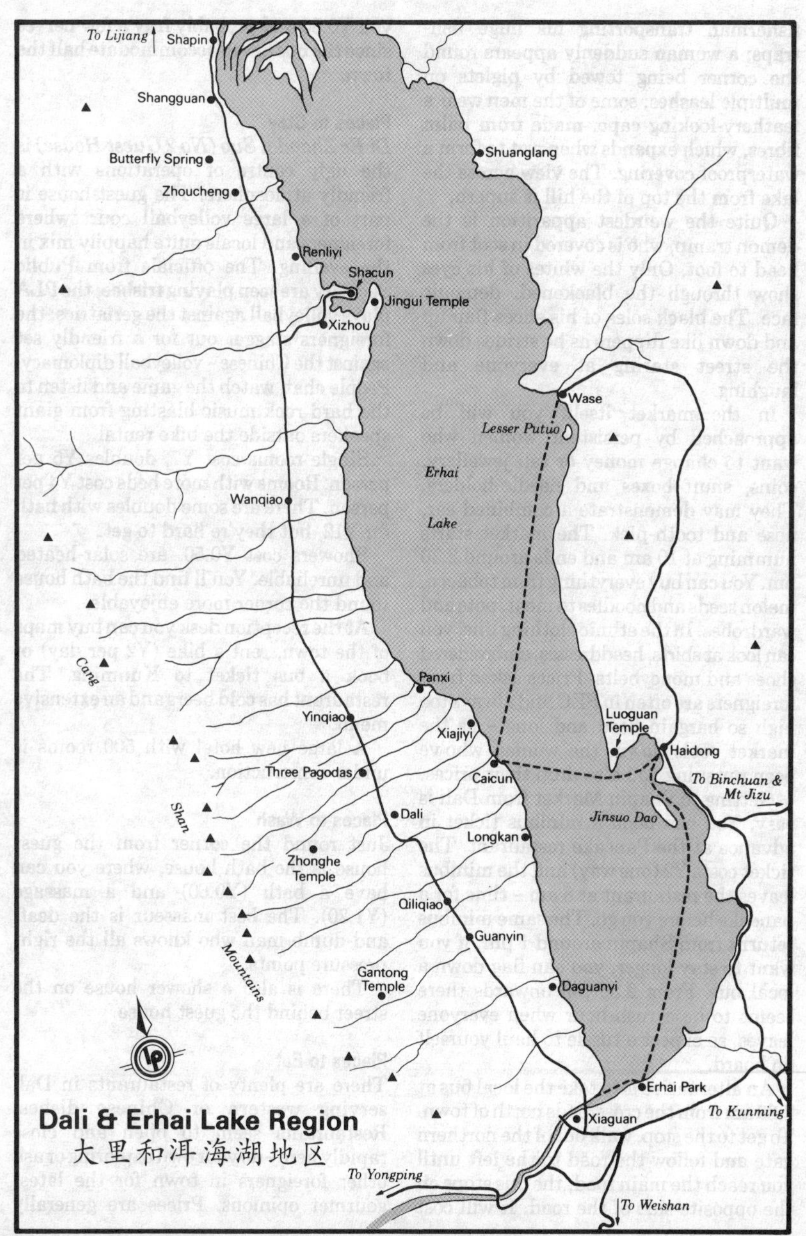

Dali & Erhai Lake Region
大理和洱海湖地区

fisherman transporting his huge fish-traps; a woman suddenly appears round the corner being towed by piglets on multiple leashes; some of the men wear a feathery-looking cape, made from palm fibres, which expands when wet to form a waterproof covering. The view across the lake from the top of the hill is superb.

Quite the weirdest apparition is the demon tramp, who is covered in soot from head to foot. Only the whites of his eyes show through the blackened, demonic face. The black soles of his shoes flap up and down like flippers as he strides down the street staring at everyone and laughing.

In the market itself, you will be approached by persistent women who want to change money or sell jewellery, coins, snuff boxes and needle-holders. They may demonstrate a combined ear, nose and tooth-pick. The market starts humming at 10 am and ends around 2.30 pm. You can buy everything from tobacco, melon seeds and noodles to meat, pots and wardrobes. In the ethnic clothing line, you can look at shirts, headdresses, embroidered shoes and moneybelts. Prices asked from foreigners are often in FEC and always too high so bargain hard and long – as the market cools down, the women who've been pursuing you also drop their prices.

Getting to Shapin Market from Dali is easy. You can book a minibus ticket in advance at the Pancake restaurant. The ticket costs Y2 (one way) and the minibus leaves the restaurant at 8 am – time for a pancake before you go. The same minibus returns from Shapin around 1 pm; if you want to stay longer, you can flag down a local bus. From 2.30 pm onwards there seems to be a rush-hour when everyone leaves, so expect a tussle to haul yourself on board.

An alternative is to take the local bus at 7.30 am from the crossroads north of town. To get to the stop, walk out of the northern gate and follow the road to the left until you reach the main road; the bus stops on the opposite side of the road. It will cost you Y0.80 and probably fray a few nerves since the bus has to accommodate half the town.

Places to Stay

Di Er Zhaodai Suo (No 2 Guest House) is the ugly centre of operations with a friendly atmosphere. The guest house is part of a large volleyball court where foreigners and locals quite happily mix in the evening. The officials from Public Security are seen playing frisbee; the PLA plays volleyball against the geriatrics; the foreigners stagger out for a friendly set against the Chinese – volleyball diplomacy. People chat, watch the game and listen to the hard rock music blasting from giant speakers outside the bike rental.

Single rooms cost Y7, doubles Y5 per person. Rooms with more beds cost Y4 per person. There are some doubles with bath for Y12, but they're hard to get.

Showers cost Y0.50, are solar-heated and unreliable. You'll find the bath house round the corner more enjoyable.

At the reception desk you can buy maps of the town, rent a bike (Y2 per day) or book a bus ticket to Kunming. The restaurant has cold beers and an extensive menu.

A large new hotel with 500 rooms is under construction.

Places to Wash

Just round the corner from the guest house is the bath house, where you can have a bath (Y0.60) and a massage (Y1.20). The best masseur is the deaf-and-dumb man who knows all the right pressure points.

There is also a shower house on the street behind the guest house.

Places to Eat

There are plenty of restaurants in Dali serving western or Chinese dishes. Restaurants seem to open and close rapidly here – do your own exploring or ask other foreigners in town for the latest gourmet opinions. Prices are generally lower at the less-frequented restaurants, which can be just as good as the trendy hang-outs where prices tend to rise with their fame.

The *Coca-Cola Restaurant* is a short walk from the guest house. This is where your dreams of pizza, potato salad, French fries, pancakes and fried cheese are translated into Chinese reality.

The *Coffee & Croquette Bar* is a few minutes from the post office. It's more a bar than a restaurant, where you can order croquettes and hard liquor from the manager. Dig deeper into your wallet if you want a shot of Remy Martin and an espresso.

The *Garden Teahouse* is a rambling, leafy place with character.

The *Garden Restaurant* is a family-run restaurant which does excellent Chinese food in its small courtyard.

The *Tea House Restaurant* does a good breakfast in the courtyard.

Festivals

Probably the best time to be here is during the San Yue Jie (Third Moon Street Fair), which begins on the 15th day of the third lunar month (usually April) and ends on the 21st day. The fair developed from the original festival of Buddhist rites into a commercial gathering which attracts thousands of people from all over Yunnan to buy, sell, dance, race and sing.

Rao Shan Lin (Walkabout Festival) is held between the 23rd and 25th days of the fourth lunar month (usually May). Villagers from the Dali area spend these days on a mass outing, dancing and singing their way from one temple to another.

Huo Ba Jie (Torch Festival) is held on the 24th day of the sixth lunar month (usually July). Flaming torches are paraded at night through homes and fields. Other events include firework displays and dragon-boat racing.

Shopping

Dali is famous for its marble. You may not want to load your backpack with marble slabs, but local entrepreneurs produce everything from ashtrays to model pagodas.

Several tailors in town are willing and able to produce clothing from local batik cloth at low cost and high speed. One such shop is diagonally opposite the Coca Cola Restaurant.

Getting There & Away

Bus Buses to Lijiang leave at 7.20 am from the bus station outside the town. Walk out of the south gate and continue about 400 metres in the direction of Xiaguan. The bus station is on your right – a shabby building across a dirt yard. Buy your ticket in advance and get there early. Tickets cost Y5.70 and the trip takes 6½ hours.

Modern Autosan (Polish) buses to Kunming leave the bus station opposite the post office at 6.20 am. The trip takes 11 hours. Tickets cost Y15.50 and should be bought in advance at the bus station. The same bus station sells tickets for a night bus which leaves from Xiaguan, not from Dali; you have to take a minibus from Dali to Xiaguan in time for your connection. The deluxe bus leaves Xiaguan at 6.30 pm and arrives in Kunming at 7 am. Tickets cost Y20 and include a couple of meals.

The No 2 Guest House sells tickets (Y13.70) for a different bus which leaves at 6.20 am from the guest house.

Minibuses to Xiaguan leave frequently (when full) during the day from the minibus station on the main street. The price varies between Y0.50 and Y1, depending on the vehicle.

Getting Around

Bikes are the best way to get around. Prices average Y2 per half day, Y3 per full day.

The No 2 Guest House rents out bikes, but requires your passport as a deposit. The Rising Sun Bike Rental, in front of the guest house, has maps of the area and doesn't require a passport as a deposit. The youth who runs it speaks good English and is helpful, even offering Chinese lessons.

Just across the street from the Coca-Cola Restaurant is the Happy Bike Shop, which also supplies maps.

DALI TO LIJIANG

Most travellers take a direct route between Dali and Lijiang. However, a couple of places visited by Chinese tourists might make interesting detours for foreigners. Transport could be a case of pot-luck with buses or hitching.

Jianchuan

This town is 92 km north of Dali on the Dali-Lijiang road. Approaching from the direction of Dali, you'll come to the small village of Diannan about eight km before Jianchuan. At Diannan, a small road branches south-west from the main road and passes through the village of Shaxi (23 km from the junction). Close to this village are the Shi Bao Shan Shiku (Shibao Shan Grottoes). There are three temple groups: Shizhong (Stone Bell), Shiziguan (Lion Pass) and Shadeng Cun (Shadeng Village).

Heqing

About 46 km south of Lijiang, Heqing is on the road which joins the main Dali-Lijiang road just above Lake Erhai at Dengchuan. In the centre of town is the Yun He Lou, a wooden structure built during the Ming Dynasty.

LIJIANG 丽江

North of Dali, bordering Tibet, is the town of Lijiang with its spectacular mountain backdrop.

Lijiang is the base of the Naxi (also spelt Nakhi) minority, who number about 245,000 in Yunnan and Sichuan. The Naxi are descended from Tibetan nomads and lived until recently in a matriarchal society. Women still seem to run the show, certainly in the old part of Lijiang.

The Naxi matriarchs maintained their hold over the men with flexible arrangements for love affairs. The *azhu* (friend) system allowed a couple to become lovers without setting up joint residence. Both partners would continue to live in their respective homes; the boyfriend would spend the nights at his girlfriend's house but return to live and work at his mother's house during the day. Any children born to the couple belonged to the woman, who was responsible for bringing them up. The father provided support, but once the relationship was over, so was the support. Children lived with their mothers; no special effort was made to recognise paternity. Women inherited all property, and disputes were adjudicated by female elders. The matriarchal system appears to have survived around Yongning, north of Lijiang.

Naxi women wear blue blouses and trousers covered by blue or black aprons. The T-shaped, traditional cape not only stops the basket always worn on the back from chafing, but also symbolises the heavens. Day and night are represented by the light and dark halves of the cape; seven embroidered circles symbolise the stars. The sun and moon used to be depicted with two larger circles, but these have gone out of fashion.

The Naxi created a written language over 1000 years ago using an extraordinary system of pictographs. The most famous Naxi text is the Dongba classic in 500 volumes. The Tibetan origins of the Naxi are confirmed by references in Naxi literature to Lake Manasarovar and Mt Kailas, both in Western Tibet.

There are strong matriarchal influences in the Naxi language. Nouns enlarge their meaning when the word for 'female' is added; conversely, the addition of the word for 'male' will decrease the meaning. For example, 'stone' plus 'female' conveys the idea of a boulder; 'stone' plus 'male' conveys the idea of a pebble.

Yunnan was a hunting ground for famous foreign plant-hunters such as

Kingdon Ward, Forrest and Joseph Rock. Joseph Rock, an Austro-American, lived almost continuously in Lijiang between 1922 and 1949. Rock is still remembered by some locals. A man of quick and violent temper, he required a special chair to accommodate his corpulent frame. He burdened his large caravans with a gold dinner service and a collapsible bathtub from Abercrombie & Fitch. He also wrote the best guide to Hawaiian flora before devoting the rest of his life to researching Naxi culture and collecting the flora of the region.

The Ancient Nakhi Kingdom of Southwest China (Harvard University Press, 1947) is Joseph Rock's definitive work; the two volumes are heavy-duty reading. For a lighter treatment of the man and his work, take a look at *In China's Border Provinces: The Turbulent Career of Joseph Rock, Botanist-Explorer* by J B Sutton (Hastings House, 1974).

One of the strangest expeditions to pass through Lijiang was that of Theodore and Kermit Roosevelt, who spent several months in 1935 searching for the giant panda. After stumbling through snow, the brothers finally hunted down an old panda which had been snoozing in a hollow tree. They fired in unison and killed it. One of their Kashmiri *shikaris* (gun-bearer) remarked that the bear was a 'sahib', a gentleman, for when hit he did not cry out as a bear would have. It was the first giant panda killed by a white man, and the Roosevelts were exultant.

In retrospect, this seems a dubious distinction: latest reports from China indicate that there are less than 700 giant pandas left in the wild and that they are heading for extinction by the end of the century.

Naxi Glossary

The transliteration used for the Naxi language is pretty mind-boggling, but you might like to try the following tongue gymnastics:

where are you going?
zeh gkv bbeu?
Lijiang
ggubbv
going to Lijiang
ggubbv bbeu
you understand Nakhi
nakhi kou chi kv
drink wine!
zhi teh

Information & Orientation

Lijiang is neatly divided into a standard, boring Chinese section and an old town full of character, cobbled streets, gushing canals and the hurly-burly of market life. The approximate line of division is a hill topped with a radio mast. Everything west of the hill is the new town, and everything east of the hill is the old town.

Information is available from the No 1 Guest House, or you might bump into some of the English-speaking locals.

Public Security is opposite the No 1 Guest House.

Bank The Bank of China is next to the bridge on the main road beside the old town. Hours are 10 am to noon, 1 to 5 pm. Closed on Mondays.

Things to See

Lijiang is a small town in a beautiful valley. The main attractions are in the surrounding area, so use a bike to get out of town to the mountains, where you can hike around. You may need time to acclimatise to the height (2400 metres).

The Old Town

Criss-crossed by canals and a maze of narrow streets, the old town is not to be missed. Arrive by mid-morning to see the market square full of Naxi women in traditional dress. Parrots and plants adorn the front porches, old women sell griddle cakes in front of tea shops, men walk past with hunting falcons (*lao ying*)

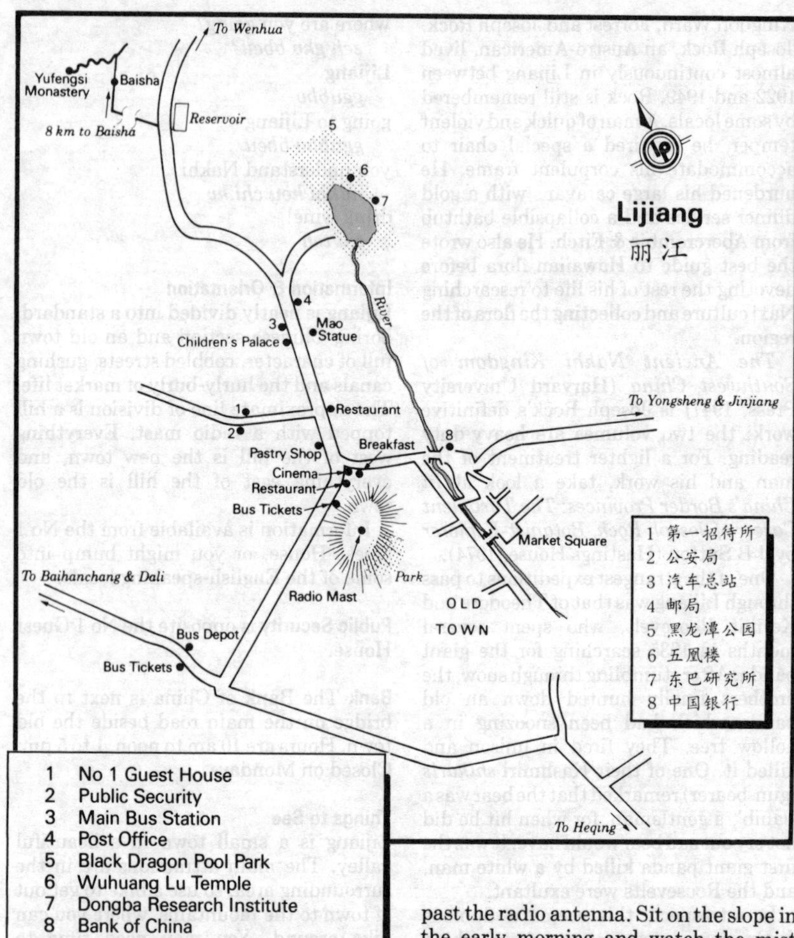

proudly keeping balance on their gloved fists, grannies energetically slam down the trumps on a card table in the middle of the street. You can buy embroidery and lengths of striped cloth in shops around the market. Some women offered intricate Tibetan locks for Y8.

Above the old town is a beautiful park which can be reached on the path leading past the radio antenna. Sit on the slope in the early morning and watch the mist clearing as the old town comes to life.

Heilong Tan Gongyuan (Black Dragon Pool Park)

The park is on the northern edge of town. Apart from strolling around the pool, you can visit the Dongba Research Institute, which is part of a renovated complex on the hillside. At the far side of the pond are renovated buildings used for an art exhibition, a pavilion with its own bridge across the water and the Ming Dynasty Wuhuang Lou temple. I like the atmosphere of this park, which escaped the standard refurbishing of steel railings, concrete runways and luminous paint.

Baisha

Baisha is a small village on the plain north of Lijiang. If you're going there on a bike, follow Lijiang's main street past the Mao statue and keep to the left. About two km out of town you'll see a reservoir on your right. Turn left off the main road and follow the trail for another eight km.

The star attraction of Baisha will probably hail you in the street. Doctor He looks like the stereotype of a Taoist physician and there's a sign outside his door: 'The Clinic of Chinese Herbs in Jade-Dragon Mountains of Lijiang'. The doctor speaks English and is keen to catch up on foreign contacts. Over a cup of healthy tea, you can discuss herbal medicine and sign his visitors' book. He can give you directions for **Dabaoji Palace**, which has some interesting frescoes. The temple, dedicated to Saddok, the patron god of Lijiang, is currently being renovated.

On the hillside, about five km past Baisha, is **Yufeng Si** monastery. The last three km of the track require a steep climb. If you decide to leave your bike at the foot of the hill, don't leave it too close to the village below – the local kids like to let the air out of the tyres!

The monastery has a magnificent view across the valley to Lijiang. The Cultural Revolution ejected the monks and destroyed the original religious objects. A large statue of Sakyamuni was heaved out of the main temple and smashed in front of the horrified monks. The temples are all silent shells and quiet courtyards filled with orchids, hydrangeas and camellias. Above the temple is a building containing the famous camellia tree which produces hundreds of flowers between February and April. This tree is a favourite with the occasional group of noisy Han tourists. A stone-faced old monk patiently explains its 500-year history; he risked his life during the Cultural Revolution to water the tree secretly at night.

Soaring 5500 metres above Lijiang is **Mt Satseto**, also known as Yulong Shan (Jade Dragon Mt). In 1963, the peak was climbed for the first time by a research team from Beijing. You can reach the snow-line on one of the adjoining peaks if you continue along the base of the hillside, but ignore the track to Yufengsi. On the other side of the next obvious valley, a well-worn path leads uphill to a lake.

Places to Stay & Eat

The *Di Yi Zhaodai Suo (No 1 Guest House)* is the official place to stay. It has comfortable, four-bed dorms at Y4.50 per bed. A double without bath costs Y20, double with bath Y44. The hotel has two blocks; the one at the back is deluxe.

The Hotel Service Bureau is on your left when you come out of the lobby. This is the place to ask about hiring a vehicle, and you might like to look at the excellent map on their wall. A map of Lijiang is 'in preparation'. Next door to the Service Bureau is the shower room – ask at the reception desk for the precise opening time. To the right of the showers, a few doors down, is the bike depot.

A new, multi-storey hotel being built in the centre of the old town should be a more exciting place to stay. Some foreigners have managed to stay in the *lüshe* (hostels), which are basic and plentiful.

The No 1 Guest House food was not a taste-bud experience – I tried it twice and then gave it a miss. Turn left out of the guest house gates and walk until you hit main street. Across the street is a restaurant (in fact, it's a cooking school) with reasonable food. There are several smaller restaurants just before the entrance to the Black Dragon Lake Park. The main street has several pastry shops with sponge cakes. In the old town, you can buy griddle cakes from street vendors. Close to the cinema is a place which serves breakfast – *baba*, a type of doughnut with oodles of sugar, and *doujiang*, the standard soybean drink.

Festivals

The 13th day of the third moon (late March or early April) is the traditional day to hold a Fertility Festival.

July brings Huopao Jie (Jumping Over Fire Festival), also celebrated as the Torch Festival by the Bai in the Dali region. The origin of this festival is traced back to the Nanzhao Kingdom.

The King of Nanzhao, intent on securing more power, invited all the kings from the surrounding area to a feast. Amongst those invited was the King of Eryuan. The Queen of Eryuan suspected the motives for such a feast and did all she could to dissuade her husband from going. He insisted he was honour-bound to accept the invitation and went to the feast.

When the kings had become properly drunk, the King of Nanzhao withdrew from the scene, ordered his servants to lock the doors of the banquet hall and then set it alight. All the kings were burnt to a cinder. The Queen of Eryuan had had premonitions of treachery and had given her husband engraved metal rings to wear around his wrists and ankles. On the basis of these rings she was able to identify the remains of her husband, who was then buried with full honours. The King of Nanzhao kept sending marriage proposals to the bereaved queen. Finally, she realised she had no option so she accepted on condition that she could dispose of her husband's ceremonial robes first. A huge fire was prepared for the robes; as the flames rose higher and higher to consume them, the queen leapt into the heart of the fire.

Getting There & Away

Bus Buses run daily between Lijiang and Dali. The trip takes 6½ hours and the fare is Y5.70. Buses to Dali and Xiaguan leave at 7 and 11 am from the bus station in front of the Mao statue. This appears to be the main bus station. A couple of other places serve as bus depots or sell tickets.

There is a bus connection between Lijiang and Jinjiang, a town on the Kunming-Chengdu railway. The trip takes nine hours and the ticket costs Y8.90. The bus leaves at 6.30 am from the bus station in front of the Mao statue, where train tickets from Jinjiang to Kunming or Chengdu can be booked in advance as well. The bus arrives in Jinjiang in time to connect with the train departing for Chengdu at 7 pm.

At the bus station, PSB has posted a plaintive sign which says the Tibet route via Zhongdian is not open, and then requests foreigners to 'respect minority consciousness'. Well, wouldn't it be great if we all practised what we preach!

AROUND LIJIANG

Monasteries

Lijiang originally had five monasteries, which all belonged to the Karmapa (Red Hat sect) of Tibetan Buddhism introduced to Lijiang in the 16th century by Lama Chuchin Chone. This lama founded the Chinyunsi monastery close to Lashiba Lake.

About 16 km south of Lijiang is **Shangri Moupo**, a mountain considered sacred by the Tibetans. Half-way up the mountain there was once a large monastery, **Yunfengsi**, which was a popular destination for pilgrims. The present condition of the monastery might be worth investigating. Behind the mountain is a large white cliff where shamanistic rites were once performed by *dtombas* (Naxi shamans).

Shigu (Stone Drum)

The marble drum is housed in a small pavilion overlooking a bend in the Yangtse, 70 km west of Lijiang. In April 1936 the Red Army crossed the river at Shigu on the Long March. During the Cultural Revolution, Red Guards split the drum in defiance of an old prophesy that calamity would befall the country when the drum split. The parts have since been patched together again.

To reach Shigu, you can either hire a jeep from Lijiang or try your luck with local transport. You should try to catch a local bus going in the direction of Judian and make it clear that you want to get off at Shigu. Another useful place to pick up a lift to Shigu is Baihanchang, an important road junction about 24 km before Shigu. If you want to make the sortie, be patient and prepared with warm clothes, food and water.

Hutiaoxia (Tiger Leap Gorge)

At this 15-km gorge the Yangtse drops nearly 300 metres. A narrow path clings to vertical cliffs at a height over 3700 metres – take it easy if you're susceptible to vertigo.

To reach Hutiaoxia, 94 km from Lijiang, you can either hire a jeep or take local transport. Buses leaving Lijiang for Zhongdian or Deqen will take about three hours to reach Xiaqiaotou, where you should get off the bus. Cross the bridge towards the cliff and follow a track to the left. It takes about 2½ hours to reach the gorge. Warm clothes, food, water and sturdy footwear are recommended.

Zhongdian

Located 104 km north of Xiaqiaotou, Zhongdian is not officially open to foreigners yet, but I have seen a CITS brochure in English about the area. PSB are starting to fine any Tibet-bound foreigners found on this closed route.

The nearby lake region of Baishuitang is said to approach the splendour of Jiuzhaigou in northern Sichuan.

JINJIANG 金江

Jinjiang is the tiny railhead for the large town of Dukou. To reach it from Chengdu, one of the best trains is the No 91 which leaves Chengdu at 7.53 pm and reaches Jinjiang at 10.40 am – for some reason, this train is not in the timetable. A local-price hard-sleeper for this trip costs Y25.50. At Jinjiang station ticket-sellers usually meet the train and sell tickets to Lijiang for the next day.

You can then turn right as you exit the station, and continue 50 metres down the street. Cross the street to the start of a road going uphill. The *Zhaodai Suo* is in a courtyard to the right, leading off this road. It's a clean, friendly place to stay, charging Y2.20 per person or Y6 for a double. They also sell bus tickets. Their food is not the best: after paying for the set lunch, I was handed a bowl of rice, a very skinny duck, a cleaver and a chopping board.

In the square outside Jinjiang station there are several open-air restaurants serving excellent food. Try their *doufu huoguo* (doufu hotpot) and the small pots of beef or pork in batter. They were also cooking a more expensive snake hotpot.

Passengers on the bus I took included a mildly retarded woman with a trio of infants who spent most of the time puking, crapping or wailing in chorus. At Dukou, a group of Tibetans boarded the bus, which promptly broke down within a few metres of the bus station. This gave me more than enough time to contemplate Dukou, a modern city composed mainly of high-rise buildings perched on either side of a deep valley carved by the Jinsha Jiang. Shortly after leaving Dukou, the bus enters Yunnan Province. The landscape changes to banana groves, terraced fields and small villages of brown mudbrick houses with grey tiled roofs. After several hours of giddy and dramatic climbing above the Jinsha Jiang (upper reaches of the Yangtse River), the bus continues through Yongsheng to Lijiang.

Getting Around

The modern part of town is a tedious place to walk around. The old town, however, is best seen on foot. The No 1 Guest House rents out bikes for Y0.60 per hour or Y5 per day. Bikes are good for anything within a radius of 15 km, but after that you'd be better off hiring a vehicle. The No 1 Guest House rents Beijing jeeps at Y0.60 per km and Y2 for each hour of waiting time.

Lijiang is also famous for its easily trained horses, which are usually white or chestnut with distinctive white stripes on the back. It might be possible to arrange an excursion on horseback.

XISHUANGBANNA 西双版纳

Located in the deep south of Yunnan Province, next to the Burmese and Laotian borders, is the region of Xishuangbanna. The name Xishuangbanna is a Chinese approximation of the original Dai name Sip Sawng Panna (12 districts). Xishuangbanna Dai Autonomous Prefecture, as it is known officially, is subdivided into the three counties of Jinghong, Menghai and Mengla. Mengla County is closed to foreign tourists at present.

The Han Chinese and the Dai each make up a third of the 650,000-strong population of this region; the other third is a hotch-potch of minorities which includes the Miao, Zhuang, Yao and lesser-known hill tribes such as the Aini, Jinuo, Bulang, Lahu and Wa.

The Dai people are concentrated in this pocket of Yunnan and exercise a clear upper hand in the economy of Xishuangbanna. During the Cultural Revolution many Dai simply voted with their feet and slipped across the border to join their fellow Dai who are sprinkled throughout Thailand, Laos, Burma and Vietnam. Not only the Dai but also most of the other minorities in these areas display a nonchalant disregard for borders and authority in general.

The Dais are Buddhists driven southwards by the Mongol invasion of the 13th century. The Dai state of Xishuangbanna was annexed by the Mongols and then by the Chinese, and a Chinese governor was installed in the regional capital of Jinglan (present-day Jinghong). Countless Buddhist temples were built in the early days of the Dai state and now lie in the jungles in ruins. During the Cultural Revolution Xishuangbanna's temples were desecrated and destroyed. Some were saved by being used as granaries, but many are now being rebuilt from scratch. Temples are also recovering their role, with or without official blessing, as village schools where young children are accepted for religious training as monks.

To keep themselves off the damp earth in the tropical rain-forest weather, the Dais live in spacious wooden houses raised on stilts, with the pigs and chickens below. The common dress for the Dai women is a straw hat or towel-wrap headdress; a tight, short blouse in a bright colour; and a printed sarong with a belt of silver links. Some Dai men tattoo their bodies with animal designs. Betel-nut chewing is popular and all Dai youngsters get their teeth capped with gold; otherwise they are considered ugly.

Both Xishuangbanna and Hainan Island have fascinating collections of plant and animal life which are a unique resource for research into rare species. Unfortunately, recent scientific studies have demonstrated the devastating effect of previous government policies on land use; the tropical rainforest areas of Hainan and Xishuangbanna are now as acutely endangered as similar rainforest areas elsewhere on the planet. The jungle areas that remain still contain dwindling numbers of wild elephants (200), tigers, leopards and golden-haired monkeys. The Tropical Institute in Jinghong has gardens with a limited selection of plants which give an idea of the spectacular plant life in the deep forests, but foreign visitors are not welcome.

As for language, you can make some headway with Chinese, but you'll also find a Thai or Burmese phrasebook (Lonely Planet produce lightweight ones) useful in remoter parts.

Festivals celebrated by the Dai also attract hordes of foreigners and Han.

The Water-Splashing Festival held around mid-April (usually 13, 14 and 15 April) washes away the dirt, sorrow and demons of the old year and brings in the happiness of the new. The first day of the festival is devoted to a giant market. The second day features dragon-boat racing (races in Jinghong are held on the Mekong River below the bridge), swimming races and rocket-launching. The third day features the water-splashing freakout – be prepared to get drenched all day by the locals. In the evenings there is dancing, launching of hot-air paper balloons and game-playing.

Top: Fishing boat on Erhai Lake, Dali (RS)
Bottom Left: Lijiang valley with Mt. Satseto in the background (RS)
Bottom Right: Dai monk on his bike, Menghun (RS)

Top: Survival – Potala Palace, Lhasa (RS)
Bottom: Destruction – Ganden Monastery, Ganden (RS)

The festivities attract loaded tourists, so all the planes are booked out, but the bus may be an alternative. Hotels in Jinghong town are booked solid, but you could stay in a nearby town and commute. Festivities take place all over Xishuangbanna, so you might strike lucky further away from Jinghong.

During the Tanpa Festival in February young boys are sent to the local temple for initiation as monks. At approximately the same time (between February and March), Tan Jing Festival participants honour Buddhist sutras housed in local temples.

The Tan Ta Festival is held during the last 10-day period of October or November with temple ceremonies, rocket launches from special towers and hot-air balloons. The rockets, which often contain lucky amulets, blast off with a curious droning sound like mini-space shuttles before exploding high above; those who find the amulets are assured of good luck.

The farming season (July to October) is the time for the Closed-Door Festival, when marriages or festivals are banned. It is followed by the Open-Door Festival, when everyone lets their hair down again to celebrate the harvest.

Climate

Xishuangbanna has wet and dry seasons. The wet season falls between June and August, when it rains ferociously almost every day. September through February there is less rainfall but thick fog descends during the late evening and doesn't lift until 10 am. Between May and August there are frequent and spectacular thunderstorms.

Between November and March temperatures average about 19°C. The hottest months of the year are April to September, when you can expect an average of 25°C.

SIMAO 思茅

Until Jinghong completes its airport, Simao will remain the drab stepping-stone for Xishuangbanna. The transit town offers you a meal, a bed for the night and a bus or plane ticket out the next day.

Information

CAAC (tel 2234) is just off the main street at Hongqi Guangchang Beice. It's open 8 to 11 am and 2.30 to 5.30 pm; closed on Saturday afternoon and Sunday.

Places to Stay

The tourist joint is *Simao Binguan (Simao Guest House)*. Doubles with bath cost Y8 per person; without bath, they're Y4 per person.

The Guest House has its own pet bear who used to be housed in a tiny cage that he was unable to move about or even stand in. Australian journalist Bob Leamen reported on the bear's plight, prompting an instant reaction from the bear-loving Australian public. Hundreds of dollars were donated to a fund to build the bear a larger cage and the excess money went to a special fund for bears at the Melbourne Zoo.

There are several other hotels in Simao. One is close to the bus station; another is on the main street, close to the CAAC office. The bus from Kunming stops at a depot which is also a hotel. They are all basic and cost around Y3 per person.

Getting There & Away

Air There are flights between Kunming and Simao. The fare is Y57 and flights depart daily except Wednesday and Sunday. There are two flights on Monday and Thursday.

CAAC in Kunming is unable (unwilling?) to co-ordinate a return ticket with their counterparts in Simao. As a result, you have to make arrangements for your return flight either on-the-spot when you arrive in Simao or by telephoning from the Banna Hotel in Jinghong town. One of the women at Simao CAAC speaks English and will want to know your name, nationality and passport number before making your reservation. You are required to pick up your ticket on the day before departure. Since CAAC closes at 5 pm, it's best to take the earliest bus from Jinghong at 6.40 am to get there before the office closes.

The airport bus for the mid-day flight from Simao leaves the CAAC office at 9.30 am and takes no more than 10 minutes to reach the airport, where everyone gets thoroughly bored for several hours. The control-tower staff use binoculars to sight the incoming plane, a turboprop Antonov. The flight lasts barely an hour.

Bus There are daily buses between Kunming and Simao. The trip takes 2½ days and costs Y19.10 soft-seat.

The haul is long but not punishing. The bus leaves Kunming at 7 am. After skirting Lake Dian, it climbs hills which become increasingly less populated, but have gushing streams and waterfalls are surrounded by lush foliage. Traffic very gingerly crosses the Yuanjiang River over a rickety suspension bridge. After overnighting, probably at Anding (Y2 per bed in a three-bed room), the bus arrives in Simao at 4.45 pm.

Various private and public buses to Jinghong leave early in the morning from the bus station or from the hotel on the main road. Tickets cost around Y4.50, and the trip takes five hours, during which most passengers throw up.

At Simao bus station, PSB have posted a warning to foreigners not to take the direct bus from Simao to Xiaguan. There must be something exciting out there, but travellers who've done the route have nothing special to report except for the man at Simao CITS, who gets very agitated when you casually tell him you've taken this road. It might have something to do with dope country.

JINGHONG 景洪

Jinghong, the capital of Xishuangbanna prefecture, lies beside the Lancang Jiang (Mekong River). It's a sleepy town with palm-lined streets which help mask the Chinese-built concrete boxes until they merge with the stilt-houses in the surrounding villages.

Information

CITS (tel 2708) is on the 2nd floor of the building opposite the Banna Hotel (enter via the stairs on the left). Hours are 8 am to noon and 3 to 6 pm; closed on Sunday. Friendly staff hand round fruit and try to solve your problems. Cold beer costs Y2.20 from the CITS fridge.

Ask here about vehicle hire for excursions into the forest; Beijing jeeps cost Y0.60 per km. A private firm provides Toyota Landcruisers for Y1 per km. You can hire a vehicle to take you to Mangsha (five km north of Jinghong), engage a guide in the village and spend the day hacking your way through virgin jungle. Keep gear to a minimum so both your hands are free, and be prepared for bloodthirsty leeches.

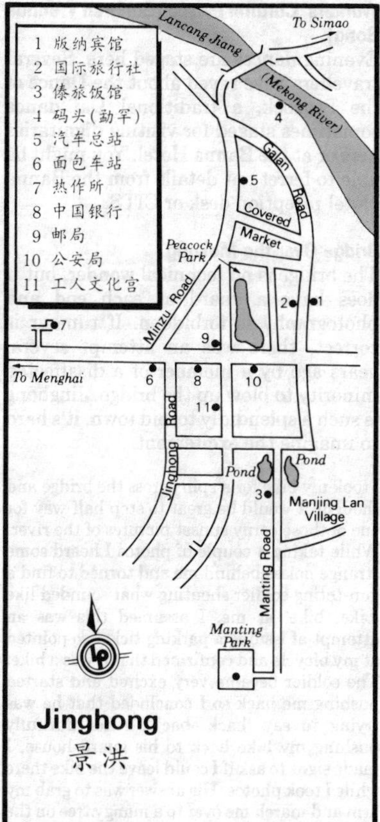

CITS will also help you book your return flight from Simao to Kunming. If you can form a small group and plan two days in advance, they may be able to arrange a visit to the Tropical Plant Research Institute.

Public Security is opposite Peacock Park in the centre of town. They seem to tolerate foreigners making side trips from open towns, providing you don't overnight in local villages. They can crack down hard on foreigners caught bushwhacking along the border.

1 Banna Hotel
2 CITS
3 Dai Minority Guest House
4 Pier for Menghan
5 Main Bus Station
6 Minibus Station
7 Tropical Plant Research Institute
8 Bank of China
9 Post Office
10 Public Security
11 Workers' Cultural Palace

Bank The Bank of China is in the centre of town, diagonally opposite the post office.

Things to See

Jinghong doesn't have much to keep you beyond a couple of days. It's more a base for operations or a place for lazing in the mid-day shade beside the river.

Villages

Manjing is a traditional Dai village in the southern part of town. You'll also find the Dai Minority Guest House here. If you continue past this village for 500 metres, you'll come to a temple under renovation. Just beyond it is **Manting Park**, which contains two imitation pagodas. The originals are further away in Xishuangbanna, so this is meant to be a chance for tour members to see the pagodas without actually going there. The gardens are full of flowers and are popular for picnics. If you go to the toilets, watch out for little boys with fireworks. While I was concentrating on business, the little buggers lobbed a couple of firecrackers into my cubicle and scared the shit out of me!

Menghan is a village on the Mekong, south of Jinghong. For details about the boat trip from Jinghong, see the separate section on Menghan.

Manjai village has a renovated temple. It's on the other side of the bridge over the Mekong. Walk there or hire a bike and explore down by the river.

Tropical Plant Research Institute

Worth a visit, but the management is too busy guiding tubby cadres on inspection tours (holidays?) to bother with foreigners. Beside a large pond there's an exclusive guest house built in imitation Dai style, that is frequented by indolent big-wigs attending 'conferences'.

You can wander through the avenue of oil palms and around the outer grounds (entrance fee Y0.10), but the inner sanctum requires special permission via CITS. After two days of valiant effort by the CITS woman, I was grudgingly granted entry. Since the minimum group size is five persons and there were two in our group, we paid the minimum price of Y5. Photography was only allowed in one part of the gardens – secret rubber plants elsewhere?

The walls of the institute building are smothered with a fantastic display of flowers. In the research gardens grow all sorts of tropical flowers and medicinal or food plants (cocoa, coffee, liquorice, cinnamon, mango). On the way out we were shown the rubber trees and the leaves of the 'sensitive' plant which curl when touched.

Peacock Garden

This small zoo and garden is next to the lake in the centre of town. Entrance costs Y0.10. The park is pleasant, but the animals in the zoo are so ferociously baited by onlookers that you can't help feeling depressed. The Gibbon monkeys just sat in their cage with no escape from the jabbing; one monkey finally pulled the stick away from its attacker, then threw up its arms and grimaced in perfect imitation of its tormentor. There's a sad bear in a tiny cage, giant salamanders and a pair of huge pythons – one appears to have been 'arrested' and then given to the zoo by the PSB.

The 'English Language Corner' takes place here every Sunday evening, so this is your chance to exchange views or practise your English with the locals.

Workers' Cultural Palace (Gongren Wenhua Gong)

Evening dances are staged here. Several travellers have raved about the Dance of the Peacock, a traditional Dai dance sometimes staged for visiting dignitaries here or at the Banna Hotel. You might be able to ferret out details from the Banna Hotel reception desk or CITS.

Bridge Over the Mekong

The bridge is no technical wonder, but it does have a guard at each end and photography is forbidden. If rumour is correct, there was an attempt several years ago by a member of a disaffected minority to blow up the bridge. Jinghong is such a splendidly torpid town, it's hard to imagine the excitement.

I took my bike for a spin across the bridge and thought it would be great to stop half-way for one of those corny sunset pictures of the river. While taking a couple of photos I heard some strange noises behind me and turned to find a gun-toting soldier shouting what sounded like 'bike, bike' at me. I assumed this was an attempt at issuing a parking ticket so pointed at my bicycle and confirmed that it was a bike. The soldier became very excited and started pushing me back so I concluded that he was trying to say 'back, back'. After dutifully pushing my bike back to his guard house, I made signs to ask if I could leave the bike there while I took photos. His answer was to grab my arm and march me over to a mangy tree on the other side of the road. I indicated that the tree was indeed impressive, and was wondering if the soldier wasn't perhaps a frustrated gardener when I discerned a tiny, rusty, mangled sign: 'No photographs'.

At the other end of the bridge was another sign, in a slightly worse state of decomposition, which was wrapped round a steel support like a piece of washing. Ten minutes later I was taking photos beneath the bridge without any signs of disapproval from above. The Chinese bridge fetish is alive and well in Jinghong.

Places to Stay

The *Banna Binguan (Banna Hotel)* close to the centre of town, about 15 minutes from the bus station on foot, is a colonial relic in a tropical garden with huge palm trees. It's a favourite of mine, one of those rare hotels in China that hasn't murdered its character – yet. The double rooms at the back are great value at Y8 per person; the balcony outside has a view across the heat haze to the Mekong. You can draw up a chair, begin your Somerset Maugham short stories and drowse through the afternoon surrounded by bougainvillea. The dorm (Y5 per person) has a complete set of wicker furniture for elegant tea parties. The showers behind the dining room are grungy affairs which start to produce hot water no earlier than 3.30 pm.

The building to the right inside the entrance is the reception office. If you want to book your flight from Simao to Kunming, you can use the phone (Y1) here to call CAAC in Simao. Bikes can be hired for Y1 per hour. Luggage storage costs Y0.10 per day. Impressionist postcards and special stamp issues are also sold. A small shop beside the entrance sells maps, brochures, ethnic clothing, wooden pipes and cigarettes.

The *Dai Minority Guest House & Restaurant* is a small family enterprise in a traditional Dai home on stilts. It is well-known as the best local restaurant in Jinghong and rents out three or four rooms as a sideline. Beds cost Y2.50 per person in small cubicles with plyboard partitions. The upstairs balcony is a pleasant place to sit with a beer in the winter and read about the sub-zero temperatures in Beijing. Watch your step at night when you head for the toilet at the back – a Dutch friend fell in the slime. The one problem with this place is that the bus station is about 30 minutes away on foot.

Places to Eat

The *Dai Minority Guest House* does tremendous Dai food and is very popular with both foreign and Chinese customers. Try their roast fish, eel or roast beef cooked with lemon grass or served with peanut-and-tomato sauce. For a different kind of rice, try the black glutinous kind. It's best to order your dinner in the morning. If you want to go the whole hog, ask about the banquet which costs about Y45 for six persons.

There are several good restaurants along the road in front of the bus station.

Street markets sell coconuts, bananas, papayas, oranges, pineapples. The covered market near the Banna Hotel is at its busiest in the morning.

Getting There & Away

Until Jinghong gets its airport (1989?) at nearby Gasa and 747s swoop daily to disgorge cargoes of day-trippers, everyone will have to use the bus.

Bus There are daily buses between Kunming and Jinghong. The trip takes three days and costs Y24.50. Buy tickets at the bus station. Buses to Simao run at 6.40 am and 1 pm from the bus station.

The minibus station, about two km past the bus station on the same road, has frequent departures to Menglong, Menghai and Mengzhe.

Getting Around

The Banna Hotel rents out bikes for Y1 an hour. If you want a jeep or a minibus, CITS can help.

AROUND XISHUANGBANNA

Menghai

This uninspiring place serves as a centre for trips into the surrounding area. Perched on top of a nearby hill is an atrocious loudspeaker system which pounds the unfortunate inhabitants with distorted noise. The Sunday market attracts members of the hill tribes and the best way to find it is to follow the early-morning crowds. This is the only time when the town shows signs of life other than the dogs, chickens, pigs and cows cruising the street. There are a couple of drab hotels (Y3 per bed); one is at the main bus station.

Frequent minibuses run from the minibus centre in Jinghong to Menghai. Minibuses to Jinghong, Menghun and Jingzhen leave from a minibus centre in Menghai, about one km down the street from the main bus station.

Menghun is a tiny village about 26 km south-west of Menghai. The Sunday market here lasts from 8 to 11 am and is a swirl of hill tribes and women sprouting fancy leggings, headdresses, earrings and bracelets. Many of the tribespeople seemed to lose their wits at the sight of a foreigner. Catch a minibus from the minibus centre in Menghai at 8.10 or 9.10 am.

In the village of **Jingzhen**, about 14 km north-west of Menghai, is the **Bajiao Ting (Octagonal Pavilion** first built in 1701. The Cultural Revolution severely damaged the original structure, so the present renovated building isn't exactly thrilling. Take a close look at the new paintings on the wall of the temple. There are some interesting scenes which appear to depict PLA soldiers causing death and destruction during the Cultural Revolution; adjoining scenes depict Buddha vanquishing PLA soldiers, one of whom is waving goodbye as he drowns in a pond!

Jingzhen is a pleasant rural spot for walks along the river or the fishponds behind the village. Frequent minibuses from the minibus centre in Menghai go via Jingzhen.

Mengzhe, 24 km west of Menghai, has a couple of temples. Take a minibus from Menghai.

Nannuo Shan (Mt Nannuo)

Nannuo Shan is on the road between Jinghong and Menghai (17 km from Menghai). It's best done as a day trip from Menghai, providing you start early and return to the main road before dusk. The bus will drop you off close to a bridge; cross the bridge and follow the dirt track about six km uphill until you join a newly constructed main road.

About one km before the junction, you'll round a bend in the road and see a fence with a stile and stone benches beyond. This is the turnoff for the steps down to the overrated **Cha Wang (King of Tea Trees)**. According to the Hani, their ancestors have been growing tea for 55 generations and this tree was the first one planted. The tree is definitely not worth descending hundreds of steps to see; it is half-dead and covered with moss, graffiti and signs forbidding graffiti. A crumbling concrete pavilion daubed with red paint completes the picture.

The new highway has been bulldozed out of the mountain for the comfort of tourists who can now visit the hill tribes further up the mountain. When I was there, the Hani and Lahu villagers were quite friendly. Repeated exposure to tour buses is certain to cause changes. If you leave the main road, there's some pleasant hiking in the area, but don't expect villagers to automatically give you a bed for the night. A Hani villager did invite us into his stilt house for an excellent meal and some firewater that left me wobbling downhill.

The Hani (also known in adjacent countries as the Akha) are of Tibetan origin but according to folklore they are descended from frogs' eyes. They stick to the hills cultivating rice, corn and the occasional poppy. Trading takes place at weekly markets where the Dai obviously dominate the Hani, who seem only too keen to scamper back to their mountain retreats. Hani women wear headdresses of beads, feathers, coins and silver rings. At one remote market the women were very nervous and it was only when their backs were turned that I could inspect their headdresses constructed with French (Vietnamese), Burmese and Indian coins from the turn of the century.

Damenglong

Damenglong is about 70 km south of Jinghong and a few km from the Burmese border. This is another sleepy village worth visiting if you want to hike around the surrounding hills.

Things to See The much-touted tourist

attraction here is the **Manfeilong Pagoda** built in 1204. According to legend, Sakyamuni once visited Xishuangbanna and left behind footprints. The Manfeilong Pagoda was built to honour a footprint which you can see under a niche below one of the nine stupas.

Old photos of the stupas show that they were once white; renovation has been effected with a hastily applied coat of silver paint which looks plain ugly. It's a peaceful spot with a handful of monks and fine views across the river towards Burma. Damenglong is worth a visit during the Tan Ta festival (late October or early November) when the Manfeilong Pagoda attracts hundreds of locals to spectacular celebrations (dancing, rockets, paper balloons).

To reach the pagoda, walk back along the main road towards Jinghong for two km until you reach a small village with a temple on your left, close to the main road. Take the track to the left, pass the temple and continue uphill for 20 minutes to reach the pagoda.

There are other temples in the area. The village of **Xiaojie**, about 15 km before Damenglong, is surrounded by Bulang, Lahu and Hani villages. Lahu women shave their heads; apparently the younger Lahu women aren't happy about this any more and use Mao caps to hide their shaven heads. The Bulang are possibly descended from the Lolo in northern Yunnan. The women wear black turbans with silver decorations; many of the designs are of shells, fish and marine life.

There's plenty of room for exploration in this area, although you're not allowed over the border.

Places to Stay & Eat There's a decrepit hotel next to the bus station or the slightly less decrepit *Zhaodai Suo (Guest House)*. To reach the guest house, turn left out of the bus station and take the next street to the right – the guest house is at the end of the street. The manager has a severe drinking problem; hold onto your receipts and complete all arrangements with him before evening, when he tends to pass out under the table. Don't keep your valuables in your room because he likes to move beds and baggage around when he's sober. Beds cost Y2 in a four-bed dorm or Y3.5 in a double. Behind the guest house is a slimy reservoir and an even more turgid toilet.

Turn left out of the bus station and continue for a couple of minutes until you see a restaurant at the foot of the slope on your left. This is probably the only restaurant in town, here food is ladled from large bowls. The market women in the street sell fruit and a type of pancake. The Sunday market is worth visiting early in the morning to see the Hani and the Burmese who are officially allowed to cross the border.

The *Ice-Cream Parlour* next to the bus station has cold bottles of beer. Chained to one of the benches is a pet monkey and its baby, both of whom suffer from the bored owner's habit of throwing firecrackers out the door. The cinema is the only source of entertainment in town. When the show's over, locals drop by the ice-cream parlour to keep the monkeys neurotic.

Getting There From the minibus centre in Jinghong there are frequent buses to Damenglong. Buses for the return trip leave the Damenglong bus station between 6.40 am and 2 pm.

Menghan

Menghan (Gao En Bang) lies on the Mekong south-east of Jinghong. Half the reason for going here is the boat ride down the Mekong; the other half is the boat ride back. Well, there is some Dai village life to watch – a market, temple and ferry on the other side of the river. Keep your eyes peeled for a glimpse of the Crim, a monster in the Mekong which is said to devour cattle and people; an explorer called Baber described it less vividly as a blanket fish.

There's a *Zhaodai Suo (Guest House)* on the edge of the village. Walk up the hill from the boat and turn right at the crossroads; keep walking for another two km until you see a couple of ponds on your left. The guest house is on your right in a large yard, a few metres further down the road. Beds cost Y5 per person. There's a restaurant on the same street, about 100 metres before the guest house.

Getting There Until the road is resurrected, the only way to get to Menghan is the boat from Jinghong. The boat leaves daily at 8 am from the pier below the bridge in Jinghong. The pier is reached via a cobbled road which branches off to the right about 20 metres before the bridge. Mornings are cold on the river so take some warm clothing. Tickets cost Y2.2 and the trip lasts about 1½ hours going downstream and three hours for the return upstream. The captain does some fancy manoeuvering to make a couple of stops en route. The return boat leaves at 1 pm. Berths are available for Y2.50 for a day trip or an overnight. Some locals take their bikes, which they lash to the railings.

A Frenchman had his money stolen in Menghan by a kid from Canton who had been travelling with him for several days. When the Frenchman went to the shower, the Canton kid escaped with Y2000 FEC. The police assumed he'd taken one of the roads to the border. I heard vague reports about individuals from other parts of China who occasionally surfaced in this region either to escape across the border region or to buy *da yan* ('big smoke').

Back in 1981, border guards near Menghan were amazed to see a raft with a foreigner perched on top rushing down the river towards them. After pursuing and intercepting the raft, they discovered that the foreigner was a Canadian intent on floating into Thailand. The Canadian was reprimanded, packed off to his embassy in Beijing and turned loose again. Within a month, mystified Chinese security guards picked up the same man on the Sichuan-Tibet borders and had him deported.

The attraction, of course, was the Golden Triangle, the famous opium-growing area on the northern borders of Burma, Thailand and Laos which is a major source of heroin.

Although the Chinese border guards don't always shoot on sight, there is firm evidence that plenty of bandits, militia or similar types on either side of the Mekong beyond the Chinese border do shoot. It is not clever to play around on the borders of the Golden Triangle.

Mengyang

Mengyang is 34 km east of Jinghong on the road to Simao. It's a centre for the Hani, Lahu and Floral-Belt Dai (there are several different types of Dai). Chinese tourists stop here to see a banyan tree shaped like an elephant.

From Mengyang it's another 19 km to Jinuo, which is home base for the Jinuo minority. One traveller reported that the Jinuo were unfriendly, so you'll probably have to stay in Mengyang. Some minorities dislike being touristed and if this is the case with the Jinuo, they should be left alone.

The Jinuo, sometimes known as the Youle, were officially 'discovered' as a minority in 1979. The women wear a white cowl, a cotton tunic with bright horizontal stripes, and a tubular black skirt. Ear-lobe decoration is an elaborate custom – the larger the hole and the more flowers it can contain the better. The teeth are sometimes painted black with the sap of the lacquer tree which serves the dual dental purpose of beautifying the mouth and preventing tooth decay or halitosis. Previously, the Jinuo lived in long-houses with as many as 27 families occupying rooms on either side of the central corridor. Each family had its own hearth, but the oldest man owned the largest hearth, which was the first at the door. Long-houses are rarely used now and it looks like the Jinuo are quickly losing their distinctive way of life.

THE NORTH AND NORTH-WEST

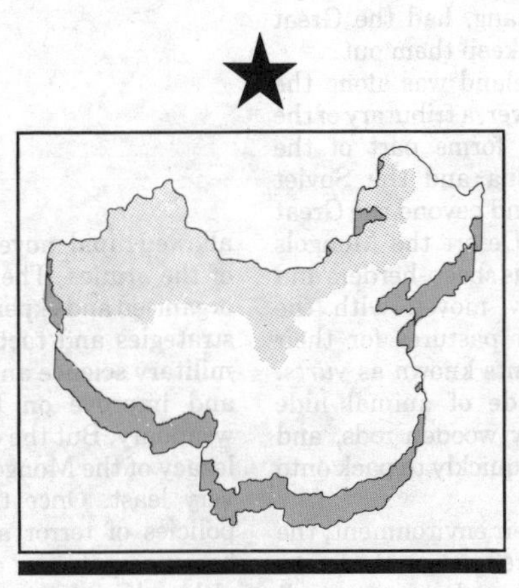

Inner Mongolia 内蒙古

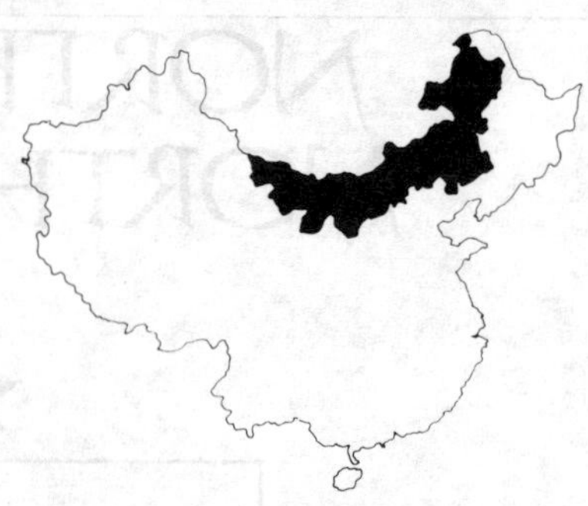

The nomadic tribes to the north of China have always been a problem for China's rulers. The first emperor of the Qin Dynasty, Qin Shihuang, had the Great Wall built simply to keep them out.

The Mongol homeland was along the banks of the Onon River, a tributary of the Amur, which today forms part of the border between China and the Soviet Union. In the grassland beyond the Great Wall and the Gobi Desert the Mongols endured a rough life as sheep-herders and horse-breeders. They moved with the seasons in search of pastures for their animals, living in tents known as *yurts*. The yurts were made of animal hide usually supported by wooden rods, and could be taken apart quickly to pack onto wagons.

At the mercy of their environment, the Mongols based their religion on the forces of nature: moon, sun and stars were all revered, as were the rivers. The gods were virtually infinite in number, signifying a universal supernatural presence; the Mongol priests could speak to the gods and communicate their orders to the tribal chief, the Khan. The story goes that Genghis Khan overcame the power of the priests by allowing one to be killed for alleging the disloyalty of the Khan's brother – a calculated act of sacrilege which proclaimed the Khan's absolute power.

The Mongols were united by Genghis Khan after 20 years of warfare; by the year 1206 all opposition to his rule among the tribes had surrendered or been wiped out and the Mongol armies stood ready to invade China. Not only did the Mongol horde conquer China, they went on to conquer most of the known world, founding an empire which stretched from Burma to Russia.

It was an empire won on horseback; the entire Mongol army was cavalry and this allowed rapid movement and deployment of the armies. The Mongols were highly organised and expert at planning complex strategies and tactics. They excelled in military science and were quick to adopt and improve on Persian and Chinese weaponry. But the cultural and scientific legacy of the Mongols was meagre, at the very least. Once they abandoned their policies of terror and destruction, they became patrons of science and art, although not practitioners. Under the influence of the people they had conquered, they also adopted the local religions – mainly Buddhism and Islam.

The Mongol conquest of China was slow, delayed by campaigns in the west and by internal strife. Secure behind their Great Wall, the Chinese rulers had little inkling of the fury the Mongols would unleash in 1211, when the invasion of China began. For two years the Great Wall deterred them, but it was eventually penetrated through a 27-km gorge which led to the north Chinese plains. In 1215 a Chinese general went over to the Mongols and led them into Beijing. Nevertheless, the Chinese stubbornly held out, and the war in China was placed under the command of one of Genghis's generals so the Khan could turn his attention to the west.

Despite the death of Genghis Khan in 1227, the Mongols lost none of their vigour. The empire had been divided up by Genghis into separate domains, each

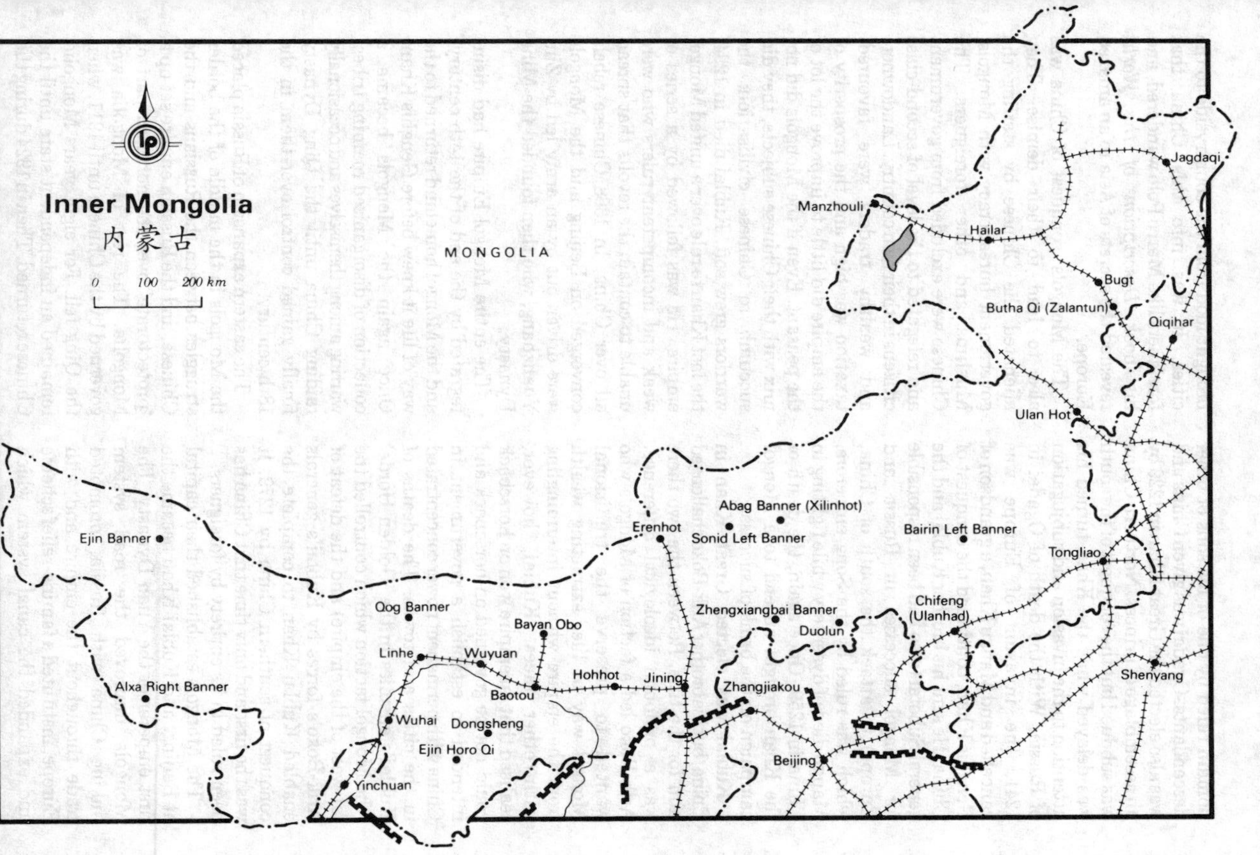
Inner Mongolia
内蒙古
0
100
200 km
MONGOLIA
Manzhouli
Hailar
Jagdaqi
Bugt
Butha Qi (Zalantun)
Qiqihar
Ulan Hot
Abag Banner (Xilinhot)
Erenhot
Sonid Left Banner
Bairin Left Banner
Ejin Banner
Tongliao
Qog Banner
Zhengxiangbai Banner
Chifeng
(Ulanhad)
Bayan Obo
Duolun
Linhe
Wuyuan
Hohhot
Jining
Shenyang
Alxa Right Banner
Baotou
Zhangjiakou
Wuhai
Dongsheng
Ejin Horo Qi
Beijing
Yinchuan

domain ruled by one of his sons or other descendants. Ogadai was given China and was also elected the Great Khan in 1229 by an assemblage of princes. Northern China was subdued but the conquest of the south was delayed while the Khan turned his attention to the invasion and subjugation of Russia. With the death of Ogadai in 1241, the invasion of Europe was cancelled and Mangu Khan, a grandson of Genghis Khan, continued the conquest of China. He sent his brother Kublai and the general Subotai (who had been responsible for Mongol successes in Russia and Europe) to attack the south of China, which was ruled by the Song emperors. Mangu died of dysentery while fighting in China in 1259. Once again, the death of the Khan brought an end to a Mongol campaign on the brink of success.

Kublai was elected Great Khan in China, but his brother Arik-Boko challenged him for the title. Between the two there was a profound ideological difference. Arik-Boko led a faction of Mongols who wanted to preserve the traditional Mongol way of life, extracting wealth from the empire without intermingling with other races. Kublai, however, realised that an empire won on horseback could not be governed on horseback and intended to establish a government in China with permanent power concentrated in the cities and towns. The deaths of Kublai's enemies in the 'Golden Horde' (the Mongol faction which controlled the far west of the empire) and the defeat of Arik-Boko's forces by Kublai's generals enabled Kublai Khan to complete the conquest of southern China by 1279. It was the first and only time that China has been ruled in its entirety by foreigners.

The Mongols established their capital at Beijing, and Kublai Khan became the first emperor of the Yuan Dynasty. The Mongols improved the road system linking China with Russia, promoted trade throughout the empire and with Europe, instituted a famine-relief scheme and expanded the canal system which brought food from the countryside to the cities. It was into this China that foreigners like Marco Polo wandered, and his book *Description of the World* revealed the secrets of Asia to an amazed Europe.

The Mongols' conquest of China was also to lead to their demise. They alienated the Chinese by staffing the government bureaucracy with Mongols, Muslims and other foreigners. The Chinese were excluded from government and relegated to the level of second-class citizens in their own country. Landowners and wealthy traders were favoured, taxation was high and the prosperity of the empire did little to improve the lot of the peasant. Even if the Mongols did not mix with their Chinese subjects, they did succumb to Chinese civilisation: the warriors grew soft. Kublai died in 1294, the last Khan to rule over a united Mongol empire. He was followed by a series of weak and incompetent rulers who were unable to contain the revolts that spread all over China. In 1368 Chinese rebels converged on Beijing and the Mongols were driven out by an army led by Zhu Yuanzhang, who then founded the Ming Dynasty.

The entire Mongol Empire had disintegrated by the end of the 14th century, and the Mongol homeland returned to the way of life it knew before Genghis Khan. Once again the Mongols became a collection of disorganised roaming tribes, warring among themselves and occasionally raiding China until the Qing Dynasty finally gained control over them in the 18th century.

The eastern expansion of Russia placed the Mongols in the middle of the border struggles between the Russians and the Chinese, and the Russian empire set up a 'protectorate' over the northern part of Mongolia. The rest of Mongolia was governed by the Chinese until 1911, when the Qing fell. For eight years Mongolia remained an independent state until the Chinese returned. Then in 1924 during the

Russian Civil War the Red Army pursued White Russian leaders to Urga (now Ulan Bator), where they helped create the Mongolian People's Republic by ousting the lama priesthood and the Mongol princes. The new republic has remained very much under Soviet domination.

During the war between China and Japan in the 1930s and 1940s, parts of what is now Inner Mongolia were occupied by the Japanese, and Communist guerrillas also operated there. In 1936 Mao Zedong told Edgar Snow in Yanan:

> As for Inner Mongolia, which is populated by both Chinese and Mongolians, we will struggle to drive Japan from there and help Inner Mongolia to establish an autonomous state . . . when the people's revolution has been victorious in China, the Outer Mongolian republic will automatically become part of the Chinese federation, at its own will.

But that was not to be. In 1945 Stalin extracted full recognition of the independence of Outer Mongolia from Chiang Kaishek when the two signed an anti-Japanese Sino-Soviet alliance. Two years later, with the resumption of the civil war in China, the Chinese Communists designated what was left to China of the Mongol territories as the 'Autonomous Region of Inner Mongolia'. With the Communist victory in 1949, Outer Mongolia did not join the People's Republic as Mao had said it would. The region remained under Soviet control.

About 1½ million people live in the Mongolian People's Republic (Outer Mongolia). Inner Mongolia stretches across half of northern China and is inhabited by almost 19 million people. About two million of these are Mongols, a predominantly Buddhist people with some Muslims among them. The rest of the population is made up of about 16 million Han Chinese (concentrated in Baotou and Hohhot) and minority Huis, Manchus, Daurs and Ewenkis. The Mongolians are very much a minority in their own land.

Since 1949 the Chinese have followed a policy of assimilation of the Mongols. The Chinese language became a compulsory subject in schools, the populace was organised into sheep-farming co-ops and communes, and new railways and roads brought in Chinese settlers. Some of the old nomadic spirit can still be seen at the annual Nadam Fair, held at various grasslands locations sometime between mid-July and early August. The fair has its origins in the ancient Obo-worshipping Festival (an *obo* is a pile of stones with a hollow space for offerings – a kind of shaman shrine). The Mongolian clans make a beeline for the fairs on any form of transport they can muster, and create an impromptu yurt city. The event is a splash of colour if you can catch up with it, with competition archery, wrestling and horsemanship – sports the Mongolians excel at, having learned them at an early age. There's also occasional camel racing. Prizes vary from a goat to a fully-equipped horse. There are signs that the fair may be staged more often with the addition of shooting, motorcycling, storytelling, dancing and more trading.

Much of the Inner Mongolia region comprises vast natural grazing land. The economy is based on stock breeding of cattle, sheep, horses and camels, and the region is the main source of tanned hides, wool and dairy products for China. The Greater Hinggan range makes up about one-sixth of the country's forests and is an important source of timber and paper pulp. The region is also rich in mineral reserves, particularly coal and iron ore. As it borders the Soviet Union, it is of paramount military importance to the Chinese.

The Mongolians are a fragmented race scattered throughout China's north-eastern provinces, as well as through Qinghai and Xinjiang. Their 'Inner Mongolia Autonomous Region' enjoys little or no autonomy at all. Outer Mongolia, ostensibly an independent nation, is dominated by the Soviet Union.

Then there's a strange little piece of land to the north-west of Outer Mongolia called the Tuva Autonomous Soviet Socialist Republic. Originally called Tannu Tuva, it emerged as a semi-autonomous Mongolian state in 1926, and was renamed in 1945. (A smattering of Chinese have also ended up on the wrong side of the borders-in-triplicate; by a Beijing count there are 10,000 ethnic Chinese residing in Outer Mongolia, 6000 of them in Ulan Bator. Back in mid-1983 more than 600 were suddenly expelled by the Mongolian government and sent to China.)

Excessive fragmentation has led to a few absurdities; the Mongolian areas remain one of the biggest headaches for cartographers. It was not until 1962 that the border with Outer Mongolia was finally settled, though parts of the far north-east were disputed by the Soviet Union. Then in 1969 the Chinese carved up Inner Mongolia and donated bits of it to other provinces – they were reinstated in 1979. The Chinese seem sufficiently confident about the assimilation of the Mongols to talk about historical absurdities like 'Genghis Khan's Chinese armies' or the 'minority assistance in building the Great Wall'.

In 1981 when an Italian film crew rented the courtyard of Beijing's Forbidden City as a Marco Polo film location (at a reported cost of US$4000 a day – the Chinese originally wanted US$10,000 a day), a splendid assembly of horses and soldiers was laid on, the soldiers portrayed by PLA troops. The Chinese claimed the money was secondary and that historical accuracy was the thing at stake. However, they didn't like the Mongols being depicted as hated by the Song Dynasty Chinese they overran – after all, that conflicts with the Communist claim that China's minorities get along famously with the Han majority. It's a rather odd claim since the Great Wall was built to keep out the minorities (referred to then less politely as 'barbarians'). More predictably, the Chinese vetoed some seduction scenes involving Chinese concubines and Mongol lechers.

Climate

Inner Mongolia is bleak. Siberian blizzards and cold currents rake the plains in winter – forget it! In winter you'll even witness the curious phenomenon of snow on the desert sand dunes. Summer (June to August) brings pleasant temperatures, but the region is prone to rainfall. May to September is feasible, but pack warm clothing for spring or autumn.

HOHHOT 呼和浩特

Hohhot (also spelt huhehaote or huhehot) became the capital of Inner Mongolia in 1952, serving as the administrative and educational centre. It was founded in the 16th century and, like the other towns, grew around its temples and lamaseries, now in ruins. Hide and wool industries are the mainstay, backed up by machine-building, a sugar refinery, fertilisation plants, a diesel-engine factory and iron and steel production. The population is around 700,000 – more than a million if the outlying areas are included.

Information

CITS (tel 24494) is in the Nei Menggu Fandian (Inner Mongolia Guest House).

CITS turns on the culture in Hohhot, from the grasslands tour to the equestrian displays at the horse-racing ground. Horse-racing, polo and stunt riding are put on for large tour groups, if you latch onto one somehow – otherwise they take place only on rare festive occasions. Likewise with song and dance soirées. Check out local entertainment, such as events at the Red Theatre near the CAAC office. Other things you might be able to wrangle out of CITS if combining in-town sights with a grasslands sortie are a visit to the carpet works, or to the underground tunnelling system built to evacuate Hohhot residents to the Daqing Mountains in the event of a Russian bear hug. Make

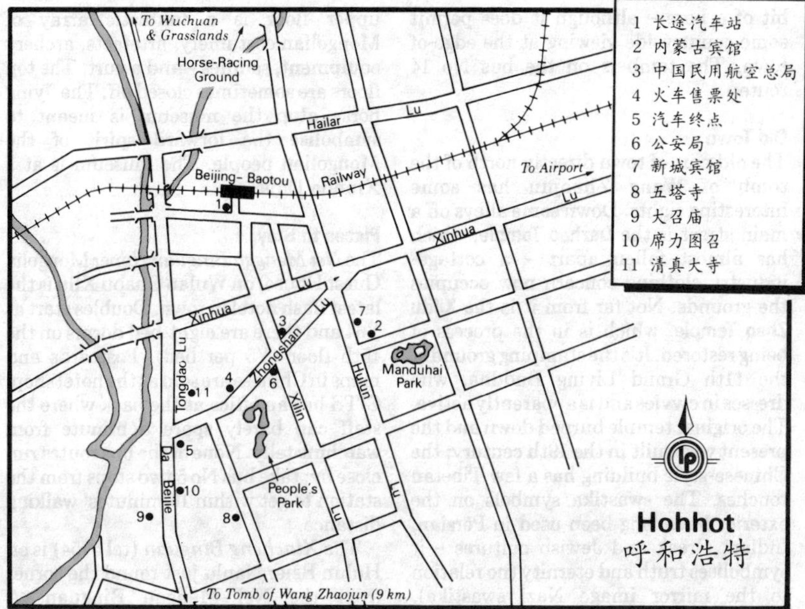

1 Long-distance Bus Station
2 Nei Menggu Fandian/CITS
3 CAAC
4 Advance Rail Ticket Office
5 Local Bus Terminus
6 Public Security
7 Xincheng Binguan
8 Five Pagoda Temple (Wutasi)
9 Dazhao Temple
10 Xilitu Zhao Temple
11 The Great Mosque

all your deals before you set off for the grasslands – it's no use trying to bargain once you get going.

Public Security is in the vicinity of the People's Park, near the corner of Zhongshan Lu and Xilin Lu.

CAAC (tel 4103) is diagonally opposite the People's Park at 6 Zhongshan Donglu. Hohhot airport is about 15 km east of the city.

Things to See

Don't be in any great hurry to see the historic vestiges of the city. They are either in bad shape, uninteresting, or inaccessible.

Wutazhao (Five-Pagoda Temple)

This miniaturised structure dating back to 1740 is now bereft of its temple, leaving the Five Pagodas standing on a rectangular block. The pagodas are built with glazed bricks and are inscribed in Mongolian, Sanskrit and Tibetan. Cut into niches are small Buddhist figures; around the back is a screen wall with an astronomical chart inscribed in Mongolian. The Five Pagodas are on the bus No 1 route.

Tomb of Wang Zhaojun

The tomb of this Han Dynasty concubine to Emperor Yuandi (1st century BC) is a bit of a bore – although it does permit some countryside viewing at the edge of town. The tomb is on the bus No 14 route.

Old Town

The old part of town directly north of the tomb of Wang Zhaojun has some interesting sights. Down some alleys off a main street is the **Dazhao Temple**, which has almost fallen apart – a cottage-industry clothing concern now occupies the grounds. Not far from it is the **Xilitu Zhao Temple**, which is in the process of being restored. It's the stamping ground of the 11th Grand Living Buddha, who dresses in civvies and is apparently active. The original temple burned down and the present was built in the 19th century; the Chinese-style building has a few Tibetan touches. The swastika symbols on the exterior have long been used in Persian, Indian, Greek and Jewish cultures – it symbolises truth and eternity (no relation to the mirror image Nazi swastika). Further north of Xilitu Zhao is **The Great Mosque**, which is not so great and is in sad shape. It dates to the Qing Dynasty, with later expansions.

These temples are incidentals; the main action is on the streets. Around the area of the Dazhao Temple are some fascinating adobe houses, low and squat with decorated glass windows. Markets in Hohhot are brisk – in summer at least. Recommended is the north-south strip running from west of the bus station (Tongdao Lu) as far as the two temples. The busy corner of Tongdao Lu and Xinhua Lu is the place for housewares and storytelling. A food market with a courtyard entrance can be found near the Museum of Inner Mongolia. There's another market on the east side of People's Park.

Museum of Inner Mongolia

Definitely worth a visit and well presented. On the lower floor is a large mammoth skeleton dug out of a coal mine; on the upper floor is a fantastic array of Mongolian costumery, artefacts, archery equipment, saddles – and a yurt. The top floors are sometimes closed off. The flying horse atop the museum is meant to symbolise the forward spirit of the Mongolian people. The museum is at 1 Xinhua Dajie.

Places to Stay

The *Nei Menggu Binguan* (Inner Mongolia Guest House) on Wulan Chabu Xilu is the latest flash hotel in town. Doubles start at Y64 and there are eight-bed dorms on the 15th floor (Y5 per bed). Postcards and maps in Chinese are sold at the hotel shop. CITS has an office at the back where the staff can barely spare a minute from watching telly. None of the bus routes run close by; take bus No 5 two stops from the station to get within 10 minutes' walking distance.

The *Xincheng Binguan* (tel 5754) is on Hulun Beier Nanlu just round the corner from the Nei Menggu Binguan. A subterranean triple in Block 9 costs Y4 per bed – at that price, who's complaining if it feels like detention? Doubles are Y20.

Places to Eat

The *Fenglin Fandian*, south of the Xilitu Zhao Temple and opposite the public toilets, is a clean, friendly restaurant. If you feel unadventurous there's always the expensive menu in the boring dining-lands of the *Nei Menggu Guest House*. Outside it's better to go snack-hunting. Yoghurt in ceramic flasks and some tasty baked goods can be found in the markets scattered around town. There's a dumpling shop (with a red front) next door to the Xilitu Zhao Temple.

Shopping

For minority handicrafts there's a store attached to the Hohhot Guest House, and you can case the Department Store in town. If you want a wider selection pay a visit to the Minority Handicraft Factory at the south side of town on the bus No 1 route. It has a retail shop for tour visits. Wares include inlaid knife and chopstick sets, daggers, boots, embroidered shoes, costumes, brassware, blankets and curios.

Getting There & Away

Air There are flights between Hohhot and Beijing (Y72), Baotou (Y166), Chifeng (Y119), Hailar (Y296), Tongliao (Y181), Xilinhot (Y96). One of the Beijing-bound planes stops off at Chifeng and Tongliao.

Bus There are sporadic bus connections between Hohhot, Datong and Baotou. A direct bus to Dongsheng at 7 am takes six hours. Another early-morning bus runs to Dongsheng via Baotou East (Dong Zhan) and takes eight hours.

Rail Hohhot is on the Beijing-Lanzhou railway line that cuts a long loop through Inner Mongolia; about 2½ hours out of Beijing you'll pass fragments of the Great Wall. On the fastest trains Beijing-Hohhot is a 12-hour trip, Datong-Hohhot is five hours, Baotou-Hohhot is three hours, Yinchuan-Hohhot is 12 hours. It's possible to buy one ticket from Beijing to Lanzhou, get off and have a look at each town and continue on with the same ticket. Train frequency is highest between Hohhot and Beijing, lower between Yinchuan and Hohhot, and very low between Lanzhou and Yinchuan, so you could be a bit pushed for time if you try to cover all these places on one ticket. There are low-frequency connections between Taiyuan and Datong, where a connection to Hohhot can be made.

Cigarette Packet with Mongolian Script

Getting Around

Hohhot is reasonably small and you can go a long way on a pair of wheels, weather permitting. Bikes can be hired at both the Xincheng and Nei Menggu guest houses, and there are numerous bike stalls along the main road to the left of the station. Prices average Y0.50 per hour, Y2 for half a day, and Y4.5 for the whole day. Passport or similar I.D. is required.

You can get a detailed city map (in Chinese only), which includes surrounding regions, from the Nei Menggu Guest House. Check with CITS or the hotel staff for bus numbers for your proposed route. Bus No 1 runs from the railway station to the old part of the city in the south-west corner.

AROUND HOHHOT

About 15 km west of Hohhot, the Sino-Tibetan monastery **Wusutuzhao** is hardly worth looking at although the surrounding arid landscape is spectacular. About 20 km east of Hohhot, along the airport road, is the topless **Wanbuhuayanjing Pagoda**, a seven-storey octagonal tower built with bricks and wood. It dates from the Liao Dynasty (10th to 12th centuries). The pagoda can be reached by a half-hour suburban train ride.

THE GRASSLANDS 草原

At present there are three officially open grasslands. About 90 km north of Hohhot (over the Daqing Mountains, through Wuchuan County, veer left) is Ulantuge Commune, alias Wulantuge, or even

Ulantoke. In a similar direction, but veering right, is Baiyunhesha Grassland (Baiyinhushao) in Siziwang Banner, about 180 km from Hohhot (a 'Banner' is a tribal county area). There is a third grassland, Huitengxile, about 120 km west of Hohhot. It is managed by China Youth Travel Service, whose office is at 9 Zhongshan Donglu, Hohhot.

Tours Tours to the grasslands are organised by the Hohhot CITS, which has a stable of vehicles ranging from jeeps to buses to take you out there. The rules of the game – negotiate! Cashing in on the magic draw of 'Mongolia' is the name of the game here, and the less you bargain the bigger the rip off. Most of Hohhot's population is Han Chinese. The Mongolians are out on the grasslands, supposedly roaming around on their horses or drinking cream tea (a mixture of camel's milk and salt) in their yurts. For pure theatre, nothing beats the CITS Grasslands Tour.

At present there are eight tour packages on offer; the shortest takes one day, the longest three days. A one-day tour to Ulantuge (including transport, yurt accommodation, guide and interpreter) will cost between Y60 and Y270 a person, depending on the size of your group and how much bargaining power you can apply. For a group of 21 people you'd be looking at Y60 per person, for a group of 10 people Y71 per person, and all on your lonesome would be Y270. Hong Kongers arrive in droves and pay about 10% less – so you should be able to negotiate a student rate.

As for visions of the descendants of the mighty Khan riding the endless plains, the herds of wild horses, the remnants of Xanadu – make sure you worm a detailed itinerary out of CITS so you can work out if it's worth the price. The 'real' country for Mongolians is closer to the border further north. Grasslands and yurt dwellings can be seen in other parts of China – in Xinjiang for example. Also, deprived of rain for a week or so, the verdant pasturelands can turn a shrivelled shade of yellow. Take warm, windproof clothing – there's a considerable wind-chill factor even at the height of summer.

Being There Here's a two-day itinerary to give you some idea of the picnics and outings in Inner Mongolia.

Day 1 2.30 pm. We discover the first day is half over – the tour is by calendar days. After a three-hour drive over the mountains to the grasslands plateau we arrive at Ulantuge commune. The major industry here seems to be shepherding tourists. It's the first commune from Hohhot, so lots of groups are processed through this meat-works. On arrival a woman pops out of a door in Mongolian costume to greet us (still, however, wearing slacks underneath and a tell-tale pair of tennis shoes). Dinner is very good – baozi and meat dishes. The guide motions toward the yurt compound at the edge of town. These are on fixed brick and concrete foundations with 75-watt lightbulbs dangling from each yurt-hole. Only for tourists – the natives live in sensibly thick-walled brick structures. The outhouse is primitive – I'm wondering if the joke is on us, and whether the locals are sitting on porcelain models with flushers. A clammy damp cold permeates the yurts, sufficient to send an arthritic into epilepsy.

Day 2 Breakfast is at 8.30, a decidedly western hour. We take advantage of the lull to poke around – post office, school, souvenir shop. There's a large temple structure, Sino-Tibetan features, probably 18th century, with colonnade, intricate windows and doorways, devilish frescoes – but entry is barred. Part of the complex around it has been turned into a dining hall for receiving the likes of us. At breakfast I ask the guide (who sits at a separate table with the driver) a few questions in relation to the tourist industry which he either ignores, evades, or pretends not to understand. Back at the yurts are two ruddy-cheeked gentlemen waiting with two moth-eaten animals. The ruddy complexion comes from wind chill – the animals have not weathered it so well. One is, I guess you might call it, yes, a horse. The other is the worst-looking excuse for a camel I've seen. I mean, camels are ugly, but this one had just about fallen apart. It's strictly a mounted picture-taking session; the attendants keep these pathetic specimens on leashes, explaining that they're too dangerous to be ridden solo.

At 9.30 am the driver whips over the grasslands – very nice, peaceful, dirt paths; it's reassuring to see some real grass in China. Hong Kongers get most enthralled about this – there isn't too much of the stuff around Kowloon. We stop to observe a flock of sheep – the shepherd poses for photos. Then, the highlight of the tour, a visit to a typical Mongolian family. They live in a three-room brick dwelling, and there, smack on the wall as you enter, is a giant poster of a koala (New South Wales Tourist Authority) which confirms my impression that perhaps I'd be better off on an Australian sheep farm. The typical family is wearing standard Han ration clothing (did we catch them with their pants down?) but they bring out Mongolian garb for dress-up photo-sessions – for us to dress up, that is. They've obviously given up. Parked out the back is their form of transport – bicycles. It puzzles me why we are brought here when there are yurt dwellers in the area. The only explanation I can think of is that they're further out from the Ulantuge commune, and the driver is too lazy or has been given other directions. Or perhaps any real Mongolian wants nothing to do with CITS – a view with which I can sympathise.

Motoring off again, we visit an *obo*, a pile of stones in the middle of nowhere. When nomads used to gather for mid-May festivals, each would bring a stone and lay it here. We go back to Ulantuge for a banquet-style lunch; a sheep is slaughtered and barbecued for a surcharge. After lunch, the guide announces that it's time for *xiuxi* – the rest period will be 2½ hours. We wave goodbye to the woman near the yurt compound (as she struggles to get into her Mongolian robes in time), and head back for Hohhot. We arrive around 4.30 that afternoon; the tour is supposed to last until 6 pm and there is a filler of sights around town that I've already seen and which don't require a guide.

In sum, the guides are lethargic and unhelpful; your real time on the grasslands amounts to about two hours, plus the drive there and back. You spend a lot of time sleeping, eating, waiting and taking pictures of each other. The three- and four-day itineraries are probably much the same, with feeble archery or song and dance routines thrown in. The best part of the trip is, unexpectedly, the food – the meals were banquet-size and tasty, something that the individual traveller is not used to.

I suppose you could try to lose your guides; horse-drawn carts seem to be a common form of transport on the communes, and of course the grassland is perfect horse country – though this suggestion would probably horrify CITS. (A Hohhot tourist leaflet shows foreigners riding in a decorated camel cart with suspension and truck tyres.) Anyway, even the small Mongolian horse is being phased out – herdsmen can now purchase motorcycles (preferred over bicycles because of substantial wind force), and helicopters and light aircraft are used to round up steers and spot grazing herds.

I met a German who'd rented a bike in Hohhot and pedalled against headwinds to one of the tourist grasslands. Helpful truckers had compassionately given him lifts and he negotiated a reasonable price for his well-earned rest in a tourist yurt.

BAOTOU 包头

The largest city in Inner Mongolia lies on the northernmost reaches of the Huang He (Yellow River), to the west of Hohhot. Previously set in an area of under-developed grasslands inhabited by the Mongols, the town underwent a radical change when the Communists came to power in 1949. In the next decade, an old 1923 railway line linking the town with Beijing was extended south-east to Yinchuan, and roads were constructed to facilitate access to the region's iron, coal and other mineral deposits. Today, Baotou is an industrial city of around 800,000 people.

If you like steel stories, you might join a CITS tour of the Baotou Iron & Steel Company which was supervised by the Soviets until their exit in 1960. The original plan foresaw use of ore from Bayan Obo (about 140 km further north). Unfortunately, the local ore couldn't make the grade and the company now imports the stuff from Australia.

Baotou is a huge town; 20 km of urban sprawl separate the eastern and western parts of the city. The station for the western section is Baotou Zhan; for the eastern section it's Baotou Dong Zhan. A minibus from Baotou to Hohhot is Y5.60 for the three hour trip.

Places to Stay & Eat

If you want to devote time to Baotou, get off at Baotou Zhan. Bus No 1 drops you off close to *Baotou Guest House (Baotou Binguan)* on Kunqu Gangtie Dajie. Doubles cost Y9. Both CITS and PSB are in the hotel compound. CITS (tel 24615) has some excellent English speakers and can provide maps. Bus No 10 stops close to the Baotou Binguan and shuttles between the western and eastern sections of Baotou in 45 minutes.

If you are not staying long, but are stopping to see Wudang Zhao Temple or Genghis Khan's Tomb near Dongsheng, get off at Baotou Dong Zhan. The *Dong He Binguan*, which charges Y18 for a double, is about a 15-minute walk (or take bus No 5) up the street in front of the station. There's a convenient, run-down hostel on the right of the square in front of the station. Triples cost Y15. It may be noisy at night, but the bus station (for

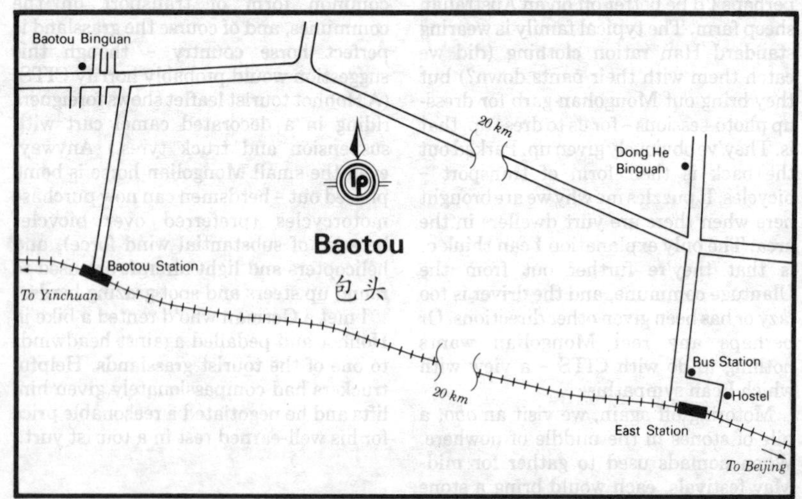

Wudang Zhao Temple, Dongsheng and Hohhot) is opposite the railway station.

AROUND BAOTOU

Wudang Zhao Monastery

The main tourist attraction is the large Wudang Zhao Monastery about 2½ hours from the city by bus. This monastery of the Gelukpa (Yellow Sect) of Tibetan Buddhism was built around 1749 in typical Tibetan style with flat-roofed buildings. It once housed 1200 monks. The ashes of seven reincarnations of the monastery's Living Buddha are kept in a special hall. Today all religious activity is restricted to a handful of pilgrims and dispirited doorkeeper monks who take the Y0.50 admission fee.

For the crowds of day-tripping, photo-clicking, screaming Han Chinese this is no place for religion. The surrounding hillsides are carpeted with hundreds of smashed bottles and piles of garbage. Try and walk into the hills away from the pandemonium; the site has a peculiar strength in its secretive, brooding atmosphere.

Bus No 7 leaves for the monastery at 7 am from the bus station at Baotou Dong Zhan. To make sure of a seat, it's best to buy tickets (Y1.40) the evening before. Only the 7 am bus goes all the way to the monastery; the other departures stop about 15 km before it, so you'd be left with some hitching or a long walk. The clapped-out bus soon leaves the sealed road and runs along a gravel riverbed. There is something of a building boom in progress and the gravel is much in demand by local builders, so the road-cum-riverbed has some diabolical holes. The bus drops you off about one km below the monastery.

For the return trip, catch the same bus from the same place at 4 pm (check with the driver when you arrive). You may also be able to get a lift back with other vehicles from the car park in front of the monastery.

There's a basic dorm with beds for Y3 on the west side of the monastery, and a slightly better deal for Y5 on the east side. CITS organises tours, but you can easily manage on your own. Take a flashlight if you want to see anything inside the monastery.

BAYAN OBO 白云鄂博

About 150 to 200 km north of Baotou is Bayan Obo, an iron-ore centre. The PSB there can't imagine what visitors are after, but you are tolerated as long as you stay away from the iron-ore mine. The train spends 5½ hours crawling between Baotou and Bayan Obo. Train No 681 leaves Baotou Dong Zhan at 5.09 pm. At Bayan Obo the bus drops you off at the local *binguan*. During the day you can explore the one street in the town. To return to Baotou, take the 6.20 am bus from the *binguan* to the station for the train leaving at 7 am. End of the Great Iron Ore Adventure. One of the western tour companies (China Passage) organises bicycle tours which make the circular trip Hohhot-Bayan Obo-Baotou-Hohhot.

DONGSHENG 东胜

Dongsheng lies south of Baotou and serves as a staging post for Ejin Horo Qi, the site of Genghis Khan's mausoleum. Buses leave in the morning from the bus station at Baotou Dong Zhan and take three hours to get to Dongsheng. There are also direct bus connections between Dongsheng and Hohhot.

The bus usually drops you off at the Dongsheng bus station. The small town has one main street. Walk out of the bus station and turn right; continue for 100 metres before joining the main street at a crossroads.

There are at least two hotels for foreigners. The *Wai Mao Binguan* is a 100-metre walk to the right of this junction on the opposite side of the road. Chinese on conference junkets and groups of foreign tourists often book out the small hotel, but independent travellers are quoted prices between Y4 and Y26 per person, depending on the room. The *Yimeng Binguan* is 150 metres to the left of the junction on the same side of the road. This is a much larger hotel with triples at Y5 per person. The receptionists seemed mighty suspicious of foreigners, and each time I returned to the hotel there was a handwritten note from the PSB requesting the name of my school, wife, business, etc – plenty of room for invention. The receptionists can put a call through to the man from CITS, who seems ill-informed about local transport – a local teacher acts as interpreter.

The best restaurant in town is the *Minzu Canting*. It's diagonally opposite the Yimeng Binguan, just past the first crossroads to the right. Restaurants on the bus station street mostly serve lashings of grease best left for the packs of ragged kids who frequent the place.

Genghis Khan's Mausoleum

Buses to Ejin Horo Qi leave Dongsheng bus station at 7 am and take three hours to get to Genghis Khan mausoleum (Cheng Jisi Han Lingyuan), but buy tickets the day before if you want to avoid hassles. It took me several attempts before I got onto a bus. The first day, the road was washed out by a storm; the second day was spent waiting for the floodwater to drop; on the third day, I arrived at 6.30 am to be told there were no more tickets. The interior of the bus station contained huge portraits of Mao, Lenin & Co which presided in the gloom over crowds of jostling passengers being herded into pens like cattle. Acting on a hunch, I watched from the entrance to the bus station while the bus was boarded inside the station in semi-orderly fashion by passengers with tickets. As soon as the bus pulled out of the entrance, it stopped and loaded on a whole group of us – extra pocket money for the driver! The bus was then packed solid, but even more passengers were added en route until the last two (one wearing a T-shirt saying 'optimist') were squeezed in head-first through the driver's window.

In 1954 what are said to be the ashes of the Khan were brought back from Qinghai (where they had been taken to prevent them from falling into the hands of the Japanese), and a large Mongolian-style mausoleum was built at Ejin Horo Qi. The Cultural Revolution did enough damage to keep the renovators busy for eight years and the result looks new. Interestingly enough, the cult of Genghis Khan has picked up again in Inner Mongolia today. Ceremonies are held four times a year at the mausoleum to honour his memory. Butter lamps are lit, *khadas* (ritual scarves) presented and whole cooked sheep piled high before the Khan's stone statue while chanting is performed by Mongolian monks and specially chosen elders from the Daur nationality.

The mausoleum has an impressive exterior consisting of three brightly coloured ceramic 'yurts' connected by halls. After puffing up the flights of stairs to the entrance, you pay a Y1 admission fee and have to register in the book. Leaflets are on sale for Y1. Outside, a photographer offers a mangy horse and Mongolian robes in case you want to pose as the Great Khan.

Inside are displays of Genghis Khan's martial gear and statue. Various yurts contain the biers of Genghis and his close relatives. The huge frescoes around the walls are done in cartoon style to depict important stages in the Khan's rise to mega-stardom – all that's missing are bubble captions with 'pow' or 'zap'. Even though I made it to the mausoleum before the 11 am busloads of day-trippers, the place seemed far too tacky.

The local hostel has erected metal-frame 'tourist' yurts close to the flights of steps leading to the mausoleum entrance. Yurts cost Y7 per person per night. Food is scarce, so take your own and a water bottle. Several buses run past the mausoleum to Dongsheng, so you might think it's easy to get back. Wrong! On the day I was there, at least three buses ignored all attempts to stop them. In the end, we formed a small group of Chinese and foreigners which trudged four km before hitching a ride on the back of an empty truck. When we overtook the last bus which had ignored us, nobody spared the abuse.

XANADU 宪那都

About 320 km north of Beijing, tucked away near Duolun in Inner Mongolia, are the remains of Xanadu, the great Kublai Khan's palace of legendary splendour. Marco Polo visited the Khan in the 13th century and recorded his impressions of the palace:

> There is at this place a very fine marble palace, the rooms of which are all gilt and painted with figures of men and beasts and birds, and with a variety of trees and flowers, all executed with such exquisite art that you regard them with delight and astonishment.
>
> Round this palace a wall is built enclosing a compass of 16 miles, and inside the Park there are fountains and rivers and brooks, and beautiful meadows, with all kinds of wild animals (excluding such as are of ferocious nature), which the Emperor has procured and placed there to supply food for his gerfalcons and hawks. Moreover (at a spot in the Park where there is a charming wood) he has another Palace built of cane. It is gilt all over, and most elaborately finished inside. The Lord abides at this Park of his, dwelling sometimes in the Marble Palace and sometimes in the Cane Palace for three months of the year, to wit, June, July and August; preferring this residence because it is by no means hot; in fact it is a very cool place. When the 28th day of August arrives, he takes his departure, and the Cane Palace is taken to pieces.

In the 18th century Samuel Taylor Coleridge (who never went near the place) stoked his imagination with some opium and composed 'Kubla Khan', a glowing poem about Xanadu that has been on the set menu for students of English literature ever since.

Over the centuries the deserted palace has crumbled back to dust and the site has been visited by very few foreigners. In 1986 a couple of British undergrads, Louisa Slack and William Hamilton-Dalrymple, followed Marco Polo's original route from Jerusalem to Xanadu. The palace remains are close to Duolun, which is off-limits to foreigners, so the local PSB ejected the British duo from the region but compassionately arranged their exit via the legendary site where all photography was forbidden. The PSB officers must have doubted the sanity of the foreigners, who proceeded to chant Coleridge's poem while pouring a small bottle of oil from the Holy Sepulchre in Jerusalem (the same gift Marco Polo had once brought for the Khan) onto the dilapidated site of the Khan's throne. According to the undergrads, very little now remains of Xanadu (locals call it Shang-du) and it is scheduled for clearance as a wheat prairie. Roll over Kublai!

XILINHOT (ABAGNAR QI) 锡林浩特

From all accounts, if you're interested in pursuing the topic of the disappearing Mongols this sounds like the best bet. Xilinhot is 500 km north-east of Hohhot as the crow flies. It is the headquarters of the large Xilin Gol League, which is subdivided into 10 districts and over 100 communes. The league covers an area of 172,000 square km, with a population of under a million – a quarter of whom are Mongolian. The Xilin Gol League was a centre of Mongolian nationalism in the 1930s but today the major occupation is the tending of sheep, cattle, goats, camels and horses – some five million of them. Industry is minimal, though petroleum deposits have been discovered. Ensconced in Xilinhot is the Beizimiao, a large, dilapidated lamasery in Chinese style dating from the Qing Dynasty.

The bus station in Hohhot is unwilling to sell tickets, so you'll probably be required to fly to Xilinhot from Hohhot; flights on Tuesday, Thursday and Saturday cost Y96. CITS has jeep excursions to communes 50 km and 130 km away, with overnight stops in yurts, tea-tasting and campfires. Should you strike a guaranteed Mongol you might get a cup of their cream tea. It's made of camel's milk and salt, and apparently tastes revolting; it's also most impolite to refuse a cup.

The frost-free period narrows at this latitude to about three months, with the best time to visit being June to August.

Footnote

Over the Great Wall and below the Bamboo Curtain is the world's most ambitious reafforestation and afforestation program – a shelter belt creeping toward its ultimate length of 6000 km. Known as 'The Green Wall', the belt is designed to protect precious farmland from the sands of the Gobi Desert when the winter winds blow. It will eventually stretch from Xinjiang to Heilongjiang (China's last great timber preserve). This huge tree-planting program is only a small part of the PRC's schedule – there's a similar belt along the south-east coast to break the force of summer typhoons. It's an attempt to reverse the effects of centuries of careless tree-cutting which, combined with slash-and-burn farming, has contributed to disastrous flooding and other ecological catastrophes.

Tree planting is the duty of every able-bodied person in China. In the early years of the PRC forest cover was decimated to about 9%, but since the formation of the communes and production brigades in 1958, the cover has been raised to almost 13%.

The goal for the year 2000 is 20% cover, which would require tree-planting on 70 million hectares. Planting in the northern frontier zones is done in one-km-wide strips; between 1978 and 1982, almost five million hectares were afforested with a survival rate of 55%, and a further 1.1 million hectares were added in 1983. Wasteland and barren hills are allocated to rural households for planting and farming (also done on a contract basis), and the government provides seeds, saplings and know-how.

Ningxia 宁夏

Ningxia was carved out as a separate administrative region in 1928 and remained a province until 1954, when it was absorbed into Gansu Province. In 1958 Ningxia re-emerged, this time as an 'Autonomous Region' with a large Hui population. The boundaries of the region have ebbed and flowed since then – Inner Mongolia was included at one time, although the borders are now somewhat reduced.

Part of the arid north-west of China, Ningxia is probably one of the poorest regions in the country. Winters are hard and cold, with plummeting temperatures; blistering summers make irrigation a necessity. The network of irrigation channels that criss-cross the region have their beginnings in the Han Dynasty, when the area was first settled by the Han Chinese in the 1st century BC.

Almost four million people live in Ningxia, but only about a third are Hui, living mostly in the south of the province. The rest are Han Chinese. The Hui minority are descended from Arab and Iranian traders who travelled to China during the Tang Dynasty. Their numbers were later increased during the Yuan Dynasty by immigrants from Central Asia. Apart from their continued adherence to Islam, the Hui have been assimilated into Han culture.

In 1958 the building of the Baotou-Lanzhou railway which cuts through Ningxia, helped relieve the area's isolation and develop some industry in this otherwise almost exclusively agricultural region.

YINCHUAN 银川

Yinchuan was once the capital of the Western Xia, a mysterious kingdom founded during the 11th century. Today it's divided into two parts: a new industrial section close to the railway station, and the old town about four km away. At the old town's centre is a large Drum Tower, from which the main streets radiate.

Things to See

Not much to rave about here, but you can spend an enjoyable day pedalling within a small radius of the town to see the following:

Bei Ta (North Pagoda)

It's easy to spot this pagoda (also known as Haibao Ta), standing like a stone spaceship to the north. Records of the structure date from the 5th century. In 1739 an earthquake knocked the lot down, but it was rebuilt in 1771 according to its original style. The pagoda is part of a monastery which has also been tarted up to complete the tourist attraction. Religion hardly moves here; the only noticeable activity comes from hundreds of wasps.

Chengtian Xi Ta (West Pagoda)

The pagoda is in the south-west of the city. Like its counterpart in the north, it is surrounded by a leafy series of sleepy courtyards. Restoration is in progress so it's not possible yet to climb this pagoda. Closed on Monday.

Nanmen (South Gate)

This is a mini-model of Tiananmen Gate in Beijing, complete with Mao portrait.

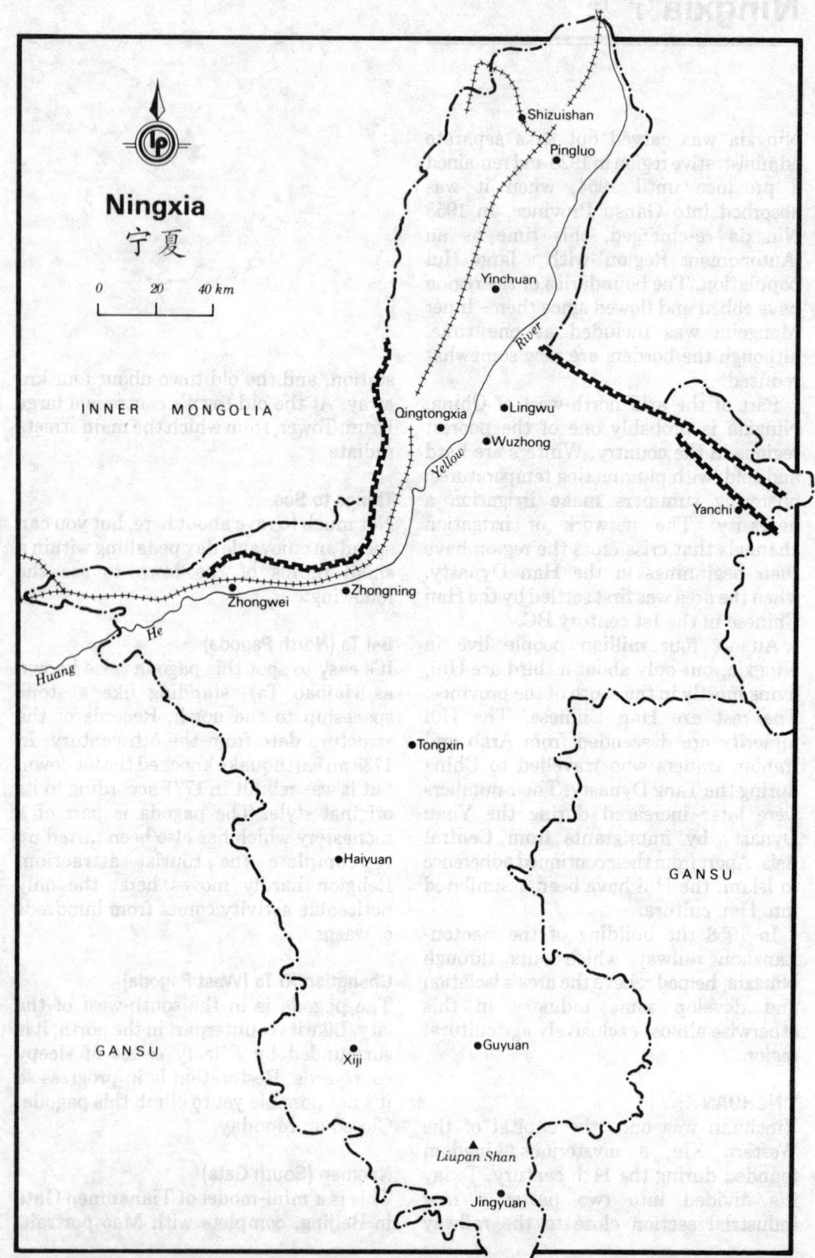
Ningxia
宁夏
0
20
40 km
Shizuishan
Pingluo
Yinchuan
River
Yellow
INNER MONGOLIA
Qingtongxia
Lingwu
Wuzhong
Yanchi
Zhongning
Zhongwei
He
Huang
Tongxin
Haiyuan
GANSU
GANSU
Xiji
Guyuan
Liupan Shan
Jingyuan

The surrounding square is being revamped, so you'll soon be able to join the local tourists and get a clean shot of yourself in front of the strange monument.

Places to Stay

The *Ningxia Binguan (Ningxia Guest House)*, sometimes also referred to as the Yi Suo (No 1 Guest House), is a classy place with prices starting at Y45 double (possibly Y26 for students). Maps and postcards are available at the reception desk, or try the Xinhua Bookstore opposite the hotel entrance. CITS has an office with maps and helpful staff on the 2nd floor of the reception building. United China Airlines (UCA) has an office just inside the entrance gate.

The *Oasis Hotel* is on the main street, just round the corner from the Ningxia Binguan. A bed in a triple costs Y7; doubles cost Y24. The coffee shop in the lobby sells yoghurt, pastries, ice cream and coffee. The roof garden is a pleasant place to relax under a sunshade.

Places to Eat

The *Ningxia Binguan* has Chinese and Islamic restaurants. The set menu for Y6 in the Islamic restaurant was poor and included an unidentifiable speciality (fried lamb's tail?) that was vile. The *Oasis Hotel* has a cavernous restaurant on the 2nd floor which provides standard dishes. Lining the main street are mutton and jiaozi restaurants. A couple of blocks from the Oasis Hotel is the Yinchuan Fandian (Yinchuan Hotel) restaurant, the *Hanmin Canting*. Although their food is usually good, the following story about overcharging might be food for thought:

Having heard reports from several foreigners about good food and blatant overcharging, our small group of foreigners, which included a Chinese speaker, tried its luck. Sure enough, the waitress charged far in excess of the menu prices. When asked to explain the difference, she said all foreigners paid double for food. Before dropping our chopsticks and marching out in disgust, we pointed out that we were eating the same food as Chinese and that this doubling of charges had not been mentioned when we ordered.

The waitress then changed tack and said that we had all received double helpings. One look at the same dishes on neighbouring tables proved that this was not true and the prices she had charged proved, on closer inspection, not to have been doubled, but raised by an arbitrary sum. When we asked for the manager, we were told (as usually happens) that she was not on duty. The insolent, sneering behaviour of the waitress stung us to take the matter higher.

Complaints of this kind are usually handled by a town's Shangye Ju (Office of Commerce). The relevant office in Yinchuan was near the restaurant and we finally located the bosses *(lingdao ren)*, who very methodically handled the problem. Finally, a cadre took us back to the restaurant where the manager and all the staff (excluding the offending waitress) were hauled out to discuss the matter. The manager kept apologising with the lame excuse that it was a case of 'mistaken percentages'. She insisted on refunding the amount that had been overcharged. After we had refused a refund on the grounds that it was the principle, not the money which was at stake, the cadre dropped a subtle hint that our acceptance would save face for the manager. So we accepted on the understanding that in future foreigners and local Chinese would receive proper treatment.

The cadre later apologised for the incident with the excuse that Yinchuan had only been opened to foreigners for a short time and the waitress didn't know there were rules. I wasn't going to waste more time arguing, but found it interesting that the waitress herself had told us it was a rule to charge foreigners double.

Getting There & Away

Air CAAC has flights connecting Yinchuan with Beijing (Y212) and Xian (Y122). United China Airlines (UCA) has an office just inside the front gate of the Ningxia Guest House and appears to be offering semi-regular flights to Beijing (Y124) and Xian (Y97) on Tuesday and Thursday.

Bus Regular buses connect Yinchuan with major towns such as Zhongwei, Tongxin and Guyuan.

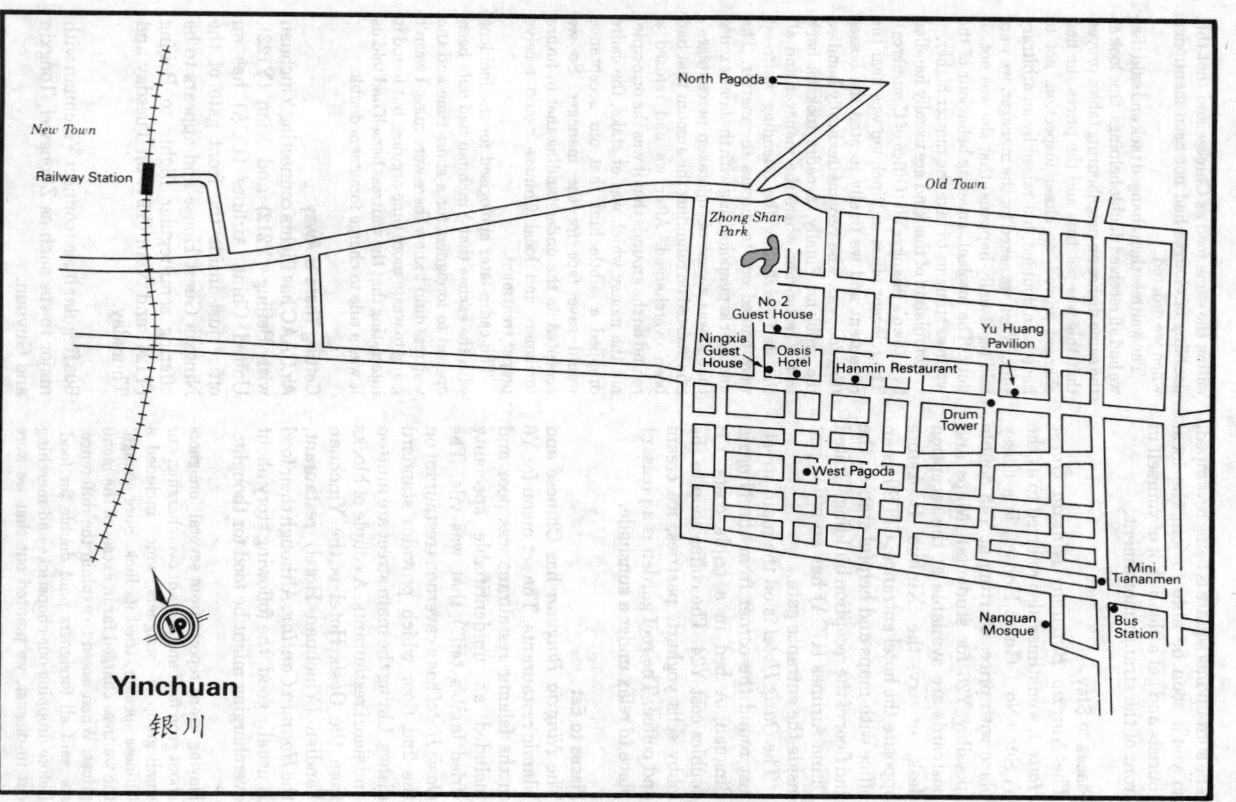
North Pagoda
New Town
Railway Station
Old Town
Zhong Shan Park
No 2 Guest House
Yu Huang Pavilion
Ningxia Guest House
Oasis Hotel
Hanmin Restaurant
Drum Tower
West Pagoda
Mini Tiananmen
Nanguan Mosque
Bus Station
Yinchuan
银川

Rail Yinchuan lies on the Lanzhou-Beijing railway which runs through Baotou, Hohhot and Datong. There are only two slow trains and one express daily in each direction, so book in advance. It takes about 10 hours to travel from Yinchuan to Lanzhou; a hard-seat ticket costs Y11.20 (tourist price).

Getting Around

Bus No 1 runs between the train station in the new town and the old town which has the hotels and sights. Ask to get off at the Ningxia Binguan near the centre of town. Minibuses charge Y1 per person on this route and are a fast, if unnerving, alternative.

I shared a minibus with some Chinese businessmen who wanted to catch a train leaving in 10 minutes. The driver loved the challenge and drove like a banshee. The driver's infant son sat in the front seat howling in panic while Dad turned on the outside loudspeaker to bludgeon the other panic-stricken road users with 'Make way, make way, we have a train to catch'. We arrived at the station just as the train pulled in.

Bikes are a good way to cover the city sights. A cheap place for bike rental is the Di Er Zhao Dai Suo (No 2 Guest House). Turn right outside the Ningxia Guest House, then right again at the next junction and continue about 70 metres down the road, looking for a gate. Ask about bikes at the office to the left beside the gate. A passport or some form of I.D. is required, and bikes cost Y0.20 per hour.

AROUND YINCHUAN

It should be possible to make a few day trips out of Yinchuan. If you pedal south-east to the Yellow River, leave your sketch-pad behind. A Canadian friend took his pad with him and sketched pastoral scenes from a quiet hillock. Unfortunately, his field of vision included a busy military airfield, and several Chinese MIGs landed in his sketches. An army patrol pounced on the Canadian and whisked him off to the local clink for 24 hours before he was released with a warning.

Helan Shan (Mt Helan)

About 17 km west of Yinchuan is the mountain resort of Gunzhongkou. It may be possible to stay here and potter around the temples and mountain trails. The highest mountain in this range, Mt Helan, is 3556 metres high.

Just north of the resort are the Baisikou Shuangta (twin pagodas), 13 and 14 storeys high and decorated with statuettes of Buddha.

South of Gunzhongkou is the Xi Xia Wangling (Western Xia Mausoleum). According to legend, the founder of the Western Xia Kingdom, Li Yuan-hao, built 72 tombs. One was for himself, others held relatives or were left empty. The Western Xia Kingdom lasted for 190 years and 10 successive emperors, but was wiped out by Genghis Khan. For some reason, the kingdom was not included in *The 24 Histories*, the standard Chinese work on the history of that era. Numerous Chinese scholars have joined the hunt to solve this mystery.

QINGTONGXIA 青铜峡

South-west of Qingtongxia, close to Xiakou, is the famous group of 108 Dagobas (Yi Bai Ling Ba Ta). It is still not known why these 12 rows of white, vase-shaped brick pagodas were built here in the shape of a giant triangle during the Yuan Dynasty.

The nearby dam was built across the Yellow River in 1962 to provide hydro-electric power.

Qingtongxia can be visited as a day trip out of Yinchuan, providing you take an early-morning bus.

ZHONGWEI 中卫

Zhongwei lies 167 km south-west of Yinchuan on the Lanzhou-Baotou railway line. It's sandwiched between the sand dunes of the Tengger Desert to the north and the Yellow River to the south. This is a market town with a plodding, peaceful pace; a complete change from the hurly-burly of Chinese cities.

Gao Miao

The main attraction in town is the Gao Miao, an eclectic, multi-purpose temple which serves Buddhism, Confucianism and Taoism. Built during the 15th century and flattened by an earthquake during the 18th century, it was later rebuilt and expanded several times until being virtually razed again by fire in 1942. Extensive repairs have been made to the present wooden structure whose dozens of towers and pavilions look like parts of a jagged wedding-cake. The temple includes a hotch-potch of statues from all three religions so you can see Gautama Buddha, bodhisattvas, the Jade Emperor and the Holy Mother under one roof.

Shui Che (Water Wheels)

If you bike or hitch west of Zhongwei down the road towards Shapotou, the road branches half-way. Take the left-hand fork to the Yellow River, where a ferry will take you across to Xia He Ye. Follow the dirt road east for about two km to reach the water wheels *(shui che)*.

Since the Han Dynasty, water wheels have been a common sight in Ningxia Province and in other regions crossed by the Yellow River. Mechanical pumps have now taken over, though water wheels are occasionally still in use to pump water from the river down a complicated system of ducts and canals to the fields.

Yangpi Fazi (Sheep-hide Rafts)

A few km due south of the town, you can see these rafts in action on the Yellow River – you might even want to have a go!

Leather rafts have been a traditional mode of transport on the Yellow River for centuries. They usually served for short crossings, although thousands of rafts were used during the '50s to freight huge loads of tobacco, herbs or people on a two-week trip covering nearly 2000 km between Lanzhou and Baotou. The largest raft then in use was made from 600 sheep-hides, measured 12 metres by seven metres and could carry loads of up to 30 tons.

The raft-making process begins with careful skinning of cattle or sheep carcasses. The skins are then soaked for several days in oil and brine before being taken out and inflated. An average of 14 hides are tied together under a wooden framework to make a strong raft capable of carrying four persons and four bikes. Single-skin rafts are also used in parts of Gansu and Qinghai, where you either lie on top of your raft or crawl inside while the rafter lies on top to direct your passage across the river. There is usually enough air inside a large cow-hide to last for 15 minutes which, reportedly, is about twice the time needed for an average crossing.

Shapotou Desert Research Centre (Shapotou Shamo Yanjiu Suo)

Shapotou lies about 16 km west of Zhongning on the fringe of the Tengger Desert. The Desert Research Centre was founded here in 1956 with the task of researching methods to fix or hold back the moving sand dunes from the railway. From 1962 onwards, the researchers have been using the 'checkerboard method' for sand blockage and fixation introduced in the '50s by a Soviet adviser. Plants are protected inside small checkerboards composed of straw bales which are replaced every five years. Even with this protection, plants still require 15 years for full growth. Several thousand hectares of land have now been reclaimed to create an impressive ribbon of greenery beside the railway.

Places to Stay

The *Xian Zhaodai Suo (County Guest House)* is in the centre of town and charges Y5 per person in a triple. CITS can be contacted here if you want to organise visits to see camels, the Shapotou Desert Research Centre, sheep-hide rafts, etc. Ask at reception about renting bikes.

Getting There & Away

Zhongwei has a couple of train connections daily to Yinchuan or Lanzhou. There are bus connections with Yinchuan and Guyuan.

TONGXIN 同心

Tongxin lies on the road between Zhongning and Guyuan. The main attraction is the Qingzhen Dasi (Great Mosque) built during the Ming Dynasty. One of the largest mosques in Ningxia Province, this is a traditional Chinese wooden structure with Islamic woodcuts and decorations of carved brick.

GUYUAN 固原

Guyuan is in the south of Ningxia Province. One of China's finest groups of Buddhist grottoes is at Xumi Shan about 50 km north-west of Guyuan. Xumi is the Chinese version of the Sanskrit word *sumeru*, which means 'treasure mountain'.

Cut into five adjacent peaks are 132 caves containing over 300 Buddhist statues dating back 1400 years, from the Northern Wei to the Sui and Tang dynasties. The finest Buddhist statues are found in Caves 14, 45, 46, 51, 67 and 70. Cave 5 contains the most famous statue on Xumi Shan: a colossal Maitreya Buddha, 19 metres high. It remains remarkably well-preserved even though the protective tower has long since collapsed and left it exposed to the elements.

Over 60 miniature Buddhist statues and tombs dating from the Han Dynasty have been found in Xiji County, about 60 km west of Guyuan. Xiji County has recently been opened to foreigners.

The trip to Guyuan from Yinchuan takes about nine hours; daily buses leave in the morning. It might be interesting to continue from Guyuan towards Tianshui in Gansu Province.

Gansu 甘肃

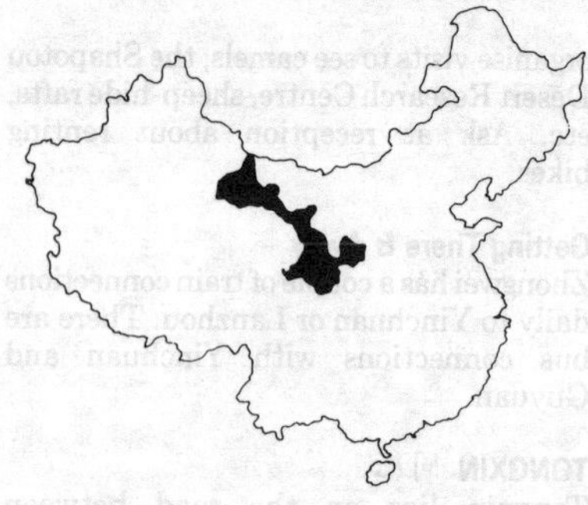

Gansu, desolate and barren, is a strange state. It's hard to imagine that through this narrow corridor China maintained political, cultural and commercial contacts with Central Asia and the lands beyond. A frontier with a semi-arid climate, liable to frequent droughts and famines, it has always been on the edge of the empire (except when that empire spilled over into Xinjiang as it did under the Han and the Qing). It was an impoverished region and its inhabitants played little part in the destiny of their country.

However, the famed 'Silk Road', along which camel caravans carried goods in and out of China, threaded its way through Gansu. The most common export was the highly prized Chinese silk, from which the road took its name. Travellers and merchants from as far away as the Roman Empire entered the Middle Kingdom via this route, using the string of oasis towns as stepping-stones through the barren wastes. Buddhism was also carried into China along the Silk Road, and the Buddhist cave temples found all the way from Xinjiang through Gansu and up through northern China are reminders of the influx of ideas the road made possible.

The Great Wall snaked its way across northern China and into Gansu, finishing up not far past the town of Jiayuguan. All was not peaceful within the wall, however. The Muslim rebellion of 1862 to 1878 was put down with incredible savagery by the Chinese; untold numbers of people, probably millions, were killed and the destruction of cities and property brought the province to ruin – and finally established Chinese control. The century was topped off by a massive famine.

Traditionally the towns of Gansu have been established in the oases along the major caravan route where agriculture is possible. With the coming of modern methods of transport some industrial development and the exploitation of oil, iron ore and coal deposits has taken place. The foothills of the mountainous regions which border Qinghai Province to the south support a pastoral economy based on horses, cattle, sheep and camels. To the north of the 'Gansu corridor' – that narrow part of Gansu that extends north-west from the capital of Lanzhou – lies a barren desert which extends into Inner Mongolia, much of it true desert, some of it sparse grassland.

Just over 19½ million people inhabit Gansu. The province has a considerable variety of minority peoples, among them the Hui, Mongols, Tibetans and Kazaks. The Han Chinese have built their own settlements, places like Jiayuguan and Jiuquan which have been Chinese outposts for centuries.

By Rail through Gansu to Xinjiang

The Lanzhou-Ürümqi rail line was completed in 1963. It is definitely one of the great achievements of the Communist regime, and has done much to relieve the isolation and backwardness of this region.

The railway line stretches north-west along the Gansu corridor from Lanzhou. The Marco Polos of the railway age can break their journey at Jiuquan, Jiayuguan and the remarkable Buddhist Caves of Dunhuang (the jumping-off point for Dunhuang is Liuyuan, and from here you

Top: Defensive Yak, Qinghai Lake (RS)
Bottom Left: Khamba rider, Bamda (RS)
Bottom Right: View from Ganden Monastery (RS)

Top Left: Debating Monk at Sera Monastery, Lhasa (RS)
Top Right: Wandering Monk chanting in the Barkhor, Lhasa (RS)
Bottom Left: Pilgrim wearing "gau" (portable shrine) in Lhasa (RS)
Bottom Right: Tibetan nomad girl with ornate hairband, Qinghai Lake (RS)

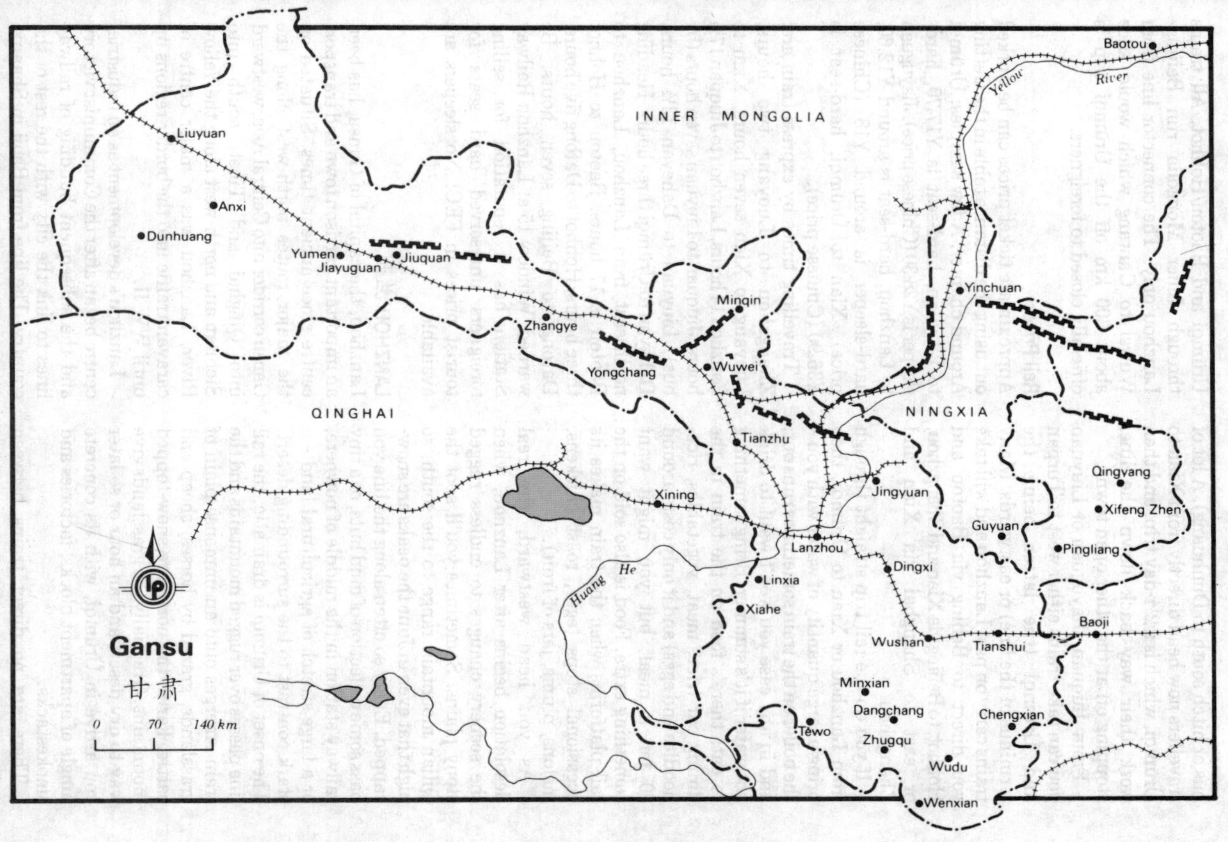
Baotou
Yellow
River
INNER MONGOLIA
Liuyuan
Anxi
Dunhuang
Yumen
Jiayuguan
Jiuquan
Yinchuan
Minqin
Zhangye
Yongchang
Wuwei
QINGHAI
NINGXIA
Tianzhu
Qingyang
Xining
Jingyuan
Xifeng Zhen
Guyuan
Lanzhou
Pingliang
Dingxi
Huang
He
Linxia
Xiahe
Baoji
Wushan
Tianshui
Gansu
甘肃
Minxian
Dangchang
Chengxian
Tewo
Zhugqu
0
70
140 km
Wudu
Wenxian

bus or hitch south to Dunhuang). A lot of travellers now head directly from Xian to Ürümqi, which is a 2½-day trip, and then work their way back down the line, stopping off at the other open towns.

From Jiuquan, Jiayuguan or Liuyuan you can take trains either west to Turpan and Ürümqi (the latter being the terminus of the line) or eastwards. Many trains carry on past Lanzhou and will take you direct to Beijing via Baotou and Hohhot, to Beijing via Xian and Zhengzhou, or east to Shanghai via Xian and Zhengzhou.

If you do the rail trip straight through from Lanzhou or Xian to Ürümqi, then bring a large quantity of water with you – the boiler on the train sometimes runs out, and in any case you won't want to drink hot water if it's summer. Bring something to eat; there's food on the train in the dining car (rice, meat, vegetables, rice-noodles and eggs) and it only costs around 80 fen a meal, but you might want something extra. Food is also sold on the rail platforms when the train makes its occasional stops (eggs, roast chickens, melons, plums, jars of fruit).

As you head westward, the real desolation begins after Lanzhou, when the scenery changes to endless rugged stony plains. Sometimes you'll spot the Qilian mountain range to the south, so high that even in June the peaks are snow-capped. Every so often along the line you pass some collection of mud huts, or a tiny railway station in the middle of nowhere, or a large stretch of agricultural land – a stark contrast to the surrounding desert. The onset of Ürümqi is dramatic; the rail line passes over rugged mountains and the train emerges onto an immense plain of grasslands, grazed by horses, sheep and cattle. Far to the north are snow-topped mountains. Gradually the grasslands give way to dry desert and an hour or so later you arrive in Ürümqi, with its concrete jungle of apartment blocks, factories and smokestacks.

There are no direct trains between Ürümqi and Baotou/Hohhot. All trains through Inner Mongolia run Beijing-Lanzhou only. The connector line from Wuwei to Gantang which would slice about 300 km off the Ürümqi trip is officially closed to foreigners.

Rail Prices

Approximate ticket prices can be worked out using the distance table in the Getting Around chapter. A few samples: Ürümqi to Liuyuan, hard-seat is Y17.70, hard-sleeper is Y28.30 (Chinese price). Jiayuguan to Lanzhou, hard-seat is around Y12.60, hard-sleeper is around Y18 (Chinese price). Xian to Ürümqi, hard-seat is Y36.90 (Chinese price).

Travelling times by express train are: Zhengzhou to Luoyang two hours, Luoyang to Xian seven hours, Xian to Lanzhou 14 hours, Lanzhou to Jiuquan 17½ hours, Jiuquan to Liuyuan seven hours (by bus), Liuyuan to Daheyan 13½ hours, Daheyan to Ürümqi three hours. Heading north-east from Lanzhou, Lanzhou to Baotou is 17 hours, Baotou to Hohhot three hours, Hohhot to Datong five hours, Datong to Beijing seven hours. Be warned: Window 15 at Lanzhou Railway Station has a reputation for selling foreigners unreserved hard seats for tourist prices in FEC! No sleepers are available.

LANZHOU 兰州

Lanzhou, the capital of Gansu, has been an important garrison town and transport centre since ancient times. Situated on the major routes north-west along the Gansu corridor into Central Asia, westward into Qinghai and Tibet, south into Sichuan and north-west along the Yellow River, Lanzhou was a major centre of caravan traffic into the border regions up until WW II.

Lanzhou's development as an industrial centre began after the Communist victory and the subsequent building of railway lines to link the city with the rest of the country. The line from Baoji in Shaanxi was extended here in 1952, another from Baotou in 1958. Construction also began on the Lanzhou-Ürümqi line, probably with the intention that it would one day join up with a Soviet Union line. Another line was built linking Lanzhou with Xining. This transformed Lanzhou into a major industrial city, destined to become the principal industrial base of north-west China. About 200,000 people lived in Lanzhou in 1949; by 1959 the number was 900,000 and today it's over two million.

Information & Orientation

Lanzhou stretches for 20 km along the southern bank of the Yellow River. The eastern segment of town, between the railway station and the large Xiguan traffic circle, is the centre of town, and in

1 火车站
2 兰州饭店
3 国际旅行社
4 金城宾馆
5 邮电大楼
6 五泉山公园
7 中国银行
8 胜利饭店
9 公安局
10 白塔山公园
11 汽车西站
12 友谊饭店
13 省博物馆
14 民航售票处
15 景杨楼
16 悦宾楼
17 邮局
18 兰州西站

1 Main Railway Station
2 Lanzhou Hotel
3 CITS
4 Jincheng Hotel
5 Main Post Office
6 Five Springs Park
7 Bank of China
8 Shengli Hotel
9 Public Security
10 White Pagoda Hill & Park
11 West Bus Station
12 Friendship Hotel
13 Gansu Museum
14 CAAC
15 Jingyang Lou
16 Yuebin Lou
17 Post Office
18 West Railway Station

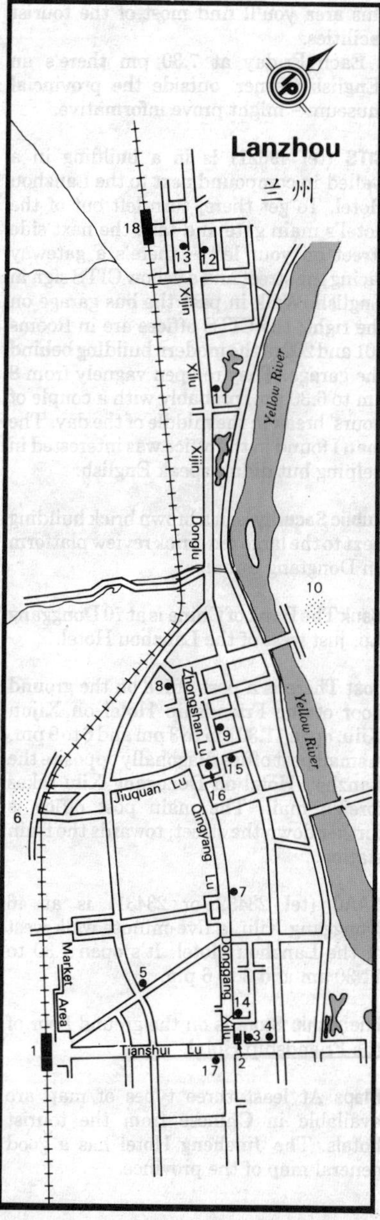

this area you'll find most of the tourist facilities.

Each Friday at 7.30 pm there's an 'English Corner' outside the provincial museum – might prove informative.

CITS (tel 49621) is in a building in a walled-in compound next to the Lanzhou Hotel. To get there, turn left out of the hotel's main gate and take the next side street on your left – there's a gateway facing the street and a yellow CITS sign in English. Walk in past the bus garage on the right; the CITS offices are in Rooms 201 and 202 of the modern building behind the garage. They're open vaguely from 8 am to 6.30 pm, probably with a couple of hours' break in the middle of the day. The man I found in the office was interested in helping but didn't speak English.

Public Security is in a brown brick building next to the large red-brick review platform on Dongfang Square.

Bank The Bank of China is at 70 Donggang Lu, just west of the Lanzhou Hotel.

Post There is a post office on the ground floor of the Friendship Hotel on Xijun Xilu, open 11.30 am to 3 pm and 6 to 9 pm. A small post office diagonally opposite the Lanzhou Hotel on Donggang Xilu takes foreign mail. The main post office is further down the street, towards the train station.

CAAC (tel 23432 or 23431) is at 46 Donggang Xilu, a five-minute walk west of the Lanzhou Hotel. It's open 7.30 to 11.30 am and 3 to 6 pm.

Friendship Store is on the ground floor of the Friendship Hotel.

Maps At least three types of map are available in Chinese from the tourist hotels. The Jincheng Hotel has a good general map of the province.

Things to See

Lanzhou has few sights, though its intrinsic interest makes it worth a stop. If you get a chance, don't miss the utterly brilliant Dance Ensemble of Gansu Province – try the People's Theatre near the Shengli Hotel or get someone at your hotel reception desk to check *Renmin Ribao (People's Daily)* for the current venue. Also not to be missed are the Binglingsi Buddhist Caves.

Provincial Museum

The museum is directly across the street from the Friendship Hotel. It's not open on Sunday and Monday and closes at 4 pm on other days.

The ground floor has now been cleared of Zhou Enlai and is devoted to exhibits on Gansu's flora, fauna, geology, minerals and natural parks – worth a visit.

On the 2nd floor there's an extensive display of decorated earthenware pottery; the Gansu painted pottery dates from the Yangshuo culture around 4000 to 2000 BC. You'll also see exhibits from the Binglingsi Caves and glazed clay statues. The model bronze chariots and mounted horsemen came from the Letai Han Tomb at Wuwei in Gansu – altogether 220 figures and chariots were unearthed, including the 'Galloping Horse of Gansu'. You can buy a replica of the galloping horse for just Y1560 from the museum shop. Also on exhibit are Jin Dynasty fresco bricks found lining the walls of a tomb at Jiayuguan; each brick is painted with a scene of hunting, cultivation or the arts. And there are the inevitable displays of bronze pots, urns and cooking vessels. The shop on this floor sells postcards and souvenirs.

Exhibits on the 3rd floor include the entire skeleton of a mammoth exhumed in 1973, as well as fragments of skeletons, teeth and tusks from other extinct members of the pachyderm family. The Long March, another mammoth event, is also the subject of a display. Photos are not permitted.

Temple of the Town Gods

The temple is a 10-minute walk east of Xiguan. It's been partially restored and is now used as a public park where old men sit around playing cards and chequers while sipping tea, often to the accompaniment of live music. There's another temple, also under restoration, just west of the bridge leading to White Pagoda Park.

Baita Shan (White Pagoda Hill)

Baita Shan lies opposite the city on the north bank of the Yellow River. The area is dotted with the usual Ming and Qing pavilions and the mountain is topped by a much older white Buddhist shrine from where energetic visitors can get a panoramic view of the heavy industrial haze below.

Binglingsi Caves

The Binglingsi Buddhist Caves are 35 km south-west of Yongjing County in Gansu Province. The oldest caves have been repaired and added to on numerous occasions since they were built during the Western Qin Dynasty of 385 to 431 AD. The 183 caves are cut into a cliff face 60 metres high and stretch for about 200 metres. They contain 694 statues, 82 clay sculptures and a number of murals. Cave 169 is the oldest and contains one buddha and two bodhisattvas; inscriptions on the wall give the date of the statues as 420 AD. Most of the other caves were completed during the prosperous Tang period. The star of the caves is the 27-metre-high seated statue of Maitreya, the coming buddha.

You probably won't be able to visit during spring and early summer because the caves must be reached by boat, and the water level is too low then. Be warned that even though the ride to the caves is beautiful and the caves themselves are magnificent, you're likely to get no more than one hour to look around them – if everything goes on time. Nor will they let you take photographs – and they do enforce that rule! Also, make sure you take food and drink with you – 10 hours can be a long time to abstain.

Getting to the Caves The Shengli Hotel runs minibuses (maximum 10 passengers) to the caves. Tickets are best booked well in advance. The price per person is Y30 for foreigners and Overseas Chinese, Y25 for locals and foreigners with Chinese student credentials. Whether you pay in RMB or FEC depends on your bargaining tenacity. Show up at 7.30 am to board the bus at 8 am.

CITS charges Y45 for a tour which may link up with one of the western or Overseas Chinese tour groups. They pick you up in a minibus from the Friendship Hotel at 7.30 am and bus you to the dusty little industrial town of Yongjing, where there's a dam and the Liujiaxia Hydro-electric Power Station.

Some travellers have managed to use public transport by taking the early-morning local bus to Yongjing from outside the Shengli Hotel. After arriving in Yongjing they boarded the tour boats to the Binglingsi Caves. Yongjing has a hotel which charges Y7 per bed.

On the way to the caves you drive through immense stretches of steep, terraced hills which grow wheat and corn. The bus ride takes about 2½ hours. Near the town you'll see one good reason for coming here if not just for the caves – wild marijuana grows in abundance on the side of the road. The bus drives over the top of the dam to a stairway leading to the boat, which takes you on a two-hour trip down the reservoir. The trip's beautiful scenery includes blue-green water, red gravel embankments and jagged grey hills on either side.

Places to Stay

The *Youyi Fandian (Friendship Hotel)* (tel 30511) is an immense Russian-built structure with huge columns in the foyer supporting the roof. The hotel has two main blocks, one facing Xijin Xilu and one behind it – the rear block is used to stow away foreigners. Triples cost Y9 per bed, dormitory accommodation Y8 FEC per bed. The post office on the ground floor stays open until 9 pm and is next to a glossy coffee shop that sells maps. To get to the hotel take bus No 1, 12 stops from the square in front of the railway station – it's a long ride. If you are on your way to Xiahe, you might prefer to stay at this hotel the night before departure since it's just a 15-minute walk from the east bus station.

The *Lanzhou Fandian (Lanzhou Hotel)* is another cavernous construction, not as nice but rather better located than the Friendship Hotel. A bed in a triple is Y10; a bed in a four-bed room is Y9. A bed in a dorm costs Y7. Dorms don't have showers, so why not use the nice ones in the main building (3rd floor for men, 2nd floor for women). Reception sells maps and will store your baggage, which is useful if you plan to spend a week or longer touring the area. On the ground floor of the main building is a coffee shop with pinkish decor. The hotel is a 20-minute walk from the railway station or you can take bus No 1 two stops.

The *Jincheng Fandian* is a new hotel a few minutes down the street past the Lanzhou Hotel. The plush part has doubles at Y108 and Y72. The dorm accommodation is on the 4th floor of the block at the back (it can also be reached via the CITS entrance). Dorm beds are Y6 FEC or Y7.80 RMB. There are several useful facilities here such as a post office, clinic, fruit stall and shop with good maps.

The *Shengli Binguan* charges Y7.70 for a bed in a four-bed room in the basement.

The railway station reportedly has a dorm upstairs with beds for Y3 – useful if your train arrives very late.

Places to Eat

The *Friendship Hotel* restaurant offers unexciting set meals at Y11 RMB per head. The *Jincheng Hotel* does an adequate set dinner for Y8. Breakfast at the *Lanzhou Hotel* was memorable for the 'butter' which the waitress spooned out of a huge tub with a label saying 'Edible Fat – a Gift of Norway'.

The restaurant street appears to be Jiuquan Lu in the city centre. Two popular restaurants are *Jing Yang Lou* and *Yue Bin Lou*.

Out on the streets, some good noodle stalls serve Lanzhou's spicy specialty, *niu rou mian* (beef noodles). There is said to be another good restaurant, the *Lanzhou Canting*, on Jiuquan Lu in the centre of town – if you can find it. The kebab sellers on the roundabout in front of the Lanzhou Hotel might be worth a try. One evening, I witnessed the sudden arrival of a battered van which disgorged the hygiene 'flying squad'. They promptly pronounced the stalls unhygienic and disbanded the vendors. Next evening everyone was grilling away again.

Getting There & Away

Air Lanzhou is connected by air to Beijing (Y258), Canton (Y371), Chengdu (Y132), Dunhuang (Y218), Jiayuguan (Y128), Nanjing (Y249), Qingyang (Y72), Shanghai (Y296), Taiyuan (Y169), Ürümqi (Y295), Xian (Y82), Xining (Y30) and Zhengzhou (Y157).

Lanzhou airport is 75 km from the city. The airport bus leaves at 7 pm from the CAAC office and costs Y2.50 one way – as opposed to Y250 quoted for a taxi! If you are booked on an early-morning flight you have to stay at an airport hotel. There are two: Hotel No 1 (Di Yi Zhaodai Suo) is cleaner and charges Y20 for a bed in a double with bath; Hotel No 2 (Di Er Zhaodai Suo) charges Y10 for a bed in a double without washing facilities. High winds often delay flights.

Bus The west bus station (Qiche Xizhan) handles departures to Linxia and Xiahe. The bus to Xiahe leaves at 6.30 am; buy your ticket in advance. There are frequent buses to Linxia hourly until noon.

Rail Trains run to Ürümqi via the Gansu corridor; to Beijing via Baotou, Hohhot and Datong; to Golmud via Xining; to Shanghai via Xian and Zhengzhou; and to Beijing via Xian and Zhengzhou.

The station has a separate window for foreigners (No 15), but one of the ticket-sellers has evidently given up. Without listening or even looking up, she just waves a slip of paper saying 'hard-seats'.

Getting Around

Apart from taxis at the Friendship Hotel, there are buses and bikes. Bus No 1 is a useful link between the station and the Friendship Hotel. Ask at the Shengli Hotel about bike hire. A word of warning: Lanzhou has a reputation among many Chinese from other provinces as a centre for proficient pickpockets and petty thieves. Be especially careful on crowded buses, at post offices and at the station.

JIUQUAN 酒泉

Jiuquan has been an administrative outpost of Chinese civilisation since the Han Dynasty. The name means 'Wine Spring' and the story goes that when the Western Han general Ho Qubing realized he lacked sufficient wine for his army to celebrate a triumphant expedition, he poured what he had into a spring and the whole army drank from that.

A glacier region in the nearby Qilian Mts has recently been opened to foreigners, who can follow a five-km path along the glacier (4300 metres).

Things to See

In the middle of the city stands the large **Drum Tower**, which was built in the 4th century. It was originally constructed as a watchman's tower at the town's eastern gate, but expansion of the town pushed it into the centre and it was renamed the Drum Tower. During the Qing Dynasty the tower was renovated, and on each of its four sides were hung tablets inscribed with cute phrases like 'Beckoning to the Hua Mountain in the east', 'Taking in a full view of the Qilian Mountains in the south', 'Westward, Yiwu can be reached' and 'The great desert stretches away in the north'. A Chinese tourist leaflet says: 'From tower, one enjoys splendid views in all directions, along with a sense of elation that comes from being face to face with the infinite and sublime'.

Clusters of tombs from the Wei Dynasty of the 3rd century AD are dispersed along a narrow strip of land, about 20 km from north to south and three km wide, that runs between Jiuquan and the Jiayu Pass. At their southern tip are a number of tombs from the Eastern Jin Dynasty (317-420 AD), decorated with murals.

Other attractions are the **Wenshushan Buddhist Cave Temples** 15 km from town. The earliest dates back to the 5th century.

Getting There & Away

Jiuquan lies on the Lanzhou-Ürümqi railway line. There are also regular buses to Jiayuguan (a one-hour drive) and a daily bus to Dunhuang.

JIAYUGUAN 嘉裕关

Jiayuguan is an ancient Han Chinese outpost. The Great Wall once extended beyond here, but in 1372, during the first few years of the Ming Dynasty, a fortress was built. From then on Jiayuguan was considered the terminus of the wall and the end of the empire.

The town lies on the Lanzhou-Ürümqi rail line, and is mainly made up of bungalows and apartment blocks interspersed with factories and smokestacks. Not an unpleasant place, but very drab and dusty. The only attraction is the fort, a worthy structure at which to stop off and have a look around.

China Daily recently reported that The Chinese State Physical Culture & Sports Commission is setting up a base near Jiayuguan for glider pilots and hot-air balloonists. Perhaps we'll soon see balloon tours following the Silk Road.

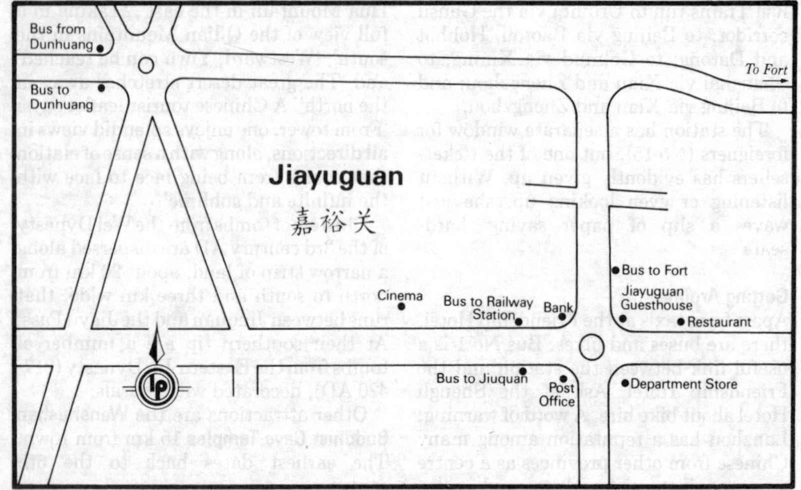

Information & Orientation
Someone has obviously given some thought to individual travellers because there are signs in English where you need them.

Jiayuguan is an easy place to find your way around since everything is easily accessible from the tourist hotel. The railway station is to the north of the town and the local bus will take you to the hotel. The bank, department store and post office are opposite the hotel, and the Public Security office is a short distance away. A bus to the fort near town leaves from outside the hotel. The pick-up point for buses to Dunhuang is a 15-minute walk from the hotel.

CITS has a rep who floats around the Jiayuguan Binguan occasionally – or ask the staff at the reception desk.

Public Security is close to the hotel. Turn right at the front gate and then right again at the first crossroads. The Public Security compound is around the corner, and the office handling foreigners is just inside the gateway.

Bank The bank is opposite the hotel.

Post There is a post office diagonally opposite the hotel.

Things to See
Jiayu Fort is the attraction of Jiayuguan. The fort guards Jiayu Pass, which lies between the snow-capped Qilian Mountains and Black Mountain of the Mazong Range. During the Ming Dynasty this was considered the terminus of the Great Wall, though fragments can be seen to the west.

The fort was dubbed by the Chinese the 'Impregnable Defile Under the Sun' or the 'Impregnable Pass Under Heaven'. Although the Chinese often controlled territory far beyond Jiayuguan, this was the last major stronghold of the empire to the west.

The fort was first built in 1372, with additional towers and battlements added in subsequent years. The outer wall is about 733 metres in circumference and almost 10 metres high. At the eastern end of the fort is the **Guanghua Men (Gate of Enlightenment)** and in the west is the

Rouyuan Men (Gate of Conciliation). Over each gate stand towers which rise to a height of 17 metres, with upturned flying eaves. On the inside of each gate are horse lanes leading up to the top of the wall. At the fort's four corners are blockhouses, bowmen's turrets and watchtowers. Outside the Guanghua Men but inside the outer wall are three interesting buildings: the **Wenchang Pavilion** and the **Guandi Temple** which have been partly restored, and the recently restored open-air theatre stage.

A local bus runs to the fort at 9.30 am, noon and 4.30 pm (extra bus at 2 pm on Sundays only). You can catch it from the stop outside the hotel. The fare is 15 fen and the ride takes about 15 minutes. Admission to the fort is 20 fen.

Places to Stay

The *Jiayuguan Binguan* is a new hotel probably destined to be packed full of tour groups. Single rooms are Y8, doubles Y16 and triples Y18. They'll readily give you a bed in a triple for just Y8 if you're on your own. The staff are extremely friendly but speak little English. To get to the hotel from the railway station, take the local bus which leaves from outside the station; it stops across the road from the hotel and the fare is 15 fen. If you're coming in on the bus from Dunhuang the hotel is within easy walking distance.

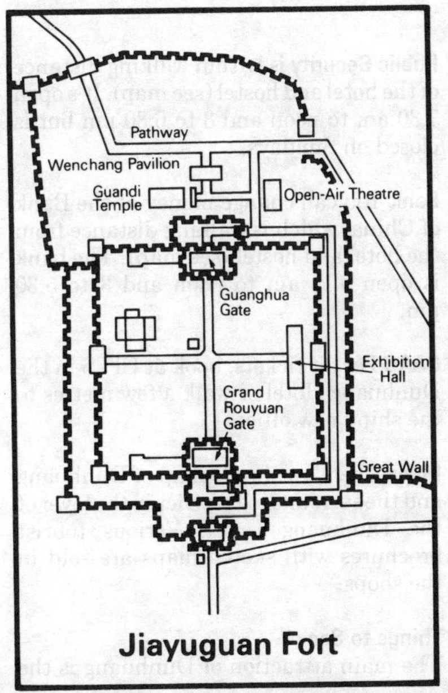

Jiayuguan Fort

Places to Eat

There are several places for good cheap eats. One restaurant is around the corner from the hotel; turn left at the front gate and then left again. Another restaurant worth trying is the one close to the cinema.

Getting There & Away

Air There are flights from Jiayuguan to Lanzhou and Dunhuang. Apparently, reservations to Dunhuang are only confirmed once the aircraft has taken off in Lanzhou.

Bus Buses to Jiuquan leave from the stop just next to the post office diagonally across the road from the guest house. The fare is 60 fen. The first bus is at 6.30 am and the last at 7.45 pm, with buses departing at half to one-hour intervals.

Buses to Dunhuang depart each morning at 7 am from the large intersection, a 15-minute walk from the guest house (refer to map).

Rail Jiayuguan lies on the Lanzhou-Ürümqi railway line. Buses to the train station depart from the stop outside the Bank of China at 5.40 am, 7.30 am, 9 am, 10 am, 11 am, noon, 1 pm, 1.50 pm, 3 pm, 3.30 pm, 4.30 pm, 5.30 pm, 6.50 pm, 8.15 pm, 9.30 pm and 11.20 pm – though these times will change to match changes in rail timetables.

LIUYUAN 柳园

Liuyuan on the Lanzhou-Ürümqi railway

line is the jumping-off point for Dunhuang. It's little more than the railway station and two dusty roads, and any traveller who comes here should bring a costume and a song-and-dance act to cheer up the Chinese.

Buses for Dunhuang wait outside the station whenever a train pulls in. The trip costs Y5 and takes 2½ to three hours. If you come later you could try hitching; otherwise you'll have to stay overnight in the town.

There are two hotels to choose from, both on the main road. The first is a whitewashed building just a few minutes' walk from the train station on the right. The second hotel is further down on the same side of the road and looks marginally better – it's a grey brick building with two columns holding up a verandah and charges Y1 for a bed.

There is one OK place to eat, a small restaurant five minutes' walk down from the second hotel. It's identifiable by a green fly-wire net hanging in the doorway. The people here are friendly.

DUNHUANG 敦煌

Dunhuang is a giant oasis stuck in the middle of the Gansu Desert, a three-hour bus ride through the oblivion end of China south of the Lanzhou-Ürümqi railway line. During the Han and Tang dynasties this was a pivotal point of interchange between China and the outside world, a major staging-post for both incoming and outgoing trading caravans. Modern visitors come to Dunhuang because of the superb Buddhist art on view in the Mogao Caves.

Information & Orientation

The centre of Dunhuang is little more than two intersecting roads. All life-support systems are within easy walking distance of each other.

CITS The staff at the Dunhuang Hotel are CITS people. One man at the front desk is extremely helpful and friendly, and gives accurate information. He speaks quite good English.

A traveller who fell sick in Dunhuang wrote to confirm the good reputation of this rare pocket of CITS angels:

> On my second day here, I went to the local hospital suffering from what turned out to be gastric bleeding. Since nobody at the hospital spoke English, they sent word to CITS who sent along an interpreter. I spent eight hours in the hospital on an assortment of drips and during this time various CITS staff fetched food and drink from the hotel, went to the bus station to refund my ticket to Golmud, and generally kept me company, finally bringing me back here at 3 am. The following day they continued to ferry me back and forth for a series of injections.
>
> On top of all that, they negotiated a reduction on my hospital bill from Y84 to Y40 and on my hotel charges from Y13 to Y8. As a result of all this, I'm just about fit enough to set off for Lhasa, leaving Mr Quan, the extremely helpful CITS interpreter, wondering why on earth I should want to go there anyway!

Public Security is within walking distance of the hotel and hostel (see map). It's open 7.30 am to noon and 3 to 6.30 pm but is closed on Sundays.

Bank You can change money at the Bank of China, which is walking distance from the hotel and hostel (see map). The bank is open 9.15 am to noon and 3 to 5.30 pm.

CAAC For air tickets, book at CITS in the Dunhuang Hotel or walk a few metres to the shiny new office.

Maps There's a simple map of Dunhuang and the surrounding district in the foyer of the Dunhuang Hotel. Various tourist brochures with sketch-maps are sold in the shops.

Things to See

The main attraction of Dunhuang is the

Mogao Caves. There is little to see in the oasis itself.

The Southern Dunes

This ridge of vast sand dunes is to the south of the oasis. You can easily bicycle out to the edge of the ridge and then climb to the top. Alternatively, a bus is often organised by the hotel and hostel to take people, mainly Hong Kongers, out there in the evening. The cost is only Y1 for the round trip. It's a steep, hard climb to the top of the dunes, but you get a great view of the oasis in one direction and the infinite stretch of desert in the other. Behind the ridge is a much-touted lake which turns out to be a putrid little pool.

Yangguan & Yumen Passes

Sixty-two km south-west of Dunhuang is the mountain pass of Yangguan. The Han Dynasty beacon towers which marked the route westwards for the camel caravans, and which warned the populace of invaders, have almost disappeared under the drifting sand. Nearby are the ruins of the ancient Han town of Shouchang. To the north-west of Dunhuang is the Yumen Pass, also noted for its ancient ruins. To get to either of these passes you'd have to try hitching up with a tour group or hire a taxi from the hotel.

Caravans heading out of China would travel up the Gansu corridor to Dunhuang; the Yumen Pass was the starting point of the road which ran across the north of what is now Xinjiang Province, and the Yangguan Pass was the start of the route which cut through the south of the region.

Mogao Caves

This is the highlight of Dunhuang and one of the highlights of north-west China. The story goes that in 366 AD the sight of a 1000 Buddhas inspired a wandering monk to cut the first of hudnreds of caves into the sandstone cliff face. Over the next 10 centuries Dunhuang became a flourishing centre of Buddhist culture on the Silk Road.

The grottoes were then abandoned and eventually forgotten. At the turn of the 20th century a Taoist monk stumbled across a cave filled with a treasure trove of documents and paintings. The cave had been bricked up to stop the contents

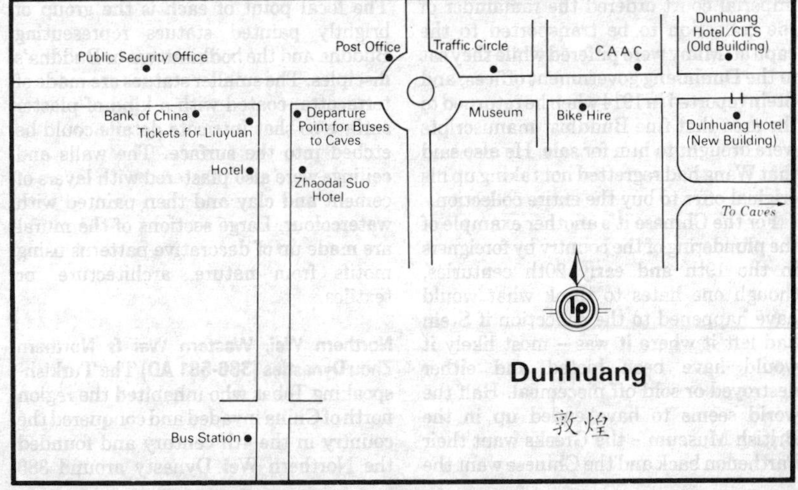

falling into the hands of invaders and the dry desert air had preserved much of the material.

Passing through the area in 1907, the British explorer Sir Aurel Stein heard a rumour of the hoard, tracked down the monk and was allowed to inspect the contents of the cave. It was an archaeological gold mine of Buddhist texts in Chinese, Tibetan and many other Central Asian languages, some known and some long forgotten. There were paintings on silk and linen, and what may be the oldest printed book in existence (dating to 868 AD).

The sacking of the caves began in earnest. Stein convinced Wang to part with a large section of the library in return for a donation towards the restoration of some of the grottoes. He carted away 24 packing cases of manuscripts and five of paintings, embroideries and art relics, all of which were deposited in the British Museum. The following year a French explorer, Pelliot, passed through Dunhuang and bought more of the manuscripts from the monk. He was followed by others from the United States, Japan and Russia, who all carted off their booty. News of the find filtered through to Beijing, and the imperial court ordered the remainder of the collection to be transported to the capital. Many were pilfered while they sat in the Dunhuang government offices, and Stein reported in 1914 when he returned to the area that fine Buddhist manuscripts were brought to him for sale. He also said that Wang had regretted not taking up his original offer to buy the entire collection.

For the Chinese it's another example of the plundering of the country by foreigners in the 19th and early 20th centuries, though one hates to think what would have happened to the collection if Stein had left it where it was – most likely it would have been looted and either destroyed or sold off piecemeal. Half the world seems to have ended up in the British Museum – the Greeks want their Parthenon back and the Chinese want the Dunhuang manuscripts back – though the manuscripts are probably better preserved where they are, and available to a far greater number of researchers than they would be in the People's Republic.

The Mogao Caves are set into desert cliffs above a river valley about 25 km south-east of Dunhuang. Unfortunately, the area is highly exposed to the elements and the erosion of wind and water have severely damaged quite a few of the caves. Cave 94, for example, is totally decimated and is now used to store junk. Today, 492 grottoes are still standing. The grottoes honeycomb the 1600-metre-long cliff face which sits on a north-south axis. Altogether they contain over 2000 statues and over 45,000 separate murals. Cave 17 is where the Taoist monk, Wang Yuan, discovered the hoard of manuscripts and artworks.

Most of the Dunhuang art dates from the Northern and Western Wei, Northern Zhou, Sui and Tang dynasties, though examples from the Five Dynasties, Northern Song, Western Xia and Yuan can also be found. The Northern Wei, Western Wei, Northern Zhou and Tang caves are in the best state of preservation.

The caves tend to be rectangular or square with recessed, decorated ceilings. The focal point of each is the group of brightly painted statues representing Buddha and the bodhisattvas or Buddha's disciples. The smaller statues are made of terracotta, coated with a kind of plaster surface so that intricate details could be etched into the surface. The walls and ceilings were also plastered with layers of cement and clay and then painted with watercolour. Large sections of the mural are made up of decorative patterns using motifs from nature, architecture, or textiles.

Northern Wei, Western Wei & Northern Zhou Dynasties (386-581 AD) The Turkish-speaking Tobas who inhabited the region north of China invaded and conquered the country in the 4th century and founded the Northern Wei Dynasty around 386

AD. They deliberately adopted a policy of copying Chinese customs and lifestyle. But friction between groups who wanted to maintain the traditional Toba lifestyle and those who wanted to assimilate with the Chinese eventually split the Toba empire in two in the middle of the 6th century; the eastern part adopted the Chinese way of life and the rulers took the dynastic name of Northern Qi. The western part took the dynastic name of Northern Zhou and tried to revert to Toba customs without success. By 567 they had defeated the Qi and taken control of all of northern China.

The fall of the Han Dynasty in 220 AD sent Confucianism into decline. With the turmoil produced by the Toba invasions, Buddhism's teachings of nirvana and personal salvation became highly appealing. The religion spread rapidly under the patronage of the new rulers, and made a new and decisive impact on Chinese art which can be seen in the Buddhist statues at Mogao.

The art of this period is characterised by its attempt to depict the spirituality of those who had achieved enlightenment and transcended the material world through their asceticism. The Wei statues are slim, ethereal figures with finely chiselled features and comparatively large heads. The bodhisattvas in Northern Wei Caves 248 and 257 are a good example of the later Wei. Like the sculptures of the same period at Luoyang, the expressions on the faces of the buddhas and bodhisattvas are benevolently saccharine – Cave 259 of the Northern Wei period is a good example.

The Wei and Zhou paintings at Mogao are some of the most interesting in the grottoes. The figures are simple, almost cartoon-like with round heads, elongated ears and puppet-like, segmented bodies which are boldly outlined. The female figures are all topless, with large breasts, which suggests an Indian influence. Northern Zhou Cave 299 shows musicians and dancers in this style, and Cave 290 shows flying celestial maidens. The paintings in Northern Zhou Cave 428 are a good example of this style.

The wall painting in Northern Wei Cave 254, done in the same style, portrays the story of Buddha vanquishing Mara. It refers to the night that Buddha sat beneath a fig tree south of the Indian city of Patna, and entered into deep meditation. Mara, the Evil One, realising that Sakyamuni was on the verge of enlightenment, rushed to the spot. Mara tempted him with desire, parading three voluptuous goddesses before him, but Sakyamuni resisted. Then Mara assailed him with hurricanes, torrential rains and showers of flaming rocks, but the missiles turned to lotus petals. Finally Mara challenged Buddha's right to do what he was doing, but Buddha touched the earth with his fingertip and the roaring it summoned up drove away Mara and his army of demons. Sakyamuni had achieved enlightenment – but Mara was waiting with one last temptation; this time it was an appeal to reason, that speech-defying revelations could not be translated into words and no one would understand so profound a truth as the Buddha had attained; but Buddha said that there would be some who would understand, and Mara was finally banished forever.

Murals tend to be highly detailed and figures are relatively small. During the Wei Dynasty portraits of noble patrons began to be depicted alongside the more religious themes that they had sponsored. These figures depict the lifestyle and fashions of the Wei nobles. The men are usually shown in the Chinese robe and the women in a tight-fitting gown with loose sleeves.

Sui Dynasty (581 AD-618 AD) The throne of the Northern Zhou Dynasty was usurped by a general of Chinese or mixed Chinese-Toba origin. Prudently putting to death all the sons of the former emperor, he embarked on a series of wars which by 589 had reunited northern and southern

China for the first time in 360 years. The Tobas simply disappeared from history, either mixing with other Turkish tribes from Central Asia or assimilating with the Chinese.

The Sui, a short-lived dynasty, was very much a transition period between the Wei and Tang periods and did not leave any great masterpieces. Again, the best Sui art was of Buddhist origin. What separates the Sui style from that of the Wei is the rigidity of its sculpture. The figures of the Buddha and bodhisattvas are stiff and immobile; their heads are curiously oversized and their torsos elongated, they wear Chinese robes and show none of the Indian-inspired softness and grace of the Wei figures.

At Mogao the Sui caves are north of the Wei caves. Buddha's disciples Ananda and Kasyapa are both seen here for the first time – see cave 419 for example. There are also a number of examples of the lotus flower symbol and designs from Middle Asian and Persian brocades. Stories from the life of Buddha provide the main themes of the wall paintings. Other Sui caves include 204, 244, 302 and 427. Some of the paintings show processions of musicians, attendants, wagons and horses.

Tang Dynasty (618-907 AD) The reign of the last Sui emperor, Yang Ti was characterised by imperial extravagance, cruelty and social injustice. Taking advantage of the inevitable peasant revolts which had arisen in eastern China, a noble family of Chinese-Turkish descent assassinated the emperor, took control of the capital, Changan, and assumed the throne, taking the dynasty name of Tang.

During the Tang period China extended its domain by force of arms into Central Asia, pushing outward as far as Lake Balkhash in what is today Soviet Kazakhstan. Trade with the outside world expanded and foreign merchants and people of diverse religions poured into the Tang capital of Changan. Tang art took on incomparable vigour, moving towards greater realism and nobility of form. Buddhism had become prominent and Buddhist art reached its peak; the proud bearing of the Buddhist figures in the Mogao Caves reflect the feelings of the times, the prevailing image of the brave Tang warrior, and the strength and steadfastness of the empire.

Extravagant robes drape many of the figures, which show an element of sensuality typical of Persian and Indian art. The Tang figures are notable for their overwhelming size and power. The best examples are the colossal buddhas of caves 96 and 130; the one in 96 stands over 30 metres. The statues can be viewed from platforms constructed in the cave wall opposite their chests and faces. The roof and walls of Cave 130 are adorned with paintings.

Portraits of nobles are considerably larger than those of the Wei and Sui Dynasties and figures tend to occupy important positions within the murals. In some cases patrons are portrayed within the same scene as the Buddha

Unlike the figures of the Wei, Zhou and Sui periods, the Tang figures are realistic with a range of very human expressions. The portrait of a Buddhist nun in cave 17 and the statue of Buddha's older disciple Kasyapa in Cave 45 are good examples of this. There are also notable exceptions such as the statues in Cave 16 with their heavy eyebrows, long slitted eyes and enormous hands.

Other Tang Dynasty caves include 45, 57, 103, 112, 156, 159, 196, 217, 220, 320, 321, 328 and 329. Cave 156 has an interesting wall mural showing a Tang army on the march and Cave 158 has a huge statue of the dead Buddha with a group of grieving 'foreigners'.

Later Dynasties The ultimate development of the cave paintings was reached under the Tang Dynasty. During the later dynasties the economy around Dunhuang went into decline and the luxuriousness and vigour typical of Tang Dynasty painting began to be replaced by simpler drawing techniques and flatter figures. However, during the Northern Song period a number of important break-throughs were made in landscape painting. Mount Wutai in Cave 61 is a a good example of this style. People are integrated into the landscape and scenery is depicted for its own sake, rather than as an abstract backdrop.

No 3 is an example of a Yuan Dynasty cave. Cave 346 is an example of a Five Dynasties cave. Cave 55 is another example of a Northern Song construction. Except for the small niches (most of them in very bad condition or bare of statues and paintings) all the caves have locked gates. Many of the locked caves are in such poor condition that they are simply not worth opening to the general public. Some, like Cave 462 – the Mizong Cave – contain Tantric art whose explicit sexual portrayals have been deemed too corrupting for the public to view. A few caves are in the process of being restored. Only 40 have been cleared for public view.

Admission now operates on a dual system: for Y0.50 you can visit no more than 10 caves; for Y6 you get a guide and access to as many of the 40 caves as you can 'do' in the two shifts (8.30 to 11.30 am; 2.30 to 5 pm). Unfortunately, all explanations posted in the caves are in Chinese.

There are few English-speakers among the staff and guides, which is no excuse for the generally apathetic attitude towards foreigners. For Y100 extra you can get an English-speaking guide whose language skills are so low you end up paying to give someone an English lesson.

If at all possible avoid going to the caves with a busload of Hong Kongers. They came to China to have fun, and while they spend half an hour having their photos taken at the front entrance, you'll be left sitting around twiddling your thumbs.

You're not allowed to take photos in the caves; you have to leave your camera and bags in the luggage hut near the entrance. Photos are sometimes permitted after payment of an appropriately vast sum of money. Banning flash photos is under-standable, but you're not even allowed to take time-exposures. Instead a shop outside the cave sells slides, postcards and books. Bring your own torch (flashlight) as most of the caves are very dark and it's hard to see much detail, particularly in the niches. Torches can be bought for a few yuan in China.

Getting to the Caves in Dunhuang is a bit of a hassle. Two buses depart from the street corner (see map) at 8 am and the trip out takes about 45 minutes. The buses leave the caves at 11.30 am, so in all you get about two hours to see what you can of the grottoes in the morning. There are also two buses leaving at 2 pm. One costs Y0.70 and returns at 4 pm; the other costs slightly more (Y1) and returns at 5 pm, which allows you an extra hour at the

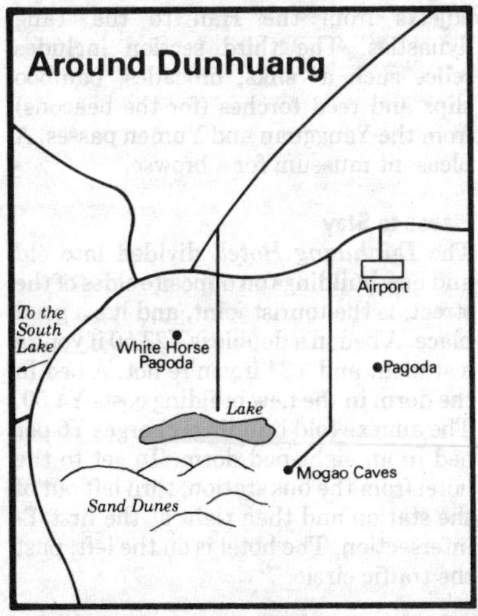

caves. Local buses do not run in the winter so you'll have to take a taxi or freeze on a bike.

Alternatively, you could hire a taxi at the Dunhuang Hotel to take you to the caves. The drive takes about 25 minutes, and if you're away for a total of about four hours then the taxi will cost you about Y44 (Y0.80 per km plus Y1 per hour waiting charge).

You could also bicycle out there, but be warned that half the ride is entirely through desert and would be absolute murder.

For Y4.50 per person you can stay in the hotel at the caves. The Y5 lunch at the hotel is served punctually at noon and is very filling.

Dunhuang Xian Bowuguan (Dunhuang County Museum)
Walk down the main street towards the Dunhuang Hotel, and the museum is on the left side, about 50 metres after the traffic circle.

The museum is divided into three sections. The first section displays some of the scriptures written in Tibetan and Chinese unearthed from Cave No 17 at Mogao. The second section shows sacrificial objects from the Han to the Tang dynasties. The third section includes relics such as silks, brocades, bamboo slips and reed torches (for the beacons) from the Yangguan and Yumen passes. A pleasant museum for a browse.

Places to Stay
The *Dunhuang Hotel*, divided into old and new buildings on opposite sides of the street, is the tourist joint, and it's a good place. A bed in a double is Y23.50 if you're a student and Y34 if you're not. A bed in the dorm in the new building costs Y4.50. The annexe (old building) charges Y6 per bed in an eight-bed dorm. To get to the hotel from the bus station, turn left out of the station and then right at the first T-intersection. The hotel is on the left, past the traffic circle.

There is a large hotel five minutes' walk down from the bus station, on the way to the Dunhuang Hotel. The large red-brick, yellow-concrete building has a wire fence and lamps on green poles. It takes foreigners. Rates are Y5 for a dorm bed.

Diagonally opposite this hotel, close to the main street, is a green building which is a new hotel, (Zhaodai Suo). Beds cost Y5 in a five-bed room and Y9 in a three-bed room. Hot showers are available from 8 to 11 pm. Bus tickets are sold at the reception desk.

Places to Eat
Food at the *Dunhuang Hotel* is good. Breakfast is Y3, lunch or dinner Y2.40; they serve you little plates of various foods. You have to tell them at each meal if you'll be eating at the next, because if you don't they won't serve you. This is fair enough if you're the only person in the hotel, but even if they've got 20 Hong Kongers and a tableload of Japanese in the restaurant they still lack the spontaneity required to serve one stray backpacker – as if they carefully weigh the food out for every meal! It's the one sore point of this hotel.

The hotel is currently restructuring *The Cafe* on the 3rd floor. Here you were once able to sit around and watch TV and get drunk on Tsingtao or Lanzhou Pijiu, or else sample such delights as 'Orong juice' 'Soole water' 'Luoky Cola' 'Ven Mouth Wine' and 'Five Smells Wine'.

There is an icecream and cold drinks shop in front of the cinema.

Getting There & Away
Air Dunhuang is connected by air to Jiayuguan (Y97) and to Lanzhou (Y218).

Bus & Rail Buses to Liuyuan depart six times daily from the bus stop on the street corner (see map) between 7.30 am and 6 pm. Tickets can be bought at the office opposite the bus stop. The trip takes about 3½ hours and costs Y5. Liuyuan is on the Lanzhou-Ürümqi railway line and is the jumping-off point for Dunhuang. It's a miserable place and you should avoid going there if possible (see the Liuyuan section for a repeat of the details).

To avoid Liuyuan, there is a direct bus from Dunhuang to Jiayuguan and then on to Jiuquan. It departs at 6.45 am. The fare to Jiayuguan is Y9.40 and the trip takes nine hours. The fare to Jiuquan is Y9.90 and takes about another hour.

Buses to Golmud leave at 6.30; the fare is Y13.90 and the trip takes 12 hours.

Getting Around

Bicycles are for hire outside the hostel at Y0.50 per hour. There's another bike-hire place on the main street almost opposite the new CAAC office.

MAIJISHAN 麦积山

Maijishan, a mountain famed for its grottoes, lies about 35 km south of Tianshui town in south-east Gansu Province. The mountain bears some resemblance to a corn rick, hence the name Maijishan (Corn Rick Mountain).

The Maijishan grottoes are rated one of China's four largest temple groups; the others are at Datong, Luoyang and Dunhuang. The caves date back to the Northern Wei and Song dynasties and contain clay figures and wall paintings. It's not certain just how the artists managed to clamber so high; one theory maintains that they piled up blocks of wood to the top of the mountain before moving down, gradually removing blocks of wood as they descended. Stone sculptures were evidently brought in from elsewhere, since the local rock is too soft for carving, as at Dunhuang. Earthquakes demolished many of the caves in the central part while murals tended to drop off due to damp or rain; fire destroyed many of the wooden structures.

Catwalks and steep spiral stairs have been built across the cliff-face but most of the remaining 194 caves can only be seen through wire netting or barred doors – take a torch. Apart from the Qifo Pavilion and the huge buddha statues which are easily accessible, you may find it hard to get a rewarding peek into many of the caves unless you take a guide.

Visitors often pause above the statue of Buddha and attempt to throw coins or even cigarettes on his head. If the objects stay there, so the story goes, the thrower's mind is pure. The visitor may be pure, but Buddha certainly cops a load of rubbish.

Admission costs Y0.50. The ticket office is about a 15-minute walk from the bus stop. Follow the road uphill, round a sharp bend to the left, and continue uphill past a statue until you see the ticket office on your right. Local squirrels wait for handouts here. Brochures, souvenirs, portrait pictures, etc are available on or around the statue. Enquire about guides in the management office just past the statue. The ticket office also has a baggage check (Y0.10 per item). The caves are open from 9 am to 5 pm.

Make sure you approach the caves from the catwalk entrance further up the mountain above the ticket office. Keep on climbing, and continue to the far end of the Buddha terrace where there is a small tunnel. Pass through the tunnel and follow the catwalks down to the exit, on the other side of the mountain.

I missed the tunnel and went down again before climbing up the exit. Within minutes I was being pursued higher and higher by a posse of attendants. By the time they had me cornered, the tunnel was in sight and we all laughed at the misunderstanding.

Places to Stay

Tianshui Binguan is meant to be the brand-new hotel for foreigners (probably groups). A local policeman told me it was 18 km from the station and suggested I'd be better off looking for something closer to hand.

At Maijishan, there's the *Luyou Fuwubu Zhusu (Tourism Services Hostel)*

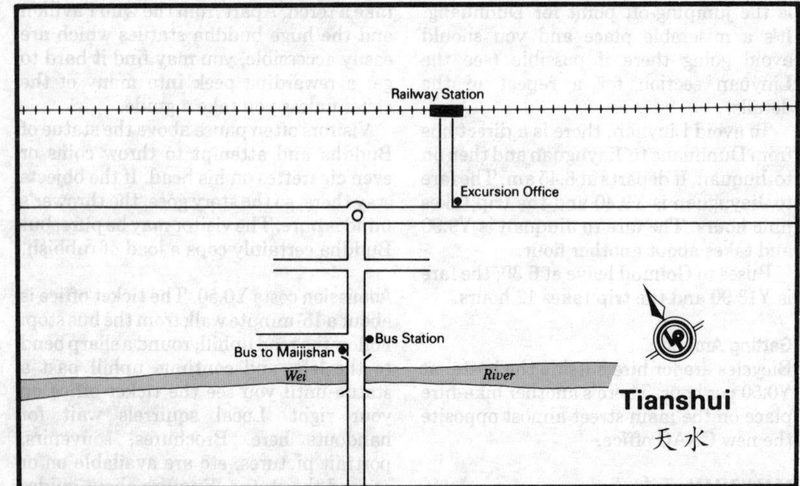

staffed by three women who were initially against harbouring foreigners and then asked a ridiculous price. The final deal was Y4 per person in a four-bed room or Y12 for two people to *baofang* (book the whole room). Most of the window-panes had shattered, so there was no air-conditioning problem. Meals cost Y2.50 for rice, peppers and meat. It's a good place to stay if you fancy a hike in hilly, densely forested country.

To reach the high ridge rising behind the ticket office, follow the road up towards the ticket office, but when you get to the sharp bend to the left, take the forest track to the right. Continue uphill along this track for about 15 minutes and then look for a track climbing off to the left. If you follow this, you'll find yourself on a dizzying, knife-edge route with fine views of the grottoes on the cliff-face.

Getting There & Away

The railway station closest to Maijishan is the one at Tianshui. Dozens of trains follow this busy line daily. If you want to make a day trip out of Maijishan, you should try to arrive early. It's probably most convenient to insert Maijishan as part of your itinerary between Lanzhou and Xian. Since trains don't start from Tianshui, you'll have to fight for a seat when you board.

At the end of the alley leading from the dungeon-like station hall to the main street is a small booking office which advertises excursions to Maijishan and other caves. The local buses for Maijishan leave about four times a day from Tianshui bus station; the last bus probably leaves Tianshui around 2 or 3 pm and returns between 5 and 6 pm. The trip takes over an hour and costs Y0.80. At weekends there are loads of buses and hordes of people.

LINXIA 临夏

Linxia, once an important town on the Silk Road route between Lanzhou and Yangguan, is now a regional centre for the Hui and Dongxiang minorities.

The Dongxiang minority speak their own Altaic language and fascinate scholars, who believe them to be descendants of Central Asians who migrated to Linxia during the 13th century. Some may have been forcibly transferred to China after Kublai Khan's conquest of Afghanistan, Iraq, Syria and Egypt. The blue eyes, high cheekbones and large noses may make you feel at home.

The Yugur minority, numbering only 8000, lives around the town of Jishishan near the Yellow River about 75 km from Linxia. The Yugur speak a language partly derived from Uighur and are followers of Tibetan Buddhism.

Not far from Jishishan, at Dahejia or San'erjia, there is reportedly an amazing form of river transport with which to cross the provincial boundary between Qinghai and Gansu. It's all done with a cowhide. The prospective 'passenger' gets inside the *pi fa* (cowhide), which is then inflated by the ferryman who ties the opening up tight. He dumps the cowhide with the passenger into the river, leaps on top and attempts to steer the contraption as it shoots across the river in six minutes flat – no, make that inflated! According to the ferryman there is enough air inside the cowhide to last for 15 minutes.

Things to See

Linxia is a fascinating slice of Arabia with the full Muslim trimmings. Apart from numerous mosques, the main attraction of the town is the markets.

If you're coming from Lanzhou, the bus station is just to the left of a large roundabout. To the left of the bus station are some market stalls. If you follow the road in front of the bus station, you'll pass a hotel about 100 metres along on the left. Opposite the hotel is a bazaar. Continue down the street and pass a mosque on your left before crossing a bridge and entering a large square. To the right of the bridge, with its entrance facing the square, is the *Dongle Qiao Canting*, an extraordinary restaurant-cum-teahouse on several floors. Pop up the spiral staircase to the top terrace, where you can sip Muslim tea and chew *guazi* (melon seeds) or order dishes such as *yangrou* (mutton) and *miantang* (noodle and meat soup).

Linxia does a thriving trade in spectacles made with ground crystal lenses and metal frames. Carved gourds, daggers and rugs are other local items in the market.

Getting There & Away

There are plenty of buses from Lanzhou (west bus station) to Linxia, but it is worth remembering that buses from Linxia to Xiahe are scarce – there is an incredible overdemand for seats. If you want to include Linxia as part of a trip to Xiahe, you should break your journey in Linxia on the way back from Xiahe. It's easy to return to Lanzhou from Linxia; take any of the buses leaving the bus station from early morning until early afternoon.

Some travellers have found a bus connection between Linxia and Xining. There are also buses from Linxia to Hezuo.

GANNAN – Southern Gansu

The southern part of Gansu Province, mostly occupied by Gannan Tibetan Autonomous Prefecture, is often referred to in Chinese as 'Gannan'. From the terraced fields of the Loess Plateau around Linxia, the landscape opens out beyond Xiahe in the south-west of the prefecture into vast grassland areas inhabited by Goloks (Tibetan nomads). Some of the heavily forested areas in the south-eastern part of the prefecture are also culturally Tibetan and have recently been opened to foreigners.

XIAHE 夏河

Xiahe is a monastery town which sprang up around Labrang Monastery, one of the six major Tibetan monasteries of the Gelugpa (Yellow Hat sect of Tibetan Buddhism). The others are Ganden, Sera and Drepung monasteries in the Lhasa area; Tashilhunpo monastery in Shigatse; and Taersi monastery in Huanzhong.

Xiahe is a great place for hiking in clean, peaceful surroundings. Take food, water, warm clothing and raingear.

Follow the river or head up into the surrounding valleys.

You may be able to organise transport (ask at the Xiahe Binguan) or hitch-and-walk to smaller monasteries in Ganjia (28 km) or Sanke (14 km). Don't expect to get anywhere quickly: traffic in this region is mostly walking-tractors, or horse-carts.

Labrang Monastery

The monastery was built in 1709 by E'angzongzhe, the first-generation Jiamuyang (living buddha), who came from the nearby town of Ganjia.

The monastery contains six institutes (Institute of Esoteric Buddhism, Higher & Lower Institutes of Theology, Institute of Medicine and Institute of Law). The sixth institute was destroyed by fire. There are also numerous temple halls, living buddha residences and living quarters for the monks.

At its peak the monastery housed nearly 4000 monks, but there are probably less than 500 today – a token complement for what was once a powerhouse of learning. Most of the monks come from Qinghai, Gansu, Sichuan or Inner Mongolia. One monk said he received Y30 per month from the government; another monk had a taste for Coca Cola, was learning how to bargain for foreign goods in English and loved roaming in a Landcruiser. There are three *tulkus* (living buddhas) in the area. One is in his 80s and lives at Ganjia; of the other two, one is in his 70s and the other in his 40s; both live at the monastery.

Many of the buildings look newly renovated. During the Cultural Revolution, monks and buildings took a heavy beating. In April 1985 the Institute of Esoteric Buddhism was razed in a fire caused by faulty electrical wiring. Apparently the fire burnt for a week and destroyed some priceless relics. Rebuilding has already started and the relics that were salvaged have been temporarily housed in another temple. As a result of the fire, monks are unwilling to use

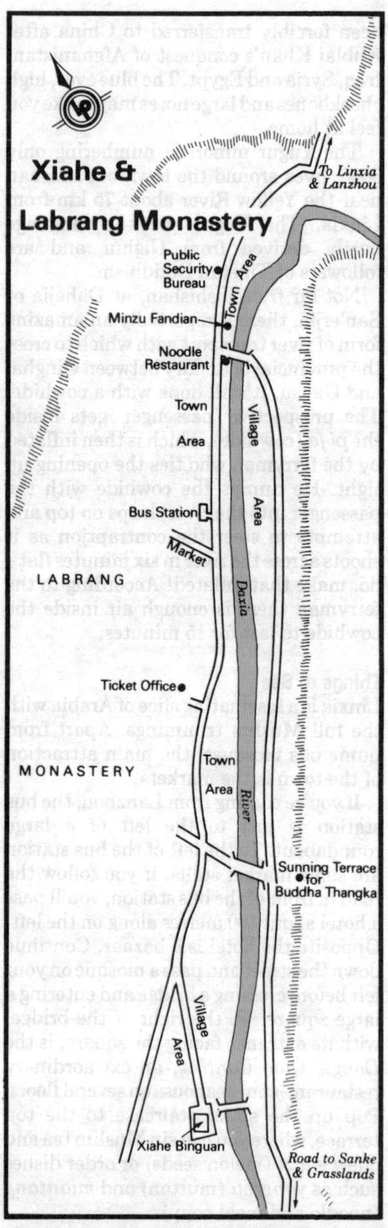

electric light anywhere in the monastery buildings, so take a flashlight (torch).

In the late afternoon, monks often sit on the grass beside the river for a 'jam-session' with trumpets and long, ceremonial horns.

Admission Tickets cost Y4 per person (Y0.80 for students) and are sold at a kiosk to the right of a large yard. The yard can be entered on the right-hand side of the main road – from the Minzu Fandian it's a two-km walk. The kiosk closes from noon to 2 pm for lunch and closes for the day at 4 pm. Postcards and brochures are on sale here.

Festivals are an important event not only for the monks but also for the nomads, who stream into town from the grasslands in multi-coloured splendour. Since the Tibetans use a lunar calendar, dates for individual festivals vary from year to year.

The Monlam (Great Prayer) Festival starts three days after the Tibetan New Year, which is usually in February or early March. On the 13th, 14th, 15th and 16th days of this month there are some spectacular ceremonies.

On the morning of the 13th a *thangka* (sacred painting on cloth) of Buddha measuring over 30 metres by 20 metres is unfurled on the other side of the Daxia River from the hillside facing the monastery. This event is accompanied by processions, bathing rituals and prayer assemblies. On the 14th there is an all-day session of Cham dances performed by 35 masked dancers with Yama, the King of Religion, playing the leading role. On the 15th there is an evening display of butter lanterns and butter sculptures. On the 16th the Maitreya statue is paraded around the monastery all day.

During the second month (usually starts in March or early April) there are several interesting festivals, especially those held on the seventh and eighth days.

The Fiend-Banishing Ceremony, which takes place on the seventh day centres around a 'fiend' who is, in fact, a villager hired to play the part of a scapegoat. The fiend, his face painted white and black, is ceremoniously driven out to the other side of the river and is forbidden to enter the monastery during the next week. On the morning of the eighth day, hundreds of monks in full regalia take part in a grand parade to display the monastery's huge collection of treasures and the paraphernalia of the living buddhas.

Scriptural debates, ritual bathing, lighting of butter lamps, collective prayers and blessings take place at other times during the year to commemorate Sakyamuni, Tsong Khapa or individual generations of the jiamuyang (living buddha).

Places to Stay

The up-market place to stay is the *Xiahe Binguan*, the former Summer Residence of living buddhas, a multi-coloured haven of peace and architectural taste. It is miles away from the bus station (allow 45 minutes for the walk). To get there from the bus station continue straight down the main street, through the village and down to the river. A bed in a four-bed dorm costs Y8. Doubles cost Y29 or Y18.30 for students – a bit pricey, but how often do you get the chance in China to wake up to birdsong and gushing water? Staff are very friendly.

Tourism officials in Lanzhou are keen to cultivate Xiahe as a destination for the tour groups which usually stay at this hotel. Last year, approximately 6000 tourists passed through here.

Closer to the bus station and less expensive is the *Minzu Fandian*, just before the bridge in the centre of town. A bed in a triple costs Y3.5. The only soul in this concrete box emanates from the Tibetan staff.

A new hotel, possibly called *Tourist Camp*, was reportedly scheduled to open soon next to the bus station. The manager, a returnee Tibetan, is knowledgeable and speaks excellent English.

In the winter, when temperatures can drop to −23°C, wood for the stove in your room is extra.

Places to Eat

The *Xiahe Binguan* has a restaurant serving good food. On the right-hand side of the bridge next to the Minzu Fandian is a noodle shop which does solid meals and is popular with the monks. There's a small bakery on the main street, just before the bus station, which sells fresh bread before the 6.30 am bus leaves.

Shopping

The main street has an abundance of shops and stalls selling patterned cloth, daggers, half-swords, yak-hair shoe-liners (to keep your feet warm), Dalai Lama pics, turquoise jewellery and trinkets. Don't take claims of authenticity too seriously, and bargain like everyone else. I was offered lynx skins and even a snow-leopard skin for Y3000 – whatever you do, don't buy these skins. If you do, you are contributing directly to the extermination of these rare beasts.

Getting There & Away

Most people reach Xiahe by bus from Lanzhou. Book your ticket (Y6.50) a day in advance. You might prefer to stay the night before departure at the Friendship Hotel, which is a lot closer to the bus station than the Lanzhou Hotel. The bus departs Lanzhou's west bus station (Xi Zhan) at 6.30 am and takes nine hours if you're lucky, 12 hours if you're not.

As our bus rumbled out of the bus station in the pre-dawn gloom, hawk-eyed staff spotted Tibetan stowaways clinging to the roof and sounded an alert which shook them off. After clambering over rough mountain terrain, the bus continues through valleys with fields of hemp, barley and beans; the occasional ruined monastery appears on a hillside with the odd snowcap towering in the background. The bus stops for lunch at Linxia.

Apart from the great scenery I found the trip memorable for several other reasons. The man sitting next to me was diligently extracting bogies which he then lined up carefully in exact rows of three on the rail in front of us. Each time passengers entered or left the bus, they unwittingly took the work of art with them.

The bus was totally overloaded and all the passengers standing in the aisle had to hit the floor when we passed through police checkpoints. At the third checkpoint, the police nabbed the driver and fined him Y5 for loading eight passengers too many (the other 15 had quickly sat down on the laps of the people in the back row).

Local farmers had the bright idea of using traffic on the road to do some free threshing. Bundles of harvested corn were strewn across the road in stacks so high that passing vehicles were forced to hurdle these obstructions in a mad steeplechase. The resulting lead content of the grain must have been startling.

On the return journey, officials stopped the bus at another checkpoint and detained a man who was transporting large bales of sheepskins on the roof of the bus. Just before reaching Lanzhou, the bus driver came face to face with an oncoming truck driver who had tried to overtake the bus on a steep gradient. Neither party would budge from their respective positions in the middle of the road and were just getting down to fisticuffs when a truce was negotiated by drivers of the vehicles snarled up behind.

To depart Xiahe, buy your bus ticket a day in advance at the bus station. Although the Lanzhou bus is meant to leave at 6 am, the driver doesn't surface until later and everyone stands outside the gates in the freezing cold. Buses sometimes leave from the Minzu Fandian and you may be able to get a lift with a truck or Landcruiser returning to Linxia or Lanzhou. Traffic in other directions (Maqu, Luqu) seems to be slow. If you're heading towards places in south-eastern Gannan such as Têwo or Zhugqu, you'll probably have to backtrack to Hezuo.

Xinjiang 新疆

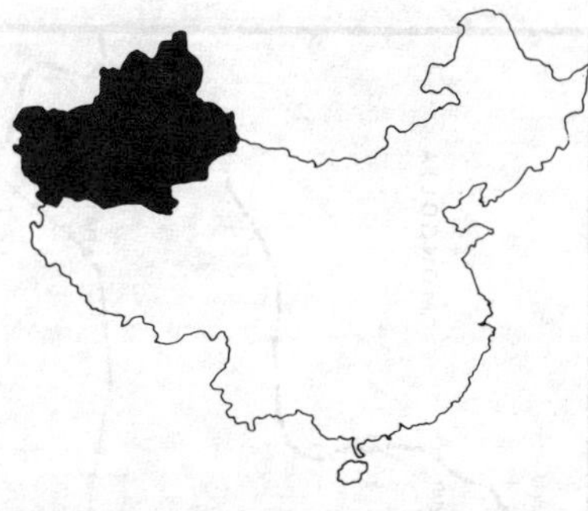

Xinjiang is one of China's 'autonomous regions', inhabited predominantly by the Turkish-speaking Muslim Uygur people whose autonomy from their Chinese overlords is in name only.

The history of this desolate north-western region has largely been one of continuing wars and conflicts between the native populations, coupled with repeated Chinese invasions and subjugations.

The Chinese were interested in the region for two reasons. First, a lucrative trade plied the 'Silk Roads' that cut through the oasis towns north and south of the Taklimakan Desert. Along this route camel caravans would carry goods from China to Central Asia (from where they eventually found their way to Europe). The trade had been going on at least since Roman days when silk, the principal Chinese export, was prized by fashionable Roman women. Whoever controlled the oasis towns could also tax the flow of goods, and so the conquest of Xinjiang was a highly profitable venture.

Second, subjugation of the region would help control the troublesome nomadic border tribes, the 'barbarians', who made frequent raids into China to carry off prisoners and booty.

The Chinese never really subdued the region and their hold over it waxed and waned with the power of the central government. The area was constantly subjected to waves of invasions by the Huns and Tibetans, as well as by the Mongols under Genghis and his descendant Tamerlane.

The Han were the first Chinese rulers to conquer Xinjiang. They did so between 73 and 97 AD, even crossing the Tian Mountains and marching a 70,000-man army as far as the Caspian Sea, although the Chinese only held onto an area slightly further east of Lake Balkash. With the demise of the Han in the 3rd century the Chinese lost control of the region until the Tang expeditions reconquered it and extended Chinese power as far as Lake Balkash.

Once again the region was lost to the Chinese with the fall of the Tang; it was not recovered until the Qing Dynasty, when the second Qing emperor, Kang-xi, came to the throne at age 16. His long rule from 1661 to 1722 allowed him enough time to conquer Mongolia and Tibet as well, giving the Chinese power over the largest area ever.

The 19th century was a bloody one for Xinjiang. If the newly arrived European barbarians were an affliction on the limbs of China, then the internal barbarians were a disease of its vitals. Unrest was everywhere. A raging rebellion had been staged between the Yellow and Yangtse rivers in 1796, followed by the massive Taiping Rebellion of 1851 to 1864. There were also two major Muslim rebellions: one in Yunnan from 1855 to 1873, and another in the north-west from 1862 to 1873 which spread across Shaanxi, Ningxia, Gansu and Xinjiang. Both were put down with extreme savagery by the Chinese. The north-western rebellion had grown out of decades of misrule by the Chinese, religious controversy and contact with the Taipings. The massacre of untold numbers of Muslims during this 11-year period represented the assertion of Chinese rule, but even as the Qing went into decline towards the end of the 19th

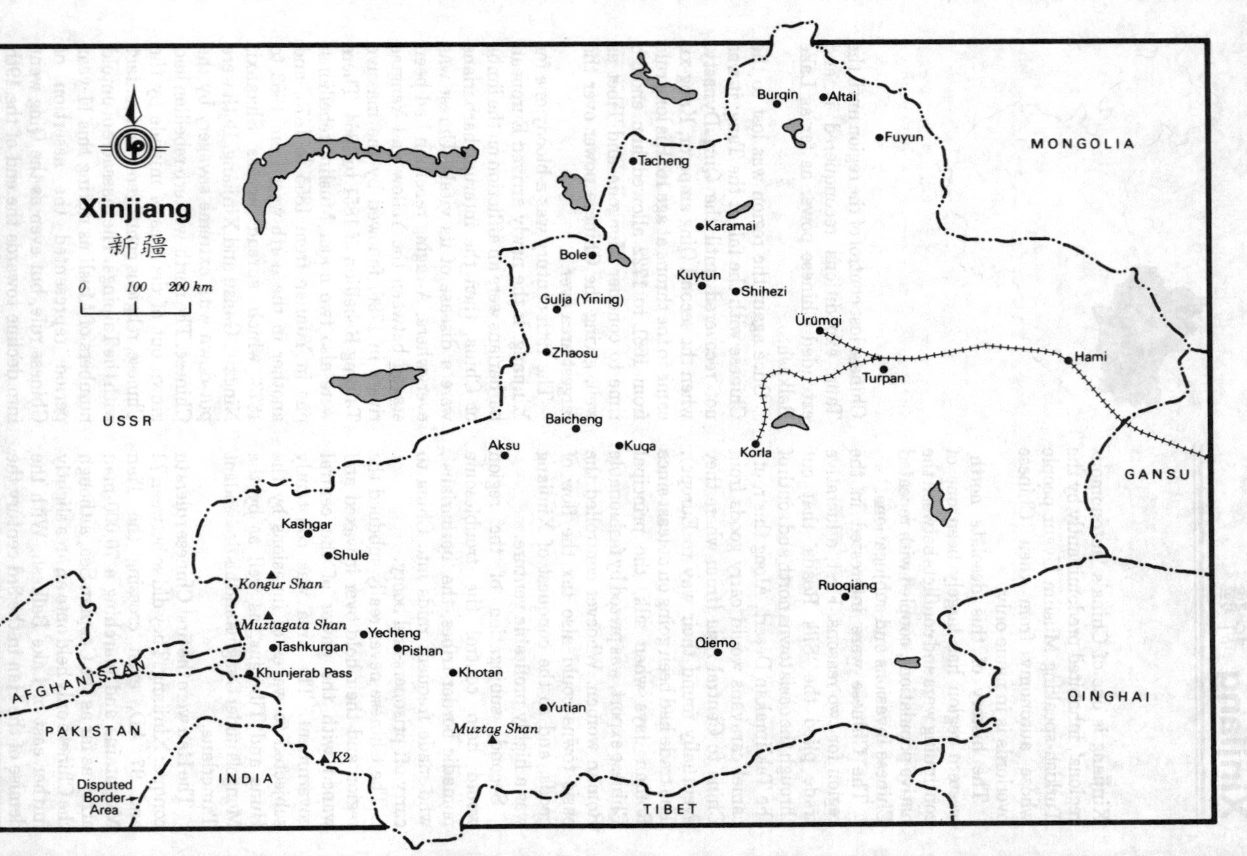
Xinjiang
新疆
0 100 200 km
MONGOLIA
GANSU
QINGHAI
TIBET
INDIA
PAKISTAN
AFGHANISTAN
USSR
Disputed Border Area
Burqin
Altai
Fuyun
Tacheng
Karamai
Bole
Kuytun
Shihezi
Gulja (Yining)
Ürümqi
Hami
Turpan
Zhaosu
Baicheng
Aksu
Kuqa
Korla
Kashgar
Shule
Kongur Shan
Muztagata Shan
Yecheng
Tashkurgan
Pishan
Khunjerab Pass
Khotan
Yutian
Muztag Shan
K2
Ruoqiang
Qiemo

century, so did their hold over the Muslim areas.

With the fall of the Qing in 1911, Xinjiang came under the rule of a succession of warlords, and the governments in Beijing and later in Nanjing had very little influence.

The first of these rulers was Yang Zhengxin, who ruled from 1911 until his assassination in 1928 at a banquet in Ürümqi (the region's traditions of hospitality are highly idiosyncratic and the death-rate at banquets is appalling). Yang had managed to maintain a somewhat unhappy peace, and his policy of isolationism had preserved the region from ideas set loose by the Chinese revolution. He was followed by a second tyrannical overlord who was forced to flee in 1933, and was replaced by a still more oppressive leader named Sheng Shizai, who remained in power almost until the end of WW II when he, too, was forced out. Sheng had initially followed a pro-Communist policy, then suddenly did a reverse and embarked on an anti-Communist purge. Among those executed was Mao Zemin, a younger brother of Mao Zedong, who had been sent by the Party to Xinjiang in 1938 to work as Sheng's financial adviser.

The only real attempt to establish an independent state was in the 1940s, when a Kazakh named Osman led a rebellion of Uygurs, Kazakhs and Mongols, took control of south-western Xinjiang and established an independent Eastern Turkestan Republic in January 1945. The Nationalist government convinced the Muslims to abolish their new republic in return for a pledge of real autonomy. The Nationalists failed to live up to their promise but soon, preoccupied with the civil war, they had little time to re-establish control over the region. They eventually appointed a Muslim named Burhan as governor of the region in 1948, unaware that he was actually a supporter of the Communists.

At the same time a Muslim league opposed to Chinese rule was formed in Xinjiang, but in August 1949 a number of its most prominent leaders died in a mysterious plane crash while on their way to Beijing to hold talks with the new Communist leaders. Muslim opposition to Chinese rule collapsed, though the Kazakh Osman continued to fight until he was captured and executed by the Chinese Communists in early 1951.

The Chinese hold over Xinjiang is certainly strong, but since 1949 the Chinese government has been faced with two problems: proximity to the Soviet Union (considered as the paramount threat), and volatile relations with the region's Muslim inhabitants.

Xinjiang & the Great Game

In the first few decades of the 20th century, the Xinjiang region looked like it was becoming another unwilling player in the 'Great Game' between the British and the Russians. It was round two of an insane power struggle which had previously afflicted Afghanistan and Tibet.

British interests in Xinjiang were obvious from a glance at a map. The region is bounded on the west by the Soviet Union, on the north by Outer Mongolia (now, for all practical purposes, an integral part of the Soviet Union) and on the east by Inner Mongolia and north-west Han China. On the south it was bordered by Tibet and British India. For centuries Indian merchants have crossed the Himalayan passes to trade in Kashgar, so the British once again saw their economic and strategic interests threatened by the Russian bear. They feared that since the Russians had now spied out the area, they might follow up with a territorial annexation. If there were any such plans, then they were stopped by the disastrous Russo-Japanese War of 1904, the revolution of 1917, the ensuing civil war and the Nazi invasion.

In the end it was the Chinese who won out in the Great Game, and they had hardly been playing. Today the region bristles with Chinese troops and weapons. Some of them are there to keep down the ever-volatile Uygurs; others hold back the real or imagined threat from the Soviet Union.

The People

Xinjiang is inhabited by something like 13 of China's official total of 55 national minorities. One problem for the Chinese is that 50% of their country isn't even inhabited by Chinese, but by minority people who mostly don't like them. What's more, these minority people inhabit regions bordering Vietnam, India, Afghanistan and the USSR – all places of past or possible future conflict.

In 1955 the province of Xinjiang was renamed the 'Uygur Autonomous Region'. At that time more than 90% of the population was non-Chinese. With the building of the Lanzhou-Ürümqi railroad and the development of industry in the region, there was a large influx of Chinese who now form a majority in the northern area while the Uygurs continue to predominate in the south.

In 1953 Xinjiang had a population of about 4.9 million, of whom 3.6 million were Uygurs and only a very small number were Han Chinese. By 1970 the number of Hans was estimated to have grown to about four million. According to the 1982 census there are now 13 million people in Xinjiang, of whom only about six million are Uygurs. It's a trend that will inevitably continue as the region develops, with the result that the Uygurs will be subjugated and pacified by sheer weight of numbers.

Relations between the Han and the minority people in the region vary. The nomadic Kazakhs were angered by the forced introduction of the communes. About 60,000 are supposed to have crossed into the Soviet Union in 1962, a figure which represents a sizeable proportion of the population (at present there are only 900,000, spread across Xinjiang, Gansu and Qinghai). Other groups of Kazakhs escaped to India or Pakistan and were granted political asylum in Turkey, where they were resettled. Chinese relations with the Tajiks (numbering 26,000) are said to be better.

Unfortunately for the Chinese, relations with the fairly numerous, minority Uygurs can be best described as volatile. The Chinese have done a great deal to relieve the backwardness of the region, building roads, railways and hospitals, and industrialising the towns. Their presence also prevents the Uygurs from fighting among themselves, a problem whenever centralised rule has toppled. So it's difficult for the Chinese to understand the hostility with which they are greeted. Part of the hostility probably originates from centuries of Chinese misrule and from the savage way in which the 19th-century rebellions were put down; part of it simply from the fact that the Uygurs don't have anything in common with the Chinese. The Uygur religion is monotheistic Islam, their written script is Arabic, their language is closely related to Turkish, and their physical features are basically Caucasian – many could easily be mistaken for Greeks, southern Italians or other southern Europeans.

Part of the problem may also stem from the intentional or unintentional policy of the Chinese to blur distinctions between Han and Uygur culture. The recent reintroduction of Arabic script in primary schools is offset by the almost exclusive use and hence requirement of Chinese language at tertiary level. Arabic script has been given a romanised form to speed up the learning process and promote literacy. The Cultural Revolution inflicted itself here by closing down the mosques, slightly more than a sore point with a devout people like the Muslims. With the death of Mao and the rise of a more liberal regime to power, the mosques have since been re-opened.

The all-out rebellions of the past may be over – the recent influx of Chinese soldiers and settlers means that it is probably out of the question. However, even now there is some sort of anti-Chinese riot or demonstration in one Xinjiang town or another every year. For many years the Lop Nur region in the Tarim Basin has been used for nuclear tests. Reports of livestock and locals suffering from radiation poisoning were recently confirmed when Uygur protesters took to the streets in Xinjiang and even Beijing. For the Uygurs the Chinese are very much a foreign occupation force.

Minorities

The minority nationalities of Xinjiang are probably some of the most interesting in China. To the west of Ürümqi, where the Tian range divides in two, is the Ili Valley. The population in the valley is a mixed bag of Kirghiz, Kazakhs and Chinese, and even includes a colony of Sibo, the descendants of the Manchu garrison which was stationed here after the conquests of the 18th century. Another peculiar army to hit Xinjiang was the refugee White Russian troops who fled after their defeat in the Russian Civil War. Some settled here and founded scattered colonies.

The most interesting minority has a population of one; in the 1930s there was a bizarre story that T E Lawrence (of Arabia fame) was active in the British cause against the Russians in Xinjiang, and had gone wandering off with a band of local tribespeople to raise hell and high sandstorms. It was a rumour which continued even after Lawrence's fatal motorcycle accident in Britain in 1936 – the Xinjiang footnote being not the least fantastic part of the Lawrence legend.

Language

Uygur Mini-Glossary If you have Caucasian features and speak Turkish, you will blend perfectly into Xinjiang. Once you leave the beaten path, Russian can sometimes prove even more useful than Chinese! Even if your command of Turkish, Russian or Uygur is minimal, the Uygurs love to hear an attempt being made at their language – helps them to forget their isolation. With no apologies for transliteration, here are some linguistic pointers for bargaining, travelling or just passing the time of day:

hello (peace be upon you)
salaam aleikum
how much?
khanj pul?
good
yakshi
not good
yok yakshi
what's your name?
sen ismi nemă?
goodbye
khosh
bus
optus
bus stop
baket
ticket
bilhet
food/restaurant
ash/ashkhana
yes
ah
no
emess

The Land

Xinjiang is divided by the east-west Tian Mountain Range into two major regions. To the south of the Tian range is the Tarim Basin, and to the north is the Junggar Basin.

The Tarim Basin is bordered to the south by the Kunlun range. It's a huge depression whose centre is occupied by the sands of the Taklimakan Desert into which streams from the surrounding mountains lose themselves.

Other streams run from the Tian range into the Tarim River, which flows eastward and empties into the vast salt marsh and lake of Lop Nur. The boundaries of Lop Nur vary greatly from year to year as a result of climatic variation; it's an area of poor grassland and semi-desert, almost uninhabited. Since 1964 the Chinese have been testing their nuclear bombs here.

The Taklimakan Desert is a true desert. Cultivation is only possible in the oases of irrigated land which centre on the streams flowing into the basin from the surrounding mountains. These oases have had flourishing cultures of their own for 2000 years and were important stopover points on the 'Silk Road', the trading route which connected China to the land further west.

The oases of Xinjiang are largely populated by Uygur people and support an irrigated agricultural industry based mainly on food grains and fruit. The grasslands of the foothills support a pastoral industry based on sheep and horses. The agriculture of places like the Turpan and Hami depressions depends entirely on irrigation, using water drawn from underground streams. Only in the Ili Valley, west of Ürümqi, is rainfall sufficient to support a flourishing agricultural and pastoral industry.

The Junggar Basin has been the centre of extensive colonisation by the Chinese since the 1950s. Large state farms have been established on formerly uncultivated land. The major towns are Ürümqi (the capital of Xinjiang), Shihezi and Manas. Their importance grew with the completion of the Xinjiang railway from Lanzhou to Ürümqi in 1963, the rapid growth in the population and the exploitation of rich oil resources in the basin.

The Junggar Basin is less arid than the Tarim Basin and most of it is grassland supporting a pastoral population. The people are primarily nomadic Kazakhs or Torgut Mongols, herding sheep, some horses, cattle and camels. The north and north-west of the Junggar Basin are bounded by the Altai mountain range of 3000 to 4000-metre-high peaks on the Mongolian border. It's an area of substantial rainfall, and the mountains are either tree-covered or form rich pastureland. The population is mainly nomadic Kazakh or Oirat Mongol herdsmen.

Climate

Try to avoid going to Xinjiang at the height of summer or the depths of winter. In summer, industrial Ürümqi is miserable and Turpan more than deserves the title of 'hottest place in China' – the maximums in Turpan get up to 47°C. In winter, though, this region is as formidably cold as anywhere else in northern China. In Ürümqi the average temperature in January is around –10°C, with minimums of around –30°C. Winter temperatures in Turpan are only slightly more favourable to human existence.

Time

Xinjiang is several time zones removed from Beijing, which prefers to ignore the fact. Officially, Beijing time applies; in practice, Xinjiang time (between one and two hours behind Beijing time) is used haphazardly for meal times in hotels, bus departures, etc. Try and straighten out any confusion by asking whether the stated time is *Beijing shijian* (Beijing time) or *Xinjiang shijian* (Xinjiang time).

HAMI 哈密

The town of Hami, known in the past as Kumul, was once an important caravanserai on the northern route of the Silk Road. It was recently opened to foreigners; a Chinese map available in Ürümqi marks various sights in town and at Shimenzi (69 km north of Hami). Hami's most famous product is the *Hami gua* (Hami melon), which is delicious and highly prized by thirsty train passengers who scramble to buy them during the short stop at Hami station.

DAHEYAN 大河沿

The jumping-off point for Turpan is a place on the railway line signposted 'Turpan Zhan'. In fact, you are actually in

Daheyan, and the Turpan oasis is an hour's drive south across the desert. Daheyan is not a place you'll want to hang around, so spare a thought for the Chinese who have to eke out a sane living here.

The bus station is a 10-minute walk from the railway station. Walk up the road leading from the railway station and turn right at the first main intersection; the bus station is a few minutes' walk ahead on the left-hand side of the road. There are three buses a day to Turpan: one at 7.30, another at 10 am and probably the final one at 3 pm, but these departure times depend on the relative positions of the sun and the moon. There are lots of trucks on these two roads and you may be able to hitch if you miss the bus; it's about an hour's drive to Turpan. If you miss the bus and can't get there hitching, you'll have to spend the night in this exotic outpost. The hotel (Y2 per bed) is behind the bus station. There's also a daily bus from Daheyan to Kashgar (Y36).

TURPAN 吐鲁番

East of Ürümqi the Tai Mountains split into a southern and a northern mountain range; between the two lies the Hami depression, falling to 200 metres below sea level, and the Turpan depression, which drops even lower to 160 metres. Both are practically rainless, with searing-hot summers.

Turpan County is inhabited by about 170,000 people, of whom about 120,000 are Uygurs and the rest mostly Chinese. The centre of the county is the large Turpan oasis. It's little more than a few main streets set in a vast tract of grain fields, and more importantly it's been spared the architectural horrors inflicted on Ürümqi. Most of the streets are planted with trees and are lined with mud-brick walls enclosing mud houses. Open channels with flowing water run down the sides of the streets; the inhabitants draw water from these as well as use them to wash their clothes, dishes and children.

Of the places in Xinjiang currently open to foreigners, Turpan and Kashgar remain closest to traditional Uygur culture; Ürümqi and Shihezi are Chinese settlements. Turpan also holds a special place in Uygur history since nearby Gaochang was once the capital of the

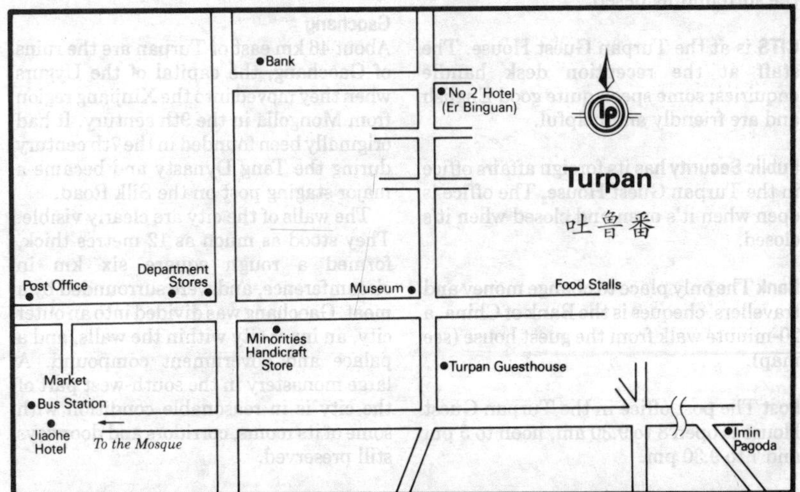

Uygurs. It was an important staging post on the Silk Road and was a centre of Buddhism before being converted to Islam in the 8th century. During the Chinese occupation it served as a garrison town.

Turpan is a quiet place (one of the few in China) and the guest house is a good place to sit underneath the vine trellises, drink beer and contemplate the moon. The living is cheap, the food is good and the people are friendly, and there are a couple of interesting 'sights' scattered around to keep you occupied. Along with Hangzhou and Yangshuo, it's one of the few places in the country where you can relax and withdraw a bit from China. It's also the hottest; temperatures in summer have been known to reach 47°C!

Information & Orientation

The 'centre' of the Turpan oasis is little more than two main roads and a couple of side streets. You'll find the shops, market, long-distance bus station, tourist guest house and a couple of plodding donkey carts all within easy walking distance of each other. Most of the sights are scattered on the outskirts of the oasis or in the surrounding desert.

CITS is at the Turpan Guest House. The staff at the reception desk handle enquiries; some speak quite good English and are friendly and helpful.

Public Security has its foreign affairs office in the Turpan Guest House. The office is open when it's open and closed when it's closed.

Bank The only place to change money and travellers' cheques is the Bank of China, a 20-minute walk from the guest house (see map).

Post The post office in the Turpan Guest House is open 8 to 9.30 am, noon to 5 pm and 7 to 9.30 pm.

CAAC There are no flights to Turpan. The nearest airport is at Ürümqi.

Maps No maps are available of the oasis itself, though there is supposed to be a large one hanging in a back room of the guest house. Their reception desk distributes a fairly good map (in Chinese) of the surrounding area, showing the little villages and the historical sites.

Imin Pagoda (Sugongta Mosque)

On the eastern outskirts of Turpan is this unusual mosque with its single minaret, designed in a simple Afghani style and built in the late 1770s by a local ruler. The pagoda is circular, 44 metres high and tapering towards the top.

The mosque is a half-hour walk from the Turpan Guest House. Turn left out of the hotel and left again at the first crossroads; this road leads straight down to the mosque. There is a hole in the wall at the side of the mosque so you can get into the main building. If you want to climb the pagoda you'll have to ask the keeper to unlock the door to the stairway; he lives in the small whitewashed building beside the mosque.

Gaochang

About 46 km east of Turpan are the ruins of Gaochang, the capital of the Uygurs when they moved into the Xinjiang region from Mongolia in the 9th century. It had originally been founded in the 7th century during the Tang Dynasty and became a major staging post on the Silk Road.

The walls of the city are clearly visible. They stood as much as 12 metres thick, formed a rough square six km in circumference, and were surrounded by a moat. Gaochang was divided into an outer city, an inner city within the walls, and a palace and government compound. A large monastery in the south-west part of the city is in reasonable condition with some of its rooms, corridors and doorways still preserved.

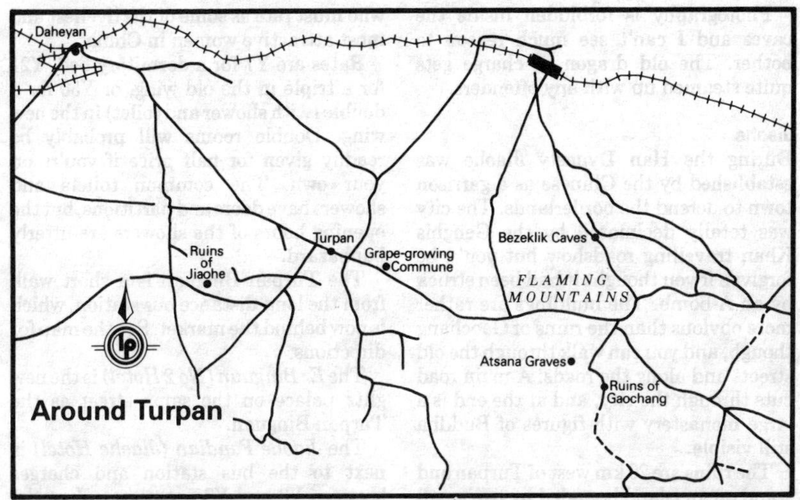

Atsana Graves

These graves where the dead of Gaochang are buried lie north-west of the ancient city. Only three of the tombs are open to tourists, and each of these is approached by a short flight of steps which leads down to the burial chamber about six metres below ground level.

One tomb contains portraits of the deceased painted on the walls, while another has paintings of birds. The third tomb holds two well-preserved corpses (one mummy from the original trio seems to have been removed to Turpan's museum) like those in the museums at Ürümqi and Hangzhou. Some of the artefacts date back as far as the Jin Dynasty of the 3rd to 5th centuries AD. The finds included silks, brocades, embroideries and many funerary objects such as shoes, hats and sashes made of recycled paper. The last turned out to be quite a find for the archaeologists, since the paper included deeds, records of slave purchases, orders for silk and other everyday transactions.

Flaming Mountains

North of Gaochang lie the aptly-named Flaming Mountains – they look like they're on fire in the mid-day sun. Purplish-brown in colour, they are 100 km long and 10 km wide.

Bezeklik Thousand Buddha Caves

On the western side of the Flaming Mountains, on a cliff face fronting a river valley, are the remains of these Buddhist cave temples. All the caves are in dreadful condition, most having been devastated by Muslims or robbed by all and sundry. The large statues which stood at the rear of each cave have been destroyed or stolen and the faces of the buddhas which ornament the walls have either been scrapped or completely gouged out. Particularly active in the export of murals was a German Albert von Le Coq, who removed whole frescoes from the stone walls and transported them back to the Berlin Museum – where Allied bombing wiped most of them out during WW II. Today the caves reveal little more than a hint of what they were like in their heyday.

Photography is forbidden inside the caves and I can't see much reason to bother. The old dragon in charge gets quite steamed up with any offenders.

Jiaohe

During the Han Dynasty Jiaohe was established by the Chinese as a garrison town to defend the borderlands. The city was totally decimated by the Genghis Khan travelling roadshow but you'd be forgiven if you thought it had been struck by an A-bomb. The buildings are rather more obvious than the ruins of Gaochang though, and you can walk through the old streets and along the roads. A main road cuts through the city, and at the end is a large monastery with figures of Buddha still visible.

The ruins are 20 km west of Turpan and stand on an island bounded by two small rivers – thus the name Jiaohe, which means 'confluence of two rivers'. You can get out to the ruins on a donkey cart; it's about a 1½-hour ride from the hotel and the return trip will only cost you Y3 (or maybe Y4 if there are two of you). There's an artificial lake close to the ruins if you want to go swimming.

Places to Stay

The *Turpan Binguan* is still the most popular hotel in Turpan, and it's one of the most pleasant in China. There are a couple of older wings as well as a new wing which takes the soya sauce as one of the worst-looking buildings in the country – imitation red pillars, white plaster relief decorations, green walls with yellow trim and domes on the roof. On the other hand, the vine trellises are good to sit under at night contemplating the moon and saturating yourself with beer. When there's a tour group in town there's a performance of Uygur music, song and dance in the courtyard under the trellises. It starts around 9.30 pm and is free to all. They're fun nights that usually end up with the front row of the audience being dragged out to dance with the performers, who must rate as some of the liveliest and most attractive women in China.

Rates are Y7 for a dormitory bed, Y21 for a triple in the old wing, or Y50 for a double (with shower and toilet) in the new wing. Double rooms will probably be readily given for half price if you're on your own. The common toilets and showers have doors and partitions, but the opening hours of the showers are utterly haphazard.

The Turpan Binguan is a short walk from the long-distance bus station, which is now behind the market. See the map for directions.

The *Er Binguan (No 2 Hotel)* is the new glitz palace on the same street as the Turpan Binguan.

The *Jiaohe Fandian (Jiaohe Hotel)* is next to the bus station and charges between Y3 and Y9 per person. Just the place to be if you like noise and action.

Places to Eat

The *Turpan Binguan* is the best place to eat – the food is excellent. Hotel meals are Y3.50 each and more than worth the money. Breakfast is very good at Y2. There is a small market down a lane approximately opposite the bus station where you can get shish kebab and flat bread; you'll also find some food stalls.

Getting There & Away

Getting out of Turpan is a confused affair but most people make it to the outside world by some means or another.

Air The nearest airport is at Ürümqi.

Bus The bus station is behind the market. The ticket windows never seem to be open, so just turn up early and buy your ticket on the day of departure from the man who stands around outside selling them. Make sure you get to the station an hour or even more before departure, because absolutely no one seems to know when the buses depart. There are buses from here to Ürümqi and to Daheyan.

Departure times for the buses to Ürümqi have been variously described as 8.30 am, 1 pm and 6 pm – although there are only supposed to be two buses a day. My bus departed at 8.30 am, stopped for an hour at 10.30 am for a meal and arrived in Ürümqi at around 1.45 pm. It's great scenery along the way – immense grey sand dunes, and snow-capped mountains visible in the distance as you approach Ürümqi. The fare is Y4.90.

Rail The nearest rail line is the Ürümqi-Lanzhou line north of Turpan. The nearest railway station is at Daheyan. Departure times for buses from Turpan to Daheyan have been given as 8 am, 8.30 am, 9 am, 5 pm, 5.30 pm and 6 pm although there are only supposed to be two buses a day. Departure times of around 7.30 or 8 am and 6 pm are probably the best bet – and apparently it can take as long as two hours for the bus to crawl to Daheyan! Try to avoid going there.

Getting Around

Public transport around Turpan is by donkey cart; there are no buses. If you walk, remember that Turpan is really spread out. You can believe those stories about this being the hottest place in China so take a water bottle with you! The middle of the day can be searing and the streets are almost bare of people.

There are several ways of getting to the sights scattered around Turpan. You can rent a taxi from the hotel at a rate of 50 fen per km. You may also be able to go with a tour group for about Y15, or you can get enough people together and hire a minivan that seats 12 people from the hotel. Outside the hotel you will be offered deals by private operators with mini-trucks. Charges for a small tour average Y10 per person for a group of six people or Y60 for two people for a whole day. Bargain their prices down to a sane level.

A trip including the Gaochang ruins, Atsana Graves, Bezeklik Caves, Flaming Mountains and Imin Pagoda will cost each person between Y10 and Y15 depending on the type of transport. (If there's time left, you might also stop off at one of the grape-growing communes.) If you want to go on a minibus trip then look for the Hong Kongers – they travel in small gangs and you should be able to tag along with them.

ÜRÜMQI 乌鲁木齐

In the centre of Ürümqi is a desolate rocky outcrop called Hong Shan. Steps to the top lead to a small pavilion from which you can get a panoramic view of the great expanse of dusty roads, shimmering apartment blocks and smokestacks that have sprung out of the surrounding desolation. Ürümqi is an interesting place to visit but it's got to be one of the ugliest cities on the face of the earth!

The capital of Xinjiang, the city boomed after the Communists built the railway line from Lanzhou across the Xinjiang desert. About 800,000 people live here now, 75% of them Han Chinese – the place has always been a Chinese island in a sea of Muslims. The inspired concrete-block architecture of socialist eastern China has been imported lock, stock and barrel, and Ürümqi essentially looks little different from its northern Han China counterparts 1500 miles east – just uglier. There are few 'sights' as such, but there's an intrinsic interest to the place which makes it worth visiting.

Two and a half days up the rail line from Xian and in the same country, you couldn't come across a people more different from the Chinese than the Uygurs. Ürümqi is the first place where you'll see these swarthy-skinned Turkic descendants in any number; larger and heavier than the Han Chinese, they have features resembling those of Caucasians and many of them could easily pass for southern Italians or Greeks. The Uygur women wear skirts or dresses and brightly coloured scarves, in contrast to the slacks and baggy trousers of the Han Chinese,

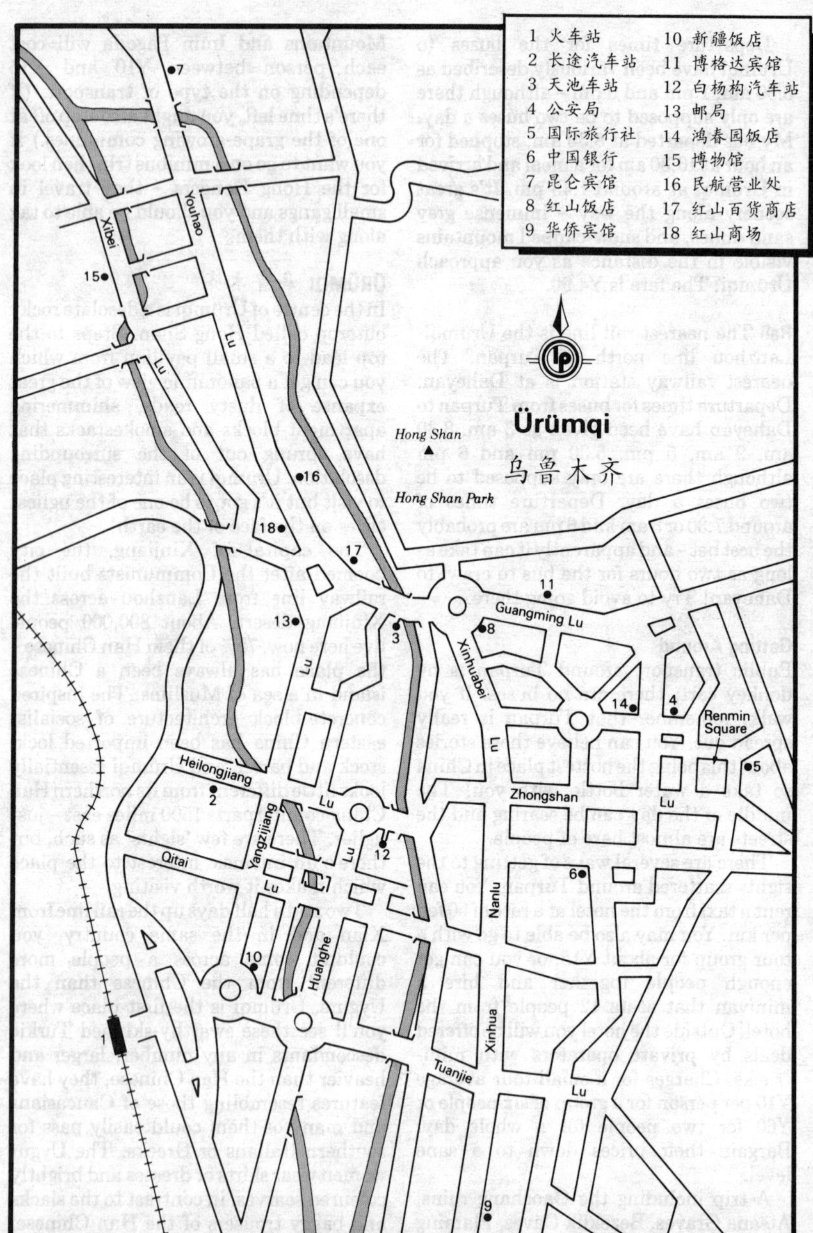
1 火车站
2 长途汽车站
3 天池车站
4 公安局
5 国际旅行社
6 中国银行
7 昆仑宾馆
8 红山饭店
9 华侨宾馆
10 新疆饭店
11 博格达宾馆
12 白杨构汽车站
13 邮局
14 鸿春园饭店
15 博物馆
16 民航营业处
17 红山百货商店
18 红山商场
Ürümqi
乌鲁木齐
Hong Shan
Hong Shan Park
Xibei
Youhao
Lu
Lu
Guangming Lu
Xinhuabei
Lu
Renmin Square
Zhongshan
Lu
Heilongjiang
Lu
Qitai
Lu
Yangzijiang
Lu
Huanghe
Nanlu
Xinhua
Tuanjie
Lu

1 Railway Station
2 Long-distance Bus Station
3 Bus to Tianchi
4 Public Security
5 CITS
6 Bank of China
7 Kunlun Guest House
8 Hong Shan Hotel
9 Overseas Chinese Hotel
10 Xinjiang Hotel
11 Bogda Hotel
12 Bus to Baiyanggou
13 Post Office
14 Hong Chun Restaurants
15 Museum
16 CAAC
17 Hong Shan Department Store
18 Hong Shan Market

and they pierce their ears – a practice which repels the Han. The Uygur men must be the only men in China capable of growing beards. Arm's distance from the Uygurs are the Han Chinese immigrants as well as the PLA soldiers who are not only there to keep the Russians at bay and maintain Chinese control over Xinjiang, but also to keep the tenuous peace between the Uygurs and the Han. It's hard not to feel you're in the provincial capital of a foreign occupation force.

Information & Orientation
Ürümqi is a blob-shaped city with an urban peninsula to the north. Most of the sights, tourist facilities and hotels are scattered across the city, though they're all easily accessible by the local buses.

The railway and long-distance bus stations are in the south-eastern corner of the city; the main tourist hotel and a couple of museums are on the northern peninsula. There are two candidates for the title of 'city centre': the first is the area around the large Hongshan Department Store where some of the major arteries intersect; the other is in the eastern part of the city, where you'll find the main shopping district, CITS office, Public Security and Bank of China.

CITS (tel 5794) is in a compound on the east side of Renmin Square, which lies in the eastern part of the city. The office is in the yellow concrete building on your left as you enter the compound. There's a sign in front of the gate.

Be thankful for any morsel of information obtained at this fount of tourist learning. The woman I spoke to in the office was quite perturbed when I told her that Hami was soon to be opened to foreigners – truck drivers had told me they'd read it in the newspaper. She explained that she couldn't divulge details of Hami's tourist wonders since CITS had no knowledge of this new opening. A couple of months later, newspapers in Hong Kong noted that Hami was open to foreigners.

The office is open Monday to Saturday, 9.30 am to 1 pm and 4 to 8 pm. It's closed on Sunday. Bus No 1 from the Kunlun Guest House will take you most of the way to the office.

There's a CTS office in the Huaqiao Fandian (Overseas Chinese Hotel) which might be able to help if you keep your questions ultra-simple.

Public Security is a 10-minute walk from the CITS office, in a large government building just to the north-west of Renmin Square (see map). To get there from the Kunlun Hotel take bus No 1 – it runs past the building.

Bank The Bank of China is housed in a new building close to Renmin Square. It's open 10 am to 2 pm and 3.30 to 4.30 pm; closed Wednesday and Friday afternoon and all day Sunday. Clambering through the building rubble of the back exit, I somehow landed up on the wrong side of the counter during siesta time, but the staff graciously changed money. International credit cards are accepted here too. The 'other' money marketeers conveniently prowl this beat. Take bus No 1 from the Huaqiao Fandian or Kunlun Binguan.

Post The main post office is a big

Corinthian-colonnaded building directly across the traffic circle from the Hongshan Department Store. The foreign section is efficient and has a packing service. Keep an eye on the customs inspection counter to see what local Uygurs send their Soviet comrades and vice-versa – the current export hit from China seems to be stockings. Outside the post office are various seal engravers keen to count you among their customers.

There is a post office on the ground floor of the Kunlun Guest House.

CAAC (tel 41536) is on Youhao Lu, the same road that the Kunlun Guest House is on, and it's open 10 am to 1.30 pm and 4 to 8 pm. Bus Nos 1 and 2 from the Kunlun Guest House go past the office.

Maps Good maps, in Chinese and showing the bus routes, are available from the train station, bus station, department stores, bookstores and most of the hotels. There are several kinds; just keep collecting until you know your way around. The Hong Shan Department Store has some excellent maps of Xinjiang on the left-hand side of the ground floor.

Things to See

As mentioned earlier, Ürümqi has few 'sights' as such and much of the interest of the city is intrinsic. Worth exploring, though, is the museum which houses some interesting exhibits. A couple of hours' drive from the city in the Tian Shan (Tian Mountains) is the stunning Lake of Heaven (Tianchi).

Museum of National Minorities & History Museum

Xinjiang covers 16% of China's total land surface. It is inhabited not only by the Han Chinese but also by 13 of China's official total of 55 minority peoples. The left wing of the museum contains an interesting exhibition relating to some of the Xinjiang minority groups and it's well worth a look.

Notable among the exhibits are the Daur hats which are made of the heads of animals and have large fur rims – the Daur number about 94,000 and are spread across Xinjiang, Inner Mongolia and Heilongjiang. The Tajik exhibition features silver and coral beads supporting silver pendants – these people number about 26,500 and are found only in Xinjiang. The Kazakhs number about 900,000 and their exhibition in the museum features a heavily furnished yurt. The Mongol exhibit includes particularly ornate silver bridles and saddles studded with semi-precious stones, stringed musical instruments and decorated riding boots.

The right wing of the museum is a fascinating section devoted to history. Prime exhibits are the preserved bodies of two men and two women discovered in tombs in Xinjiang, similar to those you may have seen in the museum at Hangzhou. Also interesting is the collection of multi-coloured clay figurines unearthed from Turpan, dating back to the Tang Dynasty. Note the collection of silk fragments with various patterns from different dynasties.

The distinctive Russian-style building with a green dome is on Xibei Lu, about 20 minutes' walk from the Kunlun Guest House. From Hong Shan Department Store take bus No 7 for four stops and ask to get off at the *bowuguan* (museum).

Places to Stay

The *Hong Shan Binguan (Hong Shan Hotel)* (tel 24761) is a good base in the centre of town even though the staff are slovenly and aggressive. Doubles start at Y26; dorm beds in an eight-bed room cost Y7. City maps and stamps are sold in a small room on the ground floor next to the door.

The reception desk hands out tickets for use in the shower unit across the yard, at the back of the compound. Plenty of hot water although you may have to wait in a long queue. The waiting room has a thought-provoking sign in Chinese: 'It is forbidden to do the big one (defecate) in the showers. Y5 fine if you do!'

From the train station, take bus No 2 for four stops. You'll then be close to the main post office, which is a short walk from the hotel. From the main bus station, turn right out of the station gates and walk about 150 metres along Heilongjiang Lu until you cross an intersection and reach the stop for bus No 8. Take this bus east for four stops and then switch to either bus Nos 7 or 17 going north for one stop.

The *Huaqiao Fandian (Overseas Chinese Hotel)* (tel 23239), formerly called the Ürümqi Hotel, is much further from the town centre than the Hong Shan Hotel, but still easy to reach from there on bus No 7. The comfortable rooms are a good place to let your bones knit after the Kashgar bus trip. Doubles cost Y44; dorm beds cost Y8 in a five-bed room.

From the train station, take bus No 10 for four stops, and then walk 50 metres east to Xinhua Nanlu and take bus No 7 south for one stop. From the main bus station, turn right out of the station gates and walk about 150 metres along Heilongjiang Lu until you cross an intersection and reach the stop for bus No 8. Take this bus east for two stops, then hop onto bus No 7 and go south for four stops.

The *Kunlun Binguan (Kunlun Guest House)* (tel 42411) used to be Ürümqi's main tourist joint, but it's only worth keeping in mind now as a second choice. Cheapest accommodation is Y10 per bed in a four-bed room – the problem is that apart from the small basin in the room there is nowhere to wash. Double rooms are Y55, with toilet and shower. From the railway station take bus No 2 (the stop is right outside the station), which will drop you off just a few minutes' walk from the hotel.

Ürümqi has several other hotels which are geared to groups and conference clientele rather than to individual travellers. Two new hotels in this category with sensible locations are the *Bogda Binguan (Bogda Hotel)* (tel 24432) and the *Xinjiang Binguan (Xinjiang Hotel)* (tel 54002). Most of the others are so far from town that you'll spend half the day getting there and back.

Places to Eat

Ürümqi is a good place to try Uygur foods such as shish kebab or *laghman* (noodles with spicy vegetables). During the summer, the markets are packed with delicious fruit, both fresh and dried.

The *Hong Chun Yuan Fandian*, close to the Public Security office, is a Chinese-only hotel with two restaurants. The one on the right of the entrance serves *Zhong can* (Chinese food), the one on the left serves *Xi can* (western food). The locals like being able to experiment with the western restaurant which some have given the nickname 'Knife & Fork Restaurant'.

Western food is surprisingly good and cheap. The menu includes hamburgers, Wiener schnitzel, ham & eggs with chips, vegetable soup, salad, chicken & peas, curry and prawns in red sauce. Ordering is best done by pointing to the relevant dishes on neighbouring tables. Beer, coffee, brandy and cakes are available. The restaurant closes around 6 pm.

Foreigners who eat here will see new variations on eating western-style. One woman speared a cream cake on a fork and stuffed it sideways into her mouth at the same time she slurped vegetable soup. It seems that the more you can pile onto your table the better your image with your friends.

The restaurant at the *Huaqiao Fandian* does a good Chinese dinner for Y6. The restaurant on the ground floor of the *Kunlun Guest House* is best avoided except by the famished. For evening munchies, turn left out of the Kunlun Guest House and walk for about 15 minutes up the main street. You'll find lots of stalls selling flat bread (20 fen) and shish kebab (10 fen). Makes a great change from rice and veggies.

For more flat bread and shish kebab try the *Hongshan Market* opposite the Hongshan Department Store. It's a bustling little covered market with innumerable food stalls and restaurants.

Getting There & Away

Escape from Ürümqi is by bus, train or plane – there are no boats.

Air Ürümqi is connected by air with Beijing (Y565), Lanzhou (Y295), Shanghai (Y633) and Xian (Y384). There are also flights from Ürümqi to the following places in Xinjiang: Fuyun, Altai, Karamai, Yining (Y117), Korla (Y77), Kuqa (Y134), Aksu (Y185), Kashgar (Y291), Khotan and Qiemo.

Bus The long-distance bus station is in the western part of town. The departure time given on your ticket is normally Beijing time; check if you're not sure. Buses depart for Shihezi at 8 am and the fare is Y4. Buses depart for Turpan at 9 am and the fare is Y4.90. Buses depart for Kashgar at 9 am and the fare is Y38.30 (good luck). Check out the small, colourful mosque opposite the bus station while you're down there.

Rail From Ürümqi there are trains running to Beijing via Lanzhou, Yinchuan, Baotou, Hohhot and Datong; to Zhengzhou via Xian; to Beijing via Xian, Zhengzhou and Shijiazhuang; to Shanghai via Xian, Zhengzhou and Nanjing.

There is intense competition for tickets at the train station, where the market has been cornered by a variety of touts both inside and outside the system. Try and book as far in advance as possible and join the queue before 8 am. If you only manage to get hard-seat, you can sometimes buy hard-sleepers on the train for at least part of your journey – providing you queue persistently within a few minutes of the train's departure.

The railway link between Ürümqi and Korla has been opened to passenger service. At present, only 500-series trains (hard-seat only) run this route, which may be scenic but is hardly worth 18 hours of hard-seat travel.

Getting Around

From the east to the west, from the north to the south, the wonders of Ürümqi are accessible by bus. Taxis are available for hire from the hotels.

AROUND ÜRÜMQI

Southern Pastures

The southern pastures are a vast expanse of grazing land south of Ürümqi. The land is inhabited by Kazakh herdsmen who graze sheep, cattle and horses here during the summer months.

Curious stories have been told of the gangs of Hong Kong Chinese who come down here by the minibus-load. Unused to vast open spaces or to the sight of animals almost in the wild, they leap from the bus and charge at the unsuspecting creatures, who scatter in all directions. A distraught Kazakh herdsman usually rides up waving his arms in the air and shouting abuse, and must be placated by the tour guide with apologies and cigarettes.

A local bus to Baiyanggou (the pasturelands) leaves from the bus station close to Lijiaoqiao (see map). There are two buses each day leaving at 8.40 am and 5.40 pm in the summer; 8.30 am and 3.30 pm in the winter. The fare is Y1.30 for the 1½-hour ride (56 km). The ticket office near Hong Shan which sells Tianchi tickets also operates trips to Baiyanggou at Y5 per person.

Tianchi – the Lake of Heaven

The Lake of Heaven is a sight you'll never forget. Half-way up a mountain in the middle of a desert, it looks like a chunk of Switzerland or Canada that's been picked up and dumped in the oblivion end of China. The small, deep-blue lake is surrounded by hills covered with fir trees and grazed by horses. Scattered around are the yurts of the Kazakh people who inhabit the mountains; in the distance are the snow-covered peaks of the Tian range and you can climb the hills right up to the snowline.

The lake is 115 km east of Ürümqi on the

5445-metre-high Bogda Feng, the Peak of God. The lake freezes over in Xinjiang's bitter winter and the roads up here are only open in the summer months.

There are daily buses from Ürümqi to Tianchi. You buy your ticket at a small booth on the northern side of the People's Park (Renmin Gongyuan), which is in the centre of Ürümqi. Buses depart from here at 7.50 am and the trip to Tianchi takes three hours. They depart Tianchi for Ürümqi at 4 pm.

A one-way ticket costs Y3. A round-trip ticket costs Y6; this ticket is valid for any day but you only have a reserved seat if you come back on the same day. If you buy a return ticket and want to come back another day but still want a reserved seat, it will cost you Y7.50.

The bus will probably drop you off at the end of the lake – from there it's a 20-minute walk to the hotel on the banks. The bus back to Ürümqi leaves from a bus park just over a low ridge at the back of the hotel. If you stay overnight then you'll have the place pretty much to yourself in the morning and after 4 pm, since most people only come here on day trips. Some people have hitched on trucks to Tianchi.

The *Heavenly Lake Hotel* on the banks of the lake is a garish building utterly out of place with the blues and greens of the surroundings. There are rooms for six people at Y4 per bed, rooms for four people at Y8 per bed and double rooms for Y10 per bed. The hotel seems to be the only place to eat. Lunch is Y5 – OK, but forgettable. The beer sells at Y1.10 a bottle, a tolerable brew but a bit tasteless. The manager speaks some English and is very friendly. A boat cruise costs Y2.

The other possibility, of course, is to hike into the hills and go camping – it's a great opportunity, and a rare one in China. And the surrounding countryside is absolutely stunning. Follow the track skirting the lake for about four km to the far end and walk up the valley. During the summer Kazakhs set up yurts in this area and charge Y5 per person. Horses are also offered at Y25 per day for a trek to the snowline. Men use felt saddles; women are given wooden ones. Bread and hot milk are usually sold by the Kazakhs but you should take as much of your own food as possible. Water is best taken from the spring gushing straight out of the mountain at the edge of the lake rather than further up the valley where humans and livestock have contributed to the liquid.

Shihezi

A couple of hours' drive north-west of Ürümqi is the town of Shihezi, or Stony Creek. It's a Chinese outpost and almost all the inhabitants are Hans. The town is officially open to foreigners. It looked dead boring when I passed through on my way to greener pastures further west.

KASHGAR 喀什

Kashgar, like Timbuktu, is one of those fabled cities that everyone seems to know about but no-one seems to get to. A thousand years ago it was a key centre on the Silk Road and Marco Polo passed through commenting that:

> The inhabitants live by trade and industry. They have fine orchards and vineyards and flourishing estates. Cotton grows here in plenty, besides flax and hemp. The soil is fruitful and productive of all the means of life. The country is the starting-point from which many merchants set out to market their wares all over the world.

In the early part of this century, Kashgar was a relatively major town on the edge of a vast nowhere and separated from the rest of China by an endless sandpit. Traders from India tramped to Kashgar via Gilgit and the Hunza Valley; in 1890 the British sent a trade agent to Kashgar to represent their interests and in 1908 they established a consulate. As with Tibet in the 1890s, the rumour machine soon spread the word that the Russians were on the verge of gobbling up Xinjiang.

To most people Kashgar, which is five or six

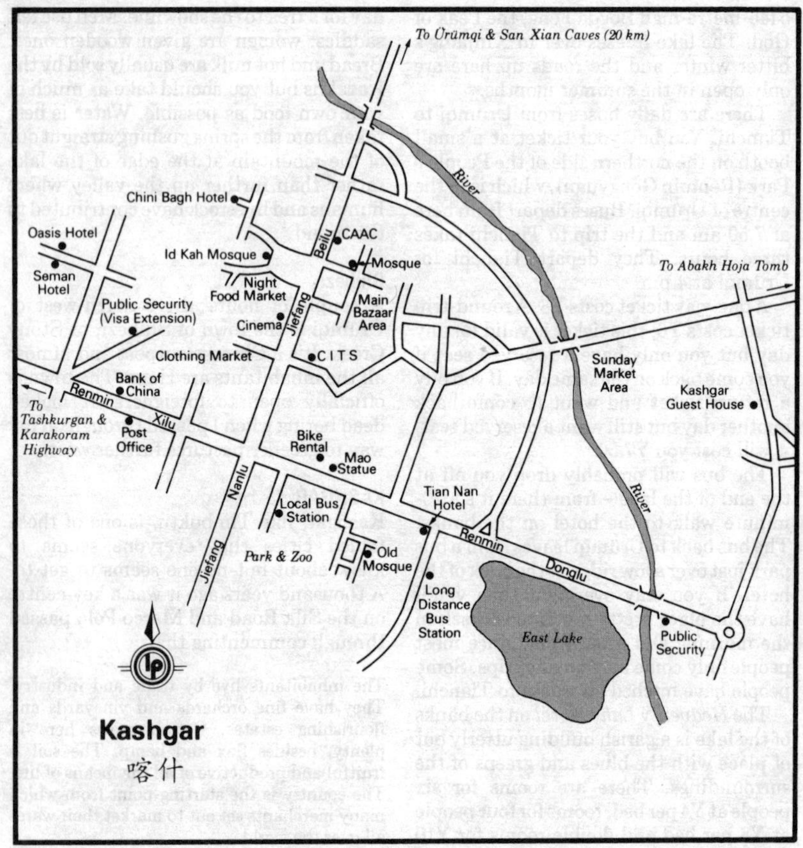

weeks' journey over 15,000-foot passes from the nearest railhead in India, must seem a place barbarously remote; but for us its outlandish name spelt civilisation. The raptures of arrival were unqualified. Discovery is a delightful process, but rediscovery is better; few people can ever have enjoyed a bath more than we did, who had not had one for 5½ months.

That is how Peter Fleming described his arrival in Kashgar back in 1935, after he and Kini Maillart had spent almost half a year on the backs of camels and donkeys getting there from Beijing. Fleming described the city as being 'in effect run by the secret police, the Russian advisers, and the Soviet Consulate, and most of the high officials were only figureheads'. The rest of the foreign community consisted of the British Consul and his wife, their 15 Hunza guards from the north of Pakistan, and a couple of Swedish missionaries.

Contact with the Soviet Union seemed to make sense given the geographical location of Kashgar. Ethnically, culturally, linguistically and theologically the inhabitants of Kashgar had absolutely nothing in common with the Chinese and everything in common with the Muslim inhabitants on the other side of the border. Whereas it took a five-month camel and donkey ride to get to Beijing and a five- or six-week hike to reach the nearest railhead in British India (although mail runners could do it in two), the Soviet railhead at Osh was more accessible, and from Kashgar strings of camels would stalk westward with their bales of wool, returning with cargoes of Russian cigarettes, matches and sugar.

Rumours and also banquets seemed to be at their peak of eccentricity in Kashgar. Fleming describes his last night there at a banquet given by the city officials 'half in their honour and half in ours . . . You never know what may happen at a banquet in Kashgar and each of our official hosts had prudently brought his own bodyguard. Turkic and Chinese soldiers lounged everywhere; automatic rifles and executioner's swords were much in evidence, and the Mauser pistols of the waiters knocked ominously against the back of your chair as they leant over you with the dishes'. Speeches were made by just about everyone, feverishly translated into English, Russian, Chinese and Turkic, and no one was assassinated.

The Kashgar of today has lost much of the 'romantic' value that made eating there in the '30s a slightly nervous experience. When the Communists came to power the city walls were ripped down and a huge, glistening white statue of Chairman Mao was erected on the main street. The statue stands today, hand (minus a thumb) outstretched to the sky above and the lands beyond, a constant reminder to the local populace of the alien regime that controls the city. About 120,000 people live here, and apart from the Uygur majority the number includes Tajiks, Kirghiz and Uzbekh. The Han Chinese are relatively small in number, nothing like the horde that dominates Ürümqi, although PLA troops are always conspicuous. Nor does it take six months to reach Kashgar now; it's a three-day bus ride from Ürümqi or you can fly out in a couple of hours if you have more consideration for your bum. No longer as remote, nor as fabled, the city sounds like a disappointment – yet the peculiar quality of Kashgar is that every so often you chance on some scene that suggests a different age and world removed from China.

In some ways times seem to have changed little for the intrepid China traveller. Fleming relates that:

> One night we slept on the floor, drank tea in mugs, ate doughy bread, argued with officials, were stared at, dreaded the next day's heat; twenty-four hours later we were sitting in comfortable arm chairs with long drinks and illustrated papers and a gramophone playing, all cares and privations banished. It was a heavenly experience.

Information & Orientation

The oasis only has two substantial thoroughfares, one running east-west and the other north-south. On the main intersection are three ugly yellow colonnaded buildings dating back to 1956, rapidly becoming ruins.

Fairly accurate maps of Kashgar are available from some of the hotels. There's one (in Chinese) in the waiting hall of the long-distance bus station which may help you orientate yourself.

Kashgar is renowned for playing diabolical tricks on the stomach; it's possibly a bug in the water, but whatever it is, your enjoyment of the place can be ruined.

Some female foreigners wandering the streets on their own have been sexually harassed. This may be remotely connected with style of dress or even the town's diet of bawdy films. Whatever the reason, it's best for women to dress as you would in any Muslim country.

Things to See

Kashgar is a giant oasis. The focus of activity is the bazaar and the Id Kah mosque and square, and the 'suburbs' are the clusters of adobe houses congregated around the centre; beyond them lie small villages scattered in huge tracts of wheatfields. The bus from the airfield takes you down the main road, where the uninspired architecture of socialist eastern China is making an impact on various stages of construction. It's hardly the bustling central Asian exotica you may have been expecting, but don't let these first impressions put you off.

Some of the best areas for walking are east of the main bazaar and north-west of the Id Kah Mosque. To the south of the centre is a large cluster of mud-brick houses covering a sort of plateau – worth a wander round. The dusty streets are lined with continuous high walls, some of them white-washed, and are clogged with children in hot pursuit of the strange foreigner. The adults don't gather round foreigners like the Han Chinese, but the Uygur children do – they come in plague proportions, and if you've got a camera then spare plenty of film for photos of every kid on the block! A foreign face, rare as it is, is usually assumed to be American, but quite often they'll ask if you're a Pakistani. Three people even asked if I was a 'Hindustani' (maybe it was the sun tan?).

The money-changing brigade will pursue you all over Kashgar. Cash US dollars are snapped up for Sino-Pakistani trade and by Kashgaris preparing for pilgrimage to Mecca.

Sunday Market

You should not miss the bumper market that takes place every Sunday on the eastern fringe of town. Hundreds of donkey carts, horsemen, pedestrians and animals thunder into town for a bargaining extravaganza. It's best to just wander at random through the huge market area and watch camels, goats, horses, melons, grapes, hats, knives, beds and door-frames being bought and sold.

Bazaar

Sundays excepted, the bazaar is the focus of activity in Kashgar. The main market-street can be reached from the lanes opposite the Id Kah Square which run off the main north-south road. Kashgar is noted for the ornate knives sold in the bazaar and by hawkers in the streets. It's also a hat-making centre, and the northern end of the street is devoted entirely to stalls selling embroidered caps and fur-lined headgear. Blacksmiths pound away on anvils, colourfully painted wooden saddles can be bought, and you can pick your dinner from a choice line-up of goats' heads and hoofs. Boots are a good buy at about Y35 per pair. The price varies with the number of soles and you should allow three days for completion. Furry hats cost between Y10 and Y15 – don't believe ridiculous prices as high as Y65.

Old Asian men with long thick beards, fur overcoats and high leather boots swelter in the sun. The Muslim Uygur women here dress in skirts and stockings like the Uygur women in Ürümqi and Turpan, but there's a much greater prevalence of faces hidden behind veils of brown gauze. In the evening the Id Kah Square is a bustling marketplace, and numerous market streets lead off from the square.

Id Kah Mosque

The Id Kah Mosque is a stark contrast to the Chinese-style mosques in eastern cities like Canton and Xian. The Id Kah looks like it's been lifted out of Pakistan or Afghanistan, and has the central dome and flanking minarets which westerners usually associate with a mosque. Prayer time is around 10 pm, though that may vary throughout the year. During the festival of Korban Bairam, usually held between September and October, pilgrims gather in front of the mosque and gradually twirl themselves into a frenzy of dancing which is driven by wailing music from a small band perched on the mosque's portal.

Smaller mosques are scattered among the houses on the streets around the centre of Kashgar.

Old Mosque

This is a mud-brick building near the park, to the east of the main intersection. You can see its dome from the main street. The mosque is completely derelict, but the dome has some of its original brilliant blue tiles and the minarets have some blue-and-white tiles.

Abakh Hoja Tomb

This strange construction is in the eastern part of the oasis. It looks something like a stubby, multi-coloured miniature of the Taj Mahal, with green tiles on the walls and dome. To one side of the mosque is the cemetery, with a rectangular base surmounted by fat, conical mud structures. The tomb is the burial place of Hidajetulla Hoja, a Muslim missionary and saint, and his 72 descendants. It's an hour's walk from the Kashgar Binguan, but you should be able to hitch a lift on a donkey cart – just show the driver a photo of where you want to go. The tomb lies on a side street off a long east-west road.

Park & Zoo

The park is a pleasant place in which to sit, but the zoo is depressing. The kindest thing you could do for some of the animals would be to put a bullet through their heads. In front of the entrance to the park is a large square and on the opposite side of the road is the massive white statue of Mao Zedong.

Hanoi

The ruins of this ancient city lie about 30 km east of Kashgar. The town reached its apex during the Tang and Song dynasties but appears to have been abandoned after the 11th century. To get out here you'll probably have to try and hire a jeep at the Kashgar Binguan – apparently it's a rough ride to see mediocre rubble.

Three Immortals (San Xian) Buddhist Caves

These Buddhist caves are on a sheer cliff on the south bank of the Qiakmakh River about 20 km north of Kashgar. There are three caves, one with frescoes which are still discernible. They make a pleasant excursion, but are not worth it just for the cave art.

Places to Stay

The *Seman Hotel* is in the former Russian consulate on the western edge of town. It's a pleasant place to stay, with relaxing grounds. A double with bath costs Y24; a dorm bed costs Y5.

The *Chini Bagh Hotel* in the former British consulate is popular with the Pakistani traders commuting along the Karakoram Highway. Doubles without bath cost Y20; a bed in a chaotic six-bed room costs Y5. The shower block is a slime pit. Barely a trace of the colonial grandeur is left.

The *Oasis Hotel* is opposite the Seman Hotel. Dorm beds cost Y6 in a four-bed room. No showers – use those at the Seman Hotel.

The *Tian Nan Hotel*, on the street corner close to the bus station, is basic, but it's convenient if you need to catch an early bus. Beds cost Y6.10 in a four-bed room.

The *Kashgar Guest House* is the best hotel in town and is up to the same good standard of any other basic Chinese tourist hotel further east. The problem with this place is that it's a good hour's walk from the town centre and there's no bus. You can usually wave down a jeep or a truck, or hitch a lift on a donkey cart. Double rooms in Building No 1 go for Y50 (with shower and toilet). A bed in a four-bed room in one of the other buildings is Y6, but the building is a real echo chamber. There's a post office, dining rooms, souvenir shops and a small store (just inside the front gate) which sells bottled fruit.

Places to Eat

You won't starve in Kashgar, but restaurant city it ain't. The *Kashgar Guest House* serves Chinese meals for Y14 each (!) and the warm beer is Y2 a bottle.

For a wide variety of Uygur foods, pop into the food market close to the Id Kah Mosque. There you can try shish kebab, rice & mutton, fried fish, *samsa* (rectangles of crisp pastry enclosing fried mince-meat) and fruit. To the left of the mosque is a tea house with a balcony above the bustling crowds. Flat bread and shish kebab are sold at the huddle of stalls on the main road, just west of the big square opposite the Mao statue. Bread is 20 fen and each kebab is 10 fen. There are a couple of excellent ice cream stalls here too – about 20 fen for a glassful – very cold and very vanilla. There are more ice cream stalls in the Id Kah Square, and you should find eggs and roast chicken being sold near the main intersection at night.

Bottled and canned fruit are available from the large food store opposite the Id Kah Square on the main north-south road. There's a smaller store next to the cinema on the main intersection selling the same. You can buy eggs near the long-distance bus station; the ones painted red are hard-boiled.

Until its recent closure, the Oasis Café (on the same street as the Seman Hotel) was *the* place for such delicacies as pizza, hamburgers, 'farmer's breakfast' or even Mom's apple pie. Rock music shook the rafters while a microwave oven (yes!) catered to western tastebuds. The Kashgar Labour Service Company cast covetous eyes at the rocketing turnover of the café and sought flimsy pretexts to oust Mr Tahir, the Uygur manager, to whom they had leased the building. Within a few days, the local Public Security Bureau co-operated by serving notice of closure for alleged 'obstruction of socialism'.

When the café's foreign clientele heard the news, they hastily collected signatures and sent a deputation to protest at the Public Security office. The officer on duty, clearly astounded by China's first tourist demo, raged at the protesters that the closure was an 'internal affair' and the security office could do as it pleased. Meanwhile, the Kashgar Labour Service Company intends to run its own café in the same building. Draw your own conclusions and vote with your feet.

Getting There & Away

Air There are daily flights from Kashgar to Ürümqi, and the fare is Y291. CAAC is on the main street north of the Id Kah Mosque. Book your ticket well in advance. You fly out in a two-engined prop plane which stops briefly at Aksu to load and unload passengers. The flight takes about four to five hours including the stop at Aksu, and is worth doing at least once just to get some grasp of the immense desolation that is north-west China.

Bus There are buses from the long-distance bus station to Daheyan, Ürümqi, Aksu, Maralbixi, Khotan, Yengisar, Payziwat, Yopuria, Makit, Yakam and Kargilik. The station is on a side street off the main east-west road, and the ticket office and waiting hall is a large white building readily identifiable by its yellow doors and the Red Star over the main entrance.

There is a daily bus to Ürümqi via Aksu, Korla and Toksun. The 3½-day trip costs Y38.90. Tickets for the bus can only be bought one day before departure and the bus is scheduled to depart Kashgar at 8 am. A young Chinese woman at the bus station speaks good English and spends the day helping foreigners obtain their tickets.

The bus to Turpan actually goes to Daheyan, stopping overnight at Aksu and Korla and going straight through Toksun on to Daheyan. The trip takes three days. Again, tickets for the bus can only be bought a day before departure. Daheyan is a small railway town on the Lanzhou-Ürümqi line, and to get to nearby Turpan there are three buses a day. See the Daheyan section for details.

The road between Xinjiang and Tibet passes through the disputed territory of Aksai Chin and is one of the roughest in the world. This route is not officially open to foreigners; some have hitched unofficially from Lhasa to Kashgar in as little as 16 days, others have taken months. Plenty of foreigners have been fined travelling towards Lhasa from Kashgar, and Public Security's worries about safety are under-standable in this instance. *Tibet – A Travel Survival Kit* (Lonely Planet Publications) contains more details on this route, which should not be attempted without full preparations for high-altitude travel. I recently heard reliable accounts of at least two foreigners dying on this route. One was thrown from the back of a truck when it hit a pothole; the other died of a combination of hypothermia and altitude sickness, also while riding on the back of a truck.

The road connection between China and Pakistan via the Karakoram Highway is described later in this chapter.

Getting Around

The city buses are of no use; to get around you have to walk or hire a bike, donkey cart or jeep. The most common transport in Kashgar is bicycle or donkey cart, and there's also the odd horse-drawn cart.

Bikes can be hired from the Oasis Hotel, but there have been numerous stories of cheating, 'misplaced' deposits and lost identity documents. It's probably better to try the bike rental close to the Seman Hotel (ask at the hotel for directions). There is another bike rental (Y0.40 per hour) in a white building inside the courtyard of the large yellow building to the left of the Mao statue.

Jeeps are available for hire at CITS and at the Kashgar Binguan. Be prepared to bargain down to a reasonable price.

KASHGAR TO TURPAN BY BUS

The baggage stored on the roof of the bus is not accessible during the trip. Take a small bag of essentials with you on board.

Day 1 The departure from Kashgar begins with a magnificent view of the Pamir Mountains spread out across the horizon. To the north of the road is the Tian mountain range with its strange stratas of red, yellow and greenish rock, and to the south is endless desert. Every so often the bus pulls into a trucking stop where you can wash down noodles and meat with a beer, watched by an ever-curious local gathering. At one of these miserable stops in the middle of nowhere stood a stone column displaying a faded portrait of Chairman Mao – reminiscent of the pillars that Emperor Ashoka erected all over India. It's a rough road, not recommended for those with bad backs.

The first big place you come to is Aksu, and you may stop here or you may go straight through and overnight at another centre. Aksu is an enormous wind-swept oasis, a stark contrast to the surrounding desert.

My bus went through Aksu and overnighted further on. The hotel is at the bus station and charges Y2.20 for a bed in an eight-bed dormitory. The bunk beds have thick quilts and you don't need a sleeping bag. Food at the hotel restaurant is surprisingly good, with none of that horrible musky odour you find in restaurants in eastern China. There's hot water for washing from two taps at the back of a shed near the hotel. Toilets are the usual partitionless squat-over holes in a block at the back of the hotel – the surrounding area has plenty of trees to hide behind if you prefer.

Day 2 Departure was at 7.20 am. Mid-way between Aksu and Korla is Kuqa. From Kuqa runs the first highway to cross the previously impassable snow-capped Tianshan range.

The asphalted highway is 532 km long and runs to Dushanzi, a new oil-drilling settlement on the north side of the range. Previously it took four days to transport oil from Dushanzi to Kuqa on the circuitous 1000-km route via Ürümqi and Korla, but the new highway cuts the travelling time down to a bit more than a day. The highway, on which construction started in 1974, crosses three rivers and tunnels through three mountains; the longest tunnel is just under 1900 metres. Most of the road is between 1000 and 3500 metres above sea level.

The bus arrives in Korla at about 8.30 pm.

Korla is a flat industrial town linked by a railway line with the Lanzhou-Ürümqi line. The hotel at the bus station charged Y1 a bed, though the beds were hard and the bedding fairly grubby. Toilets were clean and had the added luxury of concrete partitions.

Day 3 The bus leaves Korla at 8 am and passes over a low range of hills, after which the scenery is less desolate and interspersed with long stretches of pastureland. This changes dramatically as the bus begins its struggle across rocky hills which fast become increasingly desolate. We emerged on the other side into the Turpan Depression, where the first major stop is the nondescript oasis of Toksun. If you're going to Ürümqi you might stop here overnight. Buses carrying on to Daheyan go straight through Toksun with only a brief stop, and arrive in Daheyan around 6 pm – earlier or later depending on the enthusiasm of the driver and the decrepitude of the bus.

Be warned that buses don't always run on schedule. You could take four days to do the trip, driving anything between eight and 14 hours a day depending on breakdowns or other factors.

As for hitching, traffic on the road between Kashgar, Ürümqi and Daheyan is light, but there are still enough trucks to make a trip worth considering. There is a truck stop down past the Kashgar long-distance bus station from which trucks head to Ürümqi every day.

Korla and **Aksu** have now been officially opened to foreigners. The town of **Yanqi**, 52 km north of Korla, is a possible stopover (by rail or bus) for a visit to Buddhist caves in the area or to the nearby lake. Locals refer to the lake as Bagragh Kol; the Chinese call it Bosten Hu. From Yanqi to the lakeside centre of Bohu is about 12 km. Access to the lake from Bohu could involve a mud-wading expedition, but the fishing villages might be worth a visit. Prices charged for transport can be as high as Y60 per day for a motorised three-wheeler – bargaining is advised. Korla has bus and rail connections with Daheyan (Turpan station), Ürümqi and Gulja. Aksu has bus and air connections. The major problem with stopping off on the way between Kashgar and Ürümqi is that you will need great patience to commandeer a seat in buses already packed to the gills.

Kuqa, which should open soon, is the closest base for visits to nearby Buddhist caves reputed to be on a par with the Mogao grottoes at Dunhuang. Sobashi Gucheng (Sobashi Old City) is about 23 km north of Kuqa. Kyzil Qian Fo Tong (Kyzil Buddhist Grottoes) are about 130 km west of Kuqa. There are more sights within a radius of Kuqa; the short-distance trips can be done on a donkey-cart, but you'll have to bargain for a vehicle for the longer ones. The *Kuqa Xian Zhaodai Suo (Kuqa County Guest House)* might arrange vehicle hire. For a jeep or Landcruiser taking four passengers, expect to pay Y60 for half a day and Y120 for a whole day. Take food, water and a torch. There is a bus connection between Kuqa and Gulja.

THE KARAKORAM HIGHWAY 中巴公路

With the opening of the Khunjerab Pass (4800 metres) to foreigners in May 1986, it's now possible to travel along the Karakoram Highway between Pakistan and China.

For centuries this route was used by caravans plodding down the Silk Road. Back in 400 AD, the Chinese pilgrim Fa Xian recorded feelings of vertigo: 'The way was difficult and rugged, running along a bank exceedingly precipitous. When one approached the edge of it, his eyes became unsteady; and if he wished to go forward in the same direction, there was no place on which he could place his foot, and beneath were the waters of the river called the Indus'. 'Khunjerab' translates as 'valley of blood', a reference to local bandits who took advantage of the terrain to plunder caravans and slaughter the merchants.

Nearly 20 years were required to plan, push, blast and level the present road between Islamabad and Kashgar; over 400 road-builders died. The rough section between Kashgar and the Pakistan border still needs a few more years before it can be called a road. Facilities en route are being steadily improved, but take warm clothing, food and drink on board with you – once stowed on the roof of the bus your baggage is not easily accessible.

You can go from Kashgar as far as Pirali just for the trip (or some hiking en route) without crossing the border.

Information

For information or advice, contact the Pakistan Tourism Development Corporation, H-2, St. 61, F – 7/4, Islamabad, Pakistan. CITS in Ürümqi has no maps, no interest and no knowledge of the highway – other than confirmation that it does indeed exist!

A separate guide, *The Karakoram Highway – A Travel Survival Kit* (Lonely Planet Publications), will be available soon.

Visas

Pakistani visas are compulsory for visitors from most western countries. Visas are *not* given at the border; Hong Kong and Beijing are the closest places to obtain your Pakistan visa, so plan ahead if you want to enter or exit China on this road.

Chinese visas can be obtained in your own country, in Hong Kong and in Islamabad. The Chinese embassy in Islamabad takes between one and five days to issue the visa and charges 70 rupees.

Border

Opening & Closing Times are officially given as 1 May and 31 October respectively. However, the border can open late or close early depending on conditions at the Khunjerab Pass.

Formalities are performed at Sust, on the Pakistan border; the Chinese borderpost is at Pirali. Pirali now has a post office, restaurants, hotels (Y4 to Y10 per person) and a bank. You can't change Pakistan rupees at Pirali, only western currencies. Don't worry, Kashgar street marketeers love cash rupees and US dollars.

Routing

The Karakoram Highway stretches between Islamabad and Kashgar. The following chart provides a rough guide to distances and average journey times:

	distance, km	*duration*
Kashgar-Tashkurgan	280	7 hrs
Tashkurgan-Pirali	84	90 mins
Pirali-Khunjerab	35	1 hr
Sino-Pakistan border		
Khunjerab-Sust	86	2¼ hrs
Sust-Passu	35	45 mins
Passu-Gulmit	14	20 mins
Gulmit-Karimabad	37	1 hr
Karimabad (Hunza) -Gilgit	98	2 hrs
Gilgit-Rawalpindi	631	18 hrs

China to Pakistan

Buses for Pakistan leave from the bus station in Kashgar, but weekly departure dates are flexible – the normal departure day is Wednesday. Some buses only go as far as Pirali and charge Y4; others go to Sust and charge Y74. It's a good idea to traipse around hotels to see if Pakistani traders have chartered their own bus – try Chini Bagh and the Kashgar Guest House.

From Kashgar, the bus crosses the Pamir plateau (3000 metres) before overnighting just short of the foothills of Kongur mountain (7719 metres) and Muztag-Ata mountain (7546 metres). The journey on the next day passes through stunning scenery: high mountain pastures with grazing camels and yaks tended by Tajiks in yurts (Mongolian-style tents). Some travellers have stayed in yurts beside Karakol Lake, close to both these mountains. Sven Hedin, the Swedish explorer, nearly drowned in this lake!

The bus spends the second night at

Tashkurgan ('stone tower'), a predominantly Tajik town which could be used as a base to explore the nearby ruined fort, local cemeteries and surrounding high country. From Tashkurgan (3600 metres) the road climbs higher to Pirali, which wouldn't be worth a stop if it wasn't the Chinese checkpost. If you're on a Pakistani bus, you'll have no need to change buses; if you've taken the local bus from Kashgar, you'll need to change to a Pakistani bus from Pirali onwards.

Pakistan to China

From Rawalpindi to Gilgit there are five buses daily. An ordinary coach costs 85 rupees; deluxe will cost 120 rupees. If you can't stand the pace of the bus ride, the flight between Rawalpindi and Gilgit is good value at 180 rupees.

From Gilgit to Sust, there's a NATCO bus which costs 22 rupees; buy your ticket on the morning of departure at 7 am – the bus leaves at 9 am. The tourist hotel at Sust charges 25 rupees for a bed in the dormitory.

From Sust to Pirali, there's a bus for 160 rupees or US$10. At Pirali everyone changes to a Chinese bus which charges Y40 to Kashgar. This bus stops overnight at Tashkurgan; the basic hotel charges Y4 per person. Trucks offer lifts for Y40, and the starting price for a seat in a jeep is Y70. Tashkurgan to Kashgar takes aeons over an atrocious boulder-strewn road.

GULJA (YINING) 伊宁

Gulja lies close to the Soviet border, about 700 km west of Ürümqi. It is the centre of Ili Kazakh Autonomous Prefecture; the Chinese refer to it as Yining.

On the death of Genghis Khan in 1227, his four sons inherited responsibility for the Mongol empire. Chaghatai, the second eldest, took over a huge area which included Turkestan, Xinjiang and, further south, most of Khorasan. Chaghatai is said to have made his capital at Almalik, close to Gulja in the valley of the Ili River.

The Ili Valley became an easy access point for invaders and later for the northern route of the Silk Road, which stretched to the Caspian Sea. Russian and Chinese control over this borderland was at best tenuous. Gulja was occupied by the Tsar's troops in 1876 during Yakub Beg's independent rule of Kashgaria. Five years later, the Chinese cracked down on Yakub Beg and Gulja was handed back by the Russians. The border is still a nervous one; in 1962, there were major Sino-Soviet clashes along the Ili River. In late 1986, the Chinese claimed to have shot six Soviet infiltrators.

Chinese appear uneasy here and warn against staying out after dark, when knives are fast and streets unsafe. They probably do have some problems keeping order in an alien environment, but I found the local Kazakhs and Uzbekhs to be a rough bunch regularly drunk in the evenings and very friendly towards foreigners, whom they put in a different category from those in authority. One Uzbekh I met several times on the street addressed me in Russian as 'Major' and saluted. Many of the families have relatives in the Soviet Union; some are even preparing to join long-lost (and happily found!) relatives in Australia.

Things to See & Do

Gulja is a grubby, dusty place that has a few tantalising, faded remnants of Russian architecture – the rest is uninspiring. Central Asian street life is the main attraction here. The centres of action appear to be the main bus station and the cinema. Just stroll around in a wide radius. About six km south of the town centre is a bridge over the Ili River. It's worthwhile to leave the main street and follow alleys which pass the occasional Russian-style house with carved window-frames, painted shutters and plaster peeling from ornate designs. The street markets are famous for fruit (especially in August), carpets and leather (boots).

Lin Zexu, the Qing Dynasty official who played a leading role in the Opium

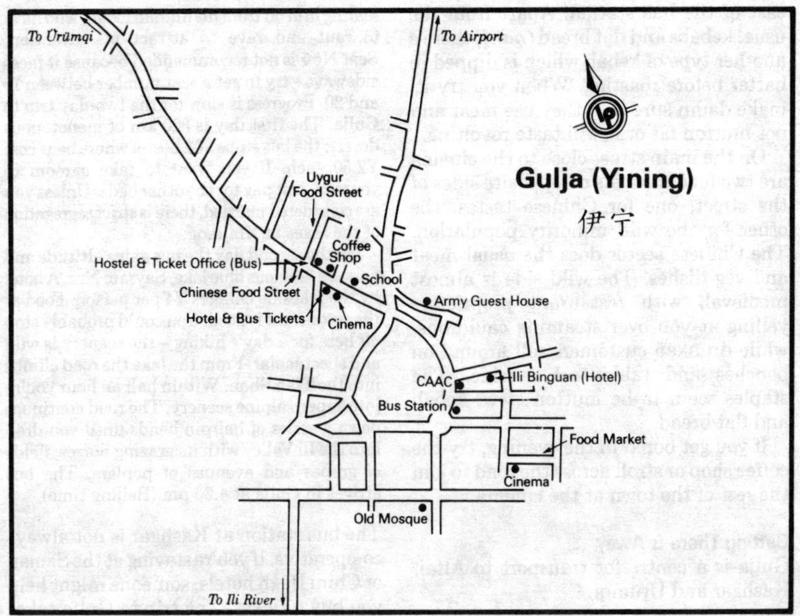

War, was exiled to Gulja. In the surrounding area are various 'sights' connected with Lin, although I'm not sure how much interest there is in his irrigation canal or the five oaks he planted.

Huiyuan, about 30 km west of Gulja, is a modern town. Further to the west of the new town are the ruins of the old town (Huiyuan Gucheng), which dates back to the Tang Dynasty.

Places to Stay & Eat

Many foreigners visit this place on the assumption it's open (Yining, the Han name for Gulja, and Xining are easily confused to untrained ears), and indeed things seem loose and easy once you're here.

The *Ili Binguan (Ili Hotel)* is close to the bus station and charges between Y6 and Y13 per person. This seems to be the standard place to stay for Hong Kongers.

The *Jiefang Jun Zhaodai Suo (Army Guest House)* is just up the street from the bus station and easily recognised by the high-walled enclosure with a sentry at the gate. Smile at the sentry and go through the parade ground to the guest house at the back. Comfortable doubles cost Y30; triples cost Y9 per bed.

Further down the main street are several hotels *(fandian)* on either side of the street. Prices start at about Y3 per night; could be some interesting activity although you might not get much sleep.

The bus station is in a dismal courtyard with a gigantic, crumbling edifice at the back serving as a hostel (Y3 per night). An endless stream of wild-eyed adults and squalling children trek in and out of dimly-lit corridors; from a window above the massive entrance columns comes drunken singing and lively accordion music. Take a look, even if you don't stay.

Food markets are the best places to eat. There's one about 10 minutes' walk south-east of the bus station. Apart from the usual kebabs and flat bread *(nan)*, there's another type of kebab which is dipped in batter before roasting. When you try it, make damn sure that they use meat and not mutton fat or it will taste revolting.

On the main street close to the cinema are two food markets on opposite sides of the street, one for Chinese tastes, the other for the wild minority population. The Chinese sector does the usual meat and veg dishes. The wild side is almost medieval, with restaurant proprietors yelling at you over steaming cauldrons, while drunken customers roll around on benches and tables set outside. The staples seem to be mutton stew, kebab and flat bread.

If you get bored in the evening, try the coffee shop or stroll across the road to join the rest of the town at the cinema.

Getting There & Away

Gulja is a centre for transport to Altai, Kashgar and Ürümqi.

Air In theory, you could present relevant papers and buy a ticket from Ürümqi to Gulja; in practice, you can expect an official knockback. From Gulja to Ürümqi should be less of a problem. Flights leave on Monday, Tuesday, Thursday and Saturday and cost Y117. This is considerably more expensive than the bus, but the flight only takes 1½ hours.

Bus Buses leave daily from Ürümqi at 9 am (Beijing time) and take two days to get to Gulja; the fare is Y18. The woman at the counter likes a nice, fancy-looking piece of paper or student card and, most importantly, FEC.

Most of the buses used in Xinjiang are constructed with a box-like cabin for the driver, sealing him off from his human cargo, who have to rant and rave to attract his attention. Seat No 1 is not recommended because it faces sideways – try to get a seat number between 10 and 20. Progress is slow for the two-day trip to Gulja. The first day is 320 km of monotonous desert; the bus stops at a hostel where beds cost Y2.50 each. If you want to take a room to yourself, just pay for the other beds. Unless you are considered married, there is strict segregation of the sexes in Xinjiang.

On the second day the bus gains altitude and passes a fabulous blue lake, Sayram Nur. A hotel by the lakeside charges Y4 per person. Food at the restaurant is good. You could probably stop off here for a day's hiking – the scenery is wild and spectacular. From the lake the road climbs into the Tian Shan. Within half an hour you're into superb alpine scenery. The road continues down a series of hairpin bends until you drop into the Ili Valley with its grazing horses, fields of grapes and avenues of poplars. The bus arrives in Gulja at 4.30 pm (Beijing time).

The bus station at Kashgar is not always co-operative. If you're staying at the Seman or Chini Bagh hotels, someone might help you buy a ticket. The trip to Gulja takes three days and the ticket costs Y38.

To buy tickets in Gulja, go to the bus companies on the main street; many of them have boards outside with prices and destinations in Chinese. Nobody worries about papers here, least of all the booking clerks, who will try hard to get you what you want.

Buses to Ürümqi leave frequently. The trip takes two days and costs Y18. Book early. If you feel like breaking the journey, you could buy a ticket to Sayram Lake or Shihezi.

Buses run daily to Kashgar via Korla, Aksu and Kuqa. The full trip to Kashgar takes three days and the ticket costs Y38.

Other interesting destinations include various towns in the Altai area.

TIBET AND QINGHAI

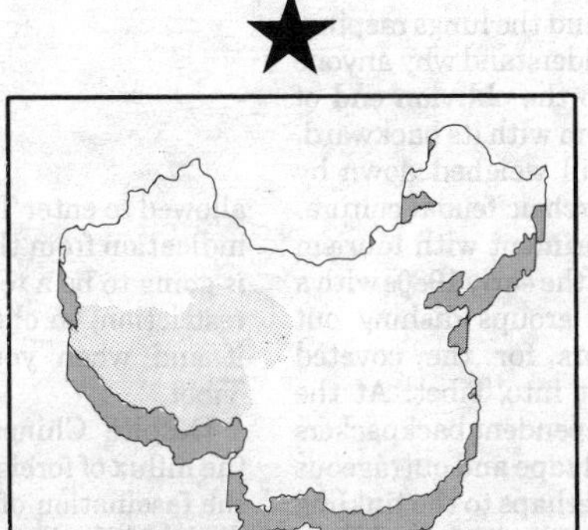

Tibet & Qinghai 西藏 青海

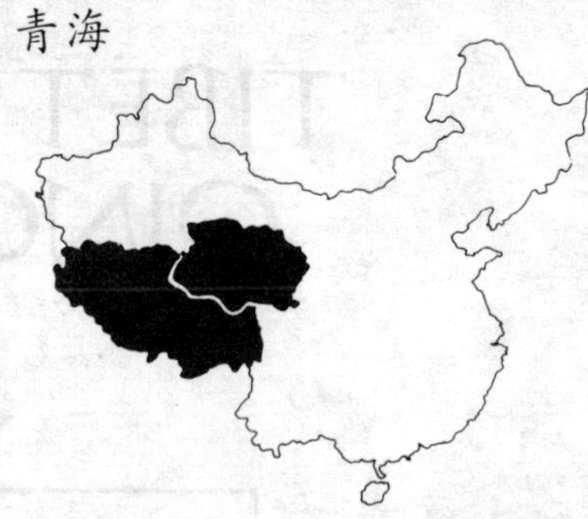

Westerners tend to imagine Tibet as some sort of Shangri-La – a strange projection of one of the world's most barren landscapes; isolated, desolate, bitterly cold in winter, a high plateau where the thin air can set the heart pounding and the lungs rasping. The Chinese can't understand why anyone would want to go to the oblivion end of their Middle Kingdom with its backward, barbarian people still weighed down by the remnants of an archaic feudal culture.

The Chinese experiment with tourism in Tibet kicked off in the early 1980s with a tiny trickle of tour groups dishing out thousands of dollars for the coveted cachet of being first into Tibet. At the same time a few independent backpackers wriggled past the red tape and outrageous prices. In response perhaps to the tinkling of the cash register and criticism of their administration, the Chinese officially opened the Roof of the World to foreigners in late 1984. In late 1987 the situation changed quite dramatically when Tibetans in Lhasa gave vent to their feelings about the Chinese and their policies. A series of demonstrations became a virtual uprising. Chinese security forces reportedly opened fire on the demonstrators, many of whom were monks from the monasteries around Lhasa. Both sides suffered casualties and at least one police station was reduced to a smoking pile of rubble. The response of the Chinese authorities was swift; Lhasa was swamped with plainclothes and uniformed security, who put an abrupt end to the uprising. The embarrassment of foreign press coverage was neatly solved when all members of the foreign media covering events in Lhasa were unceremoniously booted back into China.

Within a few weeks, it was the turn of individual travellers to be similiarly ejected. At the time of going to press, only official guests and group tours (whose movements are easily supervised) were allowed to enter Tibet. There has been no indication from the Chinese whether this is going to be a temporary or a long-term restriction, so check up on the situation if and when you intend travelling to Tibet.

Despite Chinese administration and the influx of foreign visitors, Tibet retains the fascination of a unique culture quite distinct from that of the Han Chinese. Since full-scale treatment of Tibetan regions would (and should!) take a whole book, Lonely Planet has done just that with its guide, *Tibet – A Travel Survival Kit*.

History

Recorded Tibetan history begins in the 7th century when the Tibetan armies were considered as great a scourge to their neighbours as the Huns were to Europe. Under King Songtsen Gampo the Tibetans occupied Nepal and collected tribute from parts of Yunnan Province. Shortly after the death of Gampo the armies moved north and took control of the 'Silk Road', including the great city of Kashgar. Opposed by Chinese troops, who occupied all of Xinjiang under the Tang Dynasty, the Tibetans responded by sacking the imperial city of Chang'an (present-day Xian). It was not until 842 that Tibetan expansion came to a sudden halt with the assassination of the king, and the region broke up into independent feuding principalities. Never again would the Tibetan armies leave their high plateau.

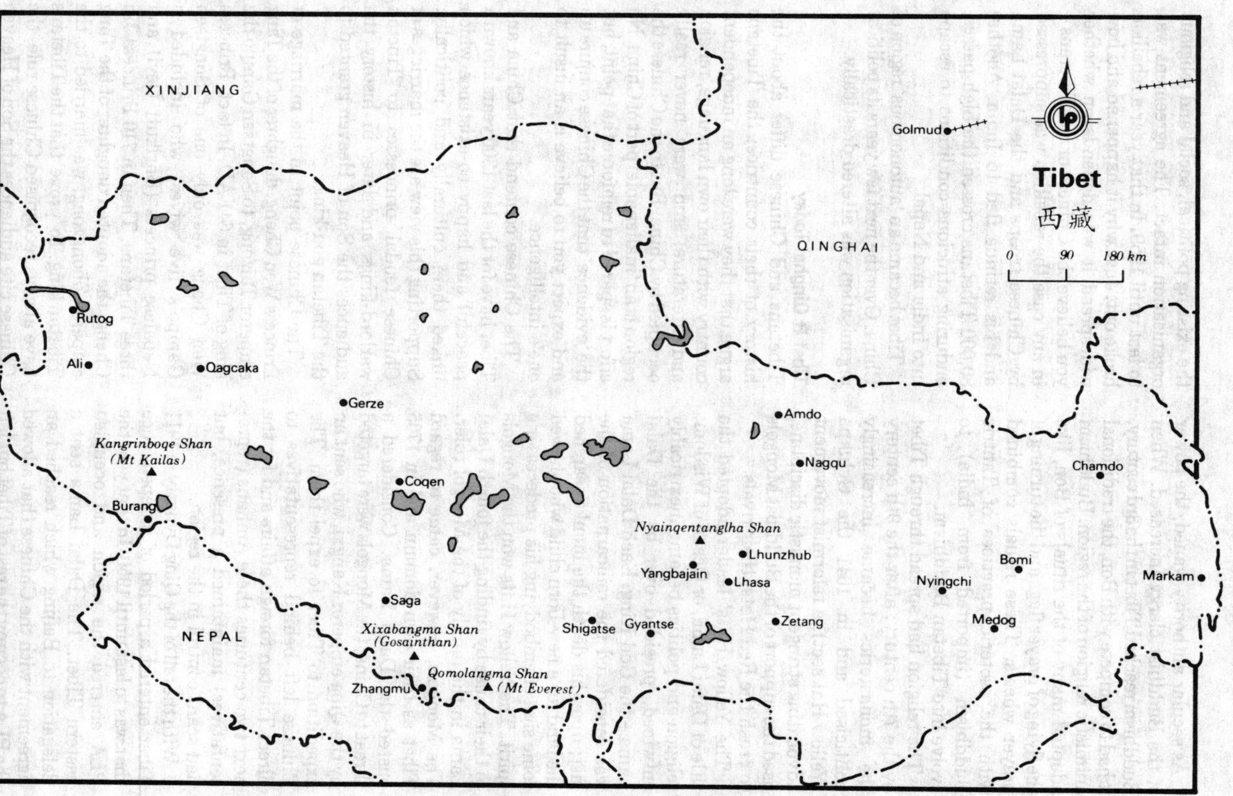
XINJIANG
Golmud
Tibet
西藏
QINGHAI
0 90 180 km
Rutog
Ali
Qagcaka
Gerze
Amdo
Kangrinboqe Shan
(Mt Kailas)
Nagqu
Chamdo
Coqen
Burang
Nyainqentanglha Shan
Lhunzhub
Bomi
Yangbajain
Markam
Lhasa
Nyingchi
Saga
Shigatse
Gyantse
Zetang
Medog
NEPAL
Xixabangma Shan
(Gosainthan)
Qomolangma Shan
Zhangmu
(Mt Everest)

As secular authority waned, the power of the Buddhist clergy increased. When Buddhism reached Tibet in the 3rd century, it had to compete with Bon, the traditional animistic religion of the region. Buddhism adopted many of the rituals of Bon, like the flying of prayer flags and the turning of prayer wheels. These rituals combined with the esoteric practices of Tantric Buddhism (imported from India) to evolve into Tibetan Buddhism.

The religion had spread through Tibet by the 7th century; after the 9th century the monasteries became increasingly politicised and in 1641 the Gelukpa (Yellow Hat sect), a reformist movement advocating stringent monastic discipline, used the support of the Buddhist Mongols to crush the Red Hats, their rivals.

The Yellow Hats' leader adopted the title of Dalai Lama, or Ocean of Wisdom; religion and politics became inextricably entwined, presided over by the Dalai Lama – the God King. Each Dalai Lama was considered the reincarnation of the last; upon his death the monks searched the land for a new-born child who showed some sign of embodying his predecessor's spirit. The Yellow Hats won the Mongols to their cause by finding the fourth Dalai Lama in the family of the Mongol ruler. The Mongols, however, came to regard Tibet as their own domain and in 1705 ousted the Dalai Lama. Considered a threat to China, the Mongols were targeted by the Qing emperor Kangxi, who sent an expedition to Tibet to expel them. The Chinese left behind representatives to direct Tibetan foreign affairs and for the next two centuries these Ambans (representatives) maintained a presence, but had scant control in the region.

With the fall of the Qing Dynasty in 1911 Tibet entered a period of independence that was to last until 1950. In that year the PLA entered the region and occupied eastern Tibet. The Dalai Lama sent a delegation to Beijing which reached an agreement with the Chinese that allowed the PLA to occupy the rest of Tibet but left the existing political, social and religious organisation intact. The agreement was to last until 1959. In that year a rebellion broke out. Just why it happened and how widespread it was depends on whether you believe the Chinese or the Tibetans – in any case the rebellion was suppressed by Chinese troops and the Dalai Lama and his retinue fled to India. Another 80,000 Tibetans crossed the high passes, enduring atrocious conditions to escape into India and Nepal.

Tibet became an 'autonomous' region of China. Over the next few years its political organisation was altered drastically.

Tibet & Qinghai Today

Tibetans and Chinese differ about the history of their countries; the Tibetans argue that they were long an independent country with their own language, religion and literature, and were never really occupied by China. But to the Chinese the region is an 'inalienable' part of China. No effort is spared to reinforce that point, but the 'evidence' that the Chinese conjure up and expect you to believe is an insult to one's intelligence.

The Chinese contend that China and Tibet have for the last 1300 years known a peaceful and happy co-existence which linked them culturally and politically. Supporting this view are the marriages of Chinese feudal princesses to Tibetan warlord-kings and later in history the audiences the Son of Heaven granted to the Tibetan god-king.

The Chinese point to the marriage of Princess Wen Cheng, daughter of the Tang emperor Taizong, to Songtsen Gampo the king of Tibet in 641 AD. In fact, Princess Wen Cheng was only one of Songtsen Gampo's five wives, who included a Nepalese princess (Bhrikuti Devi) and three Tibetans. Then in 710 Princess Jin Cheng, the adopted daughter of the Tang emperor Zhongzong, was married to the Tibetan king. To 'prove' that the Tibetans have always recognised Chinese rule, the Chinese cite audiences the Son of Heaven

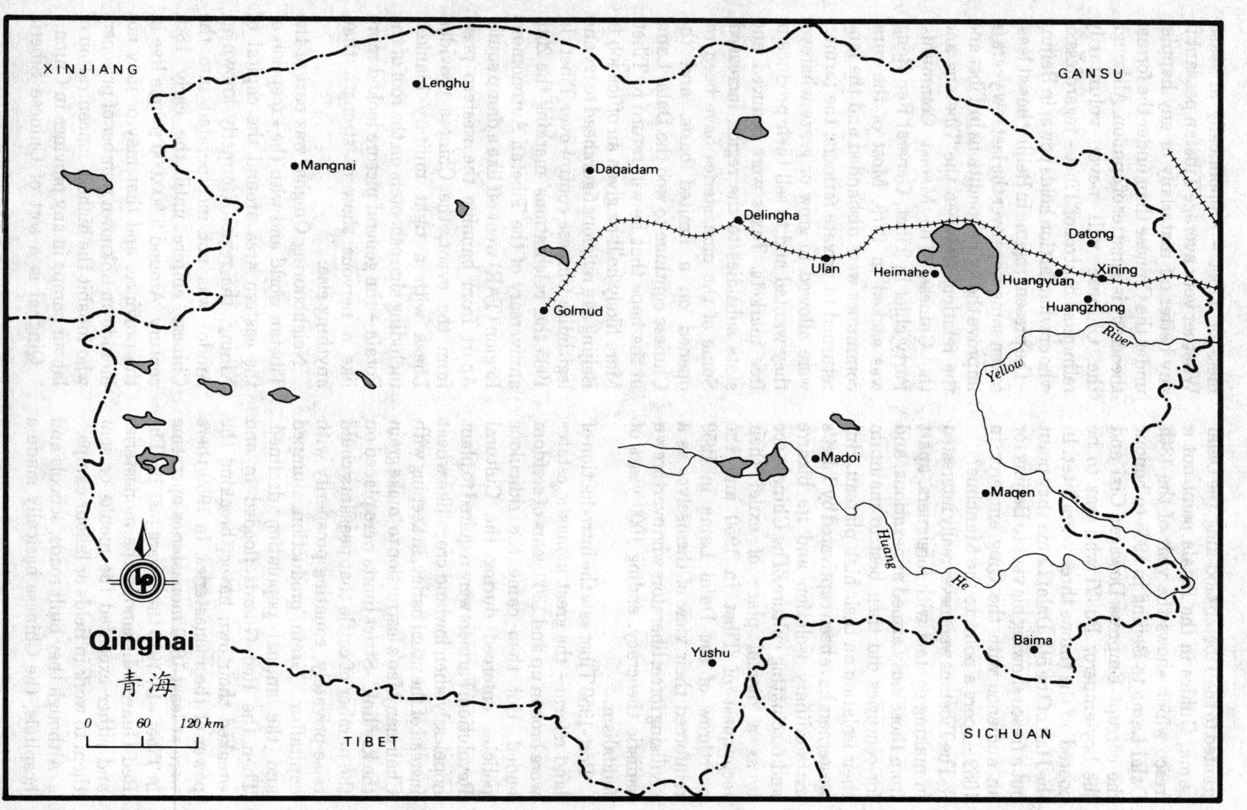
XINJIANG
GANSU
Lenghu
Mangnai
Daqaidam
Delingha
Datong
Ulan
Heimahe
Huangyuan
Xining
Huangzhong
Golmud
Yellow River
Madoi
Maqen
Huang He
Yushu
Baima
Qinghai
青海
0 60 120 km
TIBET
SICHUAN

granted to the Tibetan God-king, the Dalai Lama. Guides in the Potala point out a fresco which shows the visit of the 13th Dalai Lama to Beijing in 1908 to honour the corrupt Empress Dowager Cixi and the boy-emperor Pu Yi who was to be booted off the throne three years later. In the Hall of the 5th Dalai Lama they point out a fresco showing his visit to Beijing for an audience with the Qing emperor in 1652 – score a point to the Manchus?

The Tibetans were never really interested in making contact with foreigners, apart from those early armed annexations, and for centuries did their best to maintain their isolation on their high plateau. But westerners have been captivated by Tibet's extraordinary isolation and its bizarre and fascinating culture. The Chinese see it as a dismal place of exile; their reconquest of Tibet in 1950 and the overthrow of the Dalai Lama in 1959 reinforced their view of themselves as a civilising force, liberators who overthrew a sadistic theocracy, ending 1000 years of feudalism.

Post-1959 Tibet saw the introduction of land reform – the great monastic estates were broken up and 1300 years of serfdom ended. But then came the ridiculous policies enforced during the Cultural Revolution. Farmers were required to plant hopelessly alien lowland crops like wheat instead of the usual barley, in keeping with Chairman Mao's instruction to 'make grain the key link'. Strict limits were placed on the number of cattle that peasants could raise privately, equating prosperity with capitalism. Grain production slumped and the animal population declined. Then the Red Guards flooded in and wreaked their own havoc, breaking the power of the monasteries. In 1959 there were at least 1600 monasteries operating in Tibet – by 1979 there were just 10. The Red Guards disbanded the monasteries and either executed the monks or sent them to work in fields or labour camps.

Although they built roads, schools and hospitals, the Chinese basically made a mess of Tibet – economically at least. Whether your average Tibetan peasant is any better off materially or any happier under the Chinese than under the former theocracy is a matter of opinion. Although the Chinese will never voluntarily relinquish control of Tibet – regardless of who or what faction holds power in Beijing – the present regime in Beijing has at least taken some steps over the last few years to improve the living conditions in Tibet and the relations between the Tibetans and the Chinese. The Maoist Communist Party chief in Tibet, General Ren Rong, was sacked in 1979. Most of the rural communes were disbanded and the land returned to private farmers; the farmers were allowed to grow or graze whatever they wanted and to sell their produce in free markets. Taxes were reduced and state subsidies to the region increased. Some of the monasteries have been re-opened on a limited basis, and the Chinese continue to woo the Dalai Lama in the hope that he will return to Tibet. More likely he'll be given an office job in Beijing as a religious figurehead to try and legitimise Chinese control over Tibet. In 1985 the 'celebrations' marking the 20th anniversary of the Tibetan Autonomous Region (TAR) went off like a damp squib. Apart from banning the western press from the event, the Chinese provided Lhasa with a tight military blanket, including sharpshooters on the roof of the Potala – the general picture looked more like a nervous show of strength than anything else.

Neighbouring Qinghai was part of the Tibetan world and with the exception of the eastern area around the capital of Xining, the region (formerly known as Amdo) was not incorporated into the Chinese empire until the early 18th century. Around 3,800,000 people live in the province, and that may or may not include an unknown number of prisoners who inhabit the highest concentration of labour camps in any province in China.

Qinghai is a sort of Chinese Siberia

where common criminals as well as political prisoners are incarcerated. These prisoners have included former Kuomintang army and police officers, 'rightists' arrested in the late 1950s after the Hundred Flowers had their blooms cut off, victims of the Cultural Revolution, former Red Guards arrested for their activities during the Cultural Revolution, supporters of the 'Gang of Four' and opponents of the present regime. Many of the Han Chinese settlers of the region are former prisoners; with a prison record behind them they have little or no future in eastern China and so choose to stay in Qinghai. Oddly, the exile of a Soviet dissident to Siberia is headline news in the USA or Europe, but when a Chinese dissident is exiled to Qinghai the story might be cut to a few paragraphs or not printed at all.

Certainly the most acute problem at present for Tibet, Qinghai and Xinjiang is a policy of stealthy re-settlement. A massive influx of Han settlers from surrounding provinces threatens to oust Tibetans from employment, occupy arable land and swamp Tibetan culture with that of the Han Chinese.

Geography, Population & Climate

Most of Tibet is an immense plateau which lies at an altitude of 4000 to 5000 metres. It's a desolate region broken by a series of east-west mountain ranges, and is completely barren except for some poor grasslands to the south-east. The plateau is bounded to the north by the Kunlun range which separates Tibet from Xinjiang Province and to the south by the Himalayas and their peaks rising over 7000 metres.

The Qamdo region of Tibet in the east is a somewhat lower section of plateau, drained by the headwaters of the Salween, Mekong and Upper Yangtse rivers. It's an area of considerably greater rainfall than the rest of Tibet and the climate is less extreme. In a number of valleys in the south of the country some agriculture (such as the country's main crop, barley) is possible and most of the Tibetan population lives in this area. On the uplands surrounding these valleys the inhabitants are mainly pastoralists, raising sheep, yaks and horses.

Qinghai Province lies on the north-east border of Tibet and is one of the great cartographical constructions of our time. For centuries this was part of the Tibetan world and today it's separated from the Tibetan homeland by nothing more than the colours on a Chinese-made map.

Eastern Qinghai is a high grassy plateau rising between 2500 and 3000 metres above sea level, and slashed by a series of mountain ranges whose peaks rise to 5000 metres – the source of the Yellow River. Most of the agricultural regions are concentrated in the east around the Xining area, but the surrounding uplands and the regions west of Qinghai Lake have good pasturelands for sheep, horses and cattle.

North-west Qinghai is a great basin surrounded by mountains. It's littered with salt marshes and saline lakes and afflicted with harsh cold winters. Parts of it are barren desert, but it's also rich in mineral deposits, particularly oil.

Southern Qinghai is a high plateau 3500 metres above sea level. It's separated from Tibet by a mountain range whose peaks rise to over 6500 metres, and the Yangtse and the Mekong have their source here. Most of the region is grassland and the population is composed almost entirely of semi-nomadic Tibetan herdsmen rearing goats, sheep and yaks.

According to Chinese figures, the population of Tibet is almost 1,900,000. The number comprises Tibetans as well as the pockets of Han Chinese settlers who probably number around 150,000, although it does not include the mobile element of PLA soldiers and migrant Han workers, which could be as high as 400,000 or more. There are, in fact, a total of almost 3,900,000 Tibetans spread out over Tibet, Sichuan, Qinghai, Gansu and Yunnan.

Qinghai has a total population of

almost 3,800,000 – a number which may or may not include the unknown number of people imprisoned in the province's labour camps. The region is a mixed bag of minorities including the Kazakhs, Mongols and Hui. The Tibetans are found throughout the province and the Han settlers are concentrated around the Xining area, the capital of the province.

Climate in Tibet and Qinghai sometimes gives the impression that all four seasons have been compressed into one day. In general, summer temperatures are pleasantly warm at mid-day and drop dramatically in the shade and at night. Winter brings intense cold and fierce winds, although Lhasa sees little snow. The best time to travel is between May and September.

Health

Most visitors to Tibet and Qinghai, high-altitude regions with thin air, will suffer some symptoms of Acute Mountain Sickness (AMS). Until the body has become acclimatised to the lack of oxygen you may experience temporary symptoms such as headaches, sleeping difficulties, nausea and dizziness. If any of these persist or worsen, you should immediately descend to a lower altitude and seek medical help. It's rare for AMS to turn really nasty in Lhasa, but if it does, you should check with the hospital and consider a flight to Chengdu. Certainly, if you intend to trek or mountaineer at higher altitudes, you owe it to yourself to thoroughly understand AMS.

To prepare yourself for higher altitudes, spend the first few days taking your exercise slowly. Drink plenty of liquids (keep your urine a nice pale colour!) to avoid dehydration. Alcohol, tobacco and sedatives are best avoided.

Of the many books available on this subject, I recommend *Mountain Sickness: Prevention, Recognition & Treatment* by Peter Hackett (The American Alpine Club). If you have any doubts about your health, consult your doctor before you go.

There's no call for instant alarm, but you should not ignore AMS. I met a 65-year-old American with a pacemaker who had taken the bus from Golmud and was happily strolling the streets of Lhasa. On the other hand, Chinese Public Security have reported several foreigners dying from a combination of AMS, cold (hypothermia) and exposure.

A nasty stomach bug called giardia has travelled from Nepal to Lhasa, where it treks the intestinal paths of unfortunate foreigners – the locals seem immune. Check with your doctor on the pros and cons of anti-giardia drugs such as Tiniba or Flagyl, and take some with you since they are hard to find in Lhasa. Some of the most poignant notices in Lhasa are those by foreigners urgently seeking these magical medicines – two such foreigners in constant search of relief received the nickname of 'flagylantes'.

Coughs and colds are common among foreigners, and everyone in Tibet has a runny nose. Keep yourself well supplied with favourite medicines, vitamins and warm clothes. To beat the cold and (most importantly) the dust, join the parade of people wearing surgical or industrial face-masks – the main street in Lhasa sometimes looks like a scene from the movie *MASH*.

Finally, a word of warning about the dogs which roam in packs around monasteries and towns. Several foreigners have been badly bitten, but I haven't heard any reports of rabies yet. Keep your distance during the day, watch your step in the dark. A French friend of mine got into the habit of detonating Chinese bangers to send the hounds packing!

Transport

There is a serious shortage of transport in these regions, and drivers enjoy high status. The three main types of vehicle are bus, truck and Landcruiser. On some routes there are modern Japanese buses; other routes are covered by battered wrecks which gasp over each high pass as if it's their last. Trucks are often more comfortable, more fun and faster than the bus. Landcruisers are the chariots of the cadres and those foreigners who can afford CITS rates.

Bus prices in Tibet have been doubled for foreigners. This price hike could be considered acceptable for deluxe buses, but not for the old bangers. Trucks tend to charge the same as buses, but the Chinese government has moved to stop foreigners from hitching on trucks by threatening the drivers with fines or confiscation of their vehicle. CITS and several private taxi companies in Lhasa now hire out Landcruisers to foreigners. Whether you hire a Landcruiser or an entire bus, you should write the details into a contract.

Both in Tibet and Qinghai, your safety is entirely at the mercy of the vehicle, the driver and the condition of the road surface. Tibetans take their minds off these variables by praying, and you'd be wise to do likewise unless you want to end up a gibbering bag of nerves. Road accidents are frequent and foreigners have been injured or killed in the past.

Some foreigners have introduced their own means of transport. Small groups of mountain bikers have been commuting along the road between Lhasa and Kathmandu, stopping at the tops of passes to pose for heroic photos among the prayer flags. Chinese border officials have stopped scratching their heads and started halting the flow of bikes, collapsible kayaks, hang-gliders, rafts, skis and other tourist paraphernalia into Tibet. Although their motives for doing so are questionable they may succeed in slowing the trend towards turning Tibet into a backdrop for the sports-crazed.

Trekking

Trekking in Tibet is not officially approved, but it is feasible providing you are prepared to be self-sufficient in food, fuel and shelter.

Food

The staple diet in Tibet consists of *tsampa* (roasted barley meal) and butter tea. *Momo* (dumplings filled with meat) and *tukpa* (noodles with meat) are usually available at small restaurants. Tibetans consume large quantities of *chang*, a tangy alcoholic drink made from fermented barley.

Most of the larger towns have restaurants serving Chinese or Muslim dishes. Western foods feature on the menus of some hotels and restaurants catering to backpackers in Lhasa.

Outside the towns you should carry your own supply of food since what little is available is often highly priced and poor quality. When entering from Nepal, it's wise to bring food for the journey to Lhasa.

Clothing, Equipment & Supplies

Department stores in Xining, Golmud and Lhasa have quite a wide selection of warm clothing, but their stock fluctuates so you can't rely on them entirely. Keep the cold at bay with a down jacket, woollen sweater, long underwear, woollen socks, gloves and woolly hat. Protect yourself against the sun with lip salve, sunscreen, sunglasses and something to cover your head.

If you plan to trek, bring equipment such as a down sleeping bag, ground mat, tent, stove and fuel.

The food situation in Lhasa continues to improve, but it's still advisable to bring in any special foods or supplies – if you intend to trek, you'll appreciate the variety.

Theft

Both in Qinghai and Tibet, there has been a rise in theft from foreigners. In Xining, a nimble-fingered gang of pickpockets rides the buses. Sneak thieves operate on the train between Golmud and Xining. In Lhasa, the favourite venues for pick-pocketing are the bus station, post office, Barkhor market and hotels. Lhasa also has a chronic problem with bike theft.

Cable locks, sold in most cities in China, are useful for bikes and to secure gear on a train. Moneybelts are essential. If something is stolen, you should obtain a loss report from the nearest Public Security Bureau, though the PSB may refuse to include details of cash on the loss report.

Several foreigners trekking in the Everest base camp region have reported thefts. Apparently local villagers or nomads who possess very little find the temptation of foreign goodies too great.

Language

Although many Tibetans in the cities have a rudimentary command of Chinese, they are pleased (and try hard not to crack up!) when you make an effort to speak in Tibetan. Out on the desolate plateau, you'll have to use Tibetan. In either case, you might be able to save your bacon with a Tibetan phrasebook such as the one recently published by Lonely Planet.

Tibetan Mini-Glossary

hello
tashi delag
thank you
thuk ji chay
how are you?
kuzak de po yinpe
how much?
di gatse ray
it's very good
shidak yak po dhuk
cheers!
tamdil

LHASA 拉萨

Lhasa has long been the capital of Tibet and remains the political centre, the most important city and the showpiece of the region. It lies a mere 3683 metres above sea level.

Lhasa is actually two cities: one Chinese and one Tibetan. The Chinese part is the larger and is made up of the same sort of architecture that you see in eastern China. The lively Tibetan side is a ramshackle, scungy place, full of winding streets where the smell of yak butter clings to the air. Towering above the city and encircled by the ugly Chinese blockhouses is the Potala Palace. The other orientation point is the Jokhang Temple, which forms the nucleus of the Tibetan part of town.

Information

General information is sometimes provided by members of the staff at the Lhasa Holiday Inn. Alternatively, head for the Tibetan hotels downtown. Most of the hotels used by foreigners have noticeboards airing 1001 wishes: Tiniba is urgently sought to combat giardia, bus tickets are offered to the Nepalese border, etc.

A Traveller's Co-op might still be functioning at the Banak Shol Hotel. If it is, this is an excellent place to exchange information, consult the lending library or enquire about buying, selling or hiring trekking equipment and supplies.

CITS has an office at the Lhasa Holiday Inn (Rooms 1219 and 1238) and another branch at the No 3 Guest House (Di San Zhaodai Suo). Although CITS is expected to be the leading light for tours and vehicle hire, they continue to receive criticism for bungling inefficiency, price-gouging and lack of interest in correcting errors.

1 Jokhang Temple
2 Potala Palace
3 Norbulingka (Summer Palace)
4 Snowlands Hotel
5 Banak Shol Hotel
6 Kirey Hotel
7 Yak Hotel
8 Plateau Hotel
9 No 1 Guest House
10 No 2 Guest House
11 Lhasa Holiday Inn
12 Tibet Guest House
13 New Bus Station
14 Bank of China
15 Public Security
16 CAAC
17 Post Office
18 Old Bus Station

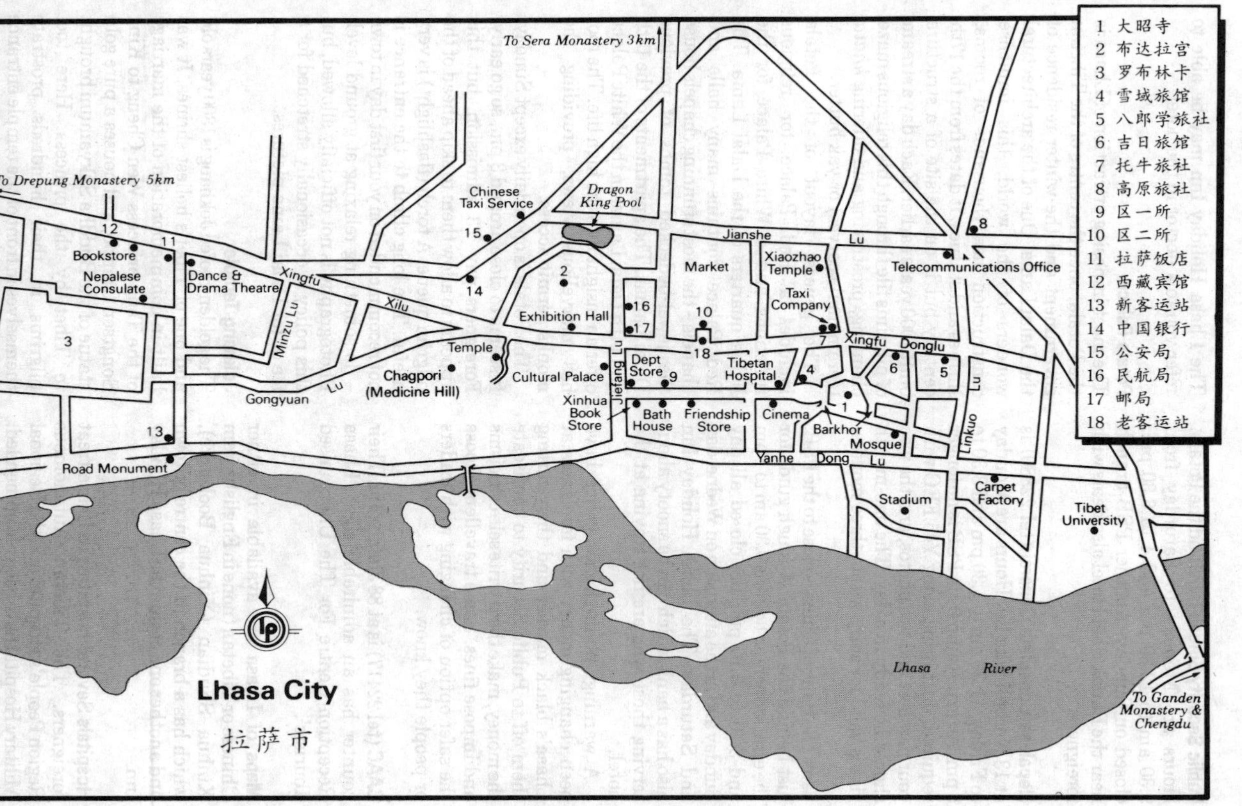
1 大昭寺
2 布达拉宫
3 罗布林卡
4 雪域旅馆
5 八郎学旅社
6 吉日旅馆
7 托牛旅社
8 高原旅社
9 区一所
10 区二所
11 拉萨饭店
12 西藏宾馆
13 新客运站
14 中国银行
15 公安局
16 民航局
17 邮局
18 老客运站
To Sera Monastery 3km
To Drepung Monastery 5km
Chinese Taxi Service
Dragon King Pool
Jianshe Lu
Market
Xiaozhao Temple
Telecommunications Office
Taxi Company
Bookstore
Nepalese Consulate
Dance & Drama Theatre
Xingfu Xilu
Minzu Lu
Exhibition Hall
Xingfu Donglu
Temple
Cultural Palace
Jiefang Lu
Dept Store
Tibetan Hospital
Chagpori (Medicine Hill)
Gongyuan Lu
Xinhua Book Store
Bath House
Friendship Store
Cinema
Barkhor
Mosque
Linkuo Lu
Road Monument
Yanhe Dong Lu
Stadium
Carpet Factory
Tibet University
Lhasa River
To Ganden Monastery & Chengdu
Lhasa City
拉萨市

Public Security Bureau is behind the Potala. Hours are Monday to Saturday from 9.30 am to 12.30 pm and 4 to 6.30 pm; closed on Sunday. Another PSB branch near the Banak Shol Hotel also deals with foreigners.

Nepalese Consulate General (tel 22880) is at 13 Norbulingka Lu. Hours are Monday to Friday, 11.30 am to 1.30 pm and 3.30 to 5 pm. An exit stamp from PSB is no longer required. Just bring along Y45 FEC with your passport and two photos, and the visa should be ready in a day. The one-month visa is valid for entry within three months.

Bank The Bank of China is close to the PSB, just behind the Potala. A rough guide for the erratic opening hours is 9.30 am to 1 pm and 3.40 to 6.10 pm. It's closed all day Sunday and in the afternoon on Wednesday and Saturday. The Lhasa Holiday Inn also has a bank which can be snooty about serving those who are not staying at the hotel.

A warning: plain-clothes police have been changing money with foreigners at Lhasa's black market and then carting them off to Public Security to confiscate the money, make them write self-criticisms and impose fines. Some travellers choose the safer option of changing with traders or people they know.

CAAC (tel 22417) is at 88 Jiefang Lu. Their counter has an admirable sign: 'Lhasa Reception Centre For The Unorganised Tourists'.

Maps of Lhasa are available in either Chinese or Tibetan (none in English) from Xinhua Shudian (Xinhua Bookstore), which has a branch in the centre of town and another one beside the Lhasa Holiday Inn.

Hospitals Several hospitals in Lhasa treat foreigners. The Tibetan Autonomous Region People's Hospital and the Regional Military Hospital have been recommended. The Lhasa Holiday Inn may be able to refer you to a doctor in the hotel.

Potala Palace

The most imposing attraction of Lhasa is the Potala, once the centre of the Tibetan government and the winter residence of the Dalai Lama. One of the architectural wonders of the world, this immense construction has thousands of rooms, shrines and statues. It dates from the 17th century but is on the site of a structure built 1000 years earlier. Each day a stream of pilgrims file through this religious maze chanting, prostrating and offering *khata* (ceremonial scarves) or yak butter.

The general layout of the Potala includes a Red Palace for religious functions and a White Palace for the living quarters of the Dalai Lama. The Red Palace contains many halls and chapels – the most stunning chapels house the jewel-bedecked tombs of previous Dalai Lamas. The apartments of the 13th and 14th Dalai Lamas in the White Palace offer an insight into the high life. The roof has marvellous views, providing the monks permit access.

The Potala is open daily except Sunday. It seems to close around 3 pm, so go early. Foreigners pay Y3 admission, but this appears to allow them to skip ahead of the pilgrim queue. A torch (flashlight) is very useful. The long climb to the entrance is not recommended on your first day in town – do something relaxing at ground level. Photography is not officially allowed, but this policy is occasionally stretched for a fee or for Dalai Lama pictures.

Jokhang Temple

The golden-roofed Jokhang is 1300 years old and one of Tibet's holiest shrines. It was built in commemoration of the marriage of the Tang princess Wen Cheng to King Songtsen Gampo, and houses a pure gold statue of the Buddha Sakyamuni brought to Tibet by the princess. Here too, pilgrims in their hundreds prostrate themselves in front of the temple entrance before continuing on their circuit. Follow the pilgrims through a labyrinth of shrines, halls and galleries containing some of the finest and oldest treasures of Tibetan art. Some were destroyed during the Cultural Revolution and have been replaced with duplicates. Take a torch if you want a closer look, and avoid getting lost by copying the nomad kids and hanging onto the tresses of the pilgrim in front.

The Jokhang is best visited early in the morning; you may not be allowed to enter after 11 am. The rules for the photography game here seem to be the same as for the Potala. Whatever you do, be considerate to the pilgrims and respect the sacred nature of these places.

Barkhor

The Barkhor is essentially a pilgrim circuit which is followed clockwise round the periphery of the Jokhang. It is also a hive of market activity, an astounding jamboree, a Tibetan-style stock exchange. All round the circuit are shops, stalls, teahouses and hawkers. There's a wide variety of items to gladden a Tibetan heart – prayer flags, block-prints of the holy scriptures, earrings, Tibetan boots, Nepalese biscuits, puffed rice, yak butter and incense.

It's worth making several visits here to see the folks who roll up from remote parts of Tibet: Khambas from Eastern Tibet braid their hair with red yarn and stride around with ornate swords or daggers; Goloks (Tibetan nomads) from the north wear ragged sheepskins and the women display incredibly ornate hairbands down their backs.

Whether you buy from a shop or a hawker, many of the Tibetan goods on sale have been imported from Nepal and you are most unlikely to find genuine antiques. The prices asked from foreigners have reached absurd heights. Whatever the starting price, be it in RMB or FEC, expect to halve it. Much of the 'turquoise' in the market is, in fact, a paste of ground turquoise and cement – some keen buyers bite the stones and reject them if the teeth leave white scratch marks. Also, bear in mind that Chinese Customs can confiscate antiques (anything made before 1959) if they think you are carrying out 'too much'.

Norbu Lingka

About three km west of the Potala is the Norbu Lingka, which used to be the summer residence of the Dalai Lama. The pleasant park contains small palaces, chapels and a zoo. For Y2 you can join pilgrims on a tour of The New Palace, built by the 14th Dalai Lama in 1956, which contains vivid murals. The gardens are a favourite spot for picnics.

The animals at the zoo stare balefully at passers-by. As I stood looking at a Himalayan brown bear, an American woman stooped close to the bars to take a picture. The bear obligingly whiffled with his nose and raised a gum to display a fine set of teeth. Then, quick as a flash, his paw zipped between the bars, passing within an inch of the woman's face before his claws ripped the camera case into the cage. The American freaked out entirely, started shaking with fright and squeaking about dangerous bears. As for the bear, he did a few victory canters round the cage before rolling onto the floor to contentedly munch the camera case. The revenge must have tasted sweet: within a few minutes he'd downed the lot and was eyeing my own camera!

Theatre & Exhibition Hall

The ungainly-looking building opposite the Lhasa Holiday Inn is The Tibetan Dance & Drama Theatre. Hopefully the shows here will be genuinely Tibetan, not a clumsy Chinese approximation.

At the foot of the Potala is the Exhibition Hall, open 10.30 am to 3.30 pm Saturday and Sunday only. The historical exhibition has some interesting photos, but draws predictable conclusions about China and Tibet. The rooms devoted to Tibetan ethnography, monastic life, handicrafts and daily life are well worth a visit. It's fun to observe the reaction of nomads on a pilgrimage to Lhasa when they see the exhibition of nomad life. Most of them get a giggle out of seeing their home in a museum – complete with stuffed dog.

Monasteries

Prior to 1959, Lhasa had three monasteries which functioned as 'pillars of the Tibetan state'. As part of a concerted effort to smash the influence of these monasteries, the Cultural Revolution wiped out the monastic population that once numbered thousands. The buildings of Ganden Monastery were demolished. Today, buildings are being reconstructed for the sake of appearances (rubble is bad for tourism and public relations) and a few hundred caretaker monks go through the motions of religious observance. Visitors who admire the shell may also sense the emptiness.

Drepung which dates back to the early 15th century, lies about seven km west of Lhasa. In 1959 there were around 7000 monks living here, whereas the present population numbers around 200 to 300. Admission to the monastery is Y2. You can visit some of the halls and colleges; the kitchen contains huge pots.

Drepung is best reached by bike. You can also take bus No 1 at 9 or 11 am from the stop close to the Banak Shol Hotel.

Sera about four km north of Lhasa was founded in 1419 by a disciple of Tsong Khapa. About 100 monks are now in residence. It's worth arriving before midday to see monks practise debate. Admission costs Y3.

At the base of a mountain, just east of the monastery, is a Tibetan 'sky burial' site where the deceased are chopped up and then served to vultures. Tourism has reduced this admittedly grisly event to an almost daily confrontation between *domden* (undertakers) and scores of photo-hungry visitors. The reactions of the *domden* have become very violent. My advice is to leave the place alone.

Bus No 10 runs direct to Sera. From the centre of Lhasa, the trip takes an hour on foot or 20 minutes by bike.

Ganden about 45 km east of Lhasa was founded in 1409 by Tsong Khapa. During the Cultural Revolution it was completely demolished. It is being rebuilt with the efforts of about 200 monks.

To reach Ganden Monastery, take a bus at 6.30 am from the Barkhor. Pilgrim trucks are now reluctant to take foreigners.

Places to Stay – bottom end

Most of the hotels in this category are clustered in the Barkhor area and managed by Tibetans.

Snowlands (tel 23687), close to the Jokhang Temple, is a friendly place – almost a legend within just a year or so – with rooms arranged around a courtyard. Beds cost Y10. Ask at reception about luggage storage and bike rental. Ignore the toilets (phew!) and enjoy the water fights.

The *Banak Shol* (tel 23829) is on Xingfu Donglu near the Barkhor. This has also achieved star ratings as a travellers' hangout in Lhasa. It's quite a warren of rooms, ladders and toilets in the ramparts. Friendly atmosphere and staff. Doubles cost Y22; a bed in a dorm costs Y10. Showers have been installed. Luggage storage costs Y0.20 per piece per day; bike hire costs Y2 per hour.

The *Kirey Hotel*, close to the Banak Shol, charges Y10 for dorm beds. Doubles start at Y12. It lacks atmosphere but has great showers for which you pay a small charge if you're not staying there.

The *Plateau Hotel* recently opened opposite the telecommunications building on the edge of town. Doubles cost Y12 per person, triples Y8 per person and a four-bed room Y5 per person. The solar-heated showers work sporadically. Ask at the desk about bike rental.

The *Yak Hotel* (formerly known by the ponderous name Beijing East Road Tribal Hostelry) is diagonally opposite the Kirey Hotel, on Xingfu Donglu. Beds cost Y10.

In the same area are two Chinese-style guest houses *(zhaodai suo)*, known as the No 1 Guest House (Di Yi Zhaodai Suo) and No 2 Guest House (Di Er Zhaodai Suo). They offer what's common elsewhere in China: uninspired, functional service. Then there are certain places which offer really cheap beds (maybe Y3 per person). Constant harassment by Public Security (who hate to see foreigners paying less than double the local rate) means that these hotels indulge in a creative game of opening and closing – now you see the foreigner, now you don't! If you want the real cheapies, ask in the traveller haunts about the Cheese Factory, Muslim Hotel or whatever the name of the hotel of the day might be.

Places to Stay – top end The *Lhasa Holiday Inn* (tel 2221) is the lap of Lhasa luxury and boasts 500 rooms. Doubles start at Y120 per room; triples cost Y90 per room. The rates in winter (1 November to 1 March) may be dropped 30%. The facilities include Chinese and western restaurants, a coffee shop, souvenir shops and a wrestling arena (practise the clinches with CITS?). A free shuttle service using slick minibuses operates between the hotel and the Barkhor. The transport desk arranges day trips to Drepung, Sera or Ganden monasteries (prices range between Y20 and Y100 per person); there's also a daily bus from the hotel to the airport (leaves 6.30 am and costs Y30 per person). If you want to hire a taxi, Landcruiser, minibus or bus, enquire at the transport desk about the amazingly autonomous prices fixed by the Tibet Autonomous Price Bureau.

The *Tibet Guest House (Xizang Binguan)* is a few metres up the road from the Lhasa Holiday Inn. Built in mock Tibetan style, it was already showing signs of dilapidation within a few months of opening. It's intended for foreign tour groups and Chinese officials on junkets. Doubles start at Y100, or you could try the tackily decorated Tibet suite for Y260. The forecourt is frequented by browsing yaks which nonchalantly obstruct the entrance ramp – about the only appealing characteristic of the place.

Places to Eat

Food can be mighty scarce out on the high plateau, but Lhasa offers Chinese, western and Tibetan cuisine.

The *Lhasa Holiday Inn* has a Chinese restaurant which is reasonable value if you eat as a small group; expect to pay Y8 per head for about five dishes. The coffee shop (open 8 am to 10 pm) serves western food such as hamburgers, French fries and Lhasa club sandwiches. Prices are relatively high, but breakfast includes endless refills of strong filter coffee.

Diagonally across from the Lhasa Holiday Inn, on the opposite side of the crossroads, is a restaurant serving excellent Chinese food.

The *Banak Shol* restaurant operates a choose-your-own ingredients system. It deserves reverence as the probable birthplace of the yakburger, and has a popular communal dining room for foreigners.

The *Kailas Restaurant* is down a side street close to the Kirey Hotel. This is a popular place run by a Tibetan returnee from Kathmandu, where he learned what makes the western tastebuds dance. The food can be a bit greasy, but the menu includes spring rolls, pancakes, chapatis, French toast and dishes for vegetarians.

Toots Restaurant, diagonally across the street from the Kirey Hotel, does good Chinese food and some western dishes such as omelettes and fried potatoes. There seem to be frequent fights here. An Aussie woman became trapped in a Sino-Tibetan brawl and had the brilliant idea of blowing her 'help' whistle. The combatants stopped immediately, although the pause (half-time?) lasted only 10 minutes before they were throwing bottles again.

There are plenty of Muslim teahouses around the Barkhor which serve good noodles.

Getting There & Away

Air Lhasa is connected by air with Chengdu (Y421). Flights to Xian (Y510) via Golmud (Y300) are not operating at present. In the past few years there have been frequent rumours about a Kathmandu-Lhasa flight – as yet, nothing has materialised.

Bus Lhasa has two bus stations. The old bus station is in the centre of town, close to the main post office. The new bus station is a deserted monstrosity four km out of town, near the Norbu Lingka. Tickets for the front of the bus are sold at the new bus station which is only convenient if you're staying at the Lhasa Holiday Inn; tickets for the back of the bus are sold at the old bus station, which is the most convenient one if you're staying downtown. Foreigners are charged double the local price. Buy your tickets several days in advance and roll up early.

Beware of well-dressed pickpockets operating around the buses, particularly in the early morning. They push up close pretending to join the scrum to get on the bus, but instead they pickpocket at lightning speed.

There are daily departures in the early morning for Shigatse (Y35), Gyantse, Zêtang (Y20) and Golmud (Y118). Buses to Zhangmu (Y84) leave on Tuesday and Saturday.

Road Routes

Although there are five major road routes to Lhasa, foreigners are officially allowed to use only the Nepal and Qinghai routes.

Nepal Route The road connecting Lhasa with Nepal is officially called the Friendship Highway and runs from Lhasa to Zhangmu (Chinese border post) via Gyantse and Shigatse. It's a spectacular trip over high passes and across the plateau. If the weather's good, you'll get a fine view of Mt Everest from the Tibetan village of Tingri. From Zhangmu, it's 11 km to the Nepalese border post at Kodari, which has transport connections to Kathmandu.

Accommodation en route is mostly basic and overpriced like the food, which can also be scarce. Whichever direction you intend to travel, take warm clothing and food.

Lhasa to Nepal Border For a six-day trip to the Nepalese border in a deluxe minibus (maximum 10 passengers), expect to pay Y380 per person. A similar trip in a Landcruiser (maximum seven passengers) costs Y450 per person; a five-day trip to the border in a modern bus (maximum 25 passengers) costs around Y175 per person. Hiring a Landcruiser will cost around Y2.10 per km, minibus Y2.50 per km, bus Y3.70 per km.

Before organising your own transport, check the noticeboards at the hotels. Most of the hotels seem to be getting into the vehicle-hire business – ask the manager. There are also several taxi services, one next to the Yak Hotel, another behind the Potala, close to PSB.

Be careful about paying deposits; it's best to write out a contract which includes exact details of your itinerary (dates, places, time required), name of driver, licence-plate number, desire to stop for photography and no price increase for technical or climatic problems. PSB may help with translation. Several readers have complained about transport managers inventing astronomical prices or drivers completely ignoring requests to keep to the agreed itinerary.

Nepal to Lhasa Despite persistent rumours to the contrary, most people manage to obtain a Chinese visa in Kathmandu for a crossing into Tibet. The system changes constantly in terms of complication, expense and time required – check with the Chinese embassy in Kathmandu for the latest in bureaucratic dance rules.

Local buses, taxis and Tibetan pilgrim buses run regularly to Barabise or as far as the Friendship Bridge. Until the bridge and the road have been restored, the steep and slippery section between the bridge and Zhangmu will have to be negotiated on foot – Sherpas will also act as porters for about Y10 or 30 rupees, but get the price straight (preferably written down!) before hiring them. At Zhangmu (Khasa) you can hunt around for buses, minibuses, Landcruisers or trucks heading towards Lhasa. Since most travellers prefer to exit Tibet via Nepal, you may be able to pay slightly less than the price asked for the trip in the opposite direction.

Qinghai Route This is the recently asphalted road connecting Xining with Lhasa via Golmud; it crosses the desolate, barren and virtually uninhabited Tibetan Plateau. Modern Japanese buses do the run between Lhasa and Golmud in 30 hours. Although they are expensive at Y116 per person, they are reasonably comfortable and include an overnight stop in Amdo.

Veteran Chinese buses attempt to do the trip in the same time by travelling day and night virtually non-stop. This is not recommended unless you want to save Y56 and like cold, brutally punishing journeys.

Take warm clothing and food on the bus, since baggage is not accessible during the trip.

Other Routes Between Lhasa and Sichuan, Yunnan or Xinjiang provinces are some of the wildest, highest and most dangerous routes in the world and they are not open to foreigners. If you do take them, don't underestimate the physical dangers – take food and warm clothing. Public Security tends to fine those heading into Tibet, but the opposite direction is controlled less. Travel on these routes usually takes several weeks of hitching on trucks which have a high accident rate. *Tibet – A Travel Survival Kit* describes these routes in detail.

Getting Around

Bicycle is an excellent way to get around. Most of the hotels hire out bikes for an expensive Y2 per hour. A passport or Y200 is required as deposit. Near the No 1 Guest House, people may pop out and offer cheaper deals.

Buses, minibuses, Landcruisers and jeeps can be hired for day excursions or trips to the Nepalese border. See the Getting There & Away section for details.

THE YARLONG VALLEY 雅鲁流域

About 190 km east of Lhasa, this valley is considered to be the birthplace of Tibetan culture. Within a radius of the adjacent towns of Zêtang and Nêdong, which form the administrative centre of the region, are several sites of religious importance.

Things to See

Samye Monastery lies about 30 km west of Zêtang, on the opposite bank of the Brahmaputra River. It was founded at the end of the 8th century by King Trisong Detsen as the first monastery in Tibet. Access is complicated, but the monastery (currently under renovation) commands a beautiful, secluded position.

To reach Samye, catch a bus from Lhasa or Zêtang. You will be dropped off close to a ferry which functions sporadically and will take you across the river. From there, a tractor, truck or horsecart freights you five km to Samye. Since there's only basic accommodation, you should plan to be self-sufficient.

Yumbu Lhakang, about 12 km south of Zêtang, is the legendary first building in Tibet. Although small in scale, it soars above the valley in recently renovated splendour. Get there by renting a bike or Landcruiser in Zêtang, or hitch on a walking-tractor.

The Tombs of the Kings at Qonggyai, about 26 km west of Zêtang, are less of a visual treat; their importance is essentially historical. To get there, rent a Landcruiser or spend half the day pedalling there and back on a bike.

Places to Stay & Eat

The *Zêtang Binguan* is the newest hotel in town. It is also the shoddiest, with fittings falling to bits and toilets leaking under the lazy gaze of insolent staff. Considering the state of the rooms, the standard charge of Y60 for a double is absurd. Student price for doubles is Y20. The restaurant food was poor. Bikes and Landcruisers may be available for hire – depends on the mood of the staff.

The *Zêtang Zhaodai Suo*, close to the Binguan, is a standard Chinese guest house which charges Y8 per person in a functional double. It may also be possible to hire Landcruisers here.

Getting There & Away

Buses for Zêtang (Y20) leave Lhasa (old bus station) every morning. Buses for Lhasa leave from the traffic circle in Zêtang every morning – buy your ticket the day before from a tin shack just south of the traffic circle.

SHIGATSE 日喀则

The second-largest urban centre in Tibet is Shigatse. This is the seat of the Panchen Lama, a reincarnation of Amitabha (Buddha of Infinite Light), who ranks close to the Dalai Lama. The present Panchen, the 10th, was taken to Beijing during the '60s. He lives a largely puppet existence there, visiting Tibet only occasionally.

Things to See

The main attraction in Shigatse is the seat of the Panchen Lama – Tashilhunpo Monastery. Built in 1447 by a nephew of Tsong Khapa, the monastery once housed over 4000 monks, but now contains only 600. Apart from a giant statue of the Maitreya Buddha (nearly 27 metres high) in the Temple of the Maitreya, the monastery is also famed for its Grand Hall with the opulent tomb (containing 85 kg of gold and masses of jewels) of the 4th Panchen Lama. Admission costs Y5 (!) and closing time is around 4 pm.

Watch out for vicious dogs, especially if you do the pilgrim circuit of the monastery.

Places to Stay & Eat

Attached to the bus station is a hostel which charges Y5 per bed. Nothing special, but useful if you want to be close to your transport. Across the road from the bus station is another hostel.

The Tibetan-run *Tensin Hotel* is popular for its roof terrace and location opposite the market in the Tibetan part of town. It charges Y7 per person in a double, Y5 in a four-bed room.

The *Chengguan Di Yi Zhaodai Suo (No 1 Guest House)* opposite the entrance to Tashilhunpo Monastery is a basic place also run by Tibetans. It's popular with pilgrims and bedbugs. A bed costs Y5.

The *Shigatse Binguan (Shigatse Hotel)*, on the outskirts of town, is a Chinese-style hotel built for group tours. Doubles for Y65 are poor value.

Shigatse has plenty of free-enterprise restaurants on the streets which serve good Chinese food. Shigatse is also a good

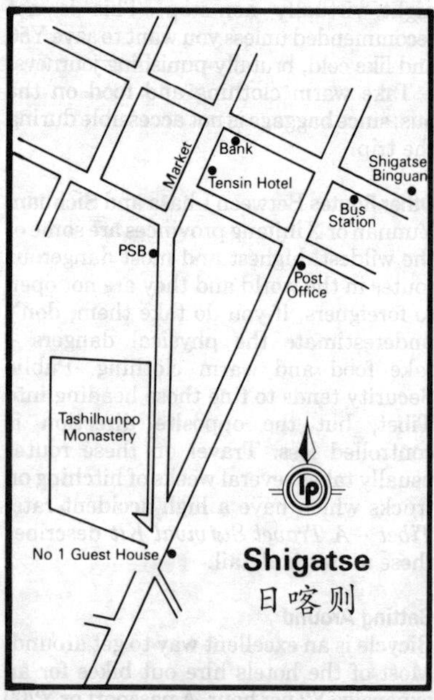

place to stock up on supplies – try the department store just round the corner from the bus station.

Getting There & Away

Bus & Truck Shigatse is an important transport centre with connections to the Nepalese border, western Tibet, Lhasa and Golmud. There are two routes linking Lhasa and Shigatse; the most popular one runs via Gyantse.

Buses to Lhasa cost Y36 and leave daily from the bus station. The bus station sometimes refuses to sell tickets (Y9) to Gyantse – cantankerous staff or policy? From Lhasa to Shigatse, there are daily departures and the trip averages nine hours.

It is proving harder and harder to find transport from Shigatse to the Nepalese border. Buses coming from Lhasa are invariably jam-packed and truck drivers are nervous about giving rides to foreigners.

Buses to Sakya leave on Tuesday and Friday from the transport depot opposite the bus station. Buy your ticket (Y16) the day before at 9 am.

GYANTSE 江孜

Gyantse is one of southern Tibet's chief centres, although its scale is that of a small village which retains some Tibetan charm.

Things to See

The **Palkhor Monastery**, built in 1427, is notable for its superb Kumbum (10,000 images) stupa which has nine tiers and, according to Buddhist tradition, 108 chapels. The monks may not allow you to complete the pilgrim circuit to the top, but the lower tiers contain excellent murals. Take a torch. Admission is Y3.

The **Dzong** (old fort) which towers above Gyantse offers a fine view over the valley. The entrance is usually locked, but you may be able to get the key (for a fee of Y2) from a small house at the foot of the steps leading up the hill; it's close to the tiny bridge on the main road.

Keep a respectful distance from the dogs in Gyantse. They rave all night and sleep until the afternoon.

Places to Stay & Eat

The bus stop has rough accommodation for Y5 per bed in a six-bed room.

There's a basic hotel closer to town. Coming from Lhasa, turn right at the crossroads and follow the road for 200 metres until you see a yellow building on your right.

If you continue straight across the crossroads, there's a hotel immediately on your right and another one about 100 metres down the road on your left.

Most of these hotels also provide basic meals.

Getting There & Away

The road from Lhasa splits here: one branch goes to Shigatse; the other heads south into Sikkim via the town of Yadong.

Buses to Lhasa are usually en route from Shigatse or elsewhere. They are often packed solid and you'll be lucky to find a seat for the five-hour ride. The fare is Y27 on a Japanese bus. Wait for the buses at the crossroads; if a bus stays overnight at the bus station in Gyantse, talk to the driver and he might let you on in the morning.

The same problems apply for travel to Shigatse (two hours, Y9) or the Nepal border.

Transport to Yadong is scarce, and a checkpoint en route turns back foreigners.

SAKYA 萨迦

Sakya is 152 km west of Shigatse and about 25 km south of the main road. The huge, brooding monastery at Sakya was Tibet's most powerful 700 years ago and once the centre for the Sakyapa sect which was founded in the 11th century. The monastery probably contains the finest collection of Tibetan religious relics remaining in Tibet – the monks may restrict you to a couple of halls. Admission costs Y5.

The bus stops at a hotel within a few metres of the monastery. Beds cost Y5 per person. A small restaurant in the hotel can provide basic food, but don't rely on it.

There's a bus from Shigatse to Sakya in the morning on Tuesday and Friday; buy your ticket (Y16) the day before. The bus returns the next day.

XINING 西宁

Xining is the only large city in Qinghai and is the capital of the province. It's a long-established Chinese city, and has been a military garrison and trading centre since the 16th century.

Nowadays, it serves as a stopover for foreigners following the route between Qinghai and Tibet. Perched on the edge of the high plateau, you can pause to consider the direction of your plunge.

Information

CITS (tel 23901 ext 700) is in the front building of the Xining Binguan. Rather sleepy service. Minibus tours can be arranged to Qinghai Lake and the surrounding area. Depending on the size of your group and the itinerary, you'll pay between Y45 and Y92 per person – excluding the cost of food and accommodation.

Public Security on Nan Dajie has several staff members who speak good English and French.

Maps Xining and Taersi Monastery maps are sold at Xinhua Bookstore and CITS.

Theft is common in Xining. Be especially careful of the pickpockets on city buses (No 9 is notorious).

Things to See

Xining has nothing exceptional to see, but

1 Railway Station
2 Xining Daxia (Xining Mansions)
3 Dongguan Mosque
4 Bank of China
5 Public Security
6 Post Office
7 Ximen Bus Station
8 Beishan Temple
9 Xining Hotel
10 Xinhua Bookstore
11 CAAC

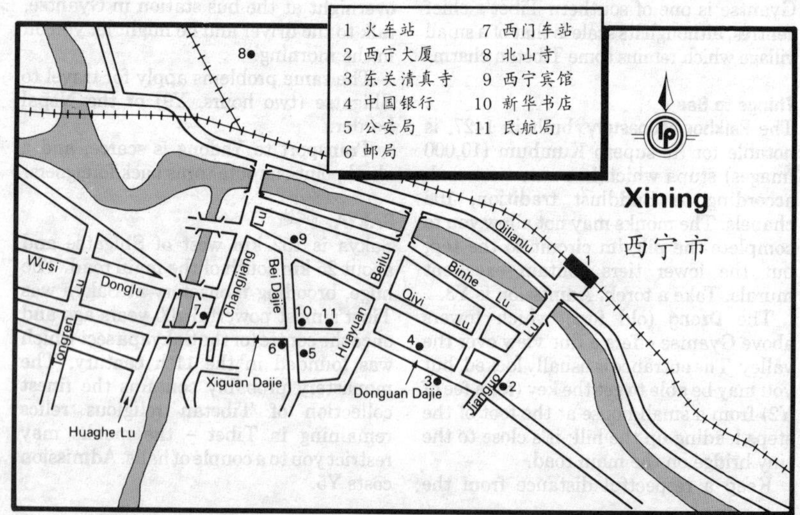

it is a convenient staging post for visiting Ta'er Monastery and Qinghai Lake. See the Around Xining section for details.

The **Dongguan Qingzhen Si (East City Gate Mosque)** is on the main street. This mosque, built during the late 14th century, is one of the largest in China's north-west and attracts large crowds of worshippers, particularly on Friday.

The **Beishan Si (Beishan Temple)** is about a 45-minute walk up the mountainside west of the Xining Hotel. The hike is pleasant and there's a good view over Xining from the temple.

Places to Stay

Xining Binguan (Xining Hotel) (tel 23901) is the main hotel for foreigners and quite comfortable once you've found your way around the many corridors. The rear building contains reception. A bed in a four-bed room costs Y6. Take bus No 9 from the stop opposite the bus station and ask to get off at the *binguan*.

Xining Daxia (Xining Mansions) is a high-falutin' name for a basic hotel. A bed in a four-bed room costs Y4. Take bus No 1 from the station and get off at the second stop.

Places to Eat

Both the hotels have standard restaurants, but the markets are far more interesting. Try the market area in the centre of town for kebabs, Muslim noodles and *hundun* (soup with a type of ravioli).

Getting There & Away

Air There are flights from Xining to Beijing (Y279), Lanzhou (Y30), Taiyuan (Y192) and Xian (Y131).

Bus The main bus station, opposite the train station, has daily departures in the morning for Qinghai Lake and Golmud (Y21.30, 1-1½ days). Buses to Taersi leave from the Ximen (West Gate) bus depot.

Rail Xining has frequent rail connections to Lanzhou in Gansu Province. There are two departures daily to Golmud; train No 303 is much faster. Foreigners have reported thefts on the train, particularly during the night.

AROUND XINING

Ta'er Lamasery (Taersi)

This is a large Tibetan monastery, one of the six great monasteries of the Yellow Hat sect of Tibetan Buddhism, located in the town of Huangzhong about 25 km south-east of Xining. It was built in 1577 on sacred ground – the birthplace of Tsong Khapa, founder of the Yellow Hat sect. Six temples are open – buy admission tickets from the window close to the row of stupas.

The monastery is noted for its extraordinary sculptures of human figures, animals and landscapes carved out of yak butter. The art of butter sculpture probably dates back 1300 years in Tibet and was taken up by the Ta'er Lamasery in the last years of the 16th century.

It's a pretty place and very popular with the local tourists – once they leave you can relax. Go hiking in the surrounding area or follow the pilgrims clockwise on a scenic circuit round the monastery.

Places to Stay & Eat The monastery has a couple of buildings which have been converted from monks' quarters into tourist accommodation. Rooms in the wooden buildings are arranged around a courtyard and come complete with gallery and murals. A bed in a three-bed room costs Y7.

The food at the monastery is good. For a change, take a wander down the hill towards town and try some noodles in a Muslim restaurant. Stalls on the approach road to the monastery sell great yoghurt and peaches.

Getting There & Away Buses to Huangzhong leave the Ximen depot in Xining at regular intervals between 7 am and 6.30 pm. The 45-minute ride costs Y0.70. Minibuses also do the trip faster for Y1.

Catch your return bus or minibus to Xining from the square in Huangzhong.

Qinghai Lake

Qinghai Lake (Koko Nor), known as the 'Western Sea' in ancient times, is a large and beautiful saline lake lying 300 km west of Xining.

The southern shore of the lake is accessible by bus or CITS tour. The small settlement of Heimahe, further west along this shore, is accessible if you take the southern bus route between Xining and Golmud. It's possible to stay at Heimahe and use it as a base for long hikes along the lake shore. To reach Niao Dao (Bird Island), take the road branching north from Heimahe – a bus goes in this direction as far as Shinaihe (40 km). From there it's a hike or a hitch for the 13 km to the Niao Dao hotel. Here you must register and pay Y3 admission before being shepherded to the island (16 km). The island is a breeding ground for thousands of wild geese, gulls, cormorants, extremely rare black-necked cranes and many other bird species. You will only see birds in any quantity during the mating and breeding season between March and early June – worth remembering if you are considering a CITS tour.

The northern shore of the lake is accessible by train. Ketu station is the jumping-off point and the lake is an hour's walk away.

In most of the small settlements around Qinghai Lake (such as Heimahe or Niao Dao) you can find a bed for between Y3 and Y6 a night. Food is simple; take supplies and warm clothing.

GOLMUD 格尔木

Golmud is a town in the centre of Qinghai which functions as a military garrison and gigantic supply station for Chinese operations in Tibet. It's a place to avoid unless you crave sandstorms, truck convoys, oil refineries and spots before your eyes – nothing to entertain the soul.

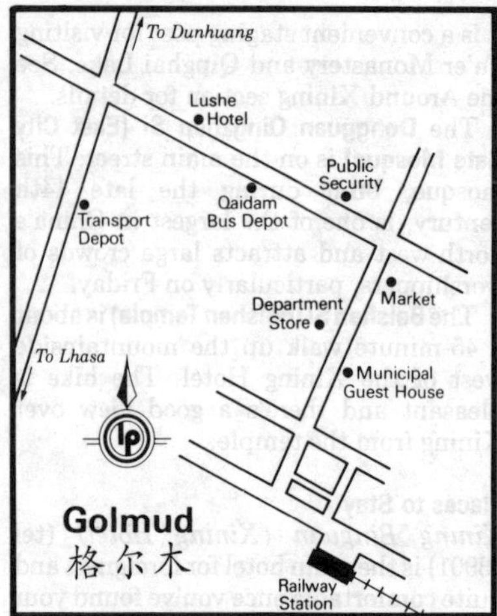

Places to Stay & Eat

The *Shi Zhaodai Suo (Municipal Guest House)* is the main place to stay even though it's miles from your connecting road transport. Doubles cost Y58, triples Y21 per person, and a bed in a seven-bed room Y4.

Showers happen around 9 pm in the building at the back – get your shower ticket for Y1 from reception. In the afternoon, bus tickets for Lhasa and Dunhuang are sold at reception. The guest house has a bus which ferries guests to the station at 9.30 am and 5 pm and waits for those arriving on the train from Xining.

At the front gate there's a bike rental. Bikes cost Y0.40 per hour or Y3 for the day. They're very useful in speeding up survival shopping or organising truck lifts and bus tickets.

The guest house has a mediocre restaurant. You'd do better at the small restaurants on the main street or in the market.

If you're on your way into Tibet, take advantage of the well-stocked shops in Golmud to load up on Snoopy hats, quilted jackets, foreign cigs and Chinese smarties.

Getting There & Away

Air The flight between Lhasa and Xian, which is routed via Golmud, is not in operation at present.

Bus & Truck There are two bus depots in Golmud. The depot on the road to Lhasa – Xizang Lhasa Yunshu Gongci – is the place to buy your ticket to Lhasa on the deluxe Japanese bus. Foreign tourists have the privilege of paying Y116, double the local price. The trip on this bus takes 30 hours, including an overnight at Amdo which is a gloomy hovel at the headache height of 4500 metres. Warm clothing, a sleeping bag, food, drink and a torch are useful on the trip – take them onto the bus since baggage is stowed out of reach on the roof.

The Chinese bus, which is not recommended because it travels non-stop, is usually waiting at the station. The fare is Y58. It's essential to take food, drink and warm clothing to survive the long, icy night.

The Chaidamu Yunshu Zhan (Qaidam bus depot) near the centre of town is the place to catch buses to Dunhuang, Qinghai Lake and Xining. Buses to Dunhuang seem to leave on alternate days at 6.40 am and arrive at 5.30 pm; the fare is Y13.90. Buses to Xining leave daily and the fare is Y21.30.

Golmud is a huge crossroads for hundreds of trucks en route to Lhasa, Shigatse, Dunhuang, Liuyuan, Xining, etc. If you want a ride on a truck, try either of the bus depots or the truck depots dotted around Golmud. As a result of an official crackdown, drivers are now less likely to make private deals and may direct you to the depot's despatch office, where you can ask for a truck ticket to your destination. The fare is often a bit higher than for the bus.

Rail There are two daily departures to Xining, but train No 304 is the fastest. Plans to extend this railway to Lhasa have been shelved in favour of the road.

Tibetan Symbols

Index

Abbreviations

Provinces, Autonomous Regions & Municipalities

Anh – Anhui
Bei – Beijing
Can – Canton
Fuj – Fujian
Gan – Gansu
G'dong – Guangdong
Gua – Guangxi
Gui – Guizhou
HI – Hainan Island
Heil – Heilongjiang
Heb – Hebei
Hen – Henan
Hub – Hubei
Hun – Hunan
InMon – Inner Mongolia
Jia – Jiangsu
J'xi – Jiangxi
Jil – Jilin
Lia – Liaoning
Nin – Ningxia
Shaa – Shaanxi
Shxi – Shanxi
S'dong – Shandong
Shang – Shanghai
Sic – Sichuan
Tia – Tianjin
T&Q – Tibet & Qinghai
Xin – Xinjiang
Yun – Yunnan
Zhe – Zhejiang

Map references in **bold** type

MAPS

Temperature

To convert °C to °F multipy by 1.8 and add 32

To convert °F to °C subtract 32 and multipy by ·55

°C	°F
50	122
45	113
40	104
35	95
30	86
25	75
20	68
15	59
10	50
5	41
0	32

Length, Distance & Area

	multipy by
inches to centimetres	2.54
centimetres to inches	0.39
feet to metres	0.30
metres to feet	3.28
yards to metres	0.91
metres to yards	1.09
miles to kilometres	1.61
kilometres to miles	0.62
acres to hectares	0.40
hectares to acres	2.47

Weight

	multipy by
ounces to grams	28.35
grams to ounces	0.035
pounds to kilograms	0.45
kilograms to pounds	2.21
British tons to kilograms	1016
US tons to kilograms	907

A British ton is 2240 lbs, a US ton is 2000 lbs

Volume

	multipy by
Imperial gallons to litres	4.55
litres to imperial gallons	0.22
US gallons to litres	3.79
litres to US gallons	0.26

5 imperial gallons equals 6 US gallons
a litre is slightly more than a US quart, slightly less than a British one

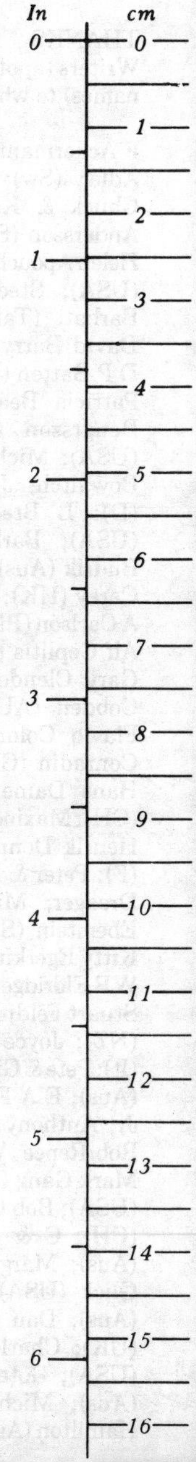

THANKS

Writers (apologies if we've mis-spelt your names) to whom thanks must go include:

F Ackermann (HK); Ralph Adam; Peter Adler (Sw); Lasse Ahvenainen (Sw); Chuck & Karen Amital (Isr); Helena Andersson (Sw); Urbanik Andrezey (P); Helen Apouchtine (Aus); Cary Appenzeller (USA); Steen Bachmann (Dk); John Barbati (Tai); Robert Barnes (USA); David Barry (UK); Rick Barson (UK); D P Batten (UK); Wendy Baylor (USA); Patricia Beach Smith (USA); Henrik Bengtsson (Sw); Donald Blackburn (USA); Michael Bond (UK); Elizabeth Bowditch; John Bowe; Ingrid Bremer (D); L Breen (Aus); Marilyn Brock (USA); Barbara Brown (USA); Udo Budrik (Aus); Sarah Capes (Aus); Geoff Carey (HK); Rachel Carlisle (UK); Cory A Carlson (PNG); Fred Carpenter (USA); Alf Ceplitis (Sw); Greg Chittick (USA); Gary Clendenon (USA); Mr & Mrs R Cobden (AUS); P J Coenraads (Nl); Flavio Colombo (It); Schloss Salaneg Conradin (CH); Neil Cunningham (C); Hans Damen (Nl); Richard Darwhall (CH); Maxine Degraaf (Aus); U Deimeter; Henrik Denmark; Francois Desbouvries (F); Peter & Maria Diedrichs (Sw); Barb Dreager; Mike Duffy; Bruce Easton; Eberstein (Sw); J & E Edwards (Aus); Kitty Egerking (Chi); Eva Ekelund (Sw); W B Eldridge (UK); Mr & Mrs Facey (HK); Stuart Feldman (USA); Mary Fitzgerald (NZ); Joyce Fitzgerald (USA); E Flax (It); Pete & Gill Fleg (UK); Robert Fletcher (Aus); E A Forster (Aus); Marcos Freire Jr; Anthony & Pauline Freeman (UK); Rob/Renee Van Gabriels/Assema (Nl); Mark Gang (USA); Paul William Garber (USA); Bob Garner (UK); Laurie Gilbert (CH); C & J Gill (USA); Jan Girdler (Aus); Margaret Girdler (Aus); Daniel Glick (USA); Jim Greig & Jane Lind (Aus); Dan Greve (Nl); Alan Griffiths (UK); Charles Gross (USA); Bill Gust (USA); Gote Gustafosson (Sw); Jim H (Aus); Michael Halpern (USA); Jane Hamilton (Aus); Helle Meldgaard Hansen (Dk); Mr Harban (UK); Rick Hardiman; R T Hardiman; Richard Harrold (UK); He Kuang Yang (Chi); B R Heitzman; Annika & Thomas Helin (Sw); Ann Henderson (Aus); Henrik (Dk); Jane Heyer (UK); Bertil Holstrom (Sw); Carsten Holz (D); Carsten Holz (Chi); Jennie Hopkins (NZ); Mary Hopkins (UK); David Hoult (UK); Linda Huetinck (USA); Bob Hyneman (Chi); Peter Ihrler (D); Bryan James (NZ); Sarah Jessup; Thomas Johansen (Dk); Susan & Murray Johnson (C); Jacqui Johnston (Chi); Mark Johnston (UK); Neil Jones (Aus); Einat & Edward Jurkevitch (F); Wren Katzalay (C); Craig Keating (Chi); George King (UK); John King (HK); John King (USA); Keith Kline; Knight & Tauber (Sw); Piet Koster (Nl); Thomas Kroger (D); Lennie Kwock (USA); Eric Larkin (Chi); Eric Larkin; Paul Law (USA); Real Leboluf (C); Ava Lee (C); Kate Leggett (C); Victorai Leighton (UK); Antero Leitzinger (Fin); Gwenola Lemoine (F); Miriam Lill (NZ); Will Lindesay (UK); W L Lindsay (UK); Jim Lindsay (Aus); Karen Lindsey (USA); Jolieske Lips (Aus); John Lister (Chi); Betsy Lloyd; Randolph Logan; Berny & Tazuko Lottner-Tanaka (Jap); Helen Loveday (UK); Cath Lovelock; Maureen Lynch; Madden-Hallett (Aus); Claudia Maher; Jenny Major (F); Bernard Maginouloux (F); K G Malvern (UK); A Margolis (USA); John Marshall (Thai); A A C Mattaei (UK); Michael McClintock (HK); Don McCort (USA); Caroline McDougall (Aus); Michael McGregor (Aus); Alex McKnight; Paul & Ruth McLean (UK); Mike McLintock (HK); Carter Mears (USA); Elisabeth Michau (F); Justine Mickle (Aus); John Mire (USA); Sue Mizen (HK); Moser (CH); Allan Murphy (C); Mary Murphy (Aus); Rev M Couve de Murville (UK); David Muskin (UK); A R Neale (Aus); Tome Newins (S); Dave Newman (USA); Ian Newton (Aus); Eva Nielsen (Dk); Naomi Nishimura (C); Joyce Noble (Aus); Lucas Noldus (Nl); Mark O'Malley (UK); John Oldale (UK); Claire L Olsen (NZ);

Richard Oyler; Cristina Paghera (It); Melissa Patrick (Aus); Keith Pearson (Aus); J Pelienburg (UK); David Pendar (UK); Dave Pidiersgill (UK); Dave Pidwell (UK); David Pierce (HK); Kurt R Rath (USA); Jesper Ravn (Dk); Pascoe Ray (UK); Susan Reiter (USA); Rebecca A Rees (USA); Beatrice Richmond (USA); Sheila Ringqvist (Sw); Espen Rinnan (N); C Ritschard (CH); Miriam Robertson (Aus); Katherine & David Rosenberg-Wohl (USA); Timothy Rowe (Jap); Henry Rowland (HK); Peter Russenberger (In); Matias Saari (USA); Lucy Sandys-Winsch (UK); Giorgio Sarti (It); Andy Saunders (USA); Michael Scher (USA); Ron Schroeder (C); Ben Schwall (USA); Deborah Sehgsohn (USA); Ken Shirley (NZ); Graham Sim; Kent Sinclair (USA); Sindre & Hans (Den); Mark Singleton (C); Vang Sisombat (Tai); Edward Smith (UK); Francois Solignac (F); Soren Sorensen (Dk); Pam Sowers (Chi); M A Spence (Aus); M Spencer; Detlef Spotter (D); Claire Staines; J S Steed (UK); Laura Stephens (USA); H P Street III (USA); Cornelius Suchy (D); Dewit Sylvie (B); Tim Temonink (Nl); Barbara Terry (USA); Leonard Thomas; Thomas; Alison Thompson (USA); Steve Throp (UK); Wouter Tiems (Nl); Nigel Tisdall (UK); Karin Torguy (Sw); Jesus Torquemada (Sp); Bjorn Tunback (Sw); Alexander Twist (UK); Tylesson (Dk); Judith Tyson (UK); Roberto Uga's; Harry Underhill; Vatche Varjabedian (USA); Irm Verburgt (Nl); Dick Vission (C); Robin Wagner (USA); Denis Qing Wang (Chi); Mark Warda (USA); L Wassenberg (Nl); Solveig Wergeland (N); Donovan Whistler (C); Karen Wilcock; Carol Wilkinson (Aus); Chris Williams (HK); Holt Williams (USA); Tim Williams (UK); Niels Willumsen (USA); Kirston Winther (Dk); Rudolf Wittsack (D); Graham Wrigley (UK); A R Young (UK); Joanne Young (UK); Gerard Yvanovich (Aus)

A – Austria, Aus – Australia, B – Belgium, C – Can, CH – Switzerland, Chi – China, Cy – Cyprus, D – West Germany, K – Denmark, F – France, Fin – Finland, G – Greece, HK – Hong Kong, I – India, Ir – Ireland, Isr – Israel, It – Italy, N – Norway, Nl – Netherlands, NZ – New Zealand, P – Poland, PNG – Papua New Guinea, S – Singapore, SL – Sri Lanka, Sw – Sweden, Tai – Taiwan, Thai – Thailand, UAE – United Arab Emirates, UK – United Kingdom, USA – United States of America

Lonely Planet

Lonely Planet published its first book in 1973. Tony and Maureen Wheeler had made a lengthy overland trip from England to Australia and, in response to numerous 'how do you do it?' questions, Tony wrote and they published *Across Asia on the Cheap*. It became an instant local best-seller and inspired thoughts of a second travel guide. A year and a half in South-East Asia resulted in their second book, *South-East Asia on a Shoestring*, which they put together in a backstreet Chinese hotel in Singapore in 1975. The 'yellow book', as it quickly became known, soon became *the* guide to the region and has gone through five editions, always with its familiar yellow cover.

Soon other writers started to come to them with ideas for similar books – books that went off the beaten track and took an adventurous approach to travel, books that 'assumed you knew how to get your luggage off the carousel,' as one reviewer described them. Lonely Planet grew from a kitchen table operation to a spare room and then to its own office. It also started to develop an international reputation as the Lonely Planet logo began to appear in more and more countries. In 1982 *India – a travel survival kit* won the Thomas Cook award for the best guidebook of the year.

These days there are over 60 Lonely Planet titles. Nearly 30 people work at our office in Melbourne, Australia and another half dozen at our US office in Oakland, California.

At first Lonely Planet specialised exclusively in the Asia region but these days we are also developing major ranges of guidebooks to the Pacific region, to South America and to Africa. The list of walking guides is growing and Lonely Planet is producing a unique series of phrasebooks to 'unusual' languages. The emphasis continues to be on travel for travellers and Tony and Maureen still manage to fit in a number of trips each year and play a very active part in the writing and updating of Lonely Planet's guides.

Keeping guidebooks up to date is a constant battle which requires an ear to the ground and lots of walking, but technology also plays its part. All Lonely Planet guidebooks are now stored and updated on computer, and some authors even take lap-top computers into the field. Lonely Planet is also using computers to draw maps and eventually many of the maps will be stored on disk.

The people at Lonely Planet strongly feel that travellers can make a positive contribution to the countries they visit both by better appreciation of cultures and by the money they spend. In addition the company tries to make a direct contribution to the countries and regions it covers. Since 1986 a percentage of the income from each book has gone to aid groups and associations. This has included donations to famine relief in Africa, to aid projects in India, to agricultural projects in Nicaragua and other Central American countries and to Greenpeace's efforts to halt French nuclear testing in the Pacific. In 1987 $30,000 was donated by Lonely Planet to these projects.

Lonely Planet Distributors

Australia & Papua New Guinea Lonely Planet Publications, PO Box 88, South Yarra, Victoria 3141.
Canada Raincoast Books, 112 East 3rd Avenue, Vancouver, British Columbia V5T 1C8.
Denmark, Finland & Norway Scanvik Books aps, Store Kongensgade 59 A, DK-1264 Copenhagen K.
Hong Kong The Book Society, GPO Box 7804.
India & Nepal UBS Distributors, 5 Ansari Rd, New Delhi – 110002
Israel Geographical Tours Ltd, 8 Tverya St, Tel Aviv 63144.
Japan Intercontinental Marketing Corp, IPO Box 5056, Tokyo 100-31.
Netherlands Nilsson & Lamm bv, Postbus 195, Pampuslaan 212, 1380 AD Weesp.
New Zealand Roulston Greene Publishing Associates Ltd, Private Bag, Takapuna, Auckland 9.
Singapore & Malaysia MPH Distributors, 601 Sims Drive, #03-21, Singapore 1438.
Spain Altair, Balmes 69, 08007 Barcelona.
Sweden Esselte Kartcentrum AB, Vasagatan 16, S-111 20 Stockholm.
Thailand Chalermnit, 108 Sukhumvit 53, Bangkok 10110.
UK Roger Lascelles, 47 York Rd, Brentford, Middlesex, TW8 0QP
USA Lonely Planet Publications, PO Box 2001A, Berkeley, CA 94702.
West Germany Buchvertrieb Gerda Schettler, Postfach 64, D3415 Hattorf a H.

Lonely Planet Guidebooks

Lonely Planet guidebooks cover virtually every accessible part of Asia as well as Australia, the Pacific, Central and South America, Africa, the Middle East and parts of North America. There are four main series: 'travel survival kits', covering a single country for a range of budgets; 'shoestring' guides with compact information for low-budget travel in a major region; trekking guides; and 'phrasebooks'.

Australia & the Pacific

Australia
Papua New Guinea
Bushwalking in Papua New Guinea
Papua New Guinea phrasebook
New Zealand
Tramping in New Zealand
Rarotonga & the Cook Islands
Tahiti & French Polynesia
Fiji
Micronesia

South-East Asia

South-East Asia on a shoestring
Malaysia, Singapore & Brunei
Indonesia
Bali & Lombok
Indonesia phrasebook
Burma
Thailand
Thailand phrasebook
Philippines

North-East Asia

North-East Asia on a shoestring
China
China phrasebook
Tibet
Tibet phrasebook
Japan
Korea & Taiwan
Hong Kong, Macau & Canton

West Asia

West Asia on a shoestring
Turkey